THE
HISTORICAL
ENCYCLOPEDIA
OF
WORLD WAR II

Originally published as
ENCYCLOPEDIE DE LA GUERRE 1939-1945
Editions Casterman, Paris et Tournai

THE
HISTORICAL
ENCYCLOPEDIA
OF
WORLD WAR II

Edited by
Marcel Baudot
Henri Bernard
Hendrik Brugmans
Michael R. D. Foot
Hans-Adolf Jacobsen

Translated from the French by
Jesse Dilson

With additional material by
Alvin D. Coox
Thomas R. H. Havens

M

Originally published as ENCYCLOPEDIE DE LA GUERRE 1939-1945 by Editions Casterman, Paris and Tournai.

First published in English in 1980 by Facts On File Inc., New York.

Illustrations by Andre Dumoulin

First published 1981 by
THE MACMILLAN PRESS LTD and MACMILLAN LONDON LTD
London and Basingstoke
Companies and representatives throughout the world

ISBN 0 333 28211 6

Printed in the United States of America
10 9 8 7 6 5 4 3 2 1

CONTENTS

List of Abbreviations

AA	Antiaircraft
AAF	Army Air Force
ABDA	Australian-British-Dutch-American Command
AEF	Allied Expeditionary Force
CCS	Combined Chiefs of Staff
CINCPAC	Commander in Chief, Pacific Area
Gestapo	*Geheime Staats Polizei*
IGHQ	Imperial General Headquarters (Japanese)
IJA	Imperial Japanese Army
IJN	Imperial Japanese Navy
OKH	*Oberkommando des Heeres*
OKL	*Oberkommando der Luftwaffe*
OKM	*Oberkommando der Kriegsmarine*
OKW	*Oberkommando der Wehrmacht*
OSS	Office of Strategic Services
RAF	Royal Air Force
RM	Reichsmark
RN	Royal Navy
SA	*Sturmabteilung* (Storm Troops)
SD	*Sicherheitsdienst* (Security Service)
SHAEF	Supreme Headquarters Allied Expeditionary Force
SS	*Schutzstaffel* (Protection Squads)
TAF	Tactical Air Force
USAAF	U.S. Army Air Force
USMC	U.S. Marine Corps
USN	U.S. Navy
USS	U.S. Ship

Throughout *The Historical Encyclopedia of World War II*, certain words, phrases or names appear in **bold face**. These are cross-references—e.g., in the article on Albania, **Malta** appears in bold face; this indicates that there is an article on Malta in the *Encyclopedia.*

INTRODUCTION
ORIGINS OF THE SECOND WORLD WAR

Those developments in the domestic and foreign policies of the major powers that contributed directly to the outbreak of war in 1939 are discussed in the following pages. No attempt is made, however, to retrace the whole history of the interwar period. This introduction covers three periods: the immediate post-World War I years, the ensuing era of hope and reconciliation and the period of new struggles and crises.

1918-1925: The Postwar Period

Two victors and future adversaries: the United States and Japan

When the Armistice ending hostilities on the Western Front was announced on November 11, 1918, it soon became obvious that the first "world" war had at least two undeniable victors: Japan and the United States. The European winners naturally felt greater relief than those overseas. But precisely because the Europeans suffered more than the non-European powers, the latter reaped greater gains from the war. Both the United States and Japan strengthened their positions in the world at a relatively modest price.

The United States did not go to war until 1917. And even after its official entry in the war, many months passed before an expeditionary force could be recruited, trained and transported to Europe. Although American troops brought great relief to the hard-pressed British and French in the final months of fighting, America's involvement was brief, and its deaths in battle were limited to 91,000. But the nation had given enormous economic assistance to the Allies and was determined to be reimbursed for it. After the war, the United States emerged more powerful than it had been in 1914.

Japan suffered virtually no losses from the time it declared war on Germany in 1914. It occupied German positions in the Chinese province of Kiaochow and expanded its foreign commerical relationships at the expense of France and Great Britain, both preoccupied with their life-and-death struggle. At the peace conference Japan found itself in a position of power without any involvement in the territorial rivalries of the European nations. In recognition of its services it received some German possessions in the Pacific, including bases that would later be useful for Japanese economic, political and military expansion. The Far Eastern equilibrium thus shifted in favor of a state that had achieved the first victory of a nonwhite nation over a white power by defeating the Russians in 1905. While the Americans were mainly interested in the Atlantic, Japanese imperialism became a powerful force in the Pacific and East Asia, where it soon laid the basis for a "Co-Prosperity Sphere" under its control. Despite their different areas of interest, the likelihood of an eventual conflict between these powers was already perceptible.

The new Russia

Russia's czarist government bore a large share of the responsibility for World War I, which it initially viewed as an opportunity to reclaim the honor lost in its defeat by Japan in 1905. Nicholas II and his ministers also hoped that an international crisis would reunite the people under the Czar's autocratic yoke. Instead they suffered military reversals and, finally, revolution. When the new Bolshevik government decided to renounce its dream of a revolution by the masses and to conclude a separate peace at almost any price, it signed the Treaty of Brest-Litovsk in March 1918, which ended fighting on the Eastern Front and allowed the Germans to mount a new offensive towards Paris.

In and out of the conflict, Russia thus weighed heavily in the balance. Officially ignored by the other great powers, the Union of Soviet Socialist Republics (a name adopted in 1922) remained a significant international factor. Although excluded from the League of Nations until 1935, the Soviet Union was nevertheless a reality, even in the eyes of the nations that refused it diplomatic recognition. Soon some discerning statesmen like Germany's Walter Rathenau began to seek its support, if not its friendship. Gradually the new Communist regime and its potent ideology assumed a principal role in the evolution of European politics following World War I.

The Soviet government had its first important dealings with two countries that had, wholly or in part, belonged to the czarist empire: Finland and Poland. Circumstances in both states raised the issue of self-government, officially endorsed by the Bolsheviks for the non-Russian peoples of the former czarist empire. Lenin himself asserted that no nation could consider itself free as long as it oppressed another.

However the cause of national autonomy in Finland was split along ideological lines. Finnish conservatives who had been quite amenable to the weak autonomy granted by St. Petersburg became separatists after 1917. On the other hand, a large part of the extreme left in Finland, whose previous political opposition to czarism had been reinforced by nationalism, refused to break with the Kremlin. The Bolsheviks, they pointed out, promised a vast socialist federation of all peoples under an egalitarian regime. This was surely preferable, in their view, to a parochial state dominated by a conservative elite.

Such arguments led to the outbreak of civil war in Finland, which ended in the establishment of a monarchy under German protection and, later, of a conservative republic. Marshal Carl Gustav von Mannerheim, who repulsed the Soviets and suppressed the Finnish Communists, founded the "Lappo" movement, based primarily on fascism, in 1930. At the same time the creation of a strong social democratic organization, supported by an efficient agricultural cooperative movement, strengthened the foundations of the country's parliamentary government and made possible a stable national democracy. Relations with the USSR, however, remained troubled. The outbreak of the "Winter War" with the Soviet Union in 1939 led Finland into an unnatural alliance with Nazi Germany.

In Poland, too, the conflict between communism and nationalism divided loyalties. To Lenin and most of his colleagues, the revolution's success hinged on its fate in the West. Although the Communists' attention centered primarily on Germany, Poland stood in their way; it could be either an obstacle or a corridor to the rest of Europe. The new Polish state, moreover, had fluid borders. Historically, it could lay claim to vast lands in central and eastern Europe. While some Poles objected to the presence of alien peoples within their boundaries, others pressed for the inclusion of as much territory as possible.

The expansionist group, led by the veteran anti-Russian freedom fighter Jozef Pilsudski, soon won out and shaped an ambitious plan of conquest. In April 1920 a Polish offensive was launched toward the south, and with the assistance of the Ukrainian separatist leader Simon Petlyura, who was operating against the Red Army, Kiev was occupied the following month. But by July the military balance began to swing the other way. While the Poles allied themselves with the Ukranian freedom movement, the Soviets not only rallied their forces around the banner of revolution, but also exploited the traditional hatred between members of the Russian Orthodox Church and the Roman Catholic population.

The Red Army, commanded by General Mikhail Nikolaevich Tukhachevsky, actually reached the gates of Warsaw. The infant republic seemed doomed only months after its birth. But in mid-August the pendulum swung once again. In a series of audacious maneuvers, the Polish general staff launched a counter-offensive that drove back the Russians, with the aid of a group of French officers led by General Maxime Weygand and a young captain named Charles de Gaulle.

The eastern Russo-Polish frontier was finally drawn along a line first proposed by the British statesman Lord Curzon in December 1919. The war that began in April 1920 ended on March 18, 1921 with the peace pact of Riga. But the wounds it left on both sides never really healed and eventually led to another war in 1939, when the Soviets invaded Poland.

The end of the Austro-Hungarian Monarchy

In southeastern Europe the Austro-Hungarian Monarchy collapsed with its surrender to the Allies in November 1918. Before World War I the monarchy had been an economically integrated entity (there were no customs barriers separating Trentino from Galicia or Bohemia from Transylvania). But intensifying ethnic loyalties eventually tore apart the multinational empire and helped set off the war. The treaties of Versailles, Trianon and Saint-Germain divided Austria-Hungary into the "Successor States," but the problem of minority disputes continued.

This problem presented certain contradictions. On the one hand, Czechoslovakia and Yugoslavia favored both nationalism and the application of the Wilsonian principle of "the free self-determination of peoples." But within each of these states were dissatisfied ethnic minorities. Quarrels soon broke out in Czechoslovakia between the dominant Czechs and the Slovaks and Sudetic Germans, and in Yugoslavia the predominantly Eastern Orthodox Serbs clashed with the Roman Catholic Croats. In 1928 the Croatian peasant leader Stepan Radich was assassinated during a session of the Yugoslavian Parliament. Continuing ethnic tensions in Yugoslavia were exploited first by Mussolini and later by Hitler.

A similar situation occurred in Rumania, a relatively old state that emerged from the war in possession of Bessarabia (formerly under Russian rule), Dobruja and Transylvania. The city of Alba Iulia in Transylvania was the center of a separatist movement that had great strength in two Rumanian provinces, Wallachia and Moldavia. The new Rumania, almost twice as large as the original area, also included an enlarged German population and a substantial Hungarian minority, which also threatened the country's unity. Bucharest therefore had every reason to oppose "revisionism," i.e., attempts to alter the terms of the Armistice. Guided by its minister of foreign affairs, Nicolae Titulescu, Rumania set out to play an influential role in the League of Nations, the caretaker of the treaties that guaranteed its boundaries.

Like Yugoslavia and Czechoslovakia, Rumania turned to France, another "victorious" power intent on preserving the status quo. Through the Little Entente, created in 1922, Paris tried to maintain order by extending its protection to these three central European countries with the greatest stake in preserving the postwar international system. Yet France lacked the military means to guarantee the safety of these territories and could offer nothing more than condolences when Germany occupied Czechoslovakia in 1938.

Among the nations frustrated by the outcome of World War I was Hungary, reduced to scanty proportions by the Treaty of Trianon. Before 1914 it had comprised half of the Hapsburg monarchy and reigned over a primarily non-Magyar population. Weaker but more homogeneous in 1919, Hungary yearned for its lost grandeur and became a leading revisionist power. This exaggerated nationalism led, after the end of Bela Kun's short-lived Communist republic, to an authoritarian regime with fascist tendencies.

The collapse of the Hapsburg empire left among its fragments one last Successor State, the humiliated "German Austria." Described by one journalist as "the state nobody wants," this rudimentary nation, stripped of its former raw materials, was barely viable. It was composed of a crowded, prestigious capital cut off from its multinational hinterland and a sharply contrasting rural population to which Vienna meant nothing. While the capital had a Social Democratic majority and a municipal government that was a model of progressive administration, the rest of the country regretted the passing of the monarchy and demanded an authoritarian regime. This polarization resulted in the civil war of February 1934, which eliminated the Austrian Social Democrats and isolated the Christian-Socialist government, too feeble by itself to resist National Socialist pressure.

Whatever their political leanings, most Austrians were dissatisfied with their state and sought alternatives to it. Some advocated a restored monarchy; many others supported unification with Germany or rallied to the Pan-European movement begun by the Austrian Count Richard von Coudenhove-Kalergi in 1922. The "Greater German" advocates included many who were neither chauvinists nor rightists. Indeed, a large number of socialists hoped to emerge from their isolation in Vienna and join their German counterparts in the Weimar Republic. The *Anschluss* movement was initially blocked by France, which regarded reinforcement of German power as a mortal threat. Yet in the end, the union denied to Austrian and German democrats before 1933 came about under the Nazis despite French objections.

The German question

Europe's greatest problem after 1918 was Germany, a country that remained hostile toward its former enemies for two important reasons. In the first place, German military leaders refused to admit that they had been vanquished on the battlefield. The Allies had virtually ended their campaign the very day German forces evacuated the territories they had occupied. It was therefore psychologically understandable but politically disastrous for Friedrich Ebert, first president of the Weimar Republic, to greet the returning troops as "unconquered." Worse yet, civilian politicians who negotiated and implemented the Armistice fostered the "stab in the back" legend that the German army would have been victorious if only those at home (Jews, socialists etc.) had not betrayed it.

A second problem was the continuation of the Allied naval blockade of Germany for three months after the Armistice. Starving German civilians conceived a hatred of the victorious powers that, in time, benefited Hitler. A generation suffering from malnutrition in infancy or adolescence matured as victims of postwar injustice.

Under these circumstances a socialist-dominated provisional government attempted to pull the country together again after the war. On November 9, 1918, after Wilhelm II had fled to the Netherlands, Philipp Scheidemann proclaimed a republic. At Weimar, home of Goethe and the symbol of a peaceful Germany, a constitutional assembly met but failed to resolve either of the two problems threatening it: communism and economic collapse.

Exploiting the confusion that followed defeat, the extreme left tried to duplicate the Bolshevik example of immediate revolution. Factory workers and military personnel returning from the war formed workers' and soldiers' councils, the German equivalent of the Russian "soviets," in which extremists commanded a sizable audience. The country seemed on the brink of a communist revolution. This threat was averted, however, due to the resolute moderation of the German Social Democrats and the absence of leadership among the extremists.

The German left, consisting of the reformist Independent Social Democratic Party and the radical Spartacus League, led by Rosa Luxemberg and Karl Lieb-knecht, was poorly organized at the war's end. The Spartacists, who advocated violent revolution, lacked the military strength to overcome the army and other right-wing organizations. Some "red" units periodically attempted sudden grabs for power, but never managed a decisive stroke. Germany thus entered a period of purposeless civil war that lasted until 1923. Luxemberg and Liebknecht had tried to give the movement greater direction, but they had been assassinated in 1919 by a band of reactionary officers. The same year right-wing forces crushed an attempt by anarchists to establish a soviet republic in Bavaria.

Following the death of Luxemberg and Liebknecht, the Spartacus League became the German Communist Party. Its only achievement, however, was to help make Germany ungovernable. Until the moment Hitler assumed power, Communist leaders denounced the Social Democrats as "Social Fascists," the "Enemy Number One" of the German working class. The division within the German left weakened the entire workers' movement and facilitated the Nazi seizure of power.

The chances of the status quo

In response to the distress of the vanquished countries, the victors of World War I offered only one solution: respect the Treaty of Versailles. Yet the Germans would never accept this "dictated" peace, a symbol of its impotence and humiliation in 1918. The German delegation at Versailles indicated its attitude by breaking the pen used to sign the treaty.

The Versailles peace agreement took large territories away from Germany, including the Polish province of Poznan and parts of Silesia and Schleswig-Holstein. The most painful loss, however, was the traditionally German port of Danzig, declared a "free city" under League of Nations supervision. East Prussia was separated from the rest of Germany by a narrow land corridor adjacent to Danzig, created to give the new Polish state an outlet on the Baltic Sea. This arbitrary division of Germany became the cause celebre of German irredentists and eventually give Hitler a pretext for starting World War II.

Germany also lost its colonies, which were placed under League of Nations mandate and administered by the victorious powers. Unlike the territorial losses in Europe, the colonial issue did not evoke deep resentment among most Germans; Hitler never sought the return of colonies either in his domestic propaganda or in his foreign policy. Yet businessmen interested in foreign trade and advocates of a strong navy, important elements in German politics, felt the colonial loss deeply and continued to hope for its rectification.

In addition to the territorial provisions of the treaty, the Germans objected to the notorious Article 241, which saddled Germany with sole responsibility for the outbreak of war in 1914. This statute was designed to justify the reparations demands of Britain and France, which intended to make Germany pay the entire cost of the war on the Western Front. The financial burden thus imposed on the German government was so onerous that it provoked debate even in the Allied countries and aided German revisionists in their demands for alteration of the entire system imposed by the treaty. British economist John Maynard Keynes, in his book *The Economic Consequences of the Peace* (1920), warned of the disastrous consequences of reparations. His predictions seemed confirmed by the inflation in Germany in 1923, which made fulfillment of the reparations demands less likely than ever.

Germany's postwar economic collapse, attributed by Keynes and others to the reparations burden, had serious social as well as economic repercussions. The entire German middle class, who normally lived on fixed incomes and accumulated savings, was financially leveled as inflation wiped out the value of bank accounts. Particularly hard hit were pensioners and others dependent on regular payments whose amounts had been set before the inflation began. Thus a former cornerstone of the German social order dissolved into a mass of frightened and rootless individuals with little stake in the existing political system, a ready audience for Nazi propaganda.

Britain and France, alarmed by the signs of growing chaos in Germany, agreed to discuss modification of reparations payments at the Genoa Conference in April and May 1922. The most noteworthy outcome of the meeting, however, had nothing to do with reparations. Walter Rathenau, head of the German delegation in Genoa, met secretly at nearby Rapallo with Soviet Foreign Minister Georgi Chicherin and agreed to an informal alignment between the two countries. Both Germany and Soviet Russia thus succeeded in overcoming the diplomatic isolation that the Western Allies had attempted to impose on them.

The Soviet connection helped German leaders evade one further provision of the Versailles Treaty: the forced disarmament of Germany. Reduced to a token force of 100,000 men, the German army was supplemented by officers and technicians trained in the Soviet Union. Germany's armaments, kept at a minimal level by the treaty, were clandestinely augmented by equipment manufactured in Soviet factories. The restricted size of its armed service also gave the German command an opportunity to impose unusually stringent entrance requirements, which produced a force of unsurpassed excellence. Officers like Heinz Guderian and Erwin Rommel, experts in the unorthodox use of armored formations, received their training in the seemingly harmless "Versailles Army." When Hitler later succeeded in tearing up the treaty, he found this cadre an excellent nucleus around which to shape his strike force.

Hope in Geneva

With an unstable Germany bent on unraveling the international order, Europe faced an uncertain future after the end of the war. One hope for the preservation of peace was the newly created League of Nations. Woodrow Wilson, disappointed by the failure of the Versailles conference to negotiate a just settlement, said of his Fourteen Points, "I lost them in the ocean, but the league will fish them out again."

The League of Nations was the first attempt in history to create a broad international government with real powers. Its Assembly, located in Geneva, was made up of representatives from all member states; the Council was comprised of delegates from the great powers and was charged with carrying out the league's decisions. An arbitration system was created to resolve and prevent quarrels, and specialized league agencies such as the International Labor Bureau (later the International Labor Organization) attempted to promote worldwide cooperation in specific fields.

Although impressive in concept and organization, the League of Nations achieved only limited success in its main task: the maintenance of peace. League mediation settled a 1923 conflict between Greece and Italy over the island of Corfu. Yet the Geneva Protocol of 1924, which required the submission of any international disagreement to arbitration by the league, was never ratified; the great powers refused to forfeit the right of military intervention where their "vital interests" were at stake. Although the idea of replacing force with law was attractive, it conflicted with the more "sacred" notion of national sovereignty.

In addition to the great powers, some of Europe's smaller countries felt this way. In 1923 war broke out between Greece and Turkey, two long-standing rivals in the eastern Mediterranean. The collapse of Turkey's Ottoman Empire in 1918 encouraged Greece, with covert support from Britain and France, to seek expansion into Asia Minor. Yet Turkish military forces, revitalized by the "Young Turk" government of Kemal Pasha Ataturk, repulsed the Greek invasion and forced Greece, in the Treaty of Lausanne, to renounce its Asian territorial claims. The league failed to prevent or even to mediate this conflict. Its involvement came only after the fighting had ceased,

when a league commission was created to supervise the exchange of Greek and Turkish minority populations.

One disappointment for pacifists in the aftermath of the Greek-Turkish war was the refusal of the British left to support the creation of a League of Nations army capable of acting against an aggressor state. The British "New Commonwealth Society," which included prominent conservatives such as Winston Churchill among its members, recognized the importance of such a force in establishing the league's credibility. But the traditionally pacifist socialists disdained what they called "international militarism." In the absence of effective sanctions and safeguards, Geneva remained a social club for diplomats.

The nationalist upsurge

With the League of Nations reduced to impotence, pacifists and internationalists hoped at least that nationalism, which had caused the carnage of World War I, would never again trouble world peace. Yet by 1923 the intensely nationalistic *fasci di combattimento*, led by former Socialist Benito Mussolini, had seized power in Italy.

Fascism was the only original political movement of the interwar period. Liberalism, socialism and Christian Democracy were survivors of an earlier era. But fascism, new and difficult to classify, had a disorienting effect on public opinion. Despite its nationalist appeal, it rejected the pillars of the extreme right in Italy: clericalism, monarchism and capitalism. Established by war veterans, the movement reflected the bitterness of those who had brought Italy into the war in the hope of territorial gains that were later denied in the Treaty of Versailles. It also rekindled the memory of the battlefield, where national solidarity overcame religious, social and political differences. Prone to violence, the fascists scorned parliamentary procedure as ineffective talk. Most of Mussolini's followers genuinely desired social change but rejected the old ideologies of communism and socialism without offering any alternative. In practice, fascism reached a fairly easy accommodation with the House of Savoy and the Vatican, symbols of the Italian establishment. Yet it remained a restless and unstable force in the nation's politics.

Outside Italy, Mussolini's political adventures were greeted with sympathy or indifference. Although the assassination of the outspoken Social Democratic deputy Giacomo Matteotti on June 10, 1924 alienated some sectors of public opinion, the killing did not upset the European right, which generally preferred demagogues to socialists. In the opinion of conservatives, Italy needed greater discipline to make the trains run on time and keep public officials honest.

Socialism had been brutally eliminated, but order was reestablished.

1925-1931: The "Good" Years

Despite the turbulence of the postwar years, the pacifists were not entirely frustrated in their desire to see nationalism reduced in importance as a political force. Passions fostered by the war ebbed, and reconciliation began to seem possible. For five years diplomats tried to lay the basis for a durable peace.

The "illegal" war

In 1923 President Raymond Poincare of France sought to force the Germans to honor their war reparations by ordering his troops to occupy the Ruhr valley. Most Frenchmen approved of this move. Socialist leader Leon Blum was in the minority when, at a congress of the Socialist International in Hamburg, he pleaded for greater flexibility in the application of the Treaty of Versailles.

The military operation, however, proved ineffective. The presence of French soldiers in the Ruhr did not improve the attitude of the German people towards reparations. The working class began a campaign of passive resistance against the French intruders. This "Battle of the Ruhr" gave the Nazis a chance to glorify their first martyr, Horst Wessel, who posthumously lent his name to the movement's hymn. French authorities aggravated the tension by using Africans as occupation troops. The resulting riots intensified Germany's renewed nationalism. Poincare was defeated in the elections of May 24 and thus forced to resign.

His failure opened the door to other solutions. Aristide Briand on one side and Gustav Stresemann on the other, two patriots who advocated Franco-German amity, succeeded in erasing one part of the Versailles system. By signing the Locarno Pact in late 1925, Germany sought to reassure French and Belgian public opinion regarding her western frontier. There would be, according to the provisions of the treaty, no dispute over its definition, nor any question of "revenge"; the Alsace-Lorraine problem was permanently resolved. Although no treaty guaranteeing the status quo of Germany's eastern frontier was ever negotiated, Locarno could at least be regarded as the dawn of Franco-German reconciliation.

Briand and Stresemann worked together for the next five years to strengthen the bond they had established. French ministers came and went, but Briand, the "man of Geneva," was constantly in his office on the Quai d'Orsay. Once he went so far as to invite his German colleague to an intimate "man-to-man" colloquy with no reporters present. And when

Stresemann entered the League of Nations Assembly on September 8, 1926, Briand welcomed him.

Germany's economic situation improved after the end of the Ruhr occupation. The investment level rose to such an extent, in fact, that Allied leaders renewed their demands for payment of reparations. On two occasions American financiers visited Europe in an effort to set German payments at a realistic level. Allied demands gradually eased, however, in the face of continued German refusal to pay.

One great obstacle to the quest for permanent peace was the foreign policy of the United States. America had not ratified the Treaty of Versailles, and the Republican Party, in power at the time, seemed bent on short-sighted isolationism. Finally, however, the leaders of the United States demonstrated that they were not completely uninterested in the fate of the world. Secretary of State Frank B. Kellogg, on Briand's suggestion, proposed an international treaty with the grand aim of outlawing war, its signatories pledging never to use armed force to settle their differences. On August 27, 1928, 15 delegations met in Paris to sign the Kellogg-Briand pact. None of the solemn speeches welcoming a new era of harmony dared raise the question, What happens if one of the signatories breaks its word?

The Federalist idea

Clarence Streit, a *New York Times* correspondent who covered the League of Nations in Geneva, became absorbed with the idea of world federalism. Bored with endless debates and resolutions, he founded the "Federal Union" movement, which envisaged not world federation but a union of the Atlantic democracies with common interests. His book *Union Now* gained some popularity in the United States but had little effect on the other side of the Atlantic.

Yet the federalist idea began to gain popularity in Europe as well. In 1923 Count Richard von Coudenhove-Kalergi published his manifesto *Paneuropa* in Vienna and with it launched a campaign for a European union. He continued to promote the movement until his death in 1972. By nationality, Coudenhove-Kalergi was Austro-Hungarian, born in Tokyo of a Japanese mother and a diplomat father. Educated in the Theresianum, where many youths who were to enter the Austrian diplomatic service spent their formative years, he was well acquainted with centrifugal nationalist tendencies. But why, he asked himself, could not different racial and religious groups live peacefully in a community with no internal boundaries under a tolerant government?

A resident of Bohemia after the war, Coudenhove-Kalergi suddenly found himself a Czech citizen. He accepted his new status uneasily, fearing that the creation of the Successor States would lead to economic fragmentation, and the emergence of new boundaries as divisive as the old ones. This ran counter to his idea of historical progress. After Coudenhove-Kalergi became convinced that the collapse of the Hapsburg monarchy had been inevitable, he concluded that the only solution was to work for the end of all frontiers and customs barriers, not only in the Danube basin but throughout Europe.

Coudenhove-Kalergi found his first followers in Austria. Following the appearance of his manifesto, he published a federalist journal in several languages. Its purpose was not to arouse the masses, but rather to sway the political and economic ruling classes. Federalist committees were formed in various countries and included spokesmen from all the democratic parties, bankers, industrialists, trade union members, writers and artists. Beginning in 1925 large conventions were organized with the support of statesmen like Stresemann and Briand.

In September 1929 Briand issued the most sensational proposal of his career, calling for creation of a "United States of Europe" within the League of Nations. The "good era" that fostered such ideas, however, was close to its end. Briand himself never quite grasped the meaning of his initiative. He talked constantly of federalism, telling one French journalist that he was inspired by the example of Switzerland. But when he was asked what would happen to the concept of national sovereignty if his dream were realized, Briand replied that there would be no question of altering it. Whether because of pragmatism or oversight, the memorandum outlining the United States of Europe was vague on many points.

European politicians reacted to the proposal courteously but without enthusiasm; it was tabled while their parliaments occupied themselves with seemingly more pressing national problems. Smaller countries agreed to participate on condition that the new federation would not be dominated by the larger nations. The stronger powers maintained that those nations with more important responsibilities should be given a greater voice. Agricultural nations spoke of a European entity that would pledge to purchase their crops, while the industrial nations demanded the benefits of free trade. Briand's plan thus resembled the fabled Spanish inn, where guests found whatever they had brought with them.

The most important responses to the idea of federation were those of Germany and Great Britain. With the Nazi threat growing, Stresemann's countrymen viewed Briand's project only as another opportunity to agitate for revision of the Versailles Treaty. British leaders, who still saw themselves as the masters of a world empire, disliked any proposal to integrate their country with the Continent. A grand unification project like the United States of Europe was not likely to win their approval. As Churchill later said of the Europeans, "We are with them, but not of them."

Shortly after Briand launched his federalist proposal, Gustav Stresemann died, exhausted by his struggle to be heard even in his own German People's Party. Almost at the same time the Great Depression struck, bringing with it the rise of trade barriers and political extremism. The United States of Europe project thus foundered. Aristide Briand continued in the struggle for several years, attempting unsuccessfully to win the French presidency. With him died the federalist idea.

Discounting Europe's ability to help itself, Britain's Laborite Prime Minister Ramsay MacDonald appealed to the United States to halt the slide into worldwide anarchy. He visited America in October 1929 but returned with nothing substantial. Unable to stem Britain's soaring unemployment rate, his socialist government fell and was replaced with a "national unity" cabinet dominated by Conservatives.

Socialism on its sickbed

The world economic crisis was unquestionably a major factor in bringing about Nazism and World War II. It ruined the confidence of Europeans in their parliamentary institutions and drove millions of them to despair. For European socialists, however, the Great Depression marked only a further stage in a decline that had begun with the collapse of the Socialist International in 1914 and continued with the rise of Italian fascism in 1922.

Italy's Socialists, strongly syndicalist in orientation, believed that the "final conflict" with employers would begin with a series of massive strikes, leading to a workers' seizure of the means of production. Italian workers actually occupied their factories, with exemplary discipline, in 1922. They discovered, however, that their leaders had no idea of what to do next. The Socialist movement in Italy was soon rent by factionalism and Socialist deputies withdrew from Parliament, just as the bourgeoisie, frightened by the workers' actions, turned to a "strong man" who seemed capable of reestablishing order. Mussolini had in fact encouraged the occupation of the factories, but his demagogic outbursts brought only knowing smiles from the propertied classes and gained him the funds he needed. It was this support that allowed him to make the "march on Rome" of October 28, 1922, when he could have been arrested easily if King Victor Emmanuel III had wanted to stop him.

As Mussolini began to consolidate his power, Italian Socialists and trade union leaders put up only weak, local resistance. Unfortunately for the future of democracy in Europe, this turn of events was far from unusual. In the period between the wars, a whole series of nations bowed before reactionary strongmen or kings, with the labor movement caught by surprise each time.

In Hungary, after the elimination of the short-lived Communist government of Bela Kun, Admiral Miklos von Horthy was elected regent on March 1, 1920. He did not immediately establish a personal power base, but his regime moved gradually toward the extreme right and into an alliance with the fascist powers. The fear of bolshevism and the aspirations of the territorial revisionists were major causes of this shift. Socialists fought bravely in rear guard actions but failed to halt the move to the right.

In Bulgaria the peasant leader Alexander Stambulisky undertook a program of agrarian reform and social legislation in cooperation with the urban proletariat. But this program collapsed when he was killed in a nationalist coup d'etat in 1923. His death was followed by a period of bloody chaos that ended only after King Boris III assumed a royal dictatorship in 1935, opening the way to collaboration with the Axis powers.

Political confusion also led to authoritarian takeovers on the Iberian Peninsula. In 1923 General Miguel Primo de Rivera established a dictatorship in Spain that ruled harshly in the beginning but eventually softened into a benevolent paternalism. Disillusioned former followers soon assembled a fascist opposition. Discouraged by his loss in a referendum and in ill health, de Rivera resigned in 1930; the way was then open for a test of strength between republicans and fascists, which culminated in the Spanish civil war. Neighboring Portugal moved slowly from a republican form of government toward a moderate dictatorship with the election of General Antonio Oscar de Fragoso Carmona as interim president in 1926 and president in 1928. Beginning in 1928, however, the government was dominated by Antonio de Oliveira Salazar, who became premier and dictator in 1932, and his conservative corporatist regime.

Democracy also failed to establish a foothold in the newly independent Baltic States. Lithuania was the first of them to adopt a fascist government, beginning in 1926 with the virtual dictatorships of Augustinas Voldemaras (1926-29) and Antanas Smetona (1929-39). In Estonia and Latvia a powerful labor movement developed, but it too submitted to fascist control in 1934.

The countries of southeastern Europe were no more receptive to democracy. In Greece, after a democratic interlude dominated by the conservative politician Eleutherios Venizelos, a military dictatorship was es-

tablished in 1936 under General Ioannis Metaxas. In February 1938 King Carol II took control of Rumania as the head of an authoritarian government. Neighboring Yugoslavia, torn by internal nationalistic strife, submitted to the rule of the Serbian King Alexander, who was assassinated in 1934 by a militant Croat, evidently armed by Italian Fascists. The country was subsequently dominated by the increasingly repressive government of Prime Minister Milan Stoyadinovich, who, like many other rightist leaders, offered his services to the Rome-Berlin Axis.

In Poland socialism also retreated before powerful nationalist forces. In 1926 the old national hero Marshal Jozef Pilsudski, a veteran of the labor movement, established an authoritarian government. His regime was far better than many others in Europe, tolerating opposition parties and a free press. To the disappointment of Socialists, however, Pilsudski pursued a conservative course; he valued national unity over social reform and refused to support any initiatives that might encourage partisan strife. Upon his death in May 1935, Pilsudski was succeeded by a military junta that shared his conservatism. Known as the "colonel's clique," this group brought the country into an uneasy coexistence with Nazi Germany.

This succession of setbacks for democracy would have been less important if the socialist parties of western Europe, with their enormous followings, had taken vigorous steps to deal with the world economic crisis. But they too remained hesitant and indecisive. Even the British Labor Party, which seemed more likely than any other socialist group to take power by parliamentary means, could offer no original remedy for the economic disarray.

A Labor government under Ramsay MacDonald, formed in June 1929, was in office when the Great Depression struck. For two years the minister of finance, Philip Snowden, watched helplessly as unemployment grew. Finally the government decided on a policy of deflation involving drastic budgetary cuts. Social services in particular were severely slashed. The result was widespread disillusionment among British workers. On August 25, 1931 the frustrated MacDonald admitted failure and resigned. A so-called National Union government was formed several days later and presided over again by MacDonald, who had broken with his party. The Laborites, severely shaken by MacDonald's defection, suffered one defeat after another in subsequent elections.

The Socialist International, which had hoped to construct a "world safe for democracy" from the ruins of World War I, was by now a spent force. In 1914 it had failed to halt the outbreak of war, and four years later it had had little effect on the peace-making process. In a number of countries the movement had proved incapable of saving parliamentary democracy. And, finally, it lacked direction in the face of the economic crisis.

In all of Europe, only the Scandinavian socialists had the energy and initiative to combat the Depression with economic controls. While German socialists wondered whether to cure the capitalist patient or let him die and pocket the legacy, the Scandinavians pragmatically applied the policies of the British economist John Maynard Keynes. Their success in alleviating unemployment and other economic hardships helped keep the Swedish socialists, under Per Albin Hanson, in power for decades. The successes of socialism in Scandinavia, however, were much less noted than its failures in Britain and other European states.

"The Great Light in the East"

As the Depression engulfed Europe, boding future catastrophes, the USSR prepared for its "great leap forward." Deeds of heroic scope had occurred there after the October Revolution, beginning with Leon Trotsky's creation of the Red Army, his defeat of the White Russians and the conclusion of peace from the Polish border to Vladivostok. The relatively liberal "New Economic Policy" then gave the Russians breathing space for several years. But in 1928, after securing absolute control over the Soviet states, Stalin decreed the first Five Year Plan—a gigantic adventure that was to affect profoundly the destinies of entire peoples.

At a time when parliamentary democracy seemed incapable of solving major problems, the Soviet government seemed to provide courageous and stable leadership. While ethnic and linguistic conflicts threatened to split apart many European states, Stalin succeeded in reuniting the diverse nationalities of the former Russian Empire. The vast, planned Soviet economy contrasted sharply with the crumbling economic systems of the West; Europeans, shocked by England's abandonment of the gold standard on September 21, 1931, watched the Soviets' coordinated industrial expansion. The USSR could proudly describe itself as a "country without unemployment," in the face of mass joblessness elsewhere.

The new prestige of the Soviet Union was dimmed by the Great Purge and the show trials of the late 1930s, with their death sentences and stories of preposterous conspiracies. Yet many Europeans remained dazzled by "the great light in the East." Certainly they saw no comparable sign of hope from the U.S., whose only notable contribution to world affairs was the Wall Street crash of 1929.

The Rising Sun of Japan

Most Europeans, preoccupied with their own economic problems, paid little attention to other parts of the world. In Asia, Japan had a free hand to expand its sphere of influence. We have already seen how World War I increased the power of Japan, like that of the United States, at the expense of the European states. From that point on, Japanese leaders worked constantly to enlarge their domain and prepare new enterprises. Like Germany in the late 19th century, Japan grew economically by flooding the world's markets with low-priced goods. Older industrial powers complained of "unfair" competition and sought to discredit Japanese products as inferior, but they could not match their low cost, enabled by cheap Japanese labor. "Made in Germany" gave way to "Made in Japan."

Here, then, was an energetic and ambitious nation on an overpopulated archipelago. If the Nazis based their propaganda on the need for "living space," Japan could make a similar claim with greater justification. In 1927 the Japanese statesman Baron Giichi Tanaka presented a memorandum outlining the necessity and plans for his country's expansion. History showed, he claimed, that empires form around vigorous nations able to bring neighboring lands under their control, to the benefit of all. His scheme involved spiritual as well as economic and military considerations, seeking as it did to preserve national unity through the Shinto religion and the cult of the emperor. With the Soviet Union absorbed in its industrialization and the United States in its isolation, Japan entered a course that would lead it through Pearl Harbor to the atomic holocaust of Hiroshima.

By 1930 the "good" years were over. Economically disorganized, politically fragmented and morally unsettled, Europe groped for solutions that only determined action could achieve. Unfortunately for the peace of the world, unscrupulous dictators and expansionist politicians were all too eager to provide their own solutions.

1931-1939: The Approaching Danger

The 1930s saw one last attempt to achieve a collective security system for Europe. This was the Geneva Disarmament Conference of 1932, presided over by former British Prime Minister Arthur Henderson.

Toward rearmament

Henderson arrived in Geneva following elections that had proved disastrous for his Labor Party. His experience at the conference hardly assured him of a satisfying end to his career. Although he obtained the Nobel Peace Prize for his efforts and asserted hopefully that the work of the conference would not be in vain, in the end it accomplished nothing.

The idea of armaments limitation was not new. After the end of World War I, a naval conference had met in Washington to codify a new equilibrium among the naval fleets of the great powers. The compromise finally accepted by all the participants provided that the British and Americans would each have a proportion of five, Japan a proportion of 3.5 and France and Italy 1.5 each. This was by no means a prelude to disarmament. The conference succeeded, however, in persuading Great Britain to renounce the principle of "two navies," which held that the British fleet must be stronger than any two following it. The United States had not yet achieved supremacy but its Navy was nevertheless on a par with Britain's.

Such arrangements found little support among pacifists, who insisted that armaments were in themselves a cause of war and that any reduction in their stockpiling would advance the prospects of peace. They asserted also that the huge expense of this unproductive materiel wasted resources that could be put to better use. Finally, they argued that since Germany had been disarmed and the safety of its neighbors consequently assured, and since the winners of World War I had promised to follow the loser in disarming themselves, there was no longer any reason for delay.

Preparations for the conference of 1932 were made with meticulous care. A number of experts tried to inventory each power's armaments. The calculations were enormously complex, especially since the conferees attempted to distinguish between offensive and defensive weapons. The meeting reached no agreement on any specific point, despite an avalanche of communiques.

If ever circumstances had favored true disarmament, the time had been immediately after World War I. By 1932 the tide had already turned, and once again the European states had begun to fear one another. No state really wanted to shoulder the burden of military budgets, but only Denmark had renounced arms, and its example had little effect. Once more the armaments manufacturers lived in luxury, as armies and navies vied to outdo each other in offensive and defensive capabilities.

Had Germany really disarmed? France began to doubt that even that proviso of the Versailles Treaty had been fulfilled. As a result, French leaders decided to set up a system of national security based not on agreements for collective action but on an impregnably fortified line of defense. Begun in 1930 the Maginot Line, named after the politician Andre Maginot, was a striking example of a military instrument that was obsolete even as it was being designed.

French military leaders based their calculations entirely on their experience in World War I, a war of position in which defensive strategy was supreme. They failed to take into account the potential of modern military technology. When the Germans attacked in 1940, the Maginot Line failed even to slow them down.

But few could foresee that the next conflict would not be fought under the same conditions as the previous one. Col. Charles de Gaulle tried to persuade several French cabinets that modern technology favored swift offensives. He failed for the most part, although he managed to convince Paul Reynaud, who in 1940 became president of the Council of the Republic. Reynaud, however, could not admit publicly that the gigantic sums spent on the Maginot Line were a complete waste and that a diametrically opposite strategy was required, nor could the National Assembly confess to its original stupidity.

Rearmament began at the crest of an economic crisis. Insecurity prevailed, for the League of Nations and international conferences were no longer thought capable of assuring a durable peace. Threats to the world order were at first vague, but came clearly into focus as time passed.

Cracks in the British Empire

These threats first appeared in the Far East. Europeans unquestionably underestimated the importance of Japanese expansion, since East Asia was far away. Although Australia alerted Britain of the danger, it doubted whether the Royal Navy, based in Singapore, was capable of defending the South Pacific and began to turn to the United States in search of naval protection in the event of Japanese aggression. The events of 1941 proved that fears for the continent were wellfounded. Ultimately, Australia was saved from invasion only because of American sea power.

The Dutch government, meanwhile, worried about Indonesia. Could this great colony stand off an extended siege with only a garrison of a few tens of thousands and a few warships based in Surabaja? Cabinet leaders had tried to convince the Dutch Parliament of the need for reinforcing the navy, but the Socialists and Communists had killed this proposal in 1923. Most citizens of the Netherlands had little interest in the colony and doubted the ability of the mother country to defend it.

The interwar period saw the decline of the British Empire which, for better or worse, became a commonwealth. Although this was not total disintegration, it was certainly a loosening of the ties binding the "white" former colonies to the mother country. In 1914 Great Britain was still able to declare war on Germany in the name of all its overseas possessions without first consulting them. Canada, New Zealand, Australia and to a lesser extent South Africa participated in the military effort. At the end of the war, however, they demanded much greater autonomy as the reward for their loyalty. In 1931 the Westminster Conference granted almost complete independence to the white dominions. The Ottawa Conference of the following year sought to cushion the effects of political decentralization by forming an economic association. A system of "imperial preferences" exempted Commonwealth members from import duties on goods shipped to Great Britain.

The Westminster and Ottawa conferences were an initial step toward decolonization. Yet they were probably not as important as observers believed at the time. For several years, trade within the Commonwealth actually fell as compared to trade between England and the Continent. The two conferences, moreover, involved only dominions speaking the English language, in which the Anglican Church was the dominant religious organization and the British parliamentary system of government prevailed. The word "Commonwealth" as used in the United Kingdom referred only to those nations. Yet problems of a different sort developed at the same time in Britain's largest nonwhite colony—India.

On the subcontinent, British rulers always followed the principle of "indirect rule," giving the greatest possible latitude to native Indian authorities in internal affairs. For many years it was common for Indians to study at British universities. The elements of an experienced national administration were gradually being assembled. Yet the Indian independence movement did not begin with this native elite. It crystallized instead around one of the most fascinating figures of the period, Mohandas Gandhi.

Both a spiritual and political leader, Gandhi ceaselessly pressed the anticolonialist struggle while attempting to elevate the morale of the country. An apostle of nonviolence and civil disobedience, he taught the Indian masses a discipline before which the British authorities were impotent. For example, groups of women would lie across railroad tracks to prevent a train from departing. Britain could not fail to be impressed by the man Churchill had called "this half-naked fakir." The world watched as Gandhi visited London to negotiate gradual decolonization; the talks failed, but his trip pricked the British conscience. Although Britain granted India complete independence only in 1947, events leading to this end were set in motion well before the war by Gandhi's constant appeals to ethics, fasting and "self-restraint." India remained quasi-neutral during World War II, emphasizing its aspiration to self-rule.

Japanese and Italian expansion

As the forces of independence gained momentum in India, the Japanese began establishing a protectorate of their own in Asia, but not without difficulty. In 1931 Japan invaded Manchuria, which had traditionally been within the Russian sphere of influence. Mukden was occupied in September. The following year Japan established a satellite state in the region called Manchukuo, ruled by a Japanese puppet who was a descendant of the old Manchu dynasty. And in 1937 an incident involving Chinese and Japanese took place in Peking, providing the Japanese with an excuse for further conquests. Japanese forces soon occupied all the large Chinese coastal centers, but they failed to gain control of the vast rural areas surrounding them. The Chinese themselves, exhausted by confusing battles among assorted warlords, managed to unite in a nationalistic fervor against the common enemy. The Communists and the Kuomintang Nationalist government concluded a truce, renouncing their "fight to the finish" until the Japanese could be driven into the sea.

Japan, however, resolutely attempted to consolidate its holdings on the Asian continent. A "New Order" for the Far East was officially proclaimed in 1938. The phrase was borrowed from the Nazi vocabulary, but it had a particular significance for Tokyo. Japanese leaders were establishing a Co-Prosperity Sphere under their control, comparable to the budding empires of Mussolini and Hitler with whom the Japanese had signed an anti-Comintern pact in 1936, forming a triumvirate known as the Axis. A government of Chinese collaborators was set up in Nanking. Japanese actions, however, aroused increasing alarm in the United States. In 1939 the federal government, prodded by the "China Lobby" in Washington, annulled a 1911 treaty guaranteeing Japan regular delivery of essential raw materials, especially oil. This was viewed as an act of economic war because of Japan's heavy dependence on foreign imports to augment its scarce mineral resources. Japanese military leaders began to consider countermeasures.

At about the same time, Italy expanded its East African possessions from Somaliland, declaring war against Emperor Haile Selassie of Ethiopia. The Italians launched a military campaign on October 3, 1936 and achieved a rapid victory, partly through the use of poison gas against defenseless Ethiopian troops. The Italian defeat of 1896 in the battle of Adowa was avenged. Fascist Italy could now consider itself a great power, especially since it also obtained favorable rectification of the frontiers of its Libyan colony.

But even an empire of this magnitude failed to satisfy Mussolini. Italian youth "spontaneously" flooded the streets, chanting "We want Corsica, Nice and Tunisia!'' Instead of these objectives, Italian leaders chose the poorly defended Kingdom of Albania. On April 7, 1939 Mussolini's troops landed in the domain of King Zog, who promptly fled his country. Once again, audacity paid off. Italy now occupied territory in Europe beyond its peninsula, with a bridgehead on the east bank of the Strait of Otranto—the springboard for a future campaign against Greece.

The world watched for the response of democratic Europe to these violations of international law. In each case, however, the League of Nations proved powerless. Japanese delegates at Geneva explained that their country's Chinese operations conformed to the league's charter. Conditions in the Far East, they said, threatened to degenerate into anarchy, and ample precedents had been set by the great democratic powers for quelling chaos in smaller or less powerful countries by colonizing them. The British and French, afraid to seem hypocritical, found this argument difficult to answer. A commission of inquiry headed by Lord Lytton was dispatched to the areas in question. Its report strongly criticized Japan, but no action was taken.

In Ethiopia, much closer to Europe, aggression was even more clear-cut. A member of the league had declared war on a fellow member, also on the pretext of internal disorder. Some rifle shots had been exchanged between Italian and Ethiopian soldiers at Wal-Wal, a point well within Ethiopian territory. After some weeks of negotiations whose only effect was to gain time for Mussolini, the conflict expanded. Emperor Haile Selassie was driven from his country and went to Geneva, where he presented his case. The embarrassed members of the league voted economic sanctions against Italy, but these proved totally ineffective. They merely provided Mussolini with an excuse for indignation, hastening his break with the league.

Expansion of Nazi Germany: The *Anschluss*
The most serious threats to peace were posed by Germany, where Hitler had assumed power in February 1933. He proceeded cautiously at first. His initial cabinet grew out of a coalition with the right, the so-called Harzburg Front, which gave him, for several months, much-needed respectability. Many observers believed that the fanatical Nazis, who had received a million fewer votes in the most recent election than in the preceding one, were finally checkmated by the conservatives. But once he had secured his position, Hitler ousted members of other parties from the cabinet and made it clear that wealthy industrialists would not determine government policies. The way was open for the construction of a totalitarian state.

The first step in this direction was the "Night of the Long Knives" in June 1934, directed against "revolutionary" elements among the brown-shirted Nazi storm troops—SA (*Sturmabteilung*). Many of the latter, including SA chief Ernst Roehm, had demanded greater emphasis on the "socialist" aspects of the Nazi program. Hitler crushed the movement with a series of executions and seized the occasion to liquidate moderate opposition groups in the same way. This brief bloodbath reassured the middle class and subdued the Nazi left, demonstrating that Germany would thenceforth have just one master.

In his foreign policy Hitler at first showed moderation. In 1934 he concluded a nonaggression pact with Poland, which was to be his first victim in World War II. For the moment, Europe was reassured; Hitler seemed less interested in foreign conquest than in domestic matters, particularly ending unemployment. Indeed, the German economy was reviving, due to a combination of factors—the slackening of the worldwide Depression, clandestine remilitarization and a far-reaching government construction program. Germany was the first country to develop a national highway system, which was admired by all of Europe. Seen in this context, the concentration camps in which the political opponents of Nazism were being "reeducated" seemed hardly to matter. This first "German miracle" was brought about largely by the modern pump-priming methods also practiced by Roosevelt's New Deal and the Scandinavian social democracies. Hjalmar Schacht, Hitler's economic adviser, was thoroughly acquainted with the principles of Lord Keynes.

Behind this facade of moderation, however, Hitler began to undermine the Versailles Treaty system and thus to alter the European balance of power. Compulsory military service was introduced in March 1935; the Locarno Pact was violated in March 1936 when Hitler sent in troops to occupy the demilitarized Rhineland. In August of that same year, the period of required military service was fixed at two years. The following month a plan for economic self-sufficiency was developed. Gradually, Germany was assembling the machinery of conquest; while building its military strength, however, it was for the moment carefully avoiding armed conflict.

The first object of Hitler's expansionist ambitions was Austria, his birthplace, where long-standing tensions erupted into civil strife in February 1934. Provoked by a local scuffle, socialist and clerico-fascist forces clashed in Vienna, whose working-class district was the target of devastating artillery fire for several days. Fighting also broke out in several provincial cities. It ended with the annihilation of the Austrian Social Democratic Party. The Christian Socialist government of Engelbert Dollfuss, deprived of the possibility of working-class support, tried vainly to mobilize a mass following through the creation of a patriotic front. The first Nazi thrust in Austria came on July 25 of the same year, when Austrian Nazis assassinated Dollfuss and attempted to seize power. But the coup failed to arouse any response in the strife-torn country. Mussolini, alarmed by the prospect of German expansion, concentrated Italian troops at the Brenner Pass on the Austrian border. Rather than risking armed conflict, Hitler backed down and dissociated himself from the coup.

Less than four years later, he was ready to try again. This time, however, there was no pretense of an internal uprising. Summoning Austrian Chancellor Kurt von Schuschnigg to his Berchtesgaden retreat, Hitler announced his intention of occupying the country. Would Schuschnigg, by ordering a military defense, seek to prevent the *Anschluss* and shed German blood? Schuschnigg capitulated. German troops marched into Austria on March 13, 1938 to the loud acclamations of crowds of Nazis. Austrian workers, traumatized by the civil war of 1934, made no move to resist.

Mussolini also accepted the *Anschluss*. Alienated from Britain and France by their resistance to his Ethiopian adventure, he felt less antipathy than earlier towards Hitler's ambitions in Central Europe.

War in Spain

The Western democracies meanwhile had other matters confronting them. Civil war had broken out in Spain, and they tried vainly to deal with its consequences. Since 1931 Spain had been a republic torn by dissension and civil strife. Conservative groups, supported by a majority of the upper class, the military and the ecclesiastic hierarchy, favored a restoration of the monarchy. This was bitterly opposed by the Spanish labor movement, itself divided among socialists, communists and anarchists. Power lay in the hands of the moderate left. In July 1936 the Spanish military rebelled against the government and moved to seize power for the conservatives. The leader of the rebel junta, Gen. Francisco Franco, enlisted most of the Army's high-ranking officers on his side and through them controlled a large part of the armed forces. The republicans, on the other hand, were unable to organize an effective defense. After a long struggle, the fighting ended in complete victory for Franco, and leading leftists fled the country.

The civil war not only set Spaniard against Spaniard, but also inflamed emotions throughout the world. Public opinion in every nation polarized on the issue of Franco's revolt; positions to be taken in the coming world war began to emerge. The USSR, seeking political advantage, shipped war materiel to the republican government. Germany supported Franco with both arms and bomber squadrons; the latter proved their destructive capacity in the bombardment of the Basque city of Guernica—the massacre immortalized in Picasso's famous painting. Italy also sent troops to fight on the rebel side. Many leftists fought for the republic, most of them in the "International Brigades" that saw action in Madrid and on the Catalan front. Even within these volunteer units, a violent and sometimes bloody rivalry developed between communists and their fellow soldiers. Experiences like these decisively affected the opinions of such leftist writers as Andre Malraux and George Orwell.

The Western democracies, for their part, tried vainly to limit the repercussions of the Spanish conflict. Britain, followed reluctantly by France, attempted to establish a policy of nonintervention that would isolate Spain from world politics. The effort failed; as one satirist noted, the democracies managed only to "refrain from intervening in the intervention of others." The League of Nations stayed aloof from the conflict, and Britain lost a little more of its prestige. That country's Conservative government, however, was in a strong position, with a solid majority in Parliament and general approval from the electorate. Such was not the case in France, where a Popular Front government had come to power in May 1936.

The Popular Front owed its origin to the events of February 1934, when a massive demonstration by fascist groups in Paris caused street fighting and shook not only the short-lived government of Edouard Daladier but the Third Republic itself. Urged on by labor leaders and workers, Communists and Socialists made common cause after the years of bitter hatred that had followed their schism at the Congress of Tours in 1920. With the republic in danger, a mass demonstration took place in Paris to support anti-fascist unity. Difficult negotiations between leaders of the two parties resulted in the formation of a Popular Front. In the elections of 1936 the front, supported by the Radical Party, won a smashing victory. Socialist leader Leon Blum became premier for the first time.

Blum's government had barely taken office before it was confronted by a wave of sit-down strikes by workers in Paris and other cities. Hurriedly conferring with union leaders and employers, Blum obtained agreement on a number of social issues, including paid holidays. With this understanding, the sit-down strikes ended, and the recently merged Socialist and Communist unions began to enroll millions of new members. Most of the new recruits, inexperienced in the politics of class struggle, were manipulated by the Communists in their effort to gain control of the unified trade union movement.

With the outbreak of war in Spain, Blum again faced a difficult situation. Politically and sentimentally he favored the Spanish republic, but he understood that French military intervention might trigger a European war. He felt, moreover, that he could not trust his own officers to move against Franco, their peer. Under these circumstances the Popular Front adopted the English policy of nonintervention. The Communists, who had refused to participate in the government, now accused the Socialists of betraying Spain. Forced into isolation, the Blum cabinet resigned.

Appeasement at Munich

At this time a more general problem confronted French Socialists: how to reconcile their traditional antimilitarism with the necessity of opposing fascism. If Hitler really wanted war, France would have to rearm. But the left was reluctant to do so, especially since the faith of many French officers in their own republic was so shaky. Rearmament, moreover, threatened several social gains won by the labor movement. A law setting the maximum work week at 40 hours had had the effect of slowing down the production of armaments, especially of military aircraft. Frequent strikes impaired production even more. The political movement most firmly opposed to fascism thus, ironically, weakened the material and psychological potential of the country's defense.

Hitler's victorious advances did not, therefore, result entirely from his leadership or the dynamism of his government. The exceptional confusion that reigned among his opponents was an important contributing factor. The hopes of the pacifists were frustrated by the failure of the League of Nations and the attempts at disarmament. Anti-fascists hesitated when forced to choose between their dread of dictatorship and their equal hatred of military violence. Socialists, defeated in Italy, Poland, Germany and Austria, were discredited in Great Britain and crushed by Franco in Spain. Communists remained suspect because of their fanatical faith in the Soviet system and their insistence on justifying even its worst aspects. Western parliamentary governments seemed paralyzed by a fatal spell inhibiting their every move and favoring the dictators. National minorities, disillusioned with democracy, drifted towards authoritarian solutions. A kind of passive nihilist mentality seized the Western world.

With circumstances so favorable, Hitler wasted no time in selecting the next target for his aggression—Czechoslovakia. Here he could exploit tensions between the dominant Czechs and other groups, most notably the German-speaking inhabitants of the Sudetenland. These frontier dwellers, who had been part of the dominant ethnic group under the Austrian Empire, had resented Czech rule from the start. During the Weimar Republic this sentiment had remained quiescent. With the rise of the dynamic Nazi regime, however, the Sudeten Germans saw their chance to escape from Czech domination. Demands for union with the Third Reich grew, and the Sudeten Party, headed by Konrad Henlein but manipulated by Hitler, welded the ethnic Germans of Czechoslovakia into a powerful force.

German agitation created a terrible dilemma for the Prague government. Its entire military defense system lay in the Sudetenland; loss of the territory would leave Czechoslovakia completely unprotected from German aggression. Soon Hitler, displaying the utmost contempt for his opponents, summoned British Prime Minister Neville Chamberlain to Berchtesgaden and Godesberg to present his demand for the annexation of the Sudetenland. The British government also sent an "expert," Lord Runciman, who concluded that Germany's complaint against Czechoslovakia was justified. Chamberlain opted to negotiate rather than fight for a doubtful cause.

After agreeing that the problem shoud be settled on an international basis, leaders of Britain, France, Italy and Germany met in Munich. On September 29, 1938 they signed an accord granting the Sudetenland to Germany. Czech representatives did not even participate in the conference; despite the guarantees of the French-sponsored Little Entente, Czechoslavokia was abandoned by the major powers.

It soon became apparent, however, that Hitler would not respect even the truncated Czechoslovakia left by the Munich Pact. German troops occupied Prague on March 16, 1939 and established a "Protectorate of Bohemia and Moravia." This time German aggression was not justified by the logic of nationalism, since it involved the occupation of a predominantly Slavic country. The unfortunate Czechs were left without even the appearance of autonomy later granted to other German puppet states.

Events then moved quickly toward war. One week after Czechoslovakia was occupied, Germany seized Memel, a former German territory granted to Lithuania after World War I. Here Hitler could also rationalize his action with nationalist arguments, for the Lithuanian administration had harshly oppressed the predominantly German population. Yet the move again demonstrated the falsity of his promise that his territorial claims would cease with the "liberation" of the Sudetenland. Those who had sincerely believed that they could save the peace by negotiating with Hitler began to realize their error. On March 17, speaking to his Conservative constituency in Birmingham, Chamberlain called upon his countrymen to be prepared to defend themselves in a long war. Britain made preparations to rearm. But Chamberlain continued to justify appeasement as a means of "gaining time" for the country's war effort.

War finally broke out less than one year after the conclusion of the Munich agreement, in a dispute over the status of Danzig. From a moral standpoint, the case was actually somewhat less clear-cut than that of the Sudetenland. The Polish government, which resisted Hitler's demand to annex Danzig, was not a democracy, as Czechoslovakia had been. Danzig's overwhelmingly German population solidly favored union with Germany, as had the Sudeten Germans. "Is it worth dying for Danzig?" the French fascist leader Marcel Deat asked insidiously. Yet for Britain and France the real question had become when to say "no" to Hitler's further demands, whatever their intrinsic justification.

The last months of peace

It is by no means certain that the democracies profited from the breathing space given them by the Munich accord, especially since Germany continued to build up its own armaments. The progress of the West's psychological preparation for war was also questionable. The British took it seriously; the French, however, floundered in despair.

The diplomacy of both countries during the last months of peace was characterized by vacillation and uncertainty. Sidney Aster, in *The Origins of the Second World War*, described French foreign policy as torn "constantly between defeatist panic and aggressive overconfidence." Britain, though ready to take the lead in dealing with Hitler, also suffered from a conflict between the pacifist Chamberlain on one side and the Foreign Office and Chiefs of Staff on the other. British war preparations took effect slowly; conscription was not introduced until May 18, 1939 and remained unpopular for some time afterwards. The stagnant indecision prevailing in the West contrasted sharply with the energy Hitler displayed in his march to war.

The military strategy of France and Britain involved enveloping Germany in a war on two fronts. Poland was the key to the eastern line of defense, but the Allies realized that in case of difficulties there they could not help the Poles to any significant extent. Even the idea of air assistance was rejected in a report by the Anglo-French Joint Planning Subcommittee, which stated, "Clearly, our primary military operations must be dictated from the outset by a search for the best means of contributing to the final defeat of Germany and not for the available means of aiding Poland, which is in fact impossible." Polish leaders, who knew in advance that they could expect little material help from the West, concluded that their best chance of survival lay in preserving peace as long as possible in keeping with their national honor. Thus they rejected the offer of an anti-German alliance with Rumania as too likely to provoke Hitler. A tight defensive alignment of Germany's neighbors never materialized. Neither Chamberlain nor the Poles, moreover, had any desire to seek Soviet help against the Nazi menace.

Soviet leaders meanwhile drew their own conclusions from these developments. Angered by his exclusion from the Munich conference and by obvious Western efforts to quarantine the USSR, Stalin decided to deal with Germany by himself. On May 4, 1939 the West was startled by the announcement that Vyacheslav Molotov had replaced Maxim Litvinov as Soviet foreign minister. Litvinov, a Jew, was closely associated with the Soviet Union's traditional anti-Nazi foreign policy. Familiar with the West and respected by his Western colleagues, he had brought the USSR into the League of Nations. Molotov was an unknown quantity, embodying the newly enigmatic Soviet policy.

Britain and France, sensing danger, slowly overcame their reluctance to negotiate with the USSR. On August 11 an Anglo-French military mission arrived in Moscow after traveling by ship to Leningrad. It was poorly prepared, however, and could not speak for Poland and Rumania, which refused to cooperate with Soviet forces under any circumstances. The gesture was too little and too late. If Britain and France had wanted to insult Stalin by demonstrating their distaste for discussions with him, they could not have chosen a better method.

Shortly afterwards the world was confronted with momentous news; the Soviet and German foreign ministers, Molotov and Joachim von Ribbentrop, had signed a friendship and nonaggression pact. Communists everywhere made a hasty about-face, dropping their efforts to consolidate anti-Nazi forces and denouncing war against Germany as an imperialist crime in which the working class must not participate. Many party members, revolted by this opportunistic policy reversal, left the movement. Yet Stalin's decision was only too comprehensible in view of the West's previous behavior.

The effect of the Nazi-Soviet Pact was to assure Hitler of noninterference from the east and to enable the USSR to establish a buffer zone on its western frontier. When Germany attacked Poland less than a month later, Soviet leaders not only refused to aid their neighbor, but took the opportunity to occupy the eastern half of the unfortunate country. Soviet forces also occupied the Baltic States and attacked Finland in an attempt to gain control of the territory north and west of Leningrad. The Finns resisted tenaciously in the so-called Winter War, costing the Red Army heavily in casualties and prestige. Overwhelming Soviet materiel superiority finally forced Finland to cede the military base of Petsamo and much of Karelia. When World War II came, however, it found Finland firmly in the German camp.

Despite its immediate advantages, the pact with Germany cost the USSR far more dearly than Stalin had anticipated. It permitted Hitler, for the moment, to send all his troops to the West; once his conquests there were completed he was able, with Operation Barbarossa in 1941, to bring the full force of the *Wehrmacht* to bear against the Soviet Union. Stalin had taken Hitler at his word; he had ignored Allied warnings of the impending invasion, and when it happened, he was taken completely by surprise.

If Britain and France had realized earlier that their attempts to "encircle" Germany through paper alliances like the Little Entente were hopeless, would they have acted in time to enlist the USSR in a viable system of collective security? Or if Hitler had listened seriously to Chamberlain's warnings that an attack on Poland would precipitate war with Britain, would he have decided to risk everything for Danzig? We can only guess. Hitler's adversaries straggled to battle poorly prepared, without a common plan of action. Even the Grand Alliance of Britain, the USSR and the United States was initially only a collection of states struggling desperately to resist defeat. The outbreak of war left many Europeans in despair. The West seemed to be in decline and the Soviet Union on the point of disintegration. Nothing appeared to stand in the way of a Nazi victory. Only the British miracle—it might better be called the Churchillian miracle—kept all of Europe from falling under Hitler's control.

Hendrik Brugmans

THE
HISTORICAL
ENCYCLOPEDIA
OF
WORLD WAR II

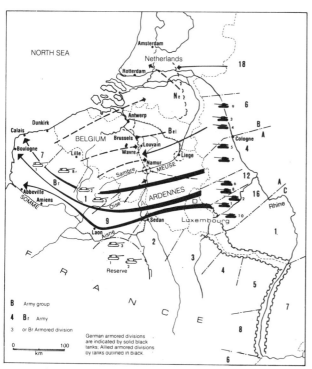

NORTH SEA

Amsterdam

Netherlands

Rotterdam

18

Ne

6

Antwerp

BELGIUM

Brussels

Louvain

Be

Cologne

B

A

Dunkirk

Calais

Boulogne

7

Lille

Wavre

Namur

Liege

4

Br

Sambre

MEUSE

12

A

16

C

Abbeville

Amiens

1

Oise

ARDENNES

D

Rhine

SOMME

9

Sedan

Luxembourg

1

Laon

Aisne

2

3

F

Reserve

R

4

5

A

N

7

B Army group

4 **Br** Army

3 or Br Armored division

C

E

8

German armored divisions
are indicated by solid black
tanks; Allied armored divisions
by tanks outlined in black.

0   100

km

6

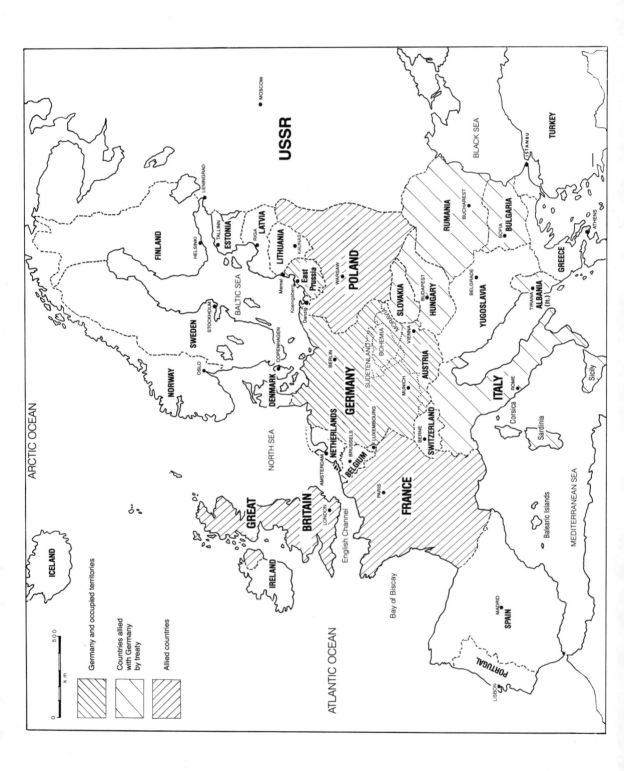

ARCTIC OCEAN

ICELAND

ATLANTIC OCEAN

GREAT
BRITAIN
LONDON

IRELAND

English Channel

Bay of Biscay

PORTUGAL
LISBON

SPAIN
MADRID

Balearic Islands

MEDITERRANEAN SEA

Sardinia

Corsica

Sicily

ITALY
ROME

FRANCE
PARIS

SWITZERLAND
BERNE

LUXEMBOURG

BELGIUM
BRUSSELS

NETHERLANDS
AMSTERDAM

NORTH SEA

GERMANY
BERLIN
MUNICH

AUSTRIA
VIENNA

BOHEMIA
SUDETENLAND

MORAVIA

SLOVAKIA

HUNGARY
BUDAPEST

YUGOSLAVIA
BELGRADE

ALBANIA
(It.)
TIRANA

GREECE
ATHENS

BULGARIA
SOFIA

RUMANIA
BUCHAREST

BLACK SEA

TURKEY
ISTANBU

DENMARK
COPENHAGEN

NORWAY
OSLO

SWEDEN
STOCKHOLM

BALTIC SEA

POLAND
WARSAW

Danzig
Koenigsberg

East
Prussia

Memel

LITHUANIA
KAUNAS

LATVIA
RIGA

ESTONIA
TALLINN

FINLAND
HELSINKI

LENINGRAD

USSR
MOSCOW

0 500
km

Germany and occupied territories

Countries allied
with Germany
by treaty

Allied countries

A

ABC PLANS.

In February and March 1941, while the **United States** was still nominally neutral, a staff mission from the **United Kingdom** visited Washington, D.C. and drafted plans for cooperation between the two countries in the event that the U.S. joined the war. The main point agreed upon was that if the two powers found themselves at war both with **Germany** and with **Japan**, Germany should be dealt with first, by **blockade**, bombing and subversion; the defeat of Japan was to take second priority.

ABDA.

The name given to the ad hoc supreme command over American, British, Dutch and Australian forces in Southeast Asia, exercised by **Archibald Wavell** during the two disastrous months of January and February 1942. The original idea was **Marshall**'s and Wavell was supposed to report directly to the Combined Chiefs of Staff; **Churchill** continued, however, from force of habit, to send him orders directly. Staff officers were delighted when ABDA was dissolved at the end of February.

ABE, Nobuyuki (1879-1953).

Japanese general, statesman and prime minister from August 1939 to January 1940. As prime minister, Abe resisted pressures from his own army to ally with **Germany** and the **USSR** against the **United States** and the **United Kingdom**. He and **Kichisaburo Nomura**, the Japanese foreign minister, tried to be more accommodating than their predecessors toward the United States and Britain concerning commerical rights in **China**. But American officials, as well as certain factions within the Japanese leadership, objected, and so the U.S. - Japanese treaty of commerce was allowed to lapse. The army, which had helped install Abe, soon withdrew its support, and his cabinet collapsed. Abe later served in the house of peers and helped lead the **Imperial Rule Assistance Association** after 1940.

ABEMAMA (APAMAMA).

See **Gilbert Islands**.

ABETZ, Otto (1903-1958).

German intellectual to whom the **Nazi Party** gave the responsibility of maintaining contacts with France in 1933. Expelled in 1938 by the French government, he returned to Paris after the German occupation in June 1940 as ambassador to the wartime government. Abetz played an important role in negotiations with **Francois Darlan** and **Laval** (see **French State**). Because of his opposition to Nazi excesses, he was recalled in October 1944 by **Ribbentrop**. The French condemned Abetz to 20 years at hard labor; he was freed in 1954. In 1951 he published *Das offene Problem*, an account of his activity in France.

ABRIAL, Jean (1879-1962).

French admiral. Abrial cooperated with the British in the evacuation from Dunkirk in 1940. In 1940-41 he was governor general of Algeria. Abrial was appointed secretary of the navy and commander of naval forces by **Laval** on November 18, 1942. In 1946 the French High Court sentenced him to 10 years at hard labor for his **collaboration** with the Nazis.

ABWEHR.

The *Abwehr (Amt Auslandsnachrichten und Abwehr)* was the information-gathering and counterespionage service of the OKW. This well-organized operation was established, in violation of the provisions of the Versailles Treaty, soon after the Nazis gained power in 1933. Naval officer **Wilhelm Canaris** was named its chief in 1935. He was promoted to vice admiral in 1936.

Under Canaris' direction the *Abwehr* rose to exceptional heights of efficiency, but it soon began to encounter interference from **Heydrich**'s **SD**, which was responsible for providing information services to the German army. The SD trespassed with increasing frequency on the *Abwehr's* private domain in the performance of special duties (see **Venlo**).

As a result of the two groups' overlapping functions, Canaris and Heydrich developed an intense rivalry. Heydrich gained the upper hand when, on September 27, 1939, he was placed in charge of the **RSHA**, the organization coodinating the police and security operations of the Reich and the **Nazi Party**, under the supervision of **SS** Reichsfuehrer **Himmler**.

Heydrich's assassination on May 27, 1942 temporarily improved Canaris' situation. Himmler, however, distrusted Canaris, and on February 18, 1944 he obtained an order from **Hitler** dismissing Canaris and incorporating the German army's information services into the RSHA; the resulting organization was called *Militarische Amt*. The expiration of the *Abwehr* was symptomatic of the constant interference by government bureaucrats in matters of intelligence, as well as the friction between the SS (of which the SD and the RSHA and, later, the *Militarische Amt* were part) and the German armed forces. The rivalry between the secret-service agencies seriously affected their efficiency.

(It was as a result of these conflicts that the spy Paul Thuemmel managed to escape the surveillance of the **Gestapo** in Prague for over six months before his arrest on March 20, 1942. A recipient of the gold medal of the Nazi Party and *Haupt-V-Mann* of the *Abwehr,* Thuemmel had anonymously offered his services to the intelligence section of the Czech army on February 8, 1936. He became its agent A-54 and subsequently furnished abundant and precise information to its staff, which had fled to London after the entry of German troops into Bohemia and Moravia (see **Bohemia-Moravia**). Thuemmel was executed on April 27, 1945 without a trial in the fortress of Terezin. Although his motives for betraying the Fuehrer were obscure, Thuemmel no doubt found the climate in the *Abwehr* hospitable to his espionage activities.)

Himmler's distrust of Canaris was, in fact, justified; Canaris had adopted a hostile attitude toward Hitler in 1938. He subsequently extended protection to plotters against the government at the same time that he pursued espionage activities against the enemies of the Third Reich. The reasons for his participation in the **Resistance** against Hitler are difficult to fathom; the contradictions in his complex maneuvers becloud his psychology.

R. Gheysens

ABYSSINIA.
See **Ethiopia**.

AIRBORNE DIVISIONS.
These large units, which made parachute jumps and glider landings only occasionally, fought as normal infantry divisions once they landed. They possessed a significant advantage: their high *strategic* mobility permitted them to mount surprise attacks, which damaged the morale of enemy troops and civilians; the threat of such attacks forced enemies to spread their defenses over large areas in order to guard vital centers. On the other hand, these divisions had weak tactical mobility; they rapidly lost their effectiveness on the ground because they did not have access to motorized transportation, their armaments were light and supplying them with provisions and reinforcements was difficult. They were completely dependent on air support, which requires air superiority and favorable meteorological conditions, and their use demanded that large air units be diverted from their normal missions. They represented, in short, an asset both dangerous and fragile.

Major missions carried out by the airborne divisions were, first, to overpower by surprise fortified positions, isolated bases, geographic points suitable for cutting off lines of enemy retreat or other nerve centers, and, second, to paralyze enemies' reserve forces, cut their communications and attack their flank or rear.

Large airborne units can only be used under certain conditions. The air cover must be strong enough to assure control of their transport, their protection and their provisioning—this last should be made available as soon as possible. The airborne operation should not be initiated unless it may prove to be decisive, either tactically or strategically. Airborne units should be used only in massive concentrations. (In 1944, on the western front, only airborne units consisting of entire divisions were used; in **Burma** it was Gen. **Orde Wingate**'s highly effective airborne force that broke the back of the Japanese defense.) The effect of surprise must be such that the enemy is incapable of disrupting the landing procedures and that the objectives can be attained; the enemy's forces, especially its armored units, the most formidable opponents for sparsely armed airborne troops, should be thin in the landing areas. (Both of these requirements obviously place a premium on **reconnaissance**.) And finally, contact between air and ground forces should be made as soon as possible, except in special cases (as in Burma, where a vast space was occupied by few enemy troops and Wingate's forces, supplied from the air, conducted rear actions for many weeks). Experience has shown as well that land communications should be established immediately. Even the three-day maximum suggested by some authorities is risky. Certainly this was true in 1939-45 (and it will probably be even more vital in the future).

In 1944 a British airborne division consisted of a headquarters (glider); a reconnaissance unit with jeeps (glider unit); an independent company of paratroopers (the "Pathfinders"); two parachute infantry brigades, each made up of three battalions; a field artillery regiment with 24 pieces; two antitank batteries and an antiaircraft battery (glider); two companies of engineers, with signal equipment, and such services as medical, transportation, orderlies, workshops and military police. The actual strength of an airborne division was rarely more than 9,000 men.

The U.S. airborne division was organized much the same way. It should be recalled that the American infantry regiment is comparable to the British brigade. Some U.S. airborne divisions had four infantry regiments, perhaps three of which were parachutists and the fourth a glider.

The combination of glider troops and infantry parachutists within the division permitted the advantages of one to compensate for the disadvantages of the other. The disadvantage of parachutists was that they arrived on the ground in a dispersed state. A company required 15 minutes—at a minimum, under ideal weather conditions—to regroup and to assemble its weapons. Lightly armed, they were defensively weak. However, parachutists had a wider choice of landing terrain (dropping zones) than glider-borne troops. The advantage of the latter was that they could land as intact groups—companies or platoons, with heavy guns at their disposal. A company could assemble in five minutes—under ideal conditions—and with the glider as a carrier of heavy equipment, its troops were fully equipped with support weapons and vehicles, which gave them more offensive and defensive power than that of the parachutists. The glider could make its approach to the landing area silently because it cut loose from the aircraft towing it at great distances from the target landing— giving its occupants the further advantage of surprise, usually denied to parachutists. Gliders needed a landing zone smaller than that needed by powered aircraft. The gliders, however, had the definite disadvantage of vulnerability while they were being towed, since they were then incapable of evasive tactics, and were utterly helpless once on the ground. Moreover, their personnel offered a compact target for enemy fire.

In 1940 the Germans had only one airborne and air-transported division but managed this reduced force with consummate skill. In **Poland**, paratroopers were dropped in small groups on the enemy rear to carry out **sabotage**. In **Norway**, they were used to capture airports, with airborne infantry arriving afterward as reinforcements. **Hitler** reserved use of the silent glider attack for the invasion of **Belgium** in May 1940; the panic induced among green troops by the sudden arrival of men armed to the teeth, a mixture of live parachutists and dummies, made possible the rapid successes of the German troops at Eben-Emael and the bridges of the Albert Canal. (See also *Fall Gelb*.)

Their lack of airborne strength and sufficient air transport kept the Germans from executing vertical envelopments en masse. Hitler regretted his inability to launch several airborne divisions followed by air-

transported divisions against the East Anglian peninsula. The Crete expedition was the last success of German airborne troops. But it proved so costly that the Fuehrer lost confidence in the airborne operation, to the point that he refused to employ it against **Malta**.

In 1945, on the other hand, the Anglo-American alliance had six airborne divisions, five of them in Europe, along with several independent brigades and regiments of parachutists. Airborne troops were always used en masse: three divisions during the **Normandy landing**, three and a half in **the Netherlands**, two to cross the Rhine. They were grouped in corps. Toward the end of the summer of 1944, an air-transported army was activated under Gen. **Lewis Brereton** with its own transport aircraft.

H. Bernard

AIRBORNE TROOPS.

The following distinctions among different categories of airborne troops used by the Allies are important: paratroop divisions, using parachutes and gliders, and **airborne divisions**, large units transported by air, both engaged in mass actions; parachute units such as the British **Special Air Service** (SAS), on the other hand, were designed for small-scale operations. A third category, the **Jedburgh** teams and operational groups, and a fourth, agents dropped by parachute for special missions, were also utilized.

AIRCRAFT—Characteristics.

Definitions of some important terms relating to aircraft must precede a discussion of the aircraft themselves. First, *theoretical range* refers to the distance an aircraft is capable of flying on a full fuel tank, assuming excellent weather conditions, a speed (that varies with altitude) resulting in optimum fuel use and no piloting or navigational error.

An airplane's *operational range* is naturally lower than its theoretical range, since the calculation of this figure takes into account the maneuvers required to get the plane into formation and to operate it tactically in a combat zone. Operational range is usually about 25% lower than theoretical range.

Radius of action is estimated at roughly three-eighths of the operational range for fighters and one-half the range for bombers or transport planes carrying paratroops or towing gliders. (Fighter planes obviously perform more evasive maneuvers than bombers.) The radius of action for transport aircraft is calculated on the assumption that they will land and refuel at their destination. It is naturally reduced when bomb or personnel loads are increased. The radius of action for bombers can, depending upon the weight of the bombs carried, be safely computed at half the operational range. If a bomber has an operational range of 1,000 miles while carrying three tons of bombs, its radius of action will be at least 500 miles. Under actual circumstances this plane's operational range would exceed 1,000 miles; before its return flight it would of course have jettisoned all its bombs.

Finally, *flight time* is the maximum time a plane can remain in the air on a full fuel tank.

The Early Years—An Overview

In 1940 no bomber used by either the Allies or the **Axis** powers had a radius of action of 1,000 kilometers (620 miles). Except for the British Wellington Mark I, none could carry a bomb load of over two tons. With the exceptions noted below, none of the bombers had four engines. The radii of action of the British single-seaters Spitfire and Hurricane and the German Messerschmitt 109 was less than 250 miles. Twin-engine two-seater fighters such as the British Blenheim Mark IV F and Beaufighter and the German Messerschmitt 110 had somewhat longer radii of action than the single-seaters. In the Middle East the British used the obsolete Gladiator fighter, equipped with four machine guns, which could fly about 240 miles per hour. The Royal Navy depended primarily on the single-engine bomber Swordfish, an aircraft-carrier plane with a radius of action of about 200 miles and a bomb load of 1.5 tons, and the four-motored seaplane Sunderland, a bomber and **reconnaissance** plane with a radius of action, when it carried no load, of about 1,000 miles.

At the beginning of the 1930s the Italian air force had acquired a brilliant reputation, reflecting the glory of **Italo Balbo's** crossing of the South Atlantic with his group of Savoya-Marchetti planes. But in the 1940s it was deplorable, in part because the Fascist government had squandered so much money on the Ethiopian campaign and the Spanish civil war. The characteristics of the Italian aircraft in World War II are consequently irrelevant.

The Development of German Aircraft

Before 1944 there were no sensational developments in German aircraft design. Among the earlier planes the following stand out: the Focke-Wulf 190 fighter, which appeared in 1942 and which had a radius of action of about 375 miles and a maximum speed of 375 miles per hour and was armed with four cannon and two machine guns; the Dornier 217 bomber, which appeared at the end of 1941, with a radius of action of 500 miles and a maximum speed of about 300 miles per hour, armed with six machine guns and capable of carrying three tons of bombs; and a transport plane, the three-engine Junker 52, with a speed of 125 miles

per hour, a range of 550 miles and a capacity of 92 passengers.

At the beginning of 1945, **Germany's** first **jet aircraft** entered combat.

The Development of British and American Aircraft

British fighters included the excellent Typhoon and the various Tempests derived from it, which had a maximum speed of 425 miles per hour. These aircraft, armed with machine guns and cannon or rocket launchers (twelve 25-pounders for the Typhoon), and capable of carrying a bomb load, were among the best of the fighter-bombers.

In 1944 the British introduced the Gloster Meteor, a twin-engine jet aircraft with a maximum speed of 600 miles per hour and a ceiling of 45,000 feet. The Gloster Meteor was armed with four 20-mm cannon and eight rockets; alternatively, it could carry a bomb load of 2,000 pounds. It was used primarily against the German V-1 rockets.

As they intensified bombing attacks against Germany and **Japan** (see **Germany, Air Battle of; Japan, Air War Against**), the Americans began manufacturing escort fighters with increasingly greater radii of action. The P-47N Thunderbolt was introduced in 1943. A twin-engine plane, its radius of action (with an auxiliary fuel tank) was 475 miles, its maximum speed 450 miles per hour and its ceiling 40,000 feet. The P-47N Thunderbolt was armed with six to eight machine guns, six to 10 rocket launchers and 2,000 pounds of bombs.

In January 1944 the **United States** introduced the P-38L Lightning. This twin-engine craft had a radius of action of 575 miles, a maximum speed of 475 miles per hour and a ceiling of 40,000 feet. It was armed with four machine guns and one 20-mm cannon; later models could also carry a bomb load of 3,200 pounds.

The single-engine P-51H Mustang, introduced in February 1944, had a radius of action of 850 miles, a maximum speed of 475 miles per hour and a ceiling of 42,000 feet. Armed with six machine guns, it was capable of carrying 2,000 pounds of bombs.

The estimated radii of action of the three airplanes listed above are calculated on the assumption that they were carrying bombs and rockets; when used as fighters, their loads were much lighter, and consequently their radii of action were much greater.

All of these aircraft were fighters that could be pressed into service as fighter-bombers when supplied with a bomb load. However, the redoubtable British twin-engine Mosquito series, the masterpiece of the British aircraft designer de Havilland, were designed for use as fighters, fighter-bombers (in some cases carrying 2.5 tons of bombs), night fighters and reconnaissance and observer craft. Their extremely long radii of action were more than sufficient to enable them to bomb Berlin with ease—the distance from London to Berlin is 540 miles. Their maximum speed was 400 miles per hour and their ceiling 40,000 feet. They were typically armed with four 20-mm cannon, eight rockets and bombs.

Allied bombers included the twin-engine American B-25 Mitchell, introduced in 1941, and B-26F Marauder, introduced in 1942, with maximum bomb loads of two tons and 1.5 tons respectively; both were designed for use solely as bombers. The U.S. Navy's twin-engine seaplane Catalina served both as a bomber and as a reconnaissance aircraft. Without bombs its radius of action was better, at 1,250 miles, than that of most others.

After 1942 both the British and Americans accelerated their production of heavy four-engine bombers. The British models were the Stirling and the Halifax, which eventually evolved into the Halifax VII, whose radius of action was 750 miles while carrying three tons of bombs and about 425 miles with six tons. Also of British manufacture was the Lancaster, the best of the bomber models. Later models of the Lancaster were capable of carrying a five-ton bomb load within a radius of action of 1,100 miles, seven tons within a radius of about 875 miles and 10 tons within a radius of 550 miles. The Americans relied most heavily on the B-17 Flying Fortress. It could carry four tons of bombs; the F and G models could carry a bomb load of two tons over a radius of action of 1,100 miles. The U.S. also had the B-24 Liberator, carrying four tons (2.5 tons in a radius of action of 1,250 miles), and the B-29 Superfortress, whose B model had a bomb-load capacity of 10 tons—7.5 tons within a 1,800-mile radius of action and four tons within a radius of 2,000 miles. Without bombs the Superfortress had a radius of 2,500 miles, its maximum speed was 400 miles per hour and it carried a crew of 11 men. Depending on the particular model, the B-29 was armed either with 10 machine guns and a 20-mm cannon or 12 machine guns.

By the end of the war the Allies were using the following aircraft as transports for materiel and men: the British Stirling, Albemarle, and Halifax (which had a range of 2,500 miles) and the American C-47B Skytrain, the military DC-3 or Dakota—a twin-engine plane capable of carrying 20 men or a jeep as well as a 75-mm cannon over a range of 1,100 miles with a maximum speed of 260 miles per hour—and the C-53 Skytrooper, for evacuating casualties. Especially long-range craft were the C-548 Skymaster and the military DC-4, carrying 50 passengers or 7.5 tons of materiel over a range of about 2,500 miles at a maximum speed of 260 miles per hour. Refitted B-24's were also used as transports.

In addition to powered aircraft, the Allies had gliders. Among them were the American CG-4A Wacco, which could carry 15 men, and the CG-10A Wacco, which could carry a jeep or artillery piece or an armored car with its personnel, as well as the British Horsa, accommodating 32 men, and the various Hamilcar models, one of which could carry a light tank or armored tractor armed with a 17-pound cannon and the vehicle's personnel.

Reconnaissance aircraft were generally fighters or bombers adapted for photography missions. The RP-38 Lightning, for example, was equipped with five or six cameras, each able to photograph land areas of nearly 2,000 square miles at a scale of 1:50,000; of 575 square miles at 1:25,000; of nearly 200 square miles at 1:12,000 and of about 100 square miles at 1:8,000.

The Development of Soviet Aircraft

By 1941 the Soviet aircraft industry had overcome its sluggishness of the 1930s and expanded considerably. The quality of its materiel was, however, not quite satisfactory.

Among the Soviet aircraft in service at the beginning of the war, the I-16 (Rata) was the fighter in greatest use, with a maximum speed of 300 miles per hour and radius of action of 250 miles. Other included the Lagg-3, with a maximum speed of 350 miles per hour and a radius of 175 miles, as well as the Mig-3 and the Yak-1, all of them simple, sturdy, but lightly armed.

Among the Soviet bombers were the single-seater IL-2 Stormovik, an assault plane of which more than 36,000 were made, and the twin-engine Pe-2, with a maximum speed of about 325 miles per hour, the plane most often used during the war both as a bomber and for reconnaissance.

On the whole, Soviet designers devoted little attention to the development of heavy and medium bombers, except as support for ground troops. Beginning in 1942-43, however, the plants dismantled in the western part of the USSR and reassembled in the Urals were highly productive; their materiel, moreover, was more modern. Anglo-American aid helped fill in the gaps. The production effort was concentrated on fighter and ground-support planes.

The La-5 and Yak-9, with maximum speeds greater than 375 miles per hour, were usually armed with machine guns and 20-mm cannon and used as fighters. The IL-2 Stormovik developed into a two-seater with heavier armament and body armor. It carried two fixed cannon of 20 or 23 mm, three machine guns, a rocket launcher and a bomb load that varied, in different situations. In 1944 the IL-10 made its appearance. Equipped with a 2,000-horsepower motor, it had a speed greater than 300 miles per hour and a bomb capacity of one ton plus cannons and rocket launchers. Another tactical bomber was the Tu-2, a twin-engine plane with a maximum speed of nearly 350 miles per hour, a radius of action of about 625 miles and a bomb load of two tons.

More modern equipment was called into service at the end of the war—the La-7, with a maximum speed of 400 miles per hour and a radius of action of 200 miles, and the fastest plane, the Yak-3, with a radius of action of more than 300 miles and the firepower of two 13-mm and one 20-mm cannon; the maximum speed of the Yak-3U was 450 miles per hour.

The only heavy Soviet bomber comparable to those of the Western Allies was the Pe-8, a four-engine aircraft with a five-ton bomb capacity and a 1,250-mile range. It was not until the war's end that the Soviets bolstered their strategic air power with the TU-4, an exact copy of the American B-29.

For transport planes, the standard Russian model was the Li-2, a version of the American Dakota craft built in the USSR.

The Development of Japanese Aircraft

The best-known Japanese fighter, in use even before the beginning of the war with the United States, was the Mitsubishi A6M, better known as the Zero. The Allies' code name for it was "Zeke." With an exceptional radius of action (some 750 miles), excellent speed (350 miles per hour) and surprising maneuverability, it was to the Japanese what the P-51 Mustang was to the Americans, the Spitfire to the British, or the Messerschmitt 109 to the *Luftwaffe*. Its armament, depending on the specific model, included one or two machine guns in the upper part of the plane's fuselage and two 20-mm cannon in the wings, as well as air-to-air rockets or a bomb load of 500 to 1,000 pounds for a **kamikaze** ("suicide") mission. By the end of the war, more than 10,000 Zeroes had been built. The Ki-27, the Japanese aircraft that had been used in Manchuria to support ground troops, was supplanted by the Hayabusa Ki-43, whose Allied code name was "Oscar." The first models of this plane required numerous modifications. The final version, however, became one of the best performers for the Japanese air force on all fronts. It was armed with two machine guns (two 20-mm cannon in the III-b model) plus two 65-pound bombs. Its maximum speed was 300-350 miles per hour, depending on the model, and its radius of action was 375-925 miles. Some 6,000 were built.

Another interceptor largely used in the battle for command of the air was the Hayate Ki-84, with excellent specifications: its maximum speed was 385

miles per hour and its radius of action 500-625 miles. Although it did not come into use until 1944, more than 3,500 were produced, in several versions.

To combat night bombing raids by American B-29s on their home islands in 1944, the Japanese had only the Kawasaki Ki-45 Toryu, known to the Allies as "Nick," a twin-engine fighter and ground-attack plane, first built in 1941 and converted to a night fighter (the Ki-45 Kai-c) in 1944. With a maximum speed of 335 miles per hour, the Ki-45 was capable of climbing to a 33,000-foot ceiling; its radius of action was 625 miles. It was armed with two machine guns or two 20-mm cannon mounted in its nose, a belly-mounted cannon of 20 or 37 mm and a machine gun aft. Some models carried two 150-pound bombs.

The interceptor aircraft J2M-5 Raiden (çode-named "Jack") appeared in 1945. Designed for naval operations, it was a modernized version of the J2M-2 and J2M-3. It had great potential for air defense, but too few came into action too late to challenge the B-29s effectively. Armed with four 20-mm wing cannon, with a maximum speed of more than 375 miles per hour, the J2M-5 could climb to an altitude of 6,000 miles in six minutes and 20 seconds. Its radius of action was 375-435 miles, depending on the model.

Among the Japanese bombers used by the naval air forces was the Mitsubishi G3M ("Nell"), which appeared in 1941. With a maximum speed of about 250 miles per hour and a radius of action in excess of 1,250 miles, it was adaptable for use as a transport. It was well armed, with six machine guns and a 20-mm cannon in retractable dorsal, ventral and side turrets, and carried an 1,750-pound load of bombs.

Best known of the Japanese bombers was the Mitsubishi G4M ("Betty"). More of these planes were manufactured than any other bomber in the Japanese air arm; it participated in actions from **Australia** to the **Aleutians**, from the first day of the war until August 19, 1945, when the Japanese delegation authorized to surrender took the final wartime flight on two G4Ms. It was ground-based; used for training, reconnaissance and transport, it had a complement of seven to 10 men, a maximum speed of 290 miles per hour and a radius of action of 1,250 to 1,850 miles, depending on the model. It carried one or two nose-mounted machine guns, one 20-mm cannon in the dorsal turret, two machine guns or 20-mm cannon in the side turrets, one 20-mm cannon in the tail, and 1,750 pounds of bombs or torpedoes, or, on occasion, an Okha suicide ship.

Another bomber was the twin-engine Mitsubishi Ki-21 ("Sally"). Considered a heavy bomber, it doubled as a transport (in this capacity it was known as the MC-1). It was the standard bomber of the Japanese army, with the following specifications:

maximum speed, 300 miles per hour; radius of action, 800 miles; armament, one machine gun in the nose, one on the side of the fuselage, another on the dorsal surface and a fourth in the tail assembly. Its maximum bomb load was 2,200 pounds.

The Mitsubishi Ki-67 Hiryu (''Peggy''), also classed as a heavy bomber, was used in both land and sea action. It had a maximum speed of 325 miles per hour and a maximum radius of action of 1,175 miles; it was armed with one machine gun each in the nose, on the sides of the fuselage and in the tail turret, as well as a 20-mm cannon in the dorsal turret. Normally loaded with up to 1,750 pounds of bombs or torpedoes, it carried about 6,400 pounds of bombs when used for a suicide mission.

An aircraft used for air-sea missions was the twin-engine Nakajima B5N bomber (''Kate''), used in the attack on **Pearl Harbor**. It was replaced in 1944 by the B6N Tenzan (''Jill''), with a maximum speed of 225 miles per hour and a maximum radius of action of 625 miles. It was armed with one machine gun and carried a bomb or torpedo load of 1,750 pounds. Another model of the B6N, used as a bomber, had two machine guns, one of them mounted on the plane's belly, and a bomb or torpedo load of 1,750 pounds. Its top speed was 290 miles per hour and its radius of action 925 miles.

H. Bernard

AIR WARFARE.

See **Airborne Divisions; Airborne Troops; Aircraft—Characteristics; Aviation, Strategic Anglo-American (in Europe); Aviation, Tactical Anglo-American (in Europe); Britain, Battle of; Civil Defense; Germany, Air Battle of; Japan, Air War Against; Jet Aircraft; Kamikaze; Radar; V-1 and V-2.**

ALAMEIN.

See **El Alamein.**

ALAM EL HALFA.

A ridge in the Egyptian desert 55 miles southwest of Alexandria, Alam el Halfa was the scene of **Rommel's** final attack of the war in the Sahara. Gen. **Claude Auchinleck** and later **Montgomery** foresaw a German offensive through the area, and a heavy line of defense was prepared to meet it. The attack lasted from August 31 through September 5, 1942. British troop and tank dispositions, deep minefields and Montgomery's personality, which inspired the defense, brought about an Allied victory. Rommel made no serious inroads and called off his attack after less than a week.

ALBANIA.

Like **Hitler, Mussolini** coveted ''living space'' and, in fact, wanted to re-create the Roman Empire. His goal was absolute domination of the Mediterranean; this required the conquest of Nice and Savoy, Corsica, **Malta, Cyprus, Greece, Albania,** Tunisia, Algeria, Morocco and even **Yugoslavia.** Significantly, Yugoslavia possessed mineral resources—copper and bauxite—for which there was considerable demand in **Italy.**

On April 7, 1939—Good Friday—Italian forces landed in Albania, a kingdom of 1,088,000 inhabitants; Italy officially annexed this country several days later. The king of Italy, who now was also emperor of **Ethiopia,** was proclaimed to be Albania's sovereign as well. The Italians thus took possession of both shores of the Strait of Otranto and gained a valuable beachhead in the Balkans.

The invasion generated a guerrilla movement in the Albanian mountains, initially rather modest in scope. When Mussolini's troops attacked Greece on October 28, 1940, the Albanian guerrillas attempted, with some success, to disrupt their communications. Two separate **resistance** movements eventually emerged. The first, *Balli Kombetar,* was liberal and anti-Communist; the second, the National Liberation Front, was Communist in orientation. The National Liberation Front alone was to survive the war. Despite immense efforts by officers of the British **Special Operations Executive** (SOE), many of whom were killed in action on Albanian soil, the two resistance movements were soon engaged in combat with each other as well as with the Italians. *Balli Kombetar* was eventually annihilated, causing the SOE to suffer its sole failure of the war in Albania. Although in neighboring Yugoslavia, **Tito,** with his brand of national communism, managed to come to an understanding with Anglo-American representatives, the fanatical, intransigent Enver Hoxha, head of the Communist Resistance in Albania, broke off all contact with the West. His National Liberation Army, well supplied with materials left behind by the Italian occupation forces after their government's surrender to the Allies in September 1943, made life difficult for the provisional governments that ruled Albania until the war's end and prepared the way for establishment of the People's Republic in 1946.

H. Bernard

ALEUTIAN ISLANDS.

The **Doolittle** raid on Japan in 1942 shook the high command of the Japanese navy, especially the Combined Fleet commander, Adm. **Yamamoto.** As a result, offensive planning against the **Midway** sector, known as Operation MI, was stepped up, and it was agreed that this operation would proceed before the envisioned thrusts against Fiji and Samoa. In a closely related compromise between the Japanese navy and the Japanese army, a simultaneous invasion of the Aleutians was planned. Although the **USSR** appeared to the Japanese to pose no threat as long as this offensive, known as Operation AL, did not violate Soviet territory, brief but intensive study was addressed to limiting the scope of the action.

The Japanese IGHQ opted for conducting only a diversionary occupation of the islands rather than a protracted campaign of destruction. Bases along the great circle (the shortest route from North America to the heart of Japan) that had the potential for enemy offensive use were to be seized. Thus, the new USN submarine and air station at Dutch Harbor on Unalaska in the eastern Aleutians was to be raided, while three islands in the westernmost part of the chain would be occupied: Attu in the Near Islands; Kiska in the Rat Islands, over 200 statute miles east of Attu; and Adak in the Andreanof Islands, over 200 statute miles further east of Kiska. This plan typified Japanese naval strategy of the time, which had already been demonstrated in the **Philippines** and the Dutch East Indies. Successful invasions of these islands had been characterized by preliminary neutralization of defenses, wide distribution of military objectives and multidirectional angles of attack. Because of limited IJN sea support capabilities, wretched terrain, few harbors and chronic bad weather—gales, snow, fog, biting cold—large-scale mobile ground action in the Aleutians would not have been possible. In addition the optimum months of operation were few.

On May 5, 1942 the jittery IGHQ directed Yamamoto to implement Operations MI and AL in conjunction with the Japanese army. The navy committed its Fifth Fleet under Vice Adm. Boshiro Hosogaya, including Rear Adm. Kakuji Kakuta's carrier strike force, which centered on two light carriers and a seaplane carrier. The army's *Hokkai* (Northern Seas) Detachment, commanded by Maj. Matsutoshi Hozumi, consisted of little more than one infantry battalion. Two transports (one for Attu, the other for Adak) were to carry 1,000-1,200 army troops of the Attu occupation force (Operation AQ) under the command of Rear Adm. Sentaro Omori. Another six transports, with 550 *Maizuru* special naval landing troops (comparable to U.S. Marines) plus a construction crew, all to be landed in Operation AOB, were the responsibility of navy Capt. Takeji Ono's Kiska occupation force. Hosogaya held his own small unit as a support force for fueling and standby beyond Paramushiro in the northern Kuril chain, 1,200 miles north of Tokyo and 650 miles west of Attu. Kakuta sortied from Ominato in northern Honshu on May

25, followed by the Kiska invasion detachment on May 27 and the Attu force, heading directly northeast for its objective, the next day.

U.S. naval defense of the Alaska sector was the assignment of Rear Adm. Robert A. Theobald's new Task Force Eight, later called the North Pacific Force, with USN and Army Alaskan Defense Command air support, all on CINCPAC-ordered "fleet opposed invasion" alert status. But although U.S. intelligence possessed considerable detail concerning Operation MI, far less was known about the Japanese drive against the Aleutians. Theobald and his associates believed that the enemy amphibious groups were not really bound for Kiska and Attu (as was reported by intelligence on May 28) but would probably strike at the Dutch Harbor region. Therefore, Task Force Eight was deployed mainly south of Kodiak to cover mainland Alaska and the eastern Aleutians, some 500 miles from Kakuta's true objective. The U.S. task force never made contact with the enemy during Operation AL, however.

In the early hours of June 3, from a point about 180 miles southwest of Dutch Harbor, Kakuta launched his strike planes, undetected by USN pickets or search aircraft. The carrier *Junyo*'s attack planes could not find the target, but 12 aircraft from the *Ryujo* located Dutch Harbor and hit the oil-tank farm, Army barracks, the hospital, the radio station and PBY **reconnaissance** planes in the anchorage. Antiaircraft fire brought down one bomber during the 20-minute raid. Following up soon afterward on the morning of June 3, Kakuta sent 45 planes against five U.S. destroyers that had been sighted at Makushin Bay on Unalaska. This time the target was obscured and the raiders returned to their carriers, having lost one Zero escort to P-40 fighters.

Yamamoto then gave orders to commence preinvasion bombardment of Adak, but the worsening weather slowed strike-force speed to nine knots and caused Kakuta to decide on a second attack at Dutch Harbor, where visibility was reportedly good. (The minor Adak mission was suspended by Hosogaya and eventually canceled for good on June 25.) On the afternoon of June 5, Kakuta launched 31 aircraft in a second raid on Dutch Harbor, something Vice Adm. **Chuichi Nagumo** had not attempted on **Pearl Harbor**. Among other targets, the oil tanks were finished off. Thirty-two Americans died in the two raids. U.S. bombers, which finally caught up with Kakuta's empty carriers, scored no hits, and two U.S. planes were lost. The Japanese pilots returned to their carriers, having lost only one fighter.

The unopposed Japanese landings on Attu (June 5) and on Kiska (June 7) proceeded according to plan, despite or because of Japanese intelligence's overestimates of the defenses. On Attu a small Aleut village was taken and two U.S. missionaries were seized; on Kiska 10 unarmed U.S. weathermen were captured. Not until June 10 did a U.S. flying boat bring word of enemy ships at Kiska and tents on Attu. Adm. Nimitz, however, resisted the temptation to divert aircraft carriers to the North Pacific after his Midway victory, while Hosogaya's greatly reinforced flotilla plied the waters southwest of Kiska unopposed until steaming away on June 24.

In the next stage the Japanese strove to retain the pair of bleak islands, while the Americans undertook to suppress and then eliminate the invaders. From mid-June till month's end, two USN and USAAF air offensives were launched against Kiska (Attu was beyond range). The scale of the effort and its results were modest. On June 30 Hosogaya shepherded 1,200 troop reinforcements and six midget submarines into Kiska under cover of a powerful task force. During the next month U.S. submarines mauled enemy destroyers and subchasers between Agattu and Kiska until the requirements for the **Guadalcanal** operation forced the withdrawal of all fleet submarines. Hosogaya's battle force was also depleted by Combined Fleet priorities. Thereupon he worked to develop bases for Japanese land-based bombers, under wretched terrain and weather conditions. Japanese offensive bombing efforts proved costly and chimerical.

Pressed to act, Theobald twice set out to bombard Kiska in July but was forced back each time by weather. On August 7 his subordinate Rear Adm. W. W. Smith carried out a naval bombardment for less than an hour, hitting barracks, barges and flying boats but striking no warships and killing few enemy personnel. At the end of the month, U.S. Army engineers landed on Adak and within a fortnight had prepared an airstrip suitable for fighter and bomber use, bringing Kiska within closer flying range in September and October. The Japanese did not discover the Adak base until early October.

Meanwhile IGHQ had decided to give up Attu and concentrate on building up and defending Kiska. In successful evacuation maneuvers, for which the Japanese navy was to become famous, transports and destroyers ferried the entire Attu garrison to Kiska in three unscathed stages between August 27 and September 16, under the protection of Hosogaya's reduced fleet. On October 24, IGHQ ordered Attu reoccupied and in early December reinforced the *Hokkai* Detachment with 1,100 more men (originally intended for Shemya island), renaming it the Garrison Unit. Maj. Gen. Junichiro Mineki now commanded a combat force of three infantry battalions.

In early January 1943 Theobald was relieved by Rear Adm. Thomas C. Kinkaid, and Rear Adm.

Charles H. McMorris replaced W. W. Smith as commander of the cruiser-destroyer force. Toward the middle of the month, the Americans came even closer to Kiska by occupying and developing air facilities on uninhabited Amchitka, only 60 miles away—an action that, although highly appropriate, had contributed to Theobald's relief because of interservice disagreement.

IGHQ decided on February 5 to cling to the western Aleutians "at all costs." Hosogaya did his best to construct airfields on Kiska and at Holtz Bay on Attu, but his resources were skimpy and the going was unsatisfactory. McMorris tried to interfere, with a direct-fire bombardment of Attu on February 18; damage was negligible, however. The Americans continued their anti-shipping patrols, while U.S. Army and Navy air squadrons pounded Kiska and Attu. On March 9 the Japanese ran the gauntlet, bringing in badly needed supplies and munitions. In another attempt on March 26, Hosogaya was intercepted by McMorris's much smaller task group. In a strictly ship-to-ship action, fought at long range for nearly four hours, the two forces engaged in a traditional but inconclusive battle off Attu, known also as the Battle of the Komandorski Islands. Concerned about the two large *Maru* merchant-cruiser transports and freighter he was convoying, Hosogaya waged a very cautious but ineffective operation and eventually turned back. McMorris had fought a bold offensive-defensive action that prevented the Japanese reinforcements from getting through. Hosogaya was retired from service the next month.

Because of the lack of logistics, sealift and manpower available for a major invasion of Kiska and because Kiska's defenses were stronger than Attu's, Adm. Kinkaid and Army Maj. Gen. John L. DeWitt had recommended on March 3 that Attu be assaulted first. Submitted through Nimitz, the proposal was approved by the Joint Chiefs of Staff on March 18. D-day was set for May 7. Rear Adm. Francis W. Rockwell was named amphibious force commander and given three old battleships to buttress his fire power and an escort carrier to supply close air support for the first time in the Pacific theater. Kinkaid also had three heavy and three light cruisers, 19 destroyers, five transports and various support craft. The landing force was to be made up of the Army's Seventh Infantry Division, which had undergone amphibious training in California.

Although IGHQ warned the new Fifth Fleet Commander, Vice Adm. Shiro Kawase, that defense of Attu should now be accorded priority, Kawase deferred a major reinforcement of the island until, from his standpoint, the time would be more propitious, at the end of May. Throughout late April, USAAF planes hammered Kiska; Attu was accorded little attention. The ubiquitous U.S. naval and aerial pickets, however, missed at least one minor Japanese navy evasion of the Aleutians blockade: a *Maru* transport bringing several scout planes to Attu around May 7, in weather so foul that Rockwell's own invasion force of 29 ships had been forced to delay its assault until May 11.

The Seventh Division came ashore unopposed in Operation Landcrab on the north shore of Attu around Holtz Bay and on the south shore at Massacre Bay. Col. Yasuyo Yamazaki had only coastal guns and a dozen AA cannons to support the defense of the island by his 2,630 troops. Although not surprised by the invasion, he had not responded to the softening-up air strikes, a battleship bombardment or the landing assault. Yamazaki instead tried to wage an inland defense of the valley between the bays on an island 15 miles wide by 35 miles long. Kawase deployed his meager naval and air resources from Paramushiro, and Adm. Mineichi Koga, the new commander of the Combined Fleet after Yamamoto's death on April 18, shifted strong formations from Truk to Tokyo Bay but was deterred from close intervention by bad weather and reports of the U.S. battleships and carriers operating offshore. Minor Japanese submarine and air counterattacks did nothing to take pressure off Yamazaki's isolated command, which put up a stubborn fight against the green Seventh Division. Indeed the U.S. ground force commander, a major general, had been relieved on May 16 after he was heard to lament that six months would be needed to take Attu.

Yamazaki's men clawed their way back to the last high ground between Chichagof and Sarana bays. At dawn on May 29, realizing that the inevitable defeat was near, Yamazaki launched a human-wave banzai charge by what one American described as "a howling mob a thousand strong" that overran a medical station and two command posts before being checked. By next morning all Japanese who had not been killed committed suicide with grenades. A total of 2,351 Japanese were recorded in the "body count"; only 28 prisoners were taken—a ratio replicated constantly in the Pacific war. Of the 11,000 American assault troops, approximately 600 had been killed and 1,200 wounded (as well as 1,500 incapacitated by illness). At the last minute IGHQ had prepared to evacuate the remnants of the Attu garrison, but events overtook them, and Kiska commanded subsequent attention.

At the Imperial Palace in Tokyo, a high-level army-navy conference had been called on May 20 to reevaluate the deteriorating situation in the Aleutians. It was now admitted that island operations lacking Japanese air and sea supremacy were foredoomed.

The conferees made the embarrassing decision to evacuate Kiska, whose garrison was twice as large as the one on Attu. Lt. Gen Kiichiro Higuchi, commanding the Northern Army, was ordered immediately to remove the troops on Kiska to the Kurils. I-class submarines, which began the process on May 26, had by June brought out 820 wounded and sick soldiers and civilians. But the evacuation was proceeding too slowly, and seven of 13 submarines had already been lost. Thereupon a destroyer squadron commander, Rear Adm. Masatomi Kimura, cleverly exploited fog cover, raced into shrouded Kiska on July 28 and extricated 5,183 men aboard six destroyers and two cruisers in a mere 55 minutes. The evacuation was aided greatly by the U.S. fleet's engagement, on the night of July 26, of a phantom flotilla that drew 1,000 real rounds in the "Battle of the Pips," caused by American radar and intelligence mistakes.

In what has been called one of the weirdest episodes in the Pacific war, the Americans failed to detect the evacuation of Kiska for more than two weeks after the last Japanese had departed, although during that time the island had been blockaded and worked over by sea and air bombardment. Conflicting or misinterpreted data from U.S. intelligence or operational sources were regarded as inconclusive or even attempts at deception. The Americans accordingly took no chances with Kiska. At Adak, Rockwell massed almost 100 ships and over 34,000 well-equipped troops, including 5,300 Canadians, all under U.S. Army Maj. Gen. Charles H. Corlett. Learning from earlier amphibious mistakes and displaying impressive levels of new leadership, the Allied army began landing on Kiska on August 15 after a softening-up bombardment of the shore defenses. The island was eerily silent, and the only troop casualties (56 killed or wounded) were caused by fire fights between friendly patrols operating in the mist. The search of empty Kiska went on until August 18; the only living things found were a few stray dogs.

Many have argued that the Japanese never should have bothered with the desolate Aleutians and that the Americans, too, should have ignored the unimportant invasion. At the time, however, IGHQ regarded the island chain as a threat to the Kurils and even to the homeland, particularly in the event of Soviet-American military collaboration. After the Japanese navy's setback at Midway, there was some thought of diverting attention from the Central to the North Pacific. A number of Americans did ponder possibilities of striking at Japan through the Aleutian aerial corridor, an unrealistic proposition, as the 1942-43 campaign demonstrated. But from the Americans' standpoint, the need for ousting the Japanese from the Aleutians—American soil within the Territory of Alaska—was undoubtedly psychological, symbolic and keenly felt. General **Marshall** advised **MacArthur** on August 10, 1942: "You should be aware that the pressures to meet the growing dangers of the situation in the Aleutians...make our problem exceedingly difficult and complex." Some Americans honestly but wrongly feared that mainland Alaska itself was in danger of invasion from the Aleutian stepping-stones; yet on September 25, 1942 MacArthur warned USAAF Gen. **Henry H. Arnold** that the Japanese "move into the Aleutians is part of the general move into Siberia."

A force of 10,000 Japanese troops, with fluctuating but generally minor naval and air assistance, eventually diverted as many as 100,000 Allied fighting men supported by sizable naval forces and air power. Still, the Japanese squandered the whole Attu garrison, 18 vessels and precious logistical and ordnance stores. Referring to Attu, Vice Adm. Takijiro Onishi admitted: "We took a foolish liking to the place and poured in too much material and unnecessary personnel, making it impossible to leave. There are...many islands like that in the south." He added, "We should have just pounded Attu and withdrawn from there." More importantly, Combined Fleet warships were deployed as backup at times when they were more needed to block U.S. operations at sites such as Guadalcanal. Additionally, the Kurils and even Hokkaido had to be reinforced after the Japanese were ousted from the Aleutians.

Whereas the Japanese revealed great skill in evacuating endangered island garrisons, their enemy was developing a more significant capability in conducting amphibious operations and leapfrogging Japanese-occupied islands, whose isolated garrisons were left to wither. Service in the Aleutians constituted "hard time" for soldiers and sailors of both sides. Many commanders lost or tarnished their reputations, or at best were relegated to anonymity. IGHQ certainly earned no luster for its conduct of Operation AL. Despite the cost in men, materiel, time and effort, the Aleutians campaign exerted scant influence on the Pacific theater as a whole, from either the Japanese or the Allied point of view. S. E. Morrison called it the "Theater of Military Frustration."

A. D. Coox

ALEXANDER, Sir Harold R. L. G. (later Earl) (1891-1969).

The son of an Irish earl, Alexander served as an officer in the Irish Guards in France during World War I. In 1939-1940 Alexander commanded the First Division of the British Expeditionary Force in France and was in charge of the evacuation of that force from Dunkirk; he oversaw the British withdrawal from Rangoon in 1942. Alexander served as commander in chief of the Allied forces in the Middle East in 1942-43; in this capacity he coordinated the Allies' capture of Tunisia. In 1944-45 Alexander was the supreme Allied commander in the Mediterranean. After the war he served as governor-general of **Canada** (1946-52).

ALGERIA.
See **French North Africa.**

ALLIED CONFERENCES.
See **Conferences, Allied.**

ALLIED MILITARY GOVERNMENT OF OCCUPIED TERRITORIES (AMGOT).
See **Anglo-American Military Administration.**

AMBROSIO, Vittorio (1897-1958).
Italian general. In April 1941 Ambrosio became commander of the Italian Second Army in **Yugoslavia.** Ambrosio was made chief of staff of the Italian army in January 1942 and chief of the general staff in February 1943. Ambrosio was instrumental in bringing about the fall of **Mussolini** and the Italian renunciation of the alliance with **Germany.** In November 1943 Ambrosio was demoted by Marshal **Pietro Badoglio** to the post of inspector general of the army.

AMERY, Leopold Stennett (1873-1955).
Amery, a British imperialist, violently attacked **Chamberlain** in the debate on **Norway** in Parliament. He served as secretary for **India** from 1940 to 1945; in 1942 he proposed eventual Indian independence. One of his sons served with the **Special Operations Executive** in **Albania;** the other was executed for aiding the Germans.

AMGOT (Allied Military Government of Occupied Territories).
See **Anglo-American Military Administration.**

ANAMI, Korechika (1887-1945).
Japanese general. Anami was the last wartime war minister. A graduate of the Army War College, he served at various times as aide de camp to Emperor **Hirohito**, superintendent of the Tokyo Military Prep School and chief of the War Ministry's Military Administration Bureau and Personnel Bureau during a period of severe intraservice factionalism. He commanded a number of Japanese armies in **China** between 1938 and 1943, and was Second Area Army commander of the Kwantung Army in Manchuria in July 1942, when the Japanese notion of invading

Siberia was still very real. Anami was transferred to the southern theater in November 1943. In this capacity he directed operations in western **New Guinea** and in the Halmahera sector. In December 1944 he was made inspector general of army aviation, chief of the army Aeronautical Department and military councilor.

With the deterioration in **Japan**'s strategic position, exemplified by the U.S. invasion of **Okinawa** on April 1, 1945, Premier **Kuniaki Koiso** resigned on April 5, to be succeeded by **Kantaro Suzuki**, in whose cabinet Anami became war minister. The relationship between the two men was respectful but extremely delicate, as the aged admiral publicly preached maximum war effort but covertly sought to obtain the peace desired by the emperor, while the fighting general struggled to control fanatical subordinates, save the army's honor, yet prevent national disgrace and disaster. On the one hand, Anami ordered the arrest of 400 suspected defeatists; on the other, he agreed, in principle, to the Supreme War Council's emerging idea of ending hostilities, though not at any price. Anami argued vigorously with Navy Minister **Mitsumasa Yonai** and Foreign Minister **Shigenori Togo** concerning Japanese military capabilities as opposed to the need to accept some kind of peace conditions. Till the end, Anami's thinking centered on improving Japan's bargaining position by delivering a smashing blow to the expected Allied invasion forces during the decisive battle for the homeland, perhaps snatching something less than victory from something more than defeat. Although this idea became increasingly unrealistic by the summer of 1945, Anami feared the threat to national institutions or even to national survival implicit in the **Potsdam Declaration** issued by the Allies in late July, which entailed disarmament and occupation of the country, victors' justice for alleged war criminals and perhaps elections to determine Japan's ultimate form of government. The Japanese army, whose spokesman in the cabinet was Anami, insisted that, unlike the navy, it remained powerful, numerous and intact in the home islands, imbued with the do-or-die **kamikaze**, or "divine wind," spirit.

After the dropping of the **atomic bomb** on Hiroshima and Nagasaki and the entry of the **USSR** into the Pacific war in early August 1945, however, the impasse between the bitter-enders and the doves in the Suzuki cabinet was resolved by the emperor's courageous decision to accept the Allied terms of capitulation. Anami was still breathing fire, exhorting the quest for life in death and striving to preserve the throne by somehow twisting unconditional into conditional surrender. Still, despite considerable vacillation and squirming, he never did perpetrate the one

deed that would have pleased his army colleagues by prolonging the war (with entirely unforeseeable consequences): he did not resign as war minister, an action that would have automatically brought down the entire Suzuki cabinet. Anami's agonized restraint was undoubtedly the product, ultimately, of his loyalty to the imperial will and of his stern sense of the samurai's honor. Junior army officer hotheads dared to defy the government's decision to surrender, hoping to convince the emperor to reconsider his decision and to rally the nation to a "glorious" last stand. The ringleaders approached Anami, who beat around the bush, sympathizing but not offering direct encouragement. In a brief, abortive and violent mutiny launched against the palace area on the night of August 14-15, hard-core patriots tried to find the imperial recording that was to announce capitulation at noon on August 15. Anami, humiliated but resolved to die in expiation, delayed his protracted suicide until the early hours, when he was sure that the plot had been foiled. A last testament stated that with his death, he "humbly apologized to the emperor for his grave offenses," an allusion not only to the army's defeat in the war but probably also to its previous misbehavior (which was known to have distressed the monarch) and to its most recent insubordination, this very night. Anami's act of suicide, one Japanese officer predicted correctly, ended "all confusion in the army and terminated any other plots." Anami deserves credit for carrying off his last and greatest role in a dangerous drama involving much subterfuge. If, as some have said, it was playacting (*haragei*), then Anami was a consummate actor.

A. D. Coox

ANDERS, Wladyslaw (1892-1970).

Anders, a Polish commander, fought both the Germans and the Russians at various times. He was wounded and captured by the Soviets in September 1939 and released in July 1941. He then formed an army of 75,000 Polish exiles in **Iran**; Anders' army participated in the capture of Monte **Cassino** in May 1944 and of Bologna in April 1945.

ANDERSON, Sir John (later Viscount Waverley) (1882-1958).

Anderson, a British administrator, served as governor of Bengal from 1932 to 1937 and as home secretary in 1939-40. He held a series of senior posts in **Churchill**'s wartime coalition, directing British home and financial affairs.

ANDERSON, Sir Kenneth A. N. (1891-1959).

British general. Anderson served in France and in **Palestine** during World War I. In 1940 he participated in the evacuation from Dunkirk. From November 1942 to May 1943, Anderson commanded the First Army in Algeria and Tunisia. From 1947 to 1952 he served as governor of **Gibraltar**.

ANGLO-AMERICAN CHAIN OF COMMAND.
See **Chain of Command, Anglo-American**.

ANGLO-AMERICAN MILITARY ADMINISTRATION.
As U.S. and British forces advanced through western Europe and Asia, the Allied command set up a vast organization known as the Allied Military Government of Occupied Territories (AMGOT) to reorganize and administer the liberated or conquered areas. The purposes of the AMGOT were to aid in maintaining order and security and to feed the population and assist it in denazification and reorganization of public health, industry, transportation, communications, agriculture, commerce, finance etc. The people in charge of this program were carefully selected and went through special training courses. Their function was to execute the orders of the administration and mobilize local resources. Civil affairs teams for a particular territory formed a special branch of the army command, or G-5, as the Americans called it.

The problems the AMGOT faced were incredibly complex, especially in friendly liberated countries, where the requirements of Allied military forces had to be satisfied without violating the sovereignty of the reestablished governments. Each liberated area was a unique case. The AMGOT underwent its first test in Sicily and southern **Italy**, where it had to deal with a starving population living under deplorable hygienic conditions. In one year, more than two million tons of food, drugs and soap were sent to the area, a feat that tied up much of the available shipping and land transport facilities to the detriment of military operations. On the other hand, hygienic measures taken by the civil affairs authorities eliminated the danger of epidemics that threatened soldiers as well as civilians.

Before the Allied invasion of France, western European **governments in exile** concluded agreements with the **United Kingdom** and the **United States** that gave Allied military commanders the powers required for smooth conduct of their operations, especially authority to requisition civilian goods and labor. French, Belgian and Dutch specialists in civil affairs were also delegated to serve as intermediaries between Allied military authorities and local functionaries. The governments of the countries to be liberated demanded, however, that they be allowed to enact any legislation considered immediately necessary. They also kept the power to try civilian lawbreakers in civil courts, leaving only crimes against military personnel or equipment to be tried by Allied courts-martial.

The governments in exile in London were certainly justified in "dotting all the i's" before the liberation of their territories to insure that their national sovereignty was not infringed upon. In France, the AMGOT was never very popular, partly because of dislike of the phrase "occupied territory." The presence of French officers newly arrived from London who were unfamiliar with the attitude of the liberated regions also aroused some dissatisfaction. General **de Gaulle's** nationalist sensitivity hardly made matters easier. In general, AMGOT interfered with the civilian administration only to replace some mayors, make arrests or liberate prisoners. Relations between the Allied authorities and the governments of **Belgium, the Netherlands, Luxembourg, Norway** and **Denmark** were much better.

On the whole, the AMGOT performed its tasks well in liberated Europe. Following the liberation of Paris, the city's military government kept it supplied with up to 10,000 tons of provisions a day, despite the continuation of large-scale fighting in the area and an acute fuel shortage. On June 30, 1945 civil affairs authorities delivered some 5,631,800 tons of provisions to satisfy the needs of France, Belgium, Luxembourg, the Netherlands, Denmark and Norway.

Aside from problems of food supply, the occupation of **Germany** and Austria presented military authorities with tasks far different from those they faced in liberated areas. German civilian officials had either vanished or were suspect, and for a time the military government exercised legislative, executive and judicial powers, established a new administration, proceeded with denazification measures, organized projects for removing rubble and saw to the care and resettlement of refugees. Most of these responsibilities fell to a British officer, Maj. Gen. **Gerald Templer**, who in March 1945 became director of civil affairs in West Germany and whose tireless energies helped preserve the region from famine and anarchy.

H. Bernard

ANNAM.
See **Indochina**.

ANSCHLUSS (Annexation).
The name given to **Hitler's** forcible integration of Austria into the Greater Reich on March 13, 1938. (See also the Introduction.)

ANTIAIRCRAFT DEFENSE (AA).
Decoys played a significant role in AA, along with camouflage, fighters, and, to a lesser degree, balloon barrages and searchlights. The two decisive weapons,

however, were **radar** and artillery.

Without radar the fighter planes' task of intercepting enemy planes would have been more difficult—practically impossible at night. Radar stations, operated by specially trained technicians, enabled each side to intercept enemy aircraft at night, often with considerable success. The British would not have been able to win the **Battle of Britain** without their many ground radar stations, which had just been installed in sufficient numbers. Radar revealed the size and direction of the air raids soon enough for fighters to intercept them (depending on where the fighters were deployed).

Antiaircraft artillery was classified roughly as heavy (over 50mm) and light. Light antiaircraft cannons were indispensable in defending warships and large airfields on the front lines, which, for combat aircraft, sometimes extended over hundreds of miles and could include both bomber and fighter bases. Columns of armored personnel carriers along the roads at the start of the **blitzkrieg** were usually accompanied by light antiaircraft cannons mounted on trucks, in case a German fighter formation pierced the defense formed by British fighters. The Germans, for their part, also considered antiaircraft artillery important for protecting armored divisions in places where they no longer had air superiority. The British armored personnel carriers that retreated under similar conditions in North Africa sometimes found themselves in a difficult situation, because their light antiaircraft cannon were mounted less effectively than the German cannons.

A dense group of antiaircraft cannons firing tracer shells posed a frightening obstacle to a pilot by day or night; at night the tracers appeared to move more slowly, but more implacably. The more the pilots saw of these cannons, and the more they returned safely from their missions with parts of their aircraft damaged or destroyed, the less they were frightened by the sight. But few pilots had the courage of **Leonard Cheshire**, who in July 1944 flew for 10 minutes in a circle around a suspected antiaircraft emplacement near Calais some 1,600 feet above the ground, while hundreds of cannons fired at him and while the 617th RAF Squadron dropped bombs in the center of his circle. He returned without a scratch.

The barrages from heavy antiaircraft guns were less spectacular, but their heavier shells inflicted more severe damage. A direct hit from an 88-mm German shell or a 103-mm British shell on the engine or the cockpit usually brought down a plane. Arranging for the shell (less than 15 inches long) and a vital airplane part (zigzagging along at more than 300 miles per hour) to meet in space, however, was hardly simple, even with the 88-mm cannon, which could fire 12 to 15 rounds a minute, or with radar-aided guidance equipment, which the major combatants started to use by 1941. This radar equipment supplemented the miniature computers known as "prophets" that estimated the direction, speed and altitude of a plane and predicted where the plane would be by the time a shell fired at it could reach it (usually within 30 seconds for a distance up to about 15,000 feet).

Pilots had different reactions to antiaircraft barrages. Inexperienced pilots often became discouraged by them, while the brave ones flew over them, hoping (or praying). An enormous amount of ammunition was needed to ensure that a barrage covered a sufficiently large portion of the sky; only important targets like London, Berlin, Moscow or Leningrad could be defended in this way. The barrages had an important indirect effect: they bolstered the morale of the population in the target cities, despite the danger of explosions from antiaircraft shells that fell back to earth.

The British produced a variant of the antiaircraft projectile: a mass of about 200 75-mm rockets launched simultaneously from a fixed position to a single point in the sky. This produced a momentary mass of explosions within 15,000 cubic feet of air and effectively prevented attacks on secondary (but still important) targets like Portsmouth.

A precise total of the airplanes felled by antiaircraft fire is impossible to give. The Imperial War Museum in London has a 40-mm Bofors Swedish antiaircraft cannon on which British troops inscribed that, with it, they brought down 101 planes during the war. This is an extraordinary total.

M. R. D. Foot

ANTI-COMMUNISM.

From an ideological point of view, the war was three-sided. On one side were the liberal Western democracies; on another the dictatorial Axis powers. But beginning on June 22, 1941, the autocratic **USSR** found itself in the Allied camp. A firm anti-communist, **Churchill** remarked, "The enemies of our enemies are our friends." Yet ideological anti-communism among Germany's enemies and suspicion of the USSR in the West remained as lively as ever.

The Nazis had always prided themselves on being the true defenders of the West against "Bolshevist barbarism." Nevertheless, after the signing of the **Nazi-Soviet Pact** of August 23, 1939, the anti-communist propaganda of the Third Reich grew almost mute, and such formulas as "No bourgeois state will survive this war," acceptable to the two countries in a common front against capitalism, gained in popularity. The watchword here was "opportunism."

In the West a significant section of the anti-communist right had always been sympathetic to fascism. Those conservatives who had never fully accepted universal suffrage feared workers' and syndicalist democracy. Occupation of the factories by the workers of **Italy** sharpened their fears; at that moment the capitalist system seemed shaken, and **Mussolini**'s appearance was greeted with sighs of relief. Besides, the "strong" new Italian state represented no threat to any foreign country.

With the outbreak of war in **Ethiopia** on October 3, 1935, anxiety gripped the **United Kingdom** concerning the security of its national interests in the Red Sea region. The British consequently adopted a firm attitude toward the aggressor. In France, on the other hand, public opinion approved the conciliatory policy of **Laval**, who, although diplomatically sympathetic to the USSR, dreaded a revolution in Italy if defeat overtook Mussolini's army. But in neither Britain nor France did the democratic response to fascism play an important role—because anti-communism was much stronger than anti-fascism.

With the growth of Nazism, the situation changed. The appearance of a resurgent German power constituted a direct threat to France, and British Prime Minister Stanley Baldwin declared that "the frontier of the United Kingdom is on the Rhine." Germany, then, was not simply the domain of a "strong man" with an anti-communist policy but was the scene of a totalitarian regime animated by aggressive nationalism. Still, many of the British and French saluted **Hitler**'s achievements. Unemployment was down, expanded public works were in progress, political street wars had been quelled, and, best of all, the Nazi policy was resolutely anti-communist.

Even German remilitarization and the occupation of the Rhineland (in violation of the Treaty of Versailles) in March 1936 opened few eyes. At this critical moment, a unique opportunity for stopping Hitler was lost. Albert Sarraut, the premier of France, declared: "Strasbourg is now within range of German artillery." This should have cleared the vision of those temporarily blinded by anti-communism.

The situation changed with the rise of the Popular Front in France in 1936 and with the beginning of the Spanish civil war the same year. In the face of the "Communist menace," a large fraction of the right supported **Franco** and his fascist and Nazi allies, the bulwarks against communism. Rare were the traditional conservatives in France (Henri de Kerillis was one of the few) who indicted German aggression as more to be feared than a victory by the "Reds." In such circles class instincts proved stronger than traditional nationalist reactions. The eventual wartime **collaboration** owed its origin to this state of mind.

Christian—especially Catholic—leaders had a particular horror of Bolshevism. Certainly the difficulties encountered by the church in Germany were well known; the 1937 encyclical of Pope Pius XI *Mit brennender Sorge* had protested some of the abuses committed by the Nazis. But such sins were much less serious than Marxist atheism. It should be noted here that during the occupation, numerous Catholics, especially in Flanders, enlisted in anti-Bolshevist ranks.

In 1936 the USSR concluded a treaty with France and **Czechoslovakia** after having joined the **League of Nations**. Military contacts between these allies had been proposed, but anti-communism within the governments and among the chiefs of staff of their armed forces aroused considerable opposition. In fact, even in the face of the ill treatment accorded them by Hitler, many members of the French bourgeoisie regarded him as a minor evil compared with the dictatorship of the proletariat. It was in this era that a popular singer in Montmartre mocked the "gorgeous gals and fancy guys who preferred victimization by Hitler to victory with **Stalin**." Such sentiments expressed by the "best people" were perhaps responsible for the Soviet about-face of 1939. Stalin was convinced that the "capitalist states" were trying to embroil him in a death struggle with Hitler, to maintain their own security.

In any case, Western public opinion was stupefied first by the Nazi-Soviet Pact, and then by the **Russo-Finnish Winter War**. Socialists especially, traumatized by the experiences of the Popular Front and the Spanish civil war, denounced the "betrayal of antifascism" by the USSR. The Communist groups that Moscow had omitted to inform of its new policy contented themselves with praising Soviet "pacifism"— until it reverted to antifascist solidarity in 1941.

After the USSR entered the war, the Nazi propaganda machine returned to its traditional anti-communism while the patriots in the **Resistance**, regardless of their political opinions, collaborated intimately with their Communist colleagues to promote the victory of the Red Army.

H. Brugmans

ANTI-SEMITISM.

The word "anti-Semitism" dates from the end of the 19th century. In its broadest sense it refers to the ideology and political concepts inspired by modern anti-Jewish thinking and should be distinguished from the religious motives that, in earlier times, fostered animosity toward Jews. The essential cause of anti-Semitism lies in the profound social and economic upheavals caused by the Industrial Revolution. The uncertainties of the free market, the dis-

15

solution of traditional social and family ties and the suffering caused by the Great Depression helped create a universal sense of insecurity, driving the public to seek explanations and justifications. Much speculation on the causes of social, economic and cultural deterioration centered on Jews.

The theories of Gregor Mendel on heredity and Charles Darwin on the origin of species, distorted and oversimplified, led some people to believe that science provided "proof" of the biological differences between human races. As a result, some students of racial theory claimed that various races have certain positive or negative peculiarities. The orientalist Ernest Renan originated the use of the terms "Semitic" and "Aryan" as racial designations. Evidently drawing on this source, the German pamphleteer Wilhelm Marr developed his notions of Jewish aggressiveness.

Anti-Semites have always founded their theories on pseudoscientific postulates. The hypothesis of Aryan and Semitic races, with opposing traits, is a distortion of fact. The two terms are properly linguistic characterizations, overlapping with ethnic and racial divisions. For example, the Hittites, historically part of the Jewish people, and the Gypsies are linguistically classified as Aryan.

The growing prevalence of anti-Semitism in the late 19th century was a European phenomenon, not restricted to any single country. The Dreyfus affair inspired outbursts in France that amounted almost to pogroms; Edouard Drumont's *Libre Parole* was for a time the most influential anti-Semitic journal in Europe. In Russia, violence against the Jews erupted after the assassination of Alexander II in 1881 and recurred periodically from 1903 through 1914. The same situation existed in the Balkans, where the population continually vented its rage on the Jews. In **Germany** and Austria, political groups sprouted up after 1880 with programs consisting almost entirely of anti-Semitic slogans. This "anti-Semitic politics" was soon absorbed by traditional conservative parties and nationalist organizations. Anti-Semitism thus grew out of the narrow area of sectarian groups and secured a foothold in influential economic and political circles. The powerful *Alldeutscherverband* (Pan-German Union), under Heinrich Class, played an important role in making anti-Semitism respectable for the upper and middle classes.

Under the cover of large parties and important organizations, obscure groups attempted continuously to propagate by slanderous and sometimes illegal means the idea that the Jew was inferior by race and by innate character. The spurious "Protocols of the Elders of Zion," a fabrication of the Russian secret police, demonstrated that any argument, even the most absurd, would be accepted as fact by "true believers." Anti-Semitic racism thus acquired a strong momentum, particularly among members of the lower middle class—clerks, shopkeepers etc.—who suffered badly in every economic crisis. Anti-Semitism offered them an explanation, in apparently valid terms, of a social and economic system that steadily reduced their status and standard of living. Even more, it flattered them by attributing to their mediocre lives a "higher moral value" than that of the rich and "upstart" Jews.

Hitler and the fledgling **Nazi Party** appealed powerfully to this sentiment after 1918 by identifying the Jew as the cause of Germany's defeat and the political and economic disasters that followed. The program of the National Socialist Workers Party (NSDAP), adopted on February 20, 1920, stated: "None but those belonging to the people *[Volksgenosse]* may be citizens; none but those of German blood, regardless of denomination, may belong to the people. It follows then that no Jew may belong to the people."

Other points of the program dealt with the elimination of Jews from all public employment and other restrictions to be placed on the principle of equal opportunity before the law. These were hardly new ideas; they had been propagated for decades by other anti-Semitic groups. Still, the hatred that Hitler bore the Jews seemed to go much further than the official claims of his party. For him the Jew was the ultimate enemy, the quintessence of evil. His propaganda constantly associated Judaism with Bolshevism in the catch-phrase "Judeo-Bolshevik world enemy." "We can see in Russian Bolshevism the drive of the Jews for domination of the world," he wrote in *Mein Kampf.* "The end of the power of Russia's Jews will also be the end of Russia as a state."

Following the Nazi seizure of power in 1933, Hitler soon made anti-Semitism an integral part of German government policy. A wave of violent anti-Jewish demonstrations in April 1933 was followed by the elimination of Jews from public employment and from the medical and legal professions. Restrictions on the admission of Jews to universities were also established. In September 1935 Hitler proclaimed the infamous "Nuremberg Laws," which stripped Jews of their civil rights and established gradations of "Jewishness." The statutes distinguished between a "full Jew," with four non-Aryan grandparents; a first-degree "mixed breed," with two non-Aryan grandparents; and a second-degree "mixed breed," with only one non-Aryan grandparent. Full Jews were deprived of German citizenship and forbidden to marry members of the Aryan race. In November 1938, following the officially sponsored pogrom known as the *Kristallnacht* ("Night of Broken Glass"), the state proceeded with the total economic exclusion of Jews; remaining Jewish businesses were expropriated, the few professions still open to Jews were closed and the Jewish community was forced to pay a *Suehnegeld* ("expiatory tax").

By the end of 1938 the Nazis had attained all the initial objectives of their racial program. Although bureaucratic inertia and economic considerations caused some delays, in the end German Jews were entirely shut out of every area of public life. **Italy** and **Hungary**, submitting to pressure from their powerful ally, also enacted measures in accord with the Nuremberg Laws. Under the vigilant eye of the party's Security Service (**SD**), German and Austrian Jews had little freedom of movement. The only possibility remaining to them (depending on individual financial means) was to accept the official policy of forced emigration, established in 1938, and leave the country.

With the outbreak of war in 1939, Nazi policy toward the Jews entered a new and more radical phase. Hitler clearly viewed the conflict as a *Volkstumskampf* ("struggle of peoples"), to be conducted with extreme violence. At the outset, however, there was no overall plan for dealing with the millions of Jews who fell into German hands in **Poland** and Western Europe. The occupiers thus restricted themselves initially to legal measures based on those in force in Germany. Since the definition of Jews was already well established, anti-Jewish ordinances could be applied quickly and ruthlessly, beginning with the exclusion of Jews from public office and university positions. Other regulations governed the seizure of Jewish property. In the **General Government for Occupied Poland**, Jews were forced to wear the star of David after November 1939. **Belgium, the Netherlands** and occupied France followed with a similar rule in October 1940.

In unoccupied France, which tried to maintain an appearance of autonomy, the **Darlan** cabinet quickly drew up a "statute for Jews." Except for **Rumania** and Hungary, where anti-Jewish regulations had already been introduced under German pressure, the countries of Central Europe enacted racial legislation between January and May of 1941. Most of these countries exerted the little sovereignty still remaining to them by delaying adoption of the decrees until forced into it by the German Ministry of Foreign Affairs.

Extension of German rule through most of Europe vastly increased the powers of the Nazi **SS** and police, which had charge of all matters relating to the "Jewish question." SS leader **Heinrich Himmler** established a tight network of SD and police units in the occupied territories, with headquarters in the regional offices of the Higher SS and Police Chiefs (HSSPF). A fairly junior official, SS *Obersturmbann-fuehrer* ("Colonel") **Adolf Eichmann,** who dealt with technical and organizational problems connected with the treatment of Jews, coordinated the work of the regional headquarters.

During the invasion of Poland, five mobile groups of the SD were created for "special assignments." Advancing behind German troops, these units rounded up and executed Polich intellectuals and others considered capable of arousing opposition to German rule. Many of the victims were Jews; some SD detachments, in fact, specialized in wiping out Jewish communities. Although SD atrocities in Poland forecast the later policy of systematic extermination, Nazi leaders had still not settled on a single course of action. Hitler obviously intended to drive all Jews out of the territories he controlled, but left the precise means to his subordinates. Even while the Polish campaign was in progress, German police leader **Reinhard Heydrich** conceived the scheme of concentrating the Jews of the occupied eastern lands in a reservation between the Vistula and Bug rivers. Any such project, however, could only intensify the chaos that prevailed in the General Government. Eichmann, appointed to make the transfers, failed to carry them out properly because of transportation difficulties. In the Misko reservation, neither food nor housing was available. After Governor General **Hans Frank** complained to **Goering** about this, the latter forced Eichmann to give up the project and dissolve the reservation in April 1940.

One month earlier, Hitler decided to replace the reservation idea with a plan for deporting four million Jews to Madagascar as soon as transportation became available. In preparation for this plan, he ordered the transportation of 6,500 Jews from southwestern Germany to camps in southern France under control of the Vichy government. In January 1941, Heydrich followed with a new deportation plan, transferring 150,000 Jews from the eastern provinces of Germany and Vienna into the Polish General Government, where they were interned in the existing ghettos of Warsaw, Krakow, Radom and Lublin or sent to SS labor camps.

The invasion of the **USSR** in June 1941 brought yet another increase in the ferocity of Nazi racial policies. Hitler's infamous *Kommissarbefehl* ("commissar order"), citing the necessities of the "decisive struggle in the East," authorized the execution of all Communists and Jews caught behind German lines. Mobile SD groups, similar to those used in the Polish campaign, followed the advancing army and began the systematic extermination of Soviet Jews. Nazi leaders also used the war against the USSR to justify new restrictive measures against the Jews of Germany and Western Europe; in addition to being required to wear a yellow star, Jews were forbidden to leave their home areas or use any communications facilities.

The year 1941 was a period of transition in German policy toward the Jews. The plan to establish a Jewish reservation had failed, and the Madagascar project was stalled. Hitler briefly considered expelling all of Europe's Jews to the interior of Russia; but the failure of German forces to win a quick victory in the east ended this plan too. Still obsessed with the idea of removing all Jews from his empire, Hitler issued an order in September 1941 for deportation of all German Jews to Poland and parts of the conquered Russian territories. Shipped hastily and without preparation to Lodz and Riga, the newly arrived Jews only compounded the chaos existing in both cities. It was clear that mass population transfers were impossible in wartime. In December 1941 the SS opened a camp at Chelmno, near Lodz, where Jews were killed upon arrival. Thus, the **Final Solution,** the organized destruction of Europe's Jewish population, became a reality.

The same month Heydrich decided to make use of a letter he had received from Goering the previous July that authorized him to "take every means of liquidating totally the Jewish question in Europe." If in July this phrase referred to deportations to Madagascar or occupied Russia, it now acquired a quite different meaning. On January 20, 1942 Heydrich called a ministerial meeting, known as the **Wannsee Conference,** of all agency heads involved in the deportation of Jews. Although he referred obliquely to a "manpower operation in the east" and claimed that "the majority of deportees will probably be eliminated in a natural way," Heydrich left no doubt as to the true nature of the Final Solution. Whether or not the other participants agreed with his plans did not interest Heydrich; he was concerned only with completing transportation arrangements and providing for the annulment of mixed marriages so that the Jewish spouses of Aryans could be deported. The conference also decided that part-Jews remaining in the Reich would be sterilized.

Although the annulment and sterilization measures were delayed by bureaucratic resistance in Germany, the extermination program proceeded according to plan. Extermination camps were quickly organized during 1942—**Bergen-Belsen** in March, Sobibor in April, **Auschwitz** (Oswiecim) in June,

The Extermination of European Judaism

(The following figures are only estimates, especially for the countries of eastern and southern Europe. They are based on the data of historians Raul Hilberg and Gerald Reitlinger.)

Country	Number of Jews in 1938	Final Solution Number of Victims	
		Minimum	Maximum
Germany and Austria	340,000	218,000	240,000
Belgium	90,000	25,000	28,000
The Netherlands	140,000	104,000	104,000
Luxembourg	3,000	2,800	3,000
France	270,000	60,000	65,000
Italy	51,000	8,500	9,500
Denmark	6,500	less than 100	—
Norway	2,000	700	700
Czechoslovakia	164,000	90,000	95,000
Poland	3,300,000	2,350,000	3,000,000
Soviet Union	5,000,000	700,000	900,000
Hungary	725,000	200,000	300,000
Yugoslavia	72,000	55,000	60,000
Bulgaria	50,000	—	—
Rumania	800,000	200,000	300,000
Greece	69,000	57,000	60,000
Total	11,082,500	4,071,000	5,165,200

Treblinka in July and Maidanek in the autumn. Eichmann and his agents in the occupied territories and countries allied with Germany sent Jews by the millions to **concentration camps** with the aid of the German Ministry of Foreign Affairs. Transports arrived regularly at Auschwitz, the main extermination center, where up to 10,000 people were sent to the gas chambers every day. While the Jews of western Europe (with the exception of the Netherlands) could not be liquidated as rapidly as SS leaders had hoped, those of Poland and the USSR were easy prey for the extermination machinery. The Polish Jews, already concentrated in ghettos or labor camps, were sent to the extermination centers. The last survivors of the Warsaw ghetto, rounded up after the revolt of April-May 1943, were murdered in Treblinka. In the USSR the Final Solution was the work of mobile SD units that separated Jews from the population, executed them in pits dug in advance and covered them with quicklime and earth.

In Central Europe, only Rumania participated actively in the Final Solution. Parts of **Yugoslavia** and **Greece** under Italian control escaped the extermination campaign until they were occupied by German troops following Mussolini's fall. Only in the autumn of 1943 did trains from Italy, Croatia and Greece begin arriving at Auschwitz and Mauthausen. The Jews of Hungary, protected by their government, survived until the spring of 1944. When German forces occupied the country in March, Eichmann began the deportation of Hungarian Jews; by June, 350,000 had been shipped to Auschwitz, where 250,000 were gassed in the space of 46 days.

Auschwitz was the last of the great death camps to cease operation in November 1944. The Jewish question in Europe, at least for the Nazi leaders, was solved.

U. D. Adam

ANTITANK WEAPONS.

In general the development of antitank weapons during the course of the war followed a cyclical pattern: weapons that were effective against an enemy's **tanks** early on became obsolete when new tanks, against which they were useless, were introduced. New antitank weapons, capable of damaging the enemy's new tanks, were subsequently developed; these, in turn, were superseded by the development of yet another generation of tanks.

It is worth noting, however, that two developments which took place during the war represented vast increases in the sophistication and effectiveness of antitank warfare. Tank destroyers—which themselves

were mounted on tank chassis—were introduced, as were rocket launchers used as portable antitank weapons. These latter utilized hollow metal explosive cones whose penetrating power was extremely high.

Early in the war the Germans relied upon their 37-mm antitank gun, which was effective against the British Mark VI tank at a range of one kilometer (3,280 feet) and against the Crusader at 500 meters (1,640 feet). It was, however, useless against the British Matilda tank. After the invasion of France, however, the Germans introduced a 50-mm cannon, which fired a 5.5-pound projectile capable of piercing the Crusader at two kilometers (1.25 miles) and the Matilda at 800 meters (2,625 feet). In 1941 they began using their 88-mm antiaircraft gun as an antitank weapon. The most powerful weapon of its type, its armor-piercing projectile weighed over 100 pounds and was capable of penetrating four inches of armor at a range of a kilometer; its muzzle velocity was one kilometer per second. The following year they began using their first tank destroyer, a 75-mm cannon on treads, which proved effective until the appearance of the Soviet KV-85 tank. Rocket launchers introduced by the Germans late in the war included the Panzerschreck, similar to the American Bazooka (see below), and the Panzerfaust, a small recoilless cannon that fired a rocket and was effective at a range of some 260 feet; both were first used in Normandy in June 1944.

As the war began, the French and the Belgians were able, with their 47-mm cannon, to pierce any armor then in use; obviously, however, these two countries' development of antitank weapons came to an abrupt end when they were occupied by the Nazis.

The British managed fairly successfully to match the pace set by the Germans in the development of new tanks with their own development of antitank weaponry. At the beginning of the war, the British 40-mm gun, a two-pounder, was effective against all the German and Italian tanks then in use; at a range of one kilometer, it was capable of penetrating metal to a depth of 1.75 inches. In 1942 they introduced the 57-mm cannon, a six-pounder, capable of penetrating nearly three inches of steel at a range of some 2,600 feet. This weapon remained effective against German tanks until the introduction of the Tiger in Tunisia at the end of 1942. The British countered the Tiger, in turn, with their 76.2-mm antitank gun, which fired a 17-pound shell at a velocity of 2,900 feet per second, as well as the Sabot shell. The first British rocket launcher—the Piat—was used initially in Sicily in July 1943; it was capable of piercing 4.75 inches of armor at a range of 325 feet. The British chose not to rely on tank destroyers.

The **United States** was the first to use a rocket launcher as an antitank weapon. Their Bazooka, capable of piercing 4.75 inches of armor at a range of 325 feet, was introduced in Tunisia at the end of 1942. The Americans were also active in the development of tank destroyers. The tank destroyer used most frequently was a 75-mm cannon mounted on a Sherman chassis; its speed was 30 miles per hour. Later, they introduced a 76.2-mm cannon and, at the beginning of 1945, a 90-mm cannon.

The 45-mm Soviet antitank gun in use when **Germany** invaded the **USSR** in 1941 proved only marginally effective against German tanks; in 1942 the Soviets introduced a 57-mm gun, which proved satisfactory until the appearance of the Tiger tank. They also transformed their 76.2-mm field gun, which fired a 14-pound projectile with a muzzle velocity of 2,250 feet per second, into an antitank gun. Later in the war the Soviets were particularly active in the development of tank destroyers. Their 85-mm gun, mounted on a 30-ton T-34 chassis, was capable of penetrating 3.6 inches of metal at a range of one kilometer. At the same range their 100-mm gun, mounted on a 40-ton T-34 chassis, could penetrate four inches of metal; their 122- and 152-mm guns, mounted on a 50-ton KV chassis, could penetrate six inches.

ANTONESCU, Ion (1886-1946).
In 1932 Antonescu, a Rumanian officer, became minister of war and in 1940 was appointed premier. He then seized power, forced the abdication of **Carol II** and restored King Michael, Carol's son, to the throne. In 1941 Antonescu brought Rumania into the war against the **USSR** on the side of **Germany**. He was arrested in August 1944 on King Michael's orders, condemned to death and executed in Bucharest.

ANTONESCU, Mihai (1899-1946).
Antonescu, a Rumanian professor, held the post of vice-prime minister during the war. After the war's end he was condemned to death by a people's tribunal.

ANVIL.
Code name for the Allied landing operation in the south of France in 1943. It was ultimately carried out under the name **Dragoon** on August 15, 1944. (See also **Normandy Landing; World War II—General Conduct.**)

AOSTA, Amedeo of Savoy, Duke of (1898-1942).
Aosta, a cousin of King **Victor Emmanuel III** of Italy, served as an air force general and as viceroy of **Ethiopia**. He was defeated and taken prisoner at Amba Alagi on May 16, 1941 and died in captivity.

APAMAMA (Abemama).
See **Gilbert Islands.**

APPEASEMENT.
This line of foreign policy was founded on the Gospel of St. Matthew 5:25, "Agree with thine adversary quickly, whiles thou art in the way with him." It was pursued by **Chamberlain** from 1937 to 1939 because the **United Kingdom** was too weak to pursue any other. It reached its apogee with the **Munich Pact** in 1938.

ARAB LEAGUE.
The core of the Arabic-speaking world, long under Turkish dominion, was conquered by the **United Kingdom** in 1917-18 and politically reorganized between 1919 and 1922 into several protectorates or mandates; all of these were—nominally, at least—independent of British or French control by 1943, though most were still occupied by British military forces. In October 1944 a protocol signed at Alexandria on behalf of **Egypt, Syria, Lebanon,** Transjordan and **Iraq** envisaged an Arab league. The league was formed by a covenant signed in Cairo on March 22, 1945 by these five states, plus Saudi Arabia and Yemen. The Arab League's objectives were, according to its covenant, to strengthen the ties between the participant states; to coordinate their political programs in such a way as to effect real collaboration between them; to preserve their independence and sovereignty; and to consider in general the affairs and interests of the Arab countries. The league has continued as a loose confederation, with no combined institutions, no president and no coherent policy. Seven more states have joined it since 1945, and it has remained a force *in posse.*

ARAKI, Sadao (1877-1966).
Araki, a Japanese general and patriotic propagandist, served as war minister from 1931 to 1934 and as education minister in 1938-39. Araki was the idol of the reformist young army officers from the time of the Manchurian incident (September 18, 1931) onward. A leading proponent of larger military budgets and Japanese expansion northward against the **USSR**, he also wanted to replace the Nine-Power Treaty with a new **United States-Japan** understanding to assure order in eastern Asia. Araki's nationalism, propounded in a series of army pamphlets, called for an "imperial way" that would "show the world our brilliant essence." As education minister he enthusiastically promoted **National Spiritual Mobilization.** Sentenced to life in prison by the International Military Tribunal for the Far East in 1948, Araki was paroled because of poor health in 1955.

ARBEITSDIENST.

In 1935, **Hitler** required a six-month period in a state-sponsored *Arbeitsdienst* ("Labor Service") camp for German youths leaving school. These camps were established by Col. Konstantin Hierl for the purpose of educating young people "in the spirit of National Socialism." Sports and group discipline were regarded as excellent preparation for military service. The *Arbeitsdienst,* initially devoted to the restoration of rural areas and forests, was frequently sent to work on military projects during the war. A women's branch, also requiring a service period of six months, functioned mainly to help rural women and the wives of workers in their kitchen duties.

ARCADIA CONFERENCE.

See **Conferences, Allied.**

ARDEATINE CAVES.

On March 24, 1944, in the caves of the Via Ardeatina, near Rome, the Germans shot 335 political and Jewish prisoners (some of whom had been pointed out by the Fascist police) in retaliation for an attack by the Italian **Resistance** on a German column in the Via Rasella the day before; the attack had claimed 32 lives. Following **Hitler**'s orders, German Field Marshal **Albert Kesselring** set the rule of shooting 10 Italians for every German killed.

ARDENNES, Battle of the.

See **Bulge, Battle of the.**

ARGENLIEU, Admiral Thierry d' (1889-1964).

Argenlieu, a French churchman, joined **de Gaulle** in London in June 1940. He was soon named high commissioner of **Free France** in the Pacific.

ARGONAUT CONFERENCE.

See **Conferences, Allied.**

ARITA, Hachiro (1884-1965).

Arita served as foreign minister of **Japan** at various times in four separate cabinets between April 1936 and July 1940. Since 1927 Arita had led the Asia (renovationist) faction, seeking more influence for the foreign ministry and a more Asian-oriented national policy. As foreign minister in November 1938, he denounced the Nine-Power Treaty, called for certain commercial restrictions on the Western countries and declared Japan's **New Order in East Asia** a strictly defensive measure. In April 1939 he opposed binding Japan too closely to **Germany** and **Italy** when others called for strengthening the Anti-Comintern Pact of 1936. Arita helped to install the puppet regime of **Wang Ching-wei** in China in 1940.

ARMAND, Louis (1905-1971).

Armand, a French mining engineer, was a member of the *Academie Francaise.* He organized the **Resistance** among railroad employees; this group was to play an important part in the **sabotage** of rail transport. After the war he became one of the most zealous promoters of the European Community.

ARNIM, Hans-Jurgen von (1889-1971).

German general. In 1941 Arnim was made a division commander, then head of the Fifth Armored Division in Africa and, in March 1943, commander in chief of the armies in Tunisia, whose surrender on May 13 ended the fighting in Africa.

ARNOLD, Henry H. ("Happy") (1886-1950).

Arnold, an American airman, learned to fly with the Wright brothers. He served during the war as chief of the USAAF and, consequently, on the Chiefs of Staff Committee from 1941 to 1946.

ARTIFICIAL PORTS (Mulberries).

When the Allies prepared for the **Normandy landing,** it became evident to them that the Germans would do everything possible to prevent their French ports from falling into enemy hands. They consequently decided on a surprise approach, which involved bypassing existing ports and landing on a bare expanse of beach. Two structures were designed to accomplish this purpose: **landing craft** of various types that were to be deliberately run aground on the beach and then opened to discharge their cargo, and artificial ports.

Churchill had conceived the idea of artificial ports as far back as 1915. In 1940, as prime minister, he thought of it again. On May 30, 1942 he elaborated on his concept in a note dispatched to **Mountbatten,** who for some time had pondered over the problems that would be posed by a military landing. During a meeting of the chiefs of staff, Mountbatten declared; "If there are no employable ports, we can build them piece by piece and tow them over." After **reconnaissance** information about Dieppe (see **Combined Operations**) confirmed the need for "mulberries" (the code name given to these artificial ports), two of them were constructed in June 1944 for use at Arromanches and Vierville. Their use came as a complete surprise to the Germans, who had never even suspected their existence. Carried over the English Channel piece by piece, these two ports, complete with breakwaters, loading platforms and mobile jetties almost ⅔ of a mile in length, had a storage capacity exceeding the port of Dover. They could handle daily cargo unloadings of 6,000 tons of equipment and 1,250 tons of vehicles. The construction of these brilliant examples of British naval engineering in-

Fig. 1

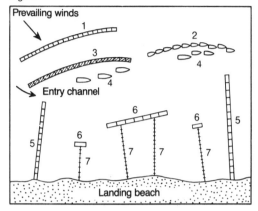

Prevailing winds

Entry channel

Landing beach

Fig. 1   Schema of the Artificial Port

1. Floating breakwaters
2. Breakwaters formed by old ships loaded with cement and sunk
3. Breakwaters formed by submerged caissons
4. Anchored cargo ships
5. Sheltering jetties made of sunken caissons
6. Wharves
7. Floating jetties

Fig. 2 A Cross-Section of the Artificial Port
The three circled segments are shown in greater detail in Fig. 3

Fig. 2

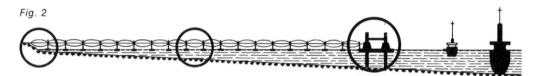

Fig. 3

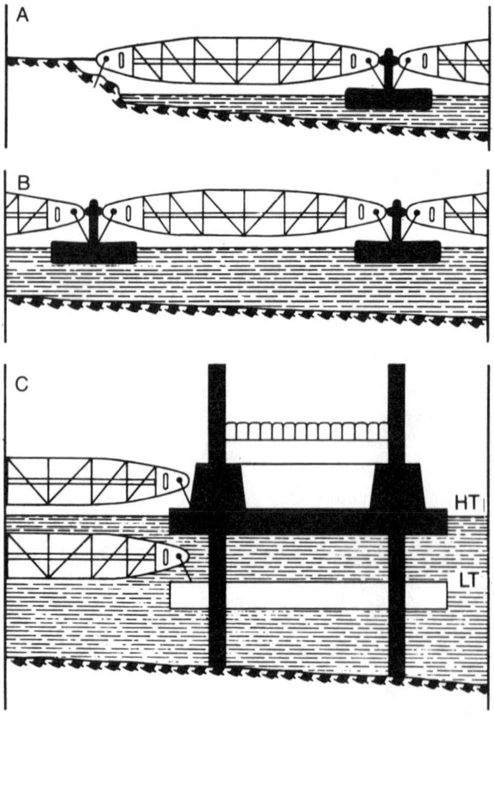

A

B

C

HT

LT

Fig. 4

A

B

A

B

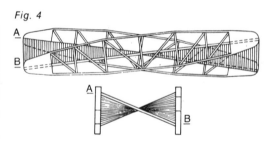

Fig. 4 Possible Damages to the Floating Jetties

Fig. 3   Details of Cross-Section
Detail C shows how the position of the wharves and, consequently, of the floating jetties could be adjusted, according to the tides
HT—High tide
LT—Low tide

genuity, weighing one million tons each, required the labor of 20,000 men over a period of eight months, as well as 100,000 tons of steel and 8.75 million cubic feet of concrete. The Vierville port, constructed under extremely bad weather conditions, turned out to be useless. So did the Cherbourg "mulberry," which was finished on June 27, 1944. But the Arromanches mulberry was able to discharge cargoes of 680,000 tons of equipment, 40,000 vehicles and 220,000 men between mid-July and October 31, 1944.

The artificial port used at Arromanches consisted of four basic elements. The first was *breakwaters* of three different sorts. One line of breakwaters was formed by filling 60 old ships with 500,000 tons of cement, which, of course, caused them to sink. Next came 146 open caissons of reinforced concrete. Six different types of caissons were made, ranging in weight from 1,672 tons to 6,044 tons; they were deployed at different levels as the depth of the ocean floor increased. The largest could be used where the ocean floor reached a depth of 30 feet. These caissons, armed with Bofors guns to protect personnel, were towed across the Channel by 1,500-horsepower tugs. At the proper moment the caissons' valves were opened; they then filled with water and sank. The outermost breakwaters, cylindrical metal floats 225 feet long and 16 feet in diameter, were assembled side by side in groups of three and supported by a concrete "keel" weighing 750 tons, the upper part of which emerged six feet from the surface of the water. Anchored at a depth of 65 feet, they were placed end to end to form a floating breakwater a mile long, which took the first shock of the waves, before they struck the caissons.

The second element of the mulberries was *fixed* or *sheltering jetties*. Floating caissons were placed end to end and sunk in lines at right angles to the shore. They protected the port from waves, and from attacking midget submarines or frogmen, and served as loading platforms for small ships.

Next were *wharves* made of pontoons. To keep the floating platforms at a steady horizontal level, which was necessary to avoid complications in unloading ships, they were anchored to steel braces on the ocean floor by a system of pulleys and cables. To compensate for the tides, pontoons were raised or lowered by winches. The winch operation was controlled by extensometers that were connected to the cables securing the pontoons to the steel braces.

The most difficult problem was how to maintain a continuous connection between the pontoons and the shore, which, at high tide, was about 3,000 feet away. In spite of the breakwaters the sea was in such constant turmoil that there was doubt as to how long *floating jetties* made up of several sections would behave. Exhaustive studies beginning in 1941 led to the construction of a jetty supported by floating caissons. Each 100-foot section was composed of two girders in an extremely rigid "bowstring" form, transversely connected at the center by an equally rigid strut and at different points on the strut by a number of articulated braces. The striated sheet metal deck was fixed to the various braces in such a way as to permit expansion. Thus, the ends of the two master girders could take various positions relative to one another. The whole structure was made of high-elasticity steel; its components were riveted together.

The variation of the tides was such that the floating jetties needed the capacity to lengthen or shorten. For this purpose they were fitted with telescoping sections, each consisting of twin girders whose ends were enclosed in a central unit into which they could slide. In this way each section could be lengthened by nine feet.

The installation of an artificial port required a graded shoreline, depending on its composition—i.e., whether it was primarily wet sand, pebbles, marsh etc. Roads in some cases needed to be constructed from prefabricated material shipped across the English Channel and swiftly laid by engineering crews. The road-building material was sometimes prefabricated metal mats, or perhaps of mineral or vegetable origin. In this last instance a British Valentine tank was sent forward with an enormous drum dispensing several hundred feet of coconut matting. A roadway laid down in this fashion over wet or dry sand proved excellent for wheeled and tractored vehicles.

H. Bernard

ASDIC.
See **Sonar**.

ASIA.
See **Greater East Asia Co-Prosperity Sphere; Japan; Pacific Theater of Operations**.

ASQ.
In this French village in the Departement du Nord, 86 people were massacred by German troops on April 2, 1944 in revenge for a **sabotage** attack on the railroads.

ASSASSINATION ATTEMPT OF JULY 20, 1944.
An unsuccessful bomb attempt on **Hitler**'s life was carried out by Col. **Claus Schenk von Stauffenberg** at the German general headquarters in Rastenburg, East Prussia.

ATLANTIC, Battle of the.

A misnomer on two counts, this term applies to a long campaign that lasted from 1939 to 1945, rather than to a single battle, and to a naval war that also extended to other seas around the world—the Mediterranean, the Arctic, the Indian Ocean and the Pacific. Sea warfare per se was limited primarily to the Atlantic, Mediterranean and Arctic, since in the Pacific, sea, air and land forces were intimately combined in a single operation. Soviet naval action in the Baltic and Black seas, although effective, was not regarded as part of the Battle of the Atlantic, because it was confined to closed bodies of water out of touch with the far-flung ocean battles.

1939-1941

In 1939 the Royal Navy was suffering from the consequences of the British government's disarmament policy, in effect since 1919. At the beginning of September the following vessels were in service: 12 battleships (five under construction), seven aircraft carriers (four under construction), 65 cruisers (13 under construction), 188 destroyers (28 under construction) and 52 submarines (24 under construction). Air protection for the RN was insufficient; the fleet did not have enough aircraft carriers or squadrons of the Fleet Air Arm (carrier aircraft operating under the Admiralty rather than the RAF). The RN had one-third the number of destroyers it had in 1918. But these small ships that protected convoys against the threat of enemy submarines were the very foundation of the navy of a country totally dependent on its merchant marine. On the other hand, the RN had **radar** for penetrating night and fog. Furthermore, its admirals were of Nelsonian stature—such men as **Bertram Ramsay**, **Andrew Cunningham**, Max Horton, Bruce Fraser and Philip Vian, to say nothing of its lower-ranking officers and sailors worthy of the navy's great traditions. The British merchant marine was first among the nations of the world, totaling over 21 million tons.

Of the three branches of the French armed forces, only the navy had completely modern equipment in 1939. It comprised seven battleships (three under construction), one aircraft carrier (another under construction), 19 cruisers, 66 destroyers and 78 submarines (16 under construction). Manned by top-notch crews and well prepared for its essential mission—to maintain contact with **French North Africa**—it played a major role in the Mediterranean supporting British naval power in the Atlantic.

The German navy, or *Kriegsmarine*, was founded in 1935 and soon became a powerful combat instrument. Its brand new ships contrasted sharply with many British vessels, refitted relics that had seen action in the

Battle of Jutland (1916). The German navy consisted of seven battleships, two aircraft carriers, 15 cruisers, 22 destroyers and 57 submarines. Most of these ships were faster than comparable Allied vessels. Yet the *Kriegsmarine* had one fatal weakness: its submarine arm. Adm. **Karl Doenitz**, commander of the **U-boat** fleet and a subordinate of Adm. **Erich Raeder**, persistently requested additional submarines but made little headway against **Hitler**'s continental mentality. The Nazi leader seemed unable to grasp the basic problem presented by war with the **United Kingdom**. For Britain, naval war meant mastery of the sea lanes—complete freedom to transport land armies and their equipment, as well as supplies for the civilian population. **Germany** had to keep Britain from attaining these goals by preventing the import and export of men, materiel and supplies. In his speeches before the war, Hitler himself stressed the importance of blockading the British Isles, dependent as they were on imports, and starving them out of the war. To achieve this goal, Doenitz demanded at least 300 submarines, with 100 earmarked for permanent patrol around Britain. At the outbreak of the war, however, only 57 submarines were in service. Doenitz expected a production rate of 29 per month. During the first half of 1940, German factories barely managed two per month; in the second half they turned out six per month. Production increased progressively during 1941, reaching 20 per month by the end of the year. But in the first months of the war, only some 20 submarines were in condition for permanent operations. Although they could sink poorly defended freighters, their success was far short of what it might have been if Doenitz had gotten the quantity he asked for.

At the outbreak of the war, the British steamer *Athenia*, carrying civilians, was sunk without warning by a U-boat 200 miles west of the Hebrides. Of the 112 passengers who perished, the first victims of the war in the Atlantic Theater, 28 were Americans. The psychological error of the torpedoing of the *Lusitania* in 1915 was thus repeated. The commander of the German submarine was severely reprimanded for violating Hitler's strict orders against provoking the neutral **United States**. On September 17 the British aircraft carrier *Courageous* was torpedoed in the North Atlantic, and on October 14 the battleship *Royal Oak* met the same fate, sunk by a submarine that daringly sneaked into Scapa Flow, a major RN harbor.

From the day the war began, the German battleship *Admiral Graf Spee*, one of the fastest and best-armed warships afloat, caused havoc among merchant ships in the South Atlantic. It was hunted down by a British squadron of four smaller ships under Commodore Henry Harwood. Despite the lesser caliber and range of its guns, the squadron, by clever maneuvering, trapped the German ship in the Rio de Plata on December 17. The captain of the *Graf Spee* scuttled the ship and shot himself; his crew was interned in Uruguay.

In the four last months of 1939, Allied merchant vessels, organized in well-escorted **convoys**, suffered relatively few losses compared to the damage inflicted on the pursuing U-boats. Large fleets sailed from **Canada** to Great Britain without incident. British technicians promptly found a countermeasure to the magnetic mines strewn by the Germans across the North Sea.

The Allies lost the Norwegian campaign of April 9-June 10, 1940, but this was not a complete disaster. German air power, operating so effectively against land forces and ports, proved incapable of wresting mastery of the sea from the British navy. The latter maintained its communications with outgoing as well as incoming vessels despite enemy air superiority. Aside from the sinking of the aircraft carrier *Glorious*, with 20 planes and 1,515 crewmen, Allied naval losses were sparse. The *Kriegsmarine*, moreover, was not left unscathed. It lost 10 modern destroyers in its naval defeat off Narvik on April 10-13. Also important was the loss of the cruisers *Bluecher* and *Karlsruhe*, which seriously diminished German naval power in the West.

With the German invasion of France in May 1940, the RN and French ships of the Pas de Calais under Adm. Ramsay accomplished what has been justly called the "Miracle of Dunkirk." Strongly supported by the RAF, which gained air superiority for the first time, the British and French overcame apparently insurmountable difficulties. With only a fraction of the ships needed to transport the huge masses of men stranded at Dunkirk, the British government called for volunteers. On the banks of the Thames and along the coast appeared the most incredible armada ever seen—fishing boats, pleasure yachts, lifeboats and trawlers. Handled by their owners or hired pilots, they threaded their way through the perils of mines, bombs and torpedoes to rescue 100,000 men. From May 26 to June 4, a total of 366,162 Allied soldiers made the crossing; of these 224,717 were British, 141,145 French and 300 Belgian, Dutch and Polish. From June 10 to June 23, the navy evacuated 242,141 people, including 50,271 civilians and 191,870 military men, 144,171 of whom were British; 18,246 French, later joining **de Gaulle**; 24,352 Polish; 4,938 Czech; and 300 Belgian and Dutch.

June 1940 was a hard month for the RN. On June 25 France capitulated. Generally loyal to Petain (see **Petain and the French State**), the French navy ignored de Gaulle's appeal for continued **resistance**. Only a few ships—notably the superb submarine *Surcouf*, the most powerful of its type in that era—went over to the British. The RN suffered an additional blow when, on June 10, **Italy** entered the war on the German side. The Italian navy at the time was a potent combat force, possessing six first-class battleships of the Cavour type that were faster than their British counterparts, 18 cruisers, 60 destroyers and 119 submarines, then the largest aggregate of underwater vessels owned by any nation. Yet despite its modern equipment and competent seamen, the Italian navy suffered from two glaring defects: it had neither radar nor naval aircraft. Its lack of aircraft carriers mattered little in view of the many Italian bases in the Mediterranean. But the fleet had no experience with land forces or in bombing land-based targets. The complex planning involved in air **reconnaissance** at sea, communication of information to the fleet and destruction of enemy warships with aircraft could not be improvised with any hope of success.

With the fall of France and Italy's entry into the war, the British situation seemed desperate. Germany controlled an arc of newly won bases from Saint-Jean-de-Luz to Narvik, the springboard of a possible attack on the United Kingdom. Submarine pens were built at Brest, **Saint-Nazaire**, Lorient and Bordeaux. Airports were constructed within range of British shipping near the coasts of **Norway**, **Denmark**, **the Netherlands**, **Belgium** and France. The RN's position was also insecure in the Mediterranean, where its bases at **Gibraltar**, **Malta**, and Alexandria were vulnerable to German attack.

At this critical juncture, when Britain could be irreparably hurt if the French fleet joined or surrendered to the **Axis**, **Churchill** reluctantly ordered the **Mers el-Kebir** operation on July 3, 1940. The Franco-German armistice specified that the French navy was to remain disarmed and at anchor in Toulon harbor, except for several squadrons assigned to protect the French colonies against British or Gaullist attacks. An important squadron consisting of the battleships *Dunkerque, Provence, Strasbourg* and *Bretagne,* under the command of Adm. Marcel Gensoul, lay at Mers el-Kebir. It was confronted by British Naval Force H from Gibraltar, commanded by Adm. James Somerville, who radioed Gensoul an ultimatum offering several alternatives: join the RN and cooperate with it in ensuing combat; enter British ports with reduced crews; or proceed to the French Antilles or neutral U.S. ports with reduced crews. If he chose internment in Britain or the U.S., Gensoul was promised repatriation of all crewmen to France and return of his ships after the war. Gensoul was also offered a fourth solution: scuttle his ships at Mers el-Kebir. Shortly after 9:30 a.m., he was given another six hours to come to a decision. He radioed the French Admiralty in unoccupied France that a British force had presented him with an ultimatum that he scuttle his vessels making no mention of the other possibilities offered. Ordered to fight and promised aid from other naval forces in the Mediterannean, the French admiral rejected the ultimatum. Somerville held his fire even after the six hours elapsed in the hope that Gensoul would order many of his crew ashore for their own safety. But London intercepted the French Admiralty's message and ordered Somerville to take action. The British ships opened fire at 5:25 p.m., sinking the *Dunkerque*, the *Provence* and the *Bretagne* together with a destroyer; 1,200 French sailors died. The *Strasbourg* managed to escape and rejoined the French fleet at Toulon.

Although the Mers el-Kebir attack was comprehensible in view of Britain's situation, it nevertheless shocked and angered many Frenchmen. Anti-British and anti-Gaullist sentiment grew among the French sailors, bringing many of them over to the side of Petain.

At Alexandria, where another French squadron, commanded by Adm. Rene Godfroy, was anchored, a much more satisfactory settlement was reached because of the personal friendship between Godfroy and the British naval commander in the Mediterranean, Adm. Andrew Cunningham. Godfroy, preferring to remain faithful to Petain but reluctant to fight his former allies, gave his word not to take his fleet out of Alexandria, in return for Cunningham's promise not to seize the French ships. London at first hesitated to accept this gentleman's agreement, but Churchill finally gave way before the arguments of Cunningham and the consideration that the French fleet at Alexandria was out of range of the Italo-German forces—certainly not the case of the French fleet at Mers el-Kebir.

The balance of naval power remained favorable to Britain in the second half of 1940. During the **Battle of Britain** (July 10-October 31), won by the RAF with the aid of radar, the Royal and merchant navies fulfilled their duties without excessive losses. Hitler was paying the penalty of his grudging expenditures for submarines. Neither Adm. Raeder nor his chiefs of staff relished the plan for invading England, known as *Seeloewe* ("Sea Lion"), which was destined to remain buried in the files of the *Oberkommando der Wehrmacht*.

In the Mediterranean the RN scored one success after another. Cunningham's ships had twice defeated the Italian fleet since July. With neither sea-air cooperation nor radar, **Mussolini**'s sea squadrons had to move cautiously despite their central position and strength as well as the advantage of numerous nearby

bases. In November 1940 Cunningham dealt the Italians a further blow. Most of the Italian fleet was concentrated at Taranto, from which it could control the central Mediterranean and protect the troop transports sailing to **Albania** following Mussolini's declaration of war against **Greece** on October 28. Sutherland hydroplanes from Malta kept the Taranto fleet under close surveillance. On the evening of November 11 two waves of Swordfish torpedo bombers totaling 21 aircraft took off from the carrier *Illustrious* 167 miles off Taranto. Achieving complete surprise, they sank the battleship *Cavour*, disabled the battleships *Littorio* and *Duilio* and badly damaged two cruisers and the Taranto arsenal. On the following days, several smaller Italian ships were destroyed. Malta could now be reinforced, and British ships entering the Adriatic to aid the Greeks encountered no resistance.

Most of the remaining Italian fleet took refuge in the Bay of Naples, where it suffered an all-night bombardment on January 8-9, 1941 before fleeing to La Spezia. Somerville's Force H arrived on February 9 from Gibraltar and hammered Genoa with impunity, while aircraft from the carrier *Ark Royal* raided Livorno and La Spezia. Rome was panic-stricken. On March 28 several British naval units engaged an Italian squadron in the battle of Cape Matapan, destroying three cruisers and several other ships and damaging the battleship *Vittorio Veneto*. While British land forces were taking **Eritrea** and **Ethiopia**, the Italian Red Sea squadron of nine destroyers, eight submarines and some smaller ships was smashed by British naval aircraft in April.

The German invasion of Greece put British naval forces in the Mediterranean to a severe test. The RN landed 57,000 men to aid Greek forces at the beginning of April but was forced to evacuate 45,000 of them at the end of the month. Air cover was weak because of the remoteness of British bases in **Egypt**, and the operation proved costly. At the end of May another 16,500 British troops had to be evacuated from Crete in the face of a second German invasion. With this island and the entire Aegean area in Axis hands, British naval units throughout the eastern and central Mediterranean became extremely vulnerable. The battleship *Nelson* and the aircraft carrier *Ark Royal* were soon destroyed. British naval strategists had to regard the sea-lanes between Sicily and Tunisia as a "dead area," routing their ships around the Cape of Good Hope to reach Egypt and the Far East. Axis convoys, on the other hand, could follow the direct line between Sicily and Cape Bon in Tunisia to reach Libyan ports; later, with the assent of the Vichy government, they had free use of Tunisian territorial waters. The fate of the British base on Malta hung by a thread. Partly cut off, the island faced incessant

German air attack. Provisioning it was a constant problem for the RN. Convoys from Gibraltar to Malta, led by Adm. Philip Vian, often lost half to two-thirds of their ships on the voyage; on one of the runs only a single ship survived to reach its destination.

Meanwhile, the United States was taking steps to help Britain despite its neutrality. In September 1940, well before passage of the **Lend-Lease** Act, **Roosevelt** initiated a series of aid measures, including transfer to the British fleet of 50 destroyers and some merchant vessels. On March 31, 1941 all German and Italian ships in U.S. harbors were seized. On April 18, Washington announced establishment of a line separating the eastern and western hemispheres; following the 30th meridian (later 26th) west, it placed Greenland in the American sphere and permitted construction of several U.S. bases on the island. U.S. warships patrolled their zone and notified London of all enemy activity they encountered. The U.S. Navy also undertook protection of convoys as far as **Iceland**. German torpedoing of the American destroyer *Robin Moor* on May 21 led to a decree of June 14 that froze German and Italian assets in the United States. Consulates and agencies of the Axis countries were closed "by virtue of their subversive attitude."

The Allies lost 3,991,641 tons of shipping in 1940, a less than catastrophic figure. The losses of the British merchant navy, the withdrawal of France and the active opposition of Italy were to some extent balanced by help from the merchant marines of smaller countries occupied by Germany but still contributing to the Allied cause—Norway, the Netherlands, Denmark, Belgium, **Poland**, **Yugoslavia** and Greece, as well as a number of Free French vessels. Small Norwegian and Dutch warships also put themselves at the RN's disposal.

The number of German submarines during 1941 increased from 89 to 198. Allied losses rose as a result, reaching 4,228,558 tons for the year; this was still within bearable limits. However, U-boat construction remained below the "critical point," despite Doenitz's insistent appeals. Two very successful raids by British and Norwegian commandos (see **Commandos and Rangers**) against German installations at Lofoten on March 3-4 and at Vaagso on December 26-28 demonstrated that the RN was still alive and kicking.

On May 21, 1941 the German pocket battleship *Bismarck* emerged from Bergen fjord with several escort ships, intent on disrupting Allied shipping in the North Atlantic. Its departure was immediately signaled to London by the alert Norwegian Resistance. With the RN increasingly harassed in the Mediterranean around Greece and Crete, the moment was well chosen by German naval strategists. The *Bismarck* was then the most powerful warship afloat, superior to the largest British dreadnoughts in displacement, speed and firepower. Off the south coast of Iceland, it sank the British battleship *Hood*, killing Vice Adm. L. E. Holland. Trapped after a furious race across the North Atlantic by the RN, the Fleet Air Arm and the Coastal Command, the *Bismarck* went to the bottom 700 miles off Brest on May 27, carrying down 2,000 men. Vice Adm. Guenther Luetjens disappeared with his ship.

With the German invasion of the **USSR**, Britain and the still neutral U.S. undertook to supply Soviet forces with desperately needed arms and materiel. Beginning in August the British navy organized convoys to the Arctic and Arkangel in the teeth of German attacks. U-boats and aircraft based in Norway inflicted heavy losses on the ships but failed to halt them. The line of supply to the Soviet Union continued along this route throughout the war.

The Japanese attack on **Pearl Harbor** brought the U.S. into the war as an active belligerent on the side of Britain. Half of the powerful U.S. Navy was allotted to the Atlantic, the other half to the Pacific, where it avenged the Pearl Harbor disaster with an important victory at **Midway** on June 3-4, 1942. The RN had suffered severely in the Far East, however, losing the superb warships *Prince of Wales* and *Repulse* in the Gulf of Siam on December 10, 1941.

1942

For the Allies the first six months of 1942 were perhaps the bleakest of the entire sea war. It was in this period that German industry attained the critical point in submarine production, much to Doenitz's satisfaction. Germany had 249 submarines in January and 365 in October, with more than 100 Italian and 65 Japanese submarines also in action. German coastal aviation cooperated efficiently with its U-boat counterpart.

On February 12, 1942 the German battleships *Scharnhorst* and *Gneisenau*, accompanied by the cruiser *Prinz Eugen*, slipped past the RN in a sudden dash from Brest to their home ports across the North Sea. A deep sense of humiliation settled on Britain, especially since this mishap coincided with military defeat in **Libya** and the disaster at **Singapore**. The new German battleship *Tirpitz*, based in Norway and escorted by cruisers, destroyers, submarines and aircraft, ravaged supply convoys to the USSR with apparent impunity.

The situation was no less alarming in the Mediterranean. At the end of 1941, *Luftwaffe* Gen. **Albert Kesselring** arrived in Italy at the head of the Second Air Fleet and the Second Flying Corps to reinforce

Axis air strength in the area. His mission was to paralyze Allied sea traffic in order to neutralize Malta preparatory to an invasion attempt and to support Axis forces in Libya. Adm. Raeder sent 21 U-boats to the Mediterranean to strengthen the Italian submarine fleet. The losses sustained by the Royal and merchant navies reached serious proportions. Adm. Vian's brilliant victory in the Gulf of Sidra on March 20-23 did not end the ordeal of Malta, which had to defend itself with 85 fighter planes and AA guns. Allied fortunes reached their nadir when Axis land forces triumphed at Gazala-Tobruk and entered Egypt between May 26 and June 25.

Despite German submarine and air attacks in the Atlantic, British commandos raided Bruneval on February 27, Saint-Nazaire on March 26 and Dieppe on August 19 (see **Combined Operations**). The Germans still retained the initiative, however. Allied merchant shipping losses increased with **Japan**'s entry into the war, totaling 7,697,905 tons for the entire year. The worst month of the war was June 1942, when 823,656 tons were lost with the fall of Tobruk. Destruction outstripped production. While submarines prowled in "wolf pack" groups and *Luftwaffe* squadrons attacked convoys to Britain, other submarines expanded their area of operations toward the American coast.

Fatalities among Allied merchant seamen were exceptionally high because of Hitler's illegal order against rescuing survivors. Ships, he reasoned, were more easily replaceable than the highly qualified personnel required to handle them. On September 17, 1942 German naval headquarters issued a confidential directive stating that "no attempt of any kind is to be made to save passengers on foundering vessels. No persons may be helped out of the water or pulled into lifeboats, capsized boats must not be righted, neither food nor water may be distributed. Rescues run counter to the elementary exigencies of war, which are to destroy enemy ships and their crews."

The tide began to turn at the end of the year, beginning in the Mediterranean. While Axis land forces were first halted and then defeated at **El Alamein** by the British Eighth Army, the RAF Middle East strategic air group under Air Chief Marshal **A. W. Tedder** won complete mastery of the skies. Aircraft of the **Bomber Command** and Coastal Command struck repeatedly and with increasing effectiveness at ships supplying Field Marshal **Rommel**. The German commander blamed Kesselring and the Italians not only for his supply difficulties but also for the complete reversal of the situation on Malta. Under its new governor, Lord **Gort**, the island changed from a defensive to an offensive base, heavily reinforced by aircraft and submarines.

On the night of November 7-8, 670 ships participating in Operation **Torch** landed American and British troops at Casablanca, Oran and Algiers. The plan was a closely kept secret and took Axis commanders by surprise. As the massive invasion force prepared to land, a feebly escorted convoy moving from Sierra Leone to England lured away submarines. The operation's success was all the more remarkable in view of the heavy losses suffered by Allied shipping in the North Atlantic from U-boat and air attacks.

On November 13 Adm. **Darlan** changed sides at his headquarters in Algeria and ordered French North Africa to reenter the war on the Allied side. Ignoring his directive the French fleet at Toulon scuttled its ships except for five submarines, three of which made their way to Algeria. The French fleet at Dakar, dominated by the powerful battleship *Richelieu*, followed the Alexandria-based ships of Adm. Godfroy in joining the Allied war effort. All overseas French possessions except for those under Japanese control did likewise.

1943-1945

Until the end of 1942, German submarines roamed freely in the North Atlantic as far south as the Azores, an area still out of range of British and American aircraft. The South Atlantic, down to the Cape of Good Hope and stretching west to the Caribbean and the Gulf of Mexico, was also dangerous for Allied ships. An offensive launched by the British Coastal Command in 1942 was only moderately effective; U-boat commanders had little fear of aircraft with long-wave radar.

German submarine production continued to soar in 1943, increasing the number of U-boats from 393 in January to 432 at the end of the year. While Britain and its dominions struggled to step up their merchant ship production, the U.S. revolutionized shipbuilding with mass production methods. Yet containing German offensive action was no longer enough for the Allies; the problem had to be solved at its roots. British Adm. Horton, commander of the western sea approaches, collaborated with the chiefs of the Coastal Command on the following countermeasures:

(1) The number of escorting vessels was substantially increased. Until the end of 1942 the British appointed escort ship groups that were sent at the desired moment to threatened convoys and then dispatched on other missions when the danger had subsided. But the enormous productive capacity of the U.S. assured victory in the battle of the convoys by permitting merchant vessels to be escorted with adequate strength over their entire voyage. Experience showed that escort ships, to be effective, had to outnumber submarines by two to one. In 1942 a convoy

of 50 merchant ships had eight destroyer escorts to ward off attacks from a submarine pack of 10 to 15; in 1944 the same number of ships had as many as 30 destroyer escorts.

(2) Under the successive leadership of Air Chief Marshals **Philip Joubert de la Ferte, John C. Slessor** and W. Sholto Douglas, the British Coastal Command became a formidable force. Liberator bombers with a range of more than 1,200 miles, operating out of Labrador and Newfoundland as well as England, patrolled the entire North Atlantic. Combined aerial and surface-escort tactics progressively throttled the German offensive in the Atlantic.

(3) Production of small aircraft carriers for escort service to extend the range of operations was stepped up. For important convoys, attack groups accompanied by escort aircraft carriers were assembled.

(4) New antisubmarine tactics were put into effect, and both aircraft pilots and sailors in the Coastal Command were thoroughly trained in their use. All convoy commanders were required to take a course at the Tactical School in Liverpool on German attack methods and how to cope with them.

(5) **Sonar** came into more widespread use as a means of detecting submerged U-boats. At the beginning of the war, the device was too primitive to do more than give the position of a detected submarine, but improvements permitted it to measure the depth of the vessel's dive. If the U-boat surfaced, it was easily spotted by escorting ships equipped with radar.

(6) Antisubmarine bombs and depth charges were continuously improved to explore at greater depth and with greater force.

(7) A system developed for intercepting radio transmissions from German submarines helped convoy commanders locate and track down lurking wolf packs.

(8) Allied air attacks on German factories manufacturing submarines and accessory equipment were extremely successful, although until 1944 bombing of submarine pens and repair facilities yielded disappointing results at a high cost.

(9) The discovery of centimeter waves led to new advances in submarine detection that ultimately proved decisive in the Battle of the Atlantic.

In addition to these developments, occupation of all of North Africa in May 1943 assured the Allies freedom of movement in the Mediterranean and sharply reduced shipping losses in the area. This made possible the landing of Anglo-American forces in Sicily, beginning July 10, 1943, and in Italy, on September 3, without the danger of naval retaliation from the enemy. The surrender of Italy and the cession of its fleet became official on September 8. Four days later Adm. Cunningham notified London that "the Italian

fleet now lies at anchor under the guns of the Malta Fortress." The island's long defense had been vindicated.

Although the existence of Allied bases in Greenland, Iceland, the Faeroes and Britain helped control the submarine threat in the North Atlantic, the central and southern Atlantic remained dangerous. The occupation of Morocco's west coast, Allied control of Dakar and **Brazil**'s entry into the war on August 22, 1942 eased the problem but did not close off all avenues of escape for the U-boats. On August 18, 1943, Allied forces occupied the Azores with the permission of the Portuguese government, establishing antisubmarine facilities on the islands of Fayal and Terceira.

In Germany Adm. Raeder fell out of favor when he failed to prevent the Allied landings in North Africa. Scorned by Hitler as strictly a "battleship admiral," he was replaced by Doenitz, who announced almost immediately that submarine construction would increase even more, that secret weapons were in preparation and that U-boats would attack convoys in successive waves of several packs rather than in a single group.

Although the number of operational German submarines continued to rise, from 425 in April 1943 to 436 in January 1944, reaching a peak of 444 the following April, the change in naval leadership failed to alter the outcome of the Battle of the Atlantic. While the Germans had lost only one submarine for every 60,000 tons of Allied merchant ships sunk in 1942, 41 U-boats were destroyed in May 1943 for 299,428 tons of Allied shipping—less than 8,000 tons per submarine. In all of 1943 the Allies manufactured 43.59 million tons of merchant shipping and lost only 3.22 million tons. U.S. and British industrial resources could then be shifted from compensating for immediate losses to the production of ships for the approaching spring and the landings on the French coasts. In the Pacific the USN reigned supreme; Japanese submarines claimed few victims. Allied losses throughout the world continued to decrease to less than 87,000 tons in April 1944 and to 27,297 tons the following May. The failure of Germany's sea effort was clearly demonstrated by the fact that, as in 1918, not a single ship transporting U.S. troops to Europe was sunk.

On June 6, 1944 the largest armada ever appeared off the coast of Normandy (see **Normandy Landing**). Under the command of British Adm. Ramsay, it included 6,939 ships of every type—1,213 warships, from battleships to midget submarines; 4,126 landing ships and landing craft; and 1,600 auxiliary and merchant vessels. The British furnished 79 percent of these ships (several of them flying the Canadian flag) and the Americans 16.5 percent; the rest were made up of French, Dutch, Norwegian, Danish, Polish, Belgian and Greek vessels. The warships passed through 12 channels that had been cleared and sounded by 12 groups of minesweepers. German aircraft and submarine resistance was practically nil. On the following August 15 an American-British-French task force under the command of U.S. Adm. H. K. Hewitt made an even smoother landing in the south of France.

The German surface fleet by this time had practically been wiped out. The battleship *Scharnhorst* was destroyed by the *Duke of York*, commanded by Adm. Bruce Fraser, on Christmas Day of 1943 off the coast of Norway. On November 12, 1944, 22 RAF Lancester bombers sank the *Tirpitz* in the Tromso fjord.

German ingenuity was still active, however. Remote-controlled bombs launched from aircraft came into increasing use. At the end of 1944, German submarines began to employ the snorkel, which was also an excellent response to Allied radar, leaving only a barely detectable line projecting above the surface of the water. In 1945 the *Kriegsmarine* introduced the powerful model XXI submarine of 1,000 tons and the model XXIII of 223 tons, with a diving speed of 17 knots, compared to seven knots in earlier models. These new types could submerge in less than 25 seconds and descend to almost 1,000 feet below the surface—an effective response to sonar. As a result of German innovations, Allied shipping losses increased slightly during the first months of 1945. But, like the V-1 and V-2 and jet aircraft, these new weapons came too late. Allied antisubmarine techniques remained adequate to contain the threat.

The principal weapon employed by Allied surface vessels and aircraft against the U-boats was the 300-pound depth charge. But most destroyers were also equipped with bombs fired forward of the bow, known as hedgehogs and squids. These were introduced at the beginning of the war in order to compensate for the loss of sonar contact during the final approach to the target submarine. For night bombing, Allied aircraft depended primarily on radar and on the Leigh light to illuminate their targets. But a new method of low-altitude bomb-sighting by radar without illumination was in the course of development for surprise attacks, and a 600-pound antisubmarine bomb became part of the naval arsenal. Allied tacticians also developed further uses of the sonobuoy, a combination hydrophone-radio transmitter that relayed to a patrolling aircraft the propeller sound of a submerged submarine. This device used American electronic systems similar to those in a small acoustic antisubmarine torpedo. Weapons such as these were fundamental innovations in the submarine-killer armory.

Beginning on May 7, 1945, the day of Germany's surrender, 156 U-boats surfaced with white flags, while 221 others were scuttled by their crews. Throughout the war 784 German submarines, of 1,161 constructed, were destroyed.

The long ocean campaign, perhaps more important to the outcome of the war than any land battle, was also costly to the Allies. Some 83,000 British sailors died in action, 52,000 in the RN and 31,000 in the merchant navy. The U.S. suffered 48,000 naval deaths, 38,000 in the Navy (not including 20,000 Marines) and 10,000 in the merchant marine. Allied losses also included 10,000 French sailors, 6,000 Norwegians, 5,000 Dutch, 700 Danes and 600 Belgians, plus Greeks, Yugoslavs, Brazilians and airmen involved in naval battles. A total of 200,000 men on the Allied side died on the seas or went down in their ships.

H. Bernard

ATLANTIC CHARTER.

This eight-point declaration of human rights and war aims was drawn up by **Roosevelt** and **Churchill** off Newfoundland, and published on August 14, 1941. It stated that neither the **United States** nor the **United Kingdom** sought any kind of territorial expansion; that all peoples deserved to choose their own governments and to live in freedom; that trade and raw materials should be freely available and that force should be abandoned as an instrument of international policy. They looked "after the final destruction of the Nazi tyranny," to a peace "which will afford assurance that all the men in all the lands may live out their lives in freedom from fear and want."

ATLANTIC WALL.

Coastal fortifications constructed by the German *Organisation Todt* between 1941 and 1944 from the north of **Norway** to Hendaye in France. (See also **Fortress Europe.**)

ATOMIC BOMB.

In 1869 the Russian chemist Dmitri Mendeleyev published *The Periodic Law of the Elements*, in which the periodic table of chemical elements first appeared. The elements in Mendeleyev's table are arranged in eight columns in order of increasing atomic weight, with that of hydrogen used as the standard. The atomic number of an element is the number of the place it occupies in the table—thus, hydrogen's atomic number is 1; helium's is 2; lithium's is 3 and so on. Certain characteristics of elements that had not yet been discovered could be predicted from the position in the table that each would occupy. These predictions were later verified with the discovery, by the British scientists Lord Rayleigh and William Ramsay, of the elements gallium, germanium and, soon afterwards, the inert gases helium, krypton, xenon and argon.

In physics classes a century ago, students were taught that the atom was the smallest, indivisible part of an element or simple body, and that it possessed the basic characteristics of the whole. Its indivisible and unalterable nature had been declared axiomatic by Marcellin Barthelot.

Then the electromagnetic theory of radiation began to unfold with the research into X-rays conducted by Sir William Bragg, Maurice de Broglie and Max von Laue, and with the discovery of radioactivity. Henri Becquerel of France had shown that heavy atoms like uranium spontaneously emitted electrified particles, as well as extremely short waves capable of penetrating opaque bodies. Investigations of cathode rays and radioactive phenomena by Sir Joseph John Thomson and Jean Baptiste Perrin yielded more precise information on the nature of matter. Cathode rays, it was found, could be deflected by an electric or magnetic field, and were composed of particles to which the name "electron" was given. X-rays, however, could not be deflected; they were electromagnetic waves, like light.

A series of studies by the Dutch scientist Hendrik Antoon Lorentz proved that the negatively charged electron was a component of all matter. It was shown that metals heated to a certain temperature emitted electrically charged particles which in fact were electrons. These electrons were also emitted by alkali metals on which light rays of the proper wavelength were directed—the so-called photoelectric effect, discovered in 1905. Since atoms are electrically neutral in their normal state, it seemed apparent that they must contain in addition to the negative electrons an equal number of positive charges.

In 1911 Ernest Rutherford represented the atom as a miniature solar system in which the "sun" at the center is a nucleus of positive charge (see Figure 1). Around the nucleus revolve planetary electrons arranged in concentric "shells." The number of electrons is equal to the atomic number of the element, and the sum of their negative charges is equal to the positive charge of the nucleus. Rutherford calculated the diameter of the nucleus at 1/12,500 of the atom's diameter. The electron revolves around the nucleus at a rate of several billion times every 1/100,000 of a second. Computations of the mass of the electron showed it to be 1/1,840 of the mass of the hydrogen atom; the diameter of the nucleus and the diameter of the hydrogen atom are 10^{-12} and 10^{-8} cm respectively. This indicates how unintentionally misleading Figure 1 can be—the emptiness of the intra-atomic space is overwhelmingly huge compared to the size of the particles in it.

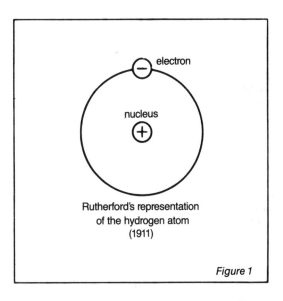

Rutherford's representation
of the hydrogen atom
(1911)

Figure 1

In the late 1890s in France, researchers Pierre Curie, Marie Curie and Andre Debierne had discovered the radioactive substances polonium, radium, then radon—produced by the disintegration of radium—and actinium. Rutherford had demonstrated the radioactivity of thorium at about the same time. Rutherford and his colleague Frederick Soddy subsequently began to investiate the radiation emitted by radioactive matter. This actually consists of three separate types of radiation known as alpha, beta and gamma rays. Alpha rays actually consist of helium atoms stripped of their two electrons, and are therefore positively charged particles. They are emitted from radioactive matter at a speed of 8,680 to 12,400 miles per second but do not penetrate matter significantly. Beta rays consist of particles of much lower mass, since they are only electrons, emitted at a speed of 62,000 to 124,000 miles per second. Their penetrating power is substantial, permitting them to enter lead to a depth of 2.8 inches. These beta rays are very similar to cathode rays. Gamma rays differ from the other two types in that they are not composed of particles but are instead electromagnetic waves of exceedingly short length. They have much greater penetrating power than X-rays.

Alpha, beta and gamma rays are easily separable. Gamma rays are not deflected in an electrical or magnetic field since they are waves rather than particles. Alpha and beta rays are, on the other hand, charged particles; they are therefore deflectable. Since they are oppositely charged, however, they are deflected in opposite directions.

In effect, radiation is the result of the disintegration of the atoms of radioactive elements. For example, an atom of radium decays to an atom of radon and an atom of helium. Radium, radon and helium are all elements. It is therefore possible to divide an atom into two other atoms. This fact became known before 1914.

The decay of a gram of radium is accompanied by a release of heat energy 300,000 times that released by a gram of carbon, indicating the enormous potential energy locked in the atom.

Some time before World War I, the English scientist Francis William Aston proposed the concept of the isotope. He had found that some elements possessed different atomic weights but the same chemical properties. All such elements should therefore occupy the same box in the Mendeleyev table—the word "isotope" is derived from the Greek, meaning the "same place." But, at the same time, they should not, since their atomic weights are different. Only later was it discovered that the reason each of these isotopes has a different atomic weight lies in the composition of its nucleus.

Along with these experimental discoveries came a prodigious step forward in theoretical physics. In 1905 Albert Einstein laid the groundwork for his Special Theory of Relativity. This remarkable work led to the creation of the space-time manifold, representing a combination of relative space and relative time. From this theory sprang the completely revolutionary concept of the *equivalence of mass and energy.*

The axiom of constant mass in classical theoretical physics corresponds to the old idea of absolute time. Einstein's idea of relative time, however, forced on theoretical physics the notion that the mass of an object varies with its velocity. The mass of a body in motion, said Einstein, is not constant but increases as the velocity of that body approaches the speed of light.

This incredible notion led to one even more fantastic. Since the mass of a body in motion increases with its acceleration, and since its motion is a form of energy, the additional mass the body acquires must be provided by that increased energy. Energy, Einstein reasoned, is therefore equivalent to mass. The equation describing this equivalence has been aptly called the most famous in history:

$$E = mc^2.$$

This simple expression indicates to the mathematical eye that small quantities of matter correspond to unimaginable quantities of energy. In it, E represents energy, m is mass and c is the speed of light. Thus, the energy contained in a particle of matter is equal to the mass of the particle multiplied by the square of the speed of light expressed in centimeters per se-

cond. One gram of matter, therefore, is equivalent to

$$E = 1 \times 9 \times 10^{20} \text{ ergs,}$$

or 25 million kilowatt-hours. And this, in turn, corresponds to the energy derived from the combustion of 3,000 tons of coal.

The mass-energy transformation equation provided the solution to a number of modern physical problems. Not only did it yield the energy content of the atom, it was later to yield the answer to another problem—how much uranium to put in a bomb to obtain a given level of destruction.

One can, in fact, redefine the atom as energy packed into an infinitesimally small volume and capable of discharging gigantic bursts of light and thermal energy into the surrounding medium, as the numerical example given above demonstrates.

Research conducted after the end of World War I delved into the secrets of the atom's nucleus. When bombarded by alpha particles and high-velocity electron beams, it released two kinds of particles: the proton, carrying an electric charge equal to but opposite in sign from that of the electron, and the neutron, isolated in Cambridge, England in 1932 by James Chadwick, a particle without an electric charge formed by the combination of a proton and an electron. It was therefore concluded that every atomic nucleus contains protons and neutrons. Since the mass of the negative electron—henceforth to be called the negatron—is negligible, the mass of the atom is equal to the sum of the masses of protons and neutrons it contains. Every atom has as many protons as it has negatrons (see Figure 2.).

The nucleus of the hydrogen atom is simply a proton; it has no neutrons. The protons in every other atom are the same as that of the hydrogen nucleus. In an atom of atomic number N and of atomic mass M, the nucleus has N protons (each of charge +1 and mass 1) and M minus N neutrons (each of charge 0 and mass 1). Thus, if the atomic mass of the most abundant type of uranium, U-238, is 238 and its atomic number is 92, it will have 92 planetary negatrons and its nucleus will contain 92 protons and 238 − 92, or 146, neutrons.

The significance of the isotope then becomes clear. The isotopes of a particular element have the same number of negatrons and the same number of protons in their atoms as the standard atom. Since they have the same atomic number, they occupy the same box in the Mendeleyev table and have the same chemical properties, because these last depend only on the number of negatrons—i.e., the atomic number—not on the atomic mass. The isotopes of a particular element differ from each other only in the number of

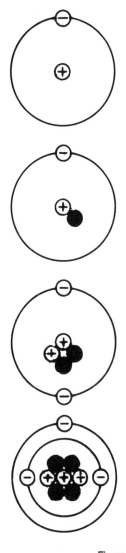

Ordinary hydrogen atom ($^1_1$H)
Nucleus: one proton
One negatron
An ordinary hydrogen nucleus is called a proton

Deuterium atom ($^2_1$H)
(Hydrogen isotope)
Nucleus: One proton and one neutron
One negatron
A deuterium nucleus is called a deuteron

Helium atom ($^4_2$He)
Nuleus: Two protons and two neutrons
Two negatrons
The helium nucleus is the alpha particle

Lithium atom ($^7_3$Li)
Nucleus: Three protons and four neutrons
Three negatrons

In a chemical symbol such as $^2_1$H, the upper number represents the atom's atomic mass and the lower number represents its atomic number.

Rutherford's representation of the atom has been modified a number of times, but will suffice for the purposes of this article.

Figure 2

neutrons their atoms contain and therefore only in their atomic mass. Deuterium, the isotope of hydrogen, for example, has a neutron in addition to the one negatron and one proton of its brother atom. One isotope of U-238 is the now famous U-235, which has three neutrons less than its heavier brother.

In the period between the two world wars, successive stages in the development of atomic physics dealt with spontaneous atomic transmutation, induced atomic transmutation and artificial radioactivity.

Spontaneous atomic transmutation refers to the natural or unassisted decay of the atomic nuclei Becquerel had discovered in the late 19th century. The nuclei of uranium, thorium and radium, for example, cannot retain all the protons and neutrons in them; as we have seen, they emit not only particles in the form of alpha and beta rays, but electromagnetic waves in the form of gamma rays as well.

The first experiment in *induced atomic transmutation* was performed in 1919 at Cambridge. Rutherford used the particles from a bit of polonium (in spontaneous decay) to bombard the nuclei of such light elements as nitrogen, boron and aluminum. He explained the result he obtained by saying that the bombarding particle first sticks to the bombarded nucleus to form a more complex and unstable one, which then expels a proton. Rutherford thus succeeded in transmuting aluminum into silicon by bombarding the aluminum nucleus, as described by the following equation:

$$ _{13}^{27}\text{Al} + {}_{2}^{4}\text{He} \rightarrow {}_{14}^{30}\text{Si} + {}_{1}^{1}\text{H}. $$

Between 1921 and 1924 Rutherford and Chadwick observed the same type of transmutation for all elements from boron to potassium in the periodic table.

Until 1932 the alpha rays of radioactive substances were the only missiles used in the transmutation of atoms. The yield of these transmutations was exceedingly slight. It was a genuine achievement if one out of 30,000 particles hit the nucleus of nitrogen. In 1932 the British researchers John Cockcroft and Ernest T. S. Walton succeeded in fragmenting the lithium nucleus by protons accelerated by an electric field of 125,000 volts in the following reaction:

$$ _{3}^{7}\text{Li} + {}_{1}^{1}\text{H} \rightarrow {}_{2}^{4}\text{He} + {}_{2}^{4}\text{He}. $$

What we see here is the division of a nucleus into two equal parts, two helium nuclei. Such a reaction was later to be called "fission." It was accompanied by the liberation of a large amount of energy. With this process, and the later use of the ions of hydrogen (protons), of deuterium (deuterons) and of helium, currents of bombarding particles 100,000 times more intense than those used by Rutherford could be obtained by using an accelerating electric field. The cyclotron, as applied by the American physicist Earnest Orlando Lawrence, was, beginning in 1930, one of the first large instruments used for this purpose.

In 1934 the French scientists Jean Frederic Joliot-Curie and Irene Joliot-Curie actually created radioactive elements of low atomic mass whose period of radioactivity lasted only a few minutes. Aluminum irradiated by alpha rays from a large source of polonium became a new element, an isotope of phosphorus. Because of its radioactivity it was given the name

radiophosphorus. In that reaction, one neutron (symbolized as $_{0}^{1}$ n) is expelled:

$$ _{13}^{27}\text{Al} + {}_{2}^{4}\text{He} \rightarrow {}_{15}^{30}\text{P} + {}_{0}^{1}\text{n}. $$

Radiophosphorus, whose radioactive period is only two minutes and 55 seconds, then becomes stable silicon by emitting a body called the positron (symbolized as $_{1}^{0}$e) which has the same properties as an electron, except that its charge is positive rather than negative. This new particle had been observed by the American physicist Carl David Anderson in 1932, its eventual discovery having been predicted by the English theoretician Paul Dirac. The positron is much rarer than the electron and has a much shorter life—of the order of 10 millionths of a second. The formula for the decay of radiophosphorus into silicon is:

$$ _{15}^{30}\text{P} \rightarrow {}_{14}^{30}\text{Si} + {}_{1}^{0}\text{e}. $$

In 1934 the Italian physicist **Enrico Fermi** discovered that the best bombarding particle for transmutations is the neutron. Since it has no electric charge, it is immune from the electric field forces exerted by the positive nucleus. A copious flow of neutrons can be obtained when a beryllium target is bombarded by alpha particles; the procedure involves placing a finely powdered mixture of beryllium and a radium salt that produces large amounts of alpha particles in an ampoule. The following reaction then takes place within the ampoule:

$$ _{4}^{9}\text{Be} + {}_{2}^{4}\text{He} \rightarrow {}_{6}^{12}\text{C} + {}_{0}^{1}\text{n}. $$

In the late 1930s the German scientist Otto Hahn bombarded uranium with neutrons obtained in this way and was remarkably successful. The uranium nucleus was split in two. But neither of the products were uranium—one was barium; the other, krypton. Thus, the bombardment of heavy nuclei like that of uranium produces a splitting or fission of the nucleus.

The next step forward was taken by Austrian scientists Lise Meitner and her nephew Otto Frisch, who had barely escaped Nazi persecution and fled to the **United States.** In 1939 they found that when the uranium nucleus split into two heavy fragments under neutron bombardment, prodigious quantities of energy were liberated. The energy released was close to six billion times that of the neutrons causing the fission. This experiment demonstrated the accuracy of

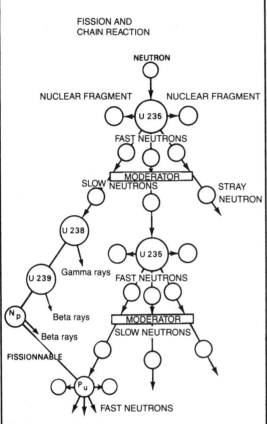

FISSION AND
CHAIN REACTION

Fission and chain reaction
A useful neutron—i.e., a neutron striking a fissionable U-235 atom—splits it, expelling three or four new neutrons. If at least one of these neutrons encounters a second U-235 atom, a chain reaction is triggered. A chain reaction is also triggered if a neutron strikes a U-238 atom. Gamma rays are liberated, and the isotope U-239 is formed. This new isotope emits beta rays, yielding the element neptunium ($^{239}_{93}$Np), which, when struck by another neutron, emits more beta rays and yields plutonium ($^{239}_{94}$Pu). The production of plutonium does not end the chain reaction; like the original U-235 isotope, plutonium can be split by a neutron to start another chain reaction.

Einstein's $E = mc^2$ equation.

The discovery was of major importance. On January 26, 1939 a conference of physicists was held in Washington. Many of them had contributed in some measure to the painfully crafted structure of atomic physics. They were of all nationalities—Americans, British and French, including **Niels Bohr** of **Denmark** and Fermi, who had escaped **Mussolini's** Fascist state. There were Germans and Austrians as well, most of them Jews who had fled the Nazis. The outcome of this conference was a proposal made in March 1939 by Fermi and Leo Szilard to President **Roosevelt** to use uranium as the explosive in an atomic bomb. After consulting Einstein, who had become an American citizen, the president appointed a Uranium Consultative Committee.

The idea then occurred to Fermi that a neutron striking a uranium nucleus could be made to liberate other neutrons which, in turn, would act on the nuclei of neighboring atoms to liberate a still greater amount of neutrons, and so on. Such a chain reaction, once started, could very well be the basis on which the atomic bomb could be designed. Fermi's notion was tested and confirmed experimentally.

As it occurs naturally, uranium is a mixture of three isotopes:

$$^{238}_{92}U, \quad ^{235}_{92}U \quad \text{and} \quad ^{234}_{92}U.$$

In each sample of uranium ore, these isotopes are present in differing relative proportions. The isotope $^{235}_{92}U$ constitutes only 0.7% of uranium ore, but it is the only one of the three with which a chain reaction can be set in motion. On a mass production basis

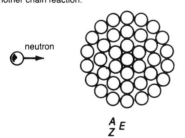
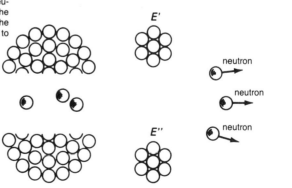

Fission: The element *E*, with an atomic weight of *A* and the atomic number *Z*, splits into two units, *E'* and *E''*, when it is struck by a neutron, emitting three or four new neutrons in the process.
Figure 3

there are several ways of developing the desired chain reaction with U-235.

Fermi in the United States, P. Thomson in London and Jean Frederic Joliot-Curie showed that the fission of U-235 can develop in raw uranium when a substance consisting of light atoms is added to the uranium sample. This added substance is known as the moderator (see Figure 3).

As we have seen, neutrons are obtained by bombarding beryllium with alpha particles in the reaction

$$_4^9 Be + _2^4 He \rightarrow _6^{12} C + _0^1 n.$$

They can be produced in even more abundant quantities by bombarding beryllium with an artificially accelerated stream of deuterons—the nuclei of deuterium—in the following reaction:

$$_4^9 Be + _1^2 D \rightarrow _5^{10} B + _0^1 n.$$

These neutrons are expelled at tremendous speed. To facilitate their capture by the uranium nucleus, they must first be slowed down for the nucleus-splitting process without at the same time being absorbed by the moderating material. The atom of the heavy hydrogen isotope deuterium is both light in mass and incapable of absorbing a neutron. It can, however, slow the neutron down sufficiently to split the U-235 nucleus; hence its use as moderator.

Split by the neutrons the U-235 nucleus breaks down to nuclei of krypton and barium, or of xenon and strontium or perhaps of bromine and lanthanum. At the same time, three or four fast neutrons are emitted in the splitting process, which is known as fission.

The energy liberated by the fission of just one gram—far less than an ounce—of U-235 was estimated to be equivalent to that yielded by burning about 28 tons of coal.

Furthermore, each of the neutrons released by the fission of one U-235 atom will in turn trigger fission of the nuclei in neighboring atoms, producing more bursts of energy and more neutrons, thus multiplying the splitting of uranium nuclei in chain reaction. Once the first nucleus splits, the chain reaction progresses spontaneously throughout the entire uranium mass.

A useful neutron—i.e., a neutron striking a fissionable U-235 nucleus—splits it, expelling three or four new neutrons. If at least one of these liberated neutrons encounters a second U-235 nucleus, a chain reaction is triggered. Neutrons hitting a U-238 nucleus

will be absorbed to form the isotope U-239, releasing gamma radiation in the process. This U-239 emits beta rays, yielding the element neptunium ($_{93}^{239}$ Np), which, when hit by a neutron, is transformed into plutonium ($_{94}^{239}$ Pu), and more beta rays are emitted. Pu-239, however, is not the end of the chain reaction; like the original U-235, this plutonium nucleus can be split by a neutron to start another chain reaction.

In 1939 Joliot-Curie and his pupils Hans Halban and Kev Kowarski, joined also by Francois Perrin, studied the conditions under which such a chain reaction could be initiated, with deuterium as the moderator.

At first the British and Americans pursued their research separately. A committee with the code name of "Tube Alloys" had been formed in the United Kingdom as a central clearing house for the atomic investigations being conducted at Oxford, Cambridge, London, Liverpool and Birmingham by Chadwick, Cockcroft and their teams, assisted by the German-Jewish scientists Rudolf Peirls and Otto Frisch, as well as some French scientists who joined them in England after June 1940. This French contingent included Kowarski and Halban, who had four months earlier transported to England 175 quarts of heavy water—whose hydrogen component is deuterium—along with some valuable papers and materials from the Jean Frederic and Irene Joliot-Curie investigations.

In Great Britain, as in the U.S., a number of scientists felt that they could derive the greatest benefit of their researches by pooling the results obtained by the British, the Americans and others. This technical brain trust, they thought, should meet in Canada or the United States, out of the reach of enemy bombers. But in 1941 some of the British experts guessed that they had outdistanced the Americans in pure research and rebelled at the idea of sharing their hard-earned secrets. The following year it was the American scientists' turn to balk at sitting down with the British, for the same reason. Actually, the Americans had been in the lead from the beginning, at least in terms of the practical details of the new bomb's design. This sore point, like many others, was amicably settled by direct communications between Roosevelt and Churchill. At the first Quebec Conference on August 19, 1943—which remained a secret until after the war—an atomic accord was firmly established between the two allies (see Conferences, Allied). A "Combined Policy Committee" was created in Washington, and under it the British and American teams were smoothly integrated under English physicist Chadwick.

Several months earlier, on December 2, 1942, Fermi and his colleagues in the U.S. had set in operation the first atomic pile devised by man.

A section of the U.S. Army Corps of Engineers called the Manhattan District (short for Manhattan Engineer District) was created to start production of the bomb. Brig. Gen. Leslie R. Groves was appointed to command the pioneer group. He got off to an excellent start when the Belgian Mining Union in the **Congo** sent its entire existing stock of some 1,140 tons of uranium ore to New York in October 1940. Without this gift the new project would have been desperately handicapped.

But the fissionable U-235 first had to be isolated. There were four ways of doing this: thermal diffusion, gaseous diffusion, separation by centrifuging and electromagnetic processing. A prime factor in choosing the method to pursue was the race against the Nazi scientists hot on the same trail. But since nobody knew precisely which of the four methods the Germans were adopting, Groves decided to use all of them. The Manhattan District was given 78 square miles of land in the Oak Ridge area in the Tennessee Valley.

Another scientific problem Groves had to face was the relative merits of U-235 and Pu-239, the plutonium isotope, which was gaining rapidly as a rival to uranium, as the fissionable material. To find the answer to this riddle, Groves set up an additional research group on a 39 square mile tract in Washington state. And to cope with further problems regarding the development of the bomb, he acquired the desert land in New Mexico that was to develop into the Los Alamos complex, where **J. Robert Oppenheimer** became research director.

On their side the Germans ardently sought to harness atomic energy for military purposes under the leadership of Werner Heisenberg. But they took the wrong turn, with disappointing results. Where the Allies were using heavy water, paraffin and especially graphite as moderators in their experiments, the German team restricted themselves to heavy water—made up of two atoms of deuterium in combination with one atom of oxygen—the chief source of which was **Norway**, where the rare substance was a by-product of chemical plants manufacturing nitrates. To the Nazis, therefore, occupied Norway became a possession of prime strategic value.

In March 1942 the Norwegian **Resistance** fighter Einer Skinnarland working for the **Special Operations Executive** (SOE) arrived in Aberdeen on a stolen German vessel with some very valuable information on the factory Norsk Hydro in **Vemork** (Rjukan), 100 miles west of Oslo, then producing heavy water. Several days later he was parachuted back into Norway with detailed instructions.

The Vemork factory was in a deep valley surrounded by mountains whose practically vertical slopes were thickly wooded. Its installations were strongly defended but not completely invulnerable. On the night of February 28, 1943, nine SOE saboteurs destroyed the Vemork plant in a daring, brilliantly planned operation.

It took the Germans five months to get the factory started up again. But on November 16, 1943, 150 American bombers struck it in broad daylight. They put its hydroelectric plant out of action, but failed to damage the heavy-water equipment, which was buried under seven layers of reinforced concrete.

At the end of January 1944, the SOE discovered that a quantity of heavy water was to be transported to **Germany**. With the secret assistance of the Norsk Hydro plant engineers, a Resistance group led by Capt. Knut Haukelid—one of the heroes of the February 28, 1943 **sabotage** attack—sent the ferry boat carrying all the available heavy water to the bottom of Lake Tinnsjoe. And with that boat disappeared all Nazi hopes of further experimentation with atomic energy.

The atomic scientist Niels Bohr was in Denmark when the German army occupied that country. Although Bohr was part Jewish, he was determined to remain in Denmark to protect his institute against German infiltration and to maintain contact with the scientists of the Third Reich, particularly with Heisenberg. At the same time, he kept London informed of the results of his research through an underground organization of Danish intelligence officers, with Swedish cooperation. At the end of the spring of 1943, Bohr passed word to the British that Germany had given up on the atomic bomb. Churchill drew a profound sigh of relief. When his situation in Denmark grew precarious in October 1943, Bohr escaped to **Sweden**, then proceeded to London with the aid of the SOE. After a short stay in London, he went on to the U.S., where he became a consultant at the Los Alamos laboratories.

The agony of **Japan** reached its zenith in April 1945. The Allies had destroyed its armies in **Burma**, annihilated its fleet and conquered Okinawa after a furious battle, and American B-29 Superfortresses were bombing the home islands almost continuously. **MacArthur** was massing his troops in the **Philippines** and in Okinawa for the assault on the island of Kyushu on D-day, planned for November 1, 1945, and shortly afterward the island of Honshu.

Japan's military situation was desperate, but Washington understood that the invading American troops would encounter fierce resistance from two million defending soldiers on a difficult terrain which would inhibit the progress of armored forces.

At 5:30 a.m. on July 16, 1945, the first atomic bomb was successfully detonated in the New Mexico desert. The most powerful weapon ever devised was now ready to be used.

President **Truman**, Roosevelt's successor, decided to use this new weapon to shorten the war and to spare the lives of thousands of Allied soldiers, as well as to end the sufferings of the peoples under Japanese rule in occupied **China, Indonesia** and the Philippines, where terrible reprisals against Europeans were foreseen. The U.S., Great Britain and China presented Japan with an ultimatum. When it expired without response, Gen. **Carl Spaatz**, head of the U.S. Strategic Air Forces in the Pacific was ordered to drop an atomic bomb after August 3, at a moment he judged suitable, on the installations of an industrial city, one of four already selected. He chose the military and industrial base of Hiroshima.

At 8:15 on the morning of August 6, 1945, Col. Paul W. Tibbets dropped the first atomic weapon, a bomb made from U-235, from the B-29 *Enola Gay*. Suspended from a parachute, the bomb weighed about four tons. It exploded in the air, several hundred feet above the surface of the Japanese soil. Some 60% of Hiroshima was destroyed and more than 150,000 people perished in the blast. The next day Truman warned the Japanese that the waste laid by this new weapon would be amplified to an unbelievable extent if they did not surrender. And on the following day, August 8, the **USSR** declared war on Japan. Emperor **Hirohito** had had enough. But his government, its backbone stiffened by the obstinacy of the military, balked at **unconditional surrender**. Soviet troops invaded Manchuria on August 9, and on the same day another atomic bomb, this time made from plutonium, was dropped on Nagasaki by Maj. Charles W. Sweeney from the B-29 *Bock's Car*. On August 10 the emperor ordered his prime minister to put an end to the war, but it was not until August 14 that the military high command gave its assent. At 4:00 p.m. on that day, the Japanese made their intentions known to Washington.

The Empire of the Rising Sun accepted the humiliation of unconditional surrender, and the war came to an end.

H. Bernard

ATTLEE, Clement Richard (later Earl) (1883-1967).

Attlee, a British labor leader, served as an officer in World War I. He led the Labor Party in the House of Commons from 1935 to 1955. During this period Attlee was deputy prime minister in the war cabinet from May 1940 to May 1945, and prime minister from July 1945 to October 1951. In his capacity as deputy

prime minister, Attlee acted for **Churchill** during the latter's frequent wartime absences; as prime minister he granted **India** its independence in 1947. Attlee's mild manner concealed a strong character.

AUCHINLECK, Sir Claude John Eyre (1884-).

Auchinleck, a British general, first gained recognition in the Indian army. He extricated British troops from **Norway** in June 1940 and became commander-in-chief in **India** in January 1941. From July 1941 to August 1942 he was commander-in-chief of the British forces in the Middle East. **Rommel's** summer attack in 1942 almost overwhelmed his Eighth Army; he went to the desert front to take personal command. He withdrew past Tobruk, where the defenses were in disrepair, and, with the aid of **Dorman-Smith**, inflicted a decisive defeat on the **Axis** forces at **El Alamein** on July 1-3, 1942. **Churchill** could not, however, forgive him the loss of Tobruk, and he was replaced by **Alexander** in mid-August. From 1943 to 1947 he again served as commander-in-chief in India, where he helped **Wavell** and **Mountbatten** ease the transition to independence.

AUSCHWITZ.

A **concentration camp** opened on June 14, 1940 at Oswiecim, a Polish town between Krakow and Katowice. In January 1942 it was turned into an extermination camp, intended to facilitate the **Final Solution**. Jews sent to Auschwitz who were considered incapable of working (infants, old people, pregnant women, the disabled and the sick) were immediately sent to the gas chambers. The others, between 20% and 40% of the new arrivals, were sent to labor camps and work details, where they remained until, exhausted by work and deprivation, they too were sent to the gas chambers. In March 1942 a second camp was opened next to Auschwitz at Brzezinska (Birkenau). This was a huge complex designed to house 200,000 prisoners and equipped with four crematoria, each with its own gas chamber. A third camp—a labor camp for a synthetic rubber plant operated by I. G. Farben—was opened in October 1942 at Monowitz. All documents relating to the camps were destroyed by the **SS**. It was therefore impossible to determine precisely how many died at Auschwitz, but the number has been estimated at four million.

AUSTRALIA.

A few hours after the **United Kingdom** entered the war, on September 3, 1939, Australia followed. Public support for it was virtually unanimous. The Conservative Sir Robert Gordon Menzies, who was prime minister when the war began, resigned in August 1941. John Curtin formed a Labor government in

September with a majority of only one vote; his majority increased greatly as a result of the general elections held in August 1943.

Australia's military contribution to the Allies was distinguished but not large; Australia had only 2,600 regular soldiers when the war began. One division was sent to the Near East before the end of 1939; another served in England in the summer crisis of 1940. Australian troops took part in **Wavell**'s westward desert advance, capturing Bardia and Tobruk in January 1941. They also fought in mainland **Greece**, Crete and **Syria**.

After **Japan** entered the war, the main Australian military efforts took place in the Far East, particularly in **New Guinea** and **Borneo**. Australia's air force and navy, however, cooperated with the British and Americans around the world. Twenty-two thousand Australians, most of them new arrivals, were lost in **Malaya** in January 1942.

Apart from some air raids near Darwin, the war left Australian home territory untouched. It did, however, cause fundamental changes in Australian life and politics. Essington Lewis, the country's leading businessman, was made virtual dictator of the Australian economy in May 1940; he brought about an industrial revolution. The country had previously exported raw materials; it began, under Lewis' direction, to consume them, in aircraft, vehicle and armament factories. Australia became the arsenal of the southwestern Pacific. Federal powers were enormously increased for the duration of the war—and the Australian states have never been fully able to reassert their authority since. Curtin's government seized the occasion to found a **welfare state** as well.

Above all, the war detached Australia—except for sentimental and formal ties—from Great Britain; the country came of age as an independent power of the second rank. It had become clear enough in Canberra that the British could do little to help the Australians at the worst moments of the war and would sacrifice Australia, if they had to, to preserve interests nearer home. This realization helped speed the severing of the umbilical cord between the two countries.

Hundreds of thousands of U.S. troops arrived in Australia on their way to fight in the southwestern Pacific. Their presence contributed to the development of an important friendship between the two powers.

M. R. D. Foot

AUSTRIA.

After the *Anschluss*, Austria ceased to exist as a separate nation.

AVIATION, Strategic Anglo-American (in Europe).

(See also **Germany, Air Battle of.**)

BOMBERS ALWAYS AVAILABLE FOR OPERATIONS (BY TYPE)

	July 1940	Jan. 1941	July 1941	Jan. 1942	July 1942	Jan. 1943	July 1943	Jan. 1944	July 1944	Jan. 1945	May 8, 1945
RAF BOMBER COMMAND											
Battle	73	——	——	——	——	——	——	——	——	——	——
Blenheim	234	176	160	58	39	——	——	——	——	——	——
Boston	——	——	——	5	47	37	——	——	——	——	——
Ventura	——	——	——	——	——	36	——	——	——	——	——
Mitchell	——	——	——	——	——	5	——	——	——	——	——
Mosquito	——	——	——	——	13	23	51	72	138	206	269
Hampden	109	111	169	161	37	——	——	——	——	——	——
Whitley	103	92	105	89	——	——	——	——	——	——	——
Wellington	148	229	391	353	256	187	124	15	——	——	——
Manchester	——	——	——	48	——	——	——	——	——	——	——
Stirling	——	——	22	38	69	104	203	139	37	——	——
Halifax	——	——	31	50	102	173	331	373	562	521	388
Lancaster	——	——	——	——	107	274	444	627	864	1,096	1,320
TOTAL RAF	667	608	878	802	670	839	1,153	1,226	1,601	1,823	1,977
EIGHTH & 15TH USAAF											
B-17 Fortress and B-24 Liberator	——	——	——	——	——	156	670	1,667	3,645	3,115	3,300
TOTAL RAF AND USAAF	667	608	878	802	670	995	1,823	2,893	5,246	4,938	5,277

TOTAL BOMB TONNAGE DROPPED ON EUROPE BY
THE RAF BOMBER COMMAND AND THE EIGHTH AND 15TH USAAF

1940	1941	1942	1943	1944	1945
14,631	35,509	53,755	256,531	1,188,577	447,051

Of this total of 1,996,054 tons, 1,047,412 tons were dropped by the RAF **Bomber Command** and 946,642 by the Eighth and 15th USAAF, which did not begin to participate in the bombing until 1943.

The tonnage indicated above includes only bombs dropped by strategic aircraft. If the tonnage dropped by medium and light bombers, as well as fighter-bombers belonging to the tactical air forces, is added, the grand total would be 2,770,540 tons: 1,307,117 by the British and 1,463,423 by the Americans.

Development of the strategic air force

In 1940 the RAF Bomber Command included 23 squadrons of medium bombers with a total useful load of 520 tons. By 1945 the command included 100 squadrons of heavy and medium bombers with a useful load of 10,000 tons. The useful load of American strategic aircraft in Europe was also 10,000 tons. The aggregate useful load in 1945 therefore amounted to almost 40 times that of 1940.

Disposition of Air Power in June 1944

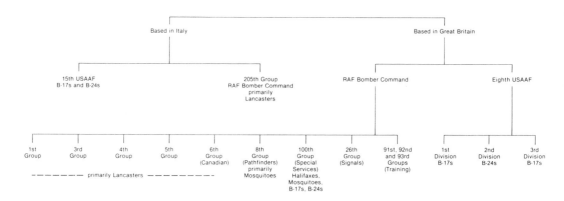

AVIATION, Tactical Anglo-American (in Europe).

When some **reconnaissance** squadrons not included in the table are added to the total, the AEAF directly controlled some 6,000 aircraft. (Within the Groups and the Tactical Air Command, each squadron consisted of 16 planes, plus one in reserve.) The AEAF also called on the resources of the organizations listed below to reinforce air support:

1. The RAF **Bomber Command**, commanded by Air Chief Marshal Sir **Arthur Harris**, and the U.S. Strategic Forces, commanded by Gen. **Carl Spaatz**. These two groups were under the overall command of the Combined Chiefs of Staff (with the exceptions noted in the article **Germany, Air Battle of**).

2. The RAF Atlantic Coast Command, commanded by Air Chief Marshal Sir Sholto Douglas. Its aircraft were based in Great Britain and, especially, Northern Ireland, with additional bases in Iceland, the Azores and **Gibraltar**. It was overseen by the British chiefs of staff, in particular Marshal of the Royal Air Force Sir **Charles Portal**.

3. The RAF Transport Command in Great Britain, commanded by Air Chief Marshal Sir Frederick W. Bowhill. It, too, fell under the purview of Sir Charles Portal and the British chiefs of staff.

4. The Fleet Air Arm, commanded by Admiral of the Fleet Sir **Andrew Cunningham** and the British chiefs of staff.

Battle Organization June 6, 1944
Allied Expeditionary Air Forces (AEAF)
Commanded by Air Chief Marshal Sir L. Trafford Leigh-Mallory
Deputy assistant: Maj. Gen. Hoyt S. Vanderberg

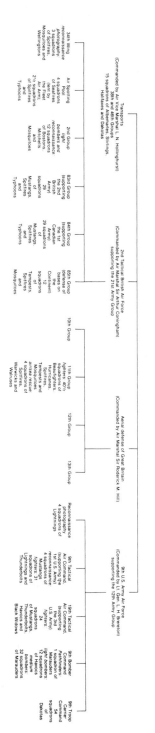

2nd Tactical British Air Force
(Commanded by Air Marshal Sir Arthur Coningham) supporting the 21st Army Group

- **Transports** (Commanded by Air Vice Marshal L. N. Hollinghurst) 38th and 46th Groups 15 squadrons of Albemarles, Stirlings, Halifaxes and Dakotas.
- **34th Wing** reconnaissance photography 3 squadrons of Spitfires, Mosquitos and Wellingtons
- **Air Spotting Pool** 4 squadrons of Seafires (lent by the Fleet Air Arm) 2½ squadrons of Spitfires and Typhoons
- **2nd Group** light bombers and reconnaissance 12 squadrons of Bostons, Mitchells and Mosquitos
- **83rd Group** (supporting the 2nd British Army) 29 squadrons of Mustangs, Spitfires and Typhoons
- **84th Group** (supporting the 1st Canadian Army) 29 squadrons of Mustangs, Spitfires and Typhoons
- **85th Group** (defense of bases on the Continent) 12 squadrons of Tempests, Spitfires and Mosquitos

Aerial defense of Great Britain
(Commanded by Air Marshal Sir Roderick M Hill)

- **10th Group**
- **11th Group** fighters, 40½ squadrons of Beaufighters, Hurricanes, Spitfires, Tempests and Mosquitos; air/sea rescue 4 squadrons of Spitfires, Warwicks and Walruses
- **12th Group**
- **13th Group**

9th U.S. Army Air Force
(Commanded by Lt. Gen. L. H. Brereton) supporting the 12th Army Group

- **Reconnaissance** photography 4 squadrons of Lightnings
- **9th Tactical Air Command** (supporting the 1st U.S. Army) reconnaissance 4 squadrons of Mustangs fighters 31 squadrons of Lightnings and Thunderbolts
- **19th Tactical Air Command** (supporting the 3rd U.S. Army) 24 squadrons of Mustangs, Thunderbolts, Havocs and Black Widows
- **9th Bomber Command** Pathfinders 1 squadron of Marauders
- **9th Bomber Command** light bombers: 12 squadrons of Havocs medium bombers 32 squadrons of Marauders
- **9th Troop Carrier Command** 54 squadrons of Dakotas

AVNOJ.

Anti-Fascist Council for the Liberation of **Yugoslavia**.

AXIS.

On October 25, 1936 **Germany** and **Italy** established the Rome-Berlin Axis with a treaty of general agreement on coordination of foreign policy. The Axis was reinforced on May 22, 1939 with a military alliance known as the **Pact of Steel**. **Japan**, which had already joined Germany and Italy in signing the Anti-Comintern Pact of 1936, allied itself closely to the Axis with the **Tripartite Pact**, signed in Berlin on September 27, 1940. From this point on, the expression "Rome-Berlin-Tokyo Axis" gained currency.

AXIS COMBAT FORCES.

Details given here concerning the strength, deployment, and composition of the armed forces of **Germany** and **Italy** are necessarily confined to certain definite periods. (See also **Military Organization and Firepower**.) Information concerning their allies—**Japan**, **Finland**, Slovakia, **Hungary**, **Croatia** and **Rumania**—is limited to the conditions that existed at the time of their entry into the war, for the sources are meager. **Bulgaria** is omitted; although it was a signatory to the **Tripartite Pact** on March 1, 1941, it did not participate in the fighting.

Germany

The German Army consisted both of men under arms in the field and their auxiliary forces, logistic and defensive, and reserve troops. It still had not reached its full potential when the war broke out. On September 11, 1939, during the invasion of **Poland**, it contained 87 divisions. Of these, 70 were infantry, four armed with light weapons, three equipped for mountain duty, four motorized and six armored. Poland was knocked out of the war with 54 of these divisions—37 of the infantry divisions and all of the others, including the six armored divisions, which were equipped with 3,195 tanks and five assault guns.

By May 10, 1940, at the beginning of the offensive in the West, the German army contained 158 divisions. These included 122 infantry divisions, four for covering, nine divisions of territorial guards, three mountain divisions, one cavalry division, four motorized infantry divisions and 10 armored divisions. There were also one police, one airborne and one paratroop division, as well as two motorized **SS** divisions. Out of this total, 137 divisions (including 117 infantry and the rest made up of cavalry, motorized infantry, and armored, airborne, paratroop and motorized SS divisions), with a total of 2,445 tanks, participated in the attack on the West.

On June 22, 1941, when its offensive in the east began, the German army deployed 205 divisions—152 infantry divisions, six for cover, six of mountain and four of light-weapons troops, plus one cavalry division, 11 motorized infantry divisions, 20 armored divisions and five SS divisions. A total of more than four million men were deployed, with 145 divisions in the east, seven in the Balkans, 38 in the west, 12 in **Norway**, one in **Denmark** and two in **Libya**. The fighting forces in the east—which included practically all the motorized infantry, armored and SS divisions—accounted for about 75% of the field troops, with a total of 3,050,000 men.

By the middle of 1943 a number of divisions, including many new units, had been badly mauled. This was true not only of the men but of their equipment as well. Also, beginning in 1943, German armaments were modified. All of these factors led to a reorganization of the forces in the field on October 4, 1943. The army was segmented into 371 divisions, most of them of reduced strength: 147 infantry divisions, 20 for covering or for manning fortifications, 12 for protection, 10 for fighter planes, 22 air divisions and nine of mountain troops. There were also 27 foreign troop formations (not counting Finnish divisions), one cavalry division, one artillery division, 17 *Panzer-Grenadiere* divisions, 22 armored divisions, four instructor divisions, 31 auxiliary divisions, 17 reserve divisions, two paratroop divisions and 15 SS divisions, in addition to 14 new formations. Of these 371 divisions, 287, or about three-fourths, were deployed on the Russian front.

When the army lost its strategic initiative, the combat-readiness of its divisions began to deteriorate because of increasing losses in men and materiel, despite the new formations, the continual reorganizations and reassignments of troops. On March 1, 1945, six weeks before the Reich capitulated, its forces included—at least nominally—291 divisions: 100 infantry divisions, one grenadier division, 27 citizen-soldier divisions, seven mountain divisions, 11 fighter divisions, three *Luftwaffe* operational divisions, seven foreign divisions, two cavalry divisions, five *Panzer-Grenadiere* divisions and 23 armored divisions. There were also one instruction division, nine of fighter-paratroops, two of *Panzer-Grenadiere* paratroops, three naval divisions and 30 SS divisions.

The disintegration of the army in the field—between September 1, 1939 and January 31, 1945, its losses amounted to 7,456,914 men—was reflected not only by the sizable drop in the number of divisions, most of them exhausted and badly equipped, but also by the fact that there were, on March 1, 1945, more than 90 "combat groups," "groups" or "brigades," vague terms applied to the remains of shattered divisions.

Even now, the strength of the *Luftwaffe* at the beginning of the war is overestimated. On September 1, 1939 it had 2,775 aircraft ready for the front—but of these only 1,182, or about 40%, were bombers. While 836 planes of every type kept watch in the west, 1,939 planes, or two-thirds of the entire *Luftwaffe*, were deployed in Poland—897 bombers, 405 fighters and **reconnaissance** and transport planes, 133 aircraft under the direct orders of the *Luftwaffe* chief, 288 observation planes and 216 fighters for defense of the eastern lands. By September 28, 285 of these 1,939 aircraft had been destroyed and 279 others were more than 10% damaged and therefore counted among the losses.

On May 10, 1940 the *Luftwaffe* could muster 3,834 aircraft over the west—342 **Stukas** (dive-bombers), 1,120 combat planes and 42 fighter-bombers, in addition to 1,016 fighters, 248 pursuit planes and 1,066 reconnaissance or transport aircraft. Unquestionably, the *Luftwaffe* contributed enormously to the success of the German armed forces in the west, but its limitations were clearly apparent in its failure to prevent the Anglo-French evacuation from Dunkirk.

On August 13, 1940 the *Luftwaffe* had a combat-ready complement of only 2,355 planes for the aerial attack on England. These included 316 Stukas and 998 combat planes, 702 fighters, 261 pursuit planes

and 78 long-range observation planes. For the *Luftwaffe*, the **Battle of Britain**, which lasted until May 11, 1941, represented a definite defeat. As early as October 30, 1940, 1,733 German aircraft had been shot down, as compared to only 915 British aircraft downed in that same period.

The onset of Operation **Barbarossa** on June 22, 1941, found the *Luftwaffe* deploying 61% of its entire power over the huge Russian front. This amounted to 1,965 aircraft, of which some 1,450 were fully outfitted. These consisted of 290 Stukas, 560 combat aircraft, 440 fighters, 40 pursuit planes and 120 long-range reconnaissance aircraft. In the initial phase of the eastern campaign, with the element of surprise in its favor, the *Luftwaffe* won a tremendous victory. It smashed the major part of the Soviet air force, much of it on the ground. But the German air force was unable to exploit this achievement, hindered as it was by the need to support the operations of the land forces not only in the **USSR** but also in the other theaters of the war as well. It thus exhausted itself and sank gradually into inferiority, from which it could not be aroused even for the defense of the homeland, which became necessary as early as 1942. Still the rate of aircraft production continued to grow, as the following table indicates:

	1939 (after September 1)	1940	1941	1942	1943	1944	1945	Totals
Bombers	737	2,852	3,373	4,337	4,649	2,287	——	18,235
Fighters	605	2,746	3,744	5,515	10,898	25,285	4,935	53,728
Fighter-bombers	134	603	507	1,249	3,266	5,496	1,104	12,359
Reconnaissance craft	163	971	1,079	1067	1,117	1,686	216	6,299
Seaplanes	100	269	183	238	259	141	——	1,190
Transport planes	145	388	502	573	1,028	443	——	3,079
Gliders (combat and transport)	——	378	1,461	745	442	111	8	3,145
Liaison craft	46	170	431	607	874	410	11	2,549
Training craft	588	1,870	1,121	1,078	2,274	3,693	318	10,942
Jets	——	——	——	——	——	1,041	947	1,988
Totals	2,518	10,247	12,401	15,409	24,807	40,593	7,539	113,514

The *Luftwaffe* lost 511,307 men between September 1, 1939 and March 3, 1945. In addition to the flight crews and their ground teams, this figure includes antiaircraft gunners, air information sections and paratroopers, although these last were technically part of the land armies.

At the beginning of the Polish campaign on September 1, 1939, the German Navy had the following vessels: two battleships, three battle cruisers, two heavy and six light cruisers, 22 destroyers, 11 torpedo boats, 57 **U-boats**, 18 patrol boats and three mine-layers.

Practically all the serviceable warships capable of offensive action, aside from three small submarines, participated in the invasions of Denmark and Norway on April 9, 1940. The vessels are listed in the following table:

Types	Existing	Serviceable	Active	Under construction	Completed or under test
Battleships	2	2	2		
Heavy cruisers	4	3	3	1	
Light cruisers	6	4	4	2	
Destroyers	20	14	14	6	
Torpedo boats	17	10	10		
Submarines (large)	9	7	5*		2
Submarines (medium)	13	11	9**	1	1
Submarines (small)	26	21	18	1	1

* Two other large submarines were launched on April 12 and 14 as transports.
** Two other medium submarines were launched on April 16 and 27 as transports.

Twelve fast patrol boats and numerous small craft also participated in the invasions. Germany ensured the success of the Polish *Weseruebung* operation by pushing its navy to the point of exhaustion. It paid a heavy price. One heavy cruiser, two light cruisers, 10 destroyers, one torpedo boat, six submarines and 15 small boats were sunk. Moreover, two battleships, two heavy cruisers and one light cruiser, as well as several destroyers, torpedo boats and minedetectors, were damaged and out of action for long periods. In fact, despite its reinforcement with new fighting units in 1940–1941, the Nazi navy found it impossible to exploit conquered Norway—or, later, France—as new bases for its offensive operations with any chance of success.

The German attacks on Allied **convoys** in the North Atlantic had to be abandoned on May 24, 1943 after repeated and costly failures. This was the turning point of the war as far as submarine warfare was concerned.

German naval losses by May 8, 1945 amounted to four battleships, five heavy cruisers, four light cruisers, two old ships of the line, 27 destroyers, 68 torpedo boats, 27 escort vessels, 106 minedetectors, 185 minesweepers, 152 patrol boats, some 525 landing ships and artillery pontoons, 968 submarines, nine auxiliary cruisers, 35 minelayers, 66 bulldozer ships, three auxiliary minesweepers, 132 auxiliary minedetectors, 137 submarine chasers, 189 reconnaissance ships, 278 coast guard cutters, 86 picket ships, 21 escort vessels and about 200 auxiliary small craft.

Of these, a number had been scuttled—one battleship, one heavy cruiser, three destroyers, eight torpedo boats, nine escort vessels, 25 patrol boats, 14 minedetectors, 59 minesweepers, 215 submarines, seven minelayers, 13 bulldozer ships, five auxiliary minedetectors, 33 submarine chasers, 13 reconnaissance ships, 146 coast guard cutters, one picket ship, and between 80 and 100 smaller craft.

More than half (630) of the 1,170 submarines the Germans launched fell victim to Allied attack, 215 were scuttled, 123 were destroyed by bombs or sunk by mines in their own waters, 38 were damaged too badly for further service, 153 gave themselves up when Germany surrendered, eight were assigned to the Japanese and three were interned.

Some 39,000 submariners served in the German U-boat fleet. Of these, 33,000 were killed or taken prisoner. The German navy had lost a total of 174,419 men by January 31, 1945.

Combining the casualties of the volunteer units—amounting to 258,692 men—with the number of dead, wounded and disappeared from the army, navy and *Luftwaffe*, the *Wehrmacht* suffered total losses of 8,333,978 men. There is no reliable data on the losses between February 1, 1945 and the date of the German surrender, but they were certainly severe.

Italy

On June 10, 1940, when Italy declared war on Great Britain and France, its army was comprised of 75 poorly equipped divisions—55 of infantry, five mountain divisions, three light divisions, three mechanized divisions, two motorized divisions, two armored divisions, three militia divisions and two colonial divisions. They were stationed in the following areas: 53 in the home country, five in **Albania**, 14 in Libya, one in the **Dodecanese** and two in Italian East Africa.

On September 13, 1940, barely four weeks after its conquest of British Somaliland, Italy mounted an offensive in North Africa with part of the troops stationed there, amounting to six infantry divisions and eight armored battalions. Several days later they were stopped only 55 miles from the Egyptian-Libyan border. The counteroffensive launched by the British on December 9, 1941 in Cyrenaica deprived the Italians of 10 divisions.

Italy attacked **Greece** with eight divisions—six of infantry, one mountain division and one armored division—on October 28, 1940. But after some scattered initial successes, they were thrown back beyond the Greco-Albanian frontier between November 14 and 21. On April 6, 1941 the Axis began the Balkan campaign against **Yugoslavia** and Greece, winning it in 18 days. In this phase of the war, the Italians contributed 38 divisions to the combined German and Hungarian troops—29 infantry divisions, four mountain divisions, three light divisions and two armored divisions.

Although **Mussolini** had not been informed by **Hitler** of the planned attack on the USSR, Italy declared war on Russia on June 22, 1941 and shortly afterward sent an expeditionary force to fight on the southern sector of the eastern front. At its maximum strength, at the end of the fall of 1942, this force included 10 divisions, of which six were infantry, three mountain and one light. They were practically wiped out in a few weeks in the Russian offensive for Stalingrad that began on December 11, 1942.

On March 1, 1943, one week after the establishment of a single command for German and Italian troops in Tunisia, the Italian army was made up of 76 mobile divisions, eight of which were in France and Corsica; 27 in the Italian boot, Sardinia and Sicily; 33 in the Balkans and the Dodecanese Islands; six in North Africa and two in the USSR.

By the time of the Allied landing in Sicily on July 10, 1943, the Italian army consisted of 64 mobile and 20 coastal divisions. Of the mobile units, five were in France, two in Corsica, 18 in the Italian peninsula, four in Sardinia, four in Sicily, and 31 in the Balkans and Dodecanese. The 20 coastal divisions, practically immobile and sparsely armed, were stationed as follows: one in France, two in Corsica, nine in the Italian peninsula, three in Sardinia and five in Sicily.

When it surrendered on September 8, 1943, Italy had under arms, outside its frontiers, 49 divisions and four brigades—33 infantry divisions, one mountain division, one motorized division and 14 coastal divisions, as well as one infantry brigade and three coastal brigades. At the same time, 29 divisions were stationed in the peninsula; they consisted of five mountain divisions, three light divisions and three mechanized divisions, plus one motorized division, two armored divisions and 14 coastal divisions, as well as one paratroop division. All of them either voluntarily laid down their arms or were forced to surrender.

After September 8, 1943 the "Italian Liberation Corps" was formed in Allied-controlled Italy. This led to the creation in 1944 of six cadres fighting against Germany along with a number of partisan units. At the same time, as the result of an agreement with the *Repubblica Sociale Italiana* government, four divisions were formed by Italian soldiers who had been interned in Germany. These troops were brought once more into the line in northern Italy in 1945, but they had no chance to prove themselves.

The Italian air force, on June 10, 1940, had 3,296 combat planes, 1,796 of them serviceable. By aircraft classification these figures break down to 783 operational bombers out of a total of 1,332 bombers, 552 fighters our of 893, 42 pursuit planes and fighter-bombers out of 267, 268 reconnaissance planes out of 497 and 151 seaplanes out of 307.

Weak in numbers and poorly armed, the Italian air force could give neither the army nor navy the support required for decisive victories. The effectiveness of Italian fighter-bomber units was negligible. This became obvious on a number of occasions—for example, when the Italian air force deployed only 110 bombers, 45 fighter-bombers and 135 fighters to support the advance of the Libyan army toward Egypt on September 13, 1940; when 75 bombers, 98 fighters and five reconnaissance planes were brought into long-range action near Brussels on October 22, 1940 to take part in the Battle of Britain; when with 320 aircraft the Italians participated in the fighting against Yugoslavia and Greece; when the Italian air force acted in the air offensive against **Malta** or the protection of convoys to North Africa.

After Italy's surrender, German forces managed to seize 200 of its aircraft as well as a number of antiaircraft batteries and to shoot down 40 planes attempting to go over to the Allies. But the Germans could not prevent some 2,500 Italian aircraft from landing in Puglia, Sardinia or Sicily, then in Allied hands.

On June 10, 1940, exclusive of ships under construction, the Italian navy consisted of five battleships, one battle cruiser, seven heavy cruisers, 12 light cruisers, 59 destroyers, 67 torpedo boats, 116 submarines, 13 gunboats, five escort vessels, 63 torpedo-launching speedboats, 13 minelayers and 40 minesweepers. It was thus twice as large as the German navy, but its effectiveness in battle was minimal. The cruisers and destroyers were of insufficient tactical value and unsuitable for night fighting; the submarines were too large and obsolete. Moreover, the Italian navy had no available sonic location devices and continually suffered from a lack of fuel.

The Italian navy also suffered from chronic defeats. In the naval battle of Cape Spada on July 19, 1940, it lost a light cruiser. On November 11–12, 1940, in a British air attack on Taranto, four battleships, one cruiser and one destroyer were lost; on March 28, 1941

45

in the naval battle of Cape Matapan, the Italians lost one battleship, two heavy cruisers and two destroyers; on November 8-9, 1941 two destroyers and seven transports were sunk in a convoy of reinforcements sailing to North Africa; on December 12, 1941 a battleship and two light cruisers were lost from a supply convoy sailing to North Africa; on March 22, 1942, in the second battle of Sidra, the navy lost one heavy cruiser and two destroyers; and in 1943 the Italians lost numerous destroyers and torpedo boats attempting to defend the supply line to the North African bridgehead.

Between June 10, 1940 and September 8, 1943, Italian naval forces lost a total of one battleship, one battle cruiser, five heavy cruisers, six light cruisers, 44 destroyers, 41 torpedo boats, 82 submarines, three gunboats, one fast escort vessel, 27 torpedo-launching speedboats, six cutters, eight submarine chasers, two minelayers and 15 minesweepers.

After Italy's surrender, the Germans seized 217 Italian warships—in addition to many commercial vessels—mainly by force. These included one aircraft carrier, two battleships, six cruisers, six auxiliary cruisers, 11 destroyers, 32 torpedo boats, 28 speedboats, 16 gunboats, 26 torpedo-launching speedboats, 11 submarines, one submarine for transporting assault boats, four small submarines, three minelayers, two minesweepers, one port monitor and 67 auxiliary small craft. Of these 217 ships, however, only 61 were operable, 42 were still under construction and the other 114 were not combat-ready. Still, a good many Italian ships managed to escape to Allied harbors. By September 21, 1943 the following had joined Allied forces: five battleships, nine light cruisers, 11 destroyers, 22 torpedo boats, 20 escort vessels, 34 submarines, five small submarines and 12 speedboats as well as other units.

Japan

On December 7, 1941, the day of the Japanese attack on **Pearl Harbor**, the Japanese army included 51 adequately equipped divisions. The navy had 10 battleships, nine aircraft carriers, one escort aircraft carrier, five seaplane carriers, 16 heavy cruisers, 17 light cruisers, two small raiders, three training cruisers, 103 destroyers, 21 torpedo boats, 13 escort destroyers, 64 submarines, seven gunboats, four frigates, 40 minelayers, and several hundred smaller ships and auxiliary vessels. The army air force possessed 3,029 aircraft and the navy 2,000.

Finland

When Finland renewed its warfare against the Soviet Union on June 26, 1941, its army had 16 small mobile divisions plus three brigades and 77 artillery platoons,

a total of 18 divisions. There were 307 aircraft; of these 41 were bombers, 36 fighter-bombers and 230 fighters.

The Finnish navy was equipped with two coast guard cutters, five submarines, seven speedboats, four gunboats, six minelayers, 18 smaller picket ships and 11 auxiliary vessels.

Slovakia

Having already sent three divisions to participate in the assault on Poland in September 1939, the Slovakian army contributed two more divisions to the attack on the USSR on June 24, 1941. These troops, however, were insufficiently equipped with rolling stock, and after losing two-thirds of their number, they reorganized as two small units—one a fully motorized "light division," the other a "safety division."

Hungary

Hungarian forces allied themselves with the German and Italian armies in the Balkan campaign. Declaring war on the USSR on June 27, 1941, Hungary immediately sent four brigades of its 24 divisions to the Russian front. On July 12, 1941 it sent three motorized divisions. Nine Hungarian divisions fought in the southern part of the front after the summer of 1942, but they were very nearly wiped out in the Battle of the Don, which began on January 12, 1943.

The Hungarian air force, with fewer than 100 bombers and fighters, attacked the Russians in June 1941.

At that time the Hungarian navy had six picket ships and seven auxiliary boats.

Croatia

In August 1941, some four months after the proclamation of Croatia's independence, its army deployed a reinforced infantry regiment on the Russian front. This was followed up, at the end of 1944, with three divisions of **Ustachis**, comprising 114,000 men, exclusive of 38,000 territorial guard troops. In addition, after 1942 three mixed divisions of the "German-Croatian Legion" under Nazi command were formed.

Very few contributions to the air battle against the Russians were made by Croatia.

Rumania

When Rumania entered the war against the USSR on June 22, 1941, its army consisted of the following units of limited capacity: 12 infantry divisions, two fortifications brigades, three mountain brigades, four cavalry divisions and one armored division. Most of these troops saw action on the southern part of the Russian front from the time the invasion began. They were continually reinforced but lost 18 of their 22 divisions in the fighting at Stalingrad in the final weeks of 1942.

On June 22, 1941 the Rumanian air force had 405 planes—80 fighter-bombers, 60 light bombers and Stukas, 225 fighters, and 40 close-range reconnaissance craft.

Patrolling the Black Sea and the Danube River, the Rumanian navy included four destroyers, three old torpedo boats, one submarine, three torpedo speedboats, three gunboats, one minelayer, seven river monitors and 46 small auxiliary vessels.

J. Schroder

AXIS CONFERENCES.
See **Conferences of the Axis Powers.**

AXIS POWERS—Military Administration.
The primary aim of military administrations in the countries occupied by the **Axis** powers was the rapid conversion of the conquered territories into suppliers of military necessities. A secondary purpose was to oversee the conquered lands during the transitional period while their political fates were being decided and until executive powers could be left to the civil authorities. The establishment of a civil administration more directly subordinate to the German or Italian dictators indicated the Germans' or Italians' desire to annex the territory in question outright. This was the case in **the Netherlands** and **Norway**, where the tendency to annexation was motivated by the behavior of their populations.

The German military adminstration of an occupied country was organized from the outset to conform with the rules governing the occupying army in exceptional situations, which include, for example, unrest in the country or foreign aggression. At first, the Nazi state adhered to the rules set on May 21, 1935 by a law on "the state of security" and a primary law on "defense of the Reich." The *Wehrmacht*, however, had no particular interest in reorganizing to adapt itself to such a situation. Its plans for the concentration of offensive forces did not take into account the possibility of war on German territory; it therefore regarded its retention of full powers as perfectly normal. This was set forth in the second law of "defense of the Reich" (September 4, 1938), which applied only to the German border territories. The sixth section of the general staff for the land forces, which in time of war was to form the "quartermaster general" service, was responsible for prospective administrative duties. A number of high officers had been chosen for it who, in case of mobilization, would form the core of superior army cadres as chiefs of the civil adminis-

tration and would appoint smaller general staffs and commissioners for regulating large communities and rural districts. Their work would be subject to the army's orders and would depend on the extent of the army's responsibility. It was in accordance with these principles that the military administration was organized after the occupation of the Sudetenland, October 1–20, 1938; after the occupation of what was left of **Czechoslovakia**, March 15 to April 15, 1939; and, for the first time in a war period, after the Polish campaign, September 1 to October 25, 1939. And it was in accordance with these same principles that on August 26, 1939, the heads of the civil administration took charge of territories that had been annexed by **Germany** in the east and west. These heads were called *Gauleiter*, who in effect were provincial governors. Later, other **Nazi Party** directors were progressively imposed on the army as heads of the civil administration in **Danzig** and West Prussia, Poznan, and other provinces whose annexation was envisaged. It was also party members who controlled the administration of Krakow, along with the eastern high command. The military executive was swiftly replaced by civil administrators, and the terrritories that were to become protectorates—or general governments—were tied to the Reich by law. Unprepared for confrontations with the party and the secret police, the army failed generally to maintain its view of how the occupation should be handled politically. The horrors in which the military was directly involved, and which it vaguely deplored, highlighted the weakness of this system, in which the civil administration acted in the name of a military authority unable to control it. To pursue the war in the west, the general staff of the army invented a novel device to maintain intact its full power: a purely military administration for recruiting its own candidates for the official administration. Those appointees were given a paramilitary status and were inserted in the military hierarchy for services in the occupied territories at all levels. In the Netherlands a civilian *Reichskommissar* quickly replaced the military administration despite the resentment evidenced by the army chief of staff. But in **Belgium** and in the north of France, as well as in the occupied French regions until just a few months before the defeat of 1944, the administration was in the army's hands. In Alsace, Lorraine and **Luxembourg**, as well as neighboring districts of the Reich, the administration was controlled by a civilian. In Serbia and **Greece**, however, where a military commander had been named for the Salonika/Aegean and southern Greek regions, the military controlled the administration.

In the occupied Soviet territories—the largest of the German-occupied lands—the administration was not under military control. Anxious to organize the living space he had conquered in accordance with his national policy as quickly as possible, **Hitler** promptly installed civil administrators. He expected them to carry out his ideological program in detail and demanded of his soldiers that they restrict themselves to strictly military matters. His first measure was to cancel the previous Soviet annexations. **Finland** regained its lost territories; the Bialystok area, formerly a Polish possession, was extended to the east and south and practically annexed under cover of a special civil administration; eastern Galicia reverted to a general government; **Rumania** obtained territory beyond the Dniester, as well as northern Bukovina and Bessarabia, which had been ceded to Moscow in 1940. The western portion of the **USSR** was so firmly managed by civilian commissars for the eastern and Ukrainian territories that the German military administration had to confine its activities to operational regions behind the front, where strictly military commanders were superfluous. Full powers remained in the hands of the commanders in chief of armies and of army groups for governing the few areas still under their authority and providing the customary territorial military services—the regional and local commands. Their number and structure depended on local needs and formed the basis of the whole military administration. The extent of their jurisdiction and their command structure changed from time to time during the course of the war as additional territories fell under military administration, in **Italy** and in the Balkans, with the retreat of the Italian armies.

The military administrations were always aware of difficulties posed by the structure of the Reich. The quartermaster-general was not in a position to keep the military administrations free from the meddling of civilian bureaucrats, especially after Hitler assumed the post of commander in chief of the army. The police, the armaments industry and the labor administration, as well as some military services, quickly quashed any autonomy in the occupied territories and took the initiative for measures that seemed appropriate to their frequently contradictory missions. This confusion concerning the responsibilities of different groups resulted in a chaotic administration. The military administration attempted to base whatever control they enjoyed on the ideology of the bureaucrats or officers directing them. It was the military commanders that carried out anti-Jewish measures, including the mass transportation of Jews to **concentration camps**. Outside the eastern territories the difference between the civil and military administrations became progressively less marked. Economic exploitation and misery, labor for the profit of the Reich and merciless reprisals characterized daily life in all the occupied regions, regardless of who was in charge. This had the

effect of arousing the population against the Germans and increasing the ranks of the **Resistance** movements to such an extent that the military administrations succeeded in exasperating Hilter. In his view, they did not take sufficiently energetic measures to profit from the populations in the occupied lands. He therefore limited the powers of the military administrations to those necessary only for prosecution of the war. After the **assassination attempt of July 20, 1944**, he put further limitations on the powers of the *Wehrmacht* even within the borders of the Reich. In the reports they drew up throughout the course of the war, the military administrations asserted that they worked for the German war effort and made considerable material contributions, thanks partly to collaborators, and partly to the realization of the vague ideas of a "Greater Germany" and, in the economic sphere, of a "**New European Order.**"

Italy's entrance into the war and its offensive in the French Alps were not as rewarding as the Italians had expected. The campaign, conducted by several Italian battalions and aided by Germans in the Rhone Valley, did not meet with Germany's approval. Under pressure from his ally to conclude an armistice with moderate conditions, and faced with the failure of his own troops, **Mussolini** renounced the occupation of a large part of French territory on the mainland and in Africa, although this had been the objective of a phase of the war that was important to the Italians. He had to be content with a band of territory he had conquered near Menton and in the region of the Alps. Disregarding the German example, he appointed military commanders for a territory of about 320 square miles, with barely 28,000 inhabitants, three-fourths of them in Menton. The president of the Armistice Commission in Turin retained administrative jurisdiction and was assisted by a special labor group under his orders. In the occupied territories—which were very scattered, some of them accessible only from France— nine commissioners performed executive functions. The measures they took, involving the extension of the Italian administration to cover the French national territory, changing the frontiers for the police and customs inspectors, the introduction of Italian currency and the evacuation of a large part of the French population from Menton, amounted to annexation. The occupation of French lands by Italian troops whom the French considered interlopers rather than a victorious army was resented more bitterly than the occupation by the Germans. But the Italians' refusal to institute anti-Semitic laws or to deport labor to their territory which, after the Allied landing in North Africa, extended to the Rhone, was generally applauded. Italy attempted, in its sphere of influence, to create faits accomplis, particularly in **Yugoslavia**. Like the Bulgarians, the Albanians and the Hungarians, the Italians considered a provisional military administration ridiculous. From its conquered territories in Yugoslavia, Rome formed the provinces of Lubiana and Fiume as well as the kingdom of Dalmatia and incorporated them into its own lands. Montenegro was named a high commissariat and given a civil Italian administration. **Croatia** was set up as an independent state under the nominal authority of a king from the House of Savoy.

Most of Greece was subjected to an Italian military administration, to the disappointment of its inhabitants who preferred Germans to Bulgarians or Italians. But Hitler had given most of Greece up to the Italian sphere of interest; German administration was limited to the Salonika/Aegean region at the south of Greece, along with most of Crete. As its share of the spoils, Bulgaria took western Macedonia and the eastern part of Thrace.

The Italian high command created, in October 1940, a special service responsible for civil affairs and administrative control of the occupied zones in **Albania**. In the summer of 1941 the high command appointed a high commissioner, responsible directly to it, as occupation administrator during the Polish campaign. The country was divided into commissariats under the supervision of civil authorities. In Albania, as in France, the Axis powers had no uniform occupation policy. In Greece a certain rivalry began to develop over the economic resources of the country. Growing internal difficulties—to name two, problems of provisioning and the Resistance—increased dissension between Germans and Italians, which came to a head with the Italian surrender and the transfer of administrative power to the Germans and Bulgarians.

Since the early 1930s the primary objective of Japanese policy had been the creation of a "**Greater East Asia Co-Prosperity Sphere.**" The strengthening of Japan's political and economic power and its lack of raw materials, as well as a sudden rise in its population, were the principal motives for military expansion. **Collaboration** with satellite governments was effected wherever possible to economize on the huge expense of occupation administrations. Hence the establishment of the ostensibly independent state of Manchukuo on February 18, 1932. The government of Manchukuo awarded Tokyo the privilege of stationing its troops on its territory, together with de facto control of its administration, after its occupation by Japanese troops in September 1931.

Japanese military branches were also set up in Peking, by virtue of the "Boxer Protocols." Japanese troops landed in Shanghai in the spring of 1932. Starting in the summer of 1937 the Japanese increased their territorial acquisitions through war with **China**. On March 30, 1940 they transferred the administration of the country to an auxiliary government at Nanking, directed by **Wang Ching-wei**. By an agreement signed on November 30, 1940, the Japanese were guaranteed their political, economic and military interests. At the end of August, Tokyo took advantage of the weakness of France to obtain similar rights from the Vichy government in **Indochina**.

Japan's expanding strength brought it into collision with the **United States**, which, by freezing Japanese assets in American banks and placing an embargo on oil shipments to Japan, only strengthened its determination to become self-sufficient. Japanese **propaganda** justified its attack on American territory on December 7, 1941 (see **Pearl Harbor**) by asserting the necessity of putting an end to the exploitation of Asia by Western capitalism. The American, British and Dutch colonial dominion would have to give way to the Greater East Asian Co-Prosperity Sphere, a "reorganization" of that part of the world under Japanese auspices. The Japanese plan called for joint advances by land and naval forces to the south and west to destroy strategic enemy positions. On December 10, 1941, **Guam** was conquered; on December 23, **Wake** Island; and on Christmas, **Hong Kong**. January 1942 saw Japanese victories in the **Philippines**, Celebes, Amboine and **Borneo**, then the tiny islands near Java. In February, Sumatra, Bali and Timor were taken, and in March, Java itself. By December 1941, Japanese troops had landed in northern **Malaya**; **Singapore** surrendered in mid-February, and **Burma** followed in May 1942. Japan had thus guaranteed its supply of raw materials from China, foodstuffs from Manchuria, oil and tin from the Dutch East Indies, and rubber and tin from Malaya.

In the conquered territories either the army or navy installed military administrations with strongly centralized bureaucracies parallelling homeland political bodies. In Java alone, which was divided into two provinces, with the territory of Djakarta in one part and 17 districts in the other, 23,000 Japanese were stationed. The territories administered by the military were sealed off from the influence of the civilian officials of the Office of Asian Development and the Ministry of Greater Asia that followed it, as well as the Ministry of Foreign Affairs, which was less rigid. Intensive cultural propaganda was instituted to encourage "Asiatic consciousness" and to impose Japanese on the populace as a second language. But the occupation administration cared nothing about ideological or racial questions. Their commanders were concerned primarily with insuring—harshly, if necessary—the military and economic interests of their troops. Political objectives as well as national movements were subordinated to military necessity. The conquered populations were obliged to accept economic exploitation by the occupying power as their contribution to the common struggle and to the development of the Co-Prosperity Sphere. The Resistance, whose original members often belonged to communist groups, were regarded as traitors and were mercilessly persecuted. Only the military defeats and the appointment of **Mamoru Shigemitsu** as head of the Ministry of Foreign Affairs brought changes in Japanese policy and more flexiblity in the military. Much more than the navy, the army encouraged the population to participate in the administration under the supervision of a ''Japanese counselor'' and permitted, at least to certain territories, a limited independence, as in **Thailand**, Manchuria and Nanking China. This independence was usually tied to the country's participation in the Japanese war effort. On August 1, 1943 the military administration in Burma ended; on October 14, 1943 the Philippines gained their independence; in March 1945 certain regions in Indochina declared the end of the French protectorate; and on August 17, 1945 Indochina proclaimed its independence, which the Japanese had long been reluctant to concede. Through such grants, Japan hoped to avoid troubles in its empire. Tokyo took its anticolonialist policy seriously in order to keep the confidence of its subject nations. But for the peoples concerned, this kind of independence meant nothing. Taking advantage of the terms of their alliances, the Japanese commanders abused their prerogatives and took advantage of their colonial subjects, which had the effect of feeding hostility toward Japan.

The situation in the occupied territories as in the allied countries showed that the Co-Prosperity Sphere was nothing but a farce. The Japanese ''New Order,'' like its German counterpart, was not based on an association of equals but was rather aimed at creating a hegemony over East Asia, which, if Tokyo's plans had been realized, would have resulted in a reshuffling of the neighboring countries into three groups: first, the annexed territories of particular strategic importance (Hong Kong, Singapore, Borneo, New Guinea, Timor); second, regions that could progressively benefit from independence (Malaya, Sumatra, Java, Madura, perhaps even the Celebes); and third, the associated states (Manchukuo, China, the Philippines, Indochina, Thailand, Burma). The New Order envisaged by Japan failed to survive the war—even the new arrangement of frontiers it had ordered or tolerated did not last. The consequences of the Japanese domination were the death of the colonial system (see **Empire**) in East Asia and, at least in part, the drift of some states into socialism.

H. Umbreit

B

BADER, Douglas R. S. (1910-   ).
After losing both legs in an air crash in 1921, Bader, a British airman, reentered the **Royal Air Force** in November 1939. After distinguishing himself as an air ace in the **Battle of Britain**, Bader was captured by the Nazis in August 1941. He managed to escape but was quickly recaptured and kept in Colditz until the war's end. After returning to England, Bader went into business.

BADOGLIO, Pietro (1871-1956).
Badoglio, an Italian marshal, was originally an enemy of the Fascists and he was consequently deprived of the post of chief of staff of the Italian army in December 1923, after **Mussolini** took power. He was, however, reappointed in May 1925. Badoglio served as governor of Tripolitania and Cyrenaica from December 1928 to the beginning of 1934. He later replaced Gen. **Emilio De Bono** as commander of the Ethiopian invasion force, notable for its appallingly brutal practices, including the use of poison gas and the aerial bombardment of a defenseless people. After having opposed Italy's entry into the war, Badoglio accepted reappointment in 1940 as army chief of staff. He resigned after the Italian defeat in the invasion of Greece. Following Mussolini's fall, he was named prime minister by King **Victor Emmanuel III** on July 25, 1943. When the armistice was signed with the Allies on September 8, he abandoned Rome and secluded himself at Brindisi with the king. Badoglio signed Italy's unconditional surrender at the end of September, and on October 30 he declared war on Germany. Distrusted by the anti-Fascist parties, which had gained control after Mussolini's fall, Badoglio resigned on June 9, 1944.

BADUNG STRAIT.
Japanese Rear Adm. Kyuji Kubo's Bali occupation force, under IJN escort, landed easily at Sanur Roads, on the southeastern coast of Bali, on February 18, 1942. In an effort to intercept the enemy, the Allied naval commander in the region, Dutch Rear Adm. Karel Doorman, committed the Dutch and American warships available to him. During the first phase of a night engagement off Bali in the Badung Strait, on February 19–20, the IJN destroyer *Asashio* sank the Dutch destroyer *Piet Hein* with torpedoes. In the next stage of the battle, the Dutch light cruiser *Tromp* was put out of action by the excellent battery firing of the *Asashio*, although the IJN destroyer *Michishio* was mauled in cross fire, especially by the U.S. destroyer *John D. Edwards*. Eight Dutch motor torpedo boats on a sortie from Surabaja accomplished nothing. Thus, after sustaining only minor damage, the Bali occupation force was able to depart without further challenge. Allied conduct of the Badung Strait sea battle was generally inept and confused, while two of the IJN destroyers, *Asashio* and *Oshio*, fought with skill and effectiveness. As a result, the Japanese were operating the airfield at Bali by February 20, and the Allied position on Java, now out of reach of reinforcement, was doomed.

BALBO, Italo (1898-1940).
Balbo, an Italian marshal, was one of the "quadrumvirs" of the "March on Rome." He was unsuccessful in convincing **Mussolini** to refrain from entering the war in June 1940. En route back to **Libya**, where he had been governor since 1935, his plane was mistakenly shot down by the Italian air defense.

BALI.
See **Badung Strait**.

BALTIC STATES.
Granted their sovereignty in 1919, the Baltic States (Estonia, Latvia and Lithuania) were included in the plan secretly arranged by **Germany** and the **USSR** for dividing spheres of interest. In the secret protocol of the **Nazi-Soviet Pact** of August 23, 1939, **Finland**, Estonia and Latvia were ceded to the Soviets. In the Nazi-Soviet friendship treaty of September 28, 1939, Lithuania was similarly brought under Soviet domination. On September 28 the USSR concluded a mutual assistance pact with Estonia; it negotiated similar pacts on October 5 with Latvia and on October 10

with Lithuania. Each of these nations provided the USSR with strategic flanking protection. Profiting from the German advance of May–June 1940 on the western front, Soviet troops overran all the Baltic States, including the Lithuanian border strip reserved for Germany by the friendship treaty. On June 15 Soviet forces entered Lithuania, and two days later they were in Latvia and Estonia. This rapid military takeover was followed by an equally swift political move. On July 21 the new national representatives of the Baltic States opted for transforming the three republics into Soviet Socialist Republics and requested admission into the USSR. The three states became the 14th, 15th and 16th republics of the USSR in August.

After the German invasion of the USSR, the three countries, together with part of White Ruthenia, constituted the *Reichskommissariat Ostland*, under the direction of *Gauleiter* **Heinrich Lohse**. From that moment the administrations of the Baltic States were deprived of their autonomy. With the end of the war, attempts to reconstitute independent governments failed. The Red Army restored the political situation of 1940 and obtained reluctant de facto recognition by France and Great Britain.

H.-A. Jacobsen

BARBAROSSA.
The German code name for the war against the **USSR**. On December 18, 1940 **Hitler** made the final decision to invade the Soviet Union. The date he originally proposed for the invasion was May 1941; the invasion did not actually begin, however, until June 22 of that year. (See also **USSR—War with Germany**.)

BARKER, Sir Evelyn Hugh (1894–   ).
Barker, a British general, fought in France in World War I. He commanded the Eighth Corps from 1944 to 1946 and served in **Palestine** in 1946–47.

BARRY, Richard Hugh (1908–   ).
A British regular officer, Barry ran the operations section of **Special Operations Executive** (SOE) from 1940 to 1942 and served as SOE's chief of staff from 1943 to 1946.

BASTIN, Jules (1889–1944).
A Belgian officer who had been a prisoner of war in 1914, he gained fame by his repeated attempts to escape, succeeding on the 10th try. Promoted to colonel, he commanded the cavalry corps in 1939–40. In May 1940 he joined the Belgian troops in France and devoted himself to the underground struggle, taking command of the Belgian Legion (see **Charles Claser; Jules Pire**.) He was made commander in chief of all

underground military forces by the Belgian government on December 30, 1942. He was arrested in April 1943, released in July for lack of proof and then rearrested in November. On December 1, 1944 he died at Gross-Rosen and was posthumously awarded the title of general in August 1946.

BATTLE OF BRITAIN.
See **Britain, Battle of**.

BATTLE OF THE ATLANTIC.
See **Atlantic, Battle of the**.

BATTLE OF THE BULGE.
See **Bulge, Battle of the**.

BAZNA, Elyesa.
See **Cicero**.

BBC.
See **British Broadcasting Corporation**.

BCRA.
See *Bureau central de renseignements et d'action*.

BEAVERBROOK, Lord (1879–1964).
A British millionaire and radical imperialist of Canadian origin, Beaverbrook, formerly Sir Max Aitken, owned several newspapers. A friend of **Churchill**, he served as minister of aircraft production from 1940 to 1941 and minister of supply from 1941 to 1942. He was a member of the War Cabinet from 1940 to 1942, when he resigned following a quarrel. From 1943 to 1945, he served as lord privy seal and a confidant of Churchill.

As minister of aircraft production, Beaverbrook achieved nearly miraculous results in the production of fighters during the summer of 1940. In great measure the success of the **Battle of Britain**—and, consequently, the Allied victory in Europe—was the result of his devotion.

BECK, Jozef (1894–1944).
Beck, a Polish officer and statesman, fought in World War I. **Poland**'s foreign minister from 1932 to 1939, Beck signed the nonaggression pact of 1934 with **Germany**. With the support of **Hitler**, he obtained for Poland the Teschen region of **Czechoslovakia** in September 1938. He objected to the cession of **Danzig** to Germany in 1939, however, and after Poland's defeat by the Nazis, he fled to **Rumania**.

BECK, Ludwig (1880–1944).
Beck, a German general, was one of the leaders of the opposition to **Hitler** within the German army. From

1933 to 1935 he was head of the military administration section in the Reich's defense ministry, and from 1935 to 1938, chief of the general staff for the land armies. He resigned his post in 1938 after warning his colleagues several times against the Nazi government's expansionist policies. A participant in the unsuccessful **assassination attempt of July 20, 1944** against Hitler's life, Beck committed suicide that same evening.

BEDA FOMM.

Beda Fomm, about 62 miles south of Benghazi, Libya, was occupied on February 5, 1941, by the British Fourth Armored Brigade, under **John Caunter**, after an advance of 170 miles in 33 hours. The next day, the brigade, 3,000 strong, took 20,000 prisoners from **Rodolfo Graziani**'s retreating army and destroyed 100 of its tanks, losing only three. This battle was the climax of Sir **Richard O'Connor**'s Cyrenaican victory.

BELGIAN CONGO.

See **Congo, Belgian**.

BELGIUM.

On September 3, 1939, Belgium, a land with a population of 8.3 million, declared itself neutral in the impending war. Three years earlier King **Leopold III** and the Belgian government had set the country's course; Belgium would engage in no alliance, defensive or otherwise, but reserved the right to increase its military strength to deter any attack on its territory. This policy of independence had been guaranteed by London, Paris and Berlin since 1937 and had been supported by an overwhelming majority in the Belgian Parliament.

In a Europe dominated by totalitarian states with an imposing record of successes, Belgium's parliamentary democracy showed signs of weakness and, on occasion, impotence. Yet the country had managed to neutralize the most violent outbreaks of the extreme right, especially of those parties following the example of Italian fascism. **Leon Degrelle**, for example, who as head of the Rex Party made no secret of his sympathy with **Mussolini**, **Franco** and **Salazar**, watched his party's representation drop from 21 to four deputies between 1936 and 1937. The National Flemish Front (*Vlaams Nationaal Verbond*, or VNV), which was to some extent an expression of the historic, social and cultural aspirations of the Flemish community, maintained a minority of 17 deputies who objected to the unified, liberal and Western-oriented structure of the Belgian state without embracing Nazism. The Communist Party succeeded in electing only nine deputies even before the **Nazi-Soviet Pact**.

The government of **Hubert Pierlot** was based on a coalition of the three traditional parties, Catholic, Socialist and Liberal. In a chamber of 202 deputies the coalition controlled 170 seats. And quite often, even in a debate on the neutrality principle, it attracted opposition votes. There were actually no clearcut differences between the parties; the opinions of one blended with those of another. Some Walloon representatives directed criticism at what they considered the excessive neutralist zeal in the leadership of **Paul-Henri Spaak**, Cardinal van Roey and the king. Was not the country "appeasing the crocodile," Jean Rey demanded, by turning its back on the threatened border and recommending a neutral conscience in the name of the necessary neutrality of the state? But the extreme right and the Flemish nationalists insisted on strict neutrality.

After January 1940 (see **Mechlin Incident**) German threats against Belgium became more audible, but the Belgian government refused to appeal for guarantees of assistance in case of invasion or bow to demands for rights of passage for foreign troops crossing its territories unless, as counseled by Gen. Raoul van Overstraeten, the king's military adviser, the Netherlands was attacked.

But by May 1940 all hopes of remaining out of the conflict had melted away. German forces overran the forts of the defense chain at the Albert Canal (Eben Emael) and drove to Sedan across the Ardennes. An immediate call went out for British and French aid, but the overwhelming imbalance of attack and defense forces impelled the Belgian army to surrender on national soil on May 28. The king, the commander of the Belgian army and the head of the government remained in the occupied territory, refusing to follow the members of the cabinet to France, where they would continue to fight at the side of the French. Even the Germans, who had apparently foreseen everything but the failure of the king to desert his country, were surprised at this decision.

Even before the Belgian army surrendered, the comparatively few administrative authorities remaining at their posts together with the country's leaders expected to resume their normal activities in the occupied land. The country could not feed itself, and the Allied governments remained aloof. Survival depended on the trade of Belgian industrial products for food staples obtainable only from Germany or the territories it controlled. The collapse of the French military made this realization especially clear. Besides the nation's elite—the bankers, the industrialists, the jurists, the ministry officials, the clerical hierarchy—vowed to avoid a repetition of the German occupation of 1914-18, when the German army kept an increasingly tight grip on the daily life of the land. These leaders were ready to make concessions if the government could remain autonomous, at least economically and administratively.

But such autonomy was exactly the aim of the German military administration, headed by **Alexander von Falkenhausen**. **Hitler**'s instructions to him were to ensure, as the priority objective, the continued production of Belgian industry for the benefit of the Nazi war economy. This insistence on the resumption of the nation's economy carried with it the implication of maintenance of civil discipline, which in turn could be assured better by obtaining the cooperation of the establishment rather than by depending on collaborators (see **Collaboration**). Essential to the success of such a policy were continuous production, an orderly populace and government by a consenting Belgian administration with real executive and legislative powers.

Beginning in June 1940, the ministerial secretariats, with the consent of the country's leaders, formed a sort of governing assembly to cope with the vital problems of the nation—food supply, reconstruction, economic recovery, justice and the like.

Certain circles entertained the idea of setting up an autocratic monarchy in the "spirit of the times"—that is, in accordance with the policies of the country's economic, social and political elite. **Henry De Man**, head of the Belgian Labor Party and a confidant of the king, devoted earnest thought to the notion. Nor was he the only one. The French defeat encouraged such considerations, for if the Reich's victory on the Continent was a certainty and if the Belgian prisoners were freed, there would be no obstacle to the establishment of an independent government in occupied Belgium, especially since the Belgian ministers in Bordeaux were willing to offer the king their resignations and accept the armistice terms.

But these prospects were abruptly changed by new events. In July 1940 Hitler banned all political activity on the part of the king and refused to make any commitment concerning Belgium's future. Furthermore he forbade any concessions to the Walloons, such as the liberation of prisoners. The king ignored the proffered resignations of his ministers, and the legal Belgian government was established in London by **Camille Gutt**, Spaak and Pierlot. The **Belgian Congo** entered the war on the side of the British, and the **Battle of Britain** cast doubts on the promise of German victory, thus reversing the trend of public opinion. But most importantly the condition of the population underwent a change for the worse. Many were unemployed, the promised provisions failed to arrive in adequate amounts despite the industrial production furnished to the Reich and the amount of calories per rationed portion was barely adequate. The

taxes imposed by the occupation were unbearably high; the military administration dismissed suspected Belgian civil servants and replaced them with admirers of the New Order; the Reich police bullied the people and even opened a concentration camp at Breendonck; Nazi propaganda blanketed the country with the aid of collaborating agents; a new system for organizing the economy was manned by submissive employees; the defense of workers by their unions was forbidden after several weeks of socialist demagogy—the list of humiliations imposed on the Belgians was seemingly endless. The first measures taken against the Jews—their forced registration—went almost unnoticed by the general population.

After a preliminary period of hesitation in the summer of 1940, the Belgians—the Walloons, in particular—became openly hostile to the occupation forces. Toward the end of the year, the Belgian establishment began to realize it had been duped. The new civil servants in the ministry secretariats (particularly in the ministries of the Interior and of Economic Affairs), or the Germans themselves when the Belgian administration refused to take direct action, grossly perverted the law. Industrial profits and distributed dividends swelled (2.9 billion and 1.8 billion Belgian francs respectively in 1942), but the Belgians could no longer be deluded into believing that the only purpose of all this economic activity was their comfort. Military collaboration with the Germans took a multiplicity of forms and grew to frightening proportions; after the war, more than 10,000 collaborators were convicted.

The German oppression then accelerated in two directions—persecution of the Jews and, beginning in March 1942, forced labor, followed by the deportation of Belgian workers to the Reich in October of that year. The Belgian reply was to contribute 80,000 guerrillas to the **Resistance**. An effective "underground railway" was organized to aid escaping Jews—notably with the complicity of parish priests and sympathetic church groups. Half of Belgium's Jews escaped deportation in this way. Aid to Belgian insurgents was provided by the maquis group known as Socrates, financed by the Pierlot government.

Isolated in the midst of their fellow countrymen who hated them even more than the detested Germans, the collaborators sensed the onset of a new battle between the military occupation administration on one side and the **Nazi Party** and **SS** on the other. The former had given its conditional blessing to the Flemish nationalists (Staf de Clercq first, then Hendrik Elias) of the VNV but with no promise of full power; the latter proposed dividing the nation into two *Gaus*—Flanders and Wallonia—and attaching them to Germany, as Austria had been in the *Ansch-*

luss. At the beginning of 1943 Degrelle led his Rex Party into the SS and announced to Brussels that the Walloons were Teutons and therefore belonged to the Nazi German peoples. To avoid being completely cut out by the extremist De Vlag group supported by **Himmler** himself, the VNV plunged deeper into military collaboration. The SS handed out bribes and favors to those accepting the Belgian form of *Anschluss.*

For less zealous collaborators—those eager for Reich domination of Europe but opposed to assimilation into Hitler's empire—the situation became extremely hazardous. VNV volunteers on the Russian front were denied the right to take orders in their own language, to have their own newspaper or to practice their Catholic religion under the guidance of Flemish priests. The De Vlag organization, on the other hand, obtained from Himmler total control over the Flemings outside Belgium—voluntary or forced laborers in the Reich and military or paramilitary personnel on the Russian front or the **Atlantic Wall.** The Flemish nationalists who had considered a German victory as Flanders' great opportunity now tried to excape from their commitment to a process leading inevitably to the erasure of the Flemish identity. What was even more important to them, however, was the fact that De Vlag was acquiring strength at their expense. It was heavily armed and was preparing a series of assassination attempts on such "Belgicists" as A. Galopin, the originator of the doctrine of 1940 providing for economic recovery and resumption of the country's administration.

Degrelle's proclamation of the Teutonic birthright of the Walloons aroused dissensions in his own Rex Party. Some of the collaborators—Latin fascists, as the Nazis called them—kept their distance from the SS but, like its members, asserted their pride in their Teutonic heritage and Hitlerite beliefs.

The Belgians, in fact, had the unique privilege of watching a confrontation between the SS activists and the German military, which as yet had not completely accepted their authority. It was not until after the Allied landing that Himmler finally subdued von Falkenhausen. A *Gauleiter* was appointed head of the civil administration but only to preside over the German panic of August-September 1944. A kind of Flemish government (De Vlag) was organized in exile for several months while the Teutonic Rex under Degrelle vainly attempted a power grab in Wallonia under cover of the last-gasp Nazi offensive of December 1944. It was then the turn of a few thousand of the 31,000 Belgian citizens who were members of the German military and paramilitary organizations of 1941-44 to undergo repression.

In 1940 resistance to the German occupation first took the form of individual initiatives—aiding in the escape of British soldiers unable to get passage across the English Channel, arranging contacts between Belgian soldiers and Belgian freedom organizations and some time afterward repatriating Allied flyers who made forced landings. The clandestine groups that engineered rescues of downed air crews—the specialty of the Belgian Resistance—included the *Comete* (see **Andree De Jongh**) and the Pat O'Leary (see **Albert Guerisse**). These were huge networks, reaching from the Netherlands to **Spain** and capable of returning 1,200 aviators to their combat groups. Information-gathering networks proliferated as well. Beginning in September 1939, at a time when Belgium was still neutral, the engineer **Walthere Dewe,** founder of the spy organization *La Dame Blanche* in World War I, repeated his activities in World War II with a new group known as *Clarence.* He worked efficiently and led an apparently charmed life until he was struck down, on January 14, 1944, at the age of 63. Two other espionage networks, *Zero* and *Luc,* were formed in the summer of 1940. Still others were spontaneously propagated by amateur agents within the country or organized by parachute-dropped professionals. Some of them became specialists in certain areas—meteorology, air bases, railroads, **radar** and the like. In 1943, some 20 such groups were welded into a single information-accumulating agency with tentacles reaching into every corner of the nation; indeed, some of them extended into France, the Netherlands, **Luxembourg** and even Germany itself. Nor were the underground newspapers far behind.

Organization of **sabotage** and a general uprising at the propitious moment was the responsibility of a number of groups receiving directives, equipment and funds from the British Secret Service. *Groupe G* in the University of Brussels, for example, specialized in scientific sabotage. The *Witte Brigade*, its nerve center at Anvers, fought both the German army and the Flemish extremists. Some of the others were the *Armee de la Liberation* based at Liege; the *Mouvement national belge;* the *Mouvement national royaliste; Service D; Les Insoumis; Les Affranchis; Nola* and the *Kempische Legioen.* The two most important were the *Front de l'Independance* and the *Legion belge,* later to change its name to *L'Armee Secrete* (the AS). Originally, the *Front de l'Independance* operated on a moral and psychological level—publishing an underground newspaper, aiding Jews and rebels—but later acquired two highly effective fighting forces known as *L'Armee belge des partisans,* whose leaders and 40 percent of whose members were Communists, and the *Milices patriotiques.* The AS recruited its cadre from among the active and reserve officers of the Belgian army, under the command of

Col. **Jules Bastin**. He was replaced, after his arrest and subsequent death at Gross-Rosen, by Gen. Ivan Gerard and then Gen. **Jules Pire**. Its adventures in continuous sabotage lasted throughout the occupation, becoming widespread on June 4, 1944. In August and September of that year, the Ardennes maquis was especially active, accomplishing the tremendous feat of preserving the harbor installations in the Escaut River by freeing both its banks of the German presence. The price paid by the Belgian Resistance was 17,000 dead, executed by shooting, decapitation or hanging; swallowed up by concentration camps; or killed in battle.

On September 2, 1944, Allied forces broke through the Belgian border, and the next day Brussels was liberated. Anvers was discovered to be miraculously intact. Returning to the capital from London to lethargic public reaction, the Pierlot government summarized its activity abroad to the Belgian Parliament on September 19. Leopold III had been sent to Germany on June 7, 1944. Having found it impossible to reign in a country overrun by the enemy, the king gave way to a regency that held title from September 20, 1944 to July 1950.

Curiously enough, the men in the government in exile, expecting to hand over the reins to those who had remained in Belgium and survived the ordeal of the occupation, now found themselves back in power. The new government naturally seated more Communists and veterans of the Resistance. But Belgium, like France, acquired no radically new regime, in the quality of its personnel, after the liberation. No really new party thrust itself forward, and the old political families other than those identified with the collaborators retained their importance with perhaps only slight changes in voting strength.

The "eastern cantons" that Germany had annexed in May 1940—without the slightest protest—were restored to the country, and Belgium was again what it had been before its fall.

J. Gerard-Libois

BELL, George Kennedy Allen (1883-1958).
Bell was Anglican bishop of Chichester from 1929. He visited Stockholm in May-June 1942 and saw **Dietrich Bonhoeffer** and other members of the German opposition, with whom **Eden** declined to negotiate.

BENES, Eduard (1884-1948).
A Czech leader of peasant origins, Benes served as first foreign minister of **Czechoslovakia** (1918-35) and succeeded Tomas Masaryk as president (1935-38). He moved to England after the signing of the **Munich Pact** in October 1938. The British recognized Benes as

president of the Czech government in exile in July 1940. In May 1945 he was restored but in uncomfortable political company. He resigned in June 1948, following the Communist coup d'etat that year.

BERGEN-BELSEN.
This camp was opened by the Germans in 1941 for ailing prisoners of war. Thousands of Soviet prisoners died at Bergen-Belsen between 1941 and 1942. In 1943 the camp came under the control of **Himmler**, who converted it into a **concentration camp** for Jews and incapacitated deportees from such other camps as Buchenwald, Dachau, Flossenburg and Natzweiler. The lack of hygiene and of care for the sick were as effective a means of extermination as the gas chambers. **Anne Frank** was one of the victims. The last camp commander was **Josef Kramer.**

BERGGRAV, Eiwind (1884-1959).
Berggrav was a Norwegian theologian, Lutheran bishop of Oslo and one of the **Resistance** commanders during the Nazi occupation. He had frequent contacts with members of the **German Resistance**.

BERIA, Lavrenti Pavlovich (1899-1953).
Beria joined the Bolsheviks in his native Georgia in 1917. From 1921 to 1931 he worked in the Transcaucasian secret police. As head of the Soviet Secret police, **NKVD**, (1938-46), Beria concluded the Stalinist **purges** and organized the home front of the **USSR** for war. After being tried secretly, he was executed.

BERNADOTTE, Count Folke (1895-1948).
As president of the Swedish **Red Cross** (1943), he was requested by **Himmler** and other German leaders in April 1945 to transmit pleas for a separate peace to Anglo-American forces. Bernadotte used these contacts to keep concentration camp prisoners from being liquidated and to obtain the immediate transfer of some of them, including a number of women, into the protection of the Swedish Red Cross. He was assassinated in **Palestine** in 1948.

BERNHARD, Prince of the Netherlands (1911-).
Born a prince of Lippe-Biesterfeld in **Germany**, in 1937 he married Juliana, the only child of Queen **Wilhelmina**. He escaped to London with the Dutch royal family in May 1940 and took command of the Dutch forces in exile, including those sent back clandestinely to the **Netherlands**. His wife became queen in 1948.

BEVAN, Aneurin (1897-1960).

A Welsh radical social-democrat, Bevan was a Laborite member of Parliament for Ebbw Vale from 1929. He led the unofficial parliamentary opposition to **Churchill** during the war. From 1945 to 1951 he served as minister of health.

BEVERIDGE, Sir William Henry (later Lord) (1879-1963).

An economist and undersecretary of labor in **Churchill's** cabinet, in 1942 he wrote the Beveridge Report on Social Insurance and Allied Services, from which the **welfare state** evolved.

BEVIN, Ernest (1881-1951).

Working his way up through the dockers' trade union, Bevin became a leader of the British trade union movement and a strong international socialist. In **Churchill's** coalition he was minister of labor and sat in the war cabinet from September 1940 to May 1945. His near-absolute powers enabled him to mobilize labor and industry for war. In July 1945 he became foreign secretary under **Attlee.**

BIDAULT, Georges (1899-1975).

French professor and editorialist of *L'Aube*, the Christian Democratic daily, from 1932 to 1940, he succeeded **Jean Moulin** as president of the *Conseil national de la resistance* in June 1943 and became minister of foreign affairs in the **de Gaulle** government in September 1944.

BLACKETT, Patrick M. S., Lord (1897-1974).

Blackett studied physics at Cambridge and made important discoveries about atomic particles. From 1939 to 1945 he applied scientific methods to warfare. He advocated control and abolition of nuclear weapons by international agreement.

BLACK MARKET.

"Black market" was the term given to the illegal trade in consumer goods, manufactured products and raw materials without regard to rationing or price-fixing statutes, practiced because of the scarcity of goods. The constantly escalating game of bidding and the risks that the traders ran pushed prices up to unbelievable levels.

In the countries occupied by the *Wehrmacht*, the black market quickly appeared. From 1932 the German people had endured privation because of sacrifices demanded to finance rearmament. Consumption of bread dropped 10 percent, oils 30 percent, dairy products 15 percent, delicatessen products 18 percent and meats 11 percent. In the occupied countries German troops enjoyed a high exchange-rate advantage—the German mark was equivalent to 20 French francs and 12.5 Belgian francs—and were thus able to acquire immense stocks of food, including agricultural produce, cereals and dairy products, and wine. Textiles and leather were abundant. The indemnity for occupation expenses also permitted the *Wehrmacht* and the Third Reich to make valuable purchases. But the situation began to deteriorate with the **evacuation** of various populations, the poor harvest of 1940, the destruction caused by air bombings and the looting of military stores. The conqueror's demands kept increasing during the occupation years.

Like the peasants the industrialists in the occupied countries had an interest in selling to the Germans. Many of them resisted the temptation either out of patriotism or fear of retaliation by the **Resistance.** Sales negotiations were conducted in secret at prices completely independent of taxes or statutes imposed by the occupying power. The secret slaughter of hogs and cattle was common everywhere.

In practice, the black market was encouraged by garrisoned troops taking advantage of the opportunity to buy stringently rationed foods for themselves or their families back in **Germany.** The city populations suffered most from the increasingly frugal rationing, which often was not even "honored" because of transportation difficulties, and were forced to make trips to the rural areas for essential food products, especially for their children. But the stabilization of salaries at a low level had the effect of barring workers and minor bureaucrats from the black market—hence, the resentment of urbanites toward their country cousins.

In December 1943 the Germans skimmed off 50 percent of France's agricultural and industrial production. That figure increased to 60 percent in 1944. An attempt was made to control the black market by economic means. Only the most unabashed black marketeers were ever caught and imprisoned; certainly those who kept the German officers supplied had little to fear. The familiar packages were openly delivered to the addresses of these officers in the large cities. It has been estimated that, depending on the particular region, 60 percent to 90 percent of the total food production was distributed through the black market.

M. Baudot

BLACK MOUNTAIN.

A plateau southeast of the Massif Central within the departments of Aveyron and Aude in France, where large groups of maquis gathered. These forces of **Resistance** fighters succeeded in conquering the entire region, effectively sustaining attacks by the

Wehrmacht and afterward taking part in the pursuit of the enemy during August-September 1944.

BLASKOWITZ, Johannes (1884-1946).

Blaskowitz was the commander in chief of the German forces in the eastern front. After the defeat of Poland in 1939, he protested the vicious measures of the SS, causing the *Wehrmacht* chiefs of staff to request Hitler to dissolve that organization. Because of the intercession of Hans Frank in favor of Himmler, commander of the SS, Blaskowitz was transferred in May 1940. From 1944 to 1945 he was placed at the head of a group of armies in the western front. He surrendered to the Allies on May 5, 1945. Following his trial before the Nuremberg Tribunal, he committed suicide.

BLITZKRIEG.

The Nazis used this term, meaning lightning war, to describe their method of rapid offensive warfare using armored forces with air support, first launched against Poland in September 1939. The British shortened the expression to ''the Blitz'' in referring to the intense air bombing of Britain by the Germans in 1940-1941. (See also Britain, Battle of.)

BLOCKADE.

In August 1940 the Germans, hoping to improve on the unrestricted submarine warfare that had almost brought them victory in 1917, declared a total blockade of the British Isles but did not have the submarine or air resources to make it fully effective. The British, later aided by the Americans, mounted a counterblockade that was somewhat more effective than the German effort, though still not complete. The Germans had access to large resources overland, which a sea blockade could hardly affect, and a few Japanese cargo ships bringing rubber and tin from Malaya managed to evade capture and slip into Biscay ports. Neutral ships whose owners agreed to cooperate with the British or Americans were supplied by them with navicerts, which entitled them to carry specified cargoes along certain routes, and were afforded convoy protection. Neither the British nor the German people suffered as much from blockade as had been the case in World War I. But some rare metal shortages (wolfram, tungsten, chrome, nickel) raised critical difficulties for the German arms industries.

M. R. D. Foot

BOCK, Fedor von (1880-1945).

In the Polish campaign, Bock was commander in chief of Army Group North. He led Army Group B in France in 1940 and was appointed field marshal that year. Bock commanded the central front in the advance into the USSR in 1941. He was given command of Army Group South in the USSR in January 1942, but was replaced in July of that year.

BOHEMIA-MORAVIA.

Declared a protectorate by Hitler on March 16, 1939. (See also Czechoslovakia.)

BOHR, Niels Henrik David (1885-1962).

A winner of the 1922 Nobel prize in physics, Bohr fled from his native Denmark to Sweden in 1942. The next year he went to the U.S. to help build the first atomic bomb, the political impact of which he foresaw. He later appealed, without success, for the international sharing of scientific data and renunciation of the bomb.

BOLERO.

Code name for the transfer of American troops to Great Britain for subsequent fighting in Europe. (See also Normandy Landing.)

BOMBER COMMAND.

British term for the United Kingdom's aerial bombardment forces. (See also Germany, Air Battle of.)

BONHOEFFER, Dietrich (1906-1945).

A noted German Protestant theologian, he opposed Hitler from the very beginning. In 1935 he was director of the Confessional Church Seminary but a year later was deprived of the right to teach. On a visit to Stockholm in 1942, he probed the possibilities of an armistice with the Allied powers. He was arrested in 1943 and hanged at Flossenburg on April 9, 1945. (See also The Church and the Third Reich.)

BOREDOM.

According to the British soldiers' proverb, ''War is 99 percent boredom and one percent fright.'' This prominent aspect of war is usually overlooked in fiction and hardly noticed even by military historians. Yet a tremendous amount of time spent by people at war is spent simply waiting: waiting for other people to arrive, waiting for the enemy to make a move, waiting for absent husbands, wives or lovers, waiting for letters from home, waiting for supplies, waiting for news. Those who could occupy their minds—by reciting poetry, going over music, composing stories in their heads—were the least bored. They formed a small minority among the hundreds of millions at war.

Boredom was generally easier to bear when news was good and morale was high. There was also less of it during active operations than during training. Yet even on operations—on watch on a calm night at sea, in the rear turret of a bomber on a long raid, on sentry duty in open country and during static war—life could be extremely boring; and boredom was not made much more tolerable by the thought that one's companions' lives depended on one's own alertness.

British troops sometimes sought simultaneously to express and to relieve their boredom by singing, to a hymn tune, "We're here because we're here because/We're here because we're here;/We're here because we're here because/We're here because we're here."

M. R. D. Foot

BORIS III (1894-1943).

As king of **Bulgaria,** Boris brought his country into the war as an ally of the **Axis** powers in 1941. No explanation has been found for his violent death on August 18, 1943.

BOR-KOMOROWSKI, Tadeusz (1895-1966).

Born a Polish count, Bor-Komorowski commanded a cavalry regiment in 1919-20. He was acting commander of the *Armia Krajowa* (Polish Home Army) in 1941-43 and in 1944 led the abortive **rebellions in Warsaw,** on orders (as he understood) from both London and Moscow. From October 1944 to May 1945, he was a prisoner of war. Thereafter he served, until 1947, as commander of the Polish army in exile and, in 1947-49, as prime minister of the government in exile.

BORMANN, Martin (1900-?).

Chief staff officer of the "Fuehrer's deputy," **Rudolf Hess,** in 1933, Bormann became head of the party Chancellery and afterward a member of the government and of the Interministerial Defense Council in 1941. He assumed the office of secretary to the Fuehrer in April 1943, working closely with **Hitler** during the last years of the war. On May 2, 1945 he vanished from the bunker of the Chancellery. In 1946 the Nuremberg Tribunal sentenced him in absentia to be hanged. Since the war's end the rumor that Bormann was alive and living in South America has circulated persistently; no hard evidence to support the rumor, however, has yet been found.

BORNEO.

The third largest island in the world. At the time of the Japanese occupation in 1941, its northern area was the British possession of North Borneo and the two British protectorates of Brunei and Sarawak. The southern part of the island, which comprised two-thirds of the total area, was a Dutch possession, part of **Indonesia.**

To the Japanese in 1941, seizure of weakly defended Borneo was closely connected to the conquest of **Malaya.** On December 16 Japanese invaders from Indochina landed at the oil fields at Miri (northern Sarawak) and Seria (Brunei), both of which had been sabotaged by the British before their abandonment. The new air facility under construction at Kuching (Sarawak) was seized by the Japanese on December 24, the last British elements falling back into Dutch Borneo. On January 19, at Sandakan, British Borneo was surrendered officially. The Japanese had lost few vessels to sporadic Dutch submarine or air attacks: two destroyers and one transport sunk, three transports damaged. Meanwhile the Japanese launched an operation from Davao, in early January 1942, designed to conquer Dutch Borneo. On January 10, 14 transports reached Tarakan Island, whose rich oil fields were set on fire and whose airfield was sabotaged by the local Dutch commander. By January 12 the 1,300-man **Netherlands** garrison had been overwhelmed. A Japanese naval air unit was operating from a repaired strip on Tarakan five days later. Thereupon, the Japanese formed a Balikpapan occupation force, which reached its objective from Tarakan on January 23 and landed troops from 15 transports the next morning. The Dutch commander, however, had defied Japanese warnings and set fire to the Balikpapan oil fields, while Allied B-17s and a Dutch submarine attacked the Japanese flotilla, sinking one transport and damaging two more. U.S. Vice Adm. W. A. Glassford had rushed a naval unit from Timor to engage the invasion force. On the night of January 23-24, four American destroyers aggressively raided the enemy and, during their second run, torpedoed and sank three transports in about 20 minutes. Understandably but wrongly waging antisubmarine tactics, the IJN commander, Adm. Shoji Nishimura, had shifted his destroyer screen east of the unexpected U.S. destroyer foray. This engagement, however, did not affect the fate of the small, retreating Dutch garrison ashore, which was finally caught by Japanese troops and forced to surrender on March 8. In the meantime, two Japanese assault forces had set out to capture the inland base of Bandjermasin, one proceeding by barges and then overland, and the second going directly overland, all the way from Balikpapan. On February 16 Bandjermasin fell. IJN aircraft were able to fly from Balikpapan by January 28 and from Bandjermasin by February 23. By overrunning Borneo expeditiously the Japanese not only acquired resource-rich areas but were also able to cover their vital sea and air lanes to **Singapore,** Sumatra and western Java. Not until 1945 did the

Allies return to Borneo, when powerful Australian amphibious forces, with U.S. naval and air support, retook Tarakan (May 5), Brunei Bay-Labuan (June) and Balikpapan (July 3). Australian casualties in these operations numbered 568 dead and 1,524 wounded. Japanese dead were estimated at 6,700; 445 prisoners were taken; and another 300 Japanese gave up after the war had ended.

A. D. Coox

BOSE, Subhas Chandra (1897-1945).

In 1938-39 the anti-British Bose was president of **India's** Congress Party. While visiting Germany in 1941 and Japan in 1943, he recruited Indian prisoners of war into his National Indian Army. The small force received little help from its Japanese allies, was depleted by desertions and proved inept. Bose died in a plane crash in Formosa in 1945.

BOUGAINVILLE.

In March 1942 the victorious armed forces of **Japan** continued to enlarge their Southwest Pacific perimeter, occupying the largest island in the Solomons— Bougainville (3,380 square miles). The island became an important sea and air refueling and supply base for subsequent Japanese operations against **Guadalcanal** and the Central Solomons. During the Allied strategic counteroffensive of 1943 in the direction of Rabaul, scarcely 200 miles away, Bougainville was a natural objective for its advanced air bases. The Japanese garrison was large, totaling 35,000 men, but concentrated mainly in the south—namely, 17th Army Headquarters built around the Sixth Division, three battalions of the Fourth Southern Garrison Unit and an IJN detachment. The Empress Augusta Bay sector, which Adm. **Halsey** and his South Pacific planners earmarked as the primary beachhead, was defended by only 3,000 troops. Coming ashore at Cape Torokina in three assault units on November 1, (Operation Dipper), the Third Marine Division, commanded by Lt. Gen. A. A. Vandegrift, encountered a mere 270 Japanese soldiers and one artillery piece. Accompanying or just preceding the Bougainville invasion were a number of diversionary raids: landings in the Treasury Islands by New Zealanders and on Choiseul by U.S. Marines; and bombardments of Buka and the Shortlands.

After debarking the troops at Bougainville, most of the U.S. transports departed immediately, in anticipation of enemy counteraction, which was soon to come. Hoping to catch the U.S. transports in transit, Vice Adm. Sentaro Omori headed for Gazelle Bay, west of Torokina Point. There, he collided with Rear Adm. A. S. Merrill's Task Force 39 in the Battle of

Empress Augusta Bay on November 1. The Japanese force consisted of two heavy and two light cruisers and six destroyers. Merrill had four light cruisers and nine destroyers. Although Omori outgunned the Americans, his complicated, high-speed maneuvers caused serious collisions in the night. From all causes, he lost one light cruiser and one destroyer sunk, and another light cruiser and two destroyers damaged. Merrill lost a destroyer to a torpedo. After the costly defeat sustained by Omori, who lost his command shortly afterward, the Bougainville invasion could proceed without interference.

Between November 8 and 11 the U.S. Army's 37th Infantry Division followed up Vandergrift's Third Marine Division, which was replaced in mid-January 1944 by the Army's Americal Division from Guadalcanal. Control of the beachhead then went to Maj. Gen. O. W. Griswold's XIV Corps. The desperate Japanese 17th Army tried new tactics of "reverse," or "counter," landings, since they could not eliminate the U.S. foothold frontally. These counteractions failed; for example, the operation of November 7, when four IJN destroyers landed 475 men, was quickly aborted by artillery. Focusing on their main mission of protecting air strike facilities, the Americans did not press far beyond their large, strong perimeter defenses, but on November 25 they finally seized steep Hellzapoppin Ridge, the site of dangerous enemy artillery emplacements. Skirmishing, patrolling and air action continued. On March 8 the Japanese stormed the 37th Division's lines. A final effort was attempted on March 24, shortly after which the Japanese fell back from the whole Empress Augusta sector.

The Americans were replaced by Australian forces: the II Australian Corps (under Maj. Gen. S. G. Savige), with one division and two brigades, supported by Fiji scouts and guerrillas. The Australians steadily pushed back the hungry, sick Japanese remnants and broke up their last, eight-day counteroffensive at the end of March and beginning of April 1944. It is estimated that, in all, 8,500 Japanese were killed on Bougainville and that 9,800 died of illness. At war's end, 23,571 men were left in the Japanese 17th Army. The neutralization of Bougainville Island in 1943-44 had eliminated "the last major obstacle—on the Solomons side—before Rabaul," in Gen. Robert Eichelberger's words. By the same token, Bougainville became the springboard for suppressing Rabaul itself, by bomber and fighter strikes launched from four good airfields within easy range. The fate of the isolated Japanese garrison on Bougainville also illustrated the validity of **MacArthur's** "wither-on-the-vine" bypassing strategy.

A. D. Coox

BRADLEY, Omar Nelson (1893-   ).
A classmate of **Eisenhower** at West Point, Bradley was selected by Eisenhower for duty in Tunisia and was soon appointed to command the II Corps there and in Sicily in 1943. He headed the First Army in the **Normandy landing**. From August 1, 1944 he led the 12th Army Group. He captured Cherbourg and moved on to cross the Rhine at Remagen. Bradley served as chairman of the Joint Chiefs of Staff from 1949 to 1953.

BRANDEBURG.
A special unit under the command of the *Abwehr*, its function, beginning in 1939, was to operate behind enemy lines or in commando operations (as at Lemberg in 1941). In 1941 it became the Brandeburg Regimental School 800 for Special Missions and in 1942 the Brandeburg Division.

BRASILLACH, Robert (1909-1945).
The literary critic of the French journal *Action Francaise* and editor in chief of *Je suis partout* from 1938 to 1945, he collaborated actively with the Nazis. He was condemned to death and executed in January 1945.

BRAUCHITSCH, Walther von (1881-1948).
The son of a Prussian general, Brauchitsch became head of the *Oberkommando des Heeres* and commander in chief of the German land armies in 1938 and was promoted to field marshal in 1940. **Hitler** relieved him of his duties in 1941 when the German army failed to take Moscow.

BRAUN, Wernher von (1912-1977).
A German engineer, von Braun was appointed technical director of the rocket research center at **Peenemuende** in 1937. He developed the V-2 prototype in 1938, but since **Hitler** had given priority in missile research to the *Luftwaffe* in 1940, von Braun was deprived of the means to proceed with his work (see **V-1 and V-2**). In 1943 Hitler demanded mass production of the V-2 rockets. Because he frustrated **Himmler's** attempt to gain control of his project, von Braun was arrested by the **Gestapo**. Released on Hitler's order, he started production of the V-2s. He fled before the advancing Russians in March 1944, escaped with 400 of his associates and surrendered to the American command. He was later invited to collaborate with American engineers on missile development and aerospace research in the **United States**.

BRAZIL.
Following the revolution of 1930, Brazil was under the benevolent dictatorship of Getulio Vargas (1883-1954). His chief aims were to increase the power of the cental government vis-a-vis the component states and to enact social legislation. In 1937 Vargas set up the *Estado Novo* (New State), with a revised constitution that gave him complete power.

Brazil broke off relations with the **Axis** powers in January 1942 and declared war on **Germany** and **Italy** (but not on **Japan**) in August 1942. A Brazilian division fought with distinction in Italy, particularly at Monte Cassino; and the Brazilian navy joined in antisubmarine patrols in the South Atlantic. Brazil was thus qualified to be a founding member of the **United Nations**.

M. R. D. Foot

BRERETON, Lewis Hyde (1890-1967).
In 1917-18 Brereton served as a pursuit plane pilot in France. In the early part of World War II, he held various U.S. Army Air Force command posts, in the Far East, India, the Middle East and Africa. In 1944-45 he commanded the Ninth Army Air Force in Normandy and then the First Allied Airborne Army.

BRETTON WOODS CONFERENCE.
See **Conferences, Allied**.

BRIDGES, Sir Edward (1892-1969).
The son of poet Robert Bridges, he served as secretary to the cabinet from 1938 to 1945 and as secretary to the treasury from 1946 to 1956 in Britain.

BRINON, Ferdinand de (1885-1947).
A French author, Brinon founded the French-German Committee in 1935 and represented the Vichy government in Paris as secretary of state. He was condemned to death by the French courts and executed.

BRITAIN.
See **United Kingdom**.

BRITAIN, Battle of.
British Preparation for the Battle of Its Life
After Dunkirk (May 26-June 3, 1940), British land forces' shortage of armaments was extreme. There was no dearth of men—although they still had to be trained—but in all of Britain there were only 500 field artillery pieces and 200 **tanks**. "Give us the tools and we will finish the job," **Churchill** was to write to **Roosevelt**. American arms began to arrive in July. The first lots were from the stock remaining from World War I and were still preserved in the original grease. In the meantime, the coastal defense, the **civil defense**, underground shelters and antiaircraft balloon barrages were being rapidly developed. The **Home**

Guard was created, enrolling those who could not be mobilized for full-time service. Its members went into training and served after office or factory hours. Equipped at first with an irregular assortment of arms, such as hunting rifles, it was charged principally with surveillance and guard duties during landing alerts, thus permitting the regular army units to pursue their training. Women of 18 to 45 were mobilized, as well. Many of them began working in factories; others formed military units in the three branches of the armed forces to fulfill all missions not allotted to men: general services, office jobs, chauffeuring, airport operational office work, antiaircraft duty, secret service, health services and welfare.

The Royal Navy was ready for battle—except for its woeful lack of destroyers. Fifty were supplied by Roosevelt early in September.

In the first week of August, the **Royal Air Force** had only 700 fighters and 500 bombers ready for combat. However, over 1,600 aircraft, 470 of which were fighters, were produced in August. The **Fighter Command** was comprised of Hurricanes and Spitfires. Their speed, approximately 360 miles per hour, did not exceed that of the enemy's aircraft, but in maneuverability and armament they were superior. Each possessed eight machine guns capable of firing 1,200 shots per minute, as against four or six guns for the enemy fighters. On July 15, Air Chief Marshal Sir **Hugh Dowding**, creator and moving spirit of the British fighter force, could muster 55 fighter squadrons. The Fighter Command was divided into four Groups: the 13th, in the north (under Richard E. Saul), with 14 squadrons; the 12th, in the center of the country (under **Keith Rodney Park**), with 22 squadrons; the 11th, in the southeast (under **Trafford Leigh-Mallory**), with 14 squadrons; and the 10th, in the southwest (under Quintin Brand), with four squadrons.

If the military forces of the **United Kingdom** were in desperate need of materiel in the face of enemy strength, the English maintained, for the moment, mastery in science and technology with **radar**, the acronym for "radio detection and ranging." Under the direction of Prof. **Frederick Alexander Lindemann,** the future Lord Cherwell, British scientists conducted a tireless war of brains. The German principle of double beaming to guide the bombers to their objectives at night as well as in daylight was discovered. Soon afterward, the method of beam deviation was found.

Even in this dark period Churchill was thinking ahead to the day when the British would assume the offensive. He evolved the ideas of **artificial ports** and **landing craft.** He invented **combined operations,** with the commandos under the direction of **Roger Keyes.**

The Council of Combined Operation Plans was placed under Churchill's direct control.

Thus, in July 1940, Britain, unaided and against all hope, was determined to fight the Italo-German **Axis,** which by then controlled practically all of Europe. As Churchill kept repeating in his incomparable speeches, Great Britain fought for a precise aim from which it would never deviate even in its darkest hours. But the safeguarding of the United Kingdom and the Commonwealth was not the only goal. The deliverance of all of Europe from the totalitarian yoke and the annihilation of Nazism was also envisioned. Few outside the island anticipated a British victory. Washington's special envoy, Ambassador Joseph P. Kennedy, the father of the future president, advised Roosevelt—who fortunately paid him no attention—not to bet on a horse that was a sure loser.

On June 30 the Germans took possession of the undefended Channel Islands, and on July 2 **Hitler** issued his first directives for the attack on England. On July 13, in the course of a conversation related in Gen. **Franz Halder**'s diary, Hitler declared that he wanted to make certain of the alliance with **Spain** to establish a united front against Great Britain from the North Cape to Morocco. **Ribbentrop** was sent to Madrid for this purpose.

Hitler did not hide his reluctance to conduct total war against England. "I see it as my obligation," he said, "to impose peace on her by force. When the United Kingdom is conquered, the British Empire will collapse. We will get nothing more out of it. Who will scramble after its fragments? The **United States** and **Japan.**"

Even before the war, Hitler thought of overcoming Great Britain by submarine activity. **Goering** expected to triumph with the air arm. But *Directive No. 16* of the *Oberkommando der Wehrmacht* (OKW) provided for a landing, if necessary. This was operation *Seeloewe* (Sea Lion).

Three air forces based in **Norway,** the **Netherlands, Belgium** and the north of France were to lead the action with 3,196 planes, of which 2,355 were initially available for combat, backed up by several Italian squadrons. In addition, the Eighth Air Corps, made up of **Stukas,** were to support the invasion troops. There were to be 7,929 **Axis** planes engaged above Great Britain on March 31, 1941.

The German bombers, designed for tactical use, were fast but poorly armed and vulnerable. The He-111 and the Ju-88 could carry at the most two tons of bombs. They would never have sufficient punch for strategic missions.

The aerial Battle of Britain actually occurred in three phases. The first, from July 10 to August 18, involved attacks on **convoys** in the English Channel and harassment of the southern ports in the hope of luring out the English fighters en masse and annihilating them—the indispensable condition for destruction or neutralization of the navy. The second, from August 24 to September 27, attempted to open the air route toward the capital, with the aim of eliminating those aircraft that had escaped in the first phase and destroying their facilities; thus, the massive bombardment of London to throw it into fatal disorder was envisaged. The third, extending through October and sporadically thereafter, when all hope of destroying the British air force and making a landing had vanished, consisted of the *Luftwaffe* blindly bombarding London and the great population centers.

On July 19, in the course of a speech made to the Reichstag, Hitler hinted at his readiness to negotiate a peace. Churchill did not respond. A simple radio message from Lord **Halifax** swept the Hitler invitation away.

The *Oberkommando des Heeres* (OKH) and the *Oberkommando der Kriegsmarine* (OKM)—high commands of the army and navy—began without much hope to prepare Operation Sea Lion. And it was then, on July 21, that Hitler confided to **Walther von Brauchitsch**, head of the OKH, his intention of attacking the **USSR**. On learning of this news, the dictator's entourage was thunderstruck. What singular leadership! Where only the previous day England was the only consideration, all other business coming to a standstill, on this day Hitler confounded the minds of his subordinates by announcing a project they could hardly anticipate, in view of the **Nazi-Soviet Pact** of August 23, 1939.

Again on July 21, Hitler told Brauchitsch that England's situation was hopeless. "In the middle of the week," he said, "I will decide, after having studied the report of Adm. **Raeder**, whether the landing will take place in the fall. If not...then next spring. But why should England pursue the struggle? Because she is putting her hopes in America and Russia. Thus, **Stalin** is flirting with London to keep Great Britain in the war, tying us up at this end, while the USSR makes off with everything she likes, something she could not hope to do in peacetime. We must therefore look ahead to war with Russia and make our preparations. According to my information the campaign will last four to six weeks. We must destroy the Soviet army or at least occupy vast Russian territories to shelter Berlin and Silesia from air attack. We will advance as deeply as possible to strike with our air force the distant industrial zones. Our political goals are the Ukraine, the Baltic States, Belorussia, **Finland**. The USSR has only 50 to 75 good divisions. We shall need 80 to 100 divisions to execute operations decisively in the east."

On July 29, **Jodl** dissuaded Hitler from attacking the Soviet Union in 1940 by demonstrating the inability of concentrating sufficient forces on the frontier of the USSR before winter. The next day Brauchitsch confided to Gen. Franz Halder his fears regarding Hitler's strategy: "As far as the landing in England is concerned, I conclude from my conversations with Raeder that we find ourselves in a dilemma: either the navy manages to mass the means of landing on Great Britain and the operation is attempted under poor weather conditions or the invasion is postponed to May of 1941 and England will have had time to be reinforced." Brauchitsch thought it senseless to become embroiled with the USSR at that moment. It would provoke war on two fronts. His idea of the best way to strike at Great Britain was to operate in the Mediterranean and cut English communications to Asia; to help **Italy** establish her *Mare Nostrum;* and, by maintaining the Soviet pact, to create an entity dominating western and northern Europe.

Hitler had a long conversation with his three chiefs of the armed forces on July 31. They discussed at length the propitious moment for the invasion; questions of the tides, the weather and visibility; and the likelihood of having sufficient ships. The pros and cons of an immediate operation were faced. It could well have begun that year, but all would not be ready before September 15. Definitely unenthusiastic, Raeder estimated that the most favorable time was May or June. It would have to be the following year. Hitler, however, pointed out that British land forces did not exist for the moment. In May 1941 they might number from 30 to 35 divisions. True, the activation of these divisions might perhaps be impeded by continuous air strikes on the production centers.

After Raeder had made an inventory of the naval forces (present and future) of Great Britain and Germany respectively, Hitler decided to take another look, in 10 days, at the opportunity for invasion. Evidently, he was seeking other means of bringing Great Britain to her knees. Submarine and aerial warfare, he said, could achieve the objective, but not before a year had passed—perhaps even two.

In any case, the Soviet Union had to be attacked. Something had to be going on between London and Moscow, Hitler guessed. And the proof was that England, which had seemed "flat on its back" only a short time before, was once more raising its head. "If we destroy the USSR, therefore, all hope will have vanished for Great Britain. And when Russia has been conquered, Germany will then be master of Europe and the Balkans."

"An irrevocable decision—we shall strike toward the East next spring," Hitler said. His incoherence was at its height. Actually, it seemed necessary to put off the invasion of Great Britain until that same spring. Some months earlier Hitler had prided himself on having achieved what no German had been able to realize since Bismarck—war on a single front. "The operations in the east," he continued, "are logical only if we can beat the USSR with a single blow. That will take five months. We must destroy the life force of Russia. The Ukraine, Belorussia and the Baltic countries will be ours."

Thus, for Hitler, the projected operation meant the conquest of *Lebensraum*. But it had a second purpose. Like Napoleon, Hitler believed he could hit Great Britain by striking at Russia.

First Phase: The Attack on the Convoys and Ports

The Battle of Britain began on July 10. By August 8, it became a total offensive. The *Luftwaffe* multiplied its attacks on convoys in waves of more than 100 planes. On August 11, while these tactics continued, Portland and Weymouth were attacked. On August 12, 200 planes struck Dover in 11 waves; another 150 hit Portsmouth and the Isle of Wight. Although German losses were heavy, the *Luftwaffe* again hammered away at Portsmouth on the following day. One radar station was demolished and four others damaged. Between July 10 and August 12 the *Luftwaffe* lost 286 planes, while the British lost 150 fighters.

The first decisive day came on August 15, the "Day of the Eagle." While hundreds of aircraft in four successive assaults attempted to break the southeast defense, a powerful air strike, leaving from Norway, was to surprise the north of Britain, which Goering thought was wide open. But Dowding foresaw everything. In the south as in the north, the RAF appeared in the nick of time and destroyed 75 German planes. On August 16 and 18, Goering resumed his pointless sorties. He lost 290 airplanes between August 13 and 23, but only 114 British fighters were downed.

The combined use of fighters, radar and antiaircraft defenses, the harassment of the continental invasion ports by bomber missions, the controlled concentrations of fighting planes, the shape taken by the battle, the attacks at all angles, the swift dogfights that established the maneuverability of the Spitfire and the bravery of its pilots totally defeated the German aerial offensive.

During the month of August, the OKM and the OKH continued to exchange views on Operation Sea Lion. Raeder supposed that after the losses sustained in Norway, the available naval forces could satisfy the requirements of only one landing on a narrow front. Brauchitsch and Halder wanted a landing on 185 miles of coastline. At the end of August, Hitler cut the figure to 75 miles. Three armies were to make the assault on the English beaches.

Second Phase: The Useless Effort to Destroy the British Air Fleet and the Attacks on London

Goering modified his plans. He decided on August 15 that the operations would be directed exclusively against enemy aircraft, including the aircraft industry. After five days of bad weather, a precious respite for the RAF, the *Luftwaffe* resumed its attacks. After a raid on London on the night of August 23, the British **Bomber Command** retaliated with a raid on Berlin the following night. Between August 24 and September 3, the Germans launched 35 massive onslaughts on airports and aircraft factories. The bomber formations were weaker and the fighter escorts had been reinforced. Between August 24 and September 6, the *Luftwaffe* lost 380 planes, but the opposing fighters were severely tested, with 286 lost and the surviving crews exhausted. By September 4, there were 706 British fighters available for combat, the replacements of personnel and materiel barely compensating for the losses.

Between September 6 and October 5, London experienced 38 heavy daylight raids as well as several night attacks with bombs dropped at random. The ratio of fighter escorts increased constantly and reached five fighters for every bomber. The climax of the offensive was September 15. Several quarters of London were in flames, from the populous East End to the aristocratic West End. The center of the city, the royal palace, numerous churches and some hospitals had been hit—all to no avail. The soul of London was unconquerable. Despite the damage it inflicted the *Luftwaffe* met disaster in the skies. Because Goering, who operated inconsistently, had pounded London for eight days, beginning on September 7, rather than air bases and radar stations, against the advice of his subordinates, the RAF was able to recover its efficiency. On September 15 the squadrons of Air Vice-Marshal Park downed 56 enemy planes in two dogfights lasting 45 minutes. And on the same day, British bombers struck at French and Belgian invasion ports.

After September 15 the *Luftwaffe* temporarily replaced its daytime assaults with night sorties. This was a concession of defeat. Actually, on September 3 the invasion had been set for September 21. But the disappointing results of the air battle postponed it to some undetermined date.

At the beginning of October, while the Home Guard watched the coasts, 13 divisions, including two from Canada, and an effective force of three armored divisions, some of them well trained and equipped, were at the disposal of the British command to repel an enemy landing. These figures are indicative of the progress made since Dunkirk. However the German navy conceded its inability to transport more than 11 divisions for the first landing waves spaced over three days. Halder affirmed, with reason, that under such conditions the operation was impossible.

On October 12 Hitler postponed Operation Sea Lion until the following spring. The top secret document *Verschiebung des Unternehmens Seeloewe auf das Fruehjahr 1941*, issued by the OKW, speaks of a landing only conditionally. It could only take place if it were absolutely necessary. In the meantime the numerous ships originally assembled for the invasion were allotted to industry, to fishermen, and to sea and river transport. Their earlier preemption for the invasion had already hurt the economic life of the German nation. The document insisted, of course, that every precaution be taken to deceive the English into thinking that the preparation for a landing on a large front was continuing.

Meanwhile, Hitler expedited his plans for the Russian campaign and resumed consideration, begun in mid-September, of a drive on French Africa by way of Spain and **Gibraltar.**

Third Phase: Pursuit of the Offensive on London and the Production Centers

In short, the Royal Navy at the beginning of October was intact, few of the factories had been hit and the situation of the RAF compared to that of the *Luftwaffe* had improved. Despite its limited means, the Bomber Command struck constantly and methodically at the western ports, the barge trains, and the enemy's naval and air bases. The German aerial offensive had not even slowed British production; during 1940 Great Britain produced 9,924 planes. Between September 7 and October 31, the *Luftwaffe* lost 433 aircraft against the Fighter Command's 242.

Since the RAF had deprived it of daylight mastery of the air, the *Luftwaffe* resorted to night bombardment. Nightly until November, 200 bombers attacked London. The material damage to the city increased, but the city's life was not in the least disorganized. **Morale** was excellent. The civil servants—the firemen in particular—worked with incredible indifference to the bombing. The king and queen remained in the beleaguered city and shared the mortal danger with their subjects.

The *Luftwaffe* extended its bombing operations to other British cities and included seagoing convoys in its scope of targets. The proximity of their bases in northern France permitted German aircraft two missions a night: attacks with normal and incendiary bombs and sometimes parachuted air mines. The destruction and loss of life were serious, as in the terrible

raid on **Coventry** on November 14; but, lacking sufficient bomb loads, concentration and mass, the *Luftwaffe* night raids were not very effective.

Gen. Werner Kreipe, chief of staff of the German Third Air Army, later wrote: "We went through this whole campaign by dispersing our efforts instead of concentrating our power, with continuity, on a single target. From Berlin, Goering incessantly interfered. In extremis, he countermanded an operation that had been carefully prepared and substituted another on the basis of information that had not even been verified.... Above all, we lacked a four-engined bomber, heavily armed, with an action radius of 1,200 miles and capable of operating at altitudes of 30,000 feet or more. Furthermore, the excellent pilots we had at the beginning became more and more rare, and were replaced by young ones who were well trained but lacked combat experience, and found themselves up against British fighter pilots clever at night maneuvering."

From July 10 to mid-November, 1,818 German planes were shot down; the British suffered 995. The RAF lost fewer pilots than the *Luftwaffe* because the German pilots who dropped safely to the ground were taken prisoner. The RAF losses among fighter pilots from July 10 to October 30 were relatively slight—450, of which 402 were British, 29 Poles, seven Czechs, six Belgians, three Canadians and three New Zealanders.

The appearance of armor on German planes at the end of 1940 inspired two immediate modifications of British planes: use of similar armor and the replacement of machine guns by cannon and heavier machine guns. The Spitfire III was armed with two 20-mm wing cannon and four machine guns, the Hurricane IIB with 16 machine guns and the Hurricane IIIC with four 20-mm cannon. The Germans followed with similar modifications.

The end of November 1940 marked the conclusion of the Battle of Britain proper. The *Luftwaffe* still tried in vain to impress their adversary with strong attacks, like that of December 9 on London, which lasted 24 hours. Despite the civilian losses (14,280 dead and 20,325 wounded, from August to October), the iron determination of the British to prevail could only grow with the intensity of the German thrusts. Running out of steam, the *Luftwaffe* weakened. Nevertheless, in the first five months of 1941, the British sustained several violent attacks. The supreme German effort, the incendiary raid on London on May 10, 1941, caused enormous damage. Six days later Birmingham underwent a heavy attack. Then came the calm. It was the eve of the onslaught on the Soviet Union.

The Consequences

It has often been said that the Germans committed a

grave error by failing to attack a "disarmed" Great Britain after Dunkirk or after the fall of France. That word "disarmed" illustrates the bias of the continental mind—reasoning in terms of land forces only. Certainly, Britain had few troops in the 1939-40 period. But such thinking overlooks the defensive potential of the Royal Navy, RAF and British radar. In this respect neither Gen. Halder nor Adm. Raeder were deceived. For a successful invasion of England, they needed a decisive victory in the sky, as the Allies were to achieve four years later, before the **Normandy landing.** If this precondition went unfulfilled, subsequent operations could not be realized.

After the Battle of Britain the Axis and Great Britain found themselves in almost parallel positions: the former had superior power on land, and the latter possessed the advantage on the seas. With the air situation stalemated, neither of the two adversaries could hope to win by arms alone. Diplomacy then came to the fore. For one of them to win, allies were needed.

By the end of June 1940, after the fall of France, the prestige of the Third Reich in the world was at its zenith. All the neutral nations of Europe were in awe of Hitler, his regime and his army. Some of these states literally fawned on Berlin. Afghanistan, **Iran** and many Latin American states did the same. Since the Germans at first adopted a mien of amiability in the countries they occupied, a good many of their inhabitants decided to be "realistic" and adapted themselves to the New Order, which did not seem all that bad. The U.S. chiefs of staff and many of the highest-ranking officers in the American armed forces believed firmly that the Axis would achieve a complete victory. In Japan the new government formed on July 17, 1940 reinforced its ties with Germany.

Hitler was at his most gleeful toward the beginning of that summer. His first disillusionment had come on September 3, 1939, when the Western powers declared war on him. But they could not prevent the collapse of **Poland**. He encountered a second check when London and Paris refused, at the beginning of the fall, to consider a peace by accepting the push to the east as a fait accompli. But his brilliant success over France induced paroxysms of pride. He had realized what the Imperial Army of 1914 could not accomplish. The forces of Wilhelm II had been beaten on the Marne, a defeat that was to lead to the surrender of Germany four years later. "If I had been the supreme ruler in 1914," Hitler affirmed, "I would have won the First World War in the first few weeks." And Field Marshal **Wilhelm Keitel** added, at the general headquarters of Bruly de Pesche, that "the Fuehrer is the greatest captain of all time." Hitler was convinced of it, and so was his immediate entourage

in the OKW. This excess of self-confidence was to bring about his ruin.

After July 1940, however, a new disappointment awaited Hitler. His entire policy after the fall of France was centered on avoiding the great conflict with the United Kingdom and the Commonwealth. Several neutral figures offered their good offices for that purpose. The British Empire, Hitler said frequently, must be preserved for the sake of world order. He remained faithful to the opinion he had expressed in *Mein Kampf:* let London permit Germany a free hand on the Continent and Berlin will allow England to do the same overseas. The two countries could have come to an understanding if any personality less intractable than Churchill had presided over the destiny of Great Britain. The *dominium mundi* would belong to this great bloc, both of whose leaders were of the same superior Germanic race! Hitler even hinted to London that the two countries could partition the French colonial empire. Imperturbably, Churchill repeated that Great Britain and the Commonwealth would pursue the struggle until Nazism was extirpated from Germany and until all the countries occupied by the Axis recovered their freedom and their territorial integrity.

On many occasions, Raeder had insisted that Hitler intensify submarine warfare and concentrate maximum industrial effort on the production of submarines. The admiral's logic was sound. The only way to conquer Great Britain, so dependent on imports, was to isolate it; to do that, enough U-boats had to be available so that some 100 of them could be continuously in operation. In 1940 the German navy had not nearly enough. Hitler, who was very soon to become obsessed by his plan to invade the USSR, was reluctant to extend the submarine offensive because he still hoped that London would accept a peace and feared Raeder's policy would lead to American entry into the war. To the great regret of the German admiralty, only five percent of steel production was reserved for submarine construction. On September 1, 1940 the number of submarines (57) was no higher than in September 1939, only enough to permit 25 to be used continuously.

In mid-September, Hitler dropped Operation Sea Lion. He had always feared its consequences. "The greatest captain of all time" on land and in the air had no taste whatever for a war on the seas.

Impressed by the British raid on Berlin of August 28 and upset by London's refusal to discuss a settlement, Hitler accepted the view of Goering. Since Operation Sea Lion would not take place, at least not that year, it was no longer necessary to pursue the aerial campaign as the preliminary to a landing. Hitler agreed that the *Luftwaffe* should undertake a series of terror bombardments that would constitute the third phase of the Battle of Britain. Yet even then he still hoped that the British would agree to a settlement with him. The only function of the new-style bombings was to make clear to Great Britain the need for arranging a peace. That was the moment at which **Rudolf Hess** and Albrecht Haushofer prepared a memorandum designed to convince London that prolongation of the war could only end in the suicide of the white race. This was a long way from that May month when Hitler was certain that the *Blitzkrieg* would mean a short war. Furious diplomatic activity was once again undertaken to set the stage for an Anglo-German accord. It met with no success.

The Battle of Britain broke Hitler's series of victories that had lasted since 1936 and smashed his plans thoroughly. Until then he was able to strike each adversary successively and locally, with everything working for him, even though the German economy was unprepared for either a general war or a long war. After the battle, the conflict, not yet worldwide, took on an aspect for Germany that her leader had not foreseen.

Churchill knew that victory was impossible for him without American aid. He also knew American opinion was divided. With consummate skill, the prime minister won Roosevelt over by assuring him constantly of his decision to pursue the struggle to the bitter end, by showing the Americans that he was fighting for them as much as for Great Britain, by persistently informing the president of his intentions and sometimes asking his advice. Churchill's political acumen and oratorical talents became a formidable psychological weapon. In his speech of June 4, he uttered the words that have become legendary: "We shall go on to the end, we shall fight in France, we shall fight on the seas and oceans, we shall fight with growing confidence and growing strength in the air, we shall defend our Island, whatever the cost may be, we shall fight on the beaches, we shall fight on the landing grounds, we shall fight in the fields and in the streets, we shall fight in the hills; we shall never surrender, and even if, which I do not for a moment believe, this Island or a large part of it were subjugated and starving, then our Empire beyond the seas, armed and guarded by the British Fleet, would carry on the struggle, until, in God's good time, the New World, with all its power and might, steps forth to the rescue and the liberation of the Old."

This was not simply an expression of courage. It was one of the most astute speeches the prime minister ever made. He assured the Americans that whatever might happen in Great Britain, the Royal Navy would pursue the stuggle in the Atlantic, from bases in Canada and the United States. This promise was of major significance to the Americans. It guaranteed their eastern flank and permitted them to concentrate a large part of the U.S. Navy in the Pacific to contain the expansionist tendencies of the Japanese. Without the Royal Navy, the U.S. naval squadrons would have to be divided between the Atlantic and the Pacific, increasing Japan's opportunities for further aggression.

After June 1940 Roosevelt seemed to be under Churchill's influence. He gave Great Britain all the aid that was in his power to give. He adroitly avoided the legal obstacles in his path and overcame the opposition of the military to satisfy the immediate necessities of the British, although this did not as yet amount to very much in the second half of 1940. But Britain's victory strengthened the position of the president vis-a-vis his chiefs of staff and those of his colleagues dazzled by the German successes. The slogan "Save America by helping Britain" gained credence in the U.S. More Americans began to believe that Great Britain was fighting for their right to exist as well as its own. The fruit of **lend-lease** was soon to ripen.

In the occupied countries the results of the Battle of Britain raised hopes and stimulated the first stirrings of the **Resistance** movement. Hitler's blunders did the rest. Certain German experts had proposed the creation of a European economic union—under the aegis of Germany, of course—but Hitler decided to do just the opposite. The Four-Year Plan, assigned to Goering, was designed to exploit all the resources of Europe for the profit of Germany alone. Only too soon did the occupied nations understand its meaning.

Meanwhile, Churchill was winning the diplomatic skirmishes. He conquered most hearts in regions temporarily enslaved by the Axis and in 1941 the U.S. began sending aid to Britain under the lend-lease program. Hitler, naturally, was to obtain the support of Japan—which threw the U.S., after **Pearl Harbor**, and **China** into the Allied camp—but he could not control Spain, pushed the USSR over to the side of his enemies and eventually lost his Italian ally. The groundwork for this was set in 1940.

The material consequences of the German defeat in the air proved to be irreparable for the Axis. From August 1, 1940 to March 31, 1941, the *Luftwaffe* lost 4,383 planes, including aircraft sustaining more than 10 percent damage and therefore unfit for combat. Of this number, 2,840 were totally destroyed. Between these two dates the *Luftwaffe* suffered 3,363 killed, 2,117 wounded and 2,641 taken prisoner or missing. The effect of these losses in highly qualified personnel was enormous, particularly as the war dragged on.

Because the Germans failed to bring down Great Britain during the summer and fall of 1940, they were forced to burden themselves with part of the air effort in the Mediterranean in compensation for Italy's weakness. On June 22, 1941, the day the Germans launched their attack on the USSR, the distribution of combat-ready *Luftwaffe* aircraft was: 2,740 (61 percent) in the east; 630 (23 percent) in the west; 310 (11 percent) reinforcing the Italian air force in the Mediterranean and less than 200 (five percent) in Germany. The figures show that 39 percent of the *Luftwaffe's* effective forces faced Great Britain or were serving in the Mediterranean theater on June 22. Counting the Italian air force, about 50 percent of the Axis flyers were drawn away from the major theater of the east. And on a front five times greater than that in the west on May 10, 1940, the *Luftwaffe* faced the Soviets with fewer combat planes.

Although a decisive victory, the Battle of Britain could not prevent the war from continuing for several years. But the only chance the Germans had had was to win the decision as quickly as possible. The British victory transformed a short war into a long one and thus sealed the fate of the Nazi Reich. It changed the course of the war. Never in the history of humanity, Churchill was to say, did so many millions of people owe so much to so few.

H. Bernard

BRITISH BORNEO.
See **Borneo.**

BRITISH BROADCASTING CORPORATION (The BBC).

The BBC, a semipublic body founded in 1922 and incorporated in 1926, had a monopoly of broadcasting within the **United Kingdom**. It was paid for partly by the treasury, partly by subscribers' license fees (10 shillings per household; 8.9 million households were licensed in 1939, 9.9 million by 1945). Already a sizable body, with 4,889 employees in September 1939, it more than doubled in strength in the first three years of the war; there were over 11,000 employees by mid-1942. The maximum, 11,663, was reached in March 1944. (Oddly enough the German broadcasting service ran at practically the same size: 4,800 people to start with, rising to over 10,000 by 1943.) They were organized in some 250 departments, scattered all over the island, with headquarters in the center of fashionable London. **John Reith**, who had created and shaped the BBC, left in 1938, but his strict and strong, if somewhat narrow, personality continued to inspire the staff. Technically, it was highly competent—fully a match for **Goebbels'** opposing networks in skill and power, if not in deceitfulness (see **Propaganda**). The BBC had 24 transmitters,

five of them long- or medium-wave, in September 1939; by May 1945 it had 121. The Germans had eight powerful stations to start with, but their total of transmitters never rose above 50.

The BBC had been one of the pioneers of television and had broadcast **George VI's** coronation in 1937; but there were only 7,000 television receivers in the country, and the service was closed down when war began. The transmitter was taken over by **Royal Air Force** intelligence and used to interfere with the navigation equipment of the *Luftwaffe* in 1940-41.

Another, longer lasting, intelligence contribution by the BBC was its exceptionally wide monitoring service, which listened to news bulletins and talks the world over and provided daily summaries of them for interested bodies in London, of which there were several. Useful as the monitoring service was, its role was secondary. In its primary role the BBC established an important bridge between the government and the people of Great Britain and between the Allied high command and the populations of occupied Europe and Asia.

The problem of who decided the direction of the BBC's wartime broadcasting policy was intricate—a point for a constitutional lawyer, much debated among politicians and journalists, few of whom really understood it. Several government departments—the Post Office, through which licenses were issued; the Home Office, traditionally responsible for public order; the Foreign Office, in charge of foreign policy; the service ministries, affected by points of security and operations; the new Ministry of Information, in charge of propaganda; and several secret services—had a right to be heard. Parliament again felt itself in a position of responsibility; and the prime minister for most of the war, **Churchill**, a consummate broadcaster, was not to be left out. From this almost inextricable tangle of overlapping authorities, the corporation eventually managed to extract a policy, making much of it by its own momentum and from within its own staff. For the first two years of the war, interdepartmental wrangles over BBC policy continued, while broadcasters carried on their work. From the autumn of 1941, things were more straightforward. The minister of information, Brendan Bracken, was in nominal charge but hardly ever exercised his authority. Consultation between committees and civil servants involved in any particular kind of broadcast usually managed to avoid any direct confrontation or stark question of control.

All through the war the BBC stuck to the motto Reith had instilled in its staff: Always, in all circumstances, tell the strict truth. As it turned out, this was an unusually powerful weapon of propaganda against an enemy who treated truth in a more cavalier way.

The BBC made no attempt to hide, in times of calamity, the size or the number of disasters that were inflicted on the British cause. It thus gained credibility when conditions improved. As it never knowingly lied, listeners came to trust in it; no such claim could be made for Radio Berlin.

The BBC's information was not always correct, and this did lead to some misrepresentation. During the Battle of Britain, for instance, it quoted figures for daily British losses that were never too high and for German losses that were never too low—misled, sometimes to a substantial extent, by pilots' reports (also honestly intended) that it had no means of verifying. German claims erred, at the same time, in precisely the opposite way. A neutral reporter, seeking reality, could make a reasonable estimation by balancing the figures presented by both sides.

Less excusably, information about the **Resistance** was sometimes imprecise, because the BBC did not have on-the-spot coverage. For example, Yugoslav partisans were particularly annoyed to hear their feats being credited to their Chetnik rivals in the months of 1943 when the British got news from partisan doings but still officially supported **Dragolyub Mihailovich** rather than the unknown **Tito**.

Serbo-Croatian was only one of some 50 languages in which, by 1944, the BBC was producing daily broadcasts. The texts for these were prepared by the BBC's own staff, on lines worked out beforehand in ad hoc committees, with people from the Foreign Office, the **Political Warfare Executive**, the **Special Operations Executive**, the British embassy (if there was one) of the country concerned and so on. Broadcasts had as their main purpose the spreading of news—true news—of the course the war was actually taking. Thus, they were able to exert a profound, worldwide influence on **morale**, as soon as the main tide of the war had turned in the winter of 1942-43, because they demonstrated the assurance of an ultimate Allied victory and **Axis** defeat, without ever needing to boast.

Before the war it had been an offense under Nazi law to listen to any foreign broadcasting station. Since the Nazis carried this law around Europe with them, to hear the BBC at all was an act of resistance. Without these broadcasts, the **underground press** would have been deprived of its principal source of information.

Newscasts were supplemented by occasional direct exhortations, particularly by Churchill (who on one occasion broadcast in characteristically anglicized French). Queen **Wilhelmina** and King **Haakon** made frequent and popular broadcasts to their own countries; and without the BBC, how many would have heard of Gen. **de Gaulle**? There were also numerous programs, such as "*Les Francais parlent aux Francais*," organized in London by Michel St. Denis and his friends, in which less known exiles talked directly to their compatriots at home. Such programs had the multiple tasks of sustaining morale on both sides of the English Channel, indicating to an occupied country that its own culture was continuing to flourish outside the Nazi umbrella and encouraging the occupied population to look forward to getting rid of the Nazis altogether. In **Denmark** especially, the BBC was able to play a leading role in organizing resistance. And during the actual campaign across a given country—**Italy** from September 1943 to April 1945, France in June-September 1944, **the Netherlands** from September 1944 to May 1945—the BBC's foreign language services were able to play an important role in administration as well as newscasting.

From the autumn of 1941 onward, the BBC provided one particular service without which a great deal of resistance activity would have been stultified: a system of coded personal messages, pure gibberish to the uninstructed listener ("The ribbon is blue," "Tony hates mutton," "Is Napoleon's hat still there?"), told certain clandestine groups that particular air or sea operations were, or were not, going to take place at prearranged hours. Tens of thousands of individuals participated in this highly public, yet almost perfectly safe, way of announcing operations.

The BBC also engaged, as a piece of straightforward journalism, in reporting from the battlefronts; from June 1944 this became a daily event. These reports, less contrived than those Goebbels had run in 1940-41 in France and the **USSR**, had a freshness and an immediacy that drew listeners' attention everywhere.

There was also, of course, a great deal of broadcasting from British transmitters (not included in the BBC's transmitter statistics) aimed at rotting the morale of the Axis forces and at sustaining that of the occupied populations. These transmissions amounted to 60 different services at least. But this was considered a matter of **psychological warfare**, with which the BBC took care to avoid any association. The corporation preferred to keep its Reithian image clean and remain ignorant of such broadcasts.

The home impact of the BBC was notable. Early feelings by the working class that the corporation represented the uppercrust were gradually dissipated by the BBC's perfectly straightforward efforts to tell the truth and explain what was happening. A highly popular series of Sunday evening talks by J. B. Priestley, the novelist, which were frankly sympathetic to socialism and not delivered with an upper-class accent, helped this process along. Churchill's broadcasts were enormous boosters of national morale, particularly during Britain's dark hours. Among the most memorable was his talk on the evening of

June 22, 1941, the very day of the German attack on the USSR, when he made it clear that he would not let his own long-standing anti-bolshevism hamper efforts to help anyone who would fight **Hitler.**

M. R. D. Foot

BRITISH CHAIN OF COMMAND.
See **Chain of Command, British.**

BROOK, Robin (1908-   ).
A British banker and merchant, Brook was a staff officer in the **Special Operations Executive** responsible in 1943-44 for all its operations in northwestern Europe. He accompanied **Eisenhower** to France as an adviser on subversion.

BROOKE, Sir Alan Francis (later Lord Alanbrooke) (1883-1963).
When war broke out, Brooke was sent to France to lead a corps of the British Expeditionary Force. He commanded the Home Forces in 1940-41. He was head of the Imperial General Staff from 1941 to 1946 and of the Chiefs of Staff Committee from 1942. When pressed, **Churchill** always deferred to his expert advice on strategy.

BROSSOLETTE, Pierre (1902-1944).
A militant French Socialist and the foreign news editor for the government radio in 1936-39, Brossolette worked for the Free French in 1942-43. After his arrest by the Germans, he killed himself on March 22, 1944 by leaping out of the window of the **Gestapo** building in Paris, thus assuring his confederates of his silence.

BROWNING, Frederick (1896-1965).
A British general and creator and guiding spirit of British **airborne troops,** Browning planned the airborne operation in **the Netherlands** that resulted in the victory of Eindhoven, at Nimegue, and a reverse at Arnhem. He was named chief of staff to Lord **Mountbatten** in **Burma** in November 1944. Having learned his lesson at Arnhem, he conducted one of the most daring and successful exploits of the war, a drive of mixed land and airborne troops over 300 miles, from Meiktila to Rangoon, where he crushed **Japan**'s Burma armies.

BROZ, Josip.
See **Tito.**

BUCKNER, Simon Bolivar (1886-1945).
An American general, Buckner commanded the 10th Army in the battle of **Okinawa** in the Spring of 1945.

He was killed in action on June 18, three days before his troops achieved a complete victory.

BUDENNY, Semyon M. (1883-1973).
Soviet marshal and vice-commissar of defense. Budenny commanded the Soviet army group in the southwestern front in 1941, but he was replaced after a major part of his army was captured by the advancing German forces. He was later given command of the army group in the northern Caucasus front.

BULGANIN, Nikolai A. (1895-1975).
In 1939 he was a member of the Central Committee of the **USSR** and political commissar in the Moscow, Belorussian, Baltic and western fronts. He became assistant commissar of defense in 1944. Appointed marshal of the Soviet Union, he was named minister of the armed forces (1947-49), a title he regained in 1953. He attained the office of premier of the Soviet Union in 1955 but was ousted by Nikita Khrushchev in 1958.

BULGARIA.
Slavic Bulgaria (6,341,000 population in 1940) and Latin **Rumania** differ in many ways. The latter sided with the Entente Powers in World War I, while the former was allied with the Central Powers. Yet the Rumanians, allied to Russia in 1917, were anti-Russian, while the Bulgarians, foes of the czar in 1915, have always felt drawn to their huge Slavic neighbor to the east.

Both nations fell into the **Axis** orbit in 1940. Both agreed to the occupation of their territories by Nazi troops, which used them as springboards for the invasion of **Yugoslavia** and **Greece** in April 1941. With **Hitler**'s permission, the Bulgarians took advantage of the opportunity to overrun and annex the Greek and Serbian provinces of Macedonia on May 18.

When **Germany** attacked the **USSR** on June 22, 1941, it brought Bulgaria into the conflict against the Western powers but failed to persuade Sofia to break with Moscow. No Bulgarian soldiers were sent to the eastern front. They did, however, join forces with the Germans against Yugoslavia's **Tito.**

The mysterious death of King **Boris III** on his return from a stormy meeting with Hitler in August 1943 strained German-Bulgarian relations. A **resistance** movement developed in the Bulgarian hinterland. At first nondescript, the organization later became Communist, although it embraced members of all the parties—notably Nikolai Petkov, head of the Agrarian Union. The **USSR** sent its agents to Bulgaria to step up resistance to the Germans and to sow confusion among the non-Communist factions in the Resistance. The **Special Operations Executive** also parachuted agents, along with arms and war materiel, to the Bulgarian partisans.

The various elements in the Bulgarian Resistance combined in the Fatherland Front, which governed the People's Liberation Army. When Soviet troops crossed the Bulgarian frontier at the beginning of September 1944, the Fatherland Front triggered a general uprising, the leaders of which seized power in Sofia. Bulgaria went over to the Allies. In Yugoslavia and **Hungary**, 450,000 Bulgarian soldiers fought at the side of the Soviet forces of Marshal **Fedor Tolbukhin**.

And once again Bulgaria and Rumania swung into the same alignment. The Fatherland Front disbanded. All dissidents were eliminated—the non-Communist Resistance fighters along with the Nazi collaborators. Petkov, one of the leaders in the Bulgarian Resistance, was executed despite protests from Washington, London and Paris. On September 8, 1946 the young king, Simeon II, was forced into exile and the Democratic People's Republic was proclaimed. **Georgi Dimitrov**, returning to his country after 10 years in the Soviet Union, assumed the office of council president.

H. Bernard

BULGE, Battle of the.

Having failed to form a spearhead across the lower Rhine in September 1944, the Allies paused for several months along the western front and prepared for a spring campaign. Faced with a threatened Soviet breakthrough in the Danube Valley, **Hitler** decided to launch a surprise attack in the hilly, densely wooded Ardennes region of **Belgium** and **Luxembourg**. Through the fall, all available **tanks** were withdrawn and refitted for fresh action, while 28 divisions of 250,000 men were assembled in utmost secrecy. The Germans were desperately short of fuel, but vast Allied gasoline stores lay waiting to be captured in Belgium.

Conceived entirely by Hitler, the plan, code-named "Operation *Greif*," called for an offensive by three armies. The largest and best-equipped of the three, the Sixth Panzer Army under SS Gen. **Sepp Dietrich**, would thrust northwestward, cross the Meuse River near Liege and race straight for the vital Belgian port of Antwerp. The tanks of the Fifth Panzer Army, commanded by Gen. Hasso von Manteuffel, were to cross the Meuse between Namur and Dinant and drive towards Brussels in order to cover Dietrich's southern flank. In the extreme south, Gen. Erich Brandenberger's Seventh Army was assigned to protect Manteuffel's thrust. As soon as the front was pierced, a special company of English-speaking commando troops in American uniforms, under SS Col. **Otto Skorzeny**, was to seize key bridges across the Meuse. Other American-uniformed units were to cut telephone wires and create confusion behind Allied lines.

Hitler's plan was a desperate gamble, given the Germans' weakened state and the overwhelming superiority of Allied air power. Seventy-year-old Field Marshal **Gerd von Rundstedt** was placed in nominal command of the operation, but he did not take part in its planning. He and other senior officers were informed of the Ardennes plan only in late October. They were appalled by the risks involved and warned that their forces were not strong enough to reach Antwerp. Rundstedt and Field Marshal **Walther Model** proposed, instead, a more limited offensive as far as the Meuse. But on November 25 Hitler announced that his decision was final. Knowing that Gen. **Eisenhower**'s command abilities were questioned by the British, he thought that a smashing blow delivered to the U.S. First Army, which held the Ardennes sector, would sow further discord within the Allied camp. "If we succeed," he told his generals, "we will have knocked out half the enemy front. Then let's see what happens!" Probably Hitler hoped that by seizing Antwerp and cutting the British off from their supply bases, he would force them to evacuate the Continent, as the British Expeditionary Force had been obliged to do at Dunkirk in 1940. With the British out of the war, even if only temporarily, German troops could be shifted to the eastern front in time to stop the Soviet offensive.

The spot chosen for the German counteroffensive seemed ideal. The Allied command thought that the rugged terrain of the Ardennes made any large-scale attack there highly unlikely. As a result Eisenhower had assembled only five American divisions in the area. Moreover, Hitler achieved the astounding feat of concealing his massive buildup from Allied intelligence. For three months the German mobilization was effectively hidden by the Ardennes forest. Special precautions were taken: potentially unreliable troops were withdrawn from the front line; deserters were threatened with reprisals against their next-of-kin; no preliminary orders were transmitted by plane or radio, even in code; and complete radio silence was maintained prior to the attack. When the assault came, at 5:30 a.m. on December 16 along an 80-mile stretch, the Allies were taken completely by surprise; indeed, they were slow to realize the full import of Hitler's move, treating it at first as a local "spoiling" operation.

Aided by fog and mist, which kept Allied air forces grounded for an entire week, the Germans advanced according to plan in the first stages of the battle. The unexpected force and timing of the attack temporarily unnerved American troops, and the activity of Skorzeny's commandos produced considerable havoc for several days. Unlike the French in 1940, however, the Americans kept up their resistance even after their lines of communication had been broken. The U.S. 99th Infantry Division, the most southerly unit of Maj. Gen. Leonard Gerow's Fifth Corps, was driven back by Dietrich's tanks and infantry, but after three days of desperate fighting at Elsenborn Ridge, it still blocked access to the direct road to Liege. Dietrich's setback severely damaged the prestige of SS troops and prompted Hitler to shift the leadership of the offensive to Manteuffel, who had quickly smashed through the U.S. 106th Division and the 14th Cavalry group defending the vital road center of **Saint-Vith**. At Schnee Eifel, in what was perhaps the most serious American defeat of the 1944-45 European campaign, Manteuffel forced two regiments of 7,000 men to surrender. However, Brandenberger's Seventh Army, after crossing the Our River and advancing as far as Wiltz, 12 miles to the west, was stopped by Maj. Gen. Troy Middleton's Eighth Corps.

On Dietrich's front, the elite First SS Panzer Division, with Lt. Col. Joachim Peiper's battle group in the lead, made rapid progress in its drive to outflank Liege from the south and seize the crossings on the Meuse at Huy. On the way, Peiper initiated a wave of terror by machine-gunning groups of American prisoners and Belgian civilians. After reaching Stavelot, located perilously close to U.S. First Army Headquarters at Spa, Peiper's advance was checked by American reinforcements. To the south, Manteuffel surrounded Saint-Vith, which was reinforced by the U.S. Seventh Armored Division. The two trapped divisions held off the Germans for one week before falling back through the last available escape route on December 21. On the 18th Manteuffel opened siege on Bastogne, another road center, which was held by the 10th Armored Division. The following day the 101st Airborne Division arrived, and the town's defense was taken over by Brig. Gen. **Anthony McAuliffe**. When Gen. Smilo von Luettwitz called on the garrison to surrender on December 22, McAuliffe simply answered "Nuts!"—a reply that struck the Germans as cryptic until it was translated as "Go to hell!"

By December 18 Eisenhower had grasped the seriousness of the situation. All U.S. forces north of the German breakthrough (the First and Ninth Armies) were placed under Field Marshal Sir **Bernard Montgomery**, leaving Gen. **Omar Bradley** in command of forces to the south. Lt. Gen. **George S. Patton, Jr.**, was ordered to give up his sector in Lorraine and drive

his Third Army northward to relieve Bastogne. Altogether more than 60,000 fresh troops were moved to the Ardennes on the 19th, and 180,000 more were sent in during the next eight days.

On the seventh day of Hitler's offensive, December 23, the skies cleared, allowing the deployment of Allied planes. Heavy damage was inflicted on German trains and armor, which were jammed solidly along the main roads. Behind the German lines, railroad stations were destroyed at Koblenz, Gerolstein and Bingen. Part of Manteuffel's army managed to go around Bastogne and push as far as Celles, near Dinant, four miles from the Meuse, on Christmas Eve, but this spearhead was destroyed the next day by the U.S. Second Armored Division. After creating a triangular "bulge" 60 miles deep and 50 miles wide at the base, the German advance was halted. On December 26 the U.S. Fourth Armored Division broke through to Bastogne.

To relieve the impasse in the Ardennes, Hitler began planning a series of rapid blows along the American front near Saarbruecken and Metz, to the south, which Patton had left dangerously exposed, and in Alsace. After the Army Group Upper Rhine, under **Heinrich Himmler**, forged a bridgehead north of Strasbourg, Eisenhower momentarily considered evacuating the city. But Allied forces moved fast enough to avoid being encircled in Alsace, and Himmler was pushed back.

On January 3 Montgomery and his 21st Army Group began their offensive along the northern flank of the Ardennes bulge, cutting the distance between themselves and Bradley from 20 to 11 miles at the western end. A week later, the bulge was reduced to 30 miles in depth, and Montgomery's and Bradley's groups stood less than eight miles apart. When the Allied counterattack began, Hitler at first refused to allow a withdrawal. Squeezed into a narrowing sector, the Germans' only recourse was to keep Allied supply lines under fire with **V-1 and V-2** launchings. Liege and Antwerp were hit hard by the flying bombs. On January 8 Hitler finally agreed to his generals' pleas for limited withdrawals. The westernmost attack spearhead, the 47th Panzer Corps, was pulled back, and the Sixth Panzer Army was withdrawn to establish a tactical reserve. It quickly became apparent that the battle was lost, however, and on January 13 Hitler permitted a general retreat. By January 21 the Germans had been driven back to the original line.

The Battle of the Bulge cost **Germany** more than 100,000 men, 1,600 planes, 700 tanks and innumerable vehicles—all desperately needed to resist the impending invasion of the Reich itself. Allied losses numbered 81,000 men. About 77,000 casualties were

American; this constituted the heaviest battle toll in U.S. history. (See also **Normandy Landing**.)

T. L. Harrison

BUREAU CENTRAL DE RENSEIGNEMENTS ET D'ACTION (BCRA).
(In English, "Central Bureau of Information and Action.") An organization created in London by Gen. **de Gaulle**. (See also **Free France; French Resistance**.)

BURGERS, Jean (1917-1944).
A Belgian engineer, Burgers was commander of the "G" group, an underground organization specializing in synchronous **sabotage** that paralyzed whole industrial sectors. Most of the group's members were recruited from among engineers at the University of Brussels. On the night of January 15, 1944, the group executed the "great cut-off," involving the destruction of 50 electric towers and halting production in a number of industrial plants in **Belgium** and as far away as the Ruhr, in addition to jamming rail communications between **Germany** and the Belgian coast. About 10 million man-hours of work were lost in the resulting confusion. Burgers was hanged in Buchenwald on September 6, 1944.

BURMA.
A strong independent **empire** in the 12th century, Burma declined, revived again and was conquered by the British in three 19th century wars; it was annexed to the Indian Empire. In 1937 the connection with **India** ended, and Burma was given some self-government, but most authority remained, as in India, with a small British-educated governing class of civil servants, who, at the outset of war, proved inadequate to their tasks. In 1940 the Japanese recruited the cadre for a Burma Independence Army and trained 30 officers, called *thakins* ("masters"), in **Japan**. U Saw, the Burmese prime minister, was detected by British security authorities making contacts with the Japanese in the autumn of 1941 and detained in the Seychelles.

The Japanese were welcomed by some Burmese as liberators in December 1941. They were followed through Burma by the Burma Independence Army, which paraded 5,000 strong in captured Rangoon in March 1942, attracted many more high-spirited and violent Burmese and precipitated a racial panic (about a quarter of Burma's population were non-Burmese). Even the Japanese found the Burma Independence Army hard to handle. In mid-1942 they weeded out most of its most troublesome elements, renamed it the Burma Defense Army and assigned it to internal security work.

In June 1942 the Japanese set up an entirely Burmese puppet government, but it had no real power. Burma was proclaimed independent in August 1943, but the proclamation was hollow and its hollowness harmed the Japanese cause all over Southeast Asia. The **Office of Strategic Services** and the **Special Operations Executive** (SOE) worked together among the dissident tribes, Karens, Kachins and Chins, to stimulate **resistance**. One of the Thakins, U Aung San, decided to change sides. He built up the Anti-Fascist People's Freedom League, a sort of popular front ranging from liberals to Communists (so far as those Western political descriptions meant anything in Burma), and was able to convince the Burma Defense Army to become its military wing. (Japanese security seems to have known little or nothing about this situation.) He then contacted the SOE. In the spring of 1945 Aung San brought the Burma Defense Army into action against the Japanese, during a critical moment in their retreat, at the same time of a large Karen uprising, also sponsored by the SOE. This helped to get the Japanese out of Burma; it also helped Aung San, who emerged as a leading figure in Burmese politics until U Saw had him killed in 1947 (and was subsequently hanged for doing so). The British gave Burma real independence in 1948.

M. R. D. Foot

BURMA CAMPAIGN.
The prestige of the **United Kingdom** in Asia was severely damaged by **Japan's** unopposed conquest of **Burma**, which cut off the only direct route by which U.S. supplies could reach **Chiang Kai-shek**, the road through the mountains between Lashio and Kunming. Although the **United States** was basically unwilling to help the British recapture Burma, they were quite eager to reopen the Lashio-Kunming route.

U.S. Gen. **Stilwell** was in command of forces on the Sino-Burmese frontier in the mountains northeast of Lashio, but he was unable to be of much help because his forces, almost all of whom were Chinese, had been virtually depleted. Stilwell was also in command of Chinese forces in Assam and elsewhere in **India**. As a result, he had to work closely with British commanders, first **Wavell**, then **Mountbatten**. At the same time, Stilwell was in direct contact with **Roosevelt** and with the U.S. general staff, and he commanded a small bomber force of USAF B-24 Liberators. His chain of command was enormously complex, and his difficult personality did not facilitate matters.

On two occasions, in the fall of 1942 and spring of 1943, the British tried to recapture Burma by launching attacks from neighboring Akyab Province in eastern Bengal. Both times they were able to make a breach in

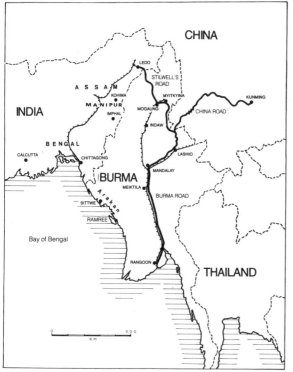

the Japanese lines, but they had to retreat because their troops were weakened by malaria.

The Japanese, ignoring the British threat from Akyab, launched an offensive in the spring of 1943 against Kohima and Imphal, two towns just inside the Indian frontier in the province of Manipur. They were met with fierce resistance from British and Indian forces. The Japanese lost 100,000 men—a quarter of their forces in Burma—and their supply lines were seriously disrupted by Gen. **Orde Wingate's** attacks. He himself lost 1,000 of the 3,000 men in his brigade, but he proved that British and Gurkha troops could fight well even in the depths of the jungle—a jungle the British army had considered impenetrable until the Japanese crossed it in the winter of 1941-42.

In the spring of 1944 the Japanese launched another offensive in northern Burma. Once more they approached Imphal. This time Wingate had a larger force—a division—and he attacked the Japanese from behind. He was unfortunately killed at the start of the attack, and the victory he had expected was not decisive. Again his losses were tremendous, especially in **Calvert's** brigade. The **Chindit** troops, meanwhile, dealt the Japanese a massive blow. With help from Stilwell's forces, they liberated Mogaung and Myitkyina in northern Burma.

The monsoon forced a halt to the fighting. By the middle of the winter of 1944-45, **landing craft** from Operations Overlord and **Dragoon** were available for Mountbatten's and **Slim's** advances. (Admiral **King** had refused to send even one landing craft from his Pacific fleet. Most Americans considered the British operations less important.) Slim's feint to the left tricked the Japanese into thinking that he wanted to free the Burma road to **China**. What his Operation Capital actually did was to strike at the Japanese in their center in January 1945. His 14th Army repulsed the Japanese 15th Army (commanded by Katamura) near Imphal and Kohima and forced them to retreat along a line from Indaw to Mandalay, which the British recaptured in March. The Burma road was more or less liberated and was put back into service by the end of February. Mandalay itself was not retaken until March 22 after an extraordinarily bloody battle at Meiktila, which was held by Honda's 33rd Army. Honda surrendered March 3. Mandalay's population had shrunk from 400,000 to 7,000 as a result of war and occupation. A British flank attack on Arakan, next to Akyab, came next. The British took the Mar and Ramree Island airfields, which enabled them to mount Operation Dracula against Rangoon. The assault was carried out by sea, land and air on May 3. **Churchill** subsequently coined the term "triphibious" to describe the operation.

The Japanese had already evacuated the city. Their strong nerves finally cracked under the combined pressure of incessant attacks, British air superiority, the inexorable increase in British forces and the unexpected British recruitment of the previously pro-Japanese Burma Defense Army camp headquarters (engineered by the **Special Operations Executive**). British control of the air enabled it to overcome most of the problems inherent in resupplying an army in swamps and trackless jungles. Malaria, the other major obstacle, was taken care of by quinine. Lacking air power the Japanese had to rely on mule trains to supply their army once it was out of reach of roads and rail routes. When they could no longer rely on mules, the troops fled to **Thailand**.

M. R. D. Foot

BURSCHE, Julius (1862-1942).

Bishop of the Evangelical Church of Augsburg in Poland, Bursche was arrested at the beginning of the occupation and imprisoned in the Oranienburg-Sachsenhausen **concentration camp** on February 15, 1940. He was held there secretly until his death in February 1942. He was kept ignorant of the fact that several yards away from his cell in the barracks, also held prisoner, were his brothers Edmond, a professor of theology; Alfred, a lawyer—both of whom died before he did—and Theodore, an architect; as well as his grandson, Wegener. His son, Stefan, had already been executed in February 1940.

BUSCH, Ernst (1885-1945).
Appointed field marshal in 1940, Busch participated in the drive on France and served on the Russian front in 1944 and in Prussia in 1945. A member of the **Doenitz** government, he died behind bars.

BYRNES, James Francis (1879-1972).
Byrnes, a South Carolina Democrat, served in the U.S. Senate from 1931 to 1941. During the war he was director of the Office of Economic Stabilization in 1942-43 and of the Office of War Mobilization from 1943 through the end of the war. He was present at the Yalta Conference (see **Conferences, Allied**), and served as **Truman**'s Secretary of State from 1945 to 1947.

C

CABINET INFORMATION BOARD.

A Japanese executive agency, created in December 1940, which was responsible for coordinating **propaganda** and **censorship** within **Japan** and **psychological warfare** abroad. The board absorbed the publicity bureaus of every government department except the IGHQ (whose information office turned out separate—and often conflicting—propaganda until the end of the war). The board supervised film studios, the *Domei* news agency and NHK, the state broadcast network, which operated Radio Tokyo, the major organ for overseas propaganda. The board censored newspapers, magazines, books and scholarly journals. Together with the home ministry's thought police and the military police *(Kenpei)*, it was responsible for suppressing rumors and politically unorthodox opinions. The board was clumsy, and some of its functions overlapped with those of the army and home ministry, so it never achieved the same efficiency as Germany's propaganda machine. It did, however, curb public discussion considerably and thus helped prevent the formation of **resistance** movements. The board was disbanded after the end of the war, in December 1945.

T. R. H. Havens

CABINET PLANNING BOARD.

An executive agency in **Japan**, which was created in October 1937 to coordinate overall economic policy during the war. While nearly every civilian ministry was represented on its staff, it was dominated by members of the naval and military affairs bureaus. The board imposed a thicket of controls, rules and regulations on domestic industry under the **National General Mobilization Law** of 1938. Corporate and financial leaders immediately attacked the board's policy companies, established for each important industrial line, because they found them too restrictive. The army, on the other hand, thought they were too flexible and pressed in 1940 to have corporate profits taxed more stiffly. With planners bickering and **production** lagging, the board soon announced a "new

economic structure" and, by September 1941, began to set up industrial control associations in place of the ineffective policy companies. This scheme, however, did not work any better, and the board was disbanded in September 1943. The army finally took direct control of economic planning in November 1943, when a new munitions ministry was established to replace the board.

T. R. H. Havens

CADORNA, Raffaele (1889-).

An Italian general, Cadorna was the son of Marshal Cadorna, who had been chief of the Italian general staff from 1914 to 1918. Raffaele Cadorna, division commander, escaped from Rome upon its occupation by the *Wehrmacht* in September 1943. He parachuted into northern **Italy** on August 11, 1944 and served as a technical consultant for the *Comitato di Liberazione nazionale dell'Alta Italia* and as chief of the **Resistance** for the Allies and the central government of Italy. He became supreme commander of the *Corpo volontari della libertà*, which brought together the armed partisans north of the Gothic Line after the November 1944 compromise.

CAIRO CONFERENCE.

See **Conferences, Allied.**

CALVERT, Michael (1913-).

A British guerrilla leader, Calvert led a column in each of the expeditions headed by Gen. **Orde Wingate**. In 1945 he took command of the **Special Air Service.**

CAMBODIA.

See **Indochina.**

CANADA.

As a mark of its independence, Canada did not enter the war until September 10, 1939—one week after the **United Kingdom**. Prime Minister **William Mackenzie King's** government secured a large majority in the general election of March 1940, indicating popular support for the war, and after the fall of France, Canadian participation became serious.

In all, just over one million Canadians served in the war, and 41,992 were killed. Canada's army did not engage in combat until the raid on Dieppe in August 1942; out of the 5,000 inexperienced Canadians engaged, 3,000 became casualties. By the time of the landing on Sicily, however, in which a division and an armored brigade from Canada took part, Canadian troops were doing much better; they continued to distinguish themselves throughout the Italian campaign. Another Canadian division and armored brigade participated in the **Normandy landing** on June 6, 1944 and took a leading part in the capture of Caen. The First Canadian Army, including five Canadian divisions as well as two British and one Polish, formed the left flank of the Overlord advance across France, **Belgium** and **the Netherlands** into **Germany** and saw heavy fighting on the lower Scheldt.

The Canadian navy was greatly expanded during the war, becoming primarily an antisubmarine force charged with **convoy** protection in the Northwest Atlantic. Canadian landing craft also took part in operations in Normandy, Provence and the **Aleutian Islands**. An extensive system of pilot training in Canada was immensely helpful to the **Royal Air Force**. The Canadian air force sent 48 squadrons overseas, including an entire group under the RAF bomber command; these squadrons accounted for two-fifths of Canada's total war dead. A few French-speaking Canadians served, with great gallantry, with the French underground.

Tensions between the French-speaking province of Quebec and the federal government were noticeably less severe than they had been during World War I, and were completely dissipated by the autumn of 1944. In any case Quebec benefited from the industrial development boom that came with the war. Most of this boom was directed, in close cooperation with the U.S., to the production of arms and military vehicles. Canada introduced the elements of a **welfare state** during the war to pacify industrial workers, and the federal election of June 1945 left King in power, although with a reduced majority.

M. R. D. Foot

CANADA—Aid to the USSR.
See **USSR—Aid from the United States, the United Kingdom and Canada.**

CANARIS, Wilhelm (1887-1945).
Canaris, a German admiral, was named head of the *Abwehr* in 1935. He was an enemy of the Nazi regime, although he served the German army devotedly, and was dismissed from the *Abwehr* on February 18, 1944. Canaris was arrested after the **assassination attempt of July 20, 1944** and hanged at Flossenburg on April 9, 1945.

CAPE ESPERANCE, Battle of.
In October 1942 the Japanese were intensifying their efforts to smash the U.S. forces on **Guadalcanal** by mid-month. This entailed constant buttressing of the Japanese garrison by means of the nightly "Tokyo Express" (destroyer-transport **convoys**, plus bombardment forces, shuttling from Rabaul and the Shortlands), neutralization of pesky Henderson airfield, destruction of U.S. Marine defenses and interdiction of American reinforcements. On October 11-12 a naval collision involving surface forces occurred between an IJN bombardment force and a U.S. task force. Rear Adm. Aritomo Goto's unit consisted of three heavy cruisers and two destroyers, which were coordinated with a large Japanese convoy headed for Kokumbona carrying the Second Infantry Division and heavy artillery. At the same time the Americans were ferrying a regiment of the Americal Division from New Caledonia, escorted by Rear Adm. Norman Scott's Task Force 64, made up of two heavy and two light cruisers and five destroyers operating northeast of Cape Esperance in "Ironbottom Sound." Scott had **radar** and **reconnaissance** advantages; the Japanese possessed a splendid visual lookout ability and sturdy vessels. Deploying in single column, TF 64 proceeded to cross Goto's "T," a classic naval maneuver that cost the Japanese admiral his life. During the fierce gunfire battle that night, which saw both good and bad use of searchlights by the Americans, TF 64 suffered damage to one destroyer and two cruisers (the USS *Boise* was severely damaged and the USS *Salt Lake City* moderately hurt). Another destroyer, USS *Duncan*, was sunk. The IJN bombardment force lost a destroyer, and one heavy cruiser (*Furutaka*) sank. Damage was sustained by the other Japanese destroyer and the two cruisers. The next morning, the IJN escort force, on its way back, lost two of its six destroyers to U.S. aircraft striking from Henderson Field. Scott's well-trained and aggressive force outfought and outmaneuvered the Japanese at Cape Esperance. Nevertheless, the Americans neither prevented the important Japanese convoy from getting through to Tassafaronga nor annihilated the surprised IJN bombardment force. The reasons were several: communications and intelligence confusion, some mechanical malfunctions and the inflexible layout of the very formation, the single column, which had so successfully crossed the Japanese "T." Goto was largely undone by his nonchalance and his dis-

belief in the intelligence reports he received. Although the Americans got their own troop convoy through safely, Scott had certainly not suppressed the depredations of the fearsome "Tokyo Express." The Battle of Cape Esperance was one of the few night engagements that the Japanese navy did not win, but the main struggle for Guadalcanal raged on with undiminished fury.

A. D. Coox

CAROL II (1883-1953).

King of **Rumania** from 1930 to 1940. He assumed dictatorial powers after suppression of the constitution in 1938, but was forced to abdicate by **Ion Antonescu** on September 5, 1940.

CASABLANCA CONFERENCE.

See **Conferences, Allied.**

CASSINO.

The Battle of Cassino, which took place around Monte Cassino in the early months of 1944, claimed so many Allied casualties that it came to be known as "the Verdun of Italy." The famous abbey crowning the hill, founded by Saint Benedict in the sixth century, was completely destroyed by Allied bombers during the battle.

CATROUX, Georges (1877-1969).

Catroux, a French general, was appointed governor general of **Indochina** in August 1939. After the occupation of France he rallied to the Free French. He became high commissioner to the Middle East in 1941 and governor general of Algeria from 1943 to 1944.

CAUNTER, John Alan Lyde (1889-   ).

Caunter had been a prisoner of war during World War I—he was captured in 1914 but escaped in 1917. He joined the British tank corps in 1924 and became a brigadier general in 1939. In 1942 Caunter commanded the victorious troops at **Beda Fomm.**

CAVALLERO, UGO (1880-1943).

Cavallero, an Italian marshal, had been, by turns, an army officer; an industrialist; under-secretary of war (beginning in 1925); again, later, an industrialist; and, in 1936-37, head of the Italian forces in West Africa. Cavallero was appointed general of the army at the beginning of the Italian campaign in **Greece.** He became chief of the general staff on December 6, 1940. He suffered several defeats in Africa; this, together with the increasing submission of the Italian command to the Germans, over which he presided, and his intrigues at the court of **Victor Emmanuel III** lost him the confidence of **Mussolini** who replaced him with General **Ambrosio** in February 1943. Arrested on orders from **Badoglio** on August 23, he committed suicide on September 12, 1943.

CENSORSHIP.

Correspondence and telephone and telegraph traffic were routinely censored under fascist and communist regimes. Letters home from those serving in the armed forces were also automatically censored by practically every country to prevent the dissemination of secret information and to preserve **morale** on the home front.

Censorship was also used, to a limited extent, for intelligence purposes. Reports could be made, on the basis of information gleaned by censors, to politicians or commanders about the state of mind of those for whom they were responsible; some economic information could also be uncovered by inspecting letters on their way to or from addresses abroad.

Censorship could be evaded only by using very simple personal codes, which no one but the writer and reader could understand, or by highly elaborate ones, in which secret agents were trained. Censors were adept at spotting such old-fashioned devices as the use of invisible ink; indeed, letters frequently arrived at their destinations bearing a large chemical "X," intended to detect any "invisible" addenda.

M. R. D. Foot

CENTRAL BUREAU OF INFORMATION AND ACTION.

See *Bureau central de renseignements et d'action.*

CFLN.

See *Comite francais de liberation nationale.*

CHAIN OF COMMAND, Anglo-American (in Europe, 1944).

Chart boxes:

- British Chiefs of Staff
- U.S. Chiefs of Staff
- Combined Chiefs of Staff (Washington)

Mediterranean Theater branch:
- Commander-in-Chief, Mediterranean Theater: Wilson (Br)
- Second in command: MacNarney (US)
- Chief of Staff: Gammell (Br)
- Combined Staff
  - Naval Forces: J. Cunningham[5] (Br)
  - 15th Army Group: Alexander (Br)
  - Middle Eastern Forces: Paget (Br)
  - Air Forces: Eaker (US)

Strategic Air Forces branch:
- British Strategic Air Forces: Harris
- US Strategic Air Forces: Spaatz
  - Eighth Strategic Air Force: Doolittle
  - 15th Strategic Air Force: Twining[4]

European Theater branch:
- Commander-in-Chief of European Theater of Operations: Eisenhower (US)
- Second in command: Tedder (Br)
- Chief of Staff: Smith (US)
- Combined Staff (SHAEF)
  - Naval Forces: Ramsay[1] (Br)
  - 21st Army Group: Montgomery (Br)
  - 12th Army Group: Bradley (US)
  - 6th Army Group: Devers[2] (US)
  - Air Forces: Leigh-Mallory[3] (Br)

(1) Killed on January 2, 1945.
(2) Landed on the Cote d'Azur August 25, 1944; subordinate to commander-in-chief in the Mediterranean until September 15, 1944, when attached to Eisenhower's command.
(3) Killed on November 14, 1944.
(4) Established in Italy; combined with 205th Group of the RAF Bomber Command to form Strategic Air Force in the Mediterranean.
(5) Adm. John Cunningham replaced Adm. Andrew Cunningham when the latter became first sea lord of the admiralty and a member of the Committee of Chiefs of Staff.

CHAIN OF COMMAND, British (Ground Forces).

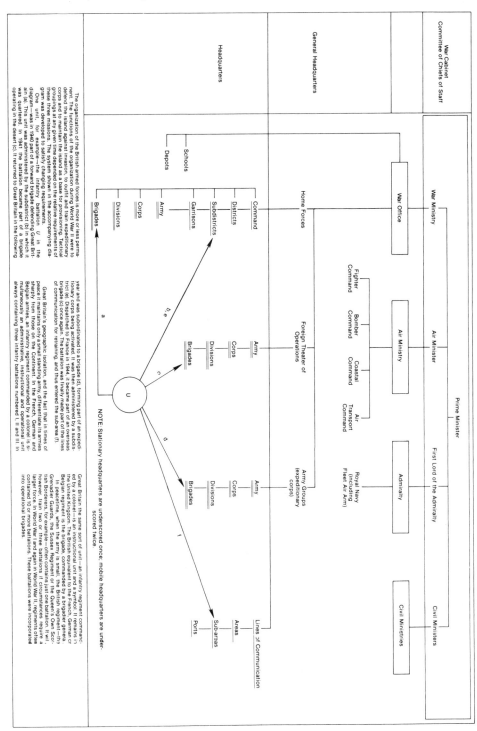

War Cabinet / Committee of Chiefs of Staff

General Headquarters

Headquarters

Prime Minister

War Ministry — War Minister

Air Ministry — Air Minister

First Lord of the Admiralty

Civil Ministers

War Office

Fighter Command · Bomber Command · Coastal Command · Air Transport Command

Royal Navy (including Fleet Air Arm)

Admiralty

Civil Ministries

Home Forces — Command · Districts · Subdistricts · Garrisons · Army · Corps · Divisions · Brigades

Depots · Schools

Foreign Theater of Operations — Army · Corps · Divisions · Brigades

Army Groups (expeditionary corps) — Army · Corps · Divisions · Brigades

Lines of Communication · Areas · Sub-areas · Ports

The organization of the British armed forces is more or less permanent. The functions of the organization during World War II were to defend the island against invasion, to outfit and train expeditionary corps and to maintain the island as a base for provisioning. Tactical groupings at any given time depended on the relative requirements of these three missions. The system shown in the accompanying diagram was developed to satisfy changing requirements.

One unit, for example—the infantry battalion U in the diagram—was in 1940 part of a forward brigade defending Great Britain (a). This unit was administered by the subdistrict (b) in which it was quartered. In 1941, the battalion became part of a brigade operating in the desert (c). It returned to Great Britain in the following year and was subordinated to a brigade (d), forming part of an expeditionary corps being activated. It was then administered by a subdistrict (e). Dispatched to France in 1944, it became part of an overseas brigade (c) once again. The battalion was finally made part of the lines of communication for retraining, and thus entered the sub-area (f).

Great Britain's geographic isolation, and the fact that in times of peace it maintains only a small standing army, differentiate its armies sharply from those on the Continent. In the French, German and Belgian armies, an infantry regiment commanded by a colonel is simultaneously an administrative, instructional and operational unit always containing three infantry battalions numbered I, II and III in Great Britain the same sort of unit—an infantry regiment commanded by a colonel—is an instructional unit and a symbol. It remains in the United Kingdom. The British equivalent to the French, German or Belgian regiment is the brigade, commanded by a brigadier general.

In peacetime, when the army is small, the British regiment—the Grenadier Guards, the Sussex Regiment or the Queen's Own Scottish Borders, for example—often contains just one battalion. It will, however, train two or three battalions if circumstances require a larger force. In World War I and again in World War II, regiments often contained 10 or more battalions. These battalions were incorporated into operational brigades.

NOTE: Stationary headquarters are underscored once; mobile headquarters are underscored twice.

CHAIN OF COMMAND, GERMAN (1939-41).

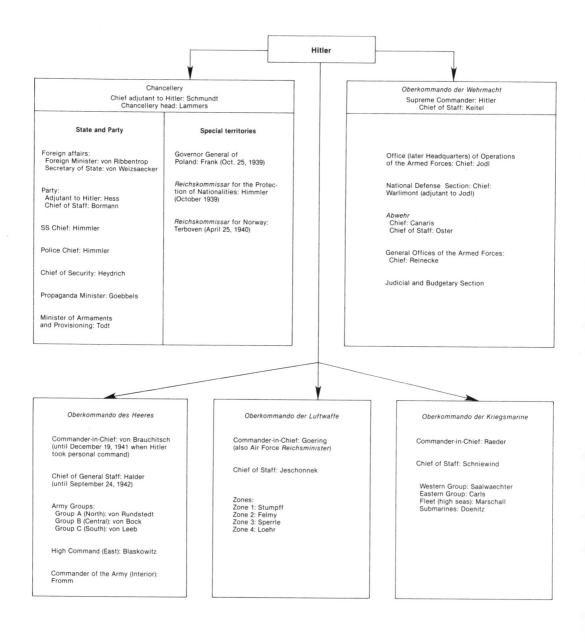

Hitler

Chancellery
Chief adjutant to Hitler: Schmundt
Chancellery head: Lammers

State and Party

Foreign affairs:
  Foreign Minister: von Ribbentrop
  Secretary of State: von Weizsaecker

Party:
  Adjutant to Hitler: Hess
  Chief of Staff: Bormann

SS Chief: Himmler

Police Chief: Himmler

Chief of Security: Heydrich

Propaganda Minister: Goebbels

Minister of Armaments
and Provisioning: Todt

Special territories

Governor General of
Poland: Frank (Oct. 25, 1939)

Reichskommissar for the Protection of Nationalities: Himmler
(October 1939)

Reichskommissar for Norway:
Terboven (April 25, 1940)

Oberkommando der Wehrmacht
Supreme Commander: Hitler
Chief of Staff: Keitel

Office (later Headquarters) of Operations
of the Armed Forces: Chief: Jodl

National Defense Section: Chief:
Warlimont (adjutant to Jodl)

Abwehr
  Chief: Canaris
  Chief of Staff: Oster

General Offices of the Armed Forces:
  Chief: Reinecke

Judicial and Budgetary Section

Oberkommando des Heeres

Commander-in-Chief: von Brauchitsch
(until December 19, 1941 when Hitler
took personal command)

Chief of General Staff: Halder
(until September 24, 1942)

Army Groups:
  Group A (North): von Rundstedt
  Group B (Central): von Bock
  Group C (South): von Leeb

High Command (East): Blaskowitz

Commander of the Army (Interior):
Fromm

Oberkommando der Luftwaffe

Commander-in-Chief: Goering
(also Air Force *Reichsminister*)

Chief of Staff: Jeschonnek

Zones:
Zone 1: Stumpff
Zone 2: Felmy
Zone 3: Sperrle
Zone 4: Loehr

Oberkommando der Kriegsmarine

Commander-in-Chief: Raeder

Chief of Staff: Schniewind

Western Group: Saalwaechter
Eastern Group: Carls
Fleet (high seas): Marschall
Submarines: Doenitz

CHAIN OF COMMAND, Soviet.

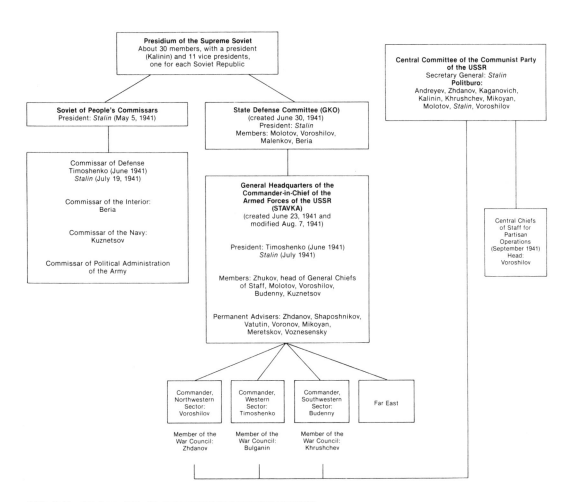

N.B.-The Presidium of the Supreme Soviet, which, together with the Soviet of Peoples' Commissars (actually ministers), formed the executive branch of the government, acted as head of state, seemingly as a group. Stalin, however, actually held the reins; he was, after July 1941, president of the Soviet of Peoples' Commissars and Generalissimo of the Armed Forces as well as Secretary General of the Communist Party. After the reorganization of August 7, 1941, the General Headquarters of the Commander-in-Chief of the Armed Forces of the USSR became the General Headquarters of the Supreme Commander with Stalin as Supreme Commander of the Armed Forces. The office of political commissar in the Red Army was abolished in 1942.

CHAMBERLAIN, (Arthur) Neville (1869-1940).

A British political leader, Chamberlain was the son of the imperialist Joseph Chamberlain. After business training in the Bahamas and Birmingham, he rose through the hierarchy of the Conservative Party and eventually became its leader. From 1931 to 1937 Chamberlain was in charge of finance, and in this capacity he restricted spending on armaments. He wanted to pursue a more active defense policy after he became prime minister in May 1937, but he found the **United Kingdom**'s military forces so weak that he felt he had no choice but to sign the **Munich Pact** in September 1938. In the face of continuing German expansion, however, he gave British guarantees to **Poland**, among other countries, and thus led the British into war with **Germany** in September 1939.

Chamberlain was an efficient administrator, but he lacked magnetism. He knew little of foreign affairs and less of **strategy**; he was, in his own phrase, "a man of peace to the depths of my soul." His parliamentary majority of some 250 seats fell to 81 as the result of a debate on May 7-8, 1940 on the **Norway** debacle; he resigned on May 10. After Chamberlain's resignation, **Churchill** made him lord president. He worked with **Dalton** to set up the **Special Operations Executive**. Soon after, however, he fell fatally ill and died on November 9, 1940.

CHAPMAN, F. Spencer (1907-1971).

An English schoolmaster, Chapman was in charge of **Special Operations Executive** guerrilla training in **Malaya**, beginning in June 1941. He stayed there through April 1944, conducted hundreds of demolitions and killed over 1,000 Japanese.

CHARLEMAGNE.

A division of the French **SS**, Charlemagne was founded in October 1944. Its members fought on the Russian front in February 1945 and on the Baltic in March 1945. In April 1945, in a last-ditch battle, they fought to save **Hitler's** bunker. (See also **Collaboration**.)

CHARLES, Prince of Belgium (1903-   ).

Charles was regent for the Belgian Kingdom from September 1944 to July 1950, until the return of his brother **Leopold III** from exile.

CHARLOTTE von Nassau-Weilburg (1896-   ).

Charlotte became grand duchess of **Luxembourg** in 1919. With her son Jean (1921-   ), she fled to London when **Germany** occupied Luxembourg in 1940 and remained there until Allied troops entered her country in 1944. She abdicated in favor of Jean in 1964.

CHATFIELD, Alfred, Lord (1873-1967).

Chatfield was a British veteran of World War I. In 1930-33 he trained the Mediterranean Fleet in night combat. From 1933 to 1938 he was naval chief of staff, and from February 1939 to March 1940 he was minister of defense coordination.

CHESHIRE, (Geoffrey) Leonard (1917-   ).

Cheshire, a British airman, succeeded **Guy Penrose Gibson** as commander of **Royal Air Force** Squadron 617 in 1943 and, with a less dashing but even more intrepid style, led its raids, including the sinking of the *Tirpitz*, for a year. Cheshire witnessed the dropping of the **atomic bomb** on Nagasaki in 1945. After the end of the war, he went into charitable work.

CHIANG KAI-SHEK (1887-1975).

In 1907 Chiang enlisted in the revolutionary movement in **China**. He broke with the Chinese Communists in 1927, but was subsequently unable to eliminate them as a political force. He became military and political leader of continental China, simultaneously fighting the Japanese, from 1937 to 1945, and the Communists, in a civil war that went on intermittently from 1934 to 1949. Eventually driven off the mainland by the Communists, he established the Republic of China on the offshore island of Taiwan (Formosa).

CHINA.

For China, World War II began on July 7, 1937. But long before then, the Japanese had established themselves in China in their search for new territories. In 1931 the Japanese army occupied Manchuria, which it transformed into a satellite state known as Manchukuo. The following year it threatened Shanghai and in 1933 occupied Jehol and Chahar, two provinces north of Peking. However, an incident took place in July 1937 that marked the true beginning of the Sino-Japanese War. On the night of July 7, a Japanese soldier from the garrison of Fengtai, a small town south of Peking, disappeared near the Marco Polo Bridge. As a result, there was a confrontation between Chinese and Japanese troops, but talks began soon thereafter at the local level. Meanwhile, the Japanese were acquiring reinforcements from Manchuria, Korea and **Japan**. Suspecting that the incident foreshadowed a grab for territory in the northern part of the country, the Chinese called up several additional divisions. By the end of July the situation had become extremely serious. A Japanese ultimatum issued on July 26 was rejected by the Chinese forces. The war began.

It remained strictly between the Japanese and Chinese from 1937 to 1941. In the first phase of the

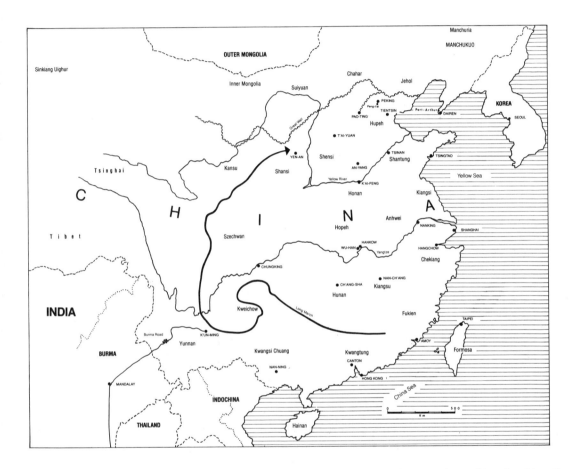

struggle, from the summer of 1937 to the end of 1938, the Japanese occupied much of northern and eastern China; the front then stabilized.

In the north the Chinese troops were menaced by three Japanese armies based on the Peking-Tientsin region. The first of these advanced rapidly to the west, north of the Great Wall, toward Suiyuan. The governor of that province abandoned it to the Japanese on October 14, 1937. Veering south, the Japanese occupied Taiyuan, the capital of Shansi Province, in November and established themselves along the Yellow River. The Second Army descended on Hopeh Province from Peking, taking Paoting on September 24, then Anyang in Honan Province and finally halting near the Yellow River. The Third Army left Tientsin, drove to the southeast and occupied

Shantung Province in December, taking the cities of Tsinan and Tsingtao. By the end of the year, the Japanese were in control of all northern China.

Meanwhile, China had to face a second Japanese offensive, this time in the central provinces. The ''Marco Polo Bridge incident'' was repeated a month later in Shanghai when a Japanese naval officer was killed by a Chinese sentinel. In mid-August 1937 the Japanese began landing heavy troop reinforcements. Not to be outdone, the Chinese concentrated more than 300,000 men in that region. For the moment, the front remained stable. On November 5, however, the power balance tipped in favor of the Japanese when they succeeded in landing two more divisions. The invaders were now in a position to penetrate to the interior and capture Nanking, the Chinese capital, which fell December 13, 1937. The government of the republic then fled to Hankow on the Yangtze River.

During the confused last days of the battle for Nanking, local Japanese navy and army elements attacked not only Chinese targets along the Yangtze but also river gunboats belonging to neutral countries, the **United States** and the **United Kingdom**, with dangerous international implications. The notorious rightist Col. Kingoro Hashimoto, then commanding a Japanese army field artillery unit on the river bank, shelled the HMS *Ladybird* near Wuhu on December 11. The HMS *Bee* was also damaged. On the same day, in the most famous of the gunboat affrays, the small, shallow-draft USS *Panay* was attacked and sunk by IJN warplanes in broad daylight near Hohsien, 25 miles upstream from Nanking, while carrying U.S. evacuees and escorting three Standard Oil barges. Three IJN bombers struck first and dropped 18 bombs. Twelve aircraft then dive-bombed and nine fighters strafed the gunboat and its helpless tanker convoy for 20 minutes. Afterward, the Japanese machine-gunned lifeboats and survivors huddling in the reeds. In all, two U.S. sailors and a civilian passenger were killed, and 11 personnel were severely wounded. A U.S. Navy court of inquiry, convened subsequently at Shanghai, concluded that the attack was "deliberately planned by responsible Japanese officers" in view of the following facts: the *Panay*'s position had been reported as required; the day was sunny and clear; the waters were still; U.S. flags were hoisted or were painted in full view and the gunboat's flimsy armaments were covered when the raid began.

American sources have wrongly thought that Col. Hashimoto, seeking "to provoke the United States into a declaration of war, which would eliminate civilian influence from the Japanese government," devised and oversaw the operation involving Japanese army artillery and IJN planes. Actually, Hashimoto was no favorite of the Japanese navy, and the IJN planes were carrier-based, operating from a flotilla at Shanghai and responding to reports that Chinese troops were fleeing Nanking aboard a string of river craft. The Japanese contend that the attack was a tragic but honest mistake stemming from problems of target identification common in warfare, especially in the early phases of the war in China, and that Japanese intelligence had not warned them that there were non-Chinese ships on the river (Chinese military deserters often fled in Chinese ships). Abuse of neutral flags by Chinese escapees was also not unknown. The IJN commanders at Shanghai immediately expressed regrets to the U.S staff stationed at that port, even before all of the details had been received. The Japanese government not only apol-

ogized but, discomfited by this unnecessary episode, also promptly and willingly paid the stipulated monetary indemnity. Certain local IJN commanders were later reprimanded by the naval ministry. Certainly no senior IJN officers or Japanese governmental authorities wanted to sink the *Panay* or to provoke all-out hostilities with the United States at a time when the bitter Sino-Japanese war was still in progress. This is not to say that the Anglo-American presence in central China, including naval patrolling, was looked upon with favor by the Japanese, but although the *Panay* case could easily have provided *casus belli*, prudence ultimately prevailed in both Tokyo and Washington in 1937.

However, the actual Japanese seizure of Nanking, the Chinese national capital, was accompanied by a breakdown of Japanese military discipline, so protracted, so barbarous and so widespread—the so-called Rape of Nanking—that foreign observers became convinced it was deliberately orchestrated as a campaign of terror and genocide designed to break the will to resist on the part of the "obstinate" Chinese Nationalist regime. For about two months, the Japanese army ran amok, their ostensible "holy war" degenerating into sordid pillage, arson, abuse and murder reminiscent of gangsters, hoodlums and pirates. Chinese males were exterminated without trial and without mercy, by a variety of means, principally by saber, bayonet and small-arms gunfire. To try to run was to be killed on the spot or hunted down like a rabbit. Women from the age of 10 to 76 were raped by individual soldiers or gangs, and sometimes killed and mutilated in the process, by day or night, in public or private. Perversion and torture were common. According to foreign estimates and war crimes data collected after the war, it is estimated that 20,000 women were raped, and that 30,000 to 50,000 male civilians and 100,000 to 150,000 male "war prisoners" were butchered. The highest total estimate of murders was 400,000. The Japanese military commanders insisted that their purpose was only to capture Chinese soldiers and deserters, punish lawless Chinese elements and collect laborers. According to official Japanese apologists at the time and later, the Japanese army's actions in the Nanking area were isolated occurrences, common in war, but exaggerated enormously abroad for propaganda reasons. The best construction that might be placed on these events is that possibly the Japanese troops were exhausted and frustrated by the long bloody battles fought from Shanghai to Nanking since August, and that the caliber of the men (especially the many reservists, the noncoms and the junior officers) was poor. With few exceptions, the officers not only failed to control criminal elements but on a number of occasions they themselves condoned or even participated in heinous actions. A few of the senior army officers seem to have been pathological sadists. Punishment was rare, erratic and generally slight—a slap on the wrist or a reprimand. The Japanese Embassy, characteristically, could exert no moderating influence on the army. Military police were few (reportedly there were only 70 for the entire occupied zone) and inefficient or even criminal on occasion. Despite Japanese denials and the sealing-off of Nanking for months, there were two dozen foreigners (American, German, British and Russian missionaries, teachers etc.) in the city who witnessed the brutality and its effects throughout the period. Indeed, some of the most telling reports came from the German observers, who condemned the Japanese behavior by a "bestial machinery." In addition, a large number of Chinese victims, often in horrible condition, somehow managed to survive the wholesale massacres and related their ordeals. In the long run, Japanese army actions during the Rape of Nanking proved to be an indelible blot on the Japanese military escutcheon.

The Japanese tried to consolidate their victory over China in 1938. Their troops in the central part attempted to join forces with those in the north, and very nearly encircled the army of Gen. Li Tsung-jen. His army escaped only by destroying the dams holding back the Yellow River near the city of Kaifeng. This maneuver halted the Japanese, but millions of peasants died in the ensuing floods. From Nanking the invaders marched the length of the Yangtze and reached Hankow in October 1938, forcing the Chinese government to flee once again to Chungking, in Szechwan Province, where it remained until the end of the war. In the south the city of Amoy, in Fukien Province, had been occupied since May. Newly landed Japanese forces took Canton the same month. By the end of 1938 the Republic of China had lost its great cities—Peking, Tientsin, Shanghai, Nanking, Wuhan, Canton—and half of its vital territory. The Japanese in the north succeeded in joining their comrades in the center, and China was split in two.

This first phase of swift Japanese successes ended in three years of stagnation, from 1939 to 1941. There were, however, more isolated defeats of the Chinese in 1939. They had to abandon the island of Hainan in February of that year, and Nanchang, the capital of Kiangsi Province, in April. But although they also lost Nanning, in Kuangsi Province, in November 1939, they regained it in October 1940. On the whole, however, 1940 and 1941 were extremely calm for the stricken country.

At the beginning of 1942, the Sino-Japanese struggle took on a completely new aspect. The assault on the American naval base at **Pearl Harbor** on December 7, 1941 marked the true start of the world war. The war in the Far East became, in effect, part of the war of Europe. Finally, China officially declared war on Japan, and on Germany and Italy as well, thus earning the right to American assistance, primarily in war materiel. Yet the Chinese front retained its almost perfect calm during 1942 and 1943, except for some important operations in the vicinity of Changsha, in Hunan Province, which was first lost, then retaken by Chinese forces. Not until the spring of 1944 did the Chinese resume their large-scale operations against the Japanese.

As we have seen, the government of Free China—**Chiang Kai-shek** and his Kuomintang Party—took refuge in Chungking in October 1938 and remained there. It governed only the western provinces of Sinkiang and Kansu, some of the central provinces—Szechwan, Shensi and fragments of Honan, Hupeh and Anhwei—and the provinces of the south and southeast, Yunnan, Kweichow, Hunnan, Kiangsi, Kuangsi and Kwangtung, except for Canton and Hainan. In all, China was shorn of its richest sections, the mines to the north and the northeast, and its most populous sections, the lower Yangtze valley and the east coast.

The shock of the Japanese attacks did little to change the Chinese regime. The complex organization of public administration included five chambers—executive, legislative, judicial, control and examinations—the governing Political Council (which was replaced in 1939 by a Supreme National Defense Council) and a national people's council. The actual reins of the government, however, were tightly held by Generalissimo Chiang Kai-shek, who was not only head of the ruling Kuomintang Party but also commander in chief of the army.

The regime was, of course, authoritarian. Neither Chiang himself nor the military situation in China, a country that had never known democracy, could tolerate any kind of liberalism. In any case the core of the Chinese problem was not the monolithic nature of its government but rather the government's inaction.

The fact is that Chiang's power rested less on the requirements of China's predicament than on several uneasy equilibria. First, the equilibrium among the great families of China—the Chiangs, the generalissimo's own family, and the Soongs, the family of his wife and her father, T. V. Soong. Second, the equilibrium among the principal political factions—the liberals, such as Sun Fo, oldest son of the father of the Republic, Sun Yat-sen; the military leaders of the Whampoa Academy, particularly Chen Cheng; the businessmen; and the Protestants, including Chiang himself. At the focal point of all these rivalries, Chiang retained control by playing off one group against another. Unfortunately, his hand was often forced by the major influence of the moment or by financial combines rather than by the judicious consideration of independent advisers. The national interest suffered as a result.

This was particularly true with respect to the conduct of the war. When the Japanese attacked in 1937, Chiang knew he was in no position to resist. Nor was he wrong. During the first few years, therefore, he was content to gain time by retreating before the invader—in the time-honored strategy of trading space for time. He quite correctly assumed that Japan would, in an effort to protect its rear, lash out at the other Pacific powers and thus mesh the China war into the world conflict. When that happened, he reasoned, the Western powers would render him substantial aid. His logic was good enough to lull him into the state of permanent immobility that he later found so costly.

The handling and even the operations of the Chinese forces had often been criticized, most severely by American military experts. The Chinese commanders were so divided by the demands of the equilibria among the various factions attempting to gain control that they were unable to follow a uniform policy. As new divisions were acquired, the diversity of command increased. In 1941 the Chinese army was made up of some 350 divisions, as against 25 for the Japanese. The pay intended for the Chinese soldier was given not to him but to higher echelon officers, which meant that little of it reached him at all. To swell the payroll, Chinese officers often claimed to command more men than they actually did. Recruits were treated with extreme cruelty; one-third of them either deserted or died before they ever came under fire. In 1942 some 15 generals abandoned their command, taking 500,000 men with them. The following year, half the men called up for service deserted. Many of the Chinese defeats in the field were caused solely by this omnipresent anarchy, and these defeats in turn led to a great deal of Chinese suffering in the war.

Aid given to the Chinese after the United States entered the war eased this situation to some extent. American **lend-lease** was extended to China, large quantities of war materiel were shipped to its armies and American military advisers were attached to their commands. The two best-known of these American generals were **"Vinegar Joe" Stilwell**, a thorn in Chiang's side, and Claire L. Chennault, whose "Flying Tigers" later decimated the Japanese air force. By 1943 the new influence began to have an effect on the Chinese situation. The opening of the **Burma** Road permitted increasing quantities of materiel to flow to the defending troops. Some 40 divisions were strengthened with modern equipment in 1944 and 1945. By

the time the war ended, the Chinese forces were far better organized and armed than they had ever been before.

Economically, the country was ruined by the war. In unoccupied China the industrial production index rose from 333 in 1939 to 376 in 1943, and a large number of enterprises that had been dismantled before the advancing Japanese were reassembled in Szechuan or other provinces. But the petty success of this "modern" sector could not hide the general desolation of the Chinese economy. It was further enervated by an incredible period of inflation, from 1937 to 1945, when the price level increased by a factor of 2,500. Nor was the economy of occupied China any better.

In fact, it would be more accurate to speak of the occupied Chinas (plural), since the Japanese set up different zones under their control with conflicting policies. In the northeast, Manchukuo remained a "state" apart under the reign of ex-Emperor Pu-Yi, now called Kang Teh. Similarly, the "Autonomous Government of Inner Mongolia," organized by the Mongol Prince Teh Wang and the Chinese Li Shuhsui, owed its existence to Japanese support.

In China proper, the grand design of the Japanese Empire was to subjugate the five northern provinces of Hopeh, Shantung, Shansi, Chahar and Suiyuan. In 1935 the Japanese set up a "Hopeh-Chahar Council" under the presidency of Gen. Sung Che-yuan. With the onset of hostilities, they went further. On December 14, 1937 the Japanese set up a "Provisional Chinese Government" in Peking, under the presidency of Wang Ke-min, which consisted of ultraconservative enemies of the Kuomintang and devotees of the rigid Confucian tradition. The official party was known as the *Hsinmin-hui*, or "Society of the New People," a political fabrication under Japanese control. The "Provisional Chinese Government" was nevertheless maintained throughout the war.

At Nanking, the former capital of Chiang Kai-shek in central China, a "Reorganized Central Government" had been set up in 1940 under the presidency of **Wang Ching-wei**, an old enemy of Chiang. A Cantonese like Sun Yat-sen and the favorite disciple of the father of the republic, Wang had been a student in Japan. He led the left-wing majority faction of the Kuomintang at Sun's death, thus breaking with Chiang. Ardently pro-Japanese, he worked for a Sino-Japanese rapprochement during the thirties, even after the beginning of hostilities. In 1938 he left the Chungking clique and returned to Nanking where, two years later, he presided over the "Reorganized Central Government." Until his death in 1944, he surrounded himself with other deserters from the Kuomintang in Chungking and even tried to organize a "purified" version of that party. In Wang's judgment, Chiang had betrayed Sun's pan-Asiatic dream by challenging the Japanese.

Actually the government of Nanking was simply another Japanese puppet. It signed a treaty in 1940 placing occupied China officially under Tokyo's control, with Japanese in charge of the major portfolios of Defense, Security, Foreign Affairs and Economy. New accords were signed in 1943 by representatives from Nanking and Tokyo providing for Japan (in theory) to abandon her old concessions, in return for which Nanking's China would retain its "sovereignty" and declare war on the Western powers. But the dependence of occupied China on Japan was in no way altered.

In these various zones, it was the Japanese army that, with the aid of the Nanking army of some 900,000 men in 1944, held complete control and imposed its "new order" (see **New Order in East Asia**). This force instituted a reign of terror everywhere which somewhat resembled that of the Nazis in Europe. But there were still vast areas that escaped its control, even in the Shanghai-Nanking-Hangchow triangle—the heart of occupied China. Toward the end of the war, guerrilla or Communist attempts at assassination, **sabotage** and train derailments increased.

As in Free China, economic and social conditions were extremely poor. Increasing quantities of raw materials and basic manufactured products were shipped to Japan in accordance with the concept of the **Greater East Asia Co-Prosperity Sphere**, and so the scarcity of goods on the continent was in no way altered. Industrial plants had been transferred to the free zones and the Japanese were not able to replace them. Industrial production dropped while unemployment rose (600,000 were unemployed in Shanghai in 1945) and inflation flourished, as in the unoccupied zones. Only the Japanese entrepreneurs, increasing constantly in numbers and arrogance, prospered, along with the privileged collaborators (see **Collaboration**).

Given this situation, it was hardly surprising that the third China, the China of the Communists, grew at an extraordinary rate during the war. The fact was fundamental; thanks to the misery of the war, the Chinese Communist Party, on the defensive in 1935-36, came to control 10 percent of the total land area in 1945.

As a result of long discussions, in which **Chou En-lai** played a significant part, Communists and Nationalists concluded an "Anti-Japanese United Front" pact in July 1937, exactly when the Japanese hostilities began. The Communist troops pledged to cease their operations against the Nationalists and merge with the latter's troops under the authority of the central government; for their part, the Nationalists promised

to end their harassment of Communist bases. This agreement, spelled out in a declaration of the Kuomintang issued on September 23, 1937, laid the groundwork for a united front of the two rival formations throughout the entire war—in theory, at least.

The 45,000 men of the Red Army were then transformed into the Eighth Route Army under the command of Gen. Chu Teh and integrated into the government defense arm, which was, in turn, commanded by the governor of Shansi Province, Gen. Yen Hsi-shan. This homogeneous organization progressively crystallized throughout the nation, and the Communist bases multiplied as the preferred weapon for combating the Japanese.

The foremost of these bases was in Shensi Province. The capital of this province, Yenan, was the base of some of the columns of the "Long March" in 1935 as well as the base of the Central Committee of the Chinese Communist Party and the Communist general staff. Yenan remained the heart of Communist China throughout the war. Quite suddenly, under cover of the anti-Japanese front and the need to strengthen the military machine, other bases took shape in northern China. Among these were the Shansi-Chahar-Hopeh base directed by Lin Piao and Nieh Jung-chen, the Shansi-Hopeh-Shantung-Honan base organized by Po Yi-po and Liu Po-cheng and the Shantung and Shansi-Suiyuan bases.

And new bases sprang up in central China toward the end of 1938. In Hopeh, Honan and Anhwei Provinces, several thousand men left behind by the "Long March" were reorganized into a new Fourth Army, under the command of the former syndicalist Hsiang Ying and the future marshal Chen Yi. This army was officially dissolved in 1941 but managed to survive just the same. Numerous other and smaller bases were created around this region but maintained themselves with difficulty. And finally, in 1939, the beginnings of Communist bases appeared in the south, especially around Canton and the Island of Hainan.

In all of these areas, the Communists never lost sight of the principles they had formerly practiced in their republic of Kiangsi. They organized the inhabitants not only for regular or guerrilla combat but for political and economic propaganda as well. By the end of the war, the Communists had enrolled 900,000 men as well as militias consisting of more than two million men and women, according to official Communist statistics. Basically, this huge reserve was used to fight troops of the Nanking or even the Chungking governments more than the Japanese, in spite of the United Front agreements. The consideration here was primarily political and only secondarily military. The peasants were given systematic instruction that was more nationalist than socialist. Also a moderate kind of agrarian reform was instituted. The farms of absentee owners or landlords who were collaborating with the Japanese were confiscated and the land taxes were reduced. At the same time, labor collectives were organized as mutual assistance or cooperative groups. For lack of capital, artisan crafts were sponsored. Personal ambitions were for the moment set aside. And gradually the results came into focus: The struggle against the Japanese and the incompetence of the Nationalist government helped the Communists gain control of the Chinese peasantry.

Under these conditions the basic differences between the government and the Communists deepened. The first conflicts occurred in 1939; subsequently, collisions between the two military forces became increasingly frequent. In January 1941 the incident of the New Fourth Army took place, when some of the Communist forces were ignominiously disarmed. The most serious of the collisions, this incident marked the beginning of a period of increasing tension. It was not until the last year of the war that relations eased between the two factions.

Actually, the year 1944 ushered in radical changes in Chinese affairs. First of all, American military assistance rose sharply. Both Chinese and American leaders began thinking of postwar Chinese-American relations. Official American circles, however, were uneasy about the Nationalist-Communist rivalry. In November 1944, Gen. Hurley was sent to Chungking as the American ambassador to try to bring about a settlement. His mission got off to a poor start, but conversations were finally begun and continued until March 15.

Military operations also took a new turn. In their last great offensive of 1944, the Japanese recaptured Changsha in June and threatened Kunming and Chungking in November. In response, the Chinese mounted counter-offensives from North Burma and Yunnan. The Burma Road was opened in January 1945, permitting supplies to flow to the entire Chinese front. By the spring, Chinese troops had scored several successes in Kwangsi Province. Diplomatic events also altered the Chinese picture. At the Yalta Conference (see **Conferences, Allied**), from February 4 to 16, 1945, the **USSR** agreed to enter the war against Japan and the Anglo-American contingent yielded to the USSR the rights Russia had lost in 1905—control of the Chinese Eastern Railroad in Manchuria and the base of Port Arthur.

After several critical months, the talks between the Chinese Nationalists and Communists were renewed in Yenan at the beginning of July 1945. At the same time, the Chinese minister of foreign affairs, T. V. Soong, arrived in Moscow to negotiate a treaty of friendship with the USSR. On July 26 China joined the United States and Great Britain in an ultimatum to Japan demanding unconditional surrender. The Japanese rejected it two days later. On August 6 the first **atomic bomb** was dropped on Hiroshima. And on its heels came the Russian declaration of war against Japan and the immediate advance into Manchuria of the Soviet troops that had been massing on the Soviet-Manchurian frontier for months.

The Japanese finally surendered on August 14. On that same day the Chungking Chinese signed a treaty of alliance with the Soviet Union providing for the restoration of Russian rights, established in the days of the czars, over the Chinese Eastern Railway. Also granted to the USSR were commercial rights in the port of Dairen and naval rights at Port Arthur. In return the Soviets pledged to defend China against any subsequent Japanese attack.

For all appearances the Nationalist Chinese government was at peace. But on August 28, the final showdown between the Kuomintang and the Chinese Communist Party began.

F. Joyaux
A. D. Coox

CHINDITS.

Inspired by the name of the stone dragon standing guard at the entrance to Burmese temples, this term was applied to the guerrilla units organized by Gen. **Orde Wingate** in 1943 to operate behind Japanese lines in **Burma**. A first expedition was in action from February to June 1943. A second, involving three brigades, contributed to the defeat of the Japanese offensive that had been launched against **India** in March 1944.

CHOLTITZ, Dietrich von (1894-1966).

Choltitz, a German general, supervised the destruction of Rotterdam in 1940 and of Sebastopol in 1942. As the last German governor of Paris, however, he disobeyed **Hitler**'s order to destroy it in August 1944 and surrendered to the Allied forces.

CHOU EN-LAI (1898-1976).

Chou was a descendant of a family of Chinese bureaucrats. He was converted to communism while a student in France. In 1927 he played an important role in the rebellion of Shanghai. He was the Communist Party delegate to **Chiang Kai-shek**'s government from 1941 to 1945 and subsequently became minister of foreign affairs of the People's Republic of China, a post he held from 1949 to 1957. He then became prime minister of the People's Republic and held that office until his death. He has been described as ''an extremely able man with great personal charm.''

CHRISTIAN X, King of Denmark (1870-1947).
Together with his government, Christian remained in his country after the German invasion as the embodiment of the passive **resistance** of the Danes. The Germans did not dare to arrest him because of his popularity.

CHUIKOV, Vasili Ivanovich (1900-   ).
Chuikov served in the war as a Soviet marshal. A factory worker, he enlisted in the Red Army in 1919, later becoming Soviet military attache to **Chiang Kai-shek**. As commander of the 62nd Army, he bore the entire pressure of the siege at Stalingrad. At the head of the Eighth Guards Army under the command of Gen. **Zhukov** in 1944-45, he penetrated **Poland** and began the final assault on Berlin.

THE CHURCH AND THE THIRD REICH.

The Ecclesiastical Policy of the Third Reich

Proponents of National Socialism regarded it as a religion, a system tying individuals to absolute points of reference: a race, a people and the Fuehrer. This definition supplies a useful basis not only for understanding the collision between religious institutions and the Nazi state but for grasping the true nature of the regime. The **Nazi Party**'s battle against the church was by no means a casual phenomenon; it sprang from the very concept of Nazism. This antagonism cannot be compared, for example, with that between the temporal state and established religion in the 19th century. The Nazi regarded his state as his religion—in **Hitler**'s words, "National Socialism is a form of conversion to a new faith." (And here we find a fundamental difference between Nazism and the Italian or Spanish variety of **fascism**. Fascism was a more purely political force, since it merely required cooperation, or at least acquiescence, from the church.)

Hitler was born into a Catholic family, but he abandoned traditional religion at an early age. Yet, he was extremely envious of an institution that had been able to maintain its influence for nearly 2,000 years. Like Nietzsche, however, he retained a certain respect for the elaborate structure of the Catholic Church: the hierarchy, the Jesuits, even the concept of celibacy— everything, in fact, that suggested the enforcement of discipline and authority. He was convinced that the sole reason for the church's survival was the acumen with which the clerics wielded power and dominated the masses. He saw it as a model for Nazism to emulate.

He was not in the least interested in Protestantism; its splintering into countless sects repelled him. Religion as such bored him. He left to his aides the mystic trappings and arcane rites of Nazism. In 1935 a Ministry of Cultural Affairs was inaugurated, but after 1937 Hitler refused to receive Hans Kerrl, his minister of ceremonies. His relations with the church were opportunistic. If reasons of policy demanded it, he could accommodate church officials because of their influence over the people, especially in the rural areas, as he proved in the concordat with Pius XI in 1933, the pretense of religious ceremony in his ascent to power in the same year and the retention of military chaplains.

His views differed from those of **Rosenberg**, the chief ideologist of the party. Hitler even prided himself on never having read *The Myth of the Twentieth Century*. But he had only scorn for the "shavelings" who, in his opinion, cared just for money and tried to deceive the credulous. For a brief interval, toward the end of 1933, he believed that a "true Christianity"—i.e., a Christianity purged of its Jewish elements—could be combined with faith in the superiority of the Aryan race. But it was only a momentary illusion. His revulsion against Christianity increased with the years. As could be deduced from his many avowals, he intended to come to terms with the church after the final victory of his Reich over its enemies.

Yet the official facade of Nazi **Germany** was quite different. Point 24 of the party's program stated: "We demand freedom for all religious denominations as long as they do not endanger the state or interfere with German traditions and mores. The party as such supports positive Christianity but is independent of any denomination in matters of faith."

Here again we find the expression "positive Christianity" that was to entice many Christians and members of the hierarchy. It could mean anything. It was, in fact, a completely empty formula to mask the immanent hostility of the system to Christianity. Hitler repeated it in his speech of March 23, 1933 after becoming chancellor: "The national government will support and defend the foundations on which the power of our nation rests. It will firmly protect Christianity as the basis of our whole morality and the family as the unit of the lives of our people and our community."

But the same year, he stated: Neither of the two faiths has any future. At least, for Germans. Fascism may make its peace with the church. I may, too. Why not? But that will not prevent me from banishing Christianity from Germany root and branch. One is either a Christian or a German. One cannot be both at the same time.

In fact, the battle against the church began immediately after the Nazis seized power. The religious societies were the first targets. If they did not spontaneously ask for integration into the unitarian associations of the Reich, they were forcibly dissolved. Thus the Centrist Party, the professional societies, the Christian unions and the youth movements were disbanded one by one. This process of *Gleichschaltung* was pursued at a faster pace among Protestants than among Catholics. For the latter, the concordat offered some protection and dampened the zeal of the party's subordinates. In 1935, just after the occupation of the Saar, for which the Nazis had not hesitated to ask the Catholic bishops of Spire and Trier to use their influence with their flocks, the national propaganda machine was thrown into high gear to demand deconfessionalization in social life. Under the pretext that the religious societies were perpetuating national discord and opposing national unification, the Nazis suppressed the surviving organizations and expropriated their property.

The Lutherans, organized in regional churches, were forced to elect one bishop for the entire Reich in May 1933. Their choice, the pastor Friedrich von Bodelschwingh, gave way after several weeks to a member of the Nazi Party. The interference of the state in the affairs of the Lutheran Church, which was much more vulnerable in this respect than the Catholic Church, provoked the birth of the "Spiritual Church." In 1935, a Reich ministry was created for the purpose of gradually subjecting the evangelical churches to the domination of the state. Government intervention in the nation's religious life became widespread. On July 26, 1935 the Vatican newspaper *Osservatore Romano* complained of a resurgence of the *Kulturkampf* in Germany. The trials of priests and religious superiors accused of money-changing began in 1936. In reprisal for the encyclical *Mit brennender Sorge* of Pius XI, the Nazis in 1937 conducted morals trials of priests and monks to "expose" the corruption in convents and boarding schools. In that same year, priests were denied the right to teach religion in the schools—a right, it should be noted, guaranteed by the concordat. The following year, all religious schools and several university Chairs of Theology were suppressed.

The total war offered new opportunities for punishing the church. The requisitioning measures forced many convents in Germany and especially in the occupied countries to close. A secret memorandum from **Martin Bormann** in June 1941 ordered the *Gauleiter* to strip the church and its priests of their last means of influencing their parishioners. "Then," it said, "the existence of only the people and the Reich will be assured for the future."

While Cardinal Baudrillart, rector of the Catholic Institute of Paris, allowed himself to be seduced by Nazi propaganda calling for a crusade to rescue the West from bolshevism in 1942, Hitler categorically denied **Franz von Papen**'s plea to open Russia to Christian missionaries. "That idea for missionary activity, the sort of thing to be expected of an old jockey, is completely out of the question," the Fuehrer said. "To allow the Christians to enter Russia would only give them the license for a battle to the death with shepherds' crooks and crucifixes." This mocking and hostile attitude never changed, although the war effort required a truce in the national interest.

The total liquidation of the church was put off until the final victory. A hint of the nature of this liquidation was afforded by the policy pursued in the Warthe *Gau*. Bormann reserved this province for an experiment in total integration with Nazism by using it as a model for the final solution of the religious question—i.e., a Protestant church reduced to the status of a private company completely at the mercy of the Reich.

The Reaction of the Churches

The Catholic Church

The papacy

The negotiations in progress since 1926 for the reconciliation of the Vatican and Rome ended in 1929 with the accords of Lateran and the concordat with Italy. But the existence of independent Catholic organizations combined under the aegis of the Catholic Action, outside the reach of **Mussolini**, was a constant source of irritation. After 1929 Pius XI sought a modus vivendi with fascism, which appealed to him in certain ways. But he vehemently protested a speech in which *Il Duce* demanded control of the education of Italy's youth. The encyclical *Non abbiamo bisogno* of June 29, 1931 denouncing the monopoly claimed by the Fascist Party indicated the extent to which relations between fascism and the papacy had deteriorated. Encouraged by the German bishops, the Pope, "after an internal struggle," concluded a concordat with the Nazis on July 20, 1933, several months after Hitler's accession to power. That Christmas, the Vatican condemned eugenics. The following year it denounced the exaltation of race. In 1935 it condemned the anti-Christian behavior of Germany. The liquidation of the Catholic youth organizations in the Reich in 1936 aroused a more vehement reaction. In concert with the German bishops—Monsignor Faulhaber of Munich dictated the text while the secretary of state for the Vatican, Cardinal Pacelli, revised it— Pius XI published the encyclical *Mit brennender Sorge* which, printed and distributed in secret, was read from the pulpit on Palm Sunday in all German churches. In it, the Pope accused the Reich of deifying a race, a people, a state and naked power in an idolatrous cult and of favoring a "new, aggressive paganism." An effort was being made to turn the face of the German people away from the church "by measures of constraint, hidden or obvious, by intimidation, by promises of economic, professional, civic advantages." The encyclical went further: "In its wretched fashion of mocking Christian humility as self-degradation, the repulsive pride of these innovators covers itself with ridicule." On Christmas, Pius XI summed up his accusations: "Germany is in a state of open persecution attaining rarely experienced heights of terror, accompanied by brutality, violence, threats and deception."

On April 30, 1938 the Pope diplomatically absented himself from Rome just three days before Hitler's visit to the capital. "The atmosphere of Rome," said the Pontiff's spokesman, "makes him ill." His announced reason was his refusal to attend "the apotheosis prepared for an enemy cross to the Cross of Christ." When it became probable that the anti-Semitic laws would be introduced into Italy, the Pope on three separate occasions—July 21, 25 and 28, 1938—condemned racism in all its forms. On September 6 of the same year, Pius XI declared before a group of Belgian pilgrims: "It is not possible to participate in **anti-Semitism**; we are spiritual Semites." An encyclical against racism and anti-Semitism that the Pope probably wanted published never made its appearance. Pius XI died February 10, 1939.

His successor, **Pius XII**, was elected several months before the war began. The new Pope was not only a diplomat of the first order, but he was intimately acquainted with Germany, where for 12 years he had been the papal nuncio. The architect of the 1933 concordat, he had fought a bitter diplomatic battle for years against the German government in reaction to the Reich's frequent violations of that agreement. If he was tempted several times to denounce the concordat and recall his nuncio, as in 1937, for example, he had second thoughts because he did not want to deprive the church of her opportunity, small as it was, to communicate by means of diplomatic channels.

In May 1939, Pius XII proposed to Hitler a peace conference that would include the great powers. Again, on August 21, he suggested an international discussion of major world problems. And on August 24 he issued a sincere plea for peace, "Nothing is lost by peace; everything may be lost by war " Finally, on August 31 he begged the German and Polish governments to make no move that would aggravate the crisis. But once the hostilities began, he had no choice but to express the hope that the laws of humanity and the international accords regarding the treatment of civilian populations and prisoners of war and the interdiction of poison gas would be respected.

Pius XII remained silent on the subject of **Poland** until after the middle of September 1939, probably because of peace discussions then in progress. But at the end of the month, he placed the Vatican radio at the disposal of Cardinal Hlond, archbishop of Gniezno and Poznan, and appointed a charge d'affaires to the Polish government-in-exile in Angers.

On October 20, 1939 he declared in his first encyclical, *Summi Pontificatus*, "The blood of many human beings, including noncombatants, raises a penetrating cry of anguish, especially in the well-beloved nation of Poland which...has the right to the humane and fraternal sympathy of the world and awaits...the hour of its resurrection in accordance with the principles of justice and true peace." In May he pointed out the tasks facing him: responding to opportunities for peace, limiting the extent of the war and offering relief for cruelty.

But there were no opportunities for peace. Diplomatic efforts to restrain Italy from entering the war met with failure. Limited to religious and charitable matters, the Pope did what he could to defend or rescue Catholic institutions, schools and convents and to solace individual misery. His letters to German and Polish bishops at that time have been compared to those sent by a priest to his parishioners; he expressed his sympathy, assured the stricken of his compassion and comforted them. Beyond that, nothing could be done except to trust to Providence.

And yet he did more. He encouraged the German bishops to speak out, to preach a credo transcending races, faiths and nationalities. Beginning in 1940, he placed the weight of his office on the Church Militant rather than on the diplomacy of the Vatican State. He praised the sermons of the bishop of Muenster against **euthanasia**, which indicated to him that there were still Germans capable of dissenting publicly and courageously. "We assure you," he wrote on September 30, 1941, "that men as brave as Monsignor von Galen will always have our support." Yet he did not think that these efforts would be of any use. In a letter to Bishop Ehrenfried of Wuerzburg, dated February 20, 1941, he described his dilemma, "Where the Pope wants to cry out loud and strong, he is enjoined to patience and silence; where he would like to act and assist, he is enjoined to watch and wait." And in a letter to his friend Monsignor Preysing in Berlin on April 30, 1943, he outlined a course of action, "We leave to the local pastor the care of weighing the extent of the danger of reprisals and the possible means of pressure in episcopal declarations, or to remain silent where the duration and atmosphere of the war make it advisable, *ad maiora mala vitanda.*"

To avert even greater evils, the Pope kept his silence

when he would have preferred to break it, or he resorted to vague terms and diluted condemnations. Weakness or subterfuge? None of the interpretations adequately explains the Pope's dilemma, which reduced him to expressions of regret and mild reproof, as in his Christmas messages of 1939, 1941 and 1944, and which forced him to keep intact the numerous humanitarian activities supported by the Vatican that saved thousands of people in Italy and elsewhere. The historian today can testify that the Pope's policy did, in fact, save lives. A solemn denunciation of Nazi crimes might have eased the conscience of those Catholics who suffered from the Pope's "silence," but in all likelihood it would have hurt those who were persecuted by the Nazis. On the other hand, the fact that the Pope did not issue an encyclical or a pontifical letter on the responsibility of the individual conscience, the right to disobey an unjust order or Christian solidarity with the Jewish people can be construed as a culpable evasion of responsiblity. Such a debate, however, belongs more appropriately to the domain of Catholic self-examination than to that of the historian.

Germany

The church hierarchy in Germany had forbidden Catholics to belong to the Nazi Party several times before 1933. After the Nazis took power, however, it changed its position. It responded to Hitler's affirmations of respect for the two great Christian faiths, made on March 23, 1933, by inviting Catholics to support the new government (March 28). Somewhat later it made an effort to cooperate loyally with the government within the limits of Christian conscience. In this spirit the German bishops chose to conclude the Reich concordat on July 20, 1933, and they continued to respect it even after it was flagrantly violated by the Nazi government. But the bishops took no definite stand against persecution, overt or subtle. In the first place the distinction between the state and the regime was not clear enough to permit such a stand. The temperament and age of the bishops were also factors—Cardinal Bertram of Breslau, president of the Episcopal Conference, was an indecisive old man who shunned decision-making. From year to year the Christian faiths lost ground. Their leaders wrapped themselves in silence when the laws distinguishing between Aryans and non-Aryans went into effect. Neither German Catholics nor Protestants protested the Nuremberg laws of 1935 or the violence of *Kristallnacht* in November 1938 (see **Anti-Semitism**). It is worth mentioning in this connection that the Belgian primate, Cardinal Van Roey, condemned these racist outbreaks at the urging of Pius XI, and that Cardinal Verdier supported his protest in a pastoral letter.

The church's hierarchy was caught between two fires. It sought frantically to save the ecclesiastical institutions menaced by the Nazi regime; at the same time, it could not count on the willingness of its communicants to resist political and propagandistic attacks. This situation robbed the German episcopate of its determination. As a force promoting the integration and solidarity of the nation, the war precluded public protest. It even choked off private objections, the only avenue for dissidence that had been available. Those church officials who distinguished themselves were Monsignor Preysing of Eichstatt (after 1935, of Berlin) for his foresighted policy, Monsignor Schulte of Cologne for his uncompromising steadfastness and his assistance to the Jews, Monsignor von Galen of Muenster for his moral courage in protesting the campaign against convents and euthanasia for the mentally ill in 1941 (at the height of the war), and Monsignor Faulhaber of Munich. Only one bishop, Monsignor Sproll of Rottenburg, was expelled from his diocese in 1938 for having refused to vote for the incorporation of Austria into the Reich. Protected by the Vatican, he shrugged off the pressure exerted on him, but he did not regain his diocese until after the fall of the Third Reich.

The sermons preached by von Galen and the defense of religious objects and ethical principles that were attacked by the Nazis aroused tremendous interest. They were printed and distributed secretly in all countries; they even reached the front. Berlin considered them the strongest onslaught against the government of Germany in several decades. Von Galen's popularity was his armor; the regime hesitated to take any action against the bishop of Muenster. As a direct result of von Galen's sermons, Hitler decided on August 28, 1941 to halt the euthanasia program. Not one German bishop was sentenced to a concentration camp, although such a move was contemplated for von Galen and then dropped as imprudent. If the general attitude of the German church officials offered little relief, their constant vigilance in repelling assaults, their protests against Nazi propaganda and their defense of "Catholic objects" made them a beacon of criticism in the darkness of the totalitarian state—possibly the only one within reach of the masses.

As that era recedes into the past, the impression grows that the church neglected certain opportunities for retaliation. If so, it was due to the situation, peculiar to Catholics, of being considered second-class citizens, to the ineradicably visceral anti-Semitism of the two Christian churches, to the naive confidence in authority, typical of the Germany of that period, and to a false interpretation of Romans 13.

Actually, the help given by the church to the victims of race prejudice or political heresy hunts was considerable, even if it was given primarily to Catholics. In isolated cases it was also extended to non-Catholics. But with the increasingly heavy pressure of the war, the views of the oppressed broadened and sensitivity to the misery of others grew. Statistics reflecting this circumstance are difficult to obtain. The heads and active members of Catholic societies who refused to collaborate were under constant police surveillance. During the war, they were picked up and with no formalities brusquely hustled off to **concentration camps**. From 400 to 500 German and Austrian priests never returned. Obviously, the number of laymen who died in the camps was much greater. Among the best known dissenters were Monsignor Bernard Lichtenberg, provost of the Berlin Cathedral, arrested for having organized public prayers for the Jews; Father M. J. Metzger, a renowned pacifist and ecumenist; and P. R. Mayer, a Munich Jesuit who escaped internment in a concentration camp only because he was a mutilated veteran of World War I. Several Catholics played minor roles in the **assassination attempt of July 20, 1944** on Hitler's life, which had been engineered by the German military. (Two churchmen, both priests, were implicated in the plot as members of the *Kreisauer Kreis*; one of them was the confessor of another conspirator. They paid for it with their lives.)

On the whole, the representatives of the Catholic Church in Germany did not encourage political opposition to the government any more than did the Protestants. Pius XII was less scrupulous than the German bishops about getting in touch with German underground groups. The German church was careful to keep its opposition in the religious sphere, partly as a precaution against "political" misinterpretation of its actions and partly because of allegiance to the state based on a complacent interpretation of Chapter 13 of Saint Paul's Epistle to the Romans.

And yet it would be wrong to dismiss as trivial the political consequences of this essentially religious opposition. Because of its influence over the mass of its congregation, the Catholic Church was a center of criticism of the state and of its Nazi leaders. Although it failed to mount a revolutionary offensive against the Nazis, it was nonetheless a counterpoint to Nazi propaganda. Extremely suspicious of the motives of the church, the Nazis watched it closely. The reports of the German police (*Regierungspraesidentenberichte*) show how seriously the regime took religious opposition.

The occupied lands

In Austria the Catholic churches published several warnings against Nazism before 1937. A pastoral letter of December 1933 condemned "the National Socialist madness that leads or must lead directly to race hatred and wars among the nations." But after the *Anschluss* of 1938, political opportunism prompted an about-face. Vienna's Cardinal Innitzer was eager to be received by Hitler and on March 21 invited his faithful to pledge their loyalty to the new regime without reserve. Summoned to Rome by Pius XI, who greeted him coldly, the cardinal published in the *Osservatore Romano* a partial retraction of his overzealous invitation. Toward the end of that year, the Nazis made their customary transition from a policy of cooperation to one of almost outright persecution. The church, which had no concordat with Austria, was divested of everything but its right to preach. It then entered an active phase of *Kirchenkampf*, sparing neither the members of the former Catholic parties nor the Christian labor unions. The lower clergy suffered the most: 115 priests either died in concentration camps or were shot. In the period from 1938 to 1942, some 300,000 Austrians officially left the church in disgust over the submissiveness of its leaders to Hitler and the Nazis.

In the other occupied countries, the attitude of the Catholic Church in general followed that of the population whose interests it defended against the occupying power. Many convents and religious homes sheltered Jews and fugitives from the Nazis, particularly soldiers of the **Resistance**. In Belgium there were outcries against the deportation of workers to Germany, persecution of the Jews, reprisals against hostages and other abuses. A large number of priests served the Resistance at great risk. Cardinal Van Roey of Malines ordered religious institutions to hide Jews. Monsignor Kerkhofs of Liege made them especially welcome. The rector of the Catholic University of Louvain, Monsignor Van Waeyenbergh, firmly opposed every attempt of the Germans to interfere with the administration of the university; he was arrested on June 4, 1943 for his refusal to deliver a list of freshmen students for submission to the **Forced Labor Battalions** (FLB). The Catholic youth clubs defended themselves effectively against all attempts to pervert the allegiance of their members. The future Cardinal Cardijn, who was first imprisoned in 1942 and narrowly escaped a second arrest just before **Belgium**'s liberation, organized many services to keep Belgian youngsters out of the FLB.

In **the Netherlands,** the bishops maintained their resentment against the invading Germans. They declared membership in the Nazi Party incompatible with the character of a communicant in the Catholic Church and possible grounds for deprivation of the sacraments. The help the Christian community gave persecuted Jews was particularly effective. In concert with other Christian sects, the Dutch bishops in 1942 extracted from Commissar **Seyss-Inquart** the concession that Catholics of Jewish ancestry baptized before January 1, 1944 would not be deported. But because they had published their demand along with Seyss-Inquart's reply, a tactic the other Christian sects had agreed not to use, the Nazis retaliated by deporting those Jewish Catholics first. The courageous action of the Dutch bishops and its tragic consequence produced a shock abroad, especially in France. Among the Dutch ecclesiastics who distinguished themselves during the occupation was the Carmelite Father Titus Brandsma, a professor in Nijmegen and adviser to the Catholic Church. He was deported to Dachau and died there heroically.

After the French defeat of 1940, the pious within the Church community were no less divided than their compatriots outside. Some Frenchmen were faithful to Vichy, some were devoted to Gen. **de Gaulle**—the first resistance fighters for whom hatred of the Nazis was the prime emotion—but the great majority of Frenchmen were uncertain of their loyalties. Vichy was the refuge for the churchman who was bitterly disappointed in the shortcomings of the Third Republic; to him the defeat by the Germans was the government's just deserve for its atheism and worldliness. Some preachers regarded Petain as the savior of France. The sycophant Catholics of Vichy were for the most part the product of Catholic rightist circles close to *Action francaise*. Extremely few of the clergy collaborated directly with the Germans. One of these exceptional few was Monsignor Mayol of Luppe, chaplain of the *Legion des volontaires francais contre le bolchevisme*. Like most of the French, the Catholic hierarchy was grateful to Petain for having, as he put it, "made himself his gift to France." Moreover, the national reformation that Vichy hoped to achieve seemed to parallel closely the basic Christian virtues. "Its motto 'Work, Family, Fatherland' is the same as ours," Cardinal Gerlier of Lyon said. Vichy changed the legislation governing church-state relationships on two points that were deemed crucial by both republicans and the laity. Teaching of the catechism was authorized within state academic institutions and was to be written into the curriculum; church schools were to be subsidized and the institution of the family was to be encouraged. These measures, doubly appreciated in contrast with the anticlerical policy of the preceding governments, represented an irresistible temptation to the church, and the hierarchy responded by affirming the legitimacy of the Vichy state. Several priests accompanied the official representative of the church, Monsignor Chappoulie, to Vichy in the hope of persuading the new government to adopt some of the projects neglected by the Third Republic.

Although the bishops' relationship with Vichy was at first cordial, it ended when their differences with the regime became public. The first disagreement concerned young people. In a collective letter the church hierarchy published its opposition to state-sponsored youth organizations. But there was no definite break over this subject until the Vichy authorities adopted the Nazis' anti-Semitic regulations. The first protest was launched by Monsignor Guerry in the name of Cardinal Gerlier in December 1940. In its declaration of June 17, 1941, the Department of Theology in Lyon decried the injustice of the anti-Semitic statute of June 2, 1941. In July 1942, when persecution took an extreme turn in Paris, the entire church rebelled, and concerted protest was sent to the government. Pastoral letters distributed by the underground press—particularly those written by Cardinal Gerlier of Lyon, Monsignor Saliege of Toulouse and Monsignor Theas of Montauban—produced an enormous public outcry. Monsignor Theas stormed: "In Paris, in tens and in thousands, Jews are being treated in the most barbarous, the most savage way. In our own area we are forced to look upon a chilling spectacle: families being torn apart, men and women abused, penned up and sent to unknown destinations of extreme danger. The indignant protest of the Christian conscience will be heard; I proclaim that all men and women, Aryans or otherwise, are brothers because they were created by God, and that all peoples, whatever their race or religion, have the right to be respected by individuals and states." Well-organized assistance, in which organizations of the Catholic Aid had a dominant role, saved 200,000 Jews from torment in France.

Lyon became a hotbed of Catholic opposition to the regime. Toulouse, urged on by Monsignor Saliege, encouraged the Resistance forces. When the free press vanished in the occupied zone and censorship became tighter in the unoccupied zone, the **underground press** gleefully restored truth to public view. The Catholic publications that circulated in secret included the *Cahiers de temoignage chretien*, founded in 1941, and the *Courrier francais du temoignage chretien*, founded in June 1943. They were widely quoted, leaving no doubt in French minds of the existence of a hard core of resistance in the church. The congregations and religious orders made the most of their mobility and became particularly active. The first chaplains of the maquis were recruited from the regular clergy.

The introduction of the FLB13 in 1943 deepened the tension between the civil authorities and the church. With the assurance that consent to deportation to Germany for forced labor was not an obligation of conscience, Cardinal Lienart of Lille, with several of his colleagues, advised disobedience. Other prelates, uneasy about the absence of any religious assistance to deported workers and aware of the possibilities of evangelization that would be open to priests accompanying them, consented to the deportations. It was seminary students and priests, in particular, who brought the deported workers the spiritual comfort afforded by the church. Hence, the origin of the worker-priest. Several such worker-priests cooperated closely with the Resistance in the underground railway to help prisoners escape from Germany, for example. At the time of the liberation, it was learned that political resistance was for the most part represented by Christians in one group and Communists in another. A Catholic journalist and former editorialist of *L'Aube* presided over the ***Conseil national de la resistance,*** beginning in 1943. Even if only a minority participated in the Resistance, it was extremely important for Catholic integration into French society. After the war, when Gen. de Gaulle and the Resistance leaders demanded a purge of the Catholic hierarchy because of the loyalty of some prelates to the Vichy government, only a few isolated cases were found, due primarily to the adroit intercession of the new nuncio Angelo Roncalli, later to become Pope John XXIII.

In Italy, many of the lower ranks of the clergy joined in the Resistance to the Germans; many of the laity, especially those in Catholic Action groups, were to pay for their daring with their lives.

The Catholic Church in Poland, for centuries the most faithful champion of the Polish nation, was singled out for persecution by the invaders. There were 2,647 such victims out of a total of 10,017 priests. While 3,646 priests were interned in concentration camps at one time or another, 1,996 died in the camps. By the end of the war, more than half the Polish church hierarchy—45 bishops—had perished, were in exile or had suffered imprisonment in some form. The tragedy of the Franciscan Maximilien Kolbe, who offered his life to save the father of a family in Auschwitz, is especially moving. The anguish of the occupation was all the more acute for Polish Catholics because the Vatican, completely cut off from the Polish hierarchy and unable to offer it any genuine assistance, felt constrained to issue no more than a general denunciation of the policy of extermination of the Polish people. The Poles in exile made more pleas for strong public statements from the Holy See than did Poles under the occupation.

Cardinal Hlond, envoy of the Holy See and a refugee at Lourdes, together with Monsignor Radonski, bishop of Wladislavia, who sought asylum first in Paris and then in London, became the spokesmen for the Polish Catholics back home. When Monsignor Radonski in September 1942 complained indignantly to the papal secretary of state, Cardinal Maglione, of the "silence" of the Pope, he was told that the Holy See could do no better than the bishops who remained in Poland. These bishops were even more silent; they failed, for example, to relay to their communicants the letters of encouragement that had been sent by the Pope. Apparently, the Holy See was allowing its policy to be designed by the local bishops. A memorandum of March 2, 1943, listing the principal appeals and duly transmitted by the nuncio of Berlin to the papal ministry of foreign affairs, was given to the latter after two days' delay but it was never answered. The papal representatives in Berlin were refused the privilege of discussing Polish affairs.

The persecution in the territories occupied first by the Soviets, then overrun by the Germans and eventually recaptured by the Soviets was especially severe. Monsignor Szeptyckyi, archbishop of Lvov, became the symbol of endurance to his martyred peoples.

No less extreme was the torture of Roman Catholics in the **Baltic States.** Exacerbating the conflicts within the local clergy were the diversity of races and languages in the region.

Determination of the role of the Catholic Church in **Czechoslovakia, Hungary** and the other Balkan countries is difficult. In addition to the collaboration—principally in Slovakia and Croatia—there was a stalwart Resistance movement that was fiercely opposed to Nazi racism. German forces entering Czechoslovakia in March 1939 transformed the occupied territory into the Protectorate of **Bohemia-Moravia**, with Slovakia remaining autonomous although submissive to Berlin. Traditionally, Roman Catholicism was the predominant faith in Slovakia, where the lower clergy shared popular resentment toward Hungary's Magyarization policy and subsequent Czech domination. A Catholic priest, Monsignor **Yosef Tiso**, became head of the Slovak government in 1940 while a second priest, Monsignor Jan Sramek, presided over the Czechoslovak government in exile meeting first in Paris, then in London. Negotiations for a concordat between the Vatican on the one hand and the Slovak government with its Catholic majority on the other were unsuccessful. When anti-Semitic legislation was forced on Slovakia by the Reich in 1941, Monsignor Tiso managed, at least in part, to soften its impact by threatening to resign. In the Bohemian-Moravian Protectorate, persecution of the Roman Catholic Church was as severe as that of the other faiths—the Czech National Church and the Church of the Friars. But this did not prevent Catholic priests from participating directly in the Resistance. By the end of the war, one-tenth of the clergy had been killed or imprisoned—a notable example was Monsignor Beran, the rector of the great seminary in Prague and the future archbishop.

The Nazis killed 155 priests by execution or torture.

In **Yugoslavia** the **Pavelich** government, supported by several members of the lower clergy, cruelly harassed thousands of Eastern Orthodox Serbs in an attempt to convert them to Roman Catholicism. Reaching its height toward the end of 1941, this persecution subsequently declined due primarily to pressure from the Vatican and from Monsignor Stepinac, archbishop of Zagreb. Hungary and **Rumania**, like Slovakia, maintained diplomatic relations with the Holy See, thus making it possible for the papal nuncios in Slovakia, in Hungary, in Rumania and in Istanbul to continue saving the lives of one million Jews together with the aid of Pinchas Lapid and humanitarian organizations.

The Protestant Churches

Germany

With congregations totaling some 43 million persons, the Protestant churches were much more subject to domination by the Nazi state than the Catholic ecclesiastics, thanks primarily to the extraterritorial protection extended by the Vatican. Fragmented into 28 autonomous sects, with no central authority, the Protestants were vulnerable to political manipulation. They were helpless in other ways as well. On the one hand, their church was rooted in nationalism and the Teutonic tradition; on the other, they adhered to a liberal theology that accentuated the contributions of Luther and the Reformation to the cultural life of Germany more than its Christian universality. It was on such soil that the slogan of "positive Christianity" could flourish. A minority of Protestants—a majority only in the Thuringian Church—believed that they could exploit Nazism to the benefit of Protestantism. These *Deutsche Christen* (German Christians) succeeded in getting appointments for their members to government posts and in some local churches. But with the introduction of racial laws into the church in July 1933, there was growing opposition to the state under the leadership of Pastor Niemoeller. At first sympathetic to the national revolution, Niemoeller founded the pastors' defense organization known as the *Pfarrernotbund* in September 1933. Theological resistance also crystallized around Professor Karl Barth of Bonn. With Niemoeller's blessing a special synod was convoked at Barmen in the Rhineland toward the end of May 1934. Under the inspiration of Barth, the synod vigorously reaffirmed the spiritual nature of the church, vertical by grace and revelation, as opposed to the racial and horizontal philosophy of the *Deutsche Christen*: "We repudiate the fictitious doctrine that the church must preach to its faithful of events, powers, entities and truths other than those vouchsafed to us by the revelation of God."

The Barmen synod refused to envisage the church as a vassal to the state. This reaffirmation of the Spiritual Church was the outcome of a real schism within the evangelical faith. The "church intact" had come into being in contrast to the "church destroyed" or the "German Christians." But the Spiritual Church stood apart from the "church intact." It constituted itself a true church with a synod, a synodal president and annual meetings; it collected assessments from its members and founded several seminaries that taught the principles of the Barmen synod. The young professor **Dietrich Bonhoeffer** was its most celebrated teacher. But the ever increasing weight of the Nazi dictatorship gradually forced the Spiritual Church's parishioners to go underground. Unfortunately, the internal disputes that divided the Lutheran from the Reformed Church as well as differences of opinion between the radicals and the moderates who tended to side with the traditional hierarchy weakened the Spiritual Church. When the war broke out, this church was gasping its last.

Meanwhile, however, the Spiritual Church was not primarily a political opponent of the Reich. Its opposition was the same as that of the traditional church—resentment toward the nationalist or racist concepts of the state which threatened its congregation. Most of its members hoped to reconcile their religious faith with their confidence in the political regime. To them it sufficed to cling to their spiritual terrain and hold out against the neo-pagan assaults. Yet even for the staunchest churchmen the lure of patriotism proved too strong. When the war broke out, Martin Niemoeller, interned in a concentration camp since 1937, volunteered for military service.

But if the Spiritual Church did not preach revolution, some of its members never relinquished the idea of political rearmament against Nazism. This, at least, was true of Bonhoeffer. Working under extremely difficult conditions, he succeeded in developing a highly original theological synthesis—a secular interpretation of a biblical approach to the modern world. He rebelled against the doctrine of Christianity apart from temporal responsibility and paying for it with complete secularization; he strove for a temporal theology to defend his church against the evils of the Third Reich.

Bonhoeffer was arrested in 1943. Apparently, he had no part in the assassination attempt of July 20, 1944 against Hitler, although he probably would have given it his ardent support.

The religious element played an important part in that attempt, even among the plotters who had abandoned religious practices. Most of those involved were descendants of the old German aristocracy or of wealthy middle-class Prussians; there were few Catholics among them. These men, who were desperate, felt completely abandoned by their churches and had no spiritual drive other than their individual conscience before God.

The Grueber Bureau, central to Berlin and with 20 branches throughout Germany, was an important organization that strove to help those who were being persecuted because of their race. It was founded under the sponsorship of the "Provisional Leadership of the Evangelical Church. Its leaders were captured and put into concentration camps. Grueber was imprisoned in 1940.

The Nazi program of euthanasia for the mentally afflicted was bitterly fought by Protestant circles, even by those who were out of touch with the church. The objections of Bishop Wurm of Wurtemberg, privately voiced in 1941, did meet with some success.

With the growing intensity of the war, interference with the regular activities of the church increased accordingly. Only the courage of the laity and the introduction of female vicars kept the clergy from disappearing completely during the final years of hostilities.

One sect that steadfastly endured the open persecution of the Nazis was Jehovah's Witnesses. In the concentration camps they had the privilege of having a triangular symbol; their firm refusal to enter military service and their patient expectation of the return of the Messiah were inspiring.

It should be stressed that the Spiritual Church was not the church of the masses. It was an elite society, especially for the youth who scorned liberal theology. Even though after the war was over, many of its members became eminent in Germany's political life—for example, Pastor Eugen Gerstenmaier, president of the Bundestag from 1954 to 1969—the fact remains that during the Nazi period the Spiritual Church almost vanished from view, and as the war progressed, it diminished in significance. At the very most, 10 percent of German pastors sympathized with it, and few of its adherents—intellectuals for the most part— were sincere churchgoers. In general, German Protestantism, because of its nationalist tradition and its less restrictive theology, had fewer qualms about collaborating with the regime than did the Catholic Church, whose international allegiance from the beginning kept it hostile to Nazism.

Perhaps the most serious moral shortcoming of the churches was their attitude toward the treatment of the Jews. In the postwar debates, frequent references were made to the "silence" of Pope Pius XII. Nevertheless, the local and regional churches bear primary responsibility for the betrayal of their Jewish fellow citizens. From the very beginning the reactions of the ecclesiastical authorities in both churches were feeble; the president of the Episcopal Conference of Germany and the president of the Protestant Confederation avoided pleas, in April 1933, to launch an official protest against discrimination aimed at Jews. While fear and political opportunism ruled on the Catholic side, the Protestants for their part believed in the right of the state to carry out such measures. Consequently, it was hardly surprising that the churches remained mute when in 1935 odious restrictions were imposed on the Jews and in 1938 all bounds on open persecution were loosed (see **Anti-Semitism**).

This abdication of Christian duty can only be understood in the context of history, when medieval anti-Semitism was raised to a higher pitch by Martin Luther's Reformation and still higher by the chauvinist mystical literature of the 19th century. Besides, the distinction between "religious" and "racial" anti-Semitism was so blurred as to be nonexistent. The warnings of a few reputable theologians against anti-Semitism as well as the appeals for moderation made by the Christian political parties of the center never had enough strength to halt the growth of secular hatred of the Jew. Similar observations could be made about the countries the Germans occupied, although there the common fate awaiting both Jew and Christian modified the traditional antagonism between them.

The Ecumenical Council

The international repercussions of the Nazi attacks on the church that led to the constitution of the Spiritual Church aroused an enormous emotional response. The sympathy it evoked in Switzerland, in England and in the United States was at once translated into expressions of comradeship with German Protestants. Furthermore, the events in Germany brought about a closer regrouping of the Protestant communities in the Ecumenical Council of the churches. This was a program established in Utrecht in 1938 although, because of the war, agreement on its execution was deferred until 1948. It was Bonhoeffer again who was instrumental in binding German Protestants to those abroad, although he was aided in this task by his personal friendship with English and American communicants. Anglican Bishop Bell of Chichester spoke out courageously against bombardment of German cities during the war and attempted unsuccessfully to obtain British sympathy for German dissidents. Until he was interned in 1942, Bishop **Berggrav** of Oslo headed the ecclesiastical opposition to the occupying Germans. A secretariat to aid refugees, established first in London in 1939 and then in Switzerland, was active in finding asylum for victims of racial persecution.

For French Protestants, the problem took on a different aspect. As a minority—800,000 out of 42 million—they were devoted to the principle of separation of church and state. They were therefore less susceptible to the blandishments of Vichy, which was bound to the Catholic Church. The Huguenots also suspected a resurgence of "clericalism"; Pastor Boegner, president of the Protestant Federation of France and one of the vice-presidents of the Ecumenical Council, believed that behind the Vichy facade in 1940-43 lurked an anti-Protestant movement. He did, however, agree to represent the Huguenots first at Vichy and then in Paris from July 1940 to March 1943, an opportunity he took advantage of to write letters of protest against racial persecution and to request intervention in favor of the persecuted—letters of March 26, 1941 to the grand rabbi of France; of June 27 and August 20 to Petain; and of August 27, 1943 to Laval. On September 22, 1942 the National Council of the Reformed Church denounced persecution of the Jews in a message to its congregations that was read from practically every Protestant pulpit. On the whole, the Protestant churches acted in a less fragmented fashion than the Catholic Church did, even though at the beginning they maintained a prudent reserve. Nor did they fail to render active assistance. Isolated at first, they quickly organized, especially in the south of France. The CIMADE—the acronym for *Comite inter-mouvements aupres des evacues*—formed by youth movements, was founded initially to help occupied Alsace-Lorraine; beginning with the fall of 1940, they devoted themselves to helping non-Aryan refugees. After the Germans extended their occupation to the southern zone of France, they continued their operations more discreetly.

Summary

The Catholic Church, the preferred target of the Nazi attack, was better prepared than the Protestants to ward off the attack. Although it was in a superior position (because of its authoritarian structure) to protect the German masses against contamination by Nazi doctrine, it was less capable of formulating a theology of political action. Protestantism, on the other hand, its doctrinal essence wounded by the Nazi heresy, was regenerated in its struggle for the "true faith" by its elite—i.e., by the solace of the Spiritual Church.

The true reflection of the churches' attitude, however, is not to be found in their "silence" but rather in their behavior within the confines of the totalitarian regime. The documentation available to us is insufficient to reveal their basic motives. Certainly, if they were cowardly, it was both individual and collective, tacit and founded perhaps on opportunistic and naive conformism. But many people were driven by their religious convictions to oppose Nazism. A renowned historian, H. Rothfels, wrote that the resistance of the churches alone had the power to achieve visible success because they "defended themselves on their own territory and lent to the active forms of the Resistance movement an urgency and strength no external revolution could have provided."

V. Conzemius

CHURCHILL, Sir Winston (Leonard Spencer) (1874-1965).

Churchill, a British war hero, was born November 30, 1874 at Blenheim Palace, the Oxfordshire home of his grandfather, the seventh duke of Marlborough. His father, who became insane, died in 1895; his mother, daughter of a New York financier, lived until 1921. Churchill never forgot the grandeur of his family and believed that his life's work was to lead free men.

He had a short career, from 1895 to 1899, as a hussar subaltern, seeing service in northwestern **India** and the Sudan. As a war correspondent in **South Africa** in 1899, Churchill was taken prisoner and escaped. He then entered politics, where he rose rapidly. By 1911 he was first lord of the admiralty and had completed renovation of the fleet, which entered World War I the strongest in the world. Churchill sponsored the Gallipoli expedition of 1915, a strategically sound concept that was ineptly handled by others. Forced to resign, he commanded an infantry battalion on the Western Front in 1916. Churchill returned to politics as minister of munitions from 1917 to 1919, war secretary from 1919 to 1921 and colonial secretary from 1921 to 1922, signing the Anglo-Irish treaty in December 1921. He was the principal proponent of armed British intervention in Russia from 1918 to 1920 and a vehement anti-Bolshevik.

After a short period out of office and Parliament, Churchill became chancellor of the exchequer in 1924, helped suppress the general strike of 1926 and saw the Grand Fleet broken up. From 1929 to 1939 he was again out of office and out of favor; he wrote a biography of his ancestor the great duke of Marlborough, opposed any increase in Indian self-government and warned of the danger of Nazism to those who did not want to hear.

In September 1939 he returned to the admiralty and electrified the navy with his energy. He defended **Chamberlain** in the debate on **Norway** and was called to replace him as prime minister on May 10, 1940. Churchill quickly formed an all-party coalition, embracing almost all of Parliament and with virtually unanimous support throughout the country. The hour and the man had found each other. As the agonies of the battles of France and the **United Kingdom** gave way to the long-drawn out task of rearmament and reconquest, Churchill's popularity waned a little, particularly among politicians; his temper was often as short as his hours were long, and he was not an easy man to work under. Militarily, he was well served by Sir **Hastings Lionel Ismay**, Sir **Ian Jacob** and a devoted secretarial staff; personally, he was lovingly cared for by his wife, nee Clementine Hozier (later Lady Spencer Churchill), whom he had married in 1908. Two of their four children saw active service, a son with the **Special Operations Executive** in **Yugoslavia** and a daughter with an antiaircraft unit in London.

Churchill's health was sometimes uncertain, and all his life he experienced fits of black depression. He had some close friendships that aroused controversy, then and later, for example, with Lord **Beaverbrook** and with **Frederick Lindemann**, who provided him with statistics. Neither was much loved elsewhere. Extreme conservatives mistrusted him as a renegade, and left-wingers as a tory. But he had, particularly during his first six months in office, tremendous popular support, and no conceivable wartime rival was ever in sight. Churchill never bore malice; he was sustained by a generous spirit, a strong heart and an abiding faith in victory.

Churchill was greatly gifted as an orator; his broadcasts did much to sustain **morale** in Britain and helped stimulate **resistance** in Western Europe. In one of them, on June 22, 1941, he publicly abandoned his anti-bolshevism and welcomed **Stalin** as an ally against **Hitler**. With **Roosevelt** he had a much closer and warmer friendship, but he was never able to bend American **strategy** to suit British interests. Churchill's personal foibles had little impact on British strategy. He met the chiefs of staff in committee daily when he was in London and was in frequent touch with them when he was away; whenever they differed on a professional point and the chiefs stood up to him, he gave way. Usually they all saw eye to eye.

Churchill was frequently abroad (see **Conferences, Allied**), or touring war factories, bomb-damaged cities or troops in training. He believed that one of his main tasks was the need to sustain the nation's will to fight, and another the need to keep the civil service on its toes. He hated bureaucratic sloth and did all he could to root it out of the government in the interests of the common man.

As a war leader, he had one cardinal advantage: he was always ready to act and believed that inaction is (as a rule) a commander's greatest mistake. He was a virtual dictator of the Roman type, charged by the country with saving it in the moment of peril, and

ready to lay down his charge when he had carried it through.

When the war with **Germany** was over and Churchill called a general election in July 1945, the electorate turned its back on him and gave a large majority to the Labor Party under the meticulous **Clement Attlee**. Churchill led the opposition from 1946 to 1951. He became prime minister again, although with a small Conservative majority and while in declining health, from 1951 to 1955. He was made a Knight of the Garter in 1953 and died on January 24, 1965.

M. R. D. Foot

CIANO, Galeazzo (1903-1944).
Ciano was **Mussolini**'s grandson. As minister of foreign affairs from June 1936 to February 1943, he was at first in favor of the Rome-Berlin **Axis** but later changed his mind and attempted vainly to keep **Italy** out of the war. He joined with the Grand Fascist Council in its motion against Mussolini of July 24, 1943. He was condemned to death in Verona by the Special Tribune of the Republic of Salo and was executed in that city in January 1944.

CICERO.
"Cicero" was the Germans' code name for Elyesa Bazna (?-1970), an Albanian who was a valet for the British ambassador in Ankara in 1942-44. Cicero stole his employer's keys and sold deciphered telegrams from the ambassador's safe for £300,000, paid in forged £5 notes. This apparently spectacular success was mishandled in Berlin: **Ribbentrop** and **Kaltenbrunner** quarreled about which of them was to lay the important intelligence gained before **Hitler** for so long that the material was rendered out of date by the **Normandy landing**.

CIRCLE OF KREISAU.
See *Kreisauer Kreis*.

CIVIL DEFENSE.
To meet the growing threat that air power posed, numerous measures were taken by the **United Kingdom**, France, **the Netherlands, Belgium, Greece, Yugoslavia**, the **USSR** and **Germany**, as well as other countries, to protect the lives, health and property of their people and the security of their industries and vital institutions. Civil defense encompassed all measures to be taken in the event of an air attack. Civil defense officials were responsible for controlling the movements of the civilian population and ensuring the proper operation of air-raid alert systems. Some of the essential services handled by the civil defense programs were the air-raid warning systems, safety and

assistance programs (firefighting, clearing of rubble, elimination of toxic material, public health etc.) and the protection of industrial centers as well as personnel. Working in close cooperation with the air-raid alert networks, the national civil defense systems helped save many lives and cultural treasures during the war.

H. A. Jacobsen

CLARK, Mark Wayne (1896-   ).

American general. Clark arrived secretly in Algeria by submarine in October 1942 to prepare for the Allied landing. In 1943-44 he was commander of the U.S. Fifth Army, which succeeded in liberating Rome. From December 1944 until the Allied victory in April 1945, he commanded the 15th Army Group in Italy.

CLASER, Charles (1901-1944).

Claser was a Belgian commander and the founder of the Belgian Legion, which sought to undermine the Nazis by sabotage, to organize teams to attack the enemy at times determined by the Allied command, to maintain order and to keep intact national institutions in preparation for the Germans' eventual departure. This organization merged in 1941 with a similar one created by Col. Robert Lentz to become the core of a new group known as the AS (see Jules Pire). Other directors of the legion at that time were A. Boereboom and Charles Van der Putten, who were arrested in 1942, as well as Jules Bastin, who commanded the mobile reserve. In 1942 Claser traveled to London to consult the Belgian government in exile, which received him icily. Claser was, however, warmly welcomed by the Special Operations Executive and obtained its promise to assist him. Claser was arrested by the Nazis in December 1942 and died in Gross-Rosen on December 12, 1944.

CLNAI.

See Comitato di Liberazione nazionale dell'Alta Italia.

CLOSTERMANN, Pierre (1921-   ).

Clostermann was an ace war pilot in France. He joined the Royal Air Force in 1940 and shot down 33 enemy aircraft before the war's end.

CNR.

See Conseil national de la resistance.

COBELLIGERENCY.

A term used to describe cooperation between two or more states in making war jointly on others that is less full or formal than an alliance.

Italy was allied with Germany by the Pact of Steel, which formed the Axis, but broke away in September 1943, made a temporary peace with the United Kingdom and the United States, and joined both in levying war against Germany as a cobelligerent, not as a full ally.

Finland and Germany were cobelligerents against the USSR; so were Hungary and Germany, but the Finns and the Hungarians hardly regarded themselves as cobelligerents.

The USSR was nominally allied with Britain, but the British found themselves treated more as cobelligerents than as allies; they were not informed of many secret Soviet plans nor of any Soviet intelligence, but were expected to expend their utmost efforts in helping the USSR to defeat Germany (see Second Front).

The U.S. was practically a cobelligerent of Britain by mid-1941, well before Pearl Harbor made it a full combatant: American and British scientists and intelligence officers exchanged plenty of secret information, J. Edgar Hoover cooperated with Sir William S. Stephenson in suppressing Axis agents in the U.S. and USN antisubmarine patrols were active in the western Atlantic. The relationship was sometimes referred to as a "common-law alliance."

M. R. D. Foot

COBRA.

"Cobra" was the code name of an operation launched July 25, 1944 by the U.S. First Army, under the command of Bradley and guided by the orders of Montgomery. It was aimed at smashing the German lines in France between Caumont and the sea in an offensive directed toward Avranches.

COCHRANE, Sir Ralph (Alexander) (1895-   ).

Cochrane, a British airman, was the chief of the British air staff in New Zealand from 1936 to 1939. As commander of the Third and Fifth Bomber Groups of the Royal Air Force from 1942 to 1945, he showed unusual qualities of enterprise and leadership.

COLLABORATION.

In Hitler's New European Order and the Japanese Greater East Asia Co-Prosperity Sphere, some satellite governments and a number of more or less important inhabitants of the occupied countries collaborated with the occupying forces—i.e., they aided the operation of the Axis war machine or its oppressive administration. This collaboration took various forms—political, military and economic,

Political Collaboration

In the countries they occupied, the Germans appealed to those sympathetic with the Nazi cause for ideological or racial reasons to assist them in their task. The sympathizers were often *Volksdeutsche*, people of German descent who lived outside the Reich. Because they often felt ill-treated by the ethnic majorities in their adopted nations, they frequently constituted a **fifth column** for the *Wehrmacht*.

These *Volksdeutsche* often received Hitler's recognition for their contributions to his cause. Except for **Hungary**, where the National League of Germans, headed by Franz Basch, never succeeded in receiving from the government the special status it sought, practically every state occupied by the Germans—notably, Slovakia, **Croatia** and **Rumania**—granted them some measure of autonomy. In Rumania the German minority in Transylvania obtained from **Ion Antonescu** a statute guaranteeing the Germans in that country the right to make their own laws. In Croatia and Slovakia the *Volksdeutsche* in effect governed themselves. In Bratislava they were represented in the ministry by a secretary of state, and the taxes they paid were used directly for their benefit.

In most cases the nationals of the occupied countries volunteered to help the Germans out of either enthusiasm for the Nazi ideology or self-interest. Some of them joined militant fascist groups, which were often subsidized by **Italy** or **Germany** (*Francisme*, the *Parti populaire français*, or *Cagoule* in France; *Rexisme* in **Belgium**; the *Nasjonal Samling* in **Norway**). For others, **anti-Semitism** or **anti-communism** was sufficient to bring them into the fascist ranks. The syndicalists allowed themselves to be taken in by the Nazis' social achievements, while writers and artists in France and other nations were carried away by the ardor of the German youth and their belief in "action." The aesthetes of Europe were drawn to Nazism for various reasons: the fascination that National Socialism held for Alphonse de Chateaubriant in his travels through Germany in 1935; **Robert Brasillach**'s taste for "romantic fascism"; Drieu La Rochelle's admiration for the virility of the Nazi man and his yearning for a united continent.

Difficult as it is to obtain a full count of those sympathetic to collaboration, the number of direct participants in the movement can easily be found. In general, only a small minority of those in occupied or satellite countries were collaborators: In France, at the beginning of 1941, the *Parti populaire français* (PPF) had 6,000 members, and the *Rassemblement national populaire* (RNP) had 20,000. In Belgium, at an unspecified point in the war, there were 20,000 members, including women and children, in *Rex* and 50,000 in *Vlaams Nationaal Verbond* (VNV). In the

Netherlands the *Nationaal socialistische Beweging* (NSB) had 30,000-50,000 members at the beginning of the occupation and 100,000 in July 1943.

The membership of these organizations melted away as the eventual defeat of the *Wehrmacht* became more likely. The opportunists in western Europe were the first to go. They had been recruited principally from among the petty bourgeois who saw in fascism "the champion of an order founded on respect for private property," from the *Lumpenproletariat*—the culturally and economically deprived—and, to a lesser degree, from the wealthy class. Aping Nazism in its parades, its uniforms and colored shirts, its ceremonies, hierarchy, symbology, and general claptrap, these "national" movements adopted the same methods of indoctrination, the same enemies to seek out and destroy, the same snarling hatred. Hitler improvised his attitude toward these groups, depending on whether they were Teutonic or not and whether the reins of government were in their hands or others'.

The attitudes of the populace in the various German-occupied countries also differed. As early as August 1943, faced with extended strikes and **sabotage**, the Germans lost confidence in the little knot of Nazis in **Denmark** and put an end to the facade of independence they had used to mask their occupation of that country. It was not the same in Norway and the Netherlands. In Oslo the head of the local Nazi party was **Quisling**, who had a following of 25,000 -35,000 in 1939. Having put together a government on the first day of the German invasion (April 9, 1940), he vainly attempted to persuade the king to return to his capital. The Germans failed to offer him any sympathy; they replaced him on April 15 with an administrative council that turned out to be less submissive than they had hoped for. But the *Nasjonal Samling* was in the majority, and it furnished cadres of collaborators and even identified itself with the **Nazi Party** in Germany. Returning to power in February 1942, Quisling sought not only to introduce the corporate state into Norway but also to encourage indoctrination with the Nazi credo by the educational system and the church. He met with such furious resistance that the occupation authorities took matters into their own hands in 1944. Ignored by Norwegians and Germans alike, torn by dissension between moderates and zealots who wanted immediate integration into the Greater Reich, the Norwegian collaborators lost all influence. Quisling and some of his henchmen were tried and executed after the war.

Anton Mussert in the Netherlands also hoped that his party, the NSB, would be called upon to play an important part in the German occupation. With the support of Hitler, whom he had met in 1936, he dreamed of heading a vast country stretching to the north of France. Nor was the NSB the only movement in 1940 supporting *Reichskommissar* **Seyss-Inquart**; the National Socialist Party of Dutch Labor and the National Fascist Front, both founded before 1940, also clamored for Hitler's attention. But in spite of several interviews with the Fuehrer between September 1940 and December 1943, Mussert obtained nothing of any importance. At the end of 1942 he was granted the title of Leader of the Dutch People and the right to appoint a secretariat of state charged with informing the *Reichskommissariat* of the execution of the principal governmental measures, but his NSB languished because of inner dissension concerning the **SS**. In the last few months of the occupation, the party underwent almost complete dismemberment. It was entrusted only with arresting Dutch Jews.

As in the Netherlands, the Germans governed Belgium with the aid of highly placed bureaucrats who remained at their posts. (King **Leopold III** considered himself a prisoner and refused to exercise his prerogatives.) The occupying forces exploited the fascist groups already in existence that had, since the 1930s, in turn exploited the rivalry between Flemings and Walloons (the VNV of Staf De Clercq on one side and the *Rex* of **Leon Degrelle** on the other). The VNV, which had since June 1940 enjoyed the financial support of the Germans, avowed its support for, and especially its consanguinity with, the invaders. And, as in Norway and the Netherlands, there was an extremist splinter group considering itself absolutely and unconditionally Teutonic, Jef van de Wiele and his De Vlag. As for *Rex*, while reiterating in 1940 its "pride in being Belgian," it fawned on the Germans even to proclaiming, four years later, its oneness with the German people "by blood and soil." In the meantime, on May 10, 1940 the military administration moved for an accord between itself and the VNV; under the pretext of ending their rivalry, it forced *Rex* to restrict its activities to the French regions of the country. *Rex Flandre* was absorbed by the VNV. This action alarmed the moderate collaborators who still hoped for national independence but underlined the insistence of the Reich on putting its confidence or its money into only those movements (*Parti populaire wallon, Cercle wallon, De Vlag*) that enabled it to win over the population while making as few concessions as possible.

Collaboration in France took on another hue. While Petain, supported primarily by **Laval** and **Darlan**, imposed a reactionary, semifascist regime on the unoccupied southern zone of France while collaborating with the Germans in his foreign policy, activists in the occupied zone exhibited open admiration for Nazism. Some of these activists crossed the line be-

tween the two zones even before it was erased in November 1942. There were at least seven such collaborationist groups, three of them born even before the war began: the PPF, led by **Jacques Doriot**; *Francisme;* and the *Parti national collectiviste*, led by Pierre Clementi. The other four made their appearance under the tenure of the German ambassador **Otto Abetz** in 1940-41. In addition to the noisy little cliques aping the Nazis—the *Front franc* of Jean Boissel and the *Ligue francaise* of Pierre Constantini—two movements of significant importance were created: the *Mouvement social revolutionnaire* (MSR), founded by a former Cagoulard, Eugene Deloncle, and especially the RNP of **Marcel Deat**, political director of the newspaper *L'Oeuvre*, who supported Laval before his return to power in April 1942 and continued to support him until the beginning of 1943. Thanks to German subsidies, these parties published organs in Paris. The PPF had two dailies, *Le Petit Parisien* and *Le Cri du peuple*, in addition to its journal for the southern French zone, *L'Emancipation nationale*. *L'Oeuvre, La France socialiste* and *Les Nouveaux Temps* were the leftist journals, as was, at least in its beginnings, the nonconformist *Aujourd'hui*. The weekly *Je suis partout*, which reappeared in February 1941, took the fascist line under the leadership of such men as Charles Lesca, Alain Laubreaux and particularly Brasillach, who left it in October 1943. The Germans used these journals to corrupt public opinion just as they used the independence movements in Brittany and Flanders to erode a country's unity and prepare it for eventual annexation.

Splintered by doctrinal or personal disputes, these movements were incapable of unifying. They were useful to the Germans for intimidating the French authorities when the Vichy government showed signs of independence. In 1942 they considered making Doriot *Gauleiter* when they lost confidence in Laval. It was not until the end of 1943, however, that collaboration "ultras" like **Darnand**, head of the *Milice* (see below), and the journalists Philippe Henriot and Marcel Deat became ministers of the Vichy rump government.

In a precautionary move before advancing with Italian troops on **Egypt** and the Suez Canal, the Nazis consulted the Grand Mufti of Jerusalem, Haj Amin el-Husseini, who had fled to Berlin after the failure of **Rashid Ali**'s revolt in **Iraq**. Recognizing the Grand Mufti as the head of the future Palestinian state, the Nazis awarded him the right to deal with the "Jewish problem" in the Middle East as they had in Europe. The British victory at **El Alamein**, however, made that project impossible, so the Mufti was forced to do battle with the British and Jews through the microphones of Radio Berlin.

The Germans used different methods in eastern and central Europe, depending on local circumstances and the credulity of the conquered. In the intoxication of his first victories on the Russian front, Hitler favored the purely colonial approach and even refused to abolish the collective farms, which might have won the Russian peasants over to the German cause.

The Fuehrer did permit at least the appearance of self-government in the protectorate of **Bohemia-Moravia** and two other states whose birth he had done so much to foster, Slovakia and Croatia. But there, too, Hitler's authority was final. Since March 1939 the government in Prague had been at least nominally Czech. It was also docile. On the pretext, however, that this administration was sympathetic to the Czech government in exile at London, the Germans installed a new ruling body with a cabinet that was composed of local Nazis plus a native of Germany.

In Slovakia, where Monsignor **Yosef Tiso**'s regime had been reorganized in accordance with the *Fuehrer prinzip* at the end of August 1940, Hitler supported devoted Slovakian Nazis—particularly Tuka, the prime minister and minister of foreign affairs, who organized the only legal party in the country on the Nazi model and used it for spreading Nazi propaganda. Although Tiso consolidated his power at the expense of certain Nazi partisans in 1943, he continued to discharge faithfully his responsibilities to his German masters.

The *poglavnik,* or prime minister, of Croatia, **Ante Pavelich**, was no less diligent a follower of the Germans, whose gangster methods he used against the Serbians of the Orthodox Church as well as the gypsy and Jewish minorities in his country. He opened two **concentration camps** in which the prisoners were periodically slaughtered. The murderous zeal of the fanatical **Ustachis**, who controlled the government, was such that even the occupying forces became uneasy about it and finally halted it in 1942. Nevertheless, the Fuehrer continued to support Pavelich and, to the great dismay of **Mussolini**, Croatia's protector, lent a sympathetic ear to the local leaders who played the Germans against the Italians.

In three other satellite states—Rumania, Hungary and **Bulgaria**—the Germans depended on less embarrassing collaborators. They had fascist parties in Bucharest and Budapest that were completely devoted to the Nazi creed but kept those of Hungary in the background, using them only when absolutely necessary. The "Iron Guard" fascists of Rumania, led by **Horia Sima**, reached their peak strength in the summer of 1940 after Hitler's successes in western Europe—some of the party's chiefs were in the Antonescu cabinet—but lost influence after the failure of the "Legionnaires' rebellion" of January 21-23, 1941.

While Horia Sima remained "in storage" in Germany, the Nazis relied on the *conducator*, Antonescu, whose regime displayed most of the fascist stigmata. He demonstrated his submissiveness by calling for "German technicians" for police and propaganda work and adjusting his foreign policy in accord with that of the Reich until August 23, 1944.

The same was true in Hungary, where the "Arrow Cross" party of Ferenc Szalasi—which was subsidized by Adm. **Miklos von Horthy**—was temporarily sidetracked while the government of the extreme right humbly carried out the Reich's foreign policy by contributing to the war on the Russian front and its domestic policy by deporting Jews. In October 1944, when Horthy requested an armistice with the Allies, the Germans, who had occupied the country since March, played their Arrow Cross card. But this party's government disappeared together with its sordid history of terror and assassinations when the Russians invaded on April 4, 1945. In the Bulgaria of **Boris III**, another puppet dictatorship, Hitler contented himself with the collaboration of rightist governments that tried, before and after the suspicious death of the king in Germany on August 28, 1943, to imitate the Nazi regime and to associate itself with the anti-**Comintern** policy. But this collaboration evoked popular resentment that the Germans could not break because they had no substitute policy and because they were otherwise occupied. Matters continued in this uncertain fashion until the collaborators were overthrown in the revolution of September 1944.

On the other side of the world, the Japanese pursued two courses—to purge the liberated territories of Western influence and to impose on them a "new order" corresponding to their original national characters (see **New Order in East Asia**). Regardless of the fate they had in mind for them, whether annexation or limited independence, the occupying forces depended on cadres of the indigenous youth, formed in Japan and free of white influence. For these young people, aid to the Japanese forces meant cooperation with fellow Asians in a struggle against Western colonialism. Nor did the Japanese hesitate to use dignitaries of the Buddhist religion to further their imperialist aims. But the Japanese superiority complex prevented them from offering responsible posts to the natives of the conquered territories, whom they angered by their arrogance. In **Burma**, for example, the nationalist leader Ba Maw' protested to Tokyo about the attitude of the Japanese military. The occupying forces could not depend on assistance in former Chinese colonies or from communists; in **Indochina, Ho Chi Minh** was as much opposed to Japanese neocolonialism as he was to the older French version.

In Indochina, particularly, the Japanese sought to

consolidate their position by every means at their disposal. In June 1943 they sent priests to Tonkin who, under the pretext of unifying Buddhist sects, launched intensive racial and xenophobic propaganda. They did the same in Cambodia, where, a short time afterward, the local clergy began an anti-French political and religious movement. A similar group appeared in Burma; known as the *Wunthann*, it proselytized among the wealthy and gained many supporters during the occupation. In **Malaya** young aristocrats from plantation and mine-owning families, educated in Cairo or Mecca, had formed, in 1940, a "Malay Union" demanding radical reforms from the British. Warmly welcoming the Japanese, they were rewarded with the responsibility of creating a national youth movement.

Such organizations, which were modeled on the Japanese Association for the National Service and had demonstrated their value in Manchukuo and in northern **China**, also sprang up in the **Philippines** and in the Dutch East Indies. In the Philippine Islands, which in October 1943 was made a puppet republic, the Japanese instituted an Association for Service to the New Philippines (*Kalibapi*) with the aim of uniting adult citizens, designed for "continuous collaboration with the Japanese Empire." Despite the best efforts of the occupation authorities, who pressured the local bureaucrats to join and approved the distribution of cigarettes and cotton goods to participants, the *Kalibapi* never enlisted more than three percent of the country's population.

In the Dutch East Indies the communities were regrouped into two rival organizations: the Islamic Federation, which was the more important, and the *Putera*, consisting of small nationalist and non-Islamic groups. "Divide and rule" was a favorite Japanese tactic. For the purpose of furthering the war effort, however, the two groups were finally welded into the *Djawa Hoko Kwai*, a multiracial unit controlled by the occupation authorities. Its achievements were negligible, especially since the Indonesians, like the Filipinos, anticipated independence after the war. In 1943 they were permitted to participate in the occupation government; **Sukarno** later presided over the Central Consultative Council. This apparently tended to encourage nationalism. The Japanese consequently preferred to rely for support on traditional Islamic groups. In January 1944 the Moslem alliance *Masjumi* was formed; it extended over all of Indonesia, which accepted protectorate status. Still, on the eve of its defeat, Japan was obliged to reconcile with the nationalists, who had taken control of all mass organizations, in order to prevent internal as well as external opposition.

Before occupying the British Indies, on the other hand, the Japanese had made certain they had the support of **Subhas Chandra Bose**, head of the anti-British progressives in **India**, who had in 1941 fled his own country and taken refuge in **Singapore**, where he had assembled a government in exile.

Military Collaboration

Chandra Bose organized a pro-Japanese army with a handful of Indian soldiers and officers who had been taken prisoner in Singapore, in February 1942. On the whole, however, the Japanese preferred to ignore supplemental troops of indigenous origin. The only other exception was the Indonesian *Peta*, organized in February 1943, which had the relatively minor function of providing garrison service to replace occupation troops sent to the front.

The Germans, on the contrary, largely relied upon the collaborators to do the dirty work of the occupation—assassinations, raids on political miscreants and the like. In Paris about 300 PPF members arrested Jews, beginning on July 16, 1942. In Norway the elite guard *Hird* participated in a number of police operations. Special tribunals were created to prosecute political dissidents in some of the occupied countries, such as the People's Tribunal in Oslo, the Special Section of the Court of Appeals in Paris and the *Milice française*.

Collaborators under the direction of **Himmler** recruited volunteers to fight in the ranks of the *Wehrmacht*. After 1940, first some of the "Germanic peoples"—Norwegians, Dutch and Flemings—and, later, in 1943 and particularly in 1944, other nationalities, contributed to the *Waffen*-SS. Some 2,000 Frenchmen entered the Seventh SS *Sturmbrigade*. The war on the Soviet Union enlisted the active participation of large numbers of anti-Bolshevik volunteers. More fortunate than Mussert, whose offer of 300,000 Dutch soldiers to fight in the **USSR** was declined by a suspicious Hitler, De Clercq and Degrelle in Belgium took command of a Legion of Flemings and a Legion of Walloons; Doriot participated extensively in the fighting of the **Legion des volontaires francais contre le bolchevisme** (LVF), an organization his party helped found. The *Phalange africaine*, which fought the Allies in Tunisia in 1943, comprised 300 men, half of them natives; all took the oath of allegiance to Hitler and fought in German uniforms. Frenchmen enlisted, at the rate of several thousand per unit, in the *Schutzkommandos* of the Todt Organization, where they trained workers for the NSKK (the National Socialist Motorized Corps); the *Kriegsmarine*, as crewmen for minesweepers and torpedo boats; and the *Luftwaffe*.

But it was in their own uniforms that the *Milice*, founded by the Vichy government on January 31,

1943 with Laval at its head, became responsible on December 30, 1943 for the maintenance of order. First limited to the southern zone of France, the *Milice* extended its authority to the northern in mid-January 1944. It contained some 15,000 zealots, young men of well-to-do families who had been won over by Vichy propaganda or ex-convicts let out of prison to join the movement. Among them were hard-core criminals—5,000 in June 1944—notably the *Franc-Garde*, remembered for its infamous attacks on the maquis in **Les Glieres** and Limousin. Bitter enemies of the **Resistance** since its creation, the *Milice* was notorious for its assassinations. Driven into Germany by the liberation of France, they supplied 2,000 young men to the **Charlemagne** Brigade—afterward the Charlemagne Division—formed with what was left of the SS *Sturmbrigade* and some auxiliary groups.

The German officers who credited the creation of a Russian liberation army and the creation of a Russian government in exile with accelerating the desertion rate of Soviet soldiers scored a small triumph with the capture of General of the Army **Andrei Vlasov** on the Leningrad front in July 1942. Vlasov had been military adviser to **Chiang Kai-shek**. After his capture he set up a committee of Russian anti-Stalinists and at the beginning of 1943 proclaimed a 14-point manifesto reestablishing the liberty of the peoples of the USSR, granting to the peasantry individual ownership of the collective farms and instituting political and religious freedom. Vlasov and his aides hoped to form eastern European divisions, under their command, manned by Soviet soldiers who had been captured by the Germans. But their hopes were shattered by the icy silence of **Rosenberg** and the open hostility of Himmler and **Keitel**, who would have liked nothing better than to dispatch Vlasov to a prison camp. In 1943 Hitler was in no mood to countenance a Russian army in the midst of his *Wehrmacht*. Vlasov was kept under guard in a Berlin suburb, made only rare public appearances and was confined to a purely propagandistic function—to encourage the desertion of Russian soldiers. The members of his proposed eastern European divisions at the end of 1943 were sent to the western front, where they were assigned to coastal defense and anti-Resistance activities and where they left bitter memories of massacre, looting and rape. It was not until a German defeat in the east seemed inevitable that Vlasov had his opportunity. He was authorized to create his Committee for the Liberation of the Russian Peoples and was even given command of an army of 50,000. But he was never to lead them into combat. Hitler, who never hesitated to call on the military forces of his collaborators in other conquered countries, felt such repugnance for the Russians that he refused their services even in the Reich's death throes.

Administrative Collaboration

Unquestionably, in Hitler's Europe the administrative personnel in the various countries lent their assistance to the occupying forces. At least one example was furnished by the magistrates in the Special Section of the Paris Court of Appeals, who agreed to try "Communist" leaders. Although the Germans imposed uncomfortable conditions on all administrators in occupied territory, their precise nature varied from country to country. In the Netherlands, where the *Reichskommissar* tolerated a national administration that limited itself to supervision, many bureaucrats judged it best to remain at their posts rather than to risk losing them to more active collaborators. It was the same in Belgium. In France the armistice agreement obliged administrators to execute punctiliously the decisions of the occupation authorities. The German grasp, which tightened in proportion to the docility of the local administration after June 1940, was particularly oppressive in the courts and the police. The German authorities assumed the right to relieve the French tribunals of certain matters that they preferred to handle themselves and increased their surveillance of French justices. The police were frequently used for arresting Communists, "Gaullists" and Jews or for selecting hostages. Were these the marks of true collaboration? Public opinion deemed them so at the time. Yet when purges were discussed after the liberation, that question was difficult to answer. Even today the controversy has continued. Where did passive obedience end and open collusion with the Germans begin?

Economic Collaboration

Of all the forms of collaboration, the economic sort is perhaps the most difficult to detect. Many industrialists insisted that by assenting to German demands they kept their workers employed and thus prevented their deportation to Germany. This seems to hint at undercover bargaining from which the occupation authorities profited either openly or in the **black market**.

In the conquered countries the Germans never lacked for money to pay their collaborators, derived of course from the enormous contributions toward the costs of occupation that they demanded from the French and Belgians, for example. First the contractors in public works who built or expanded airfields and then those involved in the construction of the **Atlantic Wall** realized handsome profits. Participants in these activities were not necessarily large companies; usually they were entrepreneurs who had been only modestly successful before 1939—which is not to say that large industrialists refused to contribute to the war chest of the Third Reich. After German occupation of France, Louis Renault offered a tank factory to the Germans of his own free will—hence the nationalization of his firm once France was liberated. And contracts were signed in September 1940 between *Aluminium Francais* and two companies in Berlin and Dessau for the sale of aluminum and aluminum oxide. The Vichy authorities failed to halt shipments of bauxite directly contracted for between firms in the southern zone of France and German industrialists. Similarly, in late 1940, agreements were signed between large German firms and the *Comptoir des phosphates* and the *Mines de l'Ouenza* for the delivery of raw materials, including iron ore. Large and medium-sized enterprises in Denmark and the Netherlands also negotiated contracts with German organizations.

Hardly a monopoly of northwest Europe, economic collaboration was also practiced in Bulgaria, where domestic producers negotiated agreements with large cartels in the Reich. Thus, the Bulgarian Special Supply Center, an organization of exporters of agricultural machinery, cigarettes, fodder, timber and construction materials, culled enormous profits by supplying German troops stationed in that country. In Slovakia, where the government authorized the exploitation of the land's resources by the great German firms, the property of expelled Czechs and deported Jews became the objects of speculation for profiteers of every kind.

It was to such speculators that the occupation authorities addressed themselves when materials of one sort or another were in short supply. Their method was to nose out and purchase hidden stocks at a price above the going local rate. The black market conducted by the Germans in France was typical. The *Kriegsmarine*, the *Luftwaffe*, the SS and later a counterespionage branch of the **Abwehr** known as Bureau Otto opened a number of purchasing offices in the Paris area. These dealt with a horde of traders—most of whom had long police records—who had managed to acquire some merchandise and wanted to resell it to their German masters. Everything could be sold: leather, metals, tools, machine tools, perfume, drugs, toys, candy. Considerable fortunes were amassed over a three-year period by means of this new form of trade under the protection of German authorities. One such short-order success was Michel Szkolnikoff. Only a moderately successful businessman before 1939, after the occupation he became the "official purchasing agent for the SS." He kept open house in his Paris apartment and in his Chatou villa and owned real estate and business firms in Paris and stores and hotels on the Cote d'Azur. When the Germans closed his purchasing offices in 1943, he retired to **Spain**

with his mistress. Another stateless individual named Joanovici—"Monsieur Joseph" to his intimates—made four billion francs by selling to Bureau Otto scrap and sheet metal, tools and automobile parts given him by "businesswomen." More anonymous traffickers included the Masuy gang and the "Gestapo of the Rue de la Pompe" and the Lafont gang (the "Gestapo of the Rue Lauriston"). Under a pseudocommercial cover, this latter group maintained a staff of the most notorious torture artists in Paris. Their side specialty was large-scale robbery, part of the loot being handed over to the Germans and the remainder—jewels, gold or merchandise—divided among the members and sold to the black marketeers. These "gestapists" were called to account after the liberation, but many of the agents for the German purchasing offices escaped. The industrialists involved in the collaboration were not much more disturbed by the postliberation purges. In France, for example, materials were needed that could not be provided by small enterprises lacking the means or experience for manufacturing them.

Japan could scarcely have waged World War II without the economic resources of Manchukuo, China and Southeast Asia. Japanese industry at the end of the 1930s was not nearly self-sufficient in iron ore, lead, crude oil or tin. Once the **United States** froze trade between the two countries in July 1941, Japan was forced to draw almost all its raw materials from the Greater East Asia Co-Prosperity Sphere. Eventually an Allied blockade snipped the sea links with Southeast Asia and crippled Japan's war output severely.

During the trade wars of the 1930s Japan sent capital, settlers and finished goods into Southeast Asia, threatening the economic position of the Western powers. When Japanese forces moved into northern Indochina in mid-1940, a trade mission soon enticed the French governor-general, Adm. Jean Decoux, into signing agreements that eventually let Japan exploit the rice, rubber, coal and heavy metal ores of Vietnam, Laos and Cambodia. These agreements were possible because Decoux was answerable to the pro-German government at Vichy. Thailand also quickly accepted Tokyo's economic demands in return for a guarantee of military protection of its status as an independent state never colonized by the West.

The Japanese seized the rest of Southeast Asia by force. They expropriated mines, plantations and plants belonging to Americans or Europeans in Burma, the Philippines, Malaya, Singapore and the Dutch East Indies. The Co-Prosperity Sphere operated each country's economy much as the colonial powers had, relying on Chinese and Indian traders to circulate consumer goods and on local cultivators to maintain farm output. But war damage, a scarcity of Japanese technicians and growing commodity shortages ended up devastating local economies everywhere in the region.

The Japanese forces directly administered economic matters in each of the occupied countries, aided by civilians sent from Tokyo. They imposed currency controls, seized the railways and established rations of rice and other scarce consumer items. The troops stationed in the Co-Prosperity Sphere lived off the local economies, which were poorly equipped to bear the burden. The inevitable black market invited bribery and corruption among the indigenous officials administering the allocations.

The occupied areas supplied Japan with key raw materials but few markets and almost no laborers (only four percent of Japan's workers came from overseas, nearly all of them from Taiwan and Korea). Manchukuo and China were the leading sources of coal and iron ore, particularly near the end of the fighting. Once the war situation worsened in 1943 and Japan's shipping grew scarce, it became harder and harder to transport fuels and ores from Southeast Asia. War production peaked in the early autumn of 1944.

Total war made it quite impossible for Japan to serve as the keystone of an economic zone it was inadequately prepared to lead even in peacetime. Having isolated the Co-Prosperity Sphere from world trade, Japan could neither absorb the region's nonstrategic exports (e.g., fruits, sugar) nor provide enough finished goods for its civilian markets. When in 1944 the Allies sank 40 percent of Japan's already depleted merchant fleet, many local industries in Southeast Asia withered. Tin production fell off 90 percent in Malaya, compared with 1940; the output of tea in the Indies was sliced in half. Nor were the economies of individual countries in the area large enough to become self-sufficient in staples as the Japanese had advocated. The result was economic stagnation and misery far beyond anything caused by previous colonial regimes.

C. Levy
T. R. H. Havens

COLLINS, Joseph ("Lightning Joe") (1896-   ).

Collins, an American general, commanded the 25th Infantry Division at Guadalcanal in 1943. As commander of the Seventh Army Corps in 1944, he landed on Utah Beach on D-day (see **Normandy Landing**). He captured Cologne on October 4. After distinguishing himself on the northern flank of the Ardennes pocket, he enveloped the Ruhr from the south and then pushed rapidly east to reach Dessau on the Elbe on April 14, 1945.

COMBINED OPERATIONS.

The British admiral Sir **Roger Keyes**, who had conquered Zeebrugge during World War I, became acutely aware in 1940 of the importance of amphibious operations to the British armed forces. He was particularly concerned with the rigidity of the separation between land forces, on the one hand, and sea forces, on the other, a major fault in strategy that had been responsible for the British defeats at Gallipoli in 1915 and in **Norway** in 1940. He therefore developed the concept of "combined operations" utilizing both land and sea power, which in his opinion would yield superior military results.

The combined operation is defined as a military maneuver in which the three major branches of the armed forces—land, sea and air—cooperate closely in striking at an enemy at a given moment and a given site with a maximum of power.

Eight days after the evacuation from Dunkirk, Sir **John Dill**, head of the Imperial Chiefs of Staff, set up plans for combined operations on a modest scale that were presented to Keyes in 1941 and to Adm. **Mountbatten** in 1943 and finally to Maj. Gen. **Robert E. Laycock**.

Combined operations were the responsibility of a commander with units of the three military branches at his disposal. Assisted by a staff of land, sea and air force officers, he developed plans for coastal (specifically, amphibious) operations, devised the best plan for arming and deploying the amphibious units under his command and issued the proper orders. The commander was required to rigorously train his units, whose land forces should be comprised of commando teams, instruct each of the branches under his command in the capabilities and needs of the other two and create an excellent *esprit de corps* among all three.

After 1941 the purpose of combined operations was essentially limited to harassing the coasts of German-occupied countries on the Atlantic and thus forcing the Nazis to spread their power thin, to gathering information concerning the enemy's troop deployment, to destroying military targets and to determining the effectiveness of innovative tactics through experimentation.

In addition to its own permanent units, the Combined Operations Command often utilized detachments placed at its disposal for a particular sortie. After each such procedure the commanders of the combined operation conducted a critique of its method, reviewed the lessons learned from the experience and used the information they yielded as well as the information about the enemy gained from the operation.

Major combined operations early in the war included commando attacks on important plants in the Lofoten Islands in March and December 1941, the destruction of mining installations in Spitzbergen in August 1941, numerous raids on Italian ports in **Libya** and a raid on **Rommel**'s headquarters. Other achievements included the destruction of the Vaagso factories in Norway in October 1941; a raid on Bruneval on February 27, 1942, in which Maj. J. D. Frost's parachutists landed behind a German **radar** station and carried off to England the essential parts of a new keying device in the German radar network; the bloody and heroic attack on **Saint-Nazaire** on March 26, 1942, in which the seaport's ship repair installations were destroyed; the conquest of Diego-Suarez in **Madagascar** in May 1942; and the raid on Dieppe on August 19, 1942.

The attack on Dieppe was more ambitious than any preceding combined operation. It had several goals. The first was to harass and discomfit the Germans and to force them to keep a heavy concentration of troops in the West, to the detriment of the Russian front. The attackers also wanted to test the power of coastal defenses; to determine the density of the troops occupying them and the means of transport and of landing required for an invasion force; and to see how tanks and other vehicles could be unloaded and readied for the attack, what obstacles often hidden by the sea might impede their deployment and the like. Another goal was to acquire information for the **Royal Air Force** on the number and disposition of fighter planes guarding western Europe. Finally, the raiders hoped to draw some of the *Luftwaffe*'s strength away from the Russian front just when the Germans needed all their resources for their drive into its southern extreme.

The Canadian Second Division took on the mission of **reconnaissance** in force, supported by aircraft and naval vessels and covered by British Commando Unit Four on the west and Commando Unit Three on the east (see **Commandos and Rangers**). A third commando team of Royal Marines followed the Canadians as rear guard.

The operation was, on the western flank, hugely successful—the 250 men in Lord Lovat's Commando Unit Four overcame and destroyed the fortified artillery position at Varangeville after an initial retreat. The operation as a whole, however, had to be considered a tactical setback, with heavy losses in proportion to the immediate material gain. Landing with 28 tanks, the Canadians fought furiously but, along with Commando Unit Four, were seriously mauled by the seasoned defense troops. A good many RAF planes failed to return.

The defect of the massive raid lay in its planning. Only Commando Unit Four was able to achieve complete surprise. A frontal assault on Dieppe could not have gone unperceived for long, and it would therefore have been more sensible to stage a preliminary naval and air bombardment of the German defensive positions. But the civilian population of the city had to be considered. The preliminary barrage was therefore withheld, and as a consequence the defending troops in that sector could man their artillery promptly. Allied intelligence was also at fault. The defense was better fortified than the attackers had anticipated, even though many aerial photos had been taken by reconnoitering aircraft.

But the precious information gained in the Dieppe raid compensated for the military defeat, for it helped prepare the road for an eventual victory. One of the lessons learned was that only the full power of naval artillery and air bombing could lay the basis for a landing in force. It was also determined that an attack on the port itself would not work; it was the beach that had to be hit and that required **landing craft** and amphibious tanks to get through the surf. Also, armored vehicles and equipment were necessary for frontal attacks on coastal defenses, with engineer units moving up behind the armor to destroy concrete outposts. A system of mats on which heavy armored vehicles could ride without bogging down in the shifting and muddy sections of the beach had to be devised, and a turretless tank over which other vehicles could pass to surmount the sea wall was considered.

The Dieppe attack had another salutary consequence for the Allies. It forced the Germans to transfer to the west several air squadrons and three strong armored groups from the Russian front. Indeed, the significance of the adventure was so badly overestimated by the German OKW that its attention for a fatal moment shifted away from North Africa, where less than three months later Gen. **Eisenhower**'s forces were to land in complete secrecy. **Hitler**, too, was deceived by the Dieppe attack; he imagined that it was an existing port the Allies were after; it apparently never occurred to him that his opponents would one day acquire the means of landing troops on beaches far from any ports. This kind of reasoning misled the Germans into concentrating on the defenses of coastal towns and considering as a deceptive feint any landing attempt at a point with no port in its vicinity. Nevertheless, Hitler ordered the construction of 15,000 permanent fortified points along the French coast six days after the Dieppe raid. He then conceived the idea that was to prove a terrible mistake in 1944—of waging the decisive battle against the invasion at the edge of the sea rather than deploying mobile reserve power in depth. Finally, the Dieppe raid implanted in the mind of the German command the erroneous notion that the Allies intended to land just north of the Seine.

But that operation was to have an unexpected sequel. Believing that it presaged a large-scale attack, the German high command panicked long enough to set in train a series of defensive maneuvers that were observed and extensively exploited by intelligence agents working for the Allies.

Hardly backward in their capacity for combined operations, the Germans executed two such feats in the first part of the war—first in Norway, in April 1940, and then in Crete, in May 1941. These, however, turned out to be of little consequence, principally because the "continental complex" of Hitler and the OKW blinded them to the possibilities for the naval exploitation of those victories. A second reason for the failure of the German strategists to follow up on these triumphs was the poor overall coordination among the OKH, OKM and OKL, although they had managed to work together well enough to achieve those successes originally. The consequences of this lack of communication among the various branches of the German military were their failure to destroy the British army at Dunkirk, their failure to hold North Africa after the French armistice and their failure to agree on the proper conduct of the **Battle of Britain**. To these one must also add their inability to conquer the strategically important island of **Malta**.

The capacity of the Japanese for combined operations was little better. From the attack on **Pearl Harbor** on December 7, 1941 to the battle of **Midway** on May 4, 1942, their adversaries offered them so little opposition anywhere that there was no point in devising elaborate plans for complex maneuvers. After Midway, however, it was the Americans who excelled in the area of combined operations. As for the Japanese, nothing was more striking than the extreme contrast between the tactical audacity of their lower echelons and the strategic timidity of their military command, unequipped as it was for air-naval collaboration.

Quite the opposite situation existed on the Allied side. The Americans, with their considerable aims in the Pacific; the British, with their much more modest aims there; and the Anglo-American combine, in its preparations for landing in Europe, mastered the art of combined operations. In the pursuit of their goals, the Allies developed the following new tools:

(1) Numerous types of boats required for a landing operation that were capable of satisfying two conditions formerly thought contradictory: they could both form an extended **convoy** in the open sea and unload their own cargo on a beach, permitting them to bypass the regular ports which were in enemy hands. To mark all coasts vulnerable to attack, whether in Europe or the Pacific, the offices of the combined operations planners set up "chart maps," atlases containing silhouettes on tracing paper of the various ships—including the bilge sections below the waterline—and sections of the sea, the beaches and the coasts, together with a diagram of the tides for days to come. By superimposing these papers, the planners were able to determine the points at which the landing ships or the larger landing craft would touch bottom and thus where the smaller assault boats would have to be let down into the sea; they could also determine the farthest points to which the assault boats could advance, where the landing party would need to leap into shallow water.

(2) Amphibious tanks, particularly the "duplex drivers" and amphibious vehicles like the DUKW—a 2.5-ton truck capable of floating or rolling on wheels—or the "landing vehicle track" (LVT), a tracked vehicle with its treads inclined at a large angle to increase its capacity for negotiating muddy terrain and enough room to accommodate 32 men in full field gear.

(3) A real novelty for landing operations—a rocket consisting of a bundle of parallel tubes, each capable of successively launching in a fraction of a second a projectile whose propulsive fuel lasted over a portion of the rocket's trajectory. The rocket was ignited electrically; the bundle of tubes was light in weight, since they served only as supports for the projectile; and the "gun" had no kick. A large number of these tubes could be set up on a boat, a tank or even a three-ton truck. Although the rocket could not be precisely aimed, it was capable of hitting the enemy at high power within a short time.

The rocket turned out to be quite effective in the Pacific when, beginning in 1943, the Americans undertook offensive landing operations. They had found that when the landing craft arrived within 3,000 feet of the beach, the men in them were endangered by the supporting artillery from their own warships. Thus, the naval guns had to cease fire, and the Japanese profited from the lull by opening heavy fire of their own. The rocket guns, or "bazookas," thus enabled the troops to land under a covering fire. They were mounted on the "landing craft tank-rocket" for that reason. There were two types of these bazookas. The smaller one carried 792 127-mm rockets, and the larger 1,080, all of which could be fired in less than 30 seconds. They were capable of covering an arc of 2,300 feet, and their range was 650 feet.

Landing operations using those methods and equipment were executed in the following way: During the night preceding the action, airborne units parachuted to the rear of the coastal defenses. Later in the night, air and sea forces bombarded enemy defenses. The landing fleet, preceded by minesweepers and sheltered by aircraft, advanced at dawn toward the coast, surrounded by its protective fleet. Amphibious tanks were then launched on the water, and the troops in their landing craft approached the beach under cover of a smoke screen while artillery guns, tank guns and bazookas fired from their emplacements. If the beach at low tide bore lines of obstacles and mines, the engineer units landed first under the protection of amphibious tanks, provided with every tool for breaking, pushing or pulling at the tank obstacles or detecting, defusing and pulling up mines to clear a path through the delaying system. (These operations, of course, had to be performed during the ebb tide.) As the tide mounted, infantry, artillery, tanks and vehicles were landed. As soon as one small beachhead was set up, engineer troops arrived with bulldozers, concrete mixers, sand, cement and other equipment for the construction of airstrips.

Every landing was a unique case, depending as it did on the nature of the coasts and the enemy's preparedness, the weather, the tide, the visibility and even the phase of the moon.

In the past all landing operations on a strongly defended coast had ended in a victory of land over sea. One of the principal causes of the defeat of each great amphibious operation in history has been the duality of land and sea commands. It was so in the peninsula of Yorktown in 1862, the Dardanelles in 1915 and in Norway in 1940.

For the first time in history the problem of a single, flexible and well-defined command over allies in war was solved by the Anglo-Americans in their amphibious operations. It made no difference whether the commander in chief was soldier, flier or sailor; he commanded an organization of chiefs of staff chosen from the three armed branches. The Americans created for this purpose, in 1942, the Army-Navy Staff College (ANSCOL), essentially a tactical course for the combined chiefs of staff. Its students were selected from land, sea and air forces, as well as from civilians in the war economy administrations. This school sharpened the taste of its students for working in a team, as part of a perfectly synchronized organization of a type that later, from 1942 to 1945, was to characterize the operational teams of **MacArthur** and **Nimitz**.

For the assault on the coasts, however, the Allies divided their combined powers into task forces. These were heavily armed raiding parties consisting of large warships with high firepower, principally in the form of naval rifles and air bombers from aircraft carriers; escort vessels; minesweepers; landing ships and landing craft loaded with troops and materiel of every type; maintenance ships; floating workshops, hospitals and warehouses; and the like. The aircraft carrier evolved into the most formidable fighting ship in re-

gions like the Pacific, where planned landing points were sometimes thousands of miles from staging bases. For each **task force** the command for the whole group was the province of the Navy until the land and air commands could set up their headquarters on a bridgehead sheltered from the enemy. This practice was feasible among American forces in the Pacific because of the Marines, land troops permanently under the command of the Navy who were often the first to debark in hostile territories. The British had their elite corps with long traditions, and their Royal Marines, infantry units that were under the command of the Admiralty and formed parts of commando units. But the Royal Marines and the British commandos never reached an echelon higher than the brigade, while the American Marines formed divisions and corps, with their own light and medium artillery, tanks, engineers and other independent services.

Three thousand years of military art and 300 years of training in the use of firearms were required to prepare for the great military revolution of the 18th century, in which land armies were grouped in divisions comprising troops specializing in different arms and thus turning a nation's army into a supple, effective body for the first time. Still another two centuries were needed to divide the various branches of the armed force into combined groups under a single command. With such a command finally realized, the harmonious coordination of the three branches, the techniques of handling the necessary instruments and tactics, the excellence of training for the landing troops, and the success of each operation—all responsible for the fine achievements of the combined operations since their modest beginnings in 1940—came about almost as a natural consequence.

Organization, strategy and tactics are experimental sciences. In the Allied landings on Sicily, Salerno and Anzio-Nettuno, the military experts seemed to be interested more in the lessons taught by every event than in the practical results of the operation. None of these engagements were particularly brilliant, any more than was the raid on Dieppe. But from their experimental results, adding to those yielded by the attempts on North Africa and Oceania, emerged the **Normandy landing**, developed with incredible precision and very likely the most ingenious maneuver in history—if it were not overshadowed in its turn by those of MacArthur and Nimitz on the other side of the world (see **Leyte**).

H. Bernard

COMINTERN.

"Comintern" is the acronym combining the initial

syllables of the two Russian words *Kommunisticheskiy internatsional* ("Communist International"). The Comintern was founded in March 1919 in response to two events: the collapse of the Socialist Second International at the beginning of World War I and the assumption of power in Russia by the Bolshevik Party, until then a member of that International. In November 1914 Nikolai Lenin, head of the Bolshevik Party, ordered the founding of a new International, the third. He attempted unsuccessfully to have this proposal adopted by the congresses of the Socialist International at Zimmerwald in Switzerland in September 1915 and at Kiental in April 1916. It was not until the November 1917 revolution in Russia that he could realize his ambition: the birth of a revolutionary communist party in every country, different from the old reformist socialist parties, and the creation of a centralized and disciplined organization directed by a "general staff of the world revolution" to replace the former Socialist International, which he scorned as a simple "mailbox."

The life of the Communist International occupied several distinct periods.

The Lenin Era

The defeat of the Central Powers in World War I, together with the disappearance of the German, Austro-Hungarian and Turkish empires, in concert with the revolutionary activity surging in many European countries, strengthened the intention of the Russian Bolsheviks to convoke the founding congress of the new International. Invitations to participate, dated January 24, 1919 and bearing the signatures of Lenin and **Leon Trotsky**, were sent out to 39 movements, assemblies and revolutionary parties. The congress opened in Moscow on March 2, 1919. The 50 or so delegates present were practically all Russians or foreigners residing in the **USSR**. On March 4 the new International was proclaimed, with Grigori Zinoviev, Lenin's lieutenant, as president. Lenin himself presented one of the reports at the congress, which discussed bourgeois democracy and the dictatorship of the proletariat. The congress itself, however, adjourned before it could define the strategy, tactics or organization of the International.

The Comintern was born in the midst of revolutionary fervor. On March 21 a Soviet republic was created in **Hungary**. Bavaria was next, with a communist experiment in April. In June, Vienna was the scene of an attempted coup d'etat. But these eruptions were of very short duration, as were later abortive efforts to found mass-supported communist parties in the major Western countries.

The second Comintern congress, in July and August of 1920, finished what the first congress started. At Lenin's urging, it adopted many fundamental resolutions on the role of communist parties, the conditions of admission into the Communist International, national and colonial matters, agricultural policy, parliamentarianism and the like. Delegations from the principal European countries attended—**Germany**, France, **Italy**, **Czechoslovakia**. Optimism was the rule, for the sessions coincided with the victorious thrust of the Red Army into **Poland**.

But this revolutionary fervor vanished abruptly. The Red Army was driven back as fast as it had advanced. The occupation of the factories by Italian workers in September did not result in a revolution, the general strike that broke out in December in Czechoslovakia was a complete loss and a riot in central Germany failed. These setbacks for the International coincided with a tactical step backward in the USSR—the New Economic Policy (NEP).

The Communist International twice modified its direction. At the Third Congress in June and July 1921, it rejected the theory and tactics of the revolutionary offensive, and in December of that year, under Lenin's direct prodding, it voiced its support for the tactic of united fronts, in which it sought the cooperation of socialist unions and parties. In April 1922 the representatives of the Socialist International and the Communist International met to find some common ground. But the negotiations, to Lenin's disappointment, led to nothing.

The fourth congress of the Comintern was held at Moscow on November and December 1922. It was the last in Lenin's lifetime, and during its course he made his last speech. Seriously ill, he took no part in the Comintern's decisions nor, particularly, in those advocated by Zinoviev, which resulted in two rebellions, one in **Bulgaria** in September 1923 and the other in Hamburg, Germany the following month. Neither one met with any success. On January 21, 1924 Lenin died.

The Struggle to Succeed Lenin

The fifth congress in June and July 1924 opened with a double innovation. On the doctrinal plane Leninism as the match for Marxism made its appearance; on the organizational plane the bolshevization of all national parties—46 were represented—was begun. Thus, the foreign communist parties lined up even more faithfully behind Moscow, and their policies took on a closer resemblance to those supported by the Kremlin. Zinoviev, the architect of bolshevization, was in his turn ejected in 1926 from the directorate of the Bolshevik Party and from the Comintern. Nikolai Bukharin then assumed the Comintern post and was himself purged in 1929. In this transitional period the political influence and the membership rolls of practically all the communist parties steadily diminished. The only revolutionary activity on a large scale was in **China**.

The sixth congress of the Comintern in August 1928 heard Bukharin's swan song. His fall ushered in the age of **Stalin** and Stalinism.

Stalin and the War Problem

Born as a result of the Second International's failure to survive the stresses of World War I, the Comintern was always preoccupied by two problems: civil war within one nation and an international "imperialist" war aimed at the Soviet Union. Before the 1930s its chief fear was an imperialist war—i.e., aggression by the democratic powers, especially France and Great Britain. Reinforcing this view was Stalin's dictum when he dominated the Comintern—that the defense of the USSR was the first duty of the working class and that every tactic toward that end, including absolute enmity toward social democracy, the minion of the bourgeoisie and the ally of fascism, was valid.

Even **Hitler**'s rise to power on January 30, 1933 had no effect on this principle; the Comintern continued until the end of the first half of 1934 to berate the Western democracies and social democracy and to predict a communist revolution in Germany. But the first in a number of startling changes in Soviet policy took place in the second half of 1934 and continued into 1935, when the USSR concluded pacts with France and Czechoslovakia. Taking its cue, the Comintern changed its attitude toward the socialists by wooing them into a "popular front" alliance along with another former target of communist abuse, the bourgeois liberals, for action against growing fascist strength.

The tactic of the popular front became obligatory for all foreign communist parties in the wake of the seventh Comintern congress, which met in Moscow in July and August 1935. It helped install the popular front government in France, in **Spain** just before the outbreak of the civil war and in Chile. China also had its version of the popular front when the Nationalist Kuomintang concluded a second alliance with the Chinese Communist Party. Everywhere else, in Europe and America, the communist parties sought partnership with socialist or liberal parties, even on a partial or provisional basis, in the name of the struggle against fascism and in defense of democracy. It was, ironically, at practically the same moment Stalin began persecuting and killing militant communists who had fled fascism in their own countries for shelter in the USSR. It was in this way that the Polish Communist Party was officially dissolved and most of its officials, like those of the Yugoslav, Hungarian and German Communist parties, were massacred by Stalinist agents.

The communist parties in all the European countries acted as anti-fascist champions until another turn-around in Soviet policy bewildered them utterly—the signing of the **Nazi-Soviet Pact** in Moscow on August 23, 1939. In ignorance of Stalin's secret plans, communists in Europe were lulled into the belief that the sole aim of the pact was to protect the USSR against attack and that they were still free to pursue their campaign to destroy fascism. Hence, the Communists in the French parliament on September 2 voted for war credits. The Socialists had done the same thing on August 4, 1914.

The Defeatist Tactic

At the end of September 1939, the war claimed Poland as its first victim. Not until that moment did the communist parties take up a new tactic born of the Nazi-Soviet Pact. Defeatism now replaced antifascism. The prime enemy was no longer fascism but the Western democracies. This was the new line of behavior for all hard-core communists—for Germans like **Walter Ulbricht**, who in the pages of the Comintern's new journal, *Die Welt*, vilified British imperialism and its "attempts to sow intrigues between the Soviet and German peoples"; for communists in neutral countries like **Norway, Belgium**, and **the Netherlands**, who condemned Franco-British imperialism with such concentrated spleen that they barely paid attention to the German occupation of their lands; for communists in democratic belligerents like France, where the party was dissolved on September 26, 1939, only a month before its secretary general, Maurice Thorez, deserted when called to the colors. The French Communist Party supported the **Russo-Finnish Winter War**, the partition of Poland and the occupation of the **Baltic States** by the Red Army. For this defeatist attitude, however, the French Reds paid a price. Prison sentences of five years each were given to 26 Communist deputies and four years each to eight others. And of the 72 Communist deputies in the French parliament, 21 resigned from the party in disgust with its policy.

The Turning Point—June 22, 1941

Hitler's aggression against the USSR caused a third violent wrench in the policy of the Soviet Union. The Comintern issued a manifesto to the communist parties throughout the world, stating that in the name of the struggle against fascism, communists in every country were obliged to form a "National Front"—i.e., a political group involving not only socialists, as in the earlier united fronts, and the democratic elements, as in the popular fronts, but also nationalist, royalist and even conservative parties.

In conformity with this directive, the communist parties of Europe mobilized for the fight against fascism. If a party's particular nation was occupied by fascist forces, the occupier was the party's target. From this moment formations flaunting national aspirations began to burgeon. In **Greece** it was the National Liberation Front, the so-called EAM; in **Albania**, the National Liberation Movement; in **Yugoslavia**, the National Liberation Movement; in Bulgaria the Patriotic Front; in **Hungary**, the National Independence Front; in France, the National Front; and in Belgium, the Independence Front.

Unlike the other parties, the communist party had a political apparatus it often applied in accordance with the dictates of the Comintern. It was a secret instrument, and since the communists had an underground tradition, they were better equipped for undercover drives against the German occupiers than other parties. But the general direction indicated by the Comintern was not limited to the national front concept. It demanded the transformation of the political eruption into a revolution, disciplined or terrorist. If all the communist parties participated in the formation of the political fronts, few succeeded in forming disciplined armies. The first to manage it was the Yugoslavian Communist Party in 1941 and then the Greeks and Albanians in 1942-43. In 1943-44 partisan armies arose in Italy, Bulgaria, France and other countries. First in Yugoslavia and then, in rapid succession, in Albania and Greece, communist factions broke with nationalists even to the point of waging civil war. Elsewhere, as in Italy and France, they embraced each other in shaky alliances that were to last until the end of the world conflict.

Yet the Comintern did not survive the war. It was officially dissolved on May 15, 1943 by Stalin himself. The members of the Presidium and the Executive Committee of the Communist International could only acquiesce. In the form of a directive, the final section of resolution said: "The Presidium of the Executive Committee of the Communist International calls on all partisans of the Communist International to continue by every means their efforts in the war of liberation of the peoples and states of the anti-Hitler coalition, to crush swiftly the mortal enemy of the workers, Nazi fascism, its allies and its vassals."

In the end, just as the Socialist International failed to resist World War I, the Communist International in its turn failed to survive World War II. To cap the paradox, it could not, in its 24 years of official existence, win to communism a single country in Europe or Asia. Not until after its demise were the first com-

munist regimes installed, in central and Balkan Europe after 1944 and in China in 1949.

B. Lazitch

COMITATO DI LIBERAZIONE NAZIONALE DELL'ALTA ITALIA (CLNAI).
"The National Committee for the Liberation of Northern Italy" was founded in Milan September 9, 1943 by the five parties of **Italy**'s Anti-fascist Coalition (Liberal, Christian Democrat, Action, Socialist and Communist).

COMITE FRANCAIS DE LIBERATION NATIONALE (CFLN).
Organized June 1942 in Algiers (see **French North Africa; Free France**).

COMMANDO PARATROOPERS.
More than 7,000 agents were parachuted into the occupied countries for the **Special Intelligence Service**, the **Special Operations Executive**, the **Political Warfare Executive**, **MI-9** and the **Office of Strategic Services**. Their point of departure was either the **United Kingdom** or **Egypt**, later Algeria or southern **Italy**, or **India**, enroute to Japanese-occupied Southeast Asia. Some of these commandos were landed on coasts by submarines or small boats; others were dropped off by Lysander or Hudson aircraft and then picked up after the completion of their missions.

These agents were nationals or former residents of the countries in which they operated. They were selected in accordance with exacting standards and underwent several months of training in isolated regions, during which they were taught radio operation, codes, the use of special weapons, police procedures of the country to which they were to be sent, the fine points of parachute jumping and tactics for dodging enemy trackers. They were also thoroughly schooled in the "cover story" they were to foist on the enemy if captured.

These agents were often grouped in pairs—the organizer and the radio operator, a two-man cell. Some were trained to work in cooperation with secret organizations to which they carried instructions and equipment. Simultaneously they maintained contact with England or some other base. Others were relied on to form new organizations. Still a third type carried out particular political missions.

Many of these agents were dropped "blind" at some prearranged spot (provided the navigator plotted the course perfectly in the night flight)—that is, nobody met them when they landed. This was generally the case with the initial landing party. Later on, most agents, especially those arriving simultaneously with parachuted materiel and provisions, were greeted at the specified rendezvous by "reception committees" furnished by **resistance** movements or espionage nets. These rendezvous were agreed upon by the **Royal Air Force** and the appropriate Allied service—the SOE, the SIS or the like. Sites were adjudged satisfactory if the terrain was flat and open and the landing area was at least 550 yards square and remote from populated places and certainly from enemy barracks or centers. The reception committee set up signal flares in a prearranged pattern, thus simultaneously providing identification and the illumination required for a safe landing. But the flares were not lit until the committee distinctly heard the plane's motors as it circled the rendezvous in a diameter of several miles. Three red lamps were lined up, about 300 feet apart, to indicate wind direction. A fourth white lamp set downwind from the first three had the double function of indicating the wind direction and emitting a repeated prearranged signal. Because of its risk—even a match flame in a totally dark area is easily distinguishable from an aircraft at high altitude—this method was abandoned in 1944 for direct communication between land and plane. Parachute drops of men or materiel were announced to the interested organizations by direct radio and often confirmed by **British Broadcasting Corporation** through the use of conventional phrases ("Charlie's aunt is resting comfortably.") at a specified time the evening before the operation.

Losses of parachuted agents were high, either because their planes were shot down or because their jumps were misplaced and the agents were captured on landing. Many were tortured or executed or interned in **concentration camps**. Between a quarter and a third of all secret agents never returned from their missions. Losses were also heavy for British pilots of the Lysander aircraft designed for parachute missions.

H. Bernard

COMMANDOS AND RANGERS.

The origin of the British commandos and their major raids before the **Normandy landing** are discussed in the article on **Combined Operations**.

In 1944 there were four commando brigades. The First Brigade and Fourth Brigade were active in the West, the Second in **Italy** and **Greece**, and the Third in **Burma**.

A commando brigade, consisting usually of 2,000 men, was formed of a certain number of commando units. There were generally four such units, each comprising 450 to 500 men. Each unit contained a headquarters troop, a heavy-arms troop and five fighting troops each of 60 men.

For the Normandy landing, the First Commando Brigade controlled Commando units 3, 4, 5 and 45, the last of these obtained from the Royal Marines. The Fourth Brigade was made up of Commando units 41, 46, 47, and 48, all of them Royal Marines.

The four commando brigades were manned only by subjects of the **United Kingdom**. In 1942, however, an international Commando Unit 10 was established, with a British headquarters and eight troops. The First and Eighth troops were French; the Second Dutch; the Third Germans, Austrians, Hungarians and Czechs, most of them Jews with Anglicized names; the Fourth Belgian; the Fifth Norwegian; the Sixth Polish and the Seventh Yugoslavian. Each of the troops in Commando Unit 10 contained 100 men rather than 60. Actually, as opposed to the purely British commando troops, these international troops had their own heavy weapons, since Commando Unit 10 was uniquely organized. Its troops were detachable for supporting the British commandos in a particular operation. Thus it was that the Dutch troop fought in the Far East, while the Belgian troop operated first in Italy and then in the west; the Norwegian troop participated in numerous raids on the coasts of its native land and was in combat at Walcheren in November 1944; the French troops landed in Normandy on June 6 and aided their Norwegian comrades in the Walcheren fighting.

When a commando brigade fought as a bloc, it was usually under a general officer of corps rank but sometimes under a division commander. In principle, commandos fought only in special terrain or in unique operations. All of their men were volunteers.

The losses sustained by these elite soldiers were very high throughout the war. After many raids on **Norway**, France, **Madagascar**, the Mediterranean, and Southeast Asia, they were involved in severe tests in Italy, Normandy, the Baltic Sea and **Burma**. By the end of the war the "Five-River Brigade"—veterans of battles on the Meuse, the Rhine, the Weser, the Aller and the Elbe in 1945—had lost 80 percent of its men.

Hitler ordered that commandos and SAS parachutists, uniformed soldiers, must be considered saboteurs and shot on sight. This was obviously in violation of all standards of military behavior in time of war. Some of the German generals, like Nikolaus von Falkenhorst in Norway, obeyed the Fuehrer's directives to the letter; many others, however, ignored them. Nevertheless, more than 200 commandos and paratroopers, often badly wounded, fell into enemy hands and were summarily shot.

Rangers were the American equivalent of the British commandos. Their operational unit was the battalion. On June 6, 1944 the Second and Fifth Ranger battalions launched the daring assaults of the Pointe du Hoc and the Pointe de la Percee in Normandy.

H. Bernard

CONCENTRATION CAMPS.

The idea of concentrating behind barbed wire a mass of people deemed dangerous to the state was not originated by the Nazis. The British had mass camps in the Boer War, and such institutions for emigrants from enemy countries proliferated among belligerents in World War I. The advantage of concentration camps is that the inmates can easily be controlled by only a few armed men. But although life in the camps of earlier wars was harsh, their prisoners were at least under the protection of the law. The Soviet, Nazi and Japanese camps were quite different. The power of their commanders over the prisoners was absolute.

Stalin based his autocracy on his "camps for reeducation through labor." The unfortunates sent to such prisons, however, never returned. Those Stalin was determined to be rid of were sent to the camps in the Arctic by the thousands.

The Japanese interned European and American civilians—men, women and children—trapped in the conquered territories. Provisioning and sanitary conditions were barbaric, accompanied by cruelty and humiliations intended to crush the pride of "the whites" systematically.

It was left to the Nazis to sink to the ultimate in bestiality in their concentration camps.

On February 28, 1933, Chancellor Hitler obtained from von Hindenburg, president of the Reich, an urgent decree "for the safety of the State" abrogating the constitutional rights of German citizens. The old man countersigned the document. On the following April 4, the Reichstag ceded full power to Hitler. Those "opposing the racial and spiritual vigor of the German people" could now be freely hunted down. The SA—Nazi storm troopers—threw themselves into the task, improvising prisons and internment camps that the SS was quick to take over. On March 21, 1933, Himmler directed the construction in Dachau of the first Konzentrationslager—officially abbreviated as KL, known to the inmates and guards as KZ—on an experimental basis. It served as the model for the camps of Sachsenhausen, near Oranienburg, established in September 1936; Buchenwald, established in July 1937; and Flossenburg, established in May 1938 and notorious for the vivisection experiments performed there on Gypsy children during the war; and Malthausen in Austria, established in 1938. The Ravensbrueck camp, opened in 1934, was, after 1938, reserved for women.

Ostensibly meant for the reeducation of the inmates, the camps were officially known as State Camps for Rehabilitation and Labor. The legend over the camp gates read Arbeit macht frei—"work is liberating." SS Reichsfuehrer Himmler considered them useful for inspiring terror and thus guaranteeing respect for the Nazi order. Between 1933 and 1944 more than a million Germans passed through those gates. Those judged "harmful" were marked for liquidation; the first victims were the mentally deranged.

In the course of the war the old camps accepted deportees from occupied countries. New camps began to open. The most prominent of these were Theresienstadt (Terezin) in Bohemia; Maidanek, Auschwitz (Oswiecim) and Stutthof in Poland; Natzweiler-Struthof in Alsace; Kaunas and Riga in the Baltic States; and Neuengamme, Gross-Rosen, Bergen-Belsen and Dora in Germany. In 1942, with their annexes and external Kommandos, the concentration camp system included more than a thousand stations of detention—or of extermination.

In the summer of 1941, Hitler decided on elimination of the Jews under cover of the war (see Anti-Semitism; Final Solution). Two camps—Auschwitz, where four million people were murdered, and Maidanek, which claimed another million victims—were equipped with extermination facilities. Four other camps designed solely for the annihilation of Jews were also created—Chelmno, where more than 340,000 were murdered; Belzec, which had the capacity to kill 15,000 people daily; Sobibor, which was responsible for 20,000 deaths every day; and Treblinka, where 25,000 were killed daily. Having given up their clothing, money and valuables, the victims were first led to the barber—human hair was especially useful for the manufacture of the special slippers worn by U-boat crews—and then, under the pretext of disinfection, were led to the gas chambers. Gold teeth were torn from mouths of the cadavers, anuses and vaginas were probed for hidden jewelry, and the bodies were then loaded into crematory furnaces. They served as the raw material for soap, fertilizer and other products.

This policy of extermination did not always sit well with the SS. Manufacturers intent on deriving as much profit as possible from forced labor were at loggerheads with security services that insisted on immediate destruction of all "racial enemies"—Jews, Gypsies, Poles and all other Slavs. The irreconcilability of these two concepts of exploitation and extermination was to become more and more manifest with the increasing need for total mobilization of the German economic machine after the Wehrmacht's defeat on the Russian front. Thousands of Jews thus escaped the gas chambers when the administration of the camps was transferred in March 1942 to the Economy and Administration Bureau of the SS. But the head of this bureau, Oswald Pohl, who preferred extermination through labor, could not induce Himmler to abandon completely the mission **Eichmann** was fulfilling with the zeal of a conscientious technocrat—rounding up as many Jews as possible for his death factories.

The same contradiction between the rational exploitation of forced labor and the determination to degrade the prisoners physically and morally—a contradiction sharpened by the fact that firms such as I. G. Farben, Krupp, and Siemens, which contributed large funds to the SS, needed that labor—characterized the administration of the camps. Undernourishment, constant beatings, lack of sleep, exposure to cold, the permanent sense of insecurity and the openly encouraged sexual attacks enervated the bodies and souls of the prisoners. Mortality was so high that Himmler ordered the camp doctors, in December 1942, to "lower it at any price" so that "the capacity for labor be the highest possible." Those the doctors deemed no longer useful for work were killed forthwith. In the last months of the war they were sent *en masse* to the *Vernichtungslager*—the death camps.

Beginning in 1936 guards provided for the camps by the SS called themselves the *Totenkopfverbande*—the Death's-Head Corps. Internal discipline was the responsiblity of camp chiefs, block chiefs and *Kapos*. To ensure respect for their authority, these "officers" carried a variety of blackjack known as the *gummi*. The camp officers were themselves often inmates who had, perhaps, been offered a choice between **collaboration** and death. In exchange for their services they were awarded special privileges—better food rations, more benign treatment and the like. They often outdid their masters in brutality.

"Divide and conquer" was the method by which a small group of SS troops could cow a horde of desperate prisoners. The inmates wore on their breasts colored triangles that indicated the cause of their internment, their serial numbers and initials identifying their nationality. The color code was violet for conscientious objectors (usually Jehovah's Witnesses), green for common criminals, pink for homosexuals, black for the antisocial and red for political sinners— although red was sometimes assigned to apolitical inmates. Jews wore two superimposed triangles, one inverted over the other in the Star of David configuration. The SS strove by every means to instigate dissension between greens and reds. Sanitation and administration personnel were generally chosen from among the common criminals or the German political prisoners. Some of the inmates received more generous treatment. Known as the *Prominenten*—the elite—they

were, in effect, hostages of the Nazi regime. Among them were personages such as Princess Mafalda of Savoy and the former French council presidents Leon Blum and **Edouard Daladier** and political figures arrested on the night of the **Normandy landing**, June 6, 1944, and on the following day. Most of them were sent to Buchenwald.

All communication between the camps and the outside was rigidly regulated—a fact that did not prevent the **Resistance** organized in Auschwitz from establishing contacts with the Resistance in Poland. Letters and packages sent to inmates by their families rarely reached the addressees. According to Hitler's decree of December 2, 1941, certain French, Belgian and Dutch Resistance operatives marked NN—*Nacht und Nebel*—were under no circumstances to be permitted communication with the outside. The International **Red Cross** was denied access to the camps on the pretext that inmates of the camp were not prisoners of war and could not therefore claim the protection of the Geneva Convention.

The influx of Resistance activists from the occupied countries and the enrollment, beginning in 1944, of able-bodied German prisoners in the *Wehrmacht* to fight on the front lines in the Soviet Union—and even in the SS, which poured antisocial and hardened criminals into its *Dirlewanger* unit, the unit charged with reprisals—forced the SS to rely, in some of the camps, on the deportees to administer the camps. These responsibilities were full of hazards and uncertainties; those discharging them had some power in appointing prisoners to various posts. What criterion was to be used to determine whether a prisoner should be given a relatively safe position or one likely to end in his death? Or was it best left to chance? The communists accepting turnkey jobs in Buchenwald decided to avoid the latter alternative for fear they might be accused of choosing political enemies for liquidation. Actually, those undertaking the terrible responsibility of making the selection gave the best posts to their closest friends. National solidarity was a typical basis for this kind of favoritism; it was logical for the members of a coherent and organized party to award each other preferential treatment. But a moral question arose, Should a prisoner accept his jailer's responsibility? Regardless of the answer to such vexing questions, the fact remained that the condition of the prisoners was better when the administration posts were occupied by political malcontents than when filled by common criminals.

The worst moments the prisoners faced were the sudden evacuations of the camps as the Soviet army approached from the east and the Allied forces from the west. The inmates incapable of walking were hurriedly destroyed. The others left on foot or in open vans in the dead of the bitter winter of 1944-45. The paths taken by these "death marches" were lined with corpses with bullet holes in the nape of the neck. The liberating troops discovered heaps of naked cadavers. Those the SS had no time to kill were in the extremes of debility. In Bergen-Belsen, liberated by the British on April 13, 1945, 10,000 corpses lay on the ground, and of the 38,500 remaining, alive but inert, barely one-third could be saved.

Those who suffered the worst were the victims of the "medical experiments," most of them women and children, performed by the SS doctors.

The total number of concentration camp victims was difficult to determine but estimated at between seven and 11 million dead.

J. Delarue

CONFERENCE OF RIO DE JANEIRO.
See **Rio de Janeiro, Conference of.**

CONFERENCES, ALLIED.
In earlier multilateral wars, no means of transport had existed to enable war leaders from different countries to consult together often. During World War II, however, the availability of aircraft made frequent meetings possible; **Churchill**'s adventurous temperament took him to many of them.

The British and French prime ministers met 16 times in 1939-40, without managing to avert the collapse of France. (Churchill would have been killed on his way back from one of these meetings had a German pilot been more alert.) Secret Anglo-American staff talks began in Washington, D.C., in January 1941 (see **ABC Plans**). In August 1941 **Roosevelt** and Churchill met at sea off Newfoundland (see **Atlantic Charter**). After **Pearl Harbor**, larger and more formal gatherings determined Allied strategy. In the first such major conference, codenamed Arcadia, which was held in Washington, D.C., from December 22, 1941 to January 14, 1942, Roosevelt, Churchill and their chief advisers set up the Combined Chiefs of Staff to coordinate future operations; issued the first **United Nations** declaration; agreed that neither would make a separate peace and envisaged landings in northwest Africa or in France.

In subsequent conferences (one attended by Churchill, **Hopkins** and **Marshall** in London in April 1942; another, attended by Roosevelt and Churchill in Washington in June 1942; and a third, attended by Churchill, Hopkins, and Marshall and **Ernest J. King** in London in July 1942) this program was clarified; the North African landing was scheduled first.

After the invasion of North Africa succeeded, another conference, codenamed "Symbol," was held

in Casablanca, Morocco on January 12-23, 1943. **Stalin** was too busy to attend. Roosevelt and Churchill agreed that an attack on Sicily, rather than France, should be next; that they would divide their resources equally between the Mediterranean and the Pacific; and that they would resume their highly secret talks, begun in June 1942, on the development of the **atomic bomb**. They also managed temporarily to reconcile generals **Giraud** and **de Gaulle**. At a concluding press conference, Roosevelt set forth the doctrine of **unconditional surrender;** a surprised Churchill promptly endorsed it.

On May 12-25 1943 a conference codenamed "Trident" was held in Washington. Shipping shortages in the Pacific were hampering **MacArthur**. At this conference Roosevelt, Churchill and their advisers decided not to strip the Mediterranean to aid him, but to follow the expected success in Sicily with a landing in **Italy** and then to build up an American army in the **United Kingdom** for an invasion of France, provisionally scheduled for May 1, 1944. Pacific strategy was discussed in detail; the British agreed to undertake a limited attack in **Burma**, and the Americans revised their Chinese policy in the direction of air operations rather than direct military aid to **Chiang Kai-shek**. In Quebec, on August 11-24, 1943 the Quadrant Conference was held. Sharp discussions on whether the invasion of northern France (Overlord) was to have first priority were inconclusive. It was agreed, as an afterthought, that a landing in southern France (**Anvil**, later **Dragoon**) was to support it. Churchill's proposal for a Southeast Asian supreme command was accepted by Roosevelt, as was his proposal that an American should command Overlord. **Mountbatten** and **Eisenhower** were appointed accordingly.

Another conference was held in Moscow, on October 18-30, 1943. **Eden** had visited Moscow in December 1941, and **Molotov** had visited London in May 1942; Churchill had visited Stalin in August 1942 to attempt to explain delays in the opening of the **second front** and the reasons why there was only a thin stream of Artic **convoys**. At the Moscow Conference, Molotov, **Hull** and Eden—the three principal Allied foreign ministers—discussed the organization of the world after the war. Their only concrete decisions were that Austria should regain its independence and that a European advisory commission should mull over the other problems in London. In Cairo, on November 23-27 and December 2-7, 1943, the Sextant Conference was held. Roosevelt and Churchill, on their way to Teheran (see below), discussed Far Eastern strategy with Chiang Kai-shek. On the military side, little was concluded. An important political declaration envisaged the expulsion of **Japan** from all territories it had conquered, including **Korea**. The

Anglo-American staff talks in December resolved remaining difficulties about Overlord.

The conference in Teheran, on November 28-December 1, 1943 was the first meeting at which Roosevelt, Stalin and Churchill were all present. The second front was discussed in detail, and Stalin put forward large claims for Polish territory at the war's end. The leaders got on amicably; beyond that, the conference achieved little.

In Quebec, on September 10-17, 1944 the Octagon Conference approved Eisenhower's plans for the advance into **Germany**; revised again the plan for Burma; agreed that the British should cooperate fully in the defeat of Japan and planned occupation zones in Germany. The **Morgenthau** Plan for "converting Germany into a country primarily agricultural and pastoral in its character" was also approved but repudiated immediately afterward.

Churchill was in Moscow again, for military talks, in October 1944; he met Roosevelt in **Malta** in February 1945, immediately before the Yalta (Argonaut) Conference, the second and most sharply controversial meeting of the "Big Three," which was held February 4-11, 1945, when Roosevelt was already mortally ill. Zones of occupation for Germany were agreed upon and a compromise was arrived at concerning U.N. membership and voting. Stalin withdrew his request for membership for all 16 republics of the **USSR**, and Roosevelt and Churchill agreed to separate membership for Belorussia and the Ukraine. Veto powers for permanent members of the U.N. Security Council were agreed. There were sharp differences on **Poland**, which were left unresolved. There were also inconclusive talks about the fate of the rest of Europe. In a secret protocol (published in 1946) Stalin agreed to enter the war against Japan "two or three months" after the defeat of Germany.

At Potsdam, formerly the imperial capital of the Second Reich, the Terminal Conference, another inconclusive Big Three meeting, was held on July 17-August 2, 1945, after the Third Reich had fallen. Stalin came; so did Roosevelt's successor, **Truman**, new to high diplomacy; and Churchill, who brought his former deputy **Attlee** with him. Both returned to England to hear the election results on July 26; Churchill did not come back to Potsdam after Attlee replaced him as prime minister. Attlee did, bringing with him **Ernest Bevin**, the new foreign secretary. Beyond victory celebrations, this conference did little: the atmosphere was cheerful, even hopeful, but nothing important was settled.

Several special conferences of diplomats and experts also deserve note. A series in London and Washington from 1940 to 1943 set up the **United Nations Relief and Rehabilitation Administration**, which did much

to help refugees in the war's aftermath. One at Hot Springs, Virginia on May 18-June 3, 1943, set up the **Food and Agriculture Organization**. Several more, inspired by **Keynes**, began in Washington in September 1943 and ended at Bretton Woods, New Hampshire in July 1944; they created the International Monetary Fund and the World Bank and established the framework that would govern world monetary policy for nearly 30 years. Conferences in Philadelphia in 1944 settled the postwar arrangements for the **International Labor Organization** and set up the International Civil Aviation Organization. Lastly, a meeting of U.S., Soviet, British and Chinese experts at Dumbarton Oaks on August 21-October 7, 1944 led to the San Francisco conference of April 25-June 26, 1945 at which the United Nations was founded.

M. R. D. Foot

CONFERENCES OF THE AXIS POWERS.

On the **Axis** side there were no conferences comparable to the **Roosevelt-Churchill** or "Big Three" encounters. The reason is that the tripartite alliance of **Germany**, **Italy** and **Japan** was not truly a coalition of equal powers. **Hitler** made all his decisions independently and presented his allies with faits accomplis. He mistrusted their leaders and offered them only the sparse information that he could not use to his own advantage. The damage resulting from this cavalier attitude reached its height in 1942-43, when the war had obviously reached a turning point. In a situation growing daily more desperate, his allies were misled by deceptive data aimed at keeping them to their alliance with the Reich. The important decisions made by **Mussolini** and the Japanese, like those of Hitler, bore the mark of pure egotism. There was no preliminary understanding among the three in making those decisions. Even at the highest level of policy making, there was nothing like the close collaboration of British and American commanding generals in the Combined Chiefs of Staff. For the German-Italian and German-small nation alliances, cooperation meant little more than the presence of representatives in the allied headquarters—a German general at Italian headquarters, for example. **Goering's** dispatch of **Keitel**, the head of the OKW, or **Jodl**, the chief of staff of the OKH, to Italy, **Finland**, **Hungary** or **Rumania** illustrated this weakness in the structure of the Axis "alliance." The concept of a global strategy against the **United States** and the **United Kingdom** to be conducted by the tripartite powers barely survived the meeting, in Berlin on February 24, 1942, of the "Permanent Council" of three commissions that had already been formed—a general commission, a military commission and an economic commission. The military commission was convoked only two or three times during the decisive months between December 1941 and early 1943. The audiences Hitler or **von Ribbentrop** granted to the diplomats and statesmen of the Axis and its allies dealt with problems that should have been handled by true councils of war. Between September 1939 and January 1945 there were more than 270 meetings between Hitler—or von Ribbentrop—and the representatives of friendly, nonbelligerent or complacent neutral states. Only a tenth of these sessions could have been considered ''councils of war,'' unless the phrase is given a very broad meaning. It is, however, worthwhile to consider the most important of them.

Negotiations conducted by von Ribbentrop with **Stalin** and **Molotov** in Moscow ended on August 24, 1939 with the **Nazi-Soviet Pact**, pledging nonaggression and dividing eastern Europe into two spheres of interest, one German and one Russian. They also insured the benevolent neutrality of the **USSR** if the western powers declared war on Germany after the planned attack on **Poland**. Subsequent negotiations between the partners, which resulted in the treaty of friendship of September 28, 1939, altering the spheres of influence—with Lithuania ceded to the USSR and the region between the Vistula and Bug rivers to Germany—was designed to demonstrate to the western powers the common viewpoint of Germany and the USSR concerning the modifications they had imposed by force on Poland. The status quo was to be considered ''definitive.''

The meetings at the Brenner Pass between Hitler and Mussolini on March 18, 1940 represented the first true war council of the Axis powers. Il Duce repeated what he had told von Ribbentrop at Rome on March 13 regarding Italy's entry into the war, at the propitious moment, against Great Britain and France. But nothing relating to German-Italian cooperation on the conduct of the war was discussed.

Toward the end of the German push into France, on June 16, 1940, Hitler received an emissary of the Spanish chief of staff, at Acoz Castle in southern Belgium. The emissary informed the Fuehrer that Franco was ready to enter the war as an Axis ally. Anticipating that the British would seek some arrangement with him, Hitler refused the offer. In the same state of mind at the time of his meeting with Mussolini in Munich on June 18, 1940, he persuaded Italy to renounce its territorial claims in expectation of an imminent armistice.

After the armistice with France on June 25, Italy's ambitions in the Mediterranean were discussed in the audiences Hitler gave the Italian ambassador, Dino Alfieri, in Berlin on July 1 and Count **Ciano** on July 7. At this second appointment Italy for the first time re-

vealed its aims in **Greece** and **Yugoslavia**, based on the divisive tensions in the Balkans. In his meetings with Hungarian, Rumanian and Bulgarian heads of state, Hitler sought a peaceful solution to the conflicts between the three nations that would not at the same time impinge on German interests. The problem was settled at Vienna on August 30 in a bargaining session between von Ribbentrop and Ciano on the partition of Transylvania, based on discussions between Hitler and Ciano at Berghof on August 28.

When it dawned on Hitler that Great Britain was in no mood to cooperate with him in ''dividing up the world,'' he plunged into conferences with Mussolini on October 4, **Laval** on October 22 and Petain on October 24, where he hoped to obtain compromises with **Spain**, Vichy France and Italy concerning their respective interests in North Africa and at the same time to convince Spain and France that entry into the war as his allies in a ''continental bloc against Great Britain'' was to their advantage.

Mussolini's decision to attack Greece and profit from victories he could not gain from the British in a separate Balkan war was communicated too late for Hitler to oppose it. When he conferred with Mussolini in Florence on October 28, the attack had already been in progress for several hours.

Hitler's lack of success in promoting harmony between Spain, Vichy France and Italy, as well as the failure of Mussolini's ''separate war,'' embarrassed him in the talks he conducted at Berlin on November 12-13, 1940, in which **Molotov** and von Ribbentrop participated. The Fuehrer and his foreign minister tried to persuade the USSR to join Germany's tripartite pact with Italy and Japan, thus becoming part of the Eurasian continental bloc. Implicit in this offer was fulfillment of the ancient Russian dream of expanding to the south into **Iran** and to the Indian Ocean. But Molotov spoke instead of Soviet expansion to the west, into Finland and Rumania, as well as south into **Turkey** for air and naval bases in the Dardanelles. Implied in this, however, was a head-on clash with German interests in the **Baltic States**, which, to Hitler and von Ribbentrop, was naturally anathema.

Failing in his meeting with the Spanish minister of foreign affairs Serrano Suner at Berghof on November 18 to get a commitment from Spain to enter the war, Hitler went to work on the Balkan countries to get them into the **Tripartite Pact**. He partly succeeded with **Hungary** in preliminary discussions with Council President Paul Teleki on November 20, 1940; with Rumania he succeeded completely, renewing the personal tie between himself and **Ion Antonescu**, the new head of the Rumanian government, in their conferences on November 22, 1940 and on January 14,

1941. But he failed with King **Boris III** of **Bulgaria** on November 18 and with Yugoslavia in his conferences with Minister of Foreign Affairs Aleksander Cincar-Marcovich on November 28 and with Prime Minister Dragisha Cvetkovich on February 14, 1941, getting nothing from any of them. Meanwhile, Italy's defeats in North Africa and **Albania** forced Mussolini to abandon his "separate war" and ask for German aid in the Mediterranean.

Although he finally won the consent of Bulgaria (on March 1, 1941) and Yugoslavia (on March 25, 1941) to join the Tripartite Pact, Hitler remained suspicious of the two countries, as evidenced by his meeting with Ciano on March 25, 1941. Immediately after the Belgrade putsch of March 27, 1941 Hitler promised Hungary and Bulgaria their share of the loot when he decided to partition Yugoslavia. This theme was further developed after the creation of the Croatian Independent State in the preliminary Hitler-Ciano dialogue in Vienna on April 20-21, 1941. It should be noted here, by the way, that Hitler conferred regularly with the Croatian leader **Ante Pavelich**, whom he protected from both domestic and foreign enemies.

In the meantime, Japan was more than ever involved in Hitler's global strategy. During a sojourn in Europe, Foreign Minister **Yosuke Matsuoka** obtained the Fuehrer's pledge "that if Japan waged war on the United States, Germany for its part would act accordingly." Matsuoka, however, was kept in complete ignorance of Hitler's definite intention to attack the USSR; he knew only that relations between Germany and the Soviet Union were worsening.

Even Mussolini was unaware of German military plans for a thrust to the east at the time of his meeting with Hitler at the Brenner Pass on June 2, 1941. Only Antonescu was informed of them, in their broad outlines, in Munich on June 18. In an exchange of views with the Japanese ambassador, **Hiroshi Oshima**, on June 3, 1941, Hitler mentioned the possibility of an onslaught on the USSR. After his initial triumph in the east, Hitler proposed on July 14, 1941 that Japan participate in the occupation of the USSR by marching from Vladivostok to Omsk, where Japanese troops would link up with German contingents. He went ever further: he unveiled a plan for an offensive alliance between Japan and Germany for war on the U.S.

On August 25-28, 1941 Mussolini remained at Hitler's headquarters and accompanied his host on a jaunt to "the front." The question of establishing a true alliance never arose. For Hitler the meeting with Ciano on October 25, 1941 concerned the distant future, while the conferences with his allies that followed it, on November 27-29, 1941, were aimed at bringing them into the Anti-Comintern Pact to compensate for the failure of the German generals to capture Moscow and to demonstrate his unshakable resolution to pursue the struggle to the bitter end.

When Japan launched its attack on the U.S. and the British and Dutch possessions in Southeast Asia on December 7, 1941 and Hitler and Mussolini followed suit with their declarations of war on the U.S., it became clear after the Fuehrer's first meeting with Oshima on December 15, 1941 that there would be no change of any importance in the method of these conferences. In his next interview with Oshima, on January 3, 1942, Hitler even went so far as to express his feeling that the Japanese could not subdue the "Anglo-Saxon powers" when they had no idea how to conquer the U.S. There was no mention now of Japanese intervention against the USSR; Hitler was not to return to that topic until January 1943.

The preliminary talks between Hitler and Mussolini and between the military chiefs of the two allies on April 29-30, 1942 at the Castle of Klessheim were the first that could be given the name "war council." Plans were roughed out for the conduct of the war in the Mediterranean in the summer of 1942—the offensive in North Africa, the conquest of **Malta**, the advance into **Egypt**—even if Hitler held his own counsel on the Malta operation and remained silent to a Japanese demand for a declaration by the Tripartite Pact nations concerning **India** and Arabia. Meetings with the Indian nationalist **Subhas Chandra Bose** on May 27, 1942 and a former minister of **Iraq** on June 15, 1942 confirmed Hitler's suspicion of entanglements in nationalist Asiatic movements that could only spoil the compromise with Great Britain that he hoped for. He did, however, make some unexpected offers to Turkey on the occasion of a conference with its representatives on May 30, July 13 and August 14, 1942, to tempt it into striking at the Russians.

Hitler's negotiations with Ciano and Laval at Munich on November 10, 1942 were dominated by the crisis provoked by the Allied landing in North Africa just three days earlier and by the measures to be taken against it—occupation of the rest of France, establishment of a bridgehead in Tunisia and the like. The even more serious crisis of the disaster suffered by the Germans at Stalingrad and in the Don loop brought Mussolini closer to the conviction of his need for a separate peace with the USSR. When Ciano informed Hitler of this at the latter's headquarters on December 18-20, 1942, Hitler answered, "There is no common ground on which Germany and Russia can meet to reconcile their essential needs in food and raw materials." In the same way, their different attitudes toward the Chetnik movement in Yugoslavia drove a wedge between Hitler and Mussolini throughout their negotiations.

From this time on, in his deliberations with the representatives of his allies at headquarters or Klessheim, Hitler tried to foster the alliances by stressing his desire to maintain them and commenting optimistically on the situation of the moment. He turned a deaf ear to German critics of the "irresponsible" ministers of the Axis countries who raised objections in his meetings with Antonescu on January 10 and April 12-13 of 1943 and with Adm. **Miklos von Horthy** on April 16-17 of the same year. These talks indicated, among other things, that Rumania and Hungary had developed wills of their own. Since their meeting at Feltre in northern Italy on July 19, 1943, Mussolini lacked the stomach to inform Hitler of the instability of his country's condition, the weakness of his own authority and his heartfelt desire to surrender.

After the fall of Il Duce on July 25, 1943, the capitulation of the **Badoglio** government on September 3, 1943 and the spectacle of a Fascist republic with little will to fight, entirely dependent on Germany, Hitler's principal worry was the specter of new defections, this time by the Hungarians and Rumanians. Bulgaria, too, showed signs of escaping the weak grip of its government after the death of King Boris III on August 28, 1943, following his meeting with the Fuehrer.

Of all these diplomatic assignations, the following stand out: Antonescu's visit of February 26-28, 1944, assuring Hitler of his devotion to the alliance; Horthy's reception of March 18, 1944, in which the regent was so severely browbeaten that he consented to the occupation of Hungary and the forced resignation of the Kallay government, which had dared recommend abandonment of the war; and a second meeting with Antonescu on March 23-24, 1944 to discuss publication of the secret cession of Transylvania to Rumania and thus prevent the collapse of Hungary's regime. As opposed to the swift treatment of these specific objectives, the extended and dreary sessions with Mussolini on April 22-23 and again immediately after the **assassination attempt of July 20, 1944** yielded only generalities. The Italian Fascist republic, after all, was nothing but a hindrance.

Even more astonishing than these last meetings with Mussolini were the discussions with Oshima on January 22, May 27 and September 4, 1944. Hitler's doubts of Japan's intentions and Oshima's ignorance of Japan's defeats in the Pacific lent these conferences a surrealist setting.

In a much different fashion the meetings with Rumanian and Hungarian representatives in the latter half of 1944—the last conference with Antonescu on

May 5, 1944, and with Szalasi, who succeeded Horthy as head of the Hungarian government after the admiral's arrest on October 16, 1944—were organized with every trick of demagogic cosmetics to keep these allies at Germany's side until the final debacle.

The conferences scheduled by the Axis and Tripartite Pact powers were enervated by their dilatory nature and by Hitler's tendencies to burst into impassioned speeches. As *Goetterdaemmerung* approached, all possible choices reduced to two: victory or immolation.

A. Hillgruber

CONGO, BELGIAN.

On May 28, 1940 the Belgian army surrendered unconditionally to **Germany**, which had occupied all of **Belgium**. Having refused to follow his ministers to France, King **Leopold III** found the presence of the enemy a hindrance to his reign. But what attitude was the Congo, a Belgian colony since 1908, with its immense economic resources, its 11 million natives and 25,000 Europeans, to take?

Rijckmans, the governor-general, did not hesitate. In his eyes, the government of **Hubert Pierlot** was the "sole voice of the nation's will." The duty of the Congo, he said, "this great Belgian land the enemy cannot and will never violate," was to work for and "hasten the day of deliverance." At the moment of the French collapse, Rijckmans decided without hesitation to keep the Congo in the war at the side of the British.

There was, however, vacillation among the colony's leaders. In Katanga, especially, there was a definite neutralist tendency, and in some quarters a desire for autonomy was expressed. The representatives of Belgian colonial society were opposed by a huge majority to the decision of General Administrator A. De Vleeschauwer, who was inclined to hold the Congo in the Allied camp. From the royal entourage in Brussels came instructions to keep the Congo out of the war or to enter it against **Italy**.

On June 18, 1940 the government adopted legislation to confirm and ensure Belgian sovereignty in the Congo. The minister of the Congo was named by decree general administrator of the colony, with executive and judicial powers that the Council of Ministers held in time of war, as provided by the colonial charter. At this time the government's position was ambiguous regarding the conduct of the war. But after his arrival in Lisbon and later in London, De Vleeschauwer, solidly supported by his general director, Robert de Muelenaere, went irrevocably over to the British and pledged the economic mobilization of the Congo in favor of the Allied war effort. On its part, London warned the Belgian ministers that it would "wash its hands of all Belgian interests" and use the power of the British navy to prevent the fall of the Congo into German hands in the event that Belgium surrendered the colony's resources to the Reich.

The essential contribution of the Congo to the Allied war effort was economic and financial—the delivery in increasing quantity of strategic metals (copper, cobalt, tungsten, tin), industrial diamonds, and agricultural and forest products such as oils and latex. Later on, the *Union Miniere* of Upper Katanga also furnished to the Allies the uranium of Shinkolobwe, with which the first **atomic bombs** were produced.

The cost of the war effort to the colonial society consisted of 60-120 days of forced labor in the fields per year; heavy reliance on native manual labor in industry, with rapid and increasing proletarization; an exodus from rural areas; and the disruption of the traditional social equilibrium. In November 1943 the papal vicar of Katanga, Monsignor de Hemptinne, frequently accused of neutralist and even defeatist attitudes, pilloried the Belgian government for excessive zeal in favor of the Allies and at the expense of the African population in expiation for its surrender in 1940.

The priority placed on economic output corresponded to the desires and needs of the Allies. The Belgians in the Congo insisted, quite strongly at times, on direct and active participation in military operations. The colony's troops intervened principally, but not exclusively, in **Ethiopia**, where they triumphed at Salo in July 1941, after the Belgian government recognized the state of war between Belgium and Italy.

Tensions surfaced in the Congo between 1940 and 1944, in African as well as European circles. For the Europeans these involved the development of social demands among salaried and appointed personnel in the form of strikes at the *Union Miniere* of Upper Katanga in October 1941, as well as the growth of demands for more autonomy for the Congo among certain groups of colonists.

Among the Africans, there was resurgence of tribal activity after May 1940 and the rural rebellion of Masisi-Lubutu in 1944; strikes and riots in Elisabethville in December 1941 and in Leopoldville and Matadi in 1945; a serious mutiny of the public security forces at Luluabourg in February 1944; and the first parapolitical demonstrations of the "evolues" of Luluabourg in March 1944.

These tensions were certainly exacerbated by conditions accompanying the war—monetary devaluation, inflation and developing fissures in the colonial bloc; and the stability forced by European labor, on one hand and the inefficiency of the territorial occupation, as well as the increased burden of forced labor and servitude, on the other. The social and political realities these tensions revealed were also the background for the movements and forces that were ultimately to determine the outcome of the struggle for the Congo.

J. Gerard-Libois

CONSCIENCE.

During the era of wars that were conducted by mercenaries without morally involving civilian populations, the problem of how to deal with the occupation of one's country by enemy troops did not arise for the ordinary citizen. But after popular patriotism embroiled individual citizens in international conflicts, the problem asserted itself. The more "total" the war, the dimmer the distinction between combatant and noncombatant became; **resistance** to the occupying power became every citizen's duty. Thus, Napoleon and his marshals were defied in **Spain** by true "guerrillas" of the people.

The people's patriotic sentiments were soon reinforced by the adoption of a particular ideology. The old crusaders' dreams were reborn in the hearts of insurgents. Under these circumstances the resultant struggle was bound to be a fight to the finish with the issues etched plainly, a fight between the "heroes" and the "villains."

Or, at least, so it seemed. But it soon became apparent that the issues were not quite so clear-cut. The ideological struggle presented the citizen with a problem of conscience: to know what he must do, to choose the road he must travel, to determine how far along it he should go. Everywhere, during World War II, in every occupied country and social group, this problem of conscience required serious choices.

Even the Resistance soldier, totally committed to the battle, was not immune to doubt, despite his apparently irrevocable choice. Would that **sabotage** operation pay off, considering the reprisals likely to follow? And there were other cases that, although less dramatic, were more subtle. Thus, the protagonist of Pierre-Henri Simon's novel *Histoire d'un amour* is a young doctor who, while looking after the wounds of a Resistance fighter in his hospital, yet feels almost a warm friendship for his colleague, a German who is not a Nazi and longs only for an end to the massacre. Should this French doctor lie to the colleague who trusts him? Yet he cannot admit that the man he is treating is an FFI maquis. He therefore faces the dilemma of betraying either his wounded comrade in arms or his German colleague, who will have to endure a terrible inquisition when his superiors discover the deception.

On the other side of the barricade, there was the relatively frequent case of non-Germans who, out of misdirected idealism, embraced the Nazi faith. In time, they realized their mistake. They could, for example, have revealed massacres of Jews they had witnessed. But what could they do then? To resign their responsibilities as collaborators could be interpreted as a cowardly act, especially when the German armies were undergoing severe setbacks. To abandon their cause would then be seen as a cover-up. Thus, often with some sense of romantic despair, some collaborators stayed to the bitter end in a cause that morally had ceased to be theirs.

Even more widespread were the moral difficulties experienced by administrators of every type whose professional obligation it was to ensure the normal functioning of some public service or enterprise. On the one hand, their task was to prevent chaos and protect the populace against disasters worse than the war and the occupation. But, on the other, they were obliged not only to confer daily with enemy authorities but also to countersign decrees they found repugnant. Yet countersign they did, in the hope that they could thereby avert the worst.

The Dutch government, for example, had left to the secretary-generals of the ministers instructions at once precise and vague when they departed the occupied country—precise, because they felt they should not have deserted their posts to avoid a change of administration, even to a Nazi government, and vague, because nobody could predict how far such "collaboration" would go.

In the winter of 1940-41, to take another example, the occupying power launched a campaign to finance the *Winterhilfe*—the "winter assistance" that for several years had already been under way in Germany. Should the government of the occupied country refuse collaboration in this kind of work? That, in effect, was equivalent to tendering its resignation. On the other hand, since the large enterprises were taxed in any case, the money thus gathered might very well end up in the Nazi coffers. Should not the Dutch people themselves profit from this windfall? Or, looking at the problem from another viewpoint, was this not an enemy propaganda operation?

The heads of businesses were placed in similar dilemmas when given the choice between equally detestable alternatives. They either had to work for the enemy—particularly in the construction of the **Atlantic Wall**—or shut their eyes to unemployment among their countrymen and their consequent likely deportation to a **Germany** under heavy bombardment. The judges who had to try such cases of collab-

oration after their country was liberated were obliged to depart from strictly juridical considerations and dwell on motives of interest to the accused. Among such judges the conviction increased that the accused should be given the "benefit of the doubt"; a man, after all, was not necessarily a traitor because he had made a decision that hindsight proved wrong. True, there were a good many cases of outright cynicism; but with them were genuine problems of conscience, in the economic sphere as well as in other areas.

Finally, there was the unique position of the Jews. The Jewish residents of the occupied countries certainly had advance knowledge of the Nazi's visceral **anti-Semitism**, but few of them, at least in the beginning, suspected its gravity. From the time they registered for deportation, first in their own countries and then in **Poland**, thousands of the victims never gave up hope. These overoptimistic hopes themselves awoke problems of conscience and caused instances of debatable collaboration.

Once the Jewish community was isolated, the Germans demanded "official spokesmen" for the ghetto. The rabbi seemed the logical choice to form a "Jewish council" and preside over it. In most cases, nothing worse ensued, at least for a time. But that was only the prelude to the tragedy, and so well was it understood that the members of the "council" resigned one by one. Others, however, remained "to save whomever they could." If ordered to deport a given number of their community, they tried first to reduce the number, then to save at least the young and healthy. But those engaged in this grisly game had become accomplices in the extermination. With the best of intentions they tried to "gain time," to "dupe" the enemy, even to warn the designated victim to allow him the opportunity of escaping if he could. The results were sometimes excellent. But at what price!

The best document testifying to such cases of conscience is perhaps the novel *L'Arche ensevelie*, the story of the annihilation of an East European ghetto and the tragic rearguard battle led by a Jew who, after concession upon concession, realizes at last that true courage for him is to persist in his task. If he is permitted to organize the cultural work of his community, he considers it a victory; then the Jews can simultaneously demonstrate their talents, their self-control and their human dignity in their crisis. But this cooperation degenerates gradually into criminal collusion. And in the end the hero of the book, having entered the last car bound for the crematory ovens, is recognized by his fellow Jews and lynched.

If the problems of "purging" that arose after the liberation were so difficult to unravel, it was largely because of the delicate nuances of judgment required of those cases uncharacterized by incontrovertible evidence of collaboration. Actually, those who had made mistakes could frequently invoke the question of conscience. Taxed with such an accusation, the Dutch minister J. A. W. Burger put it best by saying, "It is not those guilty of faults who should be punished but those who are guilty."

H. Brugmans

CONSCIENTIOUS OBJECTION.

Conscientious objection to armed action had been admitted in the British Empire and the **United States,** but hardly elsewhere, as a bar to conscription into the armed forces in World War I. From respect for the power of conscience and in deference to religious pressure groups, the same countries allowed it again in World War II. Objectors had to satisfy a lay tribunal, composed neither of officers nor of clergy, that they had serious, sincere and long-held moral principles which prohibited them from bearing arms against others. About two percent of those called up for service appeared before such tribunals; about half of these, in turn, had their objections allowed.

Those who thus registered as objectors were required to work in civil hospitals, on the land or (in the **United Kingdom**) in the fire service or on other work to protect the civil population against air raids. Many English objectors consequently had a more arduous and a more dangerous time than contemporaries who were in uniform but *embusques* in remote headquarters. They were much less unpopular than their predecessors in World War I and much less persecuted either by tribunals or by the press.

Their existence made little difference to the war efforts of the countries in which they lived and provided a **propaganda** device of some use, as an example of how a free country can work, by comparison, for example, with the German system, which sent Jehovah's Witnesses to concentration camps.

M. R. D. Foot

CONSEIL NATIONAL DE LA RESISTANCE (CNR).

The "National Resistance Council" was the parent **Resistance** organization for all of France proper, containing one representative from each of the principal Resistance movements and of the political parties opposed to the "National Revolution," as well as delegates from two labor unions. The first meeting of the council was presided over by its creator, **Jean Moulin,** afterward succeeded by **Georges Bidault** and then Louis Saillant.

CONTROL COUNCIL.
See **Interallied Control Council for Germany.**

CONVOYS.

In 1917 convoys had been proved to be the only safeguard for merchant ships against submarine attack, however incomplete. In World War II the **United Kingdom** could not survive without large imports by sea, and all the main British and Anglo-American expeditions hinged on convoys. The British, operating as before against the Germans on exterior lines with limited naval superiority, organized convoys in home waters from the earliest days of the war. These were assemblies of five to 50 merchant ships, commanded by a naval officer (usually a retired admiral called back to service), protected by as large an escort of antisubmarine vessels as could be made available—destroyers, frigates and corvettes. In 1939-40 the escort was sometimes no more than a single destroyer. The escort commander, however junior in age, had the merchant convoy commander under his orders.

Of the 114 ships sunk by German **U-boats** in 1939, only four were sailing in convoy. Early in 1940 British escorts could only reach about 250 miles west of **Ireland**, and losses were heavy; they became heavier still after the Germans gained U-boat bases on the west coast of France in June. The arrival of 50 old U.S. destroyers for use by the British in September (in exchange for the lease of British bases in the West Indies) offset the loss of the Biscay ports. By April 1941 the combined efforts of the British and Canadian navies had closed to about 300 miles the "black hole" in mid-Atlantic where U-boats could operate more or less at will. In 1941, as in 1940, the British lost some two million tons of merchant shipping to U-boats, and total Allied merchant shipping losses in 1942 were as high as 6,266,000 tons.

This was partly because U-boats had an exceptional run of success in the Caribbean and off the southeastern **United States** in the early months of 1942. By August 1942 the Americans had an efficient convoy system organized, running to New York from Key West, Florida and Guantanamo, Cuba and later extended to Aruba, Trinidad and Rio de Janeiro. A joint Anglo-American committee arranged schedules, as tight as a railway timetable, to transfer ships from these coastal convoys to transatlantic runs from New York and Halifax and from Nova Scotia to Glasgow, Liverpool or **Gibraltar**. The development of asdic, **sonar** and **radar**; improvements in methods of hurling depth charges; and the growing availability of long-range aircraft narrowed the black hole to the vanishing point.

In March and April 1943 these methods met their

principal challenge from Adm. **Doenitz**'s wolf packs, each consisting of eight to 20 U-boats hunting in a gang. The Allies won, partly because they could hear the U-boats talking to each other, partly because their antisubmarine weapons were efficient and partly because they added small escort carriers to their convoy escorts. Aircraft from these carriers forced U-boats to operate for longer hours under water and attacked them effectively. Improved U-boats, with snorkels (breathing tubes) that made them harder to detect from the air and easier to remain submerged, became available too late to secure Doenitz any important victory; by the end of 1944 he was losing submarines faster than he was sinking ships.

In all, the Germans operated nearly 1,200 U-boats, of which they lost 700 to Allied attack and nearly 100 by other causes; 32,000 German sailors died in them. The British lost just under 30,000 merchant seamen. Of the total Allied and neutral shipping losses, less than 30 percent (nearly 15 million tons) were torpedoed when sailing in convoy. Large liners—the French *Pasteur,* the Canadian *Empress of Britain*, the British *Queen Mary* and *Queen Elizabeth*—were fast enough to sail unescorted. The two *Queens* could each hold over 10,000 troops for a five- or six-day transatlantic voyage—an enormous help to the American buildup in Europe. Experience proved that any ship which could be sure of sailing faster than 14 knots throughout its voyage was practically immune to submarine attack.

Two special areas of convoy work deserve particular mention.

In 1942-43 **Malta** was so heavily beleaguered that the island nearly ran out of supplies, both of food for the inhabitants and of ammunition for the defenses. It lay much closer to air and naval bases on Italian soil than either to Gibraltar or to Alexandria. Monthly convoys were run to the island in 1942, usually with heavy losses; in August 1942 nine ships were lost out of 14, as well as two cruisers and an escort carrier, but an indispensable American tanker was brought into Valetta harbor with her decks awash, and Malta pulled through. After the invasion of Sicily in July 1943, the island was safe.

Convoys by the Arctic route to the **USSR** began in October 1941 and continued intermittently until May 1945. They carried tens of thousands of American vehicles, without which the Red Army would have been unable to perform its prodigies of supply, and much badly needed armament as well. But losses in the short summer nights in 1942 and 1943 were unacceptably high, and the British twice suspended the service—an act interpreted by Soviet leaders as malevolent weakness of will.

M. R. D. Foot

COOPER, (Alfred) Duff (later Viscount Norwich) (1890-1954).

Cooper, a British politician, served as a guards officer in 1918. After marrying a duke's daughter, he entered politics in 1924. He served in the Admiralty in 1937-38 but resigned over the **Munich Pact**. He re-entered government service after the war began, however, serving as minister of information in 1940-41; on a mission to the Far East in 1941-42; as minister resident with the Free French in Algiers in 1943-44 and as ambassador to France in 1944-47.

CORAL SEA.

In the spring of 1942, while Adm. **Isoruku Yamamoto** was envisaging a great offensive eastward that would engender the long-desired decisive battle, whose components were Operations MI against **Midway** and AL against the **Aleutian Islands**, the Japanese army was looking south, to **New Guinea**, the Solomons, and beyond to **Australia**. Operation MO was designed essentially to seize Port Moresby on the southwest tip of New Guinea and, secondarily, Tulagi on the south Solomons flank. Vice Adm. Shigeyoshi Inouye at Rabaul was given overall command of the seven groups assigned to MO. Rear Adm. Aritomo Goto, sailing with the support force, assumed tactical responsibilities. If the U.S. Pacific Fleet could be lured into a southwestern Pacific trap, so much the better, from the IJN standpoint.

Japanese fleet movements got underway at the end of April and beginning of May 1942. U.S. intelligence, with its cryptographic feats, gave Adm. **Nimitz** a tremendous edge in being able to concentrate forces at optimum locations, while the Japanese, despite greater strength at this stage of the war, were largely in the dark concerning Allied dispositions and resources. Thus, the small Japanese amphibious force at Tulagi, unloading without opposition and weakly defended, was caught by surprise when torpedo planes and dive-bombers from USS *Yorktown*, operating alone, struck three times on May 4, from morning until afternoon. The raiders sank one destroyer, one transport and two patrol craft and damaged a destroyer, a transport and a minelayer. Nimitz found the results disappointing. Task Force 17, under Rear Adm. Frank Jack Fletcher, now began searching for the enemy carrier force, while Rear Adm. Takeo Takagi did likewise with his MO carrier strike force and Adm. Inouye sent out whatever long-range flying boats he had available at Rabaul. U.S. planes sighted Goto's distant cover force and the main Port Moresby invasion flotilla on May 6. Confident that the enemy was ignorant of the carriers belonging to Takagi, Inouye allowed the operation to proceed. But the latter was duped by an erroneous **reconnaissance** report into launching a powerful two-carrier strike on May 7 against the presumed U.S. carrier force—actually the oiler *Neosho* and destroyer *Sims,* both of which were sunk, although not easily. Meanwhile, the U.S. carriers *Lexington* and *Yorktown* caught the light carrier *Shoho* from Goto's close-support force while most of its planes were away on an anticarrier strike of their own. *Shoho* was sunk, the first IJN carrier of any type to be destroyed in the Pacific war. Unknown to Fletcher, Inouye ordered the MO invasion force to fall back for the time being. Weather conditions on May 7 interfered with aerial scouting by both sides, and any ideas of night attacks were accordingly discarded. Early on May 8 the Americans finally caught sight of the two heavy carriers in the IJN carrier strike force, and *Yorktown* and *Lexington* promptly launched their planes. The former's aircraft caused some damage to *Shokaku*; the latter's accomplished little. *Zuikaku* was not even located, and *Shokaku* got away. At about the same time, *Yorktown* and *Lexington* themselves came under air attack. Poorly protected, *Lexington* was crippled by IJN torpedo planes and dive-bombers, but might have survived had it not been for internal explosions that caused her to be abandoned and finished off by a U.S. destroyer. The loss was not admitted publicly for a month. Dive-bombers damaged *Yorktown*, despite its excellent evasive action, and the carrier was driven from the scene. The Japanese lost 43 planes to all causes on May 8; the Americans, 33. Confusion at the IJN command level caused countermanding orders; in spite of Yamamoto's decisive intent, neither *Zuikaku* nor Goto's units reengaged the enemy. Operation MO had been disrupted indefinitely, and *Zuikaku* finally headed for Truk on May 11. Having lost a considerable number of planes and pilots, the Japanese carrier did not see action again for a month. Task Force 17 had also been ordered to retire from the Coral Sea on May 8, defying some temptations to linger.

The Battle of the Coral Sea had marked the first all carrier-vs.-carrier engagement in history; the entire combat was conducted by aircraft, and no surface ship even sighted an enemy surface ship. The experienced IJN pilots, flying a good mix of generally better planes, had destroyed one precious U.S. fleet carrier (33,000 tons) and two small vessels; the Japanese suffered only one light carrier (9,500 tons) sunk and one heavy carrier damaged. It had been, in Samuel Eliot Morison's view, a battle of naval errors. Poor communications, intelligence and coordination plagued the Japanese, but their plotting skill was superior and they did achieve a tactical success. The greatest consequences of the Battle of the Coral Sea, however, were strategic. First, vulnerable to the prowling Allied task force, the Japanese invaders bound for Port Moresby

with their 12 transports had turned back meekly. For this caution, Adm. Inouye has been criticized roundly, especially since British Adm. J. C. Crace had withdrawn his task force of three Australian and U.S. cruisers and three destroyers as soon as he heard that the Japanese invasion flotilla was not proceeding against Port Moresby. Inouye may have been deterred in part by USAAF aircraft, which were very active and posed a threat to any new landing effort, especially one which lacked carrier-plane support. Secondly, the Battle of the Coral Sea rendered the two IJN heavy carriers *Zuikaku* and *Shokaku* unavailable in time for the impending giant confrontation at Midway, where, some argue, their presence might have reversed the outcome. To this day pro-Allied enthusiasts celebrate the Coral Sea battle for "saving Australia." Certainly, it boosted morale after the very recent disaster at **Corregidor**, reversed the momentum of the Pacific war and warranted being called "an indispensable preliminary to the great U.S. victory at Midway."

A. D. Coox

CORAP, Andre (1878-1953).
French general. Corap was the commander of the Ninth Army, which was stationed between Sedan and Givet on May 10, 1940 and which received the shock of massed German tanks and was unable to resist them.

CORREGIDOR.
American troops under Gen. **MacArthur** held Corregidor, a fortified island in the **Philippines**, for several months against repeated Japanese assaults. The garrison finally surrendered on May 7, 1942. The island was retaken by the Americans on February 16, 1945.

COVENTRY.
This English city was heavily attacked by the German air force on November 14-15, 1940. **Churchill** said, "On the whole this was the most devastating raid which we sustained." Over 400 people were killed and much of the town's center, including the cathedral, was destroyed. The effect on the aircraft factories in the suburbs was, however, slight and temporary.

CREDIT.
During the war credit was much more readily available for military purposes and much more restricted for private uses than in peacetime. British and American banks, usually fully independent, were prepared to accept a good deal of treasury guidance about how they should lend money. **Keynes**, though

a sick man, rejoined the British Treasury as an adviser, and his ideas came to dominate British and, to a large extent, American monetary policy. The rate of price inflation in the **United Kingdom** was kept below 10 percent per annum, and adequate war production was maintained. Credit in totalitarian countries remained at the whim of the ruling party.

CRERAR, Henry Duncan Graham (1888-1965).
Crerar, a Canadian general, had served as an artillery officer in France during World War I. He was chief of the Canadian general staff in 1940-41 and subsequently commanded various Canadian formations overseas, including the First Canadian Army in 1944-45.

CRIPPS, Sir (Richard) Stafford (1889-1952).
Cripps, a British socialist leader, had, as ambassador to the **USSR** in 1940-42, predicted a Soviet defeat. He led the House of Commons in 1942 and served as minister of aircraft production from 1942 to 1945 and of economic ministries from 1945 to 1950. Cripps could be characterized as an intellectual in politics. There was no love lost between him and **Churchill**.

CROATIA.
Taking advantage of the German attack on **Yugoslavia** on April 6, 1941, Croatia declared its independence four days later. It became a kingdom under an Italo-German protectorate. (See also **Ante Pavelich**.)

CROCKATT, Norman Richard (1894-1956).
Crockatt, a British officer, had served in World War I. He organized **MI-9** and directed it, secretly and successfully, from 1940 to 1945.

CROCKER, Sir John (1896-1963).
Crocker, a British soldier, had fought in France in 1917-18. He joined the tank corps in 1922. During 1940 he managed twice to extricate an armored brigade from France. Crocker commanded a corps in Tunisia in 1943 and a corps in the **Normandy landing** in 1944.

CROSSBOW.
Code name for the bombardment of the V-1 launching sites in 1944. (See also **Germany, Air Battle of; V-1 and V-2**.)

CUNNINGHAM, Sir Alan Gordon (1887-   ).
Cunningham was a British general and a brother of Adm. **Andrew Browne Cunningham**. He commanded a British force in East Africa in 1940-41 and the Eighth Army from July to November 1941. Cunning-

ham served in Northern Ireland in 1943-44 and as high commissioner of **Palestine** in 1945-48.

CUNNINGHAM, Sir Andrew Browne (later Lord) (1883-1963).
Cunningham, a British admiral, served as commander in chief of the British naval forces in the Mediterranean from 1939 to 1943 and as first sea lord from 1943 to 1946. Cunningham was known as a sound and imperturbable sailor.

CURZON LINE.
The Curzon Line, which roughly demarcated the ethnic boundary between Poles and Russians, was worked out by H. J. Paton in 1919. The line was named after the man who was British foreign secretary at the time. In 1920 the Poles secured a frontier well to the east of it; it corresponds roughly, however, to the central third of the frontier that has been in place between **Poland** and the **USSR** since 1945.

CYPRUS.
This Mediterranean island had been taken under British protection in 1878 as a *place d'armes*, in Disraeli's words, to dominate the eastern Mediterranean; its base facilities, however, have always been slight. It was of marginal use to the British during the war as an area for training and resting troops, for mounting air cover for **convoys** and for minor operations against the Aegean islands.

CZECHOSLOVAKIA.
Before it was occupied by **Germany**, this small nation, with a population of about 14 million in 1938, had a first-class intelligence service. After 1936 an important German member of the *Abwehr* named Paul Thuemmel was in its service, thus converting Prague into a prime listening post for the western nations; it was to them that the information Thuemmel gathered was sent.

On March 15, 1939, German troops marched unopposed into Czechoslovakia. The western part of the country became the Protectorate of **Bohemia-Moravia**, while Slovakia at its eastern extreme was reduced to a vassal state of the Reich. Czechoslovakia's former president **Eduard Benes**, who went into exile after his resignation, which came as a consequence of the **Munich Pact** in October 1938, organized a National Czechoslovakian Committee with the support of France and the **United Kingdom**. In June 1940 the committee moved from France to London, where it became a provisional government recognized by Great Britain and then by the **USSR**, which was the first to guarantee Czechoslovakia its 1919 frontier. In England, Benes formed small land and air forces; as early as the summer of 1940, Czech aviators had already distinguished themselves in the **Battle of Britain**.

At the moment the German troops crossed the Czech border on March 15, 1939, a KLM plane picked up 11 Czech intelligence officers and several cases of documents for passage to England. This brilliant exploit was planned and executed by Maj. Harold Gibson of the **Special Intelligence Service**, a connoisseur of Czech intelligence, its techniques and its sources. Throughout the war the Czech espionage center in London worked with secret networks within the occupied country, which in turn cooperated closely with Thuemmel until the **Gestapo** trapped him in March 1942.

Within occupied Czechoslovakia two **Resistance** movements took root, one primarily formed of officers and the other of political activists and academics. Beginning in August 1939, the means for escape to free nations were developed. When finally Great Britain and France declared war on Germany, spectacular demonstrations surged throughout the land. Railroad strikes erupted, Czech flags were flaunted in the streets and students convoked mass meetings. The Nazi reaction was swift and brutal: 1,200 students were deported and the universities were permanently closed. "An inferior race," said the Nazis, "the Czechs are not worthy of higher education."

At the beginning of 1940, various dissident groups united to form the Central Committee of Internal Resistance (UVOD), which published its own journal as well as a secretly distributed brochure describing its program. There had been no communist movement worthy of mention in Czechoslovakia before June 22, 1941; it developed on that date—the moment Nazi tanks rumbled across the Soviet frontier.

The Czech government in London and the newly formed UVOD urged the Resistance in the direction of information-gathering rather than military action. The heavy hand of Nazi repression was making itself felt. When *Reichsprotektor* **Heydrich** was ambushed in May 1942, for example, German reprisals went beyond the bounds of reason. The villages of **Lidice** and Lezaky were leveled, their male inhabitants massacred, thousands of hostages wantonly shot, and thousands more men and women sent to **concentration camps**.

In the meantime the Czech espionage networks were acquiring a superior technique. Before 1942 they had used whatever radio operators chance threw their way until the British began dropping in experienced men by parachute. Between 1940 and 1942 some 20,000 messages had been sent and 6,000 received from outside the country. Aside from economic data, the Czechs supplied London with important information about *Seeloewe*, the code name for the projected Nazi landing in England, and its later modifications; the date of the invasion of Russia, which Stalin refused to believe; and the Germans' work on **V-1 and V-2** rockets in the **Peenemuende** laboratories.

From London, Benes appealed insistently for a unified front of all Czechs, regardless of their political leanings. The Communists responded by accusing the non-Communists of holding back on the intensive **sabotage** Moscow demanded. But Benes apparently failed to understand that as the Soviet troops drove closer to Prague after the retreating Germans, the local Communists would take firmer command in preparation for the future. The Czech president was to pay for his neglect shortly after the war.

In launching its general uprising, which did not begin until May 1945, the western end of the country was slower than the Republic of Slovakia. The latter had been forced into supplying large numbers of recruits to reinforce the Germans on the eastern front. Beginning in 1943, whole bodies of Slovak troops deserted. An entire division went over to the Russians in October; another, given the mission of wiping out Soviet partisans, joined their ranks. In eastern Slovakia there was a guerrilla uprising in which escaped French and Belgian prisoners of war fought in comradeship with the partisans. In July 1944 the Red Army parachuted 24 groups of cadre officers to the insurgents. The Slovak general insurrection erupted in August. The partisans suffered badly in the ensuing battle, but they kept large numbers of German troops pinned down. In the spring of 1945 the partisans broke into Bohemia, and the general revolt exploded there in the beginning of May. As many as 30,000 Czechs fought in the streets for the liberation of Prague until Red Army troops began streaming into the city on May 9.

Some 360,000 Czechs and Slovaks were victims of the Germans between 1938 and 1945, having met their deaths by execution or in concentration camps or combat.

H. Bernard

D

DALADIER, Edouard (1884-1970).
Daladier was premier of France at the time of the **Munich Pact**, which he signed. In 1940, while serving as minister of war, he was interned by the Vichy government. In 1943 Daladier was taken to **Germany**, where he was imprisoned until the end of the war.

DALTON, Hugh (later Lord) (1887-1962).
Dalton was a British socialist. As minister of economic warfare from May 1940 to February 1942, Dalton took charge of the formation and early work of the **Special Operations Executive**. He served as minister of trade from 1942 to 1945 and as minister of finance from 1945 to 1947.

DALUEGE, Kurt (1897-1946).
An **SS** general, Daluege took over as the executioner of **Czechoslovakia** after **Heydrich's** assassination. He was executed as a **war criminal** in Prague in 1946.

DANSEY, Sir Claude (1876-1947).
Dansey was a British secret staff officer. He served as deputy head of **MI-6** in charge of work in western Europe from 1940 to 1945. Dansey was noted for his deceptively affable manner.

DANZIG.
Given the status of a free city by the Treaty of Versailles, Danzig provided **Poland** with an outlet to the Baltic Sea. **Hitler** attacked Poland when it refused to allow Danzig to be reincorporated into **Germany** (see *Fall Weiss*).

DARLAN, Francois (1881-1942).
Darlan, a bitter enemy of England, was appointed admiral of the French fleet in 1939 and minister of the navy in June 1940. After the German occupation of France, he was named by Marshal Petain as his eventual successor. Darlan became head of the government, minister of foreign affairs and minister of the interior after **Laval's** disgrace in December 1940. He collaborated with **Germany** in the Syrian campaign, remaining in his ministry post after Laval's return in

April 1942. Surprised in Algiers by the Allied landing on November 8, 1942, he went over to the Allies. On December 24 he was executed by a student acting on the order of the **Resistance**.

DARNAND, Joseph (1897-1945).
Darnand, a militant member of the *Action francaise* party and of the fascist *Cagoule*, became head of the *Legion des Combattants des Alpes-Maritimes* in 1940. He founded the *Service d'ordre legionnaire* and, in January 1942, *Milice francaise* to organize, in cooperation with the German police, the armed battle against the **Resistance**. Darnand became an officer in the *Waffen*-**SS**, and was named general secretary to the maintenance of order in December 1943. Later he became a member of the Sigmaringen Governmental Commission. On October 3, 1945 he was condemned to death and executed.

DEAT, Marcel (1894-1955).
Deat, a French professor, was elected a Socialist deputy in 1926. He was a founder of the French Socialist Party in 1933 and became minister of the air force in 1936. In 1939 he advocated cooperation with **Germany**, opposed France's entry into the war and converted the newspaper *L'Oeuvre* into the organ of the pacifists of the left. As head of the *Rassemblement national populaire*, he embraced Nazi principles, at the same time warring against the domestic policies of Petain. In March 1944 he became minister of labor and then a member of the Sigmaringen Governmental Commission. After the Allied occupation of France, he took refuge in an Italian monastery, where he died on January 5, 1955.

DEATHS.
It is impossible to make an accounting, even an approximate one, of the human costs of the war. How, for example, can one compute the number of civilian dead in the **USSR**, in **China**, in **Malaya**, in **Burma**, in the islands of the Pacific, in the **Philippines** or in any part of the world seared by the fighting or the passions it evoked? It has been estimated that the conflict

exacted a price of between 45 million and 50 million dead, among whom some 5.7 million were regarded as members of undesirable races and another five million were political prisoners in **concentration camps**.

These figures, however, account only for those who were killed directly as a result of the war, not those for whom it was an indirect cause of death by hunger, neglect, emotional shock or despair. The number of these deaths cannot even be guessed at.

The Dutch publication *Statistisch Bulletin van het Centraal Bureau voor de Statistiek*, No 83, 48, states the problem very well for **the Netherlands** and, for that matter, any other country involved in the war: "Setting the number of Dutch victims of the war at 210,000 does not take into account those for whose death the war was indirectly responsible. The proof is the following. In our country the mortality rate was 8.6 per 1,000 inhabitants in 1938, 8.5 in 1939, 8.5 in 1946, 8.1 in 1947. If we accept the average annual rate of 8.6 per 1,000 for the years of 1940 to 1946, we arrive at the figure of 468,000 dead in the course of that period. But there actually were 747,000 deaths. There was therefore an excess of about 280,000 deaths during the war over the deaths in peacetime, or 70,000 more than the 210,000 who were the war's direct victims."

The approximate figures presented here relate only to those who died because of the war before August 15,1945. But what do we know of those who died after the end of hostilities as a result of those hostilities?

During World War I the number of noncombatants who lost their lives was very small as a percentage of the total dead. By contrast, the civil war in Russia between 1917 and 1920 and the Spanish civil war of 1936-39 claimed a very high number of innocent victims. The number of noncombatant dead during World War II was of necessity still greater, including as it must the deaths resulting from the racial persecution of the Jews, the Gypsies and the Slavs and those buried under the rubble left by air raids.

It should be borne in mind that estimates of the number of war-related deaths are often exaggerated and contradictory. Some include **Resistance** fighters killed in combat and those who were executed or died from abuse in concentration camps, as well as ordinary soldiers, under the heading of "combatants," which is logical. Others, however, confuse Resistance fighters with the innocent victims of the war, which is completely unjustified, on the assumption that most of the resisters were civilians. Still others include in the same figure active resisters who died in deportation, forced or voluntary laborers sent to **Germany** from their own countries and those killed by Allied bombs. Finally, there are lists of war casualties that for some curious reason ignore sailors in the merchant marine, so many of whom were lost (see **Atlantic, Battle of the**).

To be sure, it is often difficult to distinguish between active resisters and passive victims, especially in the smaller countries in central or southeastern Europe or in China. Clearly, in a total war, where the distinction between civilian and military is blurred or nonexistent, what makes sense is simply to list the total number of deaths in each country without classification as civilian or military. The figures given here were compiled after careful study and are presented in the order of magnitude except for the **United States** and the **United Kingdom** and their territories or dominions that did not experience occupation.

From the available data the USSR, between June 22, 1941 and August 15, 1945, lost 18 million to 20 million citizens, one-third of whom were civilians, including 1.2 million Jews.

German and Austrian losses amounted to more than six million dead, of which 3.25 million were in the armed forces. Among the civilians were 140,000 Jews and 130,000 non-Jews, resisters or victims of racial persecution.

Poland occupies third place. The exact number of her losses is not known, although it certainly exceeds five million. Among Jews alone the figure has been calculated at between 2.3 million and 2.9 million.

Between 1937 and 1945 China and **Japan** suffered 2.5 million and 2.0 million dead, respectively, between 1937 and 1945.

Yugoslavia is sixth, with 1.7 million dead.

The British Commonwealth had at least 615,000 dead, classified in the following way: the United Kingdom, 468,000, of whom 398,000 were combatants and 70,000 civilians (of the latter, 60,595 died under bombardment in Great Britain, the others in **Malta**, Malaya, etc., or in German or Japanese internment camps); **Canada**, 39,400; **Australia**, 29,400; **New Zealand**, 12,300; **South Africa**, 8,700; **India**, 36,100; the colonies, 21,100. For the dominions and the colonies, the figures are for combatants only; the number of civilian victims in Southeast Asia is unknown.

The losses of **Rumania, Hungary** and **Czechoslovakia** were 665,000, 450,000 and 380,000 respectively. There are two reasons for the relative magnitudes of these figures. The first was that Slovaks, Rumanians, and Hungarians were forced by the Germans to furnish large troop contingents to the Russian front; and second, that there were many Jews in those countries and practically all were killed. The losses in another small country, **Greece**, were also high, but for other reasons—its population endured the most terrible famine plaguing Europe during the war. Of the nation's 620,000 dead, 360,000 were victims of starvation.

The U.S. lost 323,000, of whom only 2,000 were civilians who died in Japanese concentration camps, on the seas, etc. In addition to the American dead were thousands of Filipino casualties.

The dead of France and the French Union approached 580,000, with 150,000 soldiers or sailors killed in action and 39,000 in capitivity; 24,000 Resistance fighters killed in action and 30,000 shot or massacred in France; 200,000 political, racial, or laborer deportees to Germany; and 133,000 civilian victims of military operations, half of them killed in bombing raids.

Military and civilian dead in **Italy** exceeded 400,000—250,000 while the country was allied with Germany and 150,000 after September 1943, when it joined the Allies. Of these 150,000 dead, 75,000 partisans and military personnel died in action against the enemy, 41,000 military men and political prisoners died in Germany, thousands of civilians were massacred in reprisals or killed by bombardment, and 15,000 Jews were murdered.

Dutch losses came to 209,648 at a minimum, not counting the unknown number of dead in Japanese camps. Of these, 33,948 were members of the land, air and naval forces and the merchant marine or were Resistance fighters who were killed confronting the enemy, who died in the process of deportation or who were executed. The other 175,700 were civilians, including 104,800 Jews. Several thousand nonwhite Dutch civilians also died. Belgian losses were 54,747, of whom 25,479 were in the military and 29,268 were civilians, including 1,100 Belgian Jews. To these figures should also be added 30,000 non-Belgian Jews who had lived in **Belgium** and died in deportation. Casualties in **Luxembourg** amounted to 7,000 dead, including resisters killed in the ranks of the Allied armies, Jews and other civilians.

These statistics for the French, Dutch, Belgians and Luxembourgers who fell victim to the war do not include some 50,000 nationals of these countries—38,000 of whom were French—who were killed in the *Wehrmacht* ranks as impressed soldiers or as volunteers in Nazi or collaborator auxiliaries. Several hundred Swiss, Swedes, and other western Europeans, together with a larger number of Spaniards (the *Azul* Division) and still more Russians, fell fighting on the German side. These deaths are normally counted in with the losses suffered by the armed forces of the Reich. Casualties among the French Resistance included 2,000 Italians and 1,500 Spaniards, as well as Germans, Austrians, Poles, Rumanians, Britons, Belgians, Dutch, and Luxembourgers; some Russians and other nationals died in the ranks of the Belgian Resistance movement. All these various allegiances, national and ideological, complicate the problem of categorizing the casualty lists.

The death toll in **Finland** was 90,000; in **Bulgaria**, 20,000; in **Albania**, 20,000; in **Norway**, 10,000; in **Denmark**, 7,000; and in **Brazil**, 1,200.

H. Bernard

DE BONO, Emilio (1866-1944).

An Italian general, De Bono was one of the *quadrumvirs* of the "march on Rome" of 1922. After **Mussolini** took power, De Bono became, in turn, director general of the secret police, head of the Fascist Militia, governor of Tripolitania, minister of the colonies, high commissioner of **Eritrea** and **Somalia** (in January 1935) and chief of operations against **Ethiopia** (in October 1935). He was eventually replaced in this last position by **Badoglio**. With **Italo Balbo** he opposed Italy's alliance with **Hitler**; he voted with the majority of the Fascist Grand Council against Mussolini in July 1943. De Bono was condemned to death by the tribunal of the Republic of Salo (see **Italy**) and shot in Verona on January 11, 1944.

DECEPTION.

Already an ancient device of war in the days of the Trojan horse, deception remains a most effective weapon. The British made particularly good use of deception during World War II.

Wavell, much impressed with some successful deceptions that had been carried out against the Turks in 1917, set up at his headquarters in Cairo in 1939 a body designed to startle the Italians and called, uninformatively, the "A Force." Soon it had both **Graziani** and **Aosta** thoroughly confused. (Good deceptions are usually aimed personally at an opposing commander, if enough is known about him and his prejudices.)

Another group whose name revealed little about it—"Colonel Turner's department"—contributed significantly to the air defense of the **United Kingdom** in 1939-41 by doing much to confuse **Goering**. Trick fires on the ground, for example, once encouraged the *Luftwaffe*, which thought it was raiding Portsmouth, to drop its entire bomb load on nearby Hayling Island. Three cows were killed, instead of several hundred people; no naval damage at all was done. Less obvious, more intricate damage was done to the *Luftwaffe*'s special navigating equipment by teams of wireless experts using the **British Broadcasting Corporation**'s television transmitter.

Deception units used camouflage, of course, but deception was much more than a tactical detail that could be left to a unit camouflage officer to arrange.

Whenever a commander had a choice of courses, it was to his advantage to mislead the enemy about which course he was going to take; deception, properly conceived, provided the means.

Mountbatten, as imaginative a commander as Wavell, personally took part in a major deception devised to confuse the Germans about where the Anglo-American forces were going after their conquest of Tunis and, through **Peter Fleming**, made much use of deception against the Japanese in 1944-45.

Long-term strategic aims were impossible to hide, but there was infinite room for adjusting detail. Everyone, from **Hitler** to his most junior *Hitlerjugend* private, knew, for instance, that there was going to be an Anglo-American invasion of some part of northwestern Europe some time in the spring or summer of 1944. But an elaborate deception scheme convinced him not only that the American First and British Second armies were assembling in southern and southwestern England to threaten Normandy and Brittany—which was true—but that a Fourth British Army in Scotland threatened **Norway** and that a **United States** First Army Group in Kent, under **Patton**, was aimed directly at Pas-de-Calais, where German general staff members expected the invasion to take place. So when Operation Overlord began in Normandy on June 6, 1944, the beachhead area had not been reinforced; Hitler did not, in fact, withdraw a man from Norway until June 16, nor did he send a man west of the Seine until July 1. Yet the Fourth British Army and the U.S. First Army Group had no real existence beyond a network of wireless sets broadcasting dummy traffic; the First and Second armies sufficed to break Hitler's Army Group West.

At sea there were numerous opportunities for deception, ranging from dummy battleships, which were used to show strength in harbors where none existed, to bubbles emitted by **U-boats** under attack, in an effort to deceive Allied antisubmarine craft into thinking they had blown up a target that was, in fact, still awaiting its chance to sink an Allied **convoy**.

Dummy aircraft on airfields were commonplace. Really ingenious practitioners of deception were able, from time to time, to let the enemy realize that they were dummies, replace the dummies with the real thing, conduct a raid with them and put the dummies back in place before the enemy retaliated against the airfield.

An important deceptive practice codenamed Window was used (after long deliberation) by the RAF **Bomber Command** after July 1942. It consisted simply of dropping strips of tinfoil at regular and frequent intervals from aircraft; temporarily, it baffled the German **radar** operators by choking their screens. A refined version of this device was used over the Chan-

nel on the night of the **Normandy landing**, June 5-6, 1944, by two bomber squadrons that succeeded in simulating on German naval radar a vast armada steaming toward Cape Gris-Nez, which faded away into nothing at dawn.

A department of **MI-5** carried out the most successful deception of all. It was able to recruit every single agent the Germans thought they had working for them in Britain as a double agent and thus to fill the German high command with a mass of misconceptions about the strategic intentions of the British and Americans from 1942 right through to the end of the war.

M. R. D. Foot

DE GASPERI, Alcide (1881-1954).
From the Vatican Library, where he took refuge in 1929, De Gasperi, a former secretary of Don Sturzo's *Partito popolare*, organized a **resistance** movement that became the nucleus of the Italian Christian Democratic Party. On September 8, 1943 he joined the *Comitato di Liberazione nazionale dell'Alta Italia*, a coalition of anti-Fascist political parties. Elected political secretary of the *Democrazia cristiana* at the Congress of Naples, July 31, 1944, he became minister without portfolio of the first Bonomi cabinet (June-November 1944) and then minister of foreign affairs in the second Bonomi cabinet (November 1944-June 1945) and in the Parri cabinet (June-December 1945). He served as prime minister from 1945 to 1953.

DE GAULLE, Charles. See Gaulle, Charles de.

DEGRELLE, Leon (1906-   ).
Degrelle founded *Rexism*, a political movement, in **Belgium** in 1936. Its name derived from *Christus-Rex*, the slogan of the Catholic Youth Movement, for whose publications Degrelle was responsible at the time. *Rexism* possessed nationalist, anti-communist and anti-capitalist overtones but a vague ideology. The movement was at first supported by **Mussolini**. It had, however, lost all credibility within Belgium by the beginning of the war. Degrelle was arrested on May 10, 1940 by Belgian authorities. He was, however, freed at Abbeville after the country's surrender and at once began his **collaboration** with **Germany**. In 1942 he founded the Walloon Legion and led it into battle in the **USSR**. He incorporated the legion into the *Waffen*-**SS** in 1945. After the war Degrelle took refuge in **Spain**. Having forfeited his Belgian nationality, he was forbidden to return home and was sentenced to death in absentia by his liberated country.

DE JONGH, Andree (1916-).

With her father, Frederic, the director of a school, De Jongh organized the "Comet" Belgian **Resistance** network, which had been founded by Arnold Deppe. She was arrested on January 15, 1943 while on her 37th trip to Urrugne; she had already conducted 115 Allied airmen to safety by herself. She was deported to Ravensbrueck. After the war De Jongh devoted her attentions to a leper colony in **Ethiopia**.

Deppe, who had repatriated 800 Allied flyers through **Spain**, was himself arrested in 1941; De Jongh's father was shot in Mont Valerien on March 28, 1944.

DEJUSSIEU-PONTCARRAL, Pierre (1898-).

Dejussieu-Pontcarral was a French general in command of an army corps. He became the **Resistance** leader in Auvergne in 1941, and at the end of 1943 he took command of the *Forces francaises de l'interieur*. He was deported to **Germany** in 1944, where he remained in capitivity until the end of the war.

DELESTRAINT, Eugene (1879-1945).

Delestraint, a French general, served as head of the secret army in the southern zone of France in 1942; he then became national head of the secret army. He was arrested and deported in June 1943 and was shot at Dachau on April 23, 1945.

DE MAN, Henry (1885-1953).

De Man, a socialist theoretician, became president of the Belgian Workers' Party (POB) in 1939. In June 1940 he sent a manifesto to members of his party stating that they needed to accept "the fact" of the German victory in **Belgium** and that "the role of the POB is at an end." Together with several militant socialist and Christian syndicalists he founded the Union of Manual Laborers and Intellectuals (UTMI), combining the syndicates into a single organization. After 1941 he dissociated himself from the policies the Germans had imposed on the UTMI and was forbidden to engage in any public activity in 1942 as the result of one of his protests. He retired to Savoy and in 1944 obtained political asylum in **Switzerland**.

DEMPSEY, Sir Miles Christopher (1896-1969).

Dempsey, a British general, served in France in 1940 and in **Italy** in 1943. He commanded the British Second Army in northwestern Europe in 1944 and the 14th Army in **Malaya** in 1945.

DENMARK.

Before the war, Denmark had adopted a policy of almost complete disarmament. On April 9, 1940 the country was invaded by **Germany** and occupied within a day. Berlin informed the Danish government and the 3,852,000 Danes that any resistance its armies encountered would lead to the destruction by bombing of the principal Danish cities. If, on the other hand, the German ultimatum was accepted, the invading armies would enter as friends to protect Denmark against aggression from the Allied powers, and the Germans would allow the Danish government its sovereignty as before. Aware of the futility of any attempt to halt the Nazi military machine, Copenhagen accepted.

Thus, unlike the other occupied countries—**Poland, Norway, the Netherlands, Belgium, Luxembourg,** and soon **Yugoslavia** and **Greece** —the Danish government remained where it was (**Czechoslovakia** and the **French State** have to be regarded as special cases). King **Christian X** and his court did the same. At the beginning of their occupation of the country, the Germans did not attempt to interfere with the Danish government's administration.

The **United Kingdom** countered the German occupation by landing troops on the Faeroe Islands and Iceland, Danish possessions that would prove to be of high strategic value in the forthcoming **Battle of the Atlantic**. In the **United States**, Danish ambassador **Henrik Kauffmann** rebelled at accepting the instructions of a government deprived of its freedom of action and formed the Free Denmark movement, anticipating by two months a comparable move by de Gaulle. Kauffmann's movement won Washington's support. In return, Kauffmann put another Danish possession, **Greenland**, at the disposal of the United States for the construction of air-naval bases; the hardy Danish patrol there, traveling by dog sled, pinpointed the numerous German meteorological stations on the island as targets for destruction by American aircraft or Coast Guard vessels.

Kauffmann also asked the entire Danish merchant fleet, amounting to 1.2 million tons and staffed by 5,000 experienced seamen, to assist the Allied cause. More than 90 percent of the Danish sailors responded to Kauffmann's appeal. They represented a valuable contribution to the British at a time when merchant-vessel tonnage was critical. Almost 700 of these sailors gave their lives for the Allied cause; 60 percent of the Danish tonnage in service at the start of the war was sent to the ocean floor in sea battles. Beginning in 1943 the Danish ships carried the Union Jack along with their national colors. In 1944 two new minesweepers formed the nucleus of a Danish section in the Royal Navy.

Lacking manpower, Free Denmark could not mass land or air power, but a thousand Danish exiles and emigrants enlisted in the RAF and the British army.

Some of them were members of the "Buffs" regiment, whose honorary colonel was the Danish monarch. Others enlisted in the U.S. Army. Sixty Danish paratroopers were dropped from Allied aircraft onto Danish soil.

There is not the slightest doubt that Free Denmark stimulated the formation of the **Resistance** inside the country, many of whose members, as befitted a highly cultured and technically advanced nation, were scientists, authors, pastors, engineers and skilled workingmen. Everything they did was carefully thought out and precisely executed; no pointless risks were taken, and there was virtually no political conflict among the various factions.

Denmark was the only occupied country with a clandestine news agency. Founded by Borge Outze, this **underground press** published 26 million copies of the underground newspaper *Information*. One of its most brilliant contributors was the pastor Kaj Munk, an author of worldwide reputation, who was shot in 1944.

The Danish Resistance was in direct contact with the **Special Operations Executive**, unlike the resistance movements in other countries, which had to work through their governments in London. The leader of the Danish Conservative Party, Christian Moeller, escaped to England through the efforts of the SOE. The increasing strength of the underground press, the steadily growing number of incidents of **sabotage** and the violent strikes of August 1943 enraged the Germans; in response, on August 28, the Germans presented the Danish government with an ultimatum demanding that it proclaim a state of siege, forbid all public meetings and mete out the death sentence to those guilty of subversive acts. The ultimatum was rejected; the occupation authorities deprived the government of all its functions and assumed executive power. The few ships comprising the Danish navy were scuttled by their crews.

Encouraged by Moeller's messages, which were issued periodically through the **British Broadcasting Corporation**, the Resistance stepped up its activities. The work of the secret agents on Bornholm Island in exposing German activities at **Peenemuende** in August 1943 is well-known (see **V-1 and V-2**). In September 1943 the Danish Council of Liberty was formed by seven members of the Resistance plus the SOE delegate to Denmark. The council cooperated closely with the Free Danish movement outside the country.

Although at first they had been spared, in October 1943 Danish Jews fell under the shadow of the Nazi racial laws. Institutions and individuals united to save them. An actual "naval bridge" evacuated a large number to **Sweden** with the aid of sailors and fishermen from both countries. Of some 8,000 Danish Jews, 7,200 were kept out of German hands and only 50 lost their lives.

There was no end to the general strikes; they paralyzed Denmark, particularly those industries that had been obliged to work for the enemy. Sabotage became increasingly daring and achieved spectacular results. The German air base at Aalborg, a thorn in the Allied side, was completely destroyed by three SOE saboteurs. Acting on information supplied by the Danish Resistance, the RAF, with admirable precision, bombed **Gestapo** headquarters at Aarhus, Odense and Copenhagen from low altitudes. Many Germans were killed, some of the arrested Danish resisters managed to escape in the confusion, and many German records were incinerated. As the Allies approached Denmark in March 1945, the country's railroad system was put out of service completely. And the Resistance pulled off a miracle. Every tugboat in the country headed secretly to Sweden, rendering the Danish ports useless to the Germans.

A secret Danish army, formed in Denmark and Sweden, was poised for a general upheaval at a moment set by the Allies. But the Allied advance was so rapid that the planned rebellion was called off. On May 5 the first British contingents, accompanied by Danish officers, landed at the Kastrup air field near Copenhagen. Beginning on May 7 the 280,000 Germans in Denmark surrendered to the British and to the Resistance. The king and the government returned to power, and the ministry was broadened to include Moeller, returned from England, as the representative of the Resistance.

The Free Danish, underground and in exile, did much more than help their own cause. They paved the way, with their courage and sacrifice, for the eventual arrival of the Anglo-American forces. Widely regarded as passive in 1940, the Denmark of 1945 was a full-fledged member of the Allies.

H. Bernard

DENTZ, Henri-Fernand (1881-1945).

As commander of the Paris military region Dentz, a French general, abandoned the capital to the *Wehrmacht* on June 14, 1940. As France's high commissioner to the Levant, he fought the British and the Free French in **Syria** in July 1941. He was condemned to death for high **treason** by the High Court of Justice after the liberation of France, but his sentence was commuted to imprisonment at hard labor. He died at Fresnes on December 13, 1945.

DEUTSCHVLAMISCHE ARBEITSGE-MEINSCHAFT.

See **Belgium; Collaboration**.

DEVERS, Jacob L. (1887-1979).

Devers, an American general, became deputy supreme Allied commander in the Mediterranean, under Sir **H. Maitland Wilson**, in 1944. After September 1944 he commanded the Sixth Army Group, comprised of **A. McC. Patch**'s and **Jean de Lattre de Tassigny**'s armies, which occupied Alsace and southern **Germany**.

DE VISSCHER, Charles (1884-1973).

A professor at the University of Louvain, De Visscher's reputation in international law was worldwide. He served as president of the political committee of the Belgian **Resistance**. A minister of the **Pierlot** government, De Visscher was imprisoned by the Nazis during the war; he was freed after the liberation of **Belgium**. He was one of the Belgian signatories of the **United Nations** Charter.

DeVLAG *(DeutschVlamische Arbeitsgemeinschaft)*.

See **Belgium**; **Collaboration**.

DEWE, Walthere (1880-1944).

The chief engineer of the Belgian utility *Regie des Telegraphes et Telephones*, Dewe was the greatest member of the **Resistance** in **Belgium** during two wars and one of the greatest of all European resisters. The founder and head of the information-gathering network *Dame blanche* in World War I, Dewe immediately went to work again, on May 28, 1940, to develop the spy system he had voluntarily started in September 1939; it came to be known as "Clarence." Operating in secret from the beginning, Dewe was continually on the run throughout the country, always pursued and always eluding the occupation police. On January 14, 1944 he was shot down at Ixelles. His network, which furnished an astounding amount of information to the Allies, encompassed 1,547 agents. After Dewe's death "Clarence" and its efficient personnel continued their work, under Hector Demarque, until the **Battle of the Bulge** in January 1945. Two of Dewe's daughters were caught and sent to Ravensbrueck; only one returned to Belgium.

DIETL, Eduard (1890-1944).

Dietl, a German general, was a commander of mountain troops. His division occupied and defended Narvik, in **Norway**. In 1942-44 Dietl was the commander of the German troops in Lapland.

DIETRICH, Joseph ("Sepp") (1892-1966).

Dietrich, a German general, became a member of the **Nazi Party** at its birth. Commander of the Fuehrer's personal **SS** guard, he was appointed by **Hitler** to organize the *Waffen*-**SS**. In 1942-43 he was commander of an army corps on the Russian front. Dietrich participated in the German offensive at the **Battle of the Bulge** in December 1944 and helped defend Vienna against Soviet troops in 1945. He was imprisoned by the Allies after the war but freed in 1955.

DILL, Sir John Greer (1881-1944).

Dill, an Irish-born British commander, had served in both the Boer War and World War I. In 1939-40 Dill commanded the First Corps in France. He became chief of the Imperial General Staff in 1940; in December 1941 he took over as head of the British joint staff mission in Washington, where he remained until his death in November 1944.

DIMITROV, Georgi (1882-1949).

A Bulgarian revolutionary, Dimitrov was Balkan secretary of the **Comintern** from 1923 to 1929. Dimitrov was among those accused of setting fire to the *Reichstag* in 1933, but he was acquitted of the charge. As secretary of the Comintern from 1935 to 1943, he developed the "popular front" policy of the late 1930s. Dimitrov became dictator of **Bulgaria** in 1946 and remained in power until his death.

DODECANESE.

The Dodecanese are a group of islands in the eastern Aegean; Rhodes is the largest and most important of them. The Dodecanese were controlled by **Turkey** from 1522 until their conquest by **Italy** in 1912. Their total prewar population was about 150,000; nearly all their inhabitants were Greek-speaking. Two battalions of infantry were their usual peacetime garrison; small naval stations were located on Rhodes and Leros.

During the war the Dodecanese possessed considerable strategic importance: they provided advanced air bases from which the *Luftwaffe* could strike successively at Crete and at British-held territories in the eastern Mediterranean. In return, they afforded targets for the RAF, the Royal Navy, and such raiding parties as the Special Boat Section, a maritime offshoot of the **Special Air Service** that flourished in the Aegean and Adriatic seas from 1942 to 1944. (For operations in September-November 1943, when the strategic importance of the Dodecanese was at its height, see **Mediterranean and Middle Eastern Theater of Operations**.)

Greece gained control of the islands, which had long been Greek irredenta, in 1947.

M. R. D. Foot

DOENITZ, Karl (1891-).

In 1938 Doenitz, a German admiral, became commander of the nascent German submarine fleet. He became supreme commander of **Germany**'s navy in 1943. In his will, **Hitler** named Doenitz his successor; Doenitz therefore became president of the Reich after the Fuehrer's death. On May 7 and 8, 1945 he presided over the **unconditional surrender** of the *Wehrmacht*. His government was disbanded on May 23, 1945, and its members were arrested. Doenitz was condemned to 10 years in prison at the Nuremberg war crimes trials (see **war criminals**); he regained his freedom in 1956.

DONOVAN, William J. ("Wild Bill") (1883-1959).

Donovan, an American soldier, participated in several missions to Europe between 1936 and 1941. He headed the **Office of Strategic Services** from 1942 to 1945. A favorite of **Roosevelt**'s, Donovan was known as a man of unbounded energy and resourcefulness.

DOOLITTLE, James Harold (1896-).

In early 1942, at a time when the **Pearl Harbor** debacle was still depressing American **morale**, **United States** military planners set about devising a "proper retaliation"—a strike against **Japan**'s capital, Tokyo. Very-long-range bombers had not yet been developed, and it was not possible to approach Japan close-in. The only answer was for U.S. Army bombers, specially fitted and with specially trained crews, to be launched on a one-way mission (necessitated by range limitations) from an aircraft carrier, an operation that had never before been tried. Doolittle, who had been a flyer in World War I and, between the wars, a specialist in aeronautics and a civilian test pilot, was chosen to lead the mission. After rejoining the armed forces in 1941, he had proven one of the most brilliant students of strategic and tactical bombing.

April 1942 was chosen as the date for the strike. Sixteen USAAF B-25 Mitchell bombers were lashed to the decks of the USS *Hornet*, a new carrier (the desired 20 planes could not be accommodated). Vice Adm. **William Halsey**'s Task Force 16, comprised of a second carrier, the USS *Enterprise*, and four cruisers, was sighted more than once early in the morning on April 18, several hours before the strike was to take place, by Japanese pickets operating an unexpected 650 miles east of Japan. With the element of surprise lost, Halsey and Doolittle had either to abort the mission or to run increased risks. They opted for the strike, even though the distance was considerably farther that the 500 miles that had been planned for the mission, and daylight instead of nighttime flying would be involved. Doolittle led the B-25s from the *Hornet* in high wind and strong seas. Thirteen bombers struck Tokyo without serious opposition, while, for psychological reasons, the three others went after Nagoya, Osaka and Kobe. Although none of the planes was downed over Japan, none made it to the friendly airfields in **China** as planned. One bomber was even obliged to come down in the **USSR**, where the crew was interned. The other bombers crash-landed or bailed out over China; five men were killed in the process. The Japanese army captured eight Americans; after a "trial," all were sentenced to death. Three were actually executed and one died in captivity. In other words, 71 of the 80 pilots and crewmen, including Doolittle, survived. Most of the men were saved by the Chinese, sent on to Chungking, and eventually repatriated. Halsey's task force returned to Pearl Harbor without incident.

The bold Doolittle raid caused scant physical damage to its targets, and the Japanese populace was little affected by it, but it was a sensational morale booster on the home front. While President **Roosevelt** jested that the bombers had flown from "Shangrila," **Yamamoto** and his IJN colleagues were humiliated by the impunity with which the imperial capital had been raided. Consequently, Doolittle's air strike, apart from shaking up the befuddled air defense of the homeland and causing some diversion of fighter strength, induced an immediate acceleration and overextension of Japanese offensive plans, most particularly Yamamoto's ambitious Operation MI against **Midway**.

For his role in the raid, Doolittle was promoted from lieutenant colonel to brigadier general and awarded the Medal of Honor. Halsey called the operation "one of the most courageous deeds in all military history." Subsequently Doolittle commanded the 12th Air Force during the North African landing, the Anglo-American Strategic Air Force in the Mediterranean in 1943 and the Eighth Air Force during the Allied offensives in Europe in 1944 and in the Pacific in 1945.

A. D. Coox

DORIOT, Jacques (1888-1945).

The secretary-general of the Communist Youth in France in 1923, Doriot became a deputy in 1924 and then, as a Communist, the mayor of St. Denis in 1934. In 1936 he founded the *Parti populaire francais,* a political party with a definite Nazi slant. He directed the *Legion des volontaires francais contre le bolchevisme* and fought in its ranks against the Soviets. After the **Normandy landing**, Doriot established the Committee for French Liberation in

Sigmaringen. He was killed in **Germany** on February 22, 1945.

DORMAN-SMITH, Eric E. (later Dorman O'Gowan) (1895-1969).

A British strategist, Dorman-Smith was a pupil of **John Frederick Charles Fuller** and of **Basil Liddell Hart**. After organizing the mechanization of the British cavalry in the late 1920s, Dorman-Smith became **Wavell**'s brigade major in 1930 and, in 1939, director of training in **India**. After the war began, Dorman-Smith helped Sir **Richard Nugent O'Connor** plan his victory at **Beda Fomm** in February 1942. As **Auchinleck**'s chief of staff, Dorman-Smith saved the British Empire at the first battle of **El Alamein** in July 1942. He was, however, dismissed, because he had abandoned the strategically worthless position of Tobruk. Dorman-Smith retired to **Ireland**, his homeland, to meditate on the war. Liddell Hart described him as "one of the most brilliant soldiers that the British Army has produced in modern times."

DOWDING, Sir Hugh (later Lord) (1882-1970).

As commander in chief of the RAF **Fighter Command** from 1936 to 1940, Dowding won the **Battle of Britain**. He retired in 1942 and was made a lord in 1943.

DRAGOON.

The code name of the Allied landing operation in the south of France, executed on August 15, 1944. (See also **World War II—General Conduct; Mediterranean and Middle Eastern Theater of Operations**.)

DRESDEN.

This German city was destroyed on February 13, 1945 by incendiary bombs dropped by 764 RAF Lancasters and 450 American Flying Fortresses. Some 135,000 people perished in the flames ignited by the 650,000 bombs that fell on the city.

DUCHEZ, Rene (1903-1948).

Duchez, a French dealer in paintings at Caen, was a member of the spy network *Centurie de l'OCM* and of the secret Committee for the Liberation of Calvados. He infiltrated the Todt Organization and obtained the plans, in March 1944, for the **Atlantic Wall**. These plans, like those obtained earlier by Brunet of Caen and Andre Antoine of *Les Damps*, together with Michel Hollard, of the V-1 launching ramps in Normandy, were of considerable aid to the Allies (see **V-1 and V-2**).

DULLES, Allen (1893-1969).

Dulles, a U.S. intelligence official, headed the **Office of Strategic Service**'s mission in Berne from 1942 to 1945 and negotiated the end of the war in **Italy**. Dulles subsequently became head of the Central Intelligence Agency in 1953 and remained there until 1962. **John Foster Dulles** was his brother.

DULLES, John Foster (1888-1959).

Dulles, an American statesman and specialist in international law, had served as a member of the Reparations Commission at the Versailles Conference in 1919 and as an adviser to several presidents of the **United States**. He prepared the **United Nations** Charter at Dumbarton Oaks and was a prominent participant in the San Francisco Conference. He also led the negotiations ending in the peace treaty of 1951 with **Japan**. In 1953 he became **Eisenhower**'s secretary of state and served in that capacity until his death.

DUMBARTON OAKS CONFERENCE.

See **Conferences, Allied**.

DUNKIRK.

See *Fall Gelb;* Atlantic, Battle of the.

DUTCH BORNEO.

See **Borneo**.

DUTCH EAST INDIES.

See **Indonesia**.

DUTCH UNION.

This popular movement (*Nederlandse Unie*) was launched in **the Netherlands** toward the end of 1940 after the coalition of traditional political parties failed to yield the results demanded by a population angered by **Germany**'s easy occupation of their country. It was headed by a triumvirate composed of J. Linthorst Homan, former commissoner to the queen in Groningen; Prof. Jan de Quay; and L. Einthoven, former police commissioner of Rotterdam. They immediately were flooded by demands for membership from Dutchmen who loathed the National Socialists. The leaders of the Dutch Union, however, had no choice but to negotiate with the occupation authorities and therefore to hamstring themselves with compromises that were often misinterpreted as complaisance. Moreover, the Dutch Union tended to follow, rather than lead, by adopting a vaguely socialist ideology, at some times patriotic, at others preponderantly Christian, depending on the country's spiritual climate. A serious rift developed in the triumvirate, with one party in favor of a vigorously nationalistic, militantly democratic policy and the other demanding open resistance to the invader. There were other sources of dissension too, particularly in the attitude of the union toward the **United Kingdom** after the fall of

France. Some put all their faith in **Churchill** and a swift Allied victory; others resigned themselves to a long occupation with the government in the role of gadfly to the detested Nazis. When Dutch public opinion got over the shock of defeat, there was less need of the union, but doubts concerning the course citizens should take still remained. On December 13, 1941 the occupation authorities attempted to remove all such doubts by decreeing the dissolution of the Dutch Union. But groups of citizens who, in many cases, had never made each other's acquaintance before the war and who represented various shades of political opinion, continued to meet. Other groups became the nuclei of the **Resistance** movement in Holland and inescapably suffered heavy losses. In 1942, hundreds of opposition leaders, including the triumvirate, were arrested and herded into **concentration camps**. Nevertheless, the Dutch continued to discuss the union and its declarations of 1940. One of the union's triumvirs, Jan de Quay, became minister of defense in the London cabinet after the liberation of the southern provinces.

H. Brugmans

DYLE, Operation.
A French military plan designed to prevent **Germany**'s conquest of France, by organizing the deployment of French troops in **Belgium** along a front running from the Meuse to the Dyle. The plan proved ineffective.

E

EASTERN SOLOMONS.

The Second Battle of the Solomon Sea, as the Japanese called it, took place on August 24, 1942, as part of the protracted struggle for **Guadalcanal** Island and involved only confrontations between aircraft and ships. Adm. **Yamamoto**'s powerful Combined Fleet sortied from Truk with 58 warships, including the super-battleship *Yamato* and three other battleships, 13 heavy and three light cruisers, 30 destroyers, and two fleet and three other carriers carrying 177 planes. The Combined Fleet's mission was to smash American naval forces in the southwestern Pacific, hammer U.S. positions on Guadalcanal and **convoy** three transports loaded with 1,500 troops to reinforce the Japanese garrison on the island. Badly outnumbered in warships but alerted by intelligence to the IJN sortie, Vice Adm. Frank Jack Fletcher's Task Force 61 concentrated one battleship, three heavy carriers, five heavy and two light cruisers and 18 destroyers. The Americans' numerical superiority in air power was reduced to parity (about 176 planes) when the U.S. heavy carrier *Wasp* was unhurriedly detached for refueling on August 23 and was thus removed from participation in the impending action. After some preliminaries marked by troubles with communications and plotting on both sides, the Japanese light carrier *Ryujo* (8,100 tons) was sunk by dive bombers from the heavy carrier *Enterprise* (19,800 tons). (Recent scholarship refutes the old view that the *Ryujo*, deployed 100 miles west of the Japanese heavy carriers, had been set out as a decoy.) The heavy carriers *Shokaku* and *Zuikaku* sent dive bombers and fighters against the *Enterprise*. Despite alert, improved air cover and antiaircraft barrages, the U.S. carrier was hit several times, suffered 74 killed and 95 wounded, and would probably have been finished off by a second torpedo-armed Japanese air strike. Fortunately for the *Enterprise*, the IJN pilots could not locate the wounded carrier. Fletcher pulled back southward with the *Enterprise* but was able to divert most of its planes to the inventory on Guadalcanal, while the *Wasp* hastened north. A couple of U.S. dive bombers from the *Saratoga* "got lucky" and damaged the new

seaplane tender *Chitose* (9,000 tons), which was driven from the scene. According to debriefed IJN airmen, the **United States** had suffered damage to two carriers and a battleship. (Actually, the battleship *New Jersey* had been attacked but not hit.)

On the night of August 24, Adm. Nobutake Kondo went out looking for a night battle, but when he found no important enemy warships, he abruptly retired north with his very powerful vanguard force. As for the unprotected Japanese troop convoy, the old light cruiser *Jintsu* (5,200 tons), operating with the destroyer-bombardment screen, was mauled in daylight, on the morning of August 25, by land-based U.S. planes from Guadalcanal and Espiritu Santo. One 9,300-ton transport and the old destroyer *Mutsuki* were lost in the ensuing air attacks, and the remaining two transports were ordered to retire to the Shortlands, now protected by sea and air cover. Yamamoto then had the troop reinforcements reloaded aboard destroyers for a new run to Guadalcanal.

In all, the Americans lost 20 planes shot down; the Japanese lost 60 fighters and bombers, of which half were shot down and the rest destroyed by crash-landing in the sea. It is understandable why Fletcher was so very cautious, but Yamamoto emerges strangely unaggressive in his conduct of the main operations, and Vice Adm. Gunichi Mikawa's close cover force of four heavy cruisers did not even bombard Guadalcanal. While Fletcher had been lucky to save the *Enterprise*, perhaps Yamamoto was lucky that the *Wasp*'s 82 planes were unavailable for use against him. Undoubtedly the Japanese defeat at **Midway** was very much on Yamamoto's mind and the American defeat at Savo on Fletcher's.

A. D. Coox

EBOUE, Felix (1884-1944).

Eboue, a French Guianan, was a colonial administrator. Governor of Chad since 1938, he rallied to Free France in August 1940 and became governor general of **French Equatorial Africa**. He advised Gen. **de Gaulle** to encourage participation by the native population in the administration of the **French colonies**, a policy that was confirmed by the Brazzaville Conference of January 30, 1944.

ECC.

See **European Consultative Commission**.

EDEN, Sir (Robert) Anthony (later Earl of Avon) (1897-1977).

A British politician, Eden became minister for **League of Nations** affairs in 1935 and then served as foreign secretary from 1936 to 1938 and as war secretary in 1940. In November 1940 he once again became foreign secretary—and **Churchill**'s designated successor—and continued in that post until July 1945. In October 1951, for the third time, Eden became foreign secretary. He served in that capacity until April 1955, when he became prime minister; his term as prime minister lasted until January 1957.

EDES.

A secret military organization in **Greece** with a moderate policy.

EGYPT.

Occupied by the **United Kingdom** since 1882, Egypt was a British protectorate from 1914 to 1936, when a treaty conceded independence; the British, however, retained extensive rights to military bases, particularly along the Suez Canal.

Egypt remained nominally neutral until February 1945, when it declared war on **Germany** and **Japan** (thus acquiring founder status in the **United Nations**); Egypt had broken off diplomatic relations with Germany in September 1939, with **Italy** in June 1940 and with the **French State** in January 1942.

Without the Alexandria harbor, the Nile delta airfields, vast camps and dumps in the canal zone and several headquarters in Cairo, the British could never have sustained their campaigns in the Near and Middle East. They asked only for acquiescence and labor from the Egyptians; both were grudgingly given. Private relations between the occupying forces and the locals were often bitter. Official relations were conducted through Sir **Miles Lampson**, the British ambassador, an old-fashioned imperialist who sat solid as a rock amid the rapids of political maneuver and court intrigue.

Egyptian politics, throughout the war, raged round the question of the powers of the young King Farouk (1920-65; reigned 1936-52). The government of Ali Maher, in power from August 1939 to June 1940, was friendly to him; its successors, under Hasan Sabri Pasha until November 1940 and then under Husain Sirry, were a shade more independent. A Wafdist (na-

tionalist) government, formed in February 1942 under British pressure, received a large majority in elections the following month and remained in power until October 1944.

The cost of living rose threefold during the war; by its end the Egyptians were determined to cast the British out. The **Arab League** was formed in Cairo in March 1945; nine years later the last remnants of the British garrison left.

M.R.D. Foot

EICHMANN, Adolf (1906-1962).

Eichmann, a German **SS** colonel, was made responsible for Section IV B4 of the **RSHA**, which was charged with assembling Europe's Jews under German control, in 1939. At the **Wannsee Conference** he was ordered to execute the **Final Solution** (see **Anti-Semitism**). After the war Eichmann escaped to South America, but he was eventually tracked down and kidnapped by Israeli agents in Argentina and condemned to death in Tel Aviv. He was executed in 1962; his ashes were thrown into the sea.

EISENHOWER, Dwight David (1890-1969).

Eisenhower, an American general, was supreme commander of the Allied landings in Northwest Africa in 1942 and in northwestern Europe in 1944-45.

Eisenhower was a regular officer in the U.S. Army and acted as a tank instructor in World War I. Serving under Gen. **Douglas MacArthur** in the **Philippines** from 1933 to 1939, he learned to fly. In 1941-42 he served under Gen. **George C. Marshall** in the operations division of the U.S. Army staff in Washington. Although he had never commanded troops in the field, he was put in charge of Operation **Torch**, the Anglo-American landings in Morocco and Algeria in early November 1942, and of the subsequent advances into Tunisia and **Italy**. As supreme commander of a mixed force of all arms and services and several nationalities, he devised a system of unified command. British units quickly learned to accept orders from American staff officers as readily as from British officers and vice versa. British commanders Viscount **Alexander**, Sir **Andrew Cunningham** and Sir **Arthur Tedder** all liked him and acted willingly as his subordinates. Eisenhower had some difficulties with French Adm. **Francois Darlan** and more with Free French commander **Henri Giraud**. As he wrote, "High command, particularly Allied command, in war carries with it a lot of things that were never included in our textbooks." Although a novice in politics, he pleased his political chiefs, **Roosevelt** and **Churchill**. His cooperation with Darlan annoyed the British, French and American left but pleased **Stalin** and saved many lives and much time. He got on well with **Harold Macmillan**, the minister Churchill sent to Algiers.

In January 1944 Eisenhower was moved, to his own surprise, to London to command Operation Overlord, the Allied invasion of northwestern Europe. He took over the plans for a landing in the Baie de la Seine, already prepared by COSSAC (Chief of Staff to the Supreme Allied Commander, the British Gen. F. E. Morgan), who became one of his deputies. He ran **Supreme Headquarters Allied Expeditionary Forces** (SHAEF) on the same system of unified command that he had used for the Allied North African headquarters, with equal success. Tedder moved with him as his tactical air force deputy. The strategic air striking forces remained independent under U.S. Gen. **Carl Spaatz** and British marshal Sir **Trafford Leigh-Mallory**— not a wholly satisfactory arrangement, but the best that could be made. The details of Operation Neptune, the actual landing, he left in the hands of the naval and air technicians and of Britain's Field Marshal **Montgomery**, its force commander, insisting only on adequate support by airborne troops.

After the **Normandy landing**, on June 6, 1944, Eisenhower did not move his main headquarters to France until August. He took over the general direction of Montgomery's and Gen. **Omar Bradley**'s army groups on September 1, and conducted a systematic, methodical advance on a broad front. A shortage of motor fuel and winter weather halted the advance near the German frontier at the end of September 1944. Unruffled by the German Ardennes offensive, Eisenhower waited for dry ground and clear weather (see **Battle of the Bulge**); by April 1945 there was nothing left to do but mop up.

Eisenhower's broad and original ideas, great strength of character, even temper and amiable disposition made him a strong commander. Eisenhower served as president of the **United States** from 1953 to 1961.

M.R.D. Foot

EL ALAMEIN.

This desert railway station some 60 miles west-south-west of Alexandria was the site of two important battles in 1942. On July 1 **Rommel** attacked Sir **Claude Auchinleck** at El Alamein, believing he would win a rapid victory. By July 3 he knew he had lost and by July 10 he had only 20 tanks left; his troops were skewered in the desert and his lines of communication were overextended.

Montgomery attacked Rommel on October 23 in Operation **Lightfoot** after building a superior force for 10 weeks: he had 195,000 men to Rommel's 104,000 and 1,000 tanks to Rommel's 500. Six days' attrition

made slight impact on the minefields Rommel had built between his front west of El Alamein and the impassable Quattara depression nearly 40 miles to the south; elaborate **deceptions**, however, kept Rommel guessing where the main onslaught would come. A concentrated attack led by troops from **New Zealand** on October 29 broke into the **Axis** position 10 miles from the sea; by the evening of November 2, Rommel realized he was beaten. He disobeyed an order from **Hitler** on November 3 to stand fast and began to disengage his armor on November 4. Again he had only 20 tanks left. Most of his Italian infantry formations were captured. (See also **Mediterranean and Middle Eastern Theater of Operations**.)

M.R.D. Foot

ELLINIKOS LAIKOS APELEPHTHERICON STRATOS (ELAS).

A people's army for the liberation of **Greece**, with Communist sympathies.

EMPIRE.

Four concepts of empire confronted one another during World War II. First, the long-established and far-flung colonial empires of the **United Kingdom** and France, perfectly solid in appearance in 1939, had been mortally weakened by 1945 and crumbled away during the generation after the war. Neither was strong enough to survive the disastrous campaigns in metropolitan France in 1940 or in Southeast Asia in 1941-42. The much smaller Dutch East Indian empire went the same way, less ostentatiously (see **Indonesia**); and so, after a delay, did **Belgium**'s.

The Germans, for their part, renewed in 1939 the challenge they had put to their enemies in 1914, with a new imperial style developed since 1933. A leading Nazi slogan was *Weltmacht oder Niedergang*—"World power or downfall." The rest of this book shows how they achieved their own downfall.

Two concepts of empire remained, eyeball to eyeball, though the defenders of each angrily repudiated the name of empire. The **United States** found itself in 1945 in a position to dominate the world, combining immense military power—the United States alone, so far, possessed the **atomic bomb**—with almost equally great commercial strength. It desired a world open to free enterprise, in which its own initiative and manifest good intentions would leave it in front.

By one of the great ironies of modern politics, those who mouthed the loudest anti-imperialist slogans were the greatest empire-builders; at least the facts of imperial domination and the will to power are clear. The Communists in the **USSR** believed that their understanding of the world was correct and that maximum power should therefore belong, the world over, to their party. **Stalin**'s genius—evil or good, it was genius—harnessed Russian chauvinism to the party machine to pull it through the war; his obduracy at Yalta and Potsdam (see **Conferences, Allied**) secured the Soviet Union a wide buffer zone on the west, behind which it could repair the wounds of war and prepare its next leap forward.

The emperor of **India** formally resigned his title in 1947 (though it appeared on his coins in 1948); the emperor of **Ethiopia, Haile Selassie,** retained his.

M.R.D. Foot

ENGLAND.

See **United Kingdom.**

ENGLANDSPIEL.

Englandspiel was the German code name for certain operations against the British **Special Operatons Executive** (SOE) in northwestern Europe (the operations were also called *Nordpol*, or "North Pole").

Every secret service dreams of taking over some of the other side's operatives and using their means of communication, or better still the operatives themselves, against the enemy. A combination of skill by a German *Abwehr* team led by Col. H. J. Giskes, luck and faulty staff work in London enabled the Germans to do this with some success in **the Netherlands** between 1942 and 1944. A Dutch SOE operator was caught close to his clandestine transmitter by normal wireless direction-finding methods, in March 1942. He agreed to help the Germans send messages to London on his set in good faith to the Allies, relying on the absence of prearranged mistakes in the messages to alert London to the fact that he was in German hands. London noticed nothing amiss, however, and over 40 Dutch agents were parachuted straight into *Abwehr* hands. Two of them escaped and returned to London, where they were arrested for a time on the force of apparently authentic messages from Holland, which said they were working with the **Gestapo.** The real situation was not revealed until after the **Normandy landings** in June 1944.

About half of the SOE's operatives in Holland were neutralized by this operation, and the effects of the operation spilled over into work in neighboring countries—**Belgium** and France—and into other parts of SOE, such as **Gerson**'s escape line (which survived). A similar operation, mounted by the German Security Police in France, resulted in the loss of 18 British and French agents of the SOE in early 1944; but they only constituted about one percent of the SOE agents in that country, not 50 percent, as in Holland.

Germany's successes in this field, however, paled into insignificance compared with those of the **United Kingdom.** Every single agent (with one possible exception) planted by the German secret services in Britain was, after the winter of 1941-42, working—consciously or unconsciously—under the direction of **MI-5.** This was not only a 99.9 percent professional success, it also provided the keystone of the arch of **deception** erected in the spring of 1944 to secure strategic surprise in Operation Overlord.

M.R.D. Foot

ENIGMA.

The name of a German coding machine whose prototype appeared in 1926. The model used by the land and air forces of the *Wehrmacht* was last modified in 1937. The advantage of Enigma was that even if the messages it encoded were intercepted, they could not be deciphered except with a duplicate of the machine. Its designers never considered the possibility that an enemy could reconstruct it, yet that was precisely what the French information services labored to do, in cooperation with Polish experts, for eight years. The French Commander Gustave Bertrand researched the necessary documents while Polish coworkers studied the practical aspects of the machine. They succeeded just before the war began. In July 1939 the Polish experts sent two copies of the machine to Bertrand, one for the use of his crew and the other for Gen. **Stewart Menzies** of the British **Intelligence Service.**

ERITREA.

An Italian colony on the southwestern coast of the Red Sea since 1890, Eritrea was the main base for **Italy**'s invasions of **Ethiopia** in 1896 and 1935. As part of Viscount **Wavell**'s invasion of Ethiopia, two Indian divisions under Gen. **William Platt** invaded Eritrea in January 1941. They were held up at Keren by a resolute Italian defense from February 5 to March 26 but thereafter rapidly overran Eritrea and moved on southwestward into Ethiopia. Eritrea was then occupied by the **United Kingdom** until 1952, when (by a decision of the **United Nations**) it was incorporated into Ethiopia.

ESCAPE AND EVASION.

In many countries the Nazi occupation was so oppressive that those subjected to it wanted to flee; Jews in particular needed to escape the persecution that proved fatal to millions of them. One of the tasks of the **Resistance** all over Europe was to devise and manage channels through which people might escape Nazi control. The task was intricate and difficult, but not quite impossible. In addition, the British and the

Americans (working jointly) and the Soviets (working separately) developed a series of routes along which they could try to pass highly trained people whose work had left them stranded in enemy territory: political figures, secret agents, raiding parties, and—particularly in northwestern Europe—airmen who had been shot down.

Daring and discretion saved a quarter of the Jews of **the Netherlands**, who were hidden, and most of the Jews of **Denmark**, who were spirited across the Sound into **Sweden**. In eastern Europe **anti-Semitism** was not confined to the Nazis, and a much smaller proportion of the Jews there survived. But the Poles, with 150 years' experience of occupations behind them, were accomplished at smuggling each other in and out of occupied towns and across guarded frontiers. Until 1941 it was comparatively easy to get from **Poland** into the Danube valley and thence to neutral ground in **Turkey**. When Poland became part of the Germans' route to the eastern front and again in 1944 when it became the scene of widespread fighting, free movement became more difficult, but it was hardly ever impossible.

Several hundred troops from the **United Kingdom**, **Australia** and **New Zealand** left behind in mainland **Greece** and Crete in the fighting of April-May 1941 were removed to Turkey or **Egypt** by carefully organized caique or submarine parties.

Several thousand **prisoners of war** in **Italy** managed, or were allowed, to escape in September 1943 when Italy changed sides. Some joined the partisans; some were recaptured by the Germans; the rest, some 3,000 strong, rejoined the advancing Allied forces. One hundred and fifty British officers and soldiers managed to escape from **Germany**. Fifty of these made their way back to England and thus could continue fighting; the others were interned in neutral countries. As many as 4,000 servicemen from the **United States**, Britain and British Commonwealth countries got away from France and the Low Countries to England between June 1940 and June 1944; about 1,000 of them had been left behind at Dunkirk; the rest were airmen. So efficient were the lines conveying captured airmen in these countries, in which about 12,000 ordinary citizens worked secretly, that between June and September 1944 half the airmen shot down over France returned unscathed and quite promptly. On the other hand, at least 500 of their helpers were executed; one of the officers responsible for organizing the lines postulated that "for every successful evader a Belgian, Dutch or French helper gave his or her life."

One solitary German, Baron von Werra, managed to escape from **Canada**—where he had been sent as a captured *Luftwaffe* officer—into the U.S. before it joined the war.

A myriad of private arrangements whose details will never be known enabled individuals to hide, here and there, all over Europe, from the ravages of fascism and war. The greater distances, wilder climate and variant cultures of eastern Asia made such adventures there all but inconceivable.

Little has been published on actual methods of escape, beyond personal adventure stories (which are legion): security authorities believe this is something everyone might one day need, if worse came to worst, to do again.

M.R.D. Foot

ESPIONAGE.

See **Information Services**.

ESTIENNE D'ORVES, Honore d' (1901-1941).

After escaping to London in 1940, Estienne d'Orves, a French naval officer, returned to France in December of that year to organize an espionage network. He was arrested by the **Gestapo** and executed at Mont Valerien on August 29, 1941.

ESTONIA.

See **Baltic States**.

ETHIOPIA.

An ancient imperial kingdom in eastern Africa, Ethiopia was, in the early 1930s, governed by **Haile Selassie**, its 225th successive monarch. Most of its 10 million people were engaged in primitive agriculture; it was in transition from a slave-owning to a feudal society. With **Italy's** backing, it was admitted to the **League of Nations** in 1923. Italy nevertheless provoked a frontier incident and invaded Ethiopia in October 1935. The league proved "willing to wound, but yet afraid to strike"; it imposed only annoying economic sanctions, not crippling military ones, on Italy and stood by while Ethiopia was overrun. By the autumn of 1936 Haile Selassie was an exile in London, and Ethiopia was part of the Italian **empire**.

In July 1940 Italian troops captured Kassala in the Sudan and overran British Somaliland from Ethiopia. In midwinter 1940-41 **Wavell** counterattacked. **William Platt** landed in **Eritrea**, **Alan Cunningham** advanced from Kenya, and Gen. **Orde Wingate**, accompanied by Haile Selassie, intervened from the Sudan with a small irregular force. By June 1941 the emperor was back in Addis Ababa, his capital; the last Italians surrendered at Gondar in November 1941. In 1942 the constitution of 1931 was restored, and

Ethiopia began the advance into the modern age that led to Haile Selassie's deposition in 1974.

M.R.D. Foot

EUROPE, The Concept of.

In 1923, Count Richard Coudenhove-Kalergi launched his "Pan-Europa" movement for a Continental union without the **United Kingdom** and the **USSR**. The movement was practically moribund by the time **Hitler** arrived on the scene, but the concept behind it continued to gather strength. It was hardly surprising, then, that the concept of Europe affected both sides during the war.

On the Nazi side, many of the sincere collaborators anticipated that a German victory would most likely lead to the erasure of state frontiers. They dreamed of a vast federation revolving around the strongest state in which the planets of this European solar system would nevertheless enjoy an appreciable amount of autonomy. The French writer Pierre Drieu La Rochelle even postulated in his diary that an assembly of Europe, freely elected, would one day sit either in Strasbourg or Brussels. The Belgian collaborator Pierre Daye, in his book *L'Europe aux Europeens*, argued that Pan-Europeanism was necessary to liberate the Continent at one stroke from both Russian Bolshevism and Anglo-Saxon capitalism.

Others less closely connected with the collaborators thought that Nazism could bring about certain indispensable reforms throughout Europe, something that the democracies had been unable to accomplish during the period between the two world wars. They were encouraged by the fact that during the war **Germany** had (no doubt in its own national interest) created a vast economic enclave in which manufactured products could be traded without hindrance. Drieu La Rochelle even regarded the deported laborers as the forerunners of Pan-European shock troops. *Reichsminister* **Walter Funk**, known facetiously as "Rundfunk" (a pun on the German word for "radio") because of his peripatetics around the Continent, first used the term "European Economic Community."

After their first defeats on the Russian front, the Nazis put forth a different interpretation of the concept of Europe. They now assumed the obligation to defend not only Europe but civilization itself against the "Asiatic barbarians" of the Soviet Union. In every one of the occupied countries, volunteers were recruited into the ranks of the anti-Bolshevik legions, and the *Waffen* **SS** became a European force in the service of German hegemony. Nazi propaganda lauded the cultural glories of Europe and the role of the *Wehrmacht* in preserving them. "Germany fights for Europe" was the new slogan. (See also **Fortress Europe**.)

Actually, all this was pure **propaganda**, for Hitler himself never thought in these terms. Rather than reorganizing Europe, his aim was to bring the nations surrounding Germany under his domination (see **New European Order**). Furthermore, his ambitions tended toward the east, where he hoped to drive the Ukrainians out of their fertile "breadbasket" and replace them with the German peasantry. **Franco** and **Mussolini** were to be permitted to share the Mediterranean, but always under German control. As for the "racial Germans" or "Aryans" beyond the bounds of Germany proper, they would be made part of the Greater Reich. That, at least, was Hitler's plan for the Dutch, the Flemings and the Danes. These notions bore no resemblance to the original Pan-European concept.

The Allies too paid little attention to the concept of Europe. **Roosevelt**'s ideas about Europe were naive; he even conceived the absurdity of recreating 15th century Burgundy. But few people of that era understood that the crucial postwar problem would be Germany, once it was forced to accept the **unconditional surrender** demanded by the Casablanca Conference in January 1943. Was the conquered country to be converted into an agricultural land? That was the recommendation of the Morgenthau Plan, whose fancifulness became apparent when the war regime gave way to the Allied occupation regime. But there were some who realized that only a European federalist solution could salvage the material accomplishments of the German people and at the same time end their imperialist dreams. As the final act of the war drama approached, the British diplomat **Duff Cooper**, who almost alone had voted against **Neville Chamberlain**'s **Munich Pact**, proposed a European union. He was ignored.

The federalist idea occurred to **Churchill** as well. In June 1940, as France fell, he proposed a union of the two nations with one Franco-British military force, one government, one representative assembly. The proposal had been inspired by **Jean Monnet** who, after the war, brought the French plan for reconstruction and industrial restoration into being. In 1952 Monnet also presided over the first European Common Market—that of coal and steel. But Churchill's gesture of 1940 was only the result of the desperation then prevalent among the Allies, coming too late to repair the **morale** of the French armies.

Yet Churchill did not entirely forget the concept of Europe. In May 1943 he visited Washington and discussed anticipated postwar problems with American authorities. Assuming that after winning their victory the Anglo-American forces would withdraw from the Continent, he suggested sustaining its results by setting up regional federations such as the Danubian and Balkan unions that developed to fill the vacuum left by the disintegration of the old Austro-Hungarian empire. At that time, "some dozen states" of Europe formed a regional confederation. But the discussions in Washington came to no definite conclusion on that point.

Churchill returned to it on October 11 of the same year in a note to **Eden**, then minister of foreign affairs, "We insist strongly on a **United Nations** system that would include a European Council, with an International Court and a military force capable of imposing its decisions." But the only result was the creation of the **European Consultative Commission** to advise the Allies on immediate problems. At any rate there were a number of **governments-in-exile** in London to discuss future plans for regional federations. **Poland** and **Czechoslovakia**, in particular, began exploratory conversations on the possibility of a union between the two countries. Presidents **Sikorski** and **Benes** quite clearly understood that their weakness in response to Hitler's aggressions was the logical result of their petty squabbling over territories. Those conversations, however, were halted by Sikorski's accidental death in 1943. In any case the "London Poles" soon found themselves a neglected minority when the Soviets established a rival government in Lublin.

Meetings of the governments in exile of **Belgium, the Netherlands** and **Luxembourg** produced a more lasting result. An agreement was signed on September 5, 1944 in London for the introduction of a customs union between the Netherlands and the Belgian-Luxembourg Economic Union, with the intention of expanding eventually into a complete economic union. The project was based on the assumption that the three countries would be liberated simultaneously. But this too failed to be realized. Just as liberated Belgium found itself in a position to benefit from the production of uranium in the **Congo**, the Netherlands entered the most difficult period of the war—the "winter of famine." Furthermore the proclamation of the Republic of **Indonesia** during the final phase of the Japanese occupation was to confront The Hague government with more immediate priorities. It was not until 1947 that an additional protocol allowed the Benelux union to get started.

While Allied governments remained silent on the question of European integration, the **Resistance** movements in the occupied countries raised it frequently in the **underground press**. Most non-communist national resistance movements that concerned themselves with postwar problems agreed on the necessity of a European federation. This phenomenon is particularly striking in view of the intense patriotic excitement stimulated by the struggle against the occu-

pying forces.

The most detailed project in this direction emanated from a group of Italian anti-Fascists who prepared an elaborate plan called *Manifeste de Ventotene*. The Free French, the Belgians, the Dutch and the Poles were all moving in the same direction. In September 1944 a conference in Geneva framed a federalist declaration inspired largely by the Italians— and very likely by anti-Nazi Germans as well. This idea had been evolving as the final German defeat became inevitable. Because the impending Allied victory made the question of whether the Germans and Italians would accept what they regarded not long before as inadmissible sacrifices of territory an academic one, the conferees became more and more amenable to the concept of a unified Europe.

Because the most pressing priority at the end of the war was to begin immediate reconstruction and because the Allies were not inclined to embark on any ambitious new projects, the idea of a European union was temporarily shelved. But when it resurfaced in 1946, veterans of the Resistance were its most active champions

H. Brugmans

EUROPEAN CONSULTATIVE COMMISSION (ECC).

In response to a proposal of the Soviet Union, as amended by a British proposal, the Allied foreign ministers—**Hull** from the **United States**, **Eden** from the **United Kingdom** and **Molotov** from the **USSR**— created, at the Moscow Conference of October 18-30, 1943, a political-military commission to be known as the European Consultative Commission. Its purpose was "to study European questions arising from the developments of the war and to offer common recommendations to the three governments." The commission met at Lancaster House in London on January 14, 1944 in an organizational session. Permanent representatives to the commission were John G. Winant for the U.S., Lord William Strang for Great Britain and Fedor T. Gusev for the USSR. Beginning on November 27, 1944, France was represented by Rene Massigli, participating as an equal in the commission's examination of the directives each government submitted through its representative. Ratification by the governments involved was required for adoption of the commission's recommendations.

In all, the ECC met 120 times before its abolition was ordered by the "Big Three" at the Potsdam Conference in July and August 1945.

The ECC dealt primarily with the German problem. It developed agreements concerning that nation's fate after its **unconditional surrender**—specifically, its division into zones of occupation. Its proposals of July 25, 1944 regarding **Germany**'s unconditional surrender—Article 12 of which provided for the assumption of administrative responsibilities by the principal Allied powers—were ratified by the U.S. on August 9, 1944; by Great Britain on September 21, 1944; and by the USSR on December 14, 1944. In February 1945 the Yalta Conference adopted an amendment to Article 12 for the "partition" of Germany. It generated so much parliamentary heat that the document still had not been signed when Germany's unconditonal surrender finally took place. The surrender was realized in two phases: the first was the military capitulation of May 7-9, 1945; the second was the declaration "In View of the German Defeat," issued on June 5, 1945 by the Allied supreme command. The content of this document was essentially in keeping with the ECC's proposals. Germany was divided into occupation zones in conformity with the "Protocol of the United States, Great Britain and the USSR on the Zones of Occupation in Germany and the Administration of Greater Berlin" of September 8, 1944, with the accords of September 14, 1944 supplementing the protocol. The protocol confirmed the Soviet counterproposal to the initial British offer to allow each power to occupy a particular zone exclusively, with the frontier between East and West drawn along the Luebeck-Helmstedt-Eisenach-Hof line; only Greater Berlin was to be subject to inter-Allied occupation. The final accords assigned Germany's northwest and Berlin's northwest districts to Great Britain, and the southern part of each to the U.S. After the Yalta Conference, in which the Big Three granted France equality as an occupation power, the ECC issued a "Declaration on the Occupied Zones" on May 1, 1945, recognizing equal rights of France to the occupation of Germany and Greater Berlin. It was not until July 26, 1945, however, that the ECC signed supplementary accords delineating the French occupation zone in southern Germany, which was detached from the British and American zones, and ceding two of Great Britain's districts in Berlin to France. These accords were put into operation on August 13, 1945. The ECC agreements of November 14, 1944 regarding administrative control provided for the exercise of supreme governmental power by the respective commanders for each zone and for Germany as a whole by the combined commanders. The "**Interallied Control Council for Germany**" was the supreme organ. The declaration of the Allied high command of June 5, 1945, "In View of the German Defeat," activated the accords for administrative control in their revised version after the recognition of France as the fourth victorious power.

A. Hillgruber

EUTHANASIA.

Bringing to an end, by painless and immediate means, the lives of incurably ill people who are suffering unbearable pain. Hitler's confidential decree of November 1, 1939 ordered an end to "lives without value." By the end of August 1941, as a result of this perversion of the concept of euthanasia, more than 70,000 mentally ill people had been murdered.

EVACUATION AND RESETTLEMENT.

The belligerents' concern for sheltering their civilian populations from the enemy—in particular their desire to protect them against attack from the air—marked every stage of World War II. France began its preparations before the outbreak of war with measures designed to coordinate the evacuation of densely populated areas near the German border (Alsace, in particular), the removal of the disabled and infirm from the large cities and the daily dispersion of workers in those cities. These measures were applied with some success during the mobilization period, but they faltered badly when many of those who had been evacuated returned during the ensuing "**phony war.**" The *Wehrmacht*'s drive to the west prompted the first evacutaion of the war—which became a hasty and disorganized rout because the governments of the attacked nations were so shocked by the rapidity of the **Blitzkrieg** advance. The countries west of **Germany**, better students of the Teutonic temper than **Norway** and **Poland**, took advantage of the lessons learned in 1914. First the residents of **Luxembourg** and **Belgium** and then those living in the southernmost provinces of **the Netherlands** abandoned their homes to seek shelter behind the Allied lines. The population of the French Ardennes followed their example; they were soon imitated by the citizens of Northern France, the Pas de Calais and Aisne. This was followed by a halt in the flow of refugees in the second half of May while the Germans paused to liquidate encircled pockets in the north of France before resuming the assault. Some refugees even returned to their villages south of the Somme and Aisne. The great majority, however, left their fellows at random points along the choked roads, unable to endure the fatigue and the physical punishment of horse-drawn wagons or the discomfort resulting from huddling in automobiles wrecked by inept drivers. Although there were as yet comparatively few refugees, they encountered enormous difficulties in getting **food** or arranging for lodgings.

But with the second German push into France, the thin stream of refugees swelled to a flood. Beginning on June 7 the inhabitants of the Paris area and the cities of the lower Seine were joined by people from towns along the routes they took. The enemy did not

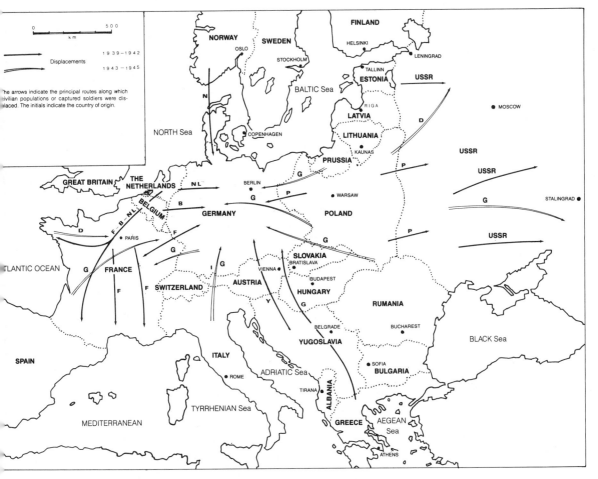

leave them unscathed; by harassing them at some points and ignoring them at others, the Germans cleverly herded the weary escapees onto the main roads, where their presence would hamper French troop movements. This harassment took deadly forms. The defenseless travelers were strafed and bombed in the small towns near the bridges over the Loire River after being trapped in the flood of vehicles and pedestrians. Many of those who had first sought refuge in these regions left them quickly for the basin of the Garonne and the mountainous southeast section of France known as the Massif Central. The fear of bombardment or even of an Italian offensive also stimulated the departure of many civilians from the large cities on the Mediterranean and in the Rhone valley. Some observers put the figure of these refugees at more than 10 million, but their initial mobility rendered an exact count impossible. Most of them returned to their homes as soon as the German authorities permitted it. The subsequent imposition of lines of demarcation cut France into several zones: the unoccupied zone, free of alien troops; the Italian-occupied zone; the German-occupied zone between the Moselle and Rhine rivers, administered by the commander of Belgium and northern France and in effect annexed by Germany; the forbidden zone of northeast France, more or less colonized by the *Ostland*; and the occupied zone administered by the German command in Paris and separated from the rest of the country by an almost impassable line. These internal boundaries impeded the resettling of the migrant population.

The reasons for the mass evacuations of May and June 1940 were numerous and complicated. The ancient European reflex of flight before the menace of an invading army was obviously a prime factor, but to it must be added systematic measures taken by the French government, ordering noncombatants to fall back to a depth of 15 kilometers (about nine miles) from the front lines and dispersing nonproductive elements of the population from densely inhabited points. The prominence given to these directives fixed in the public mind the impending need for instant departure in the face of the enemy's advance. Many of the people in Belgium and France, vividly recalling the German occupation of 1914, could not bear the thought of repeating the experience. Their departure, once begun, was accelerated by the bombardment of cities behind the combat zone and by the retreat of bureaucrats and tradesmen with the troops. The consequent development of crevices in the once solid political structure also facilitated the installation of new authorities. The frenzied fear felt by many in the face of the invasion was to foster the legend of "correct" commanders of the occupying power who paid for the goods they seized with impressive-looking, if worthless, currency. The allotments of motor fuel to permit workers dispersed by evacuation to return to their factories were also to contribute to a softening in public opinion. The populace of the invaded lands cannot be accused of willful blindness; the press was under orders to ignore any incident tending to cast doubt on this image of respectability counterfeited by the German **propaganda** services.

France again experienced such mass hegiras during the second French campaign in 1944, but they were much less widespread outside evacuated coastal zones, principally because the Germans had forbidden the civilians to leave in order to keep the roads open for their troop movements. The continual shifts in the Eastern European fronts brought about other displacements of the civilian populations, some of them beginning with the **Nazi-Soviet Pact**, like those of ethnic Germans from the **Baltic States** before the Red Army. These movements, however, were not nearly as torrential as those to the west in 1943 and especially in 1944 and 1945, when millions of civilians fled before the exceptional violence of the advancing Soviets. Many of these fleeing civilians feared retribution at the hands of the Soviets for the cruelties they themselves had perpetrated on the natives of the territory they occupied. Conducted under more haphazard conditions than those in the western theaters, the westward shift of the German or assimilated populations was most often harried by the harsh Russian winter. Consequently, the aged, the women and the children, left to themselves by the drastic mobilization measures taken by the Germans in the rural regions of the east, suffered terribly. The cities entered by the roving populations were often overburdened by refugees who had arrived before them in

search of shelter. These rootless people were, after hostilities finally ended, to fill the camps of displaced persons that proved to be such a problem for the occupying Allies. Many of them refused to return to their home villages. When they finally left the camps, it was to move in every direction; the Polish Jews took the tortuous path to Israel and the erstwhile Nazi administrators of Poland journeyed to havens in South America. In general, however, cities emptied by evacuation had larger populations by 1950 than before the war.

The largest and most disruptive consequence of the American bombing of **Japan** (see **Japan, Air War Against**) was the movement of 10 million city residents to the countryside during the last nine months of the fighting. Thanks mainly to the strong Japanese family system, rural households absorbed the evacuees through heroic cooperation at a time of fatigue, malnutrition and desperation.

The government strategy for protecting the cities against air attacks included four programs affecting civilians: dispersing factories, creating firebreaks, strengthening air defense activities in the neighborhoods and evacuating as many people as possible to the countryside. But government planning had far less to do with whether people fled the cities than the course of the war itself, since most of those escaping to the country left only after the heaviest bombings began in March 1945.

When the home ministry set up an air defense general headquarters in November 1943 to help protect civilians, there was no common view between the air defense general headquarters and the military concerning the proper attitude to take on human lives. There was less ambiguity about "structure evacuation," smashing down homes and other buildings for firebreaks. Broad strips of open land soon appeared around factories, transport centers and military bases where houses and shops had previously stood. Altogether 614,000 housing units were cleared away, usually by members of nearby **neighborhood associations** working with ropes and hand tools. One-fifth of all the housing destroyed by the war was lost in this manner, sending more than 3.5 million city residents out to hunt for new places to live.

The local associations were urged to take the lead in designating homes for destruction, resettling the homeless and providing for emergency shelter during air attacks. They showed government instructional films about how to take cover and how to stock provisions. Community leaders held lecture meetings on ways to stop fires, distributed pamphlets, drilled with bucket relay teams, and recruited a civilian air defense corps to help military spotters. The military planners called on the neighborhood associations to take charge of fire fighting, since ordinary fire companies were hopelessly understaffed. Blackouts were routine, even though nearly all the night bombings before March 10, 1945 took place by **radar**, usually through thick clouds, from about 10,000 feet. By January the alerts were so frequent and the houses so poorly heated that most city people slept in their street clothes. Until the cataclysmic destruction of Tokyo's low-lying riverside districts on March 10, the neighborhood associations managed to snuff out most fires at once.

The most important cabinet policy for the protection of citizens was a decision in October 1943 to begin evacuating persons from urban areas who were not needed in the war plants. The hope was that city leaders and the neighborhood associations could persuade the families of soldiers and conscripted laborers, mothers with small children, the elderly and the infirm to resettle in the countryside, ideally with rural relatives. Yet so long as the danger of raids seemed remote and relocation was optional, fewer people responded than the government had hoped. There are no reliable figures on how many city residents voluntarily fled before the bombings started in late November 1944, but the cabinet's dismay was evident from a report by one of its members in March of that year: "I haven't come across much public sentiment for picking up and leaving."

The only systematic evacuation ever imposed by the state was the forced removal of primary-school children from their families in the cities to group resettlement centers in the countryside, announced to the public on June 30, 1944. Under the guise of keeping the schools operating smoothly, the government was determined to preserve students as a manpower pool, despite the strains this forced separation imposed on the children and their families. Most who underwent the school group resettlement agree that they would rather have stayed home with their parents, even if it meant living through nightly American raids.

Altogether more than 450,000 primary-school pupils from national schools in a dozen major cities moved en masse to vacant inns, monasteries, community halls and hillside resorts in nearby prefectures between August 1944 and the following March. Another 300,000 city schoolchildren had already fled to the villages as voluntary evacuees. The government budgeted 241,000 yen to pay the innkeepers, cooks and helpers who fed and housed the children and their teachers.

Once they had settled in, the evacuees were expected to continue their schooling, but all of them had stiff labor obligations under the April 1944 order creating student volunteer corps. The schools in the host communities usually could not absorb the newcomers, so the children mostly studied in their lodgings. School rarely lasted more than an hour or two each day. Most students spent their time outside class gathering food for the group or working on the nearby farms as volunteers. One principal noted that "going on labor service was one of their greatest pleasures because at a time when food was very scarce they would receive sweet potatoes for working on the farms."

The towns and villages that took in the school groups welcomed the young newcomers less ambivalently than the adult refugees who soon fled to the countryside. The host-refugee relationship was cordial not only because the evacuees were young and their numbers relatively manageable but also because the government made special efforts, through entreaties and cash, to smooth the hard feelings that might occur. The students had their own lodgings, perhaps the greatest irritant in any evacuation program, and they kept pretty much to themselves. Later in the war, when everyone was weary and 20 times as many homeless city people descended on the villages, the climate turned much chillier.

Life away from home was dreary and depressing. Most children lost weight, but there is little evidence that their health suffered as a result. Epidemics were rare, among those evacuated as in Japanese society in general. Far more pupils fell ill from improper diphtheria inoculations in Nagano prefecture than from the disease itself. Parents visited their children occasionally, so long as transportation permitted it, and all the food they brought as presents was routinely shared with the other pupils. The emotional damage caused by separating small children from their anxious parents can be more easily imagined than measured.

Like most people facing disaster, the Japanese were reluctant to leave their city homes, possessions and familiar environs. Only when they were confronted with uniformed authority or the disaster itself, it seemed, would many people finally leave. Yet even then the Japanese experience in 1945 suggested that a mass exodus did not have to involve disorderly panic. More than 10 million Japanese, one-seventh of the national population, spilled out to the farms to find refuge during the last months of the war. At the end of the war, the six largest cities had lost 58 percent of their 1940 populations, and the ones with more than a million persons lost two-thirds of their residents after February 1944. More than 4.2 million persons left Tokyo during the last year of the war, four-fifths of them after the massive March 10 raid.

Apart from the school groups nearly all of this enormous flow took place voluntarily, much of it outside the state's disaster planning. Germany, with its relatively sturdy urban housing, reaccommodated twice as many bomb victims as did Japan. The Germans lost 28 percent of all their dwellings to air attacks, compared with 24 percent in Japan, yet only half as many persons relocated in the countryside (4.8 million, versus more than 10 million in Japan). Even though they tore down more than 600,000 homes, the Japanese authorities were apparently more reluctant than their British counterparts to impose a mandatory evacuation plan for adults.

After the March 10 raid the government ran special refugee trains to the mountains from Tokyo and other main centers to try to cope with the throngs who now needed no persuasion to flee. Evacuees desperately tried to make sacrifice sales of pianos, gas ovens and other items too large to carry on their backs. Others escaped in the beds of trucks if they were lucky enough to hire them. Most people, in the timeless pattern of war refugees everywhere, wordlessly left town riding bicycles, sitting atop oxcarts or trudging on foot.

Because the great majority of civilians in the largest cities migrated, the rural population of Japan bloated from 42 million in February 1944 to 52.5 million in November 1945 (two-thirds of the newcomers were females). This influx had a stunning effect on schools, housing and food supplies in the host communites. Officials in Gunma prefecture, near Tokyo, calculated that their prefecture absorbed 222,880 outsiders, about a quarter of them persons who had lost their homes to fires and the other three-fourths people who had fled to escape the same fate. More secure shelters, such as hilly Nagano and Niigata prefectures, soaked up many thousands more.

Somehow they fitted the homeless in, but villagers were often testy and suspicious toward their guests even though the great majority were relatives of somebody in the community. No one seemed eager to take in refugee mothers with small children, as was true during the British evacuation, and the hospitality soon wore thin when too many cooks shared the same kitchen. Even ties of blood could not mask the cultural and emotional gaps between city and country relatives when they were thrown together under the extreme circumstances of mass flight. The government tried to shame farmers into cooperating by means of such slogans as "Families that won't take people in are a disgrace." In the end host and guest managed to get along because they had no alternative. The refugees were there, there were millions of them, and they had nowhere to stay and nothing to eat. Basic cooperation took hold where official plans and pronouncements had not been enough.

Relations were frosty in part because most newcomers lacked the skills to help grow what they ate. Local people especially resented evacuees who "played idly" while the farmers struggled to keep up production. But most former city residents tried their best to learn farm chores such as using a hoe, cutting weeds, working land and thinning peaches. Still it seems that the evacuees were a net economic drain on the rural economy during the final months of the war, compounding a drastic shrinkage in output caused by poor fertilizer, inadequate transport, scarce fuel and, above all, cold weather.

Well before 1950 the cities of Japan had regained their normal size, as the 10 million evacuees filtered back to reconstruct their lives and many of the 6.6 million Japanese repatriated after the surrender settled down in urban districts. For a time the wartime flight from Japan's big cities interrupted the long-term trend toward urbanization, but the great postwar movement soon restored the normal patterns of city growth and congestions.

J. Vidalenc
T.R.H. Havens

F

FABIEN, Georges Pierre (alias "the Colonel") (1919-1944).
A militant member of the French Communist Party, Fabien helped found the youth movement *Bataillons de la Jeunesse* in 1941. Fabien made the first assassination attempt against a German officer, in Paris on August 21, 1941, under the name of Fredo. He was head of a brigade in the *Forces francaises de l'interieur* on the Ile de France in 1944, and was killed in action in Alsace.

FALKENHAUSEN, Alexander von (1878-1966).
A German general, Falkenhausen was military governor of **Belgium** and the north of France from 1940 to 1944. His administration attempted to spare the population under its jurisdiction many of the frustrations suffered by other occupied countries; at the same time Falkenhausen did not neglect German interests. He refused **Himmler**'s demand to divide Belgium into a Flemish *Gau*, a Walloon *Gau* and a "mixed province" that would include Brussels. Implicated in the **assassination attempt of July 20, 1944** against **Hitler**, he was recalled to Berlin and arrested by the **Gestapo**. He was, in turn, imprisoned by the Allies in May 1945. On March 9, 1951 Falkenhausen was condemned in Belgium to 12 years at hard labor for war crimes; he was freed two days later.

FALL GELB.
In English "Yellow Plan." This was the code name for the German attack on western Europe in May-June 1940.

Allied Plans
Misinterpreting the lessons of World War I, the French military command held fast, in 1939, to the doctrine of continuous fronts, as embodied by the **Maginot Line**, the heavy fortifications between the Rhine and the Moselle. The **morale** of the French army was, by 1940, after eight months of the "**phony war**," much lower than in the preceding year; this too contributed to the overall weakness of French military forces. After the declaration of war in September 1939, the **United Kingdom**'s war effort on the Continent developed more slowly than it had in 1914. The British Expeditionary Force included only a dozen divisions by May 10, 1940.

The total strength of the Dutch army was 10 divisions. **The Netherlands**' defense strategy involved primarily its traditional system of fortification in depth, based on the country's waterways and the use of deliberate flooding tactics.

Belgium had by the spring of 1940 succeeded in mobilizing 600,000 men, an exceptional feat for a country whose population was only eight million. The 22 divisions thus formed, however, were poorly equipped. The Belgian army could not possibly have halted the Germans along the initial 130-mile front. Nor could it count on any assistance from the Dutch army to the north. The only position where the Belgians could concentrate their troops with any chance of success was along the Antwerp-Namur line, known as "KW," where the French and British forces intended to make a stand in the event of a large-scale German drive into Belgium. Because both the forward movement of the Allied armies toward KW and the retreat of the Belgians from the same area had to be protected, tight control of the Albert Canal and the Meuse was necessary. If that position could not be defended, however, the Belgian army as a whole, including its units in Ardennes, intended to fall back on the Antwerp-Louvain segment of the KW line. This maneuver could be covered from an intermediate position on the Gete.

This Belgian plan, well known to the Allies, dovetailed beautifully with their Operation **Dyle**. This maneuver required the French Seventh Army to hold the mouths of the Schelde and Zeeland rivers to consolidate the Holland-Belgium weld. The British Expeditionary Force was to occupy the KW position between Louvain and Wavre. The French First Army was to hold the Wavre-Namur line, with the Namur anchor defended by Belgian troops. With the French Ninth Army pivoted on the Meuse as far as Namur, the Second Army could hold its position on the French-Belgian frontier.

Maurice Gamelin, the French commander in chief, believed, in November 1939, that if the Belgian forces managed to keep their grip on the Albert Canal for five days after a German attack, the Allies could reinforce them in time.

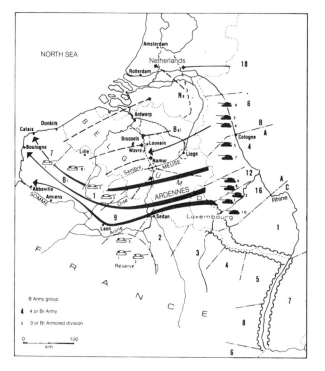

German Plans

Fall Gelb began to unfold on May 10 with a gigantic pincer movement of armor from the Dinant-Sedan line to the sea. The main push, involving most of the German armor, burst into the Ardennes, at the center, smashing through the Meuse line. Then, swiftly exploiting this breakthrough to the north, the Nazi Panzer divisions trapped masses of French and British troops in central Belgium by cutting them off from their supply lines to France. These first manifestations of the dazzling **Blitzkrieg**, the lightning-war tank tactics mastered by the *Wehrmacht*, abruptly reduced the obsolete defenses of the Allies to shambles.

With the Allied armies in the north cut to pieces, the *Wehrmacht* shifted rapidly into the second phase of the operation—the destruction of the Allied divisions south of the Somme, behind the Maginot Line.

Of the 137 divisions **Hitler** had in the west, 74 took part in this phase of the offensive. Army Group B in the north, supported by dive bombers and **airborne troops**, clashed with two Allied armies totaling 30

divisions. These German units had the multiple mission of destroying the Dutch defenders, seizing the bridges over the Albert Canal and pinning down the Allied troops in the north. After accomplishing these tasks, they joined forces with part of Army Group A to mop up the troops caught in the pincers pocket. The remainder of Group A, also aided by dive bombers and other aircraft, struck a sledgehammer blow with 44 divisions, of which seven were armored and three motorized. This spearhead broke through the Meuse between Dinant and Sedan and drove toward the lower Somme region.

This assault was covered by the German Fourth Army, based in the Sambre-Meuse furrow and acting in coordination with the armies of Group B. Following the German armor to expand the corridor it had opened, the 12th Army penetrated into Belgium through northern **Luxembourg**, and the 16th Army sent a second spearhead into Belgium through southern Luxembourg to protect the German left flank. The remainder of the Nazi troops, deployed along the Aisne, the Somme and local canals, further guaranteed the freedom of action of their comrades advancing to the north, while the armies of Group C in the south immobilized the French troops on the Maginot Line and along the Rhine.

Military Operations, May 10-14

The *Wehrmacht* launched its offensive at dawn on May 10. While the 18th Army mauled the Dutch forces opposing it, the Sixth Army advanced on the Belgian front. By 4:30 a.m. two bridges over the Albert Canal were in the hands of German airborne troops—intact. The defending Belgians apparently had no time to destroy them and delay the advance of the enemy. In the meantime, more airborne troops were landing on Fort Eben Emael. Here again, as in the Netherlands, the Germans astonished the military world with their ingenious use of a novel offensive tactic—vertical troop movements.

German tanks drove forward over the Maastricht Bridge, rebuilt on May 11, as far as Waremme, thus outflanking Liege. But Allied troops, on the march since the morning of May 10, were moving toward the Dyle. On the following day the Belgian army began its retreat to the same area to join them. The Dyle thus became the defense line on which the Germans were to be stopped.

With 40 divisions north of the Sambre-Meuse furrow facing only 30 German divisions, the Allies appeared to have the advantage. The Allied command, therefore, considered the loss of the Albert Canal only a temporary setback. Following the orders they had received, the First Division of the Ardennes Mountain Infantry retreated to the northwest after appropriate mining operations to delay the enemy, leaving that territory to French covering detachments. The French cavalry had been in contact with the enemy since May 10. On May 12 it fell back behind the Meuse, while the Germans concentrated their forces for the next day's attack. It was on this front rather than the Albert Canal that the battle unfolded.

In conformity with Operation Dyle, the Allied armies prepared their positions north of the Meuse. On the afternoon of May 12 a colloquy was held near Mons involving King **Leopold III** of Belgium; French Premier **Edouard Daladier**; Gens. **Joseph Georges** and Gaston Billotte; and the chief of staff, Lord **Gort**. It was agreed that Billotte, in command of Army Group One, "would coordinate the operations of the Allied forces on Belgian territory." This rather vague assignment of command was to cause serious difficulties.

Almost continuous north of the Meuse, the front was now formed by the Albert Canal, Diest, the Gete and the Mehaigne. At 11 a.m. on May 13 the German artillery opened up to cover the advance of two armored divisions. The opposing French tanks were deployed in small groups, confident in the superiority of their fire power and heavier armor. This first tank battle of the war was to settle once and for all the superiority of mobile over immobile fire.

In the evening the French position was broken. The exhausted troops withdrew behind the Belgian anti-tank barriers at Perwez to permit the insertion of the First Army, which had been delayed by hordes of refugees clogging the roads. As a result of the events on its right flank, the Belgian covering units fell back from the Gete toward the KW line during the night of May 13. The defense line stabilized, in the meantime, with the Allied troops occupying the following positions:

(1.) Three divisions of the French Seventh Army, from the mouth of the Schelde to north of Antwerp.

(2.) The Belgian Army, on a 30-mile front from north of Antwerp to Louvain, with three levels of divisions. A general reserve was formed from the Cavalry Corps and the First Division of the Ardennes Mountain Infantry.

(3.) Five divisions of the British Expeditionary Force, deployed in two levels on the Dyle, with one division on the Senne, one on the Dender and two on the Schelde from Louvain to Wavre.

(4.) Six divisions of the French First Army, with two seasoned mechanized divisions in reserve, from Wavre to north of the Namur. During the day a final and violent covering battle was fought in the Gembloux region.

(5.) Two Belgian divisions, supported by artillery in the fort, defended Namur.

Distributed in this fashion, the front seemed staunchly placed from the Schelde to the Meuse except for disquieting news of a rupture in the French position at the southern part of the Meuse. The French Ninth Army was deployed with difficulty along the Belgian section of the river on May 12 because of the long distances most of the troops had to cover on foot. In the Dinant region, toward 4 p.m. the defenders came into contact with **Rommel**'s division; the bridges were destroyed by Belgian sappers. At dawn on May 13 the Germans crossed the Meuse and established a bridgehead near Houx. Supported by the *Luftwaffe*, they enlarged their position and on May 14 outflanked the French lines with their armor, attacking the rear of the defending troops. The Germans also crossed the river at Montherme, but the heights at that point stymied the invaders until they overpowered the French on May 16.

The most decisive onslaught occurred at Sedan on the afternoon of May 13. It was launched on a narrow front after brutal artillery and aerial bombardments. In three hours the assault infantry established a deep bridgehead to prepare the way for a tank column crossing the river at night over a bridge built by German engineers. Taking a gamble, Gen. **Heinz Guderian** sent, on the afternoon of May 14, one division of the armored corps under his command toward the Bar Canal, where it captured two bridges intact to facilitate his advance westward. Every attempt made by the French to contain the enemy in the Sambre-Meuse sector and plug up the Sedan breakthrough failed.

Military Operations, May 15-24

Informed of the surrender of the Dutch army on the evening of May 15 and knowing that the gaping hole at Sedan was beyond mending, Gen. Billotte made the only possible decision. He ordered the retreat of the Allied forces in Belgium to the Schelde. Under the protection of a rear guard posted on the Willebroeck Canal and the Senne and Dender rivers, the Belgian and British forces fell back some 55 miles. The French First Army retreated to the Sensee-Schelde triangle, abandoning Belgian territory. Curiously enough, the Germans entered the evacuated area with a good deal of caution. Most of the units in the Sixth Army, in fact, exhibited astonishing timidity.

On May 20 the Belgian army front ranged from Terneuzen to Audenarde. British Gen. Lord Gort deployed his troops on the Schelde from Audenarde to the Franco-Belgian frontier. To guard his right flank, he concentrated small groups around Arras and on the Scarpe River, behind the French First Army, as well as along the line of the canals to the Atlantic.

The British command felt distinctly uneasy in the face of the irresolute despair gripping French head-

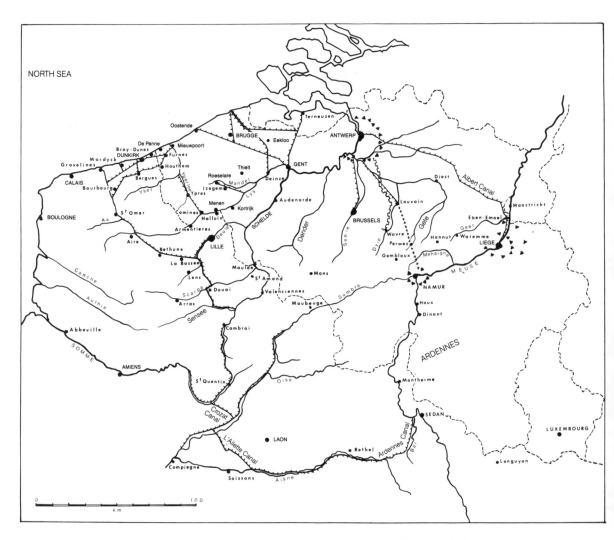

quarters. Gamelin was relieved of his command on May 19, at precisely the moment he was ordering a counteroffensive against the flank of the Panzer column. In any case his order could not be executed since there was no reserve worth speaking of to perform the operation. The aging Gen. **Maxime Weygand**, replacing Gamelin, accompanied Belgian Gen. Raoul van Overstraeten on a tour of the "front" only to discover that the Second *Panzer* Division had captured Abbeville at 9 o'clock the night before and that the encirclement of the Allied divisions in the north was now complete.

With the confusion in the Allied camp at its height on May 20, Gen. **William Ironside**, chief of the

British general staff, conferred with Gort and Billotte. They agreed that Gort was to pierce the German encircling noose to Amiens through a cooperative effort with the French and Belgians, thus reestablishing the continuity of the Allied front. The plan may have been sound in the abstract, but as Gamelin had already pointed out, with Weygand's concurrence, the Allies had neither the time nor the capability to execute it. Gort planned only a small-scale operation on both sides of Arras, an attack that would coincide with a simultaneous thrust by several neighboring French units. Another French offensive from the Somme was prepared for May 23.

The attack was in fact launched at 2 p.m. on May 21,

but relatively few troops could be put into the field. The British conducted it alone, since the French forces could not reach the staging area in time. Yet this operation, more a swift raid than a true offensive, came as an overwhelming surprise to the Germans before they beat it back at 8 p.m. Its psychological effect was prodigious. Overestimating the forces participating in the attack, the *Wehrmacht* headquarters almost panicked. **Wilhelm Keitel** at once changed his battle order, halting the armored units within the sector and driving two others back to Arras.

This same afternoon, at Ypres, Weygand opened the first conference of the chief commanders of the campaign. It was also to be the last. Only King Leopold and his military adviser, Van Overstraeten, turned up the first day. Billotte arrived later. Notified too late of the meeting, Gort missed the opportunity to talk to Weygand. The latter's plan was to initiate simultaneous counterattacks from the north and south. The necessary forces, Weygand calculated, could be assembled by having the Belgian troops retreat once more, this time to the Yser River.

Van Overstraeten objected to the scheme. This new cession of Belgian soil to the invading Germans would badly damage the morale of his troops, he insisted. Besides, the positions the army was to take up on the Yser had not been prepared, since the roads to the rear of that defense line were glutted with hundreds of thousands of refugees. In any case the Belgian forces were disheartened and some units had already broken up. Billotte then offered a realistic summary of the disastrous condition in which his group of armies found itself. Weygand proposed keeping the Belgians on the canal from Ghent to Terneuzen and on the Schelde to relieve the British troops. This plan required the concurrence of Gort. But by the time Gort finally arrived at Ypres, Weygand had already departed. With the British general came the disquieting news that the Germans had crossed the Schelde near Audenarde.

At the conclusion of the conference, the decision was made to regroup the Allied forces on a new front— Valenciennes, the Escaut (the French part of the Schelde), the old frontier line from Maulde to Halluin, the Lys River, Ghent and Terneuzen. But no more than five divisions could be provided for the attack from the south, which was not to begin until May 23.

Unfortunately, Billotte died as the result of an accident when returning to his headquarters. The major participant in the conference thus vanished from the scene without having given a single order. His successor, Gen. Georges Blanchard, did not learn until the following morning of the decisions of the conference, nor did he know what measures he was to take to put them into effect. Matters were changing so rapidly at this point, however, that neither Weygand nor Blanchard was capable of controlling the armies in the north. Each worked independently of the other until the campaign ended.

On the night of May 22, Gen. **Walther von Brauchitsch**, head of the *Oberkommando des Heeres* (OKH), ordered his army groups to tighten the noose around the encircled troops. **Gerd von Rundstedt**, commander of Army Group A, was cool to the idea. Uneasily aware of the French presence on his southern flank as well as the developing Arras counterattack, he preferred instead to halt his armor briefly and regroup on the Gravelines-St. Omer-Bethune line. Thus, the British gained breathing space during which they could consolidate their defenses along several canals. On the evening of May 23, the OKH put all the units engaged in liquidating the Allied pocket under a single command, in complete ignorance of Rundstedt's decision. This move, obviously intended to hasten the annihilation of the Allied troops, might have accomplished its purpose if Hitler had not insisted on taking a hand. On May 24, the Fuehrer countermanded Brauchitsch's instructions by ordering a halt in the German advance.

Still inside their pocket the Allied armies in the north began their retreat to Ypres on May 22. The British army dug in on the Maulde-Halluin and on the Lys as far as Menen; the units that had participated in the attack of May 21 fell back to positions behind the canal of La Bassee. During the morning of May 22, the Belgian command decided that the canal near the source of the Lys would be the final battle line from which no retreat would be made. With this maneuver completed and one British division relieved, the front extended to Menen.

On the German side, 12 divisions of Army Group B massed for the final assault. The 18th Army attacked the Terneuzen canal and crossed it in the afternoon of May 23, forcing the Belgian covering units to abandon their position that same night. Advancing further that night the *Wehrmacht* crossed the Lys as well and occupied the bridgehead at Ghent that the Allies had abandoned. The *Luftwaffe* was in complete command of the skies the entire time.

The Battle of the Lys and the Belgian Surrender

At dawn on May 24 the Belgian Army was deployed along a 60-mile arc; it was in contact with the enemy over the whole of this front. The protection the Lys river seemed to afford proved illusory. Thousands of **propaganda** leaflets dramatizing the eventual fate of the encircled armies were dropped by the *Luftwaffe*. Throngs of refugees moving aimlessly about to the rear of the troops and overflowing to the edges of the front spread an atmosphere of futility among the ranks. There was no certainty of the hoped-for meeting with the British forces. Since May 23 German artillery had been pounding Belgian positions between Courtrai and Menen, while the dive-bombing **Stukas** extended their activities to the rear on the morning of May 24.

Toward the beginning of the afternoon, four German divisions that had crossed the Lys on either side of Courtrai went on the offensive. Aiming at the hinge joining the Belgian and British troops, they threatened to wedge them asunder. The Allied command grasped the danger and rapidly closed the breach that evening on the Ypres-Izegem line with what remained of the reserve manpower plus detachments drawn from other parts of the front. On May 25 Gort tried to end the threat by creating, with the divisions earmarked for the projected offensive at Ypres, a barricade along the Comines canal to Ypres and along the Yperlee to the Yser. Further to the north, at about 7 a.m. on May 25, the German troops formed another bridgehead on the canal near Deinze.

The hours of the Belgian army were now numbered; the fatal design took shape on the following day, May 26, when the Mandel canal was crossed and the two bridgeheads previously established were joined. Another crossing was made over the canal north of Eekloo. The only reserves the Allies now possessed were the fragments of three shattered divisions that remained after a few days of fighting. This mixture of no longer identifiable units increased the difficulty of maintaining discipline; the troops were completely exhausted. On the afternoon of May 26, the king notified Blanchard that his nation was at the end of its means of resistance. Gort, too, was informed that Belgium had no more power to keep the invaders from Ypres.

The British commanders, in the meantime, made the only possible decision remaining to them—to recall their expeditionary forces home, an operation for which planning had already begun.

The principal prong of the German attack hit the center of the front, in the direction of Thielt. It broke through toward noon of May 27, clearing the path to Brugge. At this point King Leopold advised both Gort and the French military that he was nearly ready to capitulate rather than to suffer total disaster. Toward 4 p.m. the Belgian command conceded that all means of resisting the Germans had failed. Little remained but to notify the heads of the Allied missions that a truce deputation was being sent to the *Wehrmacht* command to learn the conditions for the cessations of hostilities. The response of the Germans was succinct and brutal: The Fuehrer demanded **unconditional surrender.**

At 11 p.m. the king and his chief of staff bowed to the ultimatum and proposed that firing cease at 4 a.m. on May 28. And at that hour firing ended over the whole of the Belgian front except in the Roulers-Ypres sector, where units still uninformed of the truce fought on another two hours.

The Battle of Dunkirk

On the morning of May 28, the Franco-British bridge-head around Dunkirk was under formation; the Allies still controlled the Yser, the Yperlee, the canal from Ypres to Comines, the Lys up to Armentieres and the line of canals between Gravelines and Bergues extended by a shielding group of units as far as the Lys. This defense activity was carefully watched by the German general staff. **Goering** asserted that the *Luftwaffe* would prevent evacuation of the bridgehead by sea. The night before, a German armored column punched through Allied defenses south of the Lys and cut off a half-dozen French divisions around Lille. But these trapped forces nevertheless maintained pressure on the encircling forces until May 31, thus keeping the attackers from reinforcing their comrades attempting to pierce the Dunkirk perimeter. The harried Allied command estimated that the Mardyck-Bergues-Houtem-Furnes line, protected by the canals connecting those towns, would hold fast until the British forces could embark.

On May 29, with Dunkirk under concentrated bombardment, the Allied troops in the van of the perimeter steadily gave up ground. The German advance, however, progressed at a cautious rate, with the armor replaced by infantry. The *Oberkommando der Wehrmacht* was actually in the process of assembling its power for the second phase of the "Battle of the West," designed to drive the enemy into the sea.

In the English Channel a feverish effort was under way to organize transports for the French and British soldiers. The British government attempted to make up for the shortage of troop carriers by appealing to the owners of any type of vessel to volunteer its service as a military transport. Amateur as well as professional sailors responded with such enthusiasm that the Channel swarmed with an armada of civilian craft that, in the days that followed, brought thousands of men safely back to England.

This complicated naval maneuver could never have succeeded but for the RAF, which, by wresting control of the air from the *Luftwaffe*, kept the departure of the troops in that strange assortment of boats from degenerating into a frenzied rout. By May 30 some 126,000 men had been landed in England. The French command had not issued its evacuation instructions until the night before; only by May 31 could proper Franco-British coordination be restored and an equal number of French and British soldiers be taken aboard. On that same day 68,000 men were evacuated.

When Gort embarked, early on June 1, 39,000 British troops still remained on the Continent. The Germans had reached the French-Belgian frontier in the east; at the center and the west every attempt they made to breach the canals was blocked. During the day, 65,000 men were taken off the beaches.

Violent fighting continued on June 2-3 to cover the embarcation of the last British units. The French evacuation of 53,000 men went on until the dawn of June 4. The Germans entered Bray-Dunes at 7 a.m., and at 9:30 a.m. all resistance in Dunkirk ended.

The Allies had lost tremendous stores of heavy materiel. Casualties among the ships involved were exceptionally high. But the operation succeeded beyond the most optimistic hopes. Between May 27 and June 4 some 340,000 men were taken back to England. This resounding strategic triumph was to have a profound impact on events to follow.

The Battle of France

On June 5 the French command still had 70 divisions, including three British and two Polish divisions, and the garrison of the Maginot Line. A continuous front had been established near the sea, at Longuyon, formed by the Somme, the Crozat canal, the Ailette, and the Aisne. To confront probable Italian incursions, the front on the Alps was manned by three divisions and 40 battalions of French mountain troops. Considering the length of the fronts and the scanty materiel and low morale of the French, there was no chance that an attack in strength could be repelled.

Heavily superior in numbers and in total command of the air, the *Wehrmacht* Army Group B, with 52 large units, six of them armored, went on the offensive at dawn on June 5, jumping off from bridgeheads established on the Somme. Resistance was at first effective, but by June 8 the German advance units broke through. The French commanders tried vainly to halt the offensive on the Seine, but the enemy crossed the river between Rouen and Vernon.

On June 9 the armies in the German Army Group A, reinforced by armor from their right flank—49 divisions, including 8 armored—were concentrated for the decisive offensive of Champagne. The subsequent collapse of the French defense accelerated rapidly to the point where it outran the march of events. On June 11 **Mussolini** declared war on France, and on June 13, the French forces were completely routed. Paris was occupied on June 14; having fled to Bordeaux, the ministry disbanded and Petain replaced **Paul Reynaud** as president of the *Conseil d'Etat*. While the Nazi tanks lumbered on toward Lyons and the Maginot Line was outflanked and taken from the

rear, Petain expressed, through General **Franco**, his readiness to open negotiations with the victors.

In the Maginot Line zone 500,000 men laid down their arms. Along the remainder of the front, La Rochelle, Poitiers and Chatillon were captured, and Vichy and Lyons were bypassed. In the Alps the Italians delayed their advance until the defending French were threatened from the rear by the forward German units. The tactical awkwardness and poor logistics of the Italian troops permitted the more efficient French command to keep the Alpine frontier inviolate until the armistice.

The Armistice

At 5:35 a.m. on June 25, 1940 a cease-fire was declared and the French campaign came to an end. Under the armistice conditions, all of France west and north of the line connecting Mont de Marsan, Tours, Nevers, Moulins and Chalon sur Saone was placed under German occupation. All war materiel was surrendered to the Germans, but ships and military aircraft were simply disarmed and stored away. Part of the French navy was permitted to remain in French hands to keep French overseas possessions out of British control. French forces in the unoccupied zone were reduced to 100,000 men. The 1.5 million soldiers taken prisoner in the fighting were kept as hostages until the conclusion of the armistice. Hitler permitted local administrative control in the unoccupied territory. At Vichy, on July 10, Petain became chief of the **French State**, with **Laval** as the vice-president of the *Conseil*.

While the Battle of the West was, of course, disastrous for the Allies, Hitler had lost the opportunity to destroy the British army. The political and strategic consequences of this error were to prove incalculable (see, **Britain, Battle of**).

J. L. Charles

FALL WEISS.

In English, "White Plan." This was the code name for the German attack on **Poland**. **Hitler**'s intent, since the spring of 1939, had been to resort to force to attain his territorial aims in Poland. He wanted first to generate a political situation in the east that would serve as a pretext for action in the "national defense" and then to annex **Danzig** to the Third Reich. This phase of his long-range program was limited to war on Poland. Acting on the directive of April 3, 1939 *(Fall Weiss)*, the *Oberkommando des Heeres* mobilized a land army of 53 divisions, six of them armored, with 3,000 armored vehicles, four and a fraction motorized divisions, and four light divisions, leaving a gap in the western frontier in which only 33 divisions, 11 of them active, confronted 110 French divisions. The strategy was simple—to encircle the Polish land forces, consisting of 38 infantry divisions, two motorized brigades, 11 cavalry brigades, and 600 tanks, supported by 745 planes, and destroy them at leisure. The German military potential—its men and armament, the condition of its equipment, the economic capacity of the state—was deemed adequate to the task, especially since no other great power was likely to assist the victim.

The operations were led by two army groups, the southern group under the command of Gen. **Gerd von Rundstedt** and the northern under the command of Gen. **Fedor von Bock**, supported by two fleets of 1,538 combat-ready aircraft of all types as well as naval forces. The offensive began on the morning of September 1 with a surprise attack by the *Luftwaffe* on Polish airfields. By the next day, Polish air space was totally controlled by German aircraft. The Polish army commanders, attempting to deploy their troops and resources from the east, were greatly hampered by the bombardment of rail and communications centers.

It was not until September 3 that the **United Kingdom** and France declared war on **Germany**. The **United States** proclaimed a state of armed neutrality, and **Italy** preferred to remain "nonbelligerent." Moreover, these powers failed to initiate the urgently demanded offensive that could have relieved the Polish forces; for the moment, they seemed to lack either the will or the capability to act.

The far superior German forces captured the Vistula on September 4; between September 5 and 10 they took the Narew and Bug rivers. Their victory in the battle of the Bzura between September 12 and 18 enabled them to begin their siege of Warsaw. On September 17 Brest Litovsk was in German hands, and the right and left wings of the German lines joined forces to Warsaw's rear, to enclose the Polish capital in a ring of steel. At the same time, two Soviet army groups crossed the eastern frontier of the violated country. The Polish government and chiefs of staff under Marshal Edward Smigly-Rydz escaped to **Rumania**, where they were interned.

The Red Army's mission was to march to the limits of the Russian sphere of influence (the Narew, Vistula and San rivers) granted **Stalin** by the **Nazi-Soviet Pact** of August 23, 1939. After suffering violent air and artillery punishment from its German attackers, Warsaw surrendered on September 27. The fortress of Modlin surrendered on September 28, and the military port of Hel followed on October 2. Four days later, on October 6, all local resistance ceased. Abandoned by the western powers, Poland was conquered in a **Blitzkrieg** with adroit use of armored, motorized and air tactics designed to win as quickly as possible with minimal losses. For the *Wehrmacht* the price of victory was low—10,572 killed, 30,322 wounded and some 3,000 missing. It was much higher for the Poles. To the Germans they lost 70,000 prisoners and to the Soviets 200,000. An additional 150,000 were interned

Poland on September 28, 1939

in Rumania, **Hungary**, Lithuania and Latvia. Their territory, for the fourth time in Polish history, was partitioned. In an agreement signed on September 28, 1939 by Germany and the **USSR**, Hitler left the fate of western Poland temporarily in abeyance. On October 8 some of the Polish lands he had acquired were officially designated "Incorporated Eastern Territories"; these included East Prussia and Poznan. The remaining areas fell under the aegis of the new **General Government for Occupied Poland.**

The process of Germanization was begun almost immediately in the Incorporated Eastern Territories, most of which had formerly been German; the general government, however, was subjected to brutal exploitation. Under the direction of **SS** Reichsfuehrer **Himmler**, the first measures toward racial extermination were taken in that area. Hitler for some time viewed this area as a possible hostage in an anticipated bargain with Great Britain. But when London's will to resist stiffened in July 1940, notwithstanding the loss of France, he declared the area the "Neighbor Country of the Reich," with its population theoretically permitted a national, economic and cultural life of its own but actually treated as a subordinate race, partly free, with no autonomy. In the fall of 1940 it was finally absorbed into the Reich.

H.-A. Jacobsen

FAMINE.
See **Deaths**; **Food**.

FAO.
See **Food and Agriculture Organization.**

FASCISM.
In its narrowest sense "fascism" was the term applied to the movement **Mussolini** headed when he seized power in Rome in 1922. In a broader sense it refers to political currents or parties demanding governments along the pattern of the Nazis in **Germany** or Mussolini's Fascists, which, notwithstanding certain differences, possessed similar ideological viewpoints.

There are many interpretations and theories of fascism, many of them conditioned by specific political considerations. Yet there is agreement regarding the structural conditions that brought it into being before and during World War II, even if their relative importance is debated. These conditions were, first, the crisis in industrial capitalist society induced by the social and economic revolutions that developed around the turn of the century; second, World War I and the radical transformations it set in motion; and finally, the Russian Revolution and the threat of subversion it posed to liberal and bourgeois democracy.

In countries with strong fascist movements, and especially where fascists actually gained control, other specific characteristics emerged.

Fascism enjoyed its broadest support among the middle classes, particularly in rural areas. Its adherents felt trapped between the organized workers on the one hand, and the increasingly powerful monied classes on the other. They believed that their interests were no longer guaranteed by a liberal system with little tradition. The nucleus of the movement was typically a group of nationalist extremists, militarists and rootless thugs. Sometimes it also included workers from the lower middle class with a taste for socialism. In any case fascism could not achieve a position of power without the conscious connivance of a nation's political and economic oligarchy. Unhindered by a liberal and democratic tradition, the oligarchy knew it could not resist the demands of the lower classes for emancipation and would in the end lose its social and economic influence unless it first yielded its power, at least partially, to the fascist movement. It would, however, have to deal sooner or later with the social revolutionary and anticapitalist ardor smoldering in the fascist breast.

It was from such conditions that Italian Fascism sprang in 1922, and German Nazism in 1933.

The phenomenological features of fascism were a hierarchic paramilitary organization, based on the principle of the absolute authority of a single leader; a nationalist and possibly racist ideology by which friends could easily be distinguished from enemies; respect, in principle, for private property, despite the overall anticapitalist tendency; and the exercise of power sustained by a mixture of **propaganda** and terror.

From a functional point of view, fascism was a middle-class protest movement designed to tie the hands of militant labor and limit capitalist dominance. Once in power, fascism not only subdued the labor movement effectively, it also disciplined the middle classes and stabilized the organization of private capital. It assured the maintenance of social and economic power by the traditional oligarchies, set up a one-party dictatorship and was free to pursue the kind of expansionist policy that was impossible for a limited regime.

The prototype of all the fascist movements was the *Fasci di combattimento*, founded in 1919 by the ex-socialist Benito Mussolini. It consisted for the most part of World War I veterans and attempted to terrorize the left. From its very beginnings fascism was distinguished by two contradictory tendencies: one, social-revolutionary; the other, nationalist-conservative. Their mutual antagonism persisted until the demise of Italian Fascism. At the time of the crisis in the liberal system, in 1922, it obtained control of the government with the aid of the middle class, landowners and monarchists. In 1923 it gained political respectability as the *Partito Nazionale Fascista* (the National Fascist Party). But it never managed to suppress the competing radical element nor could it attain the radicalism of the early National Socialist movement. Mussolini linked fascism with the state apparatus and with the monarchy to give his regime a conservative profile. After the fall of the regime, fascism's social-revolutionary wing tried once more to gain ascendance in the ephemeral Italian Socialist Republic.

Under cover of World War II, fascist movements managed to gain control in some countries. In 1941 the Croatian **Ustachi** movement under the direction of **Ante Pavelich** formed its own government, a feat it had been unable to accomplish under the dictatorship of King Alexander. It finally succeeded by depending on traditionally intransigent Croatian nationalism and its ally, the Catholic clergy, in a radical-fascist system that manifested its essentially destructive nature in a brutal drive against Jews and Serbians. In **Hungary**, fascist parties had combined forces around Ferenc Szalasi after 1935 to form the Arrow Cross Party. His program was a peculiarly Hungarian Magyar-imperialist melange, antifeudal in nature, which attracted both peasants and industrial workers. Despite some electoral victories and an attempted putsch, he failed to get a foothold in the government primarily because of the increasingly repressive feudal-conservative dictatorship of Adm. **Horthy**, which was allied to the **Axis** powers. The Szalasi cabinet, finally formed in the last phase of the war, in October 1944, had little political significance—perhaps because it came into being with German assistance.

Rumanian fascism was the exception, from a sociological as well as an ideological viewpoint. The "Iron Guard" of Coreliu Codreanu, controlled by intellectuals and based on peasant support, developed an ideology with a special appeal for national-religious, social-revolutionary and neomodernist loyalties, in addition to **anti-Semitism** and a taste for violence. After several electoral gains in 1932 and 1937, it was brutally suppressed. With the forced abdication of King **Carol II** in 1940, however, it formed part of the conservative government of Gen. **Ion Antonescu**. The internal struggle then taking place ended in the defeat of the Iron Guard. Antonescu's regime remained a conservative military dictatorship.

In the German satellite state of Slovakia, two rival pressure groups vied for supremacy within the controlling party. One was a quasi-fascist Catholic-conservative faction centering around President **Yosef Tiso**; the other, an extremist-totalitarian wing guided by Ferdinand Durcansky and Vojtech Tuka, totally anti-Semitic and supported by the Hlinka Guard, was unquestionably fascist and enjoyed **Hitler**'s favor.

In the German-occupied countries, fascist **collaboration** movements gained some importance where, before the war, their influence had been negligible. In **Norway**, for example, a former officer and minister of war, **Vidkun Quisling**, founded a party known as the *Nasjonal Samling* in 1933. Its ideology, based on blood and soil, was colored by anti-Western and anti-Communist sentiments associated with Greater Norway nationalism. Only with German support could Quisling, appointed ministry president in 1942, give the *Nasjonal Samling* its evanescent place in the sun. His name, however, has lasted as a symbol of collaboration.

In the Netherlands the *Nationaal-Socialistische Beweging* (NSB) of the engineer Anton Mussert owed its success in 1933 only to the fractionalization of the small parties. But the closed ranks of democratic and conservative parties, as well as the opposition of the Catholic Church, shielded the masses from its influence. The occupation authorities fostered the NSB, awarded Mussert the title of *Leider*—the Dutch equivalent of Fuehrer—and, in doing so, burdened him with the epithet of "traitor." Like Quisling, Mussert died before a firing squad.

The extremist Flemings of **Belgium**, more or less fascist, failed to breach the solid phalanx of the large parties in their search for power, as did the Walloon Rexist party, which had cut itself off from the Catholic Action group. The Rexists, led by **Leon Degrelle**, had for a short time acquired a following among lower middle class and farm people. During the occupation, small fascist groups coalesced in the *Vlaams National Verbond* (VNV), which finally became a foreign branch of the **Nazi Party**. Degrelle himself ended up enlisting in the SS with the Walloon Legion, in which he fought on the eastern front.

French fascism is somewhat difficult to pinpoint. The tradition of militant clubs on the antirepublican right, the variety of veterans' political groups and the support of dissident Socialist and Communist elements such as **Marcel Deat** and **Jacques Doriot** gave birth to formations that at first blush seemed fascist but could also be classified pro- or pseudo-fascist—such as the *Croix de Feu*, the *Jeunesse patriote*, or the *Solidarite francaise*. Some of those claiming to be fascist—*Faisceaux Francisme*, for example—were transitory phenomena of no importance. On the other hand, the *Parti populaire francais* of Doriot, the ex-leader of the Communist Party, managed between 1936 and 1938 to acquire a large number of adherents, among them a good many workers. Some well-known intellectuals enrolled in his movement as well, lending

French fascism a certain glamor. The political obstacles of the French right, the Popular Front and later the conservative-rightist Vichy regime prevented French fascism from flying very high. The policy Hitler pursued in France after 1940 depended primarily on Vichy, which had the effect of narrowing the freedom of action of the fascist extremists and preventing them from playing a decisive role.

The other European fascist movements, like the paramilitary *Heimwehr*, which figured in Austrian history in 1933-38, the middle-class groups in **Switzerland** and the unsuccessful Black Shirts of Oswald Mosley in England, paled to insignificance during the war. Another apparent casualty of the war was collaboration among fascist movements.

K. J. Muller

FEDERAL BUREAU OF INVESTIGATION (FBI).
See J. Edgar Hoover; Office of Strategic Services.

FERGUSSON, Sir Bernard Edward (later Lord Ballantrae) (1911-).
Fergusson, a British soldier, commanded a column in Gen. **Orde Wingate**'s first expedition in **Burma** and a brigade in the second. After the war he served as governor-general of **New Zealand** from 1962 to 1967.

FERMI, Enrico (1901-1954).
Fermi, an Italian physicist, won the Nobel Prize in 1938. A leading theoretician in the attempt to develop the **atomic bomb**, Fermi supervised the first atomic chain reaction in Chicago in 1942.

FESTUNG EUROPA.
See Fortress Europe.

FFI.
See *Forces francaises de l'interieur*.

FFL.
See *Forces francaises libres*.

FIFTH COLUMN.
The existence and the danger of a "fifth column" were obsessions in many European countries just before the war. Such subversive forces were, for the most part, nonexistent, but the Nazis encouraged the notion to diffuse fear and incite divisive suspicions among the populace.

The term had been invented during the Spanish civil war by the rebel Gen. Emilio Mola Vidal at the time of the four-columned attack on Madrid in October 1936. He asserted that he also had a fifth column already deployed in the besieged city. It was Mola's name for the

pro-**Franco** agents within Madrid who engaged in **propaganda** with the aims of demoralization, misinformation and sometimes outright **sabotage**.

Beginning in the fall of 1938, the term "fifth column" was increasingly used in countries threatened or attacked by the Nazis as the euphemism for activities useful to the enemy. The same vaguely used expression referred to the espionage activities conducted by the *Abwehr* and the sabotage activities of commando teams and parachutists as well as undercover tactics behind combat lines and every type of activity engaged in by all belligerents long before the idea of a fifth column originated. But the expression had a special flavor characteristic of the Nazi method—a multifaceted propaganda effort; the demoralization of a population dreading imminent attack; the infiltration of political, intellectual and even military circles; the establishment of pro-Nazi cells; and the like.

Various Nazi organs directed and financed such activity with varying degrees of success. It began after Hitler's accession to power with the creation of sections of political parties or satellite organizations in European countries with sizable German minorities. Such groups worked forcefully in **Austria, Czechoslovakia, Rumania, Hungary** and **Norway**. Pro-Nazi clubs appeared in **Switzerland**, France, **Belgium, the Netherlands, Sweden** and the **Baltic States**. Their propaganda, based on **anti-communism** and **anti-Semitism**, aroused echoes in certain layers of society. In Belgium it exploited the problem of national languages.

German minority organizations were attached to the foreign relations section of the **Nazi Party**—the *Ausland-Organisation*, or AO. Employing a staff of 700 in its central Hamburg office, the AO maintained 548 sections abroad. Its head, Ernst Wilhelm Bohle, a party *Gauleiter*, was named secretary of state for foreign affairs. The *Abwehr* recruited agents from among AO members to act as guides or support groups to prepare their countries for the reception of German occupation troops. Local AO members sometimes secreted illegal transmitters in the premises they occupied.

But if the AO can be considered a cover for a fifth column, it will also have to be classed with such propaganda mills as the *Welt Dienst* (WD), or "World Service," an Erfurt agency managed by Lt. Col. Ulrich Fleischauer, or the *Deutsche Fichte Bund* in Hamburg. The WD published a semimonthly bulletin in eight languages as a means of reaching Nazi sympathizers in foreign lands. These were used to contact intellectuals, writers, journalists, politicians—influential professionals of every type—who were asked to contribute articles or attend conferences, with travel expenses to **Germany** guaranteed. Journals and journalists were quietly bribed to perform as a Nazi claque. One of

163

the principal means of this type of infiltration was the exploitation of anti-Semitic sentiment. These sympathizers worked so assiduously as clandestine distributors of Nazi propaganda, even after the onset of hostilities, that they aroused the wrath of officials of their home countries—notably in France, Belgium and, to a lesser extent, Switzerland. Between July 1938 and June 1940 10 decrees were issued by the French government against such publicists.

If this propaganda contributed to the demoralization of the populace or their conversion to the Nazi credo, the fifth column played a comparatively minor role in military operations. But it was quite effective as a psychological tactic by rousing the people to such heights of terror that they would choke the roads in a frantic exodus. More than once the consequent paralysis of transportation was militarily convenient for invading German troops.

J. Delarue

FIGHTER COMMAND.
Commanding staff of British fighter aircraft (see **Britain, Battle of**).

FINAL SOLUTION.
At the end of 1941 Hitler decided on his "final solution" (*Endloesung*) to the "Jewish question" in Europe—the extermination of the Jews. This plan was agreed upon at the **Wannsee Conference** called by **Heydrich** on January 20, 1942 (see **anti-Semitism**).

FINLAND.
Independent since 1917, Finland became a parliamentary republic after the revolution of 1919. With the peace treaty of Moscow after the **Russo-Finnish Winter War** of 1939-40, this small nation was obliged to become more responsive to Soviet demands—for example, with the treaty of October 1940 regarding the defortification of the Aaland Islands. It subsequently pursued a prudent policy of neutrality. The government headed by Rysto Ryti, elected president of the republic in December 1940, was concerned with the increasing political isolation of the country and especially with its difficulty in maintaining economic relations with the Western powers. Finland took measures to ensure its defense: the length of military service was extended from one to two years, the frontier guards were incorporated into the army and the government increased its armaments budget. Of the European powers **Germany** seemed the most approachable to the Finns. On September 23, 1940 the two nations concluded an agreement permitting two German divisions to cross Finnish territory in the direction of **Norway**. But it was not until January 30,

1940 that the first official meeting of the Finnish chief of staff, Gen. Axel Heinrichs, and German chief of staff **Franz Halder** took place. The purpose of the German officers was to probe official Finnish opinion on Operation **Barbarossa**. The Finnish generals were cool to the idea; their first reaction was complete refusal to participate in an attack on Leningrad. But as May of 1941 faded into June, it became apparent that Finland was amenable to limited **collaboration** with the Germans once the details of the Nazi offensive plan were exposed. Finland permitted the concentration of German troops in the northern part of the country to spearhead the incursion into Murmansk, as well as the subordination of the Finnish Third Corps to the German command of Norway. On June 26, 1941 Finland took the final step of declaring war on the **USSR**, justifying its decision as the natural consequence of the de facto state of war existing between the two nations because of Soviet air force attacks on Finnish cities. It was as a "comrade-in-arms" of Germany and not as its ally that the Finns fought in the war they considered a "reengagement" or a "second defensive war," with the sole objective of regaining their lost provinces. This desire for reclamation of the territories the Russians had bludgeoned them into yielding was practically unanimous. Under the command of Marshal **Carl Gustav von Mannerheim**, 16 Finnish divisions reconquered Karelia, but their advance was halted in December 1941. A few days later, on December 6, the **United Kingdom** declared war on Finland, apparently at the insistence of Moscow. On December 7 the Finnish government officially absorbed the provinces it had ceded the USSR in 1940. Through all the heavy fighting on the Russian front from December 1941 to the spring of 1944, the action on the Finnish part of the front was limited to local skirmishes while the Finnish government several times tried to offer **peace overtures**.

In June 1944 two Soviet armies on the Leningrad front conducted the decisive operation to retake the Karelian Isthmus. The Finnish resistance swiftly collapsed. Naturally, the Reich attempted in secret negotiations to prevent the defection of the Finns by promising them increased assistance. But the latter, now led by Antti Hackzell—Mannerheim had resumed his office as president in August—sought only an end to the fighting and the departure of German troops from Finnish soil. On September 19, 1944, after long negotiations, Finland signed an armistice with the British and the Soviets. Its conditions were harsh but not unendurable. The southeastern border between Finland and the USSR, as defined by the Treaty of Moscow, was reaffirmed. Pechenga was ceded to the Soviet Union, and the Porkkala Peninsula, near Helsinki, leased to the USSR as a naval base for 50 years. Moscow also demanded the abrogation of all anti-Communist laws and the immediate reorganization of the Finnish Communist Party, as well as an indemnity of $300 million, to be paid within six years. Within a very short time the Finnish army reverted to its peacetime footing. But serious internal difficulties cropped up when the victorious powers required the Finnish government to assist in the arrest of **war criminals**. On March 3, 1945 the new head of the government, Juho Paasikivi, who had taken the post in November 1944, finally declared war on Germany retroactive to September 18, 1944.

H.-A. Jacobsen

FLAK (acronym for *Flugzeugabwehrkanone*, "antiaircraft cannon").

These German antiaircraft gun units were subordinate to the *Oberkommando der Luftwaffe* rather than the *Oberkommando des Heeres*. Consequently, they were kept under Goering's authority as part of his scheme for defending the Nazi regime against a military *putsch*.

FLEMING, Sir Alexander (1881-1955).

Fleming, a British surgeon and pathologist, accidentally discovered the antibiotic penicillin in 1929. Its manufacture in bulk was undertaken in 1941; by 1943 its use was widespread and its beneficial effects on war wounds began to be felt.

FLEMING, Peter (1907-1971).

Fleming, a British explorer, was a member of the Special Operations Executive and active in deception work in the Far East under Wavell and Mountbatten. Novelist Ian Fleming was his brother.

FLYING BOMBS.

See V-1 and V-2.

FOOD.

Food was often painfully scarce in wartime Europe and Asia. In every warring town in Europe there was less to eat than there had been before the war. Food rationing was universal (see black market for efforts to evade it). Usually the rations provided enough to sustain life and energy, but they were not universally available. Even in the unoccupied United Kingdom, meat and eggs were sometimes not to be had at all (the egg ration in 1943 was one per person per week); on the occupied Continent, townspeople learned to be hungry. Some had to learn to go very short indeed, even while they were nominally free.

Such luxuries as shellfish, fine wines and venison vanished, except for the very rich or the very well con-

nected. Ordinary bourgeois delicacies—fresh butter, fresh vegetables, white bread, coffee, oranges, bananas—became scarce or unobtainable. Biscuit factories were taken over to pack troops' rations; banana boats were filled with grain, which fed more people for longer periods of time. Such crops as mangel-wurzels, grown for cattle, were eaten by hungry men, glad to get them.

Blockade, convoy, and the concentration of shipping on the purposes of war disrupted the whole world food-distribution system, occasionally with disastrous results. Apart from the catastrophe of the Bengal famine (see **India**), which was caused as much by weather and shortage of trained administrators as by the war, there were famines in Athens and in the western **Netherlands** in 1944-45, which each directly caused several thousand deaths. Housewives who were not already economical learned to be so. Much thought was devoted to providing packaged food for the fighting forces. The Americans' lavish C rations and comparatively spartan K rations became known (through gifts and pilfering) wherever the **United States** army passed; gourmets found them uninspired, but on a battlefield they were a godsend. Techniques of dehydration, applied before the war to meat and milk, were extended to eggs, coffee (still much with us) and other foods: this saved much shipping and storage space, though it did not enhance taste. (See also **Health**.)

M. R. D. Foot

FOOD AND AGRICULTURE ORGANIZATION (FAO).

A group formed by the **United Nations** for the distribution of agricultural produce, created in June 1943 by a conference at Hot Springs, West Virginia.

FORCED LABOR BATTALIONS.

On March 23, 1939 **Hitler** declared: "The population of the non-German territories will not be called upon for military service but will be available for labor." This was the signal for the creation of obligatory labor service, known also as the Forced Labor Battalions. This organization mobilized almost 10 million Europeans from all countries between 1940 and 1945 for work in the plants and industries of the Reich. It turned **Germany** into a veritable Tower of Babel.

The "subhumans" of the east formed the majority of the laborers assembled by the Nazis. First Czechoslovaks and then Poles in 1939, Rumanians in 1940 and Yugoslavs and Russians in 1941 were forced into an existence only the deportees to the **concentration camps** delivered helpless into slavery—in the Dora plant, for example—could envy. Underpaid, undernourished, maltreated and abused, the Slavs were reduced to a wretched state. The Italians were treated somewhat better when they were transported to the Reich in 1939 in large numbers to fulfill agreements signed by **Mussolini** and renewed from 1940 to 1943. Most of them were construction workers who worked in the Todt fortification system known as the **Atlantic Wall**. After Todt's death, the German minister of armaments, **Albert Speer**, became the labor manager of Europe. As the growing demands of the German war machine dictated, he turned to other western European nations for metallurgical engineers to replace mobilized Germans. National labor offices in France, **Belgium** and **the Netherlands** first appealed for volunteers from 1940 to 1942; the collaborationist **propaganda** promised excellent opportunities. Under the additional threat of unemployment, some thousands of workers signed contracts. In June 1942 Hitler dispatched **Fritz Sauckel** to recruit additional labor, and **Pierre Laval** responded to Sauckel's demands with his system of "Relief for Prisoners." The program was a fiasco; it only made recruitment more difficult. The law for labor training, issued on September 4, 1942, furnished men between 16 and 60 years of age and women from 18 to 45 to the Reich and the French armament complexes. Finally, the Forced Labor Battalions went into operation on February 16, 1943, although they had already been in place in Belgium since March 1942, mobilizing the classes of 1939 through 1944. As many as 600,000 Frenchmen and 220,000 Belgians were involved. A good many of them refused to return after they had been given leaves, some of them escaping to Great Britain and others joining the **Resistance** in large numbers in 1943 and 1944.

To increase the labor supply, Speer arranged for better protection of the industrial plants—the so-called *Speerbetrieb*—against the prolonged bombing raids conducted by Allied aircraft. Although they were often victims of the Allied bombs and despite the close surveillance to which they were subjected, the forced laborers committed frequent acts of **sabotage** in an attempt to slow up production at considerable peril to their lives. Unfortunately, they also helped to extend the Nazi war effort.

P. Mermet

FORCES FRANCAISES DE L'INTERIEUR (FFI).

In English, the "French Interior Forces." A group of **Resistance** units operating within France under the auspices of the *Comite francais de liberation nationale*, commanded by Gen. **Marie Pierre Koenig** after March 1944. It included the *Armee secrete*, the maquis, the *Francs-Tireurs et Partisans francais* (FTP) and the *Organisation de resistance de l'armee* (ORA). Some 140,000 members of these organizations were inducted into the French First Army. The FFI were effective auxiliaries of the Allied troops, especially in Brittany, in the wake of the **Normandy landing**, and in central France.

FORCES FRANCAISES LIBRES (FFL).

In English, the "Free French Forces." A group of volunteers recruited by Gen. **de Gaulle**, with **Churchill**'s assent, in August 1940 from among the French soldiers evacuated from **Norway**, the army that had fled from Dunkirk to England and the **French colonies** loyal to **Free France**. By 1943 the FFL included the Free French First Division and the Second Armored Division, several naval units under the command of Adm. **Emile Muselier** and some air squadrons that had been in operation since the fall of 1940.

FORTRESS EUROPE.

After the autumn of 1942, when the war changed its course on all fronts in Europe and Africa, causing **Germany** and its allies to shift their strategy to defense, Nazi **propaganda** maintained its efforts to convince the German population and the enemy's that the latter would soon confront a "wall"—i.e., the **Atlantic Wall** on the western shores and the fortified Mediterranean coasts and islands—or a zone defended in depth, particularly in eastern Europe and in the North African outposts. When that happened, the propaganda predicted, all enemy attacks would shatter on the impenetrable shield of *Festung Europa*, or "Fortress Europe." This fantasy of absolute security provided by a circle of resolute defenders, the dream of a National Socialist Europe and the assurance of final victory behind impregnable ramparts were offered to the German people.

In point of fact, however, only a few strategic points had been fortified between the Nordkapp of **Norway** and the Bay of Biscay along a shoreline over 9,000 miles long, running from **Finland** to the Crimea and along the Mediterranean coast down to the bridgehead in North Africa. Moreover, the fatal weakness in *Festung Europa* was its lack of a roof. Month after month Allied air attacks increased in intensity, gradually destroying the besieged citadel's traditional advantage of the "inner line" by striking at the nerve centers of the communications network between the eastern and western fronts, from north to south. The defection of Germany's satellites toward the end of 1943 indicated how ineffective the propaganda for *Festung Europa* was. Six months later the successful Allied invasion of 1944 through the western wall demonstrated the falsity of the propaganda. If the wall of a fortress can be pierced at any one point, nothing can prevent the collapse of its defenses.

A. Hillgruber

FOURCADE, Marie-Madeleine (nee Bridou) (1909-   ).
The head of the very prestigious **Resistance** network *Alliance*, Fourcade was arrested for her opposition to the occupation of France. She made a brave escape but was retaken and later deported from France. Fourcade was president of the *Comite d'action de la resistance*.

FRANCE.
See **Free France; French Colonies; French North Africa; French Police During the Occupation; French Resistance; French Secret Services; French State; Petain and the French State; Purges; Third Republic.**

FRANCO, Francisco (1892-1975).
While leading a military revolt in Spanish Morocco, Franco, a Spanish general, plunged **Spain** into a bloody civil war. Following his victory, achieved with the assistance of **Germany** and **Italy**, he established an authoritarian clerico-fascist regime in Spain. For his policies during World War II, see also Spain.

FRANK, Anne (1929-1945).
A Jewish schoolgirl, Anne Frank was born in Frankfurt am Main. Her family escaped the Nazis and took refuge in the Netherlands in 1933. After the German occupation of Holland in 1940, they were hidden by friends in Amsterdam until 1944, when they were found and sent to **Bergen-Belsen**. Anne Frank was killed there. She left behind a harrowing diary that has become world-famous.

FRANK, Hans (1900-1946).
Frank, a Nazi leader, was the German minister of justice from 1934 to 1939 and the governor-general of **Poland** from 1939 to 1945. After the German surrender he was hanged as a **war criminal.**

FREE FRANCE.
On June 18, 1940, from London, Gen. **Charles de Gaulle**, undersecretary of state in the cabinet of **Paul Reynaud**, who had resigned only 48 hours before, made his famous radio appeal: "The new government, by alleging the defeat of our armies, has come to an understanding with the enemy to put an end to the fighting...but...is that defeat final? No! For France is not alone....This is a world war....I, General de Gaulle in London, invite the French officers and soldiers on British territory or who intend to

come here, with or without their arms, I invite the engineers and skilled workers in armaments industries on British territory or who intend to come here, to get in touch with me. Whatever the final outcome may be, the flame of French resistance must never be quenched nor shall it ever be quenched."

This call, carrying the seed of Free France, was for the most part ignored. Even less noted was his plea on June 19 to the authorities in the various **French colonies.** But its repetition on June 22 galvanized Frenchmen all over the world into joining the general. None of them were politicians. The British war cabinet, which would have preferred a "National French Committee" composed of famous statesmen and presided over by a Reynaud, an **Edouard Herriot** or a **Georges Mandel**, finally accepted de Gaulle on June 28 as the "head of the Free French" and assured him, by means of an advance that was to be repaid even before the war ended, the material means he required. On that same day the general asserted before the microphones of the **British Broadcasting Corporation:** "This engagement means that the Free French join with our Allies in a unified effort until the final victory. I have made the following decisions: (1) I take under my authority all the French who reside on British territory or intend to go there; (2) A French land, sea, and air force will immediately be formed that for the moment will be made up of volunteers...; (3) All officers, soldiers, sailors, and aviators of France, wherever they may be, are in honor bound to resist the enemy."

This speech of June 28 was decisive. It definitely cast de Gaulle in the role of the leader of Free France. And by representing his call for volunteers as a provisional one, by confronting all the French military with the requirements of their "honor," he implied that Free France, because it was the only legitimate and the only true France, must have the loyalty of the French army. In his thoughts it was France and not just a few Frenchmen who continued the fight. All his energies were, for four years, to be inspired by this idea, the sole hope for the survival of France, that **Churchill**—and still more **Roosevelt**—was reluctant to admit.

His one objective was the participation of France in the war as a full-fledged ally with the British and the great powers who were to join them until the final victory. Toward this objective, he saw two means: the loyalty of the French colonial territories and the loyalty of the French people. The July 3 drama of **Mers el-Kebir** (see **Atlantic, Battle of the**) had a chilling effect on these loyalties, but Chad on August 26 and the Cameroons on August 29 declared their allegiance to Free France. The forces of the Free French, however, remained modest in number. At the end of July they barely numbered 7,000 men, but they gradually increased with the enlistment of European and native troops stationed in the loyal territories. They were joined also by French soldiers in the reconquered territories of Gabon, **Madagascar**, and the eastern Mediterranean who refused repatriation to continental France, as well as by volunteers who spontaneously left France to enlist. By June 1942, Free French troops numbered some 70,000 men, of whom 3,600 were sailors aboard some 60 ships of various tonnages. Under the guidance of such commanders as **Leclerc**, **Marie Pierre Koenig**, **Rene de Larminat** and Paul Louis Le Gentilhomme, these men won brilliant military successes in Africa and participated bravely in naval operations.

The use of **propaganda** was possible through the facilities of the BBC, which gave the Free French broadcasters two five-minute periods daily plus the half-hour program "The French Speak to the French." De Gaulle spoke on it practically every week in place of the designated announcer, **Maurice Schumann**.

The policy of Free France was the constant concern of its leader. It progressed by stages. On October 27, 1940, when de Gaulle for the first time set foot on soil under French rule, at Brazzaville, he created the Council for the Defense of the Colonies, in which he won the support of Gen. **Georges Catroux**. On that occasion de Gaulle declared: "There is no longer any such thing as a French government. A new power must therefore take charge of directing the French war effort. Fate has imposed this sacred duty on me, and I shall not fail in it." On his return to London, he ordered Andre Dewavrin, alias Passy, to organize the Central Bureau of Information and Action (*Bureau central de renseignements et d'action*). From Churchill he obtained the guarantee that the Free French would not be subject to prosecution except by French courts.

The second stage in the development of French policy was set in motion on September 24, 1941, when de Gaulle converted the hitherto anonymous group assisting him into the National French Committee, a provisional cabinet whose ministers included Rene Pleven, Maurice Dejean, Le Gentilhomme, **Emile Muselier**, Rene Cassin, Martial Valin, and **Thierry d'Argenlieu**. At the end of October he charged **Jean Moulin** with the task of organizing the National Resistance Council (*Conseil national de la resistance*) to coordinate the activities of the various **Resistance** groups springing up on French territory under de Gaulle's acknowledged leadership. From that moment on, "Charlot" could with a clear conscience call Free France the "Fighting French." With this same concern for building a base for French sov-

ereignty, he had Adm. Muselier occupy the islands of St. Pierre and Miquelon, French possessions off the east coast of **Canada**, at the end of December 1941, just as Roosevelt, who had just declared war on **Japan** and the **Axis** powers, was about to put them under American control. In September 1942 he stepped on Britain's toes by objecting to its acquisition of Madagascar, on which they had landed without notifying him, and won his point. Less successfully, he challenged British occupation of **Syria** and **Lebanon**.

The next phase of de Gaulle's labors was the most difficult and decisive. Landing in North Africa on November 7-8, 1942, Anglo-American forces dealt with Adm. **Francois Darlan**, who happened to be there purely by chance. When he was assassinated, the Allies recognized Gen. **Henri Giraud** as civilian and military commander in chief, thus depriving de Gaulle of the glory of bringing French forces back into the war. Giraud, in turn, made no response to de Gaulle's advances. At the instance of Roosevelt and Churchill, the rival French generals met at Anfa, near Casablanca, on January 22, 1943, in a frigid atmosphere. In the months that followed, de Gaulle played his cards carefully; on June 3 he convoked the French Committee for National Liberation (*Comite francais de liberation nationale*), with himself and Giraud as the presiding officers, and after that the Provisional Consultative Assembly, whose members included 20 legislators who had refused to vote power to Petain in 1940 (see **French North Africa**). Giraud's position began to set. His French supporters—Couve de Murville and **Jean Monnet**, among others—deserted him for de Gaulle; his advocates were in the minority in the CFLN and even more so in the assembly. By November 9 it became obvious that de Gaulle alone was president of the CFLN, which, seven months later, was to become the Provisional Government of the French Republic. Thanks to de Gaulle's obstinacy and statecraft, France once again was a unified state by the time of its liberation.

E. Pognon

FREE FRENCH FORCES.
See *Forces francaises libres.*

FREE GERMANY, National Committee of.
See *National Komitee "Freies Deutschland."*

FREEMAN, Sir Wilfred Rhodes (1888-1953).
Freeman, a British airman, was in charge of British aircraft **production** from 1938 to 1940 and again from 1942 to the end of the war. In 1940-42 he served as vice-chief of the British air staff. Sir **Arthur Tedder**

said that "few people appreciate the supreme debt that we all owe to Wilfred Freeman."

FRENAY, Henri (1905-   ).

Frenay, a French officer, founded the **Resistance** movement *Combat* and its newspaper in 1941 in the unoccupied zone. He was one of the organizers of the *Armee Secrete* in the southern zone. He served as commissioner for prisoners and deportees for the French Algerian Committee in 1943 and as minister of prisoners, deportees and refugees in 1944.

FRENCH COLONIES.

In 1939 France counted among its possessions colonies, protectorates and territories under mandates on every continent. They were divided into two major blocs. The first, the African, consisted of **French North Africa** (the Algerian provinces and the Tunisian and Moroccan protectorates); **French West Africa** (Senegal, Mauritania, Niger, Upper Volta, Mali, Guinea, the Ivory Coast, Dahomey and the Togo territory, a former German colony divided, under mandate, with the **United Kingdom**); **French Equatorial Africa** (Gabon, Chad, Ubangi-Shari and Middle Congo); the Cameroons, another former German possession divided, under mandate, with Great Britain; **Madagascar**, along with the Comoro Islands. The second bloc, the Indochinese bloc, was much more populous; it included the colony of Cochin China and the protectorates of Cambodia, Laos, Annam and Tonkin. Other French possessions, in addition to the Syrian and Lebanese territories under mandate, included former Turkish provinces, Indian agencies within British territory and territories on the Gulf of Aden. France also controlled some longtime possessions in North and South America: St. Pierre and Miquelon, French Guiana, Martinique and Guadeloupe. Finally, there were the French possessions in the Pacific: Oceania, New Caledonia, the French-British condominium New Hebrides and some deserted islands in the South Pacific.

The declaration of war had stimulated defensive measures everywhere, but because the German surface fleet was too sparse to repeat the piratical raids of World War I, there was no immediate rush. In the colonies, the most pressing need was to reinforce the fortified line garrisons of southern Tunisia—the Mareth line—threatened by an attack from the Italians in Tripolitania. The French chiefs of staff had strengthened the North African and colonial contingents in France during peacetime with the formation of six Zouave regiments of Algerian and Senegalese light infantry, eight regiments of Moroccan infantry, six Tunisian regiments and six Algerian or Moroccan Spahi regiments, in addition to North African and Moroccan infantry divisions and Indochinese and Madagascan machine-gun battalions. All of these troops were in combat in May and June of 1940, sustaining severe losses and often completely encircled in Flanders or on the Somme, the Aisne, or the Loire. Some of the Senegalese infantry were massacred in Beaujolais several days before the end of the fighting, and some Spahi units were still in battle after June 20 in the Rhone valley. Those escaping imprisonment were demobilized, since no plans had been made for an enlisted army by the armistice authorities. Many of the soldiers were put into labor divisions; for example, many of the Indochinese soldiers were sent to the rice paddies of Camargue. Some of the prisoners reappeared in the service of **Germany** in North African enlisted cadres that fought against the *Forces francaises de l'interieur* in southwestern France.

The only fighting in the colonies occurred during the march of colonial forces from Tunisia to the interior of Tripolitania and their retreat after the French-Italian armistice was signed. That agreement also called for the demilitarization of a good part of Tunisia and the storage of war materiel under the control of commissions with which the numerous and well-organized Italian elements in that country efficiently cooperated. Units of the French army in the Middle East, amounting to more than 100,000 men, were also weakened by partial demobilization, which returned a number of Frenchmen to their home country. Similar measures were taken in the other colonial territories.

Few of these territories fell in with Gen. **de Gaulle** to pursue the struggle. At first only the Pacific territories, the commercial Indian agencies, and especially French Equatorial Africa joined the **Resistance** effort. Led by the examples of the governor of Chad, **Felix Eboue**, and Gen. **Leclerc** (Jacques Philippe de Hauteclocque), the Cameroons, Gabon, Middle Congo and Ubangi-Shari rallied to the Allied camp. This, in turn, helped guarantee the security of the northern part of the **Belgian Congo** and permitted Allied access to these countries' ports and particularly their roads, as well as their airports, which were used to transport trucks and aircraft from the ports of British West Africa to the Egyptian front. The troops of **Free France** were quick to join in the British effort to retake the territories in East Africa from the Italians, but their victories in **Eritrea** were still not convincing enough to convert to their cause the units occupying French Somaliland, which had been loyal to the Vichy government for some time.

The Vichy government was not satisfied with simple neutrality. The **Axis** powers continued to enjoy the support of the colonies governed by fascist administrators. In **Indochina**, Adm. Jean Decoux repelled a

Thai attack on Cambodia, but he acceded to Japanese offers of "mediation," which awarded the aggressor two Cambodian provinces. He also made available to the Japanese the Yunnan railroad, thus depriving **Chiang Kai-shek's China** of a supply route even safer than the Burma Road, as well as all the military bases in northern Tonkin and all the naval bases throughout Indochina, which were necessary to mount the offensive of December 1941 against **Malaya, Singapore** and the Dutch East Indies.

In the summer of 1940 came the **Mers el-Kebir** incident in the port of Oran. As a result of Adm. Marcel Gensoul's continuing refusal to order his battleships to a neutral harbor, beginning on June 18, and his persistent deafness to British appeals to join Gen. de Gaulle, the British sank several French ships. In what was, it would seem, the most important raid conducted by French aircraft in World War II, a retaliatory attack on **Gibraltar** followed. Several weeks later the navy at Dakar thwarted de Gaulle's attempt to win French West Africa to his cause. For long months the Free French forces in Chad were the only troops in combat besides the units that had returned from East Africa. The Vichy government, in the meantime, was planning military cooperation with the Germans to recover "dissident" territories and to support the insurgents led by **Rashid Ali**, who threatened **Iraq**'s oil wells, which were vital to the Allied navies. Vichy troops even crossed occupied Europe, from France to **Yugoslavia**, where they were halted by news of the surrender of Gen. **Henri-Fernand Dentz** in Syria; the French battleships that had intended to pick them up at Salonika headed for North Africa. There they took on board most of the units evacuated from Syria with Dentz.

The British government, justifiably afraid that the naval and air bases in Madagascar would be made available to the Japanese by Vichy authorities, began a series of operations that ended in the capture of the huge island for the Free French. The Free French troops performed admirably in the desert battles at Bir Hakeim, under **Marie Pierre Koenig**, and at Kufra and Murzuch, under Leclerc. Also, under Adm. **Emile Muselier**, Free French naval forces occupied St. Pierre and Miquelon.

The landing in North Africa was the last time Vichy troops faced Allied troops. The Germans, who always had at hand the materiel and munitions from the Tunisian warehouses, occupied the largest part of the country without opposition. A safe path of retreat therefore lay open to the *Afrikakorps* and some Italian troops in Tripolitania. The Anglo-American forces, on the other hand, had to fight at Algiers, Oran and particularly Casablanca after the Free French forces were intercepted by elements loyal to Gen. Auguste

Nogues, the commanding general in Rabat. Following the disappearance of Adm. **Francois Darlan**, the efforts of Gen. **Henri Giraud** and the Gaullists permitted the reappearance of the North African army, now reinforced by thousands of refugees from France. It is instructive that, after the reconquest of Tunisia, Moroccan elements furnished eight regiments, two of them armored Spahi, to the Italian expeditionary forces, while Algeria furnished only two infantry regiments and Tunisia just one. Other North Africans found themselves in the Free French First Motorized Infantry Division or the Second Armored Division, organized by Leclerc. The latter was afterward to take part in the **Normandy landing** and enter Paris and Strasbourg, and the French veterans of the Italian battles captured the island of Elba and then participated in the Provence landing, liberating Toulon and Marseilles before rejoining the troops coming from Normandy to Burgundy. The French First Army then mopped up the German pocket at Colmar and advanced to the Danube. Some French elements were sent to Indochina, where they joined units that had been recruited on Madagascar and Reunion island as well as in West Africa.

The political conditions in the colonies were profoundly transformed by the war. The conditions under which Vichy had governed Syria compromised the French presence and lent weight to the local nationalists' demands for immediate independence without the delays specified by accords that had been suspended since the Popular Front era. The Tunisian nationalists had cleverly obtained allies in every faction during the war, and Habib Bourguiba, liberated by Vichy France at German demand, returned to his country through Italy to assume new importance. Anti-French propaganda was to rouse bloody disturbances in eastern Algeria at the very moment of victory, in May 1945. The proposals for reform presented by the Brazzaville Conference in January 1944 were once again to be pushed to the foreground by the Indochina troubles.

J. Vidalenc

FRENCH COMMITTEE FOR NATIONAL LIBERATION.
See *Comite francais de liberation nationale*.

FRENCH EQUATORIAL AFRICA.
The French colonial holdings in central Africa, including Chad, Ubangi-Shari (later the Central African Republic), the Middle Congo and Gabon. (See also **French Colonies**.)

FRENCH INDOCHINA.
See **Indochina**.

FRENCH INTERIOR FORCES.
See *Forces francaises de l'interieur*.

FRENCH NORTH AFRICA.
The three **French colonies** in North Africa each had a special status. Algeria, subdivided into provinces, each under the authority of a governor-general, was legally responsible to the French Ministry of the Interior, while the French protectorate over Tunisia derived from the bilateral Treaty of Bardo (1881), which raised the resident general, representing the French Ministry of Foreign Affairs, to the level of the bey. The resident general of France in the Moroccan government also owed his authority to the ministry. French authority, however, was confined to the southern section of the country, which was under the reign of the sultan. The northern section was administered, in an identical fashion, by **Spain** as provided by the International Conference of Algeciras (1906). That conference had also established uniform customs regulations among the various importing states in Morocco.

These administrative diversities did not prevent the organization of a common defense among the three countries at the beginning of the war, nor did they lessen the repercussions of the French defeat of 1940. On the whole, North Africa was dominated by the joint influence of the French navy and rightists, both hostile to the Popular Front government and loyal to Marshal Petain, who was the hero not only of Verdun but also of the Riff War against Abd el-Krim (1926).

The efforts of the Armistice Commission to recruit spies were simplified by the size of the Italian colony in Tunisia and by the number of natives who had been won over by the anti-French propaganda that had emanated from Radio Bari for more than a decade. Algeria was less disciplined, and Morocco owed to its remoteness and size the fact that it was the least regimented of the three countries. Algerian opinion had, however, been profoundly affected by the incident of **Mers el-Kebir**, ingeniously exploited by Vichy **propaganda**. In any event, none of these factors could compete in effectiveness with the Germans' wide dissemination of pictures showing **Hitler** before the Eiffel Tower or, from the opposite side, leftist exploitation of the natives' discontent with the restrictions imposed on the French economy by German demands. The Tunisian chauvinist movement quickly renewed its ties with **Italy**, as was shown by the movements of Habib Bourguiba and Hadj Thamaeur, head of the Tunisian nationalist party, the *Neo-Destour*, who passed through **Germany** before entering **Egypt**, in 1942-43. The German occupation had also introduced anti-Gaullist measures similar to those enacted in the mother country. The **Resistance** elements in Tunisia were quick, nonetheless, to affirm their loyalty to **de Gaulle**'s policy, and the *Rassemblement francais democratique et social* (French Democratic and Social Mobilization), inspired particularly by the mayor of Tunis, was an important factor in the success of the Resistance in North Africa.

In Algeria the personal prestige of Gen. **Maxime Weygand**, well known among the many active or reserve cavalry officers in the three provinces, contributed a great deal to the initial popularity of the Vichy regime. But an even more important factor was the isolation of the occupied zone from Vichy France, assuring North African and especially Algerian agricultural products, closer to the French Mediterranean ports, preferential economic treatment. The operations of clandestine native political movements were facilitated by the priority assigned by Vichy to surveillance of Gaullist haunts. The *Parti populaire algerien* of Messali Hadj, affiliated at first with the Communist Party, had organized even before the war a group known as the *Etoile nord africaine* (North African Star), which was sympathetic to pan-Arabic and Egyptian groups, among Algerians working in France. The *Parti popularie algerien* had been officially dissolved in 1939. The *Mouvement des amis du Manifeste algerien* (Friends of the Algerian Manifesto) had been organized by Ferhat Abbas, a pharmacist in Setif who had been elected to the Municipal Council of Setif in 1935 with the support of the *Parti social francais* (French Social Party) of Col. Francois de la Rocque. The *Mouvement* had since its appearance in 1942-43 played a subtle game by using the good graces of the French administration to increase its influence among the native masses and flaunting the liberation of Abbas, who had been jailed for several months, as a victory for its ideas in France. This association of Moslem savants had a clearly defined religious attitude, condemning as moderates the old Algerian Islamic hierarchy, whom they accused of flouting the commands of the Koran. Somewhat xenophobic, it operated in close harmony with pan-Arabic circles in Cairo through Sheik Brahimi, another native of Setif.

Each of these groups was able to exploit the dissensions among the French caused particularly by the Vichy laws dismissing Freemason and Jewish civil servants, whether native Frenchmen or not, and the annulment by Petain's government of the Cremieux law granting to Jews the rights of French citizens—a decision that not only hurt the Jews but also made apprehensive those Moslems who suspected its application could be broadened. Algerians of European

FRENCH NORTH AFRICA

stock, whose number had been swelled by the exodus resulting from the Spanish civil war—particularly in Oran—were as divided in their political opinions as residents of France in peacetime and so were prey to the same bewilderment after the enactment of the Vichy laws.

In Morocco, nationalist movements had surfaced in 1932. They resulted both from the discontent born of the international crisis and from the ongoing competition between the native Berbers and the Arabs for the official positions the latter had believed to be their preserve. These nationalists were to find unexpected support as a result of the military operations of 1942—a trade treaty, in existence since 1836, between the **United States** and Morocco was used by the colonial government as a pretext for complicated negotiations. The European elements of the population, fewer in number than in the other two sections of French North Africa, had often been alarmed by Spain's ambitions in the Moroccan territories. As a result of doubts concerning the status of Tangier expressed in some quarters in June 1940 after the defeat of France, the Spanish threats were taken seriously.

The political fracas produced by the appearance of Adm. **Francois Darlan** in Algiers to care for his ailing son at the same moment the Allies were landing; the ambiguous situation of a military command unable to halt, despite their bluster, the fighting that was destined to end in the defeat of the Vichy supporters; the American intrigues around **Henri Giraud** after Darlan's death—all these factors conspired to facilitate the activity of de Gaulle's followers, particularly after the organization, in Algiers, of the *Comite francais de liberation nationale* (French Committee for National Liberation), which was designed to bring together the representatives of various Free French organizations. The preceding months had seen extensive negotiations among the many Free French organizations concerning the composition of the commissions that would replace the Vichy government's ministries and, in the longer term, the establishment of new institutions after the coming liberation of the mother country. An immediate problem, however, was posed by the creation of new French and colonial military units, whose equipment could be provided only by the Allies. Besides the Second Armored Division, whose command had been given to Gen. **Leclerc**, the Free French had formed the 256,000-man "B" army, consisting of two armored divisions and five infantry divisions, half of whom were to be engaged in **Italy** during the first months of 1944. The CFLN also had to settle differences among numerous commissions representing a variety of persons and parties, including moderates, radicals (notably **Pierre Mendes-France**), Socialists and Communists (notably Francois Billoux). The creation of the *Conseil*

national de la resistance (National Resistance Council) in occupied France through the efforts of **Jean Moulin**, who had contributed so effectively to raising de Gaulle's international prestige, stimulated the members of the CFLN to demand the establishment of a consultative assembly made up of delegates from the parties and organizations constituting the Resistance. Through August 26, 1944 the CFLN assumed the title of Provisional Government of the French Republic in Algeria; with the liberation of Paris it transferred its allegiance to the central government. The consensus among the exiles in London since 1941 that reforms deemed necessary in the colonies should not be discussed publicly until after the liberation of the motherland did not prevent de Gaulle from affirming, in a speech in Tunis in June 1943, the urgency of profound changes in the old political, economic and social structures of the French overseas possessions. He repeated his beliefs in a speech in October 1943 and in his declaration regarding **Indochina** in December 1943. The Conference of Brazzaville in January 1944 not only confirmed the necessity of reforming relations between the mother country and the colonies; it rejected the notion that self-government in the colonies should be regarded as a distant goal. These declarations were interpreted in contradictory ways, according to their interests of the moment, by the French in France, those in the colonies and the natives of the colonies. The return to the provisions of the Cremieux law was also used by the nationalists to crystallize resentment caused by economic difficulties and the bloody demonstrations breaking out in the Setif region and in Constantine on May of 1945, the day of the armistice.

J. Vidalenc

FRENCH POLICE DURING THE OCCUPATION.
In the spring of 1941 the Vichy government tried to remodel the structure of the French police in accordance with its own requirements. Within 10 weeks, between April 23 and July 7, 1941, 10 statutes were approved redefining the role of the police in criminal and civil matters. Police in cities with populations in excess of 10,000 were more closely controlled by the government and subordinated directly to the local prefecture. The measure originally seemed useful, but it eventually resulted in total submission to the political needs of the regime. Promotions were made and new positions were filled principally as political favors; especially noteworthy were quick promotions for well-connected bureaucrats who ostensibly "achieved remarkable results in the battle against the enemies of order." After March 1942 the early casual search for "general information" was supplanted by oppressive police procedures involving close **collabora-**

172

tion with the Germans. This trend had been fore-shadowed by a far-reaching "purge" of the more democratically minded members of police forces.

In October 1941 Minister of the Interior **Pierre Pucheu** created three new police services. The first, the *Service de Police Anticommuniste* (Anti-Com-munist Police Service), changed its name, after Pucheu's departure from the Interior Ministry in June 1942, to *Service de Repression des Menees Antina-tionales* (Service for the Repression of Anti-Nation-alist Movements), or SRMAN; no changes were made in its hierarchy or procedures. The other groups were the *Police aux Questions Juives* (Police for Jewish Questions) and the *Service des Societes secretes* (Ser-vice for Secret Societies). The supervision of these three specialized police branches was entrusted to ac-tive collaborators with the Germans as opposed to less politically oriented professional investigators. Promo-tions were based primarily on professions of ide-ological faith.

The intensification of **Resistance** activities resulted in the creation of special sections within the police ser-vices, but these did not enjoy much success. A Special Brigades team, which was at times especially effective in breaking up Resistance groups in Paris, was also put at the disposal of the general information division of the police. In general, however, the work of these unique services, which were isolated from each other by cautious bureaucrats or even by the activities of secret Resistance operatives, was very limited. When he took over as general secretary for maintenance of order in January 1944, **Joseph Darnand** endowed the Militia with supplementary police powers, which it used without hesitation. At the same time he strengthened the hand of the chief of the SRMAN, giving him the power to requisition police services, to consult all archives and the like. Some members of the Militia were integrated into the SRMAN and various "police" operations organized to counter the maquis of Savoie in the spring of 1944. These ac-tivities, conducted almost like military maneuvers, took place with the active participation of the SRMAN.

After the fall of 1942, members of the French police services were deeply divided in their sym-pathies. Some obeyed official instructions to the let-ter, becoming effective collaborators. Their political opposites refused to cooperate with the occupation authorities in tracking down Frenchmen; some even worked actively with the Resistance. Several hundred of these latter were deported or shot. This situation worsened during the final months of the occupation and was the reason for virtual seizure of power by the Militia in police affairs, which was accomplished by grouping under the authority of "regional supervisors

for the maintenance of order" Militia officers chosen by Darnand, the police services, the gendarmerie and the National Guard. These groups then cooperated with the Militia in anti-Resistance activities. But even here, patriotic French police succeeded in sabotaging pro-Nazi activity.

No other administrative organization paid as heavy a price for the occupation of France as the French police.

J. Delarue

FRENCH RESISTANCE.

Spontaneous, almost instinctive, **resistance** among French patriots angered by the surrender of French forces and by **Germany**'s seizure of France's entire economic apparatus broke out in the form of hap-hazard **sabotage** after June 1940. Officers from the general staff concealed stores of arms and munitions and proceeded to organize intelligence networks in anticipation of a later resumption of the battle against the Nazis. Other officers hastened to England at the urging of Gen. **de Gaulle** to cooperate with the **United Kingdom** in the name of **Free France**. De Gaulle's appeal to the Resistance on June 18, 1940 won the loyalty of the French troops stationed in Great Britain as part of the *Forces francaises libres* (Free French Forces) and obtained declarations of allegiance from Chad, most of **French Equatorial Africa**, the Cameroons and French installations around the Indian Ocean. Above all, his summons lent heart to every Frenchman opposed to any form of **collaboration** with Nazi Germany.

In September 1941 the *Comite national francais* (National French Committee), or CNF, was formed; by July 1942 Free France had sent delegations to 19 countries in America, Africa and Asia.

De Gaulle's speech demanding "a new republic, pure and proud"; the support of such leftists as Leon Blum, **Christian Pineau**, Pierre Brossolette and Fer-nand Grenier; the heroism of **Jean Moulin**; and the recognition of the CNF by the **USSR** helped reassure the resisters in continental France regarding the inten-tions of the Free French. The first espionage network in France was organized by the Polish army under the code names F1 and F2. The British **Intelligence Ser-vice** developed the Alliance and Gilbert networks. The first network set up by the French chiefs of staff in London was the *Confrerie Notre Dame* headed by Col. **Gilbert Renault Remy**. Resistance movements like the *Liberation-Nord*, the *Organisation civile et militaire* (OCM), *Vengeance* and the *Front National* all had their individual intelligence networks: *Cohors Asturies*, *Centurie*, *Turma-Vengeance* and *Fana*, which continuously supplied precise information concerning the *Wehrmacht* and German war production. The "underground railroad" for the rescue of Allied pilots who had been captured parachuting into France was formed. Unfortunately, **Gestapo** agents managed to infiltrate some of these networks and put an end to their usefulness.

Some of the Resistance networks for armed operations were formed by Col. Maurice Buckmaster, who was responsible for activities in France for the **Special Operations Executive** and, later, the **Office of Strategic Services**. Independent maquis groups were created, and the Allies scheduled flights for parachuting arms to them. Six hundred and sixty-eight French, English, Canadian and American agents began operating in France. Landing strips were put into service. All air operations were placed under control of the *Bureau d'operations aeriennes* (BOA) in the northern zone and of the *Centre d'operation de parachutage* in the southern. In January 1944 the Special Forces Headquarters, a joint service for all the Allies, was organized. Extensive parachuting of arms did not begin, however, until the end of June 1944. Efforts to liberate Brittany were led by Breton Resistance forces cooperating with a battalion of French paratroopers and some members of the **Jedburgh** teams of radio officers and instructors.

The principal Resistance movements in the occupied zone were the *Liberation-Nord*, which recruited its personnel from among the militant socialists and syndicalists; the OCM; the *Defense de la France;* and the *Resistance*, a church organization. Others included *Ceux de la Liberation-Vengeance* and *Ceux de la Resistance*. In the unoccupied zone *Liberation, Combat* and *Franc-Tireur,* which combined under the name of *Mouvements Unis de Resistance* (United Resistance Movements), or MUR, were active. The *Front national*, organized but not dominated by the Communist Party, and the *Organisation de resistance de l'armee* (ORA), which grew out of the Second Bureau of the armistice army but was non-Gaullist in orientation, both operated throughout France. Many parallel organizations were sponsored in various professional circles by the *Front national*, which also generated paramilitary groups specializing in sabotage and in the capture of enemy arms. The other movements at first had reserve units waiting to join anticipated Allied offensives, but they later set up maquis groups, beginning in the fall of 1943, when their ranks were swelled by Frenchmen escaping the German roundups of forced labor.

It was Jean Moulin who, as the first president of the *Conseil national de la resistance* (CNR), brought about the coordination of the many French resistance movements in May 1943 by calling for the formation of liberation committees within each *departement* representing each of the resistance movements and political parties. The training of military formations was undertaken by the *Bureau central de renseignements et d'action* (BCRA), formed in London in October 1941. Finally, a single staff was created for the underground army under the command of Gen. **Eugene Delestraint**. The COMAC—the military commission of the CNR—accelerated, with the aid of the DMR (the regional military delegates) to the BCRA, the training of the *Forces francaises de l'interieur* (FFI), under the command of Gen. **Marie Pierre Koenig**, in anticipation of the FFI's participation in a national uprising prior to the entry of Allied troops. The Resistance also operated as a search-and-destroy group against agents of the collaborationists and the Nazi-dominated Militia.

Underground leaflets and journals and secretly printed reviews were developed by the intellectuals of France as a means of resistance. Those too well known to escape enemy surveillance escaped across the Atlantic and in America spoke out against the Nazis alongside the great American writers. The Americans John Dos Passos, Theodore Dreiser, and Ernest Hemingway fled France along with such French colleagues as Andre Maurois, Jules Romains, St. John Perse, Andre Breton, Jacques Maritain, Georges Bernanos, Louis Jouvet and Rene Clair. Many of those who remained offered their services to the espionage networks and Resistance movements. Several fell into Gestapo hands and were shot or condemned to a slow death in the **concentration camps**. Marc Bloch, Jean Cavailles, Georges Politzer, Robert Desnos, Jacques Decour and Jean Prevost lost their lives in this way; Victor Basch was assassinated by the Militia.

Jacques Decour was the pseudonym of Daniel Courdemanche, distinguished professor of German and editor in chief of the Communist review *Commune*, who threw himself into the struggle very early by creating *L'Universite libre* with the cooperation of the philosopher Georges Politzer. At the same time, Jean Paulhan, director of the *Nouvelle Revue francaise*, joined hands with the *Musee de l'homme* group, which was of the same political persuasion. In December 1940 this association was betrayed by one of its members and eliminated shortly afterward; Boris Vilde, Anatole Lewitsky, Paul Rivet and Yvonne Oddon were lost. In February 1941 intellectual Communists around Politzer, Jacques Salomon and Jacques Decour circulated the underground *La Pensee libre* and were joined in June by **Vercors** and Pierre de Lescure. Catholic anti-fascists edited small journals such as *Veritas,* written by Abbe Vallee, and in the same spirit of the defense of Christian civilization and humanism P. Chaillet influenced a considerable sector of public opinion with his *Cahiers de temoignage* *chretien*. Henry de Monfort, secretary-general of the *Academie francaise*—aided by Suzanne Feingold; Emile Coornaert, a professor at the *College de France;* and Paul Petit—influenced hundreds of intellectuals with his incisive journal *La France continue*. Groups of lay educators established the secret *Ligue de l'enseignement* under the presidency of Albert Bayet.

The **propaganda** circulated by the collaborationist National Revolution was energetically rebutted by intellectuals who organized virtual universities in German prison camps.

In September 1941 the National Writers' Committee (CNE) was established by, among others, Jacques Decour, Frederic Joliot-Curie, Edith Thomas, Claude Morgan, Jacques Debu-Bridel, and, later, Francois Mauriac. After the publication of the *Manifeste du CNE* in February 1942, they were joined by Jean-Paul Sartre, Charles Vildrac, and Jean Vendal. *Les Lettres francaises* was the CNE organ in the occupied zone; Rene Tavernier and Louis Aragon published the review *Confluence* in the southern zone in 1941 and organized a CNE branch there with Stanislas Fumet, Jean Prevost, Pierre Emmanuel, Henri Malerbe, Andre Rousseaux, Jean Thomas, Pierre Courtade, Claude Roy, Georges Mounin and Alain Borde. In 1944 Pierre Emmanuel edited the review *Les Etoiles*.

In the northern zone, thanks to Vercors and Pierre de Lescure, the CNE published the *Editions de Minuit*, which printed such original works as *Le Silence de la mer*, by Vercors, in February 1942; the *Contes d'Auxois*, by Edith Thomas; the *Chroniques interdites*, by Paulhan, Julien Benda and Vercors in March 1943; the *Cahier noir*, by Mauriac; and essays by Jean Guehenno, Sartre, Gabriel Marcel, Paul Eluard, Louis Aragon, Andre Rousseaux, Raymond Queneau, Pierre Seghers, Andre Malraux, Andre Frenaud, Andre Chamson, Claude Aveline, Pierre Leyris, Louis Martin-Chauffier and Georges Adam. In October 1943 Adam gave the *Lettres francaises* a tremendous lift by obtaining for it the assistance of Max-Pol Fouchet, Pierre Binard, Claude Roy and Jean Cassou.

Nor were the only belligerents from the realm of belles lettres. The jurists from the law faculties, especially Strasbourg and, afterward, Clermont-Ferrand, grouped around Rene Capitant, Paul Coste-Floret and Francois de Menthon within the Resistance movement *Combat* in the southern zone.

Another Resistance movement, the *Front national*, was controlled by militant Communists but welcomed anyone antipathetic to collaboration with Nazi Germany. Still another was *Le Palais libre*, which appeared at the beginning of 1942 under the leadership of the eminent jurist Jacques Charpentier, aided by Mme. Yves Nordmann and Andre Boissarie.

The scientists of France, including Joliot-Curie, Robert Debre and Etienne Bernard, brought minds of the first order to the Resistance. Their assistance was often more than strictly intellectual.

And finally, the artists of France lent their ingenuity to the Resistance movement. United in the *Front national des artistes*, they published *L'Art francais*. Edouard Pignon, Julien Bertheau and Louis Daquin were among the important contributors to the Resistance in the plastic arts, theater and film.

It should be noted that without publishing houses in the free countries, the responses of the French Resistance to fascist propaganda could not have reverberated as fully as they did. The Swiss edition, in French, of the *Cahiers du Rhone*, edited by Albert Beguin at Geneva and published by Editions de la Baconniere in Neuchatel beginning in March 1942, was splendid. Other participants in this enterprise were Editions des Trois Collines and Editions Luf-Eglof, which also published the works of St. John Perse, Jacques Maritain, Jules Supervielle, Pierre Emmanuel and Emmanuel Mounier.

The **Normandy landing** began before the FFI was completely reorganized after the Gestapo's capture of many of its military leaders and most of its stocks of arms and munitions. Nevertheless, the FFI contributed significantly to the Allied effort in Brittany in particular, as well as in the Central Massif, the Alps, Provence and the Rhone valley. It fought effectively too for the liberation of southwestern France and of Paris and many other French cities. It was the FFI that mopped up the isolated German garrisons along the Atlantic coast and in Lorient, **Saint-Nazaire**, La Rochelle and Royan.

The Resistance could not have been as successful as it was without the complicity of many French citizens, which was encouraged by the **British Broadcasting Corporation**'s French broadcasts and the broadly propagated **underground press**. The guerrillas panicked the rear echelons of the retreating *Wehrmacht*, which had already been badly mauled on the Soviet front. But the reactions of the enemy were merciless; severe reprisals, directed chiefly against the rural population, were frequent. Tens of thousands of men were shot, men and woman by the thousands were sent to death camps, entire villages vanished in flames. Thanks to the swift advance of the liberating troops, the country was spared further horrors.

M. Baudot

FRENCH SECRET SERVICES.

Up until 1940 the intelligence services of the French army, air force and navy together formed the Fifth Bureau of the chiefs of staff in wartime; the Second

Bureau was charged with piecing together information fed to it by espionage agents.

At the time of the armistice, the German military staff demanded the dissolution of the Fifth Bureau, thereby expecting to deprive the Second Bureau of its information sources. The secret services, however, continued their work undercover, utilizing various means of camouflage. Depending on the Vichy government financially and materially, they met with hostility from men convinced of the final success of the Germans, like **Pierre Laval**, or profoundly Anglophobic, like **Francois Darlan** and **Pierre Pucheu**. After the **Mers el-Kebir** episode, the generally anti-Gaullist intelligence officers succumbed to the same Anglophobia that enthralled practically the entire French military.

After June 1941 the French intelligence staff twice predicted the final defeat of **Germany** and thus put themselves in a difficult position. Darlan demanded the elimination of all officers opposing the Germans, but the Special Military Services (SSM) nevertheless continued their work. Apolitical in temperament, they devoted themselves exclusively to military matters.

In London, meanwhile, the Free French considered the preparation for a politically normal life in France after the liberation one of its functions. On July 1, 1940 Gen. **de Gaulle** authorized Capt. Andre Dewavrin, alias Col. Passy, to organize an espionage service for **Free France**. This group was to change its identity from time to time; its best-known title was *Bureau central de renseignements et d'action* (Central Bureau of Information and Action), or BCRA. It created or controlled networks for intelligence-gathering, activism and assistance to Allied sympathizers escaping German vigilance. Beginning in the spring of 1941, the organization acquired a certain importance as a result of its capacity for the rapid transmission of information. Unfortunately, rivalries between groups and individuals within the leadership of Free France, as well as its serious and continual brushes with the British services, often forced the French services to operate under unfavorable conditions.

For their part, the British **Intelligence Service** and the **Special Operations Executive**, together with the American **Office of Strategic Services**, established their own networks in France, with the assistance of most of the Free French networks, for acquiring contacts with and furnishing arms and munitions to **Resistance** fighters.

After the Allied landing in North Africa and the invasion of the free zone in November 1942, the **Gestapo** and the *Abwehr* arrested SSM officers who had already been under surveillance. Continually hunted, with no funds, the heads of the SSM reached Algeria in November 1942 and there reconstituted a supervisory organization for their remaining networks in France. The French Army Intelligence Service accepted the command of Gen. **Henri Giraud**, who in turn accepted the leadership of Darlan. Curiously enough, Darlan himself was named high commissioner by the Americans, to the understandable displeasure of the Resistance. Nor did Darlan's disappearance in December 1942 allay the suspicions of the anti-Nazi French, since Giraud was still considered a representative of Petain.

The BCRA occupied its quarters in Algeria in May 1943. Giraud banned all contact with it. Thus, there were two organizations in control of the special services, both apparently on the point of exploding. Despite Giraud's departure on April 15, 1944, and the appointment of the civilian Jacques Soustelle to develop a single organization for controlling the secret services, there never was any real cooperation between the two groups.

The most important achievements of the SSM and the BCRA—the obliteration of the Hohenstaufen SS Panzer Division in May 1944 by air bombardment and the wholesale **sabotage** accompanying the **Normandy landing**—were obtained at the price of tragic losses. The further losses in time and energy consumed by all these schisms and rivalries, which were created primarily by the occupation of France, made them all the more regrettable.

J. Delarue

FRENCH STATE.

The Vichy government unanimously settled upon a policy of **collaboration** with **Germany** because it could not conceive of any other for conquered France. Following the armistice, the leaders of the French State—Petain first of all—were convinced that Germany would win the war and that France had no choice but to adapt to the new situation. They felt, in other words, that France must become a "favored province"—as William Bullitt phrased it—of the Third Reich. Thanks to the trump cards still in its possession, the **French colonies** and the fleet, France was still a colonial and naval power. Thus, Vichy could resign itself to the inevitable loss of such territories as Alsace-Lorraine.

But the collaboration changed in nature as the conflict progressed. Partly because of ideological persuasion and partly because of a desire to lighten the cost of occupation and obtain a place in the sun of the **New European Order**, the French government strove to profit from the international power shift. Their attempt, however, ran counter to **Hitler**'s intention of using the French to his advantage without any concessions from Berlin. But the British attack on the French warships at **Mers el-Kebir** on July 3, 1940 forced the Fuehrer to suspend the disarmament of the French fleet and the demobilization of the French air force in the southern zone in anticipation of a Franco-British war. On July 15 the dialogue between the French and the Germans took another turn: the French government requested an adjustment of the armistice agreement to "stem the hemorrhage of **production** and finances," while Berlin demanded access for the German military to air bases in the Casablanca region, the Rabat-Tunis railway and the ships in the Mediterranean. **Maxime Weygand**, the minister of national defense, stiffened the French position. He was willing to keep to the armistice agreement per se, with no further sacrifices—which prompted a supporting refusal from Petain, who declared that "free negotiation with France is worth more to the conqueror than a decision imposed by him." Thus, the original collaboration policy failed because the French had mistakenly expected a British surrender and a quick end to the war and because the Germans tried to escalate France's indemnity. But the dialogue did not stop there. It moved from Wiesbaden, the seat of the Armistice Commission, to Paris, where the two "croupiers," **Otto Abetz** and **Pierre Laval**, met once again. Having become, through the good offices of **von Ribbentrop**, ambassador to Paris, from which **Edouard Daladier** had him driven in 1939, Abetz decided on a pro-French policy, motivated partly by ambition and partly by his fondness for French culture and the Parisian atmosphere. He was already under fire for his ideas and therefore was in need of an immediate success. Laval, too, proved an amiable partner. First minister of state and then vice-president of the *Conseil d'Etat*, he believed that "the only path to follow is that of loyal collaboration with Germany and **Italy**." Actually, Abetz and Laval managed only to fool themselves, since one was speaking for von Ribbentrop rather than Hitler, while the other overestimated his influence on Petain and the French government.

By this time Hitler had abandoned his project for a landing in Great Britain (see **Britain, Battle of**) and was planning for his attack on the **USSR**. Still, on the advice of the German admirals, he considered a thrust toward the Suez Canal to threaten the British Empire. He therefore needed the support not only of **Mussolini** but also of **Franco** and Petain. The interview Petain had requested at the beginning of October finally took place at Montoire in Loir-et-Cher two days after a meeting between the Fuehrer and Laval. In spite of the publicity surrounding the event, it failed to produce any tangible results. Hitler was unwilling to make concessions to France; having desired the war, it had to pay the cost, in his view. Besides, he had decided that he no longer needed French aid in the

Mediterrranean basin, where he hesitated to interfere for fear of alienating Mussolini and in view of the coolness displayed toward him by Franco in their meeting at Hendaye. It soon became obvious, at least for the French, that the Montoire meeting was fruitless, for 70,000 Alsatians and Lorrainers of French origin were expelled; at Wiesbaden, the Germans rejected requests for the reduction of the occupation indemnity, the relaxation of the demarcation line and the return of prisoners. In Paris, Abetz and Gen. Walter Warlimont of the *Wehrmacht* agreed to attempt the capture of **French Equatorial Africa** and the Cameroons, then in the hands of the Free French, with the approval of Vichy. But they hesitated to give the Vichy forces the means required for the venture because they doubted French loyalty to the Nazis and feared the opening of a new front in Africa. At most, the Germans authorized Petain to visit Paris.

Did the paucity of results lead to the dismissal of Laval on December 13 or even his subsequent arrest? The reasons for his difficulties were not completely diplomatic—Petain had a profound personal aversion to Laval—but this miniature coup d'etat loosed a series of nasty measures on the part of the Germans: the expulsions from Alsace with the incorporation of mobilized Alsatians into the *Wehrmacht*, threats of seizure of French assets if payments of the indemnity established by the armistice agreement were delayed and Abetz' refusal to let Pierre Flandin take the portfolio of minister of foreign affairs, among others. Finally, **Francois Darlan** replaced Laval on February 9, 1941.

Darlan, the republican sailor who had switched sides in June 1940 and was inexperienced in politics, had enough power at his disposal to earn the respect of the Germans. He commanded the still imposing French fleet. In particular, he reassured Abetz, who remained faithful to Laval. He also reassured the other officials of the occupying forces by rushing preparations for the reconquest of the African colony of Chad and by maintaining deliveries of bauxite and Belgian gold. In May 1941, when the British were engaged in a show of force against the pro-Nazi **Rashid Ali** of **Iraq**, Darlan agreed to provide Ali with arms and to allow German transport planes to cross Syrian territory from Aleppo. The ensuing negotiations culminated in a meeting between Hitler and Darlan at Berchtesgaden, where the possibility of French participation in a war against England was raised. From the Bavarian Alps the discussions moved on to Paris, with Abetz on the German side of the table. They ended in the Paris accords of May 27-28, signed by Darlan and Warlimont. In exchange for their assistance in "strengthening the defenses of French Africa," the Germans were permitted the use of air bases in **Syria**, the port of Bizerte and the Gabes railroad to supply the *Afrika Korps*. Even the construction of a base for **U-boats** at Dakar was anticipated. Petain accepted these conditions; but Weygand, then proconsul of **French North Africa**, deemed them excessive, and his hostility stimulated the French government into demanding more. But when Darlan informed Abetz of the French counterproposals, the latter stopped him short with a flat refusal. **Rommel** was already receiving supplies brought by French trucks and vessels, and that was sufficient for the *Oberkommando der Wehrmacht*. The Germans were even more aloof to Darlan's offer to send five battalions of reinforcements to Syria in French ships; neither **Wilhelm Keitel** nor von Ribbentrop had any desire to extend the war into the Middle East at the beginning of the struggle with the Soviet Union on June 22, 1941.

After that, Darlan lost all credibility with the Germans, although he consented to the dismissal of Weygand on November 18 and the activation of a French volunteer army—the *Legion des volontaires francais contre le bolchevisme*—to fight the Soviets without getting anything in return. But toward the end of 1941, when Rommel found himself hard pressed in **Libya** and decided to fall back across Tunisia, the Germans again looked to France for help. A meeting was held between Petain and **Goering** at St. Florentin on December 1, and was followed by talks between Gen. **Alphonse Juin** and Goering. Clinging still to its fancies, the Vichy government continued to demand ''a free hand in Africa and the Mediterranean'' as the price for its concessions. Did Darlan really expect, as he asserted in January 1942, to ''declare war on England and the **United States**'' as the prerequisite to preliminary peace discussions with Germany?

The German embassy had Petain's *eminence grise*, Dr. Bernard Menetrel, dangle before the old marshal the specter of a French *Gauleiter*—perhaps **Jacques Doriot**. On April 18, 1942 Laval returned to head the government, and a new era opened—collaboration ''without reserve.'' ''I hope for the victory of Germany,'' he said, ''because without it bolshevism will flourish everywhere tomorrow.'' But the Allied landing in North Africa on November 8 reduced even further the freedom of action of the French government. The *Wehrmacht* extended its occupation to the southern zone on November 13. Darlan's about-face at Algiers frustrated the German demand for a French declaration of war on the Allies and threw the French in Africa into turbulence. On November 27 the French fleet at Toulon scuttled itself to keep from falling into German hands, the army sanctioned by the armistice agreement was disbanded, and Vichy in several weeks lost every claim to sovereignty. The occupy-ing forces fostered the myth of a southern zone in which the French government retained its power, probably because they were reduced in strength. Laval had actually become the ''head of a satellite state'' on which the Reich made exorbitant demands in the form of personnel **purges** and the arrest of insubordinate officials, and which it treated as it liked.

Even as it engaged in its rear guard battles, the government was forced to cancel the failing program for obtaining volunteer laborers for Germany—which provided for the liberation of an elderly prisoner for every three volunteers—and to replace it with the **Forced Labor Battalions**. Created on September 4, 1942 for men of 18-50 and women of 21-35, the Forced Labor Battalions were to go into operation in February 1943; those born between 1920 and 1922 were to be subject to impressment. On January 30 the government consented to the activation of the Militia ''to keep order''; it superseded the authority of the regular police. The forces at Vichy's command, the *Legion Tricolore* and the *Phalange africaine*, now took an oath of allegiance to Hitler, and French volunteers could enter the *Waffen* **SS**. Although France had respected in every particular its commitments to furnish the Reich with labor, Hitler refused to make any promises for the future. He confined himself to a few concessions on details, which primarily benefited the occupation troops—the return of the north and the Pas-de-Calais to French administration, the elimination of the demarcation line and the transformation of **prisoners of war** into ''free laborers.''

As preparations for the **Normandy landing** progressed the Germans became increasingly domineering. They had lost all confidence in Laval and indeed aroused the Parisian ultracollaborationists against him. They fought terrorism and **sabotage** at the beginning of the summer of 1943 by using *Ordnungspolizei* and the *Wehrmacht* to reinforce the collaborators and by bringing the **SD** into action against the **French Resistance**. Vichy made no attempt to interfere; it wheedled the people into remaining calm ''to avoid tears and useless agony.'' The Germans also forced Laval to invite the ultracollaborationists into the government. In December **Joseph Darnand**, head of the Militia, became secretary-general to the Ministry of Order and **Phillippe Henriot** became secretary of state for information; in March 1944 **Marcel Deat** became minister of labor. No law could be changed without German consent. The Militia, beginning in March 1944, was attached to the regional command of the *Wehrmacht*. It retained its own courts-martial, where the judicial guarantees of common law meant nothing. The fate of the country's prisoners depended on the Militia, since the administration of penitentiaries was attached—curiously enough—to the secretary-general of the Ministry of Order. Thus, nothing remained of the fiction of the "French State" except an old marshal, the head of a state recognized by the armistice agreement, whom the occupation authorities transferred from chateau to chateau before taking him to Germany and installing him in Sigmaringen.

Vichy France received practically nothing in exchange for the collaboration it had voluntarily undertaken. Deprived of Alsace-Lorraine and separated from northeastern France, which had been transformed into a "forbidden zone" for dimly understood reasons even before the peace had been signed, France was "the most important source of supplies for the Reich." But the French ate less well than people in Bohemia-Moravia, and 50 percent of the annual French revenue went to support occupation troops. Hitler was simply the wrong man to handle a conquered country. (See also **Petain and the French State**.)

C. Levy

FRENCH WEST AFRICA.
Mauritania, Mali, Niger, Senegal, Guinea, the Ivory Coast, Upper Volta and Dahomey. (See also **French Colonies**.)

FRERE, Aubert (1884-1944).
Frere, a French general and army commander, helped found the *Organisation de resistance de l'armee* (Army Resistance Organization) in 1940. He was arrested by the Germans in 1943 and died in the Struthof camp in June 1944.

FREYBERG, Bernard Cyril, 1st Baron of Wellington and Munstead (1889-1963).
A British general, Freyberg was a legendary hero, wounded ten times in World War I; at the age of 27 he was awarded the Victoria Cross and became a general. In 1945 he commanded the Second New Zealand Division brilliantly on every Mediterranean battlefield. He served as governor-general of **New Zealand** from 1946 to 1952.

FRICK, Wilhelm (1877-1946).
Frick served the Nazi government as minister of the interior. He authored anti-Semitic legislation between 1933 and 1943. From 1943 to 1944 Frick was protector of **Bohemia-Moravia**. He was condemned to death and hanged at Nuremberg.

FRITSCH, Werner von (1880-1939).
In 1934 Fritsch, a German general, was given the task of reorganizing the army. He was discharged in 1938 by **Hitler**, who was jealous of his prestige. Fritsch was killed in the German attack on Warsaw in 1939.

FROGMEN.
Various wartime experiments, conducted particularly by the British and Italian navies and by the **Special Operations Executive,** established that men suitably clothed and masked could swim for some time under water and could fasten explosive charges to ships' hulls with magnetic devices called limpet mines. They approached their targets by canoe or, more stealthily still, by midget submarine. Peculiarly steady nerves were needed for this exceptionally hazardous work; the role of luck was even larger than is usual in war. Among other notable operations in this style, the Italians sank two battleships in the Alexandria harbor in 1941; some British marines canoed up the Gironde to Bordeaux to sink two Japanese **blockade**-runners in 1942; and the British damaged, but did not sink, the *Tirpitz* in northern **Norway** in 1944.

M. R. D. Foot

FROMM, Friedrich (1888-1945).
At the time of the **assassination attempt of July 20, 1944,** against **Hitler**, Fromm, a German general, was commander in chief of the Army of the Interior. Asked to help neutralize the Nazis in Berlin, he telephoned **Wilhelm Keitel** to find out if the Fuehrer was dead. He later turned against the plotters, had participating members of his staff executed and forced **Jozef Beck** into suicide. Arrested by the **Gestapo**, however, he was himself executed in March 1945.

FTP (*Francs-Tireurs et Partisans*).
See *Forces francaises de l'interieur*.

FUJIWARA, Ginjiro (1869-1960).
Fujiwara, a Japanese business executive and wartime economic planner, served as minister of trade and industry in 1940, as state minister in 1943-44, and as munitions minister in 1944. Long identified with the Mitsui interests, Fujiwara built the Oji Paper Company into Japan's largest pulp concern before entering government service in 1938. Prime Minister **Tojo** appointed him as the first head of the Industrial Facilities Corporation in December 1941. In November 1943 he helped create the munitions ministry to snuff out army-navy factionalism over aircraft and arms **production**.

FULLER, John Frederick Charles (1878-1966).
Together with Sir **Basil Liddell Hart**, Fuller, a military theorist and historian, established the basic concepts of modern tank warfare.

FUNK, Walter (1890-1960).

In 1937 Funk became minister of economy in the Nazi government; he became president of the *Reichsbank* in 1939. Condemned to a life sentence at the Nuremberg trials, he was freed in 1957.

G

GALE, Richard (1896-   ).
Gale, a British general, was the first commander of the First Paratrooper Brigade. In 1944 he commanded the Sixth Airborne Division, which occupied and held the left flank of the bridgehead in Normandy during the night of June 6 (see **Normandy landing**). He also played an important part in the Ardennes counterattack in January 1945 (see **Bulge, Battle of the**).

GAMELIN, Maurice (1872-1958).
Gamelin, a French general, became chief of staff of the French Army in 1938 and commander in chief of the French armies in 1939. He was replaced by Gen. **Maxime Weygand** after the enemy's breakthrough on the western front on May 19, 1940. Gamelin was tried by the Court of Riom in 1942 and detained by the Germans. He was deported in 1943 and did not return until the end of the war.

GANDHI, (Mahatma) Mohandas Karamchand (1869-1948).
A Hindu saint and, in **Wavell's** words, "an extremely astute politician," Gandhi had led a movement of *Satyagraha* (civil disobedience) in protest against the **United Kingdom's** rule of **India** for 20 years before the war. He had spent much of this time in prison. In August 1942, along with other Indian National Congress leaders, Gandhi propounded the slogan "Quit India," which provoked a brief rebellion and led to his imprisonment by the British until May 1944. Gandhi participated in the negotiations that led to India's independence in 1947, a few months before he was assassinated by a fanatic.

GAULLE, Charles de (1890-1970).
Charles de Gaulle was born on November 22, 1890 in Lille. A graduate of the military college of St. Cyr, he was a brilliant infantry officer who fought with distinction in World War I until he was wounded at Verdun in March 1916 and taken prisoner. His books *Le Fil de l'epee* (1932) and especially *Vers l'armee de metier* (1934) detailed his views on the need for restructuring of the military system and creating a heavily motorized and mechanized battle corps manned by 10,000 elite professional soldiers. Despite the support of several politicians, including **Paul Reynaud**, he acquired no significant following except for several enduring friendships among the army hierarchy.

It was "completely without astonishment" that de Gaulle saw "our mobilized forces entrenching themselves in stagnancy" as the war approached. When it arrived in September 1939, the then Col. de Gaulle was in command of the tank corps in the Fifth Army, stationed in Alsace. On January 26, 1940 he addressed a memorandum to 80 prominent leaders, advocating the creation of a mechanized reserve corps and the regrouping of available materiel. It went practically ignored. Reynaud, who had replaced **Daladier** as president of the *Conseil d'Etat*, nominated de Gaulle as secretary of war toward the end of March; Daladier firmly opposed the nomination.

Five days after the onset of the German offensive against **Belgium**, on May 15, de Gaulle was ordered to take as many tanks as he could get and deploy them before Laon to protect the Sixth Army. He engaged the enemy at Montcornet, and his tanks reached the Aisne on May 19, after two days of fighting. Given the temporary rank of brigadier general, the 25th officer to be so upgraded, he was ordered to attack Abbeville, where he inflicted heavy losses on the enemy in his sector. In all other sectors, however, the German advance could not be stemmed, and his local victory was lost in the dispatches of the general defeat.

Reynaud finally succeeded in naming de Gaulle to a cabinet post, that of undersecretary of state for the national defense. Well aware that defeat was inevitable, de Gaulle exhorted the president of the *Conseil* to prepare for a continuation of the struggle from the colonies. On June 9, he went to London for his first conference with **Churchill**. The Reynaud government, now including Petain, allowed itself to be swayed toward the armistice that **Maxime Weygand** was urging on them. At about the same time, de Gaulle was convinced, in London, by Ambassador Charles Corbin and **Jean Monnet** of the desirability of an "indissoluble union" between the **United Kingdom** and France. He returned to France and attempted to gain Reynaud's enthusiasm for the plan but saw it ignored while Reynaud resigned and was replaced by Petain. Now certain that the French government would plead with the Germans for an armistice, de Gaulle fled Paris on June 17, accompanied by Gen. **Edward Spears**, for London.

Knowing that he could have no influence over the British if only a few French volunteers rallied to his cause, de Gaulle broadcast a fervent appeal on June 18. The following day he again took the microphone to assert that the "ordinary forms of power have disappeared," expressing his deep conviction that he "spoke in the name of France." Since neither Weygand nor Auguste Nogues responded to his appeals, he realized that the whole burden of redeeming France's honor had fallen on his shoulders. On June 28 the British government recognized him as the "head of all Free France...rallying to the Allied cause." And on August 7, both he and Churchill appended their names to an agreement under which de Gaulle undertook to raise a French volunteer force, comprised of air, sea and land units, whose distinctive French nature would be guaranteed and which the British government would outfit.

The **Mers el-Kebir** incident of July 3 slowed individual pledges to de Gaulle's movement, but the allegiance of Chad to **Free France**, declared on August 26, and of **French Equatorial Africa** and the Cameroons, declared on August 29, quickened them again. Jacques Philippe de Hauteclocque, afterward known as **Leclerc**, and **Georges Catroux** joined de Gaulle on July 25 and August 29, respectively. De Gaulle's defeat at Dakar on September 23 was a sharp disappointment, but he nevertheless persisted in setting up the Defense Council of the French Colonial Empire at Brazzaville on October 27. Leclerc's capture of the Italian stronghold of Kufra on March 1, 1941 and his raid on Fezzan in February 1942 were the first victories of the *Forces francaises libres* (FFL). In May and June of 1942 Gen. **Marie Pierre Koenig** won his brilliant success at Bir-Hakeim (see **Mediterranean and Middle Eastern Theater of Operations**). The attack on **Syria** by some British detachments and the FFL led to a serious break between de Gaulle and Churchill, which was never really smoothed over. **Roosevelt**, forced into the war by the Japanese attack on **Pearl Harbor** on December 7, 1941, was contemptuous of the Free French. No less scornful, the British War Office ordered the occupation of **Madagascar** by British troops in May 1942 without bothering to notify de Gaulle. The Anglo-American landing in North Africa on November 8, 1942 was in fact accomplished without the French leader's knowledge. Roosevelt felt

that **Francois Darlan** was the man to deal with, and when the French admiral was assassinated, Roosevelt turned to Gen. **Henri Giraud**, whom he recognized as the commander in chief of **French North Africa**.

Still firmly convinced that he was the sole head of France, de Gaulle by degrees undercut the naive Giraud, much to Roosevelt's disgust. On November 9, 1943 "Charlot" finally became sole president of the National Liberation Committee, which had been established on June 3. His authority was backed by the Provisional Consultative Assembly, which the committee convoked and whose 84 members included 20 delegates who had refused to vote full powers to Petain in June 1940. De Gaulle commanded all the fighting French forces—both the FFL and the larger bodies of troops stationed in French North Africa since the armistice, to which Weygand had devoted all his attention. De Gaulle even managed to obtain control of the various **Resistance** movements in continental France under the *Conseil national de la resistance* (National Resistance Council), or CNR, presided over by **Jean Moulin** beginning May 27, 1943 and then by **Georges Bidault**. It was in de Gaulle's name that the regular troops and "night fighters" contributed efficiently and gloriously to the Allied war effort despite their lack of numerical strength.

On June 2, 1944 de Gaulle had the name of the National Liberation Committee changed to the Provisional Government of the Republic of France. On June 4 Churchill informed him of the imminent **Normandy landing**. He managed, with perspicacity and persistence, to get his Anglo-American allies to allow the provisional government to exercise its authority over the liberated territories at once. On August 25 he entered Paris after Gen. Leclerc, and on August 26 he marched down the *Champs Elysees*, acclaimed by masses of Parisians. The following day he dissolved the CNR and announced that the provisional government was the sole agency empowered to rule. He was reluctantly recognized by Roosevelt and more readily by the other Allies; nevertheless, he was barred from the Yalta and Potsdam conferences (see **Conferences, Allied**). However, Gen. **Jean de Lattre de Tassigny** was later to attend the ceremonies marking the German surrender on May 9, 1945, and France obtained an occupation zone in **Germany**.

In the months that followed, de Gaulle endeavored to convince the Allies of the wisdom of transforming the centralized Reich into a federation of states and of creating an economic union including France, the Saar region and three autonomous states: the Palatinate, Hesse, and the Rhine Province. These, he suggested, could be integrated into a western European economic and strategic system, thus giving the industrial Ruhr international status. But events took a different course.

With the conquest of the common enemy, each Ally's self-interest reemerged. Beginning on May 8, 1945, Britain took advantage of French weakness to occupy Syria and **Lebanon**, which had been under French mandate since 1919. De Gaulle suffered the occupation in silence.

If he had remained in power, de Gaulle would probably have reshaped France's international status. But in 1945, when he was in effect the country's dictator, he failed to change the French social system, and in the elections of October 21 the voters ignored his exhortations for a new constitution and filled the legislature with Communists, Socialists and other advocates of views opposed to his. Finding himself unable to influence his fellow Frenchmen, he resigned January 20, 1946.

E. Pognon

GEHLEN, Reinhard (1902-1979).

From 1942 to 1945 Gehlen, a German general, led the Foreign Armies of the East in the *Oberkommando des Heeres*. His specialty was the **USSR**. In 1945 he surrendered himself and his archives to the Americans, along with some of his colleagues.

GENERAL GOVERNMENT FOR OCCUPIED POLAND.

The Polish territory that the German Reich had conquered between the new frontiers of the **USSR** on the east and the territory to be incorporated into the Reich on the west in the fall of 1939 was, on October 25, 1939, placed under the rule of the general government, a civilian administration established by **Hitler**. Certain portions of western **Poland—Danzig**, East Prussia and the Wartaland, the administrative district of Zeichenau and Upper Silesia—were incorporated into the Reich; Galicia was added on August 1, 1941. (See also **Axis Powers—Military Administration**.)

GEORGE II (1890-1947).

A nephew of Kaiser Wilhelm II, the last emperor of **Germany**, George II became king of **Greece** in 1922. He was expelled in 1922 and deposed in 1923. In 1935, however, he was recalled by a plebiscite. After his return he supported **Ioannis Metaxas**. When the **Axis** powers invaded Greece in 1941, he fled first to Cairo and then to London. He was recalled to Greece by another plebiscite in 1946.

GEORGE VI (1895-1952).

After his brother, Edward VIII, unexpectedly abdicated in 1936, George VI became king of Great Britain and the last emperor of **India**. A shy but popular monarch, he sustained British **morale** during the war with his quiet, total confidence in victory. In September 1940 he was narrowly missed by a stick of six bombs.

GEORGES, Joseph (1875-1951).

Georges was the French general in command of the northeastern theater in 1939 and 1940. In 1943 he escaped to Algeria, where he joined the *Comite francais de liberation nationale*.

GERBRANDY, Pieter Sjoerds (1885-1961).

A Dutch lawyer and politician, Gerbrandy belonged to the Anti-Revolutionary Party. He served as minister of justice in 1939 and as prime minister of the Dutch **government-in-exile** from 1940 to 1945. His voice, characterized by a marked Frisian accent, became celebrated throughout **the Netherlands** during the war as a result of his regular radio broadcasts.

GERMAN RESISTANCE.

The voluminous literature published since the end of World War II has given us a penetrating view of the multifaceted activities of the German opposition to Nazism. Nevertheless, many questions concerning details remain; this fact and the significance of the German **Resistance** as one of the most important such movements of the 20th century still require supplementary analysis, more-searching examination and more rigorous definitions. Closer observation is certainly required, for example, into all too human hesitations, indecisions and weaknesses experienced by many of the Nazi regime's opponents. And we should remember that nobody who has not undergone the trials of that period in that country has the right to make hasty judgments concerning the conflicts of **conscience** Germans experienced, or the degree of courage that was required to take a firm stand.

It is also well to remember that the term "conspiracy," as used so cleverly by the Nazis in their **propaganda**, carries a deliberate distortion. Surrounding the relatively small circle of men who planned the **assassination attempt of July 20, 1944** against **Hitler** was a much larger group of individuals and movements opposed to his regime. Capable of agreeing on the need to destroy the Nazi government, they could agree on little else. Among others there were the Socialists, the Syndicalists, the theologians both Catholic and Protestant, the Communists, the *Kreisauer Kreis*, the "White Rose" and even former Nazis. A good many people were involved in the catastrophe of July 20, 1944 only because they were related to the plotters through blood, profession or sympathy.

German opposition to Nazism, its ideology and its dictatorship began immediately after the elections of 1930, which made the **Nazi Party** the second most powerful faction in the *Reichstag*. People with profound religious convictions—among them the evangelical theologians Paul Schneider and **Dietrich Bonhoeffer** and the Catholics Rupert Mayer and Monsignor Otto Mueller—immediately saw in the Nazi regime the ultimate threat to morals, Christianity and culture. As early as 1931 Bonhoeffer understood that the greatest tragedy for the church and the German people would be an ardent and pure national sentiment coupled with a vicious neopaganism. Such a combination would be much more difficult to unmask and slay than free thought, not only because it appealed to the emotions but also because it was adopted by Christians. A National Conservative named Ewald von Kleist-Schmenzin excoriated, in a pamphlet published in 1932, the nihilist attitude of the Nazi Party, its position on religion and its intention to swallow up the state under the pretense of guarding the purity of the Aryan race. In the following year, Count Schwerin von Schwanenfeld asserted that **Germany** could be liberated from Nazism only through Hitler's violent death.

There are numerous indications that such prominent spokesmen for the Social Democrats as Julius Leber, Wilhelm Leuschner and Adolf Reichwein had no illusions about the true goal and methods of the Nazis. Although they were given long prison sentences under the Nazi regime, the **Gestapo** failed to break their inflexible will to resist. Between their liberation and rearrest, they tirelessly worked along with other opposition groups to upset the dictatorship.

Despite their clear vision and activity, however, it is true that in 1933 the only voices heard in Germany were those heralding Nazism and its "powerful popular movement" as the key to solving the social, economic and political problems of the Reich and the stimulus for restoring Germany to its rightful place as the dominant power in Europe.

The first attack on Hitler came from the political left, which had acquired a taste for fighting the Nazis during the Weimar Republic. Although they took different paths, the leftist groups worked together in secret by organizing cells of resistance in the factories, inundating the country with illegal brochures, warning the man in the street against the traps the Nazis were leading him into, but nothing was able to prevent the headlong rush to dictatorship. Moreover, the Gestapo was beginning seriously to interfere in their labors. But the Socialists in particular managed, under the most difficult conditions, to form a "front of silent reserve" behind which they developed cadres for the day of liberation. Courageous but isolated

voices took up the call for the dignity of man, while the warnings of German statesmen in exile proliferated. But they were all drowned out by the roars of a population drunk with nationalist enthusiasm. The dizzying and almost uninterrupted rise of the Third Reich, coupled with the practically "hypnotic" ease with which Hitler seemed to resolve the problems of central Europe in Germany's favor, won the admiration of the critical and the indecisive. Nothing could be heard over the shouts of "spiritual reawakening" and "new national revolution" and other Nazi slogans.

It was not until long afterward that the churches recognized the true nature of Nazism. Nor could it be honestly said that the Catholic Church, for example, exactly understood the political objectives of the Nazis from the very beginning. Finally the Nazis' open attempt to "remove piety from public life," which could only be interpreted as a disguise for an outright challenge to Christianity's right to exist, opened the eyes of many communicants and provoked protests, declarations and sermons against the false Nazi doctrine of **anti-Semitism** and the deification of the Fuehrer. Thus, the message of the church in March 1935 contained these words: "We see our people threatened by a mortal danger. This danger consists in a new religion." The racist myth elevating blood, race, the people, honor and liberty to the status of idols was a violation of the First Commandment. Pope Pius XI published the encyclical *Mit brennender Sorge*, in which he stigmatized confused pantheism and the cult of race as idolatry. The *Kirchenkampf* ("struggle for the church") reached a climax in 1937 when the Gestapo arrested and condemned a number of churchmen. Many representatives of the church fought valiantly for their freedom to preach as well as their freedom of conscience. But they failed to exorcise the evil spirit. (See also **Church and the Third Reich, The**.)

After 1933, under the pressure of events, increasing numbers of brave and wise Germans turned away from Hitler. They had concluded that spiritual arms alone were useless against despotism, injustice and terror. The desired change in Germany's situation could only come from a revolt. That, however, required the participation of the army and especially such military men as Gen. **Werner von Fritsch** and the head of the chiefs of staff, Gen. **Ludwig Beck**, who believed that a soldier's duty did not end with purely military matters but extended also to concern for the people and the nation—particularly the latter, since the political significance of the army was so clear. It was at about the end of 1937 that the generals were forced to face the fact that Hitler had reorganized the *Wehrmacht* not for purposes of defense but for wars of aggression, that he was engaged in an unscrupulous gamble that could lead the army itself, the people, the nation and all of Europe to disaster. Since Beck's warnings were ignored by the government, he felt that he had no recourse but to resign, since he could not accept the responsibility of conducting a war Hitler might start. His successor, Gen. **Franz Halder**, who held similar views, prepared to unseat the Fuehrer and bring him before a tribunal the moment he gave the order for the invasion of **Czechoslovakia**. Planned near the end of August 1938, this action was the first attempted coup d'etat. Halder could count on only a tiny minority to support him in Germany, but that group seemed determined to overthrow the dictatorship. Hitler's opposition did not intend to stop simply with elimination of the war threat; it sought peace in Europe for "reestablishing human dignity in relationships among the states as well as within them." If this hope could not be realized, the indecision of other western European powers was at least in part to blame. At Munich they greeted the German demands with admiration. After that, any opposition to Hitler was bound to fail for psychological reasons. To participate in a plot to crush the "great statesman of Europe" would be madness. Furthermore, the majority of the German people was absolutely against any change in the government.

Nevertheless, the opposition groups like those associated with Leipzig's burgomaster **Karl Goerdeler**, Gen. Beck, and Baron Ernst von Weizsaecker, the secretary of the foreign ministry, persisted in their efforts both within Germany and abroad as circumstances permitted. They warned the world of every new Nazi move, with no perceptible response. In the fall of 1939, after the Polish campaign, which gave Hitler's prestige still another boost, the first attempt on the dictator's life was planned to keep the hitherto limited war from engulfing the world. But the uncertainty of some of the generals involved in the planning, and a variety of other circumstances, foiled the plot. Most officers refused to participate because, they insisted, such a deed was contrary to the traditions of their corps—"munity," as they put it, was a word unknown in the German officer's lexicon. Above all, it would be folly to kill a successful man, and after Hitler's achievements the younger officers could no longer be depended on to do their part in such a plot. Besides, some of them hoped that Germany's military triumph in the west would satisfy the appetite of the extremists in the government. Unquestionably, they refused to consider a choice between their moral responsibility and their duty as soldiers.

After the German victories of 1940 in the north and west, the small opposition groups felt lost. Their apprehensions could not penetrate the German people's

euphoria. It was not until the number of German defeats on all fronts increased dramatically after 1941 that the anti-Nazis in Germany could return to the attack and win adherents to their cause. While some of them sought to sound out the Allies on the conditions under which they would agree to discuss peace with a new German government through intermediaries in **Sweden**, **Switzerland** or the **United States**, others tried desperately to persuade high-ranking *Wehrmacht* officers of the need to move against Hitler and his coterie. They failed. The Allies, victims of their own propaganda, refused any contact with the dissident Germans.

The situation of the German Resistance was radically different from that of other movements in Europe, and as a result, it took shape under much greater secrecy. There was no question of whether or not war was to be waged. Everything had to be prepared for the knockout punch, for the spark that would ignite the coup to eliminate Hitler. Completely isolated, ignored by the Allies, surrounded by informers in their own country, incessantly threatened by terrorists in the police system, they lived in fear. After 1942 they tried five times to kill Hitler. There were also other, unrelated attempts—that made by the **Scholls**, brother and sister, for example. An underground propaganda battle raged, started by the so-called interior emigration. Indications of official Nazi plans for the invasion of the neutral countries were furnished to the Allies. Actually, however, the opposition cabals concentrated more and more on the liquidation of Hitler and his system until the indefatigable and courageous Count **Claus Schenk von Stauffenberg** finally risked an attempt on July 20, 1944 in the Fuehrer's *Wolfsschanze* headquarters. Hitler managed, by a fluke, to escape the bomb meant for him, and the Nazi leaders launched a murderous purge. More than 200 plotters were executed. The number of victims among the German Resistance, however, was in the thousands.

The police system set up by the Nazis frustrated the organization of dissidents (see **Gestapo**; **SD**). The population was under unceasing surveillance. Informing was encouraged by the Nazis as a civic virtue; parents were often denounced by their children. Schoolboys of 14 were jailed for two weeks merely for mocking comments; their parents were carefully watched. Caretakers in large buildings, business offices, administrative agencies, schools, universities and the like became expert informers. Leuschner, the Socialist leader, wrote to an English friend: "We are locked into an enormous prison, and successful rebellion is just as impossible here as against armed guards in any penitentiary."

Figures based on Gestapo documents are suggestive of the terror in the country and of the recalcitrance the regime aroused: in just six years, the regular courts alone condemned 225,000 people to a total of 600,000 years in prison. These statistics do not include Germans thrown into **concentration camps** or killed by the police, a figure difficult to determine. Between 1933 and 1945, according to the official data, the prisons, at any one time, held three million Germans for political crimes, serving sentences as short as weeks or as long as 12 years in concentration camps or prisons. Of that total 800,000 were condemned for active resistance. In April 1939, according to a Gestapo note, there were 162,734 prisoners in protective custody (*Schutzhaeftlinge*), 27,369 accused of political crimes and 112,432 convicted of political crimes.

Compared with the Resistance movements in the other countries (**the Netherlands**, **Belgium**, France, the **USSR**, etc.), the German version fought not only its own government but the very people—fellow Germans—it attempted to liberate. In 1942 Count **Helmuth James von Moltke** wrote to an English friend that the anti-Hitlerite abroad was in a much more comfortable position than his counterpart in Germany. For the friend of democracy outside Germany, he said, "moral and national loyalties coincide; for us at home those loyalties are obviously contradictory."

An examination of the motives of the Beck-Goerdeler German Resistance group shows a "spirit of liberty" and a "revulsion of conscience." For these men life was not only a question of self-defense but also a determined stand against a system violating the conscience of man and implicating an entire people in a crime against humanity. It involved the upholding of liberty and the dignity of man facing a dehumanizing and dishonoring system. This reform movement sought not only the destruction of the Nazi regime but also the reconstruction of the republic and the state in accordance with the tradition and culture of the German people. Although many of the movement's concepts were very conservative, it nevertheless adhered to the idea that Germany's political evolution would be hindered by a national state swollen with a continental territory and saddled with a world economy.

The ideas of the *Kreisauer Kreis* (Kreisau Circle), for example, revolved around the notion of the juridical state whose obligation it was to punish violators of the law. The *Kreis* did not demand vengeance so much as it hoped for the triumph of righteousness, complete liberty of conscience, the dignity of the individual, protection of the family as the basic social unit and the organic development of communal life. One of its principal ideas was a union of the Catholic and Protestant churches. In this respect, the position of Count von Moltke on the structure of postwar Europe is significant. There must, he said, be fewer

frontiers and soldiers, fewer "hydrocephalic organizations" and grandiose plans; instead, Europeans must learn to "reestablish the image of man in the hearts of our fellow citizens." This was a "question of religion and education, of an organic liaison with one's profession and family, of a true balance between the obligation to serve and the privilege of being served."

The growing indignation and moral resistance to Nazi gangsterism, the feeling of responsibility to the people and the fatherland, the desire to reestablish the old traditional values and the urgent need to preserve Germany from total ruin in a tempest of bombings motivated the German Resistance. In spite of its failure to erase Hitler and his system, the Resistance was of great symbolic significance.

On one occasion Gen. **Henning von Tresckow** declared: "God once promised Abraham that He would not destroy Sodom if only six righteous men could be found in it. I hope God will do the same for Germany if only because of us.... The moral value of a man begins only with his readiness to sacrifice his life for his convictions."

H. A. Jacobsen

GERMANY.

On the eve of the war, the Third Reich covered an area of about 180,000 square miles; its population was approximately 70 million. The country's policies were not set by cabinet ministers, economic managers or the military, but by **Hitler** and his favorites, **SS** chief **Heinrich Himmler** and **Martin Bormann**, head of the **Nazi Party** secretariat after 1940.

The "Greater German Empire" came into being after the outbreak of the war. With Nazi conquests in **Poland**, Alsace-Lorraine, **Luxembourg** and the Eupen-Malmedy-Moresnet area of **Belgium**, it encompassed nearly 250,000 square miles. Nazi leaders attempted to restructure their state through large-scale resettlements, especially in the newly acquired territories of **Danzig** and West Prussia, where over 950,000 ethnic Germans from southern and eastern Europe were settled.

As the war progressed, measures taken to assure the "final victory" became more and more drastic; they included rationing of **food**, strict control of the economy and transportation and even the regimentation of young girls, who, after completing obligatory public service, were expected to volunteer for six months of army auxiliary duty. More than seven million foreigners drafted for compulsory labor joined some 30 million civilian workers in operating the German economic machine. In 1943 the proclamation of "total war" forced the closing of numerous commercial establishments as well as the mobilization of the country's last

reserves, organized in 1944 into the *Volkssturm* (People's Attack).

As the process of mobilization broadened, it absorbed more and more of each individual's energies, cutting him off from family, from all private associations, from every church and institution and from leisure-time activities. An unceasing emotional stimulation surrounded him, seeking to secure his absolute devotion to the Fuehrer. Huge and colorful mass demonstrations heightened their participants' zeal. Even before the outbreak of hostilities, party and government continually called for "combat" against hunger, cold and every other real or imagined discomfort. The entire German population was put on a war footing.

Hitler did not trust bureaucratic functionaries to direct public energies and mobilize the nation's resources. He preferred instead to entrust special missions to Reich commissioners or to provide his ministers with extraordinary powers, creating new procedures for every new purpose. With each new development in the "total war," a new administrative branch with new agencies and civil servants came into being. These officials, unlike their counterparts in the regular bureaucracy, could concentrate solely on the special function for which they had been assembled. Often, however, they hampered or counteracted the normal work of administration; the people and the state itself suffered from the resulting bureaucratic chaos. Although frequently lamented, confusion continued to spread; during the war, there were 58 major government agencies in addition to the nine conventional ministries of the Reich. Bureaucrats of party and state, ministers and commissioners, administrators and special envoys squabbled over power.

Hitler's motives in sponsoring such bureaucratic proliferation were a natural consequence of his character. The Nazi chief was extremely suspicious of the administration and disdained its inertia in implementing his decrees. He also disliked adding to the authority of powerful subordinates, preferring to counterbalance one service with another and thus to leave the final decision for himself. Hitler was convinced that he could achieve total power only by multiplying agencies so that areas administered by one would be surveyed by another, even if neither operated efficiently. He felt that there had to be many bodies and detachments, all of them in competition, to achieve the maximum in productivity—that the process of "natural selection" applied to state administration. Until his fall Hitler would not or could not comprehend that the constant friction produced by this system also led to a considerable waste of energy.

Only by force could the totalitarian government keep all institutions and organizations in step, hold an entire population in a permanent state of mobilization and stamp out any possibility of individual initiative or freedom. The very nature of Nazi rule demanded an enemy to fight as a justification for its excesses. Regimentation and terror were institutionalized, the process of coercion constantly refined. Dachau and Sachsenhausen, established shortly after the Nazi seizure of power, soon spawned new **concentration camps**: Buchenwald in 1936 and Flossenburg, Ravensbrueck and Mauthausen in 1938. During the war still other camps opened while the the the old ones swelled, increasing the level of terror in Germany and the conquered territories. The camp personnel, instilled with a fanatical hatred toward the inmates, saw to it that the system operated smoothly until the fall of Nazism.

Not content to imprison political opponents, the Nazis sought to eliminate anyone considered "harmful to the German people"—racial minorities, religious sects, draft resisters and many others. Hitler sought constantly to subordinate justice to ideology and expediency through new legislation, harsh sentences and political coercion of judges. The courts yielded and their judges acquiesced in this perversion of the law, going so far as to aid Hitler in his attempt to substitute for written codes an improvised series of statutes designed to fit the political needs of the moment. The severity of legal decisions often bore little relation to the crime.

The war, the extermination of Europe's Jews and other groups stigmatized as racial inferiors, the liquidation of political opponents and the massacre of eastern Europe's intellectual elite were the logical consequences of the National Socialist concept of the world. When he unleashed the war in 1939, Hitler had as his objective the complete destruction of the European legal and social order and its replacement of a new order based on the "laws of life." What he intended by this became clear when he ordered German troops and occupation officials to destroy all "life unworthy of existence."

Nazi leaders were well aware that their true objectives would meet with resentment or **resistance**. To forestall public protest, the government therefore kept its vindictive measures a closely guarded secret. Every precaution was taken to prevent the spread of information on police activities and concentration camps. Even the rough number of camp inmates remained unknown. At the same time, the Nazi Party and all its branches worked to persuade the public that the "enemies of the state" required harsh treatment. The war served as a valuable cover and justification for Nazi atrocities.

In the absence of dissenting views, the conditioning of public opinion bore fruit. Many Germans thoroughly believed that the state was threatened and therefore approved the repression of alleged troublemakers. Some were willing to go further and help detect "saboteurs of state security." Public cooperation, however, had its limits. Attempts to introduce a **euthanasia** program aimed at eliminating incurably ill patients and other social "dead weight" evoked such vehement protests from church authorities and the general public that the campaign had to be dropped inside the frontiers of the Reich.

The nationalistic furor produced by Nazi **propaganda** and the war effort welded together the most varied social groups and provided them with a common ideology. Imperialist ambitions, national frustrations, hatred of capitalism and the hopes of the oppressed masses were all encouraged by National Socialism. As a result the virtues extolled by Nazi leaders kept their persuasive power to the end; loyalty, a sense of duty, and hatred of foreigners and minorities held the system together despite the impending fall of the Reich. The process of self-immolation ended in 1945, with the disappearance of a unified Germany and more than seven million Germans dead, including 3.5 million battlefield casualties.

H.-A. Jacobsen

GERMANY, Air Battle of.

In the first five months of 1941, the *Luftwaffe* concentrated its destructive energies on the **United Kingdom** (see **Britain, Battle of**). The scientific war advanced with the perfection of **radar**. The British persisted in disrupting German directional beams despite the improvements made in them. With the invasion of the **USSR**, however, German air attacks on the United Kingdom practically ended. The German air force subsequently contented itself with harassing shipping and dropping mines.

In 1941-42 neither the **Royal Air Force** nor the *Luftwaffe* had mastery of the air. At this point British fliers began a strategic bombing campaign against **Germany**; they were soon able to intensify their efforts thanks to the **Lend-Lease** Act and, beginning in 1942, the intervention of American air power.

During the first year of the British air offensive, their aircraft carried out a series of sweeps over the Continent. The *Luftwaffe* used radar extensively in 1942; combined with the appearance of the Focke-Wulf 190 fighter, it gave them a considerable advantage. British losses edged slightly beyond the Germans.

The air war reached a turning point on May 31, 1942 with the first 1,000-bomber British raid, against Cologne. The importance of this event lay not so much in its material results, which were not terribly significant, or even in its effect on German **morale**. But the night attack of May 31 and those that followed soon afterward showed the German air staff that predictions of bombings made in **propaganda** broadcasts over the **British Broadcasting Corporation** network would be fulfilled on schedule. Moreover, the British onslaught on Cologne helped the Soviet war effort by forcing the *Luftwaffe* command to draw strength from the Russian front and transfer it to the rear for home defense. In 1941, 61 percent of the available German aircraft were supporting the armed forces in the east; in 1943 the proportion had dropped to less than 20 percent. A large number of the Messerschmidt 110, Junker 88 and Dornier 217 squadrons comprising the army's air umbrella returned to the interior of Germany for night fighter service. The **Stukas**, protected by increasingly fewer pursuit craft, became less willing to risk contact with Soviet fighters.

The British needed time, however, to perfect their methods of concentrated air attack. One important development was the creation of Pathfinder units, based on the German *Kampfgruppen 200* that had battered England during the winter of 1940-41. The Pathfinders preceded the main bomber forces to their objectives in complete darkness, marking "turning points" with flares to aid the less experienced navigators and dropping illumination flares on the target for easy identification. Red and green flares were then used to bracket the target area before the bombardiers unloaded their "eggs."

Mastery of the skies went to the Anglo-Americans in the west in the spring of 1943, by which time German air superiority had also vanished on the eastern front. At the Casablanca Conference in January 1943, U.S. and British leaders planned a strategic air campaign designed to destroy the Reich's military, economic and industrial power and to sap the morale of the German people. Under the direct authority of the Combined Chiefs of Staff, Britain's Sir **Charles Portal** was assigned to coordinate the operation. The British and Americans subsequently adopted a plan proposed by the U.S. Air Force's Gen. Ira Eaker, who divided potential targets into six groups whose destruction would end Germany's ability to resist. Most important, in Eaker's eyes, were submarine yards and construction facilities, followed by aircraft-manufacturing centers, ball-bearing plants, motor fuel refineries, synthetic rubber factories and motor vehicle **production** centers. Priorities could be altered as the situation demanded. Faced with increasing deployment of German fighters in the west, Portal named destruction of the German aircraft industry as his most important goal in a directive of June 10.

The general strategic plan (Operation **Pointblank**) called for a combined offensive by the U.S. Eighth Strategic Air Force and the RAF **Bomber Command** from British bases. Daylight bombing was assigned to the

Americans; the British bombed at night. The number of Allied squadrons increased rapidly in 1943. Twin-engine aircraft were progressively replaced by the four-engine British Stirling, Lancaster and Halifax bombers and the American B-17s and B-24s.

Following a preliminary campaign against submarine repair bases on the shores of the Bay of Biscay, the RAF Bomber Command mounted a huge air offensive that involved three successive battles—of the Ruhr, Hamburg and Berlin.

The battle of the Ruhr, involving 43 major attacks, was fought between March and July of 1943. The Bomber Command made 18,506 sorties at a cost of 872 aircraft shot down and 2,126 damaged. Despite such heavy losses more than 593 planes participated in daily bombing missions in February. In August 1943 daily missions involved up to 787 aircraft with operational crews. Heavy damage was inflicted on the cities and industrial plants of Duisburg, Essen, Cologne, Duesseldorf, Dortmund and Bochum. During the night of May 16-17, 19 Lancasters of the 617th Squadron, a crack unit commanded by **Guy Penrose Gibson**, attacked dams on the Mohne and Eder rivers that supplied power to the Ruhr industries as well as providing flood control for an enormous network of fields, rivers and canals. Gibson had invented a special type of bomb for the purpose, meant to be dropped at night from an altitude of 60 feet. The operation required intensive training. It succeeded completely, but at the loss of eight planes and their crews when the squadron ran into a terrible **flak** barrage. The precision of Gibson's raid produced striking results: electric power output dropped, the Dortmund plants lost their water supply and the valleys were flooded. By the fall, however, the dams were repaired.

The battle of Hamburg, from July 24 to August 3, involved 17,021 sorties, with 695 planes destroyed and 1,123 damaged. Economic losses suffered by the Germans were gigantic. In one of the raids conducted during this operation, the bombers for the first time used the "window" tactic of dropping clouds of metal foil strips to baffle enemy radar and thus reduce their losses. During the night of August 17-18 the RAF mounted its famous raid on the German plants at **Peenemuende** that manufactured the "V" rocket engines (see **V-1 and V-2**).

The battle of Berlin, beginning on November 23, represented a defeat for the British. In 20,224 sorties, 1,047 planes were lost and 1,682 damaged.

While the RAF Bomber Command fought its three great battles, the U.S. Eighth Strategic Air Force, headed by Gen. Eaker, also thrust at the heart of Germany, attacking key industrial cities that produced aircraft, synthetic fabrics and ball bearings. American

losses were high, however. The bombing of Schweinfurt on October 14 shattered the city's ball-bearing plants, but cost 60 of the 291 Flying Fortresses sent on the mission.

By the end of 1943, Operation Pointblank had reached a crisis point. The air offensive against Germany had produced impressive results, but at great cost. German fighter strength increased until October 1943, and their flak was merciless. Many German industrial cities, moreover, lay outside the range of protective Allied fighter cover. Stimulated by **Albert Speer**, armaments production rose in the first half of 1943, peaked for a period, dropped and then rose once more in the first few months of 1944. The hoped-for collapse of German civilian morale also failed to occur.

Allied military chiefs took several steps to improve the effectiveness of their air campaign. Beginning in November 1943, the 15th U.S. Strategic Air Force, commanded by Gen. **James Doolittle**, and the 205th Group of the RAF Bomber Command were stationed in **Italy**, considerably extending the range of the Allied air arm. New long-range fighters, especially the American P-51 Mustang, permitted Allied bombers to hit any point in Nazi-occupied Europe with sharply reduced casualties. Improved aluminum explosives also increased the destructiveness of bombing raids.

On November 7, 1943 German Propaganda Minister **Joseph Goebbels** wrote in his diary: "Yesterday we lost 30 fighter planes over Berlin. We cannot take such losses for long. In their daylight raids the American bombers are now escorted by pursuit planes of excellent quality against which our fighters are outclassed." Seven months earlier Goebbel's had noted: "The president of the German Physical Society has sent me a memorandum on the comparative status of German and Anglo-Saxon physics. Its tenor is depressing. Anglo-Saxon physics is far ahead of ours, particularly in **research** work. As a result the Anglo-Americans are also ahead in the practical application of physics discoveries to warfare. We can see that equally well in air and submarine combat."

In January 1944 Gen. **Carl Spaatz** was named commander in chief of all American strategic forces in Europe, with the Eighth Strategic Air Force put under command of Gen. Doolittle and the 15th assigned to Gen. Nathan F. Twining. Round-the-clock bombing began, with missions frequently lasting 10 to 12 hours and involving 1,000-1,200 planes. The week of February 20-25, 1944 was especially important; at this time British and American air fleets unleashed a continuous assault on the German aircraft-producing centers of Brunswick, Leipzig, Ratisbonne, Gotha, Augsburg and Stuttgart. The bombers made 6,151 sorties and dropped 19,000 tons of bombs, at a cost of 383 aircraft destroyed. The damage sustained by the targets was not irreparable, but the losses in German pilots and aircraft production could never be made up.

The bombardment of the Ploesti oil fields in April and May by the Eighth and 15th Strategic Air Forces produced spectacular results, destroying 75 percent of the facility's gasoline production capacity. The air battle of Berlin was also renewed during the first three months of 1944, with the *Luftwaffe* sustaining especially severe losses from the P-51 Mustang. Operation **Crossbow** struck at the Atlantic coast launching sites of the V-1 rockets and the stations of the German radar network.

In the face of the Allied air assault, the German armaments industry under Albert Speer performed miracles of adaptation and survival. Arms production reached its highest point in July 1944. The number of aircraft plants actually increased from 80 in 1943 to 550 in 1944, with the more important ones occupying underground installations protected by more than 30 feet of concrete. The enforced dispersion of **production** facilities, however, made the Germans extremely vulnerable to raids on transportation lines. Parts were useless when they could not be brought together and assembled.

The Allied air offensive also sapped the German war effort by forcing it to concentrate on home defense at the expense of the fighting fronts. The urgent need for fighter planes reduced the production of bombers capable of striking at Allied troop concentrations. Rising aircraft losses and the growing demand for pilots caused a sharp drop in the training and standards of the *Luftwaffe* at the same time that the Allied air forces were improving the effectiveness of their crews. Antiaircraft guns, which grew from 16 percent of German arms output in 1943 to 40 percent in 1944, took personnel and equipment away from the front-line artillery. As Speer later admitted, "There is not the slightest doubt that had there been no air raids, hundreds of thousands of men could have been spared from the armaments industry in 1943 to replace soldiers assigned to clear away the rubble of those raids at the expense of their training and efficiency." Every raid, moreover, caused the loss of millions of man-hours and slashed the efficiency of workers by depriving them of sleep. After a relatively calm night Goebbels wrote, "Absurdly enough, just 10 noisy bombers were sufficient to drive 15 million to 18 million people from their beds."

In early 1944 Allied military chiefs faced the question of how air operations could best contribute to the planned invasion of France (see **Normandy Landing**). Generals Spaatz and Eaker, in charge of the air offensive against Germany, actually considered the invasion a waste of time, claiming that bombing alone would eventually bring about the collapse of the German war effort. A proposal based on this idea, Operation Rankin, provided for a limited invasion that would only establish a beachhead on the Continent, advancing inland after the destruction of Germany's war industry had been completed. The survival and expansion of German arms production, however, strengthened the arguments of those who favored a full-scale invasion. A conference of Allied military leaders held on March 25, 1944 decided to divert part of the strategic air forces from the bombing of Germany to support the Normandy landings. The meeting assigned Allied air units the task of destroying transportation facilities in France and **Belgium**— locomotives, rolling-stock concentrations, railroad yards and repair and assembly plants for the French and Belgian railroads. Control over strategic air units in the west was temporarily transferred from the Combined Chiefs of Staff to Gen. **Dwight Eisenhower,** commander of the invasion.

Allied tactical squadrons prepared for the landings by striking at bridges across the Seine to prevent north-south movement of German troops in France. Simultaneous attacks were made on the bridges of the Albert Canal and across the Meuse as a false hint to the enemy that the landing would take place north of the Seine. Tactical aircraft also struck at the network of radar stations extending along the French coast. Nevertheless, a number of important units had to cancel their offensive plans to cope with the serious threat presented by the V-type drones. Although Allied bombers pounded 88 launching sites in France and **the Netherlands** with 40,000 tons of bombs in early 1944, the Germans constantly designed better camouflaged and less vulnerable bases.

The strategic air campaign against Germany continued with increasing intensity through the winter of 1944-45 despite adverse weather conditions. As the liberation of France and Belgium forced back German forward radar stations, Allied losses fell and the destructiveness of their raids increased. Priority targets included motor fuel refineries, communications facilities and arms factories. Bombers and tactical aircraft also sought out the bases of the new **jet aircraft,** Germany's last secret weapon, which were easily identified by their long runways. In 1944 alone, U.S. and British planes dropped 1,188,577 tons of bombs on Europe, compared to 330,446 tons in the preceding four years. During the first four months of 1945, another 447,051 tons were dropped.

Allied aircraft concentrated on western Germany in early 1945, striking at a line running from Bremen to the east of Coblenz. When U.S. and British forces crossed the Rhine in mid-March, the great Ruhr industrial area was practically isolated from the rest of the country. On March 11, 1,078 heavy bombers unloaded 4,500 tons of bombs on Essen. The following day 1,118 aircraft hit Dortmund with another 5,000 tons.

On April 16 Gen. Spaatz announced that the strategic air offensive against Germany was officially at an end. At this point he and his British counterpart, **Sir Arthur Harris**, had 28,000 combat aircraft and 1,335,000 men under their command. The total Anglo-American air campaign involved 444,000 bombing and 2,680,000 fighter sorties. More than 57,000 German civilians died in air raids.

The high cost of the air war and the failure of saturation bombing to break German civilian morale have brought charges since the war's end that the entire air offensive was a mistake. Yet the fascist dictators had clearly initiated the use of massive air raids in **Ethiopia, Spain, Poland**, the Netherlands and England. As Lecomte du Nouy wrote, "The most heinous crime of the totalitarian states was to impose on Western civilization this dilemma: to refrain from borrowing their methods of warfare and resign themselves to extinction, or to use them and revert to brutishness."

H. Bernard

GERMANY—ECONOMY OF THE THIRD REICH.

An investigation of **Germany**'s mobilization of its economic potential cannot be limited to the war period. As opposed to France, the **United States** and the **United Kingdom**, Germany was economically so well prepared for the war by September 1939 that during the first half of the war no special effort was required. It was not until the **Blitzkrieg** gave way to total mobilization of all military resources that a "war economy," in the strict sense of the term, came into being.

Economic planning in wartime is tied intimately to technical progress. The German government's first attempt to develop economic controls responsive to strategic imperatives was initiated in 1916, during World War I. It was worked out in step-by-step improvisations, without an integral plan. Because they determined the rations of raw materials each industry was to receive, the public or semipublic agencies forming this completely new war service gained control of all important aspects of **production** and distribution.

The rearmament policy pursued by Nazi Germany in the 1930s was developed with an eye to the lessons taught by experience. Well before the beginning of the war, the regime had completed a plan for economic mobilization.

The War Effort, 1933-1939

The orientation of the German economy toward rearmament between 1933 and 1939 was closely connected with the Nazi foreign policy, determined by long-term goals **Hitler** had made quite clear in his *Mein Kampf*. That policy was explained by the slogans "territorial expansion" and "conquest of *Lebensraum*" ("vital space"). These objectives were spelled out in "The Four-Year Plan" of 1936 and the Hossbach protocol of 1937.

Paralleling these goals in foreign policy was an ambitious armament program. By 1936 Germany had caught up with and even surpassed the reserve strength of its erstwhile conquerors. By the time the war broke out German military expenditures amounted to 60 billion Reichsmarks. The annual military outlay jumped from four percent of the national budget in 1932 to 50 percent, or 17 percent of the gross national product (GNP), in 1938. In the same period Great Britain devoted only four percent of its GNP to military output; the United States, just one percent. (See the following table.)

MILITARY EXPENDITURES BY GERMANY, GREAT BRITAIN AND THE UNITED STATES

	GERMANY		GREAT BRITAIN		UNITED STATES	
Year	Billions of Reichsmarks	Absolute Percentage of the GNP	Billions of Pounds	Absolute Percentage of the GNP	Billions of Dollars	Absolute Percentage of the GNP
1933	1.9	3	0.1	3	0.5	1
1934	4.1	6	0.1	3	0.7	1
1935	6.0	8	0.1	2	0.9	1
1936	10.8	13	0.2	5	0.9	1
1937	11.7	13	0.3	7	1.0	1
1938	17.2	17	0.4	8	1.0	1
Mean 1933-1938	8.6	10	0.2	4.7	0.8	1

Source: Berenice Carroll, *Design for Total War.*

An effort of this dimension required the creation of new financial procedures and institutions since the fiscal assets of the Reich (without the *Laender* and various districts) could only cover two-thirds of its expenditures between 1933 and September 1939.

Revenues and Expenditures of the Reich, 1933-September 1939, in Billions of Reichsmarks

Taxes, custom duties and other sources	81.8
Financing by ''Mefo'' notes	10.5
Tax bonds	3.1
Short-term credits	6.9
Long-term credits	16.7
	119.0
Non-military expenditures	59.0
Military expenditures	60.0
	119.0

Source: Fritz Federau, *Der Zweite Weltkrieg. Seine Finanzierung in Deutschland*, Tubingen, 1962.

To screen the huge debts (especially short-term debts) from public scrutiny, the goverment used an ingenious instrument known as ''Mefo'' notes, the name deriving from *Metallurgische Forschungsgesellschaft: GmbH* (''Metallurgical Research Institute''). This was a fictitious company whose capital was underwritten by the major armament producers in order to add a second ''valid'' signature, as required by Reichsbank regulations, to the notes with which the government covered its arms purchases. Through the end of the 1937-38 fiscal year, the face value of the notes that had been issued totaled 12 billion Reichsmarks; by the beginning of the war, only 1.5 billion Reichsmarks' worth had been redeemed. In 1939 the Mefo notes, payable at maturity, were replaced by treasury bonds bearing no interest, which the state used to pay for its orders from the armament manufacturers. These short-term credits swelled interest and redemption costs to unexpected dimensions; a long-range solution had to be found immediately since the ''new financial plan'' of 1939 was, after all, no more than a means of rapidly increasing the credit of the state. For the Reichsbank, it meant the loss of what remained of its independence. This law placing full powers of credit in the hands of the dictatorship freed the government from all institutional control over monetary and financial policy. The importance of such a law can only be understood in the framework of a wartime atmosphere; it was comparable to the financial measures that had been instituted in August 1914.

Finance was not the only area in which the German government's policies were revised in preparation for war. In 1936 the Four Year Plan introduced measures for radical economic mobilization to put the nation on a war footing. Early in Hitler's regime there had been shortages of the raw materials required for arms production as well as in agricultural production; the exhaustion of the army's gasoline reserves was feared as well. These supply crises were the result of the exigencies of foreign trade; it was virtually impossible to accommodate both military and civilian demands. Until 1935 the state could draw increasingly on the national revenue by compensating the increasing public debt through ceilings on wages. When the thousands of unemployed were reintegrated into the labor market, purchasing power increased despite the low salary levels. But the increase seemed illusory in the face of the paucity of consumer goods, especially imports. What was needed, then, was either a modification of the economic priorities through which the military machine swallowed most of the nation's resources or the maintenance of the same priorities through the imposition of heavier taxes and political pressure.

In addition to these internal economic problems, there was the deterioration of the terms of trade, which worked to the industrial nations' disadvantage. Until 1933 the German economy profited from the drop in the prices of raw materials. In 1934 and 1935, however, the price of finished products continued to drop on the world market while the price of raw materials, **food** and half-finished products either remained constant or rose. In the fall of 1935 officials of the German government began to think that rationing food might be necessary if the tempo of rearmament was to be maintained. Evidently, there could be no simultaneous rise in the level of armed strength and in the standard of living. To cope with this disturbing development **Goering** was appointed mediator, and subsequently economic coordinator, of the Division of Raw Materials and Currency.

Even more than these developments in foreign trade and the supply of raw materials, however, the problem of motor fuel was responsible for the introduction of the Four Year Plan in 1935-36. The *Wehrmacht* had vowed that it would produce synthetic gasoline in Germany; toward that end, it was pressing for the large-scale production of fuel through the liquefaction of coal, with a view of independence from foreign oil sources. The plan was designed principally to fulfill this goal, for it had been determined by 1936 that random attempts could never solve the raw material or motor fuel crises. Only a determined economic drive could maintain military priorities.

In August 1936 Hitler divulged the goals of the Four Year Plan. The task set for the economy was to create the conditions for the "self-reliance" of the German people—i.e., to furnish them with arms for an apparently inevitable war. With Germany's economic power fettered by the lack of German "living space," the means of existence of the German people could, in the long run, only be ensured by the expansion of *Lebensraum*—i.e., by acquiring sources of raw material and food products for the Reich. As matters stood, the German economy could only partially provide the people's needs; in this period its function was twofold—first, to guarantee the conditions of existence within a limited area, and second, to create the conditions of "self-reliance." The military effort was to be supplemented by an economic effort that would within four years structure the country's economy to support a costly war. The national production of fuel, synthetic rubber, ores and synthetic industrial oil would be pushed to the limit to reduce Germany's reliance on imports of raw material.

The direction Hitler gave the economic effort was part of a total strategy to make armed conflict inevitable. The plans for the acquisition of raw materials showed the influence of proposals made several years before by the Department of War Economy and IG-Farben for a German hydrocarbon and synthetic automotive fuel plant, proposals supported by the Division of Raw Materials and Currency in the spring of 1936. The goal was quite clear; there was nothing new in arming for an eventual war. What was new was the ability to forge the national economy into an instrument for armament and to connect economic self-sufficiency with expansionism. This was accomplished through the traditional bureaucracy of the Ministry of the Economy. At its head was **Hjalmar Schacht**. Despite his unorthodox methods for financing the armament program and managing foreign trade, he remained loyal to the ultimate objective: reintegration of the German economy into the world market. To this end a commission independent of the Ministry of the Economy and responsible directly to Goering was created in connection with the Four Year Plan.

The organization and goals of the plan changed several times between 1936 and 1942. Until the summer of 1938 it concentrated on planning the production of raw materials and staples. Agriculture also came under the purview of the plan during this period, as did wage and price controls, as well as labor and investments. Starting in the summer of 1938, the planners concentrated their attention exclusively on industries essential for equipping a mechanized army—industries, that is, manufacturing synthetic chemicals, light armor and finished guns. From the declaration of war until 1942, the organization of the plan developed to the point where it became the major institution for the entire war economy, capable of equipping the *Wehrmacht* and the defense and armament services. But it did not in the least put an end to the friction and delays within the bureaucracy that characterized the German mobilization system before 1939. The conflicts remained endemic within the institution and its various, badly coordinated subgroups.

The goals set in 1936-37 for raw materials, staple products and synthetic goods had to be revised frequently. The periods for their achievement were arbitrarily set, and usually too short. As a consequence, a comparison of the program with its results had little meaning. Arrangements regarding strategically important goods that should have been made by the army were added to the program for raw materials and staples. Moreover, the powers entrusted to the subgroups in the Plan were too narrow; they covered only a portion of the labor and material requirements of new industries. The various programs dealt only with production quotas, the amount of investments and the period for and sites of construction; they were not usually concerned with working capital or labor allotments, a frequent source of errors. This fragmentary

ARMS PRODUCTION IN ESSENTIAL INDUSTRIES IN 1936 AND 1942 IN THOUSANDS OF TONS

Products	1936	1942	Increase in Percent
Hydrocarbons	1,790	6,260	250
Aluminum	98	260	168
Synthetic rubber	0.7	96	13,600
Explosives	18	300	1,567
Gunpowder	20	150	650
Steel	19,216	20,480	6
Copper	61.4	41.1	− 24
Magnesium	13	30	130
Synthetic products	25.8	119.3	363

Source: Dietmar Petzina, *Autarkiepolitik.*

plan and its limited instruments posed numerous problems, which led to the inclusion of new areas under the heading of raw materials. On the other hand, this system of partial control had a certain elasticity that, by the successive concentration of resources of one branch and another of the armed forces, often procured excellent results.

It is impossible to define exactly the part played by the Four Year Plan in the war effort since it controlled specific projects for only a few industrial sectors. But an idea of the extent of its activities can be gleaned by considering the volume of its investments: 13.25 billion Reichsmarks between 1936 and 1942, or 50% of the total industrial investment in Germany for that period. Of this sum, 41% was spent on hydrocarbon production, 21% on synthetic textiles, 10% on heavy metals, 12% on powder, explosives and other finished weapons. Although the crudely drawn programs could not be fulfilled in many cases, the production figures prove that the Four Year Plan was successful, at least in the eyes of the regime. In the course of the first war years, there were never any serious shortages of hydrocarbons, rubber, light metals, chemical weapons, powder or explosives.

This economic mobilization before the war should not be confused with a true war economy. Although the level of armament it produced was far higher than in any other country, the German economy was still a long way from devising a perfectly functioning war machine. The government had to coordinate excesses in its headlong arms production by means of a still fragmentary system of controls. Domestically, the arms program aroused public anxiety that the scarcity in consumer goods would get out of hand.

Actually, the production of consumer goods increased by 25% between 1936 and 1939, although the arms plants were getting the lion's share of the industrial resources.

The change in the investment structure in 1938 and 1939 indicates the increasing load on the economic system, which from time to time required corrections by the government to equalize the imbalance among the various sectors. One cannot reasonably infer from this that, given the economic situation, war would be the unavoidable result. One can, however, understand how the strains created by the dynamism of Nazi thinking, the economic possibilities of war, and the crescendo of social pressure could, given the excessive rate of production achieved in 1938, increase the temptation to engage in military operations. The invasion of Austria, the crisis of the Sudetenland and the occupation of Czechoslovakia were not only indications of the new German military power; they also marked the limits of the system of economic mobilization which, unhindered by the opinions of the population, could only be impelled forward when triggered by a crisis.

Establishment of a War Economy, 1939-1945

At the beginning of the war, Germany benefited from an advantage in war materiel over feebler and unprepared neighbors that enabled it to score two years of victories with Blitzkrieg tactics. This does not mean that the Nazi desire for the ultimate in preparedness was satisfied. A large part of the country's resources was confined to military uses, but the war machine was not yet the irresistible colossus its propagandists made it out to be. Until 1939, two contradictory tendencies were in uneasy balance: a war economy on one side, and a higher standard of living on the other. Behind the monolithic Nazi facade seethed a divergence of views and methods. The victories at the beginning of the war seemed confirmation of the tactic, in armament as on the battlefield, of concentrating as much power as possible on the nerve center. Such moves worked out well as long as the opposing force remained inferior in strength and the Allies had not yet deployed their superior economic potential. Alan Milward justifiably notes that this tactic was better adapted to the means at the dis-

GROWTH OF INDUSTRIAL INVESTMENT

	1928	1934	1935	1936	1937	1938	1939
Manufacturing Plants:							
Value (in millions of RM)	1,717	700	1,221	1,637	2,208	2,952	3,596
Volume as percentage of 1928 figure	100	49	86	116	156	209	256
Consumer Goods Industries:							
Value (in millions of RM)	898	360	415	522	635	739	836
Volume as percentage of 1928 figure	100	59	65	80	92	106	119

Source: Dietmar Petzina, *Autarkiepolitik.*

posal of the Nazi dictatorship than a general plan like that followed by Great Britain after hostilities began. If Hitler himself insisted during the summer of 1940 on an armament reduction, it was principally for the purpose of preventing a threatened deterioration in the "**morale** of the masses."

When war was declared, bonuses for night work and holidays as well as overtime were established. The workers were even more pleased by the lengthening of the work day; in some sectors, a ten-hour day was the rule. Even the number of requisitions dropped to 0.8 million in October 1942 after having attained a maximum of 1.4 million in January 1940—particularly as the result of a judicious system of division of labor.

Other indices, like arms production levels and salary variations, confirm that there was no increase in the level of economic mobilization in 1940 and 1941. A series of laws relating to the war effort were even abrogated in September 1939, with less effect than had been hoped. Thus, a decree "limiting changes in the place of work" was only the confirmation of the existence of a prior condition inhibiting the growth of indigenous labor. The freezing of salaries, always in force, did not prevent slight increases in wages amounting to 10.4% between September 1939 and March 1941, in spite of official guidelines. Until 1941, labor mobilization was not nearly as hurried as in Great Britain, where the women's labor force, for example, increased 18% while it dropped in Germany. The manpower in the war industries rose only 11% until 1941, whereas the total rise in manpower for these industries was 36% between 1939 and 1944. The push for greater production did not really start until **Albert Speer's** time.

The second phase of the economic mobilization coincided with the establishment of a system equipped to respond to the demands of a war which was becoming much more protracted than at first envisaged.

With reluctance, Hitler had to confess that the lightning war failed to kill the Soviet colossus. By the beginning of 1942, he gave up all hope of a quick victory. A recasting of the strategic plan was necessary. The course of the war economy inside Germany as well as in the occupied territories and satellite nations veered with two appointments: of Speer as Minister of Armaments and War Industries, and, in the spring of 1942, of **Fritz Sauckel** as labor czar. Speer favored the tendency to centralize decisions, but also reinforced the autonomy of the industrial administration with a view to improving productivity. New planning methods replaced the planning procedures in use prior to 1942, which had lain incomplete due to assorted rivalries. Speer's preference for the centralization of decisions at first encountered resistance from Goering and certain circles in the *Wehrmacht*. To elude Goering's resentment, Speer had himself named "General Commissar in Charge of Armaments in the Four Year Plan," under the *Luftwaffe* commander's supervision. The arrangement was purely symbolic since Speer's appointment meant the end of the Four Year Plan, although the term remained in usage until Germany's surrender.

In 1942, the defense and armament services of the *Oberkommando der Wehrmacht* were absorbed by the Ministry of Armaments. These services in the Navy followed the same path. By 1944, Speer also managed to gain control of the *Luftwaffe* armaments service, thus providing him with a stranglehold on the Central Planning Commission, which made all the important decisions, and the Planning Service. Total mobilization of the national economy was then achieved. Speer was now in control of every administrative organ handling armaments, except those charged with labor recruitment. To him reverted all the power exercised under the Four Year Plan: the execution of existing programs, the final decision re-

PRODUCTION OF MAJOR INDUSTRIAL SECTORS
AS PERCENTAGE OF 1943 OUTPUT

	1938	1939	1940	1941	1942	1943	1944
Staple products	73	80	81	94	94	100	85
War materiel	20	25	44	44	64	100	125
Construction	325	320	208	173	173	100	88
Other production	89	102	97	107	107	100	71
Consumer goods	110	110	104	106	95	100	95
Overall industrial production	84	89	86	88	89	100	98

Source: R. Wagenfuehr, *Die deutsche Industrie im Kriege 1939-1945*, second edition, Berlin, 1963.

garding changes in plans, and the creation of new production units. Even during the transition period, when the navy and air force had their own decision-making bodies, Speer still exerted indirect control by adroitly granting or withholding raw materials.

A second characteristic of this centralized control was the stimulation of private enterprise. By instituting agencies of industrial self-management as well as commissions and pools armed with authority inside branches of industry, Germany could for the first time standardize and profit from a mass production system. The growth in armament production indicates the economic reserves that the new system of control could bring into play; between 1940 and 1944, average production tripled. Remarkably enough, the production of consumer goods in this same period dropped only slightly. Contrary to the expectations of foreign observers, total industrial production in embattled Germany continued to increase throughout the war.

After 1942, the only agency independent of Minister Speer was the General Commissariat for Employment. The order of March 27, 1942 entrusted to Sauckel supervision of the employment force, a duty hitherto shared by several commissions under the Four Year Plan—particularly the recruitment and assignment of labor, depending on the demands of the Ministry of Armaments. This system was expanded even further in the months that followed, and the labor czar had full powers that had hitherto been the privilege of the Minister of Labor under the Plan—he had the right to take all necessary measures for increasing the number of workers, conducting whatever policy he saw fit independently of the Minister of Labor. With these powers Sauckel obtained the support of the *Gauleiter*, whom he made his agents with his first decree of April 6, 1942. He became the top man on labor policy. Although he was primarily concerned with tapping labor supplies abroad, he also experimented with the German workers' ranks; his efforts at recruitment were so successful that the number of armaments workers increased by 1.3 million in 1942 alone.

This table highlights two important tendencies in the labor policy of the Reich. First, the lack of male workers was compensated, at least quantitatively, by the forced recruitment of foreign labor; second, there was a failure to increase the number of female workers primarily as a result of ideological taboos. In any case, the number of industrial workers in 1944 was practically the same as in 1939, but the rate of production was higher. Some sectors of the armament industry experienced a considerable surge in production up until 1944, as did the chemical industry (with a 30% increase), the automotive fuel industry (with an 85% increase) and electric power (with a 26% increase). Despite the rise in armaments production, the food situation for the people of the country did not deteriorate until the fifth year of the war. Until 1943, strict rationing of all consumer goods and the tributes paid by the occupied and satellite countries provided the German population with a relatively high level of

LABOR MOBILIZATION IN THE REICH
IN MILLIONS OF PEOPLE

Period	German Laborers			Foreigners and Prisoners of War	Total Civilian Labor Force
	Men	Women	Total		
May 1939	24.5	14.6	39.1	0.3	39.4
May 1940	20.4	14.4	34.8	1.2	36.0
May 1941	19.0	14.1	33.1	3.0	36.1
May 1942	16.9	14.4	31.3	4.2	35.5
May 1943	15.5	14.8	30.3	6.3	36.6
May 1944	14.2	14.8	29.0	7.1	36.1
September 1944	13.5	14.9	28.4	7.5	35.9

Source: Dietmar Petzina, *Die Mobilisierung deutscher Arbeitskraefte.*

TRIBUTES LEVIED BY THE REICH
IN BILLIONS OF REICHSMARKS

Countries Subject to Levies	2nd half 1940	1941	1942	1943	Jan. 1-Sept. 10 1944	Total
France	1.75	5.55	8.55	11.10	8.30	35.25
The Netherlands	0.80	1.90	2.20	2.20	1.65	8.75
Belgium	0.35	1.30	1.50	1.60	0.95	5.70
Denmark	0.20	0.20	0.25	0.55	0.80	2.00
Italy (after September 1943)				2.00	8.00	10.00
Other occupied countries	0.90	1.05	4.50	7.55	8.30	22.30
Total	4.00	10.00	17.00	25.00	28.00	84.00

Source: Fritz Federau, *Der Zweite Weltkrieg. Seine Finanzierung in Deutschland*, Tubingen, 1962.

consumption. The data in the table above indicates the scale of demands the Nazis made on those countries:

The occupied countries played an essential role in furnishing raw materials. In 1943, 50 to 100% of the iron ore, sulphur, silicon and nitrogen, among other materials, used by the Reich came from these regions. Beginning in the summer of 1941, trains regularly transported the booty from the **USSR** to maintain the tempo of German production. But this did not last long; the territories rich in raw materials were reclaimed by the Russians at the beginning of 1943.

The German government tried to ease the growing load of war expenses on the populace. The tax rate in the Germany of 1941 for a personal annual income of 10,000 Reichsmarks was 13.7%, as against a tax rate of 23.7% for a comparable income in Great Britain. For an annual income of 100,000 Reichsmarks, the tax rate attained a maximum of 55%, as against 75% for England. This explains the fact that of the total cost of the war to the Reich, reaching 657 billion Reichsmarks for the whole war period, only 184.7 billion RM were covered by taxes. The government preferred "silent"

financing: it forced all public centers of capital deposit to place their assets at the Reich's disposal, thus giving the populace the illusion of stability and avoiding the psychological trauma that would have been induced by sudden jumps in taxes. Until 1944, 160 billion RM of public debt bonds, corresponding to the internal tax receipts, were left with the deposit centers. To erase the remainder of the deficit, notes were issued, with the result that in 1945, the public debt was no less than 380 billion RM. Actually, this was of no importance to the conduct of the war and the manufacture of armaments since the merchandise could be obtained simply by presenting an authorization. From all appearances, the Nazis expected a collapse of the monetary system at the end of the war.

One last note on the German economic mobilization before and during the war. The Nazis succeeded in raising armament production to an astonishing level beginning in 1942 even though a considerable war effort was already in progress. The explanation for this phenomenon lies in the victories procured by the Blitzkrieg, as a result of which Germany for a short-time controlled the levers of economic potential in the

PRODUCTION OF ARMAMENTS BY THE GREAT POWERS IN 1941 AND 1943
IN BILLIONS OF DOLLARS

Allies	1941	1943	Axis Powers	1941	1943
United States	4.5	37.5	Germany	6.0	13.8
Great Britain	6.5	11.1	Japan	2.0	4.5
USSR	8.5	13.9			
Total	19.5	62.5	Total	8.0	18.3
Proportion, Allies: Axis 1941—1:2.4 1943—1:3.4					

Source: R. Wagenfuehr, *Die deutsche Industrie im Kriege 1939-1945*, second edition, Berlin, 1963.

greater part of Europe. In that brief interval Germany could imagine itself a giant industrial complex. This, of course, it was not—at least in comparison with the U.S. or the USSR. Ineluctably the military superiority of the Allies was to assert itself, for by the beginning of 1944 Germany had reached the end of its economic resources, while in America the Allies had a practically inexhaustible treasurehouse.

D. Petzina

GERMANY, FREE.
See *National Komitee "Freies Deutschland."*

GERSON, Victor (1898-).
Gerson was a French textile merchant. His wife, a Chilean, was the first female agent for the **Special Operations Executive** (SOE), beginning in May 1941. Between 1941 and 1944 Gerson organized and operated the extremely successful "Vic" escape route for the SOE.

GESTAPO.
This organization—whose name is an acronym for *Geheime Staatspolizei* ("State Secret Police")—was created in the spring of 1933 under the aegis of **Goering**, who was then minister-president of Prussia, to replace the Prussian political police. The first head of the Gestapo Bureau, the controlling section of the organization, was a jurist named Rudolf Diels. After a year in office Diels was replaced by **Reinhard Heydrich**, the head of the **SS** security services, who, under the orders of SS Reichsfuehrer **Heinrich Himmler**, had reorganized the Bavarian political police to fit the Nazi image while Himmler gradually tightened his control in all the German states.

This was the beginning of a process through which the German police fell under the influence of the SS, which would gradually absorb the police forces by detaching them from the administration of the states. At the same time, the Gestapo completely lost its judiciary character and was transformed into a powerful arm of **Hitler**'s authority. This was to become evident in 1936, when Himmler also gained the post of "chief of German Police."

Under Himmler's orders Heydrich organized and unified the political police throughout the Reich. In 1939 Himmler further consolidated his power by combining the Gestapo, under the direction of Heinrich Mueller, with the criminal police, under **Arthur Nebe**, to form the *Sicherheitspolizei*—"State Security Police"—known also as the Sipo. Heydrich was then appointed to head the parent organization, the *Reichssicherheitshauptamt*—"Central Security Office of the Reich"—often abbreviated as **RSHA**. Asso-

ciated with the RSHA was the *Sicherheitsdienst des Reichsfuehrers SS*—"Security Service of the SS Reichsfuehrer"—or **SD**, a **Nazi Party** group.

Created in 1931, the SD, under Heydrich's direction, became the Nazi spy organization for hunting down political enemies outside and dissenters inside the party. In 1933 this function was given to the Gestapo, which broadened the domain of its surveillance to include enemies of the state and the Nazi system. It had its own prisons; it maintained a presence in the "political sections" of the **concentration camps**; it could at pleasure execute or torture any of its detainees; and it conducted mass executions of **prisoners of war** as well as, in the occupied countries, groups regarded as politically dangerous. **Adolf Eichmann** and the Gestapo's Section IV B4 organized the "**Final Solution** of the Jewish question." After the **assassination attempt of July 20, 1944**, a special committee of the Gestapo brutally persecuted those who resisted the Nazi system, and the two divisions of the SD—the domestic, commanded by Otto Ohlendorf, and the foreign, commanded by **Walter Schellenberg**—took charge of secret political missions. For this purpose the SD gradually assumed control of all the other information functions of the party, including the foreign spy service and surveillance of the politics and loyalty of all social circles and media. Thus a whole web of "confidential agents" was spun to enmesh the unwary. Until 1944 Ohlendorf submitted regular reports on public opinion. They reflected the German attitude so accurately that they were condemned by the Nazi authorities as "defeatist."

The foreign division of the SD cultivated relations with fascist and other politically sympathetic groups, directed the behavior of Germans abroad and influenced the official policy of the Ministry of Foreign Affairs. It also engaged in subversive activity and **sabotage** beyond the Reich's frontiers—such as the contrived attack on the **Gleiwitz** transmitter, the independence movement in Slovakia, the Iron Guard putsch in **Rumania** and the installation of the Szalasi regime in **Hungary**. By the end of the war, the SD foreign division also controlled the *Abwehr*.

With more than 6,000 agents the SD consisted of 13 major sections with 55 lesser subsections. In each of the occupied countries and behind the front lines, a Gestapo unit was established as a surveillance team under the authority of a "commander of SD and security police." The *Einsatzgruppen*, mobile squads charged with mass executions in the occupied regions, were under the direct orders of the RSHA and were commanded, after Heydrich's death in 1943, by **Ernst Kaltenbrunner**. The Gestapo membership amounted to slightly more than 30,000.

After the war the International Military Tribunal ruled that the Gestapo and the SD were criminal organizations.

K. J. Mueller

GIBRALTAR.

In British hands since 1704, Gibraltar has repeatedly proved its strategic worth in war. A small airfield, with part of its runway built out into the sea, was added on the northern side of the rocky peninsula in 1941. The naval base, on the western side, provided vital refueling, repair and anchorage facilities for Allied warships. The straits—14.2 km wide at their narrowest point—remained under continuous British naval control, though a few U-boats and one important squadron of Vichy French ships bound for Dakar did slip through unobserved. Severe overcrowding in the town of Gibraltar did not prevent the civilian population of some 20,000 from welcoming troops, sailors and airmen resting on their way from one battle to another. Occasional air raids did little damage; the fortress remained impregnable. The number and identity of ships present was, however, visible in daylight to German agents across the bay.

GIBSON, Guy Penrose (1918-1944).

A British airman, Gibson displayed exceptional skills and daring as a pilot and leader. After commanding a bomber squadron for 11 months, he formed 617 Squadron RAF for special low-level raids on the Ruhr, which he personally led in May 1943. Gibson was killed in a minor operation in September 1944.

GILBERT ISLANDS.

It was clear to the Japanese at the beginning of the war that air facilities in the Gilbert Islands, a prewar British mandate in the Central Pacific, could threaten their strategic position in the Marshall group to the west. Under Japanese control, on the other hand, the Gilberts, athwart the lanes leading to the southwestern Pacific, could imperil vital Allied sea links. Therefore the Japanese quickly neutralized Makin Island on December 9, 1941, and Tarawa the next day.

Provoked by a small USMC Raider attack in August 1942 against Makin, the Japanese proceeded to construct enormously formidable defenses on the main atoll of Tarawa, which was reoccupied in September by Japanese forces. Secondary attention was accorded to Makin and Abemama (Apamama). The Tarawa atoll commander, Rear Adm. Keiji Shibasaki, reputedly boasted of his defense system that the enemy could not conquer the place with a million men in a hundred years.

In mid-1943, when the U.S. strategic counteroffensive got underway in the Central Pacific, Adm. **Chester W. Nimitz**'s attention shifted from the Marshall Islands to the Gilberts, presumably a less redoubtable but still very valuable objective. The resultant Operation Galvanic involved 200 vessels, 27,600 assault and 7,600 garrison troops, 6,000 vehicles and 117,000 tons of cargo. Vice Adm. Raymond A. Spruance, Fifth Fleet commander, was in overall command of the Gilbert Islands expeditionary force, with Rear Adm. Richmond K. Turner, Fifth Amphibious Force commander, in command of the assault force. Ground forces came under the command of USMC Maj. Gen. Holland M. ("Howling Mad") Smith, Fifth Amphibious Corps commander. The Northern Attack Force, bound for Makin and commanded by Turner himself, was centered on the Army's 27th Infantry Division under Maj. Gen. Ralph C. Smith. Rear Adm. Harry W. Hill commanded the Southern Attack Force against Tarawa, built around Maj. Gen. Julian C. Smith's Second Marine Division. Rear Adm. Charles A. Pownall commanded Task Force 50, the carrier force.

On November 20, 1943 the green 27th Division came ashore on Makin, with air and naval preparation, deploying a regimental combat team and a battalion landing team. The island was supposed to be taken in a day, but the 700-800 Japanese comprising the small garrison, under a mere lieutenant, and including construction men, doggedly held off 6,472 Americans, who progressed with "infuriating slowness" until November 23. Makin cost the invaders 64 killed and 150 wounded: only one Japanese soldier and 104 laborers were taken prisoner.

Also on November 20 the bloodied Second Marine Division, with air and naval support, struck at Betio on Tarawa, using amphibian tractors (amtracs) tactically for the first time. Shibasaki's force on Tarawa exceeded 4,800 men, including the tough Sasebo Seventh Special Naval Landing Force (IJN "marines") and the Third Special Base Force. While regular **landing craft** struggled in vain to negotiate the exposed reef apron, 1,500 of 5,000 Marines became casualties on the initial day of the assault. Poor or disregarded intelligence on the tide conditions contributed to the very heavy U.S. losses, as the Marines were obliged to wade 500-600 yards to shore under murderous fire. Of the 125 amtracs used at Tarawa, 90 were lost, with 323 of the 500 men operating them. Valorous USMC infantry remnants carved out a precious beachhead, aided by the facts that the main Japanese communications network had been torn up by the naval barrages and that Japanese air capabilities (weakened by major diversions to Rabaul) were negligible. (The light carrier *Independence*, however, was damaged badly and had to leave the area.) All USMC troop reserves were committed, naval gunfire support and air strikes continued, and the Americans finally brought in artillery and tanks to help the foot soldiers. The unyielding defenders were exterminated, cave by cave and bunker by bunker, through prodigious use of flame-throwers, explosive charges and gunfire. Adm. Shibasaki was apparently incinerated in his fortified bunker on November 22. When the last Japanese counterattacks were stopped and the island was conquered on November 23, the entire garrison was dead; only one officer, 16 enlisted men and 129 Koreans were taken alive. Abemama, garrisoned by merely 23 suicide-prone Japanese, was seized easily by Marines of a reconnaissance unit landed from a submarine on November 21. In all, U.S. casualties at Tarawa numbered 1,009 killed and 2,101 wounded from the total of 18,593 men committed. USN casualties were severe aboard the *Liscome Bay*, a new escort carrier torpedoed and blown up by an IJN submarine on November 24 with about 650 killed, and on the battleship *Mississippi*, which suffered 62 casualties when a turret exploded during bombardment.

There has been considerable controversy about Operation Galvanic, not only about the techniques employed but also the wisdom of having assaulted the Gilberts in the first place. Even Gen. Holland Smith later argued that the islands should have been leapfrogged in favor of the Marshalls. Other critics have suggested that the month needed to catch the next favorable tide conditions at Tarawa would have favored the invaders instead of the defenders. Certainly, heavy casualties were to be expected during the first U.S. invasion of a small atoll, brilliantly fortified and fanatically defended to the death. It is generally agreed, however, that at the cost of the blood expended so lavishly in the Gilberts operation, the Americans gleaned tactical lessons indispensable for the subsequent amphibious campaign during the long "road back" across the Central Pacific and the ultimate defeat of Japan.

A. D. Coox

GIRAUD, Henri (1879-1949).
French general. He began his career as a professor in the *Ecole de guerre* in 1927 and nine years later became military governor of Metz. He replaced Gen. **Andre Corap** as commander of the Ninth Army, was taken prisoner on May 18, 1940, escaped in April 1942 and succeeded Adm. **Francois Darlan** as civilian and military chief in Algeria toward the end of December 1942. As co-president of the *Comite francais de liberation nationale* (French Committee for National Libera-

tion) from May to October 1943, he reestablished the French army and became its commander in chief. In this capacity he succeeded in liberating Corsica in September 1943. After numerous quarrels with **de Gaulle**, he retired on April 8, 1944 (see **Free France**; **French North Africa**).

GIRAUDOUX, Jean (1882-1944).
A French writer, Giraudoux was appointed minister of information in 1938. He conducted a discreet and dignified campaign against Nazism. Extremely depressed by the French defeat in 1940, he retired from all public activity. His *Armistice a Bordeaux* was published posthumously in 1945.

GLEIWITZ.
On August 31, 1939 a German broadcasting station at Gleiwitz (now Gliwice) in Silesia, then a bit more than six miles on the German side of the German-Polish border, was attacked by a dozen men in Polish uniforms, all of whom were shot dead. Foreign journalists were shown the bodies and duly reported the attack. The incident provided **Hitler** with his excuse for invading **Poland** the next day. The dead men were in fact German **concentration camp** prisoners, acting under duress by the **SS** on orders from the summit.

GLIERES, Les.
This plateau on the Alpine foothill of Chablais in the Haute Savoie was the site on which a **Resistance** group was established. It consisted partly of the 27th Battalion of French Alpine troops and escapees from the **Forced Labor Battalions** under the French occupation authorities. Attacked in February and March 1944 by a large body of German troops aided by **SS** units, the French Militia and the *Luftwaffe*, the maquis defended themselves heroically. In spite of the arms parachuted to them, they were literally massacred during March 17-26, 1944; neither prisoners nor wounded were spared.

GLIMMER.
Code name of an Anglo-American diversion operation at Boulogne in northern France during the **Normandy landing** (see **Radar**).

GOEBBELS, Joseph (1897-1945).
Minister of information and propaganda in the Nazi government. Goebbel's weekly, *Das Reich*, was on a much higher level than the normally coarse taste of the party regulars and even earned the respect of the anti-Nazi element of the German population. In 1943 he proclaimed the principle of total war and a year later bore the title of plenipotentiary general in charge of the total war for the Reich. He and his wife

poisoned themselves and six of their seven children on April 30, 1945 in the bunker of the German Chancellery.

GOERDELER, Karl (1884-1945).
A leader of the **German Resistance** movement, Goerdeler was dismissed in 1937 from his post as burgomaster of Leipzig, which he had held since 1930. Upon the successful overthrow of **Hitler**, he was designated to become chancellor of the Reich. He was arrested on September 10, 1944 and executed at Ploetzensee on February 2, 1945.

GOERING, Hermann (1893-1946).
A confidant of **Hitler**, Goering acquired the posts of marshal of the Reich, commander of the *Luftwaffe* and president of the Council for Defense of the Reich. He founded the **Gestapo** and ran it until 1936. From 1937 to 1943 he directed **Germany**'s economy and was designated Hitler's successor by the Fuehrer himself in 1939. During the war his power dwindled rapidly after the defeats of his once-powerful *Luftwaffe* (see **Britain, Battle of**). Condemned to death by the International Tribunal of Nuremberg, he poisoned himself before the sentence could be executed.

GORT, John, Lord (1896-1946).
Known for his exceptional bravery during World War I, Gort served as chief of the Imperial General Staff from 1937 to 1939. He commanded the British Expeditionary Force in France in 1939-40 and organized the defenses of **Gibraltar** in 1941-42 and **Malta** in 1942-44.

GOTT, Sir William Henry Ewart (1897-1942).
Gott, a British general, was a corps commander in North Africa. He was appointed to lead the British Eighth Army but was killed in a plane crash before he could assume command.

GOVERNMENTS-IN-EXILE.
Most of the countries the German army occupied during the war had a government-in-exile, which competed with the occupying forces for the allegiance of the inhabitants. Most of these governments were located in London, where they usually received the support of the British government and were helped by the **Special Operations Executive** (SOE) and the **British Broadcasting Corporation** (BBC) towards the aim of recovering their homelands. The Greek government-in-exile was based in Cairo in 1941-44, as was the Rumanian in 1943-44.

The monarchs of **Norway**, **Luxembourg** and the **Netherlands** were present in the **United Kingdom** with their governments; the king of **Belgium** stayed to share the tribulations of his people, though his ministers fled. The case of **Poland** was more complicated. The Polish republic's government-in-exile moved first to Paris, then in July 1940 to London; after July 1944, however, it found itself competing not only with the Germans but also with a rival government-in-exile established under Communist control at Lublin and recognized in August as the legitimate government of Poland by the **USSR** (see **Lublin, Committee**). This rival, supported by the Red Army, seized power in Warsaw in 1945.

The case of France was also complicated. Petain's government at Vichy was still on French soil, its legality was disputable, but it was not clearly illegal. **De Gaulle**'s organization, recognized by the British in June 1940 as the focus of those Frenchmen who wished to fight on, moved to Algiers in January 1943, and on June 3, 1944 proclaimed itself the provisional government of France. The Soviet Union recognized it promptly, but not until October 1944 was it recognized by the British or the Americans.

In the Asian war none of these problems arose. Most of the territories the Japanese overran were former colonial possessions; **Thailand** submitted to **Japan**, and **China** was far too big to overrun entirely.

M. R. D. Foot

GRAND, Laurence Douglas (1898-   ).
In 1938-40 Grand, a British soldier, headed Section D, a secret organization devoted to subversion and one of the bodies from which the **Special Operations Executive** derived.

GRANDI, Dino (1895-   ).
After serving as **Italy**'s ambassador to the **United Kingdom** from 1932 to 1939, Grandi was president of the Chamber of *Fasces* and Corporations at the moment of Italy's entry into the war. Beginning in 1941 he engaged in cabals against **Mussolini** and convoked the meeting of the Grand Fascist Council on July 24, 1943 that forced *Il Duce* to submit his resignation to the king. Grandi was condemned to death in absentia by the Verona Trials of January 1944.

GRAZIANI, Rodolfo (1882-1955).
An Italian marshal, Graziani commanded the Italian forces in North Africa from July 1, 1940 to March 25, 1941. He became minister of national defense of the *Repubblica sociale italiana* at Salo (see **Italy**). An Italian military court sentenced him to 19 years of solitary confinement on May 2, 1950.

GREAT BRITAIN.
See **United Kingdom**.

GREATER EAST ASIA CO-PROSPERITY SPHERE.

A zone of economic integration, political federation and cultural cooperation under **Japan**'s leadership, the Greater East Asia Co-Prosperity Sphere was established by fiat after Japanese forces overran Southeast Asia in late 1941 and early 1942. Proclaimed as a movement to liberate Asians from Western domination, the Co-Prosperity Sphere was the final step toward Japan's long-standing goal of spreading its economic and political influence over Asia. The scheme floundered because of Japanese brutality, resistance from local peoples and economic stagnation. It finally collapsed when the Allied forces retook control of the southwestern Pacific late in the war. The Co-Prosperity Sphere created enormous resentment against the Japanese in Southeast Asia, but it also prompted nationalist feelings and moved each of the countries in the region closer to independence.

The scope of the Co-Prosperity Sphere was gigantic. In 1938 the Japanese had unveiled their **New Order in East Asia**, linking them to Manchukuo, Inner Mongolia and **China**. The Co-Prosperity Sphere embraced these areas and envisioned the addition of mainland and insular Southeast Asia, the mandated islands of the Pacific, and perhaps one day **Australia** and **New Zealand** too. By mid-1942 the entire area except for Australia and New Zealand was in Japanese hands.

Economically, the Co-Prosperity Sphere was expected to become one of three self-sufficient blocs after the war was over, along with a German zone in Europe and an American one in the western hemisphere (the **USSR** and **India**, Japan anticipated, would form a buffer region). Industries would be grouped in the north, mainly in Japan, Korea and Manchukuo. Resources would come from the south, especially **Indonesia** and **Malaya**. Each country within the bloc would be locally self-sufficient in basic necessities, and there would be free trade throughout the area. It was a textbook plan for regional autarky and **collaboration**, although temporarily the sphere would have to support Japan's war effort.

The states in the region were nominally independent but actually Japanese protectorates, with Tokyo responsible for their defense and foreign relations. They were no longer administered as colonies, once Japan's forces pushed out the Western powers. Instead they were ruled under the general authority of Japanese military commanders, augmented by civil servants from the Greater East Asia ministry in Tokyo (founded in November 1942). Beneath them were thousands of local officals who handled the routine chores, often replacing European colonial functionaries.

Japan dealt with **Thailand** and **Indochina** some-

what differently because of their unique wartime status. Thailand had never been a European colony, and the Japanese were content to rule through the established government. Tokyo continued to recognize French sovereignty over Vietnam, Laos and Cambodia, in return for which the collaborationist regime at Vichy let Japan occupy key military bases and advise the French governor-general, Adm. Jean Decoux. In March 1945 the Japanese deposed the French administration and established an "independent" Vietnamese government under Emperor Bao Dai, but immediately after Japan surrendered to the Allies, **Ho Chi Minh** seized power and proclaimed the Democratic Republic of Vietnam.

Japanese administrators kept rigid control over military matters and tried to command the economy as well. Political affairs were normally guided by a single apparatus in each occupied country, modeled after the **Imperial Rule Assistance Association** in Japan. Its aims were to control information, spread Japanese civilization and language (mainly through the schools), train local leaders, win over religious organizations, and build political and economic support for the Co-Prosperity Sphere.

Culturally the region was supposed to become a place of Pan-Asian brotherhood, peace, harmony and tolerance. It would be cleansed of capitalism, materialism, selfishness and prejudice. Japan's **psychological warfare** ceaselessly attacked white imperialism and pledged to liberate "Asia for the Asiatics." The Co-Prosperity Sphere assumed that the Japanese were entitled to lead and strongly implied that they were superior to other Asians. Tokyo spoke of uniting "the eight corners of the world under one roof" and praised Emperor **Hirohito** as moral exemplar of the new order. The Japanese touted traditional views of authority throughout the region: social hierarchy, elite rule, group loyalty and the subordination of **women**.

Although the Co-Prosperity Sphere was clearly a device designed to substitute Japanese domination for Western colonialism, many Southeast Asians did not see it as an unmitigated act of evil, especially at first. Nationalists who wanted their countries free from foreign rule were delighted to have Japan drive out the Europeans and Americans. Many political prisoners jailed by the Western colonialists were freed. Most Europeans in positions of authority were replaced by local officials, creating a new indigenous class of administrators in each of the occupied countries. The Japanese helped spread education to the poor, lifted standards of public **health**, and often improved sanitation and transport.

But the benefits of the Co-Prosperity Sphere were soon offset by grievous shortcomings. The most appalling was the arrogant, often brutal conduct of the occupying troops. Chinese living in Southeast Asia, aware that the invading army had committed countless atrocities in China, feared the worst from the Japanese and often bore it, especially in Malaya. Local elites associated with the former colonial regimes lost their livelihoods and their status, and if they were Christians, they were likely to be persecuted by the newcomers as well. Hill peoples in **Burma** and other ethnic minorities not favored by the Japanese were often treated even more poorly than under the Western regimes.

Scarcely less painful was the suffocating arrogance Japan displayed toward local populations. Prime Minister **Hideki Tojo**, in a fit of patronizing expansiveness, told his troops to "respect the opinions of the natives and to take a true, fatherly attitude towards them." Although they spoke of internal autonomy for each state in the region, the Japanese were unprepared for the pressures for independence that soon mounted.

As an economic proposition the Co-Prosperity Sphere was clumsy and ineffective from the start because the area could barely survive isolated from world markets. What finally caused it to wither was the course of the Pacific war. Except for Burma and the **Philippines**, the Allied reconquest sidestepped the region and pushed directly northward toward the home islands, severing the sea links between Japan and its supply of resources. An American **blockade** pinched off much of the trade within the area. Like the Tokyo home front, civilian commodities vanished from the shelves because goods grew scarce and transport was crippled. Although it was the operation of wartime market forces, not Japanese malevolence, that shriveled Southeast Asia back to a subsistence economy, most local residents had a lower living standard when the occupation ended than when it began.

The Co-Prosperity Sphere left behind a generation full of bitterness toward Japan. It also speeded independence for each country that had been a Western colony by stimulating nationalist feelings. By the end of the war, Japan had granted at least nominal freedom to nearly every state except Malaya—mostly because Tokyo needed to shore up popular support in light of its war losses. The Japanese trained new local elites during 1940-45 that ended up leading the independence movements in their countries after Japan's surrender. The Co-Prosperity Sphere also built large-scale political organizations that generated a much broader political consciousness among local peoples. Perhaps most importantly, the Japanese authorities trained and equipped indigenous armies in several countries, giving postwar nationalist leaders a great head start in resisting the European powers in cases where they tried to reclaim their former colonies. Although it was a diplomatic boomerang and an economic disaster, the Co-Prosperity Sphere had the unintended effect of touching off a firestorm of political change that swept through the region for many years after Japan's defeat.

T. R. H. Havens

GREECE.

When the war broke out, the Greece of **George II** had fallen under the dictatorial rule of Gen. **Ioannis Metaxas**. Although he exhibited a profound admiration for fascism and the states that had adopted it, Metaxas sought to defend the particular interests of his country in his foreign policy, and to maintain friendship with the **United Kingdom**. He thus remained on good terms not only with London, but with Rome and Berlin as well. The events of 1939-40 strengthened the judgment of the Athens government that the **Axis** powers were within easy reach of victory.

Metaxas, however, was unpopular. Like the Yugoslav government, his dictatorship failed to raise the low standard of living of the average Greek. Nor could the latter, deeply mistrustful of the Italo-German alliance, embrace the Metaxas foreign policy.

On October 28, 1940 the Greek government rejected **Mussolini**'s ultimatum. Metaxas was uneasily aware of his subjects' attitude toward the fascist powers and their consequent willingness to defend his regime against military attack. The victory of the Greek forces over Mussolini's invasion troops vindicated his assumption. In fact, the initial Italian advance reversed itself completely, and it was the Greeks who advanced into Albanian territory and swept on to the gates of Valona on January 2, 1941. To *Il Duce*'s chagrin, the German army had to rescue him from the morass he had wandered into. The forces of the Reich struck simultaneously at **Yugoslavia** and Greece. Invading Yugoslavian territory in the south, they caught the brave Greek army in a trap. Thus, the Greek victory turned into defeat; all of Greece, and shortly afterward Crete and the **Dodecanese** Islands as well, fell into the hands of the Axis powers and their allies the Hungarians, Bulgarians and Rumanians (see **Mediterranean and Middle Eastern Theater of Operations**.)

When the country was completely occupied, the king and his government fled to Cairo, leaving their country in confusion. In their haste they left no underground organization to which the people could rally. The British services, however, were farsighted enough to make certain their radio networks remained operative after their departure.

After the Germans established a satellite government in Athens, a number of **Resistance** groups did spring into existence. The most important were the EAM (National Liberation Front), whose military organization was the *Ellinikos Laikos Apelephthericon Stratos*, or ELAS ("Committee of the People's Army"), led by Communist Party stalwarts, and their polar opposites, the **EDES** ("National Democratic Greek Army"), comprised of moderates, republicans and parliamentary royalists under the command of Gen. Napoleon Zervas. Neither group lacked volunteers. Detesting **Forced Labor Battalions** and suffering from undernourishment to the point of famine, the people eagerly enlisted in any cause promising to drive out the occupiers.

In October 1942 the **Special Operations Executive** (SOE) parachuted an important British mission, led by Brig. Gen. E. C. W. Myers and Col. C. M. Woodhouse, into Greece. Another SOE mission descended on Crete. One of the principal aims of this organization, which accomplished its mission under extremely difficult conditions, was to convince these rival groups to train their hatred on the common enemy rather than on each other. This was no easy task; their reconciliation was hindered by the inept efforts of the **government-in-exile** of George II and the support the king was given in London.

Despite the king's interference, however, the Myers team pulled off a brilliant coup. The order came through from the British command at Cairo to blow up one of the major viaducts over the Gorgopotamos river on the railway line between Salonica and Athens, north of Thermopylae, just before **Montgomery**'s attack on **El Alamein** on October 23, 1942. It had been estimated that 80% of the supplies for the Axis troops in Africa traveled that route. The ELAS and EDES sappers worked together in sufficient harmony to do an excellent job.

Unfortunately, Myers' belief that he had secured the mutual friendship of the two factions turned out to be illusory. He was to discover that the ELAS had agreed to work with its rival only to ensure that it would share in the materiel dropped to them by British aircraft. Still, the two Resistance organizations managed to cooperate in another feat at the beginning of the summer of 1943. As part of the scheme of the Anglo-American command to draw the attention of the Germans to the Balkans and away from **Italy** and so to facilitate the Allied landing on Sicily, the two groups, the ELAS and the EDES, launched an all-out **sabotage** attack. They were completely victorious; the simultaneous destruction of several strategic highways and railroads delayed German movements of troops and materiel from Greece to the Italian boot. Order No. 48 to the *Oberkommando der Wehr-*

macht, dated July 26, 1943, reflects **Hitler'**s uneasiness regarding the situation in Greece and an eventual Allied landing in the Balkans.

After the surrender of Italy, the ELAS managed to acquire reinforcements from smaller Resistance groups. With these the group returned to its conflict with the EDES, which held unswervingly to its program of assistance to the British. The SOE halted the supply of arms to ELAS. The effect was an apparent reconciliation between the two organizations on March 10, 1944. Under the direction of Professor Alexander Svolos, all Resistance detachments were placed under the common command of a Provisional Committee for National Liberation, formed in the mountains of Greece. The king now understood the need for granting some concessions. He called into his government, headed by **George Papandreou**, representatives of the entire political spectrum and pledged not to reenter his country until requested to do so by a plebiscite. But the quarrels among the nation's political factions remained unpacified.

On October 3, 1944, a British **task force** commanded by Adm. T. H. Trowbridge landed several small units drawn from the Italian front in Greece, near Patras. It captured that city the following day along with 1,500 prisoners. Corinth was liberated on October 9. The Germans retreated hastily across the channel to the north of the city with the EDES guerrillas close at their heels on land and British planes of Air Vice-Marshal W. Elliott harassing them from the skies. The ELAS commanders, however, made no attempt to cut off the flight of the Germans, especially since the latter bribed the Greek Communists with arms.

On October 12 the Second British Parachute Brigade descended on the Athens airport, and soon thereafter, on November 11, all of Greece was liberated. But the political situation suddenly took a turn for the worse. The British and Greek authorities joined in demanding the demobilization of the EDES and the ELAS. The first group accepted; the second not only refused but turned the arms they had secured from the Germans on the British as well as on the Greek troops that had accompanied the original landing party. The ELAS rebels actually captured a large part of Athens and Piraeus before two British divisions taken from the Italian front arrived to quell the flare-up.

It is interesting to review the fundamental difference between the forms taken by the Yugoslav and Greek Resistance groups. In both countries Communist and non-Communist movements coexisted, and in both countries the British government simultaneously maintained relations with the royal government-in-exile and the movements hostile to it. But in Yugoslavia it was the Communists whose hatred of the Axis was unrelenting and it was the non-Communists whose amity the Axis could always purchase. In Greece exactly the reverse occurred: the Communists aided the Germans by forcing the withdrawal of British troops from the Italian front after the British had liberated their country.

Churchill arrived in Athens on Christmas Day in 1944. On January 11, 1945 the Communists were forced to accept a truce; only a few isolated holdouts remained, entrenched in the mountains. All of Greece was now truly free. After the brief regency of Monsignor Damaskinos, George II was restored to his throne by the plebiscite of September 1, 1946. He was much luckier than other Balkan monarchs.

H. Bernard

GREENLAND.
See **Denmark**.

GRU.
Central intelligence department of the Soviet army (see *Narodnyy Kommissariat Vnutrennikh Del*.).

GUADALCANAL.
The air and sea battles of **Midway** and the **Coral Sea** shook the foundations of the Japanese power structure. But even though the Japanese forces' freedom of movement was gradually constricted, their situation was in no way comparable to that of the Allies several months before. The forces of the latter had a much more difficult task ahead than the Japanese in December 1941. The distance from San Francisco to **Australia** was far greater than the distance between Tokyo and the prizes it reached for. Moreover, the Japanese ran little risk of confronting unforeseen obstacles as they advanced; indeed, they loaded their conquered territories with sufficient troops and provisions to withstand long sieges.

The Allied command had decided to make its initial move earlier, but the accumulation of materiel for Australia, Midway and Hawaii along such remotely spread stepping-stones was first priority. In amphibious operations, allowance had to be made for six tons of materiel for each man at the beginning, plus another ton each month per man. Multiplying these figures by the number of combatants and considering the distances between the continental **United States** and the battlefields yield a bare indication of the magnitude of the logistical problem involved.

In the months preceding the great offensives aimed at the heart of **Japan**, the primary objective was to clear the approaches to Australia. The first large-scale operation was the capture of Guadalcanal, the base from which Japanese long-range aircraft were within

range of New Caledonia. Japan still had hopes of isolating the Australian continent. Not only did it possess more aircraft carriers than the United States, all the islands to the northwest of Guadalcanal were at its disposal, together with their bases and air strips.

Before an attack could be launched against the "Canal," American Seabee crews had to build air bases at Espiritu Santo and in New Caledonia. D-Day for the American operation to subdue Guadalcanal and Tulagi was set for August 7, 1942. Initially, Allied strength in the Central Pacific included three American aircraft carriers as well as 14 cruisers and 30 destroyers flying the American and Australian flags. They were reinforced by the 35,000-ton battleship *North Carolina*, the first American ship of its class to reappear after **Pearl Harbor**. The assault force consisted of 11,000 men of the U.S. First Marine Division commanded by Gen. Alexander A. Vandergrift. The Japanese 11th Air Fleet waited at Rabaul for the order to take off while two battleships of 32,720 tons each, two lighter battleships of 30,000 tons, four aircraft carriers and a miscellaneous array of cruisers and torpedo boats lay ready for action in the Solomon Islands.

Both the American and Japanese battleships were formidably armed. The most powerful of their guns were eight or nine 406-mm rifles firing shells weighing some 2,640 pounds over a range of 22 miles and 148 antiaircraft guns, including 127-mm semiautomatics and 20- and 40-mm automatics capable of hurling five tons of shells in 15 seconds.

After bombardments by Allied air and naval units, the assault troops, covered by a small advance force, landed on Guadalcanal before dawn on August 7, 1942, while the bulk of the fleet remained behind to protect their rear against attack from the enemy navy. Tulagi, the site of a Japanese seaplane base, was occupied the following day, along with the airport on Guadalcanal, which the Marines took with little effort. They renamed it Henderson Field, in honor of Maj. Lofton R. Henderson who, in the defense of Midway, had sacrificed his life by deliberately smashing up his plane on an enemy aircraft carrier. At once the Marines established an "all-around defense" of the territory they had seized. With the restoration of the airfield, the first phase of the operation was complete. The Japanese reaction was not long in coming. For three months, beginning on August 8, a series of air and naval engagements raged: the battle of Savo Island on August 8-9; the battle of Stewart Islands on August 24-25, in which the American victory was secured by aircraft from the carriers *Enterprise* and *Saratoga*, reinforced by other planes from Henderson Field; and the battle of the Santa Cruz Islands on October 26. They were all indecisive ac-

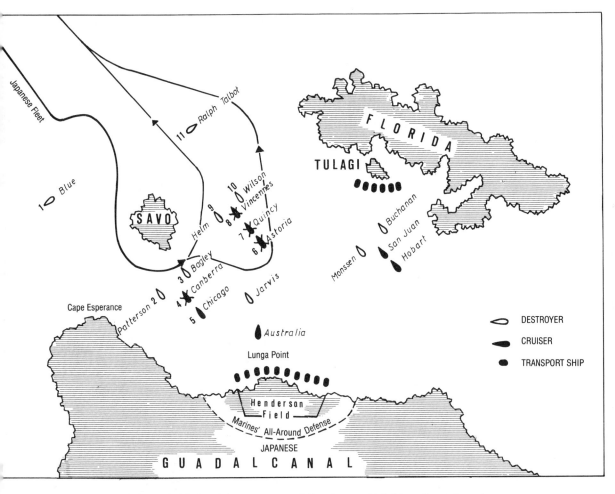

On August 7, 1942 the U.S. Marine infantry captured Henderson Airfield on Guadalcanal.
During the night of August 8-9, 11 cruisers and destroyers (numbered 1 through 11 on the map) protected the American transport flotilla while the aircraft carriers refueled. The Japanese squadron appeared; the American operators, placed on radar alert, had trouble with their new detection equipment, which was defective. The Japanese entered the channel between Savo and Guadalcanal and sank the Allied ships *Canberra, Astoria, Quincy* and *Vincennes*. To the vast astonishment of the Allied sailors, the Japanese squadron then departed to the north without attacking the unprotected American transports. The entire engagement lasted less than 30 minutes.

tions, the results of more or less accidental encounters, with mistakes on both sides. More than once the Japanese, either through strategic reluctance to commit more than a small portion of their power or through faulty intelligence, failed to exploit an initial success. The prize for the winner of this vast struggle was of major importance; each of the adversaries sought to reinforce its troops on Guadalcanal. They found themselves in a stalemate. The Japanese maintained their naval superiority in the Solomon Islands; the Americans tried without success to land reinforcements for the Marines hanging desperately onto Henderson Field. On the other hand, the superiority of American air power interfered seriously with Japanese supply lines to the island. Nevertheless, the Japanese, working at night, succeeded in landing some 900 men from small speedboats every 24 hours. Losses were heavy on both sides. The American air-

GUADALCANAL

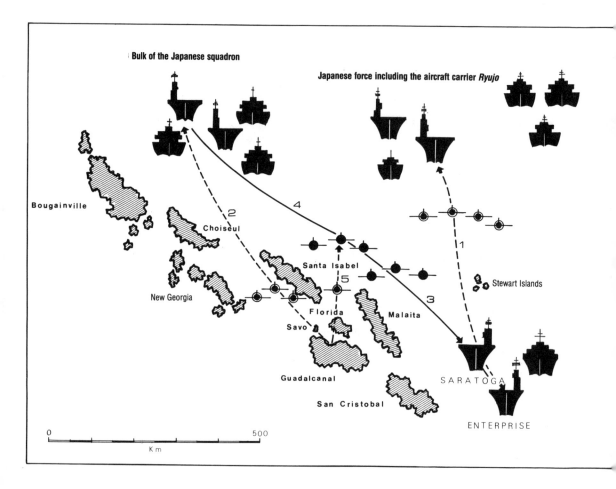

Japanese

Battleships *Nagato* and *Mutsu* (32,720 tons; 8 guns of 406 mm); battleships *Ise* and *Hyuga* (30,000 tons; 12 guns of 356 mm)

Four aircraft carriers

Numerous cruisers, destroyers and troop ships

The Japanese fleet was divided into three distinct, separate groups

Allies

Battleship *North Carolina* (35,000 tons; 9 guns of 406 mm)

Two aircraft carriers, *Saratoga* and *Enterprise*

Four cruisers and 11 destroyers

The two American task forces were fairly close together

Aircraft from the *Saratoga* and the *Enterprise* (1) destroyed the aircraft carrier *Ryujo*.
Aircraft from Henderson Field (2) heavily damaged the *Nagato*.
Two groups of 18 Japanese bombers (3), escorted by fighter planes, together with a third group of aircraft carrying torpedoes (4), attacked the *Enterprise*. The first two groups damaged the ship; the third was intercepted by American fighter planes (5) and suffered heavy losses.
Although still superior in numbers, the Japanese fleet withdrew, having lost an aircraft carrier, a destroyer, several smaller ships and 96 aircraft. Numerous ships were damaged.
The American victory was won by the aircraft from the carriers and from Henderson Field. The battleships on both sides took little part in the action.

craft carriers *Wasp* and *Hornet* were lost; they were replaced by the battleships *Washington* and *South Dakota*. Both sides acquired reinforcements.

The battle entered its decisive phase from November 12 to 15. Once again the Japanese approached the blood-soaked island. Adm. **William F.** ("Bull") **Halsey**, commander of the South Pacific naval forces, dispatched an advance **task force** of smaller vessels into the waters north of Guadalcanal to carry the battle to the enemy while the major portion of the fleet waited for the auspicious moment to deliver the finishing blow. The plan succeeded brilliantly (see also **Radar**).

The Japanese losses in ships and planes—400 of the aircraft from Rabaul were destroyed in seven weeks—were disheartening. Land forces under the command of Gen. **Alexander M. Patch** soon relieved Vandergrift's marines on Guadalcanal. It was now the turn of the Japanese troops to hang on desperately to their part of the island until being completely eliminated in the first days of February 1943.

On the world scene the battles of El Alamein, Stalingrad and Guadalcanal were all fought in that same month of November 1942. In three different theaters, scattered widely over the globe, these battles marking the turn of the tide irrevocably in favor of the Allies all occurred in one brief period.

H. Bernard

GUAM.

The most populous (60,000) and largest (212 square miles) of the Mariana Islands. A possession of the **United States**, Guam was captured by the Japanese on December 10, 1941, when the small and lightly armed U.S. garrison of less than 500 Marines and sailors and some native constabulary men were overwhelmed in a twinkling by the 5,000 Japanese troops who swarmed ashore with the Guam invasion force of the South Seas detachment. There had been Japanese air raids from **Saipan**, only 100 miles north, but naval bombardment, readily available and fully deployed, proved unnecessary. During the brief scuffle the Americans lost 17 men, the Japanese 10.

Not until the summer of 1944 did the Americans return to Guam. The recapture was coded as Operation Forager. Rear Adm. Richard L. Conolly was in overall command of the Southern Attack Force (TF 53); Rear Adm. V. H. Ragsdale commanded the Carrier Support Force. Delayed over a month by the fierce Japanese resistance on Saipan and by the presumable need to obtain greater infantry assault strength, USMC Maj. Gen. Roy S. Geiger finally landed his Third Amphibious Corps on Guam, at each side of Apra harbor, the main objective on the

west coast of the island, on July 21, shortly before the U.S. invasion of Tinian. The American spearhead forces consisted of the Third Marine Division, commanded by Maj. Gen. Allen H. Turnage, and the First Provisional Marine Brigade, commanded by Brig. Gen. Lemuel C. Shepherd, plus the Army's capable 77th Infantry Division, commanded by Maj. Gen. Andrew D. Bruce, from general reserve.

Defending the island, Lt. Gen. Hideyoshi Obata, the 31st Army Commander, unable to get back to Saipan, was supervising the construction of fixed positions. The Southern Marianas district group numbered about 19,000 men; its nucleus was Lt. Gen. Hyo Takashina's 29th Division and Maj. Gen. Kiyoshi Shigematsu's 48th Independent Mixed Brigade/Sixth Expeditionary Force.

The Americans' preliminary air and naval softening-up campaign, which lasted two weeks, was the longest and most sustained to date—28,764 rounds (from 5" to 16") were fired by warships alone. Nevertheless, Japanese underwater obstructions were remarkable. Underwater Demolition Teams (UDT's) destroyed 940 separate cribs and cubes. Still, the garrison managed to retain a formidable defensive capability, especially pronounced on the southern beaches (Agat Bay) dominated by cliff positions, where Rear Adm. L. F. Reifsnider commanded the assault sector. Once ashore, the Americans repulsed powerful Japanese counterattacks against the northern sector (Asan) on July 22 and 25. The latter action proved decisive, with the Japanese losing 3,500 dead. Driven back to the rugged northern portion of Guam, the Japanese fought on in organized fashion well into August. The unlucky Obata was killed at his last command post on August 12, two days after the island had prematurely been declared secure.

Sporadic resistance continued till the end of the war—and for years beyond. Indeed, only about 11,000 Japanese were accounted for by September 1; another 8,500 after that date. A Japanese army lieutenant colonel and 11 men surrendered on September 4, 1945. Others gave up or were killed individually, and hundreds probably died in the brush from hunger, wounds or disease. In addition to Obata (promoted to full general posthumously), Shigematsu and Takashina had fallen during the fighting, the latter by July 28. U.S. casualties in Guam amounted to 1,290 killed, 5,648 wounded and 145 missing—a total of 7,083 out of 54,891 engaged.

Japanese sources state that although the garrison tried to hold out in cave positions, the lack of antitank weapons proved fatal. While the Americans possessed considerable numbers of land-based artillery and air-spotted naval gunfire support, the Japanese on Guam were devoid of air and naval power when the final invasion came.

A. D. Coox

GUBBINS, Sir Colin McVean (1896-1976).

Serving in Russia and **Ireland** after World War I, Gubbins, an artillery officer, learned the value of guerrilla warfare. At the outbreak of the war, he fought in **Poland** in 1939 and **Norway** in 1940. He joined the **Special Operations Executive** in November 1940 as its director of operations. In September 1943 he became the organization's executive head. Throughout the war his courage, ingenuity and tenacity combined to stimulate **resistance** all over the world.

GUDERIAN, Heinz (1888-1954).

Creator of the German armored force (*Panzerwaffe*), Guderian commanded armored units in the invasions of **Poland**, **Belgium** and France and the **USSR**. He was relieved of his duties by **Hitler** in December 1941. He became inspector general of the armored troops in February 1943 and on July 21, 1944 was appointed head of the general staff of land armies. On March 28, 1945 Hitler once again relieved him of his functions.

GUERISSE, Albert-Marie (1911-).

Left behind by accident on a **Special Operations Executive** coastal operation near Perpignan in April 1941, Guerisse set up a highly efficient escape line from **Belgium** and France into **Spain**. Known as the Pat O'Leary, it passed over 600 people, including many downed airmen, before German double agents broke it up. Guerisse was able to survive imprisonment in **concentration camps**.

GUILLAUME, Augustin (1895-).

A French general, Guillaume commanded a force of North African troops. He entered Alsace at the head of his unit in 1944 and captured Stuttgart in 1945.

GUISAN, Henri (1874-1960).

In August 1939, Guisan, a Swiss general, was appointed head of **Switzerland**'s armed forces for the duration of the war by the Swiss Federation Council.

GUTT, Camille (1884-1972).

Belgian jurist, financier and statesman. A volunteer in World War I, Gutt became delegate to the Reparation Conferences of 1918-1926. In 1935 he was appointed minister of finance and in 1938 to the office of minister of finance and national defense in **Hubert Pierlot**'s **government-in-exile** in England, where he arrived in August 1940. A promoter of the Benelux union of **Belgium, the Netherlands** and **Luxembourg**, he wrote the monetary health laws in September 1944.

H

HAAKON VII (1872-1957).

An uncle of **George VI** of England, King Haakon of Norway fled to Britain in June 1940 following the invasion of his country by the Germans. During the war he encouraged Norwegian **resistance** and remained highly popular with his people.

HACHA, Emil (1872-1945).

When **Eduard Benes** went into exile in 1938 following the **Munich Pact**, Hacha succeeded him as president of the republic of **Czechoslovakia**. Hacha was summoned by **Hitler** to Berchtesgaden on March 14, 1939 and intimidated into allowing German troops to enter his country. He was appointed president of the Protectorate of **Bohemia-Moravia** on March 15, 1939. After the defeat of the **Axis**, he died in prison in Prague.

HAILE SELASSIE (1892-1975).

In 1930 Haile Selassie was crowned emperor of **Ethiopia**. When Italian troops invaded Ethiopia in 1935-36, he personally led the nation's forces against the enemy. He fled to England in 1936 and returned to Ethiopia five years later to regain his throne. Although he introduced certain political and social reforms, including the abolition of slavery in 1942, he was overthrown in a coup d'etat in 1974.

HALDER, Franz (1884-1972).

A German general, Halder succeeded Gen. **Ludwig Beck** as head of the general staff of the land armies shortly after the **Munich Pact** (1938). An enemy of **Hitler**'s policy of aggression, he plotted to unseat the Fuehrer when **Chamberlain** announced his visit to Berlin. He was directly responsible for the success of the *Wehrmacht* in 1939-1941. Deprived of his command in September 1942, he was arrested after the **assassination attempt of July 20, 1944** on Hitler's life, but he was liberated by the Americans in April 1945. In 1949 his book *Hitler als Feldherr* ("Hitler as Field Commander") was published in Munich.

HALIFAX, Lord (earlier Edward F. L. Wood) (1881-1959).

In March 1938 Halifax succeeded Sir **Anthony Eden** as British foreign secretary. He supported **Chamberlain**'s policy of **appeasement** and played a large role in negotiating the **Munich Pact** in 1938. From 1940 to 1945 he served as Britain's ambassador to the **United States**.

HALSEY, William Frederick, Jr. (1882-1959).

Halsey, an American admiral, led spectacular early raids against the Marshall Islands and the **Gilbert Islands** in February 1942 and commanded the **task force** supporting **James H. Doolittle**'s raid on **Japan** from the USS *Hornet* in April 1942. Halsey commanded the Allied South Pacific forces from October 1942 to June 1944, including the Solomons campaign. As Third Fleet commander in 1944-45 he fought from the Carolines to the **Philippines** and, by the summer of 1945, prowled Japan's own waters, hammering the country by sea and air until the war's end. Halsey participated in the V-J ceremonies of Japanese capitulation aboard the USS *Missouri* in September 1945. Halsey was promoted to the U.S. Navy's highest rank, admiral of the fleet, in 1945, after the war; he retired in 1947 for reasons of health.

During his Third Fleet command Halsey was central to three very controversial episodes: the **Leyte Gulf** naval battle in October 1944, when Adm. Jisaburo Ozawa's carrier decoy force, as the Japanese intended, enticed Task Force 38 away from vital U.S. amphibious operations; and Halsey's inept response to two fierce typhoons, in December 1944 and June 1945, which battered U.S. naval forces. Nevertheless, his reputation and fame have survived transient reversals. A tough, charismatic and scrappy sailor, "Bull" to the press and "Bill" to associates, Halsey was exactly what the U.S. Navy and the wartime American public craved, especially at the lowest points of the Pacific campaign. He has been aptly called "one of the most famous sea fighters of this or any war."

A. D. Coox

HAMBRO, Sir Charles (1897-1963).

In 1942-43 Hambro served as executive head of the **Special Operations Executive**. As chief of the British raw materials mission in the **United States**, he arranged for the exchange of information on the making of the **atomic bomb**.

HANKEY, Sir Maurice (1877-1963).

From 1912 to 1938 Hankey served as secretary of the Committee of Imperial Defense. In 1939-40 he was British war cabinet minister without portfolio.

HARDING, Sir John (later Lord) (1896-   ).

A British general, Harding served as chief of staff to Gen. **Harold Alexander** from 1943 to 1945.

HARRIMAN, (William) Averell (1891-   ).

In 1941 Harriman went to London as **Roosevelt's** special envoy to arrange the **lend-lease** program with the British. He accompanied Lord **Beaverbrook** to Moscow to discuss military aid for the Russians. He served as ambassador to the **USSR** from 1943 to 1946 and attended all the allied conferences (see **Conferences, Allied**). As ambassador he gained the respect of **Stalin**, but toward the end of the war he advised Roosevelt and later **Truman** to stand firm against Soviet domination of eastern Europe. Harriman advocated the use of economic sanctions, such as cutbacks in aid, as a means of restraining the Russians.

HARRIS, Sir Arthur T. (1892-   ).

In 1941 Harris, a British airman, became deputy chief of air staff. As commander in chief of the **Bomber Command** from 1942 to 1945, he directed the RAF air offensive that—at a cost of over 50,000 airmen's lives—helped to bring **Germany** down. His advocacy of strategic area bombing, as demonstrated in the large-scale raids on the Ruhr, Hamburg and Berlin, conflicted with the thinking of the U.S. strategic air command, which preferred attacks on specific targets considered vital to Germany's industry (see **Germany, Air Battle of**).

HEALTH.

All through World War II the poor sanitation conditions that had prevailed in earlier conflicts and often decisively influenced their outcome were completely inverted. The advances made by medical techniques during the period between the two world wars improved the medical services of the various belligerents to an extent never before achieved. Questions of military hygiene had long been discussed by members of the International Society of Military Medicine, to which all the Western nations belonged. (The organization's last meeting prior to the war was held in Washington in 1939.) There is therefore little reason to draw distinctions among the medical services that were available to each army; it is more enlightening to analyze the basic problems whose solutions depended primarily on the practical, technical, human and material resources of each of the belligerents.

In the course of a war, especially a modern one, the basic function of the medical services is to limit the losses of lives and to permit the ill and wounded to return to the firing lines as soon as possible, in the best physical and psychological condition. Hence the two aspects of medical activity: medical care for the troops and the evacuation and treatment of the wounded. Despite the advances made in the means of destruction, the significant new role of aircraft, the diverse geographic and climatic extremes of the fronts and their constantly changing locations, the medical services were able to confront each new health problem and profit from each local experience. Nor is this the least of the paradoxes posed by the war. Despite the horrible death toll of more than 50 million human beings and the incredible atrocities of the **Axis** forces, World War II provided clinicians and researchers with expectional tools for solving diagnostic, prophylactic and sickbed problems. Never in any previous war had there been such astonishing progress in the development and application of therapeutic methods, nor had each nation's scientific services cooperated so smoothly. As a result, by 1945 medicine, especially surgery, was in a position to benefit enormously from the experience gained during the war and to offer humanity the hope of increased longevity.

Hygiene and Preventive Medicine

As the military machine increased in complexity and the front grew more mobile and scattered, the greater the need for economy in the use of human resources became. Moreover, preventive measures against illness applied at its source were given absolute priority; they were more strictly observed by the *Wehrmacht* but more efficiently executed by the better-equipped Allies. These hygienic procedures— global in extent since they dealt with sterilization of water and food, sanitary kitchen facilities, the generally excellent quality of clothes and boots, parasite control, isolation of contagions and the like—transformed the conditions of the war.

Food

A soldier's daily calorie requirement is much higher than a civilian's. With war conditions redistributing food supplies and limiting exports and imports, however, specific quantitative and qualitative requirements could not be maintained. The need then arose to solve dietary problems in new ways by using substitutes. Carbohydrates can satisfy basic calorie requirements and, in a lengthy war, such demands must constantly be satisfied. Thus the **United Kingdom** increased its arable land by 50%, the **United States** in 1941 maintained a two-year reserve in its granaries, **Germany** pillaged occupied Europe—especially since it had seven million **prisoners of war** and forced laborers to feed—while **Japan** seized lands rich in rice. Fats furnish the highest percentage of potential energy and contain vitamins A, D, E and K. They were more important to the Western nations, which ordinarily used a 30% fat diet. The Germans had the foresight, before the war, to accumulate an ample reserve of fats and oils. At the end of three years of strife, however, the situation changed, and rations in occupied Europe were reduced by 30% to 40%. Japan, on the other hand, acquired an enormous surplus of animal fats and vegetables that formerly had been consumed in the United States and Great Britain. For the two latter nations therefore, there were seven to nine percent fewer such foods. Still, the United States could send the **USSR** five to seven million pounds of fats annually. Proteins are especially rare in wartime, since supplies of meat and fish are made more difficult to obtain. It was thus necessary to use various vegetable proteins to make up for the deficiency, and also to avoid slaughtering cattle, since milk production was essential. Finally, vitamins were of fundamental importance, especially natural vitamin C. Germany developed the production of synthetic ascorbic acid, transporting supplies of it by air to the eastern front, while the Allies stepped up the hunt for whales, a prime source of vitamin D, and the Soviets ingeniously extracted vitamin C from pine needles for delivery to the Red Army.

These requirements of the belligerent armies, which were regarded as priorities, forced rationing on the civilian population, on the basis of 3,000 calories daily. In the occupied territories, on the other hand, German looting of the countries' natural resources had many, often paradoxical, consequences. To this must be added the economic ravages caused by the **black market**, often with the tacit connivance of the occupying authorities, which provided an affluent few with even greater wealth while the rest of the population, particularly the city dwellers, were undernourished or close to starvation. Resistance to disease consequently diminished and the mortality rate among infants rose—to as much as 75% in **Poland**, for example. The youth of occupied Poland grew up with malnutrition and suffered the inevitable long-term results. The nations hardest hit were Poland, **Greece, Yugoslavia** and **the Netherlands**—the last in particular, where 15,000 died of starvation in the winter of 1944. Yet this redistribution of resources had its

beneficial aspects. Alcoholism, at the head of the list of typically French ailments, dropped to a spectacular low; the rate of death from cirrhosis of the liver practically vanished. The same was true of mental disturbances, the usual result of excessive drinking, thus increasing the available bed space in psychiatric hospitals and permitting their use as safe refuges for hunted **Resistance** fighters.

Prevention of epidemics and infectious diseases
One of the greatest risks to an army is the epidemic, more frequent in wartime because of overcrowding in confined places, poorer sanitation conditions and unfavorable climate.

Exanthematous typhus
This was the most serious epidemic problem of World War II, with more than two million victims. The disease was especially endemic in eastern Europe, where much of the fighting took place. In December 1939 and January 1940, 4,000 cases were reported in the Warsaw district of Poland. The problem later became more acute in cities, where the civilian population could get only 600 calories per day and hygienic conditions were in general deplorable. The typhus epidemic in Warsaw was the pretext for isolating the ghetto, the Germans doing everything possible to prevent the effective treatment of the ill. In 1941, 15,449 died of the disease in the ghetto. Infected individuals were hospitalized, and the hospitals became veritable mortuaries. After the invasion of the USSR, the German armies were struck by typhus, with 10,000 cases in the early part of 1942. Until the winter of 1944-45 the epidemic partially abated; it then broke out once more, with 80,000 to 90,000 cases and a mortality rate of 25%. The disease was practically unknown in Germany, but after 1941 it reached the civilian population and was especially rampant in the **concentration camps**, ending in the gas chambers of Auschwitz and Maidanek. At **Bergen-Belsen**, in 1945, more than 80% of the prisoners were infected, with 60,000 deaths.

For the Germans, typhus was a serious problem since, for one thing, the lice carrying the disease could not effectively be controlled at the front and in the occupied territories of the east; for another, Germany's stock of vaccines was low. The only effective deterrent, the Weigl vaccine, was very expensive, and the other products available afforded insufficient protection. This was the disturbing situation that prompted specialists, meeting at Berlin on December 29, 1941, to begin the criminal "experiments" at Buchenwald and Struthof.

The Allies applied rigorous preventive measures to their troops. Although typhus was endemic in the

USSR, Soviet troops were spared; the only danger of contagion came from the German army after the liberation of the occupied countries. British troops were several times threatened with epidemics, but managed to keep them within bounds. **Iran** experienced contagion in 1942-1943, **Egypt** in 1943, North Africa and Naples, Italy in 1943 and Germany at the time of the liberation. The American army used three million ampoules of Cox vaccine to protect its troops. The battle against lice was aided by dusting DDT into clothes and by the mass production of vaccines, proof that an army can live and work in the midst of typhus with only a few, curable cases.

Malaria

For the Allies this disease presented the greatest problem. Almost one-third of the world's population is infected but has acquired relative immunity. When troops were stationed in or moved into an endemic zone with high probability of bites from anopheles mosquitoes and no chance of eliminating the insects with DDT or similar preparations, they were not only bound to be infected but were also prey to serious variants of the disease. No vaccine against malaria exists. The only remedy is continual dosage of suppressive drugs, the protection against the disease ceasing when the treatment is suspended. A blow to the Allies was the loss of Java to the Japanese in 1942, for 90% of the world's quinine, a malaria specific, comes from that region. In compensation, the production of synthetic substitutes such as mepacrine or atabrine was accelerated. Their widespread and systematic use won the battle against malaria. Serious forms of the disease, such as the malignant tertian, became scarce and the mortality rate dropped to practically nothing. Even the convalescent period was reduced. In the Pacific, malaria was responsible for more than half the disease casualties, daily immobilizing about 0.3% of the soldiers. In the U.S. Seventh Army, operating in North Africa and Sicily, there were as many cases of the disease in July and August 1943 as there were wounded. Nevertheless, considering the number and importance of the troops transported into the endemic zone, it can be asserted that the most resounding victory over disease won by the Allies—after the discovery of penicillin, which had to come first—was the control of malaria.

Epidemic hepatitis

One of the most wicked diseases of the war, striking its victims everywhere regardless of climate, was epidemic hepatitis. Its mortality rate was only 0.2%, but it put its victims out of action for at least two months. Epidemic hepatitis was the most mysterious and the most widespread disease of the war. Its viral etiology

was—and remains—unknown. The illness arises in the digestive tract, usually through drinking water; often it is transmitted by an infected hypodermic needle or in a blood or plasma transfusion. In Germany, between one and two million people came down with the disease in the east after 1941; during the winter of 1941-1942, 60% of some German units were stricken, and in September 1943 there were 180,000 cases. Among the British, especially on the Mediterranean fronts, hepatitis cases were reported, in the Middle East at the end of 1942 and again at the end of 1943, and in the central Mediterranean at the end of 1943 and the end of 1944. For American troops the epidemic began in North Africa, with 30,000 cases in July 1943, later continuing on into **Italy**. In all, more than 250,000 American soliders fell victim to it.

Other illness

On all other epidemiological fronts, the victory was complete. For certain contagious diseases like smallpox, vaccination was obligatory in all armies, although not all the troops could be inoculated against diptheria and typhoid. Preventive vaccination against tetanus, however, was obligatory for Allied troops, while the Germans used only serotherapy for infected wounds. Smallpox, bubonic plague, tetanus and cholera—except possibly for the Japanese—were not military problems. The parasitic diseases, such as yellow fever, leishmaniasis, kala-azar, rickettsiosis, Q fever, leptospirosis, bacterial dysentery and trypanosomiasis, were only sporadically observed. Bacillary and amebic dysentry, however, continued to pose serious problems in the Middle East and in the Pacific, particularly for the Japanese. Among the contagious diseases—a civilian rather than a military health problem—pneumonia and cerebro-spinal meningitis were the most serious. In England, pneumonia deaths amounted to 20,000 to 25,000 annually, particularly in 1940-1941; in January 1940 the British had to cope with a meningitis epidemic, and in 1943 there was a similar outbreak in the American army. The use of sulfa drugs, however, lowered the death rate to five percent. Diptheria was kept in check in the United States and **Canada** through routine vaccination; vaccine was provided in England only during an epidemic. There were 29,000 cases in Great Britain in 1942 and 22,300 in 1943, with a five percent death rate; there were also numerous causes in 1944 among the army of occupation in Europe. In Germany, cases of diptheria grew six-fold from 1931 to 1941, with 175,000 in 1940 and 204,000 in 1941. Epidemics in the Netherlands and **Norway** struck more than 0.5 percent of the population in 1943. The same was true of scarlet fever, measles and whooping cough, which spread more rapidly among the less resistant civilian population. Tuberculosis was not as effectively fought; there were 105,000 cases in Germany in 1940 and 135,000 in 1941, while some 30,000 deaths from this ailment were counted in Great Britain.

For all these diseases the groundwork for modern means of prevention and treatment was laid. Research in vaccines and antibiotics accelerated, and radiological or bacteriological means of halting the progress of diseases were systematically undertaken. Progress was difficult and the means still insufficient, but the medical battlefield narrowed as the war years went by. Research into the causes of death among the civilian population of Great Britain from 1939 to 1945 showed that not only were deaths unconnected with military operations at a low rate—less than 10% in 1940-1941—but that the major causes of death were the same as today. Cardiovascular diseases caused 30-33% of all deaths unrelated to the war, and cancer, 13-15%.

Heat-induced ailments
In tropical and desert climates, troops had to compensate for their high excretion of water and salt to avoid the pathological effects of thermal imbalance—sunstroke, heat cramps, exhaustion and the like. Recruits selected for these assignments were progressively acclimated to heat, given a protein-rich diet, and forbidden the use of alcohol. Among British troops in 1942 and 1943, 17.5% were struck down by heat with a two percent mortality rate.

Two other medical problems
Apart from skin diseases, dental troubles, ear-nose-and-throat conditions and digestive upsets—in particular, the frequent gastro-duodenal ulcers—there were two disorders military medicine had to contend with frequently—venereal diseases and psychiatric disturbances. Although German and Soviet literature on the subject stressed only the "high morals" of their soldiers, the British and Americans openly discussed these serious problems.

Especially in the **Mediterranean and Middle Eastern theater of operations**, venereal diseases were the second or third most serious health problem. In the British army there were 250,000 cases, 180,000 of gonorrhea and 70,000 of syphilis. In the Middle East as in Italy, almost all prostitutes were carriers of venereal disease, but in Italy, controlling venereal disease was particularly difficult, primarily because prostitution in that country was hidden. Among American soliders in the Mediterranean, the figures for infection increased from four percent in December 1942 to eight percent in December 1943. Therapeutic measures were consequently intensified; first the sulfa drugs, then, in 1914, penicillin were called upon to halt the spread of

these diseases, which handicapped and rendered inactive a half-million men for two to three weeks.

Psychiatric disturbances mounted to such proportions that psychiatrists were quickly impressed into the American and British armies for service at the front. Seventy percent of the discharges given soldiers after their enlistment were due to psychiatric troubles. Of 10 million men examined in the United States, 700,000 were rejected for mental problems; on the battlefield, 30 percent of the men experienced psychological disorders. A distinction, however, must be made between neuroses or psychoses that overtake normal men under war conditions on the one hand and minor emotional disturbances that can be rapidly and efficiently cared for on the other. Psychiatrists found that in distant theaters of operation—the Middle or Far East, for example—a prolonged period of duty can aggravate a mental abnormality. They consequently recommended rotating troops at least every two years. It was also found that 25% of the American soldiers returning to the States from the Middle East suffered from mental disorders.

Surgery in the War
Advances in antibiotics, transfusions and resuscitation were given ample opportunity to prove their value in the war. These methods of restoring health to soldiers were unprecedented in medical history.

Evacuation of the wounded
All wartime surgical services are founded on this axiom: None of the wounded should be sent further than their physical conditions and the military situation warrant. To apply this policy in a war distinguished by the extraordinary lengths of its lines of communication and the fluidity of its fronts, well-adapted and sufficiently advanced bases had to be set up. The evacuation chain was comprised of a series of successive stages providing for the transportation and hospitalization of the wounded. As a general rule, it took about 10 to 30 minutes to get to the wounded man. "Medics" and stretcher-bearers with first-aid devices gave him plasma and attached a tag to his clothing indicating the seriousness of his condition, at the same time bringing him up to the battalion medical center less than a mile from the front. About an hour after he sustained his injury, the wounded man was examined by a surgeon who gave him "first echelon" treatment—immobilization of the wounded member, an analgesic, blood or plasma, antiseptics and an anti-tetanus or anti-gangrenous serum. He was then transferred to the division medical center, about three to seven miles to the rear, which was usually a tent equipped as a small field hospital, with an electric generator, two surgeons, an anesthetist and a nurse.

This stage was actually a selection center in which those with light wounds requiring 10 days or less of care remained before returning to the front. Those who were more seriously injured, and unable to endure further transfer, were operated on and then sent to the rear one or two weeks later. Those seriously wounded but able to be moved were taken to the army surgical center or general hospital, with 1,000 to 2,000 beds, attended by a large group of specialist surgeons. Depending on the mobility of the front and its distance from the general hospital, these wounded were transported by ambulance, train or aircraft. Convalescents were then taken to readjustment centers in which between 60 percent and 70 percent of the wounded recovered sufficiently to return to active service. This evacuation chain operated in about the same way in the Allied and German armies, except that the Germans—like the Russians—had an additional echelon between the division center and the general hospital. The basic scheme centered around the field surgical hospital later used by the American army in Korea, where it became known as MASH, the acronym for mobile army surgical hospital; its purpose was to shorten the evacuation lines.

Treatment of the wounded
Antibiotics
The first stage of the surgical revolution was antibiotic treatment. In 1932 Gerhard Domagk synthesized prontosil, the first of the sulfa drugs. The family of sulfa drugs rapidly blossomed; by 1945, 5,485 different compounds had been synthesized and tested in the United States and in Great Britain. Few of them had as yet been used in the treatment of human beings. Germany was somewhat behind the Allies in the development of sulfa drugs and depended particularly on marfanil and prontalbin as well as the sulfa drugs developed by the Swiss. But penicillin remained neglected by the Germans. This gap in the Nazis' therapeutic arsenal cost them thousands of human lives; penicillin, discovered serendipitously in 1929 by the British bacteriologist **Alexander Fleming**, had by 1940 been refined to the point where it could be used as a therapeutic agent. Arduous research in the United States and Great Britain resulted in the commercial production of purified penicillin in 1943. At first an ethical problem presented itself. The same amount of the antibiotic could cure one case of staphylococcal septicemia, 20 of gonorrhea or 400 infections of the hand. Which to treat first? Priority was finally given to fliers and war-industry labor. Beginning in 1943, during the North African campaign, penicillin came to be used widely; by June 1944 American production of the substance was practically unlimited, permitting

the treatment not only of sick and wounded Allied soldiers but also civilians and enemy prisoners.

Traumatic shock
This was the main concern of medical men in most countries. Apart from shock resulting purely from hemorrhage, traumatic shock is a complex phenomenon. It appears after several hours in patients suffering from fairly extensive wounds from which the loss of blood may be minimal but much muscular damage and multiple fractures have occurred. Such a condition, which can be fatal if allowed to continue, can be halted by controlling the loss of blood and dehydration through intravenous injection of colloidal substances, plasma or conserved serum and by protecting the patient against cold, pain or fatigue with warmth, analgesics and rest and against anoxia through oxygen therapy.

Blood transfusions
Transfusions were vital to resuscitation. There was never any lack of donors in the Allied armies, but toward the end of the Russian campaign there was not enough blood or plasma to care for the German wounded. Research was begun into means of conserving blood for a month. The first blood bank opened at Naples in July 1944. About 10% of the men wounded in the war required blood transfusions.

Anesthetics
Two general types were introduced in the war. The first was the intravenous type, such as pentothal; the second, the volatile type, particularly cyclopropane. Along with these came the closed circuit of continuous digestive aspiration, and liquid and ionic resuscitation, which transformed military surgery.

Consequences of therapeutic progress
Most wounds could be protected from infection, and gangrene, the terror of wounded soldiers in World War I, was conquerable by World War II. On the Eastern front, on the other hand, in the winter of 1941-42 and after the collapse of the German lines, there were many cases of gangrene in the *Wehrmacht*, with a mortality rate of 50 to 60%, despite local and general use of the sulfa drugs and polyvalent serum supplied by the Behring pharmaceutical plant.

Abdominal and abdominothoracic wounds, considered of primary urgency, benefited from improved conditions of evacuation and the progress made in resuscitation measures. The rates of cure were 40 to 60%, but the mortality rate was higher, at 26 to 84%, for abdominothoracic wounds, depending on the extent of visceral damage.

Victims of thoracic wounds could be operated on as emergency cases or transported to hospital centers. As time passed, the rates of cure increased.

Evacuation of soldiers with fractures was well planned; the wounded member was immobilized in a plaster cast or a splint and the patient sent to a special center. Amputations became much rarer, and were only performed in the event of complete vascular interruption. Vascular surgery, it should be noted, did not progress until later, during the Korean and Vietnamese conflicts.

Treatment of burns, which occurred more and more frequently with the increased use of armored vehicles, improved in local treatment with occlusive bandaging, the use of antibiotics and excision-grafting.

Experience with extreme cold, especially among German troops fighting in summer uniforms on the wintry steppes of the USSR, afforded medicine a better understanding of profound frostbite and its treatment by delayed amputation or sympathetic operation.

For the first time in any war, surgeons in World War II learned to organize and develop the treatment of head wounds. Given priority for evacuation by aircraft, victims were operated on within twenty-four hours. Treatment of paraplegics was radically changed, with increased accent on the prevention of scabbing and infections.

The backwardness of German surgical techniques was demonstrated by their comparative lack of success, attributable to the isolation of German doctors from the scientific world after 1939, their lack of proper equipment and medication, and particularly their inability to cope with the steadily increasing stream of wounded men, owing to their smaller number, the inferior training of surgical teams and the handicap of constant interference of politics in military matters.

Specific Medical Applications

Aeronautic medicine

The primary problem facing air force doctors was the selection of pilots, particularly by weeding out cardiac cases through strict examinations. Air personnel were regularly checked. But the rapid development of aviation and its decisive role in the Allied victory prompted medical researchers to concentrate on a more thorough comprehension of the unusual conditions under which pilots performed and how they reacted to these conditions. Such abnormalities as decompression illnesses, anoxia, the effects of high speeds, accelerations, extreme cold, fatigue and defective night vision were extensively researched. The chief problem was the safety of the pilot at high altitudes—beginning in 1940, combat aircraft flew at altitudes of more than six miles—and the American air force developed the use of oxygen masks for flights at eight miles without

syncope. Careful study was also devoted to the protection of pilots shot down into the sea with clothing enabling them to float vertically for better protection of the nape of the neck, peculiarly sensitive to low temperatures. It was in attempts to solve these problems that, after conferences on high altitudes and acute cold, the *Luftwaffe* doctors undertook their criminal experiments on the inmates of the Dachau concentration camp.

Naval medicine

Progress in this area was marked by designing naval hospitals to permit on-the-spot operations by surgical teams on arm and leg wounds, fractures and burns and to provide better conditions for saving crews in small boats or rafts furnished with food and potable water. Air attacks and the newly developed German magnetic mines at first took the navy medical services by surprise, but the doctors, particularly those in the Royal Navy, adapted to the innovations.

Protection of civilians

To deal with this problem, there was close cooperation between civilian and military health services in the evacuation of children, preferably with their mothers, the care of orphans and improved protection against air raids.

In Germany and occupied Europe, **prisoners of war**—particularly Soviet prisoners, since the USSR was not a member of the International **Red Cross**—as well as the forced laborers in the German plants, lived in exceptional squalor, although those assigned to farms were probably better fed. They were overcrowded, undernourished and lacking in water, clothing or boots, to say nothing of recreation or extended rest. German ''measures'' converted the concentration camps into extermination centers with their average daily ration of 1,700 calories. In 1945 the surviving prisoners, liberated laborers and deportees, profoundly and permanently marked by their experiences, rejoined a civilian population which was itself underfed. These sequels of the enslavement of Europe severely diminished the numbers of those ultimately responsible for reconstructing the ruins left by the Nazi cataclysm.

Hitler and his cohorts used the war to commit crimes so horrible and widespread as to distort human dignity:

Extermination in gas chambers

The first to be used were the only ones on German territory. More than 100,000 handicapped Germans were killed in them under the pretext of humanitarian **euthanasia**, but actually for hygienic purification of the race.

Experimentation on human deportees

Took place in an ethically perverted milieu where contagious diseases, especially typhus and malaria, were spreading freely. The **SS** surgeons in the camps, sometimes aided by civilian or military doctors, performed experiments on thousands of deported Europeans. To a greater extent, and this is only a rough sketch of the genocide, experiments practiced at **Auschwitz** and Ravensbrueck purported to investigate racial sterilization and genetics relating to the heredity of twins.

Organization of Health Services.

In Great Britain each of the military hygiene branches remained theoretically independent of the others. Actually, the services in the **Royal Air Force** and the land armies worked together closely. For a total of 5,700,00 men there were 16,903 doctors, or three per 1,000 men. The army medical services were reorganized. To the 14 classical units already in existence at the beginning of the war were added 19 other units born of the experience in the war, such as field laboratories, transfusion units and mobile units for treating burns, for neurosurgery, thoracic surgery, ophthalmology, maxillo-facial injuries, otorhinolaryngology and venereal disease treatment. The figure for daily admissions into the general hospitals did not exceed 0.6% of the total troop count, with an average hospital stay of 50 days.

In the United States, for each of the large fronts, medical services were under the command of a major general in turn responsible to a medical inspector. Each service was divided into four subsections: administrative; preventive medicine, also for treating the civilian population in the occupied territories; consultants inspecting the installations; and hospitalization, where in each echelon a surgeon commanded individual units.

In the Soviet Union, the most serious problem during the initial months of the war was the hasty transfer eastward of the medical sections of such great universities as Kiev and Kharkov. The commanders of the Red Army medical groups were the surgeon general, the chief physician and the director of the military medical administration. All of them kept in touch with the Health Commissar and the Red Cross. In the USSR, as in other countries, particular emphasis was laid on medical research in nutrition institutes, on blood transfusions, microbiology, labor hygiene, and neurosurgery.

In Japan, civilian hygiene was the function of the Ministry of Health, a complex organization also exercising broad control over areas other than sanitation and divided into five main offices: administration, population, hygiene, preventive medicine and the means of life. To it was also annexed a number of institutes and laboratories of hygiene and nutrition. In 1938, there were 53,000 physicians in Japan, or 8.64 per 10,000 inhabitants. In territories occupied by Japanese troops, the military health services used local medical resources.

In Germany, the civilian Ministry of Health was actually a secretariat in the Ministry of the Interior, with each of the three military branches having its own health service. A Hitler decree of July 28, 1942 regrouped the civilian health services under the direction of Leonardo Conti. The military medical services were similarly regrouped under the command of an inspector of health service, who also served as surgeon general of the army. Physician generals directed the medical services of the *Luftwaffe* and the German navy. The medical service of the *Waffen* SS were directly controlled by the inspector of health service, as were seven institutes: the Academy of Military Medicine in Berlin, the school of graduate study in Berlin, the typhus research institutes of Krakow and Lemberg, the special surgical hospital of Brussels for researching sulfa drugs, the central service of military medical archives in Berlin and the St. Johann school of mountain medicine. At the beginning of 1943 there were 25,000 physicians in the army, 10,000 in the *Luftwaffe*, 3,000 in the *Waffen* SS and about 1,000 in the navy. That same decree stipulated that Dr. Karl Brandt was to insure the cooperation of the military and the civilian sectors of the health service and report directly to Hitler. Later decrees strengthened Brandt's position and finally gave him the post of Hitler's plenipotentiary of health.

The history of sanitation services during the Second World War teaches two important lessons. First, the Allied forces used continuously improved medical methods ethically, with the least possible waste of human life. At the opposite extreme, despite the courage and desperate efforts of the majority of its medical men, Nazi Germany inexorably pursued its descent into the maelstrom of irresponsibility begun in 1933 by the mockery of medical ethics and a racist policy, ending in a desert of corpses and rubble.

The last world war involving conventional weapons had ended in a rational adaptation of health services to modern conflicts. But the bombs of Hiroshima and Nagasaki propelled humanity into the nuclear era and placed in doubt the treatment of all problems of health in future world war.

Dr. Y. Ternon

HEINCKEL, Ernst (1888-1958).

A German aircraft designer, Heinckel founded the Flugzeugwerke aircraft plant, which, during the war, produced several varieties of combat planes.

HENLEIN, Konrad (1898-1945).

The head of the German Sudeten party in

Czechoslovakia, Henlein was civil commissioner of **Bohemia-Moravia** from 1939 to 1945. He committed suicide after his arrest by the Czechs.

HENRIOT, Philippe (1889-1944).

A French statesman, Henriot acquired, in January 1944, the post of information and propaganda secretary of state in the Vichy government. An ardent advocate of **collaboration** with **Germany** to destroy Bolshevism, he was killed by members of the **French Resistance** in June 28, 1944.

HERRIOT, Edouard (1872-1957).

A French essayist and statesman, Herriot served as mayor of Lyon from 1905 to 1957 and deputy from Rhone from 1919 to 1957. He became minister of public works in 1916, and as head of the Radical Socialist Party, he acquired leadership of the government, supported by parties of the left, on May 11, 1924. Herriot recognized the **USSR** in 1924 and had the Ruhr evacuated in 1925. He was president of the Chamber of Deputies in the Popular Front government in 1936, and on July 9, 1940 he joined the Petain government. After gradually loosening his ties with the head of the **French State**, he was placed under house arrest in 1942 and arrested by the Germans two years later. He was finally liberated by **Pierre Laval** on August 12, 1944, refusing the latter's offer to form a ''transition cabinet'' with him. Arrested a second time by the Germans, he was deported to Potsdam. He was freed in April 1945 by the Red Army. A member of the French Academy, he served as president of the National Assembly from 1947 to 1954.

HESS, Rudolf (1894-   ).

A **Nazi Party** officer and one of **Hitler**'s confidants, Hess was named the Fuehrer's second successor on September 1, 1939. He parachuted into Scotland on May 10, 1941 in a vain attempt to negotiate with the **United Kingdom** before the German attack on the **USSR** (see **Peace Overtures**). He was condemned to life imprisonment in 1946 by the Nuremberg International Tribunal and has since been confined in Spandau prison; he is the only Nazi war criminal still incarcerated.

HEYDRICH, Reinhard (1904-1942).

A German naval officer, Heydrich was broken by Adm. **Raeder** in 1931 for misconduct. Upon joining the **SS**, he was given the assignment of establishing the **SD**. In August 1939, he organized the **Gleiwitz** incident which provided **Hitler** with an excuse for invading **Poland**, and in September of the same year, he became **Heinrich Himmler**'s assistant at the head of the **RSHA**. In September 1941 he was appointed pro-

tector of **Bohemia-Moravia**. He was responsible for the plan of extermination of the Jews, adopted at the **Wannsee Conference** in January 1942 (see **Anti-Semitism; Final Solution**). He died as the result of an assassination attempt by Czech parachutists trained by the **Special Operations Executive** and flown in from England. The Germans avenged his death by completely wiping out the village of **Lidice**.

HIGASHIKUNI, Naruhiko (1887-   ).

A Japanese imperial prince, Higashikuni received his military education in France and rose to the rank of general. At one time he was in charge of the Japanese army air corps. In October 1941, he was rumored to be a likely successor to Prince **Fumimaro Konoe** as prime minister, but Gen. **Hideki Tojo** was selected because he was more familiar with recent diplomatic and military developments and more likely to command the attention of the armed services. Higashikuni headed the home front defense command from 1941 to 1943 and participated in the movement to oust Tojo in July 1944. Because he was **Hirohito**'s uncle, he was a consensus choice to serve as a transitional prime minister in the wake of **Japan**'s defeat in August 1945. He held the post for 50 days.

HIMMLER, Heinrich (1900-1945).

From the war's beginning, SS Reichsfuehrer Himmler directed the policy of extermination in Europe. In 1943 he was minister of the interior in the Nazi government. The following year he became head of the Army of the Interior and in 1945 was made commander in chief of the Second Group of the land army. He attempted to negotiate the surrender of **Germany** with the Western powers to free the German army to fight only the Russians. Arrested by the Allies, he took his own life on May 23, 1945.

HIRANUMA, Kiichiro (1867-1952).

Hiranuma, a Japanese baron, justice ministry official and right-wing leader, served as head of the privy council from 1936 to 1939, prime minister from January to August 1939 and top officer of the **Imperial Rule Assistance Association** from 1940 to 1945. Hiranuma was notably friendly to military and nationalist causes. He was convicted by the International Military Tribunal for the Far East after the war and sentenced to life in prison.

Hiranuma was born in Okayama, graduated from Tokyo Imperial University and rose through the ranks to become justice minister in 1922. He opposed Japan's conciliatory foreign policies in the 1920s and founded a patriotic society to promote nationalist ideals. As chief privy councillor, he supported **Fumimaro Konoe**'s efforts in 1937-38 to draw the military and the imperial court closer together. But as an aristocrat, he excluded right-wing extremists from his brief administration in 1939 and based his programs on an elitist outlook he called "the imperial way."

His cabinet fell after the **Nazi-Soviet Pact** was concluded in August 1939, but Hiranuma remained a power behind the scenes until Japan surrendered six years later. As Konoe's right-hand man, he asserted business interests in the Imperial Rule Assistance Association after December 1940 and helped neutralize the army's efforts to take over the organization.

T. R. H. Havens

HIROHITO (1901-   ).

Emperor of **Japan** and reigning monarch since 1926, Hirohito is known to Japanese as the Showa emperor, after the official name of his reign. Hirohito was chief of state during the era of military expansion, crushing defeat and postwar reconstruction. Before 1945 he was a constitutional monarch with powers that were theoretically absolute but sharply limited in practice. Under the amended constitution of 1946, he became a "symbol of the state and of the unity of the people." Although most Japanese since 1945 have admired Hirohito and a great majority have favored retaining the imperial institution, controversy still surrounds two key points: (1) his role in the events leading to **Pearl Harbor** and (2) the refusal of the **United States** to abolish the throne after Japan's surrender in 1945.

Hirohito is the 96th monarch in an imperial line that can be traced with certainty to the sixth century (there are legends that identify another 28 emperors from the same household, beginning in 660 B.C.). Reared like all his predecessors by governesses and tutors in the austere imperial castle, Hirohito traveled to Europe as a youth, visiting the Prince of Wales in London, and became regent for his ailing father in 1921. When the latter died on Christmas day 1926, Hirohito succeeded to the throne.

Hirohito's public role before 1946 was defined partly by custom and partly by constitutional law. Like all monarchs before him, Hirohito was the chief priest of the native religion, Shinto; in this capacity his duties included reporting important matters of state to the sun goddess Amaterasu at the Ise grand shrine. Under the Meiji constitution of 1889, the emperor was also commander of the armed forces and sole source of authority for the Japanese state. As a transcendant sovereign, "far from the smoke of human habitations, no one ever to invade its sanctity," the throne was supposed to play only the ritual role of legitimizing decisions worked out by the ministers and councillors who served the emperor. As with earlier

generations of monarchs, he was expected to reign, not rule, cloaked in the legal magic of the modern Prussian system that had been borrowed by the framers of Japan's constitution.

These constraints made it nearly impossible for even the most strong-willed emperor to withhold his sanction from a course of action presented by his government. He might ask a question or express a personal view when the prime minister reported cabinet decisions to the throne, but there was no precedent for him to veto a course of action. He customarily remained mute throughout imperial conferences, when the highest affairs of state were formally approved after ritual presentations by his top civilian and military deputies. It is no wonder that so retiring and politically untutored a personality as Hirohito seemingly played only a ceremonial part in determining public policy.

However powerless and aloof he may have been, still Hirohito was far from a cipher among the prewar and wartime leadership group. David A. Titus has distinguished his public, ceremonial role as legitimizer of decisions ("emperor-in-state") from his behind-the-scenes function as a conciliator of clashing interests ("emperor-in-chambers"). In the latter role, for example, he intervened discreetly but forcefully in September 1931 to condemn the Kwantung Army after the Manchurian incident and in February 1936 to put down a revolt by 1,500 young army officers and their troops. As circumscribed as his formal powers undoubtedly were, Hirohito sometimes imposed his views informally when he found a lack of consensus among his ministers.

Since the emperor was more than a lifeless figurehead, what part, if any, did he play in the rise of the reactionary forces that waged a war in his name? There is little reason or evidence to believe that Hirohito was a megalomaniacal conspirator who maneuvered his advisers into plotting aggression in order to enhance his **empire**. However firmly he opposed headstrong army insurgents in 1931 and 1936, Hirohito may well have implicitly endorsed military expansion thereafter by his relative inaction as the world crisis grew more grave.

Japanese foreign policy from the 1890s to 1945 had two goals: (1) to provide for external security and (2) to extend Japan's political and economic influence in eastern and southeastern Asia. The first of these goals was achieved with the victory over Russia in 1905 and confirmed at Versailles. The second was pursued in the 1920s by diplomatic and economic means, but when peaceful expansion failed, Japan turned in the 1930s to military force. Now there was a much greater danger of conflict with American, British, Dutch and French interests in Asia. How to expand Japan's continental influence while avoiding war with these powers became a much more delicate diplomatic task after fighting broke out with China in 1937. In the bureaucratic struggle of elites for control of state decisions, the military outmaneuvered the cabinet and finally took it over, bouyed by the *faits accomplis* of its presence abroad and the increasing international peril created by events in Europe. In these circumstances the emperor mainly acted to reconcile different outlooks and insure a unified national policy.

One sign of Hirohito's views appeared in late August 1939, when Kiichiro Hiranuma's cabinet resigned after learning of the Nazi-Soviet Pact on August 23. Although Prince Fumimaro Konoe, head of the privy council, opposed any change in foreign policy, the emperor instructed Gen. Nobuyuki Abe, the new prime minister, to cooperate with the United Kingdom and the United States and appoint either Yoshijiro Umezu or Shunroku Hata as army minister. This remarkable intervention by the throne, together with the outbreak of war in Europe on September 1, made it more urgent than ever to come to terms with Britain and the United States.

From the diary of Marquis Koichi Kido, lord keeper of the privy seal, it is clear that the emperor worked behind the scenes throughout 1941 to be certain that all his advisers agreed on a course of action before he ratified it. Through questioning and individual audiences, he shared his misgivings about Japan's fate with the top leaders. On March 13 he told Kido he was worried about ''the subjective tendencies of the army.'' Although Yosuke Matsuoka, the foreign minister and outspoken proponent of the Axis, opposed the United States-Japan negotiations starting in April 1941, Hirohito and Kido both labored to unify the cabinet and keep the diplomatic discussions on track.

Even after the United States froze Japanese assets and shut off exports of oil in late July 1941, the emperor challenged the imperial navy's view that a war might as a consequence have to be fought promptly, before Japan's fuel reserves ran out. The emperor evidently thought the navy could not win such a desperate conflict and expressed to both Kido and Adm. Osami Nagano his doubts. At the imperial conference on September 6, when the army and navy general staff officers presented a united plan to expand the war into the Pacific, Hirohito shocked the group by reciting a poem written by his grandfather, the Meiji emperor:

> All the seas, in every quarter,
> are as brothers to one another.
> Why, then, do the winds and waves of strife
> rage so turbulently throughout the world?

Still the emperor remained little more than a skeptic, probing to test the consensus, profoundly anxious about the approaching disaster yet lacking both the strength of his convictions and the institutional authority to impose them. However much he privately resisted the army's policies, he could not afford to seem antimilitary in public because he had to elicit obedience to the government in times of crisis. For this reason even Roosevelt's eleventh-hour appeal to Hirohito to forestall war would doubtless have been unavailing, even had it arrived more promptly.

In wartime Hirohito was lionized by Japanese propaganda and psychological warfare as the patriarch of a sacred race, in whose name millions of subjects gave up their lives to win an empire described as ''the eight corners of the earth under one roof.'' His personal role in creating and disseminating such doctrines is in doubt. But it is very plain that the emperor broke the deadlock over whether to surrender in August 1945. After American atomic bombs destroyed Hiroshima and Nagasaki on August 6 and 9, he counseled surrender at two crucial imperial conferences, declaring that ''the unendurable must be endured.'' His prerecorded announcement, revealing the surrender decision to the public in unfamiliar court language on August 15, ended the era of imperial absolutism and military disaster with which Hirohito's name will always be linked.

Well before the cease-fire the Americans had decided to retain the throne as a source of political stability, without disclosing the decision until Japan surrendered unconditionally. In a uniquely American twist, the occupation authorities forced the emperor to renounce his divinity—to the puzzlement of Japanese who were unaware that he had ever been a deity. The United States found it convenient in the short term to perpetuate the imperial institution, but in the long run there was the danger that xenophobic nationalism might again one day swirl around the throne. Yet it was neither the institution itself nor the benign, fatherly figure occupying it that stirred concern. What was feared instead was a revival of the traditional moral order associated with the emperor before 1945, but there were few signs of such a trend in the increasingly secular political and social order of postwar Japan.

T. R. H. Havens

HIROTA, Koki (1878-1948).

A leading diplomat who served briefly as prime minister of Japan in 1936-1937, Hirota was foreign minister when war between Japan and China broke out in July 1937. He was the only civilian among the seven Class A war criminals sentenced to death by the International Military Tribunal for the Far East after Japan surrendered in 1945. He was found guilty of enhancing military dominance in Japanese politics, promoting Japanese expansion in China and supporting armed aggression on the continent.

Hirota was born in rural Fukuoka, a hotbed of nationalist fervor, and majored in politics at Tokyo Imperial University. From his youth onward, he took a strong interest in the patriotic Dark Ocean society, whose expansionist leader, Mitsuru Toyama (1855-1944), later abetted Hirota's rise to prime minister. After a long foreign service career, he became ambassador to the **USSR** in 1930-1932 and then foreign minister during 1933-1936.

In the wake of an unsuccessful but disquieting military revolt in February 1936, Japan's top leaders chose Hirota as premier, partly for his diplomatic skills and partly because he was acceptable to the army and navy. During his brief tenure Japan withdrew from international naval limitations agreements, signed the Anti-Comintern Pact with **Germany** and continued its military pressure on northeast China. Yet Hirota steadfastly believed that negotiation, not force, could best achieve Japan's goals. Military officials grew more prominent during his prime ministership because of weakness, not malevolence, on his part.

When he once again became foreign minister in Prince **Fumimaro Konoe**'s first cabinet in June 1937, Hirota tried unsuccessfully to solve the growing crisis in China by diplomatic means. When fighting broke out the next month near Peking, he tried to limit the emergency but soon found that the war ministry had taken matters into its own hands. Hirota fell meekly in line, defended Japan's actions to the rest of the world, and left office in May 1938 when Konoe formed a new cabinet. Although he never forthrightly opposed a strong policy in China, Hirota was a diplomatist whose career ended in failure mainly because he lacked institutional support and room to maneuver in the midst of crises abroad and military ambition at home.

T. R. H. Havens

HITLER, Adolf (1889-1945).

He was born on April 20, 1889 in Braunau, on the Inn river in **Austria**. His father was a customs officer of the Austro-Hungarian Empire. His eclectic view of the world began taking shape in his school years, at Linz and Steyr, and later in his "Viennese days," between 1908 and 1911, when he fell under the influence of a history professor who inoculated his pupils with the virus of pan-Germanism and the concept of the nobility of war and the military caste. It was then that the characteristics of his personality be-

came apparent: absolute egocentrism, the impulse to oratory, impatience with contradiction and a capacity for entertaining far-reaching projects. The struggles of the composite nationalities of the Austro-Hungarian Empire convinced Hitler that the key to world history is the yearning of peoples for a place in the sun and their trust in the preeminence of popular nationalism. He became an uncompromising anti-Semite, an enemy of Marxism, a fanatical pan-Germanist and a profound believer in the pseudo-Darwinian philosophy that life is nothing more than a struggle for existence.

Hitler went to Munich in 1913, and when World War I broke out, in the following year, enlisted in the Bavarian Army. His experiences at the front strengthened his enthusiasm for the military; "Combat fathers everything," he said. Later, he was to combine this idea with the philosophy of the struggle for national existence and the "Fuehrerprinzip." He became obsessed by the German defeat in 1918. The war, he was convinced, had to be re-ignited and waged continuously until the final victory; peace could be nothing else but the war conducted by other means.

Hitler's political career began in 1919. In 1921, he became first President of the **Nazi Party**, with dictatorial powers, and institutionalized the Fuehrer myth. Imprisoned after the failure of the putsch of November 1923 he wrote the first volume of *Mein Kampf*. After gaining amnesty, he reorganized the Nazi Party as a combat group and a fanatical mass movement. He came to power in Germany by legal means. The *Reichstag* elections in 1932 gave the Nazis a majority. On January 30, 1933, Hitler was named Chancellor of the Reich by the aged President Paul von Hindenburg. The old man's death allowed him to proclaim himself "Fuehrer and Chancellor" in August 1934, combining the functions of party chief, head of the government and leader of the state. From the Army he received an oath of unquestioning obedience. Dissolution of the *Reichstag*, a ban on rival political parties, laws guaranteeing the Fuehrer full powers and various means of terrorizing dissidents subjected Germany to a totalitarian government. In March 1935 he made military service obligatory and reaffirmed his armament policy. At the beginning of 1938 he organized his chiefs of staff, taking supreme command for himself.

Beginning in the 1920s, the central thesis of Hitler's foreign policy was the concept of *Lebensraum*— i.e., Germany's need for more territory—together with the no less important concepts of racial purity and a **new European order**, in which Germany would be foremost in the competition among the world's nations. As the creator of the conditions fixing both his domestic and foreign policies, he openly pursued a course of outright annexation based on the demands of a strong minority of pan-Germanists in Austria and the ethnic Germans in **Czechoslovakia**'s Sudetenland region. After signing the astonishing **Nazi-Soviet Pact**, he launched World War II with his attack on **Poland** September 1, 1939.

From 1939 to the winter of 1941-42, Hitler conducted a war limited in geographic scope, marked by distinct and successive campaigns which, within the framework of Clausewitz' doctrine, were only extensions of his diplomatic aims. His objectives were to crush Poland, to assure the strategic security of his northern flank and to drive the democratic taint of the Western powers from the Continent, thus leaving Europe, including the Balkans, open to reorganization under German hegemony. These operations were, in effect, to be the second act of the continuing drama in which World War I had been the curtain-raiser. But this time Germany was to be the victor, with all of Europe to compensate her for all she had sacrificed in the first act.

Both directly and through his generals and his armaments industry, Hitler applied the ultra-modern method of the **Blitzkrieg**—the lightning war—with stupefying success. It was the method of swift surprise attack on a single front with a single objective, using every means of mobility and fire power, and combining air and armored forces in land operations to achieve an immediate decision. As opposed to the classical method of warfare, Blitzkrieg tactics were designed to destroy the armies of the enemy rather than simply to acquire and occupy territories. Short campaigns, furthermore, were more profitable for the victor; economical in materiel and less injurious to the civil population, they compensated for the defects in the German economy (see also **Germany—Economy of the Third Reich**) and rendered Germany independent of the need for embarrassing economic or political liaisons with other countries. In combination with German diplomatic offers, the Blitzkrieg shifted the moral onus of continuing hostilities to the shoulders of the enemy and dovetailed neatly with the actualities of the German war industry, which, geared for offensives in depth rather than width, could, in 1939, sustain a war lasting nine to twelve months. The success of this combat tactic dissipated widespread doubts about the final victory, silenced its critics, and increasingly secured the faith of the German people in Hitler's ability to achieve the remote but fascinating goals of the "Greater German Reich."

But with his attack on the **USSR** in June 1941, Hitler completely changed his style of waging war. The large-scale battles on widely extended fronts, the territorial conquests, the wholesale looting of the occupied countries, the imposed tyrannical governments, the systematic annihilation of every ideological

enemy, the rage for killing Jews and the terror spread by Fascist goon squads were all signs of the degeneration of the war into a shambles covering the operations of avid profiteers and unscrupulous gangsters. With his declaration of war on the **United States**, Hitler drastically expanded the dimensions of his European war with the evident intention of ballooning the Reich into a superpower dominating the European continent, some strategically powerful outposts and a new colonial **empire**.

In his foreign policy since 1933, Hitler had grown tremendously in stature, apparently with little effort. Beginning in 1939 he won victory after victory in his lightning battles. He sensed wings sprouting from his shoulders; not a single misstep marred his plan. With ever-greater energy and acumen he forged each opportunity into a golden link to the next success in a gleaming chain reaching toward the fixed goal. But this chain was in the end to strangle him. Instead of exploiting his military victories politically and consolidating his gains, he used each one as a springboard to another operation still more risky until he was madly pursuing a multitude of aims with clearly limited means.

Beginning in 1939 Hitler increasingly meddled in the plans of his generals—Hitler clearly shared **Goering**'s belief that he was "the greatest of all military strategists." He had taken a decisive part in planning the French campaign and so was convinced that his intuition was worth the cold logic of all his chiefs of staff. He was served by the abundance of his ideas, the breadth of his imagination and the astonishing volume of technical erudition, all of which awed his military entourage; he had a genuine capacity for self-teaching and rapid thinking. Considering it high time to conduct Germany's military operations himself—he was suspicious of his generals who, discouraged by their defeat at the gates of Moscow, doubted their ability to win—Hitler decisively assumed command of Germany's land armies on December 19, 1941, saying "The person who takes on this petty business of commanding operations is of no importance; what is important is that men be inspired with the soul of National Socialism." Dictatorial, impulsive, deaf to the lessons of experience, he busied himself with controlling the military maneuvering, with scrupulous attention to tactical details and little regard for operational logic. The consequent relegation of his chiefs of staff to the status of observers was to lead to the complete collapse of the German Army.

Beginning in 1943, the military defeats the Nazis suffered and the decay of Germany's domestic as well as foreign affairs changed Hitler's style of command. Increasingly overworked, ever lonelier, he entered a state **Albert Speer** described as "sclerosis and hardening in the torture of indecision, bitterness and constant irritation.'' He was learning that every means of self-extrication from catastrophe had failed.

After the failure of the Blitzkrieg against the Soviet Union in 1941-42, the reverses in North Africa and in Stalingrad in 1942-43, it became obvious that Hitler could no longer hope to win the war against a coalition of the United States, the **United Kingdom** and their allies, with 75% of the world's manpower and material reserves behind them. His 1943 proclamation of total war, his successful encouragement of armaments production, his complete exploitation of the Reich's war potential, none of these could have any result but to prolong a war that could only justify his passion to dominate. He still counted on his personal magnetism, his fanatical propaganda, his hastily erected fortifications, his secret weapons and the incessant persecution of his enemies—especially after the **assassination attempt of July 20, 1944**—to quench the roaring fire threatening him and to maintain pressure on his ''cursed enemies'' until they tired of the combat. To escape the trap of war for the sake of war, Hitler saw no other way out than the voluntary ruination of Germany and the suicide of its leaders. ''The German people have not shown themselves worthy of their Fuehrer,'' he said in 1945, ''and he can only die. The future belongs to the strong—to the East.''

Hitler, his votaries, his admirers, and, indirectly, the mass who followed him wanted to attain by any means a grandiose and absolute aim that to their eyes was superior justice—the triumph of the nobler race. Yet their war was only a return to barbarism, a limitless mania for destruction demanding the death of millions of people and the debasement of many more, an enterprise in the perversion of other peoples for no other reason than scorn for ''the alien.'' By his conduct of the war, Hitler indelibly sullied the history of the 20th century with an ugly and tragic brand. The partition of Germany and the split in the heart of Europe are the direct consequences of his policy. Since the beginning, his motto had been, in effect: Germany shall be a great power or it will be destroyed.

He killed himself on April 30, 1945.

H. A. Jacobsen

HOARE, Sir Samuel John Gurney (later Lord Templewood) (1880-1950).

A British politician, Hoare served as a Conservative minister of Parliament from 1910 to 1944. He held many high offices, including foreign secretary. In that post he arranged the Hoare-**Laval** plan for the partition of **Ethiopia** in 1935. He was a strong supporter of **Chamberlain's appeasement** policy. As ambassador to

Spain from 1940 to 1944, Hoare did much to keep that country neutral.

HOBART, Sir Percy C. S. (1885-1957).

A British general and engineer, Hobart commanded the famous 79th Armored Division in Normandy and the Baltic theaters. The unit was equipped with special devices—amphibians, flame-throwing **tanks,** flailing tanks, etc.—many of which he himself developed.

HO CHI MINH (alias of Nguyen Tat Tan) (1890-1969).

At first a militant Socialist and then a Communist, Ho Chi Minh lived in France in 1921-22, in Russia in 1923-26 and in Siam in 1927-31. With the help of the **Office of Strategic Services**, he led the **Viet Minh**, which he had organized in 1941, against the Japanese. After the war he founded the Republic of Vietnam in August 1945. His followers fought French forces from 1946 to 1954, and he forced France to recognize him, according to the Geneva accords, as president of the Democratic Republic of North Vietnam. He then launched a military campaign to incorporate South Vietnam under Communist rule.

HODGES, Courtney Hicks (1887-1966).

In 1944-45 Hodges commanded the U.S. First Army during and after the **Normandy landing**.

HOESS, Rudolf (1900-1947).

As commandant of the **concentration camp** at **Auschwitz**, Hoess used the gas Zyklon B for mass extermination of the prisoners. Condemned to death, he was hanged at the scene of his crimes in April 1947.

HOLLAND, Jo Charles Francis (1897-1956).

A British soldier, Holland headed, in 1938-40, Military Intelligence Research, from which, in part, the **Special Operations Executive** evolved. He conceived of the idea of using commandos and special techniques for escape and **deception**.

HOLLARD, Michel.

A French engineer and the founder of the spy network ''Agir,'' Hollard, in 1943, conveyed information to London regarding the location of the rocket-launching sites in German-occupied Normandy as well as a sketch of the German flying bomb. He was arrested by the Germans on February 5, 1944, but escaped from his prison.

HOME GUARD.

Created in Great Britain in 1940, this territorial militia

consisted of civilian volunteers. By the end of the war, it had a corps of 170,000 men and 30,000 women (see **United Kingdom**).

HOMMA, Masaharu (1888-1946).

Homma's lifelong connections with England commenced in 1918 when he was sent to London as a military student; shortly thereafter, in September 1918, he was assigned as a Japanese observer of the British Expeditionary Force on the Western Front. He served as resident officer in **India** in 1922-25, whereupon he became U.S.-Europe Desk Chief of the Japanese Army's General Staff. In 1927 Homma began a four-year stint as Military aide to Prince Yasuhito Chichibu, Emperor **Hirohito**'s younger brother. He returned to England as Military Attache in 1930, and was subsequently decorated with the Military Cross of the British Empire. After assignment to the Geneva Conference in 1932, during the Manchurian crisis, Homma returned to **Japan**. As commander of the elite First Infantry Regiment in Tokyo from 1933-35, Homma never adhered to the intraservice cliques that typified the Japanese Army in the early and mid-1930s. He remained a loyalist during the army mutiny in Tokyo in February 1936, and accompanied Prince Chichibu to the coronation of King **George VI** in London in 1937. After the **China** Incident in 1937, Homma cooperated with General Tada in secret, ultimately futile peace feelers attempted by German Ambassador Oskar Trautmann.

Promoted to lieutenant general in 1938, Homma took command of the new 27th Division, which was sent to the China front as part of the Second Army, commanded by Prince **Naruhiko Higashikuni**. Although Homma desired a Sino-Japanese accommodation, he fought very well in the campaign to seize Hankow. In 1939, from Japanese headquarters at Tientsin, he handled local negotiations with the British during the Japanese blockade of Concession. Homma was admirably energetic in directing engineering and relief measures after great floods inundated the Tientsin area in the summer of 1939. In December 1940, Homma was made commanding general of the Formosa Army.

Against this background of staff and field ability and experience, Homma was selected in November 1941 as the 14th Army Commander in charge of the impending **Philippines** invasion, under Gen. Hisaichi Terauchi's Southern Army. But, from the outset, Homma annoyed IJA Chief of Staff Gen. **Sugiyama** by posing embarrassing questions which undoubtedly stemmed from his dissatisfaction with superficial IGHQ staff planning and, more importantly, with the fundamental notion of taking on the western powers,

especially while the China war was still dragging on. Sugiyama proved unforgiving.

Immediately upon the outbreak of the Pacific War, on December 8, the first elements of Homma's 14th Army (built around the 16th and 48th Divisions) began coming ashore on the island of Luzon. After these preliminary landings and the destruction of U.S. air power in the Philippines, Homma's main invasion of Luzon commenced on December 22. General **Douglas MacArthur**'s original intention of checking Japanese landings on the beaches ended in failure. The Americans then declared Manila an open city and, within only 22 days of the outset of the campaign, the Filipino capital was in Homma's hands. IGHQ's main objective had presumably been achieved, well before the 45- or 50-day deadline for conquering the Philippines. But the islands were far from conquered: the Filipino and American defenders had managed to retreat to the Bataan Peninsula and **Corregidor** Island, while the Japanese remained obsessed with the "crucial" importance of Manila and denigrated the significance of enemy "remnants." Although Japanese control of the Manila harbor was obviously not assured, IGHQ felt sufficiently confident to withdraw Homma's best division (the 48th) and most of the Fifth Air Group for the Java operation, one month ahead of schedule. (See also **Indonesia**.)

It soon became apparent to Homma that more than a mopping-up action lay ahead, but his requests to IGHQ for more rather than less strength earned him a reputation as a whiner. "The troops opposed to you are third class," he was told by Tokyo, "and unworthy to face us in battle." At this stage, Homma was given only the poor 65th Brigade from Formosa. IGHQ's arbitrary initial target date passed without the decisive Japanese victory in the Philippines required by **Tojo** and Sugiyama. Homma complained of his lack of men, intelligence failures and cartographic inadequacy. His men exhausted or sick, and his logistical system in disarray, he dared to suspend offensive operations, an action which inspired Sugiyama to solicit reproof of Homma by the Emperor and to consider sacking him and his chief of staff, Masami Maeda. The latter was easily replaced by Maj. Gen. Takaji Wachi, but firing a senior lieutenant general such as Homma in the midst of battle was not deemed feasible—yet. For the moment, he was given one replacement division, Lt. Gen. Kenzo Kitano's unimpressive 4th Division from Shanghai, plus artillery and aircraft. IGHQ assumed responsibility for the south Philippines, leaving Homma free to concentrate against Bataan. His powerful general offensive finally got underway on April 3, and Bataan was overrun in less than a week, not the month the now-gloomy Homma had feared. Corregidor held out somehow until May 7.

Homma had accomplished his mission, but it was four months later than IGHQ had wanted, and "excessive" strength had had to be invested. In addition, MacArthur had been "allowed" to escape to **Australia**. For all of these alleged failures, Sugiyama and IGHQ held Homma responsible. "Spies" sent to his headquarters from Tokyo, notably Col. Masanobu Tsuji, reported confidentially that Homma "lacked ability" and that his staff was "dull and stupid." Now that the main fighting was over, Homma was also reported to be too lenient toward the Filipinos, who had resisted the Japanese to the best of their ability and remained basically loyal to the Americans. Terauchi sent a negative message to IGHQ regarding Homma's "insistent tolerance." Against all advice, however, Homma released Filipino war prisoners. After a scarcely decent interval, he was relieved of his command and was retired in "semi-disgrace" in August 1942.

Homma's only subsequent wartime role was as an adviser to the Koiso Cabinet beginning in July 1944, when he was given the secret assignment of collecting data in support of the premise that hostilities had to be terminated as soon as possible. He also was connected with a complicated *sub rosa* effort by a Chinese agent, Miao Pin, designed to bring about Sino-Japanese peace, presumably with the concurrence of the Chinese Nationalist government.

Homma's courageous, patriotic actions availed him naught: within two weeks of the war's end, in September 1945, he was arrested by the U.S. Eighth Army and put on trial in Manila as a **war criminal** for offenses which had occurred in the Philippines during his 14th Army command in 1942, namely, the Bataan Death March and murders of Filipino and American prisoners. There is no doubt that such crimes occurred, but evidence indicates that Homma was personally ignorant of them, and certainly never ordered or condoned them. He was undone by certain criminal or hostile elements on his own staff, who worked behind his back to subvert his intentions. For his sloppy supervision and naive delegation of authority, while beset by the chaos and confusion of battle and the entirely unexpected circumstances of the U.S. collapse in April 1942, Homma paid with his life, the main argument of the American military prosecution being that he should have always known what was occurring under his command. Upon conviction, his death sentence was approved without hesitation by MacArthur, the general whom he had defeated in the field, and he was executed by a firing squad at Los Banos on April 3, 1946.

His U.S. defense counsel called it "a highly irregular trial, conducted in an atmosphere that left no doubt as to what the ultimate outcome would be." Other U.S. defense lawyers agreed that the conviction was unjust. Supreme Court Associate Justice Frank Murphy, protesting the verdict, spoke of the danger of "descending to the level of revengeful blood purges. . . in the natural frenzy of the aftermath of war." While the crimes of Bataan were thus avenged, Homma was scarcely the proper man to have deserved the extreme penalty: a rare Japanese officer who had opposed Tojo and stood up to Sugiyama, who had consistently worked for Sino-Japanese amity ever since the Manchurian Incident and who had not only opposed war with the **United States** and the **United Kingdom** (which he respected and knew) but also opposed the consummation of the **Tripartite Pact** with Nazi **Germany** and Fascist **Italy**.

Those who knew ill-starred Homma best have called him artistic, courageous, brillant, cultured, withdrawn, romantic, intellectual, a patrician who was probably the most Westernized of all the IJA generals. MacArthur was unrelenting in his castigation of Homma, whom he held responsible personally for the atrocities of 1942, but Homma said privately at the time: "I think of (MacArthur) as a good soldier and a good political administrator. I am quite satisfied to have fought against him for my honor." The U.S. military court in Manila sought to strip him of his honor but may have succeeded only in snuffing out his life.

A. D. Coox

HONG KONG.

A British Crown Colony with an area of approximately 400 square miles and a population, in 1941, of 1,640,000. It is a port of entry to southern **China**. Hong Kong was conquered by the Japanese on Christmas, 1941 (see also **Pacific Theater of Operations**). **Churchill**'s ringing rhetoric had claimed that the eyes of the world were on Hong Kong, which should "resist to the end." But at the time of the Japanese attack, the defense garrison, even reinforced, numbered scarcely 12,000 men under Maj. Gen. C. M. Maltby, with six infantry battalions: two British, two Indian and two new Canadian, plus the Hong Kong & **Singapore** Royal Artillery and the motley but vigorous civilian soldiers of the Hong Kong Volunteer Defense Corps. Ill-equipped and almost devoid of air or naval support, these forces, despite ample warning, had to bear the brunt of the assault by IJA air and ground units detached from the Expeditionary Army in China, namely the 38th Division (commanded by Lt. Gen. Tadayoshi Sano), which attacked on December 8. Kowloon fell on the 12th. After severe artillery and aerial bombardment, IJA amphibious forces landed on Hong Kong island beginning December 18. By the time Maltby was compelled to capitulate on the 25th, his men were worn down, short of water and ammunition and depleted by about 4,400 casualties, including nearly 800 of the 1,800 Canadians. The Japanese admitted casualties numbering 2,754. The British capitulation was followed by uncontrolled Japanese atrocities committed against the wounded and nurses. Essentially indefensible from a military standpoint, Hong Kong was the symbol of a century of British pre-eminence in China, now ruined by the quickly victorious, gloating Japanese.

HOOVER, J. Edgar (1895-1972).

From 1924 until his death, Hoover, an ardent anticommunist and anti-Nazi, headed the Federal Bureau of Investigation (FBI). In 1936 he received authority from Roosevelt to investigate espionage and sabotage. Hoover stretched this power to monitor the activities of the right and the left as well as Roosevelt's political enemies. Following Pearl Harbor Roosevelt allowed Hoover to expand the FBI's surveillance of the right, the left, labor unions, civil rights groups and the Communist Party in the United States. Under Hoover the FBI continued its monitoring of these groups after the war had ended.

HOPKINS, Harry Lloyd (1890-1946).

A special adviser and close confidant of Roosevelt, Hopkins played a major role in organizing alliances and the exchange of military supplies between the United States, Britain and the USSR. He accompanied Roosevelt to all the major conferences of the war (see Conferences, Allied). Despite ill health Hopkins went to Moscow in 1945 at President Truman's request to hold talks with Stalin. He succeeded in obtaining concessions from Stalin on the functioning of the Security Council of the United Nations and inclusion of democratic elements in the government of Poland.

HORROCKS, Sir Brian Gwynne (1895-   ).

British general. During World War I, Horrocks fought in France and Russia. From 1941 to 1945 he commanded successively the 13th, 10th, ninth and 30th corps in North Africa and northwestern Europe.

HORTHY, Miklos von (1868-1957).

Admiral and regent of Hungary. Although he began by supporting the Axis, Horthy soon made appeals to the Western Allies and the USSR. On October 15, 1944, anticipating an armistice with the advancing Soviet army, he initiated negotiations with the Soviet government that were quashed by the SS, which abducted him by force. After his abdication he was interned in Bavaria. Liberated by American troops in 1945, he took refuge in Portugal.

HOSHINO, Naoki (1892-1978).

A reform bureaucrat in the finance ministry, Hoshino was an economic planner who became the top leader in the Manchukuo government during the 1930s. Prime Minister Fumimaro Konoe appointed him head of the Cabinet Planning Board in 1940 to regularize Japan's haphazard mobilization and war production. After his appointment as minister of state in the Tojo cabinet in 1941, he served as its chief secretary until 1944. Hoshino was sentenced in 1948 to life in prison by the International Military Tribunal for the Far East.

HOT SPRINGS CONFERENCE.
See Conferences, Allied.

HULL, Cordell (1871-1955).

Hull was secretary of state of the United States from 1933 to 1944 and chief negotiator with the Japanese from April to November 1941. Hull's rigid moralism in the Japanese-American talks prevented the exploration of certain diplomatic options and brought the negotiations to a premature end. But probably no degree of American flexibility could have averted war unless each side had greatly reduced its demands.

A leading Democratic senator from Tennessee and a confidant of Franklin D. Roosevelt, Hull warned the Japanese as early as July 1939 that the U.S opposed "those who are flouting the law and order and officially threatening military conquest without limit." He began negotiations in April 1941 with the Japanese ambassador to Washington, Adm. Kichisaburo Nomura, demanding that Japan respect the territorial integrity and sovereignty of all countries—a clear indication that Japan was expected to yield its position not just in northern Indochina but in China as well.

In subsequent conversations, the Japanese were ambiguous and the Americans uncompromising. When the U.S. froze Japan's assets in July 1941 in response to Japan's occupation of Cochin China, trade between the two countries stopped and resources in Japan grew critically scarce, especially oil. Military leaders in Tokyo soon agreed on plans to seize by force the raw materials in Southeast Asia they could no longer obtain by peaceful trade with the United States, but they still believed that diplomacy would prevail because they optimistically assumed the U.S. would buy peace by resuming trade. For this reason, Nomura and top officials in Tokyo misread Hull's intransigence and saw in it the conciliatory tone they hoped to find.

Although Roosevelt was willing to meet in September with the Japanese prime minister, Prince Fumimaro Konoe, Hull vetoed the idea because he believed there could be no compromise with aggression. He likewise spurned Japan's offer of a *modus vivendi* in November and responded with a 10-point plan (the Hull note of November 26) that the Japanese regarded as an ultimatum, because it virtually called for a return to the status quo' of 1931. Hull won the Nobel Peace Prize in 1945 for his unflinching resistance to aggression.

T. R. H. Havens

HUNGARY.

The Treaty of Trianon in 1920 deprived the Kingdom of St. Stephen of an important part of its ancient territory; some 3,500,000 Hungarians were allotted to **Czechoslovakia, Rumania** and **Yugoslavia**. This error—among hundreds of others—in the treaties signed between 1919 and 1920, together with the French "Little Entente" policy, was to throw Hungary into the arms first of **Italy** and then of **Germany**.

At the head of the Hungarian government since 1919, Admiral **Miklos von Horthy** had no love for the Germans and less still for the Nazis, but his rule was totalitarian—and unpopular. The working classes strongly resented the wealthy descendants of aristocrats who supported him, and agitation by the pro-Nazi "Arrow Cross" party continually increased.

After the **Munich Pact**, on November 2, 1938, the **Axis** Powers ceded to Hungary some of the territory that had been part of Czechoslovakia. In March 1939, after Czechoslovakia ceased to exist, the Budapest government also obtained part of Ruthenia. On August 30, 1940, **Hitler** presented Hungary with the northern half of Transylvania, at Rumanian expense. These gifts, however, were the price of Budapest's increasing subservience to Berlin. In exchange, Hungary yielded to the Germans half its foreign trade.

The government adhered to the **Tripartite Pact** but had no desire for an active part in the war. The president of the Hungarian Council, Count **Pal Teleki**, committed suicide on April 3, 1941 when the *Wehrmacht* crossed his territory without his permission to attack Yugoslavia. His successor sent the Hungarian Army to the aid of Italian and German troops participating in the Balkan campaign. Six days after Germany, Budapest declared war on the **USSR**.

Hungarian losses on the steppes of the Soviet Union were exceedingly high. The destruction of the Second Hungarian Army on the Don River in January 1943 resulted in 70% casualties for the total corps. But Hitler continued to demand additional troops. During the period of the Axis retreat, however, the Hungarian Council President, Miklos Kallay, began secret negotiations with the Allies. These became known to the Germans, and the Fuehrer ordered his troops to occupy the country on March 19, 1944, in what was known as Operation **Margaretha**. At once

the Nazis began a reign of terror, and a **Resistance** movement sprang up. Arriving late in the course of the war, this movement would have been of no significance but for the fact that its activities pinned down a large proportion of the German forces on the Danube Plain, preventing their use against the Allies after the **Normandy landing** on June 6, 1944.

When the Soviets entered Hungary at the beginning of October 1944, the Germans removed Horthy for preparing to offer an armistice to the Russians and replaced him with Ferenc Szalasi. A wave of terror began, with mass deportations and the near-extermination of Hungarian Jews. A Hungarian army went over to the Soviets and its commander, General Dalnoki Miklos, presided over a provisional government that sat in Debrecen from December 21, 1944 until Budapest was liberated on February 13, 1945. Hungary then fell into the Russian sphere of influence.

H. Bernard

HUNTZIGER, Charles (1880-1941).

A French general, Huntziger commanded the French Second Army in September 1939 and the Fourth Army Group in June 1940. He presided over the delegation charged with negotiating an armistice with the victorious German forces on June 17, 1940 and became minister of war in the Vichy government in November 1940. He was killed in an airplane accident on November 12, 1941.

HUSKY.

Code name for the Allied landing on Sicily in July 1943. (See also **Mediterranean and Middle Eastern Theater of Operations**.)

HYAKUTAKE, Haruyoshi (1888-1947).

Hyakutake, a Japanese soldier, became Harbin Special Agency Chief for the Kwantung Army Headquarters in Manchuria in August 1931. During the 1930s he held a number of other positions, and commanded, in turn, the Fourth Independent Mixed Brigade, beginning in March 1939, the 18th Division, beginning in February 1940, and the 17th Army, beginning in May 1942. This last was his "army" in name only. Hyakutake was orginally given the grandiose mission of capturing strategic points on New Caledonia, Fiji and Samoa, as well as occupying Port Moresby. After the Japanese defeat at **Midway**, the 17th Army's missions were reoriented against eastern **New Guinea** and Port Moresby, complicated soon afterward by the unexpected and escalating battle for **Guadalcanal**. To cope with the new situation, IGHQ activated the Eighth Area Army in November 1942, under Lt. Gen. Hitoshi Imamura, with overall responsibility for Hyakutake's army and

Lt. Gen. Hatazo Adachi's new 18th Army. Eventually defeated on Guadalcanal, Hyakutake estimated his losses at 5,000 killed in combat, 15,000 dead of starvation and disease. He later told Imamura, with exaggeration spawned by despair: "There has never been such an instance in military history—a commander losing 20,000 men and having to be rescued by a general from another area. I swallowed my shame and kept on living until my 10,000 survivors got out safely" (in February 1943). Hyakutake wanted to commit suicide but was dissuaded by Imamura, who persuaded him that the high command needed to be told in full detail, one day, about the sacrifice of the 17th Army.

Meanwhile, commanding a much-reduced army, Hyakutake found himself surprised by enemy landings at Rendova (in the New Georgia group) in June 1943; he failed in his major counteroffensive at Empress Augusta Bay (**Bougainville**) in March 1944. His command of 17th Army was terminated in April 1945, and Hyakutake was attached to Eighth Area Army Headquarters. After his repatriation in February 1946, Hyakutake was paralyzed by a stroke and died distraught on March 10, 1947.

A. D. Coox

I

ICELAND.
Independent since 1918 but with the king of **Denmark** as its sovereign, this island of 121,000 inhabitants (in 1940) was occupied by the British on May 10, 1940. They used it as a base until June 8, 1941, when they were relieved by the Americans.

ILO.
See **International Labor Organization**.

IMPERIAL RULE ASSISTANCE ASSOCIATION.
A large-scale organization founded in **Japan** on September 27, 1940, to involve all citizens in a web of mobilization associations, the Imperial Rule Assistance Association (IRAA) was the result of Prime Minister **Fumimaro Konoe**'s ill-fated **New Structure Movement**, which tried to bring about national unity at a time of growing danger abroad. Although Konoe hoped to use the IRAA to blunt military influence over politics, the association proved to be an awkward instrument for achieving his personal political or foreign policy goals. The army took over control of the IRAA after **Pearl Harbor** but found it little more suited to its ambitions than had Konoe. The association was formally dissolved on June 13, 1945, during a last-ditch mobilization of civilians to defend the homeland with bamboo spears.

Japan was pinned down abroad and politically inert at home when Konoe resumed the prime ministership in July 1940. He announced the IRAA the same month that Japan proclaimed its **Greater East Asia Co-Prosperity Sphere** and signed the **Tripartite Pact** with **Germany** and **Italy**. Because it was confined to political and social mobilization, the IRAA made little difference to Japan's **production** efforts. Politically the IRAA absorbed the various parliamentary parties, all of which had disbanded more or less voluntarily earlier that summer in the interests of national harmony. Socially the IRAA built a massive federation of citizen's groups and smothered the media and the world of letters with much tighter controls. At the same time, the IRAA stepped up the drive to build

neighborhood associations on every street in the country.

In a superficial way the association resembled the mass organizations of wartime Germany and Italy, but politically it turned out to be a thin reed and soon played into the army's hand. The parties found it hard to resist Konoe's reform wave, but not so the Diet: it cut the IRAA budget from 50 to 8 million yen in early 1941. Neither the home ministry nor the great corporations were pleased with the menace this new organization seemed to present them. Big industry neutralized the new structure through Minister of State **Kiichiro Hiranuma**, a right-wing bureaucrat whom Konoe put in charge of the IRAA in December 1940 after it had failed to put down the army and navy. The result was a deadlock, with generals, financiers, and bureaucrats eying one another suspiciously across the void left by the dissolved parties.

As a vehicle of political integration, the IRAA broke down almost at once. Its vast efforts at social integration were more persistent but not much more effectual, because they amounted to little more than a reshuffling of the large-scale organizations already in existence. Although it was nominally a "people's movement," the IRAA was consistently used by the Konoe and **Hideki Tojo** cabinets to try to centralize the various civic associations in the civilian society and put them on a war footing. Its first chance to rally the public came at stately ceremonies held all over the **empire** on November 10, 1940, marking the enthronement of the Jinmu emperor, whose resplendent reign supposedly began in 660 B.C. and lasted 75 years. Then the IRAA started integrating the various labor groups that had been formed during the past few years, especially the patriotic industrial societies that replaced unions in the war plants.

On November 23, a date now celebrated as Labor Thanksgiving Day in Japan, the government founded the Greater Japan Patriotic Industrial Association to bring the factory units under Konoe's new structure. The number of workers in the local patriotic industrial groups continued to grow, reaching a peak of 5,514,320 members in June 1942. Although each of the unified labor associations had identical structures, managements, and budget procedures, it is unclear how smoothly they coordinated the work of their local branches. Since the IRAA itself never became politically dominant, it seems likely that its suborganizations, such as the Greater Japan Patriotic Industrial Association, drew their greatest strength from their well-established local branches in each company. Whatever its shortcomings, the patriotic industrial association poured amazing energy into its rallies, lectures and panel discussions, and it brought the war to Japan's workplaces much more systematically than had been true before Konoe began his movement.

The IRAA followed the same scenario with other key social organizations that were now made part of the new structure. One of the largest was the Greater Japan Youth Association, established on January 16, 1941, by merging four youth groups dating back to the 1920s and 1930s. By mid-1942, the IRAA reported, 14,215,837 young people belonged to the new association, an increase of nearly 10 million from the 1940 level. As with the labor associations, the individual youth clubs were apparently far sounder than the new national association, but there is no question that young people were now involved much more deeply with wartime activities than previously.

Women, too, were soon brought together by the IRAA under a huge national organization, the Greater Japan Women's Association, founded on February 2, 1942. Like the labor and youth groups, the women's association was supposedly a "people's movement," established "because voices swelled up from the masses of women seeking a national women's organization." The new association had an uncertain grip on the 19,310,000 women who officially belonged to it, especially when it competed for the allegiances of members who also belonged to the Greater Japan Youth Association units, since women between ages 20 and 25 were expected to belong to both.

One of the ironies of the organizational tightening is that the most effectual group formed under the IRAA was a namesake that came into being at least partly to undermine the parent association itself. The new body, called the Greater Japan Assistance Adult Association, began on January 16, 1942, with a good deal of help from the army. Starting with Fukui prefecture, it drew together various adult clubs, especially in the villages, into a support organization to plump for candidates favorable to the army in the forthcoming elections for the lower house of the Diet, held on April 30, 1942.

Through a separate political committee, the Tojo government also tried to manipulate the election of 1942. Tojo used the IRAA to recommend 466 candidates and mobilized the police and the bureaucracy to help them win. All but 85 were successful. Among those elected were at least 40 who were also supported by the Greater Japan Assistance Adult Association. The new association did not really offset the bureaucrats or the financial community within the parent group, but it drew on a formidable reserve of pro-military sentiment in the countryside.

Once the April elections were out of the way and a tractable lower house was in office, the Tojo cabinet decided to overhaul the IRAA by legally bringing all civic organizations under its umbrella—although in practice most were there already. The purpose of the change, the government announced, was "to strengthen their objectives and functions." The main difference was that the association now had budget access to the national treasury and uniform fiscal control over the labor, youth, women's and other similar groups.

In a classic administrative compromise, the new arrangements made the cabinet the general overseer of the newly integrated association but gave various ministers the job of supervising its activities. Now the reshuffle that began in the fall of 1940 was completed. Far from curbing the generals and admirals, the IRAA had become a giant organizational sponge, wielded at the pleasure of the military-dominated state. Its ponderous and bloated character is doubtless the main reason why the association, having absorbed all the citizens' groups, became almost useless to the authorities after mid-1942.

As the nominal overseer of the **National Spiritual Mobilization** after September 1940, the IRAA cooperated with the home ministry in urging citizens to form neighborhood associations to carry out community tasks such as defense against the air war (see also **Japan, Air War Against**), recreation, distributing rations and carrying out duties connected with local **health** and nutrition standards. Eventually the cabinet decided to put the neighborhood units under the IRAA along with the large-scale civic associations. In "Policies Regarding the Organization of the People," announced on May 15, 1942, the government made it clear that the local groups were not responsible to the IRAA, but it also decreed that the existing officers of community councils and neighborhood associations were to be confirmed in their posts by the IRAA.

The parent group now had the right to place aides in any community or neighborhood unit it wished, but in practice it decorously deferred to local leaders "to avoid duplication of effort." Exactly as with the labor, women's, and youth groups that were nominally absorbed at the same time, the IRAA became the titular organizational hinge on which the neighborhood groups turned. When the local units were actually integrated into the IRAA on August 14, 1942, the move drew a good deal of fire from below. Since the IRAA was reluctant to use its power to appoint new leaders and preferred to retain the existing local leaders, it seems very likely that most community and neighborhood groups went on settling matters, as in the past, among themselves. What they would have welcomed most from above was funding, but the IRAA did not have a big enough budget to help very significantly.

The state restructured the organizations during 1940-1942, due to its own political necessities as much as to the need for tighter social control. Neither Konoe's attempt to outflank the armed services in 1940 nor Tojo's efforts to elect a pliant lower house two years later was notably successful. Although it was hemmed in by the **National General Mobilization Law** of 1938, the Diet kept on meeting throughout the war. The semicontrolled election of 1942 had returned 85 candidates opposed by the IRAA, and as late as March 1945 by-elections were still being held to fill vacanies in the lower house. In most cases the elemental strength of the workers', young people's, and women's associations continued to reside at the plant or community level, not at the central organizational pivot.

Throughout the whole period, the IRAA proved to be a vague and cumbersome apparatus, not a smooth instrument of social mobilization in the hands of the generals and admirals who dominated the cabinets. The military services had enormous influence in Japan after 1940, but more because the simple necessity of fighting a war made standardization desirable than because of any cleverness at integrating society under mass organizations. This same necessity finally led the cabinet to dissolve the moribund IRAA on June 13, 1945 so that everyone who belonged to its subunits could join "people's volunteer corps" to defend the country against a possible American landing.

As its ultimate weapon against what might have become the bloodiest invasion by sea in history, the government organized civilian men under age 65 and women under 45 into volunteer corps in their neighborhoods or places of work. The army reluctantly undertook to train the volunteers with bamboo spears. The cabinet expected the volunteers to be home-front equivalents of the **Kamikaze** pilots, who went into battle poorly armed and fully prepared to die. The Tokyo police gloomily referred to the volunteer units as "the final people's movement." Japan's surrender decision deprived citizens of any chance to find out whether their tactics might have been any more effective against the Americans than had been the IRAA in mobilizing society for fighting this desperate war.

T. R. H. Havens

INDEPENDENCE MOVEMENTS.

The emancipation of the Asian peoples from colonial domination and economic dependence on the Western powers was clearly accelerated by the war. Aside from the fact that it was only a natural response to the provocations of the Japanese occupation, the political conscience of the peoples in question matured at a swifter pace from 1943 to 1945 than it had in the 30 years before. There were various reasons for this. When the European war became a world war in 1941, the nationalist parties in Asia had already affirmed their supreme goal—independence—before it was within their reach. They were not content simply to be anticolonialist and anti-imperialist. Thai nationalism, for example, was in large part distinguished by its anti-Chinese sentiment, whereas the anticolonialist tendencies of the Malay Chinese could be attributed to the world economic depression.

Following **Japan**'s victory over Russia in 1905, the absolute domination of the European powers in Asia began to totter, with the consequent increase in influence of the **United States** and a czar-less, renascent **USSR**. World War I and its consequences destroyed the uniformity of the European countries' approach to Asia, and at the same time gave the Japanese the opportunity to become a great economic power. President Wilson's "Fourteen Points" of 1918, with its doctrine of the self-determination of all peoples, encouraged the Asians. They were further encouraged by Lenin's assertion that he would support the struggle of the "subject" peoples for national unity and independence. Finally, some of the Asiatic peoples were already represented in the **League of Nations**— in addition to Japan, there were **China, Thailand, India** and, somewhat later, Afghanistan, **Iraq** and Egypt. In order to attain membership in the League they, like the other members, had endorsed the colonial status quo. The nationalist current gained strength in various countries, depending on the extent of their independence, their economic situation and the class in control (which was typically urban). Diverse concepts dictated the power structure of the state; they depended on the area's social ethic, which differed considerably from Chinese Confucianism to the Buddhist *hinayana* to Islam.

The sudden collapse of the colonial powers in 1941-1942 had particularly agonizing psychological consequences. The **United Kingdom**, France and **the Netherlands** lacked the sinew to protect their possessions against Japanese onslaughts. Even the proclamation of a future association of states, like that issued by the Netherlands, had no effect on the situation. Belief in the superiority of the European powers ebbed. The Asiatic people were then left with the conviction that with the loss of their colonial governors' authority, those governors had also relinquished their right to the respect and loyalty of their subjects. If the barbarous Japanese could so easily destroy the old order, what was the old order's *raison d'etre* in the first place? Could they not enter the resulting power vacuum themselves?

The awakening Asiatic nations responded enthusiastically to the audacious moves of their fellow Asiatics, the Japanese. The victorious advance of **Hirohito's** troops at first naturally aroused more pride than the conquests of **Hitler** and **Mussolini** in Europe. From the beginning, the Japanese fought for the "**Greater East Asia Co-Prosperity Sphere**" under the banner of the liberation of Asia from colonialism and the yoke of Western imperialism. They made grand economic promises and contrived the formula of Pacific cooperation. There is no doubt whatever that the initial Japanese encouragement of self-government—in **Burma**, the **Philippines** and **Indonesia**, for example—favored the **collaboration** demanded by the Japanese authorities from the heads of the nationalist parties. Nor did the populations dominated by the Rising Sun always regard the Japanese occupation as a "period of suffering." Actually, the occupied countries were not all of the same mind, and the Japanese conquerors were acclaimed as liberators for different reasons in different places. The inhabitants of **Malaya**, for example, hoped the Japanese would help them drive out the Chinese who dominated their country.

But the Japanese kept postponing the date of each country's independence and thus lost a large part of the sympathy they had been able to claim at the beginning. The remainder was dissipated by their atrocities and the looting of the occupied lands. Equally significant was the fact that despite their basically loyal collaboration, the various movements for self-advancement in these countries were exploited by the occupation forces to realize Japanese national aims. In Indonesia, for example, the ruling Samurai interned all the Dutch bureaucrats and promoted the formerly subordinate Indonesian employees to take their place. This measure increased the difficulties attendant to the reestablishment of the old colonial situation. Through mass communications, the Japanese and their native collaborators for the first time reached large masses of the population to whom they broadcast slogans of national liberation. Their use of the Indonesian language helped create a common consciousness, a symbol of unity. The proffered political and social program as well as the appeals to all patriots were not only features of collaborationist **propaganda** but also articles of faith among the **Resistance** groups. This was the nationalist policy of **Sukarno**, Thakin Nu, Ba Maw and Pibul, applied simultaneously on two different planes. Indeed, many of them even played a dangerous double game—on the one hand, they collaborated with the Japanese; on the other, they cooperated with anti-Japanese plots promoted by the Allies. It is certain that the political leaders of Burma, Thailand, Indonesia and other Pacific areas could not all be considered collaborators in the strict sense of the word. They were, in effect, serving their countries. Their devious methods were their means of preparing for the liberation of their nations in accord with the heads of the various Resistance movements led, for the most part, by Communists, and of strengthening their claim to the leadership of those nations after the Allies subdued the Japanese—which, after 1943, became inevitable. If the evolution of these countries ended in their independence after the various internal rivalries and tests of strength with the former colonial powers were finally resolved, it is equally true that the war provided the proper historical atmosphere for it. This too can be said with a good deal of justification for various parts of Africa and the Middle East.

In India, the war also brought independence closer. On many occasions violent or non-violent activity against British domination occurred while, on the battlefields, Indian volunteers fought to perpetuate the Empire. Most of the maharajahs did not bother to hide their anti-British sentiments. When the Japanese approached the Indian frontier and despair was rampant in the Indian Congress, Sir **Stafford Cripps**, in April 1942, in the name of the His Majesty's Government, presented the plan promising "solemnly" to accord "full independence" to India at the end of the war if it should be requested by a constituent assembly. But the negotiations were fruitless. In the first place, the Indian maharajahs protested that their country was not consulted on the political conduct of the war. Since the beginning of hostilities, the Congress had disapproved of the fact that the British had converted India to a belligerent without the consent of the Indian people, and **Gandhi** had, in his fashion, demonstrated against participation in the war. Later, the Congress and the Moslem League, led by Mahomed Jinnah, failed to come to an accord and once again the unbridgeable chasms dividing the country by religion, by caste and by the princes who held to their treaties with the British became obvious. In August 1942, Gandhi responded with the last "non-cooperation" campaign, which degenerated into bloody disturbances. The joint Indian-British army crushed these demonstrations. Gandhi and the other leaders of the liberation movement were arrested and held until 1944. But there was no stopping the march of history. In 1945, the British Labor Government, formed during the summer, made new offers to satisfy India's eagerness for independence.

At the same time, the Japanese proposed the convocation of a "provisional government" of "free India" under **Subhas Chandra Bose** and the creation of a liberation army. This tentative independence movement, however, was cut short by the Allied victory.

In China, the position of the Kuomintang under **Chiang Kai-shek** was systematically enfeebled by the Japanese aggression in 1937 and the later victory of **Mao Tse-tung**. It is thus reasonable to concur with the judgment of many historians that if the Japanese had no intention of sowing the seed of a Communist China, the policy they pursued nevertheless assured it. Initially, the Japanese invasion had the effect of reorienting Chinese policy, but the anti-imperialist movement was aimed primarily at the Japanese. A kind of "sacred union" or common front formed between the Communists and the Kuomintang. Yet gradually, beginning at the end of 1941, the rival forces restrained their activity against the Japanese and prepared for the final clash against each other. But demoralization and corruption enervated the Kuomintang while Mao, through rigid organization and strict discipline, maintained the fighting spirit of his Eighth Army and steeled it for the final resolution.

H.-A. Jacobsen

INDIA.
The British had proposed the "progressive realization of responsible government" in India, within the Empire, in 1917; from 1919 the system of "dyarchy" provided some degree of Indian responsibility to an Indian legislature and electorate. But the legislature's powers remained limited, even after an extending act in 1935 (which **Churchill** vehemently opposed). The sub-continent was still run by a very small, very strong network of a few hundred British district officers and their superiors—about three in a million of the total population, which rose from 338 million in 1931 to 388 million in 1941.

In 1939, the British army in India numbered some 60,000 and the Indian army, primarily British-officered, 160,000. Both forces were highly trained, but neither was heavily armed; the Indian army had no tanks and few heavy guns. Available air and sea forces were still slighter. During the war, the Indian army expanded to over two million men, the largest volunteer force ever raised anywhere; it did much work essential for British victory. Indian divisions served with distinction in the Western Desert and in eastern Africa, as well as on the eastern front in **Burma**, where they eventually proved themselves more than a match for the Japanese.

Japanese attempts to exploit Indian nationalist feeling to the point of open revolt against the occupying power had slight success. **Subhas Chandra Bose**'s Indian National Army was never a serious combat force, nor did it exercise any weighty appeal on Indian soil. But the Raj did not function in wartime with the perfect efficiency its civil service desired. Widespread shortages, particularly of railway rolling stock, led to economic distress, and in Bengal in the winter of 1942-43 to an exceptionally severe famine, in which two or even three million people died of hunger (no adequate figures are available).

The Indian National Congress, representing the Hindu majority, campaigned as actively as it could against the prospect of continued British control: "Britain's difficulty, India's opportunity," they might have said, aping the Irish slogan. A sabotage campaign in 1941-42 was put down by ordinary police methods, and the "Quit India" campaign **Mohandas Gandhi** launched was muffled by his arrest. Sir **Archibald Percival Wavell**, British viceroy from 1943 to 1947, tried to get Hindus and Moslems to agree on terms of independence which even **Leopold Stennett Amery** was willing to concede, but he had no success.

The end of the war saw India several strides nearer independence than in 1939, but with the prospect of partitions as well in full sight.

M. R. D. Foot

INDOCHINA.
France conquered Indochina gradually, beginning with the capture of Saigon in 1859 and ending with the acquisition of northwestern Cambodia from Siam in 1907. **Georges Catroux**, the governor-general in 1940, left to join **de Gaulle**, taking only an aide-de-camp with him. Adm. Jean Decoux, Catroux' successor, conceded bases to the Japanese in September 1940, on orders from the Vichy government, in exchange for recognition by **Japan** of French sovereignty. Some rubber was still exported to Europe, of which the Germans took a share under the terms of the Franco-German armistice. In the spring of 1942 the Japanese seized all French merchant shipping in Indochina; hence the reason for the British concern over, and invasion of, **Madagascar**.

Roosevelt played with the idea of handing Indochina over to **China** after the war. The Japanese got in first; on March 9, 1945 they took complete administrative control of the country, interning the French garrison (and, in a few cases, decapitating French officers in front of their paraded native troops), humiliating French civilians and running everything themselves. Thousands of imprisoned nationalists were released, but they showed no gratitude to the

Japanese (see **Burma**), who in any case were forced to surrender within six months.

The Chinese occupied northern Indochina in September 1945; the British, acting as trustees for the French, took over the rest of the country in October from a Japanese administration that remained in operation till then. The French contacted the Viet Minh through their own mission in Yunnan, but they insisted on having their colony back, thus starting down the road to their eventual ouster in 1954.

INDONESIA.

Indonesia, or the Dutch East Indies, as it was then known, remained loyal to the **government-in-exile** of **the Netherlands** in London after **Germany**'s conquest of the homeland in May 1940. In September of that year this resource-rich, 3,000-mile-long archipelago in the southwest Pacific was selected as a target of Japanese expansionist designs. The resources of the archipelago had attracted **Japan**'s attention, and, in that sense, oil and refineries helped to cause the war in the Pacific in 1941. Oil exports to Japan had been increasing for a time, but, in August 1941, they stopped on the orders of the London government.

Immediately after their attack on **Pearl Harbor**, the Japanese began preparing to invade the outlying Dutch Indies by wresting control of the main lanes north of the Macassar and Molucca passages (see also **Borneo**). Toward the end of December 1941, in fact, IGHQ moved the date for undertaking the Java invasion up by about a month, on the advice of Gen. Hisaichi Terauchi, the Southern Army Commander (GHQ Saigon). Ground forces assigned to take the Dutch Indies came under Lt. Gen. Hitoshi Imamura's 16th Army, whose core was formed by the Second Division and the 56th Independent Mixed Brigade. In the north Celebes, the Japanese landed at Menado, Kema and Bangka Roads on January 11, also dropping a total of about 500 paratroopers for the first time in an attack on the airstrip south of Menado. After overrunning their objective, the Japanese had the airfield ready for IJN use within 12 days, thus extending their strike-radius another 300 miles southward. During the battle for **Singapore** (which fell on February 15), the Japanese proceded to conquer more key points on the road to Java. Kendari in the Celebes, with its excellent air base, fell on January 24; Ambon (Amboina), by February 4; Macassar in the Celebes, on February 9; Bandjermasin in South Borneo, on the 10th. On February 14-15 Japanese paratroopers and amphibious units attacked the airbase and refineries around Palembang on south Sumatra. By the 17th, the Allied defenders of Sumatra had been driven to Java, and the next day the Japanese took Bali and Lombok. **Timor** was at-

tacked on February 19 by paratroops and landing forces. Australian and Dutch remnants fell back to the recesses of the island, where they fought as guerrillas until they were finally taken out at the beginning of 1943.

Next the Japanese hurled two invasion armies against Java in accordance with careful planning by IGHQ, which had reinforced Imamura with two infantry divisions. From the Sulu chain sailed 41 transports carrying an invasion force bound for Surabaja in the east, mainly the 48th Division, which had been transferred from the **Philippines**. From Camranh Bay in **Indochina** came the 56 transports which comprised the second invasion flotilla, headed for Batavia in the west and bearing the 16th Army Headquarters, the Second Division from the homeland, and a regiment from the 38th Division in **Hong Kong**. Overall commander of the Second Fleet's Dutch East Indies Invasion Force was Vice Adm. Ibo Takahashi. The task of defending Java fell to the Dutch Gen. Hein ter Poorten, from the Army, Maj. Gen. L. H. van Oyen, from the Air Force, and Adm. Conrad Helfrich, from the Navy. Dutch regular troops numbered only 25,000; the poorly trained territorials, another 45,000. Small Australian and British forces supported the Dutch. For air defense, van Oyen possessed fewer than 30 operational fighters and some 50 other **ABDA** (American, British, Dutch, Australian) aircraft. A similarly heterogeneous collection of old ABDA warships (eight cruisers, a dozen destroyers and 32 submarines) was all that Helfrich could commit against the powerful IJN forces, which smashed the last Allied naval units in the battle of the Java Sea. The ABDA naval command collapsed on March 1: Adm. Helfrich flew to Colombo; U.S. Adm. William Glassford and British Adm. A. F. E. Palliser, to Australia. Held up off east Java by scarcely a day, and off west Java not at all, the Japanese came ashore at both ends of the island on February 28-March 1 in a giant pincers maneuver. Sixteenth Army troops landed near the northwest cape of Java, east of Batavia and northwest of Surabaja. Batavia and Bandung fell on March 5; Kragan and Surabaja, by the 7th. Striking overland across Java, the Japanese eastern force seized Tjilatjap on March 8. The Dutch seemed confused by the diffusion and energy of the attacks. Two battleseasoned Australian battalions fought especially stubbornly for several days, but the overall effect was slight. On March 9 General ter Poorten surrendered unconditionally. Only mopping-up operations remained for IJA forces in the Indies.

A garrison of 93,000 Dutch and colonial troops, including 2,000 officers, laid down their arms; the Japanese announced that they were releasing the Indonesian soldiers. According to Japanese sources, the

Dutch losses amounted to two divisions and 15 independent battalions. About 5,000 Australian, British, and U.S. personnel were also captured, a force which the Japanese equated with one more division. Captured materiel included 732 cannon, 1,567 machine guns, and 97,384 rifles. At a time when Allied strength and fortunes were at a dangerously low ebb, such losses of men and equipment were enormous. From the Japanese standpoint, the war had moved swiftly and triumphantly into a second stage with the conquest of populous Java's oil riches. Instead of the targeted 150 days, the Japanese campaign, for all of its complexity, consumed only 90. The defenders' efforts at sabotage were pyrotechnical but not critical; the oil wells and large oil reserves were captured largely intact. (The Japanese did, however, have to ship the oil before they could use it, and their tankers were liable to Allied interception.)

With the Japanese conquest of Indonesia, the end of the European and American empires in Southeast Asia was at hand, the Malay Barrier was shattered, and Japan's vaunted Greater East Asia Co-Prosperity Sphere had become a reality. While some Dutch may have argued that the ABDA's defense of the Indies had delayed the foe for at least a month and had thwarted any Japanese notion of invading Australia, Admiral King reportedly termed the entire Southwest Pacific campaign "a magnificent display of very bad strategy." Churchill might have said of the Dutch Indies debacle as tellingly as of Singapore, "The violence, fury, skill, and might of Japan far exceeded anything we had been led to expect."

The Japanese were, in the long run, no more successful as imperialists than the Dutch had been. For several decades there had been some unrest over Dutch rule. The Japanese thus had, but failed to exploit, a considerable opportunity to pose as Asiatic liberators from European imperialism. They interned the entire Dutch population in fearsome camps where there was little food and less medical attention. But their military regime was, of course, geared to Japan's interests, not to Indonesia's. They encouraged Sukarno to develop an Indonesian nationalist movement, which did secure considerable popular support, but they made no direct concessions to it. In the end, on August 17, 1945, Sukarno was forced at pistol point by his more resolute colleagues of the Indonesian National Party to proclaim the islands' independence before the Dutch could return.

British troops attempted ineffectually to safeguard the islands for the Dutch, who eventually surrendered sovereignty in December 1949.

A. D. Coox
M. R. D. Foot

INFORMATION SERVICES.

Gathering information is not necessarily equivalent to spying. It has been carried out since antiquity by military attaches, who were not regularized until 1815, by the Congress of Vienna. Since that time, it has become common practice for military, naval and, later, air attaches stationed in foreign countries to keep their governments as well-informed as possible, within the laws of the host country. Obviously, this type of fact-gathering can only be pursued in peacetime when it is both legal and safe. Thus in the 1930s, the French Air Attache in Germany, Paul Stehlin, made sketches, in the course of authorized training flights, of air bases and aircraft factories. In addition he gathered information on the concentration of Nazi motorized troops near the Czech border, posed ready to attack, in September 1938 and again in March 1939. In wartime, however, tactical information can be gained only through direct observation or the interrogation of prisoners. Through such methods Col. Benjamin Dickson, an intelligence officer in the U.S. First Army, learned early in December 1944, that the Germans were planning a massive counteroffensive through Ardennes. Unfortunately his report was rejected and many lives were needlessly lost in the ensuing Battle of the Bulge.

In the year 500 B.C., the Chinese Sun Tzu said: "Secret operations are necessary in war, and form a solid basis for an army's movements." Thus it has always been. Information on the location and strength of the enemy's armed power and his strategic goals is of such vital importance that no state can afford to shrink from the use of reprehensible methods such as infiltration, burglary, bribery or blackmail to get it. Hence the use of "professionals"—indoctrinated agents, educated and trained in their country for all practical aspects of espionage in specific missions. After infiltration into an enemy country, they recruit local informers who are ready to cooperate in traitorous activity for various reasons—ideological devotion, frustration, a taste for adventure, cupidity, vanity, a sense of duty—motives, in short, that are far from unique but quite often complex. In time of war, "puppeteer" agents and "puppet" informers are usually shot or hanged for their sins.

Information obtained through espionage is transmitted in various ways to the interested secret services for evaluation. Thus, in World War II, every national secret service was remarkably well informed about its enemies and their plans. But a good deal of this information is so often doubtful or contradictory that the governments and military leaders receiving it often hesitate to act on such flimsy grounds. This was the case with Stalin at the beginning of 1941 when he ignored the warnings of the Soviet spy ring of the imminence of the **Barbarossa** plan for the *Wehrmacht*'s attack on the **USSR**. **Hitler**, similarly, brushed aside the secret documents **Cicero** had stolen from the British ambassador to **Turkey**.

The term ''secret services'' is used to designate all the agencies involved solely in clandestine activity devoted to espionage, counter-intelligence, counter-espionage, **sabotage**, subversion, ''black'' **propaganda**, special operations, security and the like. The history of such services throughout the centuries indicates that their collective value depends directly on the personal talent of their leaders and their willingness to abide by the rule ''the end justifies the means.''

Every country must, in the interests of self-preservation, be on the alert for espionage, sabotage and subversion on the part of agents of an enemy or potentially inimical nation.

The purpose of *counter-intelligence* is to execute preventive orders for the safety of a nation's military, diplomatic or political secrets. Among its aspects are the detection of and the collection of information on people behaving suspiciously; the constant surveillance of such suspects and the places they frequent by shadowing them, reading their mail, eavesdropping on their telephone conversations and recording them; and infiltrating other nations' networks to learn their plans, procedures and agents. This final activity requires the use of ''double agents,'' volunteers or defected enemy spies.

The purpose of *counter-espionage* is to uncover all attempts at spying and so frustrate violations of the security of the state, and to track down and arrest those responsible. Basically, then, it is a police function. Military security, in addition to police activity, played both repressive and preventive roles during World War II in connection with military information within the armed forces. (See also, for Germany, *Abwehr*, **Gestapo** and **SD**; for the **United States**, Office of Strategic Services; for France, **French Secret Services** and **French Police During the Occupation**; for the **United Kingdom**, Intelligence Service; for Italy, *Servizio Informazione Militare*; for Japan, Japanese Secret Services; for the USSR, *Narodnyy Kommissariat Vnutrennikh Del.*)

R. Gheysens

INONU, Ismet (1884-1973).

From 1923 to 1937 Inonu served as premier of **Turkey** under Kemal Ataturk. In 1938 he succeeded Ataturk as president. During World War II Inonu kept Turkey neutral until January 1945, when it joined the Allied powers.

INTELLIGENCE SERVICE.

Basically a misnomer, this term is used to describe all the British secret services.

In the period between the two world wars, the activity, energy and organizational complexity of these services very nearly paralleled their predecessors' during World War I. These characteristics of the British secret services were a consequence of the rivalry among the Foreign Office, the War Office and the Admiralty; another consequence was that they exhibited a disconcerting variety of independent facets, partly to confuse rivals.

At the time of its reorganization in 1905 by the Minister of War, Lord Haldane, British Military Intelligence, directed by the brilliant General Sir James Grierson, included in its hierarchy **MI-5**, entrusted with counter-espionage, and **MI-6**, entrusted with military espionage.

In 1939, in another reorganization, MI-5 was placed under the auspices of the Home Secretary and within the jurisdiction of the Prime Minister. MI-6 was transformed into the **Special Intelligence Service**, or SIS, attached to the Foreign Office, then under the command of Lt. Col. **Stewart Menzies**. The SIS soon introduced its section D, specializing in **sabotage** and subversion. These organizations were complemented by MIR—Military Intelligence Research—within the War Office (see **Jo Charles Francis Holland**).

In July 1940, MIR and section D were combined with the War Office to form the **Special Operations Executive** or SOE, shortly afterward to be independent, under the authority of the Ministry of Economic Warfare. Similarly, a ''black''—i.e., *sub rosa*—propaganda section created by the Foreign Office and named ''Electra House'' after the mansion sheltering it, was attached to the SOE in 1940 to become the **Political Warfare Executive** or PWE, a medium of political and **psychological warfare**. And, stimulated by the war effort, Scotland Yard developed an offshoot known as the Special Branch of Scotland Yard to cooperate with MI-5 as an executive agency.

The advent of the war took the British intelligence services by surprise. Like their peers in the French *Deuxieme Bureau* across the channel, they amounted to little more than an ineffectual group of dilettantes during the first six months of the war. The progress they had made since 1918 was minimal; compared to their much more dynamic opposite numbers in **Germany**, they had no idea of their proper function in a total war. Neither the SIS nor MI-5 were of much use in that period, as demonstrated by the **Venlo** affair on November 9, 1939, when two British agents were kidnapped by **Heydrich**'s men, and Lord **Edward Halifax**, Secretary to the Foreign Office, was deceived into believing that they were the recipients of **peace over-**

tures from a German military cabal aiming to destroy **Hitler**.

But by 1943, despite several serious blunders, the British intelligence agencies, assisted by colleagues from other Allied nations, had practically won the underground war. Their victory derived from diligent improvement of their organization and the active co-operation of the **Resistance** in all the countries occupied by German troops, to say nothing of their adversaries' gaffes, most of which were the products of intra-organizational rivalries. The Allied intelligence operatives were also the beneficiaries of unexpected assistance from sympathetic agents in such neutral countries as **Sweden** and **Switzerland**, which chose to overlook such activities.

The SOE in particular, commanded by the skillful Sir **Colin Gubbins**, was a huge organization guiding a Resistance army on the Continent that contributed substantially to the final victory. **Churchill** himself had created this new body to "set fire to Europe."

The SIS continued its labors, gathering military, political and economic information from listening posts abroad, but the number of agents it controlled in territories under *Wehrmacht* control steadily decreased. It was also handicapped by the Resistance movements which tended to confuse the activities of the SIS with the work of SOE agents.

The MI-5 was particularly effective in ferreting out German agents in the British Isles and duping them into spreading false information throughout the enemy network operating there. Double agents such as "Garbo," "Tricycle" (Dusko Popov) and "Zigzag" (Eddie Chapman, alias Fritzchen) achieved notable successes for the "Double-Cross" Committee which proved so effective in tricking German intelligence (see also **Deception**).

In the area of psychological warfare, the British went to a good deal of trouble before arriving at a systematic plan for reconquering the misty world of mass hypnotism preempted by **Goebbels**. But after this initial groping and a serious study of the ramifications of Churchill's dictum "The **morale** of the civil population is an objective of the war," they developed methods at least as effective if not more so than those of the mob-mind manipulators of the Third Reich. The "V for Victory" campaign launched by the **British Broadcasting Corporation** and blared over the radio waves along with the first four notes of Beethoven's Fifth Symphony was an incomparable psychological feat for the Allies. The PWE did its part by staging broadcasts with the aid of German emigres or prisoners hostile to the Nazi regime designed to dishearten the German armed forces. Actually, however, this counter-propaganda had a much greater influence on the inhabitants of the occupied lands than on

the ethnic Germans, among whom, in turn, civilians were more vulnerable to the British blandishments than soldiers, except during periods of military inactivity. On the whole, the British agents and their Allied counterparts, increasingly assisted by the Resistance and by their own steadily improving efficiency, became valuable auxiliaries to the fighting men in the field. The first intimations of German success in experimental **radar**, for example, came to London in 1942 by way of the Belgian Resistance. Of tremendous value to the Allied command, this information marked a long step forward in aero-naval history.

The British managed to sow a grapevine of espionage and sabotage that operated beautifully by the end of 1942. Its spectacular achievement, accomplished with the aid of Greek patriots, was the destruction of the Gorgopotamos viaduct, rendering useless the only railroad from Salonica to Piraeus, the indispensable supply link for the German troops in Africa.

In that same period in **the Netherlands**, Allied agents twice daily transmitted weather reports the British required for bombing missions.

The French Section of the SOE, directed by Maurice Buckmaster, enjoyed extraordinary success after some bad initial mistakes. By its sabotage of the Peugeot plants manufacturing tanks and trucks for the Germans, it seriously interfered with the Nazi war effort.

Beginning in May 1943, British missions were constantly in touch with **Tito** in **Yugoslavia**, supplying him and his men with weapons. It was this band of guerillas that played an increasingly important role in the strategy of General **Maitland Wilson**.

Danish radio posts responded daily to coded questions asked by London radio. And in **Norway**, one morning in February 1944, a commando team in the Norwegian section of the SOE blew up the ferryboat *Hydro*, loaded with a supply of heavy water still remaining to the Germans one year after the sabotage of the Norsk Hydro plants' facilities for producing heavy water by another Norwegian commando. It was the loss of this second store of the precious material in Lake Tinnsjoe that put an end to the experiments of the physicists of the Third Reich who sought to develop the **atomic bomb**.

The Italian boot was honeycombed with British agents, regularly transmitting information on the military and political situation in that country, from October 1943 to April 1945.

After the end of 1943, the German secret services were reduced to a merely defensive instrument and finally met an ignoble end. Its mission completed, the SOE was dissolved in 1946.

R. Gheysens

INTERALLIED CONTROL COUNCIL FOR GERMANY.

The rationale for the establishment of the Interallied Control Council for **Germany** in Berlin on August 30, 1945 had been publicly announced in the Declaration of the Four Victorious Powers of June 4, 1945. Until its de facto dissolution on March 20, 1948, the council was the highest controlling agency of the powers occupying Germany. Its mission and limitations were defined by the Accords of November 1944 regarding the control arrangements and supplemented and modified by the Accord of May 1, 1945, concerning the participation of the French Republic. The four commanders in chief sat on the Control Council, which acted as the central administrative body of the occupation government. It was responsible for planning Germany's military and economic future, in accordance with instructions each commander in chief received from his government.

The council's basic impediment to action lay in the fact that any one member could veto a decision. In case of disagreement the supreme commanders made the decisions for their particular zones in conformity with the directives of their respective governments, thus deepening rifts—especially between the Soviet zone and the zones occupied by the Western powers. Moreover, because of the veto exercised by France, the "central German administration" envisaged by the "Big Three" at Potsdam in July and August 1945 could not be instituted. The Control Council thus lacked a German infrastructure.

The proclamations, laws, directives, orders and instructions issued by the Control Council between 1945 and 1948 (which would be rendered null and void by the Proclamation of 1955 of the sovereignty of the German Democratic Republic and the Federal Republic of Germany) were particularly important for Berlin, where the council controlled the Interallied Military Command governing the city after the Western powers secured its western sectors in early July 1945. The command was a composite of the four military commands, each assuming the function of "Supreme Military Command" in turn every 15 days. Here, too, decisions could only be made unanimously. Specific issues were settled within the framework of the Interallied Coordination Measures of December 21, 1945.

The departure on March 20, 1948 of Marshal **Vasili D. Sokolovski**, the supreme Soviet commander, after the disclosure of plans for a state comprising the three Western zones during the London Conference (attended by the **United States**, the **United Kingdom**, France and the Benelux countries) put an abrupt end to the activities of the Control Council. With the introduction of the West German mark in the western sectors of Berlin, the Soviet representative left the Interallied Military Command, which suspended its activities on July 1, 1948, when the Soviet blockade of the city began. The composition of the command was then, de facto, reduced to the three Western commands in Berlin.

The agreement among the four powers regarding the "Control of Aerial Security," adopted on November 22, 1945 by the Control Council, permitted flights between the Western zones and Berlin through three reserved air corridors. It remained in effect even during the crisis resulting from the Soviet blockade, thanks to the understanding of the Soviet representatives.

The other nonmilitary funtions of the Supreme Allied Command forming the Control Council were turned over to the "high commissioners" in 1949 when the status of the Western occupation in Germany was settled. After the declaration of the sovereignty of the Federal Republic of Germany and of the German Democratic Republic in 1955, those functions went to the ambassadors of the United States, Great Britain and France in Bonn and to the ambassador of the **USSR** in Berlin.

A. Hillgruber

INTERNATIONAL LABOR ORGANIZATION (ILO).

At the beginning of the war, the **League of Nations** still existed, but it was largely paralyzed. In fact, it barely managed to stay in existence. The ILO, however, although closely connected with its parent organization, continued to operate.

It should be noted that the ILO's recruitment of members had always been independent of the league's. The **United States**, for example, joined the ILO in 1934 without ever having entered the parent organization. And other states, including **Brazil**, **China**, Peru, Venezuela and **Hungary** resigned from the league but maintained their membership in the ILO. This situation was instrumental in keeping the ILO active during the war. The International Labor Bureau (ILB) left Geneva in 1940 to take refuge in Montreal. The ratification of conventions necessarily decelerated, and information on social conditions in various parts of the world was scarce. Nevertheless, an International Labor Conference was held in New York in 1941, during which the objectives of an international policy were defined and confirmed by several resolutions.

The trend of public opinion during the war seemed to indicate the acceptance of some of the principles contained in the **Atlantic Charter** of August 1941, especially that affirming the right of peoples to self-determination. One of the conclusions of a conference held by the Institute of Pacific Relations at Mount

Tremblant in Quebec in December 1942 was that the fundamental aim of policy in Southeast Asia and in other colonies throughout the world should be to facilitate their early independence. The conference also asserted that social and economic development in colonial territories was equally important. This opinion was confirmed by a series of measures designed to promote autonomy in territories under British rule—Jamaica, Ceylon, Fiji etc. On December 6, 1942, Queen **Wilhelmina** of **the Netherlands** declared that a Dutch Commonwealth would be established after the war "on the solid ground of full association with no room for racial or national discrimination."

Taking note of all these events, the Administrative Council of the ILB met in London in December 1943 and decided that a regular session of the International Labor Conference would be convoked in April 1944. To prepare for concerted international action on post-war problems, it was necessary to examine the social problems arising during the final phases of the war and after the end of hostilities and to define the ILO's position, status and principles of action.

Having completed its deliberations, the International Labor Conference meeting in Philadelphia adopted on May 10, 1944 a declaration containing the following Section 2:

> Believing that experience has fully demonstrated the truth of the statement in the Preamble to the Constitution of the International Labor Organization that lasting peace can be established only if it is based on social justice, the Conference affirms that all human beings, irrespective of race, creed or sex, have the right to pursue both their material well-being and their spiritual development in conditions of freedom and dignity, of economic security and equal opportunity and that the attainment of the conditions in which this shall be possible must constitute the central aim of national and international policy...

In the first section of the same declaration, the conference once again affirmed the fundamental principles of the organization, especially the following:

> ...that labor is not a commodity; that freedom of expression and of association are essential to sustained progress; that poverty anywhere constitutes a danger to prosperity everywhere, and that accordingly the war against want, while it requires to be carried on with unrelenting vigor within each nation, equally requires continuous and concerted international effort in which the representatives of workers and employers, enjoying equal status with those of Governments, join with them in free discussion and democratic decision with a view to the promotion of the common welfare.

A recommendation concerning the minimum standards that should govern policy in colonial territories was appended to the declaration of Philadelphia.

These standards concerned slavery; opium; forced labor; recruitment of labor; penal correction; employment of women, children and young people; salaries; public health; housing; social security; discriminatory practices; labor inspection; professional organizations and cooperatives. Although it did not allude specifically to the granting of autonomy to colonial territories, Article 4 of the recommendation contained the following provision: "All possible initiatives will be taken to associate the peoples of the subject territories with the preparation and execution of measures for social progress in an effective manner, preferably through their own elected representatives, wherever this method is possible and appropriate."

P. de Briey

INTERNATIONAL MILITARY TRIBUNAL.
See **War Criminals.**

IRAN.
After World War I Riza Khan took control of Iran, also known as Persia, assuming the title Riza Shah Pahlavi in 1925. His home policy was aimed at reducing tribal power, emancipating **women** and introducing railways and industry; his foreign policy, playing the British off against the Russians. German influence increased in the late 1930s, and by 1940 several hundred German technicians were in Iran. Iranian neutrality was proclaimed in September 1939. But when the **United Kingdom** and the **USSR** became allies in June 1941, the shah's foreign policy collapsed. In August they jointly occupied Iran to secure safe transit of British and American arms supplies into Soviet territory. Riza Shah abdicated in September 1941 and left the country. He died in Johannesburg in July 1944.

His son, Mohammed Riza Pahlavi, tried to rule more democratically. He accepted Anglo-Russian occupation as fact, and in September 1943 Iran declared war on **Germany**. The volume of supplies crossing Iran into the USSR was important for the Soviet war machine, and due acknowledgment was made at the time of the Teheran conference (see **Conferences, Allied**) in November 1943, in which Iran played no part beyond providing the site.

The cost of living in Teheran rose tenfold during the war. Advisers from the **United States** were invited to try to provide some economic help, and some American troops also arrived to ensure the safe transit of supplies and to improve the railways. The U.S. and British troops were withdrawn within six months of the end of the war in accordance with a treaty agreement. Soviet troops remained in Azerbaijan, in northwestern Iran, until May 1946.

M. R. D. Foot

IRAQ.

After the **United Kingdom** took Mesopotamia from **Turkey** in 1918, it was made a **League of Nations** mandate under the British, who set up the Kingdom of Iraq there in 1921 and introduced Iraq to the League as an independent state in 1932. The British retained air base rights at Habbaniya, west of Baghdad, as well as large commercial interests in the Mosul and Kirkuk oil fields.

At the outbreak of the war, Iraq severed relations with **Germany**, but did not declare war. Early in 1941 a Pan-Arab group under **Rashid Ali**, who was in contact with the Germans, seized power, and in May 1941 Iraq was at war with Great Britain. The British, by a resolute show of rather slender force, won in a month, and Rashid Ali fled to **Iran**. Iraq declared war on all three **Axis** powers in January 1942. Iraqi communications and oil were important to the British war effort, but there were no further operations on Iraqi soil.

M. R. D. Foot

IRELAND.

Late in the 12th century Ireland was partly conquered by England. Over 700 years of resentment and intermittent armed resistance by the Irish culminated in the Easter Rebellion in 1916. The uprising, which took place in Dublin, was put down, but the republic then proclaimed was eventually established in 1921, after three years of armed conflict with the British. By a treaty dated December 6, 1921, Ireland was partitioned. Six of the nine counties of Ulster, called Northern Ireland, remained part of the **United Kingdom**. The other 26 counties became a virtually independent dominion called the Irish Free State (*Saorstat Eirann*) and a member of the **League of Nations**. The British retained small naval bases at Queenstown (now Cobh), Berehaven and Lough Swilly until **Chamberlain** handed them over to the Irish in April 1938 as part of his **appeasement** policy. The ports were at that time indefensible, but his action hampered British naval defenses against German submarines, sometimes severely, a few years later (see **Convoys**). But it showed enough good will towards Ireland to secure Irish neutrality (the Free State was the only dominion not to participate in the war). The Germans maintained a legation in Dublin, which was of some use to them as a channel for intelligence; it could at least send useful weather reports. They at-

tempted, without success, to foster attacks on the British by the Irish Republican Army.

Free State government policy remained neutral. Yet, several thousand citizens of the Free State fought in Britain's armed forces, out of friendship for the British and combativeness of spirit; no obstacles were placed in their way, but they had no encouragement either.

The eastern coast of Ireland was sometimes accidentally raided by the *Luftwaffe*. The British kept a garrison, usually at least two divisions strong, in Northern Ireland, and Belfast was an important aircraft and shipbuilding center; thousands of American troops also stopped off in the six northern counties on their way to Europe.

M. R. D. Foot

IRON ROAD.

The operation of the iron-rich mines of Kiruna and Gallivare in northern **Sweden** was considered essential for the Nazi war effort. Fearing an allied attempt to bar German access to the mines, **Hitler** ordered the at-

tack on April 9, 1940 on **Denmark** and then **Norway** with the consequent seizure of Narvik, the Norwegian port through which the ore was exported. The German battleships *Scharnhorst* and *Gneisenau* kept watch over Narvik from the Lofoten fjord, with 10 destroyers as escorts. On April 10 and 13 the Royal Navy replied by blasting the German destroyers. The Allies struck again on April 16, when Gen. Emile Bethouart, in command of a French detachment, landed near Narvik and overcame adverse climatic conditions and the resistance of German troops under the guidance of Gen. **Eduard Dietl** to capture the port on May 28. This maneuver, however, had been designed to accompany a pincers attack under the direction of Lt. Gen. Hugh Massy on Namsos to the north and Andalsnes to the south, ending in the liberation of Trondheim. The pincers failed to form. Directing one of its arms, Maj. Bernard Paget reached his target, Dombas, but Gen. Carton de Wiart, in charge of the other, was blocked by a German counterattack, to the detriment of the entire operation. The Allies were then forced to land at Mosjoen, Mo-i-Rana and Bodo in order to reinforce precariously held Narvik, but they failed again when the Germans repossessed Mosjoen on May 11 and Mo-i-Rana on May 18. With the Allied evacuation of the ports of Namsos and Andalsnes, the German armies, supported by aircraft and naval forces, could not be stopped, and Gen. Bethouart's corps of 24,000 men had to abandon Narvik and Norway itself on June 8, 1940 to escape the German trap. The whole episode constituted a severe rebuff to **Paul Reynaud**, president of the French *Conseil d'Etat*, who had proudly announced Narvik's capture and claimed the closing of the Iron Road to the Nazis.

M. Baudot

IRONSIDE, Sir William Edward (1880-1959).
At the beginning of World War II, Ironside, a British general, succeeded **John Gort** as chief of the Imperial General Staff and held that post in 1939-40.

ISHIWARA, Kanji (1889-1949).
Ishiwara, a Japanese lieutenant general, was a noted Pan-Asian propagandist and archrival of Gen. **Hideki Tojo**. Ishiwara planned the Japanese seizure of Manchuria in September 1931 and developed an elaborate scheme for its semiautonomous development. He founded the East Asian League in 1933 to bring about racial harmony, economic integration and political federalism among Asian states so that they could throw off Western imperialism. His plans for domestic unification provoked great hostility from various political factions in Tokyo, and Tojo finally suppressed the East Asian League in 1941, ending

Ishiwara's military career on the eve of **Pearl Harbor**.

Ishiwara graduated from the military academy and the war college. He rose to top positions in the Japanese Kwantung Army and plotted its takeover of Manchuria. He believed that Japan faced an eventual war of attrition with the Western powers and regarded Manchuria as the cornerstone of a self-sufficient economic zone to match **Germany**'s in Europe and America's in the western hemisphere. He worked, unsuccessfully in the end, to establish Manchukuo as an autonomous region free of political or economic interference from Tokyo.

As a right-wing spokesman, Ishiwara, a devout Nichiren Buddist, announced that **Japan** had a moral duty to rescue Asia from Western values. His East Asian League, which was intended to include Manchukuo, **China**, Southeast Asia and **Australia**, was to be a loose political federation led by Emperor **Hirohito**. The West could be defeated, he thought, if Japan unified its own leadership elites and integrated the economies of all the states belonging to the league. But domestic divisiveness undercut Ishiwara's scheme, and no true economic regionalization took place. After Tojo cashiered him in 1941, Ishiwara called for the former's arrest and execution; he managed to escape imprisonment for his outspokenness by going into retirement to promote patriotic societies.

T. R. H. Havens.

ISMAY, Sir Hastings Lionel (later Lord) (1887-1965).
In 1938 Ismay, a British general, became secretary of the Committee of Imperial Defense and served as **Churchill**'s personal chief of staff from 1940 to 1945. He was the principal intermediary between Churchill and the British chiefs of staff.

ISRAEL.
See Palestine.

ITALY.
Italy, which had 49,840,000 inhabitants in 1940, emerged from World War I impoverished, cynical in outlook and spiritually and morally unstable. Italy was bitterly disappointed by the Allies' failure to keep their promises of April 26, 1915, when they had wooed it into joining their cause, in the treaties of Versailles and St. Germain. But the disappointment caused by the peace treaties was not the immediate reason for the masses' unrest. The riots that erupted in 1919 were stimulated by the militant left. These disorders were further inflamed by the stark contrast between the wretchedness of the working class and peasantry at one extreme and the insolent luxury of

the wealthy war profiteers and landowners at the other. Inflation was rampant; the cost of living soared at a fearful rate. The governments that succeeded each other, too weak to accomplish much, shared the blame, in the eyes of the populace, for the tottering peace structure, the economic situation and the violence in the streets. It was then that **fascism** took the offensive against the rising demand for socialism and against the parliamentary regime.

Conceived in 1919 by **Mussolini**, fascism presented no well-defined program except the subordination of the individual to the state and of freedom to authority. Its basic principle was the control of the government by the Fascist Party. "Everything is in the State; nothing spiritual exists and, *a fortiori*, nothing of value can exist outside the State," *Il Duce* declared with super-Hegelian flamboyance. "The Fascist State, in every way synthesized and united, develops and dominates the lives of the people. The State is the absolute before which the individual is only relative."

In October 1922, 60,000 members of the Fascist militia and the Black Shirts, financed by the wealthy of the industrial north, participated in the famous "March on Rome." The Eternal City was cut off from the outside by the cessation of railroad and telephone services; Fascist activists took over provincial and municipal administrations. Before entering Rome, Mussolini dispatched a bold ultimatum to King **Victor Emmanuel III**. The monarch accepted it, in effect elevating Mussolini to control of the government. On October 31 the Fascist legions paraded triumphantly before the Quirinal—named for the ancient Roman god of war.

Mussolini assumed power illegally, with the assent of a king who 22 years later would pay for violating his constitutional oath with his throne, and steadily acquired dictatorial sway. He began by appearing before the legislative chamber on November 16, 1922 and declaring that he would dismiss the deputies forthwith unless they granted him absolute power. They granted it to him. Only the Socialist opposition refused to be cowed; the others proclaimed their devotion to fascism for fear of reprisals. Ignoring the threats of *Il Duce*'s followers, the Socialist deputy Giacomo Matteotti ringingly denounced the Mussolini government on May 24, 1924. Several days later he disappeared. His colleagues feared the worst and went into seclusion—a foolish tactic, as it turned out.

Maintaining a discreet silence concerning Matteotti's fate, Mussolini revealed his true nature following the discovery of Matteotti's corpse on August 14. The assassination of the deputy aroused furious protests in Italy and, indeed, throughout the world when it was discovered that his murderer was one of *Il Duce*'s press attaches. But the militia suppressed the incip-

ient rebellion, and Mussolini seized on a subsequent attempt on his life as the pretext for the law of April 25, 1925 that extended his power even further. A month later he forbade the return to the Italian parliament of the opposition deputies by simply relieving them of their office. Freedom of press and of assembly were abolished, as were the workers' rights to strike and to occupy the plants in which they labored; the privilege of municipal administrations to act independently of the central government was canceled. A secret police known as the *Organizzazione di Vigilanza e Repressione dell'Antifascismo*, commonly known as the OVRA, was formed as much to stifle domestic dissidence as to keep a close watch on anti-Fascist emigre circles or guard the nation's frontiers. Arrests and arbitrary detention flourished, a special tribunal was set up to condemn the enemies of fascism to prison sentences or death and government control over the activities of Italian citizens was firmly established.

Many among the elite of Italian society went voluntarily into exile: former Prime Minister Francesco Nittti, Secretary General of the Catholic Party Luigi Sturzo and Count Carlo Sforza, among others. From beyond the border they denounced the crimes of the Mussolini regime and sought to combat the myth of its efficiency in "making the trains run on time," propagated by Western observers who considered the Italian dictator "the man of the century." Among themselves, they organized the *Concentrazione Antifascista*, which held its first conference in France in April 1927 and issued a weekly organ, *La Liberta*, secretly circulated in Italy. In 1929 Carlo Rosselli founded the republican movement *Giustizia e Liberta*, which bravely continued to fight the Mussolini regime despite the arrest of dozens of its members.

But these opposition movements could not make themselves heard. *Concentrazione Antifascista* vanished in 1934. In Italy itself, most anti-Fascist liberals and Catholics practiced a passive **resistance**, cautiously avoiding provocation of the authorities. Many hoped that the king would some day bring about the return to a constitutional government or that the Vatican would change its tolerant attitude toward the regime. The center of this nonviolent opposition was Senator Benedetto Croce; so universally popular was this brilliant statesman that Mussolini would never dare harm him. Opposed to such extremely patient moderates were the Communists under the leadership of Palmiro Togliatti. Many of the Communist Party officers were arrested and given life sentences; one of them was executed.

Although Mussolini's Fascists did not hesitate to choose murder as a means of getting rid of recalcitrant parliamentarians, they were not nearly as bloodthirsty as **Hitler**'s Nazis. Between 1927 and 1943 some 5,000 people were condemned officially by the Fascists for political sins, 29 of them to death and seven to life imprisonment. It has been estimated that 10,000 Italians were deported without a trial during the same period and another 15,000 kept under government surveillance. These figures are high, but they are trifling compared to the number of victims claimed by the Nazis.

When **Stalin** suspended the traditional hostility between Communists and Socialists to encourage the formation of Popular Fronts in 1934, there were reconciliations throughout the left. The two Marxist parties in Italy even began to fraternize with liberals and Christian Democrats. A journal published in Paris entitled *Grido del Popolo* ("The Cry of the People") was secretly distributed in Italy.

In an attempt to coordinate Italy's economic requirements with his policy of prestige—exemplified by his renaming the Mediterranean the *Mare Nostrum*, as in ancient Rome—Mussolini succeeded in conquering **Ethiopia** between October 1935 and May 1936. He thereby avenged an old Italian defeat, but he also aroused the hostility of the **League of Nations**, which, in its customary fashion, slapped Italy with ineffective economic sanctions. On December 11, 1937 he led his nation out of that body after consulting with Hitler, whom he had hitherto kept at arm's length. Having opposed the *Anschluss* in 1934, even to the extent of massing troops on the Brenner Pass at the Austro-Italian frontier, he now conceded to the Fuehrer a free hand in Austria. The *Anschluss* was actually carried out in March 1938. Despite the Italian victory over Ethiopia, despite the bloodless conquest of **Albania** on April 7, 1939, despite the resounding titles their monarch could now flaunt—king of Italy, Ethiopia and Albania—resentment gripped Italy's masses and even a segment of the Fascist Party when Mussolini added his signature to that of the Fuehrer on the "**Pact of Steel**" that formed the Rome-Berlin **Axis** on May 22, 1939. Many of them gloomily saw it as the first definite step toward a war few wanted.

On the other hand, the Spanish revolution of 1936-1939 offered the enemies of fascism an opportunity to fight it directly. The Italian volunteer brigade that sided with the loyalists in Spain found themselves firing at their compatriots in the regular units Mussolini had sent to reinforce **Franco**'s rebel army. This fact—aggravated by the slogan written everywhere on the walls of Italian cities, "Today in Spain, Tomorrow in Italy"—infuriated Mussolini. Nor was he appeased by the victory of Generalissimo Franco, for the revolution hurt rather than helped Italy. Not only did the Ethiopian and Spanish campaigns undercut Italy's finances; they seasoned soldiers who would

one day reenlist in the fight against fascism and trained the people back in Italy in the art of subverting a despised government.

Among the Italian intellectuals who chose to emigrate from Mussolini's domain were the historian Guglielmo Ferrero and the atomic physicist **Enrico Fermi**. The latter's escape to the **United States** was an outstanding example of the aid the Axis dictator's malice lent to the Allies, for Fermi's genius assisted in the creation of the ultimate weapon of the war to come, the **atomic bomb**.

In Italy, as everywhere else in the civilized world, the announcement of the **Nazi-Soviet Pact** on August 23, 1939, had a stupefying effect. Its immediate result was the breakdown of the anti-Fascist coalition. The Italian Communists for a time abstained from political activity, perhaps out of bewilderment. Had Stalin played into the hands of the Nazi and Fascist regimes?

At the end of August 1939, Count **Galeazzo Ciano**, minister of foreign affairs, who opposed the assistance Italy was rendering Hitler, managed to arouse somewhat the resentment of his father-in-law Mussolini toward the Reich. *Il Duce* learned to his astonishment that his army required 17 million tons of materiel, necessitating 17,000 trains for transportation! Always inclined to believe flattery and optimistic estimates of the strength of his regime, he now was forced to confront the extreme distress of the armed forces under his command. On August 25 he informed Hitler that Italy could not for the moment lend itself to any military adventure. Ciano's heartfelt appeal on September 2 for an international conference to halt the German-Polish hostilities that had begun the day before remained inaudible amidst the thunder of guns.

But encouraged by the swift liquidation of **the Netherlands** and **Belgium** and the subsequent defeat of the French army, Mussolini brought Italy into the war on the side of the Nazis on June 10, 1940. He thought of it as a minor skirmish, well within Italy's capacities, that would rapidly burn itself out. The fall of France and the **United Kingdom**'s isolation damaged the hopes of Italy's anti-Fascist bloc. On October 28, 1940 Mussolini, still convinced that the war would rapidly end, invaded **Greece** from his Albanian outpost. His grand notions collapsed at once. The victory of the **Royal Air Force** in the **Battle of Britain**, the murderous blow dealt to his battleships on November 11, 1940 by British air and naval attacks at Taranto (see **Atlantic, Battle of the**), the disastrous campaigns in Albania and **Egypt** and **Libya** at the end of the year and the rapid loss of **Eritrea**, **Somalia** and Ethiopia to the British forces under **Wavell** in the spring of 1941 (see **Mediterranean and Middle Eastern Theater of**

Operations), to say nothing of the constantly exacerbated privations, rendered the regime increasingly unpopular and very soon odious to the Italian people. When the German army crossed into the USSR on June 22, 1941, the Communists resumed their underground activity, encouraged by Togliatti, speaking from Moscow. Strikes broke out in 1942 and 1943, frequently in Italy's industrial north, to the great disgust of the Germans. The underground press flourished. Many of the Italians in France joined the Resistance—some 2,000 of whom died in action. Americans of Italian descent enlisted in large numbers in the military forces of the United States.

In April 1943 an Italian who had served as prime minister before 1922, Ivanoe Bonomi, founded the Unified Anti-Fascist Front. Aided by *Il Duce*'s enemies in the king's entourage and among the Fascist officers, it took the lead in the internal struggle that was to end in the fall of Mussolini on July 25. The Italian activists submerged their political differences in the common effort to get their country out of the war and to turn on the Germans and Fascists who had led it astray. They failed to agree, however, in their plans for the country's future. Some were monarchists; more were moderate republicans; still a third group consisted primarily of radical leftists.

The destruction of the Italo-German armies in Tunisia in May 1943 and the Allied invasion of Sicily two months later were the death blows to Italian fascism. Three plots, in fact, had been hatched to rid Italy of Mussolini. The first, inspired by the militant anti-Fascists led by Bonomi, was designed to persuade the king to replace Mussolini with **Pietro Badoglio**, then to break immediately with the Reich and open negotiations with the Allies. A second conspiracy centered around the fanatically anti-German **Vittorio Ambrosio**, chief of staff of the Italian army, who, with his adjutant, Gen. Giuseppe Castellano, kept in close touch with Duke Pietro Acquarone, head of the king's own troops. They too sought to force out Mussolini in favor of Badoglio. The third cabal was made up of important members of the Fascist Party. Some of them, like Ciano, wanted to eliminate Mussolini in order to regenerate the party. Having learned to detest the Nazis, Ciano himself demanded peace at once; the others, like Carlo Scorza, recently appointed party secretary, and Roberto Farinacci, both ardent admirers of the Germans, considered Mussolini the betrayer of his great ally. These two men demanded convocation of the Grand Fascist Council as soon as possible, although it had not met since 1939. On July 16 Mussolini agreed to summon the council for a meeting a week later, on the 24th.

Between these two dates, Victor Emmanuel promised Acquarone, Castellano, Badoglio and the chief of police that he would have *Il Duce* arrested the next time Mussolini left an audience with the king. At its meeting on July 24, the Grand Council voted against Scorza and his fellow reactionaries, 19 to seven, refusing to restore full power to the king. Mussolini was chosen to bear this news to Victor Emmanuel on the 25th. After spending 20 minutes with the monarch, Mussolini was arrested as he attempted to leave.

The Italian radio announced the formation of a new government by Badoglio that same evening. A short time afterward Badoglio was in contact with the Allies through the **Special Operations Executive** (SOE) radio link. The armistice between Italy and the Allies was made public on September 8, five days after the landing of the British Eighth Army in the southern area of the peninsula. The chaos then reigning in Italy allowed the Germans, who had for some time been aware of the Italian attempts to renounce their alliance, to substitute their own troops for the Italians and establish a front. While the king and the government concluded formalities to enter the Allied camp, Mussolini, rescued from prison by **Otto Skorzeny**'s daring raid, which Hitler had ordered, established the so-called Republic of Salo on Lake di Garda and there instituted a reign of terror. He ordered the execution of his son-in-law Ciano, his former political crony Marshal **Emilio De Bono** and several others who in his eyes were guilty of having betrayed him at that fateful meeting of the Grand Council on July 24. With Marshal **Rodolfo Graziani** he then proceeded to activate regular units in order to reinforce German combat troops and to organize militia detachments to fight ''terrorism'' at a level of cruelty even the **Gestapo** could barely match.

Badoglio, on the other hand, was reactivating troop units that were later to fight bravely in Allied ranks, while the members of the Italian Resistance daily proved their toughness in the field. Hitler issued detailed orders on the handling of Italian troops, dividing them into three categories: those ready to fight alongside the Germans, whom he would greet with affection; those who resisted, who would be placed in labor battalions in the east after their officers were shot; and those who wanted to return home, whom he would deport to the Reich as forced laborers. The members of the first group were pressed into the service of the Republic of Salo, those in the second and third were, for the most part, sent, under horrible conditions, to Germany and the USSR. But many of the men in the last two groups managed to escape into the mountains, swelling the numbers of the Resistance.

Not until December 1942, when the first British SOE operatives parachuted into Italy, did the Allied command succeed in making contact with the Italian

Resistance. The American **Office of Strategic Services** (OSS) established some listening posts by way of **Switzerland** at the beginning of 1943. In general, however, the Allies approached the Italian Resistance gingerly because its political tendencies were so uncertain. Neither the British nor American services, not even the Resistance, played a part in Mussolini's ruin; the July revolution was carried out by *Il Duce*'s peers and not by the people. It was the direct consequence of his defeats on the battlefield. In the final collapse of his regime, Mussolini was utterly abandoned even by his closest companions.

The changes his fall triggered were broad and fast. His opposition in the parliament could as a consequence see its way to its objectives. The political situation was further clarified when the king made his about-face and a large part of the country fell under German occupation. The Resistance abandoned its quarrel with the established regime and turned its guns on the Nazis and the puppet Salo regime. From October 1942 to September 1943, the Italian Resistance, seeking to destroy fascism, became the ally of the **German Resistance**, seeking to destroy Hitler. In fact, it became as militant as the Resistance movements in other countries under German domination. The workers of Milan, Genoa and Turin participated by means of strikes and **sabotage**. Allied **prisoners of war**, escaping in large numbers from Italian camps in the chaotic armistice period, received aid and lodging not only from the Italian Resistance but from humble peasants as well. Some of these escapees managed to slip through the German lines and rejoin their armies, thanks to mountain guerrilla units and Italian guides; others enlisted in the Resistance movements.

Gen. **Colin Gubbins** established a new SOE section in the Italian peninsula near Bari. It had its own training schools, radio stations and ammunition dumps; it was supplied by air and sea. Meeting growing enthusiasm from the people, it extended its range of activity over northern Italy, the Balkans and even **Poland**. Commander G. Holdsworth of the Royal Navy made Italy the special focus of his section. Even before the section was really organized, Holdsworth's officers had already infiltrated into enemy territory at Sorrento to evacuate Benedetto Croce and his family. It was inevitable that the eminent statesman and philospher, given his rigid distaste for totalitarian rule, would be arrested by the Nazis.

While Rome was still beyond the reach of Allied forces, a Committee for National Liberation was formed there under the leadership of Bonomi. The members of this committee combined with Badoglio's government, which was recognized by the Allies, to form the *Comitato di Liberazione nazionale dell'Alta Italia* (CLNAI), or National Committee for the Liberation of Northern Italy. All parties, including the Communist Party, were welcome to participate. This new organization immediately rebuked the Committee of Rome for remaining in contact with a king and prime minister long since reconciled with fascism. It was a situation the Allies—**Churchill**, in particular—found unpleasant, especially since they had supported both the king and Badoglio. Anglo-American aid to Italy in the beginning was kept low. Fears arose in Washington and London that communism had too strong a hold on the northern industrial part of the country and that its followers would behave as nastily there as they had in Greece. The Allies therefore expected to equip only a few groups of saboteurs. Nevertheless, in 1944, they dropped 513 tons of materiel to the Italian Resistance by parachute through the SOE and another 290 tons through the OSS.

On June 4 Allied troops entered Rome. Bonomi supplanted Badoglio as the head of the government. During the months that followed, strikes broke out with increasing frequency in the cities, as did attacks by Resistance units on German positions from the mountains. These assaults on the occupiers continued in spite of the terrible reprisals the **SS** and the Salo militia exacted from the populace in return.

On August 21, 1944 Gen. **Albert Kesselring**, the German commander in chief on the Italian front, sent the following message to the supreme chief of the SS and the Italian police as well as the general director of transportation: "Destruction of railroad bridges by the guerrillas has mounted to such an extent that their reconstruction, indispensable for our operations, will shortly become impossible. These acts of sabotage are the work of powerful groups following minutely detailed plans. For example, to blow up a bridge between Turin and Milan, the Resistance engineers detonated charges of several hundred kilograms. As a result, important bridges must be guarded in force by the supreme chief of the SS and the police, with the latter required to supply all necessary personnel to the director of transportation."

Kesselring's letter did not achieve his aims, evidently, for it was followed by the following order to the units under his command on October 1: "The activity of the guerrillas keeps increasing. They are now operating in hitherto inviolate regions. Their acts of sabotage become more and more frequent, and our transportation facilities are in danger. This plague must cease forthwith. What is more, these partisan bands have excellent intelligence services and are dependent on the population for information on the preparations and movements of our troops. As a first measure, I order a week of antipartisan operations from October 8 to 14 to go into effect; the details of the order follow. This antipartisan week should show these bands the extent of our power and the relentlessness of our retaliation."

But Kesselring's order could not stop the spreading violence perpetrated by the Italian underground. The Allies were impressed by the exploits of the Italian Resistance. In November 1944 a CLNAI mission infiltrated into southern Italy with the help of the SOE. Its members were four major Resistance leaders: Alfredo Pizzoni, Ferruccio Parri, Giancarlo Pajetta and Edgardo Sogno. After some discussion the delegation signed an agreement with the Supreme Allied Command in the Mediterranean and then with the representatives of the Bonomi government. Under its provisions the CLNAI was to exercise all government functions in the occupied part of the country until its final liberation, with the Bonomi government temporarily relinquishing its powers to the CLNAI. The underground forces, known as the Corps of Volunteers for Liberation (CVL), were to carry out, in the name of the CLNAI, the instructions given by the Allied command. In return the Allies agreed to furnish the CLNAI with the material means for continuing its secret activities.

Thus strengthened by the respect of Allied leaders, the ardor of the Italian maquis and the people of northern Italy increased. The SOE and the OSS responded by parachuting 48 missions of British and American officers into occupied territory. The heroic Gen. Raffaele Cadorna, son of the distinguished general of World War I, dropped into Italy from an SOE plane in August 1944 to take command of the CVL.

Impatient over the long delay of Allied forces before the "Gothic Line," the Italian Resistance was finally recompensed by additional stores parachuted into their territory. In the first four months of 1945, the OSS and SOE succeeded in 551 such airborne provisioning missions, dropping a total of 1,229 tons of war materiel, including 666 tons of arms and ammunition, 292 tons of explosives and 271 tons of miscellaneous supplies. Through miscalculations of one kind or another, however, 305 other deliveries fell into the hands of the Germans or the Fascists. All the Italian territory under German control was divided up by grid lines, as on a military map, with information arriving for the resisters from every town and village. The enemy was never alone; it could keep no secrets nor pull any surprises. Through the Partisan Information Service, the Allied command followed the maneuvers and deployment of German troops with perfect confidence in the reliability of the data they obtained. With the British Col. Hedley Vincent as senior officer, the network of Allied military missions completely covered northern Italy. Busily expanding

his local activities during the winter of 1944-45, Gen. Cadorna and his underground army awaited the call for a general uprising.

On April 9, 1945 Field Marshal Sir Harold Alexander, commander in chief of the Mediterranean theater, signaled the final offensive of the army group commanded by Gen. Mark Clark on the Italian front. General strikes, perfectly synchronized, broke out in Turin, Biella, Vercelli, Novara and Milan, while the maquis harassed the Germans with sabotage and raids. On April 21, British and American forces broke up the German front, and three days later at 10:30 p.m., the precise moment fixed by Gen. Alexander, Cadorna initiated the phase of general upheaval. In the words of the Resistance journal La Resistenza italiana:

> Snow melts in the sun and liberty descends from the mountains with the brigades of our Resistance. A superb dawn breaks on our 25th of April. The march of the Allied armies cannot be resisted, but we must not permit our assaults on the enemy to flag because our lives may be required up to the last minute. The first British or Americans to come must find northern Italy completely cleansed, its industry healthy and normal, the Germans defeated, the tyrant crushed.
>
> But see how the villages in the mountain valleys disgorge their people! The dead remain unwatched. Huge fires leap from peak to peak. The mountain brigades encircle the hills and, continually descending, not in patrols but by well-planned mass maneuvers, approach the great arteries over which flow thick and feverish hordes of Germans.

The cities liberated by the Resistance teams grew rapidly in number, as their German and Fascist garrisons surrendered. On April 26 the broadcasting station "Milan Radio Liberty" began transmissions. The "soft underbelly" of Europe gave way to the fan-shaped drive of the Allied armies: the right wing aimed at Trieste, the center focusing on the Brenner Pass leading to Austria, the left slicing into the French Alps. According to a British report the Italian Resistance, unaided, killed or captured 50,000 Germans between April 24 and May 2. Mussolini attempted to escape the jaws of the closing trap into Switzerland but was arrested by vigilant guerrillas at Dongo, on the shore of Lake Como, on April 27. The following day he was executed, his corpse hung by the heels. Three days later his friend Hitler was to die in flames.

About 60,000 Italian maquis were killed in action between September 1943 and May 1945; 8,000 of them never returned from concentration camps. In addition, thousands of nonbelligerent Italians were murdered by German troops in reprisal for guerrilla attacks. The Nazi, Fascist and collaborationist press spread the legend that the Italian Resistance movement was Communist in orientation. This was a monstrous lie. The Communists in the movement were numerous and active, but they fought no less uncompromisingly than their blood brothers from every social class and political party. Among their dead were aristocrats, bourgeois, officers and priests.

But if the Communists were far from a majority in the movement, they were seriously preparing to take power at the end of the war. In April 1945 the number of Communist Party members swelled abruptly. With its many seasoned warriors, the party proselytized a number of "last ditch" resisters to ensure as many votes as possible in coming elections and thus bring about a Communist state. The party began an active and convincing propaganda campaign, naturally appropriating for itself the name "the Party of the Resistance."

But events in Greece and **Yugoslavia** had prepared Anglo-American political strategists for this eventuality, and the southern and central part of the country were kept firmly in British and American hands. It was this political fact that kept the Communists in check. Furthermore, Allied troops and the spread of the Allied occupation to the northern provinces in April and May of 1945 warded off the threat of a repetition of the civil war in Greece. Nor was there any doubt that the operations of SOE and OSS officers, who shared the battles and risks of the guerrillas, played a decisive part in pacifying the country's political temper. After June 1944 these officers were sent on their missions with instructions to detect and report on the political tendencies of the maquis groups in their domains of operation. They knew, consequently, that a good portion of the materiel and arms dropped by Allied supply planes to these men were cached by their chiefs with an eye to their future use after the liberation.

The SOE and OSS officers did their work brilliantly. But the British and American civil affairs personnel who arrived with the victorious troops to establish the Allied Military Government of Occupied Territories had little understanding of northern Italian attitudes and mores. The newcomers lacked the finesse in dealing with the Resistance elements of the SOE and OSS men, who had shared the rough lives and daring of the guerrillas. To make matters worse, large quantities of weapons were still hidden in heavily Communist areas such as Massa-Carrara, La Spezia or the Emilian Plain. One of the favorite sites for such caches was the local cemetery in a mountain village.

In the meantime, the Italian government sent a newly formed body of carabinieri into northern Italy. These policemen, new to the ways of industrial Italy and the Resistance, coming as they did from Sicily, Calabria and other southern provinces, were received

cooly by the sophisticated industrial workers. Realizing its mistake in time, the government replaced them with northerners chosen from among the reliable elements of the Resistance. These superior carabinieri did their work tactfully and sympathetically. Much of the credit for the final reestablishment of order in Italy belongs to this elite corps.

The largest part of the Italian people were hostile to communism. Nor could the Communist Party rely for comfort on the proximity of its sphere of activity to the mainland of Stalinism, as the Greek Communists did. Moscow, too, was aware that the SOE teams had long known about Soviet intentions. In fact, the SOE missions dispatched from 1943 on and the swarm of Allied troops in Italy at the end of the war formed an effective deterrent to the western expansion of Communist influence.

Italy was not to fall under the curse of civil war. The veteran Resistance fighter **Alcide De Gasperi** presided over the reconstruction of his country. Smoothly, he substituted a republic for the monarchy and assured his Christian Democratic Party a solid majority in parliament.

In the midst of all the contrary currents engenderd by the liberation, the firm course of the Italian Resistance stands out. Its vigorous activity in effect constituted the core of a new *Risorgimento* among the Italian people. It contributed enormously to the democratic reformation of Italy, the territorial unity of the country and the restoration of its feeling for democracy. It was to the services and patriotism of the Resistance that Italy owed the respect accorded it by the Allies as a partner in the victory. Regenerated by its agony, the great Mediterranean nation cleansed its spirit of the shadow cast upon it by fascism and by the humiliating alliance with the Reich that Mussolini had forced upon it.

H. Bernard

IWO JIMA.

Iwo Jima is the largest island in the Volcano group, which with the Bonin Islands and the Izut Shoto to the north make up the Nanpo Shoto, a chain of islands extending southward from Tokyo Bay for about 750 miles to within 300 miles of the Marianas. Iwo Jima means Sulfur Island; sulfur deposits extend upward to its surface, and sulfur dioxide permeates its northern plateau. The island is shaped like an elongated pear (or, more vividly, a dripping ice cream cone), and is less than five miles from northeast to southwest, varying in width from two and a half miles in the north to half a mile in the south. Its total area is less than eight square miles. Iwo Jima is utterly bereft of fresh water and is covered with brown volcanic ash and black cinders, across which men and tracked vehicles move only with considerable difficulty, and wheeled vehicles not at all. An extinct volcano, Mount Suribachi, lies near the southern tip of Iwo, rising to a height of 550 feet and dominating the rest of the island. The northern plateau contains various hills, ridges and deep gorges: the elevation of the highest hill is 382 feet; two others reach a height of 362 feet. The island possesses no anchorages or useful inlets and the surf conditions are unfavorable for amphibious operations. Maj. Yoshitaka Horie of the Imperial Japanese Army described Iwo Jima as an "island of sulfur, no water, no sparrow, and no swallow"; it is by all accounts a hideously ugly place.

Iwo Jima possessed strategic importance solely because of the projected aerial campaign against the Japanese home islands, which became possible after American victories in the Marianas. The most destructive aircraft employed against **Japan** was the B-29 Superfortress, a four-engine bomber that with a fourton bomb load had a range of 3,500 miles. During the latter half of 1944 about 100 B-29s had operated from airfields in **China** under the Army Air Force's 20th Bomber Command, occasionally striking the Japanese home islands. Very long-range bombing of Japan was also possible from **Saipan** or Formosa, roughly equidistant from Tokyo (at a range of 1,500 miles). A landing on Formosa was originally planned, with the additional purpose of facilitating landings on the Chinese coast. When Japanese advances on the Chinese mainland rendered American landings impractical and forced the evacuation of the 20th Bomber Command to the Marianas, the Joint Chiefs of Staff determined to seize Iwo Jima as an emergency landing strip for Saipan-based B-29s and as a site for fighter bases; P-51 Mustangs on Iwo could escort B-29s to Japan. A somewhat prompter invasion in late 1944, when the Joint Chiefs were still debating where to strike, would have been far less bloody than the campaign that eventually opened in February 1945, further delayed by the protracted fighting on Luzon.

Between June 8 and 10, 1944 Gen. Tadamichi Kuribayashi had arrived on Iwo Jima and taken command of its defense. He arrived in time to witness air strikes and air battles initiated by seven American carriers, which over the course of June and the first days of July destroyed 213 Japanese aircraft on Iwo and Chichi Jima, leaving four Japanese fighters and one bomber for the air defense of the Volcano and Bonin groups. On July 6, following the last Japanese sorties, a prolonged naval bombardment destroyed the four remaining fighters and all above-ground structures on Iwo. American submarines torpedoed three Japanese transports within sight of land a few days later. Depressed and frustrated, the Japanese awaited an in-

vasion; to their surprise, they waited for seven and a half months, a gift of time which Gen. Kuribayashi put to devastatingly effective use.

Lt. Gen. Hideyoshi Obata, charged with the defense of Iwo earlier in 1944, had been faithful to prevailing Japanese doctrine and planned to meet the invasion at the water's edge, emplacing artillery and constructing pillboxes on the beaches. Kuribayashi had different and deadlier notions. Lightly manning the beaches, he emplaced artillery, mortars and rockets at the foot and on the slopes of Mount Suribachi and on the high ground to the north of Chidori airfield, one of three on Iwo. Noting the effectiveness of naval bombardment against surface installations, he imported mining engineers from Japan and constructed elaborate tunnels and underground fortifications, well-ventilated, interconnected and provided with multiple exits. Iwo was honeycombed with caves, which the Japanese extensively improved; one-fourth of the garrison was detailed to tunneling. Iwo's black volcanic ash made excellent concrete when mixed with cement, and many works had steel-reinforced walls and roofs four to 10 feet thick. Subterranean works, sometimes 75 feet below the surface, were virtually immune to air attack. Kuribayashi's defensive works were profuse, brilliantly sited, heavily gunned and immensely strong.

By February 1945 Iwo's garrison had been reinforced to a total strength of between 21,000 and 23,000 men, 361 artillery pieces of 75-mm or larger caliber, a dozen 320-mm mortars, 65 medium (150-mm) and light (81-mm) mortars, 33 naval guns and 94 antiaircraft guns 75-mm or larger. He had in addition more than 200 lighter AA guns and 69 antitank guns, more than 70 rocket guns and 22 **tanks**, which were concealed and partially buried. Kuribayashi ordered his guns to remain silent during the preliminary American bombardment, intending to use them to devastating effect against the landing beaches and then to move them north. Banzai charges were forbidden, although local counterattacks were not. His static defense plan was intended to inflict maximum casualties in a protracted campaign; it succeeded brilliantly.

The preliminary naval and air bombardment of Iwo was the heaviest in the **Pacific theater of operations** up to that point. It utilized 6,800 tons of bombs and 22,000 rounds of shell from guns of 5" to 16" caliber, but was disappointingly ineffective. The decision to launch carrier strikes against Honshu reduced the period of naval bombardment from 10 to three days, over bitter Marine Corps protests, which were vindicated in the ensuing slaughter, where Marine courage, skill and blood substituted for more extensive softening up of the Japanese works. Total American casualties in the campaign reached 27,499, compared to the

24,761 B-29 crewmen who eventually used Iwo in emergency landings, and were in excess of the total Japanese garrison. Japanese casualties are unknown, but were in the neighborhood of 20,000. Although bombed around the clock for two weeks prior to the invasion, air attacks were impeded by poor visibility and superb camouflage, much of which was not flammable and little affected by blast. American **recon-naissance** revealed that Kuribayashi's works progressed throughout the bombardment.

Operation Detachment, the Iwo campaign, was under the overall command of Adm. Raymond A. Spruance, the commander of the Fifth Fleet, with Vice Adm. Richmond K. Turner commanding the Joint Expeditionary Force, Task Force 51. Gen. Holland Smith was the commanding general of the Expeditionary Troops, Task Force 56, with 70,647 marines, consisting chiefly of the Third, Fourth and Fifth Marine divisions under Gen. Graves Erskine, Clifton Cates and Keller Rockey. The initial landing force was made up of the Fourth and Fifth divisions, less the 26th Marine Division, held in reserve, with the Third Marine Division in reserve as well. The planning for Detachment can fairly be called superb; it was a task of staggering complexity. In addition to the foreshortened naval bombardment, however, four intelligence failures should be noted: Japanese strength was underestimated by 70 percent; the character of Iwo's soil was not discovered; the new Japanese **tactics** were not predicted; and American casualties were underestimated by 80 percent.

At 8:59 a.m. on February 19, 1945 (D-day), the first Marines landed on Iwo Jima. They had breakfasted on the traditional steak and eggs, and the initial waves were not subjected to anti-boat fire. Some men were briefly optimistic about the effect of the naval and air bombardments. The first unpleasant surprise consisted of Iwo's steeply terraced shores, which blocked Marine fields of fire and impeded movement. The second shock was the volcanic sand, which made movement up a steep incline all but impossible for men carrying 100-pound loads. The third surprise was the astonishing volume of mortar fire that began at 9:15 a.m. Japanese artillery was well registered on Iwo and extraordinarily well coordinated and massed. The beaches were strewn with antitank mines and Japanese fire was murderous, concentrating on LVTs (landing vehicle, tracked); landing craft and beaches.

The character of warfare on Iwo Jima was not established. Hellish terrain had to be negotiated in the face of vicious and massive direct and indirect fire from a brilliantly entrenched and camouflaged foe. In addition to these novelties the Marines encountered one familiar if unloved feature of Pacific theater combat: the fantastically tenacious and extraordinarily skillfull

Imperial Japanese infantry. The Japanese generally abandoned their works only under extreme provocation, specifically flame weapons and large rockets. They expressed their dislike of flame weapons by immediately concentrating their fire on them; as a result, flame tanks were disguised as ordinary armor with elaborate fake gun barrels, a tactic whose success was partially vitiated by the status of tanks as the second favorite target of the Japanese. Tanks were as often as not disabled by the terrain, and frequently fell victim to mines, prepared obstacles and Kuribayashi's 69 antitank guns. Until Mount Suribachi fell, most Marine positions sustained fire from guns to their front, flanks and rear. Extremely heavy fire directed at the congested beaches sometimes inflicted heavier casualties on Seabees and engineers than those suffered at the fronts, and the casualties at the fronts were massive.

By the first night the Marines controlled far less than half their territorial goal for the day, but they had secured a solid beachhead. They had landed almost 30,000 men and tons of supplies in preparation for night banzai charges that never came; Kuribayashi sold lives dearer than that. On the 20th, D + 1, the Marines advanced on Mount Suribachi to the south and toward the airfields to their north. The 28th Marine Divison took the crest of Suribachi by the 23rd and controlled the slopes by the 24th, pouring gasoline into ravines and igniting it when all else failed. The famous flag raisings took place at 10:20 a.m. and three hours later on the 23rd; Joseph Rosenthal's photograph is of the latter event.

The drive to the north was a horrifying slaughter. If anything, the ground became steadily worse. On the 21st, 50 **kamikazes** attacked the fleet, sinking the carrier *Bismarck Sea*, damaging the carrier *Saratoga* and setting afire the net tender *Keokuk*. The ground fighting was not a battle of maneuver, although the Japanese attacked unit flanks exposed in the course of uneven advances and repeatedly attempted to infiltrate Marine lines, sometimes successfully. In the face of almost insuperable obstacles, the Marines advanced with extraordinary courage; in the face of certain defeat, the Japanese fought in kind. Famous names evoke particularly well-remembered carnage: Turkey Knob, the Amphitheater, Charlie-Dog Ridge, and most explicitly, Death Valley and the Meat Grinder. The official Marine Corps history is a series of phrases like "...through even more nightmarish terrain...." The landing force revived the rolling barrage, dormant since World War I, but the mainstay of the Marine response to Kuribayashi's labyrinth was great bravery and extreme endurance. The last Japanese attack, in which Gen. Kuribayashi may have perished, took place on March 26; the general's body was never identified. Fighting continued through June.

Adm. **Chester W. Nimitz**'s tribute to the Americans who fought on Iwo Jima is an eloquent understatement applicable to the troops on both sides: ''uncommon valor was a common virtue.''

F. Smoler

J

JACOB, Ian (1899-   ).

Jacob was on the staff of the British Committee of Imperial Defense from 1938 to 1946. From 1940 to 1945 he functioned as **Churchill**'s link with the army. Jacob became know as the personification of tact.

JAPAN.

Foreign Policy

On December 7, 1941 several carrier-based Japanese aircraft squadrons attacked the Pacific Fleet of the **United States**, which was anchored at **Pearl Harbor**. That same day, Japanese troops landed in British **Malaya**, and the Asiatic war, previously confined to **China**, combined with the war in Europe to cover the globe. The daring and success of the Japanese aggression was a shocking surprise; the final outbreak of hostilities, however, had long been expected. The occupation of Manchuria in 1931 and the even more provocative invasion of China, which had begun in 1937, as well as Japanese infiltration into **Indochina** in 1940 and 1941, had indicated that the expansionist policy of Japan's ruling military clique aimed at domination of the entire Far East and the Pacific. Until then, at least in Western eyes, the "**New Order in East Asia**" proclaimed by the Empire of the Rising Sun had seemed nothing more than inane **propaganda**. But by its adherence to the **Tripartite Pact**, Japan finally made known its intention to join **Germany** and **Italy** in partitioning the earth. Japan's policy of aggression in the Far East met with Western disapproval— it refused, in effect, to be content with the modest role assigned it—and as a consequence, collision with the European colonial **empires**, which, along with the United States, had vital interests in the Pacific, was inevitable.

In December 1941 the Western democracies and imperial Japan represented two opposing spheres whose sole connecting link was a technically based and standardized war machine. At one extreme was the imperialist principle of colonial powers and the associated American concept of an "informal empire"; the latter was exemplified by the "Open-Door Policy" in China. At the other extreme was Japanese economic imperialism, based upon a mystique of the supremacy of the state and personified by a nation seeking sources of raw materials abroad, in the manner of a feudal society, to feed its growing industrial complex. What did a war against the United States, **the Netherlands** and the **United Kingdom** offer this new empire, isolated in Asia and tied only by a fragile defensive alliance to the Rome-Berlin **Axis** half a world away? Exactly what were the aims of the rival groups at the head of the empire? Tenuous though it was, the alliance with the Axis powers offered Japan the best opportunity to smash the Western nations that hampered its program of conquest. Within the framework of this **strategy**, its most urgent task was to coax Germany into declaring war on the United States, Japan's principal enemy. A Japanese feeler in that direction was extended in Berlin some 60 hours before the attack on Pearl Harbor. **Hitler** indicated his agreement without any idea when, where or how the war with the United States would be triggered. It was no more than a blank check given Japan, minus the Fuehrer's endorsement, when Germany was for the first time encountering serious military difficulties, with the **Blitzkrieg** grinding to an impotent halt at the gates of Moscow. It was a guarantee Germany could hardly make good.

The prospects of cooperation between the two nations were dimmed by the difference in their relations with the **USSR**. The Japanese were bound to the USSR by a neutrality treaty, while Germany was engaged with the Soviets in a death struggle, further aggravated by ideological and racial hatred. Apart from a potential land bridge across the vast expanse of a conquered or neutralized Soviet Union, there was no way for Japan and Germany to assist each other, except through naval operations in the Indian Ocean. Nor could the two countries exchange war materiel on anything like a grand scale. If close political and strategic cooperation between the Japanese general staff and the commands of the Axis powers had been possible, it might have been the key to Japanese and German invincibility. But a war for itself alone, within the confines of the Pacific and Southeast Asia, could at best conclude with no more gain for Japan than a compromise forcing the "white" colonial powers to abandon some of their positions while the Japanese Empire was left the onerous task of guarding a far-flung and captious patchwork of little nations.

The complexity of the situation and its strategic significance were never fully explored by the Japanese rulers. The Japanese were hindered from making decisions by the very structure of the government; as a result, their discussions of strategy and policy often ended inconclusively. Emperor **Hirohito**, by reason of his position as the resident deity and as provided by the constitution of 1889, left the exercise of governmental powers to a triumvirate of the imperial court, the cabinet and the chiefs of the armed forces. This oligarchy, unrestrained by any parliamentary control, was responsible only to the emperor while he, by custom, was forbidden to participate in their deliberations. The cancellation of civil rights by the parliament's laws of March 26, 1938 authorizing prosecution of the war and the usurpation of power by the military were also responsible for the political paralysis of this feudal society, which had no real comprehension of Western attitudes. Japan's traditional elite patterned their behavior on the patriarchal system of the ancient clans and could not adapt to the freedoms characterizing a liberal system. Thus, every clique pursued its own rigid dogma—the armed forces, themselves strictly divided into navy and army, the cabinet and the court.

The army, whose cadre of lower officers was recruited from among the impoverished peasantry, remained faithful to a socialist-agrarian philosophy of "living space" on the Asiatic continent. The navy was by contrast highly technical and, consequently, more sophisticated; closely associated with the country's heavy industries and with the court, it was more interested in the conquest of sources of raw materials—the oil fields of Southeast Asia, for the most part—and feared the American Pacific Fleet as its most formidable rival. With the exception of the minister of foreign affairs, the cabinet members allowed themselves to be guided by the prime minister who, throughout the war, was either a general or an admiral. In the summer of 1940 all political parties were obliged to fuse into a martially coordinated group. In view of this distinctly Oriental discipline, the policy of the nation could only be dictated by the military in "liaison conferences" involving the highest ranking officers of the army and navy. The only civilians or political specialists participating were the ministers of foreign affairs, **Shigenori Togo** and **Mamoru Shigemitsu**. Neither one ever bid for support among the others of any concept of policy adaptable to

particular situations, especially in the USSR or the occupied territories.

The divergence of views among the various governing agencies became apparent in the first weeks of the war in the Pacific. The plan of conquest was simple: to annihilate American, British and Dutch bases in Asia and thus fence off this geographic entity as a Japanese domain. Such a localized and practically solipsistic concept of war deliberately shut out strategic operation in concert with the European partners. Similarly, Japan's rulers never considered possible bases for peaceful compromises after their domain was occupied. Blinded by deep conviction of the righteousness of Japan's mission and the irresistibility of its might, the military chained itself to the illusory hope that the "white" industrial nations, once deprived of their colonies, would never return to the offensive. This self-indulgent limitation of strategic planning was typical of Japan's war policy. One might also attribute it to the prestige complex of a ruling military junta.

In the preliminary talks with their European counterparts after Pearl Harbor, the Japanese diplomats concentrated on defining their claims in the Pacific and warning against any intrusion on them by either Rome or Berlin, with few requests for political or military cooperation. Naturally, conceding any territories to the exclusive control of Japan collided with Hitler's intention to endow Germany with world power second to none—and certainly superior to the upstart "yellow" race—thus finally revealing the impossibility of cooperation between totalitarian states flushed with pretensions to preeminence. If the heads of the Japanese state were incapable of a single will and if that single will belonged only to the Fuehrer, both parties were also incapable of—or unconcerned about—understanding the need for a world strategy in the war they had provoked. Without a common plan, the assurances exchanged by the Japanese with Germany and Italy that none would ever conclude a separate peace with the Anglo-American command could amount only to a simple guarantee by the Germans that they would declare war on the United States and thus prevent the concentration of the American fleet in the Pacific.

Several days after the signature of the "Treaty to Exclude a Separate Peace," Berlin was presented with a Japanese proposal for a military agreement involving separation of the spheres of influence of the two states by longitude, with obvious indications of the curious Japanese narcissism in the other points it specified. It was nothing less than a plan for partitioning the world, conceived and urged on Tokyo by the Japanese navy. It was designed to forestall the concerted German-Japanese action against the Soviet Union that had been recommended by a faction of the Japanese army chiefs of staff. The proposed line of separation, accepted by the Germans with some political and economic reservations, was 70° east longitude. That cleavage placed **India** squarely in the Japanese sphere and, apparently for the first time, revealed territorial aspirations beyond the initial war plan. Actually, these more extravagant hopes had been widely rumored within the upper reaches of the Japanese government since the summer of 1940, when the negotiations leading to the Tripartite Pact had been held. In 1942, however, the Germans included this same area in their military plans. The result was a rivalry between the two powers over the question of a "declaration of independence" for India.

The Japanese claimed for themselves the right to conduct the war independently in the southwestern Pacific. Furthermore, both they and the Germans were very serious about their respective dividing lines; any attempt by either side to cross the other's line, if only with auxiliary cruisers, provoked tedious negotiations that thwarted a swift and supple response to emergencies. The councils provided for by the Tripartite Pact sat in Tokyo and in Berlin after Japan's involvement in the war began, but their function was limited to projecting a false image of concerted conduct of hostilities for the benefit of public opinion in their respective countries and abroad.

The first successes of the Japanese forces were even more impressive than those won by the Germans' Blitzkrieg. On February 15, 1942 the British garrison in **Singapore** surrendered this keystone of Great Britain's power structure in the Pacific to an attacking Japanese force, which was outnumbered by three to one. Besides infuriating **Churchill**, this shocking defeat signaled the retreat of the British from the Pacific and transferred the main burden of the war against the Japanese to American shoulders. It seemed also to herald the sunset of the British Empire. Incomprehensibly, however, this brilliant coup of the Japanese was not exploited politically. Their minister of foreign affairs suggested opening negotiations with the British to obtain the conquered territory under the seal of an accord. The proposal was ignored by the general staff. Infused with overconfidence, the Japanese commanders drew up elaborate plans to expand their original territorial aims. Emboldened by their rising sense of prestige and the enthusiasm of their acquiescent populace, the leaders of the state embarked on a mania of conquest. It seemed to them that they had only to consolidate their hold on the newly acquired territory and, from this firmer position of strength, continue their global negotiations with Germany.

But the divergent opinions of the military regarding targets and the rivalry between its two branches prevented Japan from exploiting these initial victories with combined land and sea thrusts. About a month after the beginning of the war, the occupation of territories that were still far from being conquered were divided into two zones. The Asiatic continent and the islands to the south were allotted to the army, while the Pacific and the eastern islands of the Dutch Indies were allotted to the navy. After that, India was to be the focal point of army operations, while the navy would converge on **Australia**. Unfortunately for the Japanese neither arm was capable of realizing maneuvers on so gargantuan a scale. They therefore contented themselves with incomplete strategic decisions and painfully contrived compromises. The result was an ineffective dispersion of forces, unable to contain the swift American counteroffensive. The advance of the Japanese fleet into the Indian Ocean, which had not even been announced to the German command, aroused fears in London that the British position in the Middle East and the main channel for the shipment of supplies to the USSR were in danger, and for a time an urgent call to the American fleet for reinforcements was meditated. But this Japanese operation turned out to be merely a show of force. Making no attempt to force a fight on the British Eastern Fleet, of much inferior strength, the Japanese ships withdrew to mount a raid on Australia to the south and to steam in the direction of the island of **Midway**, where Adm. **Isoruku Yamamoto** hoped to inflict a decisive defeat on the American Navy. Both projects failed.

After eight months of war, Japan was on the defensive in the **Pacific theater of operations**. Yet the military oligarchy that controlled the government summarily refused to initiate diplomatic maneuvers or strengthen the national economy—the real foundation of the war effort—even though these alternatives were feasible. Recognizing that, the Ministry of Foreign Affairs made some abortive attempts to stave off the clearly emerging possibility of the Empire's defeat. But, ironically, Japan's growing military weakness undercut these attempts, since the Japanese ruling clique insisted on a purely military solution up to the moment of capitulation.

Because the Allies would consider nothing less than the **unconditional surrender** of the Tripartite Pact powers, the Japanese felt that they could turn for help to the Soviet Union, the single ally of the Western nations not at war with Tokyo. Only the Japanese navy had had the resources to attempt to detach the USSR from the Allies by diplomatic means rather than by a military attack, which would have been useless from an economic point of view. Furthermore, any such military attempt was likely to end in failure—the Japanese had not forgotten the army's poor showing in the border clashes with Siberian troops in 1939. Since an armistice between the USSR and Germany was always possible, Tokyo did put out some feelers toward Moscow, less with the idea of remaining in close collaboration with the Germans than out of a desire to concentrate the power of the two countries on the main enemy of Japan, the Anglo-American alliance, and to receive the industrial products Japan so badly needed once again from Russia via the Trans-Siberian Railroad.

Even before Japan's entry into the war, its navy had been preoccupied with a political solution to the Blitzkrieg's lack of progress against the Soviet Union. With that in mind, the navy kept the seaway to the USSR unmined and absolutely refused to halt the transportation of war materiel to Vladivostok. The Japanese army, on the other hand, turned its energies in the opposite direction. Once its operations in the South Pacific ended, it resurrected its plans for an attack on the USSR, with the encouragement of the German Ministry of Foreign Affairs—but not, it should be noted, with Hitler's. At almost the same time, the Japanese navy was making its first official overtures to mediate the Nazi-Soviet war. It was met with rebuffs—from the apolitical German admiralty and especially from the Ministry of Foreign Affairs. Since the possibility of Germany's winning the "battle of destiny" on its eastern front appeared to blossom once again in the summer of 1942, other attempts by the Japanese navy along the same line remained fruitless, as did similar appeals to Moscow. Even the Japanese army advocates of an anti-Bolshevik crusade, as well as **Hiroshi Oshima**, the Japanese ambassador to Berlin, criticized the Nazi strategy of extermination before officials of the German government and recommended an occupation policy similar to that of the Japanese, which, at least according to its propaganda, was designed to liberate the peoples of Asia from oppression by the colonial powers. Thus, both sections of the Japanese armed forces envisaged a Eurasian bloc defending its eastern and western flanks against Anglo-American attacks. But they differed on the means for attaining that aim. A Japanese attack on the Soviet positions in the Far East, at least to the shores of Lake Baikal in Central Asia, might have been successful after the land operations in the South Pacific at the end of the spring of 1942. Such an adventure, coordinated with the summer offensive planned by the *Wehrmacht*, represented the last chance for the Japanese and Germans of collaborating closely in the war. Indeed, in view of the Japanese naval catastrophe at Midway, it seemed all the more practicable. But the opportunity for collaboration was

dashed—on the one hand by Hitler's race fixation, as evidenced by his reluctance to contract firm obligations with the "yellow" Japanese, and on the other by the obstinacy of the Japanese navy in pursuing its grandiose ambitions in the Pacific.

But toward the end of 1942, the forces of the Tripartite Pact suffered a second catastrophe—the battle of Stalingrad. The idea of a Eurasian continental bloc now seemed much more attractive to Hitler, and he asked officially for Japanese cooperation in the destruction of the Soviet Union. And this time, Tokyo rejected the offer with the complete approval of the Japanese army. Shigemitsu, the new Japanese minister of foreign affairs, even assigned priority to Japanese mediation of the Russo-German conflict. But the steps taken in this direction at what seemed to be favorable moments, such as the failure of the *Wehrmacht*'s summer offensive in 1943 and the defection of Italy, were stalled by Berlin and Moscow, although both sides had in the meantime begun serious negotiations for a separate peace at Stockholm. Apparently, the Russians deemed the Japanese proposal of mediation inopportune because they wanted restoration of the sphere of influence in the Far East they had lost to Japan in 1905. Very likely, too, they wanted to see Japan enfeebled by the war, without the strengthened prestige the role of mediator would give it.

After the failure of the mediation attempt of September 1943, the Japanese command decided on a change in political and military strategy. The Asian theater was subsequently to be considered independent of the European, and Japan's association with Germany was to be nothing more than a propaganda device. Since the Reich refused to form the Eurasian bloc by ending the war with Russia, Tokyo, in its own interests and against those of Germany, began seeking a rapprochement with the USSR against the anticipated American counteroffensive. It was urgent from a military point of view to establish a line along the Kuril Islands, the Bonins, the Marianas and western **New Guinea** as the "zone of absolute national defense" against the Americans.

In several agreements concluded in March 1944, Japan for the first time agreed to treat its huge Communist neighbor as a partner with equal rights. The Japanese oil and coal concessions in the northern part of Sakhalin Island were returned to the USSR, in accordance with the principles already accepted by **Yosuke Matsuoka** in April 1941, when he signed a treaty of neutrality with the Soviets. A second pact was negotiated on fishing rights, without disadvantage to the USSR. Discussions aimed at augmenting trade were energetically conducted by the Japanese. But these concessions failed to move **Stalin** from his promise to the Allies at Teheran (see **Conferences,**

Allied) to cooperate in the war against Japan. On the contrary, when Tokyo, fearing the imminent collapse of the Third Reich, offered to redraw the Manchurian frontier in the Russians' favor and to denounce both the Anti-Comintern Pact and the Tripartite Pact, the Soviet government replied by condemning Japan as an aggressor and refusing to extend their neutrality pact. As the Rising Sun sank lower in military strength, the goal of an Asiatic association of nations, which might have had a chance in 1941-42 except for the objections of the Japanese army, became all the more unrealistic.

Developments on the war fronts determined Japanese policy in the occupied territories. The New Order in East Asia proposed by the Ministry of Foreign Affairs shortly after the attack on Pearl Harbor remained buried in its files as long as these territories were out of the reach of Anglo-American forces.

In the minds of its statesmen, Japan was to occupy only key strategic positions such as **Hong Kong**, Singapore, North Borneo, New Guinea and **Timor**, permitting the other countries self-government. The former colonies of Malaya and the Dutch East Indies (see **Indonesia**), lower on the political evolutionary scale and possessing no well-organized national movements, were scheduled for semiautonomy under Japanese supervision. The **Philippines, Burma** and Indochina were to be allowed the status of independent allies on the model of Manchukuo, Nanking China and **Thailand**. During the first year and a half of the war in the Pacific, however, the "**Greater East Asia Co-Prosperity Sphere**"—the successor to the New Order in East Asia—existed only in Japanese propaganda. The occupation troops of the army and navy independently used their authority as conquerors to take what they liked in the occupied territories, with no regard to the demands of Tokyo. With the creation of the Ministry of Greater Asia in September 1943, the military even succeeded in wresting official control of the occupied territories from the Ministry of Foreign Affairs, in spite of Minister Togo's resignation in protest. On the whole, systematic exploitation of these territories failed for lack of an adequately detailed plan and because of the ever-present rivalries within the military and the Tokyo regime—and, most importantly, because of the insufficiency of Japanese naval strength. Each territorial governor pursued his own occupation policy and often mobilized auxiliary native troops—exiled Indians in Malaya, for example—to fight the former colonial powers and to ensure profitable **collaboration**. The Japanese never encountered **resistance** movements on any appreciable scale; the peoples they conquered accepted them as liberators despite instances of oppression and mistreatment by the arrogant soldiery. This state of af-

fairs also helped them in acquiring collaborators in the countries under their rule. But for lack of the concept of a regional occupation, the Japanese command failed to profit from the anti-British riots that erupted in India during the summer of 1942.

It was not until Shigemitsu took control of the Ministry of Foreign Affairs in Tokyo that the occupation policy was reviewed and its supervision restored to the Ministry's aegis. This was a natural outgrowth of the work he had done as ambassador to the puppet government of **Wang Ching-wei**, when he had revamped Japan's policy in occupied China. Burma and the Philippines, both of which had been largely autonomous before the war, were granted independence on August 1 and October 14, 1943, respectively. They nevertheless recognized Japan's predominance in Asia and its right to keep garrisons on their territories for the duration of the war. In October 1943 a **government-in-exile** for "Free India" was set up in Singapore under the direction of **Subhas Chandra Bose**, head of the radical wing of the Indian independence movement. He had come there from Germany, presumably to spearhead the Japanese expedition against British India, projected for the spring of 1944.

As prelude to the "Greater East Asia Conference" in Tokyo at the beginning of November 1943, Japan concluded a friendship treaty with Nanking China, promising to withdraw occupation troops at the end of the war in the Pacific. Military exigencies, however, dictated otherwise. The army in particular began to treat neighboring Asiatic nations as equal partners only when it could no longer impose its leadership on them by force. The credo of Japan's dominance in Asia and the superiority of the Japanese over other Asiatics were sacrosanct; in the minds of the military elite, all of Tokyo's notions of equality had to fall before it.

The whole patriarchal structure of the Empire's social system was closely intertwined with the privileged position of the warrior caste. This was the real reason for Japan's reluctance to yield independence to Indochina and Indonesia. In spite of this rigid occupation policy, the Japanese managed, with their Greater East Asia Co-Prosperity Sphere, to eliminate the "white man" from East Asia; they failed, however, to attain supremacy in Asia because of their occupation policy. (See **Independence Movements**.)

During the entire war the Japanese grappled incompetently with the problem of the war economy. Given the divergence of the strategic aims of the Japanese army and navy and the intrigues within the home government, it was impossible to establish priorities. There was simply no way to choose between the competing demands of the army and navy, each of which had its own aircraft, while the army had its own fleet of **landing craft**. The home islands, with no oil, metals or coal, had struck at the United States to break the embargo Washington had imposed on it. Curiously enough, however, the Japanese army in the course of its victorious advance took little time to exploit or transport the enormous wealth in raw materials within its new domain. Both the armed forces were primarily in pursuit of glory. With practically all the means for transportation devoted to hauling the materiel of war that pursuit demanded, there was little left to furnish the industrial plants at home with rubber, oil, iron, tin, nickel, bauxite and coal. Completely ignorant of the economic basis of the war and the need for catering to it, the war lords at the head of the government were blind to industrial bottlenecks and the low output of the shipyards until after they lost mastery of the seas in the disaster at Midway. It seems absurd that barely four months after the onset of hostilities, Japan started experimenting with ships made of wood and concrete, and that in August of 1942 it asked Germany for a half-million tons of vessels, including the crews, a million tons of steel and 20 thousand tons of aluminum instead of reorganizing its own economy and improving its sea lanes. These steps alone could have insured the cohesion of the occupied territories by placing them under the protection of the navy before the depredations of American submarines increased to the danger point. Until 1943 the Japanese showed no interest in hunting down enemy merchant ships. The natural effect was the considerable easing of the logistics problem for American planners. The **convoy** system, the most frequently used method of shipping protection in other war theaters, was not taken up by the Japanese until American warships had sunk a million tons of merchant vessels. Nowhere did the ignorance of the Japanese command seem more apparent than in their lack of attention to the safety of sea lanes for proper supply of the armaments industry. The absence of an adequate plan for the war economy, in a wretched state since 1942 for lack of raw materials, assisted the Anglo-American counterattack. A country continuously in need of everything from **food** staples to machine tools and from aircraft engines to eyeglass lenses could never compete with a highly industrialized and richly endowed nation like the United States. Japan's war economy was hopelessly inferior to the "white" productive capacity, with its limitless potential, especially in the face of white soldiers' greater familiarity with machinery of all types. To their dismay the Japanese suddenly realized that the model of Western technology they had so assiduously constructed was only superficial; they had no comprehension of how to mobilize it effectively for a war.

The strictly hierarchical order that blocked individual initiative and the indecision and inflexibility of both the supreme military command and the officers at the various fronts, who knew no other mode of behavior under fire but heroic death, were part of the feudal, preindustrial past. Its effect was fatal for the Japanese defense and increased the relative strength of the American forces, which were often weaker in numbers than the Japanese, but compensated for that with much greater efficiency in the use of their equipment.

With the fall of **Saipan** in July 1944, the home islands of Japan were within range of American strategic bombers. In this area the lack of coordination between the two arms of the Japanese military was again clearly highlighted. This time, however, it produced political repercussions. The pressure of the *Jushin*, a loose group of former prime ministers, forced the resignation of **Tojo**, who then occupied the post. His place was taken by two heads of government, one of them a general, **Kuniaki Koiso**, the other an admiral, **Mitsumasu Yonai**. This shake-up represented a victory for the navy and for moderate political forces. The Japanese defense zone fell back to the line formed by the Kurils, the home islands and the Ryukyus. The supreme governmental body, the Coordination Conference, was recognized as the "Supreme War Council," with six members. For the first time, the admiralty considered the possibility of concluding a peace.

While the navy counted the political costs of its military defeats, the army undertook large-scale offensives against India and China. The push across the Burmese frontier became stalled at Imphal, in India, but it regained the land bridge between Hankow and Canton. The American air bases in that region fell to the Japanese, with the result that the Japanese army's faith in itself swelled to the point where it envisaged a final battle in which it would wipe out invading American troops on the home islands themselves, if necessary. Although the Japanese command mobilized all available reserves of the army and navy along with the new suicide aircraft units (see **Kamikaze**) for the decisive battle anticipated in the Philippines, the American fleet first delivered a body blow to the Japanese navy and then landed troops on the island of **Leyte**.

The invasion of the island of **Okinawa**, often considered part of the Japanese home islands, brought down the Koiso-Yonai government and raised Adm. **Kantaro Suzuki** to the seat of power. The new government devoted no more thought to the conclusion of a peace than had the old. Even after the German surrender, the realities of the Japanese military situation in the Pacific were ignored in favor of irrational samurai dreams. To ingratiate itself with the USSR,

Tokyo voided all agreements concluded with Germany—at a time when the Soviets were still insisting on the return of the old, pre-1905 Russian sphere of influence as the price for their assistance to the Allies in crushing Hirohito's empire. The extreme secrecy of the **peace overtures** extended in June and July 1945 to the United States by way of the Soviet Union, the blindness of the military to the consequences of the incessant defeats and the impenetrable muddle of the Tokyo bureaucracy all testified to the fact that the old Japanese elite was far behind the swift march of events. Through the messages from the Japanese delivered by way of **Sweden** and **Switzerland**, American officials knew Japan was ready to surrender before the **atomic bombs** were dropped on Hiroshima and Nagasaki—cities, incidentally, of no particular military significance that had been deliberately spared until then. But it was practically impossible for the Japanese leaders to agree to unconditional surrender without the intervention of the emperor. It finally came in mid-August. By abandoning his aloofness from politics, Hirohito deprived himself of the majesty of heaven and cast doubt on the divine origin of the Japanese state.

Neither the American atomic bombs nor the Soviet declaration of war, but rather their own inability to cope with the war and the problems it created, compelled the Japanese people and, above all, their leaders, to surrender on August 15, 1945. It may even have been the impossibility of fusing Western techniques and ideas then governing world politics with the spiritual and social life of Japan. The collapse of the state and the American occupation that followed it deeply offended the Japanese and are still resented today, less as a military defeat than as a profound spiritual rebuke and an imposed social revolution.

The Home Front

Japanese society
The family in wartime

Fierce and brutalizing though it was, World War II did not devastate the structures underlying society in any of the major nations involved in the fighting. The most important of these structures in Japan was the family, both as an elemental social institution and as a pattern for organizing other small groups. The family was the firmest source of continuity and security for the Japanese during wartime. Living in the city and taking part in **neighborhood associations** made people rely more on others nearby, but in the catastrophe of the air war (see **Japan, Air War Against**) in 1944-1945 it was the family that usually offered refuge through relatives in the villages. Wartime made little dif-

ference in Japan's long-term patterns of marriage, fertility, divorce or juvenile crime, in contrast to the United States or Britain.

The **National Spiritual Mobilization** of 1937-40 depended mostly on the efforts of Japanese **women** to make people more aware of the war in China. The state encouraged motherhood as a positive state, typified by the mother in the ideal family, to supply nurture and support to those who were lonely, injured, bereaved or newly drafted. After 1940, when the cabinet extended the network of neighborhood associations to every town and village in the country, it usually turned out that the family system was more effective in providing wartime labor than the new neighborhood units, especially in rural areas.

Even in the big cities the government was careful to use the family as a building block of neighborhood solidarity, rather than smashing it. Unlike their counterparts in the Soviet Union, who used wartime to undertake social reconstruction, Japanese authorities fought the war by encouraging the preservation of the family tradition. Members of Japanese city households led a relatively independent, self-reliant life, separate from those around them. Although households no longer necessarily included a large number of relatives from several generations under one roof, the family was still the basic social unit to be mobilized for home front activities in support of the fighting abroad.

"The weakening of the family system would be the weakening of the nation," Prime Minister Tojo told the Diet in October 1943. In spite of a growing labor shortage, with so many men absent from home in the services, Tojo deferred to conventional social expectations about women's roles and exalted the family system rather than resorting to a labor draft of women for the war plants.

Instead the state launched a nationwide fertility campaign to raise the birth rate by 50 percent, but despite patriotic encouragements and financial inducements to bear more babies the campaign had very little effect on the demography of wartime. Nor was there a discernible change in long-term marriage or divorce rates. The number of marriages each year stayed just below 10 per thousand through 1943, remarkably close to the annual rate since 1900. The divorce figure remained steady between 0.6 and 0.7 per thousand through 1943, the last wartime year for which statistics are available, and it rose along with the marriage rate after 1945.

The cabinet suddenly violated the spirit of familism on June 30, 1944, when it announced that schoolchildren would be taken from their families in the cities and resettled en masse in the countryside. The state's motive was to protect the students as a human resource through **evacuation and resettlement**, no matter how they or their parents felt about being separated from one another. More than 350,000 third-through sixth-graders from the public schools in a dozen major cities were taken in groups to vacant inns, meeting halls, temples and resorts in nearby prefectures. Already 300,000 urban schoolchildren were living in the villages as voluntary evacuees. Another 100,000 first- and second-graders were sent out in March 1945, raising the number of students who relocated in groups to more than 450,000. There is no gauge that can measure the emotional damage that occurred when children were separated from their anxious families, but it seems likely that not even the frightful air raids were as traumatic as the compulsory detachment of young children from their homes.

In the last months of the war, more than 10 million city residents sought refuge in the mountains and farm villages, two-thirds of them women and children. Frictions between host families and refugees, as in the British evacuation, were especially great in the case of mothers with small children. Although the great majority of evacuees settled in with rural relatives, not even ties of blood could mask the cultural and emotional gaps between city and country life styles. But simple necessity eventually crowded out all other considerations, and basic human cooperation prevailed in the emergency conditions of desperate need.

Minota village in Saitama prefecture, near Tokyo, found in a June 1945 survey that its population had swollen by 30 percent since January 1944. About a quarter of the newcomers were direct victims of bombing, and the rest had fled the cities as a precaution. Three-quarters of the host families were relatives of the refugees they housed, and proportionately as many poor homes accepted evacuees as rich ones. Almost none of the visitors had any experience in the fields, a source of misunderstanding and misgiving wherever city people relocated.

It is hard to know whether host or guest was inconvenienced more when 10 million outsiders piggybacked on 42 million country people. But in the end the two groups learned to get along because the wreckage resulting from a lost war deprived them of any other choice. The state played its part, as it had with its earlier policies toward the family, by appealing to the collective tradition of Japanese society. The government used school groups to relocate young people and neighborhood associations to ease the stress of moving. Above all it tried to cajole or even shame farmers into taking in their city cousins. Nearly all did so voluntarily, if reluctantly, less because their state demanded it than because family ties remained very durable even during total war.

The demography of war

Although three million Japanese lost their lives in World War II, wartime had surprisingly minor effects on the nation's population in the long run. Japan had 72,540,000 residents in the home islands in 1940. A decade later the population was 83,200,000, almost precisely what it would have been without the war.

Birth rates fell steadily from 36.1 per thousand in 1920 to 30.8 in 1937, a normal decline for an industrializing country. By 1938-39 the rate was down to 26.8 per thousand, reflecting a dropoff in marriages. The absence of 1.1 million men abroad on military duty had little effect on births, since most soldiers and sailors were in their early twenties and not yet ready for marriage. Even when the armed forces swelled to their peak of 8.2 million men, the impact on birth rates was surprisingly modest.

The military authorities nonetheless trumpeted family solidarity and operated marriage-counseling centers, "to cause women to move from an individualistic view of marriage to a national one and to make young women recognize motherhood as the national destiny." A marriage improvement movement was launched in connection with Prime Minister Tojo's fertility campaign. For many years Japan had complained that it was land-poor and needed more living space. Now that war had broken out, the government decided more babies were needed and passed a national eugenics law to promote child-bearing by outlawing birth control.

The goal was to raise birth rates by nearly 50 percent, to three million per year. Tojo's wife, the mother of seven, declared that "having babies is fun" and urged Japanese women to raise large families. The government encouraged early marriages, set up match-making agencies and instructed companies to pay baby bonuses to their employees. Families with ten or more children were promised free higher education when they reached college age.

The incentives and exhortations had little effect. Between 1941 and 1943, when the state promoted natalism most strongly, the marriage rate rose to about 10 per thousand, up from 8.1 during 1935-39. The jump was partly a product of inducements offered to soldiers for registering informal marriages promptly. But the main reason marriages increased was that young men could now afford to marry somewhat earlier because of wartime economic expansion.

Births themselves stayed almost constant at the 1940-41 level of about 2.2 million per annum through the year ending September 30, 1944. The live birth rate hovered around 30.2 per thousand, only slightly higher than the depressed figure of 26.8 for 1938-39. Then births plunged more than 10 percent in 1944-45 and another 15 percent the following year, reflecting larger draft calls of potential fathers, migration to flee air raids, economic deterioration and reduced levels of nutrition.

Natalist campaigns proved to be no more successful in Japan than elsewhere during World War II. Despite ceaseless discomforts and the three million war deaths, the long-term fertility of Japan's population proved to be quite resistant to the ravages of warfare. The birth rate was erratic in the mid-1940s, but the gradual downward pattern of fertility evident since World War I continued throughout the decade as a whole. Unlike the Soviet Union, where the war dead may have been outnumbered by babies not conceived because of the conflict, Japan's postsurrender baby boom soon offset the decline in 1944-46.

After Japan was defeated, the Allies repatriated 3.1 million Japanese civilians and 3.5 million troops from abroad. At the same time, 1.2 million noncitizens, mainly Koreans, emigrated from Japan. The fate of 237,000 other Japanese in Siberia, 79,000 in Karafuto and the Kurils and 60,000 in Manchuria was less clear, but presumably few of them survived the war. Perhaps a half-million civilians lost their lives on the home front and more than two million troops died abroad. To avoid this grim fate, more than 10 million civilians took part in evacuation and resettlement schemes in the countryside, temporarily interrupting the longstanding trend toward urbanization, but well before 1950 the cities regained their usual size.

Although there was no permanent damage to childbearing in the abstract, three million individuals did die sooner because of the war. Age structures and male-female ratios were disarrayed. Schools, labor forces and old-age homes would be alternately crowded and undersupplied for decades into the future. Just as the percentage of young workers in the Japanese work force during the 1950s and 1960s was disproportionately large because of wartime wiggles in the fertility slope, outlays for a more mature labor pool and expanded facilities for care of the elderly that are required today as a result of those same wartime fertility variations crimp the national economy.

The role of women

Women were the mainstay of home front society in Japan just as much as they were elsewhere during World War II, but they participated in the war economy somewhat less fully than in any other major country involved in the conflict except Germany. Women were indispensable for the stability of the Japanese family, community councils, neighborhood associations and commodity rations. They were the chief agents of the National Spiritual Mobilization in making civilians aware of the war emergency in China and the Pacific. Women also played a leading part in ceremonies to see off soldiers bound for the war front, comforting the wounded and bereaved and receiving the ashes of those who died in battle. Women worked in the swollen war economy in unprecedented numbers; without their labor Japanese forces could not possibly have put up the stiff fight that they did. Yet the Japanese authorities never fully or systematically mobilized the potential female work force, either by inducement or by compulsion, so women ended up as Japan's greatest underutilized asset of the wartime era.

One of the first actions of Prime Minister **Fumimaro Konoe**'s **New Structure Movement** was to combine the three prewar federations of women's organizations into a single Greater Japan Women's Association, subsuming all private groups. After a good deal of bureaucratic jostling, the new association began operations on February 2, 1942. All married women, and single women over age 20 as well, were expected to join "to fulfill all the responsibilities of women in wartime." The press put it more succinctly: "Its main purpose is to make good mothers." The association was expected to promote Tojo's campaign to lift the birth rate by 50 percent, but its efforts had little impact.

Like the youth groups and labor federations that formed in 1940-1941, the Greater Japan Women's Association was nominally a "people's movement" under the auspices of the **Imperial Rule Assistance Association**, an umbrella organization for political and social mobilization founded by Konoe in September 1940. Altogether 19,310,000 women supposedly joined the new women's unit, but it seems that local chapters were far stronger than the national association. By all accounts the women's groups served most effectively throughout the war at their familiar tasks from before the merger, particularly comforting injured soldiers and the families of men killed at the front.

Women made an important contribution to Japanese wartime **production**, but they were never offered the financial incentives used in America and elsewhere. Labor enrollment for men and women began in November 1941, when unmarried women ages 16-25 had to register for possible service, but only the men were actually drafted for war work. In February 1944 the registry was expanded to include unmarried women ages 12-39, but once again only the men were called for service. Unmarried women and students of both sexes were mobilized in various volunteer corps during the last year of the war, but the Japanese were never fully coercive in dealing with their labor needs.

Part of the reason for this reluctance to conscript women workers was that their labor was badly needed on the farms. Both farm output and the rural work force held steady through 1944, primarily because women and some older persons replaced the 2.8

million men and 650,000 young women who, it is estimated, had left farming for the services or the factories. Women formed 52.2 percent of the rural work force in 1940, a figure that rose to 57.6 percent by 1944. When farm production finally dropped off in 1945, inadequate supplies of fertilizer, worn-out equipment, smaller areas under cultivation and disastrously cold weather were more to blame for the dismal harvest than any lack of hard work on the part of the field hands, most of them women.

As the buildup for war production moved along, the cabinet induced old men to join the work force, and by February 1944 more than two-thirds of all males over age 60 were working. They were joined by most **prisoners of war**, who numbered more than 30,000 by the surrender, and nearly 1.3 million Koreans who came to Japan between 1937 and 1945. Japan also imported more than 38,000 contract Chinese laborers. The authorities tapped all these sources before mustering the labor of unmarried women, and they never systematically mobilized those who were married.

By 1944 more women held jobs in Japan than ever before, but they remained the most underemployed social group. The number of working women eventually exceeded 14 million, which was 42 percent of the civilian labor supply in 1944. But in spite of the heavy military draft, the female portion of the work force in that year was only three percent larger than in 1940 and just seven percent larger than in the depression year of 1930.

Between 1940 and 1944, the loss of 300,000 men from the nonmilitary labor supply was more than offset by the gain of 1.4 million women (including students); still, this represented only a modest 10 percent increase in the number of female workers. In America, by contrast, the number of working women jumped by more than one-third. The Japanese state did not put women to work more methodically partly because the wages they received for their toil if they took jobs in the war plants were low but also partly because of old attitudes about what constituted appropriate work for females.

It is tempting, but too simple, to blame patriarchal officials for not mobilizing women more promptly and thoroughly. In fact the state was reluctant to conscript workers of either sex, and it never resorted to an outright labor draft of women at any point. The result was that relatively modest numbers of women took jobs outside the occupations traditionally open to them: farming, shopkeeping, clerical duties and kitchen work. Although young unmarried women had to register for possible factory service after November 1941, the government enlisted them only by random exhortation until early 1944 and by systematic inducement thereafter.

The cabinet's attitude in 1942 was that "in Japan, out of consideration for the family system, we will not draft" women workers. By early 1943 the war had bogged down, the economy was showing signs of strain, and there was a labor shortage. Still the mobilization plan issued that spring merely "urged" women to work in industry, a sign that the government remained ambivalent about the place of female labor.

By late 1943 women who were not working were being criticized as "women of leisure" or as "unpatriotic," but Tojo's idyll of Japanese womanhood by the hearth seemingly still underlay the state's policy. The prime minister told the Diet in October that "there is no need for our nation to labor-draft women just because America and Britain are doing so." He said that "we are able to do our duties here in the Diet only because we have wives and mothers at home." Rather than raising wages and improving conditions for those who worked, the government and big industry regarded the woman as temporary help, someone who should return home as soon as she was married. This was no change from prewar days.

The second phase of enlisting women workers, starting January 23, 1944, finally made something of a break with the past. Women's volunteer labor corps were created for aircraft manufacturing and other essential industries, and a new labor registration was conducted. Neighborhood associations prodded unmarried women into joining the corps. Those who did so had to serve a full year, later extended to two. It was hard for single women to refuse, but the new plan fell short of being a compulsory labor system. The national mobilization program for the spring of 1944 provided for these corps but cautioned that "due consideration shall be given to the limitations of women." In practice, women who were badly needed at home were often excused, and at all times single women were urged to marry (escaping further service). In spite of such prevailing attitudes, the state labor enrollment program functioned reasonably efficiently, considering that it was confined by statute to the unmarried minority of adult females. By March 1945 about 472,000 women had gone to work through the volunteer corps, although half had been working elsewhere before.

Japan's war production and labor force peaked at the end of the summer of 1944, when a cabinet inventory of resources pointed out that male workers were scarce but that there was still a huge supply of potential female laborers. In October the nearly four million women who were working in the war industries were frozen in their jobs by state decree, the last major step taken to mobilize women. Thereafter materiel shortages slowed industrial production more and more. After large-scale bombing raids began in November 1944 and people started to flee the cities en masse, the state quite simply lost control over the movement of workers in its war plants.

The shrinking war economy at the end of the conflict made conditions grim for most women who worked in the plants. Some had to sleep in their factories, which were plunged into cold by the complete lack of heating fuel. Workers often received for lunch only a bowl of broth with a few noodles. When materials, equipment and parts grew scarce, the laborers were demoralized by having to stand idly for hours on end without even being permitted to read. For women who lived in company dormitories, fatigue and filth depressed their spirits further. Living close to a noisy plant made sleep fitful at best, and the American bombardment often meant that rest was impossible. Women volunteers who served far from home often grew lonely for their families. As one of them later wrote: "what pleasures were there those days? Love-making was impossible, there was no time for reading and foreign music was prohibited."

Japan's labor needs during World War II were met primarily by redeploying male workers from nonessential industries, supplemented by three million students, a million older men, more than a million Koreans and Chinese and fewer than a million new female workers who were not students. Nor were many of the women who were already employed when war broke out shifted into important positions of executive or production-line responsibility. Instead, most of them worked in the fields, the marketplace, the kitchen, the stockroom—wherever low-paid, light labor was needed. Women had actually outnumbered men in the factories before 1930, because of jobs in the spinning mills, but now they represented less than a quarter of the industrial work force. Another sign that women were less than fully mobilized for war was the continuing presence of domestic servants, nearly all of whom were females. There were still enough well-to-do families in February 1944 to provide employment for 600,000 domestics.

The state was skittish about putting women to work in good part because public opinion—male and female alike—was frosty toward the idea of compulsory women's labor. It is true that women often lacked technical ability to perform industrial occupations, but the nub of the matter was that traditional ideas of appropriate activity for women were economic disincentives throughout the war.

Time-honored values within the culture undoubtedly constrained the state's capacity to put women to work on behalf of the war. Yet in the absence of so many men, economic necessity forced more women to work than ever before, mocking the government's policy of keeping the married ones at home. The war made wage earners of many women for the first time and caused changes in their roles within the family that would have been difficult to imagine a decade earlier.

Youth groups

As a part of its New Structure Movement in 1940-41, the Japanese government set up the Greater Japan Youth Association to absorb young people's organizations of all sorts and rally the nation's youth to support the war. Whether they enthusiastically endorsed the military expansion or not, persons in their teens and early twenties rarely resisted taking part in war-related activities through local chapters of the association because for decades young people had been expected to join age-group organizations in their home towns.

Young men's and women's clubs arose in the late 19th century in rural areas, designed for recreation and community service. Starting in 1915 the education and home ministries began to encourage their spread throughout the country. After World War I, four major youth-group councils were formed, to bring the local units under a measure of state leadership. At the same time such foreign organizations as the Boy Scouts, Girl Scouts, 4-H clubs, YMCA, YWCA and sports groups became well established in Japan, particularly in the cities. Their growth added to the government's determination to bring all young people's organizations under a single umbrella.

The Japanese authorities were well aware of the Hitler youth movement in Germany, but they preferred to centralize Japan's youth groups organizationally rather than regiment them ideologically. The Greater Japan Youth Association was officially established on January 16, 1941, by merging the four councils of young people's clubs dating back to the 1920s and 1930s. The association, in turn, was an important structural element of the Imperial Rule Assistance Association, which Prime Minister Konoe had created to streamline wartime administration and to prevent the armed services from taking over domestic politics.

The Greater Japan Youth Association consisted of 36,299 local chapters at the outset. In the next year and a half, these groups increased their combined membership from 4,428,239 to 14,215,837, mainly by hounding nearly all young people between 10 and 25 into joining, especially those in the relatively underorganized cities. Most clubs kept up the same voluntary activities as before the unification: cleaning nearby parks, planning field days, helping with community festivals. But the state also used them to spread the aims of the war and to marshal work teams for spot jobs in neighborhoods and on the farms.

Wartime schools were more useful to the state than the youth groups for indoctrinating the young, and as the fighting wore on the Greater Japan Youth Association grew less useful in mobilizing the sentiments and the labor of young people than the education system, volunteer work corps and the draft. The association often worked at cross purposes with the Greater Japan Women's Association, to which young women were also normally forced to belong. Although the local youth clubs were usually stronger than the unwieldy central organization into which they had been merged, there is no question that young people were now plunged into wartime activities far different from the games, fairs and shrine festivals of earlier years. Only the disruptions of large-scale bombing raids and urban resettlement in the countryside in early 1945 halted the work of the youth groups.

Schools and education

Japan's school system was a key agency for propaganda during World War II, particularly through the National Spiritual Mobilization movement. Curricular reforms brought increased attention to the Greater East Asia Co-Prosperity Sphere and Japan's war aims, and students were obliged to show respect for the monarchy by listening to the imperial rescript on education of 1890 and bowing to portraits of Emperor Hirohito. In the end, state **propaganda** and curricular revisions frayed the schools less seriously than did certain ancillary programs brought about by the war: military drill, student labor service, volunteer corps and especially evacuation and resettlement in the countryside to escape the American air raids late in the conflict.

The education ministry, proud of its autonomy and often wary of the army, cabinet and home ministry, nonetheless let schooling fall in step with the National Spiritual Mobilization soon after Japan went to war with China in 1937. Already new ethics texts (*Shushin*) and a propagandistic volume called *Basic Principles of the National Essence* had been introduced to play up Japan's cultural distinctiveness among elementary pupils. In January 1938 the education ministry sent around instructions to teachers showing how to work the China crisis into each subject area.

Schoolchildren had to join in new activities to correct the earlier "overemphasis on intellectual training," and classroom hours were shortened correspondingly. They had to undergo more physical training. School sports grew more martial, with baseball displaced by marching, judo and kendo. Boys in the upper elementary and secondary levels had to take frequent military training, which the army admitted was intended "to build up the morale of the nation, rather than to serve primarily as a measure of preparedness."

The obligation to perform school labor service cut still further into class time as a result of the spiritual campaign. Students had to give as much as 10 days at a time for gathering charcoal, picking up leaves or cleaning out parks—jobs no longer routinely performed in a slowly tightening war economy.

Radio broadcasts to the schools, first developed by the national air network (NHK) in 1935, were systematized during wartime despite the education ministry's fears about losing control over their content. By 1941 direct broadcasts to pupils in class were legally incorporated into the curriculum. Their themes grew more militaristic after Pearl Harbor ("Front Line Diary," "Greater East Asia Co-Prosperity Sphere Lectures"), yet it seems that many students regarded them as entertaining diversions rather than as classroom material to be taken seriously.

Once they graduated from elementary school, most children kept on pursuing their spiritual training in a form of continuing education devised for young working people. Since only a minority of prewar Japanese boys and girls studied beyond the compulsory six years of grammar school, the government set up youth schools for teenagers so they could get part-time vocational and military training. Classes met for three hours or so each day while the pupils also held jobs. About three-quarters of the 13-15 age group enrolled in youth schools during the war.

Starting in 1938 the national education commission recommended that primary schools be revamped to offer not only ordinary skills but also "basic training of the people in comformity with the moral principles of the Japanese empire." The reforms, which took effect in April 1941, required students to attend elementary schools (renamed national schools) for eight years and youth schools part-time for another five. Even more military training was wedged into the daily schedule, and secondary education was more tightly integrated. These structural changes were never fully implemented because of wartime conditions, but the shift in curricular content was weighty. Although classwork in the national schools was nominally split into four teaching categories, the education ministry insisted that "there is to be no division of learning, nor any separation of subjects of study, and the bulk of the instructional content will deal with training imperial countrymen."

The national texts of 1933 were revised twice during the war, once in 1940-41 and again in 1943. All editions between 1903 and 1943 stressed the national essence, Japan's rise to prominence and pressures from abroad. But the new versions were needed to keep up with the empire's expansion and world diplomatic events, and the manner of presentation grew more romantic and less formal by 1943. Schoolchildren were now taught that the Shinto sun goddess would protect her divine land through mystical powers that drew man and nature together. In the same vein was *The Way of Subjects*, issued by the education ministry in August 1941 as a handbook for young persons. This remarkable document attacked "individualism, liberalism, utilitarianism and materialism" and offered an elaborate rationale for Japan's overseas activities.

Most of the state's energies were expended on younger pupils, but not even university students were free from the program of spiritual mobilization. Tokyo and Kyoto Imperial Universities announced courses on "The History of Japanese Ideology" and "The History of the Japanese Spirit." Starting in August 1940, instructors were forbidden to use the Bible as a text because it was "detrimental to the moral education of the Japanese."

Although the curriculum was lyrical about Japan's destiny, its aura of fantasy did not stand in the way of badly needed technical education during wartime. Rather like the Nazis, certain officials talked vaguely of a "Japanese science" based on "the imperial way." But the government soon shifted more students into technical areas, and it converted most public commercial institutes into technical schools. The result was that there were three times as many science and engineering graduates in 1941-1945 as a decade earlier. To encourage basic **research**, the state formed a series of federations and societies in 1940, capped by a technology agency two years later to coordinate policy. Japan's scientific and technical shortcomings in wartime stemmed from inadequate financing, equipment and leadership much more than from a preoccupation with ideology or propaganda.

The government's language-instruction policies, however, were as short-sighted as its science policy was practical. Zealous officials in the spiritual mobilization branded English as the language of the enemy in 1937, and soon citizens found that Japanese terms derived from European languages had been replaced in official announcements by ersatz native equivalents. Although it was not unsympathetic to these efforts, the education ministry treated the matter with discreet inaction. It issued no national ban against teaching English, in deference to those who knew how vital it was for scientific research, but instead left the question to the local school districts. Faced with demands for more military drill and student labor service, the local authorities usually took the ministry's silence as consent to eliminate English classes from the middle schools, and by 1943 the language had virtually disappeared from the curriculum below the university level.

Through that same year, the last for which there are reliable records, well over 99 percent of the age group was enrolled in Japan's elementary schools. What turned the education system to tatters by 1945 was a combination of factory labor needs, flight from the largest cities and finally a huge dearth of supplies and equipment. To release students sooner for war work, the education ministry cut back most secondary curricula in April 1943 by a full year. Once schooling was out of the way, every one was expected to go to work, and after April 1944 all students over age 10 were soon mobilized for labor in the fields or war plants, practically on a full-time basis.

Because family ties stayed pretty much intact and young people were busy learning or working, the rise in juvenile crime was much slower in Japan than in most other countries that joined in the fighting. Arrests increased 40 percent between 1941 and 1944, then fell back precisely to their 1941 level the next year. But records were poorly kept at the end of the war, and it is hard to weigh arrest figures against the knowledge that the police harassed many young people, especially university students, when the state controls were tightest. Crime in general seems to have diminished in Japan's tightly organized wartime society, although most statistics are untrustworthy because of poor reporting and undermanned local police.

Education was a serious enterprise for the country's 18 million students, one that forced them to adapt to the national emergency. Primary students returning from the summer vacation in 1942 were fed roasted sparrows for lunch, part of a govenment campaign to protect the rice crop from the birds. College men and women soon grew used to seeing pyramid markers on top of empty desks, honoring their classmates who had gone off to war. During alerts the pupils wore air-raid bonnets, covering the head and shoulders like the upper half of a hooded sweatshirt, to ward off sparks and debris symbolically if not in fact.

Labor service became a much larger requirement for students above the third grade after June 1943. Their vacations and holidays were given over to war work, and the school year was shortened by as much as a third in some areas to keep children on the job longer. One teacher remembered taking her class two hours into the mountains near Nagoya to cultivate new fields: "all 600 pupils or so from the school cut down thick weeds and pulled out rocks and tree stumps. This severe work went on for thirteen days. . . . I was so tired that my hoe dropped, and I forget whether all this had any effect in the war zone."

Student deferments finally ended in the autumn of 1943 for most young men over nineteen in the universities and higher level schools. Only students in engineering or the sciences were excused from the call-up. Altogether 130,000 men were inducted en masse, removing about a quarter of those enrolled in higher education at a stroke. To mark the occasion, the cabinet sponsored a supremely somber parade in the Meiji stadium in Tokyo. "Thousands and tens of thousands gathered in a drizzle," wrote an observer, "to see off the uniformed students with rifles on their shoulders." Each school group, led by a flag bearer, chanted "naturally we don't expect to return alive."

By the spring of 1944 most students at other levels found their schoolwork more and more disrupted as well. All of them who were older than 10 had to join "volunteer labor corps," beginning in April, for nearly full-time war work. "Sometimes we still went to class," wrote a fourth-year high school student, "but it was in name only. There were only fragments of instruction." Learning by doing turned out to be a particulary bitter lesson for an 11-year-old school volunteer in a large chocolate factory. He was caught helping himself to a piece of candy and forced to stand in front of Kawasaki station with a big sign saying "I am a thief."

The last year of the war affected teachers as greatly as their students. If they were not in the services or involved in war production, instructors were often asked to supervise the student volunteer corps or accompany school groups who evacuated to the mountains from big cities after August 1944. Because so many men teachers were being drafted, women took over for them even in the older grades, which heretofore were strongholds of male authority. Textbooks at all levels were so scarce by April 1945 that old ones had to be copied over by hand. There were no writing tablets and no sheets of paper for art classes, and students "used old newspapers for practicing characters until they turned completely black." That same month classes at the public secondary schools were suspended, since 70 percent of the students were away as labor volunteers, but the primary schools and universities struggled on, despite the air war and evacuation, right to the brief summer vacation in August.

Minority groups

Neither the one million Burakumin outcasts nor the Korean and Chinese residents of Japan improved their status during wartime, despite the booming factory economy and full employment. Unlike black Americans during the same period, who overcame some barriers by participating quite fully in industry and the services, minorities in Japan benefited very little from the national mobilization. Koreans and Chinese who came from the colonies to work in Japanese factories were subjected to appalling abuse, and many thousands of them died from the treatment they

received in Japanese hands. But compared with the fate of minorities in Germany or the USSR, they generally emerged from the war bloodied but unbowed.

The Japanese had discriminated against Koreans for centuries, never more so than during 1910-45 when they ruled Korea as a colony. Local self-rule and voting rights were only nominal, wages were poor, education doctrinaire and housing substandard. On the other hand, Japan modernized the Korean economy, extended the school system and built modern transport facilities. The Japanese governed their other main overseas colony, Taiwan, somewhat less harshly from 1895 to 1945 while it was part of their empire.

During the wartime labor mobilization, Japan used nearly 1.3 million Korean workers in mining, construction and stevedoring. Most were lured across the Tsushima straits by the promise of higher wages, but thousands were conscripted against their will to work under conditions little better than slavery. They were supplemented by more than 38,000 contract Chinese laborers, of whom 564 are believed to have perished on shipboard en route to Japan. Foreign workers comprised about 4 percent of the labor supply, compared with the 20 percent of Germany's wartime work force that came from occupied areas.

"Koreans were the hardest workers," a Japanese student recruited to build an airfield recalled, but "they were frequently beaten with wooden clubs." Because inflation outstripped wages for all industrial employees in Japan, these foreign workers did not prosper from their jobs. Usually they worked in segregated units under police guard. Housing, diet and sanitation were hardly better than in Korea or Taiwan.

The government ordered employers to watch their Chinese workers carefully, 24 hours a day, because "the more kindly you are toward them, the more presumptuous they'll grow." It is said that high-voltage lines strung outside their barracks kept the Chinese from fleeing. Several thousand Koreans were sent to build an underground command headquarters in Nagano prefecture late in the war. Their fate remains unknown, and some persons claim they were massacred to hush up the project. In June 1945, 418 rebellious Chinese workers died in a work-camp riot, the majority of whom are believed to have been flogged to death by the police. The foreign ministry estimates that 6,830 of the more than 38,000 Chinese contract laborers died in Japanese hands. There are no official figures for Koreans, but a reliable estimate puts their deaths above 60,000.

Burakumin participated somewhat more fully in the swollen economy than during the depressed 1920s and early 1930s, but their status rose very little. They served in considerable numbers, subtly segregated, in the Japanese forces, almost always in the enlisted ranks. Koreans could volunteer for the Japanese army after 1938 and were conscripted for military duty after Pearl Harbor. Roughly 187,000 soldiers and 22,000 sailors came from the colony under the draft. Wartime ended up as a bitter experience for all citizens throughout the Japanese empire, above all for minorities.

Religious groups

The wartime Japanese government interfered with citizens' freedom of worship mainly when religious organizations seemed to threaten public order. Heterodox beliefs and ceremonials were tolerated so long as priests and their followers accepted the authority of the state. Yet it is also true that many persons were persecuted because their faith led them to speak out against the war. The government promoted a system called State Shinto to invoke the native deities in support of the war effort. Its propaganda trumpeted Japan's "holy war" to spread Shinto.

The government restructured the major religions under centralized bureaucratic rule in 1940. The religious organizations law gave the home ministry jurisdiction over all denominations and faiths. In November 1940 the ministry set up a new bureau of religious ceremonies, reminiscent of earlier state agencies serving the same purpose in the seventh and the nineteenth centuries.

Within a year the many sects of Shinto were reduced to 13 groups, Buddhist denominations were merged into 28 branches, and Christian communions were cut down to just two, one of them a merger of 33 Protestant churches. Newer religious faiths, such as Tenrikyo and certain neo-Nichiren bodies, were suspect not because of their theology but because of their potential for creating disorder among the less well educated. The police forced these newly-risen sects to show their loyalty by modifying teachings that seemed to conflict with imperial supremacy.

Some Shinto sects dating back more than a thousand years chafed under the yoke of wartime State Shinto, which stood at the top of the religious hierarchy. But most sects as well as State shrines supported the war actively. Millions of pilgrims prayed and celebrated at Ise, Meiji and the other grand shrines early in the war. Great numbers also turned out at the Yasukuni shrine in Tokyo to pray for the spirits of the war dead. Schoolchildren were taken to worship the deities regularly, and Shinto was a staple in their textbooks. In the final wartime revision of the national history text, published in 1943, factual accounts of the war for empire in East and Southeast Asia were supplanted by lyrical fantasies about the legendary Shinto deities who created "the land of the gods."

For citizens of all ages the national propaganda urged loyalty and devotion to Emperor Hirohito as the descendant of the Sun Goddess and chief priest of Shinto.

Japanese Buddhism, never headstrong in the face of state power after the early seventeeth century, actively supported World War II. The enormous and highly respected Nishi Honganji temple in Kyoto put its priests into the war plants as counselors and laborers. The temple set up recreation centers for servicemen and workers in its buildings and even collected funds for aircraft that went into battle christened with the temple's name. The even more austere and venerable Kongobuji temple on Mt. Koya, for the first time in its 1,100-year history, ordained 55 women in 1944 to replace priests who had gone off to the front or to the war plants. Japan was in no sense unique: organized religions in all the major countries fighting the war nearly always cooperated with the military policies of the state.

Even Christian groups rallied behind the war, often to show their loyalty despite the alien origins of their creed. Christians were asked the rhetorical question, "which is greater, Christ or the emperor?" and sometimes treated harshly by the thought police if they wavered. Members of the Plymouth Brethren and the Holiness Church were persecuted. Many Jehovah's Witnesses and members of the Salvation Army were jailed for refusing military or factory labor service. Most Japanese Christians reconciled themselves to the war in the spirit of the Christian philosopher Tadao Yanaihara, who wrote in 1941 that "the storm will not rage forever, the fire will not spread everywhere." In the end "righteousness always triumphs over injustice." For convictions such as these, Yanaihara lost his professorship but kept his conscience.

Entertainment

Soon after Japan began fighting China in July 1937, the government launched its National Spiritual Mobilization campaign to make civilians familiar with the military's aims and involve people in war-related activities on the home front. Through propaganda and systematic organization, the state encouraged frugality and sobermindedness in light of the national effort in China. The combination of moralistic exhortations and steady reductions of consumer goods in a shrinking civilian economy crimped Japan's normally thriving entertainment industry and eventually made it almost impossible for the exhausted public to have even an occasional good time.

Matches, sugar, fabrics and fuels were all growing scarce a year before Pearl Harbor. Gasoline consumption was limited to 30 liters a month for private cars, and taxis could no longer be found after midnight to take late revelers to their unheated homes. There were fewer places by 1940 to go for amusement, since restaurants had been hit by food shortages and by limits on their prices and hours of operation. The government began to save rice by brewing sake from sweet potatoes, and drinking hours in the bars were confined to the period from 5 p.m. to midnight.

To expand the nation's production, golf courses were plowed under for farmland, and those who played the remaining ones were allowed to buy just two new balls per season. Citizens were discouraged from driving to places of amusement, so theatergoers parked a bit short of their destinations to elude the police. Although golf was deemed self-indulgent and caddies banned as "an unnecessary luxury," skiing suddenly became popular because the government ruled it was good for people's health, and thus permissible recreation.

The cabinet took a dim view of dance halls, whose records already suffered from the effects of bamboo phonograph needles now that steel ones had disappeared. On Hallowe'en night 1940, most dance halls hired live bands to play "Auld Lang Syne" because at midnight, by government edict, they closed their doors forever.

Through the **Cabinet Information Board**, the police and controls on the liquor industry, the governments of Prime Minister Hideki Tojo and his successors had enormous leverage over how people used their spare time once Japan went to war with the United States. The authorities found that they had to balance their ideological disdain for frivolous entertainments and the organizational demand to conserve resources against the basic need of the weary public to have fun now and then. The result was a melange of inconsistent prohibitions and diverse popular amusements until the last year of the war. Then the pinch of an impoverished economy and an understaffed entertainment industry meant that even during the off-hours life simply was not very much fun.

Promptly after Pearl Harbor the information board cut the hours at movie theaters to keep civilians off the streets at night, but admissions jumped anyway because other amusements were disappearing. As in America and elsewhere, library circulations nearly doubled between 1941 and 1943. Radio programming grew more patriotic—and also more boring. Life in Tokyo's night quarters was still very plush in 1942, with restaurants open until 11 p.m., when customers spilled out to catch the last train home.

People who wanted to travel could still reach their favorite mountain hot springs in 1943, despite rules against long trips. In the major cities, jazz was banned because it was considered decadent, but German and Italian pop music was deemed praiseworthy. Fewer concerts took place after 1941 because the information

board ruled that half the selections had to be works by Japanese artists. Exceptions were made for certain German composers late in the war, particularly when all-Beethoven programs drew crowds to Tokyo's Hibiya public hall in January and February 1945. Even ballet adapted itself to total war in March 1944 with a dance called "Decisive Aerial Warfare Ballet," billed as "an artistic contribution to the national drive for heightening the air consciousness of the people."

Nighttime sobriety set in during 1943 in the urban amusement centers. In March the government added a 90 percent surcharge on theater admissions, not to raise revenue but to cut the hours they were open. But audiences flocked to the few remaining performances. "When we farmers occasionally went to Tokyo," one said in early 1943, "people would be gathered in a huge crowd in front of the kabuki theater trying to buy tickets. We could not bear the idea of sweating so hard to produce rice to be sent to city people who amused themselves like this."

Soon entertainment grew even more scarce. As athletes were conscripted, Japan's professional baseball teams had to make do with substitutes until partway through the 1944 season. Sumo wrestling stayed immune to the war until 1945, but the state broke up entertainment troupes starting in 1943 and closed more than 10,000 geisha houses and other amusement centers. Prostitutes were obliged to become factory workers, lest they turn into "accomplices of the Anglo-American ideological strategy." Clever bartenders early in the fighting evaded the restrictions on selling sake before nightfall by decanting it into fresh bottles and selling it as cider. Then the fear of grain shortages led the government to close most of the bars by 1943, but small amounts of beer, sake and wine were distributed regularly through the neighborhood associations. Presumably the public was relieved to learn in February 1945 that sweet potatoes would no longer be used for artificial sake, since they were now needed for synthetic fuel.

The government disapproved of unseemly entertainments in the midst of a national emergency, but the real reason for its puritanism was to conserve resources. In February 1944 the cabinet closed all the remaining expensive restaurants, geisha houses, stage shows, kabuki dramas, high-price bars and top-line theaters. Movie theaters, by now showing almost nothing but war films and historical episodes, were allowed to operate only by daylight. The state made these moves partly to shift entertainers to the factories but also partly to conserve fuel. The rich still had the solace of Karuizawa, a mountain resort where lectures on wood block prints and the annual summer tennis championships went on as usual in August 1944.

Once the B-29s began devastating Japan's cities in the spring of 1945, the government decided to open "people's bars" once or twice a week. These rough-and-ready establishments sold a single shot of whiskey, a bottle of beer, or a few cups of low-grade sake—known as bombs because they made one's mouth explode. Whatever small lift the government's bars may have given public morale, the spartan climate accompanying a losing war had reduced the entertainment centers to a handful of frugal taverns offering little refreshment and even less cheer.

Wartime shortages, not moral injunctions from the authorities, finally brought the world of entertainment and mass culture to a halt. Restaurants stayed open, legally or not, only so long as they could get food and drink from their suppliers. In the arts there was a retreat from criticism like that in America and Europe, with strict media censorship, ludicrous controls on music and a great deal of hero worship in films and the dance. Writers, musicians, and the Kyoto school of philosophers (who professed to detect a new spirit of "moral energy" in Japan's East Asian war) made the period one of cultural nationalism, but avant-garde painting remained thriving and unmolested because of its slender audiences. Finally both the mass amusements and higher culture were reduced to a shambles by a desiccated consumer economy and frightful American air raids; there was little joy and even less safety to be found in the few entertainment districts that still remained.

Health in wartime
Health and nutrition
Like many countries, Japan underwent a partial but significant improvement in the health care available to its citizens during World War II, especially during the early months of the conflict. At the same time, civilian diets began to deteriorate because of food scarcities, an Allied naval blockade and fertilizer shortages. During the last months of the war, bad weather and the American air war against Japan cut deeply into food production. Despite considerable malnutrition in 1945 and 1946, Japanese civilians were spared the ravages of major epidemics, although many members of the imperial forces lost their lives to contagious diseases while serving in Southeast Asia and the Western Pacific.

The Japanese parliament passed more social welfare legislation during the military emergency than in the two decades before World War II. The motive was instrumental, not humanitarian. The army was so concerned about the condition of its recruits that it persuaded the government to create a new welfare ministry in 1938, to protect the health of the country "with

a view to strengthening the nation's military potential." Whatever the intent, the government quickly adopted laws improving health care for nearly all civilians.

One was a national health insurance law, effective in July 1938, protecting many persons not previously assured against illness, especially farmers. Health insurance associations were mandated for each community. By the end of 1938, more than a half-million persons belonged to 168 local associations; by 1945, the plan had been extended to 41.4 million civilians through more than 10,000 local health insurance associations. Although it was incomplete and uneven in its scope, the wartime plan was a vast step forward and laid the foundation for the comprehensive health-care insurance scheme adopted soon after the surrender.

Another law prompted by the fighting abroad provided for public health centers throughout Japan, to teach residents first aid, sanitation and nutrition as well as to provide physical examinations and inoculations. Eventually 133 health centers were set up, at least one in every prefecture. Public health nurses were systematically trained and sent to rural areas, where doctors were scarce and health care spotty. Although the military draft claimed most younger doctors, the supply of medical practitioners in Japan was generally adequate throughout the war, never falling below the ratio of one physician per 2,000 citizens considered the minimum norm.

The wartime government took steps to regulate the price and quality of medicines, establish gymnasiums, playgrounds and physical training programs for children and provide postal life annuities along with the existing postal life insurance plan. The state also promoted medical as well as other scientific research through several federations and councils created between 1940 and 1942, although the military authorities offered only lukewarm support because they distrusted many civilian researchers.

After Pearl Harbor a lack of personnel, facilities and especially medicines made decent care a good deal harder to come by. During the last two years of the war, plain good luck helped the country avoid any big epidemics. The government depended increasingly on local cooperation to keep its citizens well. Community councils and neighborhood associations were told in 1942 to set up public health divisions to help the local public health centers by encouraging "good physical and spiritual" standards. The community organizations conducted simple physical tests, promoted good nutrition, insured adequate sanitation and sent citizens to nearby health centers for immunizations and tuberculin skin tests or X-rays.

Food grew scarce after 1943, but slimmer diets apparently did not bring on waves of epidemic diseases.

Deaths from tuberculosis rose from 203 per 100,000 in 1937 to 225 in 1943, mainly because of higher disease rates among the elderly. (The disease actually killed fewer persons under age 20 each year between 1940 and 1943; a majority of its young victims were girls.) Japan was the only major country involved in World War II with a higher TB death rate in 1940 than at the beginning of the century. The disease was a problem common to all industrializing countries, not one peculiar to the war years, and Japan's rate was higher partly because urbanization and economic development occurred later there than in the other wartime societies. Crowded city living spread the disease faster than the health officials could contain it, and reduced nourishment alone was probably less responsible for the rise in TB rates than poor housing, bad sanitation and long hours in dank factories.

From spotty statistics compiled by the welfare ministry, it appears that local outbreaks of malaria and typhus occurred near the end of the war, the latter because lice were so common. Dysentery, paratyphoid and diphtheria cases rose substantially between 1941 and 1945, but cholera, smallpox and typhus all grew much worse after the surrender, presumably because more than 6.6 million Japanese were repatriated from abroad. Scarlet fever cases dropped steadily from 1941 to 1945 and remained uncommon after the war. Penicillin became available in late 1944, helping the fight against diseases.

Young people suffered graphically from inadequate diets during the war. Both boys and girls averaged three centimeters shorter in 1946 than their counterparts in 1937, and one to four kilograms lighter, depending on their ages. The lack of nourishment made children especially vulnerable to myopia, trachoma and rickets—the latter a result of inadequate calcium because milk was scarce. Presumably because of poor diets during gestation, boys born in 1942 averaged 1.8 centimeters shorter and 209.4 grams lighter at birth than those born in 1940. For girls the figures were 2.3 centimeters shorter and 235.3 grams lighter.

By 1943 mealtime was certainly less pleasurable for most citizens, but it is uncertain how much nutrition was lost from the ordinary diet during the last two years of the fighting. Fish catches were cut in half by the lack of gasoline for the fleets, although the reduction hurt the fertilizer industry hardest. Cattle and dairy production, minor sources of food for most Japanese, dropped even further. The Bank of Japan calculated in April 1944 that the average daily intake was 1,927 calories and 61.2 grams of protein, more than a quarter of it from the **black market**. This represented a 17 percent drop since the start of the war, compared with a 2 percent loss in Britain and gains of

1 and 4 percent in Germany and the United States. The actual amount ordinary civilians ate remained between 1,925 and 1,975 calories and 60 to 62 grams of protein during 1942, 1943 and 1944. Then in the year Japan surrendered people took in just 1,793 calories a day, although they ate slightly more protein, 65.3 grams.

Through 1944 the state's rice purchasing and distribution system worked well enough, and crops stayed abundant enough, to keep the nation adequately fed. As late as March 1945 the offical allocations and total intake in Osaka were almost precisely at their April 1942 levels. Then the B-29 raids, coupled with a relentless shipping blockade, made the food situation by summertime very stingy. Of five cities surveyed by the welfare ministry in June 1945, only Yamaguchi reported that its residents were consuming more calories than the 1944 national daily level of 1,927. Kyoto was worst off, at just 1,677 calories a day. It is no coincidence that the U.S. Strategic Bombing Survey found after the surrender that nearly two-thirds of the adult population of the old capital had lost nine kilograms or more from inadequate diets.

All who endured the hardships of wartime in Japan concur that food grew scarce, particularly delicious food, but all agree too that the malnutrition found in Kyoto and elsewhere did not amount to mass starvation. In some respects the winter after the surrender was even more difficult for food supplies because bad weather made 1945 a poor crop year. Already the government had stepped in to create "hodgepodge dining halls," equivalent to the wartime "British restaurants" and the community kitchens in Germany. When hungry civilians started gathering weeds for soup, the state handed out pumpkin seeds so city residents could cultivate burned-out lots. Starting in mid-April 1945, office workers were given bags of dried biscuits as lunch substitutes. Soon the government distributed 20 million seedlings so people could grow sweet potatoes for food and also for airplane fuel. Finally the authorities announced a program to collect 5 billion liters of acorns for flour, because they "have just as much nutritive value as whole rice."

The war era was a time of psychological as well as physical malnutrition and stress. Families were separated, people kept shifting jobs and residences, women often took over men's duties, and bombs destroyed the major cities. Hardest of all was dealing with the unknowable: the fate of loved ones in battle and the future beyond the war. Mental health statistics are crude and unreliable gauges of the psychological toll in wartime, especially since personnel shortages forced four-fifths of Japan's psychiatric hospitals to close between 1941 and 1945. As a result, the number of inpatients plunged, after a steadily rising trend in mental diseases in the 1930s. Deaths by suicide dropped from a yearly average of 14,000 in 1930-1935 to 9,851 in 1940 and 8,784 in 1943, then regained their prewar level by 1949. Full employment and general public participation in an all-consuming national effort may have helped individuals disregard or palliate their anxieties so long as the war was still on. But the relatively immature recognition of mental disease at the time, together with poor record-keeping and inadequate care for the ill, make it risky to infer that wartime was less upsetting to most Japanese than the peaceful years before or since.

Unlike most of the major countries involved in the war, Japan seems to have suffered from relatively little drug abuse and even less venereal disease than before 1941. Little is known about illegal drug consumption during wartime, although rigid laws and strong social pressures apparently kept the number of addicts at the modest level of 3,600 after 1938. The government took a generally realistic approach to the problem of venereal disease, even though its fervent natalism contradicted efforts to distribute preventive devices. The separation of millions of men from their usual sexual partners, a consequence of war rather than official health policy, probably had a greater bearing on both demography and disease rates among civilians than the public health and population programs of the state.

As a potential menace to staying well, sanitation worried local officials throughout the whole war. Neighborhood associations were helpful with burning rubbish, but sewage disposal became a problem when private contractors ran short of manpower to haul the accumulation to nearby farms, where it was used as fertilizer. By 1944 the head of sanitation in Tokyo reported that broken-down trucks, aging equipment and gasoline shortages meant that city workers could not handle more than 70 percent of the sewage produced each day. The city government persuaded private railways to haul some of it on "filth trains" in the dead of night to farmers in the surrounding prefectures. But because of personnel and transport difficulties, many tons ended up untreated in Tokyo Bay.

The health and sanitation policies of the wartime Japanese government were practical but very inadequate. More significant than official programs was the plain adversity of living on a home front mobilized for a losing war. Poor food, clothing and shelter, crowded workplaces and the scarcity of doctors and medical supplies were the results of a wartime footing that compromised a person's chances of avoiding illness. The wonder is that people's health stayed as sound as it did, considering the fearsome capacity of a total war for disrupting life and limb.

Rations

Only Great Britain among the major countries involved in the fighting entered World War II with food resources as modest as Japan's. There was no starvation in Japan during wartime, although famine was a minor threat in the early months of the American occupation after the surrender. But there were plenty of individuals who were poorly fed and clothed, especially in the last phase of the war when there were just not enough commodities to go around. To head off undernourishment and dispiritedness, the government in early 1941 began rationing basic foods, clothing, fuel and other necessities to every home in the country. The official distribution program was plagued by almost endless snags but did its tough job quite well for most of the war. When it finally floundered and a black market grew rampant, the reason was less a lack of will or equity on the part of the state than a simple shortage of things to eat and wear.

Despite price controls imposed in September 1939, shopkeepers began gouging their patrons as goods became harder to find now that the country was at war with China. Rice suddenly grew scarce late in 1939, partly because of distribution problems and partly because poor harvests in Korea reduced the supply. Matches and sugar were rationed starting in June 1940, the latter at half a kilogram per person per month, and charcoal was added to the list in December. Clothes made of staple fiber (bark and wood pulp woven with small amounts of wool and cotton) began to appear that year, and shoes—especially leather— were hardly available at any price. As in America during the war, shoe repairmen were swamped with trade. Gasoline was rationed for private cars, and taxis could no longer be found after midnight.

On Christmas Day 1940, the first rice controls were imposed on the festive rice cakes for the New Year's season. Formal rations began the next April in the six largest cities, and by Pearl Harbor the network of distribution centers covered the whole country. The aim was fairness, so that rich and poor could have an equal chance to buy necessities. The means was a dual allocation system, to neighborhoods and companies, that helped keep laborers placated while assuring everyone a basic ration of 330 grams of rice a day. Adjustments were made for age, sex, fertility, veteran's status and occupation. Other grains and potatoes were occasionally substituted for rice, but somehow the state managed to meet this basic ration though thick and thin until the last months of the war.

"The rations are in," a runner from the neighborhood association would shout up and down the block. Residents knew it was time to report to the captain's home or the local distribution center to pick up foodstuffs or other restricted items. Once the neighborhood units were officially integrated into the national distribution system in October 1942, the captain would ask for a consensus and instruct the local grocer which vegetables the group wanted—so long as there was still a variety to choose from.

Inevitably, there were abuses. Two or three times a month, depending on the size of the family's ration, someone would bring the household passbook, have it inscribed and lug home the standard 14-kilogram sack. Women who were not pregnant frequently got caught putting cushions under their kimonos to extract the additional allocations for expectant mothers. Men just as frequently were accused of falsifying their veteran's status or listing "phantom" family members on their allotment sheets.

Shopkeepers complained about the intricate ticket system used to ration salt, clothes, soap and other items. By 1942 the bureaucrats had managed to devise 35 separate ticket books for controlled commodities. Because they were relatively nonperishable, rice, soy sauce and bean paste could be precisely rationed. Most other foodstuffs were distributed to neighborhood associations without formal per capita rations, and unavoidably some people got more than others. At first most consumers expected the shortages to end as soon as shipping tangles were combed out, but soon the neighborhood groups began distributing seeds for vegetable gardens and warning of a long period of scarcity.

When housewives grew annoyed at the long lines and skimpy allocations at local food centers, the authorities responded with high-minded appeals to "patriotism for all" and "sacrifice yourself to the public good." Tokyo tried to shame the city's ration chislers with several "kindness and gratitude" campaigns in 1942, posting notices on storefronts: "sellers and buyers are comrades in arms; we are all soldiers on the home front." But it was hard to be altruistic, the economist Hajime Kawakami noted in January 1943, when everyone was "thinking from morning to night only of food."

Clothing shortages were so severe that the government set up a point system for rations. Men quite often wore the national civilian uniform first adopted during the National Spiritual Mobilization in the late 1930s, and women were usually seen in the standard peasant pantaloons. To make new purchases, each city resident had a yearly ticket allowance worth 100 points, but rural people had to settle for merely 80. A three-piece men's suit took 50 points but a civilian uniform only 32. Shirts were 12 points, underpants 4, socks just 1, but overcoats 50. In the first year of the system, 29 percent of the points reportedly went unused, giving the state an excuse to cut the rations in half when textiles grew even more scarce in 1944.

To conserve leather and rubber, the government urged people to wear clogs rather than shoes or sneakers. Shark skin and "sea leather" were temporarily tried as substitutes. In June 1943 the cabinet announced an "Outline for Implementing Simplified Wartime Clothing Habits," which regulated styles still further, with short sleeves now the norm even for winter, and restricted made-to-order clothing.

A year later the neighborhood associations were made responsible for apportioning the most essential clothing items, a silent confession that the ticket method no longer worked because very few new clothes could still be had. In May 1944, Tokyo's leading newspaper, the *Asahi*, reported that "recently everything from the distribution of cotton thread, socks and toilet paper to repairing shoes, umbrellas and pots and pans is being carried out by the neighborhood associations." With supplies so short, understandably the government preferred to let neighbors decide among themselves how to divide them up. Almost everywhere it was settled by raffle, leaving to fate what neither a free market nor the state system could accomplish: how to distribute too few commodities to too many customers.

Coal and charcoal were already so scarce by 1941 that hotels had to regulate hot water for their guests. During the winter of 1941-42 citizens saved fuel by heating their home bathtubs only once every three days or so, a hardship that by 1944 seemed a luxury when the charcoal rations often weren't available at all. The last winter of the war was when some city people began burning their libraries for fuel, figuring that the books might soon be destroyed in an air raid anyway. Early in 1945 neighborhood associations began felling trees in the gardens of great mansions for firewood. Gas, propane and charcoal were scarcely to be had. Tokyo's first fuel distribution after the 1944-45 winter began took place on May 21, 1945, long after the city had been half-destroyed by bombs.

When Japan's prospects abroad and way of life at home turned gloomy in 1943, most people were realistic enough to see that shopping on the black market was the only way to get enough to eat. Even before Pearl Harbor, the home ministry admitted, there had been a good deal of profiteering in controlled goods. By mid-1943 city people regularly went out to nearby truck farms to buy sweet potatoes and other items at several times the official prices. The **Cabinet Planning Board** was anxious enough about people's livelihoods to prepare a report in September 1943 concluding that food was the number one problem—its sufficiency, adulteration, clumsy distribution and high price on the black market. When black market prices shot up the next spring, the justice ministry spelled out new rules about how each neighborhood unit should receive its allocations and how the fish and vegetable stores were to account for their sales. But the state found it impossible to stamp out the illegal transactions, as someone later recalled, because "it is plain to anyone that without them, it would have been impossible to go on living."

Statistics on black marketing are almost as haphazard as those for gambling or other social vices. The Japanese wartime black market peaked in mid-1944, when fewer goods became available through any channel. One private research group estimated that Tokyo workers' families used the black market in September and October 1944 for 9 percent of their rice, 38 percent of their fish and 69 percent of their vegetables. In Osaka, according to another survey, the proportion of food that people bought on the black market rose from 18 percent in April 1942 to 24 percent two years later—then fell back again to 18 percent in March 1945 because even black marketeers could not obtain supplies. By June, as war-end disorganization spread, the average daily amounts obtained from nonofficial sources ranged from 15.7 percent in Kyoto and 20.1 percent in Tokyo to as much as 35.9 percent in the prefectural capital of Yamaguchi. Between them, the regular distribution and the black market managed to keep people reasonably fed until air raids and mass flight from the cities skewed the allocation system in the last few months of the war.

For the millions of city office workers who regularly ate out at least once each day, there was no black market to replace the restaurants that had closed by 1943 for lack of food or help. Finally the government itself stepped in to create "hodgepodge dining halls." Workers could register to eat "lunches" that usually consisted of a thin porridge garnished with potato fragments, a radish leaf, a bit of snail, or a few grains of rice. As of April 1944, 335 of these dining halls had been opened in Tokyo, and eventually thousands more were provided throughout the country. Although these establishments by no means served elegant meals, the government was edgy enough about its food policies in mid-1944 to suppress its long-time critic, the progressive monthly *Kaizo*, for calling the hodgepodge soup "not nutrition but fat."

Through 1944 domestic food production held up pretty well, especially rice, but the amounts reaching consumers were pared down by several factors. One was a 90 percent drop in rice imports by 1945 compared with the prewar period, a result of shipping losses. Another was the expansion of the armed forces. In 1945 there were 3.5 million troops posted in Japan, up from one million at the start of the war. The basic military ration was cut from 900 to 600 grams of rice per day in 1944, then to 400 grams in 1945, when civilians had to make do with just 300

(down from 330 earlier). Through 1944 the national rate of substitutes in the basic rice ration stayed below 15 percent. Even as late as May 1945, only 13 percent of the Tokyo ration was filled by potatoes or grains other than rice. Then in June, July and August, the substitutes suddenly formed half the total allocation.

The B-29 raids during the American air war against Japan threw food deliveries into great confusion during the last months of the conflict. By springtime at least 130,000 tons of staples had been destroyed in air raids on warehouses. When Tokyo announced plans in late March 1945 to hand out pumpkin seeds and fertilizer so that neighborhood associations could cultivate burned-out lots, the authorities found that resourceful citizens had planted many of the areas already.

When the basic civilian ration was cut 10 percent in the early summer of 1945, people were urged to eat plantain, mugwort, chickweed and thistle. Tons of pulverized food were manufactured from potato stems, mulberry leaves, wild plants and the residue of soy beans, peanuts, apples and grapes. Pumpkin became a mainstay of most persons' diets. Although there was a good deal of malnutrition once the ration system and the black market could no longer meet the nation's food needs, most citizens' health was not permanently ravaged by the temporary scarcities of Japan's desiccated war economy.

Government controls
The police
Wartime Japanese society was tightly policed. There were relatively few incidents of resistance to the war policies of the government. Juvenile crime rose less quickly than in the other major countries for which there are statistics, and other offenses seem to have stayed at about their prewar levels.

Ordinary municipal and prefectural forces handled routine police work. The military police, known as *Kenpei*, supervised Japanese troops at home and abroad. Overseas they also routinely harassed civilians in occupied countries. *Kenpei* units in Tunhua, China, seized suspected anti-Japanese guerrillas: their "shrieks of pain and the sound of whipping continued for an hour or so" every night. In Japan the military police also did political dirty work for the army, supreme command and cabinet by intimidating election candidates, apprehending suspected terrorists and threatening judges.

Just as notorious were the special higher police, or *Tokko*, established in 1911 under the home ministry to control "dangerous thoughts." Such thoughts were usually concrete movements that threatened political order, not intellectual or ideological heresy in the abstract. After World War I the special higher police suppressed leftist social movements of all sorts, but especially the Japan Communist Party and its sympathizers. By 1932, *Tokko* units existed in every prefecture and acted as the state's principal intelligence network. There were 380 thought police in the Tokyo headquarters, up from just 70 four years earlier.

During the war *Tokko* spies helped watch for left- and right-wing political activity, checked on religious organizations and spied even on academic societies. Under the peace preservation law of 1925, thousands of suspects were arrested and turned over to the justice ministry's prosecutors each year for "anti-military" or "anti-war" activities. The brutality of the special higher police matched that of the *Kenpei*. The Kanagawa prefectural unit framed the editorial staffs of two progressive monthlies in 1942, accusing them of communist agitation. A woman prisoner suffered from "erotic terror" inflicted by the Kanagawa thought police. At least three other persons died from the torture they received in the incident.

The wartime Japanese police were ruthlessly efficient and often cruelly repressive, yet only one person, the spy Hotsumi Ozaki, was executed for treason. By comparison with Germany, the Japanese police treated citizens rather mildly. Although they were purged from their jobs by the Americans in 1945, many former *Tokko* and *Kenpei* officers found their way back into police work in the postwar period.

Propaganda and censorship
Japan's wartime efforts at thought control were more effective on the home front than abroad. Like the other major countries involved in the war, Japan accomplished better results with its propaganda during the early months of the fighting than after the imperial forces began losing battles overseas. But censorship remained strict until the last stages of the war, and the state managed to manipulate opinion within the country fairly successfully because the authorities retained strong organizational controls over the media, the schools, religious groups and neighborhood associations almost until the surrender. Both the myth and the cudgel turned out to be effective instruments for getting citizens to accept the war.

Before 1940 the army, navy, foreign ministry and imperial general headquarters each had a separate press service, and the cabinet set up an information bureau of its own in September 1937 after war broke out in China. The army news office issued a pamphlet showing how the military was cooperating with the National Spiritual Mobilization, which was by then under way. In 1937 the army declared that "a spirit of self-sacrifice must be fostered and internationalism, egoism and individualism which lead to forgetfulness

of the State, to evasion of control essential to the State and to conduct contrary to the interests of the country must be eradicated." This meant that "we must regulate and control the benefits and liberties of the individual," added the diplomat Yosuke Matsuoka in 1938, because the "State is the totality and the individual is a part."

Most news management, in the sense of positive manipulations of information, took place through the single news agency that had been created by merging earlier wire services into one public corporation in January 1936. Known as *Domei*, it received all its political directives from the Cabinet Information Bureau and was the only official source for out-of-town and international news. Aided by *Domei*, the daily newspapers cooperated actively with the authorities (they had little choice in the matter). But Japan's propaganda before Pearl Harbor was mainly directed at other Asians and its future adversaries in the west, and most of the state's dealings with the press before December 1941 employed the negative manacles of suppression.

The government uncovered acts dating back to 1893 that permitted wartime censorship. The police peace law of 1900 and the peace preservation act of 1925 were supplemented by a series of acts in 1935, 1939 and 1941 that were designed to control publications and protect defense secrets. Additional regulations were announced from time to time under the general authority of the National General Mobilization Law, passed in 1938. The army used its police, the *Kenpei*, to enforce strict controls over military information and troop movements. Sensitive political and economic topics were checked by the home ministry's thought police, the *Tokko*. Newspaper editors began submitting stories to the home ministry for advance approval during the war rather than risking punishment after an unwelcome item appeared in print. Nevertheless, fines and imprisonment were often imposed, and most papers had "jail editors" to represent them behind bars when sentences were handed down.

Censorship, like most forms of psychological terror, is probably most effective when it is arbitrarily imposed. Its randomness and unpredictability are far more intimidating than a blue pencil or a blackout uniformly applied. Yet the authorities decided to take even more direct steps than mere news management in order to control what people read. On the pretext of conserving paper, the home ministry and local police forces drummed hundreds of newspapers out of existence between 1937 and 1939, consolidating local dailies in most prefectures into a single regional paper. The number of women's magazines by 1941 had dropped from 80 to 17; art magazines fell from 39 to 8. The victims of these blunt shears had no support from the judiciary. Even if they could have afforded lawyers, the freedom to publish was not available at any price.

"Dangerous thoughts" are what most proscribed outlooks were branded, yet the erratic manner in which dissent was purged suggests that ideas were most dangerous when they seemed to threaten how power was organized. Before 1937, the state usually harassed authors rather than editors or publishers, but once the war in China broke out the bureaucrats caused endless headaches for publishing houses when they insisted on inspecting proofs before publication. More than 20,000 books a year were appearing in the late 1930s, and normally the censors had just five days to disapprove of a title. Understandably enough, their favorite method of control continued to be hounding certain authors who were offensive to the government.

The liberal economists Tadao Yanaihara and Eijiro Kawai were driven from their professorships at Tokyo Imperial University for speaking out when the institution cooperated with the war. The state suppressed the works of both, along with the fiction of such popular writers as Fumio Niwa, Fumiko Hayashi and Jun'ichiro Tanizaki. The collected works of Marx and Engels, Lenin and modern Japanese Marxist scholars were banned from sale. Even love stories seemed decadent to the censors.

Radio was much easier to maneuver than the print media, and it soon became the main propaganda vehicle for both the home front and Japan's **psychological warfare** overseas. After 1934 all stations in Japan had been absorbed by the public broadcasting corporation, NHK. Once the war began, the state expanded radio audiences by waiving the monthly subscriber fee of one yen (about 30¢) for large families and those with men at the front. The authorities gave away AM radios in poor villages—but banned shortwave sets, assuring a monopoly on what people could hear. Beginning in January 1938, the government broadcast ten minutes of war dispatches and further news each evening at 7:30. Like Japan's newspapers during the war, NHK carried few reports of the European theater, and the *Domei* press agency remained its only official source of news. Controversial political developments were never reported, and starting the day Japan bombed Pearl Harbor listeners could no longer even hear weather broadcasts because they might aid the enemy.

Since movies, of all the media, are the most absorbing for the audience and the least subject to distractions, it is surprising how little heed the government paid them during the early mobilization. The censors had always scanned films from abroad for signs of socialism as well as kissing, and no Soviet productions could be shown. When the home ministry began to withdraw American and British films, there were still plenty of domestic movies to replace them. In 1937, a record year, Japanese studios poured out 580 features and nearly 2,000 newsreels and other short films. Yet there was still a market for foreign movies, especially ones from France while they were still available early in the war.

The state ordered producers to support the national effort by depicting "truly Japanese emotions" and portraying respect for the family system, under the motion picture law of April 1939 that imposed both negative controls on film distribution and positive guidelines for producing propaganda. Gradually such items as *Japan Stands Alone* appeared, showing the country as the defender of Asia against the aggressive U.S. Navy. After 1940 the home ministry insisted on censoring all movie scripts in advance.

The government's news policy became much more smoothly coordinated after the information bureau was upgraded to the Cabinet Information Board in December 1940. The board absorbed both the publicity and the censorship duties scattered among various agencies—except for the imperial general headquarters, whose outrageous untruths only complicated the board's work throughout the war. *Domei* was the board's chief means of spreading war news written to show Japan's position to its people in the best possible light. Stories from abroad were carefully trimmed to remove anything offensive to the military services or other ministries. Severe as it often was, the correspondent Otto D. Tolischus observed, at least the screening was "open, official censorship." Although its negative, repressive activities were usually more dramatic, the board stepped up its positive management of the news after Pearl Harbor and, under a new president, Eiji Amau, it became a rather suave propaganda unit until the war turned against Japan.

"Japan's war aims are the liberation of Asia and the destruction of America and Britain," one commentator proclaimed in 1942. Another said it was necessary to establish "a world peace which reflects the light of the power and glory of the Emperor." Prime Minister Tojo boldly told the Diet on May 27, 1942, in a speech widely quoted by the government's propagandists, that "it has been and will remain the inflexible determination of our entire nation never to sheathe the sword of righteousness unless and until the influence of the Anglo-American Powers, with their dream of dominating the world, has been completely uprooted." Like the Germans, the Japanese leaders rarely spoke of "victory" but often of "struggle'' against the west to attain a future peace for Asia's ''new order.''

Schoolchildren were taught the parable of a sailor who received a letter from his mother: ''you were in the August 10 attack on Weihaiwel but you didn't distinguish yourself with an individual exploit. To me this is deplorable. Why have you gone to war? Your life is to be offered up to requite your obligations to our benevolent Emperor.'' The sailor was comforted by an officer who said ''there'll surely be another glorious war before long'' in which he could redeem himself. Students' knowledge of ethics was tested with examination questions such as ''why are loyalty and filial piety united in our country,'' ''why is Japan's Constitution superior to those of other nations,'' and ''what kind of spirit is required to overcome the present difficulties facing the nation?''

The pivot of Japanese propaganda was the emperor, not just in the official textbooks but in the information board's broadcast announcements as well. The authorities were fond of quoting Foreign Minister Matsuoka, who declared that ''without the Emperor, neither Japan nor the Japanese people could be imagined. Thence a Japanese government would also be inconceivable. The instant the Emperor were removed, both Japan and the Japanese people would cease to be. No country outside of Japan has this national constitution. This is the greatest thing we have to boast of in the world.''

Despite such bombast, it appears that Hirohito was important mostly as a symbol of the nation, not as a law-giver or object of worship. Because every large organization needs a set of principles to keep it from splintering, the state's imperial propaganda was useful for cementing Japan's inumerable social groupings into a mosaic that could sustain war. All the main countries that fought World War II centralized their governments and economies enormously, regardless of ideological differences. To fortify the mobilization, what counted most was that Japan have a dogma, not its precise content. For historical and religious reasons the best choice was imperial loyalism, but the political, military and economic apparatus it legitimized was indispensable for fighting the war. In effect, the organization became its own ideology. Like soldiers and sailors everywhere, the 12 million Japanese who went on military duty served an institution, not just a doctrine. The same held true for people on the home front, all of whom participated in some way in waging total war.

One key task was to tell them why the country was mobilizing its economy for war production rather than consumer goods. The government propagandists admitted that Japan had ''in the past adopted capitalism, considering it advisable, or rather inevitable,

to do so for the sake of her economic advance.'' But now ''she is about to replace liberalism, individualism and capitalism with the totalitarian economic structure in which the object of the state must be given primary attention.'' In short, the economy was gearing up to fight the enemy.

Likewise Prime Minister Konoe felt constrained to say why the political parties were being dissolved as a part of his New Structure Movement in 1941: ''there is no need of political parties which establish their own policies and conduct campaigns for power at a time when the Government has the fixed policy of establishing a highly organized national defense state and a Greater East Asia Co-Prosperity Sphere.'' Instead, the parties were brought under the umbrella of the Imperial Rule Assistance Association, which Konoe intended as a foil to the power of the military but publicly heralded as ''a national movement to cooperate with the Government'' to enable ''the entire nation to practice the Way of Subjects of the Throne.'' Duty, in short, meant obedience, not selfish economic desires or divisive political demands.

Along with the propaganda came renewed efforts to trim the media's sails. On the pretext of saving newsprint once again, the government created a Newspaper League in November 1941 to allocate paper under instructions from the information board. Within two years the number of dailies shrank from 454 to just 54, but their circulation swelled to nearly 13 million, virtually one per household. The wartime state not only blanketed the country with a controlled press but also speeded the drift toward oligopoly that made the top three dailies into giants after the surrender.

The day after Pearl Harbor the Cabinet Information Board called a rushed meeting of news executives to explain which types of stories they could report and which they could not. The latter included ''views that intentionally distort our true war aims or slander the imperial government's legitimate policies.'' Both NHK and the papers were warned that news must now be prepared ''as much as possible in cooperation with the government.'' By coloring the news to its taste, rationing stocks of paper and badgering journalists to join various federations, the information board unquestionably weighted the flow of news in the state's favor from late 1940 onward. But there are hints that the controls were far from absolute. The cabinet needed journalists and printers if its messages were to reach the public, and few writers apparently lost their credentials. A good deal of war news continued to be printed, however much of it was shaped to throw favorable light on the imperial forces.

In the last year of the war the information board apparently used its cudgel less often, to build confidence in its reports at a time when the military general headquarters was issuing war reports based on fancy rather than fact. The state realistically understood that a news-management operation, to keep on working, has to maintain the hypocrisy gap between the ideal and the actual at a reasonable level. Even then, as became apparent in 1944-45, it was impossible to hide a losing war from the public for very long.

Book publishers, reorganized as the Japan Publishers' Council under the Imperial Rule Assistance Association, found their supplies of stock scarce at best and sometimes absent altogether if they ran afoul of the information board. The number of titles published tumbled from 28,138 in 1941 to just 5,354 the next year and only 875 during 1945, among them such improbable volumes as Hegel's *Theory of Dialectic Change*, Hesse's complete works and works by Henri Bergson and T. S. Eliot. The number of book publishers was reduced from 3,664 to 204 within a year, presumably by forcing all but the most powerful to suspend their operations or merge with larger firms. The survivors were instructed by the publishers' association to become "fighters in the ideological war and producers of paper bullets."

In any event, the war was a poor time for quality manuscripts. Even if they were not conscripted for factory or military duty, authors had to make do under the controls on news and academic freedom. Often there was neither the leisure for reflection nor the prospect of finding a publisher when one's book was completed. Nearly all writers, as in America and Britain, cooperated with the war out of a sense of civic duty, and most joined the Japan Patriotic Literary Association after it was started by the information board in May 1942. One member stated after the war that the association "always obeyed the wishes of the state. It took the lead in disseminating publicity." At the same time, a well-known group of scholars in Kyoto contrived to justify Japan's expansionism by calling for "a new world view and a new moral energy." By the very nature of the book trade, however, the Patriotic Literary Association was less directly propagandistic than other writers' groups, and in some ways it may have helped protect the interests of authors against the state. Still it nurtured uniformity and a distinct policy viewpoint rather than the creativity and liberating environment that usually lead to good books.

The state saved its sharpest blade for the magazines, with their huge circulations that made them especially inviting to the censors and their leisurely deadlines that made them easy to control. The number of magazines was cut from 1,970 in 1940 to only 965 in 1944—many of them tiny or irregular special-interest journals. The most spectacular repressions affected two of the largest monthlies, *Chuo koron* and *Kaizo*, whose top editors were replaced with persons more acceptable to the government after a series of police raids on the offices of the two magazines in September 1942.

By comparison with Germany, the Japanese government treated its press critics rather mildly during World War II. Only one person, the spy Ozaki Hotsumi, was executed for treason. But the September 1942 incidents left at least three persons dead as a result of the torture they received in prison. *Kaizo* and *Chuo koron* struggled on until mid-1944, when they were suddenly closed down by the state because, said Radio Tokyo, "their policies were incompatible with the proper guidance of public thought." Prime Minister Tojo was more peremptory: "the masses are foolish. If we tell them the facts, morale will collapse."

The facts nevertheless made very striking propaganda in Japan's movie theaters, as the information board discovered after Pearl Harbor. Even composers were urged to produce patriotic marches and war songs for broadcast on NHK. The combination of print, radio and film served the state's propagandists well in wartime, and the negative shackles of censorship, backed up by an efficient police network, helped snuff out any organized resistance efforts by ordinary citizens against the war policies of their government.

Production

Japan entered World War II better prepared than the United States but undermobilized to fight a total war. Four years of desultory conflict in China had drained manpower, resources and morale. Japan went to war in December 1941 mainly to seize in Southeast Asia the resources it needed to maintain and expand its army and navy, its economy and its empire, now that vital raw materials had been shut off by the American decision to freeze Japanese assets on July 26, 1941. Japan's leaders apparently gambled that the imperial forces could knock out the American seventh fleet at Pearl Harbor, quickly overrun Southeast Asia and sue for a negotiatied peace before the Allies could muster for an all-out war of attrition. The choice of tactics meant that Japan delayed full-scale economic mobilization until after Pearl Harbor. In the end, a scarcity of liquid fuels and metal ores, caused mostly by the U.S. naval **blockade** of the main Japanese islands, was more responsible than poor planning or tardy mobilization for the inadequacies of Japan's wartime production.

Japan began war with China in 1937 riding the crest of economic recovery from the worldwide depression. Industrial production in that year was 83 percent higher than in 1931, lifting both workers' wages and the number of strikes. Wholesale farm prices were up 58 percent over 1931, raising farm income much faster than the overall rate of inflation. A good deal of the prosperity was attributable to the eight-fold rise in defense spending during 1931-37. The army and navy now claimed 70 percent of national expenditures, compared with less than 30 percent in 1931.

With so vigorous an army, Japan confidently expected to settle the "China incident," as the fighting near Peking in July 1937 was called, with a prompt show of force. No one expected the war to drag on for eight years or to tap Japan's productive capacity so thoroughly. Most early efforts to rally the home front centered on the National Spiritual Mobilization of September 1937, a movement with more propaganda than economic purposes. But the spiritual mobilizers used neighborhood associations, youth groups and labor organizations to collect scrap metal and sell savings bonds. The most concrete step taken in 1937 was establishing the Cabinet Planning Board in October to coordinate wartime economic policy.

By 1940, it was evident to everyone that Japan was involved in a real war on the mainland. With Europe now in conflict and the Americans increasingly hostile to Japan's expansion, the Japanese government decided that the opportunities and the risks abroad demanded an even firmer industrial base at home. As a consequence, the New Order in East Asia, proclaimed in November 1938, was redefined as a zone of autarky and extended to include Southeast Asia in September 1940. Raw materials from the south would be sent north for manufacturing in the war plants, and the munitions produced were to be sent back south for use at the front.

By 1940 military expenditures in Japan were double their 1937 level (6.81 versus 3.27 billion yen), and arms procurements helped to drive up the output of durable goods 36 percent in the same period. Heavy industry, which had accounted for 58 percent of industrial production when the war with China began, climbed to 73 percent by the end of 1941. The new factory openings drew hundreds of thousands of workers from the farms, and by 1940 the proportion of civilians employed in agriculture had dropped to 42 percent from 48 percent a decade earlier. Not included were many people still listed as farmers who had taken jobs moonlighting in the war plants.

Despite the urgent situation abroad, heavy industry in Japan expanded as it had before—through inducements resulting from the political process, not by military fiat. The army and navy still had to have their budgets approved each year, and imperial ordinances under the March 1938 National General Mobilization Law had to be screened by a 50-member council not notably partial to the military. As late as

1940-1941, "Japan's economy was financed and operated by private enterprise, which disposed of profits and dividends with relatively slight government interference. Control, in the sense of comprehensive state plans enforced on industry, was still in embryonic form." (T. A. Bisson)

Inflation was so severe during 1937-40 that real consumption per capita fell 17 percent, despite the seemingly good wages in the munitions factories. With the year 1936 as 100, the retail price index had risen by 1940 in the U.S. to 101, in Germany to 104, in the United Kingdom to 125—and in Japan to the shocking figure of 175. The state had announced an excess profits ordinance in August 1937 and set price ceilings in certain product lines the following summer. But it was easy to evade the rules, and the fired-up manufacturing sector kept on driving prices higher. When war broke out in Europe, the cabinet knew that inflation would probably become contagious, as it had during World War I, so the government suddenly announced a price freeze on September 19, 1939, fixing rents, wages and general consumer prices at their September 18 levels. This step had little effect in slowing inflation.

Soon after the war with China began, the social affairs bureau of the home ministry ordered employers to stop overworking their laborers on the pretext of the crisis abroad. In October the ministry set 12 hours as the legal work limit and directed employers to give their workers rest breaks, two days off each month and a shift system. In spite of the demand for their labor and the price controls imposed in September 1939, factory workers' wages rose less quickly than inflation between July 1937 and July 1940, slicing their real earnings by 8 percent.

At the same time the government set about eviscerating the Japanese labor movement through an official campaign during 1938-40 to establish patriotic industrial associations in every plant and enterprise in the country. With slogans such as "labor and capital are one" and "the plant is one family," the patriotic industrial campaign encouraged working people to accept the paternalism of their companies in lieu of unions. By December 1940, 4,815,478 workers (about two-thirds of the industrial labor force) belonged to 60,495 patriotic industrial associations. In the meantime, the labor unions had been pressured to dissolve, and by 1944 they ceased to exist at all.

Although most employers were delighted to see the labor movement wither away, they were unhappy to have the state intervene in management-employee relations. This was especially true after the Imperial Rule Assistance Association took nominal control of the patriotic industrial associations in 1942. Both capital and labor "showed reluctance to form patriotic industrial societies, but the bureaucracy took a completely unbending attitude and finally used the power of the police to establish them semiforcibly.'' (Y. Shimonaka) It is not surprising that big business proved to be so stubborn in the overall economic buildup for war. Labor was scarcely happier with the government's directives. But the main aims of the patriotic industrial societies were practical, not merely political. The government set them up not to crush unionism, which it had long accepted as inevitable, but to deal with a wartime economic emergency.

Pearl Harbor was the decisive event for the country's overall economic mobilization, even though the cabinet did not expect a dragged-out war. Conversion had begun in earnest in the spring of 1941, when many of the textile mills were turned into munitions plants, at a time when big business, the military services and the civil bureaucracy could not otherwise agree about how to plan the buildup. Prime Minister Fumimaro Konoe appointed the head of the Sumitomo empire, Masatsune Ogura, to his cabinet in April 1941 to help coordinate the industrial expansion. By the end of 1941, control boards had been set up in a dozen major industries, and early the next year the state announced eight plans for raising output by mobilizing labor, capital, energy, transport and the like. These programs foundered less because they were laggardly than because they were not fully integrated and required more resources than were available. Although the Americans overrated Japan's economic potential, the wonder is that production held up as long and as well as it did.

Between 1940 (the base year in many Japanese statistical analyses) and 1944, when war production peaked, total real output rose about one-fourth. In the United States, the growth was about two-thirds during the same period, although the 1940 base was different because the American economy was still depressed, whereas Japan had virtually regained full employment by that year. Rather than further expanding the entire economy, Japan's planners elected to divert resources from civilian to military production. Private capital formation, construction and consumer expenditures fell between 1940 and 1942 in response to the government's policy of economic adaptation as war outlays grew from 17 percent of gross national product to 30.5 percent. By mid-1942, Japan's forces had seized most of Southeast Asia and the western Pacific, and the tactic of economic adjustment, rather than overall expansion, seemed justified.

Once the war bogged down after the battle of Midway in June 1942, Japan paid much more heed to lifting its production. With 1940 as 100, the index of the gross national product rose from 102 in 1942 to 113 the next year and 124 in 1944—a rise of 10 billion yen

in real terms between 1942 and 1944, to a peak figure of 49.3 billion yen for the latter year. War expenditures represented 30 percent of the GNP in 1942 and 51 percent two years later. One Japanese estimate after the surrender put war costs at 94 percent of national income during the econmically chaotic first eight months of 1945.

Much of the reason Japan could keep up the fight is that more citizens took jobs and worked longer hours than ever before. Civilian employment grew from just over 31 million in 1937, a boom year, to nearly 33 million in 1942. Then the heavy military draft cut the adult work force slightly, but 1.8 million students mobilized for full-time war work raised the total number who were employed in February 1944 to roughly 33.5 million—averaging 11 hours a day in the factories and, during busy seasons, even longer in the fields.

Much of the increase resulted from national population growth, not a mass flight from the countryside. The number of agricultural workers held nearly steady throughout the war at about 14 million, although many of them by the end were women and the aged, replacing men drafted for factory or military service. Millions of persons shifted jobs as well: the number working in commerce dropped from 4.9 million in 1937 to 2.5 million in 1944, whereas manufacturing gained 2.3 million workers and mining an additional 290,000.

Workers were mobilized through a combination of inducement and coercion. Incentive pay was offered in certain key industries, and patriotic appeals were issued to get people to change jobs. Outright conscription of males (women were never drafted) accounted for only 8 percent of civilian employment at its peak, but the threat of being called presumably forced a lot of reluctant men into the war plants. Altogether perhaps 1.5 million men were conscripted for factory duty, mainly from small family enterprises. Various labor enrollment schemes were implemented to obtain a registry of potential women workers, but they were never activated. Perhaps more compulsion would have been beside the point, since the production downturn in late 1944 resulted mostly from deficiencies in raw materials, not labor.

After Pearl Harbor wages continued to climb more slowly than inflation. Japan's war workers actually earned a third less in 1944 than in 1939 as a result. By August 1945, the Japanese factory employee was receiving only two-fifths as much as in 1934-36—and working longer hours to earn it. Taxes were up 250 percent between 1940 and 1944. Because it expected a brief war, the state financed the munitions output mainly through bonds, which speeded up inflation. Then, in 1943 and 1944, it raised both direct and in-

JAPAN

direct taxes, further squeezing the worker, whose real wages were already diminished by rising consumer prices. As commodities grew scarce and rations proved to be inadequate, the inevitable black market claimed orbital prices for daily necessities.

Unlike the Nazis, the Japanese made hardly any effort to keep consumer goods in the stores during their buildup for war. In 1941 consumer goods accounted for approximately 40 percent of national income, a figure that plunged to just 17 percent by March 1945. Yet despite rising costs, lower rewards, higher taxes and commodity shortages, very few workers went out on strike. **Sabotage** was only a minor concern, and absenteeism did not seriously harm output. Most workers stayed on the job because they had no real choice. If not fit for military duty, adult males still faced the labor draft—enforced by the police—if they did not voluntarily pick a war job. And nearly every family needed wage-earners to pay the steep taxes and high prices for daily necessities.

Farming paid somewhat better than factory work during 1937-45, but the cultivators hardly benefited more than city people because of uncontrolled inflation at the end of the fighting. Women formed a majority of the farm work force in 1940, accounting for 57.6 percent by 1944. Most of the rest were children or old people. Output stayed high through 1944, although a drop in rice imports from Korea and Taiwan after 1943 caused shortages for city consumers. Only in 1945 did production in the rural sector fall significantly below prewar levels. The government enforced a rice delivery system to assure adequate distribution to urban families and paid farmers rather well for their harvests. But inflation cut the value of their savings by 90 percent at the end of 1945.

When the labor pinch began to hurt the overall Japanese economy in late 1943 and especially 1944, the government turned to students, the elderly, minority groups including Koreans and Taiwanese, convicts, prisoners of war and women volunteers to boost the basic civilian work force of approximately 18.5 million adult males and 12.7 million adult females. These persons formed a crazy-quilt pattern of employment near the end of the war, one that was complicated in 1944 by excepting farmers from conscription on the one hand but drafting hundreds of thousands of the most highly skilled laborers out of the factories for military duty on the other.

Many workers were forced into the munitions plants when their employers were put out of business by the state. Dressmaking, typing and art schools were closed down, as were most of the prep schools that tutored students for entrance examinations. Small enterprises that managed to stay open had to spare an employee twice a week for labor service, a duty

that also faced children in the nation's schools. In September 1943 the authorities banned men from working in several occupations, including sales clerks, railway ticket-punchers and conductors and barbers. As in the wartime United States, munitions contracts helped the largest corporations grow even bigger by swallowing up small companies. The four richest industrial concerns doubled their share of corporate and partnership capital between 1941 and 1945.

The military draft was heaviest by far during the last year and a half of the war, and the tightest civilian labor squeeze took place between April and October 1944. By October nearly two million students above age 10 had been put to work in volunteer units, often full-time. In February 1945 the figure reached three million, which was more than two-thirds of the age group and nearly a tenth of the entire civilian labor force. More than two-thirds of the men and nearly a third of the women aged 60 or older were working in February 1944, mostly in the fields. More than half the nation's convicts, who numbered about 50,000, were put to work in heavy industry, joined by most of Japan's prisoners of war. A much greater help were the nearly 1.3 million Koreans who came to Japan during 1937-45, mainly to work in mining and heavy industry, and more than 38,000 contract Chinese laborers from Taiwan. For nearly all the new factory workers, housing, transport and health care facilities were substandard, but their living arrangements grew truly deplorable only during the American air war against the major cities during the last eight months of the fighting.

Women were the most underutilized resource of all in Japan's wartime production efforts. At its peak the number of working women exceeded 14 million, which was 42 percent of the civilian labor supply in 1944. But despite the military draft, the female share of the work force in that year was only three percent greater than in 1940 and just seven percent higher than in the depression year of 1930. Not until January 1944 did the state exhort unmarried women to join women's volunteer labor corps, a duty that was hard to refuse because of strong social pressures, but the new plan fell short of being a compulsory labor system, and married women were never systematically put to work.

Whatever its inadequacies, the government's labor planning met the needs of wartime production adequately until materiel shortages began to crimp output in the autumn of 1944. The American blockade slowly starved the main islands, and then devastating air attacks by B-29s based in the Marianas starting in November 1944 drove the gross national product down by one-quarter between 1944 and 1945. As much as half the industrial capacity in key product lines was destroyed by the air war, and without enor-

280

mous American aid after 1945 the economy would have taken far longer than until the mid-1950s to regain its 1934-36 level of output.

T. R. H. Havens
B. Martin

JAPAN, Air War Against.

As soon as the U.S. naval force was knocked out of action in the attack on **Pearl Harbor**, American military leaders began to consider potential means of counteroffensive action. The range of possibilities was limited by the immense distance to the enemy homeland, the secondary strategic priority accorded the **Pacific theater of operations**, the vulnerability of transoceanic supply routes and the feebleness of the Allied military forces early in the war, especially in the air. Pinprick raids were mounted as early as January 1942 by U.S. carrier-based aircraft, striking at such peripheral targets as the Marshall and the **Gilbert Islands**. In April 1942 Lt. Col. **James H. Doolittle** led U.S. Army B-25 bombers in a one-way attack on Honshu island launched from an aircraft carrier. The real struggle for air superiority, however, did not occur until later in the war with the appearance of long-range fighter planes (the P-38 Lightning, with a range of 800 miles and a maximum speed of over 350 mph) and powerful land-based bombers (the B-29 Superfortress, with a range in excess of 3,000 miles, a maximum altitude of 25,000 feet, a speed of 350 mph and a bomb load capacity of 16,500 pounds).

At the Quadrant Conference held in Quebec in August 1943, American air planners proposed the bombardment of Japanese heavy industries, such as steelworks, by B-29 squadrons based in central **China**. The plan, known as Operation Matterhorn, would have required staging at Kunming in China and a huge base effort from a complex of as yet unbuilt airfields, oil depots and port facilities in Calcutta. These impractical plans had been scaled down appreciably and redirected by the time of the Sextant Conference in Cairo in November 1943, when the Combined Chiefs of Staff (CCS) reconsidered the Matterhorn project. The American Joint Chiefs of Staff (JCS) had by now created the 20th USAAF in Washington, embracing the new 20th Bomber Command, which itself consisted of two wings, the 58th and the 73rd. Each wing controlled 112 B-29s (the number to be increased eventually to 192 as bombers became available) destined for **India** but under JCS direction. In China Gen. **Joseph Stilwell** was expected to build four airfields to accommodate B-29s near Chengtu, 200 miles northwest of Chungking, as well as fuel and ammunition depots. The Allied Supreme Commander in Southeast Asia, Lord **Mountbatten**, reported that the

airfields which were needed in the Calcutta area could be ready for the B-29s by May 1944. The Quadrant conferees decided that Ceylon should also be developed as a base area for bombing raids against the Palembang oil fields in Sumatra by summer 1944.

The 20th Bomber Command began bombing raids from its bases in India against industrial objectives in Japan in mid-1944 (northern Kyushu was attacked on June 16 and Sasebo on July 8) and against targets in southern Manchuria (where the Anshan iron works were attacked on July 29) shortly thereafter. Intervals between raids were reduced gradually, and the number of bombers participating in attacks was increased on occasion to about 100. Nevertheless, logistical difficulties involved in the airlift across the "hump" of the Himalayas limited the level and scope of the bombing operations. In addition the maximum range of the B-29s allowed them to hit only Kyushu, the farthest of the major Japanese islands from the core of the country, Honshu.

As it had done after the Doolittle raid in 1942, the Japanese army immediately initiated ground offensive operations to extirpate American bomber bases in China, especially those in Kweilin and Liuchow. Beginning in May 1944 a series of USAAF installations were overrun: Hengyang, Lingling and, on November 24, Nanning—the last American base in Kwangsi province. Other Japanese army units wiped out advance air installations to the east in Kiangsi and Fukien provinces, from which Japanese shipping in the South China Sea had been bombed. With the seizure of Suichuan air base in late January 1945, all the U.S. air strips in the region had fallen in succession. Two months later new Japanese ground actions were undertaken to eliminate American air bases elsewhere in China. Laohokow, a 14th USAAF site, fell in early April, but an assault on Chihchiang, location of the largest American forward base south of the Yangtze River, was checked in May. Against the important long-range Chengtu complex, the Japanese had to resort to air strikes of limited strength.

The Americans explored the possibility of leasing Siberian bases for bomber raids against Japanese targets, but as long as the **USSR** remained nominally neutral in the Pacific war, nothing came of the idea. Clearly the Americans needed "unsinkable aircraft carriers"—Pacific islands on the road to Japan, such as the Marianas chain, 1,200 miles from Tokyo—to bring Japan's industrial centers within range of bombing attacks. After the seizure of the Marianas in June and July 1944, work began there on the construction of major air bases. The Advance Headquarters of the 21st Bomber Command was established on **Saipan** in August, followed by the arrival of the 73rd Wing in October. The 313th Wing went to Tinian in

December; the 314th set up on **Guam** in January. (In October 1944 the JCS had directed that the B-29 campaign against Japan from the Marianas be intensified.)

Adm. **Chester Nimitz** was instructed in early 1945 to capture the Bonins, to provide emergency landing installations for B-29s as well as sites for fighters escorting bomber raids against Japan, and the Ryukyus, to be used for advanced air and naval facilities. The latter were to support the planned invasion of the homeland by ground forces (Operation Olympic, scheduled for autumn 1945). The initial objective was achieved with the seizure of **Iwo Jima** in February and March 1945; the second by the conquest of **Okinawa**, which took from April until June of that year.

Meanwhile the 21st Bomber Command had commenced daylight, high-altitude B-29 raids, dropping 500-pound high-explosive bombs on aircraft factories in the Tokyo-Yokohama district and in Nagoya, Kobe and Osaka. On November 24, 1944, in the first bomber attack on Tokyo since Doolittle's raid, about 110 B-29s made an ineffective strike. Although raids of increasing strength were conducted through De-

cember, it became apparent to American intelligence analysts that most of the main targets were not being knocked out. Maj. Gen. Curtis LeMay, head of the 21st Bomber Command since January 1945, suggested that the "soft" and congested Japanese industrial targets were vulnerable to low-level attacks with incendiary bombs. Consequently on February 4 a force of 70 B-29s conducted an "experimental" raid on Kobe, dropping 160 tons of incendiaries in the process. The encouraging results led to a much heavier trial raid on February 25, when 172 B-29s hit Tokyo in broad daylight with about 450 tons of fire bombs, destroying some 28,000 buildings.

The effectiveness of the low-altitude B-29 raids against Koge and Tokyo induced the JCS to begin incendiary raids against selected industrial targets throughout the country. The monthly tonnage of bombs increased from 13,800 in March to 42,700 in July. With the establishment of the Eighth Air Force on Okinawa, the figure would ultimately have reached 115,000 tons per month if the war had continued. As it was, from May 1945 the B-29s struck Japan on an enormous scales:

B-29 Raids on Japan

	Date:	Target:	Number of B-29s
May	23	Tokyo	520
	25	Tokyo	564
	29	Yokohama	450
July	3-4	Honshu island	470 +
	8-10	Sendai etc.	497
		Yokkaichi	63 (special radar-equipped B-29s)
		Inland Sea	30 (sea mining)
	12-13	Utsunomiya etc.	506
	16-17	Numazu etc.	471
	18-20	Fukui etc.	547
	21-23	Ube	77 (radar-equipped)
	24	Osaka-Nagoya	599
	25	Kawasaki	76 (radar-equipped)
	26	Omuta etc.	305
	28	Tsu etc.	562
August	1-2	Nagaoka etc.	766
	6	Other than Hiroshima	604
	8	Tokyo	412
	9-10	Other than Nagasaki	165 (escorted by 102 P-51s)

On August 14 a total of 833 B-29s struck industrial and urban targets in the largest—and last—of the bombing raids. These attacks were complemented by numerous, massive raids involving swarms of U.S. and British carrier-based aircraft throughout the summer of 1945.

Despite the scale of the bombing missions, few of the B-29s that participated in the raids on Japan were lost: only 1.47% (nine bombers) in 611 sorties flown in November 1944; 0.86% (eight bombers) in 930 sorties in December and 1.29% (13 bombers) in 1,000 sorties in January 1945. Losses remained well under one percent per month through the war's end. In March and July 1945 no B-29s were downed in 3,013 and 6,464 sorties respectively. In Europe the loss rate of the U.S. Eighth Air Force to German interceptors was approximately three times that of the 20th Air Force in the Pacific throughout the period of hostilities. The worst monthly rate of lost planes for the Eighth Air Force (in April 1943) was more than 3.5 times the lost plane rate for the 20th Air Force in November 1944, its worst month except for August 1944, when three planes were lost in 171 sorties—a loss rate of 1.75%. A total of 74 B-29s were downed in 31,387 sorties between June 1944 and August 1945—an overall loss percentage of 0.24%.

In all fairness to the Japanese defense command, however, it should be noted that IGHQ had ordered, beginning in April 1945, the conservation of aircraft for protection against the anticipated invasion of the main islands. Thereafter until July the Japanese army and navy ordered their fighters to engage only unescorted B-29s under extremely favorable conditions. The decline in the scale of effort by Japanese fighters against the 20th Air Force is suggested by the number of interceptor attacks per bomber sortie:

Japanese Interceptor Attacks per Sortie

November 1944	1.1
December	5.1
January 1945	7.9
February	2.2
March	0.2
April	0.8
May	0.3
June	0.3
July	0.02
August	0.04

As a percentage of the total Japanese fighter force, no more than 26.47% (450 planes) was ever assigned to defense of the homeland. The figure was only 16.82% as late as December 1944. The largest number of fighters (535) was assigned at the end of the

war, but this amounted to merely 16.46% of the 3,250 planes then available.

For Japanese civilians the most violent phase of the war was the strategic bombing of 66 cities by the 20th Air Force, beginning in late November 1944 and continuing to the day Japan surrendered, August 15, 1945. Fearsome and devastating though they undoubtedly were, the fire raids and explosive attacks on Japan involved fewer than one-eighth the number of bombs dropped on **Germany** during the war (160,000 tons, versus 1,360,000). The level of destruction was not nearly so great as that inflicted by the saturation bombings of Vietnam by American B-52s some two decades later. Conventional bombs killed nearly as many people during the air war against Japan as the **atomic bomb** attacks of August 1945, but the explosions in Hiroshima and Nagasaki were different from all others, before or since.

The best estimate is that a half million persons died from the American bombings of Japan proper (the figure for Germany is 300,000). The attacks on Japan occurred during the last months of the war, when the economy was already in tatters, and only 22 percent of the bombs were dropped on precision industrial targets. Because Japanese city dwellings were dense and very flammable, almost as much housing was destroyed in Japan as in Germany (24 percent versus 28), even though the total tonnage dropped on Japan was much less. U.S. naval shelling of the Japanese coastline caused relatively negligible damage; 99.5 percent of the civilian casualties resulted from the air raids.

The air attacks burned out some 64 square miles in five main cities, including 10 square miles in Tokyo on the night of March 10, 1945 alone. About 42 percent of Japan's urban industrial zones were demolished, further depressing **production** in factories that were already starved for resources. More than half the country's manufacturing capacity in vacuum tubes, ammonium sulfate and oil refining was destroyed during the war, as was a fourth of its aluminum and pig iron production capability. Half of the telephones and national railway repair shops were wrecked by the air raids, and the output of wheat flour dropped by 50 percent because of the bombings. Soon after the surrender the Japanese government calculated that the Boeing Superfortresses had ruined 40 percent of Osaka and Nagoya; 50 percent of Tokyo, Kobe and Yokohama; 90 percent of Aomori and almost 100 percent of Hiroshima.

The U.S. turned to incendiary **tactics**, sometimes called area bombings, when it became apparent that the earlier precision raids on strategic and industrial sites had not produced the desired effect. Now the aim was to cripple the cities and perhaps frighten the Japanese people into giving up the war effort or even

283

revolting against the government. Before March 10 most attacks took place in midday, dropping relatively small bomb loads because the planes had to carry huge amounts of fuel to operate at high altitudes from bases in the Marianas. All this changed late on the night of March 9 when Gen. LeMay dispatched more than 300 B-29s toward Tokyo, each carrying six tons of incendiaries and almost no fuel reserves. Flying at night and at low altitudes, the planes released their bombs over the packed residential districts along the Sumida River in eastern Tokyo. The result was a conflagration that burned an area as large as Manhattan Island from the Battery to Central Park.

After a two and a half hour attack, the departing air crews could see flames from 150 miles (250 kilometers) out at sea. Some of the fires took four days to burn out. The lanes, canals and rivers of the low-lying districts trapped many thousands in the holocaust. Most of the dead suffocated because the flames consumed so much oxygen. At the Meijiza theater the bodies of suffocated victims were reportedly stacked more than six feet high. An army surgeon wrote: "In the black Sumida River countless bodies were floating, clothed bodies, naked bodies, all as black as charcoal. It was unreal. These were dead people, but you couldn't tell whether they were men or women. You couldn't even tell if the objects floating by were arms and legs or pieces of burnt wood."

Carbon monoxide poisoning and other forms of oxygen deficiency were obvious among the survivors who reported to emergency medical centers. The only official disaster personnel still available in Tokyo were nine physicians and 11 nurses, because many doctors had been drafted and most of the rest had already moved their equipment and patients to the countryside. Japanese **Red Cross** teams coped as best they could at first aid stations in the ruined area. No water pressure remained in the broken mains, and no gas or electric service was available for days.

Eastern Tokyo was obliterated. Nearly one-fifth of the city's industrial areas and an astounding 63 percent of its commercial districts had disappeared overnight. More than a quarter of a million buildings burned down, driving at least a million survivors into hasty **evacuation and resettlement**. The U.S. Strategic Bombing Survey calculated that 83,793 persons died in the March 10 raid, but the actual figure was probably at least 90,000, and it may have exceeded 100,000— greater than the 73,000 who lost their lives in the Kanto earthquake of September 1, 1923 and surpassed among modern Japanese disasters only by the agony at Hiroshima.

The Americans justified the fire bombings as a tactic to shorten the war and insure that industrial centers not identifiable by air **reconnaissance** were demolished. After the indifferent results of the high-explosive attacks from November to February, the March 10 raid was an unqualified success by any military definition. The American forces presumably fire-bombed more targets in Japan than in Germany because the closely built Japanese wooden houses burned very easily and because the precision attacks on German factories and bases had been much more effective (especially after mid-1944). There is no reason to think that the Americans would not have used incendiary tactics more frequently in Europe if conditions had warranted.

In short order the B-29s returned to Saipan and Tinian, refueled and rearmed and then dropped 1,790 tons of high explosives on Nagoya. Two days later they hit Osaka, followed by Kobe, and Nagoya again with incendiaries, dynamite and jelly bombs. In 10 days the Americans flew 1,595 sorties, unloaded two million bombs (9,373 tons) and destroyed nearly 20 square miles of Tokyo, Nagoya, Osaka and Kobe, at a cost of 22 planes. By mid-April, the Japanese government announced, three million persons had been forced to take refuge because fire raids had burned down their homes during the previous six weeks.

One of the most intensive fire raids took place on May 26, when 500 Superfortresses dropped 4,000 tons of bombs (more than twice the amount dropped on March 10) on residential sections in northern and western Tokyo. "Oil turning to fire rained down," one observer wrote in his diary. "Down the road to the south was a sea of flames in which the high roofs were floating." As soon as residents reached safety and the flames died down, officials from the **neighborhood associations** helped resettle the victims temporarily and distributed **food** rations. Captains patrolled their blocks during subsequent night raids and took roll by the light of flares. The energy and vitality that have long characterized the work habits of the Japanese and the organizational strength of the local associations were great assets to Japan in confronting the destruction and beginning to overcome it.

The B-29s returned to Japan with bigger and bigger loads, especially after Okinawa was captured in late June 1945. They bombarded Yokohama on May 29 and Osaka two days later, dropping 3,200 tons of high explosives on each city, causing considerable damage. The busiest day of the entire air operation against Japan was July 10, when 2,000 Superfortresses and fighters attacked cities from Kyushu to Tokyo. In the last weeks of the war, once the main centers had been smashed so badly that they could not recover, many smaller communities became targets.

Part of the reason the bombings did not disrupt Japanese **society** totally is that the nation was already inured to exhausting war work, shortages of food and clothing, and separation from family and friends. The raids were yet another heavy burden imposed by wartime, although a particularly cruel one. Little looting took place in the burned-out districts because there was almot nothing left to be plundered in an economy characterized by great consumer scarcities. The cities also remained fairly orderly because their neighborhoods were sufficiently coherent to avoid complete chaos, except in the most extreme circumstances, as on March 10. Some citizens stayed calm under attack by remembering the old supersition that they could protect themselves by eating good-luck foods like pickled plums or red beans with rice. Certainly the major comfort for most city residents was the knowledge that they could escape to the countryside, where most still had family, if things got bad enough.

The bombings damaged **morale**, but they had surprisingly slight effect on people's outward conduct. Society remained reasonably stable, and citizens still needed their wages from the war plants, so most civilians carried on with their duties. The army noted, however, in an internal memorandum on June 8 that "criticism of the military and government has steadily increased." Such grumbling, the memo concluded, was "a sign of the deterioration of public morality."

Most persons kept their reservations to themselves or confined them to their diaries. An 18-year-old girl wrote on July 21, 1945: "Everything considered, I wish I had ended up dying during the bombings. If only there weren't a war, we wouldn't have to pretend we were happy." When the Americans began dropping leaflets announcing bomb targets in advance, the public could see how powerless to protect them the state had become. War weariness grew even greater after the army admitted an American raid on Hiroshima: "As a result of an attack by a small number of enemy B-29s yesterday, August 6, the city of Hiroshima was considerably damaged. In this raid the enemy apparently used a new type of bomb. Details are now under investigation." When the government revealed a second raid on Nagasaki three days later, one diarist noted, "It is reported in today's paper that Japan's destiny has become the worst imaginable."

The American air war on Japan succeeded in demolishing a war economy already starved for resources by years of sacrifice, improvisation and substitution—and by the U.S. naval **blockade** of the home islands. But strategic bombings, whether precision or saturation, conventional or nuclear, failed to destroy morale, provoke rebellion or demolish the social fabric. The fear of more atomic bombings after Nagasaki led to wild rumors that Tokyo, Kyoto or other cities would be the next to be obliterated (no one in Japan knew that the **United States** had no more atomic bombs ready to be used or that it would be another month before the next one could be assembled). Despite this threat, civilians kept on battling until the emperor himself chose peace. They probably did so most of all because they dreaded the alternative—whether "the sound of the shoes of Russian troops" once the USSR had entered the war, on August 9, or simply the unknown future that lay beyond surrender.

T. R. H. Havens

JAPANESE ELECTION OF APRIL 30, 1942.

At the height of **Japan**'s military successes in the Pacific, Prime Minister **Hideki Tojo** revived the flagging **Imperial Rule Assistance Association** to help candidates favorable to the government in the parliamentary elections of April 1942. The army, the civil bureacracy and the financial community competed for advantage at the polls, but the outcome was a triumph for Tojo's cabinet. All but 85 of the 466 winners had been endorsed by the IRAA election committee.

By law seats in the lower house of the Diet were contested at least once every four years, although the average since 1890 was closer to three. A general election was due on April 30, 1941, but Prince **Fumimaro Konoe**'s second cabinet forced through a bill delaying the election one year. Well before the 1942 poll, the army set up an adult association to support candidates sympathetic to its policies. Soon the association claimed 1.3 million members, mostly in the villages. In the unruly climate of wartime politics, this was a menacing auxiliary weapon for the generals to brandish.

To foil these efforts and others by corporate and bureaucratic interests, Tojo put Gen. **Nobuyuki Abe** in charge of an IRAA political committee to recommend candidates and give them 5,000 yen ($2,000) each. The cabinet ordered the police to round up opposition candidates if they challenged Tojo's policies, and dozens of them were arrested for doing so. Understandably, 381 of the winners were supported by the IRAA. Forty had also been endorsed by the army's adult association.

Through massive interference, the cabinet outmaneuvered its bureaucratic, corporate and military competitors in the balloting. Perhaps more significant was the fact that there were elections at all. Rather than contriving emergency powers to stall the vote further, Tojo gambled that he could shore up support for his government from the voters. The Diet continued to meet throughout the war, the 1889 constitution remained in force, by-elections were held and all military appropriations were debated and voted in the lower house. In the 1942 election the military-dominated Tojo cabinet used parliamentary channels skill-fully to its advantage rather than subverting them and imposing martial law.

T. R. H. Havens

JAPANESE RESISTANCE.

Ordinary Japanese offered far less **resistance** to their government's wartime policies than the Germans or Italians. There were many sporadic outbursts of in-dividual opposition but no collective uprisings, even though a premise of the American air war on **Japan** (see **Japan, Air War Against**) was that demoralized ci-vilians would turn against their state once the cities lay ruined. The only counterpart to the German gen-erals' **assassination attempt of July 20, 1944** on Hitler's life was a successful movement led by senior statesmen and imperial courtiers to topple the cabinet of Gen. **Hideki Tojo** in July 1944.

As war weariness set in and Japan's forces were pushed back in the Pacific, individuals sometimes cursed soldiers who were passing by or scrawled epi-thets of frustration in public places. A few criticized Emperor **Hirohito** for his apparent aloofness and lack of concern for the families of those who died under his command. But fear was doubtless an even more powerful means of standardization than **propaganda**, **censorship** or the tightly-organized **neighborhood as-sociations**. Dissenters generally had no group support because all groups were structured by the state; they were as a consequence unlikely to speak out alone in the face of brutal police power. Those who did were usually jailed.

The prosecutors picked up 866 persons for allegedly violating the peace preservation law in 1943. Of these, 215 were indicted and the rest apparently either repented or were released because they were obviously innocent. The incomplete figures for 1944 suggest that about the same number were indicted from among 700 or so who were detained. The police bureau of the home ministry reported in August 1945 that incidents of public unrest had risen from 308 in the year ending March 1943 to 406 the next year and 607 in the year ending March 1945. Outright antiwar and antimilitary acts grew from 51 in 1942 to 56 a year later and 224 in 1944. Virtually all were individual outbursts, not group efforts.

These were remarkably small figures for a country of 70 million persons. Fatigue with a losing war effort accounted for the rising number of cases late in the war. But the noisiest critics were already in jail, cowed into silence or converted into supporting the govern-ment. Most potential resisters took refuge in silence, such as the novelist Kafu Nagai, who could not sup-port the war but did not wish to risk jail by saying so.

For writers accustomed to speaking their minds, silence became its own prison. Among persons of con-science the moral burden of remaining quiet was a very heavy one.

As early as January 1943 the thought police evalu-ated the public mood very realistically in a report list-ing reasons for discontent: battle reverses, air raids, consumer shortages, long hours in the factories and social frictions with minority groups. The way to deal with unrest, the home ministry decided, was to insist on total obedience. Any sign of discontent, if not sup-pressed, could lead to greater protests. This is why the state harassed citizens even in the last months of the war. Once the chain of repression was in place, it could not be loosened—only snapped.

Aristocrats, former prime ministers and imperial courtiers had more license than ordinary civilians to resist the Tojo government once it became plain in 1943 that the war had bogged down. Led by Prince **Fumimaro Konoe**, a handful of prestigious nobles and politicians began to maneuver secretly to bring down Tojo's cabinet in the summer of 1943. Right-wingers such as retired Gen. **Kanji Ishiwara**, Tojo's lifelong rival, began separate but insignificant move-ments to replace the prime minister. The military police blunted many of these efforts, and Tojo tight-ened his control in March 1944 by making himself chief of the army general staff while retaining his other offices. Only when **Saipan** fell in July 1944 and public confidence in Tojo's leadership sagged did the movement to oust him succeed, a sign of how weak the resistance even from the most eminent nobles in the land really was.

Ordinary Japanese were powerless to establish an organized resistance for two reasons. One is that the state had a monopoly on the instruments of violence. There was no way for citizens to resist the power of the police and the army. The other is that until very late in the war the government had enough organizational control, through civic associations and the media, to snuff out any sort of collective action against its pol-icies.

T. R. H. Havens

JAPANESE SECRET SERVICES.

After 1938-39, control of the Japanese secret services was entrusted to the embassies and consulates, depending on the specific work of the agents in each location. Although they were under the control of of-ficers trained for this purpose, these espionage services collapsed almost completely—in the **United States**, at least—once hostilities began.

Counter-espionage activities were under the super-vision of the Ministry of War and extended into the

286

occupied territories in order to facilitate the detection of enemy spy operations and **sabotage** networks. The secret information-gathering service, an army organization, was responsible for performing espionage services, pacifying occupied territories and continuing the work of political and military subversion.

The contribution of the Japanese espionage service to the success of the attack on **Pearl Harbor** was enormous. Several months before the event, Organization F had already completed its spying activities in **Indonesia** and extended them to **Malaya**. In **Burma** the way was cleared for the advance of the Japanese by the Army of Burmese Independence, which also organized various guerilla groups for the anticipated attack on **India**.

Besides the military security services, organized on the Western model, Japan had a special police section, the *Tokko*, created in 1911 as part of the Ministry of the Interior to suppress leftist political movements and later charged with counter-espionage. It was the *Tokko* organization that broke up the Soviet spy network **Richard Sorge** had established in Japan in October 1941.

J. Schroder

JEBB, Sir Gladwyn (later Lord Gladwyn) (1900-   ).

A British diplomat, Jebb served as private secretary to **Anthony Eden** and **Edward Halifax** in 1937-40. He became the first political director of the **Special Operations Executive** in 1940 and continued in that capacity until 1942. After the war Jebb served as acting secretary-general of the **United Nations** in 1946 and as British ambassador to France from 1954 to 1960. Jebb became known as a prominent supporter of a closer European union.

JEDBURGH.

Jedburgh and the Operational Group were intelligence-gathering teams under the authority of the Special Forces headquarters attached to **Eisenhower's** general headquarters before the **Normandy landing**, and dependent on the **Special Operations Executive** and the **Office of Strategic Services**. Just before June 6, 1944, 93 Jedburgh crews in uniform parachuted to the French interior. Each was composed of one British, one French and one American soldier. Of these three, two were officers and one a radio operator. Their mission was to furnish a headquarters for local **Resistance** groups, to coordinate individual efforts into collective maneuvers, to inventory existing war materiel in maquis hands and to arrange for supplemental supplies via radio. The Special Forces also parachuted American "Operational Groups" of 32

men each, with precise missions of **sabotage** or protection. Their particular tasks completed, the groups were required to join the nearest branch of the *Forces francaises de l'interieur* and fight with them.

JET AIRCRAFT.

World War II was the last war fought by aircraft using internal combustion engines. Jet aircraft did not appear until 1945. Yet the basic idea of the jet engine was not new. In 1930 a **Royal Air Force** officer named **Frank Whittle** sent the Air Ministry a report stating that the internal combustion engine had reached its greatest efficiency and that there was little possiblity of further improvement. In fact, he insisted, it was a mechanical freak—pistons, crankshafts and valves constituting an unjustifiably expensive system that wasted energy. Any attempt to increase the power of this type of engine in future aircraft would produce an enormous mass of metal that could only add to its inertia. In addition, the propeller took a great deal of punishment and should therefore be dispensed with. It would be better, Whittle concluded, to scrap the internal combustion engine altogether and subsitute a device thrusting the aircraft forward with reactive jets powered by the combustion of gases in a chamber.

With their usual resistance to change, the authorities ignored the idea of jet propulsion and its implications for aeronautical engineering. As a result, Whittle's creation, the experimental prototype of the British jet aircraft Gloster E 28/39, did not come into being until May 1941. A short time later, the first practical model was sent to the **United States** for examination by a Jet Propulsion Committee.

Others besides the British were active in the new field. First a Frenchman named **Maxime Guillaume** in the 1920s, then two German students at the University of Tuebingen, Hans von Ohain and Max Hahn, had proposed the development of a jet engine. Guillaume had no luck in his country; the two Germans had a more attentive audience in theirs. The authorities of the Third Reich and the **Heinkel** aircraft firm took the invention more seriously than their British counterparts. The first flight of a German turbojet aircraft occurred on August 27, 1939, four days before the war broke out.

Why did the British, Americans and Germans take so long to get the new type of craft into the air? In the confusion that naturally arose as they began the mass **production** of fighters, fighter-bombers and heavy and light bombers, the Allies hesitated to complicate matters by tooling up for the new version, convinced that they could win with conventional types. The Germans, on the other hand, alarmed by their air defeats at the end of 1942, realized that only by devising new and terrible weapons could they still win the war. Hence their production of the **V-1 and V-2** and other remote-controlled or automatically guided rockets. Hence, too, their production of the schnorkel and the powerful class XXI and XXIII submarines (see **Atlantic, Battle of the**). These arms came too late to decide the issue. So did the turbojet aircraft—but only because of **Hitler**.

The Messerschmitt-262 made its maiden flight in July 1942. But it was not until the end of 1943 that the Nazi leaders opted for the mass production of this remarkable craft. With its speed of 575 miles per hour—the fastest Allied fighter could do no better than 475—its four 30-mm cannons and 24 50-mm rockets and its two Junker Junio jet engines with nearly one ton of thrust, it could easily have knocked its lumbering internal combustion opponents out of the skies. But Hitler's thirst for vengeance demanded that the Me-262 be held in reserve to smash the RAF in its home skies rather than fighting on the Continent. The plane therefore had to be modified. A further delay was necessary to convince the Fuehrer that it should be used to fight invading bombers. But when the first group of Me-262 jet fighters made its appearance in 1944, Hitler could still not bring himself to give jet engine production top priority. He was not to make up his mind until January 1945.

German factories finally built 1,433 Me-262's, but only 200 were allowed into action. The performance of these craft left no doubt of what they could have done if supplied in greater numbers. **Pierre Clostermann** later remarked that in March 1945 six of these planes shot down 14 B-17 Fortresses in a single fight. Each of the German fighters was armed with 48 rockets. Another of the German jets was the Arado-234, with two or four engines, for high-altitude **reconnaissance** and tactical bombing. It had a speed of about 490 miles per hour and carried four 30-mm cannon and two bombs—one weighing a ton, the other 1,100 pounds. Only a few Arados saw action, however.

To hinder the proliferation of German jet aircraft in the skies, a primary function of Allied flyers in the last weeks of the war was to destroy the enemy's landing and takeoff strips as well as his gasoline depots, hangars and auxiliary installations (see **Germany, Air Battle of**).

If hostilities had lasted just a few days longer, the first groups of the British Gloster Meteors, Whittle's creation, would have made their debut. This twin-engine aircraft, with its maximum speed of 600 miles per hour, had already been used effectively against the V-1 rockets. It was far superior to the Me-262. The Gloster Meteor of Air Commodore Sir Frank Whittle was to demonstrate its full powers after the war.

H. Bernard

JODL, Alfred (1890-1946).

From 1939 to 1945, Jodl, a German general, was head of the *Oberkommando der Wehrmacht*'s Bureau of Operations. He signed the surrender at Reims on May 7, 1945, as head of the chiefs of staff in **Karl Doenitz**'s government. He was condemned by the Nuremberg court and hanged (see **War Criminals**).

JOUBERT DE LA FERTE, Sir Philip Bennett (1887-1965).

Joubert de la Ferte, an airplane pilot who became British air chief marshal, was already a flier in 1914. He served in World War I as a pilot in the British air force. On August 31, 1914, on an air **reconnaissance** mission, he noted the deviation of German columns toward the northeast section of Paris. His report was an important factor in the Allied victory of the Marne. From 1939 to 1945 he served as chief of the Coastal Command in the **Battle of the Atlantic**, and then as head of the chiefs of staff and head of Lord **Mountbatten**'s staff in Southeast Asia.

JUIN, Alphonse (1888-1967).

Juin, a French marshal, was commander of the 15th Motorized Brigade. He was taken prisoner by the Germans in May 1940 and freed in June 1941. Succeeding Gen. **Maxime Weygand** as commander in chief of the forces of North Africa in November 1941, he went over to the Allies in November 1942. He became resident general in Tunisia in 1943, then obtained command of the French Expeditionary Corps in Italy in November 1943. In May 1944 he won the battle of Garigliano. He was appointed head of the chiefs of staff for national defense in 1944.

K

KALININ, Mikhail S. (1875-1946).
President of the **USSR** from 1938 to just before his death.

KALTENBRUNNER, Ernst (1903-1946).
At the time of the *Anschluss* (1938), Kaltenbrunner was appointed secretary of state for the Austrian secret police. In January 1943 he succeeded **Reinhard Heydrich** as head of the **RSHA**, participating energetically in implementing the **Final Solution**. He was condemned to death at Nuremberg and hanged in 1946.

KAMIKAZE.
This suicidal air squadron was developed by the Japanese toward the end of the war, when all hope of victory had vanished. The pilot of an aircraft loaded with explosives zeroing in on a target and colliding with it head-on was known as a kamikaze, the Japanese word for "divine wind." The most famous of these aircraft was the *Okha*—"cherry flower"—better know as the *Baka*, the name given it by the Americans. The *Okha* was a small wooden single-seater driven by three rockets and carrying a maximum of 1,000 kilograms (2,205 pounds) of explosives. It was launched from a bomber some 12.5 miles from the target and guided by radio signals. It crashed into its target at a velocity of about 375 miles per hour under the thrust of its rockets. Its charge was not detonated on contact but was delayed to exploit the effect of penetration. Kamikaze pilots were endowed with a mystique deriving from the ancient warrior code of *Bushido*, based on Buddhism and the "profoundly rooted belief that the nation, society, and heaven itself formed a single unit incarnated in the Mikado."

Faced with utter defeat the Japanese gave the kamikaze pilots not only special planes like the *Okha 11* and the *Nakajima Ki-115*, but any type of aircraft capable of flight. Incredibly, they also used human torpedoes, known as *Kaiten*, fired by submarines, and suicide speedboats called *Shinyo*. The latter carried a single helmsman, with two tons of TNT in its prow.

Speeding into the target at 30 knots, the charge exploded on contact.

These devices were costly to the Allies in the Pacific, but their force was on the whole blunted because they were insufficiently massed for large-scale destruction; they came into use too late, when **Japan**'s air force was badly depleted and its navy impotent to exploit their effect; the explosive charges were in general too weak and the American proximity fuse (see **Radar**) was an effective riposte.

H. Bernard

KATYN.
On April 12, 1943 a mass grave containing the bodies of 4,500 Polish officers was discovered at Katyn, a village in the **USSR** near Smolensk. This massacre has been attributed successively to the Russians and the Germans. The American Committee of Inquest in 1953 concluded that it was an act of reprisal conducted by **Stalin**'s political police in 1939.

KAUFMANN, Henrik (1885-1963).
When the Nazis occupied **Denmark** in April 1940, Kaufmann, the Danish ambassador to Washington, refused to recognize the resignation of the court and government of Copenhagen. He immediately organized Free Denmark, made **Greenland** available to the Allies and brought the important Danish merchant marine into the Allied camp. He directed the Free Denmark movement throughout the war and was quite influential in stimulating the **Resistance** movement inside Denmark.

KAYA, Okinori (1889-   ).
A bureaucrat without direct ties to big business, Kaya was Japanese minister of finance during 1937-38 and 1941-44. He believed that continued good relations with the **United States** were essential, especially after the outbreak of war with **China** in 1937, because **Japan** depended on the U.S. for raw materials. In a dispute over economic mobiliziaton in 1938, corporate interests had him removed from the cabinet.

After heading the North China Development Corporation during 1939-41, Kaya returned as wartime finance minister under Prime Minister **Tojo**. He incorrectly predicted that inflation would be modest during the war, and he gradually lost control over planning and **production** to the armed forces. In 1948 he was sentenced to life in prison by the International Military Tribunal for the Far East for his part in leading Japan's war effort (see **War Criminals**).

KEITEL, Wilhelm (1888-1946).
German field marshal. In 1938 Keitel was named head of the *Oberkommando der Wehrmacht*. Throughout the war he obeyed **Hitler's** orders, even those repugnant to the honor of an officer, in servile fashion. On May 8, 1945 he signed **Germany's** surrender on behalf of the *Wehrmacht*. He was condemned to death in the Nuremberg trials of **war criminals** and was hanged.

KELL, Sir Vernon (1873-1942).
The first head of **MI-5** (1909-14), Kell resumed the post in 1924 and served until 1940.

KERSTEN, Felix (1898-1960).
A chiropractor of Estonian origin, Kersten was able to obtain the freedom of numerous prisoners through the influence he had over **SS Reichsfuehrer Heinrich Himmler**, his patient from March 1939 to April 1945. On March 12, 1945 he secured a written pledge that the **concentration camps** would not be dynamited, that the execution of Jews would cease and that the Swedish **Red Cross** would be permitted to send packages to concentration camp inmates. He was awarded the decoration of Grand Officer of the Order of Orange-Nassau by Prince **Bernhard** of **the Netherlands** in 1950 and Swedish citizenship in 1953 for having insured the success of the Red Cross expedition of assistance to **Germany** in April 1945.

KESSELRING, Albert (1885-1960).
From 1939 to 1940 Kesselring, a German field marshal, commanded the First and Second Air Fleets and from 1941 to March 1945 was commander in chief of the Southwest Army in the Italian and Mediterranean theaters. He was commander in chief of the western theater from March to May 1945. Condemned to death by a British military court in 1947, he was pardoned in 1952.

KEYES, Sir Roger (later Lord) (1872-1945).
A British admiral, Keyes, who had led the Zeebrugge raid in World War I, became the British liaison officer with King **Leopold III** of **Belgium** in May 1940. In July of that year he was appointed Britain's first head of **combined operations**. Full of bright but impractical ideas, he was dismissed in October 1941.

KEYNES, John Maynard, Lord (1883-1946).
British economist. Keynes, a Cambridge intellectual, possessed one of the sharpest brains of his age. His *Economic Consequences of Peace* (1919) shattered confidence in the peace settlement of World War I and his *General Theory of Employment, Interest and Money* (1936) enabled capitalism to survive. He was financial adviser to the British treasury during the war, organized the International Monetary Fund and, in September-December 1945, negotiated a loan from the **United States**.

KIDO, Koichi (1889-1977).
Kido was a Japanese marquis, cabinet official and top imperial adviser during World War II. As lord keeper of the privy seal from 1940 to 1945, he asserted the influence of the imperial court and aristocracy and tried to curb the military leadership. He was a central figure in making **peace overtures** early in 1945. After the surrender the International Military Tribunal for the Far East sentenced him to life in prison for war crimes, but he was paroled because of poor health in 1953 (see **War Criminals**).

After graduating from Tokyo Imperial University, Kido held posts in the ministries of agriculture and commerce, trade and industry and home affairs before serving successively as minister of education, welfare and home affairs between 1937 and 1939.

A close associate of Prince **Fumimaro Konoe**, Kido became lord keeper of the privy seal in 1940. When Konoe's cabinet fell in October 1941, he convinced the other senior statesmen to name Gen. **Hideki Tojo** as prime minister in order to keep the army operating within established institutions, but the move had little impact on the events leading to **Pearl Harbor**.

When the war turned against **Japan**, Kido helped force Tojo from office in July 1944 and pressed actively to bring the fighting to an end the following spring. As the emperor's chief source of information about war and politics, Kido played a major part in persuading **Hirohito** to work for peace in 1945.

T. R. H. Havens

KING, Ernest J. (1878-1956).
Following Pearl Harbor, Adm. King became commander-in-chief of the **United States** Atlantic Fleet in 1941 and chief of naval operations in 1942. He was responsible for coordinating U.S. joint force operations and joint operations with the Allies. King oversaw such major innovations in naval warfare as the use of carrier-based air power and amphibious operations.

He attended the major wartime conferences (see **Conferences, Allied**) and was a member of the Combined Chiefs of Staff Committee. In 1944 he was given the new five-star rank of fleet admiral. The fleet commanded by King was the largest ever assembled, surpassing the combined strength of all other navies in the world.

KING, W. L. Mackenzie (1874-1950).
A Canadian liberal politician, King was prime minister of **Canada** from 1921 to 1930 and from 1935 to 1948 and foreign minister from 1935 to 1946, during which time he concluded a defense pact with the **United States** (August 1940).

KLEIST, Paul von (1885-1954).
German field marshal. In the invasion of France, Kleist commanded a force that broke through the Allied lines at Sedan, opening the way to the English Channel in a lightning advance. On the eastern front he captured Belgrade in 1941, and took part in the battles of Kiev and Stalingrad. He was commander of a group of German and Rumanian armies but was relieved of his duties by **Hitler** in 1944 for his refusal to follow blindly the Fuehrer's orders.

KLUGE, Guenther von (1882-1944).
In 1941 Kluge, a German field marshal, was the commander in chief of the group of armies in the central part of the eastern front, and in 1944 he commanded the German army in the west, including Army Group D in France. Implicated in the **assassination attempt of July 20, 1944** against **Hitler**, Kluge was relieved of his duties by the Fuehrer. He killed himself on August 18, 1944.

KOCH, Erich (1896-1959).
German *Gauleiter* and *Reichskommissar* of the Ukraine, Koch was responsible for the policy of exploitation and extermination in that region of the **USSR**. He was turned over to **Poland** in 1950 and condemned to death in 1959.

KOENIG, Marie Pierre (1898-1973).
A general in the **Free France** movement and commander of the French brigade in **Libya**, Koenig was the hero in the fighting at Bir-Hakeim from May 27 to June 11, 1942 (see **Mediterranean and Middle Eastern Theater of Operations**). He was made national commander of the *Forces francaises de l'interieur* in March 1944 and military governor of Paris in August 1944. From 1945 to 1949 he commanded the French occupation troops in **Germany**.

KOISO, Kuniaki (1880-1950).
Koiso, a Japanese general, served as minister of colonial development in 1939-40 and as prime minister from July 1944 to April 1945. A brusque advocate of military rule at home and anti-Western expansionism abroad, Koiso was a key figure in the control faction of the imperial army. His cabinet had the hopeless task of prosecuting a losing war while seeking a negotiated peace in the face of Allied demands for an **unconditional surrender**. After the war he was sentenced to life in prison by the International Military Tribunal for the Far East (see **War Criminals**).

Born in Yamagata and educated at the war college, Koiso became staff chief of the Japanese Kwantung Army, posted in Manchuria, during 1932-34. He steadfastly sought a military coup in Tokyo so that efficient economic and military mobilization could occur. As a cabinet minister in 1939-40, he demanded full national economic management and immediate expansion to seize resources in Southeast Asia. He supported **Kanji Ishiwara**'s East Asian League.

After a term as governor-general of Korea, Koiso became a compromise prime minister following the ouster of Gen. **Hideki Tojo**. He helped create the supreme war council in August 1944 to link the cabinet, imperial court and high command more closely. During his term in office, the war situation grew steadily worse, and Koiso gave way to Adm. **Kantaro Suzuki** in April 1945.

KOLBE, Maximilien (1894-1941).
At **Auschwitz**, Kolbe, a Polish churchman, volunteered to take the place of the father of a family who was condemned to death. He was tortured and then murdered on August 14, 1941. On August 17, 1971 he was beatified by Pope Paul VI in homage to the victims of Nazi **concentration camps**.

KOMMISSARBEFEHL.
The "Order of Commissars" was the instructions of the *Oberkommando der Wehrmacht* issued by direction of **Hitler** on June 6, 1941 to the German troops in the **USSR**. It dictated that Red Army political commissars be liquidated rather than treated as **prisoners of war**, because of the ideological conflict and hatred between Nazis and Bolshevists. Only partially obeyed, the order had the effect of stiffening Russian resistance.

KONIEV, Ivan S. (1897-1973).
From 1941 to 1945 Koniev, a Soviet marshal, was the commander in chief of several army groups (designated "fronts" by the Russians)—the West, Northwest, First and Second Ukrainian. He captured **Dresden** and Prague. The forces under his command joined the American troops led by Gen. **Omar Bradley** at Torgau on April 25, 1945.

KONOE, Fumimaro (Konoye Ayamaro) (1891-1945).

Konoe was an imperial adviser, a prince of the blood and prime minister of Japan for most of the period between the outbreak of war in China on July 7, 1937 and Pearl Harbor, December 7, 1941. Although Konoe wanted to avoid war with the United States and tried to give civilians the upper hand in policy-making, during his rule Japan moved closer to all-out war abroad and complete military dominance at home. In October 1941 his third cabinet fell, like the two before it, because of pressures from the armed services.

Konoe once again became a key official at the imperial court and later had a hand in toppling the cabinet of his successor, Gen. Hideki Tojo, in July 1944. He also joined in peace overtures the following spring. Rather than face trial as a war criminal, he took cyanide at his Ogikubo home in Tokyo on December 16, 1945.

Because he possessed neither great strength of character nor any discernible ideology, Konoe was scarcely less an enigma to the Japanese than he was to foreigners. His impeccable manners, broad learning and wide travel (he sent his son to Lawrenceville and Princeton) persuaded many Americans that he was a liberal who wanted peace. His bellicose rhetoric and coziness with the military convinced many Chinese that he intended to subjugate them by force. Within Japan he was most often regarded as the high-born son of the noblest family in the land, an aristocrat intimate with the throne who could resolve domestic turmoil and international crises because of his unique position above politics and his great skill at reconciling conflicting interests.

Because so much was expected of him, by both the powerful and the humble, when Konoe came to office, his resignation in October 1941, when Japan was at the brink of cataclysm, was both discouraging and disillusioning. Since the war he has been chiefly remembered for his indecisiveness and vacillation. But the real flaw of prewar Japanese politics was institutional, not personal. The cabinet and the parliamentary system placed only very weak restraints on the powerful and surprisingly autonomous interest groups that arose in the 1930s—above all the military, which by constitutional law reported to the emperor alone. Few if any statesmen could have coped with these handicaps more successfully than Konoe.

Prince Konoe was born in Tokyo on October 12, 1891 and was educated at the imperial university in Kyoto, the ancient capital where his Fujiwara ancestors had ruled the worlds of taste and politics a thousand years before. Although he served briefly in the home ministry, Konoe spent nearly all his career in the house of peers and at court. He had neither talent nor experience as an administrator when he formed his first cabinet in June 1937. But he had exceptional skills as a political mediator, aided by his prestigious lineage and his ties to the emperor. His most steadfast domestic goal was to enhance the influence of the court and hereditary nobility amid the many competing interest groups of newly made men: businessmen, party politicians and bureaucrats, but above all the armed services.

Precisely these skills at building consensus, rather than marking out bold new policies, won Konoe the prime ministership in June 1937. The country was still staggering from the effects of an army revolt the previous year that paralyzed Tokyo for three snowy days in February and disrupted national politics for weeks thereafter. Abroad the USSR, China and even the United States were becoming more hostile, now that Japan had withdrawn from the old world order of naval agreements and the League of Nations and tried to construct a new one by signing the Anti-Comintern Pact with Germany in November 1936. Both the governmental establishment and the public expected that if anyone could surmount these crises, it would be the gracious, aristocratic, conciliatory Konoe.

Although his elitist aims in domestic politics were kept carefully shrouded, Konoe made no secret of his outlook on world affairs. Together with his eventual ambassador to Washington, Adm. Kichisaburo Nomura, Konoe attended the Versailles peace conference in 1919 and blasted the victors for imposing their standards without abolishing colonialism or recognizing Japan's "legitimate right of survival." In the 1930s he demanded an end to the rich nations' monopoly of world wealth, and he praised Japan's continental expansion after the Manchurian incident in September 1931 as an axiom of national destiny. Yet despite his earnest anti-imperialism and support for a strong foreign policy, Konoe had scant experience with foreign affairs and a surprisingly incomplete knowledge of world issues. His fate as a leader was deeply colored by the fact that he understood the politics of how to form a policy far better than what policy was appropriate in the subtle realm of international relations.

His cabinet had barely taken office when the Marco Polo Bridge incident touched off war with China on July 7, 1937. Konoe did little to restrain the generals who wanted to broaden the fighting in the absence of clear war aims. He rebuffed Roosevelt's October 5, 1937 "quarantine" speech with an attack on America's discriminatory immigration laws and warned that if the rich "nations continue to refuse to yield some of their vested interests to the have-not nations, what solution is there except war?"

In January 1938 Konoe cut off relations with the Chinese Nationalists and laid plans for an economic bloc among Japan, Manchukuo and China. This grandiose scheme, known as the **New Order in East Asia**, was officially proclaimed on November 3, 1938. By the end of his cabinet the following January, Konoe had managed to drive Japan deeper into crisis with China without checking the power of the military at home. His ministers were prestigious figures who generally resented the army's influence, but Konoe provided little cohesive leadership to assert his cabinet over the armed forces. It was they who drove him from office and back to the privy council, of which he now became the head.

By mid-1940 Germany had overrun France and Japanese troops were entering northern **Indochina**. Domestically the economy was in disarray and political elites—most of all the war ministry—competed fiercely for control of the cabinet. When the army brought down the government of Adm. **Mitsumasa Yonai** in July 1940, once again Konoe seemed best suited to mediate between factions and guide the country as events abroad grew more dangerous.

Before he took office on July 22, Konoe was certain to win cooperation from the army and navy. As soon as he resumed power, the prince unveiled his **New Structure Movement**, a mass political base he could use to rebuff the military, mobilize the public and design an unfaltering foreign policy. The new structure, expressed mainly through the amorphous **Imperial Rule Assistance Association**, stirred such wrangling that Konoe soon found himself conciliating again rather than leading. Although the prime ministership stayed in civilian hands until Konoe resigned on October 16, 1941, his new structure was a failure and the armed services increased their influence over policy-making as the crisis with the United States deepened.

Konoe turned out to be no more adept at sizing up foreign affairs than he had been at political reform. He miscalculated the effect Japan's increasingly pro-Nazi policies would have on relations with the U.S. Konoe brushed aside warnings from several advisers that the **Tripartite Pact** with Germany and **Italy**, signed by Foreign Minister **Yosuke Matsuoka** on September 27, 1940, would antagonize rather than restrain the Americans. In a curious twist of the logic of the **Munich Pact**, Konoe declared that any hint of conciliation would only make the United States more unyielding and that Japan would not compromise its position in China in the slightest. Since **Cordell Hull**, the American secretary of state, was equally inflexible, it is not surprising that the U.S.-Japan negotiations of April 1941 soon bogged down.

Only when Germany attacked the Soviet Union on June 22, 1941 did Konoe abandon the premise of German-Japanese cooperation with the Soviets on which the Tripartite Pact had been implicitly based. He realized too late that the **Axis** was a thin shell and that a way must be found to reach an understanding with the United States. He dissolved his second cabinet on July 18, 1941 to remove Matsuoka and formed a third one the same day, with the hope of continuing the talks with the U.S. indefinitely.

Although Konoe had now grown more conciliatory, neither Hull nor the Japanese generals scaled down their demands. The war ministry pressed Konoe to wind up the negotiations quickly. Still convinced that the Americans wanted peace at almost any price, Konoe suggested a summit conference with Roosevelt in September—a scheme quickly vetoed by Hull as too compromising and too risky. Although he worked tirelessly through private as well as official contacts to prolong the negotiations, in the end Konoe could satisfy neither the Americans nor the Japanese army that diplomacy was likely to produce promising results. When Konoe left office on October 16 to rejoin the imperial court as an adviser, the government was turned over to the man who led Japan to war against America, Tojo. Neither of them could have prevented the catastrophe that befell Japan, even if either had foreseen it in time.

T. R. H. Havens.

KRAGUJEVAC.

From 1818 to 1841 this city was the capital of the young Serbian state, an important communications and industrial center. With 30,000 inhabitants in 1941, it was also a stronghold of the labor movement. The Communists used it as a base for an energetic **Resistance** campaign. During the Serbian insurrection in mid-October 1941, they inflicted heavy losses on Nazi occupation troops in the city's suburbs. On the order of Field Marshal **Wilhelm Keitel** to execute 100 Serbs for every German killed and 50 Serbs for every German wounded, the Germans massacred many of its people. The male population between the ages of 17 and 70 was exterminated; schoolboys were rounded up and shot along with their professors. The victims of the Nazi horror—3,500 men, according to German sources, 7,000 according to local records—were slaughtered between October 21 and 23. Kragujevac became the bloody symbol of **Yugoslavia**'s resistance to the invader.

J. Marjanovic

KRAMER, Josef (1906-1945).

A member of the SS, Kramer was a deputy at **Auschwitz** before becoming commandant of **Bergen-Belsen** (see concentration camps). He was condemned as a war criminal and executed in November 1945.

KREISAUER KREIS.

In English, "Kreisau Circle." This group of German Christian intellectual resisters led by Count Helmuth James von Moltke and Count P. Yorck von Wartenburg (see German Resistance) opposed Hitler and sought to regenerate Germany through means other than assassination of the Fuehrer. Many of the group's leaders were accused of participation in the assassination attempt of July 20, 1944 and executed.

KRUEGER, Walter (1881-1967).

A veteran of combat in France in World War I, Gen. Krueger was commander of the U.S. Sixth Army in World War II from 1943 until the end of the war. He led almost all southwestern Pacific ground operations in New Guinea, the Bismarck Archipelago and the Philippines. In October 1944 Krueger commanded the Sixth Army in the invasion of Leyte.

KRUPP von BOHLEN und HALBACH, Gustav (1870-1950) and Alfried (1907-1967).

German armaments industry magnates, Gustav Krupp and his son Alfried had no scruples about employing thousands of prisoners of war and inmates of concentration camps as forced laborers in their factories. Gustav was not tried at Nuremberg for reasons of poor health; Alfried was sentenced to 12 years of solitary confinement but later paroled (see War Criminals).

KUECHLER, Georg von (1881-1968).

In 1940, Kuechler, a German field marshal and commander in chief of the 18th Army, was responsible for the air bombardment of Rotterdam. In 1942 he was commander in chief of Army Group North on the Russian front. Two years later he was placed on reserve at Hitler's order. Condemned to 20 years of imprisonment at the Nuremberg trials, he was freed in 1953 (see War Criminals).

L

LABOR CHARTER.

This ordinance, passed by the **French State** (see also **Petain and the French State**) on October 26, 1941, provided for the regulation of labor conflicts between various professional groups, outlawed lockouts and strikes, specified a minimum-existence salary level and created social enterprise commissions. Heavily criticized by both employers and the working class and rarely put into practice, it was finally abolished on July 27, 1944.

LAMPSON, Sir Miles (later Lord Killearn) (1880-1964).

British ambassador to **Egypt** from 1936-1946.

LANDING CRAFT.

About 80 types of ships and boats designed for landing troops and/or materiel were used during World War II. Some of the best known are described below:

Self-Powered Vessels

Landing ship infantry (LSI)

These were transports designed to ferry personnel rapidly. Their displacements ranged from 3,000 to 10,000 tons. They were designed not to run aground on beaches and were capable of carrying small boats such as the LCA (see below).

Landing ship tank (LST)

This was the largest ship capable of grounding itself and then retracting from the beach; it was manufactured by mass **production**. With a hull that could be opened at the bow, the LST was designed for transporting and for landing 40 to 70 **tanks** weighing 25 to 40 tons each, as well as other vehicles, on beaches by ramps and pontoons; it could, however, navigate the high seas. There were three types of LST, varying in displacement from 1,100 to 3,065 tons. One of these, the LST-2, was about 325 feet long and 50 feet wide; it had two 900-horsepower engines and a top speed of 10 knots.

Landing ship headquarters (LSH)

This vessel had every convenience for the efficient operations of combined land, naval and air chiefs of staff. It served as a seagoing corps and division general headquarters until the latter could be transferred to a land installation.

Landing craft infantry (LCI)

This self-propelled boat, with a speed of 15 knots, carried 250 men, fully equipped. With a bridge in the form of a ramp to the shore, it could be run aground in ¾ of a meter of water. Its displacement was 300 tons.

Landing craft tank (LCT)

There were nine different varieties of this vessel, with capacities ranging from three 40-ton tanks to eight heavy tanks, or from 250 to 350 tons of materiel. One model, the LCT-2, was 160 feet long and 31 feet wide. Its top speed was 11 knots. The LCT-2 carried two 40-mm cannon; its crew consisted of two officers and 10 seamen. Tanks transported by the LCT-2 landed directly on the beach.

Support landing craft

These included the landing craft tank (Rocket) [LCT (R)]; the landing craft flak (LCF), which was heavily armed against aircraft; and the landing craft gun (LCG). This last vessel was designed to destroy tanks and enemy coastal defenses, as well as to furnish artillery support to landed troops until field artillery support was available. It was 155 feet long and 22 feet wide, and carried howitzers of 77 or 88 mm, 11 Oerlikons of 20 mm and 11 machine guns and a crew of three officers and 27 seamen.

The landing ships were capable of making any kind of crossing. The possibilities of the landing craft, however, were limited. Landing craft infantry vessels were generally limited to 24-hour voyages and were thus perfect for the Channel crossing from England to Normandy.

Small Craft Launched from Larger Vessels
Landing craft personnel (LCP)
About 37 feet long and 11 feet wide, these had wooden hulls and gasoline or diesel engines with 150 to 250 horsepower. Their speed was seven to eight knots. They carried a crew of three men and three tons of materiel, or 26-36 men.

Landing craft assault (LCA)
About 41 feet long and 10 feet wide, these had two Ford V-8 engines of 65 horsepower each. With a speed of seven to ten knots, their crews normally numbered four men; their capacity, however, was 35 men with 880 pounds of materiel. The LCA had a plated hull, armored gunwales, an armored gate at the top of the ramp and elevated gunwale armor to protect the heads of its passengers. It was valued for its low silhouette and silent engines.

Landing craft vehicle and personnel (LCVP)
This craft was faster than the LCA, but did not have its armor.

Landing craft mechanized (LCM)
This was a small barge designed for carrying vehicles. There were about a half-dozen varieties. The LCM-3, the most common type, could carry a 30-ton tank, or 30 tons of cargo or 60 men.

Other Landing Craft
Along with these landing and support vessels, there were broad arrays of specialized accompanying barges: the landing barge engineering (LBE) and landing craft emergency repairs (LCER), which were used as service centers; the landing craft kitchen (LCK), which was employed for feeding troops about to land; and various others.

In addition to these were the huge landing ships career (LSC), used to transport the landing craft and their crews, their construction scaffolding or their hulls, to all theaters of operation in the world.

LAOS.
See **Indochina**.

LA PORTE DU THEIL, Paul de (1884-   ).
A French general and founder of the *Chantiers de la jeunesse*, youth camps run by the Vichy government, de La Porte du Theil was arrested by the **Gestapo** in January 1944 for **sabotage** of the **Forced Labor Battalions** and aid to the maquis and sent to a **concentration camp**. He was indicted by the High Court of Justice in November 1947 and acquitted.

LARMINAT, Rene de (1896-1962).
A French officer, Larminat was head of Gen. **Maxime Weygand**'s chiefs of staff in May 1940. He served as high commissioner of **French Equatorial Africa** in 1942 and became chief of the First Free French Division in 1943. He fought in **Italy** and was then named commander of the *Forces francaises de l'interieur* on the Atlantic shore; he captured Royan in April 1945.

LATTRE de TASSIGNY, Jean de (1889-1952).
In 1939 de Lattre headed the chiefs of staff of the Fifth Army in Alsace. He commanded the 14th Infantry Division in 1940 against the German thrust into France. In 1942 he became chief officer of the 17th Military Division in Montpellier. He was arrested in November 1942 when he attempted to resist the entry of the German army into the free zone. A French war council condemned him to a prison sentence of 10 years, but he escaped in September 1943 and joined Gen. **Henri Giraud**, who gave him the command of Army Group B in the army of **French North Africa**. He formed the First French Army, which landed at Saint-Tropez on August 16, 1944; took Toulon and Marseilles; fought northward toward Alsace; and captured Stuttgart, Ulm and Constance. On May 9, 1945 he signed the *Wehrmacht* surrender on behalf of France. He was named inspector general of the army in 1945. He died in 1952 and was posthumously named marshal of France.

LATVIA.
See **Baltic States**.

LAVAL, Pierre (1883-1945).
Former deputy of ''pacifist'' tendencies, he represented Aubervilliers between 1914 and 1919, during which time he shifted to Right Center. In the 1930s Laval served as foreign minister and was president of the *Conseil d'Etat* three times—from 1931 to 1932, again in 1932 and from June 1935 to January 1936. As minister of foreign affairs, he was a staunch anti-communist, delaying the signing of the Franco-Soviet Pact of May 2, 1935, and sought to align France with Fascist **Italy**, as evidenced by his trip to Rome in January 1935, the **Hoare**-Laval plan designed to put an end to the war in **Ethiopia** by appeasing Italy and his policy of ''encouraging the aggressor'' in December. Hostile both to the Popular Front and to the declaration of war on Germany, he encouraged the antiwar faction and in June 1940 used his politicking talents to force the armistice on France and offer full power to Marshal Petain on July 10, 1940. (See also **French State** and **Petain and the French State** for Laval's policy during the occupation.)

Condemned to death by the High Court of Justice, Laval tried to poison himself but was saved, with difficulty, only to be executed on October 9, 1945 (see **Purges**).

C. Levy

LAYCOCK, Sir Robert Edward (1907-1968).
One of the initial commando leaders, Laycock, a British general, was chief of **combined operations** from 1943 to 1947, succeeding Lord **Mountbatten**.

LEAGUE OF NATIONS.
In 1941 only Great Britain remained a permanent member of this international organization created after World War I. On April 18, 1946 the league gave way to the **United Nations**. (See also Introduction.)

LEAHY, William D. (1875-1959).
After serving as chief of naval operations for two years, Adm. Leahy retired from the U.S. Navy in 1939, but a year later he was appointed ambassador to Vichy France. In 1942 **Roosevelt** made Leahy his chief of staff and for the rest of the war he headed the Joint Chiefs of Staff. He was one of the president's closest advisers and accompanied him to the wartime conferences (see **Conferences, Allied**). He continued to serve as chief of staff under President **Truman** until 1949.

LEBANON.
A small Christian Arab state, Lebanon was separated from the Ottoman Empire after conquest by the British in 1918. In 1920 it became (following a secret Franco-British pact in 1917) a French mandate under the **League of Nations** and received a republican constitution in 1926. In 1940 the governor sided with Vichy France. In the summer of 1941, in a brief and bitter campaign, British troops supported by Free French forces conquered both **Syria** and Lebanon. The Free French took over the civil administration, promising independence soon (it was granted in 1943). Lebanon joined the **Arab League** in March 1945. From 1942 to 1945 Lebanon provided a haven where allied troops on leave from active fighting could rest and refresh themselves.

LEBRUN, Albert (1871-1950).
A French politician, Lebrun served successively as deputy, minister and senator. He was the last president of the **Third Republic** (1931-40). He was interned in 1943-44.

LECLERC (Jacques Philippe de Hauteclocque) (1902-1947).
Hauteclocque was the chief of staff for the Fourth French Division in the Ardennes in September 1939. During the German invasion in 1940, he fought in the forest of Warndt and later, from June 10 to 15, in Champagne with the Second Armored Group. After France's capitulation he responded to **de Gaulle**'s appeal on June 18, 1940 and joined him in London on July 25. He left there on August 6 for Cameroon, which he succeeded in allying with **Free France**, and organized a small military unit to detach Gabon from the Vichy government. On December 2 Leclerc, as he had begun to call himself, was appointed military commander of Chad; from there he led two expeditions that were to enhance the renown of Free France—the capture of Koufra in **Libya**, on March 1, 1941, and the raid on Fezzan, which lasted from February 27 to March 14, 1942. By then a brigadier general, he organized the defense of Tibesti; he then left on December 16, 1942, with 3,000 men and a badly depleted store of materiel, to conquer Fezzan, then Oum el Araneb on January 4, 1943 and Ghadames on January 26; from there he went on to join **Montgomery**'s army in Tripoli. He operated in Tunisia at the head of Force L and knit the *Forces francaises libres* volunteers and the North African troops of the Armistice Army into a cohesive organization. He later took command of the 18,000 men of the Second Armored Division, equipped and motorized by the U.S. Army, in England in April-May 1944. Landing in Normandy on July 31, 1944, he led the Second Armored Division in the capture of Le Mans on August 9 and Alencon two days later. After the fighting at Ecouche on the following day, he launched a drive toward Paris, then in the grip of rebellion, to aid the **Resistance** and force the surrender of Gen. **Dietrich von Choltitz** on August 25. As part of the American Third Army under the command of Gen. **Omar Bradley**, he led his troops in hard fighting in eastern France from September to November 1944, taking Strasbourg on November 25. In the spring of 1945 Leclerc resumed pursuit of the enemy as far as Berchtesgaden, **Hitler**'s mountain retreat, which he captured on May 5, 1945.

Leclerc was the symbol of the French army's rebirth. His bravery, his spectacular victories in Africa, the liberation of Paris and Strasbourg and the capture of Hitler's hideaway made him a legendary hero. Just before his death in an airplane crash on November 28, 1947, he was made a marshal of France.

E. Pognon

LEEB, Wilhelm von (1876-1956).
In 1939-40 Leeb was commander of Army Group C in the west. In July 1940 **Hitler** promoted Leeb to field marshal for his role in the defeat of the French at

Alsace-Lorraine. In the invasion of the **USSR**, he led Army Group North. He was relieved of his command on January 16, 1942 and expelled from the army in 1944.

LEGION DES VOLONTAIRES FRANCAIS CONTRE LE BOLCHEVISME (LVF).

In English, "Legion of French Volunteers Against Bolshevism." This organization, founded in July 1942, received its insignia from **Laval**, who on that occasion was the target of an attempted assassination. It fought on the Russian front and was decimated. In October 1944 it became the nucleus of the **Charlemagne** Brigade under the **SS**.

LEGION FRANCAISE DES COMBATTANTS.

In English, "French Veterans' Legion." This organization was created by Marshal Petain in August 1940 to weld into a single group the veterans of both world wars as the moral support and inspiration of the national revolution. Banned by the Germans in the occupied zone, it was considerably influential in the free zone, often to the detriment of the mayors of municipal councils. **Joseph Darnand** combined this organization with the *Service d'ordre legionnaire*, a paramilitary brigade devoted to **collaboration** with Nazi **Germany** and later to be organized into the French *Milice* and the *Francs-Gardes*.

LEIGH-MALLORY, Sir Trafford Leigh (1892-1944).

A British airman, Leigh-Mallory headed the 12th Fighter Group during the **Battle of Britain** in 1940, the 11th Fighter Group in 1940-42 and the **Fighter Command** in 1942-43. At the end of 1943 he was appointed to command the Allied Expeditionary Air Force during the **Normandy landing**. In that position he was in charge of 9,000 aircraft supporting the invasion. He was killed in a plane crash in November 1944.

LEND-LEASE.

On March 11, 1941, while the **United States** was still neutral, **Roosevelt** signed the Lend-Lease Act, which permitted the president to sell, lend, lease or otherwise provide services and material to a country whose defense he considered vital to the defense of the United States. The United States was to be paid or repaid in kind, or by direct or indirect gain, as the president deemed satisfactory.

Thus, the countries benefiting from these loans or services—the **United Kingdom**, its allies, later the **USSR** and **neutral countries** like **Turkey** that were threatened by the **Axis** powers—were not indebted to the United States for the full value of the goods they received as a borrower would be under normal circumstances. The intent of the act was that the conditions and the type of compensation would later be negotiated, in light of the importance of the assistance and of the general economic situation. Lend-lease, then, was far from the "cash and carry" policy of the past. The Lend-Lease Act, an important factor in the victory, saved Great Britain from imminent bankruptcy under the financial load of the war. Although the law expired on September 27, 1945, lend-lease was continued in another form by the **Truman** Doctrine, one application of which was the **Marshall** Plan.

H. Bernard

LENTZ, Robert (1885-1949).

A veteran of World War I, Lentz was called back to active service in 1939 as chief of staff of the Belgian 17th Infantry Division. After the surrender of **Belgium**, he organized officers and enlisted men for underground action, combining his movement with the Belgian Legion of **Charles Claser**. He was arrested on May 8, 1942 and in September 1943 sent to a **concentration camp**. He went through the "death march" from Oranienburg to the Schwerin Bridge, where a small group of those still alive was rescued by the Russians.

LEOPOLD III (1901-   ).

The wartime king of **Belgium**, Leopold occupied defensive positions in the field with his troops to share in their fate "come what may." His refusal to follow his ministers to France created considerable tension in his relations with them. On May 28 the Belgian army surrendered. Adm. **Roger Keyes**, the British liaison officer to the king from May 10 to May 28, later refuted **Churchill**'s accusations of **treason** on Leopold's part. Held prisoner in Belgium, the king remained politically inactive despite popular protests against German requisitions, deportation of his subjects and other acts in violation of their civil rights. He did, however, express his resentment in letters to **Hitler** and the resident military governor. The attitude of the royal entourage was frequently criticized by the **Resistance** and members of the Belgian **government-in-exile** in London.

At his request, on November 19, 1940, Leopold was received by Hitler at Berchtesgaden to discuss the situation of his people as well as the future of Belgium and the dynasty. A widower since the death of Queen Astrid in 1935, he married Liliane Baels, daughter of the governor of West Flanders, on September 11, 1941. The marriage was announced to the populace on December 6. On January 25, 1944 the king dictated his political will, to be given to Prime Minister

Hubert Pierlot after Belgium was liberated. It demanded that the ministers publicly recognize their guilt. On June 7, 1944 the king was deported to the Reich; on May 7, 1945 he was freed at Strobl by American troops. When he undertook once more to exercise his preogatives of state, he ran into the opposition of the Socialist, Liberal, Communist and Udebist parties. Leopold then retired to **Switzerland**. On March 12, 1950 a popular referendum showed 57.7 percent to be in favor of the king's return, but with a regional imbalance of 72 percent in Flanders, 48 percent in Brussels and 42 percent among the Walloons. The king returned on July 22, 1950. To appease the disturbances his reappearance aroused, he endowed Prince Baudouin with his powers, finally giving up everything except his title on July 16, 1951.

LEY, Robert (1890-1945).

In 1933 Ley, an early Nazi leader, suppressed the labor unions and replaced them with the *Deutsche Arbeitsfront* ("German Labor Front"), which included practically all of **Germany**'s manpower. He also founded the *Kraft durch Freude* ("Strength Through Joy") organization. During the war he organized the recruitment of laborers from territories occupied by the Reich, at first on a voluntary basis and then by force. In 1945 he was in command of the **Adolf Hitler** corps of volunteer soldiers. Arrested by the Allies, he hanged himself in his cell at Nuremberg, leaving a letter in which he recommended the reconciliation of Germans and Jews (see also **War Criminals**).

LEYTE.
Allied Progress Toward the Philippines Between February 1943 and October 1944

After February 1943, when all Japanese resistance ceased at **Guadalcanal**, the initiative never returned to the empire's forces. The American occupiers would spend the first seven months of 1944 building up the island of Guadalcanal as a staging base. While materiel accumulated in the embarcation area, they continued to improve their positions in the South Pacific. At the end of 1942, Australian troops moving through the jungles of **New Guinea** had taken Gona and Buna. Between March 1 and 3, 1943, American and Australian aircraft destroyed a **convoy** of eight enemy supply transports in the Bismarck Sea, escorted by destroyers and bound for Lae and Salamaua. Heavy aerial fighting involved both sides around Rabaul from April to July.

On the Allied side, Gen. **Douglas MacArthur** was in command of the South Pacific theater and Adm. **Chester Nimitz** of the Central Pacific. On March 28 the Third Fleet of Vice Adm. **William "Bull" Halsey**, operating in the Solomon Islands, which had pre-

viously been under Nimitz's command, passed temporarily into MacArthur's domain. Halsey's fleet included the aircraft carriers *Enterprise* and *Saratoga*, two escort carriers and a protective complement and the Third Amphibious Force under Rear Adm. Richmond K. Turner. MacArthur's Seventh Amphibious Force contained five Australian divisions in addition to three American divisions, which were commanded by Gen. **Walter Krueger**.

The Allied naval successes of the first days in March provided MacArthur with broader freedom of action at sea, thus sparing his troops the trials of jungle marches. During the summer the Allies captured New Georgia and the air base of Munda.

At the beginning of September, MacArthur began an attack on the fortified zone of Salamaua, defended by the Japanese 18th Army, which included three divisions. The Third Australian Division, reinforced by an American division arriving by sea, completed the encirclement of Salamaua. On September 4, while fighting in the zone still continued, the Australian Ninth Division landed east of Lae. Almost simultaneously, supported by aircraft and under cover of a smoke screen, 1,700 paratroopers from the 11th Airborne Division landed near the Nadzab air base, about 20 miles northwest of Lae. The capture of this base permitted the arrival by air of the Australian Seventh Division, which had taken off from Port Moresby. Lae fell under the convergence of the Seventh Division and the forces that had landed to the east of the city. All resistance in Salamaua had ceased five days before.

At the other extreme of the immense front, in the Aleutian Islands, American and Canadian forces recaptured the islands of Attu and Agattu in the spring of 1943. These prizes had been taken by the Japanese the year before and were indispensable to the Allies for the planned converging air attack. In August the Japanese evacuated the Aleutian island of Kiska as well.

Supplies could now arrive in quantity. Rather than trying to take the islands one by one, wasting time and effort, the Allies thrust toward **Japan** with combined power, attempting to capture only those points necessary for the establishment of bases and airports and neutralizing or simply ignoring islands of no immediate importance, which might contain hundreds of thousands of isolated defenders. Already revealed at Casablanca in January 1943, the broad outlines of the operations were confirmed at the "Quadrant" Conference in Quebec in August 1943 (see **Conferences, Allied**). In **Burma** Adm. **Mountbatten**'s forces took the offensive with the aim of reopening the supply route to **China**. In the South Pacific, forces from the **United States**, **Australia** and **New Zealand**, led by

MacArthur, continued their penetration of New Guinea, the Solomon and Bismarck Islands and beyond, in preparation for a thrust at the **Philippines** in the fall of 1944. In the Central Pacific, Adm. Nimitz's forces pressed on toward the Marshall, Mariana and **Gilbert Islands** and toward the Philippines, in anticipation of a concerted attack, with MacArthur, on that archipelago.

The **strategy** of the Allied command was to force the Japanese navy to accept battle. Once in Allied hands, the Marianas could serve as bases for B-29 strategic bombers within range of Japan itself. The military problems arising in the Pacific were more complex than those in Europe, where the British Isles themselves were, in effect, natural aircraft carriers. Land bases in the Pacific, however, were often thousands of miles from the objective, a distance that exceeded the range of most bombers. Hence the development of aircraft carriers and the essential functions of the "**task force**," a self-sufficient, flexible, powerful and fast-moving unit. The vast range of its **reconnaissance** aircraft contributed considerably to the task force's freedom of action, as did its ability to concentrate the power of its individual components on a single target far enough from the original base to serve as a "stepping stone" for an attack on still another potential base. The task force was capable, too, of creating diversions, neutralizing enemy bases, covering troop landings and defending against enemy raids.

From Lae to the Philippines, MacArthur had to cover nearly 2,250 miles. Nimitz' first objective was some 2,500 miles from his home base, and his ultimate goal, the Ryukyu Islands, was some 5,450 miles away. To complicate the situation further, MacArthur's point of departure was 4,000 miles from Nimitz'. Nevertheless, cooperation between the two was secure. The Japanese defenders, on the other hand, were established along a primary front line marked by **Wake Island**, the Marshall Islands, the Gilberts, the Bismarcks, and western New Guinea, with their secondary line of defense based on the Bonin Islands, the Marianas, Yap, the Palaus, Morotai and **Timor**. The keystone of the first line of defense, its air-naval center of gravity, was the island of Truk.

Beginning in October 1943 the Allies initiated the action leading to the convergence on the Philippines. MacArthur established two axes for the operations in the South Pacific—the first in New Guinea under Gen. Krueger, the second in the Solomon Islands under Adm. Halsey. Krueger took Finschhafen on October 2, 1943, and followed it up with the capture of Aitape and Hollandia, with its numerous airfields, in April 1944, Biak shortly afterwards and Sansapor in

July. In Halsey's zone, a detachment from New Zealand overran the island of Vella Lavella in September. The Treasury Islands fell in October. On November 1 the American Third Marine Division landed on **Bougainville**. These conquests put airfields capable of handling fighter planes in the hands of the Allies less than 200 miles from Rabaul, the large base in New Britain held by 60,000 Japanese soldiers and a heavy concentration of aircraft. In addition to these conquests, the landings on the Green and St. Matthias Islands as well as on the western part of New Britain completed the isolation of Rabaul. MacArthur had covered a stretch of 1,500 miles in 10 months and completely cut the supply routes of 135,000 Japanese in New Guinea and the southern islands. The Caroline Islands were blockaded by Nimitz on the north and MacArthur on the south, working closely together, despite the great distances separating them, to tighten the noose around the enemy and narrow his maneuverability. That action isolated another 100,000 Japanese.

The air-naval war conducted by Nimitz was electrifying, not only for the immense area in which he deployed his forces—the Seventh Air Force under his command patrolled a patch of the Pacific five times the area of continental United States—but also for the defensive power of the Japanese bases caught in his net, the bases of Jaluit, Ponape (Ascension), **Saipan** and the Bonins, which had been part of the Empire of the Rising Sun and had been continually fortified since before the war began. This was the greatest achievement of the **combined operations** of the two American chiefs. Their task forces amply demonstrated their flexibility and strength. In November 1943, the islands of Tarawa and Makin in the Gilbert group were captured; a month later, they were equipped with four airfields. Majuro, Kwajalein and Eniwetok in the Marshalls were taken in February 1944. To the amazement of the Japanese, Wake Island and the Carolines were simply bypassed. On June 15 the Marianas came under attack. A defending Japanese fleet was badly defeated, and the garrison of two large units on Saipan was assaulted by the Second and Fourth Marine Divisions, followed by the 27th Division. After 20 days of fierce fighting, the island succumbed; 26,000 Japanese were killed and 1,800 taken prisoner, while 3,500 Americans were killed and four times as many wounded. Nimitz's capture of Saipan, Tinian and **Guam** marked nearly 3,750 miles covered in nine months. The high price paid for the conquest of Saipan was not spent in vain; from it, B-29s could easily reach the heart of the Japanese Empire and return.

The Philippines, defended by 350,000 Japanese, the last obstacle in the path to Japan herself, were

MacArthur's and Nimitz's Offensives Toward Japan, November 1943-August 1945

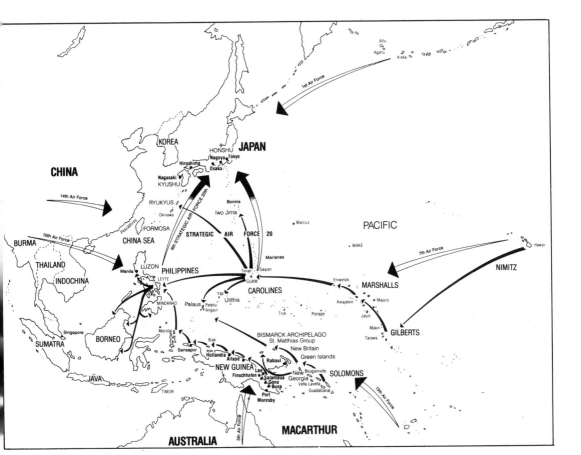

now the focal point of Nimitz's and MacArthur's power. A secure grasp on this far-flung archipelago was required for the final assault on the empire's home islands. The Philippines were to become the natural aircraft carriers from which Japanese communications lines in the China Sea could be destroyed. In the meantime, British, Indian, American and Chinese forces under Mountbatten were going ahead with the offensive they had begun in Burma at the end of 1943.

By September, Morotai was in MacArthur's possession, while Nimitz took the islands of Peleliu and Angaur in the Palau chain as well as the Ulithi Islands, to protect the flank of the offensive on the island of Leyte. At the same time the 11th Air Force, from Alaska, the Seventh Air Force, from Nimitz's group and the Fifth and 13th, from MacArthur's, converged on the enemy in continuous waves.

Before the attack on Leyte, American bombers had inflicted heavy damage to the air bases on **Okinawa** and **Luzon** and, between October 12 and 13, on Formosa. This last pass provoked the greatest air battle in history, between American planes based on aircraft carriers and Japanese aircraft based on the home islands, the Ryukyus and Formosa. For the 110 American planes lost in that epic struggle, the Japanese squandered 660. These losses were to prove fatal to the defenders of Leyte, the next goal of the Allies in their march toward the Japanese heartland.

The American Landing on Leyte and the Japanese Counteroffensive

MacArthur and Nimitz successfully combined their forces on Leyte in October 1944. For about a year they continually kept pushing ahead, enclosing hundreds of thousands of Japanese troops in pincer movements, maneuvering ceaselessly and attacking simultaneously with increasingly powerful blows as their lines of communications lengthened. The Japanese command had been caught napping. Completely unaware that the American attack was bearing on Leyte, they had deplored six divisions in Mindanao, five in Luzon and only four spread between Leyte and Cebu. Misled by a furious American air bombardment of Luzon, they believed that this largest island of the Philippine group would surely be the landing point of American troops, rather than the much smaller Leyte. But it was Leyte, defended by only one Japanese division, where Krueger's Sixth Army came ashore.

The American fleet was divided into two groups. The task force commanded by Marc A. Mitscher, which was part of the Third Fleet, included six battleships, 16 aircraft carriers, 15 cruisers and 58 destroyers. Its mission was to protect the landing troops by warding off enemy attacks from air or sea. The Seventh Fleet, commanded by Thomas Kinkaid, included a support squadron under the command of Jesse B. Oldendorf and an escort aircraft carrier squadron under Thomas L. Sprague. The total power of the fleet, including several Australian units, amounted to six old battleships, four heavy cruisers, four light cruisers, 18 small escort carriers and 60 destroyers. Its function was to provide direct support to the landing parties.

At dawn on October 20, the troops landed under Kinkaid's naval barrage blasting enemy positions. This time the hesitant Japanese commanders gambled their fleet to save the Philippines by breaking past the American ships and landing reinforcements for the defending garrison on the island. On that same day four Japanese squadrons headed for Leyte's waters. Jisaburo Ozawa's group, drawn from patrol duty around the Japanese home islands, included two mixed cruisers—which combined the functions of a battleship and an aircraft carrier—one heavy aircraft carrier, three escort carriers, three cruisers and eight destroyers. Takeo Kurita's group, coming from **Singapore**, had five battleships—including the powerful *Yamato* and *Musashi*, 18,000 tons heavier than the biggest American ships, whose superior fire power was supplied by nine 457-mm naval rifles and 140 antiaircraft guns—10 heavy cruisers, two light cruisers and 15 destroyers. Shoji Nishimura's group, also from Singapore and also under Kurita's command, had two battleships, one heavy cruiser and four destroyers. Finally, Adm. Kiyohide Shima's group arriving from the Pescadores Islands just west of Formosa included one light cruiser and four destroyers.

On October 23 the Japanese navy was reinforced by the Second Air Fleet with 450 planes. These had been sent to Luzon to join 250 army planes. To these surface and air fleets were added the Japanese subsurface fighters—the submarine fleet based on the Philippines.

Adm. **Soemu Toyoda**, in command of this Japanese array, first used Ozawa's group to attack the American fleet, attempting to draw it away from the landing zone. Kurita's group was then to pass through the San Bernardino Straits while Nishimura's group moved through the Surigao Strait; both units were then to attack the fleet supporting the disembarking American troops. Kurita, who had no aircraft carriers, was to get help from the air fleets based on Luzon. Shima was to take his naval group through the Surigao Straits a few hours after Nishimura; his mission was to sink all the American troop transports after the more heavily armed groups ahead of him had destroyed the American fighting ships. Thus, with the Leyte bridgeheads sealed off, the American invading force on the island could be cut up at leisure.

This strategy of moving separately and attacking in force might have succeeded if the Americans had reacted as Toyoda expected them to. They did not; the separately-deployed columns were not given time to join forces but were attacked singly, in raids in which submarines, aircraft and the new weapon of **radar** were all utilized. Perhaps the chief reason for the Japanese defeat, however, was the fact that Adm. Toyoda, commander in chief of the operation, directed the battle from his offices in Tokyo, while the American command coordinated operations locally, with all the threads of communication securely in its grasp.

Kurita's powerful battleships had no air umbrella. Beginning on the 23rd they were attacked by the American submarines *Darter* and *Dace*, which patrolled the passage to the south of Mindoro. Kurita lost two cruisers, one of which was the flagship, in the Sibuyan Sea. The next day at 6:00 a.m., Mitscher's task force loosed its aircraft to search out and destroy the enemy. They spotted Nishimura's and Shima's squadrons and hit the battleship *Musashi*, which until then had been kept out of action, with 21 torpedoes. The huge vessel was swallowed by the waves. A heavy cruiser was damaged in that fight. In the afternoon Kurita lost heart as a result of the poor coordination between the navy and the army flyers and turned back in his wake. This retreat was signaled to Adm. Halsey, who was also informed of the approach of Ozawa's aircraft carriers. This information, plus the unduly optimistic American pilots' reports of the damage to Kurita's ships, led Halsey to drive north with the entire Third Fleet and challenge Ozawa; in doing so, he left unprotected the San Bernardino Strait and the flank of the Leyte bridgehead. This slip was perhaps the consequence of the split in command between the

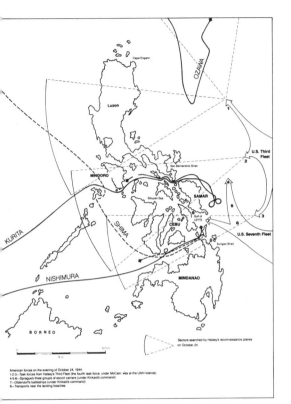

American forces on the evening of October 24, 1944.
1-2-3—Task forces from Halsey's Third Fleet (the fourth task force, under McCain, was at the Ulithi Islands)
4-5-6—Sprague's three groups of escort carriers (under Kinkaid's command)
7—Oldendorf's battleships (under Kinkaid's command)
8—Transports near the landing beaches

Third Fleet, under Nimitz's orders, and the Seventh Fleet, under MacArthur's. But the Japanese suffered from the same disease in an even more virulent form; the single battle that Tokyo had planned for turned out to be three isolated battles fought simultaneously on October 25, 1944.

The battle of the Surigao Strait

At 2:00 a.m. on October 25, Nishimura led his squadron into the Surigao Strait. Oldendorf's ships blocked his path. The American vessels were deployed in depth, with the fast torpedo boats in front, then the destroyers concealed in the coastal folds and finally six old battleships strung across the narrows. Assailed first by torpedoes, Nishimura rushed into the wily Oldendorf's trap. The American ships' radar-controlled guns opened fire at a range of nearly 12 miles. At 4:30, after two hours of fighting in almost complete darkness, Nishimura's fleet was wiped out, with only one torpedo boat still on the surface. The Americans had lost just one speedboat.

But Oldendorf's radar screen showed blips, indicating an enemy presence elsewhere. This was Shima's

flotilla, trailing Nishimura's squadron, according to Toyoda's plan, into the Surigao Strait. Adm. Shima, however, was under Tokyo's direct orders, while Nishimura had been under Kurita's command. There had been no liaison between the two before the battle. Although he was only 50 miles behind his fellow admiral, Shima had no knowledge of the disaster that had just befallen Nishimura, and ran into Oldendorf's ships. He made a swift retreat, but not until he had lost his light cruiser and two destroyers.

The battle of Cape Engano

During the night of October 24-25, as we have seen, Halsey left Leyte with Mitscher's task force to battle Ozawa. The morning of the 25th a cloud of American planes attacked the enemy ships 100 miles east of Cape Engano. Ozawa's pilots were inexperienced; a good many of them who had taken off the night before had to go back to Luzon to land because they were not sufficiently trained to land on a carrier flight deck in a heaving sea. Ozawa was further handicapped by poor radiomen. He steamed north to entice Halsey away from Kurita.

In the meantime, Adm. Kinkaid was sending desperate calls for help. His opposite number, Kurita, had entered San Bernardino Strait and was advancing into the Leyte Gulf. At 11:00 a.m. Halsey changed his plan, deciding to return south with battleships borrowed from Mitscher's task force while Mitscher continued northward after Ozawa with only two groups of aircraft carriers. This could have resulted in the sacrifice of the task force, but Halsey was betting on the superiority of the American fighter pilots.

Left to himself, Mitscher engaged Ozawa and continued to pour destructive fire on the Japanese. Ozawa's four aircraft carriers were sent to the bottom, along with a cruiser and three torpedo boats. The Japanese admiral limped back to his home base with the remnants of his fleet, but he had accomplished his mission. When Halsey turned south on October 25, he radioed Kinkaid that he could not reach their rendezvous until the following morning at 8:00.

The battle of Samar

In an attempt to make up for the six-hour delay caused by his abrupt retreat, Kurita and his fleet rounded Cape Engano eastward and sped at 20 knots through narrow channels along the coast of Luzon during the night, in a brilliant demonstration of seamanship. He seemed to be shaping a victory. With no information to the contrary at dawn on the 25th, Adm. Kinkaid was under the impression that Halsey still guarded the San Bernardino Strait. Oldendorf at that moment had ended the battle of the Surigao Strait; Kinkaid's fleet of aircraft carriers was divided into three groups 120 miles east of Samar and Leyte. These carriers, actually refitted merchant vessels protected by destroyers, should have been easy prey for Kurita. If he decided to attack, they would be unable to flee. Laboring through the seas at a maximum speed of 17 knots, they could hardly hope to outrun a Japanese ship capable of 30 knots. The superbattleship *Yamato* opened fire at a range of 15 miles. For the only time in naval history, ships were under fire from 457-mm guns.

At 6:58 a.m. on October 25, the northern group of six escort carriers and seven destroyers took the opening salvos from the *Yamato*'s guns. The planes took off from their flight decks in spite of them. As the Japanese ships approached, the northern group retired behind a smoke screen. The American destroyers opened fire, sacrificing themselves to delay the enemy fleet. Three of them were sunk. An escort carrier also went down, its aircraft maneuvering capably although they were designed primarily for supporting landing troops rather than for attacking naval vessels.

But then a startling development occurred at 9:25 a.m. Kurita, no more than two hours away from the landing beaches, turned north once again. The reasons for this unexpected retreat are still obscure. Had the damage caused some of his ships to reduce their speed? Had they scattered to the point where radio communication was difficult and air protection nonexistent? Did Kurita think Halsey's squadron was 250 miles further south than it actually was? Or did he fear Oldendorf's battleships, which only hours before had ended their fighting in Surigao and were now out of ammunition—a fact Kurita obviously could not have known? Whatever his motives, he missed a golden oppourtunity and the trapped Kinkaid miraculously escaped disaster.

Pursued by enemy aircraft, Kurita suffered more losses in his retreat. The task group commanded by John S. McCain, in Halsey's fleet, had come to Kinkaid's assistance. At 1:10 p.m. its planes assaulted the Japanese ships. Later in the afternoon the Japanese admiral once again passed through the San Bernardino Strait before Halsey's fleet could intercept him. Leaving their land base that same day, some **Kamikaze** pilots destroyed the escort carrier *Saint Lo*. The following day, U.S. Army and Navy planes again subjected Kurita to a terrible bombing that cost him three cruisers and damaged the great ship *Yamato*. More fortunate than his colleagues, the Japanese admiral managed to save a good part of his fleet.

By the evening of the 26th, at the close of the greatest air-naval battle in history, the Japanese had lost three battleships, four aircraft carriers, 10 cruisers, nine destroyers and one submarine. American losses were only one light carrier, two escort carriers, three destroyers, one torpedo boat and one submarine. The victory could have been even more decisive if a single naval command had coordinated Halsey's and Kinkaid's activities and seen to it that the San Bernardino Strait remained sealed to the enemy. In any event, after this battle the Japanese fleet ceased to exist as a powerful and organized force. There were no further encounters between suface fleets, and never again was any landing beach threatened from the rear by a hostile fleet or by aircraft from a carrier.

After Leyte

After Japan lost the Battle of Leyte, its final agony commenced. The Philippines were gone. So were other strategically vital points: **Borneo, Iwo Jima** and Okinawa, which fell after a long and bloody battle, lasting from April 1 to June 21, 1945. Allied bombers struck repeatedly at the heart of Japan (see **Japan, Air War Against**). On July 24 a British squadron under Adm. Bernard H. Rawlings launched a murderous air-naval offensive against Nagoya, Osaka and Nagasaki. A total **blockade** was thrown around the home islands. Cities flamed, munitions dumps exploded and nothing remained of the Japanese fleet. Yet there were well-preserved aircraft in the country that had not been used; they were held in reserve against an enemy landing. In the home islands, in China, in Southeast Asia and in the islands by-passed by MacArthur and Nimitz, the Japanese land forces still numbered five million men.

The Allied landings were set for November 1, 1945 on the island of Kyushu and for March 1, 1946 on the island of Honshu. But after the **atomic bombs** were dropped on Hiroshima and Nagasaki, Japan surrendered on August 14, 1945.

H. Bernard

LIBYA.

Italy conquered Libya in 1911-12, driving out the occupying forces of **Turkey**. By 1939 the colony had a population of nearly 900,000, of whom 95,000 were Europeans, who lived in the coastal towns. Two of these were sizable: Tripoli with over 100,000 people and Benghazi, only half as large. The coastal zone was indeed declared, in January 1939, to be a part of Italian national territory. South of that zone lay cultivable steppe, which Italian colonists started to occupy, and south of that, a sand desert scattered with oases. In and across that desert the bulk of the population lived as nomads—camel-borne bedouin.

Libya provided an almost bare stage across which in 1940-43 German, Italian and British imperial troops (and a few anti-fascist units in exile) marched and countermarched as fast as the terrain, the presence of enemies, and the lack of water and gasoline allowed (see **Mediterranean and Middle Eastern Theaters of Operations; Long-Range Desert Group**). Although gasoline was seldom far from any fighting man's mind during these campaigns, at the time Libya's vast petroleum reserves were still undiscovered.

LIDDELL HART, Sir Basil (1895-1970).
British military theorist and historian, Liddell Hart conceived the **tactic** of an "expanding torrent" attack, as opposed to the static warfare that had characterized the fighting on the Western Front in 1917-18. Although for many years he remained a prophet crying unheeded in his own country, he was carefully read by the German military; Gen. **Heinz Guderian** called him "the inventor of modern tank warfare." His advocacy of mechanized forces and air power to penetrate deep into enemy territory was implemented by the Germans in their **Blitzkrieg**.

LIDICE.
This village near Kladno, in Bohemia, **Czechoslovakia**, was destroyed on June 10, 1942 in reprisal for the assassination of Nazi official **Reinhard Heydrich**. All males of the village over the age of 16 were shot, the children were deported to a **concentration camp** at Gneisenau and the women were imprisoned at Ravensbrueck. Lidice became the symbol of the criminal acts of revenge committed by the Nazi regime in World War II (see **Bohemia-Moravia**).

LIE, Trygve Halvdan (1896-1968).
A Norwegian diplomat, Lie served as foreign minister of **Norway**'s **government-in-exile** (1940-45) and secured Norwegian shipping for Allied use. Lie was secretary-general of the **United Nations** from 1946 to 1953.

LIGHTFOOT.
Code name for **Montgomery**'s offensive against **Rommel** at **El Alamein** in October 1942 (see **Mediterranean and Middle Eastern Theater of Operations**).

LINDEMANN, Frederick Alexander (later Lord Cherwell) (1886-1957).
Beginning in 1921 Lindemann was **Churchill**'s lifelong friend and scientific adviser. He advised the prime minister on such matters as bombing effectiveness and supply needs and backed original research and projects like the bending of German navigational beams. However, his recommendation of aerial bombardment of German cities was carried out with questionable results. Lindemann was variously regarded as Churchill's inspiration and his evil genius.

LINGE, Martin Jensen (1894-1941).
A Norwegian actor and military officer, Linge fought in the south of **Norway** in April 1940 and then escaped to England. He participated in the raid on the Lofoten Islands in March 1941 and Nordfjord, where he was killed on December 27, 1941.

LIST, Wilhelm (1880-1970).
In 1940 List was promoted to field marshal for his role in commanding the 14th Army in the German invasion of **Poland**. A year later he led the 12th Army in France, where he used infantry in support of armored troops. In 1941 he invaded the Balkans and conquered **Greece** after the Italian defeats there. He was given command of Army Group A on the Russian front in 1941 but dismissed from his post in September 1942. Although condemned to life imprisonment by the Nuremberg tribunal in 1948, he was freed in 1952 (see **War Criminals**).

LITHUANIA.
See **Baltic States**.

LITVINOV, Maxim (1876-1951).
As Soviet minister of foreign affairs from 1930 to 1939, Litvinov pursued a policy of friendly cooperation with the Western democracies until he was replaced by **Molotov**. He was a member of the Central Committee of the Communist Party of the **USSR** until 1941. From 1941 to 1946 Litvinov was vice-commissar for foreign affairs, and from 1941 to 1943 he was the Soviet ambassador to Washington.

LOEHR, Alexander (1885-1947).
Following the *Anschluss*, Loehr, an Austrian air officer, became a general in the *Luftwaffe* and commander of the Fourth Air Fleet, which he led in **Poland**, the Balkans and the **USSR**. In 1944 he was commander in chief of Army Group E in the Balkans. He was executed by the Yugoslavians as a **war criminal**.

LOGISTICS.
The theory and practice of providing **food**, evacuation facilities, hospitalization, medical supplies and transportation to military positions over large distances. Its purpose is to furnish personnel and materiel adequate in quality and quanity to the proper point and in sufficient time.

LOHSE, Heinrich (1896-1964).
From 1941 to 1944 Lohse was responsible for the Nazi occupation policy in the Balkans and Belorussia. He held the ranks of *Gauleiter* and *Reichskommissar* for the "countries of the east."

LONGMORE, Sir Arthur Murray (1885-1970).

During World War I Longmore served in the British navy. He was commander in chief of the **Royal Air Force** in the Middle East in 1940-41 and RAF inspector-general from 1941 to 1942, when he retired.

LONG-RANGE DESERT GROUP.

This British irregular unit was formed in June 1940 in **Egypt** by R. A. Bagnold for operations in the Western Desert. Made up largely of New Zealanders, the volunteers-only group led a life that was extremely tough and lonely, but rewarding. The group's tasks were to reconnoiter far west of the main fighting lines and report on enemy movements and dispositions. Sometimes a traffic count on the only main road, parallel with the coast, was kept for weeks on end from a hiding place nearby. The information, sent back immediately by wireless if necessary, was invaluable to the British Eighth Army right through to March 1943, when the group discovered that the right of the Mareth Line in Tunisia could be turned.

The group was organized in a dozen truck-borne patrols, with 10 trucks to a patrol and about a half dozen men to a truck. Its **tactics** and administration were fluid and successful. Over 50 of its members were decorated for gallantry, and only 16 were killed. Considering its size, it exercised a wholly disproportionate influence on the desert war.

LUBLIN COMMITTEE.

The Polish Committee for National Liberation was created in Chelm on July 21, 1944 and transferred to Lublin on July 25. It was the nucleus of **Poland's** Communist government of 1944-45. On July 22, 1944 it created the Polish People's Army, combining the Polish Army formed in 1943 in the USSR and the clandestine People's Army founded in 1942 under the name People's Guard by the Polish Workers' Party and changed in 1944 to People's Army.

LUFTWAFFE.

The German air force (see **Britain, Battle of; Germany, Air Battle of; Aircraft—Characteristics**).

LUXEMBOURG.

The neutrality of this little country, which had neither an army nor a navy, was guaranteed by the signatories to the Treaty of London in 1867. It was nevertheless invaded twice by German armed forces within one generation. During World War I many of its inhabitants enlisted in the French and Belgian armies and later in the American Army.

On May 10, 1940, after the second invasion, the royal family and the government left the country and later went to England, thus making known their desire to remain in the Allied camp. The Luxembourgers, whose national language is German, were fanatically anti-German and refused to "surrender their souls."

With expansive **propaganda**, the Nazi area commander announced that a census would be held on October 10, 1941; Luxembourgers would be expected to sign a clause amounting to a pledge of allegiance to **Germany**. The **underground** press immediately began its own propaganda campaign against it. Overwhelmed by the practically unanimous negative response of Luxembourg's citizens to its annexation by **Hitler**, the area commander was forced to rescind the census. This, however, did not prevent the Nazis from pressing the country's youth into the *Arbeitsdienst*—the labor service—and later into the *Wehrmacht*.

When the order for obligatory military service was made official on August 30, 1942, strikes broke out in the factories and the country's economy was partially paralyzed. A spontaneous rebellion sprang up among other groups throughout the country—merchants, artisans, bureaucrats and students—who defied the Germans publicly in the cities. Many peasants in the countryside refused to supply the occupation troops with produce.

Suppression was brutal. In less than 48 hours a summary court condemned to death 21 patriots chosen at random. They were immediately executed. Hundreds of Luxembourgers arrested in the days that followed were hauled off to **concentration camps**.

Despite the cruelty of the Germans, the spirit of the oppressed little country remained unconquerable and its will to resist firm, as evidenced by the widespread upsurge of protest in the period of the industrial strikes. The movement for self-defense among the Luxembourgers was to bear fruit. The Germans could not go back on their decision to enlist the youth by force, but they understood that they could never count on the Luxembourgers' loyalty. Nevertheless, 11,168 young men from the duchy were pressed into military service. The dilemma posed for them was horrible. If they attempted to hide, their families were punished by the Germans; to surrender themselves meekly meant likely death on the Russian front, which was to claim 2,848 dead or missing. Many of the impressed youth were shot for desertion. In the prison of Sonnenburg—now Slonsk, in **Poland**—the killers of the Frankfurt-an-der-Oder **SD** engaged in a bloody orgy on the night of January 31, 1945. Of the 819 prisoners massacred, 89 were Luxembourgers forced into the ranks of the German army.

By the thousands the youngsters found individual or collective hideouts or escaped to French or Belgian **Resistance** units. Some managed to cross the Channel to England. Clandestine espionage nets developed.

Agents from Luxembourg often attached themselves to Belgian underground groups. Other patriots concealed **prisoners of war** who had escaped from Germany. Not one of these was denounced to the Nazi police, as a report based on the testimony of these escapees indicated. Hundreds of French and Belgian citizens passing through the tiny country were helped by its people despite the consequent risks. For Allied pilots parachuting from planes shot down by the Germans, Luxembourg became an important link in the secret British chain responsible for their return to duty. Expert guides smuggled the escapees into **Belgium**, from where they were taken across France and **Spain** to return to England by way of **Gibraltar** or Lisbon.

In the **United Kingdom** a small unit of Luxembourgers was organized within the first Belgian "Liberation" brigade to fight on western battlefields. A military mission of the Allied command liaison officers was headed by the Prince Consort, Felix of Luxembourg, and the Prince Royal, Jean, served in the Irish Guards. Luxembourgers fought in the **Royal Air Force** and the Royal Navy as well as in French and American units. Several were agents parachuting into occupied territories for the **Special Operations Executive** or the **Special Intelligence Service**. Luxembourg paid its share of the war costs with 5,259 deaths out of a total population of 293,000, or 1.8 percent.

On September 10, 1944, American troops crossed into Luxembourg. The country was still to undergo some painful times during the **Battle of the Bulge**, which began on December 16. By mid-February 1945, however, it was completely liberated.

It was not only the final offensive of the Germans that seared Luxembourg. In the course of military operations along the length of the Moselle and the Sure rivers, a good part of the frontier region had become a shambles. These, in addition to the ruins created in May and June 1940 by the artillery on the **Maginot Line**, ravaged more than one-quarter of the total real estate on which structures were built in the country. At the beginning of the war, thousands of the inhabitants of the southern part of Luxembourg were evacuated to the central and northern areas. Another 45,000 people, it has been estimated, took refuge in France. At the end of hostilities, part of the Ardennes population, cut off from their countrymen by the German advance, were accepted by Belgium.

Between September 10, 1944 and December 31, 1972, the Grand Ducal government disbursed almost 10 billion francs in compensation for bodily and material damage to Luxembourgers during the war, the equivalent of the entire national budget for 1969.

H. Bernard and H. Koch-Kent

LVF.
See *Legion des Volontaires Francais contre le Bolchevisme*.

LYTTELTON, Oliver (later Lord Chandos) (1893-1972).
From 1915 to 1918 Lyttelton served in the Grenadier Guards. He was controller of nonferrous metals (1930-40) and president of the Board of Trade (1940-41). After a brief term as minister resident in Cairo (1941-42), he became minister of **production** (1942-45) and cochairman of the Anglo-American Production and Resources Board. He combined aristocratic charm and courage with a sound business sense.

M

MacARTHUR, Douglas (1880-1964).

American general. MacArthur commanded a division in France in 1918 and then became superintendent of West Point until 1922. Thereafter he held commands in the **Philippines** until 1930, when he was named Army chief of staff. In 1935 he stepped down and two years later retired, but he was recalled in 1941 to assume command of U.S. Army forces in the Far East. He moved to **Australia** in March 1942 as commander of the Allied forces in the southwestern Pacific. He reconquered **New Guinea** (1943-44) and the Philippines (1944-45). MacArthur received **Japan**'s surrender on September 2, 1945 and was made Supreme Allied Commander of occupied Japan. During the Korean War he led U.S. and **United Nations** forces in 1950-51, until he was relieved of his command by President **Truman**.

McAULIFFE, Anthony C. (1898-1975).

In the defense of Bastogne against the Germans, Gen. McAuliffe, as temporary commander of the encircled 101st Airborne Division, fought on stubbornly from December 18, 1944 until his unit was rescued on December 26. His answer to the Germans' demand for surrender, which has since become legendary, was the single word "Nuts!" (see **Battle of the Bulge**). As commander of the 103rd Division he joined the Allied forces advancing from **Italy** at a point near the Brenner Pass on May 4, 1945.

McCREERY, Sir Richard (1898-1967).

After service in France in World War I, McCreery, a British cavalry general, returned with the British Expeditionary Force in 1940. Two years later he became chief of the general staff in the Middle East and in 1944-45 commander of the British Eighth Army in Italy. After the war he commanded occupation forces in Austria in 1945-46 and on the Rhine in 1946-48.

McLEOD, Sir Roderick W. (1905-   ).

In 1944-45 McLeod, a British officer, commanded the **Special Air Service**.

MACMILLAN, (Maurice) Harold (1894-   ).

A British politician, Macmillan was in the army during World War I. As a progressive conservative, he served in Parliament from 1924 to 1929 and from 1931 to 1964. Macmillan was a junior minister in 1940-42 and minister resident in Algiers from 1942 to 1945. He took part in political settlements throughout the Mediterranean. From 1957 to 1963 he was prime minister.

McNAIR, Lesley James (1883-1944).

A veteran of combat in France during World War I, he served as Gen. **George Marshall**'s right-hand man from 1942 to 1944 and has been credited as the man who trained the U.S. Army for combat in World War II, using a system that simulated actual battlefield conditions. He was killed in a tour of inspection on the Normandy front on July 25, 1944 at the time of the Cobra attack near St. Lo.

MADAGASCAR.

This huge island, off the east coast of Africa in the Indian Ocean, had a population of 4,087,000 in 1940. France annexed it to its colonial **empire** in 1896 in accordance with the desire of Queen Ranovalona III. After France's defeat in 1940 the island's government remained faithful to Marshal Petain. For a time **Hitler** regarded Madagascar as a likely place to which the Jews of Europe could be deported. Alarmed by the Tokyo-Vichy treaty of July 29, 1941 and the free hand it permitted **Japan** in Southeast Asia, the **United Kingdom** took the precaution of landing British and South African troops at Diego-Suarez, on the northernmost tip of Madagascar, on May 5, 1942, and again at Majunga on September 16. Resistance to these landings was ended by the island's governor on November 6. The attitude of the Zulus toward military service under Marshal **Jan Smuts** exasperated the French colonials and met with a harsh reaction from Gen. **de Gaulle**. **Churchill** turned the island over to the Free French, who entrusted its defense to Gen. Paul Legentilhomme. But serious economic difficulties lent credence to nationalist **propaganda** encouraged by the

Anglo-American Protestant missionaries on the island and the racial and religious rancor between the Merina and Sakalava tribesmen. The major anticolonialist movement, known as the MDRM (*Mouvement democratique de renovation malgache*, or "Democratic Movement for Malagasy Renewal"), won the election of 1946. This was followed by bloody rebellions organized by the PA.NA.MA (*Parti nationalist malgache*, or Malagasy Nationalist Party) in March 1947 and December 1948, which were rigorously suppressed.

M. Baudot

MAGINOT LINE.

Named after Andre Maginot, minister of defense from 1929 to 1932, this French system of fortifications stretched along the 200-mile Franco-German frontier from Thionville to just south of Belfort; it was considered impregnable. By advancing through **Belgium** the Germans swept around it from the rear in 1940. It has since become the symbol of fixed defensive systems—the Mareth Line in Tunisia, the Gustav Line in southern **Italy**, the **Mannerheim** Line in **Finland**—fallen victim to the tactic of swiftly moving armored columns.

MAISKY, Ivan (1884-1975).

A Soviet diplomat, Maisky was ambassador to Britain from 1932. In 1943 he was appointed deputy commissar for foreign affairs, and he participated in the Yalta and Potsdam conferences of 1945 (see **Conferences, Allied**).

MAKIN.

See **Gilbert Islands**.

MALAN, Adolph Gysbert ("Sailor") (1910-63).

A South African airman who joined the **Royal Air Force** in 1936, Malan became an ace pilot in the **Battle of Britain**. He was the first man to fly a Spitfire at night, shooting down an enemy bomber within 10 minutes. In 1944 he commanded a tactical wing in France.

MALAYA.

The **United Kingdom** gradually took over the Malay Peninsula in the first half of the 19th century. A dozen sultanates were brought under colonial suzerainty. **Singapore** was founded, by the private enterprise of Stamford Raffles, as a port in 1819, and by a century later had become one of the world's principal entrepots. By 1939 Malayan rubber and tin were of central importance to the world economy. The British admiralty envisaged a large base at Singapore, but perennial shortage of money hindered a develop-

ment; all the defenses, which were believed very strong, faced out to sea.

On December 7, 1941 the Japanese suddenly advanced toward Malaya from **Indochina**. **Thailand** offered no resistance; the first troops crossed into Malayan territory on December 9. A force of two divisions—less than 35,000 men, including only half a dozen experts on Malayan affairs—advanced down the peninsula with such verve and originality that in five weeks, with fewer than 1,800 dead, it had reached the outskirts of Singapore. A mixed Australian-British force under Arthur F. Percival, reluctant to leave the few roads, was time and time again outflanked in a jungle wrongly believed to be impassable for armor or even for infantry. Two British ships, sallying from Singapore to subdue the Japanese, left their air cover behind and were sunk by air attack on December 11. An Irish sky enabled the Japanese air force to catch the still weaker **Royal Air Force** on the ground.

Two unused divisions reached Singapore from **Egypt** late in January 1942; they disembarked and surrendered without firing a shot; these were among the 80,000 men the Japanese took prisoner when a general surrender was negotiated on February 15. It was a striking, even scandalous, instance of the apathy into which an **empire** can decay. The local inhabitants did not stir a finger to assist the British, who were in no state to ask for their help.

As occupiers, the Japanese at once found themselves at odds with the large Chinese colony. The Chinese formed a Malayan People's Anti-Japanese Army and, with some help from the **Special Operations Executive** (see also **F. Spencer Chapman**), conducted guerrilla warfare from the jungle. The bulk of the Malayan population cooperated with the Japanese occupiers. There were no further formal operations during the war, only clandestine ones. Lord **Mountbatten**'s staff made elaborate plans for the reconquest of the peninsula, which were never used: **Japan** surrendered first.

M. R. D. Foot

MALINOVSKI, Rodion J. (1898-1967).

Soviet marshal. After commanding a sharp-shooting corps, Malinovski was promoted to the command of the Second Army of the Guard at Stalingrad, then to commander in chief of the Second and Third Ukrainian Fronts and in 1945 to commander of the Baikal Front. He also led military operations against the Japanese in Manchuria.

MALLERET, Alfred (1911-1960).

A militant French Communist, Malleret (alias Gen. Joinville) was one of the leaders of the *Francs-Tireurs et Partisans francais*, a maquis group. He was also head of the *Forces francaises de l' interieur* in August 1944.

MALRAUX, Andre (1901-1976).

A French writer, Malraux was an anti-fascist militant who fought in the Spanish civil war on the side of the loyalists. He took a prominent part in underground combat operations in Limousin and Perigord in 1944 and continued to fight in the French First Army in Franche-Comte and Alsace. In 1944 he became first minister of information under Gen. de Gaulle.

MALTA.

Along with Gozo and Comino, Malta had been in British hands since 1800; in 1939 it was a crown colony under direct rule. Restoration of representative government was promised for July 1943. A national assembly met in January 1945 to discuss details; the new constitution became effective in 1947, and in 1964 Malta became independent.

The islands' area is about 75 square miles; at its nearest point, Sicily is only about 50 miles away. The wartime Maltese population was some 280,000. Control of Malta implied control of the central Mediterranean; Valletta, the capital, contained the only major Mediterranean fleet base for the British navy. The base was hardly used until late 1943, except by submarines and convoy escorts, because it was judged too near the 14 main airfields of Sicily. (Indeed, Admiralty anxiety about Malta's vulnerability to air attack had been one of the two main factors that discouraged the United Kingdom from leading opposition to Italy's attack on Ethiopia in the League of Nations in 1935; the other was alarm about Japan.)

An army garrison, 14,000 strong, and three squadrons of Royal Air Force fighters, two of light bombers and one of torpedo bombers were stationed on Malta. Air activity over to and from Malta was constant, almost incessant, in 1941-42. It had six airfields with interlocking runways; they were frequently damaged by bombing, and just as frequently repaired. One airfield alone received, as a daily average, throughout the month of April 1942, as many bombs as fell on Coventry in the famous raid of November 1940. Food, fuel, even water ran short; the whole population was under severe strain, living a troglodytic existence in caves. The strain was worst for antiaircraft crews and airfield ground staff, along with fighter pilots, who might regularly have to fly four or five sorties a day, for weeks on end, from makeshift bases.

One convoy a month from Gibraltar, sent under heavy escort and often furiously opposed, just sufficed to maintain supplies. The RAF lost nearly 1,000 aircraft from Malta—shooting down in retaliation some 900 German and 500 Italian aircraft, a favorable

balance. Still more favorable was the naval-air balance: the bombers on Malta exercised a crippling effect on Axis communications with North Africa. Their attacks, combined with those of the navy and the RAF, operating from Egypt and Libya, and powerfully aided (unknown to the pilots concerned) by Ultra, eventually kept the Axis armies in Libya and Tunisia from receiving fuel, reinforcements, ammunition and supplies and hastened their defeat in May 1943.

Albert Kesselring frequently contemplated the conquest of Malta but, being an airman, he thought—wrongly—that an air attack alone would suffice. His error was fatal to his cause.

In April 1942 George VI awarded the island the George Cross, the highest British award for civilian heroism in conditions of extreme danger; this was the only time it was ever awarded collectively.

M. R. D. Foot

MANDEL, Georges (1895-1944).

A former secretary to Georges Clemenceau, Mandel was an influential parliamentarian between the two world wars. As minister of the interior in May 1940, he recommended prosecuting the war and setting up the government in Africa. He resigned in July after Paul Reynaud was replaced by Marshal Petain. He was arrested by the French at Meknes and eventually turned over to the Germans. Taken into custody by the Vichy *Milice* on July 1, 1944, he was assassinated.

MANNERHEIM, Baron Carl Gustav von (1867-1951).

Appointed field marshal in 1933, Mannerheim reorganized the Finnish army and built a line of defense extending about 80 miles across the Karelian Isthmus on Finland's southeastern border. He led Finnish armed forces against the Soviets in the Winter War in 1939-40 and again from 1941 to 1944. Appointed president, he concluded an armistice with the USSR in 1944. (See also Introduction.)

MANSTEIN, Erich von (1887-1973).

Author of the plan for invading western Europe, Manstein led a corps in the invasion of France in 1940 and commanded the 11th Army in their defeat of the Russians in the Crimea in 1941. He made a valiant but vain attempt to extricate Gen. Friedrich von Paulus's army from its encirclement at Stalingrad in 1942. Manstein was relieved of his duties in 1944 for criticizing Hitler's decisions in the Russian campaign. In 1949 he was condemned by a British tribunal to 18 years in prison; he was freed in 1953.

MAO TSE-TUNG (1893-1976).

Of peasant origins, Mao became a socialist in the 1911 revolution. He was a founding member of the Chinese Communist Party in 1921 and became chairman of the politburo in 1935. In the late 1920s he conceived the theory of the peasantry as the base of revolution and sustained it in a controversy with **Stalin**. In 1934-36 he led the "Long March" of the peasant-based Communist army from central to northern **China**, where he set up a base in Yenan. He joined his army with **Chiang Kai-shek**'s Nationalist forces in a front against the Japanese and in 1944-45 accepted aid from the **Office of Strategic Services** in fighting the invaders. After the defeat of **Japan**, he had a complete falling out with Chiang Kai-shek and in three years secured control of mainland China, proclaiming the People's Republic of China in 1949. Mao was a poet and scholar as well as a revolutionary theorist, experienced guerrilla commander and exceptionally capable politician.

MARGARETHA.

Code name for the *Wehrmacht*'s occupation of **Hungary** on March 19, 1944.

MARIN, Louis (1871-1960).

Head of the French right-liberal movement and minister of state in the last cabinet of the **Third Republic** under **Paul Reynaud** from May to June 1940, Marin joined the **de Gaulle** cause and became an advocate of **resistance**. He went to London in the spring of 1944 and appealed to the patriotism of the French people via the **British Broadcasting Corporation**.

MARITA.

Code name for German intervention in **Greece** on April 6, 1941.

MARSHALL, George Catlett (1880-1959).

As Army chief of staff from 1939 to 1945, Marshall directed U.S. **strategy** with consummate skill. He was at the Potsdam Conference and, as secretary of state (1947-49), implemented the Marshall Plan, a massive program of aid to postwar Europe. Marshall was responsible for augmenting the Army's manpower and aircraft throughout the war. Although opposed by **MacArthur**, the U.S. Navy and the Chinese, among others, he prevailed in his goal to concentrate the Allied attack on **Germany** first and then turn to conquest of the Japanese in the Pacific.

MARSHALL-CORNWALL, Sir James (1888-).

A British general and military historian, Marshall-Cornwall had a brilliant combat record in both world wars. He held a permanent office for exercising upper-echelon functions, principally the coordination of British and French forces in June 1940.

MARTEL, Sir Giffard le Q. (1889-1958).

British lieutenant general. During World War I, Martel saw combat with the Tank Corps, and from 1919 to 1930 he was one of the pioneers in the development of armored **tactics**. In 1940 he led the Arras counterattack of May 21 (see *Fall Gelb*). Between 1940 and 1942 he activated the British armored force. In 1942-43 he served as British military attache in the **USSR**.

MASON-MacFARLANE, Sir Noel F. (1889-1953).

An outspoken British general, Mason-MacFarlane was military attache in Berlin in 1937-39 and **John Gort's** chief of military intelligence in 1939-40. He was in charge of the military mission to the **USSR** in 1941-42, governed **Gibraltar** in 1942-43 and headed the Allied Control Commission in **Italy** in 1944, which oversaw the establishment of that country's democratic government.

MATSUOKA, Yosuke (1880-1946).

A leading diplomat and spokesman for **Japan**'s interests in **China**, Matsuoka served as foreign minister during the critical year from July 1940 to July 1941, when Japan redefined its treaty relations with most of the major powers in Europe. After the surrender he was indicted by the International Military Tribunal for the Far East as a main architect of Japan's military expansion, but he died, crushed and insane, before he could be tried.

Matsuoka was born in Yamaguchi prefecture but went to Oregon at age 13. He graduated second in his class at the University of Oregon and soon joined the Japanese foreign service. In 1921 he moved to the South Manchurian Railway Company, a creature of the Japanese government, where he became a principal adviser to the Japanese Kwantung Army, posted in Manchuria. Matsuoka was elected to the lower house of the imperial Diet in 1930 as a member of the *Seiyukai* party, but he quit his seat and renounced electoral politics three years later.

As Japan's chief representative to the **League of Nations** in 1932-33, Matsuoka gave an able and carefully reasoned defense of Japan's actions in Manchuria in September 1931, when the Kwantung Army seized control. After the League censured Japan by adopting the sharply critical report of the Lytton commission in February 1933, he castigated his fellow delegates, announced Japan's withdrawal and stormed out of the hall. His next major assignment took him back to the

South Manchurian Railway, which he headed from 1935 to 1939.

Matsuoka was appointed foreign minister in Prince **Fumimaro Konoe**'s second cabinet in July 1940, partly because each powerful faction in the government thought he might support its interests and partly because Konoe thought his nerve, style and diplomacy of bluster could achieve goals the two men shared: solving the China crisis, avoiding war in the Pacific, winning favors from **Germany** (whose victory seemed certain) and wresting control of foreign policy from the army. Matsuoka was the loudest advocate of dreams held by Pan-Asianists in Japan for decades: a new world order with three spheres. America would control the western hemisphere, Germany would control Europe and Africa and Japan would control East and Southeast Asia. **India** and the **USSR** east of the Urals would form a buffer. What Matsuoka most wanted was to replace the Western powers as colonialists in Asia; what he most feared was that Japan would be left isolated in a postwar world dominated by Germany and the **United States**.

His first major step was to conclude the **Tripartite Pact** with Germany and **Italy** in September 1940, an alliance that Matsuoka expected would keep the Americans at bay and guarantee Japanese control of French, Dutch and British colonies in Asia after the war. To resolve the Chinese dilemma, he recognized a puppet regime under **Wang Ching-wei** in Nanking in November 1940. Each of these moves, however, only antagonized the Americans and the Chinese further. In March 1941 Matsuoka visited **Hitler**, hoping to intimidate the United States by demonstrating the solidarity of the **Axis**. Despite Hitler's urgings, he refused to commit Japan to attacking **Singapore**. In April he signed a neutrality treaty with **Stalin**, even though he almost surely knew that Operation **Barbarossa** was in the offing. The result was that Japan sat idly by when the German armies rolled eastward in June 1941.

Matsuoka was undercut by Konoe in April when the prime minister began negotiations with the United States, and he was forced from office when the third Konoe cabinet was formed in July. His policies, which assumed the likelihood of a smashing German victory, had sought peace and room for diplomatic maneuver. Instead they had brought war closer and boxed Japan in. Having dashed the hopes of the factions who sponsored him, Matsuoka became an unstable personality after he left public life, his dreams unfulfilled and his career ruined.

T. R. H. Havens

MAURRAS, Charles (1868-1952).

The French founder of the *Ecole romane* (a literary movement with neoclassical ideals), Maurras was an enemy of democracy and an activist for integral nationalism with a tendency to monarchism. An editorialist for *L'Action francaise* beginning in 1908, he was considerably influential among young French intellectuals. As an advocate of **fascism** and provisional understanding with the Nazis, he inspired the technocrats of the *Revolution nationale* and contended simultaneously with the **Resistance** and **collaboration** movements such as **Marcel Deat**'s *Rassemblement national populaire*. He was condemned to life imprisonment and expelled from the *Academie francaise*. In 1952 he received a pardon.

MECHLIN INCIDENT.

In November 1939 a German light aircraft carrying a liaison officer and his pilot was blown off course and made a forced landing at Mechlin, just inside the eastern frontier of **Belgium**. A gendarme approached it and found the officer trying to set fire to some papers, which the gendarme seized. The papers turned out to be the German general staff plan for the invasion of the Low Countries and France. The papers' content was clandestinely communicated to the British and French governments and military staffs, all of which assumed that this was a clumsy German attempt at **deception**. No countermeasures were taken or even envisaged.

MEDITERRANEAN AND MIDDLE EASTERN THEATER OF OPERATIONS.

At the beginning of the war this theater was quiet, apart from some local Arab-Jewish tension in **Palestine**, and even that was not at the time more than a police problem of internal security. Commercial traffic between England, **India** and the Far East continued through the Suez Canal until **Italy** entered the war in June 1940. Thereafter most shipping was diverted around the Cape of Good Hope until late 1943, when **convoys** through the Mediterranean began again. The British kept small battle fleets at **Gibraltar** and Alexandria, regarding their main prewar naval base, **Malta**, as dangerously close to Italy. They had a small army in **Egypt** for the defense of the Suez Canal. Their only actual possessions in the area were Gibraltar, Malta, Aden and British Somaliland, but as a mandatory or protecting power they also occupied **Cyprus**, Egypt, Palestine, Transjordan and **Iraq**. All but Egypt, the most important, were lightly held.

Italy had geographical dominance over the central Mediterranean, and, as a result of recent conquests, a sizeable colonial **empire**, composed of **Albania, Libya,** the **Dodecanese**, **Eritrea**, **Ethiopia** and a larger slice of Somaliland. But **Mussolini** felt himself unready for war; he had not desired one until 1942. He was painfully aware that his air force, the strongest in the world in 1934, was obsolescent, that his navy could not fight after dark and that his large army's **morale** was uncertain. He had a force of over 200,000 men under **Rodolfo Graziani** in Libya and one nominally about half as large again under the Duke of **Aosta** in eastern Africa.

The first operation in the Mediterranean was, even for a war, a tragic one: the attack that the British found it necessary to make on their allies of a few days before, the French naval squadron at **Mers el-Kebir** near Oran, on July 3, 1940. This was the first occasion since 1815 that French and British forces had fired on each other. As a result of the attack, the western Mediterranean was left clear for the British and Italian navies to confront each other.

East Africa
In July 1940 Aosta moved northwestward into the Sudan to occupy Kassala, and, in August northeast-

ward for an easy conquest of British Somaliland. He had neither ammunition nor an opportunity to advance further; Mussolini ordered him to remain on the defensive. At the end of the year, he was attacked. **William Platt** advanced into Eritrea from the Sudan, with two Indian divisions and the Sudan Defense Force. He was held up for seven weeks by a stubborn and gallant defense of an almost impregnable position at Keren, but was able to secure a squadron of heavy infantry **tanks**, which broke through at the end of March 1941. The rest of Eritrea was under his control within two weeks.

Meanwhile **Alan Cunningham**, with one South African and two African divisions and ample air support, had invaded Italian Somaliland from Kenya. He captured the port of Kismayu on February 18 and Mogadishu, the capital, which held large supplies of oil, on the 25th. He and Platt then both advanced into Ethiopia, hoping to join up with **Orde Wingate**'s Gideon Force of irregular Ethiopian warriors, who were accompanied by the Emperor **Haile Selassie** himself, returning from exile: the Gideon Force had been operating from the upper Sudan since December 1940. The capital fell on April 6; Aosta, surrounded at Ras Dasham, surrendered on May 19. Italian resistance continued for five months more in the province of Gonder; it was over by November 27, 1941.

The Opening of the Desert Campaign
Spurred on by Mussolini, Graziani advanced gingerly to the Egyptian frontier in September 1940, crossed it and sat down 60 miles further on, at Sidi Barrani, having inflicted 40 casualties on his heavily outnumbered opponents. **Archibald Wavell**, the British commander-in-chief, let him be for the moment.

The Balkans
On October 28, 1940, without adequate notice even to **Hitler**, Mussolini sent his army in Albania to invade **Greece**, on false assurances from his staffs that everything was ready. By mid-November the surviving attackers were all back behind the Albanian frontier. All through the winter of 1940-41, under **Ioannis Metaxas**, Greece maintained a fighting front in the severe terrain of southern Albania. The Italian fleet, assembled at Taranto to operate against Corfu, was routed on November 11-12 by British torpedo-carrying biplanes, which sank three battleships and did much other damage, while only two British aircraft were lost. A little British technical help was provided during the winter for the Greeks. **Anthony Eden** and **John Dill** visited Athens in February 1941, and under the influence of their reports, **Churchill** pressed Wavell and **Arthur Longmore** strongly, for political

reasons, to increase the amount of aid they could give. They did so; this became a noticeable drain on operations in the North African desert.

O'Connor's Coups

In December 1940, with Wavell's approval, **Richard O'Connor**, who commanded in the Western Desert under **Maitland Wilson**'s supervision, adopted a suggestion of **Eric Dorman-Smith**'s—he suddenly broke the Italian position at Sidi Barrani. A two nights' march entirely around the Italians' flank, followed by a tank attack from the rear at dawn, wholly disorganized them. There was no time to count prisoners, but one British report said there were ''about five acres of officers and 200 acres of other ranks.'' Some 38,000 prisoners were taken in a week, for the loss of 133 killed. This was the reward of the British cabinet's daring in sending the only available reserve of tanks to Egypt in July 1940, all the rest having just been lost in France.

Not only were the Italians knocked out of Egypt; they were all but chased out of Cyrenaica as well. Three Italian divisions disintegrated in Egypt; four more surrendered to Australians in El Bardi early in January 1941. The Australians took Tobruk on January 22 and Benghazi on February 6. Close naval and air support reinforced their advance. South of Benghazi

John Caunter's Fourth Armored Brigade brought off the astounding victory of **Beda Fomm** on February 5-7, 1941, destroying 100 tanks for the loss of three and disrupting the surviving Italians' attempts to break out to El Agheila on the provincial frontier.

Balkan Disruption

Yet the tide of British success, which had risen high, was about to ebb. Already in mid-December 1940, as soon as victory in Egypt was assured, Wavell had withdrawn one Indian division from the desert to join Platt's force in the Sudan. By mid-February 1941 the lines of supply across Cyrenaica were stretched uncomfortably far; the calls of Greece and Iraq as well as Ethiopia on Wavell's attention and resources became more and more insistent.

On March 28, 1941, in a night action off the southern tip of Greece, Cape Matapan, Andrew Cunningham's fleet inflicted a decisive defeat on the Italian navy, which lost two cruisers, and did not again venture seriously into the Aegean.

On the previous day a coup d'etat in Belgrade had proclaimed **Peter II** of **Yugoslavia** old enough to reign; the Germans' retaliation was swift. On April 6 they bombed Belgrade, on April 7 Skopje, April 9 Salonika. They captured Belgrade on April 13 and Athens two weeks later. Staff muddles and inferior force hampered British efforts to help the Greeks: air inferiority in particular. Two successive lines, in Macedonia and in Thessaly, were lost; Thermopylae was turned, as Xerxes had turned it. The kings of Yugoslavia and Greece escaped, in British warships, to exile.

Crete

Over 30,000 of the troops who got away from the mainland were taken to Crete, against which, **Ultra** sources at once made it clear, an immediate attack impended. The data were passed on to **Bernard Freyberg**, the force commander, and others on the island, who were told nothing of the source. They found the information incredible and ignored it. They swiftly regretted that decision. Crete is within 125 miles of Rhodes, where the Italians' airfields were available for the *Luftwaffe*. On May 20 **Kurt Student**'s 11th Airborne Corps launched its attack. By May 23 he had operational control of the Maleme airfield at the western end of the island, thanks to a reckless onslaught by his parachutists and glider-borne troops, the elite of the new German army, who pressed on regardless of huge casualties. They were fresh; their enemies from **New Zealand** and the **United Kingdom** were already half-exhausted. Freshness and air superiority brought victory fast.

Not a single German soldier reached Crete that May by sea: the British navy, acting as recklessly as the

Luftwaffe, saw to that, at heavy loss. But the airborne effort sufficed; the Germans were masters of Crete by the end of the month. The effort had burned Student's corps out; it was never again usable as an airborne force. This, though, was unknown to **Germany**'s enemies, who were duly depressed by another defeat.

About 3,000 troops were left at large in the Cretan mountains, of whom about a third were brought off, by caique and submarine, in a series of escape operations later in the year. Many were captured; some joined the **Resistance**, which was tough.

It is often argued that the value of the fighting in Greece and Crete was that it dislocated the plan for **Barbarossa**, the German invasion of the **USSR**, and thus determined the fate of the war. There is not enough evidence to bear this out; on the contrary, it appears that the date for Barbarossa was never altered after the end of March 1941.

Wavell's troubles did not come singly. While the Balkans were in tumult, the activities of **Rashid Ali** in Iraq caused him such concern that he had to supervise that country's invasion in May—Iraqi oil being indispensable to the whole British war effort. Five weeks of brisk operations were enough, but the Germans' attempts to counter them involved the British in another, tougher five-week campaign in **Syria**.

Rommel Arrives

Meanwhile, there were also difficulties in the Western Desert. In October 1940 Hitler had considered the possibility of joining in the desert war, but postponed a decision. He now sent **Erwin Rommel**, who had made his name as a Panzer divisional commander in France in 1940, to stiffen the Italians in Libya. Rommel landed within a week of Beda Fomm and was soon joined by elements of five light and 15 Panzer divisions. By an elegant **deception**, mounting cardboard replicas of tanks on Volkswagon cars, he bluffed the British into thinking he was much stronger than he was. In April 1941 he probed into Cyrenaica. The best British troops had been withdrawn to Egypt for a rest, or had been sent to Greece; by a stroke of German luck, O'Connor was taken prisoner. Inexperienced troops and commanders were no match for Rommel; by May 1941 the British had lost almost all their winter gains and were back on the Egyptian frontier leaving only an Australian garrison in Tobruk, a thorn behind Rommel's left flank that hindered his further advance. The navy's inshore squadron kept Tobruk supplied, and ran in 35,000 troops during the course of the summer to replace the Australians, who were recalled for service in the Far East by their government.

Both Churchill and Wavell were affronted at the retreat, but the two had much else on their minds.

Churchill forced on a reluctant Admiralty a plan to send 300 tanks by convoy straight through the Mediterranean to Egypt—this saved six weeks on the Cape route, and took place in April 1942 (57 tanks were lost in a ship sunk by mines near Sicily). With these tanks Wavell mounted an attack ("Battleaxe") in mid-June, but he lost 90 of them, in tank traps baited by Rommel for the 88-mm antiaircraft gun, which had been modified—at Hitler's personal suggestion—to work against tanks also. It could pierce the armor of the stoutest British tank, the Matilda, at 1.25 miles; the British did not know what had hit them.

Wavell was thereupon replaced by **Claude Auchinleck**, who brought Cunningham over from eastern Africa to command the newly constituted Eighth Army in the desert, consisting of the 13th and 30th Corps. Rommel's *Afrika Korps*, meanwhile, was reinforced: the Fifth Light became the 21st *Panzer* Division, and a new division, the 90th Light, was added to the *Korps*.

After a pause for reorganization, Cunningham mounted Operation "Crusader" on November 18, 1941. The operation was to relieve Tobruk, against which Rommel was preparing an all-out attack, which "Crusader" just anticipated. Five days of confused tank battles around Sidi Rezegh were indecisive. Auchinleck, visiting the front, found his friend Cunningham excessively put out by a raid of Rommel's on Eighth Army's communications; with a heavy heart, he replaced him with **Neil Ritchie**. Ritchie's army persevered; by the end of November, Tobruk was relieved and Rommel, reduced to 30 tanks, withdrew. Both sides had suffered from faulty radio links, which made it hard for commanders to coordinate their scattered units. Air superiority rested, on the whole, with the British, a change from the situation in Crete.

Several British attempts to outflank Rommel, as he had outflanked them in his raid of late November 1941, fell short of their objectives; the **Axis** forces withdrew right back into Tripolitania. Thirty more tanks, received just before they left Benghazi, enabled the Germans to hold Beda Fomm this time against a raid in late December.

That was a bad month for the Royal Navy in this theater: it lost three battleships; the *Barham*, torpedoed and sank at sea; and the *Valiant* and the *Queen Elizabeth*, disabled for months by Italian **frogmen** in the Alexandria harbor.

The British believed themselves simply to be checked at El Agheila, the southernmost point on the gulf of Sirte, where their advance had stopped, and busied themselves with bringing up supplies and preparing for the next movement forward. This time it was their turn to have their impending attack anticipated. For, on January 21, 1942, Rommel suddenly struck back. He caught the British First Armored Division, a comparatively inexperienced formation new to desert war, at Antelat, some 25 miles east of Beda Fomm. His opponents, much less skilled than he in armored warfare, dissipated their tank strength in piecemeal attacks and lost nearly half of it in a few hours. He had difficulty in persuading his Italian allies to accompany his advance (the *Afrika Korps* cooperated with six Italian divisions, one of them—the *Ariete*—armored). The difficulty was resolved when Rommel, after a feint northeast towards Mekili, struck toward the northwest and easily recaptured Benghazi, well stocked with stores.

Each side in the desert war was, of course, used to employing captured stores. **Food** will warm almost any stomach; gasoline will burn in almost any carburetor. Rommel indeed owed his own survival, on the night of November 24-25, 1941, to the fact that he was riding in a captured British command vehicle and was therefore taken for a British general and left alone when he found himself momentarily surrounded by troops of the Fourth Indian Division.

It was now Rommel's turn to organize his supply lines, while the British established themselves after February 4 on a position running southward from Gazala, about 20 miles west of Tobruk. The Gazala Line, as it came to be called, was too new and too shallow to afford a secure defense against a modern mobile enemy and too strung out for adequate mutual support between its strong points. The southernmost and most isolated of these, at Bir Hakeim, some 35 miles inland, was held by a Free French brigade under **Marie Pierre Koenig**.

Churchill pressed insistently for an attack, both to relieve the Russians, who were under severe pressure, and to divert enemy attention from Malta, which was under particularly close siege. Again it was Rommel who struck first. On the night of May 26-27, he led his armor entirely around the Eighth Army's left and struck towards the sea at its rear. He got within 20 miles of his objective but ran into unexpected opposition from "Grant" tanks, recently and secretly brought from the **United States** and equipped with better guns than his own. The British believed the German tanks were uniformly superior to theirs; this engagement, among others, proved them wrong. The Germans, Rommel particularly, simply had a clearer understanding of armored tactics and of army-air cooperation and a better organized and more efficient force. The British and their allies gradually learned, through hard experience, to give as good as they got, but it took time.

Meanwhile, the scales of skill and fortune were still laden in favor of the Axis. Ritchie's forces continued to use their armor piecemeal, and Rommel's continued to destroy it, in three weeks' of confused fighting. During the first 10 days of June, the Bir Hakeim redoubt sustained and survived continual attacks. "Nowhere in Africa was I given a stiffer fight" said Rommel. Koenig, acting on orders from above, withdrew most of his men on the night of June 10-11, after a defense that placed the Free French movement, and its leader, **de Gaulle**, firmly on the world map. Rommel then repeated his sally around the British left flank, this time with more success against the British armor. On June 14 Ritchie started to retreat, much farther than Auchinleck had intended. A South African garrison, left behind in Tobruk, was suddenly overwhelmed by a concentrated attack on June 20, and 35,000 men surrendered. So much materiel was captured there that the next month 80 percent of the *Afrika Korps* rode in British vehicles.

This was a severe moral blow for the Allies. The town's defenses had been allowed to fall into neglect over the preceding months. And while Auchinleck realized that in strict strategic theory Tobruk was worthless, so much **propaganda** had been made out of its successful defense in 1941 that it had acquired a symbolic value far beyond its real worth. Ordinary citizens the world over, who could not tell **strategy** from strabismus, had heard of its glorious defense and were correspondingly depressed—or elated—when they heard that this time it had hardly held out a day. Auchinleck thenceforward was a marked man.

On June 23 Rommel, with only 58 tanks left fit to fight, closed with the Eighth Army on the Egyptian frontier; he was elated by his own promotion to field marshal and determined—this, again, was strict strategic theory—to pursue a rout hard. **Albert Kesselring**, his theater commander, had intended to invade Malta; Hitler, dubious of Italian support, persuaded him to let Rommel press on instead. Mussolini flew over to Africa with a white horse, on which he proposed to ride in triumph into Alexandria.

Ritchie had decided on the 20th that even the frontier position was untenable and ordered a retreat to Mersa Matruh, nearly 125 miles east of it. From this position, though by now far superior in strength and in tanks to Rommel, the Eighth Army was driven by the German commander's audacity. Without pausing to prepare, he flung in the 2,500 men to which the *Afrika Korps* had been reduced by June 26, and with them took 6,000 prisoners, huge supplies and the whole Matruh position.

The Tide's Last Turn

By this time Ritchie had been superseded. Auchinleck flew up to the front to take over himself on June 25, accompanied by Dorman-Smith; during the flight

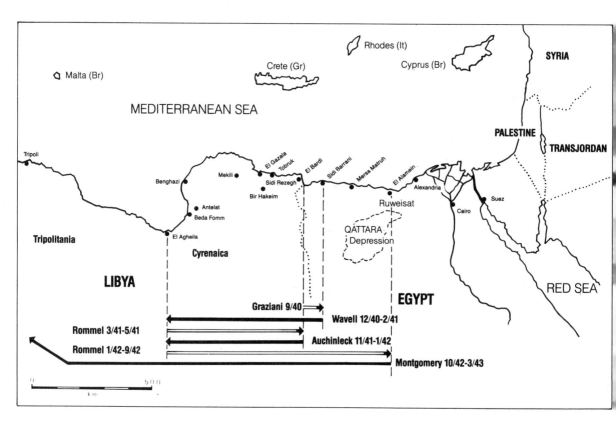

they reread appropriate sections of **Basil Liddell Hart's** *Strategy of Indirect Approach* and decided to apply its principles. Part of Rommel's success against the Matruh position was due to the fact that Auchinleck had already ordered a further withdrawal, to **El Alamein,** where his army stood.

El Alamein, a desert railway station some 60 miles west-southwest of Alexandria, gave its name to a famous battle the following October, but the engagement fought there on July 1-3, 1942, officially as yet quite unrecognized, was still more important. There were four heavily defended ''boxes'' between El Alamein and the impassable Qattara depression, 35 miles to the south; the Germans did not know of one of them, at Deir el Shein beyond the western end of the Ruweisat ridge. Between the boxes, mobile columns of all arms operated.

Rommel stumbled on the Deir el Shein box on July 1 and lost all day reducing it. The British fleet abandoned Alexandria that day for the Red Sea; the files at the general headquarters in Cairo were burned (thus much increasing its later efficiency); in both cities there was some civilian alarm. In the desert the soldiers held firm; the airmen spent the night bombarding Rommel's columns, so that the Germans got no sleep. By July 4 his troops were so exhausted that he had to call off his attack. The 15th *Panzer* Division, for instance, was reduced to 15 tanks and 200 riflemen, who panicked at the sight of a slight advance by the British Seventh Armored Division.

The British troops were tired also, too tired to carry through Auchinleck's order for immediate counterattack; his application of Liddell Hart's principles, however, saved the day, the army and the empire. Rommel, with 20 tanks left fit to fight, was pinned down in the desert at the end of over-stretched communications; Mussolini went back to Rome. Whereupon Auchinleck was himself dismissed. Churchill and **Alan Brooke**, disturbed by the hurried retreat and by rumors of disquiet in the ex-cavalry regiments over Dorman-Smith's unfamiliar methods, visited Cairo themselves in early August and did not like what they saw. Auchinleck was informed that his command was too large; would he take over the eastern half of it, covering **Iran** and Iraq? He would not, so he was sent on leave. **Harold Alexander** was

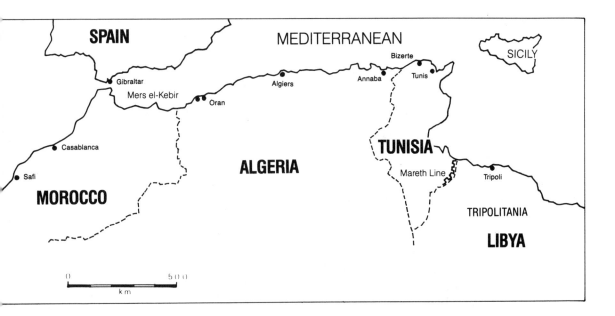

brought in to succeed him, and **Bernard Montgomery** (following **William Gott**, who was killed on his way to take up the appointment) to command the Eighth Army. The troops meanwhile were busily wiring and mining themselves into a whole series of boxes around El Alamein. On August 31 Rommel, in desperation, launched his last desert attack, at **Alam el Halfa**; Auchinleck's dispositions, deep minefields and Montgomery's personality, which engendered plenty of confidence, defeated him in a week. On September 5 he called off the attack, and was in no position to retreat.

Churchill had been calling for an offensive since June, but Montgomery was determined never to start an attack he was not sure he would win. By October 23 he had accumulated 195,000 men to his enemy's 104,000, and 1,000 tanks to 500. He then launched operation "Lightfoot," which began with six days of frontal attrition against Rommel's minefields west of El Alamein, which were now also deep. Elaborate deceptions kept the Germans and Italians guessing about where the main onslaught would come. On October 29 Operation "Supercharge," a concentrated attack led by troops from New Zealand, broke into the Axis positions about 10 miles from the sea; by the evening of November 2 Rommel realized he was beaten. He disobeyed an order from Hitler the next day to stand fast (he was known to be fond of going well forward himself, to control events on the spot as generals in much earlier wars had done; this sometimes made it possible to evade instructions). On

November 4 he began to disengage his armor; again it was reduced to some 20 tanks. Most of his Italian infantry formations were captured.

This was a victory for the strategy of direct approach, but Montgomery's inexorable caution hampered pursuit. Rommel himself and the bulk of his armored units' personnel escaped westward.

North African Pincers

The *Afrika Korps*, retreating from El Alamein, at once found itself retreating into danger. On November 8, 1942, Operation "Torch," some 650 ships cooperating in the largest **combined operation** yet attempted, put ashore in **French North Africa** a force of some four American and British divisions. Elaborate feints had persuaded the Germans that a fresh threat to Dakar was developing, and they believed the 14 fighter squadrons concentrated at Gibraltar were meant for Malta.

American troops, sailing straight from the United States, landed at three points on the coast of Morocco; British and American troops landed near Oran and Algiers. In each of these two cases an attempt to land right in the harbor was bloodily repulsed, and there was sharp fighting in Morocco also—the only occasion French and American units have ever fired on each other—for a few hours. After some extreme political confusion, in which almost all the senior French officers present were arrested and then released, French resistance ceased, all the more readily because the German riposte to "Torch," Operation "Attila," consisted of occupying Marshal Petain's hitherto "free" two-fifths of southern France.

By accident, Petain's deputy **Francois Darlan** happened to be in Algiers at the time, at his sick son's bedside. **Eisenhower,** Operation Torch's overall commander, decided to ask for Darlan's cooperation; he secured it, and began to work through him and the established French colonial regimes. This decision, approved by **Roosevelt** and **Stalin**, was much less well thought of by the British, and greatly dismayed resisters of every complexion. De Gaulle, who had been kept entirely in the dark about Operation Torch, was furious; so was **Henri Giraud**, who believed that he should have stood in Darlan's shoes himself and indeed in Eisenhower's as well, but could convince no one else of his own capacity, and soon faded out. Working with Darlan did at least mean that the Anglo-American forces could establish themselves rapidly and peacefully ashore. On hearing of Operation Attila, Darlan, as commander in chief of Vichy's navy, ordered the fleet in Toulon to join him in Algiers; this the fleet refused to do, but it sank itself at its moorings on November 27 when the Germans arrived to take it over. And the political difficulty solved itself in a few weeks' time, when a young French royalist fanatic assassinated Darlan on Christmas Eve. (To his great surprise, the young man was himself executed two days later on Giraud's order.)

Eisenhower was kept too busy by these political distractions to have much time for warfare, which was put in **Kenneth Anderson**'s charge. Anderson's weak First Army pressed on for Tunis, assisted by a small airborne operation at Bone; by November 28 it was only 12.5 miles short of its objective. But German reaction was prompt and thorough. **Hans-Jurgen von Arnim,** acting under Kesselring's close direction, pushed Anderson back towards the Algerian frontier; winter weather soon set in.

Rommel meanwhile was withdrawing westward without any grave difficulty. Montgomery's Eighth Army was not in Tripoli until January 23, 1943; their advance patrols crossed the Tunisian frontier six days later, but the main body was in no hurry to outrun its supplies. Rommel was even able to put in a sharp strike, in mid-February, behind his own right flank against the American Second Corps holding the Kasserine Pass. His tanks secured his last victory, against a keen but inexperienced and ill-organized enemy. In the middle of the Kasserine battle, Alexander took over—under Eisenhower, who confined himself to overall control—the coordination of the First and Eighth Armies' moves against the Axis troops in Tunisia. The Germans proposed to retain a permanent bridgehead into Africa there; in fact, they stayed for less than three months. Montgomery, for once

hastened by an Ultra report out of his plodding progress westward, closed up his main body on his advance guard in a hurry and thus nipped a sudden attack by Rommel in the bud. Montgomery next, forewarned by the **Long-Range Desert Group**, started to outflank the Mareth Line of old French fortifications in southern Tunisia on March 21. Alexander skillfully coordinated his and Anderson's attacks on Arnim (Rommel was on sick leave), with ample air support; by May 13 Africa was entirely clear of uncaptured Axis forces. Over 150,000 prisoners were taken, nearly as many as had surrendered at Stalingrad.

Sicily and After

The Casablanca Conference (see **Conferences, Allied**) had selected Sicily as the next objective. Particularly intricate deceptions, including the washing up of what appeared to be a dead staff officer's body—with his papers—on the coast of **Spain**, persuaded the Germans to divide their resources between Greece and Sardinia, in spite of a pointer provided by the capture of the islets of Pantellaria and Lampedusa in mid-June. The Germans had only 40,000 men in Sicily when the Anglo-American attack, Operation "Husky," began on July 9-10. A force of 140,000 troops was put ashore near the southeastern corner of the island. The presence of 230,000 Italian troops meant they were outnumbered by two to one, but the Italians' fighting value was by then slight, and they did not oppose the British landing south of Syracuse at all at the start. An airborne element in the landing force mostly went astray, because the pilots had little experience, a fault that would be remedied later.

Part of the importance of the Sicilian campaign centered on the lessons learned from it for later and larger combined landings; part from the speed with which the island was taken over. Gen. **George Patton** distinguished himself on the left, American flank; he led his armored force across the island to Messina, and by taking it on August 17 he brought Operation Husky to an end. By that time the landing's success had already precipitated the fall of Mussolini. The Fascist Grand Council met, for the first time since the war began, on July 24 and passed a resolution hostile to *Il Duce*. The next day he went to see King **Victor Emmanuel III**. He learned in a 20-minute interview (of which no details are known) that he had been dismissed, and he was quietly driven away in an ambulance to a prison cell. **Pietro Badoglio,** his successor, at once began, through a captured **Special Operations Executive** radio operator, to negotiate an Italian change of sides. For the Allies this raised the question of how were they going to administer lands they conquered. Libya had been too sparsely populated to raise serious problems. The French had used their accustomed channels in northwestern Africa. Sicily was handed over to Americans who spoke fluent Italian; they turned out to be *mafiosi*, who reimposed Mafia rule on the province where Mussolini had crushed it. For the rest of Italy the Allied staffs devised the AMGOT—the Allied Military Government of Occupied Territory—which issued currency, transported food, cleared drains and dustbins and did the rest of the routine work of local government. It worked well enough but was hardly less authoritarian than the system it displaced. De Gaulle took early warning, and he determined to allow nothing of the sort in metropolitan France.

The Italian Campaign: 1943

Badoglio finally signed an act of surrender on September 3, 1943; the demand for **unconditional surrender** put forward at Casablanca made this a necessary formality, though six weeks had passed in working out the conditions. On the same day the Eighth Army crossed the Strait of Messina and began another of its methodical approach marches, along the bad roads of Calabria. A British **airborne division** arrived by sea at Taranto and pressed on by jeep for the airfields at Bari and Foggia.

The secret of the surrender talks had been well kept. Although Badoglio asked for a further delay, Eisenhower insisted that the news be published on September 8. That night the Germans took over the airfields around Rome, on which a parachute landing was cancelled. Victor Emmanuel and Badoglio fled to Brindisi. An Anglo-American seaborne landing at Salerno, some 30 miles southeast of Naples, took place on the 9th and ran at once into thin but stiff German opposition—so stiff that Gen. **Mark Clark**, its commander, almost withdrew his Fifth Army. He was operating at the limit of fighter cover from Sicily, but the Eighth Army captured Foggia on September 27, relieving the air pressure on Clark, and his opponents withdrew, although not far.

The populace of Naples tried, without arms or preparation, to rise against the Germans during the last three days of September, suffering terrible reprisals before the Fifth Army arrived on October 1. But the Allied advance to the northwest was soon halted at the Gustav Line, which held the Eighth Army in the Sangro valley and the Fifth Army along the Garigliano all through the winter. This was siege warfare, much as it had raged on the Western Front in France and Flanders in World War I. It was what the commanders on both sides had known as young officers; it was what the troops on both sides had been brought up to abominate as a waste of time and spirit. The answer to it was known—the tank. But much of

the terrain in the Apennines was too tough even for tanks.

Fourteen German divisions held this Gustav Line against a truly international force: not only Americans and British, but Indians, Frenchmen, Poles, Italians, Greeks, Brazilians, New Zealanders and even some Japanese from California made up the 21 divisions of Alexander's force.

Side Effects

The capture of the south Italian airfields enabled the SOE to extend its operations considerably in eastern and southeastern Europe. It coincided with the installation in Germany of a big antiaircraft block, stretching from **Denmark** to Bavaria, to shield Berlin from the **Royal Air Force** and the U.S. Army Air Force; this made lone flights from England to **Poland** impossibly dangerous. The SOE turned out to be better placed for supplying the Polish Home Army from Bari. A great deal more supply work could now be done for guerrillas in the Balkan states, but they were now in less drastic need of supplies, because they seized much Italian war material in mid-September. A commando brigade, based near Bari, began to operate in support of **Tito**'s partisans among the Adriatic islands.

Simultaneously with the Salerno landing, the use of a few **landing craft** were found to enable the Free French, with the SOE's help, to seize Corsica. The Germans left for the mainland unmolested, and the Italians were quickly overpowered. Much the same happened when a small Allied expedition landed in Sardinia in October.

The pressure on Malta vanished; the pressure on **Portugal** to yield bases in the Azores became irresistible. Convoys to the Far East could pass through the Mediterranean and the Suez Canal with little difficulty.

Mussolini's rescue from a mountain camp by **Otto Skorzeny** on September 16, a brilliant operation in itself, was of slight political importance. *Il Duce* ran a shadow government at Salo, but his state had no real power.

Several thousand British **prisoners of war** who were in camps in Italy were released; others found that they had a much better chance to escape than usual. Many were recaptured in mid-September 1943, when the Germans included as part of the business of turning Italy into an occupied country a sharp police action against strangers. Many more escaped to the southeast, Allied territory. A few tried to hide up in the Apennines; winter drove them down again, and nearly all were caught. And some of the more adventurous made contact with the partisan bands who now seized the opportunity to take to the hills.

Some of these bands had roots reaching back to the time of Austrian occupation, over 80 years before; there was a vigorous Italian tradition of resistance to tyranny, even after 21 years of Fascist rule. But so far they had little in the way of arms or organization. They had a good deal of popular support, but it needed to be channeled to have any effect. The *Comitato di Liberazione nazionale dell'Alta Italia* ("National Committee for the Liberation of Northern Italy") set to work on this task.

An Aegean Front?
Churchill had long coveted air bases in the Dodecanese from which to attack oil refineries in **Rumania** and to widen the air front against Germany: "It seemed to me a rebuff to fortune," he said, "not to pick up these treasures" when Italy changed sides. **Special Air Service** Maj. George (Lord) Jellicoe parachuted into Rhodes on September 9, 1943 to try to persuade the Italians to subdue the smaller German garrison there. He had no success and had to leave hurriedly. On September 15 British battalions were landed on Cos, Leros and Samos.

There were not enough landing craft to send more, and the Americans, who controlled the only reserves, were not prepared to weaken the **Normandy landing**— still far in the future—by lending any at all. They sus-pected Churchill, perhaps rightly, of wishing to revive his project of 1915, when the British had attempted to force through the Dardanelles and open a warm-water route to Russia. It was less sound to reject a project that, in 1943 as in 1915, was of brilliant originality, simply because when first attempted it had narrowly failed. Churchill was not going to imperil his relations with Roosevelt, or the main chance of Overlord, for a secondary point; after repeated protests he fell silent.

So Rhodes remained in German hands, as did local air superiority. It was therefore comparatively easy for the Germans to reduce the three British invading battalions, recapturing Cos by a parachute assault in the first week of October and reconquering Leros and Samos in the course of October and November.

The Italian Campaign: 1944-45
In January 1944 Clark decided to try to turn his enemy's right flank and landed two divisions at Anzio on the 22nd; it was only 30 miles southeast of Rome, and Kesselring for a moment thought himself in danger. But the landing was not pressed with much vigor; only naval artillery fire saved it from a disastrous defeat in a counterattack. For four months Anzio remained a beachhead, nothing more.

Clark's main attention was concentrated on Monte **Cassino**, an evacuated monastery—founded by Saint Benedict—on a mountaintop that barred his road to Rome. Repeated attacks reduced it to rubble, but the Allies could never quite capture it until a corps of French mountaineers got around its left flank in mid-May, and Poles took it on the 18th. Kesselring thereupon withdrew past Rome—which the allies entered on June 4—to another even stronger position, the Gothic Line, which ran from Pisa past Lake Trasimene to Rimini on the Adriatic.

By this time there were 26 German divisions in Italy, eight of them preoccupied with the struggle against the partisans. A million men and women were out on strike for a week in March 1944 in towns throughout the Po valley. By midsummer about 100,000 partisans were living *en maquis* in the Apennine or Alpine foothills; they were frequently exposed to attack but inflicted heavy casualties in return as well. All told, they caused about 50,000 German casualties; 35,000 of them were killed, and another 20,000 wounded. Attacks on them intensified in the summer of 1944, because Alexander had to give up seven divisions for Operation **Dragoon**, on which the Americans and the French insisted but which was no longer of much strategic use. He did his best to keep German attention concentrated on his main fighting front, and broke into the Gothic Line on September 2, when the Greeks took Rimini; but by December 5 his right had advanced no farther than Ravenna, and the Americans on his left were not far north of Pisa. He instructed the partisans to go home for the winter, in a broadcast that gave much unintended offense, for the partisans felt themselves to be under no foreigner's command; the cry of 1848, *L'Italia fara da se*, was raised again, and again with little immediate effect. Committees of liberation proliferated, in an atmosphere close to that of civil war. Politics went on, though still without elections, for which the dominating Allies could not yet see an opportunity. In April 1944 Badoglio formed a new government, with six parties represented in it. After the fall of Rome, the king handed his powers over to his son Umberto, who secured the replacement of Badoglio by Ivanoe Bonomi, a figure from the prefascist past. The communists, on directions brought fresh from Moscow by Palmiro Togliatti, supported his government of national anti-fascist union and bided their time.

In April 1945 the northern cities revolted to meet the advancing Allied armies, who took Bologna on April 22 and reached the Po on the 23rd. By then surrender negotiations were well under way. They were conducted from **Switzerland** by **Allen Dulles**, the European head of the **Office of Strategic Services** with **Karl Wolff**, the supreme **SS** commander in Italy (who was acting in defiance of **Himmler**) and with Kesselring, who signed a document of surrender on April 29 calling for an end to hostilities (so heavily had his forces suffered from air and partisan attack) at noon on May 2.

Mussolini heard of these negotiations in Milan on April 25. He set off in disguise for Switzerland with his mistress but was recognized by partisans on the 27th, shot the next day and hung up by the heels from a meathook in a Milan garage.

Dragoon

On August 15, 1944 the U.S. Seventh Army under Gen. **Alexander Patch** landed on the Riviera in southern France and started to fight its way up the Rhone valley. **Jean de Lattre de Tassigny**'s First French Army landed with it and soon took both Toulon and Marseilles. Resistance forces held open the old *Route Napoleon*, from Nice through Grasse and Digne to Grenoble, which fell months earlier than had been foreseen. On September 2 Dragoon's forces made contact with Overlord's.

Commentators continue to debate whether Dragoon was worth mounting at all. For the Free French it was a political necessity: the French army had to take a prominent part in the liberation of France, and **Leclerc**'s armored division, which freed Paris on August 23-25, was not enough. For the Americans it also seemed a political necessity, as a means of keeping Churchill from pursuing some imperialist adven

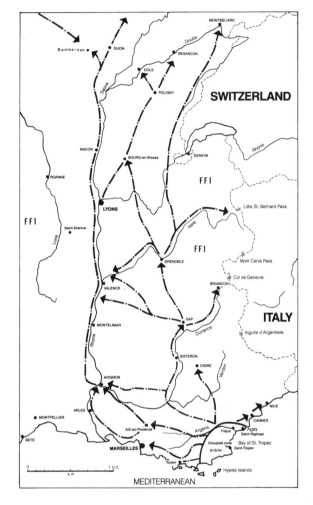

ture in the Balkans. And there were never enough landing craft for Dragoon to have been mounted simultaneously with Overlord.

The Balkans were in fact conquered by the Soviet army, which was in Belgrade by October 1944, squeezing the Germans out of Greece, which the British promptly occupied with a small holding force that soon found itself involved in a civil war. Churchill's dream of an advance through the Ljubljana gap onto the central Danube remained a dream.

M. R. D. Foot

MEENSEL-KIEZEGEM.

Inhabitants of Meensel-Kiezegem, a Belgian village, attempted to conceal the Canadian pilot Edward

Blankinsop. All the participants in the action were captured in **SS** raids on August 1 and 11, 1944. In retaliation the Germans killed 68 people—one-sixteenth of the village's population—and the flier as well.

MENDES-FRANCE, Pierre (1907-   ).
A French lawyer, Mendes-France was a deputy from Louviers in 1932, undersecretary of the treasury and the inventor of a bold plan for budgetary reform in 1938. In 1940 he was imprisoned while attempting to flee by ship to North Africa, where he intended to continue his fight against the Nazis. He escaped and then volunteered as a pilot for **Free France**. In November 1943 he became commissioner of finances for the Algiers French Committee and in September 1944 minister of the national economy in the **de Gaulle** government. He resigned on April 5, 1945 because of the failure of the head of the state to adopt his plan for a special tax on capital that was designed to confiscate illicit profits.

MENZIES, Sir Stewart (1890-1968).
A British cavalry officer, Menzies fought in France in 1914-18. On Adm. Hugh Sinclair's death in November 1939, he succeeded as chief of **MI-6**.

MERS EL-KEBIR.
Naval base on the Gulf of Oran where the Royal Navy on July 3, 1940 sank the French fleet anchored there (see **Atlantic, Battle of the; Mediterranean and Middle Eastern Theater of Operations**).

MESSE, Giovanni (1883-1968).
An Italian general, Messe participated in Italy's invasions of **Ethiopia** (1935-36) and **Albania** (1939). In 1941 he commanded the Italian expeditionary force on the Russian front. At the beginning of 1943 he was made commander in chief of the Italian First Army in Tunisia, but the **Axis** situation there was hopeless. In May 1943 he surrendered his forces and himself to the Allies.

MESSERSCHMITT, Willy (1898-1978).
German engineer and founder and director of the Augsburg aircraft manufacturing plant of the Messerschmitt Werke, AG. A designer of many planes, he was also head of the war economy.

METAXAS, Ioannis (1871-1941).
From 1913 to 1917 Metaxas, a Greek general, was army chief of staff. He was then exiled on two occasions (1917-21 and 1923-25). In April 1936 he became prime minister of **Greece** and on August 4 seized dictatorial power, wielding it until he died on January

29, 1941. Under his severe but well-intentioned despotism, Greeks united to fight **Italy** beginning in October 1940.

MI.
See **Military Intelligence**.

MI-5.
Counterespionage section of British military information (see **Intelligence Service**).

MI-6.
Espionage service of the British military (see **Intelligence Service**).

MI-9.
British service responsible for repatriation of fliers parachuting into enemy territory and escaped prisoners.

MICHELET, Edmond (1899-1970).
A veteran of World War I and a militant Christian Democrat in 1932, he represented the *Liberte* and *Combat* **Resistance** movements from 1941 to 1943. He was arrested in February 1943 and deported to Dachau in July. In 1945 he became minister of the armies. An enthusiastic follower of **de Gaulle**, he wrote an excellent book on the Nazi practice of deportation, *Rue de la Liberte*.

MIDDLE EAST.
See **Mediterranean and Middle Eastern Theater of Operations**.

MIDWAY.
Following the attack on **Pearl Harbor**, the Japanese armed forces stretched like a gigantic octopus in every direction and won easy successes against feeble opposing forces. After March 1942, however, the first signs of Allied resurgence appeared. The dikes that finally halted the Japanese flood were the frontier between **Burma** and **India** on one side and the **Australia-New Zealand** bloc on the other. Up until then the Japanese had conquered only populations indifferent to the struggle and even welcoming their intrusion—as in Java. The **Philippines** and Burma were two exceptions; guerrilla warfare against the occupier continued there. Gen. **Harold Alexander** stopped the enemy at the foot of the Manipur hills. Australia and New Zealand, the cradle of hardy fighters, were eager to stave off the Japanese hand reaching for their throats.

The Japanese were in control of all the Philippines except for the Bataan peninsula and the island of **Corregidor** off Luzon, where Gen. **Douglas MacArthur's** forces hung on desperately. On February 23, 1942

Roosevelt ordered MacArthur to take supreme command of the Allied forces in the Southwest Pacific, in accordance with a decision the president had reached with **Churchill**. On March 12 he turned the defense of Bataan over to Gen. Jonathan N. Wainwright and left for Australia. Bataan continued to resist the numerically superior enemy until April 8, and Corregidor held out until May 6, both serving as breakwaters against the Japanese tide.

On March 10 the Allies achieved an important victory when a fleet of bombers escorted by fighters destroyed several Japanese warships and transports assembling at Lae and Salamaua on the northeast coast of **New Guinea**. The purpose of the naval grouping was to supply the contemplated attack on Port Moresby, on the island's southeastern coast. The effect of this feat was to delay the Japanese assault on the city by two months. And, on April 19, 16 B-25 bombers under the command of Lt. Col. **James H. Doolittle**, taking off from the flight deck of the aircraft carrier *Hornet*, 668 miles from Tokyo, dropped their explosives on the Japanese capital—to the surprise of the home island defense command, which considered itself outside of striking range. Reinforcements of American troops arrived in Australia some time afterward, while two Australian divisions in the Middle East came back home.

The Battle of the **Coral Sea**, one of the epic struggles in the Allied march to Japan, took place May 4-8. American planes from the carriers *Yorktown* and *Lexington* converged on a large Japanese fleet. These vessels had rounded the eastern cape of New Guinea and were entering the Coral Sea with the intention of depositing troops to occupy Port Moresby, thus posing a serious threat to Australia. The battle was a confused affair, with heavy losses on both sides. A bad blow to the Allied cause was the sinking of the *Lexington*, but the remnants of the Japanese fleet were forced to withdraw and Australia was saved. The Battle of the Coral Sea was the first in naval history in which aircraft carriers played a major role; neither fleet was within sight of the other.

In possession of the northern coast of New Guinea, the Japanese attempted by a series of land and sea maneuvers to take Port Moresby. But their movements on sea were severely restricted and finally stopped by Australian and American forces. Port Moresby remained forever out of reach. The Japanese did, however, capture **Guadalcanal** in July, thereby acquiring for themselves a valuable natural aircraft carrier for their operations in the direction of the Hebrides Islands and New Caledonia.

Impressed by the American strength displayed in the Battle of the Coral Sea and in the earlier attack on their home islands by Doolittle, the Japanese kept on-

ly a secondary naval force in the South Pacific and concentrated their major strength in the direction of the Midway Islands, an archipelago in the Hawaiian group. Possession of one of these atolls would give them a base a little more than a thousand miles from Pearl Harbor and Hawaii itself. And with this American outpost in Japanese hands, all of the Central Pacific would be in the emperor's pocket.

The Japanese admiralty subdivided the fleet into five groups:

—The advance group, consisting of four forces with a total of 16 submarines.

—The shock group, with four large aircraft carriers and 261 planes, two battleships, two heavy cruisers, one light cruiser, 12 destroyers and five oilers.

—The occupation group, with a covering force and a close-support force, totaling two battleships, eight heavy cruisers, one light cruiser, one aircraft carrier with 24 planes, 11 destroyers and two hydroplane carriers with 32 aircraft. (Also in this group were a transport force of 12 troop ships containing 5,000 soldiers, one light cruiser, 10 destroyers and one oiler; a third force consisting of minesweepers; and a fourth force, a maintenance flotilla with four oilers and a floating machine shop for naval repairs.)

—The main group of three battleships, one light cruiser, one light aircraft carrier with eight planes, nine destroyers, two oilers and two hydroplane carriers.

—The **Aleutian Islands** diversionary group, with two aircraft carriers holding 101 planes, four battleships, three heavy cruisers, five light cruisers, 24 destroyers, six submarines, some minelayers and minesweepers and three troop transports carrying 2,250 soldiers.

The Aleutian diversionary group bombed Dutch Harbor on Unalaska Island. The shock group preceded the main group by two days. These two groups headed in the direction of the Aleutians and did not veer toward Midway until just before the attack was launched on June 5. Two hundred miles from the island fortress, aircraft took off from the shock group's aircraft carriers, bombed the island's defenses and attempted to destroy the American planes there. The troop transports and minesweepers of the occupation group left from **Saipan** and Eniwetok with their close-support force, while the covering force left from **Japan**. The distinctive feature of Adm. **Isoruku Yamamoto's** plan was the dispersion of his strength. He spread a large array of submarines in an arc east and northeast of Midway to ward off enemy interference with his operation against the island and with the diversionary detachment to the Aleutians. There was no question of the effectiveness of the Aleutian attack, for the Japanese managed to take Attu and Kiska, two of the islands in the Alaskan chain. But it represented a waste of naval and air power.

The selection of Adm. **Chester Nimitz** as commander in chief of the naval forces in the Pacific was an especially smart one. The job he assumed, that of commanding a fleet whose ships were either in repair or under constructiona after Pearl Harbor, was hardly enviable. But he showed by the scope of his **strategy**, the accuracy of his intuition, the swift execution of his decisions and the effective combination of his tactical and technical perceptions that he was one of the great figures of the war. Nimitz was, furthermore, ably seconded by his team of Raymond A. Spruance, **William F. Halsey**, Marc A. Mitscher, Frank J. Fletcher, Willis A. ("Ching") Lee, Jr. and Thomas C. Kinkaid, who carried air-naval strategy to heights that would have been unattainable before 1941.

He was also aided by the fact that Americans had broken the Japanese code. Intercepted by American antennae, the messages transmitted within the enemy fleet were deciphered to inform Nimitz in the middle of May that Midway and the Aleutians were to be targets of attacks. Unable to match the power available to the enemy, he assigned only a small fleet to defend Australia and an even weaker one, well over 4,000 miles away, to guard the Aleutians. He secretly concentrated three aircraft carriers with 233 planes, seven heavy cruisers, one light cruiser, 17 destroyers and 19 submarines in the Central Pacific. Also, he added reinforcements to the air defense on Midway until it included 121 aircraft, among them 19 Flying Fortresses, the redoubtable B-17s.

Beginning in the last few days of May, the air patrols taking off from the island surveyed a patch of the sea with a radius of about 800 miles while American submarines kept watch on the west and north. The **task force** "Sugar" included the aircraft carriers *Enterprise* and *Hornet*, six cruisers and 11 destroyers under the command of Adm. Spruance. It lay off the northern coast of Midway, ready either to defend the island or to speed to the Aleutians in the event of a large-scale attack on the latter. The aircraft carrier *Yorktown* was being refitted at Pearl Harbor; extra crews were working to prepare her for service by May 30 as the nucleus of Adm. Fletcher's "Fox" task force. Also included in Fox were two cruisers and six destroyers. His ships finally ready, Fletcher joined Spruance off Midway.

On June 3 just before 9:00 a.m., a **reconnaissance** plane from Midway sighted the Japanese occupation group steaming 700 miles southwest of the island.

The commander of the air unit based on Midway dispatched nine B-17s to intercept the occupation group. Starting at 4:24 p.m., 570 miles out to sea,

they attacked the Japanese three times. The bombers were followed by a wave of four Catalina hydroplanes, each armed with one torpedo. The losses to the Japanese were negligible; the American commander was holding the bulk of his striking force for the main enemy fleet with its big carriers.

On the same day at 6:00 p.m., Fox and Sugar were 300 miles east-northeast of Midway. Receiving his signal to make contact with the enemy, Fletcher guessed that the ships he was to engage consisted only of troop transports and their escorts. Nimitz's intelligence officers advised him that the carriers approaching the island from the northwest intended to attack it on the morning of June 4. As for the Aleutian attack, Fletcher considered it no more than a feint or a secondary operation. At 7:15 p.m. on June 3, Fox and Sugar steamed southwest to take up their positions 200 miles north of the island at dawn on June 4, from which their planes were to attack the Japanese carriers once their positions were found.

At 5:34 a.m. on June 4, an American reconnaissance plane sighted the enemy carriers 180 miles northwest of Midway. At 6:07 Fletcher, in command of both task forces, ordered Spruance to lead Sugar southwest to attack the Japanese carriers the moment their position was definitely ascertained. Fox followed in Sugar's wake. It was Fletcher's brilliant assessment of the situation that set up the Midway victory.

Almost immediately after the Japanese aircraft carriers were sighted, 72 Japanese bombers escorted by 36 Zeros pounced on the island. The B-17s and the 10 torpedo-carrying hydroplanes took to the air to intercept the aircraft carriers. And at the same time, from the island of Midway itself, 27 American fighters rose to meet the oncoming enemy aircraft. It was perhaps the most unequal battle in the whole of World War II. In their briefing the American fighter pilots had been told that their mission was one of self-sacrifice on which the fate of the Central Pacific and perhaps the entire war depended. They fulfilled this sacrifice to the bitter end—27 of them against 108 of the enemy. With the help of the island's antiaircraft guns, they destroyed 43 Japanese planes, but only 12 returned to the island base. All the installations on Midway were destroyed except for the air base and its landing strips. The bombers and torpedo planes based on the island attacked the Japanese fleet but suffered heavy losses from the Zeros and the ships' antiaircraft gunnery. At 6:50 a.m. the first phase of the battle ended.

In the meantime, 200 miles to the northeast, the second phase was beginning. Completely surprising the Japanese, the two task forces, Fox and Sugar, bore down on them at full speed. The Japanese had had no idea of their existence.

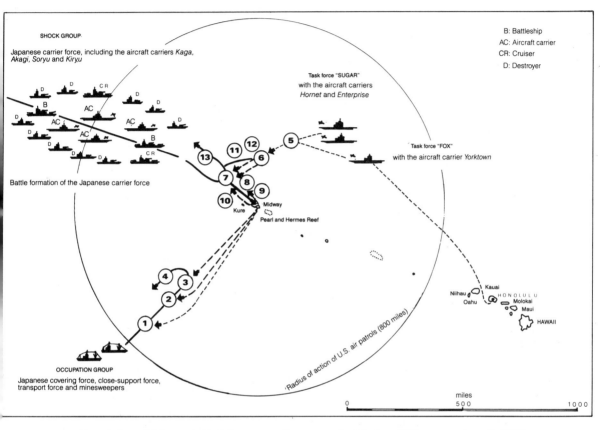

1. Aircraft from Midway sighted the occupation group just before 9:00 a.m. on June 3, 1942.
2. Nine B-17s from Midway attacked the group at 4:24 p.m. on June 3.
3. On the evening of the same day four torpedo planes from Midway attacked the group again.
4. The group withdrew that evening.
5. Positions of "Sugar" and "Fox" at 6:00 p.m. on June 3 (300 miles north-northeast of Midway).
6. Positions of "Sugar" and "Fox" at dawn on June 4 (200 miles north of Midway).
7. Japanese shock group sighted at 5:34 a.m. on June 4 (180 miles northwest of Midway).
8. Seventy-two Japanese bombers and 30 fighters attacked Midway before 6:00 a.m. on June 4.
9. Twenty-seven fighters from Midway intercepted the Japanese aircraft.
10. B-17s and torpedo planes from Midway hit the Japanese aircraft carriers.
11. Aircraft from "Sugar" and "Fox" hit the Japanese aircraft carriers at 8:06 a.m. on June 4.
12. Planes from the *Hiryu* attacked "Sugar" and "Fox."
13. The Japanese shock group withdrew on the evening of June 4.

The first planes, which took off from the *Hornet*'s deck at 8:06 a.m. could not locate the enemy until 9:25. They attacked in a rather scattered fashion and suffered severe casualties. Three squadrons of torpedo planes drove at the Japanese aircraft carriers and were almost entirely wiped out. Of 41 American planes involved in the combat, 35 were shot down. But they accomplished the important feat of throwing the enemy shock group into confusion. The American attacks intensified at about 10:15, with wave after wave of aircraft aiming their explosives at the Japanese ships. This operation represented a new tactic—mass strikes by dive bombers against enemy surface vessels, assisted by planes launching torpedoes. Unwittingly, Adm. Yamamoto lent some assistance of his own to the Americans by placing his aircraft carriers in compact formation. His purpose was to increase the concentration of his antiaircraft fire power and his carriers' defending planes. But although he took the precaution of surrounding the carriers with other warships, they were still vulnerable from the air. Of the four aircraft carriers in the shock group, three were sunk. The sole survivor, the *Hiryu*, loosed all its fliers against the American task forces. But in this instance Fletcher and Spruance proved wiser than their opponents, for their forces were six miles apart; they were close enough to benefit from the support lent by the other's air power without being perilously concentrated. Despite these precautions, however, the carrier *Yorktown* was hopelessly damaged. By way of compensation, however, the only remaining Japanese carrier, the *Hiryu*, had been so badly crippled by the *Enterprise*'s aircraft that it was deliberately scuttled by its officers. Adm. Yamamoto then issued the order to retreat in an effort to husband his resources.

Bad weather on the next day, June 5, gave the shock group a respite. But its agony resumed on the following day with the return of good flight conditions. A Japanese cruiser went to the bottom while two others were damaged. However, the main Japanese force, commanded by Yamamoto himself, remained aloof from the melee. Although his advantage in firepower was overwhelming, he ordered his fleet to retire without having challenged the enemy. His reason? Simply that Fletcher and Spruance had between them destroyed his air power while preserving theirs.

In this battle the Americans kept rigidly to the principle of economy of power. Quite to the contrary the Japanese command had dispersed its forces strategically and concentrated them tactically, thus contributing to its own downfall. Japan's naval might was exhausting itself with the loss of four heavy aircraft carriers, two cruisers, three destroyers and numerous small boats—and what was even worse, the loss of the battle-seasoned crews in the four carriers. The American fleet had lost one carrier, one destroyer and 150 planes.

The Battle of Midway was one of those rare conflicts in history won by the side inferior in number but superior in tactical wisdom and flexibility.

The naval equilibrium between the two great opponents in the Pacific was slowly reestablishing itself, although the Japanese fleet still had six heavy aircraft carriers against the American four. Adm. Yamamoto had lost the opportunity at Midway to tilt this balance even further in the direction of Japan. He was never again to have it. Moreover, the continuing drop in Japanese naval strength was reflected in increasing losses of transports and merchant vessels to Allied submarines and aircraft. Unlike seven months before,

when they had been short compared to the Allied lines of communications, the Japanese arteries became much longer and more tenuous as a result of this battle. Furthermore, the shipyards in the home islands were incapable of compensating for the casualties sustained by the Japanese supply ships.

In Europe the Allies had experienced three years of setbacks before snatching from the **Axis** bloc and its satellites the decisive victories of **El Alamein** and Stalingrad to reverse the current. But all the Americans needed to reverse the war in the Pacific was six months. Apparently, Roosevelt and Churchill's judgment at the Arcadia Conference of December 22, 1941 (see **Conferences, Allied; World War II—General Conduct**) was vindicated—the enemy to be feared was **Germany**. Japan, its initial victories notwithstanding, was little more than a muscle-bound dwarf.

H. Bernard

MIHAILOVICH, Dragolyub (Draza) (1893-1946).

A royaltist army officer and Serbian nationalist, Mihailovich organized a resistance group known as the Chetniks after **Germany** invaded **Yugoslavia** in 1941. Almost from the start his group clashed with **Tito**'s partisans, and through an understanding with the Nazi occupation forces, his army drove the partisans out of Serbia. Although initially backed by the British and the Yugoslav **government-in-exile**, the British warned him in 1943 against cooperating with the Nazis and a year later threw all their support to Tito, who eventually gained control of the country. Mihailovich was captured by the Communists and executed in 1946.

MILITARY INTELLIGENCE.

British agency for gathering military information (see **Intelligence Service**).

MILITARY ORGANIZATION AND FIREPOWER.
Land Forces

The fundamental unit of the land forces of most countries was the division.

Infantry divisions

With a typical strength of 16,000 to 18,000 men, infantry divisions usually included a general headquarters, a **reconnaissance** unit, three regiments ("brigades," in the British army) of infantry, each regiment containing three battalions of about 800 men. The battalion was further subdivided into three or four companies, depending on the country, and a heavy artillery unit armed with mortars, heavy machine guns, motorized artillery and the like. Also included in the division were a number of field artillery batteries, **antitank weapons** and antiaircraft guns, engineer companies, signal companies and all the services necessary for the life of a large assembly of men—medical, transportation and maintenance services, military police and so on.

As the war progressed, the number of men in a division was never increased and often diminished. But because the designers of the weapons they used were working overtime to improve them, their total firepower increased. In 1944 the British infantry division was equipped with 3,347 vehicles; 1,000 motorcycles; 18,790 rifles, carbines and pistols; 1,262 light machine guns; 40 heavy machine guns; 359 infantry mortars (formidable weapons); 72 field guns; 110 antitank guns; and 145 antiaircraft guns—altogether, more than five times the firepower of a similar division in 1940. Each of the rather rare motorized infantry divisions in the armies of the major countries had its own "motor pool" for transporting personnel and equipment.

Cavalry divisions
Comparatively few in number at the beginning of the war, these large units were gradually disappearing, except in the **USSR**, where the terrain suited this type of warfare. The Soviets used the cavalry in conjunction with their armor to good effect.

Airborne divisions
See **Airborne Divisions**.

Armored divisions
The armored force was to undergo considerable change during the course of the conflict. Between 1939 and 1941 the Germans used their 10 armored divisions with astonishing success, massed in depth or combined with air support. Including only 2,683 tanks in all, however, these Panzer divisions were not as formidable either in armor or firepower as those developed later by the Allies (see **Tanks**). In 1944 a British armored division of 15,000 men comprised a headquarters; a reconnaissance unit; a tank brigade of three armored regiments and an infantry battalion on motorized vehicles operable in any terrain; a motorized infantry brigade of three battalions and a heavy machine gun company; two regiments of field artillery, one motorized, the other drawn; a regiment equipped with antitank weapons; a regiment of antiaircraft gunners; a battalion of engineers; and various units for communications and other services. It contained a total of 3,414 vehicles, of which 246 were medium tanks, 44 light tanks, 261 armored half-tracks, 100 armored cars, and 2,098 trucks. Not

counting tank-mounted cannon and machine guns, its firepower included 15,000 rifles, carbines and pistols; 1,400 light machine guns; 22 medium machine guns; 160 mortars; 302 portable antitank weapons (Piats); 48 field guns; 78 antitank guns and 141 antiaircraft guns. The 1944 armored division stretched out over 90 miles if spread in convoy form along a road, with 40 meters (about 130 feet) between vehicles. Actually, this huge caravan, covered by its deployed reconnaissance unit, typically split up into two or three groups, each taking a separate route, while its various services, well in the rear, moved in large jumps. All these machines together consumed over 150,000 gallons of gasoline for each 100 miles they traveled.

In addition to their armored divisions, consisting principally of Cromwell medium tanks and designed for pincer movements or swift pursuit, the British had independent armored brigades of heavy tanks—the Churchills—designed for breakthrough in cooperation with armored infantry. Another consideration was the need for a compromise between swiftness and safety: the former was possible only with light armor; the latter, with heavy armor. This dilemma naturally influenced the evolution of tank design as the war continued.

Corps, armies and groups
The corps was a group of divisions. But there was a qualitative as well as a quantitative difference between the two terms. The division was the permanent whole; regiments and other units were parts of it. The corps, as it operated in World War II, was simply a framework whose inner components could be detached or replaced as needed. It had fewer organs than the division—a headquarters; a corps reconnaissance unit; on occasion, artillery; but always engineers, signal troops and other services, each containing some 3,000 men. Its top command, depending on the mission of the corps, could temporarily assume leadership of a variable number of infantry and armored divisions in addition to artillery, engineering and transportation reinforcements in the form of general reserves. Ordinarily the corps contained from two to four divisions; occasionally, five or six.

In the same way, corps were the separate components of an even bigger group, the army. An army included a headquarters and its own army troops, supplemented by a variable number of corps, usually from two to four, but on occasion as many as five or six. Finally, two to four and sometimes five armies were put together to form an army "group," with its own headquarters and army group troops.

Special units

Only part of the general reserves were assigned to the larger units described above; some were used as reinforcements, including large masses of artillery and engineer corps, special equipment and transport units and tank and airborne forces.

The general artillery reserves deserve special mention. In the confusion of battle, the lines separating divisions and corps became vague or vanished altogether. Some fluidity was required to meet the demands of combat conditions. To divide the available artillery equally among the various corps and divisions, for example, would be to violate the principle of maximum materiel at the proper time—or as an American general in the Civil War once put it, "gittin' thar fustest with the mostest"—for to achieve certain missions, some units required tremendous firepower while others required none. The general reserve was the pool from which the commander in chief could draw men and equipment for temporary use by one of the larger units, the better to accomplish its mission; it constituted the firepower always available to the headquarters command.

The same rationale applied to the corps of engineers. It was similarly convenient to centralize engineering personnel, because there were maneuvers for engineers just as there were maneuvers for artillery men. That, in turn, required that reserves be available and that they be ready to move. Why else encumber the progress of the columns with engineers, especially since the weight of the unwieldy equipment they used often exceeded that of the artillery? Besides, the organization required for engineers was much less bulky since it involved relatively simple tasks like building rudimentary bridges for crossing obstacles, planting mines or blowing up structures the enemy might use. In any case, commanders could dip into their engineering pool and, on a provisional basis, avail themselves of bridge builders, trailblazers or mine neutralizers.

Divisional strength vs. actual strength

It would be misleading to judge a land army's contributions to the war effort by the number of divisions it contained, as some military experts attempt to do all too often. Actually, in modern armies, the divisions, with 9,000 to 18,000 men each, depending on the nature of the division and on the country, constitute only a relatively modest percentage of the entire land forces. It is true that divisions often act as a spearhead, but this does not mean that all troops in divisions are necessarily combatants and those not in divisions are not. Within the divisions themselves, there are service personnel who are not truly combatants. On the other hand, among the corps, the armies, the army groups and the general reserves many nondivisional combatants are found. These include corps reconnaissance units, British independent armored brigades and American independent tank battalions, **commandos and rangers**, the **Special Air Service**, general artillery reserves and others. On the whole, however, the higher the echelon, the fewer combatants it includes, especially in communications and in the rear guard. The number and nature of the units to be provided in each of these specialties for a particular operation depend on the mission, the enemy, the terrain, the communications system and the transportation, equipment and provisions of all kinds that are available in the theater of operations. The number obtained by dividing the total strength of the land forces in a given theater by the number of divisions in action there may be defined as the division ratio. Armies arriving from overseas, which had to bring everything with them, had a much higher division ratio than the forces of the continental countries, which could use civilian labor for some activities.

By way of example, the Allied land forces in the European theater under **Eisenhower**'s command totaled about 4,581,000 men in the heart of **Germany** on May 7, 1945. There were 93 Allied divisions at that time. The division ratio was therefore about 50,000. Some 10 months earlier, when the Allies had barely crossed the western frontier of the Reich, the division ratio was 40,000. It should be borne in mind that the higher a particular army's standard of living is, the higher its division ratio tends to be. The Americans were accustomed to a standard of living superior to that of the British, the French or the Germans; the standard of the Soviet troops, who were unaccustomed to choice **food** or extensive medical services, was clearly lower than that of the other European armies; the division ratio for the Chinese and Vietnamese was at the practical minimum. Evidently, the less developed countries had the advantage in this respect. After the Korean War, for example, Gen. **Maxwell D. Taylor** insisted on the need for reducing the American division ratio, to the advantage of the troops in actual combat.

Naval Forces

See **Task Force; Combined Operations; Warships**.

Air Forces

The air superiority of the German *Luftwaffe* was the result of its superior tactics even more than of its edge in equipment. While the Allied air commanders launched their planes in the amorphous form of a dust cloud, the Nazi aircraft kept tight formations under strict discipline imposed by a central authority. They were organized into *Luftflotten*—air fleets—which in turn, were made up of one to three *Flieger-*

korps—flying corps—of 250 to 300 planes each. The *Luftflotte* was generally assigned to the support of an army group, but was not under its orders. The number of *Fliegerkorps* it contained, and their structure, varied according to the urgency of the mission of the army group it supported. Aside from these *Luftflotten*, there was an autonomous *Fliegerkorps* that included dive-bombers of the **Stuka** type in temporary squadron form for offensive cooperation with large land units—particularly armor—in need of the additional firepower they supplied.

But if German air **tactics** were mature and remarkably well organized, German air **strategy** had never developed. The *Luftwaffe* chiefs sought to develop a strategic pattern which would enable them to use their available air power to its fullest potential, but they were as inept at contriving a workable strategy as they were adept at tactics.

The British found themselves at the opposite end of the seesaw where aircraft were concerned. Deficient in the number of planes it could get off the ground, the **Royal Air Force** was nevertheless exceptionally well organized. Its flying schools were excellent and its air and ground cadres experienced. The RAF divided its men into "commands": the **Fighter Command**, the **Bomber Command**, the Coastal Command, the Balloon Command, the Training Command, the Maintenance Command and, later, the Transport Command.

Although their names would seem to indicate a duplication of purpose, the Coastal Command should not be confused with the Fleet Air Arm. The latter was independent of the RAF, subordinate instead to the Admiralty, and was an elite group trained in aircraft carrier disciplines. The Coastal Command, an RAF subdivision, patrolled the seas for signs of enemy naval, submarine or air activity.

With the increase in the intensity of the fighting, first British, then Anglo-American air power began to grow astonishingly in 1942. Strategic aviation, relying upon heavy bombers (see **Aircraft—Characteristics**; **Aviation, Strategic Anglo-American [in Europe]**; **Germany, Air Battle of**), tactical aviation (see **Aviation, Tactical Anglo-American [in Europe]**), transport aviation and other forms of air presence grew to formidable proportions.

The eventual aims of strategic and tactical air power were identical—to destroy the enemy. The first, however, extended the havoc of the second both in space and in time, aiming at annihilating enemy industrial **production**, paralyzing enemy communications and fracturing enemy **morale**. The function of tactical air power was to assure complete mastery of the skies over the battle theater, prepare the field and support the thrust of the land forces, and attempt to cut enemy communications through strikes at his lines, depots and bases.

Beginning in February 1943, in North Africa, the Allied air arm came under centralized control. The tactical air units were detached from the land forces command and turned over to the control of Air Chief Marshal Arthur Coningham. The Mediterranean strategic air forces under the direct command of U.S. Gen. **James H. Doolittle** and the tactical forces of Marshal Coningham were placed under the general command of Air Chief Marshal **Arthur W. Tedder**, who in turn was subordinate to Gen. Eisenhower, commander in chief of the European Theater of Operations.

Like the artillery the air force obeyed a centralized command. Based in North Africa, it was given the responsibility of supporting the land forces on the front line of the Italian battlefield, as well as those farther to the rear, and striking at Mediterranean lines of communication and enemy bases. Such a mass operation, in which none of the missions involved were deprived of any strength for the benefit of any other, operated under a centralized direction and could therefore fulfill its full potential for adaptability, concentration, mobility and economy of power. In the last phase of the Tunisian campaign, Allied air superiority was complete, leading to a total victory.

The headquarters for tactical air operations was located near the land operations headquarters, permitting close contact among the officers of the two branches. Air officers maintained close liaison with subordinate land units, while army officers were attached to air headquarters and lower echelon units to allow the latter to keep in touch with the disposition of the land forces, as well as to learn of the intentions of the commanders. This close relationship between the two branches also permitted the airmen to keep the army informed, quickly and efficiently, of the data supplied by air reconnaissance. An effective system of liaison and information exchange among all the air and land units was organized to draw every possible advantage from the mobility and versatility of the tactical air force. This was the purpose of the Air Support Signal Unit (ASSU), army radio operators under the direct supervision of air force headquarters—to transmit messages on every aspect of the direct support available from the air fleets.

In the desert the land and air forces diligently perfected their cooperation. There was later to be a British tactical air force (TAF) on the army group level and U.S. Army air force (AAF). Both of these were used to support ground troops but were not under the command of the army group leadership, taking their orders instead from the air chief in the combined headquarters of the theater of operations. They included a headquarters located near the army group headquarters; a reconnaissance wing; a medium-bomber unit; a unit for the defense of the base; a repair and maintenance unit and as many tactical units as there were armies in the group. Thus, the tactical air force was equipped with fighter planes, fighter-bombers and medium bombers. It had no heavy bombers but was in a position to borrow some from the strategic air command for particular tactical missions. In the west, in 1944, a tactical or Army air force with two tactical groups could deploy 1,500 aircraft, 20,000 vehicles and from 70,000 to 80,000 men.

Still, the tactical group supported an army—it was not part of it. For maximum efficiency the two branches integrated their activities. Each member of the partnership had to be aware of the needs, capabilities and limitations of the other. Both the planning and the execution of particular operations were integrated within a central organization in the tactical army group known as the joint operation center (JOC). An army's tactical group contained a headquarters close to the army's; an air control center (ACC), which was the executive section of the group, with an alert system involving radar, a radio listening post and reconnaissance as well as a control system; fighter aircraft and fighter bombers; radio operators; and such auxiliary units as airstrip builders and maintenance and defense troops. The tactical group had, in 1944, some 20,000 men, 4,000 vehicles and 400 to 500 permanently attached aircraft. Of the available manpower in the center, 50% were signal and radar troops.

Military Command

World War I ended before the problem of the general command of the conflict could be completely solved. But for the Allies in World War II it ceased to be a problem with **Roosevelt** and **Churchill**'s creation of the Combined Chiefs of Staff (see **World War II—General Conduct**) and the combined and integrated general staffs in each of the theaters of operation.

The *combined general staff* was composed of representatives of the three armed forces—air, sea and land (see **Combined Operations**). The *integrated general staff* was an inter-Allied organization whose duties were assigned to various members, irrespective of nationality. Between the British and American delegations, it should be remembered, the sometimes formidable impediment of different languages did not exist.

The **Normandy landing**, on June 6, 1944, serves as an example of the operation of this mixed chain of command. The commander in chief of all air, sea and land forces was Gen. D. Eisenhower. His second-in-command and eventual replacement was British Air Chief Marshal Tedder. The simultaneously combined and integrated general staff was the **Supreme Headquarters Allied Expeditionary Forces** or SHAEF, led by U.S. Gen. **Walter Bedell Smith**. The officers in each of its component staffs were both American and British, the commander of the Anglo-American naval forces in the European theater was British Adm. Sir **Bertram Ramsay** and the head of Allied tactical air fleets was British Air Marshal Sir **Trafford Leigh-Mallory**.

A similar chain of command was instituted in the other theaters of operation (see **Chain of Command, Anglo-American**).

Atomic Weapons

The prime military innovation of World War II was the **atomic bomb**. An example of how this overwhelming weapon revolutionized military and tactical organization is provided by the attack on the Siegfried Line by the British 30th Corps under Gen. **Brian Horrocks** on February 7, 1945. The offensive was mounted between the Maas and the Rhine, south of Nijmegen, and backed up by more than a thousand artillery pieces deployed in depth over a narrow sector. This arrangement was at the time considered a textbook model of its kind. But 10 years later it would have constituted a horrible example. Just one or two tactical atomic bombs would have reduced that awesome assemblage of firepower to so much scrap metal in minutes.

If firearms had been allowed to develop normally between, say, the French Revolution and the end of World War II, there would be no need to change the structure of the larger military units. At the level of the infantry division, for example, artillery, engineering and other services were all under the direct control of the division commander. This method of organization was necessary if the division was to function as an independent, viable and spirited combat group. With the arrival of the atomic bomb in 1945 and the nuclear weapons derived from it, however, the armored division that accomplished such wonders on the battlefields in World War II now appears too cumbersome and too centralized to cope with nuclear warfare. In short, the entire organizational system of the armies of the world's great powers has had to undergo drastic revision.

The present-day division of the "Landcent" type, with a complement of 15,700 men and 4,000 vehicles, represents an abrupt divagation in the evolution of military organization. Besides its headquarters and reconnaissance unit, it has two brigades of armored infantry and one of tanks; for support, it has conventional and atomic artillery as well as engineers and logistic units. But each of the brigades has its own firepower and logistic services, permitting it to operate in complete independence for three to five days. The division of former days was much more cohesive. The modern brigade of about 3,000 men and 1,000 vehicles is a division in miniature. It can easily be shifted from one divison to another with no logistical difficulties.

H. Bernard

MILORG.
A secret military organization in **Norway** during the war.

MIR (Military Intelligence Research).
See **Intelligence Service.**

MITCHELL, Reginald Joseph (1895-1937).
A British aircraft designer, Mitchell developed several innovative planes, like the S-4 Floatplane that won the Schneider Cup in 1927, 1929 and 1931. Although stricken with a mortal illness Mitchell, who dreaded the rising potential of the *Luftwaffe*, designed the famous eight-gun Spitfire fighter plane that was to contribute so enormously to the victory over the Germans in the **Battle of Britain**; the plane first appeared in 1936. He died after this achievement and received **Churchill's** accolade ''The First of the Few.''

MITCHELL, William (1879-1936).
An American general and commander of the air forces of the American Expeditionary Force in 1917-18, Mitchell was the foremost advocate of a strategic, independent air force, which, he insisted, could be the determining factor of victory in a future war. Truly a prophet, he foresaw in 1920 the importance of the polar regions and particularly the Arctic route in the age of flight. Opposed by officers in the Army and Navy hierarchy, he was courtmartialed in 1925 for insubordination, convicted and suspended from the service for five years, but he chose to retire. He continued to defend his ideas passionately until his death. His principal convert in this concept of air strategy was Alexander Seversky, a former czarist pilot who emigrated to the **United States** and designed the famous Boeing aircraft. Like the earlier American military leaders, the *Luftwaffe* experts ignored Mitchell's concepts and concentrated on a tactical rather than a strategic air force (see **Britain, Battle of**). The great pioneer was to prove his point posthumously with the RAF **Bomber Command** and the U.S. Strategic Air Command of 1941-45 (see **Aviation, Strategic Anglo-American [in Europe]; Germany, Air Battle of**).

MODEL, Walther (1891-1945).
One of **Hitler's** favorite officers Model was chief of staff to German units in **Poland** and France. He held various commands on the Russian front; the most notable was that of Army Group Center, which halted the Russian offensive near Warsaw in 1944. Following the **Normandy landing** he was sent to the western front to hold back the Allies and as head of Army Group B was able to prevent them from establishing a bridgehead at Arnhem. Finding his troops encircled in the Ruhr in April 1945, he shot himself.

MOLOTOV, Vyacheslav (1890-   ).
Minister of foreign affairs for the **USSR** from 1939 to 1945 and signatory to the **Nazi-Soviet Pact** on August 23, 1939. From 1930 to 1941 he served as president of the Peoples' Council of Commissars and vice-president of the Committee for Defense of the State. He negotiated a mutual assistance agreement with Britain following the German invasion of Russia. He worked tirelessly to promote the war effort and attended the major wartime conferences (see **Conferences, Allied**), urging the Western Allies to open the **Second Front.**

MOLTKE, Count Helmuth James von (1907-1945).
German aristocrat, jurist and Christian intellectual, Moltke was an anti-Nazi from the **Nazi Party's** beginning, although he was opposed to any violent overthrow of **Hitler.** He became one of the heads of the *Kreisauer Kreis.* In January 1944 he was arrested and hanged a year later at Berlin-Ploetzensee.

MONNET, Jean (1888-1979).
Frenchman, former deputy secretary-general of the **League of Nations** (1919-1923). A businessman and financier, he became chairman of the Anglo-French Coordinating Committee in London, in September 1939. In June 1940 he participated with Lord Vansittart and Gen. **Edward Spears** in crafting the plan for fusion of the French and British empires proposed by **de Gaulle** and **Churchill** to **Paul Reynaud.** He vainly appealed to Petain in 1940 to take refuge in **French North Africa.** In August 1940 he was appointed a member of the British Supply Council's mission to the **United States** in spite of his French nationality, but he resigned this post at the beginning of 1943 to take the position of economic adviser to Gen. **Henri Giraud** in Algiers. He later entered the *Comite francais de liberation nationale* as armaments commissioner. In September 1944 he became minister of commerce in the first French provisional government and in December 1945 was in charge of the plan for modernization and equipment.

MONTGOMERY, Bernard Law, Viscount (1887-1976).

In 1940 Montgomery, a British commander, extricated his division from Dunkirk; in 1940-42 he trained troops energetically in England. After **William Gott**'s death in August 1942, he was appointed to command the British Eighth Army in **Egypt** and ordered to attack **Rommel** forthwith. He delayed his attack at **El Alamein** until late October, however, by which time he had built up material and moral superiority; within seven months, under **Harold Alexander**'s guidance, he had driven the last **Axis** forces out of North Africa at Tunis. He led his army forward into Sicily and southern **Italy**, and was then withdrawn to England.

In the **Normandy landing** he commanded (under Gen. **Eisenhower**'s supervision) all the ground forces from June 6 to July 31, 1944; he then led the 21st Army Group, on the Allies' left and seaward flank, for the rest of the war. Eisenhower did not accept his plan for a single thrust north of the Ruhr, which in any case was checked at Arnhem in mid-September. American troops came again temporarily under his command when he stemmed the Ardennes offensive during Christmas 1944. He accepted the surrender of the German armies in northwestern Europe on the Lueneburger Heide on May 4, 1945.

Montgomery's success as a commander derived partly from his iron will, partly from a refusal ever to attack unless he had a firm base and a strong chance of winning and partly from a well-developed cult of personality: he had good relations with the press, and his men knew he would run no unnecessary risks with them.

MONTMOUCHET.

Heights at the intersection of the French departments of Haute-Loire, Cantal, and Lozere where thousands of *Forces francaises de l'interieur* members from Auvergne, Velay and Gevaudan gathered in June 1944. They were attacked and dispersed by heavily armed German forces after putting up heroic resistance.

MONTOIRE.

On October 24, 1940 Montoire, a village in the French department of Loir-et-Cher, was the site of the meeting between **Hitler** and Marshal Petain of France in which the **collaboration of the French State** with **Germany** was planned (see **Petain and the French State**).

MORALE.

The problems of why people will fight and die for an idea, and what ideas they will fight and die for, are difficult ones, on the borderline between political and ethical theory; they can receive no more than glancing treatment here.

World wars involving industrial states, of comparable strength, that are not promptly settled by a **Blitzkrieg** usually turn into slogging matches, in which each side holds grimly on, hoping the other will break first (see **Boredom**). This had happened in World War I, in 1915-17; it happened again in 1942-43. Morale, in such cases, can be the deciding factor. To undermine the enemy's morale is the aim of **psychological warfare**. Morale is high or low according to whether those who have it accept the dangers and discomforts that are a necessary part of war cheerfully or gloomily. As a rule, the winning side is cheerful and has high morale and the losing side is gloomy and has low morale. But neither side may know whether it is winning, and high morale is not found only when one's own side seems to be winning. British morale, for instance, probably touched its highest point in the late summer and early fall of 1940, immediately after the disasters of the collapse of France and the Dunkirk evacuation. The realization that the country was all but devoid of friends outside the **empire**, and that it could be saved only by its own exertions, acted as a stimulus rather than as a depressant. Everbody worked exceptionally hard, and the period of greatest danger was safely endured. In **Churchill**'s phrase, "the nation was as sound as the sea is salt." Gloomy individuals could of course be found then, as always; some people will no doubt complain that the cushions are uncomfortable in paradise. But the general tone of life—this is an infallible sign of high morale—was to treat difficulties with good temper and to look for a way around them or through them, instead of complaining and thus making things worse.

Fighting troops' morale tends to be the higher the more they have to do (until, after several days' battle, exhaustion sets in from sleeplessness). Idleness is an even greater depressant than defeat (as the experience of the garrison on the **Maginot Line** in 1939-40 demonstrated). Good commanders make a point of keeping their men busy, and of getting themselves seen and known by their men, who thus trust them more. This was where **Bernard Montgomery** had an advantage over **Claude Auchinleck**, who was shy, and **Erwin Rommel** over all the other **Axis** commanders in Africa, who were less glamorous than he. Although there are reasons for regarding Auchinleck as a greater general than Montgomery, it is clear that the Eighth Army's morale improved after Montgomery assumed its command in August 1942, because he generated more confidence among the people around him.

Civilian morale is often more important than military. In the short run, it is affected by such comparative trivia as the size of the **food** ration or the number of nights' uninterrupted sleep one can get in a week; in the long run, it is the product of a people's history, not to be tampered with lightly. Such nations as the Poles or the Serbs, who had centuries of **resistance** to oppression behind them, nations in which every child learned at its mother's knee the duty to resist, were almost impossible to hold down indefinitely, irrespective of what military disasters might overtake their formal armed forces. The Jews are sometimes accused of having gone like lambs to the slaughter, but when they did stand and fight, in the Warsaw ghetto, was their morale low?

By an ingenious combination of **propaganda** and terror, **Goebbels** and **Himmler** managed to sustain morale in **Germany** through the shortages, casualties and catastrophes of the winter of 1944-45, to the bitter end of the Third Reich. Terror can act to keep morale up, if all else fails: people carry on willingly enough with the war, or the mine, or the canal, or whatever other task is set under their nose if they know that something worse still awaits them if they falter. **Lavrenti P. Beria** had mastered this technique in the **USSR**, where it was sometimes necessary to keep the non-Russian nationalities in line—at least until they came in contact with the Nazi occupation policy, a fate so appalling for non-Aryans that they were quickly ready to do whatever Beria bid. Russian morale remained stout almost all through the war, thanks largely to memories of 1812.

Japan entered World War II without cheering crowds, spirited brass bands or any great surge of public emotion. Like the other nations involved in the fighting, Japan was well aware that a wildly popular conflict 25 years earlier had turned into the most brutal war of all time. The Japanese leaders, who knew that their forces were doomed in any lengthy war of attrition, gambled on lightning victories in Southeast Asia and the Pacific, after which they would reach a negotiated peace with the hard-pressed Allies. As a result, the authorities in Tokyo mobilized their country's economic resources carelessly at first, depending on propaganda in the form of **National Spiritual Mobilization** to sustain the home front. As the war lengthened, economic controls tightened and the propaganda wore thin, public morale was buffeted by anxiety, fatigue and a growing economy of scarcity in the marketplace. Then in late 1944 people's spirits were dampened further by air raids, **evacuation and resettlement** in the countryside and impending defeat. Yet nearly all of them carried on, whatever their inner moods, to the very end of the war.

Many citizens were already tired of the four-year-old war in **China** by the time Japan attacked **Pearl Harbor** in December 1941. Their worries about taking on the formidable **United States** eased once the im-

perial forces swept across Southeast Asia and the western Pacific in the winter and spring of 1942. Despite **censorship** and state propaganda, news of the military stalemate and eventually the deteriorating Japanese position abroad spread to many civilians at home. Bad news from the front, especially when **Saipan** fell in July 1944, aggravated the burdens placed on public morale by declining diets, poor clothing, long hours in the fields or war plants and fear for the safety of loved ones in the armed services. But tight organizational controls and the state's monopoly on weapons prevented any organized resistance from forming, even amid the disruptions of the last three months before Japan surrendered.

At the same time that the cabinet was preparing **peace overtures** in early June 1945, the army insisted on mobilizing civilians into "people's volunteer corps" for defending the country with bamboo spears against a possible American landing. Most citizens knew that they would have little chance of success if they faced American flame throwers and machine guns with such tools, but they dutifully took part in the drills.

Society was still well enough ordered in mid-1945 to let the government set up such volunteer units, and the repeated air raids did not prevent people from carrying on with their duties. But war weariness was unavoidable, as the cabinet acknowledged on June 8: "Criticism of the military and government has steadily increased. This trend is apt to shake faith in the leadership class. This is also a sign of the deterioration of public morality." The authorities did what they could to help people keep their chins up, but no one imagined that serving in volunteer corps was a cheerful task.

However resolutely they kept on working, civilians were particularly dispirited by the American air attacks. The air war on the home islands (see **Japan, Air War Against**) began in earnest with B-29 raids from fields in the Mariana Islands in late November 1944. Two months later the Foreign Morale Analysis Division of the U.S. Office of War Information reported that popular morale in Japan was already low, even before the most concentrated American attacks began. After the surrender, Maj. Gen. Masamichi Amano said that the air raids "had strengthened the people's enmity toward the United States and the will to carry the war through to a successful conclusion." About the same time Adm. Sadatoshi Tomioka noted that "the damage wrought was immense owing to the self-spreading nature of the incendiaries. Therefore, the people lost their desire for the continuation of the war." Judging from the German experience, both leaders were probably right. Strategic bombings seemed to lower the public's "passive morale," or inner feelings, without necessarily making them more reluctant to stick to their jobs. Their "active morale," or devotion to duty, remained high even if they felt miserable inside.

Right after the war a U.S. Strategic Bombing Survey team, working through interpreters at a time when many Japanese were emotionally flat, concluded that well-educated citizens had been both less certain of victory and less willing to stop the war than other civilians. The fire bombs helped to convince even the most optimistic citizens that Japan's position was desperate. Young people, and particularly individuals with a secondary school education or more, expressed the most consistent criticism of the country's war leaders. These findings seemed to confirm that people's hopes were dimmed by the bombings but also that they were willing to carry on the battle.

Civilians may have been fed up, and the volunteers may have felt foolish training with spears, but nearly everyone on the home front kept up the fight to the very end. One reason for persisting was that no one wanted to be blamed for quitting, as Hisako Yoshizawa, a home economist, noted: "Most people already believe that we won't win. They just think about how miserable it will be if we lose.... Still the public listens to the government and meekly keeps on working. This is so that if we lose, it won't have been the people's fault." Another reason was that civilians were not fully aware of the grim situation in Okinawa, the Pacific or even the Japanese cities unless they happened to be there.

More war workers would have fled to the countryside if they had not needed their wages. No doubt a natural patriotism, in the elemental sense of love for the homeland, impelled many persons to pick up spears to defend their territory. Some certainly felt an obligation to loved ones at the front. Other stuck it out until the fate of Japan's political system could be determined. The threat of force also cowed many citizens into staying at their jobs, since the army and police remained awesome. But probably the biggest incentive to keep on battling was a basic fear of what would happen if people stopped. Whether public morale, high or low, had much to do with the surrender decision seems doubtful, since only the supreme war council, meeting in the imperial caves during the second week of August, was in a position to choose peace. When the top civil and military leaders reached an impasse, it was Emperor Hirohito, not the exhausted public, who chose surrender. (See also Surrender Decision by Japan.)

M. R. D. Foot
T. R. H. Havens

MORGENTHAU, Henry (1891-1967).

Secretary of the treasury from 1934 to 1944, Morgenthau devised the sale of Defense (later War) Savings Bonds to finance the U.S. war effort. He also oversaw the freezing of Japan's assets in the United States. In his last year in office, he suggested at the Quebec Conference that Germany be transformed into an agrarian nation (the Morgenthau Plan).

MOROCCO.

See French North Africa; French Colonies.

MORTON, Sir Desmond (1891-1971).

A British governmental official, Morton investigated other powers' armaments from 1930 to 1940 and was Churchill's assistant in secret matters from 1940 to 1945.

MOULIN, Jean (1899-1943).

Head of the Popular Front in the French department of Eure-et-Loir, Moulin in July 1940 resisted the demands of the enemy to the point of attempting suicide. Dismissed on November 2, he fled to London and was then sent as a delegate of the French National Committee in 1942 to combine the Resistance movements Combat, Francs-Tireurs and Liberation. In November 1942 he became president of the Committee for Coordinating Movements in the southern zone and organized, in turn, the Secret Army under the command of Gen. Eugene Delestraint in April 1943; the Central Services of the French Resistance in both the occupied and southern zones; the General Committee of Studies for the Reform of French Institutions; and the Noyautages des Administrations Publiques (NAP), charged with infiltrating the Vichy government. He also allotted funds for the various needs of the Resistance. In the spring of 1943 he was entrusted with the mission of uniting the representatives of the major political movements, the trade unions and the political parties of the Third Republic into the Conseil National de la Resistance (CNR). He became president of the CNR on May 27 but was betrayed to the enemy three weeks later, on June 21, at Caluire. On July 8, 1943 he died as the result of extended torture.

MOUNTBATTEN, Lord Louis (later Earl) (1900-1979).

A British admiral and second cousin of King George VI, Mountbatten was a wireless specialist by training but possessed great powers of leadership. In May 1941 he narrowly escaped drowning when his ship was sunk in acton off Crete. As chief of combined operations between October 1941 and August 1943, he sponsored a vigorous raiding program including pre-Normandy invasion attacks on the coast of France, and oversaw the development of artificial ports. Churchill appointed Mountbatten to the Chiefs of Staff Committee in early 1942 and took him to some of the major wartime conferences as an adviser (see Conferences, Allied). As supreme Allied commander in Southeast Asia, he coordinated the defeat of Japan in Burma, Malaya and the Dutch East Indies. As last viceroy of India, he oversaw the withdrawal of the British in 1947.

MULBERRY.
See Artificial Ports.

MULTILATERAL WARS.
Conventionally, wars are supposed to be two-sided: "our side" against "the enemy." But World War II (see World Wars) provided several examples of campaigns in which at least three sides, each inimical to both (or all) of the others, were involved.

An old-fashioned Marxist's class interpretation of the war would show the working class, acting through communist parties the world over and particularly through the Communist Party of the USSR, on one side, and rival combinations of aggressive capitalist states, the Axis powers and their Western enemies, on two others. As a matter of expediency, the working class could work with the Western powers against the Axis; but, once the Axis was beaten locally, it must be ready to exert itself against the next class enemy. (Events in Greece in December 1944 provide an apt illustration.)

In Poland, a patriotic Pole had two enemies, the Germans and the Russians, who combined from August 1939 to June 1941, but then fought each other, largely on Polish soil (see Warsaw, Rebellions in.)

In Yugoslavia, things were more complicated still. Parts of the royal army stayed behind after the German invasion of April 1941, to combat it secretly. They also found themselves opposed by Tito's partisans, who had different views concerning their country's future, but shared their anti-German feelings, and by the Croatian Ustachi separatists, who embarked (with German and Italian connivance) on a program of systematic genocide which—had it succeeded—would have broken Yugoslavia up entirely.

In Czechoslovakia, Hungary and France there were similar conflicts of interest and loyalty; a prefect in southwestern France was stopped one day in August 1944 by five different bodies of armed men, each of them ready at a pinch to open fire on any of the other four.

In Burma, Indochina and Indonesia the Japanese posed as the friends of the local inhabitants against their former imperialist masters, the British, French and Dutch: the pose did not always carry conviction. In China, Chiang Kai-shek did his best to wear the mantle of a national leader against Japan, while arming himself as best he could against the Chinese Communist Party. He was so weakened by fighting the Japanese that he could not hold out long after the end of the war against his other, nearer enemy.

M. R. D. Foot

MUNICH PACT.
On September 29, 1938 Munich, the cradle of Nazism, was the scene of a conference on the future of Czechoslovakia. At Mussolini's suggestion, Hitler and himself met with Neville Chamberlain and Edouard Daladier. They agreed that the Germans could invade Czechoslovakia on October 1 (as Hitler had intended all along), to take over the Sudetenland, which thus had its frontier changed for the first time since the 12th century. Neither the Czechoslovakian nor the Soviet government was represented at the conference; Czech diplomats summoned to hear the decision of the conference were arrested upon their arrival by the Gestapo. Hitler and Chamberlain signed an amiable form of words next morning.

MURPHY, Robert Daniel (1894-1978).
American diplomat. As consul to Algiers, he prepared the way for the Allied landing in North Africa in November 1942 (see Torch). He played a part in the surrender of Italy in September 1943 and was a political adviser in the United States zone of occupied Germany from September 1944 to March 1949.

MUSELIER, Emile (1882-1965).
A French admiral whose initial allegiance was to de Gaulle. Muselier traveled to St. Pierre et Miquelon, south of Newfoundland, which became the first territory of Free France in 1942. After a misunderstanding with de Gaulle, he changed his loyalty to Gen. Henri Giraud, who charged him with restoring order in Algiers in 1943. He was the author of two books, *Marine et resistance* and *De Gaulle contre le gaullisme*.

MUSSOLINI, Benito (1883-1945).
He was born on July 29, 1883 in Predappio, in Emilia Romagna, a violently anti-clerical and "Red" district which had formerly been part of the Papal States. His father, a blacksmith, was a Socialist who christened him with the name of Benito Suarez, the Mexican revolutionary. His mother, a devout Catholic, was a schoolteacher. Intending at first to become a teacher himself, the young Mussolini entered the oppositon movement. He spent years of exile and poverty in

Switzerland, where he wrote articles for the leftist press. He was arrested for vagrancy, then returned to **Italy**, where he edited the weekly *Lotta di Classe*. Noted for his biting wit, he played a dominant part in the extremist wing of the Socialist Party Congress in Reggio nell'Emilia. Appointed editor of the daily *Avanti*, he quickly turned it into a prominent journal.

When war broke out in 1914, he at first championed the cause of peace. But after founding the newspaper *Il Popolo d'Italia*, he made a complete about-face and screamed in editorials for Italy's intervention on the side of the Allies with the same vehemence he had displayed earlier in the cause of peace. The reasons for this abrupt turnabout were partially financial—the French government, in particular, liberally supported the pro-French press. Or perhaps Mussolini felt that pacifism was too effeminate a sentiment for his brutal instincts. At any rate, he was read out of the Socialist Party in 1914, but, thanks in considerable part to his speeches and articles, Italy entered the war on May 24, 1915. Mussolini was drafted on August 15 as a private; he was eventually wounded on the Isonzo.

After full recovery, he took up his newspaper once again. His experiences at the front and his sense of loyalty to his former comrades-at-arms lured him more and more toward a nationalism inspired by a sense of the cohesion of all classes of the Italian people. For the first time, the relatively young nation of Italy could sustain a people's party. Thus the *Fasci di combattimento* or "fighting bands," whose name was borrowed from the peasant bands of the preceding century who had revolted against the Italian establishment, was born. At the time this "**Fascism**" seemed to be nothing more than just another extremist group simultaneously crying patriotic and revolutionary slogans. But it was to throw the conventional political parties into disarray.

The new party seemed to signal a growth in the political significance of the Italian proletariat, but this was of short duration. For one thing, the Socialists had split into three factions—reformist, extremist, and Communist—and exhausted themselves in fratricidal strife. For another, the trade union movement had adopted the extreme tactic of occupying factories, which the alarmed middle class regarded as the prelude to revolution. This was the so-called "Red Year" of 1920. In their panic, the businessmen and the centrist parties began offering concessions, but these pointless and hysterical strikes left a bitter taste in the workers' mouths: they failed to produce the longed-for "New Dawn" of revolution. Furthermore, the middle class promptly forgot its promises once the excitement died down. Thus the working-class movement temporarily lost its impetus. It is therefore misleading to pretend, as Mussolini did, that Fascism saved

the country from Bolshevism. Besides, the future *Duce* had himself urged the occupation of the factories in order to keep the loyalty of his working-class following.

Confronted by the "*Fasci*," the Socialists founded the "*Arditi del popolo*"—the heroism of the people. The consequences were a series of attempted assassinations, reprisals, "punitive expeditions" and attacts on leftist institutions. The number of dead and wounded increased, as did the number of Italians demanding the restoration of "order." Although he himself was head of an army, Mussolini insisted that his adversaries were responsible for the violence; once they were silenced, as he proposed to do, the streets would again be peaceful.

On October 28, 1922, the "Fasci" marched on Rome. Encouraged rather than frightened, since he had little faith in the parliamentary form of government, King **Victor Emmanuel III** received the "providential man." Mussolini then became Prime Minister at the head of a cabinet which included only three ministers of his own party. But he was soon to acquire full power as the nation's dictator with the help of the powerful "Militia," his iron-fisted police organization.

His government experienced a serious crisis after the elections of 1924, when the Socialist deputy Giacomo Matteotti, who had complained bitterly of "irregularities" in the election process, was assassinated. A wave of revulsion swept Italy. Mussolini was shaken for the moment. But his self-confidence was soon restored by a childish error on the part of his opposition. They walked out of the Parliament in a pout, thus permitting their power-hungry Prime Minister the opportunity to impose his leadership on the nation in quasi-legal fashion. On January 3, 1925, the Fascist State was proclaimed, and with it the dictatorship.

A period of consolidation followed. Influenced by his mistress Margarita Sarfatti, Mussolini developed a doctrine of discipline, national cooperation and corporate "representation." It was directly opposed to pacifism, liberal democracy, individualism and socialism. A number of institutions posed as the incarnations of this chimera, but they could never be more than artificial facades controlled by "*Il Duce*" with one hand while he leashed the Fascist Grand Council, created on September 9, 1928, with the other. The only non-Fascist organization Mussolini was willing to tolerate was the Vatican, perhaps because it had viewed his usurpation of power benevolently. Irreligious himself, he saw in the Church a factor for order and a relic of "Roman glory." He imposed on the Pontiff the Lateran Accord of February 11, 1929, which limited the "prisoner of the Vatican" to a miniature fief known as the "*Citta del Vaticano*." On March 24,

1929, Mussolini was confirmed in office by a huge majority of votes in a plebiscite.

He viewed the burgeoning Nazi movement in **Germany** with contempt and **Hitler** with suspicion; hence his order to mass Italian troops in the Brenner Pass the first time Hitler attempted the Austrian *Anschluss*. For several years he sought the friendship of the Western powers and especially of Italy's "Latin sister," France. He signed the treaty of the Stresa Conference, which maintained the status quo in Europe and thwarted Hitler's policy, in an apparent attempt to aid in containing the Nazi menace. But these gestures toward the West were immediately forgotten in *Il Duce*'s eagerness to conquer **Ethiopia**. Addis Ababa was captured on May 5, 1936 by Italian troops under Marshal **Pietro Badoglio**. While France hesitated, the **United Kingdom** urged the **League of Nations** to declare economic sanctions against Italy. The only real effect of the League's action was to arouse feelings of national solidarity in Italy, affecting even the anti-Fascists. The **women** of the country pledged Mussolini their love. His break with the West was complete, although he did later attempt to mend it.

The final step in cementing the bond of sympathy between Fascism and Nazism was the Spanish Civil War of 1936 to 1938, in which the armed forces of both dictatorships intervened. The Rome-Berlin **Axis** was fomed on October 25, 1936; Italy joined **Japan** and Germany in the Anti-Comintern Pact on November 6, 1937; and, on December 11 of that same year, *Il Duce* removed Italy from the League of Nations. Invited to Germany, Mussolini was once and for all convinced that his host's power, growing at a feverish pace, would be irresistible. Hitler returned the visit in May 1938, and Mussolini seized the occasion to display his navy while keeping his less impressive army in the background.

It was also 1938 that Hitler provoked the Czech crisis. With war imminent, Mussolini took the initiative and set up a "peace conference" at the request of Britain and France. This was the scene of the infamous **Munich Pact**, from which Hitler emerged in a sullen mood even though he had mastered it completely. His invasion of **Czechoslovakia** followed, and when he had accomplishd this bloodless coup, he declared that country a German protectorate without consulting his Italian ally. *Il Duce* meekly accepted the snub by signing the so-called **Pact of Steel** on May 22, 1939, establishing a military alliance with the Reich.

In September 1939, however, Italy avowed its non-belligerence, refraining from invading France until its "Latin sister" had already been raped. The Italian army, poorly equipped and trained for fighting in difficult terrain, failed to cover itself with glory either in France or **Greece**—which it attacked on October 28, 1940, after its conquest of **Albania** in April 1939. Only German assistance permitted Mussolini to achieve some bitter victories in Epirus and North Africa. In **Libya**, for example, the Italians committed the gaffe of delaying their invasion of **Egypt** until the British had received reinforcements. After Hitler's attack on the **USSR**, Mussolini sent several contingents of Italian troops to assist the *Wehrmacht*. They fought bravely but were severely mauled. Vainly, *Il Duce* urged Hitler to seek a separate peace either on the Western or Eastern front. After the battle of **El Alamein** on November 5, 1942, the Axis grip on North Africa weakened. Tunis fell to the Allies on May 7, 1943. Sicily was invaded several weeks later when the fortress of Pantelleria yielded meekly, with barely a struggle. Quite contrary to Mussolini's hopes, the Italian soldier did not have the "homeland in danger" reflex. It became obvious that Mussolini's Italy had lost the war, especially after *Il Duce* himself lost face when the Grand Fascist Council rejected him on July 24, 1943. He was arrested on the following day and transferred to *Gran Sasso d'Italia*, from which he escaped with the help of a daring **SS** commando team sent by Hitler on September 12.

Physically and morally dwarfed, the inventor of Fascism lingered in the shadow of his imitator Hitler as the Fuehrer occupied the Italian mainland with **Albert Kesselring**'s troops. But in a final burst of political energy, Mussolini founded the "Republican State" in North Italy to oppose the Badoglio government, which was cooperating with the Allies. On December 1, 1943, the infant nation was rechristened the "Italian Social Republic"; a set of anti-Semitic statutes was its first legislative gesture. Established at Salo on the shores of Lake di Garda, the neo-Fascist state immediately became the target of furious guerrilla assaults. In retaliation, Mussolini ordered the execution of those who had "betrayed" him at that fateful Grand Fascist Council meeting on July 24. One of the men who fell was Count **Galeazzo Ciano**, the husband of Mussolini's daughter and *Il Duce*'s former Minister of Foreign Affairs. Another was General **Emilio De Bono**, who had participated in the March on Rome.

Fleeing the approaching Allied armies, Mussolini wavered between taking refuge in Switzerland and making a heroic last stand. In Milan, Archbishop Schuster tried vainly to shield him from a lynching by meeting with moderate **Resistance** leaders. Mussolini resorted once more to flight northward. Attempting to disguise himself as a German officer, he was recognized by chance and put to death on April 27, 1945. His cadaver and that of his mistress Clara Petacci were hung like carrion in the Square of Martyrs in Milan. Twelve years later his remains were buried in the family vault he had had built at San Cassiano in his native province.

H. Brugmans

N

NACHT UND NEBEL.
In English, "Night and Fog." On December 7, 1941 **Hitler** issued a decree that under normal circumstances no information was to be given about arrested persons and that no contact between them and people outside was to be permitted. There were to be no exceptions, and such persons were not to be brought before a war council unless "special circumstances so required." Thus the Night and Fog category of prisoners was created.

NAGANO, Osami (1880-1947).
A Japanese admiral, Nagano served as navy minister in (1936-37) and as chief of the naval general staff from 1941 to 1944. Nagano walked out of the London naval conference in January 1936 over the issue of parity for **Japan**, and rammed through a one billion yen appropriation the next fall for 66 new ships and 14 flying corps. Long friendly toward **Germany**, he had concluded by April 1941 that war with the **United States** was inevitable. Nagano pressed hard for the Japanese drive into southern **Indochina** in July 1941 because there was "no choice left but to break the iron fetters strangling Japan." At the crucial imperial conference of September 6, when Japan took the final steps toward war, he contended that the Japanese should attack at once, before the enemy could muster its strength, and establish an "impregnable sphere" in Southeast Asia. Nagano died while awaiting trial after the surrender on war crimes charges brought against him at the International Military Tribunal for the Far East.

NAGUMO, Chuichi (1887-1944).
A Japanese vice-admiral at the start of the war in the Pacific, Nagumo commanded the IJN's First Air Fleet, containing aircraft carriers. He led the attack on **Pearl Harbor** as well as subsequent operations in support of naval action in the South Pacific, particularly the attack on Ceylon in March-April 1942. He was in command of the aircraft carrier formation destroyed by the U.S. Navy in the Battle of **Midway**. Beginning in August 1942 and throughout the course of the

various naval operations in the Battle of **Guadalcanal**—the site of the important air battles in August and October—he directed the combined air and naval fleet, which had been reorganized to include the aircraft carriers that had escaped damage. Nagumo was appointed to the command of the Central Pacific Fleet for the defense of the Mariana Islands. He committed suicide on July 6, 1944, when American forces landed on **Saipan** and threatened his headquarters there.

NARODNYY KOMMISSARIAT VNUTRENNIKH DEL (NKVD).
(In English, "People's Commissariat for Domestic Affairs.") After the Bolsheviks seized power in Russia at the end of 1917, the Soviet secret services, descendants of the Tsarist *Okhrana*, pursued a policy of mass terror under the official pretext of defending the endangered "Socialist Fatherland." They fought the counterrevolutionaries, liquidated the wealthy *kulak* peasants as part of the policy of forced collectivization and carried out a number of successful **purges** within the party apparatus.

Created in July 1934, the *Narodnyy Kommissariat Vnutrennikh Del*, or NKVD, succeeded the GPU, or State Political Administration. **Stalin** appointed Genrikh Yagoda as its head. On September 25, 1936, Yagoda was supplanted by Nikolai Yezhov. **Lavrenti P. Beria**, named chief adjutant of the NKVD on July 20, 1938, replaced Yezhov on December 8, when the latter mysteriously disappeared —most likely to be executed in secret.

After Beria took over, the changes made in the organization and functions of the government police over the course of the subsequent fifteen years were such that even a specialist would find it difficult to find his way through the maze of successive administrative modifications Beria adopted to mold the responsibilities of the state police to his own liking.

On February 3, 1941, the NKVD developed a new section known as the NKGB, or People's Commissariat of Public Safety. With the onset of the Russo-German war (See **USSR—War with Germany**), the

NKVD lost that section on July 20, 1941. In April 1943, the NKGB reappeared, this time as a distinct agency at the same level as the NKVD. Both organizations controlled Soviet espionage and counterespionage activities, even to the extent of exercising equal authority over the *Glavnoye Razvedyvatel'noye Upravleniye* (GRU) or Central Intelligence Administration, an extension of the Fourth Bureau of the Red Army which was in charge of military espionage. This duality created rivalries and clashes of jurisdiction which were inevitably settled by Stalin. The Kremlin was the prime mover of the investigations which were conducted, and the Kremlin passed judgment on the information obtained.

The efficiency of Soviet intelligence was well known. It was the outgrowth of its singleness of purpose and its fixed concern for security. The experience of the NKGB heads enabled them to avoid a good many blunders. The agents recruited were all extremely valuable, and the Soviet intelligence networks were better at escaping surveillance than their Allied colleagues. Intelligence policy was directly controlled by Moscow and followed a long-term plan.

On September 6, 1933 a German journalist named **Richard Sorge**, recruited on January 29 by the Red Army's Fourth Bureau, landed at Yokohama. Sorge had contracted to work for the *Frankfurter Zeitung*, the best German newspaper of the day, as well as the *Zeitschrift fuer Geopolitik*, a Nazi journal founded by Karl Haushofer, and had received his professional journalist's credentials. He was to create the "Ramsay" espionage network.

In 1937, a certain Leopold Trepper, alias Leib Domb, a Polish Jew, established a Brussels-Paris-Amsterdam network under the cover of an importing and exporting firm. After the German invasion of western Europe in 1940, it was quite ready to cooperate with **Fritz Todt**'s organization, from which it obtained orders for construction materials.

In similar fashion Sandor Rado, born in **Hungary**, a former comrade of the communist Bela Kun, organized the *Societe Geo-Presse* in Geneva which supplied the Swiss press with excellent maps.

Even in Berlin itself, a network directed by *Luftwaffe* Captain Harro Schulze-Boysen, an intellectual of communist leanings who had become wholeheartedly pro-Soviet out of loathing for Nazism, had been planted in December 1940 by the Soviet Ambassador to the Third Reich, Vladimir Dekanozov.

The networks of Trepper and Schulze-Boysen merged under the code name of *Rote Kapelle*—Red Orchestra. When Rado's network began operating just before Operation **Barbarossa** was launched, it was known as *Rote Drei* (Red Three). From all of these networks a stream of precious information was fed to the **USSR** by radio. But the evaluation of this data was the nub of the problem, and the deeply suspicious Stalin misread the secrets these agents had obtained at the risk of their lives. His preconceived ideas of **Hitler**'s intentions, his tendency to mistake his wishes for reality and his cynicism respecting the capitalist intrigues of the Western democracies drove him to brush aside the revelations laid before him. In Tokyo, Sorge had become a close friend of General Eugene Ott, first the German military attache and, later, the Ambassador to Tokyo. Sorge learned enough from Ott to advise Max Klausen in Moscow of the massing of 170 to 190 German divisions on the Soviet frontier on May 12, 1941. And on June 15 he notified the GRU that the date for the German offensive had been set: "War will break out on June 22...." These warnings were confirmed by Harro Schulze-Boysen's network in Berlin and by Sandor Rado in Geneva, who got his information from **Rudolf Roessler**, a German refugee who was in touch with highly placed informers in **Germany** whose identity is still unknown. This warning to Stalin was further confirmed by messages from **Roosevelt**, from **Churchill** and from the intelligence division of the French Army of the Armistice. Yet Stalin remained unconvinced. The master of the Red Army only made some trivial redeployments of troops, promoted a few officers and called up some reservists. When the German army finally made its move at dawn on June 22, 1941, the Russian defenders were taken completely by surprise.

Much later, after Stalin's death, while the so-called de-Stalinization process was underway in the Soviet Union, the Communist Party organ *Pravda* published a posthumous appreciation of Sorge in its September 4, 1964 issue. That article pointed out that "Stalin paid no attention to the reports [from Sorge] any more than to the others." Also revealed was the fact that some of Sorge's reports bore such marginal notations as "doubtful and imaginary information." According to the work of the Soviet historian Roy Medvedev, later sealed from public view by the Central Committee but published abroad in 1971, it was rumored in the USSR that Stalin and Gen. Fillipp I. Golikov, head of the *Razvedupr* (the GRU), wanted to recall Sorge and punish him as an "inciter to panic" as well as a "double agent." If Stalin can be charged with much of the responsibility for the helplessness of the Red Army in the weeks preceding the **Blitzkrieg** against the Soviet Union, evidently others such as Golikov and **Kliment Voroshilov** shared in it.

But Stalin knew how to profit from his errors. The military information that continued to make its way to his desk was thereafter examined respectfully and acted upon with dispatch. When Sorge reported, beginning in September 1941, that the Japanese had decided to honor the neutrality pact they had signed with the USSR in Moscow on April 13, 1941 and that they would not attack Siberia because they were worried about defeat at the hands of the Allies, Stalin promptly withdrew the Soviet troops massed in the Far East and brought them to Moscow and Stalingrad to reinforce the battle-weary veterans of those fronts.

From the Schulze-Boysen network came information regarding the *Luftwaffe* and German troop movements as well as exact estimates of gains or losses in attacks and counterattacks. Trepper himself assembled a wealth of documents on the German army. Thanks to his still unknown sources, Roessler furnished Rado and, through him, the USSR with intelligence reports. We have the testimony of journalist Otto Puenter, who in the spring of 1942 helped decipher Rado's telegrams that would in the end find their way to Moscow: "Qualitatively and quantitatively," said Puenter, "Roessler's information was invaluable to both the Swiss and Russian Intelligence services," and "Moscow was informed in great detail of operations like the offensive of **Friedrich von Paulus'** Sixth Army against Stalingrad and the *Zitadelle* plan of July 1943." There is no question of the value of the information these networks transmitted to Moscow, but it is difficult to assess their importance to military **strategy** because the Soviets refuse to publish the details of their espionage activities during the war, tending instead to attribute their military successes to the Red Army and the brilliance of its commanding officers.

Nor did German counterespionage remain inactive at that time. In December 1941 the *Funkabwehr*—the radio surveillance agency—located the transmitters of the *Rote Kapelle* in Brussels, arrested Trepper's aides, seized the coded messages and broke the code in July 1942 to discover the address of "Coro," the alias of Schulze-Boysen. The latter was caught on August 30, 1942 and his network destroyed. The *Abwehr* and the *Funkabwehr* continued to track the *Rote Kapelle*, following its tentacles into **Belgium, the Netherlands** and France. Trepper was the next to fall into Nazi hands, in Paris on November 19, 1942. By the end of 1942 practically all of the "Red Orchestra" had vanished. The Soviet network in **Switzerland** then took over and itself became the central instrument in that spy apparatus.

Sorge was arrested in Tokyo on October 18, 1941 through an indiscretion on the part of a militant Communist named Ritsu Ito. The "Ramsay" network was erased. As for Sandor Rado's ring, *Rote Drei*, it was caught by the Swiss Federated Police in the act of secretly transmitting some messages to Moscow—a flagrant violation of Swiss neutrality—on the night of October 13, 1943. Rado's assistants, the married cou-

ple Edmond and Olga Hamel, were seized, along with a store of documents relating to the organization's activities. A second transmitter in the network, used by a young woman in Bale named Margrit Bolli, was also located. Getting wind of these developments, Rado disappeared. On November 20, 1943, the radio operator Alexander Foote, who worked for Rado's ring, was captured by the Swiss police, who also nabbed the remaining members, including Roessler—much to the annoyance of the Swiss secret service.

In the USSR, the counterespionage agents of the NKVD allowed German spies no chance to become active on Soviet soil. Only in territory occupied by the *Wehrmacht*, where agents could be recruited from among the disenchanted minorities, did the *Abwehr* or the **RSHA** have any success in uncovering the intentions of the Red Army high command. The *Fremde Heere Ost* (Foreign Armies of the East), a unit of the *Oberkommando der Wehrmacht* under the command of Gen. **Reinhard Gehlen**, did manage some real achievements in espionage; most of them, however, were tactical in nature.

R. Gheysens

NATIONAL COMMITTEE FOR THE LIBERATION OF NORTHERN ITALY.
See *Comitato de Liberazione nationale dell'Alta Italia.*

NATIONAL GENERAL MOBILIZATION LAW.
This law was the basic legislation permitting the mobilization of **Japan**'s civilian **society** and economy during World War II. It provided the overall legal authority for deploying "manpower and material resources for the highest and most efficient development of the total power of the state in time of war."

The mobilization law, which replaced earlier statutes controlling the munitions industries and **production**, was drafted by the **Cabinet Planning Board** under Prince **Fumimaro Konoe**'s cabinet soon after Japan went to war with **China** in July 1937. Although the law was similar to ones passed earlier with little opposition in France and the **United Kingdom**, its critics attacked the bill as unconstitutional when it was introduced to the 73rd Diet in January 1938. Under pressure from the military, legislators finally approved the law without amendment on March 24, 1938. It was officially promulgated on April 1 and took effect May 5.

Twenty-five of its 50 articles provided for controls on civilian organizations, labor, industrial and consumer commodities, corporations, contracts, prices and the news media. The law empowered the government to subsidize war production and to indemnify manufacturers for losses caused by mobilization. It also contained 18 articles setting penalties for violations.

Wartime restrictions were to be imposed by imperial ordinance, without going before the Diet, but each ordinance had to be sent for advice to a 50-person mobilization screening council representing business, party politics, the bureaucracy and the armed forces. Few ordinances were issued before 1941; until then the state was still primarily the chief customer, rather than the designer, of the economic buildup that remained under the leadership of private industry. But citizen's daily lives were already straitened by the National Spiritual Mobilization, propaganda and censorship and forced savings campaigns. The national muster was speeded by Konoe's New Structure Movement in September 1940, which placed tighter controls on labor and community organizations under the mobilization law.

The December 7, 1941 attack on Pearl Harbor was the turning point for Japan's overall mobilization. Shortly before, the 76th Diet had revised the mobilization law to expand the state's powers. Preparations for an all-out war grew intense: civilian factories were turned into war plants, control boards were set up in a dozen major industries, a labor registry was established and eight plans for raising output were announced. The full authority of the mobilization law was brought to bear on home front society as well as the economy during 1942-45. The law was formally abolished on September 29, 1945.

T. R. H. Havens

NATIONAL KOMITEE "FREIES DEUTSCHLAND."

An anti-fascist organization founded at Krasnogorsk, near Moscow, on July 12-13, 1943, by German emigres and the Supreme Political Administration of the Red Army. Numerous German prisoners of war joined it. Combined in September 1943 with the German Officers' Circle, it attempted through propaganda pamphlets and broadcasts to bring about Hitler's fall, prevent the collapse of Germany and end the war while favorable terms could still be obtained. Completely unsuccessful, it was dissolved on November 2, 1945.

NATIONAL RESISTANCE COUNCIL.

See *Conseil National de la Resistance.*

NATIONAL SOCIALIST WORKERS' PARTY.

See Nazi Party.

NATIONALSOZIALISTISCHE KRAFTFAHRKORPS (NSKK).

A Nazi organization of motorists. Its membership on

the eve of the war was 500,000. An official branch of the Nazi Party, it was used for providing transportation services in military operations.

NATIONAL SPIRITUAL MOBILIZATION.

This was the name of a broad program of propaganda directed toward the Japanese home front early in the war, designed to make citizens aware of the nation's military aims and get them involved in war-related activities. Soon after fighting broke out with China in July 1937, the Japanese government realized that the conflict was likely to require a full-scale effort. Early the next year a National General Mobilization Law was enacted, authorizing economic and political controls to draw together the country's full resources to carry out the war. Even before this law took effect, the authorities started rallying public support for the conflict in China when Prime Minister Fumimaro Konoe announced the National Spiritual Mobilization campaign on September 10, 1937.

The state began mobilizing opinion even before the economy because in July 1937 the country was more ready for war militarily than psychologically. The government was also aware that the tight-knit social groups comprising the nation at large were not instantly tractable when orders came from above. The war at home began with ideological standardization because in the 1930s it was so notably absent among the general public.

Japan entered the war with little enthusiasm. There were few posters, little bunting, hardly any marching bands. Citizens were preoccupied with recovering from the recent depression and the disturbing political violence of the mid-30s. They also knew that there had been no real provocation in China and that Japan's likely enemies were elsewhere. The lack of public exhilaration explains why the government labored so hard at spiritual mobilization, both before and after Pearl Harbor. And, like citizens of the other major nations involved in World War II, the Japanese also felt little war fever because they remembered the grim carnage of World War I.

Konoe kicked off the National Spiritual Mobilization in September 1937 with such somber slogans as "national unity," "loyalty and patriotism," "protect the imperial country" and "work, work for the sake of the country." The cabinet devoted the next three years to an extensive campaign to make citizens aware of the war through pamphlets, lecture meetings, pilgrimages to shrines and tombs and ceremonies to see men off to the front and welcome the injured home. Like so many Japanese movements, the spiritual mobilization relied on careful organization as much as persuasive ideology for its success. It used local subcommittees, veterans' groups and civic women's associations to reach nearly every household.

Although many civilians found the campaign little more than "inane, empty phrases," its vagueness was probably the movement's greatest strength. It was easy for people to remain indifferent to the slogans but hard to oppose them. Like many effective ideologies, the spiritual mobilization was flexible enough to excuse almost any exercise of public power, regardless of its doctrinal aridity. Most importantly, the campaign laid the basis for organizing people into community councils and **neighborhood associations** once the fighting in China bogged down and a long war stretched ahead.

By 1938 the spiritual mobilization provided children's brass bands to send off soldiers with the plaintive melody, "Protecting the Home Front." The focus of the spiritual campaign became the emperor. "Group pressures arose," recalled the essayist Yoshimi Takeuchi, "such as the compulsion to remove their hats felt by passengers riding streetcars in front of the imperial palace and the Meiji shrine." After Pearl Harbor, Tokyo streetcars stopped at the point nearest the palace on their routes so that passengers could rise and bow deeply in worship. No law required people to do so, but social pressure insured that they did.

The spiritual campaign's main message for citizens' daily lives was "extravagance is the enemy." The authorities warned people not to be wasteful and urged them to avoid luxuries. The finance ministry started a savings campaign in June 1938 through the spiritual mobilization movement, exhorting citizens to "let the housewife save for her family" and "save for yourself and for the state." Although Japan's overseas propagandists smoothly assured the world that frugality and savings were "purely precautionary measures," already rationing of gasoline and copper had been imposed.

To mark the first anniversary of the Marco Polo Bridge incident, the spiritual mobilizers held a somber parade on July 7, 1938, when more than 10,000 marchers walked from the Yasukuni shrine to the imperial palace to "guard the home front." The first of each month was designated Public Service Day for Asia, when the bars closed, people ate modest lunches and citizens' groups worshiped at shrines. Later the authorities switched the observances to the eighth of each month and renamed it Imperial Edict Day, marking the declaration of war against the **United States** on December 8, 1941. Ceremonies of all sorts helped Japan rally for war by drawing large numbers of people into rituals held in the open. Sad as they were, the brass-band sendoffs made soldiers feel appreciated and those staying behind feel involved. The spiritual mobilization used rituals shrewdly to reduce the gap between public and private feelings, deflecting the hostility and resentment that people might otherwise have let burst forth.

Extravagance became more of an enemy as war with the United States approached. The spiritual campaign ostracized showy dress starting in 1939, urging men to wear a national civilian uniform and women to exchange their dresses and kimonos for *monpe*, the drab peasant pantaloons worn in the northeast. Cosmetics and permanent waves were banned in 1939, but many women continued to have their hair done even when charcoal replaced electric dryers late in the war. The national defense women's associations sent their members, clad in white aprons, to see soldiers off at dockside or to ask passersby on downtown streets to sew one loop each in: "thousand-stitch bands" to be given to departing servicemen. These same matrons distributed handbills to stylishly dressed women, urging greater sober-mindedness in light of the national emergency. The drive for self-restraint was ineffectual, and no amount of moralizing could conceal the huge textile shortages by 1940. The tightening war economy, not stern streetside dowagers, eventually drove citizens into the approved styles.

The program to rally civic-mindedness spread to the media and the schools by the end of the 1930s. Cabinet propagandists used the press, book publishers, film makers and broadcasters to spread the spiritual mobilization movement. An army pamphlet declared that "a firm belief in the ideals of the **Empire** and its mission must be implanted." Publishers were warned that "Japan's unique civilization must be promoted," and teachers were reminded that "education of a very intellectual type must be abandoned; stress must be laid upon moral training." The state ordered film producers to support the spiritual campaign by depicting truly Japanese emotions and promoting respect for the family system. Like most other aspects of the spiritual mobilization, media policy during the war against China was more hortatory than harsh, but the legal and organizational apparatus built during this period made it easier to apply much stricter controls after Pearl Harbor.

Most of the activities of the national spiritual program were hurry-up enterprises: parades, pamphlets, ceremonies, nightly broadcasts on the national radio network (NHK). But the campaign also affected millions of Japanese schoolchildren in the long run through military drill, student labor service, educational broadcasts and a showy curricular reform in 1941. In January 1938 the education ministry issued pamphlets showing teachers how to work the China crisis into each subject area, a practice that continued right to the surrender in 1945. School sports grew more martial. Those who had completed their compulsory six years of primary schooling were now required to attend "youth schools" part-time, and by 1941 three-quarters of the 13-15 age group was enrolled for further vocational and military training. Textbooks and courses grew more moralistic after the education revisions of April 1941, emphasizing the unique aspects of Japanese history rather than the nation's current ideology of Asian conquest. In this respect Japan's spiritual mobilization resembled both Soviet and German propaganda in wartime: all three gradually deemphasized potentially divisive ideological issues and turned instead to patriotic themes based in their national past.

In and out of school, the spiritual movement prodded citizens to read special reprints of early Japanese literary classics as well as books such as *The History of Japanese Thought* by Tsunetsugu Muraoka and *The History of the Japanese Spirit* by the philosopher Tetsuro Watsuji. The authorities also tried to root out English loan-words and replace them with ersatz Japanese equivalents. Radio announcers suddenly had to give up English-derived terms in their baseball broadcasts because they were no longer permitted to say *sutoraiku, boru* or *hitto endo ran* (strike, ball, hit and run). Most ludicrous of all was the attempt to discourage small children from calling their parents *mama* and *papa*, as though the state could root out many generations' usage in the most elemental social unit of all.

Japan had scarcely defeated the twin enemies, extravagance and the English language, when the most prominent phase of the spiritual mobilization ended in September 1940. The campaign was taken over by Konoe's **New Structure Movement**, which turned to neighborhood associations and community councils to carry on the work of rallying people's sentiments and involving them in public ceremonies. After December 1940 the new **Cabinet Information Board** took charge of most propaganda and **censorship**. Thanks to the spiritual movement, by Pearl Harbor the country had fallen into a routine of parades, ceremonies, slogans and savings subscriptions that made it almost impossible to ignore the war. The press was under restraint, radio was completely controlled and the schools had been gently but firmly bent to serve the state. It might still not be easy for a citizen to accept the war in **conscience**, but it was now much harder to oppose it in public.

T. R. H. Havens

NAZI PARTY.
Acronym for *Nationalsozialistische Deutsche Arbeiterpartei* (NSDAP)—in English, "National Socialist German Workers' Party" (see **Hitler**).

NAZI-SOVIET PACT.
The accord with secret clauses signed on August 23, 1939 by **Joachim von Ribbentrop** and **Vyacheslav Molotov**, foreign ministers of Nazi **Germany** and the **USSR**, respectively. (See also Introduction.)

NAZI TREASURE.
On August 10, 1944 some representatives of the German industrial cartels and the **Nazi Party** met secretly at Strasbourg in northern France to develop a plan permitting the elite members of the regime to find themselves a safe refuge in the event of **Germany**'s defeat. Important sums for this purpose—\$500 million, according to some accounts—were to be transferred to banks in **neutral countries** or to friends in Europe or South America. One of the most active networks for the escape of the Nazi hierarchy was that provided by **Otto Skorzeny** for the **SS**.

NEBE, Arthur (1894-1945).
Chief of the German criminal investigation department of the **SS**. After becoming an SS general, Nebe abandoned the Nazi ideology out of disgust with the cruelty of the government and was a party to the **assasination attempt of July 20, 1944** against **Hitler**. He was hanged in March 1945.

NEDERLANDSE UNIE.
See **Dutch Union**.

NEIGHBORHOOD ASSOCIATIONS.
Community organizations and block associations were formed in every city and village in wartime **Japan** to carry out local administrative functions on the home front. As the war emergency deepened, citizens cooperated through their neighborhood associations to assure sanitation, equitable rations and mutual aid to combat the fearsome air war (see **Japan, Air War Against**) waged by the **United States** after November 1944. These civic units helped to prevent Japanese **society** from turning chaotic as millions of urban residents took part in **evacuation and resettlement** in the countryside.

Soon after Japan went to war with **China** in 1937 and Prime Minister **Fumimaro Konoe** launched the **National Spiritual Mobilization**, the cabinet extended a movement begun in the early 1930s to strengthen local administration by forming community councils and neighborhood associations in every city, town, and village throughout the country. A community council normally included several hundred households or an entire village, and the neighborhood association was designed as a subunit of the council, with 10 to 20 families. Both were supposed to be informal citizen's organizations to plan local affairs beneath the ward, town or village assembly and salaried bureaucracy.

The cabinet was eager to build neighborhood units after 1937 in the relatively underorganized cities as an adjunct of its spiritual mobilization campaign. Soon the associations took on more administrative than political functions, canvassing for savings subscriptions, keeping parks clean, drilling for air raids and sometimes even collecting taxes. They also worked with police and fire officials, arranged for festivals, took on sanitation and public **health** duties and looked after the aged—many of the services of local government—at no pay.

Japan's wartime community councils and neighborhood associations are sometimes portrayed as instruments of repression and authoritarian social control. In the months after **Pearl Harbor**, these organizations took on so many duties, and drew so many people into their activities, that so concise a description is a poor fit. Without some measure of local cooperation from ordinary citizens, it would have been impossible to thrust such organizations on the people from above. Especially in rural areas, the authorities deferred to village tradition by letting men with local influence guide the new associations rather than imposing new leaders. By the time the neighborhood groups were absorbed into Konoe's **New Structure Movement** in September 1940, the authorities had managed to establish 79,028 councils in cities and towns and another 118,430 of them in the countryside.

When the home ministry issued Order No. 17, "Essentials of Providing for Community Councils," on September 11, the government began a gigantic piece of social engineering to prepare everybody for a concentrated war buildup. Its main targets were the residential districts of the largest cities, where community solidarity was weakest. The edict restated why active community councils were needed, and it also set out the framework for building neighborhood associations beneath them. Without forgetting its ties to local elites, the government reached beyond them to draw in every citizen by the strongest sort of urging short of legal compulsion. The state deferred to the group nature of Japanese society by deliberately trying to mobilize people in units of ten or fifteen households, not as individuals or isolated families.

The scheme of community and neighborhood organizations was highly structured, yet the group conventions on which they were built suggested something different from sheer authoritarianism. Participating was not the same as having an equal voice, but it meant belonging to a tangible organization of neighbors who needed to get along with one another too much to tolerate heavy-handed authority. In a country that has long preferred interminable discussions and consensual decisions, it was *de rigueur* to accommodate everyone's views at least occasionally. When war forced the wealthy to rub elbows with the poor, the social pyramid grew a little less steep. Japan's neighborhood associations were something less than agents of democracy, but as time passed they took on more and more practical duties and often had to improvise on their own, beyond the discretion of the increasingly embattled state.

The **Imperial Rule Assistance Association** calculated that in July 1942 there were 1,323,473 neighborhood associations in Japan and additional ones in Taiwan and Korea as well. In the six largest cities, where the government's efforts were greatest, there were 282,175 associations by April 1942, with an average of eleven families in each. On top of their earlier duties, the local units were now expected to undertake crime prevention, counterespionage and honoring soldiers and their families.

By hounding city-dwellers into working together, the authorities hoped to manufacture enough community sentiment to get Japan through the crisis. As one of their most lyrical apologists explained to foreigners in 1944, life in the neighborhood associations made "living collectively much more comfortable than living alone...life can be very pleasant even during the stringent period of war! The hostile, icy atmosphere of the immediate past has given way to friendliness and helpfulness." If the ice had melted, it was doubtless because people anywhere unite in a crisis, not just because the state had nourished a hothouse "spirit of neighborhood solidarity."

After August 1942 the neighborhood and community associations were nominally integrated into the imperial rule association, but the local groups went on settling most matters, as in the past, among themselves. One of the touchiest was financing the community organizations, a problem that the state never fully resolved before the surrender. In 1940 a general tax reform increased central revenues at the cost of regional fiscal autonomy, just when wartime chores for local bureaucrats were piling up. Some cities took in fewer taxes after 1940 despite a steadily growing economy, and local aid payments from the national treasury did not make up the difference. In the meantime, expenses grew enormously for all Japanese cities during the war—especially municipal office costs, whose proportion of the swollen 1945 urban budgets was 59 percent higher than in 1939. At the same time, the neighborhood and community organizations were carrying a big administrative load, without pay for their officers or much help with their expenses apart from the dues paid by each household. Not until 1943 was public aid funding regularized, but even then the neighborhood associations and community councils could not stay afloat without the spirit of voluntarism.

The event that transformed these groups most of all came on October 29, 1942, when the government officially made them responsible for distributing **food** and clothing rations—an action propelled by the course of the war, not the leadership or financing policies of the state. Every community council was told to form a distribution department to watch over allocations to the neighborhood associations. The intention was to reduce hoarding and assure that everyone had an equal chance to buy necessities. Until then, for most citizens the neighborhood association had involved air defense drills and other occasional wartime obligations. From that point on, it meant an intimate daily relationship to each household's purchasing habits for the rest of the war.

These new duties were a tremendous drain on the councils and their neighborhood associations, and they created a need for more leaders. In the villages the old leadership class of local officeholders, teachers, landlords and veterans' association officers dominated the community councils. Finding natural leaders for the urban councils was much more complex. Right to the end of the war, the government was never fully satisfied with the quality of local leadership and constantly issued edicts to encourage good persons to step forward, a further sign of how imperfectly the community and neighborhood groups were fitted to the apparatus of state. In Tokyo, Osaka and Kobe the top officials were overwhelmingly male, representing the more well-established city occupations, such as merchants, manufacturers and owners of urban rental properties. Company employees, lawyers, doctors, accountants and clergymen were disproportionately underrepresented. Families who had lived in their city neighborhoods for a relatively long time formed the pool from which most leaders were chosen. Most were men over forty years of age. In short, they were the urban counterparts of the local men of influence in the villages. Leading a council or a neighborhood association was an emotional outlet for older, well-established men with time on their hands who were ineligible for service at the front.

The notice clipboard, passed from door to door with space for each family to stamp its red-ink seal by way of acknowledgment, was the voice of the neighborhood association in wartime. It blanketed the residential districts as effectively as any of the mass media, linking the households during the intervals between the monthly meetings of the group and the regularly scheduled activities like air raid drills. The national radio corporation (NHK) broadcast a half-hour program for the regular meetings of the neigh-

borhood units, held at a member's home with at least one delegate from every household in the association. The most time-consuming monthly chores were settling unfair food distributions, especially late in the war when there wasn't enough for everybody. The larger community councils operated somewhat more formally, but they too met monthly and dealt with the same sorts of local administrative problems as the neighborhood associations.

Not everyone was happy with such forced togetherness. Some people resented supporting group functions they would rather do for themselves, such as the doctor who refused to pay his assessment for inoculations and insecticide. But the wartime emergency eventually drove virtually all residents into cooperating to cope with their common quandary.

This was particularly true once American B-29s began pounding the cities from bases in the Marianas in November 1944. Until then, air defense in the neighborhoods had consisted mainly of bucket relay drills, digging trenches for shelter in back yards and supplying containers of sand to throw on the flames. Now the local units helped to tear down buildings to create firebreaks and encouraged residents whose labor was not needed in the war plants to resettle in the countryside. Neighborhood leaders also helped find new housing for people whose homes had been ripped down or burned out. With local fire companies hopelessly understaffed, the community groups also took charge of firefighting and usually managed to snuff out the fires at once until the great incendiary raids began in March 1945.

Local people were the first to help resettle the victims after the unprecedented holocaust in Tokyo on March 10, in which nearly 100,000 citizens died in a single fire raid. Each neighborhood association in districts outside the target area was asked to contribute bedding and dishware to tide over the survivors until they could relocate more permanently somewhere else. Without the help of countless ordinary residents, the central government and city authorities could not possibly have coped with the flood of evacuees after the raids. Still, the only permanent answer was to take shelter with one's family in the countryside, where ties of blood kept people together while the cities burned.

Despite all the hunger, the air raids and the migrations of millions to the countryside, the community councils and neighborhood associations kept on functioning remarkably well. Notice boards came around in many neighborhoods right to the surrender, with routine announcements about food, draft examinations and evacuation procedures. Even during the early months of the American occupation, the local groups kept at their duties, the most important of which was allocating scarce food and clothing. As the grim war situation impoverished people's lives more and more greatly, the local organizations kept on working in the face of a true emergency because citizens needed them, not just because the state continued to rely on the neighborhood groups as administrative units.

T. R. H. Havens

NELSON, Sir Frank (1883-1966).

A British businessman, Nelson spent his early career in **India**. He became the first head of the **Special Operations Executive** (SOE) in July 1940. He got Whitehall to accept the SOE, but at the cost of his own health; he retired in May 1942.

NENNI, Pietro (1891-1980).

An Italian anti-Fascist, Nenni was arrested in France by the **Gestapo**, deported to **Italy** and finally freed by the **Badoglio** goverment. He played an important part as general secretary of the Socialist Party in the policy Italy pursued after the surrender.

NEPTUNE.

See **Normandy Landing**.

NETHERLANDS, The.

The Netherlands' constitution of 1917, providing for universal male suffrage and proportional representation by lists, created a succession of coalition governments. Dirk Jan de Geer became prime minister for a second time in August 1939; his left-center government included, for the first time, two socialists, and followed a policy of complete official neutrality (but see **Venlo**).

At dawn on May 10, 1940, the German army and air force launched a massive assault on the Netherlands, as well as on **Belgium** and France. The attack was led by *Waffen*-SS units, one of which covered 70 miles on the first day, and by **airborne troops**. Its *Schwerpunkt* was directed on Rotterdam, where Dutch troops fought stubbornly against a better trained and much better equipped enemy. They had no **tanks** at all; sheer weight of superior training and metal rapidly crushed them. Queen **Wilhelmina** narrowly escaped to England on a British warship; her family and ministers did the same. On May 14 the center of Rotterdam underwent the fate of Warsaw: a massive German air bombardment killed nearly 1,000 people and broke the local will to resist. (**Kurt Student** and **Dietrich von Choltitz**, the local commanders, tried to call it off as unnecessary; **Goering** and **Albert Kesselring** did not comply). By the evening of May 15

organized **resistance** had ceased throughout the country; the whole coast and frontier line was in German hands, and under strict watch, by May 19. Parliament and parties were dissolved, and **Arthur Seyss-Inquart** instituted an administrative regime that became more and more severe. He extracted as much **food** and manufactured goods from the Netherlands, for **Germany**'s benefit, as he possibly could. The Nazis took for granted that the Dutch, as fellow Aryans, would happily cooperate with their "**New European Order**;" they were wrong. There was no extremist tradition in the Netherlands; as witness the 4% each of votes secured by the Communists and by Anton Mussert's **Nazi Party** in the 1937 elections. The remaining eleven-twelfths of the population liked a quiet life, and did not like being ordered about; there was (and remains) intense resentment at the occupation.

Mussert's party, 30,000 strong when war began, rose only to 50,000. Seyss-Inquart showed it little favor. Over 6,000 of its members joined the *Waffen*-SS, in which they formed a weak division; another 54,000 Dutchmen joined various other sorts of German military forces.

The rest of the population saw things differently. Resistance was reborn at once after defeat—so far, at least, as it can begin at all without weapons. The Dutch were masters of a simple, devastating technique: when Germans entered a bar, all the Dutch in it drank up and left. There was a large printing industry in Holland, which soon produced an active **underground press**; there were about 1,000 separate clandestine newpapers by the end of the war. Among them five are worth mention: *Trouw*, run by the Calvinists; *De Waarheid*, thoroughly decentralized by the Communists; and three progressive papers, *Parool*, *Vrij Nederland*, and *Je Maintiendrai* (the royal family's motto). This last came to publish 80,000 copies of each issue, working from four separate centers. These papers were supplemented by much poetry and some historial pamphlets, reprinted from the fight against Spanish occupation three and a half centuries before, which the Germans were imperceptive enough to permit.

But no arrangements for underground work had been preconcerted. The **Special Operations Executive**'s subversion and **sabotage** were unravelled, with skill as well as luck, by H. J. Giskes, the *Abwehr* colonel responsible for counter-espionage at The Hague; of over 40 highly trained Dutch agents who were parachuted unknowingly into the hands of Germans in 1942-43, only two survived. The SOE recovered eventually, and dropped about 30,000 light arms, hardly any of which had to be used. There was clandestine radio contact between London and the Netherlands continuously after the autumn of 1940, and a dozen first-class intelligence networks were in operation in 1943-44.

Three local movements, the right-wing *Ordedienst*, the leftwing *Raad van Verzet* (RVV) and the left-of-center *Knokploegen* were effective; they were grouped together in the autumn of 1944 as the *Binnenlandse Strijdkrachten* (forces of the interior). The *Raad van Verzet*, for instance, destroyed the provincial registers in Amsterdam in March 1943, with the object of hindering German efforts to trace Jews and others; it also helped those 85% of students who refused in April 1943 to accept German rules for the universities to vanish. The *Ordedienst*, largely staffed by army officers, prepared for administration after the Germans had gone, and the *Knokploegen*, besides sabotage, looked after the *onderduikers*, people who had gone into hiding, as did the RVV. Dutch geography militated against maquis, but hiding people in towns, even from the **Gestapo**, was not impossible. One *onderduiker* is world famous: **Anne Frank**. Of the 140,000 Jews in the Netherlands at the time of the occupation, some 104,000 were found by the Germans, deported and killed. Most of the rest were successfully hidden.

The Dutch churches, both Catholic and Protestant, were active in public protests against Nazi methods. The first big round-up of Jews in Amsterdam in February 1941 produced a general strike there, which was ferociously suppressed. There was another mass strike in most industrial centers and in parts of the countryside also in late April and early May 1943, when the Germans proposed to rearrest Dutch **prisoners of war** they had released; the strike cost 150 dead, but the prisoners stayed out of camps.

The exiled queen often broadcast to the Dutch, and greatly heartened them. Her government, under **Pieter S. Gerbrandy** from September 1940, was less popular, but was universally accepted as the legitimate authority. (De Geer, meanwhile, returned to the Netherlands and made his peace with **Hitler**.) On September 17, 1944, when **Bernard Montgomery** launched his airborne assault on Nijmegen and Arnhem, London issued a call for a general Dutch railway strike, which was obeyed. It had been expected that the operation would succeed, thus relieving the strikers promptly, but it just failed, and the strike could not be called off. The resistance movements issued strike pay, including a Christmas bonus, to the railwaymen; not a florin went astray. The Germans, in retaliation, hindered the shipment of farm produce from the rural east to the industrial west of the country; in the last, dreadful winter of 1944-45 in parts of Holland there was nothing at all to eat but sugar beets and tulip bulbs. About 15,000 people died of starvation.

The end came suddenly, when the German right flank broke at Wesel in late March 1945; the troops remaining in the Netherlands were rapidly withdrawn.

M. R. D. Foot

NETHERLANDS EAST INDIES.
See **Indonesia**.

NEURATH, Baron Konstantin von (1873-1956).
From 1932 to 1938 Neurath, a German diplomat, was minister of foreign affairs. In 1939 he became minister without portfolio and between 1939 and 1943 served as "protector" of **Bohemia-Moravia**. He was given a 15-year sentence at the war crimes trials in Nuremberg; he received his freedom in 1954.

NEUTRAL COUNTRIES.
The fighting in World War II took place over a very wide area of the world, but a few states did manage to remain outside it, though none were unaffected by it. Several neutral states were close to main combat zones for years, yet managed not to get directly involved. Several more—**Turkey** and **Portugal**, for example—maintained the best pretense of neutrality they could until Allied pressure or their own self-interest drove them into declaring war on the **Axis** powers at a very late stage. **Sweden** and Turkey both had secretly pro-Allied governments but were unable to avoid selling to **Germany** metals without which the German arms industry could not have worked. The Swedes managed to remain neutral to the end. Both Sweden and **Switzerland** provided (by closing official eyes) springboards for Allied secret services attempting to infiltrate Germany and **Italy**. Portugal for a time supplied Germany with a springboard aimed in the opposite direction. **Spain** favored the Axis but was persuaded to stay neutral by the British ambassador, Sir **Samuel Hoare**.

NEW EUROPEAN ORDER.
The Nazi policy aimed at establishing a new European order on a racial basis; World War II was seen as its essential precursor. The boundary lines of the German sphere of influence were to be the Arctic Ocean to the north, the Mediterranean Sea to the south, the Atlantic to the west and the Ural Mountains to the east. On the eastern side a garrison of soldier-peasants was to guard against Asian attack. Within this Greater European domain, assuming a German victory in the war, the Latin countries, **Italy**, France, **Spain** and **Portugal**, would be permitted to exist, provided they recognized their subservience to **Germany**. The same would apply to **Finland**, **Turkey** and perhaps a few of the Balkan

states. In northern, central and eastern Europe, however, at least within the area where **Hitler's** version of the "superior Nordic race" lived and which "the Greater German Reich" was destined to encompass as the nucleus of Europe, there was to be no question of Germany's dominance. In that region, only the privileged people capable of being incorporated into the Reich, assimilating the Nazi ideology and accepting the protection of the German military might be permitted to have their own state. For the Slavic "subhumans," exploitation and finally eviction was to be their fate, their rich territories reserved for feeding the nobler Teutons.

In 1939, as the unquestioned leader of a country in a state of war, Hitler decreed on September 1 a project of **euthanasia** for the "sanitization of the social organism," demanded, apparently, by the Nazi *Weltanschauung*. Such a project could not have been realized in peace time; it would have met with horror at home and abroad. Thus the war was considered a new step toward the "Nazi revolution" and the total revision of the social architecture. Hitler also regarded the liquidation of his political opponents as a measure necessary for the "biological health" of the people. By no means were these decisions to apply only to the Reich; they were to invade the conquered territories along with the *Wehrmacht* and the swastika in conformity with the ideology of Nazi Europe.

In April 1940, *Reichsminister* **Goebbels** declared to representatives of the German press: "Now in Europe we are continuing the same revolution we began on a smaller scale in Germany. Only its dimension has changed. The principles, experiences and methods of that earlier time are still in force today. They are still applicable everywhere." But at that moment the Nazis considered it more useful to conceal their ultimate aims for tactical reasons. As Goebbels put it: "If anyone should ask today, 'How do you picture the New Europe?' we would have to admit that we do not know. Naturally, we have an idea of what it might be. But if we were to explain it, our enemies would be aroused and resistance to us would grow. When we have the power, everyone will see and we ourselves will see what there is we can do." "We speak today of vital living space. Anyone can draw whatever conclusions he likes. As for what we want, that we shall know at the proper time."

When the war broke out, the **concentration camp** system was extended and the number of arrests of enemies of the state of every conceivable sort rose swiftly. Foreigners and **prisoners of war** alike were flung into the camps. After 1941, in accordance with the *Nacht und Nebel* decree, their families were given no information. From September 1939 to March 1942, the population of the camps soared from 25,000 to 100,000 in spite of a mortality rate of 50%, on the average, through exhaustion, epidemics, injections and abuse. By August 1943, the figure was 224,000. On August 15 of the following year, the camps held 524,286 people, including 145,119 **women**. The maximum was reached at the beginning of 1945 with 714,200, of whom more than 30% died along with the flaming, crumbling Reich.

According to a report of **SS** *Obergruppenfuehrer* Oswald Pohl, the director of the economic administration, which controlled the camps after March 1942, there were 20 concentration camps, with 165 annexed labor camps, in April 1944. The names of **Auschwitz, Maidanek, Treblinka, Bergen-Belsen** and Sobibor have in particular become symbols of the Nazi policy of extermination. By the fall of 1941 the Nazi command had made the decision in principle to implement the "**final solution**" of "the Jewish question" by systematic extermination by means of shooting or gas chambers and crematoria—despite the intention of some of the influential Nazis to return to the initial plan of using the prisoners as a reservoir of labor for German war industries.

A particularly cruel aspect of Nazi domination in Europe was its occupation policy in the **USSR**. It was the logical consequence of the program the Nazis had developed since the '20s for the application of their philosophy. Never doubting that the USSR would also fall victim to their **Blitzkrieg**, the Nazi government had developed no plan, apart from the murder of undesirables, for obtaining and using the cooperation of the peoples of the Soviet Union in its conquest and liberation of the country from Bolshevik control. Instead, the Nazi occupation policy, with its theories of race and *Lebensraum* evoked great loathing that, in the last analysis, contributed decisively to the German defeat.

On the whole, there were three different concepts of what the Germans hoped to achieve in the USSR. The extremists—**Himmler, Bormann** and the *Gauleiter* of the Ukraine, **Erich Koch**—won out with Hitler's full approval. Their notions were inspired by the basic idea of supermen and subhumans. The mission of the Germans in the occupied countries, as they viewed it, was to pillage and dominate. They utterly rejected the idea of fair treatment of the Russians. The SS Reichsfuehrer summed up the official attitude in this way: "How the Russians or Czechs get along is a matter of complete indifference to me. Whether they live in luxury or perish in want does not interest me in the least except where we need them for our culture." Nor did the German services or other executive organizations place any limits on the behavior of the Nazi officials toward the populace.

In this connection, an American postwar survey of the opinions of a thousand "displaced persons" is worth summarizing. To the question of whether the attitude of the population toward the Germans had changed between the invaders' arrival and their departure, 728 answered "Yes" and 85 "No." The change of mind, most of them said, occurred in 1942 when there was no longer any doubt of German objectives, when instead of liberty the captive Russians found themselves in a state of servitude far worse than any **Stalin** had imposed. It was then that any notion of German-Russian **collaboration** to overthrow the Communist regime expired, never to be reborn. The growth of the vast **resistance** movement in the USSR, culminating in an organized military operation, was to a large extent the result of Nazi callousness. Also interesting was the displaced persons' responses to another question: "Who, in your opinion, behaved best among the Germans?" Of the replies, 162 chose the German civilians, 545 the German front-line soldiers, 69 the garrison troops, and only 10 the SS and **SD**.

The proposals of **Alfred Rosenberg** and his followers for "the solution of the Eastern problem" were slightly more moderate but met with Hitler's veto. Rosenberg, the *Reichsminister* for the eastern occupied territories, the Fuehrer's race expert and an avowed antagonist of the Kremlin and Pan-Slavism, thought that some autonomy could be given to the various nationalities in Russia's west—the Baltic peoples, the White Russians, the Ukrainians and the Caucasians—albeit with direct political and economic subservience to Germany.

As it happened, there were still some foreign affairs experts and a number of highly placed officers in the *Wehrmacht* who argued for a more reasonable policy. They had from the beginning advocated a constructive occupation policy. Germany's mission should have been to drive a wedge between the Soviet population and its regime by treating the Russians decently and offering them, as a specific reward, release from the shackles of Stalinism. It could not be realized by sponsoring a combat group of volunteers like that headed by General **Andrei A. Vlasov**, for the Nazi ideology and Hitler's notions of racial purity could not tolerate subhumans fighting alongside supermen. By 1944, when the defeat of Germany was clearly foreshadowed and the Nazis had reconciled themselves to accepting the Russian liberation army in their ranks, the anti-Bolshevik slogans had naturally lost their convincing ring.

Adding to the list of grievances the Russians had against the Germans was the fate of the prisoners of war. With the exception of the "Hiwis" (the *Hilfswillige*, or auxiliary volunteers) and Vlasov's Russian troops, Russian soldiers falling into the hands of the Germans were treated as subhumans, and more than one-third of the six million Russian prisoners of war died of hunger, disease or want, another million were shot or otherwise liquidated, and more than 280,000 died in transition camps. The infamous *Einsatzgruppen*, distinguished by the letters A, B, C and D, established by Himmler and **Reinhard Heydrich** in the fall of 1939, had a special mission in the East. They followed closely the progress of the combat units, proceeding with the "preliminary phases of the final solution" and the policy of extermination in the *Wehrmacht*'s wake.

In western and northern Europe, the German occupation policy was somewhat more tolerant but not sufficiently so to pacify the countries occupied. The little nations like **the Netherlands** and **Belgium** were, for Hitler, "dung states" which only managed to survive because a "pair of European countries could not agree on a way to swallow them up." They had "no sense of honor," in his estimation. But it was not long until the Germans introduced the systematic reign of terror they had launched in the East and increased its pitch, with growing hatred on both sides. Large numbers of hostages were shot in the Western countries in reprisal for assassinations of German officers and soldiers. The count for France alone at the end of the war was about 70,000 victims, including those who died in prison. One of the most inhuman of the vicious German actions was the work of the SS division "Das Reich," which in the French town of **Oradour-sur-Glane** in 1944 burned to death or machine-gunned 642 villagers. Two years before, the SS had avenged the assassination of *Reichsprotektor* Heydrich by wiping out the Czech village of **Lidice**.

This occupation policy was accompanied by systematic looting of the territories and the unscrupulous deportation of forced laborers to Germany to fulfill **Goering**'s four-year plan and the economic demands of the Reich's war machine. The burden on France for occupation expenses was particularly severe—some 60 billion marks out of the 104 billions paid to Germany by all the occupied countries. But this sum in no way included the value of the commodities the German occupation officials shipped off to the Reich, such as farm harvests, oats, oil, steel, fodder, livestock, etc. Even today, only a very rough estimate can be put on the value of these contributions. Nor should the priceless artistic treasures extracted by Rosenberg's *Einsatsstab*, particularly from France, for the private collections of Hitler and Goering be forgotten. A 1944 figure mentions 137 trainloads of merchandise with 4,174 crates containing 21,903 works of art, including 10,890 paintings.

The German records for forced labor in 1944 show that by September 30, 1944, more than 7.5 million foreigners and civilian prisoners were harnessed to German industry or the Reich's economic mobilization of manpower. The conditions under which men, women and sometimes children worked in Holland, Belgium, **Poland** and especially the occupied Russian territories were so debased as to recall the worst methods of imperialist exploitation of centuries past. The fact that prisoners from such Western countries as France and the **United Kingdom** received better treatment than the millions of laborers from the East hardly lessened this aspect of Nazi bestiality.

The theory and practice of Nazi domination in Europe between 1939 and 1944 revealed the essential characteristics of Hitler's plans for his New Order. The "Greater German Reich" of the future, inspired by the taste of its designers for a Teutonic Holy Roman Empire flavored by Nazi sauce, with a swollen Berlin as its "world capital," was to be a self-contained economic **empire** impervious to blockade and superior to the Anglo-Saxon world economic system. With **Japan**, the dominant power in Asia, it could contain the **United States** in an iron vise. Its laws and constitution were only different facets of its core creed: the "will of the Fuehrer." This empire, reigning by virtue of the violence of the Fuehrer-State, wanted nothing less than the systematic extirpation of all alien races; in particular the Jews. The victory of the "master race" over "God's chosen people" was to demonstrate once and for all the natural heirarchy of races. The "theological fact" was to give way to the "biological myth." The misfits were to be expunged and the recalcitrants cordoned off in concentration camps, there to serve as experimental animals for "progressive" scientists, or to be deported to Siberia. What survived of the "alien peoples" were destined to serve as a kind of helot to the blond and blue-eyed. As the SS Reichsfuehrer expressed it in a memorandum on the treatment to be given the "subject peoples in the East": "A fundamental question in the solution to problems of this sort is the education and testing of the youth. For the non-Germanic population of the East, there should be no schooling above the fourth-grade grammar-school level. The curriculum of this grammar school should be restricted to simple calculations up to 500, the ability to write one's name and the doctrine that it is divine commandment to obey Germans and to be honest and submissive workers. I do not consider literacy advisable. Other than this, there should be absolutely no education."

The enormous expanse of the USSR could serve as a training ground for maneuvers and military field problems. In place of Christian principles, the rules of order of the SS would be the moral guide since Hitler

wanted to substitute the comforting doctrine of submission of the individual to the majesty of the state for the Christian doctrine of the infinite importance of the individual human soul. Instead of "an upper layer of economic privilege," the Party leaders, permeated by a new morality and married to specially educated aristocratic ladies, were to establish the standard for the minds and behavior of the "master race." For the victorious heroes of the war Hitler promised the delights of multiple marriage to guarantee the multiplication of the Germanic peoples. "The victory of childbirth" must follow the victory of arms, as *Reichsminister* Bormann noted in a document written at the end of January 1944 after an interview with Hitler.

Again, on May 8, 1943, Hitler expressed his "unshakeable conviction" that the Reich would one day dominate all of Europe. "To do that," the Fuehrer continued, "we shall have to continue fighting, but it will no doubt lead to the most splendid of military achievements. After that, the path to world domination will follow as a matter of course. With Europe securely in our hands we can surely possess the whole world...Under these conditions, naturally, we cannot consider questions of law or injustice..." Hitler was determined that this time Germany would not abandon the battle before the last round.

H.-A. Jacobsen

NEW GUINEA.

Except for **Greenland**, New Guinea, 306,600 square miles, is the largest island on earth. It lies in the eastern part of the Malay Archipelago and north of **Australia**. Barely penetrable and sparsely populated, it was divided between Dutch and Australian administrations. From 1942 to 1945 the Japanese military occupied its western and northern coasts. The island was the farthest point south reached by the Japanese in their conquest of the Pacific. A solid defensive effort by mostly Australian forces, backed by U.S. troops, repulsed the Japanese attempt, begun in 1942, to take Port Moresby in the southeastern portion of the island, which would have given them a base for launching air attacks on Australia. Under Gen. **MacArthur**, the Allied forces then mounted a series of counteroffensives that by May 1945 had succeeded in eliminating Japanese control of the island.

NEW ORDER IN EAST ASIA.

This Japanese program of economic, political and cultural coordination to bring peace and stability to **China**, Manchukuo and **Japan** was in effect from November 1938 to September 1940. Prime Minister **Fumimaro Konoe**, who applauded the Japanese army's expansionism in China after fighting broke out in July 1937, proclaimed the new order on November 3, 1938 as a replacement for the treaty system imposed earlier by the Western powers. He called for mutual aid among the three states, under Japanese guidance, to establish a self-reliant zone free of Western interference.

Because the **USSR** menaced Japan's position from Siberia, the Japanese army under the new order kept its main strength in north China and seized only the major cities and railroads in the interior, conceding Chungking and the southwest to the Chinese Nationalists under **Chiang Kai-shek**. The Japanese government set up development corporations in north China to exploit coal and iron ore resources. Culturally the new order fostered the common brotherhood of Chinese and Japanese in the face of Western imperialism.

The new order attracted Asian nationalists who were eager to get rid of colonialism, but soon they saw that the plan was just a shroud behind which Japan was replacing the **United States** and Europe as overlord. Arrogant and often ruthless conduct by Japanese troops quickly disillusioned citizens living in the area and soured them on the puppet regime of **Wang Ching-wei**, set up at Nanking in March 1940. The new order was replaced in September 1940 by an even more grandiose scheme, the **Greater East Asia Co-Prosperity Sphere**.

T. R. H. Havens

NEW STRUCTURE MOVEMENT.

Once war with **China** broke out in July 1937, **Japan** acted quickly to reorganize its economic exploitation of Manchukuo and the occupied areas of north China. The Manchurian Industrial Development Corporation, led by the parvenu manufacturer and friend of the Japanese Kwantung Army, Gisuke Aikawa, started up in March 1938 and soon established new iron and steel mills, aircraft factories and automobile plants. The new economic structure on the continent was rounded out by the North and Central China Development Corporations. By 1940 China and Manchukuo were producing 39 million tons of coal per annum, and the following year they met 30 percent of Japan's pig iron needs.

Under the terms of the **National General Mobilization Law** of 1938, the cabinet had the authority to restructure the domestic economy as well. But opposition from big business, bureaucratic rivalries, the surprisingly fast economic development of the continent and the uncertain duration of the war with China all helped to postpone a major reorganization of the economy at home. **Production** lagged as a result. Finally **Naoki Hoshino**, president of the

Cabinet Planning Board, led the New Structure Movement to place key industries under the same types of controls that were in effect on the continent. Not until September 1941 did the war crisis seem great enough to persuade private industry to surrender its authority to the army's economic strategists, working through industrial control boards established by the Cabinet Planning Board.

The main goals of the New Structure Movement were as much political as economic. While industrial planning was gradually growing more integrated, senior statemen, headed by Prince **Fumimaro Konoe**, called for a supra-party organization that would absorb all political factions, national societies and business groups. The new transcendant association was intended to solidify the home front and block any extremists from seizing control of a fragmented polity.

Between Konoe's resignation as premier in January 1939 and his return in July 1940, Japanese politics were almost paralyzed. During this interval three cabinets grappled unsuccessfully with economic mobilization, ambitious militarists, a bogged-down war in China and the outbreak of fighting in Europe. At exactly the same time, Japan's parliamentary political parties, never models of stability, suddenly grew wobbly because of factional splits and threatened to disintegrate. By the spring of 1940 Japan was dangerously vulnerable to a coup by military radicals. To head off this possiblity, the New Structure Movement called for a national unity organization embracing all groups and interests in the country. Such a structure would also speed economic preparedness.

Many party politicians joined the movement in order to try to stop the army from snuffing them out entirely. Others battled to retain their autonomy within the lower house of the Diet, which continued to meet throughout the war. Once Konoe returned as prime minister in July 1940, the major parties quickly voted themselves out of existence in favor of the new scheme for national unity. On September 27, the same day Japan signed the **Tripartite Pact** with **Germany** and **Italy**, the New Structure Movement reached its climax when Konoe announced the creation of the **Imperial Rule Assistance Association**.

T. R. H. Havens

NEW ZEALAND.

A virtually independent British dominion since 1901, New Zealand entered the war on September 3, 1939 out of longstanding loyalty to Britain. New Zealand troops, first consisting of only one division, which was later joined by another and by an armored brigade, went to **Egypt** for advanced training and saw action there and in **Greece**, **Libya**, **Tunisia** and **Italy**. They were reckoned among the most spirited and reliable troops in the British Eighth Army. Additional forces were raised by conscription and worked under the **United States** command in the southwestern Pacific, operating against the Japanese.

In home politics the Labour government, in power since 1935 under M. J. Savage, intensified the economic controls it had already begun to operate before the war, when Peter Fraser had set up the framework of a **welfare state** in 1938. War **production** increased, but prices remained fairly stable. Fraser succeeded Savage as prime minister in 1940 and held the post till 1949. He played a leading part, as spokesman for the small nations, in the drawing up of the **United Nations** Charter at San Francisco in 1945. New Zealand by the end of the war had had its ties with the **United Kingdom** loosened, but not broken; it was somewhat closer to the U.S. and a good deal closer to its nearest neighbor, **Australia**.

NIGHT AND FOG.
See *Nacht und Nebel*.

NIMITZ, Chester W. (1885-1966).
American admiral. Appointed commander in chief of the **United States** Pacific Fleet shortly after the Japanese attack on **Pearl Harbor**, he was responsible for the U.S. victory at **Midway** in June 1942 and for the subsequent undermining of Japanese naval power. He was among those receiving **Japan**'s surrender aboard the USS *Missouri* on September 2, 1945.

NKVD.
See *Narodnyy Kommissariat Vnutrennikh Del*.

NOMURA, Kichisaburo (1877-1964).
An admiral, diplomat and Japanese ambassador to the **United States** at the time of **Pearl Harbor**, Nomura abrogated **Japan**'s treaty of commerce with the U.S. as foreign minister in late 1939. Together with Saburo Kurusu, he negotiated with **Cordell Hull**, the American secretary of state, from April through November 1941. He tried earnestly to avert war without compromising Japan's position on the Asian mainland. Both Hull and Nomura wanted to turn Japan away from the **Axis** and toward an accommodation with the United States. Nomura's ambiguity and vacillation, which greatly imperiled the negotiations, were caused by his imperfect English, his diplomatic inexperience and the uncertain political climate in Tokyo, and also by his hope of forestalling war by letting the talks drag on as long as possible. This tactic failed when the Japanese government took the Hull note of November 26 as an ultimatum. Through confusion and communications

delays that were symbolic of the entire negotiations, Nomura met with Hull to announce the impending attack on Pearl Harbor more than an hour after it had already begun.

NORDPOL.
See *Englandspiel*.

NORMANDY LANDING.
Four years' preparation went into the Allied re-entry onto the continent after the near-disaster of Dunkirk. Four years' raiding experience by **Louis Mountbatten**'s and **Robert F. Laycock**'s commandos, including the disastrous dress rehearsal at Dieppe; four years' pounding, often ineffectual, by the **Royal Air Force**'s **Bomber Command** at industrial and communications targets; two and a half years of the same by the USAAF; a year's meticulous planning, done in dead secrecy in London by a joint Anglo-American staff; a year's administrative build-up (Operation **Bolero**) by the Americans of troops, aircraft and ammunition in England, without which the operation could never have been mounted at all; the protracted **battle of the Atlantic**, over which all Bolero's supplies came; the struggle to design and assemble adequate **landing craft**; and the work of all the secret services that sought to foster **resistance**; all these were combined in the largest amphibious operation ever mounted. Bolero assembled 21 U.S. divisions; there were 26 British-Canadian and Polish divisions as well. The Germans had 36 infantry and six *Panzer* divisions between Brest and the Rhine, and about 15 more infantry and three more *Panzer* divisions readily available.

The major Anglo-American attack on northwestern Europe, long anticipated by the Germans on the beaches south of Boulogne, took place instead in the Baie de la Seine at dawn on June 6, 1944. This was Operation Neptune, the assault phase of Operation Overlord. **Eisenhower** had postponed it for 24 hours, awaiting more favorable weather; no longer a postponement was feasible without risking the essential element of surprise. As it was, the armada was so large that by dusk on June 5 a few ships were already in sight of the shore; they spent the night disturbed only by a moderate sea.

Eisenhower decided to call out resistance forces for maximum activity on the night of the landing and to undertake an intricate program of road and rail interdiction bombing in the first days of June, which cut every bridge over the Seine below Paris and every bridge but one on the Loire below Briare. The **French Resistance** added 950 rail cuts and a myriad of road blocks and acts of minor **sabotage** on the critical night. Massive bombardment of the landing area, from sea and air, began at midnight. **Bernard Mont-**

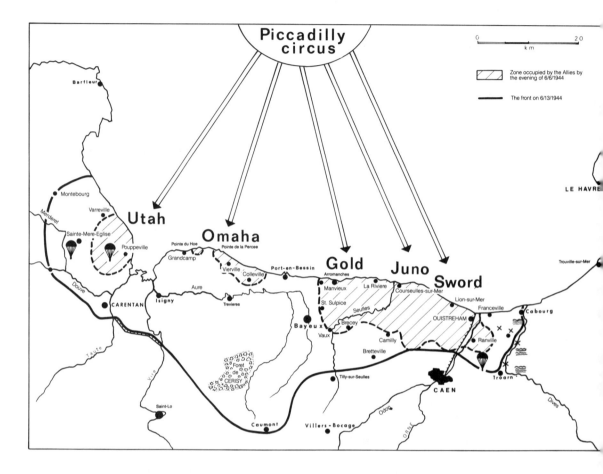

gomery, the force commander, put three divisions ashore from the air in the early hours of the morning, and five from the sea after dawn, on the first day (D-day). Two American **airborne divisions**, aiming for the base of the Cotentin peninsula, were widely scattered in their first drop. The seaborne landing just east of the peninsula (Omaha beach) nearly failed, but was rescued by the evening of the first day; all the rest succeeded. A British airborne division seized and held the crossing of the Ouistreham-Caen canal, on the operation's left flank, in its earliest hours. Caen was to have been captured on the first day; the Germans held it till July 9. But by June 11 all Neptune's landing areas had been built into a single solid front; 326,000 troops were ashore, and the work of Overlord went ahead. **Erwin Rommel**, the defending general (who was away on leave at the critical moment), had kept his strength well forward, and had no immediate reserves available. An exceptionally elaborate and suc-

cessful **deception** plan led the Germans to believe that the main landing, under Gen. **George S. Patton**, was going to take place south of Boulogne after all; thinking Neptune itself was a feint, they did not react fast.

The success of the landing gave enormous encouragement to the populations of occupied Europe: the end of the war was at last clearly in sight. Still, there was far to go. Montgomery pursued for the next month his intended **strategy**, of hammering away on his left flank—to which he attracted all the available German armor—with British and Canadian troops, while the Americans on the right cleared the Cotentin peninsula. Cherbourg was taken on June 26, but German demolitions delayed its re-opening as a port until July 19. **Artificial ports** meanwhile supplied the forces ashore, though the one serving the Americans was severely damaged by a storm in the third week of June. There was no German naval and virtually no air

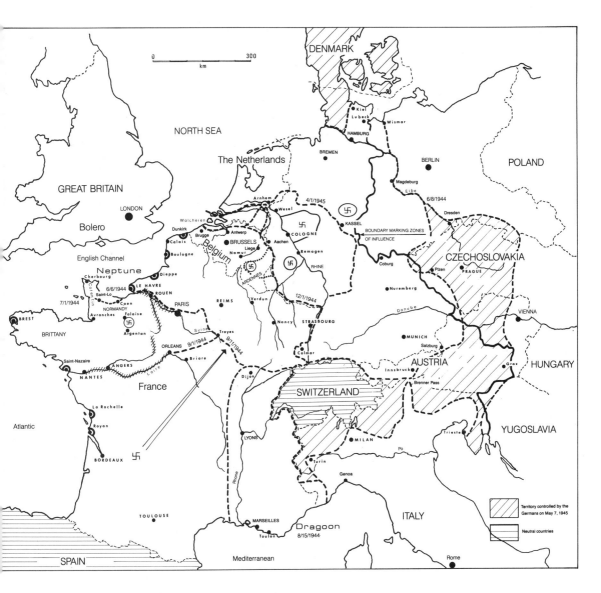

interference, but the German army fought stubbornly for every inch of the close Norman countryside.

On July 25 Gen. **Omar Bradley** launched his First Army in an offensive southward from St. Lo, which reached Avranches in a week. Patton's Third Army then passed through the First, fanned out across Brittany—where the French **Special Air Service** had fomented a popular rising—and swept round in a left-handed half-circle through Mayenne and Alencon, behind the Germans' left rear.

Rommel by this time had been wounded, and **Gerd von Rundstedt**, his superior, had been replaced by **Guenther von Kluge**. Von Kluge attempted a counter-offensive westward from Mortain; but Bradley, fore-warned by **Ultra**, stopped him in his tracks. The German Seventh Army was thereupon encircled in a vast pocket between Falaise and Argentan; it lost half a million men, most of them as prisoners.

By now France outside the battle areas was teeming with resistance groups, many of them with SAS troops

357

or SOE or OSS officers from the **Special Operations Executive** or **Office of Strategic Services** as their fighting core; the Germans were losing control over their own rear. On August 15 **Lucian Truscott's** Sixth Army Group—moved in landing craft sent around from Normandy to the Tyrrhenian—disembarked on the coast of the Riviera and began its advance up the Rhone. This was made much easier by resisters, who opened a route through the lower Alps, again around the Germans' left flank. In the last week of August the isolated German garrisons in southwestern France headed back for the Reich—by road, as the railways were no longer in service—and lost heavily in resistance ambushes on the way. Five Free French divisions were by now in action, four under **Jean de Lattre de Tassigny** in the Sixth Army Group and one under **Leclerc** in Patton's Third Army.

As the Allied armies moved northeastward, Eisenhower had intended to bypass Paris; feeding its population would further strain his already tenuous lines of supply. But resisters in the city forced his hand. Communists and Gaullists initiated an insurrection on August 19; **Dietrich von Choltitz**, the German governor, could have repressed it but did not, and surrendered to Leclerc on the 25th.

Meanwhile the Canadians were advancing rapidly along the coast. They took Dieppe on September 1 and were in Brugge by the 9th. The British reached Antwerp on September 4 to find that the Belgian resistance had secured the port installations virtually intact, although no ship could unload at Antwerp until November 26, after fierce fighting on Walcheren had cleared the mouth of the Schelde.

This advance overran several hundred V-1 launching sites, from which the Germans had been bombarding London with pilotless aircraft (each carrying a ton of explosive) since June 13. These attacks had been much less destructive than had at first been feared—the **V-1 and V-2** between them caused about 31,000 casualties in England—but were highly disagreeable; they also gave the population of southeastern England a direct feeling of personal participation in the war once again. After they lost Antwerp, the Germans directed their V-weapons on that city as well; indeed, of 3,000 V-2s fired between September 8, 1944 and March 29, 1945, 1,750 were aimed at Antwerp and 1,250 at London. Belgian casualties were quite as large as the British. There was no defense against a V-2, but over half the 7,840 V-1s fired at England were destroyed in the air by fighters or **anti-aircraft defenses**. The Americans meanwhile had also pressed forward vigorously, taking Verdun on September 1, Liege on the 8th and **Luxembourg** on the 10th. But they ran out of gasoline and impetus as

they neared the Siegfried Line, just inside the west German frontier, where, for a short time, they stuck.

One attempt to break the deadlock, turn the Germans' new right flank and bring the war to a sudden end narrowly failed. Allied **airborne troops** had repeatedly prepared to drop in key areas behind the battle front, only to find their dropping zones overrun by the swiftness of the ground troops' advance. On September 17 two U.S. airborne divisions seized the bridges at Nijmegen and Eindhoven, and the First British airborne division dropped at Arnhem. Intelligence that there were two **SS** Panzer divisions near Arnhem was ignored, but proved true: the British parachutists were too lightly armed to secure their objective against such oppostion, and a drive to link up with them overland was checked by tough German defenses. The remnant withdrew on September 25.

While the British and Canadians fought to open the Schelde, the Americans and French tackled the left bank of the Rhine. Nancy fell on September 15, Aachen on October 21, Belfort on November 22 and Strasbourg on the 23rd, but the autumn rains were unusually heavy, and progress was slow. The opening of Antwerp enabled Eisenhower to shorten his supply lines, which had hitherto run from Brest (captured, damaged, on September 18), Cherbourg and the Channel ports; but Antwerp was on his extreme left flank. German garrisons held out in the Channel Islands, Lorient, **St. Nazaire** and the mouth of the Gironde, but were easily enough contained. Submarine operations from the Biscay coast came almost to a standstill: a distinct subsidiary gain for the Allies.

The sudden German offensive in the Ardennes on December 16 achieved tactical surprise—partly because complete radio silence prevented Ultra from giving any warning—but it never shook Eisenhower's nerve. By Christmas Eve it had been mastered. It never even reached Namur, the halfway mark towards its goal of Antwerp, and it cost the Germans a quarter of a million men, as well as 1,600 aircraft and 600 **tanks** (the Allies lost some 60,000 men in it). (See also **Battle of the Bulge.**)

In January the Ardennes salient was finally reduced, and in February and early March Eisenhower's armies pinched out the German forces west of the Rhine. On March 7 an American armored spearhead seized a bridge, accidentally left undestroyed, at Remagen between Cologne and Coblenz. By March 23 Bradley had three corps east of the Rhine there, in a bridgehead 25 miles wide; on that day Montgomery's armies launched a major crossing of the Rhine near Wesel, downstream of the Ruhr. Over 40,000 tactical support sorties were flown in four days. Resistance to the land attack was comparatively slight, and by April 18 the Ruhr in-

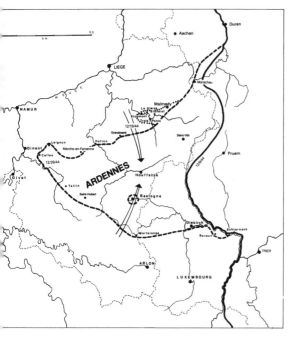

economy (see **Germany—Economy of the Third Reich**). For the most part the ore was extracted from the Kiruna and Gallivare basins in the north. Carried by a single railroad line, it could be unloaded at the Swedish port of Lulea, ice-bound for most of the year, or at the Norwegian port of Narvik, kept ice-free all year round by the Gulf Stream. German vessels had sailed freely into Norwegian territorial waters to pick up the iron ore at Narvik since the beginning of the war (see **Iron Road**), a practice the British wanted stopped. Despite appeals and maneuvers by **Churchill**, as yet only first lord of the Admiralty in **Neville Chamberlain**'s cabinet, the British government balked at forcing the hand of a small **neutral country**—although at one time it considered conspiring with **Finland** to grab Narvik and Lulea. The course finally agreed upon, with the consent of France, was to lay mines in Narvik's waters to impede the transportation of the ore to Germany. Naturally, the British anticipated a violent reaction from the Reich, so they planned to occupy Narvik, from which they would be in a position to blockade Lulea with mines dropped by plane.

But while the Allied powers vacillated and conferred, **Hitler** was carefully preparing to steal their fire by occupying **Denmark** and Norway. The conquest of Norway would not only improve his access to Swedish iron ore, the Fuehrer reasoned, it would also give him an immense strategic and economic advantage. **Alfred Rosenberg** and **Vidkun Quisling**, the leader of Norway's Nazis, had known each other for a long time and had between them conceived the notion of including both Norway and Denmark in the "Greater Germanic Union." In Nazi hands, Norway could be the northern sector of a powerful arc stretching from Narvik in Norway to Saint-Jean-de-Luz in France, with England as its focus. Moreover, Norway's economic resources would be of considerable value to the Reich's war machine—its fisheries and the canning and other industries that had sprung up around them; its cod liver oil refineries; its **production** of wood, paper, cellulose, molybdenum and titanium; and its hydro-electric energy, which could contribute vitally to the development of electrochemical and electrometallurgical industries and to the production of iron alloys, ferrosilicates, aluminum, nitrates, calcium carbide, ammonium and, indirectly, "heavy water," the precious by-product of the manufacture of nitrates (see **Atomic Bomb**).

Attacked without a declaration of war, by the German navy, army and air forces on April 8, 1940, Norway could react with only feeble resistance. The Germans were aided by a **fifth column** consisting of a handful of well-organized men led by Quisling, fresh from a briefing in Berlin. The Norwegian Nazis seized

dustrial area had been encircled, costing the Germans a further 325,000 prisoners.

The Bomber Command and the Eighth USAAF resumed their strategic onslaught on a much weakened Germany; the Third Reich altogether broke up. On April 25 American and Soviet troops met at Torgau on the Elbe. The British took Bremen on April 26 and Hamburg on May 3. The Americans reached Nuremberg on April 20 and Munich on April 30; they arrived in Salzburg on May 4, and made contact with their own Fifth Army south of the Brenner the same day. **Alfred Jodl** signed an act of **unconditional surrender** on May 7.

M. R. D. Foot

NORTH AFRICA.
See **French North Africa; Mediterranean and Middle Eastern Theater of Operations.**

NORWAY.
Germany vitally needed Swedish iron. Despite its efforts to achieve self-sufficiency, the Reich had to import about 22 million tons of iron in 1938. Of this amount, 9.5 million tons were provided by countries cut off from the Reich after the Allies imposed a **blockade** in 1939, and nine million by **Sweden**. Obviously, the loss of the high-quality Swedish ore would have been an irreparable disaster for Germany's war

the country's nerve centers, handed the military bases over to the invader, spread false rumors and guided German vessels into the country's fjords. The tiny Norwegian fleet and coastal batteries cost the enemy some losses, but these did not prevent the German troops, arriving by sea and air, from taking the important industrial centers and principal ports. Norway had taken no measures against the aggression; they were pointless since, with typical foresight and attention to detail, Hitler's forces had captured munitions dumps and military supply centers on the very first day of hostilities.

Their plans suddenly confounded by this carefully engineered operation, the Allies had to improvise. They landed their hastily assembled troops in Norway's fishing ports. The two victories of the Royal Navy near Narvik on April 10 and 13 and the feat of French mountain troops in taking the city on May 28 were the only bright spots. By June 10 the last Allied forces had been driven out of the country. The Germans had won a huge victory, but in doing so they had sacrificed a good third of their cargo aircraft and more warships than they could afford, especially since the campaign in the west had yet to be completed. Furthermore, effective as it was against land forces and seaports, German air power was in no position to contest the Royal Navy's mastery of the open seas. Apart from the British aircraft carrier *Glorious*, sunk with 20 fighter planes and 1,515 sailors and airmen aboard, Allied naval losses were minor.

French forces managed to leave Norway with a valuable prize—nearly 45 gallons of deuterium (heavy hydrogen) in the form of "heavy water." The **United Kingdom** maintained many contacts in Norway, thanks to the long history of amicable trade relations between the two countries. Among the British veterans of the Norwegian campaign were five small companies that were later to form the nucleus of commando teams under the leadership of Col. **Colin Gubbins**, who was to head the **Special Operations Executive** (SOE). Thus other contacts with men who were soon to work for the SOE and the **Special Intelligence Service** (SIS) were made during the brief Norwegian campaign.

The king, **Haakon VII**, his family and his government retired to Great Britain. In addition to small land forces consisting of an infantry brigade, an airborne unit, commando teams and special-assignment troops, some airforce squadrons and a tiny navy, Norway gave the British and their Allies its huge merchant fleet—the third largest in the world. Of the Norwegian crew members of these ships, 4,647 were to sacrifice their lives in the fighting at sea. Thus, the significant part Norway played in the war was out of all proportion to its population of barely three million

people. To this, one must add the abundant revenues the Norwegian government-in-exile received for the voyages of its freighters and the consequent respect it enjoyed among the **governments-in-exile** sheltered in the British Isles.

By far the major part of Norway's people were violently opposed to the Nazis. Quisling was profoundly detested—his name was to become synonymous with "traitor" in just about every language in the world— as were his henchmen. The opposition of the Norwegians was so outspoken, in fact, that it was not until February 1942 that the Nazi leader could form his puppet government in Oslo. Under the authority of *Reichskommissar* **Josef Terboven**, Quisling set up a repressive regime, merciless to those who defied it. Nevertheless, the collective Norwegian **conscience** refused to be stifled. Administrative personnel snubbed Quisling outright, and the youth, sports and veterans' associations fought him constantly.

Clandestine activity in Norway was particularly suitable because of the country's geographical characteristics. Norway's area was tremendous, given its small population; the long, winding fjords indenting its coast seemed to offer haven to Nazi ships but failed to shelter them from the eyes of the **Resistance**; the interior of the country was filled with mountains, snow, waterfalls, secluded valleys, reindeer, hunters and skiers. Few Germans would venture there and, as a consequence, members of the Resistance could hide there after their sorties. The Resistance too had the great advantage of a long frontier with Sweden, a friendly neutral country; the frontier was too extensive for the Germans to patrol successfully, so rebels escaping German pursuit could easily slip across it.

As opposed to their counterparts in the European countries to the south, the Resistance groups in Norway and Denmark occupied only a narrow section of the political spectrum. Actually there were only two, and they differed more in modus operandi than in politics. One of these movements, inspired by the SOE, trained particularly for **sabotage**. Its headquarters, under the direction of the heroic Norwegian officer **Martin Linge**, was in England. The other was the better known **Milorg**—an acronym for military organization—which typically assembled at some secret spot for training and arming and then attacked a planned target in a surprise operation. Led by the former commander in chief of the regular Norwegian army, Gen. Otto Ruge, Milorg established listening posts in five sectors of the country and employed SIS couriers in Sweden to convey the information they acquired to London.

The first attempts at sabotage were promoted by the SOE. It established a continuous liaison between the Shetland Islands to the northeast of Scotland and the Norwegian islands just to their east. Over this line, known as the "Shetland Bus," agents and materiel passed into Norway to aid the escape of rebels who were fleeing the Nazi police or who aspired to fight in the ranks of a Norwegian detachment forming in England. Beginning in June 1940, 12 Norwegians were dispatched by the SOE to cut the railroad and blow up bridges in the vicinity of Bergen, a large seaport on the west coast of Norway. In May 1941 a young radio operator named Odd Starheim was deposited on Norwegian soil by a British submarine. Searching for information, he stumbled on startling news—the German pocket battleship *Bismarck* had ventured out of the Bergen fjord. This precious bit of rumor set in motion a chain of events that ended in the powerful ship's sinking (see **Atlantic, Battle of the**). As 1941 unfolded, acts of sabotage increased in scope and daring. A raid on the Lofoten Islands, a large archipelago off Norway's northwest coast, was carried out by British and Norwegian commando squads together with some SOE men on March 3. It was a huge success: 19,000 tons of German shipping were sunk, 18 cod liver oil refining plants were blown to rubble and 225 Germans and collaborators were hustled off as prisoners. The Vaagso raid, begun on December 26, resulted in extensive destruction of German installations and the capture of 98 soldiers, but cost the life of Martin Linge, its leader. His place was taken by a group of saboteurs in England and Norway who adopted his name in tribute to his memory.

The Lofoten raids evoked harsh reprisals from the Germans and, consequently, the disapprobation of the Milorg and King Haakon in London, which in turn led to friction between the Norwegian government-in-exile and the British. But Col. J. S. Wilson, commander of the Norway section of the SOE, resolved these differences at the beginning of 1943. An agreement was reached, establishing an Anglo-Norwegian Collaboration Committee (ANCC), with Col. Gubbins as its first chairman, to resolve future problems. Also established was the principle that the SOE was to do nothing in Norway without first consulting Milorg, which, with the aid of the SOE, was to have sole responsibility for sabotage operations and the training of the underground army. The intramural quarrel now over, the materials parachuted to the Resistance fighters in the field grew in quality and quantity, as did the underground radio communications networks. The Norwegian branch was now the most effective of the European Resistance movements, as it demonstrated with the destruction of the Norsk Hydro plant, which produced heavy water, and with the sinking of the ferryboat carrying the last heavy water the Germans possessed across Lake Tinnsjoe.

By the summer of 1944 the Shetland Bus had smuggled 190 agents and 400 tons of explosives into Norway, while Allied aircraft had dropped 208 agents and more than 12,000 crates of materiel in 717 successful flights, out of a total 1,241 attempted. These hazardous missions armed the 35,000 resisters Milorg had under arms by the time of the **Normandy landing**. These men had been trained in the mountains. In 1944, 110 radio operators had been equipped, sending 7,034 messages to London and receiving 8,720 during the occupation. The sabotage teams continued their attacks on factories, mines and ports, keeping large segments of the *Wehrmacht* pinned down guarding valuable installations.

Infuriated by the mounting toll exacted by the Resistance, the Germans retaliated with atrocities, beginning in 1941. In February 1942, after the Lofoten escapade, they shot 43 people caught boarding a ship for England. The following April, after the arrest of a group of British and Norwegians near Televaag, 300 houses in that city were burned and their inhabitants deported. In December, 50 members of Milorg were shot. The next year, 1,100 officials, then 1,200 students and 30 professors were arrested. However, the geographic peculiarities of Norway inhibited German harassment of the population. For all the effectiveness of German helicopters in searching an area for fugitives, they could not possibly cover the immense and rugged interior of the country. The forests, aided by every variety of natural cover, formed a near-perfect camouflage.

After June 1944 the Resistance changed its targets. It contrived a plan for blasting roads and railways to delay if not altogether halt the movement of German troops. Four teams that had undergone special training for that purpose were returned to Norway. Another three such teams arrived at the end of 1944. Nor did Milorg fail to sabotage German transportation through the sea lanes. Under orders from the British Admiralty, it struck at the enemy's stores of submarine fuel. During the winter of 1944-45 the Resistance burned some 330,000 gallons of gasoline, 1,250,000 gallons of diesel oil and 86 tanker trucks. They destroyed the entire supply of torpedoes for the **U-boats** in the Norwegian base of Herten.

At the request of the Resistance, the SOE arranged for an attack by the **Royal Air Force**'s **Bomber Command** on **Gestapo** headquarters in Oslo. The operation was an unqualified success, killing more than 100 German police and quislings.

When Finland surrendered to the Allies in September 1944, a number of German units left it for Norway by the northern route, swelling the number of occupation troups. A bare three months later, on December 16, the *Wehrmacht* mounted its last offensive in the Ardennes (see **Bulge, Battle of the**). To prevent the German troops in Norway from making their way south to reinforce their comrades in the combat zone, Milorg began striking at railroads and other German military installations; this effort continued into the first few months of 1945, climaxing on the night of March 14, when 1,000 acts of sabotage against the country's railroad system were carried out simultaneously. But the chiefs of Milorg were wise enough to protect fortifications, harbor installations and vital industrial combines in anticipation of the day when Norway would once again be free. It was during a protective mission that the eminent chemist Major Leif Tronstad, transferred from London to Norway at his own request, was killed by one of Quisling's men.

Milorg created, in three practically inaccessible locations, large bases that had a multiplicity of purposes—to serve as a refuge for those seeking to evade enemy pursuers, as an enclave for training enlistees in the Resistance movement and as a launching ground for aggressive operations. Two cleverly planned raids from these bases mauled enemy units badly in April 1945. In a scheme to convince the Germans that an Allied landing would be attempted in Norway, the Norwegian brigade in England remained at their station in northern Scotland, ostensibly to train with British mountain troops, while rumors of an impending embarkment were subtly spread. This maneuver fooled the German command into keeping 17 *Wehrmacht* divisions in a tense but idle alert for the remainder of the war.

On the night of May 6, Churchill's radio call for action triggered the Milorg forces' attempt to seize all strategic locations, a feat they accomplished without a fight. The Reich's military command was taken by surprise—it had been misled by a recent report of the Gestapo denying the existence of a Norwegian underground. The German troops put forth no resistance, and on May 8 meekly accepted **unconditional surrender**. The following day Allied advance parties descended on the air bases in the country, and on May 10 the British First Airborne Division—the survivors of Arnhem—entered Oslo along with Norwegian paratroopers from England. The Resistance and Allied forces stripped 342,000 German officers and enlisted men of their arms.

As it turned out, there was no need for a general uprising in Norway, just as none was required in Denmark. And for that reason, as in Denmark, the losses suffered by the Norwegian Resistance were disproportionately low compared to its achievements.

H. Bernard

NSDAP.
See **Nazi Party**.

NSKK.
See *Nationalsozialistische Kraftfahrkorps*.

NUREMBERG TRIALS.
See **War Criminals**.

NYGAARDSVOLD, Johan (1879-1952).
Norwegian prime minister from 1935, Nygaardsvold arrived in London as a refugee in 1940 and there served as prime minister of **Norway's government-in-exile**.

O

OBERG, Carl (1897-1965).

Between 1942 and 1945 Oberg, an **SS** officer, served as head of security police in France. He was condemned to death in Paris in 1954 but was pardoned in 1963.

OBERKOMMANDO DER KRIEGSMARINE (OKM).

High command of the German navy (see **World War II—General Conduct**).

OBERKOMMANDO DER LUFTWAFFE (OKL).

High command of the German air force (see **World War II—General Conduct**).

OBERKOMMANDO DER WEHRMACHT (OKW).

High command of the German armed forces. Beginning in 1938 the chiefs of staff of the *Wehrmacht* commander in chief, **Hitler**, were directly concerned with the "OKW" war theaters," e.g., **Norway** and the southern and western fronts (see **World War II—General Conduct**).

OBERKOMMANDO DES HEERES (OKH).

High command of the German army (see **World War II—General Conduct**).

O'CONNOR, Sir Richard Nugent (1889-   ).

In World War I, O'Connor had served with exceptional bravery. He was commander of the Seventh Division and military governor of Jerusalem in 1938-39, but with the advent of war, he became a corps commander in the Western Desert (1940-41) and routed the Italians at **Beda Fomm**. While on **reconnaissance** in April 1941, he was taken prisoner by a German patrol. After his escape in December 1943, he assumed command of the Eighth Corps in France.

OCTAGON CONFERENCE.

See **Conferences, Allied**.

ODER-NEISSE FRONTIER.

The boundary line between the eastern and western German provinces along the Oder and Neisse rivers established in 1945 by the Potsdam Conference (see **Conferences, Allied**).

ODESSA.

Acronym for *Organisation der SS Angehoerigen* ("Organization of **SS** members"). A secret network set up to arrange the escape of several SS members from prosecution for war crimes. (See also **Nazi Treasure; War Criminals**.)

OFFICE OF STRATEGIC SERVICES (OSS).

Reduced to a skeleton staff after the Armistice of 1918, the American secret services remained in a cataleptic state until after the onset of World War II. At the beginning of 1941, President **Roosevelt**'s special envoy Col. **William J. Donovan** returned to Washington to report on information he had gathered during a three-month tour of Europe. He informed the president that the **United Kingdom** had no intention of surrendering, that **Hitler** meant to attack Suez, that the **United States** must prepare for war and that a large portion of the proposed war effort should be devoted to regenerating the country's moribund secret services. Roosevelt was convinced by Donovan's logic. In July 1941 Col. Donovan was made a general and entrusted with organizing the Office of the Coordination of Information (COI), which in June 1942 became the Office of Strategic Services or OSS—which, said the irreverent, stood for Oh, So Secret!—whose mission was to gather and analyze strategic data and to prepare and launch special services. An object of gentle mockery at the beginning, the OSS was to become an efficient weapon of war.

At first a small group of enthusiastic amateurs based in New York's Rockefeller Center, it acquired a staff under the supervision of Gen. Donovan, George Bowden, **Allen W. Dulles** and David K. E. Bruce. (Recruiting its first agents from among the social elite of New York and Washington—particularly graduates of Harvard, Yale and Princeton—the OSS soon acquired another nickname: Oh, So Social.)

The intelligence services, particularly G-2 in the

Army, and the Office of Naval Intelligence (ONI), did the best they could with severely limited means. In 1935, for example, the ONI managed to filch the Japanese "type 91A" coding machine, in an operation conducted by a Navy officer named Ellis M. Zacharias. With this device Laurence F. Safford and his Navy Communications Security Section (OP-20-G), in coordination with William F. Friedman, an expert cryptologist and head of the Army's Signal Intelligence Service, were able to deduce the operation of the revised model, "type 97B," in 1940. Unfortunately for the United States, however, this brilliant code-breaking exploit and the knowledge it conveyed to the American military of **Japan**'s naval and diplomatic preparations for war failed to prevent the attack on **Pearl Harbor**. That failure was the result of a breakdown of communications among the intelligence services and an incredible display of indecision on the part of the American command. But it was later compensated by American victories in the Pacific that resulted at least in part from information furnished by intercepted Japanese coded messages regarding the concentrations and deployment of the IJN fleet. It was this stolen data that enabled the U.S. Navy to win the decisive Battle of **Midway** in June 1942. It also enabled American pilots in Lockheed P-38 Lightnings from the **Guadalcanal** airfield, to shoot down two Mitsubishi bombers, one of which was carrying the commander in chief of the Japanese Combined Fleet, Adm. **Isoruku Yamamoto**, over the island of **Bougainville** on April 18, 1943.

The attack of December 7, 1941 on Pearl Harbor was painstakingly planned by the Washington-watchers in the Third Bureau, Section 5 of the Japanese Navy Department, who were very much aware of the inadequacy of the U.S. Army's intelligence services. After the attack, first the COI and later the OSS developed swiftly. By the end of 1943, OSS agents could be found in practically every part of the globe except for Latin America, which remained the province of the Federal Bureau of Investigation (FBI), and the Far East theater, where Gen. **Douglas MacArthur** insisted that his own G-2 be the sole intelligence service.

No discussion of American secret services could be complete without a word about the FBI. The single federal police agency of the United States, it was organized, under the name "Bureau of Investigation," as a division of the U.S. Department of Justice in July 1908 to keep a close watch on the activities of spies, saboteurs and potentially violent political activists, among its other labors; it was renamed the Federal Bureau of Investigation in 1935. After May 10, 1924 its director was **J. Edgar Hoover**, a controversial figure who remained in office through a number of presi-

dential administrations until his death. In his tenure at the FBI—nearly 50 years—he molded the bureau to suit his own tastes and continually added to its investigative staff. In June 1941 it smashed a German espionage ring in the United States. About a year later it captured eight expert saboteurs who had been brought secretly into the country from **Germany** by submarine.

Germany's espionage was also a prominent aspect of underground activities in World War II. After his selection as head of the **Abwehr**, Adm. **Wilhelm Canaris** tried to implant a spy ring on the other side of the Atlantic on the assumption that the United States was likely, as in 1917, to enter the war against his country on the side of the Allied powers. Canaris's directives were executed by those naturalized German immigrants to the United States who were ready and willing to aid the Fuehrer's information gleaners—for a share of the Reich's treasury, of course. Toward the end of 1939 a naturalized American named William G. Sebold traveled to Germany to visit his family. He returned to his adopted land, went immediately to the FBI and revealed that by using blackmail the Nazis had recruited him for the *Abwehr* as a shortwave radio operator. With Sebold as its willing pawn, the FBI devised a counter-gambit in which he would, as a double agent, pass on to the *Abwehr* messages dictated to him by the FBI, with the approval of Army and Marine intelligence officers. In response to the impressive information fed to them by Sebold—he had adopted the alias "William G. Sawyer" in accordance with the *Abwehr*'s orders—his correspondents in Hamburg asked for still further material. Sebold and his FBI mentors enthusiastically complied. He became so much the darling of the German espionage network, in fact, that the Nazi spymasters wanted "Sawyer" to act as their contact with agents they had already planted in the U.S. Armed with the identities of these agents, and with the mountain of evidence required to satisfy the American courts, the FBI swooped down on them on the evening of June 28, 1941 in a coordinated raid. This one shattering defeat deprived the Germans of all their American agents at a critical time—just before the attack on Pearl Harbor. Thus William Sebold, a brave and honest man acting in the defense of his adopted country, was instrumental in changing the course of history.

With the United States in the war, the OSS went to work with doubled energy. George Bowden, a Chicago lawyer, brought a professional colleague with him to the Rockefeller Center office. The colleague was Arthur Goldberg, then a young labor attorney. These men agreed that an OSS network could be created in Germany based on the labor organizations that had been dissolved by Nazi edict but that still remained active underground. This branch of the OSS organized rapidly and would eventually acquire valuable information concerning German troop movements, concentrations of **food** and munitions and the sites of important industrial plants whose function the Germans tried to keep secret. Dulles stationed himself in Berne, **Switzerland** at the beginning of November 1942 to recruit agents who would infiltrate Germany and its satellites. At the same time Bruce, in London, took control of OSS activities in the European theater—activities that included guidance to the maquis in southern France, espionage and **sabotage**. To correct several blind spots in the OSS system of surveillance, Donovan assigned an OSS man to work as liaison officer with the SOE and thus avoid duplication of effort.

Dulles, who had, in the course of his prior professional work, dealt with many German businessmen, renewed his acquaintance with them to extend OSS feelers into Germany and so keep up with developments in the enemy land. By reestablishing and reinforcing contacts with devoted anti-Nazis within Germany, he thus devised a remarkable espionage apparatus against the **Axis**. Unfortunately, little is known about the aid the OSS lent them. By extending his net further into Europe, Dulles was able to get into touch with the French maquis operating in the Jura province and in Savoy, as well as with Italian guerrillas; to finance operations of various kinds; to supply lists of friendly sites in enemy-held territory where parachute drops could be made safely; and to determine the effectiveness of Allied air raids on Germany, **Italy** and the Balkans. Among the great achievements of the Berne listening post was the report of May 1943 on **Peenemuende**, where the murderous **V-1 and V-2** were manufactured, along with several valuable notes on the bomb-launching ramps on the French coast, just opposite Dover. As his crowning achievement Dulles undertook secret negotiations between the fall of 1944 and April 29, 1945 with German Gen. Heinrich Gottfried von Vietinghoff for the **unconditional surrender** of the Reich's air, sea and land forces in Italy.

As the war's momentum swung more and more toward the Allies, suspicion and mutual mistrust increased between the **USSR** and the Western Allies. Soviet espionage activity was intense after the end of the fighting; the **atomic bomb** was the prime target of Soviet inquisitiveness. On November 2, 1945 Hoover gave President **Truman** a full report on the secret information furnished Soviet authorities by American bureaucrats during the last years of the war. On September 20, 1945, the OSS was officially dissolved, but on July 26, 1947, the Central Intelligence Agency

(CIA) made its appearance as the chief intelligence branch of the United States government.

R. Gheysens

OKAWA, Shumei (1886-1957).

A Japanese jurist, Pan-Asian ideologue and civilian pamphleteer for the nationalist movement in the 1930s, Okawa wrote that "heaven has decided on **Japan** as its choice for the champion of the East...a truly grand and magnificent mission." He propounded expansionist views through patriotic societies and close military connections. He took part in several terrorist plots in the 1930s and was indicted for war crimes by the International Military Tribunal for the Far East after Japan surrendered in 1945. The court found him unfit to stand trial, and the charges were dropped.

OKH.
See *Oberkommando des Heeres*.

OKINAWA.

Beginning in January 1945 the American high command prepared for an amphibious assault on Okinawa, the largest of the Ryukyu Islands. Located approximately midway between Formosa and **Japan** and 360 miles from the coast of **China**, the island was 67 miles long and, on the average, eight miles wide: it was thus large enough to provide a base for an invasion of Japan itself. Once in American hands, moreover, it could be used to cut off sea communication with Japanese positions in South China, **Burma** and the Dutch East Indies (see **Indonesia**).

Okinawa was defended by Lt. Gen. Mitsuru Ushijima's 32nd Army, whose strength had been built up to 77,000 combat troops and 20,000 service troops. Deeply entrenched in the island's rugged and densely forested interior, the Japanese had placed large amounts of artillery in fortified limestone caves. For air support a force of 2,000 planes had been assembled on bases in Japan and Formosa.

With the code name Operation Iceberg, D-day for the American invasion was set for April 1, Easter Sunday. The Navy put Vice Adm. Marc Mitscher in charge of the fast carriers; Vice Adm. Richmond K. Turner was to manage the amphibious operation. The landing itself was to be carried out by the recently formed 10th Army under Lt. Gen. **Simon B. Buckner**. Altogether, more than 170,000 American combat troops would take part in the invasion, including the First, Second and Sixth Marine Divisions, four infantry divisions of the Army 24th Corps under Maj. Gen. John R. Hodge and a fifth division in reserve. They would be put ashore by eight transport squadrons of

57 ships each.

To weaken the Japanese defenses prior to the American landing, and to reduce the threat of a counterattack from the air, Mitscher's fast carrier group, Task Force 58, began "softening up" the island on March 18. At the same time the American B-29 Superfortresses from **Guam** shifted their attacks from Japanese cities on the main island of Honshu to the airfields on Kyushu (see **Japan, Air War Against**). The British Pacific Fleet, consisting of two battleships, four carriers, six cruisers and 15 destroyers, under Adm. Sir Bruce Fraser also arrived on the scene in mid-March to cover the area southwest of Okinawa. American raids destroyed 160 Japanese aircraft in this preliminary phase, but the fleet suffered considerably from **kamikaze** attacks, which were mounted on an unprecedented scale. The carriers *Intrepid, Franklin* and *Wasp* were severely damaged, while the *Yorktown* was sunk by a regular Japanese bomber.

Bombardment of Okinawa began on March 25. From that day on the Americans had to contend with daily massed waves of kamikazes. Sixteen **radar** picket ships were established around the island to intercept and report incoming flights. Only about one in 10 kamikaze planes got through American fire, but a total of 34 ships were sunk and 368 damaged by Japanese suicide missions before Okinawa was taken.

The main landings took place at 8:30 a.m. on the southern part of Okinawa's western coast. Two Japanese airfields in the area were quickly occupied. These operations proved relatively easy, since Ushijima had decided to avoid combat along the exposed beaches and instead wait until the invaders were outside the range of their naval gunfire support. By evening on April 1, 60,000 troops had come ashore, and the American beachhead had been expanded to a width of nine miles. Not until April 4, when their drive toward the south end of the island ran up against two and a half Japanese divisions, did the American Army encounter serious resistance.

On the other hand, Japanese air attacks continued without interruption and intensified greatly from April 6 onward. On the 6th and 7th nearly 700 planes, half of them kamikazes, were dispatched to Okinawa. They were to precede a sortie by the 73,000-ton Japanese battleship *Yamato*, which, however, had been sent with only a small naval escort, no air cover and only enough fuel for the outward journey. On the 7th Mitscher's **task forces** attacked the *Yamato* as it passed through Van Diemen Strait. After a two-hour bomb and torpedo onslaught, the giant ship went down with 2,488 on board; it had never even had a chance to fire its big guns.

The Army's land campaign soon became protracted. Pushing north, the Sixth Marine Division clashed on April 6 with two Japanese battalions, which were dug into the rocky Motubu Peninsula. The Japanese lost some 2,500 men before they were overcome on the 17th; Marine losses were only one-tenth of that number. Meanwhile, on April 13, a Marine detachment reached the northern tip of Okinawa.

On April 19 an intense sea, air, and land bombardment was launched against Japanese positions in the southern part of the island, but it did little damage to the system of cave defense. Hodge then attacked with three divisions of his 24th Corps. Still, progress was slight and American casualties high. After Ushijima mounted an aborted counter-offensive at the beginning of May, the American advance was bogged down by heavy rain. It was renewed early in June, pushing the Japanese back into the extreme southern end of the island, where their positions along the Yaeju-Dake escarpment were destroyed with flamethrowers. On June 21 organized resistance came to an end. The following day Ushijima and his chief of staff, Lt. Gen. Cho, committed suicide, along with many troops. About 7,400 Japanese surrendered during the final phase of the battle.

Altogether, the Japanese probably lost around 110,000 men in the Battle of Okinawa. The kamikaze raids, which were dubbed *Kikusui*—"floating chrysanthemums"—brought death to more than 1,500 flyers, and there were probably an equal number of suicidal attacks by other Japanese aircraft. The American 10th Army suffered 7,613 dead and 31,800 wounded during the three-month campaign. The Navy suffered 4,900 killed and 4,800 wounded. These figures constituted the heaviest American toll of the war in the Pacific.

T. L. Harrison

OKL.

See *Oberkommando der Luftwaffe*.

OKM.

See *Oberkommando der Kriegsmarine*.

OKW.

See *Oberkommando der Wehrmacht*.

OP 25.

Code name for the German operations against **Yugoslavia** on April 6, 1941.

OPPENHEIMER, J. Robert (1904-1967).

An American nuclear physicist, Oppenheimer was director of the laboratory at Los Alamos, New Mexico, where the **United States** developed the first **atomic bomb**.

ORA.

Organisation de Resistance de l'Armee (see **Forces Francaises de l'Interieur;** **French Resistance**).

ORADOUR-SUR-GLANE.

A village in the French departement of Haute Vienne where, on June 10, 1944, the population of about 700, including children and the aged, were herded by a unit of the *Das Reich* division of Gen. Heinz Lammerding into the parish church and burned alive in reprisal for a **Resistance** raid on another locality.

ORDER OF COMMISSARS.

See *Kommissarbefehl.*

ORGANISATION DE RESISTANCE DE L'ARMEE (ORA).

See *Forces Francaises de l'Interieur;* French Resistance.

ORGANIZZAZIONE DI VIGILANZA E REPRESSIONE DELL'ANTIFASCISMO (OVRA).

The political police created in **Italy** in November 1926 by the laws ''in defense of the state,'' or the ''Fascist statutes.'' During the war OVRA functionaries demonstrated their capacity for extreme brutality in the French Alps and the Balkans.

OSHIMA, Hiroshi (1886-1948).

Japanese diplomat. Oshima was the Japanese ambassador to **Germany** in 1938-39 and from 1941 to 1945.

OSS.

See **Office of Strategic Services.**

OVERLORD.

See **Normandy Landing.**

OVRA.

See *Organizzazione di Vigilanza e Repressione dell' Antifascismo.*

P

PACIFIC THEATER OF OPERATIONS.
The war in the Far East and Pacific was fought primarily in the following areas: **China**, which was attacked by **Japan** in 1937 and deprived of huge territories, but which was able to neutralize large masses of enemy troops by virtue of unrelenting guerrilla warfare and financial as well as technical aid from the **United States**; the Malay States and **Burma**, important objectives for the Japanese, not only because of the British bases of **Singapore** and Rangoon but also because of the Burma Road, the sole land route for provisioning a hungry China; and the Pacific, including Japan, **Indonesia**, the **Philippines**, Australasia and Polynesia.

The Pacific is immense, extending from the British base of **Hong Kong** to San Francisco and from the **Aleutian Islands** off the Alaskan coast to the Tropic of Capricorn. It extends over 6,000 miles from east to west and some 5,500 miles from north to south. The Pacific Ocean's surface is ruffled by the winds constantly blowing between the two tropics. It is also the domain of the monsoon, the wind that blows in one direction for six months of the year and then veers to the opposite direction for the other six months, toward Southeast Asia and the East Indies. True to its name, it is generally calm. The sky over the Pacific is typically cloudless; so during the day visibility is high and at night the constellations can easily be read by navigators. Sometimes, however, the ocean's gentle heaving is abruptly ripped by terrible storms and typhoons. The ensuing deluges are seasonal, and therefore military events on it or on its shores are affected by the time of year. During the month of November, for example, Sumatra is pelted by an average of 20 inches of rain.

The major island groups of the Pacific are Japan, the East Indies, the Australasian group and the Polynesian group. They are all volcanic in origin. The islands are actually peaks of chains of volcanoes and submerged mountains, covered with the lush flora of the tropics. This basic structure has been radically altered by the coral-building madrepores that for eons have been patiently building barrier reefs and atolls.

These have posed hazards to the naval activities of the Pacific nations but have also provided natural landing quays, harbors and airports.

The Japanese Empire consisted of a central nucleus, including the Ryukyu Archipelago; the home islands of Kyushu, Shikoku, Honshu and Hokkaido; a "belt" formed by Korea and Manchukuo—territories wrested from China after 1937; nearby islands—Formosa, the Bonins, the Kurils and the southern half of the island of Sakhalin; and some advance posts in the Marianas, the Carolines and the Marshalls.

This far-flung and populous empire, with 130 million inhabitants (including Manchukuo but exclusive of the Chinese territories occupied after 1937) is poor in coal, oil and minerals—serious deficiencies in view of the heavy industrialization of the home islands. But whatever Japan lacked in oil was, as a result of Japanese conquests early in the war, abundantly compensated by the huge reserves in Indonesia and the Philippines, territories that had been controlled by the United States (the Philippines), the **United Kingdom** (the northern third of **Borneo**), **Portugal** (the eastern part of **Timor**) and **the Netherlands** (Sumatra, Java, Bali, the western part of Timor, the Celebes, the Moluccas and two-thirds of Borneo).

The Australasian group includes **Australia, New Zealand, New Guinea,** and the Solomon Islands. Australia is a British dominion about three-quarters the size of Europe. It is developed primarily on the eastern coast and to a lesser extent on the southwest. At the extreme north is the important base of Darwin. The immense central area is mostly desert. New Zealand is also a British dominion. New Guinea, whose western half was controlled by the Netherlands before the war, and whose eastern half by Australia, is a forbidding and mountainous island, heavily forested, with low and swampy shores. On the southeast coast is Port Moresby, formerly the capital of the Australian portion of the island (and now of Papua New Guinea). The Solomon Archipelago includes myriad islands, among which are **Guadalcanal**, the Louisiade Islands and New Britain.

The Polynesian group is a scattering of volcanic and

Pacific Theater of Operations

Extent of Japanese conquests (August 1942)

coral islets surrounding the larger islands already mentioned. Before World War II the Marianas, the Carolines and the Marshall Islands in the Polynesian group were Japanese possessions; Hawaii, with Honolulu and **Pearl Harbor**, and the island bases of **Midway**, **Wake** and **Guam** were American; Tahiti, the Marquises, New Caledonia (outside the theater of operations) and New Hebrides (divided with Great Britain) were French (all of them elected to side with **de Gaulle** after 1940); and finally, Tonga, part of the New Hebrides, the **Gilbert Islands,** Fiji, Samoa and some others were British.

The American Aleutians, the stepping stones between North America and Asia, marked the northern bounds of military operations. These islands are completely different from those where most major operations of the war took place—their climate is polar rather than tropical.

Some Pacific islands, like Java, can be said to be completely settled, since they have well-defined roads, ports, cities and means of transportation into the interior. Islands like Borneo and New Guinea, on the other hand, cannot be completely settled, since their interiors are virgin jungle. Only the coastal areas are truly accessible. A small Polynesian island may be entirely settled or not at all. Total occupation generally transformed it into a formidable fortress and a "stationary aircraft carrier"—i.e., a base for launching air offensives.

There are no islands of any significance between Hawaii and the continental United States. The 3,000 miles separating Hawaii from San Francisco thus constituted a safety belt.

Troops in Burma, **Malaya**, Indonesia and parts of Australia required medical attention as much because of the sun, the tornadoes, the heavy floods, the foul mud, the hot and humid climate, the endless variety of insects and such diseases as malaria, yellow fever and dysentery as because of enemy soldiers. But no particular precautions had to be taken in most of the Polynesian islands, caressed by the trade winds and the offshore breezes. (See also **Health**.)

The Japanese held the advantage of basing their military operations on their home islands—no mean advantage, considering the distance to their objectives as compared to the distance between those objectives and the United States. The distance from San Francisco to Manila is nearly 7,500 miles; it is less than 2,000 miles from Yokohama to Manila. In addition, Japan held excellent bases, which it had assiduously fortified since 1919, on the Marianas, the Carolines and the Marshalls. Finally, it could concentrate its entire fighting strength against the United States, which, along with its Allies, was also battling the **Axis** powers in Europe.

In addition to grabbing **Thailand**, Japan took advantage of the French by obtaining from Vichy the use of French air bases in **Indochina**, notably in Saigon, from which the British base on Singapore was easily reached. In July 1941 Japan imposed an "accord on common defense" on Indochina and seized a number of anchorages in the French colony. (See also **Badung Strait; Bougainville; Cape Esperance; Coral Sea; Eastern Solomons; Leyte; Okinawa; World War II—General Conduct**.)

H. Bernard

PACT OF STEEL.
The military accord of May 22, 1939 between **Italy** and **Germany** (see Introduction).

PALESTINE.
On November 2, 1917 the British government proposed "the establishment in Palestine of a national home for the Jewish people." This proposal became known as the Balfour Declaration. Five weeks later an Anglo-Australian army took Jerusalem from the Turks, with the help of a guerrilla force of Arabs on their desert flank. The last Turks left Palestine in September 1917, and the **League of Nations** granted the British a mandate over it in 1920. The Balfour Declaration and the mandate both included assur-

ances that the local inhabitants' rights would be safeguarded, but there was continual tension between the local Arabs and the ever-growing number of Jewish immigrants. Persecution of Jews in the mid-1930s by the Nazis and others increased the number of immigrants and heightened the tension. Haj Amin el Husseini, the Mufti of Jerusalem, organized Arab terrorism effectively, but fled to **Lebanon** for his own safety in October 1937. By December 1937 Arabs and Jews had started to fight each other in Palestine and they continued to do so through 1938 in spite of the efforts of the British occupying forces to keep them apart (see **Orde C. Wingate**).

In May 1939 the British government promised eventual independence for Palestine—which had already seemed implicit in the terms of the mandate. The promise was ill received. The Mufti, moving successively to **Iraq, Iran, Italy** and **Germany**, made as much trouble as he could; **Churchill** once called him "the deadliest enemy of the British **Empire**." But during the war Palestine was quiet; the Arabs put up with things as they were, Jewish immigration being necessarily at a standstill (no ships were available), and the Jews in any event did not want to multiply obstacles for any enemy of the Nazis. There were also substantial and intelligent British security forces on the spot. Palestine came under the aegis of the British Middle Eastern Command headquarters at Cairo; the command had a staff college at Haifa, of which **Eric Dorman-Smith** was commandant in 1940-42. Troops were sent to Palestine to rest and to train when they could be spared from more active fronts. A brigade recruited from the Jewish part of the population fought with some distinction in North Africa and Italy. Unnoticed by the British, the Jews devoted much effort during the war to the organization of the *Haganah*, the secret citizens army that secured in 1948 the independence of the state of Israel and the partition of Palestine.

M. R. D. Foot

PAPAGOS, Alexandros (1883-1955).
A Greek general, Papagos was chief of staff under Gen. **Ioannis Metaxas**. He successfully counterattacked the Italian invasion of **Greece** in a bitter winter war in Epirus during 1940-41, driving the enemy back to **Albania**. In April 1941 the Germans overcame his resistance and conquered mainland Greece despite British intervention; in the process Papagos was taken prisoner and eventually sent to Dachau. He was freed by the Americans in 1945. He became prime minister of Greece in 1952.

371

PAPANDREOU, George (1888-1968).
A former leader of the Greek Social Democratic Party, Papandreou in April 1944 was named prime minister of the Greek **government-in-exile**, set up in Cairo by the Allies. He entered Athens in October 1944 to preside over the National Union government.

PAPEN, Franz von (1879-1969).
In 1933 Papen, a German politican, was instumental in securing President Paul von Hindenburg's selection of **Hitler** as chancellor and was himself named vice-chancellor. He spent the 1936-38 period as ambassador to Vienna, in which position he prepared for the *Anschluss* with **Austria**. He was the German ambassador to **Turkey** between 1939 and 1945, and although he concluded a Turko-German friendship treaty (1941), he could not draw that country into the war on the German side. In 1946 he won acquittal at the Nuremberg trials, but a year later he was imprisoned by a German court (see **War Criminals**).

PARK, Sir Keith Rodney (1892-1975).
A British airman, Park commanded the 11th Fighter Group of the **Royal Air Force** under **Hugh Dowding** in 1940 and bore the brunt of the **Battle of Britain**. He was air commander in chief in the Middle East in 1944 and in Southeast Asia in 1945-46.

PATCH, Alexander McCarrell (1889-1945).
A veteran of World War I, Gen. Patch first saw action in New Caledonia in 1942 and took command in **Guadalcanal** at the end of the year. After the defeat of the Japanese there in 1943, Patch commanded the U.S. Seventh Army in the invasion of Southern France on August 15, 1944, making contact with Gen. **George Patton**'s Third Army near Epinal four weeks later. Following the **Normandy landing**, his troops moved east. By the end of 1944 they had taken northern Alsace from the Germans, and in March 1945 they crossed the Rhine.

PATTON, George Smith (1885-1945).
Patton, an American general, had been a **tank** officer in France during World War I, just after the birth of the tank as a military weapon. Those experiences, and his studies of the American Civil War, led Patton to adopt the British military analyst **Basil Liddell Hart**'s theories on the utility of the tank as an effective weapon for piercing static enemy defense formations. Patton commanded the U.S. Seventh Army in Sicily in 1943 and the U.S. Third Army in France in 1944. It was not long before he gained a worldwide reputation for his almost reckless daring, the depths to which his armored units broke through enemy defenses, and the facility with which his troops could counterattack,

as they did against the German offensive in the **Battle of the Bulge**. Patton brilliantly demonstrated his mastery of armor as a tactical weapon by the astonishing speed with which his units sprinted across **Germany** at the end of 1944. A short time later he was killed in an accident.

PAUL-BONCOUR, Joseph (1873-1972).
A former minister and president of the *Conseil d'Etat*, Paul-Boncour was against the grant of power to Marshal Petain in 1940 and formed a secret group of French parliamentarians opposed to Vichy. On June 26, 1945 **de Gaulle** gave him the honor of signing the **United Nations** Charter in the name of France.

PAULUS, Friedrich von (1890-1957).
A German field marshal, Paulus commanded the German Sixth Army that was forced to surrender to the Soviet defenders of Stalingrad in early 1943. As a **prisoner of war,** he joined the *National Komitee "Freies Deutschland."* He was freed by the USSR in 1953.

PAVELICH, Ante (1889-1959).
Croatian dictator. Pavelich led the **Ustachi** beginning in 1929. In 1941, with the aid of **Germany** and **Italy**, he seized power in **Croatia**, which was declared independent of **Yugoslavia**, and retained it until 1945 (see **Collaboration**). Thereafter he led the Ustachi from his Argentine exile; he died in Madrid.

PEACE OVERTURES.
The search for peace during the Second World War, unlike the first, was regarded as less important by all parties than attempts to secure positions of strength in the postwar world. Intermediaries, operating officially or on their own initiative, sounded out the great powers with proposals aimed at securing peace but worked mostly in the dark, and typically with only one purpose: to permit a particular nation to acquire a more favorable position for the next phase of the conflict. For the Nazis, as for the Western Allies—in particular the **United States**—any treaty or separate peace would represent only a truce, not a final peace agreement. As long as one of the two opposing alliances refused to yield to the other, peace was, in the view of both parties, not to be considered. Three successive phases can be distinguished in the slide toward world war: the "phony war," the Germans' switch from an offensive toward the west to an offensive toward the east, and finally the world war itself.

The Phony War
During the first eight months of the war there were oc-

casional direct contacts between the opposing armies—in particular **Germany** and the **United Kingdom**. In France, despite several abortive moves toward arriving at a settlement at lower ministerial levels, the government refused to consider a new accord with **Hitler**. The domestic situation in France was unstable, there was little enthusiasm for a war and the official position was to reject any proposal for peace or eventual mediation by some neutral state that was not predicated upon the dismemberment of Germany after the anticipated total victory of the Allied powers. In England, on the other hand, the mass media adopted a more restrained tone. Prime Minister **Neville Chamberlain**—the popular pun on his name was "J'aime Berlin" ("I love Berlin")—had not yet clearly announced any intention on his part to pursue the war until the Nazi regime fell. His reserve, inspired by hope for a relaxation of tensions and also by fear of the social upheavals that would inevitably occur in the wake of a world war, was perfectly consonant with German intentions to avoid operations in the west until the conquest of **Poland** (see *Fall Weiss*) was complete. The Swedish industrialist Birger Dahlerus twice attempted to mediate after the beginning of the war, but gave up at the end of 1939. Before that, however, he conferred with **Goering** and Hitler and managed to secure an extremely vague German proposal, which he duly transmitted to London. Depending on the events in Poland and the role the **USSR** would play, the proposal indicated, Germany was ready to accept peace and recognize a Polish state much reduced in size, with the territories taken from it entering the Reich's sphere of influence. Similar assurances were reaching London simultaneously through **Alfred Rosenberg**"s foreign policy department of the **Nazi Party** and from **Franz von Papen**, then ambassador to Turkey.

In his speeches on September 19 at **Danzig** and on October 6 before the *Reichstag* in Berlin, Hitler declared that he was prepared to discuss a compromise. His offers, however, were deliberately imprecise. The British government was skeptical but hoped to use them as a wedge to split the Nazi leadership and lead to a new government more amenable to a truce. Toward the end of September a crisis did come about in the German regime as a result of the formation of a coalition of members of the military, diplomats and industrialists opposed to Hitler's plans for waging war on the western European Allies (see *Fall Gelb*). A rift even appeared within the Nazi Party itself, prompted by the revulsion of the hard-liners against the **Nazi-Soviet Pact** allying the nation of supermen with the subhuman Bolsheviks of the USSR. There then emerged the possibility that the popular Goering might qualify as the alternative to Hitler.

With the amateur Swedish diplomat Dahlerus as his intermediary, Chamberlain endeavored to encourage Goering at Hitler's expense. But the Fuehrer's suspicions were aroused. He guessed the British intentions of cutting him off from the German masses and dealing directly with the more accessible Goering and foiled it by assuming tighter control of the talks with the Chamberlain government. When Dahlerus asked **Edward Halifax** and Chamberlain whether they wanted a change in Germany's government, they replied that they would prefer "important changes within the regime"—i.e., they did not require Hitler's departure as a condition for entering negotiations with Germany. As October drew to a close, the British concluded that these preliminary maneuvers had ended in failure since the Fuehrer would not trust his lieutenant to deal with them on his own. The truth, however, was that Goering was quite content to obey Hitler's directions loyally.

Nevertheless, when the "**Russo-Finnish Winter War**" broke out, Goering made one last attempt to dicker with the Chamberlain government, probably without his chief's knowledge. His messenger Dahlerus was told on December 28, 1939 by Sir Alexander Cadogan, undersecretary of state at the Foreign Office, that the British government could not sanction the violence Germany had committed against Poland. Hitler had to be banished from the government and the German people made to see that a policy of international aggression could lead only to disaster. Chamberlain thus put an abrupt end to the dialogue. He was thenceforth to identify the German government with the Nazi Party and its philosophy, as his Conservative opposition in Parliament, their leader **Churchill**, and the British press were already doing.

The states that were still neutral had few opportunities to offer their services as arbitrators to the belligerents during the first two months of the war. Acting alone, each with an eye to possible gains for themselves, they made no attempt to form a third bloc to be interposed between the other two. Even the signatories to the Oslo Convention—**Belgium, Denmark, Finland, Luxembourg, the Netherlands, Norway** and **Sweden**—refrained from any concerted move to counter the menacing sword the belligerents hung above their heads. Only the Scandinavian countries tried to act, but the moment they seemed amenable to German offers, those offers were quickly withdrawn.

The conference of the Scandinavian heads of state, announced with tremendous fanfare, fizzled ignominiously on October 18. It had neither general support nor a genuine desire for action on behalf of Finland, threatened by the Soviet Union. The impotence of these governments, all of them social-democratic, appalled the people of Europe. They put more faith in the efforts of individuals and particularly in the peace movement mounted by various church denominations in the Scandinavian countries. The Danish businessman Carl Kai Pless-Schmidt and the Norwegian bishop **Eiwind Berggrav** visited London and Berlin with official approval, gaining access to the most importat personages in both capitals. Their labors, too, ended in failure.

The Channel countries of Belgium and the Netherlands, facing the Hobson's choice of a German attack or a Franco-British occupation, separately sought a formula to please both sides. In particular Eelco van Kleffens, minister of foreign affairs in the Dutch government, tried, with the aid of Papen, to effect the change in the German government so much desired by the British, while his Belgian counterpart **Paul-Henri Spaak** contented himself with trying to occupy several positions at once. On November 7, 1939 King **Leopold III** of Belgium and Queen **Wilhelmina** of the Netherlands attempted a diplomatic approach of their own. They were in a desperate situation. Hitler had overcome his opposition within Germany and there was no further impediment to his aggressive plans; Belgium would certainly be the first target. The British, moreover, were growing impatient with Dahlerus' fruitless efforts. The offer of the royal pair was rejected, but Hitler waited until the Allies had rejected it first, thereby hoping to convince the French that he had made a secret deal with the Belgian and Dutch governments.

Other states found it more convenient to engage in preliminary peace talks simply because, as the allies or ideological acolytes of one side or the other, they found an extended, exhausting war much less desirable. The USSR, **Italy** and **Spain** watched the victorious German march at the end of 1939 with anxiety or approval, but without any desire to expand the conflict. These governments actively supported the peace Hitler continually claimed to desire in his speeches, and sought the Allies' consent. In particular, they encouraged some political circles in France, principally that surrounding Petain, then the French ambassador to Madrid, and some men in England's Conservative Party, to break with their governments' negative responses to the Fuehrer's blandishments. On September 2, Italy attempted, by means of a second mediation offer, to persuade him to accept a partially dismembered Poland as an independent neighbor. **Mussolini** was for a while content to let **Galeazzo Ciano**, his minister of foreign affairs, do the negotiating, but when Ciano's policy began to diverge from the Italo-German **Axis** pact and Italy faced the prospect of isolation, he intervened directly with a letter to Hitler on January 3, 1940. In

it, he proposed to join Germany in a war to destroy bolshevism, suggesting that Germany demonstrate its good will toward the western European democracies by re-creating the Polish state. The Germans were offended; they saw in this proposal a lack of faith in their military prowess.

With the Polish campaign ended, the opposing armies settled down to wait. Only Mussolini continued his efforts to appease Hitler, not so much to obtain a total cessation of hostilities as to delay to some extent the frightening progress of the German juggernaut. In this effort he aroused some sympathy among highly placed Americans, especially the wealthy businessmen of the Liberty League and diplomats in the State Department. But they were powerless against **Roosevelt**. The president had decided to make no mediation attempts even while the Polish campaign was still underway, nor was he moved by repeated appeals from **neutral countries** like Belgium, Finland and **Rumania** to intervene. For its part, the German government intimated that it might listen to an American proposal, but Roosevelt personally rebuffed its advances. He found the increasing pressure of public opinion, however, difficult to resist, especially since 1940 was an election year. He therefore relented, at least to the extent of permitting two prominent businessmen, Texas oil magnate William Rhodes Davis and one of General Motors' presidents, James D. Mooney, to negotiate semiofficially in Berlin, London and Washington. Another attempt was made by the Undersecretary of State Sumner Welles, who was sent to Rome and other important European capitals at the end of February 1940. His negotiations showed him clearly that Chamberlain and the French premier **Edouard Daladier**, like Mussolini, would have consented to a peaceful settlement guaranteed by the United States. Hitler's attitude, however, was demonstrated by his refusal to discuss with Welles necessary steps toward peace, although he did consent at least to give the undersecretary an audience. Examining the results obtained by his emissary, Roosevelt could see no way to prevent war, or even to give the western democracies a respite in which to complete their rearmament program or to put Hitler in an untenable position. Even though there were indications that the U.S. could have stepped in to prevent war, Roosevelt chose to consider Welles's journey a regrettable failure, and he used this decision to justify his original intent—to abstain from meddling in the European crisis. To the American public he insisted that he had done everything he could to maintain the peace.

The War in Europe

On May 10, 1940, when Hitler launched the attack on the west, while Churchill presided over his new cabinet for the first time, the possibility of a political solution grew even dimmer. The new prime minister based his war policy on the assumption that he could obtain an alliance with the United States and establish a personal friendship with the president. Losing no time, he asked the Americans for practical assistance. But it was not until the middle of July, after he had given ample proof of his determination to continue the battle against Hitler, that Churchill obtained Washington's support. In his speeches Roosevelt urged the Western democracies to stand fast against the Hitler typhoon, thus implying that the United States would go to the limit in assisting the Allies, but he was waiting for the results of the military operations, the collapse of France and the critical enfeeblement of Great Britain before placing America at the head of the coalition against Hitler. Italy was prey to the same reservations. As the Allies continued to retreat in France, Italian neutrality became more and more valuable. Yet Roosevelt supported the diplomatic drive by France, Great Britain and the Vatican to detach Mussolini from Hitler by territorial and economic concessions with words alone. At the beginning of the German offensive in the west, Mussolini had ended his offers to mediate, but he waited until June 10, 1940 to plunge Italy into the war—exactly when Germany no longer wanted Italian assistance, under the apprehension that Italy's presence in the conflict would keep the French from accepting a separate peace.

The underlying reason for Hitler's attack on the west was to force the British into isolation by demanding that the French sign a separate armistice. That done, he would deprive England of its foothold on the Continent and finally compel it to submit to German hegemony in Europe. To further this plan, the Nazis concentrated their diplomatic efforts and propaganda on the neutral capitals, with the intent of encouraging the politically powerful groups in France and England clamoring for peace—especially individuals like Petain; the advocate of appeasement Sir Samuel Hoare, whom Churchill had exiled by appointing him Britain's ambassador to Madrid; English conservatives such as Lord Lothian, the ambassador to Washington; and the American ambassador to London, Joseph Kennedy. These men, among others, had privately acknowledged the inevitability of an Allied military defeat and were therefore likely to support making concessions to Berlin. One can then easily understand why Hitler, in a casual conversation with his officers a week after the French campaign began, expressed a warm desire for an accord with Great Britain. Again, before his chiefs of staff on June 2, he spoke enthusiastically of England's "mission for the white race," implying that his next war aim would be

the liquidation of bolshevism. But the Fuehrer refrained deliberately from making his views official, for fear of jeopardizing the anticipated peace. In his imagination, domination of the Continent was only the prelude to mastery of the world. But first he had to crush France and humiliate Britain.

In London and Paris the diplomatic corps feared nothing more than a magnanimous peace offer from Germany. The public was tired of the war, especially in view of the apparent invincibility of the *Wehrmacht*. Churchill and **Paul Reynaud**, pleading with Roosevelt for help, raised the specter of an imposed German peace and urged the president to take a decisive step—if only to threaten America's entry into the war. To these pathetic appeals Roosevelt responded with demands—that France refuse to turn over its fleet to the Germans, that Britain continue fighting from **Canada**. It was immediately thereafter, on May 25, that the French war cabinet discussed the possibility of an armistice for the first time. Reynaud tried, several days later, to convince Churchill to accept Italian mediation. He was met with a firm refusal, but the suggestion aroused a passionate debate in London. On a proposal by Chamberlain, however, the British war cabinet declared itself open to negotiations, provided that any agreement would guarantee national independence. Churchill himself adamantly opposed negotiations of any kind, but at the same time he had to consider the possibility that a government succeeding his might be forced by the military situation to take such a step. He called upon Roosevelt to avert this possibility by granting immediate and unlimited aid. To preclude a deep split between the doves and hawks in his government like that fragmenting French public opinion, Churchill made several efforts to enroll David Lloyd George in his cabinet. The old man, who had been prime minister during World War I, was the only public figure in England to come out publicly for reaching an agreement with the Germans. Had he accepted Churchill's invitation and negotiated with Hitler, he might have replaced Churchill as prime minister. But he was afraid of being relegated to the minority and obscured in Churchill's shadow. He therefore refused and lost the opportunity to tilt the government toward appeasement.

Apparently ignorant of the momentous struggle over the war policy of the British **Empire**, Hitler was content to wait until France was successfully neutralized, an event expected to take place at the beginning of June, after which the British could be similarly pacified. The only problem remaining would be the possibility of American intervention, which so far had been purely verbal. When Roosevelt issued a warning to the fascist powers in a speech in Charlottesville, the

Fuehrer replied immediately by means of an interview with the American journalist Karl von Wiegand on June 13, 1940. "Europe for the Europeans, America for the Americans," he said, adding that he would make no attempt to influence Americans politically or militarily and that he would continue to seek peace with Great Britain.

The French request for an armistice on June 17, 1940 unleashed another crisis within the British government. Lord Halifax, minister of foreign affairs, and his undersecretary of foreign affairs, Richard Butler, hinted to Germany through Swedish diplomats that they were ready to consider a compromise. Churchill managed to end these approaches via Stockholm, but they indicated that he had not won support for his policy of resistance to the Germans at any price from everybody in the administration. German propaganda insisted that Churchill was dismantling the British Empire and giving it piece by piece to the Americans. The charge aroused sympathy in some conservative circles. A rumor that a cabinet reshuffling was due and that it would be reflected in peace offers emanating from Chamberlain, Halifax and Hoare began to spread. Diplomats and **information services** dutifully repeated it. News of the incident at **Mers el-Kebir** on July 3, 1940 put an end to it by demonstrating that Churchill and the hard-liners had won out.

Reverting to his intention to force the English into accepting his terms, Hitler ceased his peace offers. But his entourage kept in touch with British officialdom, going even to the extent of sending a semi-official emissary, Prince Max Egon zu Hohenlohe-Langenburg, to **Switzerland** at the beginning of July 1940 to meet Carl J. Burckhardt, former **League of Nations** high commissioner, and a representative of the British government. Hohenlohe showed his interlocutors a letter from Hitler's permanent representative for foreign affairs, Ambassador Walther Hewel. It asserted that Hitler had no desire to destroy the British Empire and, in this spirit, offered a final opportunity. The prince presented its terms as a basis for negotiations and sent an abbreviated version of it to the papal nuncio who, through the good offices of the Vatican, conveyed it to the British government. The Foreign Office instructed its plenipotentiary to receive it coldly, and when the German document finally reached London after a long delay, it was given no notice.

Undaunted, the Germans appealed to the Duke of Windsor, who made no secret of his pro-German sympathies. The duke had been arrested in an attempted flight from France, and since he openly castigated London's war policy, he was recommended to Berlin by the Spanish government as the perfect intermediary for German-British contacts. But somehow the Germans let slip the opportunity. Yet, when the duke was first sent to Lisbon and then named governor of the Bahamas, **Joachim von Ribbentrop** conceived the notion of kidnapping the one-time king and setting him up as a sort of antimonarch to his brother **George VI**. But British counter-espionage and the duke's loyalty to the reigning sovereign put an end to that romantic project.

Goering's clique included some economists who acted to halt the war out of the conviction that Germany was economically too weak to ride out a long war (see **Germany—Economy of the Third Reich**). Goering then borrowed the plan developed by Albert Plesman, director general of the Dutch Air Company, proposing that the great powers divide the world into economic spheres of influence, with Africa to be exploited by an international body. This notion of a condominium formed by the advance industrial nations to control colonial imports and exports seemed, in 1940, a viable and realistic plan even in some British circles. In any case, it was defeated by Sweden's refusal to act as intermediary and by the outbreak of the **Battle of Britain**. In fact, some influential German businessmen suggested to Washington that since German hegemony had become an accomplished fact on the Continent, should not the American government advise its British confreres to submit? The State Department took the proposal seriously, but Roosevelt rejected it out of hand. The president was preparing for his third election campaign with the idea of spearheading the Allied drive against Hitler. In a fireside chat he declared himself ready to pick up the challenge the Nazis had flung at him. And again, in a public speech just before Hitler's address to the *Reichstag* that was scheduled for July 19, he denounced the totalitarian states in a fashion designed to stiffen the resistance of Great Britain and the neutral states to the continual promises of peace held out by the Fuehrer.

Hitler's speech was a masterpiece of propaganda, reflecting the firm coalition of the party, the army and the people, but his final "appeal to reason" failed to arouse the response he had hoped for in England. British radio received it with acid comments. Churchill selected Lord Halifax to compose the official reply, since the latter was known to be a proponent of compromise with Germany. Another unforeseen effect of Hitler's speech was to put an end to talks that were then in progress between the British ambassador to Washington and the German charge d'affaires Hans Thomsen.

By the end of July 1940 it became obvious that direct meetings between the belligerents or a mediation offer from Roosevelt were no longer possible. The choices of the neutral states narrowed considerably. They therefore intensified their efforts to induce the opposing sides to meet around a conference table, but the differences between them were much deeper than they had been in the fall of 1939. An offer from the king of Sweden, Gustav V, in August 1940 was scorned by Churchill and snubbed by the Nazis. The Swedes persisted until December 1940 in their attempts to find a solution through the intervention of trusted men in the diplomatic world, but without success.

Especially disturbed by their country's awkward position between belligerents, and apprehensive of a possible occupation by their Nazi neighbor, some prominent Swiss politicians tried their hand at effecting a reconciliation. By lending a patient ear to the Germans' vows and their promises for a "**New European Order**," the Swiss minister of foreign affairs, Marcel Pilet-Golaz, hoped to wheedle the Nazis into talking with the British, but he was frustrated by his own commander in chief, Gen. **Henri Guisan**, who deprecated these pacifist efforts.

Occupying a strategic location on the Mediterranean, **Turkey** no less than Switzerland scrambled about for a means of bringing the antagonists to an international bargaining session. Spain, too, in its equally vital position at the opposite end of the Continent, declared itself officially nonbelligerent and continued to urge both the Germans and English to negotiate. **Franco**, however, was definitely the wrong choice for mediator; he owed Hitler too much for the invaluable assistance the Fuehrer had given him during the Spanish Civil War and had no doubt that the days of the British lion were numbered. Nevertheless, Spain worked harder at seeking a solution to the burgeoning conflict than any other country.

During the American elections in late 1940, the isolationists called insistently for peace in Europe. Roosevelt, however, convinced public opinion that the isolationist spokesman, the America First Committee, was pro-German. After his election he proclaimed the United States the arsenal of democracy and undercut his isolationist opposition and its support for mediation until the beginning of the Nazi-Soviet war (see **USSR—War with Germany**).

In its turn, the Japanese government entered the game in February 1941 with an offer of its good offices. Its motives for doing so were primarily to resolve certain domestic tensions and to reach a quick solution to its own six-year old conflict with **China**. The Japanese foreign minister, **Yosuke Matsuoka**, met with a humiliating refusal by the British and complete indifference by the Germans. All the same, when he arrived in Europe two months later, the Germans tried to convince him of Japan's need to begin hostilities against Britain.

Of greater import than these attempts to secure peace after the defeat of France were those proposed by the Holy See. All sides, the United States among them, made every effort to win the advantage of the Pope's enormous prestige. They could hardly afford to reject with just a cursory glance the offer the prudent **Pius XII** made on June 28, 1940. Nevertheless, Hitler failed to react, the British replied only after a long delay and Mussolini waited in vain for a move he could endorse. Rapidly breaking political and military events pushed the papal plea into obsolescence. Undiscouraged, the Pope transmitted to the British a letter containing German terms by way of his nuncio in Switzerland, but Churchill refused on principle to use any contacts through the Vatican. Consisting mostly of Italians, the Curia in general supported Mussolini's ambitious plans of conquest, but British suggestions the Vatican could have used to obtain a separate peace for Italy were not withheld. But after the German attack on the Soviet Union, the Curia, considering Nazism a lesser evil than communism, made less of an attempt to hide its partiality to the Axis. When, in 1942, the Allies began to appear stronger, however, the Vatican returned to its policy of neutrality and threw all of its efforts into preventing the collapse of Italy.

On May 11, 1941 the startling news of **Rudolf Hess'** parachute jump into Scotland was made public. There is no evidence that he made the jump on Hitler's order, yet the motives for the mission corresponded closely to the Fuehrer's political credo—to rescue the Nordic and Aryan British from the mongrel camp into which they had fallen, or at least to neutralize them, dissipating the menace of the West and permitting the Nazis to pursue their mission of destroying the Bolshevik dragon. Hess' madcap act was inspired by a conversation he had with the two exponents of the Nazi theory of geopolitics, Karl Haushofer and his son Albert, in August 1940. The subject of their talk was the method of obtaining an accord with Great Britain. It was the junior Haushofer's idea to contact the Duke of Hamilton, a Scottish peer he knew, on the neutral soil of **Portugal**. A letter to this effect, addressed to the duke, was intercepted by British intelligence agents. When rumors of an impending Nazi offensive to the east began to multiply and the British government was desperate for information, pressure was applied to the duke to keep his appointment in Lisbon with the younger Haushofer. But the appointment was never made, for Hess decided to take matters into his own hands by taking to the air. Whatever the British learned from Hess after they interrogated him was kept strictly secret, on Churchill's orders to prevent additional public debate on German peace offers. The official German explanation that

Hess fell victim to a spell of lunacy dovetailed nicely with British plans to isolate the Nazi bigwig from all public discussion and keep him in reserve for future political maneuvering. His arrogance still intact, he presented the German conditions for peace—among others, the enforced dismissal of Churchill—but kept an obstinate silence on a possible war against the USSR. When the Germans thrust eastward finally came on June 22, 1941, the Soviet government suspected Hess of having negotiated a secret pact with the British for a capitalist drive on the Communist citadel, and **Stalin** demanded a solemn agreement between the two countries that neither would conclude a separate peace with Germany. Questioned a second time by a member of the cabinet, Hess unequivocally asserted that he had only come to sue for peace on Germany's western flank while it engaged the Soviet Union on the east. This information was transmitted to Stalin, who received it, not with gratitude, but with heightened suspicions regarding British motives. The presence of the Nazi emissary on English soil was constantly to poison relations between the British and the Russians—aside, that is, from the animus Stalin already bore Churchill for the latter's dispatch of British troops to Russia to fight the infant Red Army in 1918. The Soviet leader obviously feared that Hess was being groomed to replace Hitler and promote an Allied-German combination against the USSR.

The World War
The war in Europe
The surprise attack on the USSR on June 22, 1941 and the equally surprising attack on **Pearl Harbor** on December 7 extended the war across the world. The opposing coalitions had hardened to the point where no dialogue was possible beyond the fronts. The simple fact that the USSR was at war with only two signatories of the **Tripartite Pact**, however, held out one possiblity for separate peace talks. Most attempts to break the opposing coalition were merely politico-strategic ploys designed to trip the enemy rather than to convince it of the folly of continuing the fight. During the **Blitzkrieg** against the Soviet Union, Hitler forbad any peace feelers. That order derived obviously from the Nazi mythology of Germany as the Siegfried destined to cut the heart out of the Bolshevik dragon. The true aim of the march into the Soviet Union was not the surrender of the enemy, as it had been in the campaign against the west, but the total erasure of the "Slavic subhumans." Faithful always to the theme of his *Mein Kampf*, that the "living space" of eastern Europe was fated for Germanization, Hitler remained stone deaf to any proposal for reaching an understanding with the Soviets under any conditions. All that was necessary for him to attain his dream of world

hegemony under the swastika was this one critical victory. It seized his imagination so completely that he devoted little thought to the British or the few remaining neutral states. Imbued with their bleakly Darwinian view of the restructuring of **society** and shaped by the military ethic of "all or nothing," the Nazis left unused the political treasure represented by the acquiescence of the neutral states, including the Vatican, to the idea of German domination.

The Nazi propaganda accompanying the "Anti-Bolshevik Crusade" awakened echoes everywhere in Europe. On such a basis the diplomats could finally see the possibility of a German-British accord. The Turkish government made offers, as did Franco from Spain, always ready—orally, at any rate—to lend his services to anti-communism. He established a distinction between the superfluous war in the west and the war to the death in the east, indispensable to a united Europe. Berlin treated these proposals as so many testimonials that these countries had renounced all freedom of political choice and recognized the soundness of Hitler's steadfast faith in a German victory. The same motive was visible behind the proposals of the Swiss, the Swedes and the Vichy French—or so, at least, the Nazis hoped. To the Anglo-American Allies, however, German military success in the East and the prospect of a Europe revolving around Berlin was an alarming prospect. In the face of a securely fortified Europe, backed by the awesome economic and agricultural resources of the USSR under German *Gleichschaltung*, an Anglo-American challenge in 1941 or 1942 seemed hopeless.

The Germans received repeated peace feelers from British industrial and commercial interests. The probability of the American aid on which Churchill was counting seemed to recede as the Germans advanced eastward. Moreover, Roosevelt was involved in a desperate struggle with his isolationist opposition to make good his promises of assistance to the Russians. American military experts almost to a man insisted that the Soviets could hold out no more than six weeks against the murderous Blitzkrieg, and what American could visualize himself marching side by side with Bolshevik atheists? Few in Washington, as in London, doubted that the fall of Stalin, and the subsequent disappearance of Communism, was imminent. Plans were underway for a democratic **government-in-exile** under Alexander Kerensky, the former prime minister of the Russian Provisional Government. Thus the air over England was full of political guesses, especially after the British-Soviet mutual assistance pact was signed on July 12, 1941. In the Soviet Union after a German victory, there would be little opportunity to resurrect **resistance** among Russian social democrats, simply because too few had survived the **revolution** and the ensuing civil war. Of this fact the Allies were well aware, which is why they did not ask the USSR for a program to oppose the Nazi-led European Union they so much feared. The **Atlantic Charter**, the declaration of Western freedoms negotiated between the British and Americans on August 14, 1941, was designed to forestall a German peace offensive. The charter aroused little response from Europeans, who were fascinated by the twists and turns of the war in the east. When he publicly affirmed on October 2, 1941 that the days of USSR were numbered, Hitler loosed a public panic in Great Britain. The press flaunted stories of the bleak future confronting the island, with only the slim Channel between it and a German continental bloc, and criticism of Churchill was rekindled in the Labor Party. London itself was irritated by the constant offers of mediation from the neutral states. To avoid a concerted drive for peace stimulated by Nazi propaganda, Churchill formally denied any possibility of peace in a special address. He was seconded by Roosevelt's attacks on American isolationists. The Anglo-Americans' fear of a Europe united under the hooked cross of Nazism was as little understood in Berlin as young Haushofer's project of a New Europe, presented in November 1941 and then entirely forgotten. But, quite suddenly, the hesitation of the German army before Moscow, the strong Soviet counterattack, and especially the entry of Japan into the war in December 1941 all clamored for swift recomputation of the chances for a peace.

The beginning of the Pacific war and the surprising initial successes of the Japanese shifted the center of gravity of the conflict much further toward the east than the fighting in the USSR. The Japanese had a closely plotted plan of conquest. They wanted to create a "**Greater East Asia Co-Prosperity Sphere.**" After having driven the whites out of East and Southeast Asia, they would conclude a compromise peace, assuring them hegemony in their new zone of influence. But their initial logic went awry in the intoxication of victory; **India, Australia** and the entire Far East became long-term objectives of the war. Thus the opportunities for peace talks after the most serious British defeat, the surrender of **Singapore**, were squandered.

Great Britain's position was poor after it had lost its support points in continental Europe; it began to have visions of a lost Asian and Near Eastern empire. It is against this backdrop that one must view the peace offers launched toward Germany from Switzerland and Portugal. The originators of these appeals were usually politicians of the second rank, most likely acting on signals provided by Lord **Beaverbrook**, who was regrouping the "loyal opposition." The German Foreign Ministry forbade the development of contacts between the British consul in Zurich and the German legation there, for which a Swiss armaments manufacturer had already begun to act as an intermediary. Out of a petty Anglophobia, Ribbentrop acted with even more intransigence than Hitler, who had wanted to maintain this means of communication with the British for information purposes. By a heavy majority on July 1, 1942, the House of Commons killed a vote of no confidence in the government. Churchill and his refusal to negotiate with the enemy were upheld; the opposition of the "appeasers" was defeated. From that moment until the final shot of the war, peace probes were no longer transmitted through minor diplomats.

It was now the turn of the Germans who opposed Hitler to seek contacts with the Allies. The military defeats stimulated the disaffection of some of the generals, *Abwehr* agents, some isolated diplomats and even some factions of the **SS**. But it was at the United States that they aimed their appeals, since that nation was at the head of the Allied camp, and the only power capable of resisting the Soviet drive into central Europe, now gaining momentum. Papen, whose sentiments regarding Nazi domination were mixed, had been trying various approaches since the summer of 1942, when he became convinced of the impossibility of a Blitzkrieg victory in the USSR and of the inevitable disintegration of Germany. He vainly tried to obtain the good offices of the Vatican.

At the Casablanca Conference (see **Conferences, Allied**) on January 24, 1943, Roosevelt asserted that the goal of the war was "**unconditional surrender.**" This formula stiffened official policy. But it also put excellent arguments into the mouths of opposition circles in Italy, Germany and, later, Japan. These circles took some tentative steps, but without much hope, since the Americans absolutely refused to revise the formula, even in the event of a change in regime. In Turkey since February 1943 the German Adm. **Wilhelm Canaris** had been urging former minister to Bulgaria and assistant naval attache George H. Earle, one of Roosevelt's cronies, to try for the abandonment of this formula in exchange for an understanding between Germany and the West. In his speech of March 21, 1943, Papen emphasized the danger of Soviet expansion, highlighted the political support America could give Europe and indirectly recognized the principles of the Atlantic Charter. His appeal was clear. It was featured by the foreign press but was ignored by official circles. Vainly, Papen attempted to interest Earle in his plea. Vainly also, a peace probe was transmitted to London, although Churchill was beginning to have second thoughts about the need for an unconditional surrender. In the meantime even the intelligence service of the SS associated itself with Papen's fruitless attempts.

No doubt for tactical reasons, the first of which was to prevent German-Soviet negotiations for a separate peace, the American intelligence services went on the alert to determine the intensity of the opposition to Hitler and the stability of the German government. There was another reason, too, originating in American espionage circles that considered Roosevelt's attitude too pro-Soviet. Those circles, which would come into prominence under **Truman**, never considered dealing with Germany, but were aware of the need to preserve its political and military potential in order to contain the rapidly growing Soviet threat. They therefore were eager to abet a coup d'etat against the Nazi regime.

In the spring of 1943, there were three conferences between **Allen Dulles**, head of the European section of American intelligence, and semiofficial German emissaries in Switzerland. One of the latter was Prince Max von Hohenlohe; a second, Reinhard Siptzy, an agent of **Walter Schellenberg**. They discussed with Dulles Hitler's shortcomings as a field commander and American war aims. A salient element in these discussions, as in the later conference of Roosevelt's personal envoy with the Vatican, was the American government's concern that German and Soviet diplomats were preparing a treaty to end the war in the east. A new Nazi-Soviet Pact would have resulted in a Eurasian continental bloc. The concessions made verbally to the Germans during these talks and in a meeting with Papen at the beginning of October 1943 were certainly dictated by this fear and were meant to counter similar offers from the Soviets.

At the foreign ministers' conference in Moscow in late October 1943, mutual and immediate exchanges of information on German peace offers were proposed. This was insisted upon by the British representative, who felt that his government had depended too heavily on the promise of a separate peace after the Hess incident and that everything should be done to prevent a new Stalin-Hitler combine.

The story of German-Soviet contacts after June 22, 1941 is among the most fascinating and least understood of the entire war. It had a much greater effect on the course of the war and on the behavior of the Tripartite Pact signatories than is generally known. Of all the nations involved, it was the USSR most of all that toyed with the idea of a separate peace. Among all the motives for these maneuvers, it is sometimes difficult to differentiate those stemming from a long-term plan from those inspired by the day-to-day tactical situation. The seriousness of these propositions can be judged only for certain periods of the war, but the most frequent motif running through them was the fear of encirclement by the capitalist nations.

Several weeks after the German invasion of the USSR, in a move paralleling that of Rudolf Hess, the Soviet ambassador to Sweden, Alexandra Kollontay, tried to defect to the Germans. The news was announced to Hitler by the *Abwehr*, whose Kremlin experts were concentrated in Stockholm. He was at first inclined to follow it up, but apparently decided it was a waste of time, since the German armies were then progressing well into the Soviet Union, and a possible security risk in any event. The whole project was finally dropped by the *Abwehr*. In the meantime, the international press was full of rumors of an imminent armistice. In his conference with the British envoy **Anthony Eden** in December 1941, Stalin insisted that the western frontier of the Soviet Union should be identical with that of Imperial Russia in 1914. Furthermore, he made a distinction between Hitler and the Germans, thus apparently confirming the rumor then current—that if the Western powers denied Soviet territorial demands, he would reach an agreement once again either with Hitler or some other Nazi government to obtain satisfaction. In March 1942 the Soviets renewed their offer of an immediate armistice that had already been formulated in September 1941 through secret agents in Stockholm. The Germans made no attempt to pursue it, but contact was maintained. The renewed German offensives in the summer of 1942 seemed to doom the negotiations, but when Soviet resistance stiffened at Stalingrad, they entered a new phase. After some preliminaries, the attache to the German minister of foreign affairs, Peter Kleist, received an offer based on maintenance of the Soviet frontiers of 1939—the era of the Nazi-Soviet Pact—in Stockholm on December 11, 1942. Toward the end of the battle of Stalingrad, the Soviets addressed themselves directly to the German legation in Sweden, but received no reply from Berlin. In the meantime Semyonov, the Soviet specialist on Berlin, was appointed to the Stockholm legation and undertook to talk with the Germans, probably on orders from his superiors.

Germany's two allies intensified their efforts to halt this absurd and wasteful ideological war. Before their entry into the hostilities, the Japanese had made no secret of the fact that they deplored the military operations in the USSR, which curtailed their economic dealings with the Reich. With a rare unanimity of opinion among the army, navy and civil authorities, the Japanese recognized the German defeats by suggesting an armistice to Moscow and Berlin. The Soviet government preferred to deal directly with the Germans, and did not bother to reply to the Japanese. In Berlin the Japanese offer was impatiently swept aside by Ribbentrop.

Hitler's refusal to consider an armistice in the east grieved the Italians. After positions held by Italian troops at Stalingrad were penetrated, Ciano proposed a separate peace at the end of December 1942. Hitler rejected the proposal with disdain. Mussolini tried again in April 1943, when the Allied successes in Africa began to pose a serious threat to Italy (see **Mediterranean and Middle Eastern Theater of Operations**.) But Hitler regarded the war against the Communists as the mission he had been created to fulfill, turning his back not only on negotiations with the Russians but on the European Charter Mussolini proposed as well. The Italians then offered a separate peace to the Western Allies, reminding them of earlier British and American offers to distinguish between Italians and Germans in preliminary armistice talks. Mussolini's ouster on July 25, 1943 only accelerated the process. On September 3 **Pietro Badoglio** broke the Italo-German "**Pact of Steel**"and signed a separate armistice with the Western Powers. This was the inevitable consequence of Hitler's fanatical devotion to the eastern campaign and his refusal to unite the Japanese, German and Italian forces against the Western Allies.

Relations between Germany and Japan cooled in the fall of 1943. Japan was to continue its mediation between Berlin and Moscow until July 1944, in combination with a little flirtation of its own with the Soviets, aimed at luring them into Asiatic bloc. But Japan failed to interest the USSR, which had just succumbed to American pressure to participate in the war effort against those same indefatigable peacemakers, the Japanese.

At this same moment the German-Soviet talks in Stockholm had reached their climax. In June 1943 a high official in the Soviet Ministry of Foreign Affairs waited vainly for his German opposite, with whom he was to discuss, through channels, restoring the Soviet frontiers of 1939. Once again the Germans had turned a deaf ear to the east. The only news they wanted from that direction was the success of their "*Zitadelle*" offensive. But "*Zitadelle*" came to grief, and even the most cautious of the Soviet leaders understood that they now had the initiative. The possibilities for contact with the Germans had radically changed. The founding of the *National Komitee "Freies Deutschland"* on July 12, 1943 heralded the birth of a Nazi-free German republic. It also permitted the Soviets to play at both ends of the same table. On the one hand they addressed themselves to a committee of **prisoners of war** and refugees; on the other, they remained in contact with Nazi officials in Berlin. Stalin could now exploit these two lines of communication to get the **Second Front** he had so long demanded.

Hitler paid no more attention to his minister of foreign affairs, who wanted to follow up the Soviet proposal, than did his allies. In any case, Ribbentrop was not the type to act on his own initiative. **Himmler**, however, had acquired means of communicating personally with the two opposing sides during the summer of 1943, and even went so far as to use liaisons established by the **German Resistance**. In September 1943 the USSR established another means of contact, this time in the person of V. G. Dekanozov, the former Soviet ambassador to Berlin. Through him, Stalin now demanded a return to the Russian frontiers of 1914. But the Germans refused even to glance at the offer.

Hitler's continuing refusal to consider a dialogue with the Soviets was simply another facet of the Nazi blind spot that was in the end to lead Germany almost to destruction. What appears to us today as incomprehensible generosity on Stalin's part was perhaps only a maneuver to get the Germans to sit at a conference table. It can hardly be doubted that the Soviets in 1943 truly wanted an accord with the Germans under conditions the Western Allies would never grant. After the Moscow conference and the meeting of the "Big Three" at Teheran, the secret agents at Stockholm kept in contact as a prospective means of putting pressure on the Western powers. The chances of an entente between the Nazis and the Communists in 1944 diminished rapidly with the promise of a **Normandy landing** and the unexpectedly hurried retreat of the Germans before the Red Army. As long as the Fuehrer remained in charge of the war, no further miracles of diplomacy could be expected in the East. His ineradicable faith in the mission of the "Nordic race" to dominate the "Slavic hordes" and his application everywhere of the Nazi "might makes right" creed would not permit him to seek a political compromise either in the East or West. He was equally obdurate toward his Balkan collaborators when they urged a less rigid policy, if only to counter the partisans' appeal to the conquered populations. When the Germans were forced to evacuate **Greece**, they considered joining the British, on the basis of common anti-Communist sentiments, to swing Anglo-American policy to the German side. The proposal vanished under Hitler's frown. Local discussions among Allied officers—and Churchill's growing revulsion for the Russian appetite for territory—showed only too clearly that as late as 1944 it might still have been possible for the Anglo-American and German governments to reach an understanding if Hitler had not ruled out any compromise of any kind.

Certain Americans opposed Roosevelt's policies, hoping for a unified Germany as a rampart against communism. This view dovetailed with that of a rebel clique in Germany, attempting like their Italian brethren to overthrow their dictator. Strangely enough, these German rebels found a friend in Franco. Plans were feverishly being made in Madrid to kidnap Hitler and keep him out of the way long enough to arrange a separate peace with the Catholic bloc in southern Germany. In the meantime the Red Army in the east and the Anglo-American armies in the west had crossed the Reich's 1938 frontiers. Proposals for surrender now seemed more popular than proposals for a separate peace. Ribbentrop now made an offer, with the apparent approval of Hitler, that might have been taken seriously had it been submitted two years earlier. Under its terms Germany was to retain its independence, with the Nazi government intact, and in alliance with the Western powers would help repel the Communist invader. In the absence of a suitable response from the Western Allies, Ribbentrop intended to make the same offer to the Soviets, with the direction of battle reversed. Envoys extraordinary were dispatched with this proposal to Sweden, Switzerland and Spain, but the whole explosive mixture misfired. Communications were blocked, and Germany's enemies, hot in pursuit of a total victory, would not be diverted from it.

With the reins of power slipping out of their grasp, Himmler, Goering and **Goebbels** were busy drafting peace offers of their own, each designed to protect its writer personally against the inevitable **purges** and general settling of accounts. Finally, when **Karl Doenitz'** government failed to gain approval of its offer of partial surrender—i.e., to the Anglo-Americans but not the Russians—Germany capitulated unconditionally on May 8, 1945.

The war in the Pacific

At the beginning of the war in the Pacific, the Japanese government exhibited the same reaction to peace offers as the Germans. No official initiatives toward suspension of hostilities emanated from the **Tojo** cabinet. The prime minister was too preoccupied with military conquest and the formation of an Asiatic empire. He expected that the war would force the Americans and British to accept a dictated settlement that would rid Asia of their presence once and for all. Any dialogue with the enemy, even in secret, was viewed by the Japanese army with disdain.

More amenable was the navy, generally more sophisticated in its approach to international affairs. Through its attache to the Japanese embassy at Berlin it established a liaison with Switzerland for the transmission of diplomatic information. After the fall of Singapore on February 15, 1942, Adm. **Kichisaburo Nomura**, head of the Japanese Military Commission in Germany and the highest-ranking Japanese officer then in Europe, discussed methods of establishing a peace treaty with an Allied agent in Switzerland. Prominent Japanese civilians with similar intentions, unable to exert any influence over the warlords, wanted to send former premier **Fumimaro Konoe** to Switzerland to conduct peace talks. But when the fortunes of the war in the Pacific turned, especially with the Japanese defeat at **Midway** early in June 1942, which was accompanied by other evil portents, notably the dead halt of the German offensive into the USSR, Tokyo's appetite for fresher and more detailed information from Europe increased. During the summer of 1943 a high-ranking delegation was sent to Germany, and then to Switzerland, presumably to broaden the channels of information. Like their colleagues in the navy, the Japanese army officers were beginning to face the need for a diplomatic staff in Switzerland.

In November 1943 the Japanese admiralty established a committee for examining the unfolding of the war and the prospects for further operations. It collaborated closely with opposition circles dissatisfied with the bellicose Tojo. Its findings were melancholy—Japan could not obtain a decisive victory for lack of war materiel. In September 1943, with **Hirohito**'s support, talks were conducted with agents of **Chiang Kai-shek** as the first step toward ending hostilities on the Asian continent. The tentative move was immediately halted by Tojo. A similarly strangled peace attempt was the suggestion of the most influential of the Emperor's counselors, **Koichi Kido**, the Keeper of the Seal, who proposed to declare Southeast Asia neutral territory. The Allied formula of "unconditional surrender" voided such a move.

The overthrow of Tojo by the committee of former premiers on July 18, 1944 freed the hands of the peace-seekers. The new co-premier, Adm. **Mitsumasa Yonai**, immediately ordered the navy research section to develop specific proposals for a cessation of hostilities. The plan then contrived was for Japan to surrender without sacrificing its imperial mode of government and give up all its conquests except Formosa and Korea. But such a concept had first to be fed in gradually increasing doses to an army fanatically convinced that it would eventually triumph and to a completely ignorant public. This plan served as the basis for action for the Japanese navy, to which cessation of the war was an absolute necessity. It was not until the accession of Adm. **Kantaro Suzuki**'s government on April 7, 1945, however, that the navy could begin to follow it.

Japan had made peace overtures to various European countries as early as August 1944, but only in June 1945 was the war situation critical enough to force the supreme war council in Tokyo to drop most of its demands and seek an end to the war in earnest. Japan's peace initiatives fizzled not just because they came too late and conceded too little. They were doomed from the start by Stalin's secret promise to the Allies at Cairo in December 1943 to enter the war against Japan after Germany fell, an intention secured at Yalta in February 1945 with large territorial concessions to the Soviets. Peace feelers were also fated to fail because of the Allies' oft-expressed resolve to avoid the mistakes of Versailles by achieving unconditional surrender.

Japan had begun the war with the United States hoping to negotiate a peace when the Americans grew tired of fighting, perhaps as early as mid-1942. In August 1944 the Japanese foreign minister, **Mamoru Shigemitsu**, asked his ambassador to the Soviet Union, Naotake Sato, to determine whether the Soviets would be willing to negotiate peace with Germany, now that the Red Army was advancing and the Germans were retreating. Tokyo also instructed its ambassador to Berlin, **Hiroshi Oshima**, to sound out Hitler about a settlement with the Soviets. Had such an agreement been reached, German forces could have been redeployed on the western front, stalling the Allied drive begun at Normandy the preceding June. This might in turn have forced the United States and Great Britain to transfer troops from the Pacific and thus relieved the pressure on Japan. By mid-September **Vyacheslav M. Molotov**, the Soviet foreign commissar, von Ribbentrop, the German foreign minister and Hitler himself had all told Japanese diplomats that a negotiated settlement was out of the question—for the Germans because they were losing in the east, for the Soviets because they were winning and wanted to destroy Germany's power completely.

Eager as a handful of Japan's leaders were to end the war in the late summer of 1944, once the discussions with Moscow and Berlin came to naught the senior statesmen and imperial courtiers who had ousted Prime Minister Hideki Tojo in July in order to seek peace now seemed indecisive about how to proceed and fearful that army extremists might terrorize the court and the country. By late September munitions **production** was peaking, civilian livelihoods were straitened and the imperial forces were retreating, but the leadership stalemate persisted.

A Tokyo news executive, Bunshiro Suzuki, broached peace to the Swedish minister to Japan, Widar Bagge, in September. Suzuki said he was speaking for Prince Fumimaro Konoe, the former prime minister, who regarded unconditional surrender as a key sticking point. But the conversations soon stalled, and no further initiatives of importance took place until early the next year.

The idea of peace came into favor at court on St. Valentine's Day 1945, when Konoe made a discursive but forceful speech to Emperor Hirohito about the likelihood of defeat and the possibility of a communist revolution if Japan did not surrender soon. Konoe was particularly worried that the imperial army might ally with Japanese communists to threaten the court and aristocracy. Peace was now not only a military inevitability abroad but also a political necessity at home.

In early March the Americans began pounding major Japanese cities with B-29s in their frightful air war against the home islands (see **Japan, Air War Against**). With the war now at the palace doorstep, the Swedish minister in late March advised Tadashi Sakaya, a top Japanese diplomat, that the Allies might yield on unconditional surrender if the Japanese initiated peace. Bagge soon departed for Stockholm, the Japanese cabinet fell, and follow-up inquiries in April and May from the new foreign minister, **Shigenori Togo**, were unavailing.

At about the same time a Japanese naval attache in Berne, Cdr. Yoshiro Fujimura, believed Japan's war prospects were so parlous that he contacted the American **Office of Strategic Services** in Switzerland to see if discussions might be started. The Americans received approval from Washington to listen to anything the Japanese might say, but Fujimura got little' support from his naval superiors in Tokyo, despite repeated urgent cables. The Japanese also extended parallel feelers in Zurich and Basel in May, but none of these moves bore fruit. By now Tokyo had elected to turn to the USSR once again as an intermediary, nullifying the Switzerland initiatives, and the Americans were bent on exerting "maximum force with maximum speed," in **Henry L. Stimson**'s words, knowing that the Soviets had promised to enter the war against Japan three months after the German surrender of May 8, 1945.

In the Pacific the Battle for **Okinawa** had begun on April 1, bringing down the Koiso cabinet four days later. The senior statesmen chose Adm. Suzuki, the immensely respected head of the privy council, to form the new cabinet for the frank purpose of ending the war. But to win support from the army, Suzuki had to pledge publicly to continue the fighting, and a modest purge of 400 peace advocates took place. On the other hand, Suzuki picked Togo as his foreign minister because he was known as an opponent of the war.

The Soviet Union informed Japan on April 5 that the neutrality pact between the two countries would be allowed to lapse in April 1946, as scheduled. This disturbing news led the army and navy to insist on fresh negotiations with Moscow to try to keep the USSR from attacking Japan and to try to barter naval cruisers for Soviet oil. Togo correctly suspected that the Allies had already conceded territories in East Asia to Stalin in return for Soviet intervention in the war, but he worked out plans for approaching the USSR to seek its friendship, a non-aggression pact and mediation of a surrender favorable to Japan.

Germany surrendered before Togo's overtures could be set in motion. At a series of crucial meetings on May 11-14, the supreme war council (whose members included the prime minister, the army, navy and foreign ministers, the chiefs of the army and navy general staffs and sometimes the emperor) reaffirmed its resolve to seek a treaty that would keep Moscow out of the war, without directly confronting Tojo's suggestion that Soviet assistance be obtained to seek a negotiated peace. In the strict sense, Japan was not yet officially committed to seeking peace, but rather to obtaining an understanding that would prolong the war.

Had Tokyo been unambiguously determined to discuss a negotiated peace, various other options might have been considered in the spring of 1945. Neutrals such as Sweden, Switzerland or the Vatican were likely intermediaries, and brief talks with Chinese diplomats did take place in March, but apparently the Japanese regarded none of these sufficiently important in world diplomacy to use them for peace talks (assuming the supreme war council had been eager to hold talks). Direct contacts with the United States and Great Britain seemed likely to antagonize the Japanese armed services and unlikely to get the Allies to budge from their goal of unconditional surrender. For these reasons, Togo—without a mandate to discuss peace directly—prepared to contact the Soviets in late May.

Former Prime Minister **Koki Hirota,** who once was ambassador to the USSR, was appointed to start talks with the Soviet ambassador to Japan, Jacob A. Malik, at a hotel at Gora near Tokyo. Hirota proposed an improvement of friendship between the two countries and a nonaggression treaty, but the Soviets were unenthusiastic. Meanwhile Okinawa was on the verge of surrender to the Americans and the USSR was strengthening its forces along the Amur river in preparation for an attack on Japan.

The supreme war council met hastily on June 6, the first anniversary of the Normandy landing, to adopt plans for a final home front mobilization to resist the American seaborne invasion expected later in the year. Some of the generals and admirals knew that the June 6 plans for civilian "volunteer corps," armed only with bamboo spears, would not produce victory, but they remained unyielding in their determination

to fight to the end so that the military could retain the upper hand amid the domestic chaos that was certain to follow the surrender. Just as personal advantage had led Konoe to seek peace, the same motive prompted the armed services to shirk it.

As soon as the military's plans for civilian mobilization had been ratified by an imperial conference on June 8, Koichi Kido began urging "peace with honor," which virtually meant unconditional surrender. American bombers were now destroying Japanese cities almost without resistance, a naval **blockade** was starving the home islands and the home front economy was sapped to its core. When Okinawa fell on June 21, Kido and others convened an imperial conference the next day at which Hirohito, well briefed by Foreign Minister Togo, asked when a representative could be sent to Moscow to seek a negotiated peace. War Minister **Korechika Anami** and Army Chief of Staff Yoshijiro Umezu expressed reservations, but the emperor chastened them into silence. At last Japan was officially committed to making peace overtures, long after its position in the war zone had deteriorated into hopelessness. By waiting so long, Tokyo had defaulted any real chance of a negotiated settlement because it had long since run out of cards to play.

Hirota went to see Malik again on June 24, this time to offer very extensive resources and territorial concessions if the Soviets would sign a nonaggression pact. The Soviets were no more receptive to these plans than they had been to Hirota's suggestions earlier in the month, and Malik ended up refusing to see his counterpart for two weeks on the pretext of illness.

Hirohito instructed Prime Minister Suzuki to send someone to Moscow to break the logjam and seek Soviet mediation before the Allies met in Potsdam in late July. On July 10 the supreme war council chose Konoe as the emissary, and the prince agreed after a conference with the emperor. Working through ambassador Sato in Moscow, Togo told Molotov on July 13 that Konoe would arrive bearing the emperor's request that a Soviet-Japanese treaty be concluded with particular attention to Manchuria. No mention was made of mediating a surrender. Moscow stalled for time, seeking clarifications from Togo. Not until July 21 did Togo authorize Sato to tell the Soviets that the Konoe mission would ask Stalin to help bring the war to an end. Yet that same day Togo made it clear that under no circumstance could Japan accept an unconditional surrender. Whether this assertion represented stubbornness, myopia or mere bravura cannot be known, for already the Allied leaders were gathering at Potsdam to seal Japan's fate.

The overtures to the USSR fell flat because Japan

had nothing of value with which to buy Soviet nonintervention and because Tokyo waited far too long to broach the question of mediating peace. Although the subject had arisen as early as August 1944, no Japanese leader took concrete steps to seek peace until Konoe's conference with the emperor in February 1945 and Togo's appointment as foreign minister seven weeks later. Exploring peace initiatives became official state policy only on June 22, and no foreign government was formally notified of Japan's willingness to surrender, even if conditionally, until July 21. It is small wonder that these ill-timed, unrealistic and inadequate efforts bore such bitter fruit. Had they succeeded and led to a prompt surrender decision, even as late as Potsdam, the world might have been spared the agony of Hiroshima and Nagasaki. (See also **Surrender Decision by Japan**.)

In the whole course of the Second World War, the traditional sources of power were impotent to bring about one fruitful conversation regarding the methodology of obtaining a peace. With the resources of the major powers completely mobilized, the conflict was in essence an ideological struggle between two mutually antipathetic concepts of the world in which little in the way of sympathetic dialogue could be exchanged. All the peace attempts had this in common: they had no effect on the actual military progress of the war. They only contributed, within the context of the primacy of force, to a hardening of political attitudes that persists even now.

B. Martin
T. R. H. Havens

PEARL HARBOR.

On Sunday, December 7, 1941, while talks between Japanese and American diplomats were still going on in Washington, a U.S. naval squadron of 94 warships and auxiliary vessels lay at anchor in Pearl Harbor, in the territory of Hawaii. Eight battleships were grouped together, separated from each other by no more than 50-100 feet, in two lines. The sky was heavily overcast. At about 6:00 a.m., in a customary morning maneuver, ant antitorpedo gate guarding the 2,500-foot harbor entrance was opened. At 7:02 a.m., two of the local **radar** operators saw blips on their screens, indicating large groups of aircraft in flight toward the island from the north. They reported the sighting to their superior officer. His guess was that they were American craft from the continent, and there the matter was dropped as a trivial break in the customary routine.

A rift in the clouds suddenly opened, and at 7:55 a.m., swarms of aircraft poured through it, hurling bombs at the American ships. The attacking planes,

360 of them, had zoomed off the flight decks of six aircraft carriers, which, with some submarine carriers and the five small, special-purpose submarines they launched, stood about 200 miles from their target.

The first wave of Japanese bombers smashed or disabled most of the American planes in their hangars or on the open airfields. It was followed with an attack, in several waves, by torpedo planes and dive-bombers. The submarines that had managed to slip into the port contributed to the destruction by sinking some of the vessels already damaged by the initial bombing waves and damaging others. The eight American battleships, three cruisers and a great number of smaller vessels were sunk or crippled. The Japanese losses, amounting to some 30 planes and the five submarines, were minor given the magnitude of the victory. By 9:45 a.m., less than two hours after the initial onslaught, practically the entire U.S. Pacific Fleet was either on the ocean floor or drifting helplessly on its surface. Once again the civilized world was accorded the view of a democratic country unscrupulously violated by a totalitarian power even before a break in diplomatic relations. Nor was this the first time the Japanese had committed such an act; it was equally successful against the Russian Imperial Navy in 1905.

The results of the surprise attack would have been much less serious had the Americans exercised more vigilance. With a probable enemy in the habit of striking at neighbor nations without making formal declarations of war, the inability of a powerful nation to protect itself is hardly understandable. As if in indifference to the "war warning" issued by Washington on November 27, less than two weeks before the disaster, the officials of the base treated that particular Sunday just as any other Sunday; the military personnel on the base had been given passes to attend religious services outside the base. The heroism displayed by the fliers, the sailors, and the antiaircraft gunners in this hell of exploding gunpowder, manning their stations until they were swallowed by the ocean with their ships or crushed under cascading rubble, could never erase the image of a huge, shameful blunder.

Nor was it the last of the military tragedies to pursue the Anglo-American alliance. Just three days later, 5,000 miles from Hawaii, the British dreadnoughts *Repulse* (32,000 tons) and *Prince of Wales* (35,000 tons) were sent to the bottom by a Japanese attack. Based at **Singapore**, they had departed on a mission to destroy a fleet of Japanese transport vessels in the Gulf of Siam. They had no air cover—a fatal mistake. They were attacked by about a hundred Japanese bombers and torpedo planes. Both ships foundered; with them and their crews died their commanding officer, Adm. Sir Tom Philips.

This punishing loss was more than a personal tragedy for the British. Not one ship of the line was left to them to oppose Japanese power. For the first time in centuries, the British flag had vanished from the seas of Asia. **Japan** now supplanted the **United Kingdom** as absolute mistress of the waves as the result of a carefully planned and promptly executed series of maneuvers. It had begun by depriving its enemy of all freedom of motion and therefore of any opportunity to reinforce its isolated garrisons. The Japanese, in fact, made the best of their central position and their proximity to the mother country to insure numerical superiority in each of its conquests without committing heavy land forces and having to contend with commensurate logistic difficulties.

Their initial successes, however, fell short of their goal. The land installations at Pearl Harbor, overlooked by the rampaging attackers, were intact. The power stations servicing the base were still operable, stores of gasoline remained untouched and the shipyards at once began work on the ships that were salvageable. None of the American submarines were hit. The one piece of good fortune was the absence from the base at the time of the attack of the two large carriers *Lexington* and *Saratoga*, (33,000 tons each) and the smaller carrier *Enterprise* (19,000 tons). They should have been at Pearl on December 7 but had not as yet completed their deep-sea training maneuvers. In the Battle of **Midway**, six months after the Japanese attack, these three giants, reinforced by the aircraft carriers *Hornet* and *Yorktown* arriving from the Atlantic, were to avenge the sinking of their sister ships.

The disaster of December 7 was partially intended by the Japanese to depress American **morale**. It had the opposite effect. The indignation and sense of mortal danger it aroused in the **United States** unified the country behind its president as no other act could have. With few exceptions the entire nation was possessed with the single aim of humiliating the Japanese for their act of infamy.

In the meantime, the Japanese swept from one conquest to another. After taking **Wake** Island and **Hong Kong**, they invaded **Thailand** and the Malay Peninsula. They landed their army on the **Philippines** and, in the naval battle of Surabaja, destroyed a combined British-Dutch-American fleet commanded by the Dutch Adm. Karel W. Doorman on February 27, 1942. Not long afterward, Sumatra, Java and the Solomon Islands were overrun by the Japanese. They made a successful landing on **New Guinea**, with their sights aimed at **Australia**, their ultimate target. These victories, however, could not have been so easily accomplished if the Japanese had not first deprived Great Britain of its great base of Singapore on February 15, 1942. The last of the British bastions in the

Pacific, its loss was a bitter blow for London—especially since, like Pearl Harbor, it was the victim of an inefficient, hopelessly inadequate defense. Its fall removed the last obstacle to the Japanese, who occupied all of **Burma** and thus cut the famous Burma Road on which **China** relied for supplies.

Strange as it may seem, these individually conclusive victories did not add up to total military superiority. **Hitler** urged the Japanese to press on toward **India** as the third arm of the gigantic pincer whose other two arms the **Axis** troops advancing through the Caucasus and Suez would form after May 1942. There were obviously no limits to the Nazi or Japanese dreams. Not only did the Rising Sun pursue its fruitless war over the vast Chinese front, in which it had been bogged down since 1937, it persisted in scattering its meager resources in all directions. (See also **Pacific Theater of Operations**.)

H. Bernard

PEENEMUENDE.
Built at the mouth of the Peene River, Peenemuende was the rocket **research** center that produced the **V-1** and **V-2** rockets fired at England by the Nazis toward the end of the war. American bombers heavily damaged Peenemuende on August 4 and 25, 1944.

PENIAKOFF, Vladimir ("Popski") (1897-1951).
A Belgian merchant of Russian descent and an accomplished desert navigator, he fought in the Libyan Arab Force Commando in 1940-42. He formed a small strike force—officially called Popski's Private Army—in November 1942 and operated with it in Tunisia and **Italy**, causing disproportionate casualties and alarm. His initiative saved Ravenna's churches.

PEOPLE'S COMMISSARIAT FOR DOMESTIC AFFAIRS.
See *Narodnyy Kommissariat Vnutrennikh Del*.

PETAIN AND THE FRENCH STATE.
On May 18, 1941, while the Panzer divisions made their dash to the Straits of Dover, the president of the *Conseil d'Etat*, **Paul Reynaud**, reconstituted his cabinet. From Madrid he recalled Marshal Petain, then French ambassador to **Spain**, where he had been for the past 14 months, and appointed him vice president of the *Conseil*. Reynaud hoped that the old "conqueror of Verdun" would revive the self-confidence of the French. But Petain considered the war as good as lost. By June 13, the situation had become exceedingly grave. The old marshal declared to the *Conseil* that France had no choice but agree to an armistice, and that he himself would never leave the soil

of continental France. Gen. **Maxime Weygand**, commander in chief since May 18, was not far behind him in recommending an armistice. On June 16 Reynaud resigned in despair at his inability to prosecute the war and at the flight of the government to **French North Africa**. President **Albert Lebrun** then called on Petain to form a government. On the following day the new premier announced to his people: "I give myself to France to ease her misfortunes," and, "the fighting must cease." The armistice, for which Spain served as the intermediary, was signed on the evening of June 21 with **Germany** and on June 24 with **Italy**.

The new Petain government moved from Bordeaux, to which it had retreated on June 14, to Vichy in central France on the 29th. Enter **Pierre Laval**, recently promoted to the post of vice president of the *Conseil*. Within 10 days, both chambers voted Petain, by a thundering majority of 569 to 80, the power to draw up a new constitution (see **Third Republic**). Even the word "republic" disappeared from the title of the new regime. It was known simply as the **French State**.

The head of the French State was 84. For several years Frenchmen like Gustave Herve, disheartened by the impotence of the preceding French parliamentary governments, supported him as the best available chief of state. In almost all Frenchmen, Petain inspired a blind confidence. But his thinking was essentially defeatist: to him France's defeat was final and irrevocable, and the **United Kingdom** had therefore to fall as well. Prey to the same belief, Laval used the marshal's prestige to persuade the French to accept Nazi and fascist ways in the hope of salvaging what remained of French sovereignty. Petain loathed him, yet named him his political heir.

While the new constitution was being written—it never was to be published—a de facto regime was installed. Without realizing that the defeat and occupation could hardly inspire confidence in his government, Petain went to the absurd length of launching, under the auspices of the conqueror, a "National Revolution" founded on the slogan Work, Family, and Country. Measures that might have been considered beneficial if France were free became law—assistance to "the woman in the kitchen," jobs for youth, aid to agriculture and small shopkeepers, reclamation projects for the provinces and the like. He defined the new regime in these words: "National in foreign policy, hierarchical in domestic policy, coordinated and controlled in economy, and above all, social in spirit."

But France was, by virtue of the armistice terms, three-fifths occupied; Petain's government controlled the remainder—the poorest part of the land. The Germans pillaged it at their leisure, despoiling it of money, foodstuffs, industrial products. On the very doorstep of this "state," it exercised surveillance and constraint. Laval decided that submission was inevitable. He persuaded Petain to meet Hitler at **Montoire** on October 24 and promise him his **collaboration**. To the marshal, "collaboration" was merely a word that might secure the return of 1.9 million **prisoners of war**. To Laval, it was a policy. On December 13, therefore, Petain dismissed Laval as his chief minister in favor of Pierre Etienne Flandin. But barely two months later the new minister was replaced, at the Germans insistence, by Adm. **Francois Darlan**. Like Laval, the admiral began by collaborating. He placed the Syrian airports at the disposal of German aircraft, an act which led the British and *Forces francaises libres* to occupy **Syria** and **Lebanon** between June 8 and July 14, when that part of the Middle East was still under the French mandate. But he emerged from his submissiveness by degrees. From Paris, the German "ambassador" **Otto Abetz** demanded that Petain summon Laval back to his old job. The marshal gave in to his pressure on April 17, 1942. "I am no better than a messenger boy," he privately told an intimate. On November 11, just after the Allied landing in North Africa, the Germans spread their occupation into the Free Zone. Despite pleas from Weygand and others, Petain refused to leave France to take refuge in Algeria.

All the diplomatic missions left Vichy, and on November 18, 1942, Petain ceded all his powers to Laval. But the swarthy "Pierrot" was completely in the power of the *Gauleiter*, **Fritz Sauckel**, appointed to control France in June 1942. His principal occupation was to argue against Sauckel's demands for Frenchmen by the hundreds of thousands to go to Germany as forced laborers—of the 1,575,000 demanded, Laval supplied only 785,000. The Jews, lacking any defense, and the **Resistance** forces, whose numbers were swelled by the men escaping the forced-labor dragnet, were pursued by the French police (see **French Police During the Occupation**) as well as the **Gestapo**. Captured, often by betrayal, they were first tortured, then sent to **concentration camps** to be destroyed.

The Allies landed in Normandy on June 6, 1944 (see **Normandy Landing**) and began a victorious campaign, aided by the Resistance. Petain was now convinced of Germany's eventual defeat. He therefore considered turning over his powers without hindrance to **de Gaulle**, forgetting that **Free France** had never acknowledged that he had any. In Paris, Laval wangled a return to the Third Republic, availing himself of the services of **Edouard Herriot** and Jules Jeanneney, former presidents of the Chamber of Deputies and the Senate respectively, who finally went into hiding. On August 17, he was transferred by the Germans to

Belfort. The next day Petain, in turn, was forced to flee Vichy. Both men, together with several collaborating ministers, were, on September 7, brought to the Sigmaringen Chateau. The "French State" still survived. France, now swept practically clean of its omnivorous occupiers, came under the jurisdiction of the "Provisional Government of the Republic"—the government of de Gaulle.

On April 26, 1945 Petain, permitted to leave Sigmaringen for **Switzerland**, returned to France out of his own desire. He was tried by the High Court of Justice and sentenced to death, but de Gaulle commuted the sentence to life imprisonment. He died on the Isle of Yeu in 1953.

E. Pognon

PETER II Karageorgevich (1923-1970).

King of **Yugoslavia**, Peter II ascended to the throne under a regency when his father was assassinated in 1934. On March 27, 1941 he assumed full royal powers when a coup d'etat in Belgrade overthrew the regency, but on April 6 he had to flee before the German attack. He reached England in June 1941 and headed an increasingly ineffective **government-in-exile** that supported **Dragolyub Mihailovich** and his Chetniks. He made an accommodation with **Tito** in August 1944 but was deposed in November 1945.

PETRIE, Sir David (1879-1961).

An official of the Indian police from 1900 to 1936, Petrie was head of **MI-5** from 1940 to 1945.

PHANTOM.

In World War I errors of command had repeatedly prevented a break-in from becoming a breakthrough; generals were too remote from the battle to understand what was going on in time to react. Phantom was a British signals unit formed to remedy this. It worked by shortwave wireless telegraphy over ranges of up to 500 miles, using portable transmitters. Its patrols traveled by armored car, by jeep, on foot or by parachute. Liaison officers of the commander in chief could accompany Phantom patrols, or the patrols could go alone and report what they saw. **Montgomery** found them useful at the second battle of **El Alamein** and in the advance to Tunis. The **Special Air Service** could not have operated in northwestern Europe without them.

PHILBY, Harold Adrian Russell ("Kim") (1912-).

Double agent. Born in **India** of British parents, Philby attended Cambridge, where he was secretly converted to communism. He taught at the **Special Operations** Executive's school at Beaulieu in 1940-41. He then transferred to the **Intelligence Service** and, by 1945, was head of its security section and already passing data to the **NKVD**.

PHILIPPINES, The.

The islands were Spanish by the end of the 16th century and became the principal Christian community in the Far East. They were ceded by **Spain** to the **United States** in 1898. The constitution of 1935 gave them a large measure of self-government. The Japanese invaded them on December 8, 1941. Combined U.S. and Filipino forces under Gen. **MacArthur,** outnumbered and outgunned, held out on the Bataan peninsula, west of Manila, until April 1942 and on Corregidor island at the mouth of Manila Bay for a month longer. The Japanese made extensive use of airfield and port facilities in the islands in 1942-44. The inhabitants, cool in turn toward the Spaniards and the Americans, were hardly warmer to their fellow Asiatics. On October 20, 1944 MacArthur returned, by a **combined operation**, to **Leyte** in the south of the island group. He brought substantial forces and retook most of the islands by the end of February 1945. A few Japanese pockets were still holding out in August 1945; one or two individual tough-minded officers may still be hiding in the hills. The islands became an independent republic on July 4, 1946.

M. R. D. Foot

PHONY WAR.

This term was used to describe the brief era, from the end of 1939 through the first few months of 1940, when the governments and chiefs of staff of the Franco-British alliance fell into a curious form of lethargy in the face of **Hitler**'s army on the western front. The phrase is a British invention. This paralytic response to the aggressiveness of the Third Reich had manifested itself before, with the remilitarization of the Rhine's left bank, the *Anschluss* and the dismemberment of **Czechoslovakia**. The Left's commitment to pacifism; the World War I veterans' revulsion against that experience and their desire to avoid its repetition in an even worse form; a bad **conscience** about the Draconian conditions imposed on the Weimar Republic of **Germany** in 1919; the fear of bolshevism and the consequent sympathy with an opposing ideology, **fascism**; the **propaganda** spread by **Mussolini**'s secret funds and **Otto Abetz'** forays into the world of high society and political influence; the lack of preparedness of the western European armed forces and armament industries; the refusal of military officers to believe in the need for such a war—all these factors added to a general feeling of helplessness and to a **strategy** that would, it seemed, remain purely defensive in nature until the labor supply for accelerating the manufacture of arms, **tanks,** aircraft and munitions could be replenished. Time was needed to extend the **Maginot Line** along the Belgian frontier. The attitude of the **USSR,** suspicious of an "imperialist" war, affected the factory workers, who were encouraged by militant communists to slow down plant operation. Franco-British military cooperation, resumed only in March 1939, was hurt by Gen. **Maurice Gamelin,** who opposed a staff organization that would combine the commanders of both countries; by the snail's pace of British rearmament after the Conscription Law of April 27, 1939 was enacted; by the extreme weakness of the French air force; by the shortage of skilled workers; by the lack of any coordination in arms **production**; by poor economic conditions—the feebleness of the French franc, the exodus of capital during the *Front populaire* period, the trade balance deficit; and by the opposition of the financial services to any massive rise in military expenditures. Also contributing to this malaise were the defeatist attitude of many active and reserve officers, the obsolete training methods and doctrines of the war college, the delay in mobilization, the anti-British prejudice of the French navy and the false but persistent rumors of an invincible German might. Those who spread these rumors, however, failed to take into account that the French had a greater force at the front, excellent artillery and first-rate tanks in practically the same numbers as the Germans, if poorly deployed. But problems of supply and the requirements of a genuine war economy had been neglected.

The annihilation of the Polish defenses; the rejection of Hitler's offers of peace on September 19 and October 6, 1939; the indifference of the British dominions, particularly the French Canadians; the failure of the attempts of the Pope and the American envoy, Sumner Welles, to mediate (see **Peace Overtures**); the rift between the French generals Gamelin and **Joseph Georges** (the latter was the commander in chief of the northeast European theater of operations); the underground activity of *Abwehr* agents planted in France by **Goebbels** and **Himmler**; the petty spite of the Volunteer Corps in publicly doubting the Allies' military effectiveness; and the Belgian government's unwillingness to create a secondary Namur-Antwerp defense line even after the chiefs of staff agreed to its necessity all contributed to the paralysis of the western European powers.

On January 20, 1940 Col. **Charles de Gaulle** addressed a memorandum to 80 high-ranking officers in the French army, pointing out the dangers of armored attack and the urgency of acquiring **antitank weapons**.

It was a second fruitless appeal; the first, written November 11, had also met with no perceptible response. While **Edouard Daladier**'s government took severe measures against the Communists, pacifist propaganda at the front, the restlessness of the troops, the frequent furloughs granted among units in contact with the enemy and the relaxation of discipline sapped the **morale** of the French troops. Promised British reinforcements, moreover, failed to arrive. Nor was there any apparent air cover. The serendipitous discovery of the German plans for the attack on **Belgium** in the plane shot down on January 10, 1940 in the **Mechlin incident** led to both the hasty revision of the plans by **Erich von Manstein** and the *Oberkommando der Wehrmacht* on one side and the reinforcement of Allied defenses on the other. Its cost to the Germans was only a few weeks of delay; its reward to the Allies came too late to improve their position.

The impotence of the defending forces brought about the fall of Daladier's government and his replacement by **Paul Reynaud**. A plan was adopted to strike at Germany by depriving it of Rumanian oil and cutting of its access to Swedish steel (see **Iron Road**; **Norway**). But the German attack on Scandinavia on April 9 ended both that plan and the Phony War.

M. Baudot

PIECK, Wilhelm (1876-1960).

A German Communist Party deputy to the *Reichstag*, Pieck fled to the **USSR** when **Hitler** was invested with full power. In Moscow he founded the *National Komitee "Freies Deutschland"* in 1943 and, after the partition of **Germany**, became the first president of the German Democratic Republic in 1949.

PIERLOT, Hubert (1883-1964).

Belgian statesman of the Catholic Party. As prime minister, Pierlot and three members of his cabinet met with King **Leopold III** on May 25 at Wynendaele in a vain attempt to prevail upon the king to flee to France and continue the struggle at the side of the Allies. On May 31 he declared his opposition to the Belgian parliamentarians at Limoge who tried to bring to a vote the question of the king's dethronement. After the surrender of France, he decided to leave for London with two colleagues but was arrested by Spanish authorities on August 24. He escaped toward the end of October. Thanks to the **government-in-exile** over which he presided in London, **Belgium** remained officially a partner in the Allied victory. He returned to Brussels in September 1944 and formed a National Union government from which he resigned in February 1945.

PINEAU, Christian (1904-).

A French economist, Pineau was a militant member of the French labor union organization *Confederation General du Travail* from 1934 to 1940. An editorialist of the French journal *Peuple*, he was one of the founders of the *Liberation-Nord* **Resistance** movement. He was deported to Buchenwald but survived and, after gaining his freedom, became minister of **food** in 1945. He authored *La Simple Verite*, a history of the **French Resistance**.

PIRE, Jules (alias "Pygmalion") (1878-1953).

A Belgian general, Pire was in command of the 10th Infantry Division in May 1940. In 1941 he entered the Belgian Legion of **Charles Claser**. In February 1944, as head of the legion, which had grown to a membership of 54,000 and became the *Armee de Belgique* on June 1, 1944, he executed an order of the **Supreme Headquarters Allied Expeditionary Forces** to touch off a series of **sabotage** raids designed to delay the concentration of German units in Normandy. On September 1 he led his group in guerrilla activity. Working with other **Resistance** movements, he prevented the retreating Germans from destroying installations—particularly the port facilities of Antwerp—that the advancing Allies would need. Beginning on September 4, his army protected the flanks of Belgian armored divisions supporting the Allies. On October 15, acting on the instructions of Gen. **Eisenhower** and the Belgian government, Pire dissolved his movement.

PIRON, Jean (1896-1974).

A Belgian officer, Piron commanded the Belgian brigade *Liberation* formed in Great Britain. This unit, landing in Normandy on August 3, 1944, liberated Honfleur and entered Brussels on September 4 with the Guards Armored Division, to which it was attached. It later campaigned in the Belgian province of Limbourg and in **the Netherlands**.

PIUS XII (Eugenio Pacelli) (1876-1958).

Papal nuncio to Munich in 1917 and the first nuncio to Berlin in 1925, Pacelli became cardinal in 1929 and secretary to Pius XI in 1930. In 1933 he negotiated the concordat with **Hitler** and was elected Pope on March 2, 1939 (see **Church and the Third Reich, The**).

PLATT, Sir William (1885-).

A British general, Platt was commandant of the Sudan Defense Force from 1938 to 1941. That year he played a major role in defeating the numerically superior Italian froces in eastern Africa, under the Duke of **Aosta**. From 1941 to 1945 he was commander in chief of the East Africa Command.

POINTBLANK.

The code name for the Allied air offensive against **Germany**, established in 1943 by the American general Ira C. Eaker (see **Germany, Air Battle of; World War II—General Conduct**).

POLAND.

Briefing his top generals on August 22, 1939, **Hitler** explained that the previous plans, to attack the West first, had been changed. Poland would be the first target. Were France attacked first, Poland would open military operations, and **Germany** would face military opposition on two fronts. Instead, Hitler wanted to isolate and destroy Poland before France and the **United Kingdom** moved. The attack was scheduled for August 26. The next evening, the **Nazi-Soviet Pact** was signed by **Ribbentrop** and **Molotov**.

Last-minute efforts to dissuade Nazi Germany from war continued. Poland was required to postpone its general mobilization until August 31. Upon the signature of a British-Polish treaty of alliance on August 25, Hitler postponed the invasion of Poland by a few days.

At dawn on September 1, 1939, without a declaration of war, the German attack on Poland began from the sea, air and ground along the entire 1,250-mile frontier (see *Fall Weiss*). A "fifth column" operated from inside. From the beginning this was a total war, directed against all elements of the Polish armed forces and civilian population and conducted with utmost cruelty. Misinformation, diplomatic action and attempts to blame Poland, the very victim of aggression, for the war were designed to foster acceptance of this new fait accompli by Great Britain and France. This time Hitler failed. On September 3, a British ultimatum declared, at 11:00 a.m., a state of war would exist between Britain and Germany if Hitler failed to withdraw his troops; France followed suit with a 5:00 p.m. deadline. The deadlines passed, and war was declared.

The Germans thrust 58 divisions and higher formations, including seven armored, four light armored and four motorized divisions, with a total of around 2,800 **tanks**, into Poland. They used over 2,000 planes, including 900 bombers and 230 divebombers. Against this power, Poland threw 32 infantry divisions, 11 cavalry brigades and one armored brigade, in total 49 higher formations, with some 433 planes, many of them obsolete. A small navy of 15 major vessels was overpowered in the German-controlled Baltic Sea; some of its vessels reached safety in British ports. The Germans outnumbered the Poles seven to one in planes and 20 to one in tanks. Additionally, they had the strategic advantage of the **Blitzkrieg**, whose force was unfamiliar—and awesome—not only in 1939, but even in 1940 and 1941.

According to a pact signed by Gens. **Maurice Gamelin** and Tadeusz Kasprzycki on May 19, 1939, French troops were bound to start air attacks and local operations immediatley after mobilization, with a full offensive foreseen within two weeks of mobilization. The validity of this convention was conditioned by a political protocol that remained unsigned on September 4, but an offensive of 110 available Franco-British divisions was nonetheless expected. In 1939, the Germans were not ready for a European war on two fronts. They had only 20-23 divisions on the Western front in September 1939; only a few of these were combat-ready. According to the Nuremberg depositions, at the end of the Polish campaign the Germans had only a two weeks' supply of ammunition.

The task of the Polish armed forces was to hold the line until an offensive could be mounted in the West—in mid-September, it was anticipated—tying up the main body of the German troops. The Poles held more than two weeks; they held for 36 days. The Polish force at Westerplatte, 182 men strong, resisted attacks from sea, air and ground until September 7. Warsaw surrendered on September 27. The Hel Peninsula crews defended themselves until October 2; The fortress Modlin fell the same day. The campaign's last battle was fought to the last cartridge at Kock by Gen. Franciszek Kleeberg's group, which capitualted on October 5. Maj. ''Hubal'' (Henryk Dobrzanski) fought a guerrilla action until June 1940.

Some major counterattacks were fought by Polish troops with strategic and tactical success. One was the battle at Bzura, led by Gen. Tadeusz Kutrzeba. The Germans called it ''the greatest battle in military history.'' The Poles held the enemy through September 20, when some withdrew to join Warsaw's defenses.

When the front moved east beyond the Vistula River to the Bug River on September 17, however, the Red Army marched into Polish territory. On the eve of the Soviet invasion, about 25 Polish higher formations were still fighting and fully engaging the enemy. By that time the western front was inactive; the ''phony war'' had begun. The Soviet invasion forced Polish units to surrender either to the Germans or to the Red Army.

Terrible losses were suffered by the civilian population, additionally affected from the first day by repression and exterminations. The hero of Warsaw defense, Mayor Stefan Starzynski, soon was sent to a **concentration camp**. Millions followed.

A new division of the Soviet and German spheres of influence was agreed upon by Ribbontrep and Molotov on September 28, 1939. Poland was divided along Narva-Bug-San Rivers, roughly, that is, along the

''**Curzon line**.'' In the German sphere, some territories were incorporated directly into the Reich, and the central part of the country was organized under the **General Government for Occupied Poland**. Attempts to create a Polish puppet government failed and were followed by oppressive German administration. The eastern part of prewar Poland was meanwhile absorbed by the **USSR**. Polish national leaders were deported en masse into the Soviet Union and dispersed, together with war internees, throughout labor camps, prisons and other places of confinement.

The day after Poland's invasion by the Red Army, the president of the Polish Republic, the governor and the supreme commander crossed the Polish-Rumanian boundary and were interned in **Rumania**. President Ignacy Moscicki designated **Wladyslaw Raczkiewicz** his successor and resigned from office, as did the supreme commander in chief, Marshal Edward Smigly-Rydz, and the whole government.

Gen. **Wladyslaw Sikorski**, one of the leaders of the opposition, was appointed prime minister and formed a new Polish **government-in-exile** in Paris on September 30. On November 7 he was appointed supreme commander-in-chief of the Polish armed forces. His government represented four major democratic political parties and was responsible to a national council, a parliament in exile, presided over by Ignacy Paderewski. The first tasks of the government included reestablishment of the Polish armed forces abroad. It was recognized by all western European Allied countries. The government was located first in Angers, and subsequently in London.

The organized **Resistance** movement in Poland included a delegate from the Polish government-in-exile, who was its vice prime minister, some other ministers and a secret Council of National Unity, based on major political parties. Its agencies were developed down to townships and villages.

An essential branch of the Resistance movement was the underground Home Army, started in September 1939. Political parties also formed military organizations, the most numerous being Peasant Battalions (BCh). The Communists, confused by **Stalin** and Hitler's cooperation in 1939-41, began their organizational activities more than two years later than the Home Army and the BCh. All such military organizations were eventually combined into one underground Home Army (the ''Armia Krajowa,'' or ''AK''), which became part of the Polish armed forces. Only extremist groups remained outside it.

The Home Army network covered the entire nation; its commanders were, successively, Gen. Michal Karasiewicz-Tokarzewski; Gen. Stefan Rowecki, who perished in Sachsenhausen; Gen. **Tadeusz Bor-Komorowski**; and Gen. Leopold Okulicki, who died in a Soviet prison. The Home Army organized **deceptions** and **sabotage**, conducted intelligence operations, produced arms and ammunition and retaliated for German atrocities. It played a significant part in total war effort. Its intelligence provided the Allied command with documentation and pieces of **V-1 and V-2** rockets. (The action to protect the population against its compulsory displacement in Zamosc and Bilgoraj counties, however, forced an end to this project.) Aid for inmates of prisons and concentration camps was developed. Incarcerated people were freed. Another aspect of Home Army activities was information, **propaganda** and **psychological warfare**. Centered mainly in the Office of Information and Propaganda ("BIP"), in cooperation with the **information services** of the government-in-exile, peasant battalions and political parties, it brought to naught Nazi efforts in Poland. It conducted daily radio monitoring, mostly of the **British Broadcasting Corporation**; its **underground press** publications included secret radio releases, journals, periodicals and pamphlets. It carried out, together with the underground boy scout movement, "a small sabotage," full of the esprit and determination of the nation in its struggle. The Polish radio station *Swit* operated clandestinely. Liaison was maintained between the occupied country and the government in the West; couriers were regularly parachuted or otherwise smuggled into the country. Arms were delivered by air. "Help to Soldiers" and the "Green Cross" successfully operated.

Another service was aid to Jews, whom Hitler had condemned to extermination in the **Final Solution**. Jews themselves, and leaders of the Free World, refused to give in to this plan to the tragic end. For helping Jews hide or encouraging anyone in this process, Poles were subjected to a regime of unparalleled repressiveness; whole families were punished by death. Jews were mesmerized by hope and, all too often, submitted to concentration in ghettos, isolation and gradual extermination. Gen. Sikorski appealed for help. The Jewish Service in the Home Army and in the Department of Interior of the London government-in-exile maintained liaisons with Jewish fighting organizations. The civil resistance under Stefan Korbonski issued appeals for help for Jews and punished renegades. The 1943 Warsaw ghetto uprising (see **Warsaw, Rebellions in**) was supported by agencies of the underground. Information and documentation was sent to the West. Thousand of families risked all to help those Jews within their reach, as did numerous priests and religious orders. Forty thousand to 50,000 Jews (according to Filip Friedman), or 100,000 to 120,000 (according to Jozef Kermisz) were saved in Poland's territory.

In the meantime, Gen. Sikorski built up a part of Poland's armed forces in the West: four infantry divisions, the Independent Brigade of Sub-Carpathian (Podhale) Rifles and the 10th Armored Brigade. The Independent Brigade of Carpathian Rifles was organized in **Syria**, under the command of Col. Stanislaw Kopanski. Polish units participated in the expedition to **Norway** beginning on April 24, 1940. All available forces participated in the French campaign. The Second Division of Infantry Rifles, however, was interned in **Switzerland**.

In Britain, the Polish navy and air force were rebuilt. The Polish air force participated in the **Battle of Britain**, in which one hundred Poles, one-eighth of the **Royal Air Force** fighter pilots, shot down at least 203 German aircraft and probably another 35 and damaged 36, losing 33 pilots. With six other squadrons they constituted an independent Polish fighter wing. In 1940 two bomber squadrons were organized. About 9,000 Polish soldiers thus served in the RAF under their own colors.

In eastern Poland, the soldiers and officers who surrendered to the Red Army after its invasion on September 17, 1939, expected the internment due soldiers of **neutral countries**. Poland had signed a non-aggression pact with the Soviet Union in 1932 and renewed it through 1945. The Soviet government, however, treated captured Polish soldiers harshly. They were joined in labor camps and prisons by masses of deportees: 1,500,000 civilians from eastern Poland. Officers were kept in separate camps. After the end of June 1940, no information reached families of friends of some 14,500 of them. In that period, the *Narodnyy Kommissariat Vnutrennikh Del* (NKVD) and the **Gestapo** cooperated in a common action against the Polish underground. Also some Jewish intellectuals were exchanged by the NKVD for their agents in German prisons.

With the German attack on the Soviet Union on June 22, 1941, the situation changed. An agreement on July 30, 1941, signed by Sikorski and **Ivan Maisky**, reestablished diplomatic relations between the Soviet government and the Polish government in London. The Nazi-Soviet Pact was annulled. The common determination to fight against the Nazi invader was stressed. The reestablished Polish Embassy in Kiubyshev, with Stanislaw Kot as ambassador, was permitted to set up agencies to take care of deportees who were granted "amnesty" and released from their confinements. On August 19, 1947 a Polish army was established in the Soviet Union. Gen. **Wladyslaw Anders**, just released from Lubianka Prison, was appointed commander in chief of that army under the supreme command of Gen. Sikorski, who confirmed all arrangements in his personal visit with Stalin, in November-December 1941. Those officers who had disappeared in 1940, however, could not be found.

This new Polish army faced considerable difficulties from its inception. **Food** was insufficient; supplies were meager; restrictions multiplied. Two concepts of the army's use developed: to organize in the Soviet Union and to fight within the Red Army or to leave the Soviet Union for **Iran** and eventually to return to or fight from the West. The last concept prevailed, with Stalin's support. The Polish army and a portion of the civilian population left the Soviet Union on August 5-25, 1942. Gen. Anders became commander-in-chief of the Polish armed forces in the Near East, where the Second and Third Corps were created. The Independent Brigade of Carpathian Rifles, which had already been organized in Syria, successfully participated in African operations against the Italians and the Germans, particularly in the defense of Tobruk. It was then incorporated into the Second Corps. Together they participated in the invasion of **Italy** at the beginning of 1944. Outstanding achievements by the Second Corps were the capture of Monte **Cassino** and Ancona, a significant contribution to the defeat of the **Axis** powers.

After visiting the Second Corps in the Near East, Gen. Sikorski's plane crashed in **Gibraltar**, on his return flight from **Egypt**, on July 4, 1943, killing all on board except the pilot. Sikorski was succeeded as prime minister by Stanislaw Mikolajczyk, leader of the Peasant Party. Gen. Kazimierz Sosnkowski became supreme commander-in-chief of the Polish armed forces.

In the meantime, the Soviet government supported the organization of the Union of Polish Patriots and the creation of the Polish Tadeusz Kosciuszko Division, commanded by Gen. Zygmunt Berling and subordinate to the Soviet Union. The activity of Communist and Soviet partisans in Poland intensified as well.

In April 1943, Germans discovered the collective graves of Polish officers in the forest of **Katyn** near Smolensk and accused Soviet authorities of the mass murder. The grave site contained a part of the officer corps which the Polish government was looking for. The government requested that the International **Red Cross** examine the graves and appealed to the Allies for assistance. The Soviet government took offense and broke diplomatic relations with the Polish government-in-exile on April 25, 1943.

A secret, Moscow-oriented Country's National Council was subsequently organized in Poland by a group of Communists and sympathizers. The Polish Worker's Party and Communist People's Army increased their activities.

The First Infantry Division and, subsequently, the First Corps of the Polish armed forces was organized in the Soviet Union. Red Army officers were assigned to Polish units. In August 1943 the First Division participated in front-line operations. It engaged in a battle at Lenino on October 12-14, 1943 and suffered heavy casualties—502 killed, 1,776 wounded and 663 lost.

The Home Army in Poland was eager to enter common operations with the Allies as they approached from the west. Such attempts—in fact, the mere existence of the pro-London Polish underground—were interpreted by Moscow as contrary to its interests. Home Army troops, as well as civilian or political authorities connected with the Polish government-in-exile in London were, if apprehended east of the Curzon Line, disarmed, arrested, deported to Siberia and in some cases executed. But terror was also visited upon the pro-London underground west of the Curzon Line; the London government's delegate to Lublin province was deported to the USSR with his staff and the commander-in-chief of the Home Army in September 1944, together with thousands of rank and file, mostly peasants and workers.

When the Red Army reached the Vistula River on August 1, 1944, an uprising broke out against the Germans in Warsaw. At the order of Stalin himself, it was allowed to run its course. No planes from the West were permitted to land. After 63 days of fighting, the insurgents surrendered. Some 250,000 inhabitants were killed, and all the treasures of Warsaw lay in ruins. What was left intact was looted and burned by German demolition squads.

Under the auspices of Moscow, from the Country's National Council emerged the Polish Committee of National Liberation (the **Lublin Committee**), which assumed the administration of the country on July 22, 1944. On December 31, 1944 this committee declared itself a temporary government and soon was recognized by Moscow. To allow members of the pro-London Resistance movement to decide their individual allegiance, the Home Army was dissolved in February 1945 and only the delegate of the armed forces remained, together with part of the London government. In March 1945 these representatives were invited for conversations with Soviet aurthorities and then arrested and deported to a prison in Moscow. At the June 1945 Moscow trial of 16 Polish leaders, they were condemned up to 10 years in prison. The delegate Stanislaw Jankowski, vice prime minister of the London government, recognized at that time by Great Britain and the **United States**, died in a Soviet prison, and Gen. Leopold Okulicki, the last commander-in-chief of the Home Army, died in the Soviet Union under unknown circumstances.

In the last stage of war, a 351,000-strong Polish army, which had been created in the Soviet Union in July

1944, participated in the Red Army's operations against the German enemy, fighting on German soil and contributing to the capture of Berlin.

In the West, some 195,000 Poles were by then under arms, in the Polish navy and air force and in the Second Corps in Italy; in addition, the Polish First Independent Airborne Brigade helped capture Arnhem. The First Armored Division under the command of Gen. Stanislaw Maczek fought in France and in **Belgium**, contributing to freeing several cities and regions, including Breda in **the Netherlands**. It accepted the surrender of Wilhemshaven. In all the countries of western Europe, Poles, particularly in France, were active in Resistance movements.

The day the Germans capitulated, Poland was split between a Polish government recognized by the Western Allies and a Polish Committee of National Liberation, stubbornly supported by the Soviet Union. A precarious solution was worked out with the creation of the Provisional Government of National Unity in Moscow in June 1945. On July 5, 1945 recognition of the Polish government-in-exile in London was withdrawn by the major democratic powers of the West.

W. W. Soroka

POLAND—General Government.
See **General Government for Occupied Poland**.

POLISH COMMITTEE FOR NATIONAL LIBERATION.
See **Lublin Committee**.

POLITICAL WARFARE EXECUTIVE (PWE).
A British service for political and psychological warfare (see **Intelligence Service**).

PORTAL, Sir Charles Frederick Algernon (later Viscount) (1893-1971).
A British air marshal, Portal was chief of the air staff from 1940 to 1945. He was a member of the Combined Chiefs of Staff and played a major part in the Allied conferences (see **Conferences, Allied**).

PORTUGAL.
Portugese policy during the war was entirely in the hands of **Antonio Salazar**, who was foreign minister from 1936 through 1947, as well as prime minister, beginning in 1932. He was determined to remain neutral as long as he could, more to save expense than because of particular devotion to either side. He ruled through the National Unity Party, which occupied every seat in parliament, and a fairly efficient police force. Untroubled elections took place in 1942.

Lisbon held legations (upgraded to embassies in 1941-42) from several warring powers, and thus provided opportunities for informal and secret contacts; the Italian surrender negotiations, for example, began there in August 1943. Such civilian air travel as there was between the **United Kingdom** and the **United States** was staged mostly by way of Lisbon; many people spent weeks there waiting for passage. It also provided the terminal for several escape routes running out of **Belgium** and France.

Portugal's main strategic importance derived from its ownership of the Azores, possession of which by either side would be decisive in the **convoy** battles which characterized the **battle of the Atlantic**. **Roosevelt** contemplated occupying them in the spring of 1941, but the U.S. was not yet a belligerent. **Churchill** maintained constant pressure on Salazar, in the name of the alliance of 1373; in October 1943 Salazar at last gave way. Joint Anglo-American occupation of Azores bases was thenceforth allowed, with marked results. Air cover against German submarines could now extend right across the Atlantic. Portugal thus became in effect a cobelligerent, and was admitted to the founding circle of the **United Nations**.

M. R. D. Foot

POTSDAM CONFERENCE.
See **Conferences, Allied**.

POTSDAM DECLARATION.
A policy statement issued on July 26, 1945 by the **United States**, the **United Kingdom** and **China** that demanded the **unconditional surrender** of Japan, threatened utter destruction if Japan did not yield and spelled out Allied goals in Japan after the ceasefire. Drafted in Washington and amended slightly at Yalta to suit Britain, the declaration warned that both the imperial forces and the Japanese homeland would be crushed if Tokyo did not surrender unconditionally. (Unknown to the Japanese, the Americans now had the **atomic bomb** and were ready to use it if this stiff declaration was not accepted.) The document said that the Allies would dissolve the Japanese empire, demobilize the army and navy, mete out "stern justice" to **war criminals**, conduct a military occupation and reestablish democratic principles. The occupation would end when "a peacefully inclined and responsible government" was established by "the freely expressed will of the Japanese people." The declaration complicated Japan's surrender decision because it did not specify the fate of the emperor. After two atomic attacks, the **USSR**'s entry into the war and **Hirohito**'s personal intervention, the Japanese leaders accepted the declaration on August 14, 1945 (see **Surrender Decision by Japan**).

T. R. H. Havens

POUND, Sir Dudley (1877-1943).

As first sea lord from 1939, Pound, a British admiral, directed Great Britain's naval **strategy** and presided over the chiefs of staff.

POWNALL, Sir Henry Royds (1887-1961).

A veteran of World War I, Pownall, a British general, was chief of staff to **John Gort** (1939-40), commander in chief in the Far East (December 1941 to February 1942) and in **Iran** and **Iraq** (1943), and chief of staff to Lord **Mountbatten** (1943-44).

PRESS, Underground.

See **Underground Press**.

PRISONERS OF WAR.

The prisoner of war phenomenon was a much more significant factor in the Second World War than in the first for a number of reasons. One important reason was that the number of those prisoners was much greater. According to the American historian Gregory Franklin, counting only those prisoners held for long periods, there were 1,800,000 French soldiers, 4,545,000 Germans, 7,800,000 Russians, 1,336,000 Italians, 130,000 Hungarians and 100,000 Rumanians; information on prisoners of other nationalities is lacking. In the second place, these prisoners were relatively better treated than those who were "deported." Finally, the provisions of the Geneva Convention were much less generally heeded than in World War I. At least insofar as the French were concerned, this was primarily a result of the carelessly conducted Scapini mission, which had the effect of keeping the International **Red Cross** away from the prisoners, and thus permitting all sorts of abuses: the mixture of prisoners of all nationalities in the same camp, the treatment of noncommissioned officers as common laborers and the failure to protect the camps against air bombardment. In Oflag XB, for example, 100 prisoners died in bombing raids in February 1945.

Dutch prisoners were, in 1940, considered fellow Teutons by the Germans and were therefore accorded preferential treatment. For the first weeks after the surrender, they were authorized to move about freely and in uniform. They nevertheless remained irreconcilably hostile. The infuriated Germans then determined to imprison them, but most of the intended victims got wind of the move and vanished from view. The few career officers who gave themselves up voluntarily to the Nazis found themselves in severe difficulty after the liberation.

At the beginning of the war many prisoners were confined in the "frontstalags" in France and **Belgium**. There was ample opportunity to escape, but,

on the advice of superior authorities in the camps, few attempts were made. Beginning in 1941, these men were sent to **Germany**, where they rejoined their brothers-in-arms already there. Officers among them were placed in the "oflags" while enlisted men occupied the "stalags." Germany was divided into various regions, and each had its "oflags" and "stalags" with suffixes indicating their site—for example Oflag XB was the Hanover officers' camp, while Stalag XVIIB was in the Austrian section. There were, of course, special camps for those who refused to submit—e.g., Rawa-Ruska and Luebeck.

Stalag prisoners were registered in a base camp where they were locked in only during the night. With the coming of day, they were sent in crews to work in the mines, in factories, in forests or on farms. Men in the last group were better off than the others; **food** was plentiful and their labor less arduous. At the end of the war, in fact, they were often the only healthy men in the villages, where they were given minor administrative tasks like distributing food ration cards and even driving trains on spur lines. Often, too, they quietly became part of the community through marriage.

The other prisoners were not nearly as lucky; they did, however, understand the art of passive resistance to the demands of their masters. In such prison camps, the cigarettes received by the American inmates were a valuable commodity on the **black market**. Furthermore, in 1942, the "relief" system (see **Forced Labor Battalions**) was instituted, and some French prisoners were forced to work as civilian laborers in German industrial plants.

The officers in the "Oflags" occupied a different station. They were kept under lock and key at all times and, although they were not forced to work, they were the least favored category where food rationing was concerned—the same as Germans who were 70 and older. Until September 1944 gift packages sent to these men were allowed to reach them to compensate for their short rations; this practice was discontinued, however, in the final months of their captivity, and their situation became extremely trying. To occupy their enforced leisure, the imprisoned officers engaged in artistic and intellectual pursuits. In some of these camps crude universities were organized. A few officers—very few, fortunately—were attracted by the siren songs of the Scapini mission and volunteered for work in Germany.

Conditions were especially bad for Soviet and Italian prisoners who for various reasons could not claim the protection of the International Red Cross. About 2,800,000 out of a total 7,800,000 Soviet prisoners died in Germany. They had, however, the benefit of periodic visits from representatives of Gen. **Andrei A.**

Vlasov's volunteers, who tried to induce them to serve in the armed forces of the Third Reich. The Italian prisoners who began arriving in German prison camps in October 1943 were regarded by the Fascist government as political detainees under guard in Germany. Badly nourished and ill-treated, they led a wretched existence. They were visited from time to time by Fascist officers promising them a world of delights if only they consented to reenlist in **Mussolini**'s army. Many of them died of exhaustion and want. The French prisoners often shared their own meager diet with them.

British and American prisoners of the Japanese suffered under horrible conditions. Judging from the accounts given by the prisoners, torture was common. A. G. Allbury has described the terrible ordeal imposed on the prisoners who built a railroad in **Burma** under Japanese taskmasters. That project cost the lives of 15,000, and the Japanese had the incredible gall to erect a monument in their honor.

Quite different was the treatment accorded German prisoners sent to the **United States** and **Canada**. They enjoyed their stay in the Americas so much, in fact, that many of them sought American brides while still prisoners of war and so become citizens of their host countries the easy way. Others returned to western Canada after the war as permanent colonists. But the Nazi combatants who fell into the hands of the Russians and even the French at the end of the war had ample reason to regret their fate. In a prison camp in the French *departement* of Indre, the mortality rate among the German prisoners was so high that Frenchmen who had been prisoners of war themselves advised the *departement* prefecture to end the abuse.

To escape imprisonment, a captive had to prove that he deserved freedom, as a member of the medical corps, the father of four or more children, a World War I veteran in the reserves or the like. Once one was interned in a German prisoner of war (PW) camp, escape was difficult, especially for officers with no particular knowledge of the local dialect or of German mores. Yet there were many attempts, either through the classic tunnel or by **deception**, which naturally met with success much less often. In some of the "Oflags" elaborate methods of evasion were developed. The PWs patiently saved money; mended and stored away civilian clothes; set up crude tool shops with wire cutters, files and saws; in short, did everything possible to prepare themselves for the opportunity to escape. As nearly as can be determined, some two to three thousand British, French, Belgian,

Dutch, Polish and Scandinavian soldiers managed to escape from PW camps and find their way either to some **Resistance** group or to a more conventional army through **Switzerland** or Belgium, and later through France, **Spain** or **Sweden**. An outstanding example was the liberation of the French general **Henri Giraud** by a coup planned on the outside.

Captivity for PWs generally ended in a great migration. Ahead of advancing Allied forces, the PWs were transferred by stages to the German interior. Beginning in mid-April 1945, often as the result of barter agreements between Allied and German commanders occupying the sector, prisoners were freed and allowed to return home.

R. Lacour

PRODUCTION.

In every industrial country, means of production were, or became, concentrated on providing arms and fighting vehicles of every kind. **Japan** and **Germany** had a start over the other combatants. The Japanese social, industrial and political system concentrated on war and on preparations for it. Since 1904 Japan's ruling class had contemplated dominating East Asia, and since 1931 its armed forces had been getting plenty of practice in **China**. The Nazi leaders also saw war as a necessary means to the world domination they sought. After the spring of 1933 German factories were converted to war production, often secretly. The tale of the man who thought he was making parts for children's strollers, stole an item from each section of his factory and found that they could be assembled into a machine gun may only be a barroom anecdote. But it is true that Lufthansa's principal medium-range air liner was so constructed that it only took an hour's work to convert it into a Heinkel III medium bomber, by removing the seats, opening three panels in the fuselage and clipping in the bomb bay and two gunners' positions, all of them kept ready in a secret storage area.

German war planning relied on the concept of the **Blitzkrieg**. A sizeable proportion of the gross national product regularly went into armaments production (see **Germany—Economy of the Third Reich**). But the armaments the Germans produced were enough to sustain them through a few brisk campaigns only, not through a long war.

Certainly war preparations solved the German unemployment problem, which had been one of the worst in the world during the Great Depression of 1930-33, by putting skilled workers into arms production and the less skilled into making roads. Germany's highway network, the first in Europe, was planned with military uses in mind—it facilitated the march of motorized units toward the country's frontiers. (No one foresaw that in the closing weeks of the Reich the roads would provide usable tactical landing strips for fighter aircraft.) But there was a considerable element of **propaganda**, and indeed of mere bluff, in the prewar German armament effort. The Nazis believed, correctly, that if they shouted loud enough, people would be frightened of them, and might thus make important concessions without a struggle. This proved to be the case in 1936 and 1938. **Goering** said that Germany had to choose between guns and butter, but the real goal of the Nazi leaders was both guns and butter: military success and glory, without the effort, exhaustion and weariness Germany had endured in World War I.

German production was in fact enough for a short war, but not for a long one. It was not until the winter of 1941-42 that **Hitler** realized his mistake—after the **USSR** survived a five-month Blitzkrieg attack without surrendering it was clear that the Blitzkrieg alone would not do. For the next two years arms production concentrated on quality. It was supposed that, in German hands, high quality weapons would automatically bring victory. Some remarkable weapons were indeed produced. But they did not suffice against the ineluctable quantity of arms piled up against them—by the Soviets, who knew that their own backs were against the wall; by the British, who worked double or even triple shifts so that machines were seldom left idle (the Germans hardly ever went beyond single shifts); by such powers as **Canada** and **Australia**, embarking on large-scale metallurgical manufacture for the first time; and, above all, by the seemingly inexhaustible resources of the **United States**. American industrialist Henry Kaiser, for example, applied mass production methods to shipbuilding, of which he had known nothing beforehand; by 1944 he was producing "liberty ships." These unwieldy—but seaworthy tubs, displacing 10,000 tons, were constructed in four days each. These ships made Operation Overlord (see **Normandy Landing**) feasible. During the last winter of the war, Hitler simply prevailed upon the Germans to produce as much as they could, in the teeth of the Allied pincers that were gradually throttling their economy.

It would be interesting to reduce all this to a series of tables, but complete data are still unavailable, and may in some cases be irrecoverable. One set of comparative figures is worth presenting:

Annual Production of Aircraft

	1939	1940	1941	1942	1943	1944
Germany	2,518	10,247	12,401	15,409	34,807	40,593[1]
Japan	—	—	5,090	8,861	16,693	28,180
United States	2,141	6,019	19,433	48,000	86,000	96,000
Great Britain	2,400	11,100	17,300	20,750	24,800	26,500

[1]This figure is for aircraft which left the factories. Many of these were destroyed by Allied bombs before they ever saw action.

M. R. D. Foot

PROPAGANDA.

Propaganda played an important role in the last year of World War I. The German general staff, unable to admit that it had (as was indeed the case) been defeated in the field by the British, fostered the myth that the Second Reich had been "stabbed in the back" by Marxist propaganda. The **Comintern**, founded the next year, certainly made lavish use of propaganda in the 1920s and 1930s, establishing a degree of world confidence in the intentions of the **USSR** that (in the face of all evidence) survives to this day. And **Hitler**'s rise to power was much aided by propaganda, in the hands of a master of the art, **Joseph Goebbels**. Power once attained, **Ribbentrop** tried, in vain, to wrest control over Nazi propaganda from Goebbels.

Much of the work of the German armies in the 1940 campaign in the West (see *Fall Gelb*) had been done for them in advance by propaganda. The Belgians and the Dutch were eager to believe in a purely mythical **fifth column**; such rumors spread dangerous confusion. French troops, pinned on the inactive **Maginot Line**, were subjected both to Nazi broadcasts—which were easy to pick up on their small radio sets—about the irresistible might of the *Wehrmacht*, and to more insidious and more effective propaganda, spread by newspaper innuendo and a whispering campaign by Communists in their own ranks. This encouraged them to believe that the war was only a plot among a lot of businessmen to make themselves still richer at the people's expense. **Maxime Weygand**'s army was three-quarters beaten before a shot had been fired.

Why the same techniques had so much less effect on the British is a question that awaits an answer. In the summer of 1940 German broadcasts to the **United Kingdom** reached a large but skeptical audience. So great was the hunger for news that millions of people listened, occasionally, to the enemy; but hardly anybody believed a word said by the Germans, unless it was confirmed by some better source. Everyone could see where the German self-interest lay.

With the formation of the **Political Warfare Executive**—originally a part of the **Special Operations Executive**—in August 1941, British propaganda authorities, whose efforts had been hindered for a year by interdepartmental bickerings (similar to the Goebbels-Ribbentrop dispute, but more diffuse), were able to start serious work. Some ingenious journalists began a series of "black" broadcasts to Germany, called *Soldatensender Calais*, full of extraordinarily detailed intelligence about the German armed forces—some of it culled from **Ultra**—which gave them credibility, and shot through with lurid and scabrous detail about the private lives of the German army and **Nazi Party** high command, pure propagandists' invention (if pure is the proper adjective). Most of these inventions were fiction, but they sapped the Germans' confidence in their leadership—or at least were meant to do so. Equally scabrous accounts of what foreign workers transported to Germany were doing to and with absent soldiers' wives sapped their confidence in themselves (see **Morale**). There are no authoritative published assessments of how effective this propaganda was. But there was a lot of it, under various names and in various languages, from over 60 different stations. Most of these stations purported to work from inside German-held territory, but did not.

The Americans in the **Office of Strategic Services** joined in "black" and "gray" broadcasting with joyful zest as well. A more important part of the American propaganda effort lay in straight reporting, especially from European battlefields before the **United States** entered the war. These reports reinforced the propaganda message carried by the **British Broadcasting Corporation**'s "white" broadcasts: they simply told the truth about the non-Nazi world's efforts to remain non-Nazi, and truth carries its own conviction.

Japanese propaganda even more strongly pro-Japanese than it was anti-American or anti-imperialist, persuaded few in southeast Asia and none elsewhere. The rottenness of some of the imperial regimes the Japanese toppled was self-evident; the excellence of their proposed replacement was less so. Common sense sufficed to show that the Japanese were only another kind of imperialist.

Soviet propaganda brought off one of the most remarkable propaganda coups of the war. Working on a population drilled for centuries to accept what those in authority said without question, and for over 20 years to follow the gyrations of the Communist Party line—often as straight as a corkscrew—without perceptible complaint, the Soviet propaganda machine was able to assert the party's control of the population more tightly than ever, utilizing the slogan "The Great Patriotic War," the name by which the campaigns of 1941-45 are still known in the USSR. This was a paradox to make Goebbels seem a simpleton. The initiative for it must have come from **Stalin**, who had been trained in propaganda in his teens at Tiflis seminary, and had clearly forgotten nothing.

M. R. D. Foot

PSYCHOLOGICAL WARFARE.

Since ancient times, commanders have known that the shortest way to victory lies in unsettling the mind of the opposing commander; next to that comes unsettling the minds of his men. Capital cities, main government offices and main headquarters thus make obvious targets. Dispersal and camouflage were the obvious counters: e.g., the administrative capital of the **USSR** was moved from Moscow to Kuibyshev. **Hitler** left **Germany**'s administrative capital in Berlin, where it was severely bombed, but removed himself to the forest fortress of Rastenburg in East Prussia, where he spent most of 1943 and 1944 isolated from the realities of the war he thought he was directing.

Bombing was generally regarded as an efficient means of psychological warfare. On the whole, retrospect suggests, this was a mistake. Bombing terrifies those who are timid and downhearted already, but it makes the brave braver and bloodier-minded. From Catalonia in 1936-37 onward, there are plenty of examples of **morale** being raised, not lowered, by sustained air attacks. In the earliest stages of **Blitzkrieg**, however, sudden air attack does have a stunning psychological impact. The German and Japanese air forces both sought to add to this effect by using attachments to the bombs dropped which intensified the falling weapons' scream. This was exceedingly unpleasant the first time one heard it, and might break weak troops at once. But the effect soon enough wore off; it was easy to see through it.

Bombing towns was sometimes more effective as psychological warfare through its indirect results than through the actual damage it caused to civilian life, property, and morale. Soldiers far from home could have their own morale shattered by thoughts of what their own close relatives might be suffering. Hence both sides tried to make the other's flesh creep with tales of fire and slaughter. These were probably more effective than the ingenious attempts of the **Political Warfare Executive** to persuade the German Army that its womenfolk were being seduced by foreign workers (see **Propaganda**).

The weapons of psychological warfare were those of the ordinary news media, plus graffiti and the leaflet. Over 8,000,000,000 leaflets were printed and distributed by the British and the Americans during the war—with what results, none can say. In the winter of

1939-40 the British, reluctant to trigger off a fiercer air war than they could manage against Germany, confined their bomber effort to the dropping of leaflets. In 1941-43, aircraft flying low over occupied Europe to parachute clandestine agents and supplies made a habit of carrying leaflets also, which they could drop some distance away from the target zone to provide a comparatively innocent explanation for the aircraft's presence in the neighborhood.

Only one successful slogan was launched during the war on an international scale, and that by accident. The symbol of "V" for an Allied victory was mentioned on January 14, 1941 by Victor de Laveleye during a BBC broadcast to **Belgium**, as standing both for *victoire* and for *vrijheid*, and therefore something Belgians of both tongues might approve. Suddenly, unexpectedly, the idea of writing "V" everywhere with chalk caught on, and was taken up enthusiastically in several occupied countries and in the **United Kingdom**. The Germans were so taken aback by the "V" campaign ("V" to them had meant hitherto *Vertrauensmann*, a collaborationist stool pigeon) that they tried to take the cry over as "V" for *Viktoria*, accompanied by the opening bars of the great German Beethoven's Fifth Symphony; on the **Axis** side, the slogan did not catch on. The Fifth Symphony became extraordinarily popular; the BBC took up the short-short-short-long rhythm of the Morse "V" as an interval signal in broadcasts to occupied Europe for the rest of the war. Innumerable Vs chalked on western and northern Europe's walls signaled to the German occupiers that they were not loved.

Japan modeled its psychological warfare campaign on those used by Britain in World War I and Germany in World War II. Japanese propaganda toward the home front and the imperial forces usually had far more impact than did the psychological warfare directed at prospective allies in the **Greater East Asia Co-Prosperity Sphere**. Least effective was the psychological warfare waged on neutrals, such as the USSR, and the enemy.

Japanese propaganda at home and abroad was coordinated by the **Cabinet Information Board**, although the army general headquarters insisted on issuing its own information. Both on the air and in print, Japanese propagandists relied mainly on selected quotations from the world press and carefully doctored statements from **prisoners of war**. The aim was to drive a wedge between the Allies and weaken their will. By the end of 1942, with the removal of Great Britain from Southeast Asia, anti-British propaganda virtually disappeared and the material was now almost entirely directed against the **United States**.

Radio Tokyo, a branch of the state network (NHK), was the tireless voice of Japan's psychological combat

with the Allies. On the day of the attack on **Pearl Harbor** it proclaimed "though we negotiated with America for eight months, it absolutely did not attempt to comprehend matters in our light, in the just light." A year later, as American Marines stormed **Guadalcanal**, the announcer said that the island "has been serving as a precious bait to lure the United States naval forces" into a trap so the imperial navy could dispatch them "to the bottom of the sea."

Even as late as October 26, 1944 Radio Tokyo declared that "one thing is now clear: America has lost the war" because "all the Japanese have to do in future operations is to project their indomitable spirits at the enemy." Such bravado, like all propaganda, lost credibility as it became more and more grounded in fantasy. Still, it is true that the half-dozen Nisei announcers who played the part of **Tokyo Rose** toyed with the emotions of countless American troops in the Pacific until late in the war.

Most of Japan's psychological warfare was aimed at the peoples of East and Southeast Asia who lived within the Co-Prosperity Sphere. The aim was to win their cooperation in building a new economic zone under Japan's leadership. This was to be accomplished by humiliating the white colonial powers and liberating oppressed peoples. "Already Japan," one propagandist gloated in 1941, "has rescued Manchuria from the ambitions of the Soviets, and set **China** free from the extortions of the Anglo-Americans. Her next great mission is to assist towards the freedom of the Thais, the Annamese and the Filipinos and to bring the blessing of freedom to the natives of South Asia."

Three abstract but closely connected themes ran through Japan's messages to fellow Asians. One was "the world as one family," or in a more ominous translation, "the eight corners of the world under one roof." Another was the emperor as the spiritual leader of all mankind. He, not the Japanese state, would guide the Asian people to freedom. The third was the new postwar economic bloc represented by the Co-Prosperity Sphere. Germany would head a second bloc in Europe and the United States a third in the Western Hemisphere. When Japan spoke of "Asia for the Asiatics," naturally many Asians thought it meant "Asia for the Japanese."

Japan's defeat of the seemingly invincible colonial powers in 1941-42 was easily the most effective propaganda weapon in the campaign to win local support for the Co-Prosperity Sphere. The Japanese tried to eliminate all traces of the Westerners. Not only did they impose wartime **censorship** and forbid people to listen to enemy broadcasts in the countries they occupied; they also introduced new pro-Japanese textbooks in the schools, trained local nationalist leaders to succeed the disgraced colonial administrators and made an astounding effort to replace European languages with Japanese throughout the area. Japanese cultural propagandists concentrated especially on **Malaya** and **Indonesia**, with their rich resources for the empire's economy. They encouraged the region's Chinese residents to support the Nanking government of **Wang Ching-wei**, but met with no more success than in China itself.

Japan also used religion to win allegiance in Southeast Asia, particularly among Muslims. Radio Tokyo declared on March 12, 1943 that "the Jews are the greatest enemies of the Moslems. London and Washington Jews are responsible for the blood of the poor Moslems." Such appeals helped gain the loyalties of village leaders in areas where Islam was strong, such as Java and the Malay peninsula. Likewise the Japanese sponsored Pan-Asian conferences of Buddhists to drum up support for the Co-Prosperity Sphere. Just as they did on the home front, Japan's propagandists used an ingenious combination of technology (radio, film, print media, loudspeakers) and organizations (schools, churches, temples, political groups, lecture societies, village associations) to try to win hearts and minds.

Eventually Japan's fortunes in war blunted the impact of these psychological tactics. Already the Burmese and Filipinos had denounced a good deal of the Japanese propaganda as too crude and obvious. When the imperial forces were being pushed back in the Pacific, Radio Tokyo kept up a bold front toward the enemy, but in Southeast Asia the propagandists stopped promoting Japanese language and culture by 1944 and instead encouraged anti-colonialist nationalism to prevent the European powers from reclaiming their colonies. Although it was bedeviled by poor coordination, inept linguists, technical breakdowns and much naivete, Japan's overseas propaganda had its greatest effect in building nationalist sentiments throughout the area it once hoped to rule as the Co-Prosperity Sphere.

M. R. D. Foot
T. R. H. Havens

PUCHEU, Pierre (1890-1944).

A French economist and bitter enemy of parliamentarianism, he joined the *Parti populaire francais*, led by **Jacques Doriot**. He became secretary to the minister of industrial production in February 1941 and then to the ministry of the interior in July 1941. Pucheu designated the 27 hostages to be shot by the Germans in Chateaubriant in retaliation for the murder of a Nazi officer. He was French ambassador to **Switzerland** in 1942, and he joined the entourage of Gen. **Henri Giraud** in Algeria in November of that

year. Arrested in August 1943, he was condemned to death by a military court and executed on March 20, 1944.

PURGES.

An Overview
Postwar purges resulted from the two deepest desires of the people in the occupied countries who had resented their invaders: first, to drive those who had collaborated with the enemy from all administrative posts; second, to punish those who had rallied to the racist banner of the "**New European Order.**"

After the creation of the first **Resistance** movements, every occupied country was the home of at least one group bent on revenging their nation's honor by threatening and sometimes even executing on sight the most enthusiastic exponents of **collaboration**, whether they were paid agents of the invading forces or propagandists for them. The **governments-in-exile** encouraged their followers to take any necessary steps to liquidate the most dangerous traitors. The Resistance battled the collaborators who denounced their fellow citizens, out of vengeance, hatred or greed, by doing everything in their power to reduce the native Nazis to impotence. The number of summary executions staged by loyalist groups increased in 1943 and again in 1944. Examples were made of **black market** operators, of those who abused forced laborers, even of those who refused to aid militant dissidents. Local police and court officials generally did all they could to impede investigations into the activities of these revenge-seekers, although sometimes ordinary criminals took advantage of their reluctance by posing as maquis.

During attacks by Soviet guerrillas on the German rear, as well as in **Yugoslavia** and in France just after the **Normady landing**, collaborators, citizens of the **Axis** countries in the pay of the **Gestapo** and captured soldiers alike were shot after summary trials. Members of Resistance groups who were found guilty of serious crimes against the honor of their movements were hailed before courts-martial and executed. But as the hour of liberation approached, the commanders of the armed forces in the Resistance ordered the end of summary punishment by firing squads, and asked the citizens of liberated territories, by means of posters, to refrain from any form of mob violence impelled by patriotic passion, so that the execution of justice could be left to the legally constituted courts and, in cases of spying for the enemy or activity against the national interest, military or civil tribunals. These instructions were not universally followed. The snail's pace of the courts, encumbered as usual with minor judgments, and their ineffectiveness in dealing with offenders against whom no witnesses could be found to testify, incited the most enthusiastic members of the Resistance to return to summary executions.

Moreover, the judicial machine was unprepared for the suppression of the various forms of collaboration. The number of persons executed summarily was relatively insignificant—amounting to between 1/600 and 1/1500 of the total population—except where fighting between military units of the Resistance and occupation troops occurred. Elsewhere, the proportion of purge victims amounted to less than one in 6,000; in other regions it was much less still. None of the Western countries had legislation adequate to punish the many forms of collaboration that had occurred during the course of prolonged enemy occupation. In fact, it became necessary to introduce laws which went into effect retroactively in **Norway, the Netherlands** and **Denmark**, where the death penalty had been banned for many years but was reintroduced after the liberation for crimes committed in connection with the occupation. In Norway, the royal decree of October 3, 1941 reestablishing capital punishment was publicized by radio and printed notices. The Dutch government-in-exile did the same on December 22, 1943; so did the Danish Parliament, with a law passed on June 7, 1945, with the cooperation of the Danish Socialist Party.

In **Belgium**, laws against civil disorder were suspended after the liberation; in France, similar legislation was passed on August 26, 1944. In the Netherlands, the hunt was on not only for members of Nazi or fascist groups but also for people simply suspected of pro-German sympathies. Disgrace and the loss of civil rights were the penalties meted out to such outcasts in Norway, Denmark, the Netherlands, Belgium and France. This type of punishment was especially severe in the Netherlands, where sentences of ten years in prison were the rule for those guilty of crimes against the nation. As many as 60,000 Dutch collaborators were deprived of their civil rights; members of the Nazi police or of fascist military organizations lost their citizenship and had their property confiscated. Similar penalties were imposed in Norway and France.

Special tribunals were set up. Belgium set up courts-martial composed of two civil judges and three military officers. Thirty-five special courts were created in the Netherlands, in which two out of five judges were required to have served as officers in the armed forces. These men presided over the trials of the most active collaborators. For lesser crimes, there were 100 tribunals, each including one civil judge and two members of a Resistance group. Norway and France conducted trials with a jury drawn by lots from a list compiled by Resistance groups; three judges passed sentences. In France, members of the *Milice*

and similar armed groups were judged summarily by courts-martial of the *Forces francaises de l'interieur* or by Resistance fighters and guerrillas, and later by ordinary military courts. The Danes kept their judicial procedures intact. In Belgium, Holland, Norway and France, because of the enormous number of people suspected of collaboration, single prisoners were chosen for trial as representatives of their groups.

The accused in Norway, the Netherlands and Denmark were allowed to plea-bargain with the prosecution—a privilege exercised by 60% of those found guilty in the Netherlands and still more in Norway. The most serious cases in France—those of Marshal Petain, **Pierre Laval, Joseph Darnand** and 105 others —were judged by a high court appointed by the National Consultative Assembly. The Norwegians were the harshest in imposing penalties on the collaborators: in Denmark and the Netherlands, prison sentences were, proportionately, issued to four times as many culprits as in France; in Belgium, to six times as many; and in Norway, to more than seven times as many. Belgium pronounced the death penalty on 4,170 people, of whom 230 were executed; France executed 783 out of the 2,086 people against whom death sentences were pronounced, out of a population five times Belgium's. The figures for other countries are as follows: the Netherlands carried out 36 out of 130 death sentences; Denmark, 23 out of 46; and Norway, 25 out of 30. The proportions of pardons for those sentenced to death were 17% in Norway, 50% in Denmark, 63% in France, 73% in the Netherlands and 94% in Belgium.

The effects of judicial vengeance subsided quickly, first through individual reductions of penalties, and then by collective pardons or amnesty laws. Ten years after the liberation, the number of collaborators still in jail was negligible. Only the memory remained, along with the shame of a prison record for disloyalty and, sometimes, anger at unwarranted punishment by harsh and biased judges drunk with vindictiveness. The sentences were not always proper; it was the small fry, driven by ignorance or misery into the arms of the enemy, rather than the upper classes who suffered most.

The second objective of the purges, to oust collaborators from positions of authority, was the responsibility of administrative commissions at regional and national levels. The commendations presented to the national commissions resulted generally in transfers from one administrative body to another. Only some of the police, the magistrates and semi-public officials were actually dismissed.

Sentences for economic collaboration were levied against only a few enterprises; for the most part these were satisfied by fines or the confiscation of illicit profits. They were severe only for the masters of the press.

Some of the mayors unseated by the purge committees were subsequently returned to office by voters in municiple elections.

Purges in France

The purges carried out in France merit closer examination as fairly representative of those carried out throughout occupied Europe after its liberation. The great majority of the French people had been, from the very beginnings of the Vichy Government, hostile to the official aid given Nazi **Germany**. They disapproved completely of those who took the easy path, especially when profits were the motive. The National Front, whose members represented every profession, including the police, magistrates and attorneys, began the first punitive operations against accomplices of the Germans and, particularly, against the informers and judges who contributed to the efforts of the special panels which were instituted to pass summary judgment on members of the Resistance. Broadcasting from London through **British Broadcasting Corporation** facilities, **Free France** issued threats of imminent punishment for collaborators.

Actually, the Resistance carried out very few summary executions before the final months of 1943. Actions against collaborators intensified in the wake of the Normandy landing, when Joseph Darnand's *Milice* and other paramilitary groups aided the Gestapo and the *Wehrmacht* in tracking down French patriots. The maquis then began setting up courts-martial to try members of the *Milice* and other auxiliaries of the occupying army who were caught possessing arms. City dwellers raged against peasants dealing in the black market and trading with German troops. Heavy fines were often imposed on the farms and their offending operators; in addition, the peasants were sometimes beaten or even murdered and their possessions confiscated. In some regions in which the *Legion francaise des combattants* established a counter-policy of revenge against leftist militants, violence ran rampant. Such cases, however, were relatively rare.

The need for discipline among the ranks of Resistance fighters stimulated the formation of councils of war among underground units. They devised rigid rules of conduct for their members, with especially harsh penalties for looting, abandoning sentry posts and rape. The heads of **women** accused of having cohabited with German soldiers were shaved amid the jeers of mobs gone mad in the hours just after the liberation. Delays in trials due to crowded court dockets, mild sentences imposed on the guilty, pardons issued to administrative internees and liberal terms of amnesty sometimes aroused riots which ended in the lynching of the beneficiary of the judicial error.

Ordinances enacted on June 26 and September 14, 1944 added to the courts of appeals courts of justice, each responsible for one or more sections within a department of France. These new courts were charged with judging those accused of collaboration with the enemy and acts inimical to the national defense. The rage of the country focused on those who had associated with collaborationist groups or indulged in racial slurs; more restraint was exercised by civil courts whose responsibility it was to sentence offenders to national disgrace, to prison or to loss of civil rights.

The courts of justice began their deliberations early in October 1944, with juries drawn by lots from lists proposed by the departmental liberation committees. By the time their task was completed, they had judged 124,751 cases. The Paris court remained in session until the end of 1951; the cases then remaining to be heard were turned over to a military tribunal.

Of the 50,095 judgments handed down by the courts of justice between October 1944 and the end of 1948, 8,603 were acquittals; 2,640 were death sentences (of which only 791 were carried out), along with 4,357 death sentences passed *in absentia*; 2,777 were life sentences at hard labor; and 10,434 were shorter prison terms. Of the 67,965 judgments handed down by the civil courts, 19,881 were acquittals and 48,486 were sentences to national disgrace. The numerous reductions of penalties, the no less numerous pardons and the amnesty laws liberated 68% of the convicted collaborators in December 1948; only about 1% remained in prison by October 1952. All those convicted by the civil courts were granted amnesty on August 6, 1953.

The High Court of Justice had been created to judge the principal architects of the policy of collaboration. It was paired with the State Tribunal, which had been established by Petain; its members were elected by the National Assembly, by majority vote in 1945 and by proportional representation in 1947. It judged 108 people between 1945 and 1949. In 42 cases it chose not to prosecute, and in 16 it pronounced sentences *in absentia*. Three acquittals, eight death sentences (of which only three were carried out) and 17 prison sentences were among its verdicts. Public opinion in France was concerned only about the trials of Petain, Laval and Darnand. At first favorable to the former chief of state, most of the French came to agree that stringent punishment was in order. When Petain's death sentence was pronounced, a public poll showed that only 16% of the French people favored his acquittal. Laval, who had given himself up, was judged in a highly emotional atmosphere and died dramatically.

The purge of administrative collaborators was finally accomplished within each department. Sentences were, in general, light.

The difficulty of determining the circumstances surrounding illicit profiteering largely thwarted attempts to punish merchants dealing with the enemy, or traders in the black market.

Revenge-seekers among the public were bitterly disappointed by the lack of zeal among the purgers, who spared a great many of the leaders and parasites who had profited from the collaborationist policy. As for those who were purged, or feared that they would be, they raised such a loud cry about the "Red Terror" that many people came to believe that the Resistance had killed at least 100,000 Frenchmen. But carefully conducted official inquiries in 1948 and 1952 fixed the total number of executions at about 15,000.

M. Baudot

PUTTEN.

A Dutch village in the province of Gelderland. On October 2, 1944, in reprisal for what they considered a crime against them, the Germans burned part of the town and deported most of its male population to Neuengamme and other points in **Germany**. Practically none of the deportees returned.

PWE.

See **Political Warfare Executive**.

Q–R

QUADRANT CONFERENCE.
See **Conferences, Allied.**

QUISLING, Vidkun (1887-1945).
The head of the Norwegian *Nasjonal Samling* and a collaborator with the Nazi administration in **Norway,** Quisling served as prime minister from 1942 to 1945 under the control of **Josef Terboven.** He was sentenced to death for **collaboration** after the liberation of Norway and executed.

RACZKIEWICZ, WLADYSLAW (1885-1947).
Raczkiewicz was president of **Poland's governments-in-exile,** first in Angers, France in 1939 and then in London in 1940.

RADAR.
Radar (an acronym for ''RAdio Detection And Ranging'') was invented in 1932. Two properties of electromagnetic waves in general—their tendencies to move in a straight line and to be reflected from the surface of an electrically conductive body—govern radar's operation and use. When the waves in question are of high frequency, they have the additional property of being easy to direct. Using these properties, the British physicist Edward Appleton determined the altitude of the ionosphere in the earth's upper atmosphere. Armed with Appleton's findings, **Robert Watson-Watt** found experimentally that moving objects could be detected by picking up the waves they reflected when a radio transmitter was trained on them. Thus radar, a powerful military instrument in World War II and an even more powerful military and research tool now, was born. Developed by Watt and Sir **Henry Tizard,** it contributed significantly to the defense of their country in the **Battle of Britain.**

In 1940 the British coast was protected by a chain of radar stations along the shore, their antennae directed at prospective enemies. At a range of 60 miles and more, the radar chain could locate attacking aircraft, measure their distance from the coast, count their number and, through successive and coordinated observations, plot their routes. All this information was fed to a central agency, the **Fighter Command,** which instantly assigned the defense—or attack—mission to one of the four fighter groups guarding the British Isles. Thus the radar equipment introduced an economy of forces into the British defense. Not one plane took to the skies unless a *definite* emergency arose, at a *definite* moment, at a *definite* point in space, and in *definite* strength. Guided by radio-telephony, the **Royal Air Force** was capable of delivering a surprise attack. Without radar, a permanent and exhausting patrol system would have been necessary. With the scanty materiel then available to the British, that need could never have been met. To the **United Kingdom,** radar was a God-given miracle in its hour of crisis.

Furnished with the AIMk IV, an airborne radar set capable of detecting enemy aircraft at distances ranging from 600 to 20,000 feet, British night fighters once shot down 32 German bombers in one engagement. The next radar generation, the AIMk X, had an improved range of 325 to 525,000 feet (100 miles).

The first British bombing raids on **Germany** in 1941 yielded poor results in proportion to the heavy losses involved, principally because of an inability to concentrate the assault. The RAF took measures to improve itself, one of which was the creation of the Pathfinder Corps which relied upon the Mosquito aircraft, masterpiece of the British designer Geoffrey de Havilland. Preceding bomber fleets, the Pathfinders reconnoitered targets at night, in absolute darkness, illuminated them with rocket flares and, after identifying them, indicated the targets for the bombers by framing them with red and green lights. It was through radar that the RAF pilots could ''see'' in a pitch-black medium; first the GEE radar model in March 1942, then its successors OBOE and H2S and, a short time afterward, Rebecca-Eureka.

GEE was a range-finding device utilizing the assistance of three land stations. It measured distance by determining the time required for a radar signal to travel to its target and return. It was used in the British bombing of the Ruhr valley, where German industry was concentrated, but central Germany was out of its reach.

OBOE made blind bombing possible as far as 300 miles from the ground radar station; the bombers were guided to their targets by two land stations. The first of these continuously measured its own distance from the aircraft. Depending on whether this distance was greater or less than the distance between the station and the target, the station sent out one of two different signals—dashes or dots. Thus the bomber was guided to the circumference of a huge circle centered at the radar station and passing through a point in space directly above the target. The only function of the second station was to determine the direction from the bomber to the target, thus enabling the pilot to fix the point on this circumference at which to let loose his "eggs." The maximum range of the system was 230 miles at an altitude of 25,000 feet.

Built into the aircraft, H2S was a completely self-sufficient device independent of ground stations. It consisted of a transmitter-receiver combination with a rotating antenna for both transmission and reception, and a luminescent screen highlighting "blips" representing objects reflecting the radar signal. Properly used, H2S provided information regarding coastal contours, large cities, lakes and ships at sea. A special type of the device known as ASV (Air-Sea Vessel) was used by coastal planes for reconnoitering unknown surface craft.

Rebecca-Eureka was designed to keep an airplane headed in a particular direction, simultaneously providing information on the distance between a point on land and the plane. Essentially, Eureka was a land beacon fixed at a particular point and capable of emitting a response signal when queried by an initial triggering signal from Rebecca on board the plane. From this reply, Rebecca deduced and displayed information to the aircraft pilot regarding not only the range between the land beacon and the plane but also the direction of the beacon with respect to the plane.

Radar was also an invaluable tool in naval warfare. Beginning in the second half of 1942, the American forces in the Pacific were able, by complex radar instruments much more sophisticated than Japan's, to compensate for their numerical inferiority in ships, which had resulted from the Pearl Harbor fiasco (see also Task Force).

But it was in anti-submarine warfare against the Germans that radar played a decisive role. In 1942, the Allies were in trouble. They had lost 7,788,468 tons of shipping in a single year. At that rate, they would soon have been so crippled that defeat would be inevitable. Toward the end of 1942, therefore, the Allied admiralties (see Atlantic, Battle of the) undertook a series of measures that soon began to reduce the number of marine casualties. None of those measures, however, would have been of the slightest use

had it not been for the research of the British scientists in the Transmission Research Establishments. It was they who developed the cavity magnetron tube that was the heart of the radar system, generating electromagnetic waves only inches in length. The new invention proved to be the death blow to the U-boat, for it sped the development of a more compact radar system easily carried by anti-submarine aircraft. The ray emitted by the radar antenna had to be sufficiently fine to determine with precision the angular coordinates of the object detected. To obtain a sufficiently thin beam of radar waves, the antenna had to be about ten times as long as the wavelength. Furthermore, the maximum range of the radar, the dimensions of the reflecting object being equal, varied inversely with the length of the radar wave. Hence the advantage of using short waves.

In addition to radar, the British Coastal Command was equipped with the "Leigh Light" with short waves U-boats could not detect. It thus afforded Allied submarine hunters a weapon with the advantage of surprise, by night and by day.

The Allies' ability to generate and control ultra-short waves was unquestionably one of the decisive factors contributing to their victory. It has been said that the hertzian short wave was more important to the West than the Soviet front, for it was the real conqueror of the Battle in the Atlantic. Radar was also to play a tremendous part in the design of anti-aircraft shells. It had been difficult to determine the altitude at which shells should be set to detonate, since enemy planes often alternated between high- and low-level flight. This problem was solved by the development of the "proximity fuse"—one of the secret weapons introduced by the Allies during the last months of the war. Connected to the shell's charge, this fuse contained a miniature transmitter-receiver emitting a continuous stream of waves. As the shell neared the enemy plane, the waves reflected back to the shell by the plane itself were received and amplified, and detonated the charge in the shell exactly at the desired distance from the enemy aircraft.

The proximity fuse, used at Antwerp to shoot down the German V-1 rockets (see V-1 and V-2), was used with equal success to combat the Japanese Baka bombs, which were explosive jet aircraft with human pilots. It also proved effective in aborting rockets launched from aircraft. Employed for the first time by American field artillery in the Battle of the Bulge in December 1944, the proximity fuse was the major factor in the Allies' defeat of the German counteroffensive, Gen. George S. Patton noted.

Both sides eventually developed equipment to neutralize radar, and subsequently counter-countermeasures to defeat these countermeasures. The purpose of active countermeasures was to confuse enemy radar by generating waves of the same frequency which covered their radar screens with false "blips" camouflaging the true target "blip," a trick that could be trumped by the counter-countermeasure of changing the radar frequency. Passive anti-radar devices either produced false radar echoes or prevented the reflection of waves from their targets. One example of this type of countermeasure was the procedure known as Window, which involved dropping a screen of metal-foil strips, known as "chaff," which were about as long as the enemy's radar waves; this maneuver was guaranteed to baffle German beams attempting to fix on Allied bombers. "Chaff" was used before the **Normandy landing** to delude the Germans into thinking that the landing would take place on the Straits of Dover.

The improvement of the radar system to the point where it could distinguish accurately between fixed and moving targets put an end to Window as a successful countermeasure. But the competition of electronic warfare, with its countermeasures and counter-countermeasures, still continues unabated.

For all its success, radar has one glaring flaw: its "eye" is limited to line-of-sight viewing and is therefore blind to low-flying aircraft masked by slight rises in the ground. The famous bombing of Augsburg on February 25, 1944 by RAF Lancasters was a resounding achievement with astonishingly low losses because of the hedge-hopping flight of the British planes over France and part of Germany. Imitating this procedure, the *Luftwaffe* was similarly successful in its last gasp, on January 1, 1945 during the Battle of the Bulge.

H. Bernard

RAEDER, Erich (1876-1960).

Appointed commander in chief of the German navy in 1933, Raeder was responsible for the buildup of **Germany**'s naval forces before the war began. He planned the invasion of **Norway** (1942) but succeeded in convincing **Hitler** to shelve Operation *Seeloewe*, the proposed invasion of England. He constantly pressed for enlargement of the navy and advocated unrestricted submarine warfare. In 1943 Raeder was replaced by Adm. **Karl Doenitz**. He served 10 years in prison as a **war criminal**.

RAF.

See **Royal Air Force**.

RAMSAY, Sir Bertram (1883-1945).

A British admiral, Ramsay was in charge of the British Expeditionary Force in the evacuation of Dunkirk in May 1940. He helped plan and direct the landing of British armed forces in Algeria in 1942 and Sicily in 1943. The following year he became naval commander in chief of the Allied Expeditionary Force in the **Normandy landing**, with almost 5,000 ships of every type under his command. Ramsay was killed in an air accident on January 1, 1945.

RANGERS.

See **Commandos and Rangers**.

RASHID ALI AL-GAYLANI (1892-   ).

In 1941 Rashid Ali, a former Iraqi prime minister, joined the pan-Arabists and led a coup d'etat supported by the **Axis**. His forces attacked British troops stationed in **Iraq** in April 1941. At the end of May he fled to **Iran**.

REBELLIONS IN WARSAW.

See **Warsaw, Rebellions in**.

RECONNAISSANCE.

"Time spent in reconnaissance is seldom wasted," says an old officers' proverb, "if you know what you are reconnoitering for." Armored cars conducted reconnaissance for most armies in phases of mobile warfare. Jeeps were sometimes better in cross-country performance, and so had horses, but both were vulnerable to machine gun fire. British infantry units might use their bren gun carriers, small armored cars which were not vulnerable to small arms fire and low in profile but noisy.

Surface warships of any size did not like to sail far without an air reconnaissance screen ahead of them until longer-ranging naval **radar** was generally available, by the middle of 1942. The pattern of sea warfare changed thereafter (see **Midway**).

Air reconnaissance, first used in World War I, took enormous strides forward in World War II. One of the reasons air superiority was vital was that it permitted the side that held it to obtain an enormous quantity of information from reconnaissance and denied the equivalent opportunity to the opponent. Every major air force had special squadrons devoted to air reconnaissance and air photography. Their aircraft usually operated unarmed at great altitudes, out of range of **anti-aircraft defenses** and relied on speed to escape if attempts were made to intercept them.

M. R. D. Foot

RED CROSS.

An international organization for the relief of suffering, the Red Cross was founded in 1864 by the Swiss Henri Dunant, who had been a horrified eyewitness of the sufferings of the wounded at Solferino five years earlier. Its flag—the Swiss flag with the colors reversed—became accepted in World War I as the international symbol for hospitals and hospital ships; in World War II it was generally used and respected as such.

The organization has affiliated branches in most countries, except for the Moslem world, where the Red Crescent performs similar tasks, and the **USSR**, which has never recognized it. The membership of the branch in the **United States** exceeded 36,000,000 in 1944. Subscriptions and donations from members provide the main income.

Through national branches, field and base hospital staffs were provided on many fronts to care for wounded of any nationality. Red Cross teams devoted themselves also to providing comforts—tobacco, books, writing paper, etc.—to wounded convalescents.

The other, and still more important, branch of Red Cross activity concerned **prisoners of war**. The Geneva convention of 1929 laid down the main principles for their treatment, and teams of Red Cross inspectors—usually Swiss—regularly inspected all the main camps that included prisoners from the signatory powers, among which the USSR was not included. Belligerent powers (except, again, the USSR) provided the names and serial numbers of prisoners of war to a central Red Cross bureau in **Switzerland**, which passed the data on to the captive's country. The process usually took several months. Substantial comforts for prisoners were also arranged under Red Cross auspices.

The USSR paid a heavy price for the lack of Red Cross protection for its prisoners, five-sixths of whom died in enemy hands. On the other hand, the USSR was not bothered by teams of visiting Swiss, and its forces could treat the prisoners they took exactly as they chose.

One group of prisoners, most in need of Red Cross aid, hardly ever got it: **concentration camps**, nominally an internal and not an international affair, were excluded as a rule from the Red Cross' purview. In **Germany**, in the spring of 1945, Red Cross teams were able to mitigate the sufferings of a few prisoners in them and to remove sick prisoners to **neutral countries**.

REFUGEES.
See **Evacuation and Resettlement**.

REICHENAU, Walter von (1884-1942).
A German field marshal, Reichenau commanded the 10th Army in **Poland** and the Sixth Army in **Belgium**, France and the **USSR**. In December 1941 he took over command of Army Group South on the Russian front. He remained in that post until his death as the result of a heart attack.

REICHSSICHERHEITSHAUPTAMT.
See **RSHA**.

REITH, Sir John (later Lord) (1889-1971).
British official. He was first director general of the **British Broadcasting Corporation** from 1927 to 1938, minister of information in 1940 and minister of works in 1941-42. His strong character clashed with that of **Churchill**.

REMY (Gilbert Renault) (1904-   ).
A French film specialist and writer, Remy founded one of the first espionage networks, known as the *Confrerie Notre-Dame*, in November 1940. "Col. Remy" was active in the **Free France** delegation in London and in the development of intelligence and **Resistance** organizations in both French zones. His books on the work of the resisters and the films he produced for television were extremely successful.

REPARATIONS.
It is a tradition as ancient as war itself that a conqueror is entitled to crush and despoil its antagonist. Tributes and booty have always been the regular consequences of a military conflict. "Reparations" are quite similar, but differ from earlier forms of compensation by their amount and duration on the one hand, and by their justification—that the fallen enemy must pay for all the war damage it caused—on the other.

The concept of reparations arose during World War I. In defiance of President Woodrow Wilson, who wanted **Germany** to pay only the amount of the damages caused directly by the war, the French adopted the much broader interpretation specified in the Versailles Treaties. The Reich in principle was deemed responsible for all material damage caused by the war and for its consequences. This translated into an astronomical sum of hundreds of billions of gold marks, to be paid in installments over 60 years, according to the Young Plan.

The battering taken by the reparations policy during the 1920s demonstrated that placing the crushing cost of a conflict in an age of world wars on the shoulders of a single country runs counter to the essential structure of the world economy and the interdependence of the industrialized states. None of these states was in a position to risk the unfavorable balance of trade and the massive unemployment that would have resulted from an enormous transfer of funds to the victors, even if Germany had the sum demanded. It also demonstrated that the economic problems posed by the continuous transfer of money were aggravated by the political results of such an extended period of payments, stretching over more than a generation. The moral force of a war debt to be repaid was bound to diminish as time went on.

The victorious powers of the Second World War, however, remembered the lesson taught by the First, and from the very beginning limited the amounts they demanded and time period over which the money was to be paid. In place of currency transfers they required grants in kind and the disassembly of German industrial plants. At the Yalta Conference (see **Conferences, Allied**) in February 1945, the Allies stipulated that Germany, as the major aggressor, was to compensate in kind those countries that had suffered the heaviest losses in the war. Three forms of reparation were established: claims on German goods by foreign countries, the disassembly of industrial plants and a levy on current **production** in the particular form of a requisition on German labor. The sum due in reparations was limited to 20 billion marks, of which the **USSR** claimed half.

The Potsdam agreement of August 1945 did more than simply set the method of payment. The reparations and the limitations placed on the German economy were to be sufficiently stringent that Germany could not wage another war. The proposals crystallized in the form of an Allied plan for reparations and for the German economy, which was instituted in March 1946. According to this plan, Germany's industrial production could reach no more than 75% of its level in 1936. To that must be added the claims on German goods by foreign countries, the abandonment of the merchant fleet and the selection of the disassembly of selected industrial plants. This plan put the stamp of approval on the principles of preventive enfeeblement and of penalty before reparations.

None of the points in this plan were ever applied, because one condition essential to its realization remained unfulfilled—the condition that Germany's economic unity be maintained. The advisability of such a severe drain on German economic strength came into question, and differences between the **United States** and the USSR deepened. As a consequence, the Western Zones decided to revise the plan, drastically reducing the number of plants to be dismantled, from 1,800 to 859. The final figures were established by the Petersberg Accord of 1949, which further reduced the disassembly operations, practically ending this policy.

For lack of suitable criteria, it is impossible to evaluate the amount the Germans gave up in Reparations. The Inter-Allied Commission on Reparations estimated the value of the disassembly operations at 700 million marks, or 1.5 billion 1938 marks. Germans estimated that reparations amounted to three or four times that figure. According to the Commission, the losses due to the disassembly in the reconstitution of West German industry amounted to only 3%. German economists, on the other hand, estimated the average drop in industrial capacity at 5.3% up until the end of 1949. If the disassembly policy was not too energetically pursued, claims on their goods by foreign countries would total something like 10 billion marks, according to the Germans. Adding to this the losses of taxes and the merchant fleet—1.4 million tons at the end of the war—the reparation damages were estimated at 20.18 billion marks for West Germany. Although a considerable sum in absolute terms, it is relatively insignificant within the framework of the expenses—measurable and otherwise—resulting from the war: the social costs, the costs of reconstruction, the costs attendant to the treaty with Israel and the like. Actually, the reparations did not restrain West German economic development nearly as much as the disassembly policy just after the end of the war.

The consequences were much more serious in the Soviet-occupied zone. In the first few years after the end of hostilities, the USSR systematically and extensively dismantled plants. The Soviet estimates of the reparations costs for the German Democratic Republic alone ran to 7.5 billion marks; the German estimates varied from three to four times that amount. In addition to the disassembly and removal of the German industrial plants to the USSR, the claims on German labor—the **prisoners of war**—were high. To keep proper control over these transfers of workmen to the USSR, the Soviets set up "Soviet action societies" (SAG) in the most strategically significant regions of East Germany.

Compared to the German expenditures, the contributions of the other nations were small. The former German allies—**Italy, Hungary, Bulgaria, Rumania, Finland** and **Japan**—were compelled to pay reparations. **Austria**, although officially considered an occupied country, was required to pay in kind—actually, 7.5 million tons of crude oil—while Finland was assessed a total of 300 million dollars. Japan's share, set by the peace treaty of 1951, was two billion dollars; only half that sum was, strictly speaking, for reparations.

It is difficult to estimate how much the countries collecting the reparations gained. Certainly, it was much less than the damage to the German economy, for the disassembled plants which were relocated could not in general be fully exploited at their new sites. In any case, the reparations after World War II had nothing like the disastrous economic or political consequences of those levied in the 1920s.

D. Petzina

RESEARCH.

Pure research, not unexpectedly, was slowed down by the war. Elderly scholars were interrupted by bombing and distracted by rationing; they had trouble finding or keeping secretaries or assistants. Younger scholars were swept up into the war, usually as intelligence officers, sometimes in more combative roles. (The leader of the Allied **Resistance** in Crete, for example, T. J. Dunbabin, was a classical archaeologist and a fellow of All Souls College at Oxford.) Code-making and breaking employed a great many mathematicians, and usually kept them too busy to pursue any work not directly connected with the war.

Computer design advanced somewhat during the war in the **United States**; aeronautics, a subject with direct military implications, progressed enormously. Front-line fighter speeds doubled between 1939 and 1945; the British and Americans pursued the conventional aircraft designs they had been working on before the war, while the Germans broke new ground with an operational **jet aircraft**, the He 262, whose main disadvantage was that it could fly for only ten minutes. The Germans also introduced the pilotless jet, the V-1, and with the V-2 inaugurated the age of ballistic missiles. (See **V-1 and V-2**.)

Radio research produced miniature transmitters for use by clandestine agents, about the size of a cigarette pack—ancestors of the minute devices now used in space research. Transistors, and the whole development of modern electronics, developed out of radio research conducted during the war. In medicine there were great advances, as is usual in wars (see **Health**); improved field surgery and antibiotic drugs were, from the ordinary patient's point of view, the most beneficial. Finally, fundamental research in physics was of central importance to the development of the **atomic bomb**. The eminent scientists who staffed the Manhattan Project established, in the course of creating the bomb, a number of serious advances in our understanding of how matter is constructed. On a more mundane level, their work opened up the eventual possibility of solving, through nuclear fission, the world's problems of energy supply.

M. R. D. Foot

RESISTANCE.

In the modern political and military lexicon, "resistance" refers to the rebellious attitude that a peremptory and greedy authority established by a foreign government, an authority that scorns funda-

mental rights and violates democratic principles, typically arouses.

The Declaration of the Rights of Man and of the Citizen in 1789 specified resistance to oppression as one of those rights, in its Article 2. This right was affirmed by Comte de Mirabeau, one of the declaration's authors, in these words: "When authority becomes arbitrary and oppressive, resistance is a duty and cannot be called rebellion." During World War II the Resistance was led by citizens of the countries occupied by the armies of Fascist **Italy**, Nazi **Germany**, or jingoist **Japan**, clandestinely at first, and later more overtly.

In the period between the two world wars, the intellectual elite and the Marxist proletariat throughout Europe banded together in vigorous opposition to **fascism**. The struggle agains **Mussolini**'s Fascists began in 1922, against **Hitler**'s Nazis in 1932 and against **Ioannis Metaxas**'s dictatorship in **Greece** in the mid-1930s, although in none of these countries was it as bitter and savage as the civil war in **Spain**. Those who opposed the **Munich Pact** in 1938 were to be the first resisters in 1940.

The **Nazi-Soviet Pact** in 1939 and the **Russo-Finnish Winter War** the same year dismayed liberal Europe and for a time paralyzed it. Not until after the **Blitzkrieg** assault on the the west (see *Fall Gelb*) and the *Wehrmacht*'s occupation of **Norway, Denmark the Netherlands, Belgium, Luxembourg**, and half of France, following the tragedies of **Austria, Czechoslovakia** and **Poland** (see **Fall Weiss**), did an ardent faith, a strengthening hope and the first stirrings of resistance come to the aid of the prostrate democracies.

Gen. **de Gaulle**'s appeal on June 18, 1940 did not bring Europe's dormant energy to the immediate aid of the **United Kingdom**, the only power left to face the **Axis**. There was little response from those countries that were still free from totalitarian terror or from latent resistance sentiment in the occupied territories, but it was a beginning. Encouraged by the **British Broadcasting Corporation**'s transmission of hopeful messages from the various **governments-in-exile** and political organizations in London and by leaflets dropped over Europe, the spirit of the Resistance began to flare. The memory of the underground networks during World War I returned to French and Belgian minds, and with it the desire to re-create a people's army.

In De Gaulle's *Memoires de guerre*, the leader of **Free France** defined the role of the Resistance in this way:

We envision nothing less than an organization that will permit us simultaneously to inform Allied operations by providing intelligence about the enemy, to arouse resistance to the enemy in every region and to equip every sympathetic force that will, at the proper time, participate, at the Germans' rear, in the battle for liberation in order to prepare for our country's restoration to health once victory has been achieved. France must be brought back into the war, thus to participate in the final victory. During the first stage information networks must be established for the benefit of the Allied chiefs of staff. A second should consist in sabotage of the enemy war machine wherever it may be and rejection of any compromise with the occupying authority and its accomplices. A third should see the organization and training of military forces to attack the enemy as the Allies advance, to hinder his defense and to promote a climate of national unanimity for the restoration of the nation's economy and of fundamental freedoms.

That was one of the facets of the Resistance: patriots refusing to surrender. There were others: humanists committed to defending their ideals of liberty, equality and fraternity, and Christians who abhorred totalitarianism, racism and neo-pagan Hitlerism. For them the goal was to counteract **Goebbels' propaganda**, along with the stream of hate that echoed from the satellite states: from the French devotees of the *Revolution nationale* (see **Petain and the French State**), the supporters of the **New European Order** and the servile press.

The **underground press** and a vast array of literature circulated sub rosa contributed importantly to the Resistance.

Perhaps the most striking aspect of the Resistance movement was that it sprang up simultaneously in all the occupied countries. Yet the different guerrilla movements in the eastern and western parts of Europe never sought to coordinate their activities or to elaborate a common strategy. The Resistance's spontaneous growth came first; organization, communication and cooperation came later. The Resistance sprouted haphazardly in the beginning, its participants unconcerned with each others' past opinions, political or religious associations or social status. Each group was usually small in number but determined and active, capable of performing major feats either on its own or in cooperation with related groups. But everywhere it stimulated among the populace a spirit of disobedience, a constant indifference to the orders issued by the enemy and the governments under enemy control and a permanent condition of tacit complicity with the Resistance. The Resistance groups were intent on exacerbating any possible difficulties for the occupying power in the economic sphere, especially those connected with rationing and requisitioning. They took advantage of the confusion—and the resentment—that arose out of the establishment of occupied and unoccupied zones, the restrictions on

movement and the conscription of labor. They undermined official strictures on local newspapers or expropriations of radio receivers. In most cases the organized Resistance had aims beyond simply expelling the army of occupation and ousting governments and administrators installed or supported by the enemy. They hoped for nothing less than the complete revamping of local institutions to make them more democratic, the establishment of an economy free from the constraints of monopoly or trusts, nationalization of the means of **production**, and freedom of opinion in the press.

The Resistance flourished everywhere. The attack on the **USSR** in June 1941 drove the revolutionary energy of the Communist Party and extreme leftist organizations into the Resistance. In some countries, like **Yugoslavia**, that energy derived from only a handful of highly trained men, thoroughly seasoned by combat service in the International Brigades during the Spanish civil war. The part played by the Communist Party was all the more decisive since the party gave absolute priority to the patriotic battle for liberation, recruiting people from all political and social backgrounds for the Resistance and taking the lead in audacious operations that younger Resistance fighters found much more attractive than the more cautious efforts of the other factions. In the political as well as the military arena, Resistance groups animated by the Communist Party offered a tight organization and a singleness of purpose, enhancing their efficiency and minimizing the risks.

At its very beginning the Resistance displayed nothing more than a multiplicity of personal reactions reflected in improvised deeds—hiding arms and munitions, printing and distributing leaflets, harboring escaped prisoners. There were even some isolated instances of **sabotage**. But the most effective and well-coordinated work was done by the general staffs of the occupied countries' armed forces, which prepared for an eventual offensive by setting up depots for armaments, materiel and men or listening posts that gathered as much information as possible on the enemy's battle plans.

Then the first secret networks were formed. They specialized in obtaining military or economic information, assisting in the escape and evacuation of prisoners or Allied pilots who had parachuted from crippled planes, massing reserves of arms, printing propaganda leaflets or journals and engaging in acts of sabotage.

In the recruitment of espionage agents, chance encounters or the ties of friendship were more effective than political or professional contacts. On the other hand, Resistance movements that engaged at first in propaganda without being too closely tied to a political party usually ended up with a definite political orientation to the left or extreme left. But after a time simple propaganda opposing **collaboration** with the Nazis no longer sufficed. It became necessary to establish, with or without the aid of the Resistance movements, means of acquiring information that the chiefs of staff in Moscow, London, Cairo and Algiers could coordinate through central agencies.

As hope was reborn with the first Axis defeats, the Resistance turned more and more toward the use of arms, as the Communists had originally recommended. Caution was shrugged off, and the more determined guerrillas organized sabotage operations or trained, usually in groups of 30 each, for armed action at the critical moment, in concert with the movements of Allied troops. The bravest of these were incorporated into the maquis and provided with arms by parachute. The others were held temporarily in reserve for use in mop-up procedures in liberated sectors.

The creation of the **Forced Labor Battalions** swelled the ranks of the maquis with escapees from the German labor draft, who were moved more by fear of the increasingly frequent bombings of German factories than by patriotic reflex. The Anglo-American landing in North Africa in November 1942 was followed by the Germans' total military occupation of both French zones and the consequent dissolution of the French armistice army. But this demobilization had a beneficial effect in that arms and materiel were clandestinely turned over to the Resistance. In addition, the Resistance obtained reinforcements from maquis in the mountainous regions of southern France, where the *Wehrmacht* was numerically weak.

In all the occupied countries, 1943 saw an accelerated growth of armed Resistance groups. The administrative and military arms of the occupying power were thus forced to divert their attention from the war itself to formerly secret groups of troublemakers that had become disciplined armies fighting in the open. Within the Resistance groups, tables of organization and chains of command were drawn up, regrouping of forces for special purposes was arranged and general staffs were established. In many cases, however, individual groups within the Resistance insisted on retaining a measure of autonomy. As a result, coordination of the various guerrilla groups on the local level was often purely theoretical.

When the Allied command recognized, at the end of 1944, that the Resistance within the occupied countries was powerful enough to contribute significantly in the last phase of the war, it stepped up its efforts to supply the guerrilla groups with weapons and military instructors. The Allies continued, however, to depend primarily on the **Special Operations Executive**, even though that organization was peppered with double agents. The **Jedburgh** groups, each containing three British, American or French officers, were dropped by parachute to pick up information on enemy activity accumulated by the Resistance and to aid in operations in the enemy rear. These groups were under orders to keep away from the regional cadres and the local Resistance groups, but they actually made contact with the cadres as soon as they possibly could. The Sussex teams had a similar function.

As the occupied countries were liberated by the Allied troops, the Resistance cooperated closely with them. In many locations armed Resistance formations had already taken possession of cities and controlled large areas. They were often assigned to mop-up tasks at the rear of the retreating German forces. Administration of the liberated lands was immediately assumed by liberation committees appointed several weeks or months before. Alleged traitors or collaborationists were arrested and tried.

The Resistance was later to contribute heavily to the work of reorganizing the administration and economy of the liberated countries. Once **purges** and the installation of new personnel were well under way, they began the work of reconstruction, often nationalizing certain industries.

Neither the offensive **strategy** of the Allies nor the defensive **tactics** of the occupation armies initially took into account the efforts of the Resistance. Both commands preferred to use well-trained military intelligence agents to spy on troop deployments and war industry production. The use of Resistance men and facilities for sabotage, in order to spare the civilian population of the occupied countries the risks of bombardment, had been recommended by the British command in the summer of 1940; this advice was generally ignored.

The Allies wanted to receive the intelligence Resistance groups had gathered as much as they wanted assistance from these groups in countering procollaborationist propaganda. **Churchill**, and **Roosevelt** even more, insisted on assuaging the feelings of the de facto authorities of the countries the Germans had defeated by letting them share in the encouragement directed toward the Resistance. Allied hopes for a sudden change in attitude on the part of occupation authorities gradually dissipated, but the Allied command remained suspicious of the Resistance and its guerrillas. Policy makers feared that Resistance movements would support communist revolutions or military putsches. Arms, munitions and money were therefore offered in small amounts. It is also true, of course, that possible means of assistance were often limited and that priority could not always be awarded to a Resistance group that was as yet untried. The victory achieved by the Yugoslavian partisans and, later, the cooperation of the *Forces francaises de l'interieur* with the American Third Army in Brittany and Seventh Army in Provence completely altered the views of the Allied command. After August 1944 parachute drops of arms and officers were much more frequent and generous.

Beginning in 1944 Gen. **William Donovan**, the head of the **Office of Strategic Services**, and, later, Gen. **Eisenhower** attached more value to the achievements of the Resistance. Similarly, the Red Army chiefs of staff began to appreciate the worth of Russian partisans in 1943 after having long been oblivious to it.

Nonetheless, an inaccurate interpretation of the facts caused the Allied command to repeat their earlier error. The Resistance was seen as an unwieldy mass of mobilized volunteers, organized around a core of maquis to whom arms were periodically parachuted. This unfortunate notion led the Allies to continue their neglect of the Resistance, which in turn led to their worst defeats at the hands of enemy aircraft and **tanks**.

But failure to recognize the efficiency and extent of the contributions of auxiliary forces was by no means restricted to the Allies. The Axis powers were only mildly concerned about the resisters, assuming that their functions were confined to espionage and propaganda. The fear that these uniformless combatants and saboteurs would appear on other fronts steadily grew as the implacable battle waged by Yugoslav and Russian partisans increased in intensity. This, together with the emerging fear of the terrorists, contributed vastly to the demoralization of the Axis troops. At first, the rivalry among the various secret services responsible for detecting seditious groups impeded the hunt for Resistance fighters. The **Gestapo** was finally entrusted with this duty. Thanks to the auxiliary police recruited in each of the occupied countries and the employment of double agents who infiltrated the Resistance, the networks and movements were undermined, large quantities of parachuted arms and munitions were captured and many parachutists were apprehended. Many of the radio transmitters communicating with London were actually operated by Axis agents or had passed into Axis control. This operation was known as *Englandspiel* in the Netherlands. The counterespionage efforts of the *Abwehr* and the Gestapo hurt the Resistance badly. In fact, at the moment the **Normandy landing** was launched, the officers of the *Forces francaises le l'interieur* who preceded it were arrested and could not immediately be replaced.

Perhaps it was because the Allies failed to understand and consequently misused the Resistance that its members were quickly detected and constantly imperiled by the German secret services. Still, it managed to contribute significantly to the Allied victory, surviving with the active or passive complicity of the very great majority of the occupied nations' inhabitants. Many of the resisters were shot or died in Germany as deportees. The civilian population around them suffered casualties, too, in the merciless German reprisals. The losses the Resistance inflicted on the enemy were nonetheless considerable. Moreover it elevated the **morale** of the population and sowed panic in enemy ranks.

Most of the governments installed or tolerated by the occupation authorities—the administrators of central or regional services and the mayors of the cities—insisted that by avoiding the worst, by obtaining the liberation of prisoners or pardons for resisters and by seeking to ameliorate the more Draconian measures of the Germans in the occupied countries, they were more effective than they would have been by consistently refusing to collaborate in any way. Nor is there any doubt that the passive resistance of an enormous number of magistrates, government officials, police officers, railroad workers and, particularly, postal clerks was more effective against the occupying power than any other type of activity. It was reflected in numerous delays, mistakes in routing, misinterpretations of orders and manufactured goods that were damaged or of poor quality. It was responsible for the complete silence that greeted the activities of the maquis as well as the unceasing help that was given imperiled patriots who sought to escape or to find refuge and the lies that were told to the police who pursued them.

Intellectual and spiritual resistance substantially influenced the morale of the populace. It began with the circulation of leaflets inimical to Nazism; the reluctance of some newspapers to disseminate official propaganda; the development of an underground press, national, regional or local in orientation; and the appearance of books lauding the spirit of the Resistance and promising stern retribution for collaborators or proponents of Nazi racism. Religious authorities in Germany, Norway, the Netherlands and Belgium fought racial persecution and state control of the youth movements. Many priests and pastors, acting on their own, joined Resistance groups.

The governments-in-exile in London used the facilities provided by the BBC to encourage the resisters at home in their native languages.

In spite of the often heavy losses caused by Allied bombers, most of the people retained their political faith and assisted fliers parachuting to the earth by offering them refuge and an opportunity to escape pursuers.

Amassing information on the strength and movements of enemy troops, submarines or air forces and on production in enemy war industries constituted the major task of the intelligence networks. Listening posts were numerous and far-flung, but the heavy message traffic, together with the complications of encoding, decoding and selecting and matching large quantities of data, resulted in exasperating delays.

In the beginning, telephone lines used by the enemy were sabotaged; afterwards, locomotives were destroyed and rail switching was hindered. Derailments were arranged, with railroad workers assisting in the work of misdirecting convoys. Enemy telephone lines were wiretapped and letters mailed to German field commanders and the Gestapo were opened and even confiscated. In the midst of military operations, in addition to cutting off rail service at strategic points to paralyze transportation almost everywhere, tree trunks were flung across rails and large numbers of automobiles were disabled, their panel indicators set wrong to mislead convoy drivers, while isolated vehicles were attacked.

Individual assassination attempts on officers in the army of occupation were the exclusive province of free-lance operators or partisans, forced to accumulate arms by this method since they were not the beneficiaries of gifts via parachute. To discourage agents in the pay of the enemy, individuals convicted of **treason** were executed after summary trials. Occasionally, robbery and other criminal acts were performed by men pretending to be Resistance members.

Gradually, however, individual operations gave way to concerted, cooperatively planned ventures, carried out according to precise instructions broadcast by intelligence networks. Later, when the Resistance groups were organized and unified by national Resistance councils and the military committees subordinate to them, they, together with military delegates sent from London with orders from the Allied command, worked out a coordinated strategy and tactical procedures. Arrests of cadre members, difficulties in communication, insubordination and the high command's misjudgment of various situations all impeded the smooth execution of plans.

Guerrilla warfare was most feared by the occupying troops, who completely abandoned particular sectors or avoided unsafe roads rather than running the risk of succumbing to an ambush. The guerrillas specialized in attacks on isolated vehicles or small convoys, strafing detachments on the march or assaulting small posts. They were few in number but well seasoned in the art, armed with small machine guns, automatic rifles, bazookas, grenades and sometimes mortars. They struck swiftly and without warning, then retreated rapidly to bases safe from the enemy. Opera-

tions of this sort required large stores of munitions for the continuous harassment of occupation troops. (See also **French Resistance**; **German Resistance**; **Japanese Resistance**.)

M. Baudot

REVERS, Georges (1891-   ).
In June 1940 Revers, a French general, was head of the **Darlan** military cabinet. He was national leader of the *Organisation de resistance de l'armee* from 1942 to 1943.

REVOLUTION.
Most analyses of the National Socialist revolution in **Germany** indicate that it was bound to lead to war—that without war, Nazism made no sense, and that even so nonsensical a doctrine had to seek sense in some way. And just as revolutions cause wars, wars cause revolutions.

Strictly political revolutions were few during World War II until near its end. **Mao Tse-tung** used the disruptions of the war to forward the revolutionary cause in **China**; he ended the war stronger, by comparison with either of his opponents (see **Multilateral Wars**), than he had entered it. Indeed the war, by knocking out **Japan** and weakening the Kuomintang, made his eventual success more likely.

Tito successfully led the only authentic new revolutionary movement of the war in **Yugoslavia**, having carried it on from the mountains of Bosnia and Montenegro since 1941. He owed more to **Special Operations Executive** (SOE) than to the **USSR**, and more to his own countrymen than to either. Although a Croat, he was able to transcend Croatian feelings and achieve a southern Slavic communist view of war and **society**. **Ante Pavelich** was not, but Pavelich's attempt at a national revolution was swept away along with **fascism**, as was Marshal Petain's much milder one in France (see **Petain and the French State**).

Several countries in eastern Europe found a revolution imposed on them as the Red Army advanced in 1944-45. The degree of popular support this commanded became clear in 1953 in East Germany, in 1956 in **Poland** and **Hungary** and in 1968 in **Czechoslovakia**. **Bulgaria** alone appears to have accepted communism with a degree of enthusiasm.

In the USSR the nominally revolutionary regime survived on the strength of an old-fashioned chauvinistic appeal (see **Propaganda**). National revolution got its opportunity in **Indonesia** at the end of the war; the **Philippines**, **Burma**, **Malaya** and other Southeast Asian countries soon followed on the way to independence (see **Independence Movements**).

The war's most interesting legacy to revolution was

the demonstration repeatedly given by **resistance** movements of the value of individual armed action against an established system, however harsh the system. This was not an aim the SOE had set for itself in 1940, but it may have been an unavoidable consequence of the SOE's work.

On the strictly military side, did the war see any revolutions? **Heinz Guderian**'s applications of **Basil Liddell Hart**'s doctrines felt revolutionary at the receiving end, but he did no more than Gen. William Tecumseh Sherman had done marching through Georgia in 1864. Gen. **Kurt Student** did something quite new in May 1941 when he captured Crete with a wholly airborne German force; the coup, however, could have been foreseen at least 10 years earlier. Ultra was striking, but no more so, or hardly more so, than the achievements of Room 40 in World War I. **Arthur Harris** applied **Hugh Trenchard**'s doctrines, bombing populated areas in western Germany with devastating, but not quite decisive, results. The **atomic bomb** that brought the war to an end in August 1945 appeared revolutionary then; retrospect, however, reveals it to be an extension of artillery.

M. R. D. Foot

REYNAUD, Paul (1878-1966).
Following World War I, Reynaud, a French statesman, was deputy from Brasses-Alpes in 1919, minister of finance in 1930 and an advocate of the military innovations proposed by **de Gaulle** and of the Franco-Soviet alliance. He was keeper of the seals and then minister of finance in the cabinet of **Edouard Daladier** in 1938, stubbornly refusing any compromise with the Nazis. He became president of the *Conseil d'Etat* and minister of foreign affairs on March 21, 1940. Neither his attempt to improve the military posture of the country or to gain his government's approval for an Anglo-French union succeeded, and he resigned on June 16. Arrested in September by the Petain government (see **Petain and the French State**), he was sentenced to life imprisonment in October 1941 and then deported by the Germans to Oranienburg in November 1942. He was released in 1945 and was one of the principal witnesses against Petain at the marshal's trial.

RIBBENTROP, Joachim von (1893-1946).
After serving as ambassador to the **United Kingdom** from 1936-1938, Ribbentrop was German minister of foreign affairs from 1938 to 1945. In 1939 he signed the **Nazi-Soviet Pact**. He was condemned to death as a **war criminal** by the Nuremburg tribunal and hanged.

RIDGWAY, Matthew B. (1895-   ).
In July 1943 Ridgway, an American general, commanded the 82nd Airborne Division in the invasion of Sicily and in the Salerno landing in September. On June 6, 1944 he parachuted with his division on the Cotentin Peninsula (see **Normandy Landing**). As commander of the 18th Airborne Corps, he successfully led his 82nd and 101st Airborne Divisions in the capture of Eindhoven and Nijmegen. On December 18 he was called upon to reinforce the northern flank of the Ardennes pocket. In March 1945 his divisions executed the huge airborne operation at Wesel, across the Rhine. They finally crossed the Elbe in April 1945 and joined up with Russian forces on the Baltic.

RIO DE JANEIRO, Conference of.
The foreign ministers of all American states—10 of which were already at war with **Germany** and **Japan**—met at Rio de Janeiro in January 1942 to consider a **United States** proposal that they should all join the war. Opposition by Ecuador (because of a boundary quarrel with Peru) and by Argentina (on principle) prevented agreement on the proposal, but those present agreed to share various rights of **cobelligerency** when at war with a non-American state. Useful economic arrangements were also made.

RITCHIE, Sir Neil Methuen (1897-   ).
In 1941 Ritchie, a British general, was deputy chief of staff in the Middle East to Sir **Claude Auchinleck**, the commander in chief, and led the Eighth Army in 1941-42. In 1944-45 Ritchie commanded the 12th Corps.

ROESSLER, RUDOLF (1897-1958).
A German spy for the **USSR**, Roessler operated under the pseudonym "Lucy." He was a resident of **Switzerland** after 1933. He delivered vital information on the *Oberkommando des Heeres* to the Soviets (see *Narodnyy Kommissariat Vnutrennikh Del*).

ROKOSSOVSKI, Konstantin K. (1896-1968).
Rokossovski, a Soviet marshal, was commander in chief of several army groups on a number of different fronts; at Bryansk, on the Don and at the Center and White Russian fronts (see **USSR—War with Germany**). Rokossovski captured Warsaw in 1944 and East Prussia in 1945. He signed the German surrender for the **USSR** at Berlin on May 8, 1945.

ROL-TANGUY (nickname of Henri Tanguy) (1908-   ).
Rol-Tanguy, a French Communist, was the chief of the *Forces francaises de l'interieur* in Paris. He launched the insurrection in Paris on August 19, 1944, denoun-

cing the truce the *Conseil national de la resistance* had concluded with **Dietrich von Choltitz**. With **Leclerc**, Rol-Tanguy received the surrender of the German commander of the Paris region on August 25, 1944.

ROMMEL, Erwin (1891-1944).
Rommel, a German soldier, took command of a division in 1940; from 1941 through 1943 he commanded the German and Italian forces in Africa (see **Mediterranean and Middle Eastern Theater of Operations**). In 1943 and 1944 Rommel was commander in chief of Army Group B, first in **Italy**, then in northwestern Europe, along the Atlantic coast from **the Netherlands** to the Loire, where he led the battle against the Allies after the **Normandy landing**. **Hitler** came to suspect his participation in the **assassination attempt of July 20, 1944** and forced him to commit suicide; he received a state funeral.

ROOSEVELT, Franklin Delano (1882-1945).
Roosevelt was president of the **United States** from 1933 to 1945 and joint leader, with **Stalin** and **Churchill**, of the alliance that defeated **Hitler**. His family was of Dutch origin, and he was born into the unofficial aristocracy of New York State, where he was a state senator from 1910 to 1913. He served Woodrow Wilson as assistant secretary of the Navy from 1913 to 1920 and was an unsuccessful Democratic candidate for the vice-presidency in 1920. In 1921 he suffered a severe attack of poliomyelitis and never fully recovered the use of his legs. His wife Eleanor, whom he had married in 1905, acted as his "political eyes and ears," keeping him in touch with American public life. By 1928 Roosevelt was fit enough to reenter the political arena, and he was elected governor of New York.

In November 1932, in the trough of the Great Depression, when over 13,000,000 Americans were unemployed, he was elected president, succeeding Herbert Hoover; he took office in March 1933. Thereupon, in his "first 100 days" in office he galvanized American business life from slump into fresh activity. His "New Deal" revitalized agriculture, business and labor alike; his personality inspired confidence. A large number of the measures he introduced, such as the highly successful Tennessee Valley Authority for developing a hitherto backward region through hydroelectric power, would have been called socialist in other contexts, but he secured their acceptance as part of the American way of life.

He was one of the earliest to appreciate the political uses of radio, and in a series of "fireside chats" — begun before, and continued during, the war— he projected his personality and his ideas into millions of American homes. Although he was thus more widely known than any of his predecessors, he was not by any means universally loved: many Americans, in fact, detested him.

The Supreme Court raised some objections to the New Deal, but by and large, ceased to oppose it within a few years of his reelection, by a crushing majority, in 1936. He instituted diplomatic relations with the **USSR** in 1933, and in the late 1930s moved American foreign policy toward support of the **United Kingdom** and France and against the **Axis** powers. His long-standing friendship with Churchill led to close Anglo-American cooperation from the summer of 1940 onward. Convinced by **William Donovan** and **Carl Spaatz** that the British were not about to be beaten, Roosevelt lent them substantial quantities of American arms, including fighter aircraft and 50 old destroyers through the **lend-lease** program. Breaking with precedent he ran for a third term as president in November 1940 and was again reelected, with a comfortable (though less enormous) majority. His lend-lease legislation, enacted in Mach 1941, brought the United States almost to the point of **cobelligerency**; in August 1941 Roosevelt signed the strongly worded **Atlantic Charter**. In December 1941 the **Pearl Harbor** attack—which he may well have foreseen but could not prevent or forestall—brought the United States into the war. As president, Roosevelt was commander in chief of all American armed forces. He left all questions of **tactics** to his chiefs of staff, Gen. **George C. Marshall**, Adm. **Ernest V. King** and Gen. **Henry H. Arnold**; they, in turn, followed his directions on grand **strategy**. His forte was providing leadership on moral issues; he had always regarded Nazism as evil and threw himself into organizing the American national war effort with the zeal of a crusader. Besides his efforts at home, devoted to organization and oratory, he traveled repeatedly to wartime conferences (see **Conferences, Allied**), and at Teheran took a liking to Stalin, with whom he was inclined to side, in order to keep a check on what he believed to be Churchill's often imperialist ambitions. In November 1944 he was reelected president for the fourth time, with a reduced majority and a dubious Congress. But his health, never tremendously robust, was undermined by the strains of war. He was far from his best form at Yalta in February 1945; many people who saw him there thought him ill. He died suddenly, of a stroke, on April 12, 1945.

Hitler thought, even at that impossibly late moment, that Roosevelt's death was a stroke of fate that presaged a German victory after all. But a well-wound clock in proper working order that reaches 11:59 cannot be stopped from striking 12:00.

M. R. D. Foot

ROSENBERG, Alfred (1893-1946).

In December 1919 Rosenberg joined the **Nazi Party**. He headed the party's foreign relations department in 1933 and was for the most part responsible for shaping the ideology of National Socialism. In 1941 he became minister of the occupied eastern territories. As official party "philosopher," he was a leading proponent of the Nazi theory of races and of the Fuehrer mystique. Condemned to death as a **war criminal** by the Nuremberg tribunal, he was executed in 1946.

ROTE KAPELLE.

(In English "Red Orchestra.") See *Narodnyy Kommissariat Vnutrennikh Del.*

ROUNDUP.

Established in April and abandoned in July of 1942, Roundup was the code name for an Allied landing in France, planned for the summer of 1943 (see **World War II—General Conduct**).

ROYAL AIR FORCE (RAF).

The British air force. (See **Airborne Divisions; Britain, Battle of; Germany, Air Battle of.**)

RSHA (Reichssicherheitshauptamt).

The central organization for security of the Reich. Created on September 27, 1939 by **Hitler's** decree, it was controlled by **Heinrich Himmler**, who later added to its responsibility the direction of the **SS** and the state police departments (see **Gestapo; SD**).

RUMANIA.

In 1919 the Treaty of Trianon detached Transylvania and Timisoara from **Hungary** and transferred them to Rumania. The Treaty of Neuilly confirmed Rumania's annexation of the Bulgarian portion of Dobruja, acquired in 1913 after the Second Balkan War. In 1920 the Allies approved plebiscites in Bessarabia and Russian Bukovina, in which the people had voted to remain part of Rumania. The kingdom of Ferdinand I thus doubled its territory; its population came to include 1.5 million Hungarians, 780,000 Jews, 723,000 Germans, 448,000 Ukrainians, 358,000 Bulgarians, 308,000 Russians and 57,000 Serbs.

The growth of "Greater Rumania" was not the success the western European Allies—particularly France, which lavished friendship on its "Latin sister"—hoped it would be. The Bucharest government never intended to institute social reforms or guarantee the rights of its minorities as the peace treaties of 1919 and the **League of Nations** required. The agrarian reform law of 1921, breaking up and distributing close to 25,000 square miles from the great aristocrats' estates, did nothing to improve the lives of the peas-

ants. Wretched and illiterate, lacking farm equipment or animals, with no means of getting loans, they could do nothing with their parcels of land. Some sold their meager property; others became the prey of unscrupulous usurers and lost everything. What little industrial expansion the swollen state experienced derived from foreign capital invested in the Ploesti oil fields.

Rumania's political system was the fabrication of King Ferdinand and his ministers. The new constitution of 1923, purporting to grant universal suffrage, was a fraud. Deep dissensions in the country, indeed in the very heart of the royal family, muddled matters still further. Ferdinand's eldest son, Carol, lost his claim on the throne because of his marriage to Madame Magda Lupescu. On Ferdinand's death, in 1927, Carol's son Michael, then six years old, succeeded to the monarchy. But three years later, Carol became King **Carol II**, easing himself into the throne by edging his son out.

The Great Depression in the early 1930s affected the country profoundly. A railroad workers' strike, an effort to increase their scanty salaries, spread to other sectors of the economy. It was fiercely suppressed. The head of the Central Committee for Strike Action, railroad worker and Communist Gheorghe Gheorghiu-Dej, was sentenced, along with his assistants, to long sentences in the Doftana prison. They were to remain there until liberation in 1944.

The Rumanian Communist Party, legally nonexistent, grew. So did the extreme rightist movement known as the Iron Guard, founded by Corneliu Codreanu. Aping the Nazi method, Codreanu declared himself the mortal enemy of democracy and the Jews. Inspired by **Hitler's** accession to power, he dreamed of a regenerated Rumania under the political and economic aegis of Nazi **Germany**. He mimicked Nazi methods, terrorizing the populace through political gangsterism. Prime Minister Jon Duca, head of the Liberal Party, and the great historian Nicolas Jorga died at the hands of the Iron Guard.

After a long flirtation with each of the political parties in his country and an equally lengthy period of indifference to Codreanu's campaign of hate, King Carol finally established a de facto dictatorship in 1938 by instituting a new and authoritarian constitution. All political parties were declared illegal, including the Iron Guard, although it continued its depredations just the same. Still, with the exception of the Communists, bowing toward Moscow, and the Iron Guard, captivated by Berlin, most Rumanians remained faithful to their Allies from World War I. To the nation's intellectuals, France remained the country most worthy of respect.

The **Munich Pact** in 1938 was as catastrophic for

Rumania as it was for the other European states. It marked the irreparable break between west and east. The submissiveness of the statesmen from Paris and London before Hitler's browbeating shattered Franco-British influence in Bucharest after September 1938. Now isolated from western Europe, Rumania fell into Germany's orbit and made available to the Reich its wheat and corn and especially the precious Ploesti oil wells, on which the Nazi war machine was to depend until its destruction.

The **Nazi-Soviet Pact** in August 1939 was even a more punishing blow for Rumania, caught as it was between the two strongest powers in Europe, which were now allied. As the new, if unofficial, master of the country, Hitler forced Rumania to cede Bessarabia and northern Bukovina to his strange new ally, the Soviet Union. The Fuehrer and his **Axis** partner, **Mussolini**, meeting in Vienna the following August 30, then required Bucharest to cede northern Transylvania to Hungary.

The Rumanian people, by no means enamored of Germans in general and Nazis in particular, rebelled at this amputation of practically all their territorial gains of 1919. Mass demonstrations were organized against the Vienna *Diktat*. Seizing the opportunity offered by this unrest, Gen. **Ion Antonescu** unseated Carol and placed Michael on the throne once again and then established his own dictatorship with Hitler's approval. A former military attache in London, Antonescu promptly forgot his former affection for the British and threw his country wholeheartedly into Berlin's embrace. But his "good intentions" meant nothing to the Fuehrer, who continued his dismemberment of Rumania by compelling it, in accordance with the accords of Craiova, to yield southern Dobruja to **Bulgaria**.

Events moved rapidly. Antonescu assumed the title of "*Conducator*," the Rumanian equivalent of "Fuehrer" or "*Duce*"—to say nothing of the Russian "*Vozhd*," used for **Stalin**—and, at the beginning of October 1940, allowed his country to be occupied by the *Wehrmacht*. Twelve German divisions became the unwanted guests of the Rumanian people. The Iron Guard was reconstituted, in a no less brutal form; its adherents killed a great many political recalcitrants and Jews. On June 22, 1941 the armies of Antonescu, newly titled marshal, attacked Soviet territory in company with their German allies. Nowhere did the Nazi policy prove as cynical as it did in Rumania. In 1940, during the period of "friendship" between Germany and the Soviet Union, Hitler forced Rumania to give Bessarabia up to the **USSR**. In June 1941, just one year later, he was forcing Rumania into the bloody war against the USSR to "recover" Bessarabia! (See also **Collaboration**.)

At that instant Rumania was in a truly paradoxical position. In World War I, it fought in the Allied ranks. In World War II, of all the satellites of the Reich, it was the one most deeply opposed to the Allies. Almost a million Rumanians served on the eastern front, getting as far as the Volga, the high-water mark of Germany's surge into Russia (see **USSR—War with Germany**). And still another paradox: Antonescu, indebted as he was to the Fuehrer for his position at Rumania's helm, interposed himself between the Nazis and his people as a protective force by dissolving the vicious Iron Guard. Moreover, the **concentration camps** in Rumania were not the death camps found in other occupied countries. The Rumanian press refrained from printing Nazi orders, and the number of losses among Rumanian Jews was half what it was in most other occupied lands.

Rumanian forces suffered tremendous losses under fire, principally because they were not as well equipped as the Germans; the terrible privations they endured on the Russian steppes and harassment by Russian guerrillas also played havoc among their ranks. Their misery increased at an accelerated pace. Because of the immense value of Ploesti, German garrisons were plentiful, with one battalion stationed in every Rumanian village. Eleven Nazi espionage and reprisal services were constantly in action.

Nevertheless, demonstrations, strikes, labor agitation, **sabotage** and the **underground press** all proliferated. The working class and the Communists provided the stimuli, and the **Resistance** united Rumanians of all political allegiances, of all social classes, of all faiths. There were frequent acts of sabotage in industrial plants, metallurgical mills, shipyards, railroad workshops and on the rails themselves. Beginning in November 1941 the Germans became acutely aware that the damage wrought by saboteurs on the Ploesti petroleum refineries and wells had reduced **production** by 15% to 20%. The workers in the factories manufacturing aircraft, **tanks** and artillery equipment developed a technical form of sabotage that involved introducing minor defects into these products that would, in no time, render them useless. On June 12, 1942 a raging fire broke out in the Tirgoviste arsenal. In the winter of 1943 the warehouse of the Mirsa armament plants went up in flames, destroying 70,000 artillery shells. The peasants undercut the forced delivery of agricultural products to the Germans, hid farm animals and cereals and sheltered and assisted insurgents, dissidents and deserters. Even more numerous than these were the escaped Russian **prisoners of war** who were also sheltered by the Rumanians. A campaign was conducted among the Axis units on the eastern front to provoke desertions and mutiny. The hostility between German troops and Rumanians was continuous, especially after the battle of Stalingrad.

The United Anti-Hitler Front was formed in June 1943, integrating the Communist Party, the Organized Hungarian Workers in Rumania, the Peasant Socialist Party and some cells of the Social Democratic Party. By every indication there was constant and direct contact between the Rumanian Resistance and the Soviets, through parachuted agents and other means. It is definitely known that the **Special Operations Executive** (SOE) sought to establish a similar relationship with the Rumanian Resistance.

Beginning in 1941 Rumanian statesmen at odds with Antonescu and his regime conferred with British and American representatives in Lisbon, Stockholm, Berne and Instanbul. London pinned its hopes on the leader of the National Agrarian party, Juliu Maniu; he responded by sending it amicable messages from time to time, notifying the British on one occasion, in the spring of 1943, that he was preparing a coup d'etat, to be led by Gen. Constantin Sanatescu. In August of that year a mission dispatched by the Cairo section of the SOE parachuted into **Yugoslavia** and crossed into Rumania. Maj. David Russell, in command of the SOE detachment, was killed shortly afterward. His radio operator, who managed to escape the assassins, continued to transmit messages to Cairo asking for reinforcements. These calls were answered by the arrival, just before Christmas 1943, of SOE agents Gardyne de Chastellain and Ivor Porter, who parachuted into Rumania. Both were arrested a few days later, and Russell's operator informed Cairo that the newly arrived agents were in a Bucharest jail.

London then understood that Maniu was an undependable dilettante. The coup d'etat he had promised never came off. By the spring of 1944, however, the continuous defeats that sent the German army staggering back across the Soviet Union convinced Antonescu that **fascism** was no longer a reliable instrument. Together with Maniu he authorized Prince Barbu Stirbey, a political liberal, to meet Allied representatives in Cairo for discussion of a Rumanian armistice. Stirbey's mission produced no results, nor was a later mission conducted by Constantin Visoianu any more effective. Maniu seemed to be an impotent dreamer. As the price for a Rumanian cease-fire, he demanded that British airborne units be sent to Rumania to protect it from the Soviets, an impossibility from every point of view. Again, on April 16, 1944, Maniu asked Gen. **Maitland Wilson**, commander in chief of the Mediterranean theater (see **Mediterranean and Middle Eastern Theater of Operations**), to dispatch two **airborne divisions** to Rumania. That demand could no more be satisfied than the first. The Allies attempts to pry Rumania out of the war were unsuccessful. If substantive negotiations

with the Rumanians had taken place at that time, London and Washington, both in a mood to placate Moscow, would have tried in every way to be fair to the Soviets. Yet, when de Chastellain and Porter were let out of jail after the Rumanian rebellion in August 1944, the Soviets accused them of secretly negotiating with Antonescu for a separate peace.

The information gathered by British and American services in Rumania was extremely valuable. Acting on that information, British and American bombers converged on the Ploesti petroleum complex. Leaving from **Italy**, the American 15th Strategic Air Force and the 205th **Royal Air Force** Group flew bombing missions on April 5, 15 and 24, 1944, and the American Eighth Strategic Air Force, based in England, hit the oil fields in May. They achieved spectacular results. The total production of Rumanian motor fuel dropped by 85% in May compared to April, by 50% in June and by 25% in September.

Before the summer of 1944, Rumanian guerrillas failed to exhibit as much elan as those in other occupied countries, although they were active in some of the mountainous regions and in the Danube delta. But in August they pulled off a major coup. After Soviet troops mounted furious offensives on August 20 from Iasi, just inside the Rumanian border, and from Kishinev, on Soviet territory, Rumanian guerrillas staged an armed revolt in Bucharest on August 23, four days after the Paris insurrection. In less than half a day, all vital points in the Rumanian capital had been captured, the Antonescu government had been overthrown, and the dictator himself had been put under arrest. The rebellion spread into the countryside, particularly to Ploesti and other important economic centers, which the Rumanians took before the retreating Germans could destroy them. The regular Rumanian army made its political about-face; the king formed a new government and successfully negotiated an armistice with the Allies. As a departing gift, the *Luftwaffe* bombed Bucharest; Rumania responded by declaring war on the Reich. By August 28 not only Bucharest but all the surrounding territory was free of occupation troops. The Rumanians took 5,437 prisoners, including seven generals. On August 30 Soviet troops entered the city without having fired a shot.

The Rumanian revolt was most significant. It tore the whole country and its valuable resources out of the German grasp with comparatively little bloodshed and opened the door to central Europe. Furthermore, it added 14 Rumanian divisions—365,000 soldiers— to Soviet forces, contributing importantly to the liberation of Transylvania, Hungary and Slovakia.

Nor was the Rumanian Resistance restricted by its national frontiers. Rumanians of Yugoslavian origin crossed the Danube to fight under **Tito's** banner. In Slovakia, peasants from northern Transylvania who had been forced into Hungarian labor camps deserted to join the Rumanian guerrillas. In the USSR, deserters from Antonescu's army rallied to the Soviet partisans. Many of the Rumanians who lived in France enlisted individually in the **French Resistance** while others formed the Rumanian National Front, a recognized part of the *Forces francaises de l'interieur.* Among the Rumanians who offered up their lives were Olga Bancic, a member of the *Manouchian* group, who was decapitated on her 32nd birthday in the Stuttgart prison for refusing to talk, even under torture.

Having fallen into the Soviet sphere of influence, Rumania witnessed, between 1945 and 1947, the classical Soviet process—the elimination of all political parties except the Communist Party. On December 30, 1947 King Michael abdicated and the Rumanian People's Republic was proclaimed.

H. Bernard

RUNDSTEDT, Gerd von (1875-1953).

In 1939 Rundstedt was commander in chief of an army group during the German offensive in **Poland** and then led Army Group A in the invasion of France, after which he was promoted to field marshal. Transferred to the Russian front, he commanded Army Group South in 1941-1942. Except for the period between July and September 1944, he was commander in chief of the western front from 1942 to March 1945. Captured in 1945, he was freed four years later.

RUSSIA.

See **USSR.**

RUSSO-FINNISH WINTER WAR.

A secret clause of the **Nazi-Soviet Pact,** which was concluded on August 23, 1939, assigned **Finland** to the Soviet sphere of influence. The **USSR** subsequently forced the **Baltic States** to sign a mutual assistance agreement with it. On Oct. 5, 1939, the Finnish minister of foreign affairs, Eljas Erkko, was invited to Moscow for talks on "specific political questions." In the ensuing discussions, which began on Oct. 12, **Stalin** demanded that Finland follow the example of the Baltic States in signing a mutual assistance pact and that it cede several forward posts on Finnish territory to the USSR for the defense of Leningrad. These demands were rejected; Finland had no intention of giving up either its policy of neutrality of its independence. But Moscow seized on a frontier incident, ostensibly provoked by Finland, as the pretext for renouncing the two countries' nonaggression pact of 1932. On Nov. 30, 1939, Soviet forces attacked at var-

ious points on the Russo-Finnish frontier. Fifteen Finnish divisions under the command of Marshal **Carl Gustav von Mannerheim** repelled 45 Red Army divisions, relying on forest combat to inflict heavy losses on the invaders.

On December 14, 1939 the **League of Nations** declared the USSR an aggressor and excluded it from the collective security system. **Sweden** remained neutral in the conflict, rejecting a league recommendation to aid the Finns. France and the **United Kingdom,** however, shipped arms to the embattled country. On February 5, 1940 the Allied War Council decided to support Finland's defensive struggle by sending an expeditionary army of 50,000 men, but the tide of battle suddenly turned in favor of the Soviets and the point of the gesture was lost. Toward the end of February, overwhelmingly superior Soviet forces breached Mannerheim's secondary defenses and forced the Finns to sue for peace. In return, Moscow withdrew its support from Otto Kuusinen's regime, a puppet communist government that had been established in Terijoki, a frontier town the Red Army had captured earlier in the war. The "Peace of Moscow" was signed on March 15, 1940, ceding the Karelian Isthmus, the city of Vyborg and other Finnish territories in the north, as well as some islands in the Gulf of Finland to the USSR. Hanko, a port on the Baltic, was leased to the Soviets as a naval base.

H.-A. Jacobsen

RUYTER van STEVENINCK, Albert Cornelis de (1895-1949).

A Dutch officer, Ruyter van Steveninck was commander of the *Prinses Irene* Brigade, formed in England. The brigade participated in the fighting in Normandy, **Belgium** and **the Netherlands** from 1944 to 1945. He was promoted to major general in 1949.

S

SABOTAGE.

As its name suggests, sabotage can be a pretty rough business: hurling a sabot (a wooden shoe) into a complicated machine can do a lot of damage quickly, and may not always be traceable. In practice armaments factories were so carefully supervised during the war that such incidents were almost unknown.

An alternative technique, less obtrusive and often more efficient, was used by a great many people who did not wish well to the war effort of the state that controlled their labor. The Czechs were best at this; they applied the technique of their fictional compatriot, Jaroslav Hasek's "Good Soldier Schweik." That is, they were affable and courteous to their taskmasters but hopelessly inefficient. Doing everything much too slowly and not quite the right way, they produced exasperation instead of progress. Railway workers all over western Europe outside **Germany** were almost up to Czech standards of incompetence. The Germans were baffled by go-slow techniques, and lacked the manpower to run all the conquered lines themselves. Repeated appeals by the **British Broadcasting Corporation** and by Radio Moscow to foreign workers in Germany to sabotage the plants they worked in do not seem to have had any noticeable effect, at least none that was noticed at the ministerial level; German Armaments Minister **Albert Speer** was unaware, when interrogated long after the war, that anything of the sort had even been attempted.

Britain's **Special Operations Executive** (SOE) embarked on a much more serious, professional program of sabotage in various occupied countries; highly professional training was given at an SOE school near London by George T. Rheam, the originator of most modern sabotage techniques. Rheam taught his pupils how to examine a factory to check which machines were really indispensable to its working, and then to check these machines to see which part of each of them in turn was decisive. A small plastic bomb (plastic explosives had been invented by one of SOE's organizational forebears), making quite a small bang, could then put a whole factory out of action for months.

The plastic would be exploded by an igniter called a time pencil; a good saboteur would have a pocketful of these, timed to go off at predetermined intervals, ranging from five minutes to 48 hours of their activation. Armed with Rheam's training and SOE's explosives, agents carried out numerous significant acts of sabotage. The destruction of the Gorgopotamos bridge in **Greece** on November 25, 1942 had a significant effect on the movement of German troops around the eastern Mediterranean. Important railway and bridge demolitions were carried out in **Yugoslavia**, **Italy** and **Denmark**. In France the railway system was thoroughly infiltrated by SOE-inspired sabotage teams, and became virtually useless to the Germans. A crack sabotage party (one of whose members, Andre Jarrot, served several times as minister for the quality of life of the Fifth Republic) devastated the canals of northeastern France in the summer of 1943, cutting all those that connected the Rhine to the Mediterranean; it returned in the spring of 1944, neutralizing a chain of electric power stations and thus forcing the Germans to overuse their limited stocks of coal. In France, **Belgium** and **the Netherlands** sabotage of telephone systems advanced so far that the Germans had to do most of their business by radio, resulting in considerable gains for Allied intelligence, especially for **Ultra**. And in **Norway** a party of nine SOE saboteurs brought to an end the entire German attempt to construct an **atomic bomb**—a startling example of the power of sabotage.

Sabotage provided an important element of a grand principle of **strategy**, economy of effort. The trouble was that the high command did not trust saboteurs. Sir **Colin Gubbins**, with all his force of character, could never get his senior British colleagues to treat SOE as they treated, for example, corps artillery. Since they could not themselves go out and watch an operation, or have a photograph brought to them the next morning showing exactly where a bomb had gone off and with what effect, they regarded sabotage as a "bonus," not as an integral part of the war machine.

The Red Army learned better; the consequences are with us today, in the current wave of terrorism.

Sabotage behind the eastern front was kept strictly under Red Army staff control, but one would do well to remember the tale of the sorcerer's apprentice.

M. R. D. Foot

SAINT-NAZAIRE.
This French seaport on the Atlantic was used by the Germans as a submarine base. On March 27, 1942 the British raided it and succeeded, with severe losses, in blowing up the sea gate closing off the entrance to the port.

SAINT-VITH.
Heroically defended by the American Seventh Armored Division, commanded by Maj. Gen. Robert W. Hasbrouck and Brig. Gen. Bruce C. Clarke, this little city in **Belgium** was, from December 18 to 22, 1944, the scene of a climactic engagement in the **Battle of the Bulge**, the decisive event of the winter campaign.

SAIPAN.
Saipan is some 1,250 nautical miles south-southeast of Tokyo. It is one of the principal islands of the Marianas, a group which stretches for 425 miles from Farallon de Pajaros, 335 miles southeast of **Iwo Jima**, to **Guam**, 250 miles north of the Carolines. Saipan is approximately 14 miles long and six and a half miles wide, its long axis running generally north-south; it is irregularly shaped, and its total area is roughly 72 square miles. The east coast is free of reefs, the west coast fringed with them; the east and north shores are marked by steep cliffs that plunge to the water's edge, while the western coast is low-lying and offers few obstacles to movement. American landings thus, unsurprisingly, occurred on the western shores. Mount Tapotchau is the highest point on Saipan and is located almost exactly in the center of the island; it is 1,552 feet high and extremely steep. Northern and eastern Saipan is hilly and rolling.

The Allies invaded the Marianas in order to acquire secure bases for the long-range aerial bombardment of the Japanese home islands. The B-29 bases in **China** proved vulnerable to Japanese overland advances, as Gen. **Henry H. Arnold** had predicted; in anticipation of this development the Army Air Force threw its support to Adm. **Ernest J. King**'s proposal for an Allied advance through the Central Pacific. Gen. **MacArthur** had opposed this offensive orientation, arguing instead for a line of advance through the southwestern Pacific. The eventual compromise included two concurrent, mutually supporting series of operations: MacArthur's route was through **New Guinea** and **Indonesia** to the **Philippines**; Adm.

Chester W. Nimitz's was through the Central Pacific. Nimitz's route was to receive priority, as it was expected to provide a more rapid advance toward **Japan**, sever vital lines of communication, provide swifter acquisition of strategic air bases and provoke a decisive battle with the Japanese fleet. Campaign Plan Granite II, inaugurated by the seizure of Saipan, would achieve all of these objectives.

The Japanese anticipated an American invasion but misjudged its timing. The original American plans targeted Saipan for November 15, 1944, and this was the approximate date by which Japanese defenses were scheduled for completion. The invasion was moved up to November 1, then to September 1; when the decision was made to neutralize Truk and leapfrog it, the final date of June 15 was selected. The speed of the American advance through the **Gilbert Islands** and the Marshall Islands, and the leapfrogging of the central Carolines, left little time for the shipment of lumber, steel, cement and barbed wire from Japan; the devastating American submarine campaign destroyed much of what was shipped. The Japanese planned to meet the invasion at the water's edge, in strict adherence to their military doctrine, and defensive works were sited accordingly. Saipan's natural obstacles, which canalized movement, its long fields of fire, its good cover and excellent observation points were not fully exploited; troops were frequently frittered away in wasteful counterattacks. The brilliance that characterized the defense of Peleliu, Iwo Jima and **Okinawa** was yet to come.

The Japanese garrison included the 43rd Division (reinforced), the 47th Mixed Brigade (three infantry and three artillery battalions plus an engineer company), the 55th Naval Guard Force, the First Yokosuka Special Naval Landing Force, a **tank** regiment, an antiaircraft regiment, two regiments of engineers, two transportation companies, an independent infantry battalion and numerous other units stranded on Saipan at the time of the invasion, for a total of 29,662 troops. Although well equipped with field artillery, the Japanese lacked sufficient means to move their large pieces and were forced to abandon guns in the course of withdrawals. The strategic surprise achieved by the invasion resulted in the capture of considerable quantities of heavy weapons left in naval depots, on railroad flat cars and near incompletely excavated gun positions. In spite of every shortcoming the commanders of the Saipan force, Lt. Gen. Yoshitsugu Saito and Vice Adm. **Chuichi Nagumo**, possessed one considerable asset: their tenacious, enterprising and brave troops.

Adm. Raymond A. Spruance, commander of the Fifth Fleet, directed all forces involved in Granite II, under Nimitz's overall command. Vice Adm. Richmond K. Turner commanded the Joint Expeditionary Force employed in the amphibious operations in the Marianas, and Gen. Holland M. Smith led the expeditionary troops—the Second and Fourth Marine Divisions under Maj. Gens. Thomas E. Watson and Harry Schmidt, the First Provisional Marine Brigade and the 27th and 77th Army Infantry Divisions. The pre-invasion bombardment of Saipan lasted three and a half days and destroyed the bulk of Japanese air and seapower in the vicinity, but it was less effective against defensive works. The seven fast battleships arrived before the minesweepers and were forced to fire at ranges in excess of 10,000 yards, precluding direct fire. Area fire was far less effective against fortifications, and the survival of Japanese shore batteries acted as a magnet for naval gunfire and air strikes, further diverting attention from infantry works. The old battleships, more accomplished in shore bombardment, arrived on D-1, and had only a single day to employ their superior skills. Air-spotter training was inadequate, and ammunition had to be conserved for use against Guam. The shortcomings of the bombardment were partially offset by the incomplete state of the Japanese works, but the inevitable tradeoff was naval firepower for Marine blood.

On June 15 the Second and Fourth Marine Divisions began landing on Saipan's western shore, while a demonstration off Tanapag Harbor pinned down one Japanese regiment to their north. By nightfall two shallow beachheads, half the day's territorial goal, had been established in the face of stiff resistance, at a cost of over 2,000 casualties. The expected nocturnal counterattacks were poorly coordinated, as Japanese artillery had been by day. Star shells and naval gunfire, along with the firepower already established within the Marine perimeters, made the attacks a costly failure. On D+1 Marines linked up and modestly expanded their beachheads, built up artillery, armor and troops and were further reinforced by elements of the 27th Infantry Division. By D-Day, however, the invasion of Saipan had already achieved one of its primary objectives; it had lured the Japanese Combined Fleet from Philippine waters, and on D+1 Spruance postponed the Guam landing and moved to meet the Japanese. The remainder of the Marianas campaign was predetermined: the Japanese on Saipan were doomed.

The Japanese contested the inevitable yard by yard. Aslito airfield fell on June 18 and Hill 500 on June 20, D+5, although the Japanese breakout from Nafutan Point reached both areas before extinction. The American rear was harassed by artillery, snipers, boobytraps and mines, and was pocketed with holdouts ensconced in caves and spider holes. Infiltrators were persistent and sometimes successful; on the

night of June 21-22 an ammunition dump was blown up on beach Green 1, with considerable loss. By D+5 the southern quarter of Saipan, with the exception of Nafutan Point, had been secured, within the limits described above. On D+7 the drive to the north began with the capture of Mount Tipo Pale; on D+8 the Marines advanced through the evocatively named Death Valley and against Purple Heart Ridge. Infantry and armor counterattacks and harrowing terrain delayed the capture of Mount Tapotchau until D+12, after which the Americans enjoyed the advantages of superior observation. Savage fighting continued through the first week of July, culminating in the most devastating banzai attack of the war, on the night of July 6-7. Saipan was declared secured on July 9, although hundreds of Japanese continued to resist, some for over a year. The announcement of American victory provoked mass suicides among the Japanese civilian population in the north; hundreds jumped to their death from the sea cliffs. Total American casualties on Saipan were 14,224; about 24,000 Japanese were killed and 1,780 prisoners were taken, over half of whom were Korean. The Japanese studied their mistakes on Saipan, drew the appropriate conclusions and applied them to lethal effect: a smaller garrison on Iwo Jima inflicted twice the number of casualties.

F. Smoler

SALAZAR, Antonio de Oliveira (1889-1970).
After becoming prime minister of **Portugal** in 1932, Salazar ran the country with dictatorial powers for the next 36 years (see the Introduction). He secured Portugal's neutrality throughout the war but eventually allowed the Allies to build a base in the Azores.

SALO, Republic of.
See **Italy; Mussolini.**

SAS.
See **Special Air Service.**

SAUCKEL, Fritz (1894-1946).
A German *Gauleiter*, Sauckel was appointed high commissioner of labor in 1942. He was ordered by **Hitler** to requisition workers in the occupied countries (see **Forced Labor Battalions**). He was condemned to death at Nuremberg as a **war criminal** and executed.

SCAVENIUS, Erik (1877-1962).
Denmark's foreign minister from 1940 to 1943 and prime minister in 1942-43, Scavenius tried to cooperate with **Germany** in the best interests of his country but gave up when he judged German demands too insistent.

425

SCHACHT, Hjalmar (1877-1970).
From 1924 to 1930 and 1933 to 1939, Schacht was president of the Reichsbank. He became **Germany's** minister of ecnmics in 1934 and plenipotentiary of war economy in 1935. By using methods similar to those employed by **Roosevelt** in the **United States**, attributable to the theories of the British economist **John Maynard Keynes**, he engineered the financing of Germany's rearmament. A political neutral, although once a member of the democratic *Deutsche Staatspartei*, he resigned from his ministerial functions when **Hitler** refused to reduce the military expenditures he deemed inflationary, and he warned that the German economy could not support a lengthy war. After joining the opposition to the Fuehrer, he was arrested in 1944 and imprisoned in Ravensbrueck. He was tried as a **war criminal** by the Nuremberg tribunal in 1946 and acquitted.

SCHELLENBERG, Walter (1911-1952).
The head of the **SD** *Ausland*, Schellenberg was involved in the numerous intrigues of the Nazi regime. Toward the end of the war, Schellenberg, who had developed contacts with the Swiss and the Allies, urged **Heinrich Himmler** to negotiate a peace treaty. Although sentenced in 1949 to six years in prison as a **war criminal**, he was freed in 1951.

SCHOERNER, Ferdinand (1892-1973).
Schoerner, a German field marshal, was commander in chief of the 17th Army. In 1945 he was appointed commander in chief of the south, center and north army groups.

SCHOLL, Hans (1918-1943) and Sophie (1921-1943).
Brother and sister, they were leaders of the "White Rose" **German Resistance** movement. Driven by a completely unselfish faith in their country and humanity, they were arrested for distributing leaflets at the University of Munich and condemned to death by the People's Tribunal. They were beheaded.

SCHUMAN, Robert (1886-1963).
A French jurist and deputy from the Moselle, Schuman was undersecretary of state for refugees in 1940. Deported in 1942, he escaped, became an advocate of a united Europe and in 1950 began the movement for a European common market for coal and steel.

SCHUMANN, Maurice (1911-   ).
A French official, Schumann joined the Free French in 1940 and was the **British Broadcasting Coporation** spokesman for **Free France**. He served in Gen. **Leclerc's** division in 1944. From 1944 to 1945 he was a member of the Consultative Assembly.

SCHUSCHNIGG, Kurt von (1897-1978).
Schuschnigg became chancellor of Austria after the assassination of Engelbert Dollfuss in July 1934. Although he initially resisted **Hitler's** effort to incorporate **Austria** under German rule, he was intimidated by the Fuehrer's demands for a closer union between **Germany** and Austria in a February 1938 meeting. After an unsuccessful attempt to have the question of Austria's independence resolved by a plebiscite, he was forced to resign. Arrested after the *Anschluss* on March 13, 1938 (see also the Introduction), he was imprisoned by the Nazis until 1945. At the Nuremberg **war criminals** trials in 1946, he testified for the prosecution.

SCHUTZSTAFFEL.
See **SS**.

SCOBIE, Sir Ronald (1893-1969).
Scobie, a British general, headed the Tobruk garrison in 1941, the **Malta** garrison in 1942-43, the Middle East Command in 1943-44 and British troops in **Greece** in 1944-46.

SD (Sicherheitsdienst).
The security service of the **SS** under the orders of **Heinrich Himmler** (see **Gestapo**).

SECOND FRONT.
During the first year of **Germany's** attack on the **USSR** (see **USSR—War with Germany**), the **United States** was preoccupied with the war in the Pacific and the **United Kingdom** with its precarious hold on northeastern Africa and the catastrophe in its Southeast Asian **empire**. The Western Desert front, with its wide oscillations, did not occupy as many as 20 divisions of all nationalities; on the eastern front hundreds were locked in combat. Basic fairness seemed to suggest that the Americans and the British should take some of the load of slaughter off the Soviets' shoulders.

The Dieppe raid on August 19, 1942 was widely acclaimed as a dress rehearsal. The better informed people were about the reasons for the raid's failures, the less optimistic they were about mounting a second front quickly. The traditonal difficulties of operating with ships against a fortified coast (see **Atlantic Wall**) were multiplied in the days of **radar**, long-range artillery and dive bombers.

A brisk **propaganda** campaign for a "second front

now,'' which may have originated on Communist initiative, and certainly preoccupied many who sincerely sympathized with the Communists, raged in Britain and the United States from the summer of 1943 to the summer of 1944. The will to create a second front on the European mainland, and so relieve the USSR's burden, was there; **Roosevelt, Churchill** and the Combined Chiefs of Staff all felt it acutely. The real obstacle was a technical one, known only to a select few and angrily brushed aside as unimportant by the Soviets whenever it was mentioned to them: lack of shipping, especially of **landing craft. Hitler** had abandoned his attempt to invade England in September 1940 because he could not win the aerial **Battle of Britain**; even had he won it, Adm. **Erich Raeder** presented a formidable list of naval difficulties, headed by the impossibility of securing enough troop-carrying barges (the barges of Europe's inland waterways were hopelessly unsuitable for operations in tidal waters). The raiding experience of the **commandos and rangers** in 1941-42 gave the British and Americans something to go on, but not until autumn 1942 could adequate shipping be assembled for the Northwest African landing of November 8 (**Torch**). Even during this operation difficulties and defects were encountered. Adequate landing craft were available for the landings in Sicily and at Salerno and Anzio in the second half of 1943, and the opening of the Italian front did take a little pressure off the USSR.

A fleet of landing craft and transports, whose size was unprecedented, was assembled in Britain during the winter of 1943-44, and at last on June 6, 1944 a formal Second Front was opened (see **Normandy Landing**). By this time about 60 German divisions were stationed in western Europe waiting for it; so were almost all the German navy's forces and over a third of the *Luftwaffe*'s.

M. R. D. Foot

SECRET SERVICES.
See **Information Services**.

SEELOEWE.
(In English, ''Sea Lion.'') Code name of the German plan for a landing in Great Britain to be carried out in the fall of 1940. It was put off until the spring of 1941 and finally abandoned altogether because of the defeat of the *Luftwaffe* in the **Battle of Britain**. (See also **United Kingdom; World War II—General Conduct.**)

SELBORNE, Third Earl of (Roundell Cecil Palmer) (1887-1971).
As minister of economic warfare from 1942 to 1945, Selborne, a British Conservative leader, took political responsibility for the **Special Operations Executive**.

SERVIZIO INFORMAZIONE MILITARE (SIM).
Italy's SIM organization was responsible for gathering, controlling and exploiting useful information concerning foreign armies and states. It also developed the counterespionage services for the preparation of its own military forays. With its various sections it was a branch of the Italian army and, at the time of **Mussolini**'s entry into the war, was joined not only by the parallel autonomous organizations of the navy and air force but also by an independent organization for counterespionage and special services. This peculiar structure of information-gathering agencies led to difficulties in coordination that repeated reorganization failed to resolve.

Rarely informed of the intentions of the Italian command, the SIM furnished precise data on the ''order of battle of the enemy'' before Mussolini's assaults on France, **Greece** and **Yugoslavia**. Despite its relative precision, however, this data was either misinterpreted or completely ignored. The same was true during the African campaign and the Soviet offensive in the winter of 1941. But **Germany**'s intentions in the event of Italy's abandonment of the struggle—of which Mussolini was well aware—were not neglected.

J. Schroder

SEXTANT CONFERENCE.
See **Conferences, Allied.**

SEYSS-INQUART, Arthur (1892-1946).
An Austrian Nazi, Seyss-Inquart briefly succeeded **Kurt von Schuschnigg** as chancellor of **Austria** in March 1938. He became deputy governor-general of the **General Government for Occupied Poland** in October 1939. From May 1940 until his arrest by the Canadian army in May 1945, he was *Reichskommissar* for the **Netherlands**. He was hanged after being sentenced to death by the Nuremberg **war criminals** tribunal.

SHAPOSHNIKOV, Boris (1882-1945).
A former staff officer of the czar, Shaposhnikov entered the Red Army in 1917 and directed its Operations Office during the Russian civil war. He became **Stalin**'s military adviser and assistant commissar for defense. As chief of the general staff from 1937 to 1942, he organized the army by converting it to combat readiness.

SHIGEMITSU, Mamoru (1887-1957).
Shigemitsu, a Japanese diplomat and a cabinet minister, graduated from Tokyo Imperial University, with

a specialty in German law, in 1911; in April 1912 he was sent to Berlin as a member of the diplomatic corps. Upon the outbreak of World War I, in August 1914, Shigemitsu was transferred to London, where his sympathy for Anglo-Saxon institutions, his life-long friendships with prominent Britons and his an-tipathy to militarism took root. He became Japanese consul in Portland, Oregon in 1918; in 1919 he was assigned to Japan's delegation to the Versailles Peace Conference.

Except for a six-month stint in Berlin in 1928, Shigemitsu was stationed in China from 1925 through 1933, where he worked long and hard for improved Sino-Japanese relations. During the Shanghai inci-dent, in April 1932, he managed to induce uncooper-ative local Japanese army commanders to accept a cease-fire, leading to a full-scale truce. He was severe-ly injured by a Korean bomb-thrower the following day at a ceremony in Shanghai celebrating the agree-ment; nevertheless he managed to sign the final ac-cord a week later from his hospital bed.

After one of his legs was amputated, Shigemitsu re-turned to duty in May 1933 as vice-minister for for-eign affairs under Count Yasuyu Uhida and **Koki Hirota**. During this period he encountered mounting army hostility, particularly because of his benign at-titude toward China and the **United Kingdom**, and was consequently prevented from receiving an ap-pointment as ambassador to China. Despite such hos-tility he became ambassador to the **USSR**; he served in Moscow from 1936 through 1938. A great test of his abilities occurred in July-August 1938, when Japanese and Soviet armies clashed in strength over disputed Korean-Siberian boundary at Changkufeng Hill (in what became known to the Soviets as the Lake Khasan affair). During negotiations in Moscow that he him-self termed "extremely unpleasant and severe," Shigemitsu and Foreign Commissar **Maxim Litvinov** finally hammered out a cease-fire ending the crisis, ef-fective August 11. For his stubborn, stern handling of the parleys, he earned the Soviets' enmity, as would be seen after World War II.

In September 1938 Shigemitsu was transferred to London as ambassador, at a time when Anglo-Japa-nese relations were at an especially delicate stage. He served with distinction in England until the war broke out, against his wishes, in December 1941. During the war Shigemitsu served as ambassador to "puppet" China from 1941 to 1943; as foreign minister from April 1943 to April 1945, in the cabinets of **Hideki Tojo**, **Kuniaki Koiso** and **Mitsumasa Yonai**; and again as foreign minister in the first postsurrender cabinet under Prince **Naruhiko Higashikuni**, in August-Sep-tember 1945.

It was Shigemitsu who limped aboard the USS *Mis-*

souri in Tokyo Bay on September 2, 1945 to sign the instrument of surrender "by command and in behalf of the emperor of Japan and the Japanese govern-ment"—a painful duty, for his army counterpart despised him as "a detestable '**Badoglio**,'" and Allied spectators aboard the *Missouri* regarded his discomfiture with "savage satisfaction." Soon after-ward, he was arrested by occupation authorities as a suspected **war criminal**, reportedly only at Soviet behest. In 1948 he was sentenced to seven years' im-prisonment, although he was exonerated on three main counts, including the crucial Count 1, overall conspiracy, and Count 55, conspiracy to wage aggres-sive war at Changkufeng. His was the lightest sentence imposed on any of the 25 surviving Japanese Class A defendants (none went free). Sixteen eminent Britons and Americans, including Lord **Hankey** and U.S. dip-lomat Joseph Davies, spontaneously volunteered to send statements on his behalf to the unrelenting In-ternational Military Tribunal for the Far East. He was released on parole in 1950; his jail term, commuted to five years, expired in 1951.

In the liberal postwar climate, he reentered politics after the occupation ended. He became president of the new Progressive Party in 1952; on the merger of the Progressives with the new Japan Democratic Party in November 1954, Shigemitsu became vice-president and Ichiro Hatoyama president. Shigemitsu served as foreign minister once more in Prime Minister Hatoyama's cabinet, from 1955 to 1956. Ironically he negotiated the restoration of Soviet-Japanese diplomatic relations in autumn 1956 under Hatoyama's aegis.

Shigemitsu's long, distinguished career earned him a reputation for being methodical, deliberate, self-assured, orthodox and ardently loyal to the throne. Some critics in Japan called him a cold, inflexible, petty bureaucrat of limited vision and, surprisingly, even a tool of the army. Few, however, would take issue with **Yosuke Matsuoka**'s characterization of him as "a type who can endure boiling water in the bathtub."

A. D. Coox

SHIRATORI, Toshio (1887-1949).

A Japanese diplomat and nationalist spokesman, Shiratori was associated with the renovationist clique in the bureaucracy. He joined the foreign ministry in 1929 and established close ties with the military. After urging expansion into Manchuria, he argued that the Slavic peoples and the Japanese were fated to clash over Asia. In April 1937 he scoffed at democracy as "obsolete" and declared that "surely totalitarianism will be the political philosophy of the future." Shiratori became ambassador to **Italy** in 1939 and helped negotiate the **Tripartite Pact** in September 1940. He was tried as a **war criminal** by the International Military Tribunal for the Far East and found guilty in 1948; the following year he died in jail.

SIAM.
See **Thailand**.

SICHERHEITSDIENST.
See **SD**.

SICILY, Invasion of.
See **Mediterranean** and **Middle Eastern Theater of Operations**.

SIKORSKI, Wladyslaw (1881-1943).
After serving as **Poland**'s prime minister in 1922-23 and war minister in 1924-25, Sikorski, beginning on September 30, 1939, was again prime minister and commander in chief of the Polish **government-in-exile**. In July 1941 he and **Stalin** entered an agreement bringing an end to the state of war between Poland and the **USSR** and abrogating the Soviet-German partition of Poland. Sikorski was killed on July 4, 1943, when his plane crashed taking off from **Gibraltar**.

SIKORSKY, Igor (1889-1972).
Sikorsky, a Russian-born American aircraft engineer, invented the helicopter in 1939.

SIMA, Horia (1906-?).
A Rumanian fascist, Sima served in the Rumanian government in 1940-41. Thereafter he fled to **Germany**. He ran a German-dominated puppet regime from Vienna between August 1944 and April 1945, when he vanished.

SIMPSON, William (1888-1980).
Commander of the American Ninth Army operating in the region of Aachen and later on the Rur, Simpson, a lieutenant general, crossed the Rhine on March 24, 1945 to conquer Magdeburg and Wittenberg, and forced passage of the Elbe River on April 13.

SINGAPORE.
Singapore (225 square miles including Singapore Island and the smaller adjacent islands) was, in 1940, a British crown colony with a strategic naval base; it was captured by the Japanese on February 5, 1942.

SIS.
See **Special Intelligence Service**.

SKORZENY, Otto (1908-1975).
A German **SS** officer, Skorzeny performed several special missions under orders from the **RSHA**. In 1943 he liberated **Mussolini** from imprisonment by Italian **Resistance** forces and in 1944 kidnapped the son of Adm. **Miklos von Horthy** of Hungary in order to force the regent to end his secret negotiations with the **USSR** and **Yugoslavia** and then to resign. During the **Battle of the Bulge** he disguised German soldiers as Americans to cause trouble in Allied lines. He was acquitted in the Nuremberg **war criminals** trial in 1946. (See also **Nazi Treasure**.)

SLEDGEHAMMER.
Code name for a limited Anglo-American landing in France in 1942. It was replaced by Operation Torch, the landing in North Africa on November 7, 1942. (See **World War II—General Conduct**.)

SLESSOR, Sir John C. (1897-   ).
A British air officer, Slessor was director of plans from 1937 to 1939 and participated in the talks leading to the **ABC Plans** in 1941. Slessor headed the **Royal Air Force** Coastal Command in 1943 and commanded the RAF in the Middle East in 1944-45. In 1950 he became chief of air staff.

SLIM, Sir William Joseph (later Viscount) (1891-1970).
After service in World War I, Slim joined the Indian army. He led Indian units in North Africa, **Iran** and **Iraq**. In 1942 he was sent to **Burma** to command the First Corps, which was forced by the Japanese to retreat into **India**. In late 1943 he was put in charge of the 14th Army and in 1944-45 led it in the Allied counteroffensive in Burma. His force succeeded in driving the Japanese from Imphal and Kohima. An exceptionally good general, Slim was strategically sound and logistically brilliant.

SMITH, Walter Bedell (1895-1961).
Smith, who had served with the U.S. Army in France in 1918, was selected in 1942 to be Gen. **Eisenhower**'s chief of staff. He helped plan the **Normandy landing**, negotiated the surrender of **Italy** and arranged for Germany's surrender. Eisenhower called him a master of detail with a clear understanding of important issues. Smith served as American ambassador to the **USSR** from 1946 to 1949 and as head of the Central Intelligence Agency from 1950 to 1953.

SMUTS, Jan Christiaan (1870-1950).
A South African political leader, Smuts fought the British from 1899 to 1902 but was later reconciled with them and became a friend of **Churchill**. He

fought the Germans in 1916-17 and was a member of the British war cabinet in 1917-18. During his second term as prime minister of **South Africa**, from 1939 to 1948, Smuts brought his country into the war on the Allied side. He was a strong advocate of the **United Nations**.

SOCIETY.
Society was necessarily much shaken by the war, with its scale and with the casualties, disruption and ruin it caused. In a few areas (eastern Europe, Southeast Asia) the war brought a complete social **revolution**, though in most the fundamentals of society remained the same.

The family is still the world's basic social unit; people still wear clothes in public; people still need to work for a living. But myriad individual families were disrupted by war casualties or by the strains of prolonged separation of partners. And millions of young men and women who had hardly been separated from their families before had to learn to live apart from them, usually under conditions of discipline that did not much endear collective systems to them.

World War I had proved the possibility of state action, on a very large scale, both nationally and internationally; such a body as the Allied Maritime Transport Council was the envy of later shipping controllers. Manipulation of very large bodies of men and machines advanced further; operations as complex as Gen. **Douglas MacArthur**'s multiple landings in the **Philippines** or "Neptune," the invasion of Normandy (see **Normandy Landing**), were far more intricate than any general staff in World War I, even Max Hoffman's, could have managed to control. Paradoxically, to have played a part in one of these gigantic combinations did not necessarily prejudice people in favor of very large-scale action. After six years of being ordered about, people valued their individuality more than ever.

The war saw the end, or at least the diminution, of a number of social prejudices: that **women** are in any sense the inferior sex; that government always knows best; that there is anything admirable in **empire**, or ranting, or slaughter. Enormous social sacrifices had been made to get rid of **fascism** and Nazism, and the revelations concerning the **concentration camps** in the closing weeks of the European war satisfied everybody that this war, at least, had been one worth fighting. Those who fought learned something about courage, and comradeship, and the worth of joint action. On the whole, those who learned most, and were most frightened, say least about it.

M. R. D. Foot

SOE.
See **Special Operations Executive**.

SOKOLOVSKI, Vasili D. (1897-1968).
A Soviet general, Sokolovski was head of the chiefs of staff of various army groups ("fronts") and commander of the western front in 1943-44.

SOLOMON SEA, Second Battle of the.
See **Eastern Solomons**.

SOMALIA.
In the mid-1890s Somalia was divided into three colonial states: a semicircular French portion around Djibouti, a British strip running nearly 450 miles eastward towards Cape Gardafui and an Italian strip running southwestward from the British portion along the coast to the Kenyan border.

In July 1940 the **French State** indicated it would no longer cooperate with the **United Kingdom**, whose plans for the defense of British Somaliland had hinged on French support. **Italy** occupied the British colony in August 1940. **Archibald Wavell**'s expedition into **Ethiopia** in January 1941 squeezed the Italians out of both British and Italian Somaliland; they thereupon surrendered.

The two colonies were fused into the Somali Democratic Republic in 1960.

M. R. D. Foot

SONAR.
An acronym for Sound Navigation Ranging. During World War I, Paul Langevin used the piezoelectric properties of quartz crystals for tracing the movements of submarines and other underwater objects through ultrasonics. In the period between the wars, this technique was employed in a system for preventing collisions between vessels in fog. The efficient propagation of ultrasonic waves in water was also used in a device for continuous sounding of sea depths. Improved considerably by the British before 1939 and the U.S. Department of the Navy during the war, sonar, in combination with **radar**, contributed significantly to an Allied victory in the sea war, notably the **Battle of the Atlantic**, by increasing the Allies' ability to defect German and Japanese submarines.

SORGE, Richard (1895-1944).
Sorge was a grandson of one of Karl Marx's correspondents and the son of one of the founders of **Germany**'s Communist Party. Under cover of the *Frankfurter Zeitung*, for which he was the Japanese correspondent since 1933, Sorge was a spy in the service of the **USSR**, using the pseudonym "Ika." Ar-

rested in October 1941, he was hanged in 1944 (see *Narodnyy Kommissariat Vnutrennikh Del*).

SOUTH AFRICA.

South Africa joined the war on the Allied side on September 4, 1939 on the motion of **Jan Smuts**, who then became prime minister and went on to receive a large majority in the general election of 1943. Opposition to the war was widespread in the Afrikaner community, but Smuts refused to prosecute opponents. Two divisions of volunteers fought in **Ethiopia** and the Western Desert; over a third of all South Africans then serving were taken prisoner at Tobruk in July 1942. The South African air force and various technical services fought with distinction in the Mediterranean. South African port facilities were important to **convoys** en route to **Egypt** and **India**.

SOVIET CHAIN OF COMMAND.

See **Chain of Command, Soviet.**

SOVIET UNION.

See **USSR.**

SPAAK, Paul-Henri (1899-1973).

Belgian minister of foreign affairs from 1939 to 1944, Spaak left for London with Premier **Hubert Pierlot** in August 1940, three months after the German invasion of **Belgium**. At the time of the invasion, Spaak and Pierlot had strongly urged King **Leopold III** to continue the struggle against the Nazis in France at the side of the Allies, but Leopold refused to leave Belgium. The two ministers eventually set up a Belgian **government-in-exile** in England. Spaak returned to Belgium in 1944.

SPAATZ, Carl (1891-1974).

With **William Donovan**'s help, Spaatz, an American airman, convinced **Roosevelt** that the British would survive in 1940. Following **Pearl Harbor** he was chief of the Air Force Combat Command and in 1942 became head of the U.S. Eighth Air Force. In the summer of that year, he and his units were sent to England. In 1943 Spaatz led the Northwest African Air Forces and then the Mediterranean Allied Air Forces. He commanded the U.S. Strategic Air Forces in Europe (1944-45). In that post he secured air superiority over **Germany** and German-held territory by concentrating attacks on vital industrial targets, particularly oil refineries and related installations which the Germans had to defend (see **Germany, Air Battle of**). In 1945-46 Spaatz held command of U.S. Strategic Air Forces in the Pacific.

SPAIN.

The Spanish civil war ended in 1939, after **Franco**'s nationalist troops entered Barcelona on January 25 and Madrid on March 28. They had succeeded in conquering republican Spain with the aid of the Italian Fascists and German Nazis. In February 1939 France and the **United Kingdom**, recognized the new state; they were joined by the **United States** in April 1939. In March 1939 "*El Caudillo*" signed the Anti-Comintern Pact. When the war broke out, the Spanish chief of state unsuccessfully attempted to mediate. But in June 1940 he changed from "neutral" to "nonbelligerent," his sympathies drawing him ever closer to the **Axis** powers, whose military triumphs in the west evidently impressed him. He took advantage of the situation by occupying the international zone of Tangier on June 14 without regard to the protests of the western European powers. When France asked **Germany** for an armistice, Franco informed the German government that he was prepared, "after a brief interval for convincing public opinion," to enter the war. In exchange, he demanded **Gibraltar**, Morocco and various territories in West Africa, including Guinea. He also requested delivery of war materiel, raw materials and **food** products. Out of consideration for France, however, Berlin refused to commit itself.

On October 23 Franco and **Hitler** met at Hendaye. Franco did not repeat his proposal; he indicated that he would not enter the war, nor would he permit German troops to traverse Spanish territory for an attack on Gibraltar. As long as Great Britain remained unconquered, he could not place in jeopardy the power he had just won unless absolutely necessary. In a protocol, *El Caudillo* simply said that he was ready to join the Axis and that, eventually, he would participate in the war. He saw in the German invasion of the **USSR** in June 1941 a convenient occasion to restate, at least symbolically, his sympathy with the Nazi cause. On June 22 the Spanish government declared its readiness to engage in the war "against Russian Communism." A division of volunteers (the *Azul*) was activated under the command of Gen. Munoz Grandes and sent to the eastern front (from which it was to retire in March 1944). From the Axis point of view, this was hardly adequate compensation for the cancellation of operation "Isabella-Felix"—the attack the Germans had planned on Gibraltar.

After the Allied landing in North Africa in November 1942, Franco decreed partial mobilization to guarantee Spanish neutrality. As the military balance began to shift, and with the encouragement of Sir **Samuel Hoare**, the British ambassador to Madrid, Franco reoriented his policy toward the Allies. He closed the German consulate general in Tangier and expelled all German nationals from Morocco in May

1944. At the same time he reduced tungsten exports to Germany. Finally, on May 7, 1945 Spain severed diplomatic relations with Germany. The Franco government was, nevertheless, not among the signatories to the **United Nations** Charter.

H. A. Jacobsen

SPEARS, Sir Edward Louis (1886-1974).

A British soldier and politician, Spears was active in liaison work between the British and French armies in May-June 1940. He got **de Gaulle** out of France on June 16, 1940 and led the British mission to **Syria** and **Lebanon** from 1941 to 1945. Spears was a close friend of **Churchill**.

SPECIAL AIR SERVICE (SAS).

The SAS was formed as a regiment of the British army in **Egypt** at the end of 1941 to conduct raids in the western Sahara. It developed, under **David Stirling** and R. B. Mayne, into a small but redoubtable combat force. Each of its members was a volunteer; each was trained in **sabotage**.

SAS members typically parachuted into occupied countries in small groups of about 10 men each. Their goal was to create as much confusion as possible among enemy forces without being discovered. The only factor limiting the length of their missions was the possibility of capture.

The SAS sought information, hindered enemy communications and telecommunications, attacked vital objectives and identified targets for Allied bombers. Offensively they infiltrated specific areas in large numbers, spreading false rumors and working with local **Resistance** units; later in the war they prepared landing areas for **airborne divisions**. Defensively they specialized in information gathering and in undermining the war economy (notably in **Norway**). They conducted raids against airfields, depots etc.

The original SAS unit operated in Libya, meeting with considerable success—Mayne, for example, destroyed 47 Italian aircraft in a single night—and an occasional failure: Stirling was taken prisoner. The unit subsequently fought in Sicily and in Calabria. A second SAS battalion was eventually formed, and both were brought back to Scotland at the beginning of 1944 to form the SAS Brigade. Commanded by **Roderick W. McLeod**, it included a British general staff; four small regiments of about 600 men each—two British and two Free French; a Belgian company; and a **Phantom** radio company.

The SAS was particularly effective in western Europe in 1944-45. On the night of June 6, 1944 (see **Normandy Landing**), the Second French Regiment of parachutists landed in Brittany and brought about a general insurrection throughout the peninsula, resulting in the rupture of all communications with the interior of France and delaying considerably the transfer of German units from Brittany to Normandy. The First and Second British SAS regiments, the First French Regiment and the Belgian company were landed, over the next few weeks, in the hills of Perche, along the Seine, in the Eure-et-Loir department southwest of Paris and in the Morvan mountain range and, later, in the Ardennes and the Vosges. Everywhere they acted in conjunction with the local Resistance, harassing retreating enemy troops, furnishing information on the movements of enemy units and on targets to the Allied air forces and rescuing hundreds of downed Allied aviators. In August 1944 the Second British SAS Regiment carried out the memorable Operation **Wallace**, crossing France from Rennes to Epinal in 20 armored jeeps, spreading havoc among the enemy's rear guard with the aid of the Resistance. In the Vosges in September 1944, 90 SAS troops held out against an entie **SS** division for three weeks. An SAS group in the Morvan forest used, with considerable effect, a 57-mm antitank cannon that had been parachuted to them.

The SAS experienced heavy losses: around 40 percent. Over 100 captured SAS members fell under the *Nacht und Nebel* decree, although they were wearing uniforms; of these, only four returned unharmed. The damages the SAS inflicted on the enemy were considerable; it was especially effective in creating diversions and undercutting German plans. The officers and men of the SAS possessed enormous impetuosity, enterprising spirit and mobility—so much so that some of them managed to liberate the northern part of **the Netherlands** and all of Norway, overcoming the flabbergasted German garrisons there largely by force of personality.

H. Bernard
M. R. D. Foot

SPECIAL INTELLIGENCE SERVICE (SIS).

British military espionage service, earlier known as **MI-6** (see **Intelligence Service**).

SPECIAL OPERATIONS EXECUTIVE (SOE).

The SOE was a British secret service intended to stimulate **resistance**. It was formed in July 1940 by the fusion of a **propaganda** branch of the Foreign Office, a research branch of the War Office and a small but lively section of the **Intelligence Service** that had recently been created "to investigate every possibility of attacking potential enemies by means other than the operations of military forces," particularly by clandestine means in **Germany**. In August 1941 the SOE shed its propaganda element, which became the separate **Political Warfare Executive**. By that time it was already a worldwide organization.

Constitutional responsibility for the SOE was accepted by the minister of economic warfare—first **Hugh Dalton**, then **Lord Selborne**; from time to time it received directives from the chiefs of staff or the prime minister, **Churchill** himself. But the work was necessarily too intricate for ordinary ministerial control to apply; Parliament was given no chance to discuss it. A succession of executive heads—**Gladwyn Jebb, Frank Nelson, Charles Hambro** and **Colin Gubbins**—did have some direct personal control over policy and a little power over operations. They stood at the peak of a staff pyramid. Next below them came a council of heads of departments and advisers from other organizations, numbering nearly 20 and meeting, with the executive head, every day. Then, sometimes with intervening controllers, came "country sections," each responsible for work in a particular occupied country, and technical sections, who dealt with such problems as the forging of false identity cards or the devising of secure ciphers or of time fuses (plastic explosives were invented by the SOE). Large intermediate headquarters were located in Cairo, Kandy and New York and later in Algiers and Bari; there were also offices in Berne, Stockholm, Madrid, Lisbon, Tangier and elsewhere in **neutral countries**. At the pyramid's base, besides the clerks, drivers and orderlies without whom no wartime unit could exist, were the secret agents themselves, either waiting to go abroad or already at work in occupied lands.

The SOE's total size was unknown. It probably reached a maximum of about 13,000 (including 3,000 **women**) in the spring of 1944; the influence it exercised on the war was proportionately much greated than its strength. Most of the women were cipher or signals operators or drivers. A few, exceptionally competent, were staff officers; a few, exceptionally brave, were agents, some highly successful.

Recruitment was more or less haphazard. **Jo C. F. Holland**, the agency's real founder, had conceived of it in **Ireland** as far back as 1920. He brought Gubbins, a lifelong friend, in to run it; each invited other friends to join, and they in turn recommended their own friends and so on. **Laurence Grand** followed a similar path through extensive contacts in London. The council was composed partly of senior businessmen, partly of regular officers. The bulk of the staff were younger professionals or businessmen, with a sprinkling of regulars (see **Richard Hugh Barry**) and a few people who had spent their lives in intelligence work. It was no more an "amateur" staff than was that of its opponent, the **SD**.

The agents were from much more varied back-grounds: they ranged from dukes and princesses to burglars and brothel owners, through every conceivable intermediate class. Most, though not all, were natives of the country they were to work in; nearly all had to be fluent enough in its language to pass as natives. Almost all were trained in the **United Kingdom**.

Training schools in southern England and on the west coast of Scotland gave agents paramilitary training in small arms, **sabotage**, unarmed combat, climbing, boating, parachuting, propaganda and the elements of clandestine behavior—how to change identity (be thorough), how to follow a suspect (be inconspicuous), how to be interrogated (be silent), how to escape (be quick).

The SOE's main troubles stemmed from poor communications with occupied countries as much as from difficulties in finding reliable cohorts in local Resistance movements. The agency had a small navy of its own, which operated into **Norway** (the "Shetland Bus"), France, **Italy, Yugoslavia, Greece** and Southeast Asia, but only with boats, small ships and midget submarines. Air transport was the more usual way of moving agents in and out of enemy-held territory, but the aircraft available were always too few. Moreover, they had to be shared with any other secret services operating into the same area, and from time to time the SOE's relations with some of these services were strained. There were only two **Royal Air Force** bomber squadrons (nos. 138 and 161) based in England permanently that were available for secret service work, and they could seldom mount as many as 25 sorties a night between them.

What strained the SOE's relations with other secret services—aside from questions of personal jealousy and suspicion, which seemed endemic in that world—was the simple fact that the SOE's agents went abroad to promote unrest, disquiet, dissatisfaction, even **revolution**, while the troubled circumstances the SOE favored provided the worst conditions possible for escape or intelligence agents, who needed plenty of calm and the minimum of police presence. Often there were also crossed wires and misunderstandings that arose from the dense cloak of security in which the SOE found it indispensable to work.

People in the SOE were expected not to tell their parents or wives or husbands what they were doing, even in the barest outline. Officers on small boats in Cornwall, for example, operating into Brittany, let it be known locally that they were engaged in naval signals training (thus accounting for the festoons of **radar** aerials on their craft); one was told by his wife that it was time for him "to do something dangerous, like other boys." The main headquarters, at 64 Baker Street, London, was labeled "Inter-Services Research

Bureau''; there were several other cover titles, such as the Union Trading Company (compare James Bond's Universal Export), or N I D (Q) or M O 1 (S P), all in use at once. This served to create confusion, as well as to divert or at least diffuse suspicion. None of the German efforts to penetrate the SOE appear to have succeeded in placing anyone at any SOE headquarters.

The leading members of the SOE combined with their passion for secrecy enormous vitality, real imaginative power, a strong sense of humor and a thorough grasp of the nature, purposes and limits of clandestine war. Not all the staff, nor all the agents, were brilliant, but the best of them carried out work of real distinction. **William ("Little Bill") Stephenson**, for instance, who coordinated the work of the SOE and the **Special Intelligence Service** in the **United States**, made possible the Allied naval victory of Cape Matapan by the raids he supervised on codebooks in Washington, D.C. At a lesser level the SOE sections working into France issued their circuits there a new type of ration book on the day the Vichy government brought it into use; one of those circuits deprived northeastern France of electric power for two months; another brought main line rail traffic between Toulouse and Limoges to a stop for three months.

Of the SOE's work in Asia and Africa very little is yet known. It played a substantial part in sustaining resistance in Norway, in creating and sustaining it in **Denmark** and in arming and sustaining it in **Belgium** and France. Some 1,800 agents and 10,000 tons of stores—mostly arms—were sent into France alone. In **the Netherlands** there was a disaster, discovered rather late (see *Englandspiel*). In Italy little was done before the fall of **Mussolini**, but much was accomplished thereafter. In Germany and **Austria** hardly anything could be done at all; some degree of cooperation on the part of the bulk of the inhabitants was indispensable for work by the SOE on any sort of wide scale. **Poland**, at the extreme limit of the RAF's range—permission was given only once, too late, for supply aircraft to land in Soviet territory—presented the SOE with a series of agonized choices; the organization did what it could to support the Home Army, a course to which its council felt it was honor-bound. In Greece SOE agents tried to hold various bands of mutually antipathetic resisters together and ended by supporting the monarchist bands against the Communist groups. Simultaneously, across the frontier in Yugoslavia, the same SOE headquarters in Cairo came to support **Tito**'s Communist partisans against **Dragolyub Mihailovich**'s Chetniks. These apparently contradictory decisions were taken because in each particular case the course followed seemed the one most likely to lead to the swift defeat of **Hitler**. The SOE's politics can in fact be summed up in a word:

anti-Nazi.

The SOE had plenty of cooperation from the **Office of Strategic Services**, which was in part modeled on it; the two bodies ran several combined staffs. From the *Narodnyy Kommissariat Vnutrennikh Del*, it got virtually nothing; it gave virtually nothing in return (see **Cobelligerency**). With the **governments-in-exile** in London and Cairo, its relations were of course constant, though seldom altogether smooth and occasionally difficult indeed. Most Continentals were profoundly suspicious of any British secret service and often bemused by the security precautions as well.

The SOE represented an acknowledgment by the British government that war was no longer entirely a gentleman's affair; a raffish, amateurish, disreputable air has stuck to it. At the time, people in the SOE welcomed being thought of as disreputable; it made a good cover for hiding their real efficiency.

The body was disbanded in January 1946.

M. R. D. Foot

SPEER, Albert (1905-   ).

German architect and inspector general of Berlin buildings in 1937, Speer succeeded **Fritz Todt** as minister of armaments and munitions in 1942 and in 1943 became commissar general of the Four-Year Plan in charge of armaments. A technocrat and hence a political outsider, he entered a field he knew little about and in it managed to raise the German **production** of armaments to an extent never before achieved. When he realized in the second half of 1944 that the military situation was hopeless, he attempted to convince **Hitler**, with whom he could always obtain an audience, that it would be tragic to go on with the war. In the beginning of 1945 he opposed Hitler's orders demanding the annihilation of Germany's industry and agriculture; in every way possible he tried to prevent the execution of such plans, apparently having gone so far as to consider killing Hilter with poison gas. In May 1945 he was made minister of the economy in the **Doenitz** government. He was condemned by the Nuremberg **war criminals** court to 20 years in prison and was freed in 1966. He was one of the few Nazis to admit his share of the responsibility for the Nazi horrors. In his memoirs, first published in 1969, he freely admitted his weaknesses and faults during the 1933-45 period.

H.-A. Jacobsen

SPEIDEL, Hans (1898-   ).

A German general, Speidel was head of the chiefs of staff of the occupation troops in France. In 1943 he commanded an army corps on the Russian front and was **Rommel**'s chief of staff at the time of the **Normandy landing**. Arrested by the **Gestapo** after the assassination attempt of July 20, 1944 against **Hitler**, he was liberated by the Allies in 1945.

SPERRLE, Hugo (1885-1953).
As commander of the Condor Legion, Speerle was sent to assist **Franco** in the Spanish civil war in 1936-38. Field Marshal Speerle was chief of the *Luftwaffe* Third Air Fleet, which provided air support for the German armored offensives in the western campaign and carried out bombing missions in the **Battle of Britain**.

SS (*Schutzstaffel*).
The SS was created in 1925 by the merger of the *Stabswache*, a guard organization, and the **Hitler** *Stosstruppe*, the shock troops, to form the elite striking arm of the **Nazi Party**. At first limited in numbers, its primary function was to protect the heads of the Nazi Party and to defend the party itself against armed attack. **Himmler**, who had been named SS Reichsfuehrer in 1929, brought the strength of the SS up to 50,000 men, giving it its status as the Nazi Party elite corps, with its own uniform—black instead of the Nazi brown—its distinctive symbols of a death's head and the double runic S and a rigorous discipline. It gradually became the security arm of the Nazi Party, protecting it against subversion from within as well as without. On April 13, 1931 the SS took a decisive part in the bloody repression of the rebellious *Sturmabteilung*—the storm troopers, the street fighters of the Nazi Party, who were led by Ernst Roehm—in the so-called "Night of the Long Knives," June 30, 1934. Led by Hitler himself, this **purge** of the more "unsavory" Nazis claimed a good many lives, including Roehm's. The Fuehrer then accorded the SS a measure of autonomy within the Nazi Party. When the Nazis came to power, the SS became the dominant—and most dangerous—instrument of the Nazi system. In 1934 Himmler was made commander of all the political police of the German *Laender*, and in 1936 he became chief of the German police. He organized the police state and the infiltration of the state police by the SS. The **RSHA**, combining the state police and the Security Service (**SD**) of the Nazi Party under **Reinhard Heydrich's** authority, was created in September 1939. The territory of the Reich was divided into SS sections, each headed by a combined SS officer and police chief.

The SS also sought to infiltrate other areas with varying results. The "Circle of Friends of the Reichsfuehrer SS" established connections with the country's economic and financial powers; through the SD *Ausland* and the *Volksdeutsche Mittelstelle*, it succeeded in influencing foreign policy. The SS also had economic interests in construction and armaments. The war undoubtedly advanced the power and importance of the SS.

In the course of the war, the pursuit of political and racial enemies became brutally oppressive in the occupied countries and went as far as liquidation of their elite, as in **Poland** and the **USSR**, culminating in the extermination of Jews (see **Anti-Semitism**; **Final Solution**), organized after 1941 by mobile SS groups, and the administration of **concentration camps**.

The policy of colonization and population shifts, based on racist notions, for which Himmler had been responsible since 1939 in his official position as "*Reichskommissar* to Preserve German Ethnicity," was not limited to organizing the return of German ethnic groups to the homeland, but provided also for the removal of populations from the annexed territories and for the mass deportation of foreign labor into **Germany**. Like the prisoners of the SS concentration camps, the forced laborers became part of the German war **production** machine and the economic enterprises of the SS (see **Forced Labor Battalions**).

Before the war began, the SS broke the state's monopoly on arms in order to become Hitler's personal troops and to serve the Nazi state as guards for concentration camps. In addition to these units—special purpose groups and the concentration camp guards—two SS divisions were formed within the regular army in 1939. Directly after their activation, they were allowed to institute their own courts-martial, independent of those of the *Wehrmacht*. This was the beginning of the *Waffen* SS within the Reich's armed forces. Toward the end of the war, there were 38 SS divisions—with a full general at the head of the SS army—and several SS corps commanders. Of its 900,000 men, almost 200,000 were foreigners. If that statistic was proof of the Reich's urgent need for fighting men, it also indicated that a specific anticommunist ideology and a racial obsession can unite men of divergent backgrounds. Extremely well-equipped, the *Waffen* SS were as reckless as they were brutal; their name is plainly stamped on such eruptions of bestiality as the massacres of **Oradour-Sur-Glane** and **Lidice**.

Near the war's end Himmler even controlled part of the *Wehrmacht*—the reserve, the officer candidate schools, the *Abwehr*, armaments and **prisoners of war**. While the *Waffen* SS far overreached its original function as the state police, it cannot be considered a fourth branch of the *Wehrmacht*. It had begun as a competitor of the army and always kept its identity as the "*Fuehrertruppe*"—the leader's bodyguard—even after its elite status eroded. As the result of its expansion, a sort of "State SS" formed in the Third Reich, but with it the original SS lost its homogeneity.

K.-J. Muller

SS CHAIN OF COMMAND.

Himmler, the SS Reichsfuehrer and German chief of police, was responsible to **Hitler** alone. A *"Hoeherer SS und Polizeifuehrer"*—a superior SS and police leader—headed each of 30 territorial sections and reported to Himmler. At the end of 1944 Himmler ruled his "empire" with the assistance of the following 12 major adminstrative groups. (The precise structure of the SS was changed periodically; this arrangement, however, was fairly typical.)

Personal Staff of the Reichsfuehrer SS

Karl Wolff, who was also responsible for the *Ahnererbe* association and the *Lebensborn* program, headed this group.

Central Administration of the SS

This group was headed by Gottlob Berger, one of those responsible for the recruitment of the *Waffen* SS.

SS Central Command

Headed by Hans Juettner, the SS Central Command encompassed two subsidiary units:

Command bureau of the regular SS

Membership in the regular SS amounted to 240,000 men in 1939; by 1945 its strength had declined to 40,000.

Command bureau of the *Waffen* SS

Two units fell under this bureau's jurisdiction. The *Waffen* SS was created in 1940 as the *Verfuegungstruppen*, units for special missions, reinforced by "death's head" formations (*Totenkopfverbaende*). At the end of 1944 the total strength of the *Waffen* SS was 910,000 men. The death's head units (**concentration camp** guards) included 30,000 men at the end of 1944.

"Race and Population Resettlement" Administration (RUSHA, or *Rasse und Siedlungshauptamt*)

Headed by Richard Hildebrandt, this administration was responsible for all questions relating to "purity of blood" both within the SS and outside it.

SS Administration of Justice

This group, headed by Franz Breithaupt, administered the high court of the SS and the police, the regular SS and police courts, and the SS and police courts in the field.

Administration of SS Personnel

Maximilian von Herff headed this group.

Central Security Administration (RSHA, or *Reichssicherheitshauptamt*)

Ernst Kaltenbrunner, the successor to Reinhard Heydrich, administered the **RSHA**. Its subdivisions included:

Personnel, formation, organization

Administration—economy

SD

The **SD** encompassed both the SD *Inland* (Interior SD), headed by Otto Ohlendorf, and the SD *Ausland* (External SD), headed by **Walter Schellenberg**.

Security (Sipo, or *Sicherheitspolizei*)

Included under the jurisdiction of this group were the secret state police (**Gestapo**, or *Geheime Staatspolizei*), headed by Heinrich Mueller, and the criminal police (Kripo, or *Kriminalpolizei*).

Ideological investigations

General Administration of Civil Police (Orpo, or *Ordnungspolizei*)

This group, headed by **Kurt Daluege**, was the central administrative bureau for conventional local and regional police.

"Economy and Administration" Organization (WVHA, or *Wirtschafts und Verwaltungs Hauptamt*)

Oswald Pohl, the chief of this group, was responsible for concentration camps, construction, various industries (among others, 296 brick factories, porcelain plants and 75 percent of the nonalcoholic drink industry) and the administration and finances of the *Waffen* SS.

Department of the *Obergruppenfuehrer* Heissmeyer

This group was responsible for national educational policy and for the boarding schools.

General Administration for German Minorities (Vomi, or *Volksdeutsche Mittelstelle*)

Werner Lorenz administered this group, which was responsible for the techniques and organization of population transfers.

Department of the Reich Commissariat for Consolidating the German Nation

Ulrich Greifelt headed this department, which oversaw the planning and realization of population transfers.

STALIN, Iosef Vissarionovich (1879-1953).

Stalin was born on December 21, 1879, in Gori in what is now the Soviet Republic of Georgia, to a Georgian shoemaker; he died March 5, 1953 in Moscow. In 1899 he became a professional revolutionary; he was first arrested in 1902. He later pursued his subversive work in the Caucasus region under various pseudonyms—Koba, among others. In 1912 he was elected in absentia to the Central Committee of the Bolshevik Party and of the Russian section of the committee. In the first Soviet government, from 1917 to 1923, he was commissar of the people for the nationalities of Russia. His rise to power began in earnest with his nomination as secretary general of the Central Committee of the Communist Party of the **USSR** on April 3, 1922. After Lenin's death he drove all his political rivals out of the party, one after the other. When he succeeded in expelling his enemy **Leon Trotsky** from the USSR in 1929, he attained his first major aim. With his accurate instinct for knowing where and when to exert a maximum of force, he became dictator. Gradually he attained unlimited power, permitting him to attempt, in accordance with his theories, the construction of socialism in a single nation, since the achievement of international socialism, the final aim of Leninism, was still beyond his means. Forced collectivism and forced industrialization through several Five-Year Plans changed the USSR from an agrarian and backward country to a modern industrial state. At the same time, Stalin put into effect a system of treaties, designed to protect the socialist exeperiment. From 1936 to 1938, through a spectacular series of **treason** trials, he succeeded in liquidating his most dangerous rivals in the first of what became known as "great **purges**." Thus, through an iron-fisted reign of terror he acquired exactly the type of government he wanted—a bureaucratic totalitarian dictatorship reinforced by an extraordinary "personality cult." At the same time he kept the **Comintern** firmly in hand. From the beginning of the 1930s, his entire policy depended on the arousal of Soviet patriotism; he justified this ideologically as a consequence of international proletarian solidarity.

Before World War II Stalin's foreign policy centered on the defense of the USSR against Nazi expansion. But neither the formation of a popular front, the treaties he consummated with France and **Czechoslovakia**, nor the policy of collective security could limit Nazi aggression. Stalin then concluded that it was necessary to deal directly with **Germany**. Consequently he signed the **Nazi-Soviet Pact**, which granted him substantial economic advantages plus additional territory in **Poland**, the **Baltic States**, and, in 1940, Bessarabia. With the successful invasion of **Finland** (see **Russo-Finnish Winter War**), he obtained an advanced strategic position. In further negotiations with **Hitler** he demanded the complete annexation of Finland, expansion of Soviet holdings in **Rumania** with the acquisition of southern Bukovina, the recognition of **Bulgaria** as part of the Russian sphere of influence and the installation of Soviet bases in the Dardanelles and portions of **Turkey**. Stalin also contemplated other, long-term projects: using neutral **Sweden** as a buffer state to protect the Soviet frontier, controlling the Baltic Sea through a Soviet-Danish committee under his control and extending Soviet influence over **Hungary, Yugoslavia, Greece** and western Poland. When, in 1940-41, Germany began planning its invasion of the USSR, Stalin tried desperately to reach a new understanding with Hitler and simultaneously brushed aside overtures from British diplomats. The sudden German incursion into Soviet territory on June 22, 1941 (see **USSR—War with Germany**) was the "greatest shock" of Stalin's life.

Stalin became president of the peoples' commissars on May 5, 1941; he promoted himself, on July 1, 1941, to president of the defense committee, then to commander in chief of the Soviet armed forces; he added the titles of marshal in 1943 and generalissimo in 1945. Whatever his title, Stalin plunged energetically and devotedly into planning military operations and conducting negotiations with the Allies. He proclaimed the "Great Patriotic War," identifying the defense of socialism with the defense of the fatherland, and imbued the Russian people with a new sense of patriotism. In order to lift spiritual elan, he restored the Russian Orthodox Church to a position of honor. To lessen the irritation displayed by certain groups in the **United Kingdom** and the **United States** at finding themselves allied with a Communist state, he dissolved the Comintern in May 1943. Stalin held numerous conferences with his allies, allowing some insight into his long-term plans. In a parley with **Anthony Eden**, the British minister of foreign affairs, in 1941, he proposed the recognition of the Soviet frontiers of June 1941, Soviet annexation of the Finnish territory of Petsamo and the installation of Soviet bases in Rumania. In 1943 and 1944 he requested a bulwark for further defense in the form of German disarmament, close ties between the USSR and Poland, the liberation of oppressed peoples and the reinforcement of Soviet influence in Asia. The powerful westward drive of the Red Army and his clever diplomatic techniques lent Stalin a strong postwar influence over the maps of Europe and Asia, especially with the Soviet declaration of war against **Japan** on August 8, 1945. The USSR's present-day position as the second most powerful **empire** in the world, in the wake of the most important Russian victory ever achieved, is Stalin's greatest legacy.

H.-A. Jacobsen

STALINGRAD, Battle of.
See **USSR—War with Germany**.

STAUFFENBERG, Count Claus Schenk von (1907-1944).
A wounded hero of the war with a first-class intelligence and a soul of iron, Stauffenberg, a German staff officer, became a true leader of the **German Resistance** toward the end of 1943. He was the central figure of the **assassination attempt of July 20, 1944**, preparing and executing the scheme to kill **Hitler** and rescue his country with no thought to his own welfare. The bomb he planted, however, only shocked and blackened the Fuehrer, although it mortally wounded some of his assistants. Stauffenberg paid for it with his life on the same day; he was killed by order of his superior, Gen. **Friedrich Fromm**.

STAUNING, Thorwald (1873-1942).
A Danish politician, Stauning was president of the Social Democratic Party from 1910 and prime minister from 1924 to 1926 and from 1929 to 1942. In the 1930s he built the Danish **welfare state**. After April 1940 he did what he could to preserve **Denmark** from the excesses of the Nazis.

STEPHENSON, Sir William S. ("Little Bill") (1896-   ).
A Canadian millionaire, Stephenson headed British Security Coordination from 1940 to 1945. This office, based in New York, handled all British secret service affairs in North America and carried out several espionage schemes.

STETTINIUS, Edward R., Jr. (1900-1949).
An American businessman, Stettinius was a steel industry executive until 1940, when he left the business world to devote full-time to his work on the National Defense Advisory Commission. He also served on the War Resources Board, set up to determine which raw materials would be needed in the event of war, and later with the new Office of Production Management. In 1941 he became **lend-lease** administrator, a post he held until 1943. He served as undersecretary of state in 1943-44 and secretary of state in 1944-45. Stettinius took part in the discussions leading to the creation of the **United Nations** and was appointed the first **United States** ambassador to that body in June 1945.

STILWELL, Joseph W. ("Vinegar Joe") (1883-1946).
An American general, Stilwell became an expert on **China** in the interwar period. He led Chinese troops and then U.S. Army forces in China, **Burma** and **India** and was chief of staff to **Chiang Kai-shek** from 1942 to 1944.

After the Japanese overran U.S. airbases in eastern China in 1944, the Joint Chiefs of Staff wanted Stilwell to take command of all Chinese forces, but Chiang had him recalled.

STIMSON, Henry Lewis (1867-1950).
An American politician, Stimson was twice secretary of war, from 1911 to 1913 and from 1940 to 1945, and was secretary of state from 1929 to 1933. In spite of political differences—Stimson was a Republican—he ably helped **Roosevelt**'s war effort. He oversaw war mobilization and military training and advocated **lend-lease**, greater aid to Britain and compulsory military service. During the war he gave great support to scientific **research**, particularly the development of the **atomic bomb**. Yet he expressed serious reservations about the use of the bomb against the Japanese.

STIRLING, (Archibald) David (1915-   ).
A British officer, Stirling was a commando and founder, in 1941, of the **Special Air Service**. From 1943 to 1945 he was a **prisoner of war**.

STOPFORD, Sir Montagu G. N. (1892-1971).
A British general, Stopford fought in France in 1940. Three years later he took command of the 33rd Indian Corps in **Burma** which lifted the siege of Kohima by the Japanese and reopened the road to Imphal. The corps then chased the Japanese into central Burma.

STRATEGY.
A distinction should be made between *general strategy* or *political strategy*, on one hand, and *operational strategy*, on the other. In the British and American military lexicon, the first was often called *grand strategy*.

General strategy is the art of concentrating all the military power, regular as well as auxiliary, of one state or a coalition of states on the principal objective: defeat of the enemy. This was the level at which **Churchill**, **Roosevelt**, **Stalin** and **Hitler**, assisted by their military and civilian advisers, operated during World War II.

Operational strategy is determined primarily within each theater of operations. It is in the hands of the commander in chief of each theater of operations—Gen. **Eisenhower**, for example, in the western European theater in 1944-45, when he controlled the land, sea and air forces as well as the **Resistance** fighters in the occupied territories.

STREICHER, Julius (1885-1946).
From 1923 to 1945 Streicher was editor in chief of the obsessively anti-Semitic journal *Der Stuermer*. He was also a *Gauleiter* of the **Nazi Party**. Streicher was con-

demned to death as a **war criminal** and hanged in 1946.

STUART, Sir Campbell (1885-1972).

A Canadian publicist, Stuart directed British war **propaganda** in 1918 and from 1938 to 1940.

STUDENT, Kurt (1890-1978).

A *Luftwaffe* general, Student led German airborne units in the campaigns in **the Netherlands** and **Belgium** in 1940 and Crete in 1941 (see **Airborne Divisions**). Despite earlier successes, the raid on Crete was judged too costly by **Hitler**, and Student's troops then became an elite ground force. His knowledge of airborne operations enabled the Germans to stifle the Allied thrust in the battle of Arnhem in September 1944.

STUELPNAGEL, Karl Heinrich von (1886-1944).

A German general bitterly opposed to Nazism, Stuelpnagel was one of the cabal who attempted a coup d'etat in 1938. He succeeded his cousin Otto as the commander of occupation troops in France. An active supporter of the **assassination attempt of July 20, 1944** against **Hitler**, he successfully conducted his part in the plot, the arrest of all **SS** and **SD** members in Paris. He was abandoned by his superior, Gen. **Guenther von Kluge**, and failed in a suicide attempt that deprived him of his vision. Cared for until he could stand trial, he was strangled at Ploetzensee on August 30.

STUELPNAGEL, Otto von (1878-1948).

A German general, Stuelpnagel was commander of occupation troops in France from 1940 to 1942. He was arrested by the French in 1946 and tried in Paris but committed suicide in his prison cell.

STUKA *(Sturzkampffugzeug Stuka)*.

Dive-bombing aircraft (see **Britain, Battle of**).

SUETSUGU, Nobumasa (1880-1944).

A Japanese admiral, a political organizer and minister of home affairs from 1937 to 1939, Suetsugu sought huge navy budgets in the 1930s to modernize the fleet for the almost certain war to come. He was a noted advocate of submarine warfare. As home minister, he helped draft the **National General Mobilization Law** of 1938 and called for strict controls on profits as well as wages. He was pushed aside by big corporate interests in 1939 but reemerged in 1940 as president of the National Federation for the Construction of East Asia, a supraparty organization of rightist groups that was superseded later the same year by the **Imperial Rule Assistance Association**.

SUGIYAMA, Hajime (1880-1945).

Japanese war minister (1937-38) and chief of the general staff (1940-44), Sugiyama, a general, helped to restore discipline in the army after the February 1936 revolt by young officers. In 1943, when he was promoted to field marshal, he became a member of the supreme military command and was placed in charge of mainland defense forces in preparation for an enemy invasion. After the surrender he and his wife committed suicide.

SUKARNO (1901-1970).

In 1927 Sukarno founded the Indonesian National Party. Because of his political activities he was imprisoned by the Dutch in 1929-31 and placed under house arrest from 1934 to 1942. He was released by and worked with the Japanese in 1942. In July 1945 he announced his five principles—nationalism; internationalism and humanism; understanding and democracy; welfare; and belief in one God—and on August 17, 1945 proclaimed the independence of the Republic of **Indonesia**, with himself as president. **The Netherlands** refused to recognize the new status of its colony until 1949.

SUNER, R. Serrano (1901-   ).

Suner was Spanish minister of foreign affairs in 1940-42.

SUPREME HEADQUARTERS ALLIED EXPEDITIONARY FORCES (SHAEF).

The supreme chiefs of staff of the Allied forces in Europe after 1944, under the command of Gen. **Dwight D. Eisenhower** (see **Military Organization and Firepower**).

SURRENDER DECISION BY JAPAN.

Japan's tortuous surrender process in August 1945 reflected almost perfectly the clash of interests and the ponderous decision-making by consensus that had led the country into war with the **United States** in December 1941. To speed the proceedings, the U.S. dropped two **atomic bombs** on Japan, but it is uncertain how decisive they were in forcing complete surrender. The chief sticking point for the Japanese was the future sovereignty of their emperor. Ironically it was **Hirohito** himself who broke the deadlock when the conflicting interests could not be resolved by voluntarily subjecting his authority to the Americans and choosing peace.

Earlier **peace overtures** by Japan, in the spring and summer of 1945, had been ineffectual, and the Allies gathered at Potsdam in mid-July (see **Conferences, Allied**) fully expecting the imperial Japanese forces to fight on. Late on July 16, on the eve of the conference, U.S. Secretary of War **Henry L. Stimson** handed **Churchill** a slip of paper at the prime minister's cottage: "Babies satisfactorily born." The atomic test in New Mexico earlier that day had been a success. Japan could now be told to surrender or pay the consequences, which included atomic warfare—a fact only the Americans and British at Potsdam knew.

The **Potsdam Declaration**, issued on July 26 by the United States, **China** and the **United Kingdom** (the **USSR** was not yet at war with Japan), demanded the "**unconditional surrender** of all the Japanese armed forces." Failure to comply would mean "the inevitable and complete destruction of the Japanese armed forces and just as inevitably the utter devastation of the Japanese homeland." The declaration listed what would happen after the surrender: the influence of nationalists and militarists would be brought to an end, **war criminals** would be punished, the **empire** would be dismantled and a military occupation would be imposed until the people freely chose a peaceful and responsible government. Nowhere did it spell out the fate of the emperor.

The Americans had already set in motion plans to drop both of the atomic bombs available to them, and nothing Tokyo said during the next 10 days caused them to change their minds. The Japanese supreme war council met immediately on July 27 to discuss the declaration. The council consisted of Prime Minister **Kantaro Suzuki**, foreign minister **Shigenori Togo**, war minister **Korechika Anami**, navy minister **Mitsumasa Yonai**, army chief of staff Yoshijiro Umezu, navy chief of staff **Soemu Toyoda** and, sometimes, Emperor Hirohito. Suzuki and Togo wanted to accept the declaration; Toyoda and Anami wanted to brush it aside and asked the emperor to make a strong statement to the nation urging people to carry on.

Caught in a dilemma, Prime Minister Suzuki bowed to pressure from the army and navy. Officially Japan was committed "to press forward resolutely to carry the war to a successful conclusion," and Postdam had not altered this pledge. He told the press on July 28: "The government holds that the declaration is by no means an important issue. We are simply paying no attention to it." The phrase he used for "paying no attention" was translated literally as "killing it with silence." Suzuki apparently meant "no comment" on the declaration, but in print the phrase suggested that Japan was "ignoring" the Allies' ultimatum. When no official response came forth to clarify the press accounts, the Allies assumed Japan had rejected the document. The atomic attack proceeded as planned, and on August 6 Hiroshima was obliterated.

The raid rekindled the search for consensus among the key elites in Japan's wartime leadership: veteran bureaucrats, senior active duty military officers, top courtiers, aristocrats and the imperial family itself.

Foreign minister Togo conferred with Hirohito as soon as he heard the news and urged him to surrender at once. But the stalemate continued. Then, on August 8, the Soviet Union declared war on Japan, an even greater shock than Hiroshima. The futility of Japan's earlier peace initiatives to Moscow was an embarrassment, and most importantly Manchuria was almost defenseless because much of the Kwantung Army had been withdrawn to defend the Japanese homeland. The decision-making process came to its climax on August 9.

Early that morning Suzuki and the emperor agreed that Japan should accept the Potsdam Declaration without further delay. At 10:30 a.m. the supreme war council split three to three on the issue—Suzuki, Togo and Yonai in favor; Anami, Umezu and Toyoda against unless four conditions could be met: they wanted to ensure that the emperor would remain sovereign, that war criminals would be tried by Japanese authorities, that surrender and disarmament would be carried out on Japanese orders and that the enemy forces would conduct only a limited military occupation of designated areas for a temporary transition period. The diehard trio apparently knew the Americans would never agree to these provisions. Yonai accused the holdouts of clinging to a mentality that foolishly sought a "seashore confrontation" with invading Americans. The real reason for not yielding probably was that the military hoped to retain the upper hand amid the defeatism that was likely to follow a chaotic surrender.

The news from Nagasaki at midday that a second atomic bomb had shattered that picturesque seaport did not resolve the impasse in Tokyo. The cabinet met from 2:30 to 10:30 p.m. without reaching an agreement. The time had come for an imperial conference in the musty air raid shelter deep beneath the emperor's palace in Tokyo. Such conferences were the most solemn occasions imaginable, when high decisions of state were formally ratified after they had been reached by the cabinet and (after it was created in August 1944) the supreme war council. Present were all cabinet ministers, the army and navy chiefs of staff and chiefs of military affairs and the president of the privy council—23 men in all, convoked in audience by the emperor at 11:00 p.m. on August 9.

For three and one-half hours the pro- and anti-surrender factions debated without agreement. Prime Minister Suzuki modified his pro-surrender position to include the demand that "the prerogatives of his majesty as a sovereign ruler" not be affected. With that one condition, he said, Japan could live with surrender as specified at Potsdam. Pressing for a decision, and fearful that Tokyo would be the next to be attacked with an atomic bomb, at 2:30 a.m. Suzuki broke precedent by appealing to the emperor to settle the matter. In a moment of deep emotion and high drama possibly without parallel in the nation's history, Hirohito said the time had come to bear the unbearable, that Japan should accept peace as Suzuki had outlined it. The emperor had chosen peace, and the cabinet and supreme war council accepted his command.

But Japan had still not agreed to quit unconditionally. Suzuki immediately cabled the Swiss and Swedish governments that his country accepted the Potsdam statement "with the understanding that the said declaration does not comprise any demand which prejudices prerogatives of His Majesty as a Sovereign Ruler." The Americans, sensing victory and lacking any more atomic bombs to drop, sidestepped Suzuki's qualification and answered on August 11 that "from the moment of surrender, the authority of the Emperor and the Japanese Government to rule the state shall be subject to the Supreme Commander for the Allied Powers." The American reply, which reached Tokyo at 12:45 a.m. on August 12, made no mention of the long-term fate of the throne.

At an informal cabinet meeting convened at 3:00 that afternoon, Gen. Anami was outraged at the American response. He demanded to know what "subject to" the supreme commander meant, whether this was an attack on the emperor's sovereignty. Togo reported that Hirohito himself was satisfied with the answer from Washington and suggested that the phrase meant "restricted by" rather than "subordinate to" the Allied commander. Once again no decision was reached. It may well be that this semantic debate was only a diversionary tactic forced on him by intractable generals jostling for advantage in the impending post-surrender vacuum of power. But the question of imperial sovereignty touched the very core of Japanese political practice and national ideology, and it is easy to imagine that millions of Japanese who had sacrificed so much to fight a bitter war in the emperor's name shared Anami's reluctance to yield the throne's authority.

By Monday, August 13, pressures for a decision had become intense. Washington cabled the foreign office that afternoon to protest that Japan was dragging its feet. Gen. Anami felt trapped in an impossible quandary. A man of huge ambition and great strength of character, he did not know how to admit defeat. He was ripped by the conflict between loyalty to the emperor's wishes and his own sense of duty to keep up the fight. On August 13 his own subordinate, the 33-year-old Maj. Kenji Hatanaka, demanded that Anami sanction a coup led by army patriots in the war ministry against the traitors who wanted peace. Although Anami held firm and stalled Hatanaka for 24

hours, nearly everyone in the top leadership was frightened by the prospect of a military revolt on the one hand and of more atomic bombs on the other.

The supreme war council and the cabinet discussed the American position again early on August 14. At 10:50 that morning the emperor brushed aside the nuances contained in the American text and declared that peace was preferable to destruction. He directed the cabinet to prepare a rescript accepting the Potsdam terms and announcing surrender. Once again the solemn occasion prompted many to cry. The conference was over within an hour, and what has become known as Japan's "longest day" began at noon August 14.

The cabinet ministers felt they had failed their sovereign in war, so they could at least obey him in peace. Gen. Anami labored to head off Maj. Hatanaka's imminent rebellion while the cabinet thrashed around for nine hours before agreeing on a surrender text. At 9:00 p.m. the state radio network (NHK) threw the country into confusion with a report: "Very important news will be broadcast at noon tomorrow. Every citizen is requested to turn on the radio and listen." It would be the first time a Japanese emperor had ever addressed the whole nation.

An NHK crew recorded the emperor's announcement twice, on separate disks, at 11:30 p.m. and left the castle at midnight. Suddenly they were confronted by imperial guards under rebel command who demanded the recordings; they had, however, been safely hidden inside the palace. Ignoring Anami's advice, Maj. Hatanaka and his fellow insurgents had murdered Lt. Gen. Takeshi Mori, head of the palace guards, and seized control of the castle. By 2:00 a.m. the rebels had entered the palace and begun searching for **Koichi Kido**, the lord keeper of the privy seal, and the records. Kido was in hiding and the disks had been safely stored by the grand chamberlain, Yoshihiro Tokugawa, in a locker in the room of the empress's secretary. Nevertheless the palace was securely under rebel control throughout the night.

At the same time other followers of Hatanaka tried to torch the official residence of Prime Minister Suzuki. They used heavy oil rather than gasoline and did little damage. They did manage to burn down his private residence, but Suzuki, who had miraculously escaped assassination in a similar coup nine years earlier, once again eluded his enemies. At 5:10 a.m. the insurgents seized the NHK studios in order to make an announcement to the nation, but the network's announcers and engineers refused to cooperate.

Gen. Shizuichi Tanaka, the commander of the eastern army district, who had once served in London and Washington, boldly put down the revolt early on the morning of August 15. He rode directly to the palace, put the imperial guards under his command and liberated the court from its captors. Gen. Anami, meanwhile, committed ritual suicide to atone for Japan's defeat in battle. Maj. Hatanaka, having been turned away from NHK at daybreak, learned of Anami's suicide and shot himself to death in the outer plaza of the castle. Nine days later Gen. Tanaka, in a final act of loyalty to his emperor, also shot himself to death. A number of other military suicides took place after the surrender, but Hatanaka's rebellion was the only serious threat to political order.

"To our good and loyal subjects," the emperor's voice began the broadcast at noon. He spoke in refined court language scarcely intelligible to many of his listeners. "The war situation has developed not necessarily to Japan's advantage," he continued: this was the closest he came to admitting that Japan had lost. Without mentioning unconditional surrender, and with little hint of what lay ahead for the people, the emperor said that "we have resolved to pave the way for a grand peace for all the generations to come by enduring the unendurable and suffering what is insufferable." While the Japanese wept with sorrow, relief and anxiety about the future, President **Truman** accepted the Japanese surrender at once. The bloodiest war in history had ended.

How decisive the atomic bomb was in forcing the surrender may never be known. In a military sense, Japan's forces were defeated as early as the spring of 1945, but this did not keep them from fighting on. Repeated fire raids in the spring on city neighborhoods (see **Japan, Air War Against**) had inflicted terrible suffering without accomplishing their goal, of weakening **morale** to the point where citizens would pull down their government. Just as the air war was inconclusive, so too were the naval operations. The U.S. **blockade** had sealed off the home islands so effectively that both the civilian economy and war **production** were starved for resources, yet the Japanese fought on.

There is no question that an American invasion of the Japanese mainland, set for Kyushu in November 1945 (Operation Olympic) and the Kanto plain near Tokyo the following March (Operation Coronet), would have been the bloodiest seaborne attack of all time. It is understandable, perhaps, that a war-weary United States did not more carefully consider the consequences of atomic warfare before bombing Hiroshima. Whatever the merits, if any, of this attack, there was no evident justification for the second raid on Nagasaki before the diplomatic effects of the first explosion could be gauged.

Did the atomic bombs speed the surrender? The

first attack clearly led Japan's leaders to reconsider their wait-and-see attitude toward the Potsdam Declaration. Yet the intervention by the Soviet Union seems to have had an even greater impact among the dozen or so men who finally accepted peace. Throughout the tortured process, their greatest concern was the ultimate fate of the throne. Despite the advice of the former ambassador to Japan, Joseph L. Grew, and other top statesmen, President Truman elected not to compromise the Allies' firm insistence on unconditional surrender by disclosing to the Japanese what the Americans had long known—that they had no intention whatsoever of abolishing the throne. It can never be known whether reassurances from Washington on this crucial point at some date before August 6 might have convinced the Japanese to surrender before the age of nuclear warfare ever began.

T. R. H. Havens

SURRENDER, Unconditional.
See **Unconditional Surrender**.

SUZUKI, Kantaro (1896-1948).
Suzuki, a Japanese baron, served his country as an admiral, member of the privy council and prime minister of the cabinet that surrendered on August 15, 1945. Born in Chiba, Suzuki distinguished himself in the Russo-Japanese War in 1904-05 and became admiral and chief of the general staff in 1923. As grand chamberlain of the imperial court, he was gravely wounded by a would-be assassin's knife during the military revolt in February 1936. Only his wife's desperate plea to the attacker prevented his murder. Suzuki served as a privy councillor throughout the war and became head of the council in 1944.

When **Kuniaki Koiso**'s cabinet fell in April 1945 because of the deteriorating war situation, Emperor **Hirohito** and several senior statesmen turned to Suzuki because he was a universally respected leader who could bring the war to an acceptable end. But the price of army support for the new cabinet was his pledge to continue the war and his willingness to round up 400 peace sympathizers.

Suzuki, foreign minister **Shigenori Togo** and eventually the emperor all realized the situation was hopeless and encouraged **peace overtures**. At 2:30 a.m. on August 10, an imperial conference, meeting in the imperial caves for shelter, reconsidered accepting the **Potsdam Declaration** in light of the atomic bombings and the Soviet entry into the war but found itself deadlocked. Quite without precedent, Suzuki asked the emperor to settle the matter. The emperor spoke for peace, initiating the surrender decision that was announced to the nation on August 15 (see **Surrender Decision by Japan**). Two days later the Suzuki cabinet resigned, its chief mission fulfilled.

T. R. H. Havens

SUZUKI, Teiichi (1888-).
From 1941 to 1943 Suzuki, a Japanese general, was minister of state and director of the **Cabinet Planning Board** under the third **Konoe** and the **Tojo** cabinets. He was appointed head of the cabinet research bureau in 1937 to plan wartime mobilization, and in December 1938 he joined the Asia Development Board with responsibility for guiding the new Nanking government of **Wang Ching-wei**. In April 1943 when **production** snags cropped up and workers' **morale** fell in the munitions plants, Suzuki headed the first of a number of blue-ribbon investigations into wartime factory efficiency and resource allocations. After the surrender he was sentenced as a **war criminal** to life in prison by the International Military Tribunal for the Far East; he was paroled in 1956.

SWEDEN.
Sweden's Social Democratic government declared its neutrality in September 1939. An all-party coalition, founded in mid-November 1939, lasted until 1945. Neutrality lasted also, but with difficulty. Like **Switzerland**, Sweden owed its immunity to attack largely to its population's visible, resolute readiness to defend it.

There was general support for **Finland** in the **Russo-Finnish Winter War** in 1939-40, in which some thousands of Swedish volunteers took part, but only as volunteers. Sweden continued to sell iron ore to **Germany** (see **Iron Road**); this was a proximate cause of the Anglo-French and German expeditions to **Norway** in April 1940. After the German occupation of Norway and **Denmark**, Sweden was less well placed to resist German pressure.

From June 1940 to August 1943, the Germans received transit rights for goods, and occasionally for troops, between Norway and Finland; a whole division once passed, with its arms, through Sweden. By August 1943 the German strength had diminished so much, and British and Soviet pressure had increased so much, that the rights were withdrawn.

Sweden provided shelter for refugees from both German and Soviet oppression (see **Evacuation and Resettlement**). Most of the Jews from Denmark were smuggled across the Sound into Sweden; a few escaped **prisoners of war**, and thousands of refugees from the **Baltic States**, reached Sweden also. The British maintained a regular, though uncomfortable, air service by light bomber between Scotland and Stockholm from 1941 through 1945; otherwise, Sweden was largely isolated.

M. R. D. Foot

SWINTON, Lord (Sir Philip Cunliffe-Lister) (1884-1972).
A British statesman, Swinton was chairman of the Security Executive in 1940-42.

SWITZERLAND.
Switzerland managed to escape being dragged into World War II as miraculously as it had avoided involvement in World War I; it owed this fact to the cleverness of its Federal Council and especially to the devotion of Gen. **Henri Guisan** to defending Swiss territory before giving any thought to a policy of neutrality.

Caught in the nutcracker formed by **Germany** to the north and **Italy** to the south, Switzerland was simultaneously an annoyance and a temptation for the **Axis** powers. Germany in particular had no patience with the independent spirit of the Swiss and especially the outspoken Swiss press, which, while demanding that the Swiss federal government respect the country's traditional neutrality, never concealed its resentment of the high-handed directives aimed at it by the German-dominated cantons of the Swiss federation.

On the other hand, the presence of the **League of Nations**, abandoned by Rome, Berlin and Tokyo, on Swiss territory put Switzerland in danger of becoming a source of righteous indignation, admonishing the totalitarian states for their failure to behave. Such a position could hardly square with conventional notions of neutrality.

Conscious of these various dangers, the Federal Council proclaimed the neutrality of the Swiss Federation on March 21, 1938, barely 10 days after the violation of **Austria**'s territory (see *Anschluss*; Introduction). The declaration took the form of a "Memorandum on the Neutrality of Switzerland Within the League of Nations." When war became inevitable at the end of August 1939, the memorandum was followed up by a firm Swiss declaration that its desire for neutrality must be respected.

On August 28 Switzerland alerted its frontier troops. On August 30 a clause in the Swiss Constitution calling for the election of a general as commander in chief in case of a national emergency was put into effect; Gen. Guisan was chosen by the Federal Assembly by a vote of 229 to 204. When **Hitler** invaded **Poland** on September 2, Guisan demanded a decree of general mobilization from the Federal Council and the call-up of 450,000 men. Regulations then required that every citizen keep his arms and equipment at home, ready to act on orders when required. Thus, where the great western powers hesitated, bewildered, in the face of Hitler's reckless actions, Switzerland was the first nation in Europe to be on a complete war footing. It should be remembered, however, that the Swiss army in 1939 consisted of largely untrained, unseasoned troops with obsolete equipment. There was a bare **antiaircraft defense**, no military information sources, not even a master plan. The miniscule Swiss army could not possibly offer much resistance to an attack.

The state of the "inner front" was, if anything, even more disquieting. Switzerland counted more than 200,000 ethnic Germans among its citizens. Thousands of them, staunch Nazis, massed at strategic points awaiting only a signal from their consular leader. In the Italian cantons, the "cultural" agitation could take a dangerous turn. Less given to puppet-like behavior, the ethnic French in Switzerland were discontented as a result of the French experiment with the Popular Front of 1936 and were doubtful about the effects of the **New European Order** Hitler and **Mussolini** had begun to impose.

From September 1939 to June 1940 Guisan erected defensive curtains along the entire frontier. After France was knocked out of the war he decided to change his **tactics** by reorganizing his defense to adjust to the new situation and forming a "national redoubt," with the formidable Alps as his ramparts. To rouse public opinion he assembled the army cadres at Ruetli, where several centuries before the Swiss federation had been born, and, speaking "as a soldier to soldiers," he announced his decision to the country. Throughout the war Guisan was careful to remind his countrymen that they could only escape belligerence by making any invasion of their nation more expensive than its occupation warranted. To support his argument he reasserted his intentions to defend the country at any cost and to exploit every possibility for turning the Alps themselves into an impregnable fortress.

The national redoubt formed a natural wall, running along the breadth of the country from west to east. The best defense, it was decided, would be to abandon the flatlands in front of the mountains and to destroy every installation there that could be of any use to the enemy. Preparations were made to blow up more than 1,000 such installations of every type. Guisan understood that his **strategy** demanded considerable sacrifices of the Swiss living on the flatland and that he must therefore ask their consent. He organized thousands of meetings with special officers; at each one he explained the need for the redoubt. For two months the Swiss worked furiously at their

fortifications, erecting **tank** obstacles, planting artillery of every type, mining all the passages and laying in provisions, medical supplies and munitions to enable the border guard to maintain their positions for months.

The Swiss heeded Guisan with the same fascinated eagerness with which the British heeded **Churchill**. This was a comparable demonstration of the heights to which a democratic people can rise when galvanized into action by a resolute chief.

The Swiss exhibited the same determination in nonmilitary affairs. Depending on the surrounding nations for vital supplies of coal, minerals and raw materials and on what their merchant shipping could bring in via the Italian ports, they were compelled eventually to come to terms with the Germans and Italians. Switzerland consequently had to make concessions hardly consonant with the typical policies of **neutral countries**—authorizing the passage of German and Italian military trains except for troop transports through the Simplon and Saint-Gothard railroad tunnels, delivering various commodities, including war materiel, granting important **credits**, particularly to Italy, and the like. The Allies, of course, protested vigorously, but they understood that these arrangements would also be to their benefit, since the two Axis nations had no choice but to respect Swiss territory if they wanted to keep the tie between them intact.

Italy and especially Germany continually complained of the delay the Swiss took in filling their orders and the pro-Allied sentiments of the Swiss population, press and radio. The Federal Council defended itself against these allegations with increasing brusqueness as the war progressed.

The Swiss radio kept dark a good many secrets it could have exposed—for example, the rumors in Switzerland about the hideousness of daily occurrences in the **concentration camps**—to avoid displeasing the Germans. In any case, it was always objective. At the same time, the citizens of the occupied countries continually tuned in the Swiss stations, in defiance of the German ban on illegal radio reception, paying particular attention to the international commentators Rene Payot and Van Sain.

Swiss neutrality did not prevent any of the nation's editors from paying tribute to the writers in occupied countries who fought the totalitarian Nazi doctrines. The most daring thrust in this direction was made by Albert Beguin in his "Cahiers du Rhone," honoring such authors as Andre Rousseaux, Stanislas Fumet, Emmanuel Mounier and Pierre Emmanuel.

The story of espionage in Switzerland during the war remains obscure. It is certain that services for the **USSR** and the **United Kingdom** operated out of Swiss territory, notably the **Roessler**, Rado and Puenter networks (see also *Narodnyy Kommissariat Vnutrennikh Del*), unknown to the Swiss authorities, who broke up the underground groups they did discover.

Almost 400,000 refugees flooded into Switzerland during the war (see **Evacuation and Resettlement**). With the assistance of the Swiss government, the International **Red Cross** performed many services for prisoners and their families. These Red Cross representatives, generally Swiss citizens, were often heroic. During the infernal debacle of the Third Reich, the Swiss Red Cross saved thousands of concentration camp inmates. But none of this could completely efface the memory of the merciless refusal of asylum to thousands of Jews in 1942 and 1943.

At the end of the war, the Swiss government was the object of bitter criticism from many of its citizens who regarded its policy of neutrality and of countering threats against its territory, economic life and democratic regime as a moral surrender. Actually, in a war in which the survival of democracy was at stake, the Swiss never compromised it.

M. Herman

SYMBOL CONFERENCE.
See **Conferences, Allied**.

SYRIA.
Syria had been the center of a vast Arab **empire** in the eighth century and part of the Turkish empire from 1515 to 1918. Napoleon failed to conquer it in 1799, and the French coveted Syria from then on. The **United Kingdom**, with Arab help, occupied the country in 1918. A national congress declared Syria independent in 1920, but the French took control and drove out Faisal, the newly elected king (who became king of **Iraq** in 1921). The **League of Nations** imposed a French mandate in 1922. Eighteen years of tension between Paris and Damascus followed; nationalist protests and uprisings forced a series of concessions from France, including a 1936 treaty that looked toward Syrian independence, but which the French never ratified. Alexandretta (Hatay) was ceded to **Turkey** in June 1939, to the annoyance of Syrian nationalists.

On July 10, 1939, the French high commissioner suspended the Syrian constitution, which had gone into effect in 1932. He proclaimed on June 28, 1940 that his regime would cease hostilities against **Germany** and **Italy** and accept orders from Vichy. The Vichy government subsequently appointed Gen. **Henri-Fernand Dentz** its high commissioner for the area. In March 1941 renewed Syrian nationalist uprisings led first to repression, then to concessions by local French authorities, who in May allowed *Luftwaffe* aircraft to refuel on their way to fight the British in Iraq. On June 8, 1941 British and Free French forces under **Maitland Wilson** and **Georges Catroux** invaded Syria and conquered the country after five weeks' bitter fighting. The British favored Syrian independence but conceded control to the Free French; in September Catroux proclaimed the country's independence, provided that its policies did not diverge from those of **Free France**. Elections held in 1943 under the restored 1932 constitution returned a very large nationalist majority, and Syria, along with **Lebanon**, was invited, in March 1945, to send delegates to the **United Nations** founding conference in San Francisco. Despite this de facto recognition of Syrian independence, the French made a last attempt to control Damascus by bombarding the city on May 29-30, 1945. They were stopped by the British. The last foreign troops left Syria in April 1946.

M. R. D. Foot

T

TACTICS.

Tactics is the art of obtaining the best distribution of the means of combat on the battlefield—troops, arms and other materiel—at the right time. It involves the preparation of plans, preferably new and better than the enemy's, with advantageous deployment of available means. A distinction should be made between *general tactics* and the *tactics of arms*, the former referring to efficient use of arms and services to insure their smoothest operation and the latter to the same but in connection with a particular branch of the military forces—infantry, armor, airborne etc.

TANCREMONT.

A fort in a belt of redoubts in Liege, **Belgium**. Although completely isolated, it held out until May 29, 1940.

TANKS.

The charts on pages 447-449 trace the evolution of Soviet, German and Anglo-American tanks during World War II.

TARAWA.

See **Gilbert Islands**.

TASK FORCE.

In the course of their air and naval operations in the immense **Pacific theater of operations** and within the limits of their modest means—modest, at least, in 1943, although they swelled rapidly thereafter—American forces formulated the rule of *concentration*. At the same time they were increasing the flexibility of their combat capability, which shortly grew to awesome proportions. The Americans solved their logistical problems in the Pacific, which were considerable because of its vast size, with the task force, a supple striking arm of variable power, depending on its mission. Several task forces could pursue widely separated targets and yet maintain their unity by regrouping immediately afterward. While the terms "squadron" or "fleet" are essentially administrative, the task force organization is much looser. Until the summer of 1942, task forces of limited power, developed for

SOVIET TANKS

Year	Type	Weight in tons	Armor thickness in millimeters	Armament	Speed in kilometers per hour	Cruising range in kilometers
1942-43	T 34/76	28.5	65	one 76.2-mm cannon; two machine guns	55	300
	T 34/85	32	100	one 85-mm cannon; two machine guns	55	300
	KV 85	46	110	one 85-mm cannon; three machine guns	35	250
1944	Joseph Stalin	46	115	one 122-mm cannon; three machine guns	37	150
1945	Pike	50	105	one 100-mm cannon; three machine guns		

N.B. The T-34 was one of the best tanks in the war because of its ease in handling, which resulted from its excellent 300-horsepower diesel engine, which gave it a rated power of 20 horses per ton and a speed of 53 kilometers per hour; its Christie treads, which permtted easy adaptation to high speeds and poor terrain; and its 12-hour range of action. The tank was well profiled. Like all Soviet tanks, its smooth lines and depressed silhouette made it a poor target; the slanted or rounded surfaces of its armor caused enemy projectiles to glance off rather than meeting the tank head-on. In general the treads of Soviet tanks were one-third larger than those of the Germans'. Since their pressure per square unit of area was consequently lower, they were less prone to entrapment in the frozen waterways or bogs which characterize the terrain of eastern Europe.

GERMAN TANKS

Year	Type	Weight in tons	Armor thickness in millimeters — Turret Front	Turret Side	Hull Front	Hull Side	Armament — Cannon — Caliber in millimeters	Weight of shell in kilograms	Muzzle velocity in meters per second	Depth of penetration in millimeters at 500 meter range	Number of machine guns	Maximum speed in kilometers per hour	Cruising range in kilometers	Crew—number of men
1940	Mark I	5.8	15	13	12	15					2	51	139	2
1940	Mark II	10	15	15	15	15	20		800		1	48	200	3
1942	Mark III	12	30	15	30	20	50	1.950	825	56	1	48	200	3
1940	Mark III	18	30	20	30	20	37	0.679	750	30	2	40	160	5
1941		20	30	30	30	30	50 (short)	2.721	750	55	2	40	168	5
1942		22	30	30	50	30	50 (long)	2.721	825	76	2	40	168	5
1940	Mark IV	20	40	30	40	30	75 (short)		385	41	2	40	200	5
1941		22	35	40	60	40	75 (short)	6.500	385	55	2	40	200	5
1942		24	50	30	50	30	75 (long)	6.800	797	89	2	44	200	5
1943		27	80	30	60	30	75 (long)	6.800	797	100	2	44	200	5
End 1942	Mark VI Tiger	56.8	100	82	102	82	88 (70 calibers)	9.000	810	110	2	36	136	5
End 1944	Mark VI Royal Tiger	67	185	80	150	80	88 (71 calibers)	9.970	1,025	182	3	32	168	5
	Mark V Panther	45	110	45	80	40	75	6.525	940	141	2	56	168	5

N.B. "70 calibers" means that the length of the cannon barrel is 70 times the caliber.

BRITISH AND AMERICAN TANKS

| Year | Type | Weight in tons | Armor thickness in millimeters | | | | Armament - Cannon | | | | Number of machine guns | Maximum speed in kilometers per hour | Cruising range in kilometers | Crew—number of men |
| | | | Turret | | Hull | | | | | | | | | |
			Front	Side	Front	Side	Caliber in millimeters	Weight of shell in kilograms	Muzzle velocity in meters per second	Depth of penetration in millimeters at 500 meter range				
1940	Mark VI (British)	5.5	14	12	12	8					1	56	208	3
	Tetrarch (British)	7.5	16	16	16	14	40 (two pounds)	0.908	793	56	1	60	227	3
1941	Matilda (British)	26.5	75	75	78	65	40 (two pounds)	0.908	793	56	1	25	148	4
	Crusader (British)	20	49	24	47	28	40 (two pounds)	0.908	793	56	1	45	320	4
	Valentine (British)	17	65	60	60	43	40 (two pounds)	0.908	793	56	1	23	143	3 or 4
1942	Grant (U.S.)	29.5	76	50	50	38	one 75; one 37	6.700	725	74	1	32	212	6
	Stuart (U.S.)	12.5	44	25	44	25	37	0.870	884	63	2	58	312	4
	Sherman (U.S.)	30	76	51	75	45	75[1]	6.700	725	75	2	40	230	5
1943	Churchill (British)	38.5	90	75	101	75	57 (six pounds)[2]	3.200; 1.500	854; 1,160	80	2	24	198	5
1944	Cromwell (British)	30	76	63	76	46	75	6.550	870	107	2	55	264	5
	Comet (British)	33	101	64	76	43	77	3.500 (armor-piercing)	1,083	202	2	47	198	5
1945	Pershing (U.S.)	43	100	100	100	76	90	11.000; 7.500 (armor-piercing)	910; 1,100	120; 200	2	50	200	5
	Centurion (British)[3]	46	127	76	76	57	76.2 (17 pounds) (armor-piercing)	7.700; 3.500	884; 1,100	162; 253	1	37	145	4

[1] Replaced in 1944 by a 76.2 (17-pound) cannon for, at first, 25 percent, then 50 percent of the Sherman tanks used in the British Army. The new cannon fired a shell weighing 7.7 kilograms with a muzzle velocity of 884 meters per second and an armor-piercing shell weighing 5.5 kilograms with a muzzle velocity of 1,100 meters per second. The armor-piercing shell is a powerful anitank weapon. The diameter of its core is less than that of the launching gun. The shell itself is made of light metal, permitting it to be fired easily. When it strikes its target, the shell separates into fragments from the core as the result of centrifugal force.

[2] Replaced in 1944 by a 75-mm cannon. Ten percent of the Churchills, Shermans and Cromwells had a 95-mm "close support" howitzer.

particular missions, comprised one or two aircraft carriers escorted by cruisers. The "eyes" of the task force were destroyers equipped with search radar, sweeping out a circle 250 miles in diameter. The task force's "vision" was extended further by reconnaissance aircraft. It compensated for its inferiority in firepower by the accuracy of its radar-computer firing system, whose range was 25 miles. This gave the Americans a huge advantage over the Japanese, to whom such sophisticated electronic equipment was practically unknown. After August 1942 American shipyards were able to furnish the task forces with their first high-speed battleships, and in 1943 each task force was reinforced with several aircraft carriers, a number of battleships with considerable antiaircraft firepower and every type of attending vessel necessary for its existence as an independent unit—hospital ships, repair tenders and the like.

The urgent need for aircraft in combat transformed the naval engagement into aero-naval battles. Most of the great sea operations reached their climax with the arrival of bombers and fighters from carriers or land bases. The tactic of ship versus ship gave way to more complex duels between aero-naval combinations. With the increasing effectiveness of battleships' antiaircraft guns, the battle picture was further complicated, with sea-air as well as air-air combat.

Beginning in 1943 the use of task forces became as general among the British as among the Americans. (See the article on **Combined Operations** for a discussion of task forces' role in transporting ground troops for landings on Sicily, Normandy, the **Philippines** and **Okinawa**, among other battlefields.)

H. Bernard

TAXABLE.
Code name for the Anglo-American diversion operation on Boulogne during the **Normandy landing**.

TAYLOR, Maxwell D. (1901-   ).
An American general, Taylor commanded the 101st Airborne Division in the **Normandy landing**, at Eindhoven and in the **Battle of the Bulge**. He was an early advocate of the use of airborne forces. His postwar assignments included superintendent of West Point, Army chief of staff and military adviser to Presidents John F. Kennedy and Lyndon B. Johnson.

TEDDER, Sir Arthur William (later Lord) (1890-1967).
A British airman, Tedder flew in France in 1915-17. He commanded the **Royal Air Force** in the Middle East in 1941-43. In January 1943 he was appointed commander in chief of the Mediterranean Air Command. He oversaw the integration of land, sea and air forces in the Allied drives through Tunisia, Sicily and mainland **Italy**. A farsighted strategist, he was **Eisenhower's** deputy commander for the **Normandy landing**.

TEHERAN CONFERENCE.
See **Conferences, Allied**.

TELEKI, Count Pal (1879-1941).
Hungarian prime minister. Teleki took his own life to protest the passage of German troops through his country to attack **Yugoslavia**.

TEMPLER, Sir Gerald W. R. (1898-1979).
A British general, Templer served in World War I. In 1942-44 he commanded several divisions and the Second Corps. He was chief of the Imperial General Staff from 1955 to 1958.

TERBOVEN, Josef (1898-1945).
A German politician and an ardent member of the **Nazi Party**, Terboven was *Gauleiter* of Essen from 1928 to 1940. As *Reichskommissar* for **Norway** from 1940 to 1945, he pursued a brutal policy. He committed suicide on May 9, 1945 rather than be taken by the Allies.

TERMINAL CONFERENCE.
See **Conferences, Allied**.

TERROR AND COUNTER-TERROR.
In planning their conquest of Europe, the Nazis did not foresee a war in the classic pattern, aimed only at the acquisition of territory. The military aspect of World War II was accompanied by an attempt at ideological conquest to insure a truly "totalitarian" grasp of the conquered regions. The domestication of minds and souls was to accompany the annexation of the territory containing them, and dissidents were promised a quick death—or perhaps a slower, more painful one. This new concept, giving the war the aspect of religious conversion by fire and sword, motivated the unchecked hatred and violence that quickly filled the occupied countries and escalated the ensuing repression and extermination.

In all European countries the Nazi occupation rested on a policy of terror from the very first. Summary executions, trials by "kangaroo courts" followed by executions on flimsy charges and the seizure of hostages became commonplace everywhere. On February 15, 1940 a secret general directive of the *Oberkommando der Wehrmacht* ordered the periodic capture of hostages, and successive decrees recommended the greatest severity for offenders. Lending assistance to or sheltering escaped prisoners, secretly crossing a demarcation line, disobeying or neglecting an order to keep watch on some suspect or brawling with a German soldier were often punishable by death.

As such policies became generally recognized, a sullen rage settled in among the populations subject to these senseless and disproportionate reprisals. Attacks on German soldiers in the summer of 1941 marked the first appearance of counter-terror as a means of retaliations. The occupation authorities responded in turn, with mass executions. On September 16, 1941 an order issued by **Wilhelm Keitel** called for the execution of 50 to 100 hostages for every German soldier killed in all the occupied countries of Europe from **Norway** to **Greece**. Local authorities everywhere posted "hostage laws." From that time on, all residents of an occupied country detained for any reason by the authorities were to be considered hostages. For every attempt to murder a member of the occupation army there was an execution of hostages, and every such execution launched a new series of attempts to murder occupiers. The escalation was beginning. Thus it was that on September 17, 1942, 116 hostages were executed in retaliation for the death of a single German soldier in Paris.

Resentment of the Germans was exacerbated by the *Nacht und Nebel* decree, providing for deportations into the unknown, the legalization of "hard interrogation," reprisals against fugitives' family members or fellow employees, sudden police raids and the wanton destruction of homes and villages. Hatred of the occupiers became general, and that facilitated and provoked more attempts to kill Germans. On May 27, 1942 the Czech Resistance mortally wounded **Reinhard Heydrich**, **Himmler**'s right hand and the head of the Central Security Service as well as vice protector of **Bohemia-Moravia**. He died on June 4. In reprisal the Czech villages of **Lidice** and Lezaky were annihilated and their inhabitants massacred or deported.

On October 18, 1942, to stifle the activity of **Resistance** groups in western European countries, **Hitler** issued a directive to army commanders authorizing the extermination to the last man of "gangs of English saboteurs and their valets," in uniform or out, armed or not, or their delivery to the **SS** if they were captured alive. Some German officers ignored the order; **Erwin Rommel** burned his the moment he received it. In any event, resistance to the Germans continued; so did Nazi atrocities—provoked and otherwise.

In September 1941, 33,000 Russian Jews were slaughtered in the gorges of Babi Yar, near Kiev. In October 1941 seven Greek villages were razed and 416 male inhabitants shot. In **Yugoslavia** the towns of Kriva Reka, Machkovae and Skela were set afire and their inhabitants murdered. In the Ukraine and the Crimea, dozens of Soviet villages suffered the same fate. In Marseilles 25,000 inhabitants of the Vieux Port quarter were expelled in January 1943 and the

quarter destroyed. Near Rome 335 men 15- to 74-years-old were massacred in the **Ardeatine Caves** in March 1944, and in June of that year Filetto in the Abruzzi Apennines was burned to the ground and 17 of its inhabitants shot.

In the last months of the occupation of Europe, political and military events synchronized with reprisals. In June and July 1944, in the wake of the **Normandy landing**, dozens of French villages fell victim to such reprisals, among them Tulle, where 99 hostages were hanged, Argenton-sur-Creuse and **Oradour-sur-Glane**, which was reduced to ashes, leaving 642 dead. In August and September the Germans carried out massacres in Zaguiez and Udora in Yugoslavia and in de Foret, Marcourt, Ghlin and Jemappes in **Belgium**. **Gerd von Rundstedt**'s offensive in December in the Ardennes (see **Bulge, Battle of the**) was accompanied by wholesale murder in 31 villages in the Belgian Ardennes, notably Bande and Stavelot, where the Germans murdered 140 civilians. On March 7, 1945, German commanders in **the Netherlands** gave orders to shoot 80 hostages and destroy their homes. As usual the results were absolutely contrary to the effect sought.

J. Delarue

THAILAND.

Thailand has been independent since the Thais conquered it from the Khmers in the 13th century, except for the Japanese occupation from 1941-45. Anglo-French strength and rivalry kept Thailand from being occupied by either power, or any other, during the European empires' expansion into the Far East. Over four-fifths of the population are Buddhist peasants, little interested in politics or war.

Col. (later Marshal) Pibul Songgram, Thailand's prime minister from 1938-44, was strongly pro-Japanese, having come to admire **Mussolini**, and **fascism** in general, while studying in France. When **Japan** attacked the **United States** (see **Pearl Harbor**), he facilitated a Japanese invasion of Thailand. No defense was offered, and in a matter of days Japanese forces passed straight through Thailand to attack **Burma** and **Malaya**. As a reward, Thailand was given the two Shan states of Burma and the four most northerly states of Malaya.

Pibul's political rival, Pridi Phanomyong, was made regent of the young King Ananda in 1942; he secretly got in touch with the **Office of Strategic Services** (OSS) and the **Special Operations Executive** (SOE). In Thailand these two services were rivals rather than allies (see **multilateral wars**), the Americans—and indeed the Thais—being suspicious of British imperialism. After Pibul was forced from power in July 1944 by a parliamentary vote, which the Japanese ignored, Pridi held power behind the scenes. The OSS and the SOE both parachuted in a few agents and radio operators; there was much talk but no actual shooting. The Japanese in Thailand surrendered, with the rest of Japan's forces, in September 1945, and Thailand's independence quietly resumed. Just as quietly the areas taken over in 1942 were handed back to the British.

M. R. D. Foot

THEUNIS, Georges (1873-1966).
A Belgian officer, engineer, financier and statesman, Theunis was **Belgium**'s minister of finance in 1920, prime minister from 1921 to 1924 and ambassador extraordinary to Washington in October 1939. When, in September 1940, the dean of the Belgian diplomatic corps abroad notified his colleagues that the war was over for Belgium and the **Congo**, Theunis responded with a scathing letter that Belgium and the Congo would remain in the war at the side of the **United Kingdom**. When a portion of the Belgian gold held in France was delivered by Vichy to the Germans, Theunis obtained a lien on the equivalent of that sum in French gold for delivery to the **United States**.

THIRD REICH.
See **Germany**.

THIRD REPUBLIC.
After the elections of 1936, the members of the Popular Front in the French Chamber of Deputies, who had been elected on the slogan "bread, peace, liberty," saw extensive changes in political configurations. The radicals, under the influence of **Edouard Herriot**, president of the Chamber, and **Edouard Daladier**, president of *Conseil d'Etat*, allied themselves with the right center majority, as they had so many times after a leftist victory. Diplomatic setbacks, particularly the Czechoslovakian crisis and the **Munich Pact** in September 1938, profoundly divided the various parties that constituted the Popular Front. More than the others, the Communists vehemently asserted their wholehearted espousal of the struggle against **fascism**. They protested, with no result, when **Germany** occupied **Bohemia-Moravia** in March 1939, and again in April when **Mussolini** invaded **Albania**. They also criticized the Daladier government bitterly for its moves to establish diplomatic relations with **Franco**, now ensconced in Madrid after winning the Spanish civil war, and opposed the appointment of Marshal Petain as ambassador to **Spain**. Fears aroused by the international crisis were great enough to bring about the reelection of Pres. **Albert Lebrun** for

another seven-year term. The introduction of a new candidate, it was feared, would have divided the country.

The relative peace occasioned by an adjourned parliament and paid leaves was abruptly shattered by Polish-German border incidents and especially by the news of the conclusion of the **Nazi-Soviet Pact**. The French in particular regarded the pact as a cruel blow because most of them, the Communists in particular, had hoped for a French entente with the **USSR** as the medicine **Hitler** needed to keep him quiet. The politicians were all the more divided since **Stalin**'s astonishing about-face seemed to many of them a betrayal of the anti-fascist ideal the Soviet dictator had professed to personify. The Communist deputies who remained faithful to him soon found themselves pursued, and sometimes jailed, first in France and then in Algeria, while the secretary of the Communist Party, Maurice Thorez, fled to Moscow. Armed, in the form of the pact, with additional ammunition against the Communists, the right demanded that broader measures be directed against the party, which was held responsible not only for acts of **sabotage** against French factories but also for the undeniably poor **morale** of the French troops. In fact, after the raids in the Warndt Forest left French troops in position from **Luxembourg** to the Rhine, the inaction of the **Phony War** would in itself have been enough to destroy the fighting spirit of the army totally, badly housed as it was in an especially severe winter.

The intrigues continued. The advocates of compromise, negotiating sporadically, with **Italy** as a mediator, were at odds with those demanding greater diplomatic activity. The Soviet demands on **Finland** (see **Russo-Finnish Winter War**) presented opportunities for both sides, but these came to naught in the face of the need to deprive the USSR of oil to prevent its being given to the Germans under the provisions of the pact. This situation in turn meant that French troops in the Middle East could not be moved. The political rivalries within the French parliament ended with the disappearance of the Daladier cabinet. Reinforced by the support of several Socialists, **Paul Reynaud** attempted to bring France's strategic paralysis to an end, without success. The speed with which the Germans took **Denmark** and soon thereafter all of **Norway**—by May 1940—was stupefying. The failure of the western European Allies to stop them weakened Reynaud, who tried to gain the support of the right by bringing Petain and **Georges Mandel** into his cabinet. He also gave command of the army to Gen. **Maxime Weygand**, recalling him from **Syria** to save the military situation endangered by the German offensive toward the Meuse through Luxembourg and **Belgium** (see *Fall Gelb*). In 10 days the *Wehrmacht* arrived at the estuary of the Somme river, encircling Belgian, British and French troops deprived of possible aid from the Dutch and Belgian armies, both of which had surrendered. The flight of the population from the countryside before the advancing menace of German troops (see **Evacuation and Resettlement**) spread panic to Paris. Several weeks later, whatever hope remained was blasted by Italy's entrance into the war. The evacuation of the French government first to Touraine and then to Bordeaux set in motion a variety of intrigues among the regime's opponents—Weygand, in particular, who imagined he could salvage the prestige and authority of the French army as well as preserve public order by getting the civil authorities to surrender. In the meantime, the French troops, harassed by a seasoned, well-equipped enemy, were paralyzed by a thick stream of civilians running frantically from strafing German aircraft, while administrative officers abandoned their posts.

Reynaud gave way to Petain as head of the government. Several hours later the public learned from the radio of the request for an armistice, worded to give the impression that the negotiations were already complete and that there was consequently no point in further fighting. The inclusion of Bordeaux in the occupied zone forced the politicians to move to Vichy.

The perennially ambitious **Pierre Laval** was intent on resuming the ministerial career the Popular Front had interrupted. He was an expert in political strategy as well as Petain's adviser, and was thus in an excellent position to use the state of siege under which France found itself to discourage politicians who opposed his policies. Some unexpected demonstrations by French military groups that had escaped disbandment scared the hesitant deputies into throwing their support to the "Republican Marshal" of 1934 to ward off a military dictatorship. As a result, only 80 deputies had the nerve to vote against granting Petain full power to organize the **French State** in the vote taken on July 10. Laval accumulated a supporting chorus of generals, admirals, politicians, businessmen and technocrats whose loyalty was rewarded with positions of power which were secure from administrative or parliamentary interference. These men proceeded to guarantee their positions by enacting a series of measures to control potential enemies of their "national revolution" (see **Petain and the French State**) while permitting their exploitation of the economic consequences of the defeat.

J. Vidalenc

TIMOR.
An island with about 900,000 inhabitants in the

Timor Sea at the eastern tip of the Malay Archipelago. Its western portion was part of the Dutch East Indies and its eastern portion was under Portuguese control. In February 1942 it was captured by Japanese forces.

TIMOSHENKO, Semion K. (1895-1970).
In 1940-41 Timoshenko was a marshal of the USSR, commissar of defense and commander in chief of several army groups; from 1941 to 1945 he was vice-commissar of defense.

TISO, Yosef (1887-1947).
After the **Munich Pact** in 1938, Tiso, a Czechoslovak priest, became president of the Federal Slovak Government. On March 14, 1939, with the approval of **Hitler**, he proclaimed the independence of Slovakia and from October 1939 to 1945 served as president of the Slovak Republic. He was condemned to death in a people's court and was hanged at Bratislava.

TITO (real name Josip Broz) (1892-1980).
Tito, a Yugoslavian Communist leader and a Croatian, was a **prisoner of war** in Russia from 1915 to 1917. He fought in the Red Army from 1917 to 20; shortly thereafter he joined the Yugoslavian Communist Party, for which he was imprisoned from 1928 to 1933. In 1936-37 he arranged, from Paris, clandestine recruiting for the International Brigades in republican **Spain**; in 1937 he became the secretary-general of the Yugoslavian Communist Party.

When, in April 1941, **Yugoslavia** was invaded, Tito at once began to organize a **resistance** movement; from the end of June he set out to build a revolutionary state independent of the occupier. He had 12,000 Communists to help him, including 300 who had fought in Spain. Tito set up his first base at Uzice, in western Serbia. He insisted on Serbo-Croatian cooperation, and fought Germans, Italians, **Ustachi** (Croatian terrorists: see also **Ante Pavelich**) and Chetniks (see **Dragolyub Mihailovich**). In 1942-43 his army, which had risen to 20,000 people—**women** fought in it alongside men—was harried through Bosnia and Montenegro but never cornered. In November 1942 he set up a national assembly at Bihac; it traveled through the mountains with the rest of the force. His stamina, determination and leadership were vital to the partisan movement, as was the toughness of the southern Slavs. The movement's strength rose tenfold after the Italian surrender in September 1943. By this time the British, on the advice of **Special Operations Executive** officers on the spot, were supplying him with arms by air and flying out his wounded, most of whom he had carried with him on the march. The **Office of Strategic Services** followed the SOE's example. **Stalin** had recommended

TITO

that Tito cooperate with the Chetniks and sent him hardly any supplies until April 1944.

In December 1943 he was proclaimed marshal and became president of the liberation council, a de facto though as yet unrecognized government. In the autumn of 1944 Tito's partisans cooperated with the Red Army's left wing in clearing the Germans out of Yugoslavia, capturing Belgrade on October 20. The Red Army moved on; Tito remained in charge of the Federal People's Republic of Yugoslavia.

M. R. D. Foot

TIZARD, Sir Henry Thomas (1885-1959).
A British scientist, Tizard served as an airman in World War I. As chairman of the Aeronautical Research Committee from 1933, he encouraged the development of **radar** and other devices. He visited **Canada** and the **United States** in 1940 and **Australia** in 1943 to promote scientific **research. Churchill's** preference for **Frederick Lindemann's** advice led to Tizard's return to academic life. He later served as chairman of the Defense Research Council (1947-52).

TODT, Fritz (1891-1942).
A Nazi engineer, Todt was founder in 1938 of the Todt Organization, a military group with the responsibility of capital construction projects of high strategic value, such as the Siegfried Line, railroad facilities in the rear of the German army in Russia and the **Atlantic Wall.** From March 1940 to his accidental death in 1942, he was minister for armaments and munitions.

TOGO, Shigenori (1882-1950).
Togo was foreign minister of **Japan** both when **Pearl Harbor** was attacked on December 7, 1941 and when Japan surrendered on August 15, 1945. Togo opposed the war but also resisted major concessions to the **United States** in 1941. He returned to office four years later expressly to help end the war. He died while serving a 20-year sentence imposed by the International Military Tribunal for the Far East for his part in a conspiracy to bring about war with the U.S.

Togo was born in Kagoshima prefecture, graduated from Tokyo Imperial University in 1908 and entered the foreign ministry. He represented Japan at the **League of Nations** in 1930 and served as ambassador to the **USSR** in 1938. He joined the new **Tojo** cabinet as foreign minister on October 18, 1941 and strove to find a diplomatic solution with America without modifying Japan's basic demands. There is little weight to the charge that Togo deliberately delayed notifying the Americans of the attack on Pearl Harbor.

When **Kantaro Suzuki,** the aging admiral, formed his cabinet on April 7, 1945, he appointed Togo foreign minister once again because "he was a man who was clearly opposed to the war" and could bring about peace. Togo tentatively made **peace overtures** to the Soviet Union, despite many misgivings, in May. He correctly imagined that the Soviets had reached an agreement with their allies (at Yalta—see **Conferences, Allied)** about the postwar disposition of territories in East Asia, making them immune to concessions from Japan in return for mediating a negotiated peace. With support from **Hirohito,** expressed at an imperial conference on June 22, Togo, **Koki Hirota** and eventually **Fumimaro Konoe** all vainly sought Soviet intervention.

When the Allies called on Japan to surrender at Potsdam on July 26, Togo tried without success to prevent the supreme war council from dismissing the call. After Hiroshima was destroyed on August 6 and the USSR entered the war two days later, he urgently pressed the emperor and the supreme war council to capitulate (see **Surrender Decision by Japan).** With the emperor's forthright concurrence, this view prevailed and Japan capitulated on August 15.

T. R. H. Havens

TOJO, Hideki (1884-1948).
Tojo, a Japanese army career officer, became war minister under Prince **Fumimaro Konoe** in July 1940; he became prime minister in his own right before **Pearl Harbor,** serving in that capacity from October 1941-July 1944. In his junior days Tojo was heard to say, "I am not intelligent, so unless I study hard I shall not become a great man." As a senior officer he remarked: "Endeavor and hard work have been my friends throughout life, as I am just an ordinary man possessing no brilliant talents." While not physically big, even as a schoolboy he was pugnacious, fearless and stubborn, his brawls earning him the nickname of "Roughneck." His later sobriquet, "The Razor," referred to his rapier-like mind and mannerisms. Possessed of an all-business attitude, he was not given to vague, complicated or indirect behavior. A man of action, not a profound thinker, he was precise, decisive, forthright, devoted and simple, a good executive instead of a genius or broad-visioned statesman. Critics called him self-righteous, impatient, intolerant, short-sighted, tactless, hot-tempered, vain, hasty, high-strung and increasingly conceited and tyrannical, though, for better or worse, he was known to keep his word. In later life he was less direct and simple, more morose and arrogant. Despite his undoubted strength and unforgiving memory, however, he was never the dictator, even in wartime, that was

454

imagined in Western countries. Given the Japanese style of governing by consensus, he more nearly resembled a forceful chairman of the board, whose sanctions included surveillance, pressure and personal reprisals such as induction into military service, banishments and transfers.

From a family of 10, Tojo was the son of Hidenori, a man of great ability from rather humble feudal stock, not from one of the traditional main provinces but from a minor outside fief in remote northern Japan. Tojo's father rose from a noncommissioned cadet rank in the 1870s to retirement as a lieutenant general in 1908 at the age of only 53. With the death of his father at an early age and the demise of his older brothers, Hideki had to assume serious family responsibilities. His early life was humdrum. After attending military prep school, he graduated in the 17th military academy class of 1905, ranking a highly respectable 10th among 363 graduates. Commissioned a second lieutenant near the end of the Russo-Japanese War, he spent seven years in the infantry. He married the well-educated, strong-willed Katsuko Ito, by whom he had seven children between 1911 and 1932. He graduated from the prestigious army war college, indispensable for high military position, with honors in 1915 as a captain. His colleagues in the 27th Class included future Gens. **Massaharu Homma** and **Hiroshi Oshima**. When World War I ended he was sent to **Switzerland**, where he spent two years as an assistant military attache, holding the rank of major after 1920. In the summer of 1921 he visited **Germany**, his only direct and sustained exposure to a non-Asian milieu in his life. He returned to Japan late in 1921, rushing across the **United States** by train after visiting the Washington conference. It is highly probable that he was more impressed by his months in postwar Germany (with whose language he was acquainted) than by his brief trip to the United States (whose language he could not speak and which he seemed very anxious to leave).

The next years brought Tojo promotions and important assignments, at the army war college, the war ministry and the army general staff. He became a colonel in 1928 at the age of 44, after being on active duty for 23 years; five years later he was promoted to the general-officer rank (major general, there being no brigadier rank in the Imperial Japanese Army). In the highly political atmosphere that permeated the military during the 1930s, when Japan was often termed a "government by assassination," Tojo threaded the shoals, upsetting some Army luminaries, impressing other important personages by his indisputable ability and drive. After loyally carrying out a number of unpopular assignments designed to get him away from military politics at the center in Tokyo, he was saved

from oblivion by the commander of the powerful Kwantung Army in Manchuria, Gen. Minami, who invited him to become the *Kempei* chief of the field army. This proved to be a turning point in Tojo's life, a stepping-stone to bigger and better posts of authority. As one commentator later put it, "Getting kicked out of Tokyo was about as vexing for Tojo as falling down a sewer and finding a gold watch."

From 1935 until 1937, when he became chief of staff of the Kwantung Army, Tojo played a dominant role in Manchuria, where he earned such epithets as "a forerunner of **Himmler**" and "the bogeyman of Manchukuo." Promoted to lieutenant general at the end of 1936, he commented, "Now I can face my father without shame." Tojo was an adherent of the *Tosei-ha* or control faction in the army, and he enthusiastically cracked down on the rival imperial way faction (*Kodo-ha*), instigators of the short-lived 2-26 mutiny in Tokyo in February 1936, an insurrection that Tojo termed "unpardonable." Pursuing "military police politics," for which he was well known, Tojo kept the Kwantung Army quiet, arresting 500 to 600 imperial way suspects and heartening the loyalists in Japan. During this last major domestic disturbance of the 1930s, Tojo had the good fortune or the good sense to emerge on the winning side.

As Kwantung Army chief of staff, Tojo was the kingpin, surrounding himself with loyal and ambitious subordinates. When hostilities broke out between Chinese and Japanese forces at the Marco Polo Bridge in Peking in July 1937, Tojo was quick to rush reinforcements to northern **China** from Manchuria. The next month, in his only real combat experience (at the age of 53), he led the Tojo Corps into Chahar Province in Inner Mongolia, conducting a *fait accompli* with lightning success. Reward for his services in Manchuria ensued: appointment to his most important post to date—vice minister of war under Seishiro Itagaki, from May 1938. His tenure was marked by its brevity (six months) and belligerent public utterances. At the end of the year, he was put on ice as inspector general of army aviation and chief of the air headquarters. After one and a half years in these undramatic posts, Tojo returned to center stage, as war minister in the Konoe cabinet from July 1940. The prince-prime minister would live to regret Tojo's association with him, but at the time the general had demonstrated his suitability for the position by his administrative skills, his aggressive patriotism and political steadiness, his persuasiveness and sincerity, his quickness and decisiveness and his closeness to high military circles in Tokyo. By all accounts he was the ablest and the most successful war minister in modern times, during a period of 15 months of mounting tension on the international scene. Tojo became the spokesman for the hawkish elements in Japan, espousing a get-tough policy in the face of American diplomatic maneuvering. Intoxicated by the success of the *Wehrmacht* in Europe and the attendant weakening of the Western powers' imperial stance in Asia, Tojo and his associates strengthened ties with the **Axis** dictatorships, culminating in the **Tripartite Pact** signed in Berlin in September 1940. Tojo was influential in the deliberations on "north vs. south" **strategy** that raged in high command circles during 1940-41.

Konoe's increasing difficulties with Tojo regarding the feasibility of a Japanese-American diplomatic settlement led to an irreconcilable impasse. In October 1941 Konoe fell, to be replaced as prime minister by a general whose cabinet "reeked of gunpowder." Tojo had been selected by the imperial advisers with indispensable military recommendation, not because he was popular (which he was not) or jingoistic (which he was) but because he was dedicated to military discipline and was expected to be able to control the hotheaded army in a time of national crisis. In addition he was known to be loyal to the throne, vigorous and knowledgeable.

It became easier for Tojo to chair the board as prime minister because he retained his army commission, unlike all previous officers who had held that government post. He continued to serve simultaneously as army minister throughout his 33-month-long cabinet, and for the first three months of his administration he also held the home ministry portfolio. When the munitions ministry was founded in November 1943, he headed it as well. Still, Tojo was no dictator. His aim was to moderate the fierce competition among wartime elites and coordinate not only the desperate war abroad but also **production** at home. That he failed is less remarkable than that he took on far greater duties than any Japanese prime minister before or since.

Although he was poorly cast for the part, Tojo was undone in the end by twin flaws he could not mend: institutional weaknesses in the Japanese polity and a deteriorating war situation. Politicians, industrialists, bureaucrats and military leaders muted their rivalries during the wartime emergency, but no Japanese leader had the force of personality to transcend the lack of institutionalized policy-coordination mechanisms and assure consensus. Tojo never got the upper hand over the navy, even when he took full control of munitions production and simultaneously became army chief of staff late in his cabinet. The campaigns abroad suffered as a result, although even the most unified command and well-planned mobilization could not have withstood the loss of shipping lifelines to the U.S. Navy or the destruction of Japanese cities by the Army Air Corps. His narrow outlook and stubborn refusal to

modify Japan's war policies in the face of growing Allied strength led to his forced resignation on July 18, 1944.

Soon after Japan surrendered, Tojo learned that he and other top Japanese leaders would be tried for war crimes before an international military court (see **war criminals**). When police arrived to arrest him at his Ikenoue home in Tokyo on September 11, 1945, Tojo tried to kill himself with a revolver. He survived, faced his court trial with great composure, and argued unsuccessfully that he had led Japan on a course that was both legal and proper, given the hostility and growing encirclement of the Allied powers. Sentenced to death, he chanted the Buddhist rosary en route to his execution by hanging two days before Christmas 1948.

A. D. Coox
T. R. H. Havens

TOKYO ROSE.
As a part of its **psychological warfare** against the **United States**, Radio Tokyo broadcast programs of dance music and nostalgic reminiscences about life back home to American troops stationed in the southwestern Pacific during World War II. The most widely known announcer, an American citizen of Japanese descent named Iva Ikuko Toguri, was dubbed "Tokyo Rose" by her audience. Other clear-voiced women with impeccable English also entertained American troops with broadcasts from the Tokyo headquarters of NHK, the state-owned radio network that was controlled by the **Cabinet Information Board.** There is little evidence to suggest that the programs were successful in demoralizing the American troops, but they were extremely popular in war zones where few other diversions could be found.

Toguri was arrested after the war by U.S. officials and charged with **treason.** Her defense was that she was caught in **Japan** at the time of **Pearl Harbor**, visiting her sick aunt, and originally went to work for NHK as a secretary to support herself. The court fined her $10,000 and sentenced her to 10 years in prison. She was released after six years and waged a tireless campaign, together with her husband Philip D'Aquino, to clear her name. She was pardoned by President Gerald Ford on January 19, 1977.

TOLBUKHIN, Fedor I. (1894-1949).
Tolbukhin was commander in chief of the 57th Army in the battle of Stalingrad and then of the Third Ukrainian Front. He was promoted to marshal in 1944 and commanded occupation troops in **Austria** in 1945.

TORCH.
Code name for the Anglo-American landing in North

Africa in November 1942 (see **World War II—General Conduct**).

TOYODA, Soemu (1885-1957).

A Japanese admiral, Toyoda became commander in chief of the Japanese Combined Fleet in 1944. Toyoda was condemned to imprisonment as a **war criminal** by the International Military Tribunal for the Far East; he was liberated in 1949. After his appointment as navy chief of staff in 1945, he sided with the army leaders—Gens. **Korechika Anami** and Yoshijiro Umezu—who wanted Japan to continue fighting (see **Surrender Decision by Japan**).

TREASON.

By the mid-1930s the problems of treason and loyalty had again become as acute as they were in the 16th and 17th centuries. **Fascism** and communism provided fresh ways of looking at the world, comparable to the doctrines of the Reformation and the counter-Reformation, and the civil war in **Spain** showed that these were doctrines for which men would kill and be killed, as they had done in earlier, religious wars.

Yet earlier allegiances remained firm in many strata of **society**, and the concept that it was a moral imperative to obey duly constituted authority remained strong. Intense difficulties arose for men of the utmost integrity and good will who found themselves facing in opposite directions. The French will long argue, for example, who was the traitor and who the patriot, **de Gaulle** or Petain? The Vichy regime did not hesitate to prosecute for treason Communists who sought to work with the Nazis in 1940-41. In **Poland**, **Czechoslovakia** and **Yugoslavia**, what constituted treasonable conduct depended on which side one took in a many-sided war and what army of occupation was in one's village, city etc.

In many countries released from German occupation, there were witch-hunts, sometimes inspired as much by petty personal motives as by grand (or ignoble) political ones. In France the **purges** that followed the liberation are reliably reported to have killed about one in a thousand of the population. Even in the unoccupied **United Kingdom**, there were several trials, and two men were hanged for having given aid and comfort to the king's enemies.

In the **USSR** authorities took an even sterner view. Every returned **prisoner of war**—1.2 million managed to survive and return, out of some six million taken prisoner—was automatically held to have become a "traitor" to the Soviet Union by the act of surrender and was given a long sentence in a labor camp, irrespective of the circumstances of his surrender or return.

The matter may be summed up in an English epigram of over 300 years ago:

Treason doth never prosper. What's the reason?
If it doth prosper, none dare call it treason.

M. R. D. Foot

TRENCHARD, Hugh Montague (Viscount) (1873-1956).

Chief of staff of the **Royal Air Force** in 1918, Trenchard planned a massive bombing of Berlin with the new Super Handley-Page aircraft, but the armistice ending hostilities was signed before the raid could be carried out. The first RAF general to be promoted to marshal in 1927, Trenchard unsuccessfully sought the creation of a strategic air force in the **United Kingdom**. He nevertheless managed, through education, training and the schools he founded, to form the nucleus of the powerful **Bomber Command** of the future. (See **Germany, Air Battle of; Aviation, Strategic Anglo-American [in Europe]**.)

TRESCKOW, Henning von (1901-1944).

A German general and chief of staff under Gens. **Fedor von Bock** and **Guenther von Kluge**, Tresckow had a bomb planted in **Hitler**'s plane after the Fuehrer's visit to the eastern front on March 13, 1943, but the bomb failed to explode. Several other times in the 1943-44 period he made attempts on Hitler's life. When the **assassination attempt of July 20, 1944** failed, Tresckow took his own life in despair.

TRIDENT CONFERENCE.

See **Conferences, Allied**.

TRIESTE.

The port of Trieste and the surrounding territory had been returned to **Italy** in 1918. It was taken by the Germans at the time of the Italian surender to the Allies in 1943. In May 1945, according to the terms of the Yalta agreement, the Anglo-American forces occupied the primarily Italian city and the northern region of the Gulf of Trieste, mostly Slovenian, known as Zone A. **Tito**, who claimed the entire region including the city of Trieste, occupied the littoral to the south, mainly Croatian, called Zone B. The peace treaty with Italy, effective in February 1947, stipulated that both zones combined constituted the Free Territory of Trieste, guaranteed by the **United Nations**. For lack of unanimous consent by the Security Council, the proposal was never consummated. In 1954, however, Italy and **Yugoslavia** signed a provisional de facto accord awarding Zone A to Italy and Zone B to Yugoslavia, with guarantees to minority nationalities in both zones.

TRIPARTITE PACT.

In Article I of this pact, which was signed in Berlin on September 27, 1940, binding **Germany, Italy** and **Japan** as comrades-in-arms, Japan recognized the right of Germany and Italy to "create a **new European order**," while Germany and Italy recognized the right of Japan to "create a new order in all the Asiatic space" (see **New Order in East Asia**). The most significant portions of this document—at least, for the citizens of the three powers—were Article 3, in which the signatories pledged "to sustain each other mutually by every political, economic and military means if any one of the three contracting parties is attacked by a power not now engaged in the European war or the Sino-Japanese conflict," and Article 5, providing that "none of the foregoing provisions in any way affect the political status between each of the three contracting parties and the Soviet Union." No great effort of the imagination was required to realize that the mysterious "power" referred to in Article 3 was the **United States**.

The participants in the actual writing of the treaty indicated, however, that during the secret conferences in Tokyo in August 1940 between the Japanese foreign minister **Yosuke Matsuoka** and the German envoy—in which Italy did not participate—ancillary agreements stipulated that in case of war Japan was to keep its freedom of action. The effect of this, naturally, was to vitiate the clause that would have seemed automatically to embroil the other two participants if the third should be attacked. The contract, in effect, had built-in loopholes.

The Japanese government and the German government, represented by **Joachim von Ribbentrop**, hoped to divide the eastern hemisphere into four great regions. Southern Asia, including **India**, was to go to the **USSR**—thus included in the treaty—in accordance with the old concept of a "continental bloc" which, with the Eurasian bloc, would enclose the two Anglo-Saxon naval powers in a gargantuan pincers forged by the three powers of the pact plus the USSR. But this scheme did not appeal to **Hitler**, and in his talks with **Molotov** during November 12-13, 1940 in Berlin it was abandoned. In place of this great power, several small powers were brought into the Tripartite Pact—**Hungary**, on November 20, 1940; **Rumania**, on November 22, 1940; Slovakia, on November 23, 1940; **Bulgaria**, on March 1, 1941; and **Yugoslavia**, on March 25, 1941. Yugoslavia, however, dropped out of the pact after the Belgrade revolt of March 27, 1941; it was replaced by **Croatia** on June 15, 1941.

In secret negotiations conducted with the United States in the summer and fall of 1941 regarding a detente between the two powers in the Pacific and East Asia, the Japanese government seemed ready to forget the pact in exchange for some concessions from the Americans. But Washington hardened its position, and the Japanese embraced the pact with renewed enthusiasm at the end of November 1941. Although Germany and Italy were not enjoined to participate in the attack on the United States on December 7, 1941, Hitler and **Mussolini** declared war on their associate's new enemy four days later. The smaller signatories to the Tripartite Pact followed suit reluctantly after several days under prodding from Germany.

The pact was supplemented by a German-Japanese-Italian protocol signed in Berlin on December 11, 1941 forbidding any separate armistice or peace agreement with any one of the Anglo-Saxon powers. Article 3 of that protocol called for the close cooperation of the three signatories "even after the end of a victorious war, with the coming of the new order in the sense of the Tripartite Pact of September 27, 1940." But such coordination was impossible in view of the divergence of interests and the pretenses to superiority of each of the three nations. The pact therefore took its place among the ranks of the many forgotten proposals of the past to divide up the world.

On May 6, 1945, just before the surrender of its exhausted German comrades, the Japanese government disavowed all treaties concluded with the Reich.

A. Hillgruber

TROTSKY, Leon (Lev Davidovitch Bronstein) (1879-1940).

A Russian revolutionary, Trotsky advocated permanent revolution in Russia beginning in 1906. With Lenin he seized power in November 1917. He was exiled from the **USSR** by **Stalin** in 1929. Trotsky founded the Fourth International in Mexico but not long after was assassinated by a NKVD agent (see *Narodnyy Kommissariat Vnutrennikh Del*).

TROTT ZU SOLZ, Adam von (1907-1944).

A German jurist opposed to the Nazis, Trott was an indefatigable seeker of peace from 1939 to 1944. In this cause, he traveled to the **United Kingdom**, the **United States, Sweden, Switzerland** and **Italy**. He was hanged at Ploetzensee on August 25, 1944.

TRUMAN, Harry S (1884-1972).

Truman grew up on a farm in Missouri. He graduated from high school but a lack of funds prevented him from attending college. Before serving in France during World War I, he held various jobs, including mailroom clerk and bookkeeper. After the war he married Mary Elizabeth (Bess) Wallace in 1919. In the early 1920s Truman entered local politics in Kansas City and was elected to two terms as county court judge. Running on the Democratic ticket, he won a seat in the Senate in 1934. Six years later he was chairman of a special "watchdog" committee that uncovered instances of mismanagement and fraud in national defense expenditures. His work on the committee saved the government millions of dollars, gained him national prominence and eventually led to his nomination and election as vice-president in 1944. Truman succeeded to the presidency upon **Roosevelt's** death in April 1945. Excluded from major policy discussions while vice-president, he relied heavily on his close advisers.

Truman was determined to obtain **Japan's unconditional surrender** as soon as possible and without further loss of American lives (see **Surrender Decision by Japan**). When told of the first successful **atomic bomb** test at the Potsdam Conference (see **Conferences, Allied**) in July, he authorized its use a month later. Following the war the **United States** was faced with such major international problems as stemming the tide of Soviet expansion and rebuilding the ruins left by the war. Truman decided to use America's economic power to stop the Soviets' advance and to rebuild Europe. Under the Truman Doctrine the U.S. provided economic aid to **Greece** and **Turkey** in 1947 to prevent Communist takeovers there. That year **George Marshall** announced the European Recovery Program—known as the Marshall Plan—which called for massive assistance to reconstruct Europe and reestablish its prosperity. During his second presidential term Truman supported the formation of the North Atlantic Treaty Organization in 1949 and authorized the U.S. entry into the Korean conflict the following year.

TRUSCOTT, Lucien King (1895-1965).
An American general, Truscott led the Sixth Army Group in Operation **Dragoon** in 1944, moving his troops into Alsace, southern **Germany** and **Austria** in the year following.

TUCK, Robert Roland Stanford (1916-).
A British airman, Tuck was an ace pilot in the **Battle of Britain**. Made a **prisoner of war** in 1942, he escaped in 1945.

TUNISIA.
See **French North Africa; French Colonies**.

TURKEY.
This ancient **empire**, which once stretched from Baghdad to Casablanca and from Budapest to the upper Nile, was finally cut down to its modern size by the treaty of Lausanne in 1923. Kemal Ataturk (1881?-1938), a supporter of the "Young Turk" revolution of 1908 and a successful commander against the British and Australians in 1915, forced the truncated country into the modern world. As president from late 1923 until his death in November 1938, he increased literacy by romanizing the alphabet, liberated **women** from complete social seclusion, set up the elements of a modern state machine and encouraged a little industry.

Ismet Inonu took over on Ataturk's death and pursued a policy of resolute neutrality. Turkey signed pacts of nonaggression with the British and French in 1939 and with the Germans in 1941; the Turks did not wish to fight alongside the Russians, their secular enemy, or for the Nazis, or against their allies from World War I, the Germans. Their mines supplied **Germany** with chrome, vital for industry—steelmaking in particular. In 1944 British protests persuaded the Turks to reduce the amount of chrome they sold to the Germans; eventually, in February 1945, they declared war on Germany, realizing that they could not otherwise qualify for founder status in the **United Nations**. No operations resulted. (See also **Cicero**.)

M. R. D. Foot

U

U-BOAT.

From *Unterseeboot*, the German word for "underwater boat" or "submarine" (see **Axis Combat Forces**).

UDET, Ernst (1896-1941).

An aviation ace in World War I, Udet, a German general, was director general of equipment for the *Luftwaffe*. He gave priority to speed and maneuverability and was largely responsible for the *Luftwaffe*'s concentration on single-engine fighter planes and light- and medium-range bombers in the early part of World War II (see **Aircraft—Characteristics**). He committed suicide in November 1941.

ULBRICHT, Walter (1893-1973).

Head of the German Communist Party, in 1933 Ulbricht emigrated to the **USSR**, where, as a member of the political commissariat in the Red Army, he helped to organize the *National Komitee "Freies Deutschland."* Returning to **Germany** after the war, he headed the Socialist Unity Party and from 1960 was chairman of the Council of State of the German Democratic Republic.

ULTRA.

Code name of a special British interception effort. With Polish help, **MI-6** obtained a copy of the Germans' most secret cipher machine and broke the codes used on it in 1939. Throughout the war **Churchill** and a few senior British and American commanders could thus read many of **Hitler**'s personal instructions on highly secret matters as soon as they were issued.

UNCONDITIONAL SURRENDER.

The term "unconditional surrender" had originated in the American Civil War. On January 24, 1943, at a press conference held in the aftermath of the Casablanca Conference (see **Conferences, Allied**), **Roosevelt** and **Churchill** demanded the unconditional surrender of **Germany, Italy** and **Japan**. Going much further than simple military surrender, this demand specified something new in international law: "total and political capitulation." It implied that the enemy would not be admitted to the subsequent negotiations as a full partner, and it rejected outright the concept of an accord as in the "normal European wars" of the past. Formulated toward the end of 1941 by the Americans, the demand did not win the agreement of the British until the beginning of 1943, and then only at Churchill's insistence. Roosevelt refused under any circumstances to countenance a repetition of the stalemate with which World War I had ended, when Germany had claimed that Woodrow Wilson's Fourteen Points established its absolute right to erect a lasting new order.

The principal motive for demanding unconditional surrender was to guarantee the durability of a peace dictated by the victors to the vanquished. A second justification was consideration for the feelings of the **USSR**, which were strained by the absence of a **Second Front**, and the fear that it would conclude a separate peace with **Hitler**. It also served as a hint to **Stalin** that the **United States** and the **United Kingdom** would disregard any armistice or **peace overtures** from any German government, with or without Hitler at its head. When Stalin declared in his order of the day on May 1, 1943 that the principle of unconditional surrender must be the rule for a policy of collective war, he was attempting to counter not only any peace feelers on Hitler's part but also any unwarranted ambitions on the part of the *National Komitee "Freies Deutschland."*

Italy's surrender on September 3, 1943 was in principle unconditional, although it had been prepared by negotiations with **Pietro Badoglio**'s government, which remained in power. The principle was still in force even after Italy's declaration of war on Germany October 13, 1943, which the Americans and British recognized as participation in the war on their side.

The draft of a document for Germany's unconditional surrender was sent by the **European Consultative Commission** to the American, British and Soviet governments. In the last weeks of the war, a proposal for "partition," added to the document during the Yalta Conference of February 4 to 11, 1945, aroused

461

certain differences of opinion among the Allies. But the document signed at Reims on May 7, 1945 and at Berlin-Karlshorst on May 8 was only a military surrender. It did, however, contain a passage that was to create difficulties. After the arrest of **Karl Doenitz** and his government on May 23, 1945, the four great powers took it upon themselves to proclaim, on June 5, 1945, the "total political capitulation of Germany in view of its defeat."

Nazi **propaganda** had attempted, in the last days of the war, to use the demand for unconditional surrender to goad the German people into a final desperate thrust. Its effect, however, remains unclear.

In the case of Japan, unconditional surrender was obtained (see **Surrender Decision by Japan**). But it was, in a sense, incomplete, since it permitted Emperor **Hirohito** to retain his throne, although his powers were strictly limited.

A. Hillgruber

UNDERGROUND.

See **Resistance**.

UNDERGROUND PRESS.

The underground press was the voice of the **Resistance** and the medium it used to communicate with the public. Perhaps the best way to evaluate it is to examine the motivations of the Resistance movement itself. Certainly the most important was the desire to liberate one's oppressed country. But that desire was rarely the only motivation. Nazi **Germany** and Fascist **Italy** were more than simply predatory nations; they espoused and imposed an ideology that denied human rights, opposed liberal democracy and betrayed socialism. For these reasons, more than out of mere patriotism, they were worth opposing. Many of the resisters were indifferent to their nation's fate; many others were willing to betray it. Ideology and political faith, in effect, so freely crossed national boundaries as to render them indistinct. Because of this combination of factors, the Resistance and the underground press found a secure place not only in the countries under the domination of the **Axis** powers but in Italy and Germany themselves.

Until November 1926 the Italian press had only been controlled and censored by the **Mussolini** regime. At that time, however, it was subjected to discriminatory statutes forbidding the publication of opposition—particularly Communist—journals. Some of these proscribed journals continued to publish and were distributed in secret. The most important was the Communist Party organ *L'Ordine Nuovo*. Fly-by-night newspapers, little more than **propaganda** leaflets, appeared and vanished—*L'Officina, Il Martello,*

Il Contadino povero, Il Pungolo, Il Galletto, L'Avanguardia. January 1925 marked the appearance of a new publication, *Non mollare*—"Do Not Yield." Sponsored by a group of independent anti-Fascists, it soon went underground. The Communist *L'Unita* illegally published its first copy on January 1, 1927. It was soon succeeded by *La Liberta*, an Italian-language journal written by young exiled Communists set on French presses and circulated under Mussolini's nose. A similar publication was *Lo Stato operaio*, under the direction of Palmiro Togliatti. The labor unions, once the distributors of more than 100 periodicals, continued to publish *Bataglie sindicali* even after they were dissolved by the Fascist government. Reform Socialists had the *Rinascita socialista* and *L'Operaio italiano*, and the extremists circulated *Avanti*. In 1927 the anti-Fascists who were also anti-Communist regrouped to form the organization *Giustizia e Liberta*, which put out the newspaper *Umanita Nova*. Another opposition group calling itself *La Giovane Italia* regularly printed their paper *L'Altoparlante*. The 1930s gave birth to the *Soccorso rosso* (1931), *L'Appello del recluso* (1932), *La Catena* (1933) and *L'Aiuto del popolo* (1935). In the fall of 1939, as the war was beginning, the Communist *Lettere di Spartaco* appeared. And in 1943 *Il Proletario* was introduced in Naples while *La Voce del Lavoro* surfaced in Ancona. Despite all this competition from the entire spectrum of the political opposition, *L'Unita* remained the major underground newspaper during the war years.

Quite naturally, most of the Resistance press in Fascist Italy emanated from the most fanatical of the anti-Fascists, the Communists. Of the 300 publications that emerged at various times, at least 200 were sponsored by the ultraleft.

During the first years of the Nazi regime in Germany, virtually no clandestine publications arose to counteract the official propaganda organs. Catholic and Protestant clerics expressed their views cautiously from the pulpit (see **Church and the Third Reich, The**), and the resisters among the middle class and in the army felt no need to address the public. The working-class Germans who refused to be seduced or intimidated by the dictatorship relied largely on the spoken word to convince their compatriots; on occasion they used leaflets. But the beginning of hostilities and especially the first few German defeats started the hidden presses. Two of the journals dominating the opposition were the Communist *Die Innere Front*—"The Domestic Front"—and the basically Catholic *Die Weisse Rose*—"The White Rose." The first appeared after the invasion of the **USSR** by German troops and was controlled by Harro Schulze-Boysen and those around him (see also *Narodnyy Kommissariat Vnutrennikh Del*); the second cost the lives of its founders, **Hans and Sophie Scholl**. Some of the others were *Friedens-Kaempfer* ("Fighter for Peace"); *Gegen-Angriff* ("Counterattack"); *Rote Fahne* ("Red Flag"); *Neuer Vorwaerts* ("New Forward"), which was printed in Berlin, Breslau and Hamburg; the organ of Catholics in the south, *Kirchenstimme* ("Voice of the Church"); *Freiheit* ("Freedom"), a newspaper for the workers of the Rhineland; and the *Ruhr Echo*, for workers in the Ruhr Valley. The *Friedens-Kaempfer* staff even managed to publish a deluxe illustrated edition, printed outside Germany and featuring articles by such well-known emigres as Thomas Mann, Heinrich Mann and Lion Feuchtwanger, under the title *Neue Deutsche Blatter* ("New German Pages").

The status of the Resistance and its press was technically and morally precarious in the Axis countries. In the first place, at least during the war, the prospect of helping to hamstring his own country in its hour of peril posed a serious dilemma for the German patriot. Besides, the resister working against his own government within his own country was likely to find many more betrayers than aides. (See also **German Resistance**.) Conditions were obviously different in countries occupied by a totalitarian enemy. Here patriotism was the prime motive, and the local activist could count on many friends and few informers—especially in view of the atrocities committed by the invaders. Nevertheless, underground work, offering ample opportunity for heroism, was always dangerous. The risk of detection in the act of printing an underground journal was high at all levels—editing, makeup and distribution; the final stage was particularly hazardous. Unfortunately, the **Gestapo** never lacked accomplices to set traps for opposition journalists. Once caught, they faced torture, deportation and brutal death. But the publications survived; their staffs could always be replaced.

The first country to begin nationwide resistance against the German conquerors was **Czechoslovakia**, occupied by the Nazis on March 14, 1939 before the war even began. Yet only one title in its underground press has been preserved by history. That was *V Boj*—"In the Struggle"—led by the heroic Joseph Skalpe, who died defending it. **Poland**'s turn came in September of that same year. A nation with a long tradition of resistance, usually to aggression on its eastern frontier, Poland published a good many underground newspapers. One of the largest of these was *Glos Polski*, "The Voice of Poland," although it did not begin publishing until July 6, 1941. Other voices of the Polish Resistance were *Warta* ("The Guard"), *Insurekcja* ("Rebellion"), *Robotnik w Walce* ("The Embattled Worker"), *Pochodnia* ("The Torch"), *Sprawa* ("The Cause"), *Mlodziez*

("Youth"), *Wolna Polska* ("Free Poland"), *Jutra* ("Tomorrow"), *Do Broni* ("To Arms"), and *Wiadomosci Polskie* ("Polish News"). Judging only from these titles, it is immediately obvious that in Poland, at least, patriotism rather than Marxist dogma inspired the revulsion against German rule.

Norway was invaded on April 9, 1940. The most widely circulated Norwegian journal opposing the "master race" was the *Vi vil oss et land*—"We Want Our Own Country." Other secretly printed newspapers were *Kongs Posten* ("Royal Courier"), *Tilden Tegn* ("Signs of the Times") and the labor union paper *Fri Fagbevegelse* ("Free Syndicalism"). The Germans also overran **Denmark**, arousing just as much antipathy there, judging from the incredible proliferation of *sub rosa* publications. The Danish were even enterprising enough to set up an underground press agency, the only occupied country with the single exception of France to do so. It has been calculated that the Danish rebel newspapers enjoyed a total circulation of 26 million copies, an extraordinary figure for so small a nation.

Having overcome their northern neighbors, the rampaging Nazis inundated the west on May 10, 1940 (see *Fall Gelb*). That same day **Luxembourg** was occupied; very soon thereafter Resistance journals began to sprout. The first was the *Ligue des patriotes* ("League of Patriots"), the work of Jean Vercel. Three underground newpapers soon began to circulate. The largest of these was *De Freie Letzburger* ("The Free Luxembourger"), whose publishers were in regular radio contact with London. **The Netherlands** was next on the Nazi schedule, and there too the response of the Resistance movement was not long in coming. The first underground newspaper to publish was *Het Parool* ("The Password"), with a circulation of 20,000. Later arrivals were *Vrij Nederland* ("Free Holland") and *Je maintiendrai* ("I Will Stand Fast"), both of which, along with *Het Parool*, were Socialist. Another, *De Waarheid* ("The Truth"), was Communist; *Trouw* ("Constancy') was a Calvinist paper; *Christofor* was Catholic. Other publications were *De Geus*, *Oranje Krant* and *Ons Volk* ("Our People").

With the surrender of the Belgian army on May 28, 1940, the conquered nation's Resistance movement came alive. Like all the nations on Germany's periphery, the Belgians had been through a similar ordeal a generation before. The first secretly published paper, therefore, was the one that had serviced practically the same people in World War I. Its name was *La Libre Belgique* ("Free Belgium"); its first issue after the new German occupation was distributed on August 15, 1940. And, as in the other countries bordering Germany, the hobby of baiting the occupying power by printing the truth acquired an enormous following in **Belgium**—some 650 journals of various political faiths were passed from hand to hand. There were Communist papers such as *Les Temps nouveaux* ("New Times"), *Clarte* ("Light"), *Jeunesse nouvelle* ("New Youth") and *Le Drapeau rouge* ("The Red Flag"), with its Flemish edition *De Roode Vaan*. The Socialist papers included *L'Espoir* ("Hope"), *Combattre* ("Battle"), and *Le Monde au travail* ("The World at Work"). Various other political sects published *Sous la botte* ("Under the Jackboot Heel"), *La Brabanconne* (which is the name of the Belgian national anthem), *Feux de barrage* ("Barrages"), *La Legion noire* ("The Black Legion"), *La Voix des Femmes* ("Women's Voice"), *Vrij* ("Free"), *Het Belfort* ("The Alarm"), *Jong Belgie* ("Young Belgium") and the satirical *Coup de queue de Doudou Montois* ("A Flick of Doudou Montois' Tail"), which was distributed in the Belgian industrial city of Mons. It should be remembered that these journals were, in the occupied countries, often the only forums in which public opinion and the patriotic spirit found voice.

In June 1940 France, humiliated by defeat, received another blow to its pride when the Petain government acquiesced in the occupation of three-fifths of France by foreign troops. It provided the impetus for a surge of journalistic activity in the form of handwritten sheets, typewritten pages or screeds printed on coarse paper by stamp pads or toy presses; these were slipped under doors, sent through the mails or simply strewn on the streets. Then some anonymous genius invented the chain letter, in which the recipient is invited to make several copies of the text and send one to someone else who will, in turn, send a number of copies to his correspondents and so on. Several of these chain letters had formal titles: *Appel du Gaulois* ("Gallic Call"), *Chaine nationale* ("National Chain") and the like. Some of them actually flowered as regular periodicals, even in the occupied zone, where being caught with such material was punishable by torture and worse.

The first issue of the underground paper *Quand Meme* ("Nevertheless") made its appearance in Eaubonne in August 1940. *France, libere-toi* ("France, Free Yourself!") had published its second edition by October 1940, a month which gave birth to six other clandestine periodicals: *Pantagruel*, named for Rabelais' genial giant; *En captivite, organe de fils de France* ("In Captivity: The Voice of the Sons of France"), expressing the Catholic viewpoint; *L'Universite libre* ("The Free University"), a Communist journal that continued publication until France's liberation; *La revolution francaise* ("The French Revolution"), written by the Socialist extremists Henri Barre, Le Bourre and Jean Rous; *L'Homme*

libre, bulletin d'informations ouvrieres ("Free Man; The Worker's News Bulletin"), which appeared in the forbidden zone under the direction of Jean Lebas, the mayor of Roubaix; and *Notre droit* ("Our Right"), published by Edmond Lablenie.

In Paris, **Christian Pineau**'s *Liberation (nord)* ("Liberation [North]") appeared toward the end of 1940. Boris Vilde and Anatole Lewitsky, two members of the **French Resistance** movement *Musee de l'Homme* ("Museum of Man") paid with their lives for their audacity in publishing their journal *Resistance, bulletin officiel du comite national de Salut public* ("Resistance: The Official Bulletin of the National Committee for the Public Welfare"). On January 1, 1941 *Valmy*, the organ of the militant Resistance unit *Jeune Republique* ("Young Republic"), came into being. The new year also saw the publication of the *Bulletins d'information et de propagande* ("News and Propaganda Bulletins"), by Capt. **Henri Frenay** and Berty Albrecht in both French zones. In June that paper, which was directed at the clergy, became *Les petites ailes* ("Little Wings"); later it changed its name once more, to *Veritas* ("Truth"). In that same year *La Voix de Nord* ("The Voice of the North"), which enjoyed especially wide readership; *Liberation (sud)* ("Liberation [South]"), published by Emmanuel d'Astier; *Defense de la France* ("French Resistance"), published by Philippe Viannay; *Cahiers du temoignage chretien* ("Notebooks on Christian Witness"), published by R. P. Chaillet; and *Socialisme et liberte* ("Socialism and Liberty"), published by Robert Verdier, Raoul Evrard and Elie Bloncourt, all appeared in the northern zone. In the southern zone the *Franc-Tireur* ("Sniper") and Henri Frenay and Francois de Menthon's *Combat* were published, along with *L'Humanite* ("Mankind"), *La Vie ouvriere* ("The Working Life") and *L'Avant-Garde*, Communist journals printed on a press furnished by a Resistance group, the National Front. After that most of the secret journals, which had until then been motivated solely by patriotism, took on a more political tone.

In 1942 the Socialist newspaper *Le Populaire* ("The People"), published by Daniel Mayer, reappeared in the southern zone; Nicolas Hobam and Marcel Leroy published *Lorraine*. At the end of the year, *Resistance* became the organ of *Musee de l'Homme*. The *Cahiers* ("Notebooks") were published by the *Organisation civile et militaire*, or OCM (Civilian and Military Organization); the *Etoiles* ("Stars"), by Aragon; *La France Interieure* ("Inside France"), by Georges Oudard; and *Les Lettres francaises* ("French Letters"), by Claude Morgan and the *Comite des ecrivains* (Writers' Committee).

In addition to the generally circulated Resistance

journals like *Franc-Tireur, Liberation, Combat, Resistance, Defense de la France* and *Les Lettres francaises*, which began to appear throughout France after the German occupation of the southern zone and the subsequent coordination of the various Resistance movements by **Jean Moulin**, a number of special, professional and local organs of different types appeared beginning in 1943. In an effort to preserve the memory of the underground press after the liberation, the National Library of France collected some 1,035 different mastheads of newspapers circulated in France. Dozens of these were printed in Polish, Serbo-Croatian and Spanish.

At the beginning of 1944 the press run of the big underground papers was at its peak. *Defense de la France*, for example, published 450,000 copies while *Combat* published 300,000. The especially brutal crackdown by the Germans on these activities in the spring hurt this circulation. On the other hand, the approach of the liberators gave the underground papers a tremendous lift. The presses of the sports daily *L'Auto* also ran off copies of *Ceux de la liberation* ("The Liberators"), *France libre* ("Free France"), *Liberation (nord)* ("Liberation [North]"), the bulletins of the *Office de publicite generale* (Information Office) and the *Cahiers* (Notebooks) of the OCM, among others.

By 1944 the underground press operated relatively unfettered. It was, however, controlled to an extent by central organizations, which in turn were directed by **Comite francais de liberation nationale** and the **Conseil national de la resistance**. One important source of information was the *Bureau de presse de la France combattante* (Press Bureau of Wartime France), with offices first in Lyon and then in Paris, for which **Georges Bidault** and Pierre Corval, chief editor of the *Bulletin d'informations generales* ("General New Bulletin") wrote a great deal. Another was the *Journal de minuit* ("Midnight Journal"), the news daily published by *France d'abord* ("France First"), the agency that disseminated information derived from the Information Center and the united resistance movements. Most of the underground papers were edited by the central committee of an individual Resistance movement, with several members alternating as editor in chief. In addition to their day-to-day concerns, the journals pushed the idea of a unified Europe (see **Europe [The Concept of]**) to succeed the crumbling "**New European Order**" foisted on the tired Continent by the Nazis.

In April 1941 **Yugoslavia** fell to the invading Germans. The Resistance in that country was divided into two major factions. The first, on the political right, published many periodicals in Slovenia: *Svoboda asi Smrt* ("Liberty or Death"), *Svoboda Slovenija* ("Free Slovenia"), *Slovenija in Europa* ("Slovenia and Europe"), *Zarja Svobode* ("The Dawn of Liberty"), *Slovenski Porocevalec* ("The Slovenian Observer") and *Teti Kolumnista* ("Fifth Column"). The second, of course, reflected **Tito**'s Communist views. But Tito apparently had more faith in the sword than in the pen, for the list of underground journals in occupied Europe contains the name of not a single Titoist publication.

E. Pognon

UNION OF SOVIET SOCIALIST REPUBLICS.
See **USSR**.

UNITED KINGDOM.
At the start of the war the United Kingdom was among the world's great powers; by the end, it was the leading world power of the second rank. Feudal features still survived in the political system, which was crowned by a monarchy that could trace its ancestry back to the Dark Ages. **George VI**'s duties, however, were hardly more than formal. The country was governed by a large, efficient civil service, nominally dependent on Parliament but in practice autonomous on most matters. In Parliament the House of Commons, the lower and more influential chamber, had last been elected in 1935, with a Conservative majority of some 250, reduced from the 500-odd majority it had enjoyed after the election of 1931, during the Great Depression. The House perpetuated itself until June 1945, since a general election was thought inadvisable in the midst of a war against a nearby neighbor.

Neville Chamberlain, prime minister when the war began, was in his own phrase of September 1938 "a man of peace to the depths of my soul," and quite unsuited to the conduct of a great war. He brought **Churchill** into the government, in charge of the Navy, when the war began; Churchill was practically the only combative figure in a cabinet of elderly Conservatives who longed for a quiet life. During debate on the bungled Norwegian expedition, Chamberlain's majority fell to 80; he resigned, and Churchill replaced him on May 10, 1940, the very day the main German attack in the West began (see *Fall Gelb*).

Churchill at once formed an all-party coalition, bringing in Labor and Liberal ministers and parting with some of Chamberlain's stodgiest colleagues; Sir **Samuel Hoare**, for example, went to Madrid and **Lord Halifax** to Washington as ambassadors. For all important purposes Churchill was a dictator of the Roman type; he had immense authority as well as energy, and a personality like a sledgehammer. He could do more or less what he wanted.

Political life was at a virtual standstill. At the low point of the war, in the spring of 1942, there were a few murmurings against Churchill's leadership because not even he could bring success swiftly. Laborite **Aneurin Bevan** needled him in the House of Commons; Sir **Stafford Cripps**, a much more considerable figure in the Labor party, emerged for a moment as a possible rival to the prime minister. (Cripps had been British ambassador in Moscow until the Soviet regime asked for his withdrawal after he signed a report from his military attache suggesting that the **USSR** would hold off the *Wehrmacht* for about eight weeks.) The Cripps-Churchill rivalry came to nothing; Cripps, a desiccated intellectual, had only ideas to offer a public that liked Churchill as a man.

A decision fatal to Great Britain's future was taken at about that time, the result of debate among civil servants rather than consideration by the war cabinet. Churchill as minister of defense initiated and approved the measure, which was to fight all-out against **Japan** as well as **Germany**. Though this was the only honorable course, economically it turned out to be ruinous.

A new party, the Commonwealth Party, was formed in 1943, advocating ideal socialism, Sir **William Beveridge**'s plan for a welfare state and a **second front**. It won three by-elections but made no serious impact. The main parties, Conservative, Labor and Liberal, observed a truce during the war by not running candidates against each other. Gradually the impression spread that Churchill, though a splendid galvanizer of bureaucrats and a superbly gallant war leader, had a much less certain touch with problems of peace. These problems had been brought home to a large part of the population in the winter of 1939-40. Over a million mothers and small children from the big industrial towns had been evacuated to the countryside to protect them from bombing in the first weeks of war; they brought with them vermin, disease, and the smell of real poverty. The astonished countryfolk who had to accommodate them resolved that people ought never be made to live under such conditions and the idea stuck. (See **Britain, Battle of; Evacuation and Resettlement**.)

At the end of the war with Germany, Churchill proposed that the parliamentary coalition continue until the defeat of Japan. The Labor Party refused. A caretaker, purely Conservative, government held office from May to July 1945. Parliament was dissolved in June, and on July 5, 1945 there was a general election.

During the election campaign (if we may adapt a quip by John Stuart Mill from 80 years before), the Conservatives fought on a slogan of gratitude to Mr. Churchill, and the electorate replied, Thank you Mr.

Attlee. There was widespread, overwhelming gratitude to Churchill for having held the sky suspended for five years and beaten **Hitler**, but this was coupled with an equally widespread feeling that his gifts for wartime leadership were unsuited to the tasks of economic reconstruction that had to follow. The votes of servicemen scattered all over the world took a long time to reach their constituencies; the election result was not declared until July 26. To the general surprise, there was a large Labor majority of 146 seats—the first and so far the largest majority that party has ever enjoyed. Clement Attlee formed a government, took Churchill's seat at Potsdam (see **Conferences, Allied**) and saw the war out.

M. R. D. Foot

UNITED KINGDOM—Aid to the USSR.
See **USSR—Aid from the United States, the United Kingdom and Canada**.

UNITED KINGDOM—The War Effort.
The **United Kingdom** made the decision to liberate the Continent in June 1940. It was then that **combined operations** came into being. The principal architect of the military preparation and operational planning system, a man who could be relied upon in bad times as well as good, was Sir **Alan Brooke**, later to become Field Marshal Lord Alanbrooke, the head of the Imperial Chiefs of Staff. Working patiently in **Churchill**'s shadow, he forged the successful defense of the **Empire**. Very little was said about him at the time. Looking back, it is clear that his was one of the great minds behind Allied strategy.

In 1940, however, it was plain to everyone, for several reasons, that a long struggle lay ahead. First was the problem of ships: until the end of 1942, the tonnage sunk on the high seas exceeded the tonnage built. Second was the problem of limited manpower: in view of the fact that the forces of **Australia**, **New Zealand**, **South Africa** and **India** would soon be absorbed by the African, Asian and Pacific theaters of operations, there remained only the United Kingdom, with 44,000,000 inhabitants, and **Canada**, with 10,000,000, to face the **Axis** powers in Europe. The Royal Navy and the merchant fleet had some 1,500,000 men, the **Royal Air Force**, 1,000,000, and the coastal and **anti-aircraft defenses**, 300,000; the need to send large units to overseas theaters made it obvious that the number of British divisions available for landings on the Continent would be reduced. The final problem was presented by the need to develop a significant expeditionary force from scratch.

On October 5, 1940, at the height of the **Battle of Britain**, Churchill ordered the planning of a landing on the French coast. The invasion was to take place in four phases: first, landings and consolidations of beachheads; second, strengthening the consolidated beachhead in anticipation of a large-scale enemy counterattack; third, landings of cleanup forces; and fourth, enlargement of the beachhead.

With this basic plan agreed upon, the tasks of the command were to create a general headquarters for the invasion troops; to develop the plans and equipment necessary for the expeditionary forces' success; to concentrate these forces for the invasion; and finally, to load, ship and land troops and equipment on the beaches.

Military Instruction and Administration

In 1940 the British saw that their role had three aspects. Their home territory constituted the natural center of the imperial communications network; they were in the best position to serve as base for the invasion forces; and their territory was itself a possible theater of operations. During 1940-41 the German threat was especially severe and the most important function of the British land army was to fortify the home islands against a cross-Channel attack.

The British military organization in 1940-41 (see **Chain of Command, British**) was effective enough for the armed formations to fulfill their defensive functions while preparing for their ultimate offensive activities. This preparatory activity pivoted around *military instruction* and *logistics*. The creation of the **Home Guard** and the **women**'s military services relieved the combat units of missions and functions that might have slowed their training and activation.

Military instruction was realized through the standardization of functions for all echelons and the inclusion of appropriate special courses in well-established schools, careful selection of personnel and of instructional materials and checks on the adequacy of exercises conducted by unit commanders and the accuracy of exercise conditions in such subjects as field firing or battle conduct.

For a complex undertaking like a landing of trained troops, the dominant problem was *logistics*—in particular, provisioning, repairs, accommodations, transport and matters relating to personnel (branch A) and to materiel (branch Q). This system, patiently worked out on paper, was subjected to several experiments in the course of the large-scale exercises to expose defects in the logistical methods. The exercises were conducted with special attention to their realism, and huge tracts of land, whether inhabited or not, were expropriated for them. The "Bumper" exercise, involving experimental measures for dealing with an attempted enemy invasion, was perfected in 1941. The "Spartan" maneuver in 1943 highlighted the useful-

ness of the new system of administrative zones. Amphibious exercises on a grand scale were also conducted in the first few months of 1944. This entire instructional program was complicated by the need to furnish units for unrelated operations. The best fields for acquiring seasoning were the **Mediterranean and-Middle Eastern Theater of Operations**, the Far East, Dieppe, Tunisia and Italy. The lessons of each day were applied profitably, and men were then exchanged between the units with some experience in the war and those formed in Great Britain. A sturdy military tool was thus fashioned. The excellent training provided by the Chiefs of Staff, the officers and underofficers, the Battle School, the endless maneuvers with real ammunition in all types of weapons, the psychological tests and the detailed organization of services were all to bear fruit.

In World War I the constant need to reinforce a stable front threw into the fighting whole British armies whose bravery and discipline could not compensate for the lack of professional general officers or for the perfunctory training of artillerists. Circumstances in the World War II were different: England took the steps that were necessary to achieve victory. For three years the British patiently studied the lessons of every defeat. There was nothing more instructive in the tactical realm than reading the *Current Reports from Overseas* and *Notes of Theatres of War*, published periodically during the war, which demonstrated with each day's information the flexibility brought about by variations in tactical procedures, according to whether they were designed for the European theater, the mountains, the desert or the jungle.

Materiel

Only science and technology can bring new forms of materiel into being. As early as the end of World War I, when England was militarily feeble, an elite group of scientists and engineers threw themselves into the work of designing weapons that, by their quality, would compensate for the lack of quantity of conventional arms. In this task they succeeded triumphantly, inspired by their knowledge, their persistence, the discipline of the scientific method and their sense of patriotism.

One member of this elite was **Reginald Mitchell**, the designer of the first low-winged monoplane, which had won first prize in the Venice Competition of 1927. Taking advantage of a trip to **Germany** to note the growing power of Nazi fighting planes, he began, despite ill health, the arduous task of developing a new design that could counter the terrible bombers that had destroyed Guernica with such cruel efficiency in the Spanish civil war. The fruit of his efforts was the Spitfire, a fighter aircraft whose maneuverability and firepower were to defeat the *Luftwaffe* in the Battle of Britain. It also took its inventor's life; he did not survive to celebrate his triumph.

In the field of military electronics, Edward Appleton and **Robert Watson-Watt** perfected **radar**, that brilliant application of the principle of the conservation of energy. It was Randall who, under the direction of Professor Oliphant, invented the cavity magnetron vacuum tube to provide radar with its centimeter waves, the study of which was continued by Bee, Skinner, and others at the Transmission Research Establishment. The new domain of thermoplastics was conquered by the Merriam brothers. Air Commodore Patrick Huskinson, totally blinded in the bombardment of London on April 16, 1941, brought to maturity his concept of the four-ton airborne bomb. There were innovations introduced by groups rather than individuals—the **artificial ports** and the Pluto pipeline, for example—which had seemed utopian not long before. Perhaps most wonderful of all was the serendipitous discovery of penicillin by **Alexander Fleming**, who revolutionized treatment of the wounded to such an extent that men who would otherwise have lost their lives or remained permanently disabled were often completely cured within a month.

But there was a long and worrisome road between the preliminary **research** and the eventual mass production, especially in a country that had for so long remained unprepared for total war. The energy expended by the British after Dunkirk was gargantuan; every obstacle along the road was surmounted in one way or another. Frequently, manufactured materiel required some modification that could hold up **production** until it was completed. At times a newly developed weapon would prove inferior to its enemy counterpart on the field of battle and had to be junked. There were problems peculiar to industry itself—the delay involved in retooling for mass production, for example. Even more vexatious was the frequent complaint of a dearth of some raw materials, such as rubber. Necessity stimulated inventions: a system for raising vehicles to load them aboard ships; new methods for packaging **food** in sealed containers; equipment for storing gasoline and other fuels.

With the incessant generation of new weapons or new defenses against newly-developed weapons came the need to train the men in the field in their use and maintenance as well as their tactical potential. There were continuous amphibious exercises at the Special Training Center in Scotland, for example, in which both men and materiel were worked to the limit of endurance. It was from such repeated experimentation that the logistics agencies learned how to deal with the problems faced by the **convoys** plying the

Atlantic routes.

Aircraft

The accompanying diagram shows the levels of British aircraft production throughout the war. It very clearly indicates that the United Kingdom, unlike Germany, did not initiate its wartime industrial effort until after it officially entered the war; that regardless of the dangers to which the British were exposed, they never sacrificed their production of training planes in favor of combat aircraft, which contributed significantly to the superiority of RAF pilots and crews; and that not until 1942, as the program for destruction of German industry progressed, did the production of heavy bombers enter its accelerated phase.

The total figure of 128,835 aircraft emerging from the Commonwealth's factories between 1939 and 1945 hints at the formidable power available in the last two years of the war to the RAF marshal, Sir **Charles Portal**.

The Navy

The shipyards of the British Empire built, between 1940 and 1945, two million tons of **warships**, including 722 combat vessels and 5,000 others, among them landing ships, as well as eight million tons of merchant vessels. The table below shows the Royal Navy's increase in strength in each class of fighting ships. Aside from the numerous battles it engaged in and its essential role in the landing operations in the Mediterranean theater and in Normandy, His Majesty's Navy escorted more than 220,000 ships in 9,000 convoys between 1939 and the end of 1944. During this period the convoys logged a total of 219,000 nautical miles. British navy and air ships sank 600 of the 868 German and Italian submarines lost in the course of the war; the Navy seized or destroyed 10,056,000 tons of enemy merchant vessels and swept 200,000 mines. This battle of the oceans, lasting more than six years, cost the Royal Navy 47,000 lives and the merchant marine 31,000 (see **Atlantic, Battle of the**).

THE DEVELOPMENT OF THE ROYAL NAVY, 1939-1944

	1939	1944	Losses
Battleships and battle cruisers	15	15	5
Aircraft carriers	6	13	8
Light and escort carriers	0	45	
Heavy and light cruisers	78	91	25
Destroyers	193	325	129
Submarines	61	128	77

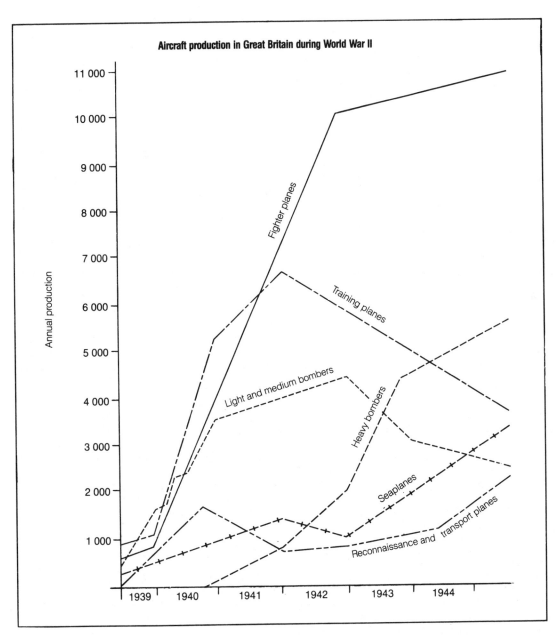

Aircraft production in Great Britain during World War II

The Great Effort

After the Dunkirk defeat, when Great Britain was quite alone, the superhuman effort began. Resources were accumulated through growth in the volume of production, reduction in civilian consumption and the mobilization of domestic and foreign capital.

The placidity with which the harshest measures were received highlights the importance of public **morale**. On a year's wages of 1,000 pounds, the average British subject paid 380 pounds in taxes; unearned income of 1,000 pounds was taxed at a 94% rate for a household with two children; luxury articles were taxed at 100% of their value. Despite these overwhelming tax rates, more than 8.467 billion pounds worth of national bonds were subscribed for an average of 177 pounds per capita. Meat, eggs, sugar and fruit were rationed, the consumption of these items dropping by 27%, 56%, 35%, and 56% respectively. Butter, margarine, tea and candy were rationed parsimoniously. On the other hand, consumption of potatoes rose 54% as a result of measures adopted to expand agricultural production, in which women and Italian prisoners participated. The growth in agricultural production permitted a 43.5% reduction in sugar imports thus freeing a substantial number of merchant vessels for other uses. Gasoline was strictly rationed. Products of little use to the war effort—private automobiles, refrigerators, vacuum cleaners, pianos and the like—were not again to be manufactured until the war ended.

The output of the British industrial plants before 1945 was 100,000 cannon, 900,000 naval mines, 18,000 torpedoes, 26,000 tanks, 75,000 armored half-tracks, 920,000 wheeled vehicles, 500,000 telephone sets, 500,000 radio posts, two artificial ports and 3,000 miles of pipeline (see also **USSR—Aid from the United States, the United Kingdom and Canada**).

In 1939 there were fewer than 500,000 men in the three branches of the armed forces. In 1944 about 15,000,000 men and 7,000,000 women toiled in the war effort; the armed forces included 4,500,000 men and 467,000 women. (The figures given for production are for the entire Commonwealth; the personnel figures are for the United Kingdom only.)

Logistics

Landing techniques required shipping superior armaments at the proper time and to the proper ports. No local operation, however brilliantly it began, could succeed if it were not regularly supplied with reinforcements. The problem was complicated if it involved crossing the ocean. The secret of logistical success lay in the organization of transport.

Solutions to the logistical problem were sought in the War Office by a group of logistics control experts; the whole organization, with its various ramifications, was known as Movement Control. Its mission was first, to construct the installations required for transport and landings, and second, to send the designated units into the bridgeheads according to plan. There must be no general formula to be followed; only the results of a succession of experiments, which were used to formulate a method adapted to the circumstances. In sum, the organization was essentially experimental.

A good many complications arose. The movement of a million men, with perhaps half that number of vehicles, in a single general direction was bound to cause bottlenecks which required attention; furthermore, this mass transportation had to be accomplished

without disturbing the national economy. Units transported by ship were divided into loads adapted to the nature of the specific landing. The rule of cargo balancing always had to be observed; for example, in the hastily organized expedition to **Norway** in 1940, anti-aircraft guns were shipped on one boat and their shells on another; the second vessel was sunk, and although the first arrived intact, the guns it carried were useless because of the failure to observe the cargo-balancing rule; after that, a ship hauling cannon also contained their shells and the men to fire them, the vessel transporting trucks also carried their drivers and fuel. The possibility of delays caused by rough seas and storms had to be taken into account. Vehicles shipped with full gasoline tanks had to be protected against contamination by sea water. Troops had to be landed in the best physical and psychological condition possible.

The process can be summarized in the following way: the units were sent into the *concentration zone*, in the northern part of England, to continue their training. The function of the zone was to reinforce the *formation zones*; it operated as a kind of spigot, turning on or off the supply of military units, which were then sent to the south of England. There they engaged in the pre-landing formalities. The men were settled in camps providing them with every possible comfort while they were briefed in detail on the operations they were to carry out. They were given maps and aerial photos of the landing site terrain for study; false names were given for the geographical features shown on the maps in the interests of secrecy. The actual maps and photos were submitted in sealed packages to the Battalion Intelligence Officer, who distributed them after the landing was accomplished, through the chain of command. The units' military vehicles were inspected, waterproofed and loaded on the landing ships by the Movement Control under the command of the Chiefs of Staff rather than by the unit personnel themselves. Coordination of the units' movements was also the function of the Movement Control up to the loading zone.

The vastness of this perpetually changing effort is all the more impressive when, in addition to the preparatory organizational labor, one takes into account the effects of unforeseen circumstances—and particularly the decision to send the units off to some alternative site which they sometimes occasioned—as well as the periodic need to mount a false invasion in order to deceive the enemy as the Allies did in 1943.

H. Bernard

UNITED NATIONS.

Twenty-six states at war with the **Axis** powers issued a

declaration on January 1, 1942, setting out their war aims. They and others arranged, at the San Francisco conference of April-June 1945, to set up the United Nations; its charter became effective on October 24, 1945, with 51 founder-members.

The organization is devoted to the maintenance of international peace and security, and works through six main parts:
1) The Security Council, with 15 members, five of which—the **United Kingdom, China**, France, the **United States** and the **USSR**—have permanent seats and permanent veto power, by a compromise reached beforehand at Yalta (see **Conferences, Allied**); the rest are elected for two-year terms by the General Assembly.
2) The General Assembly, in which every member state has a single vote (except the USSR, which by a further Yalta compromise has three, Belorussia and the Ukraine counting for this purpose only as independent states).
3) The Trusteeship Council, which has taken over the work of the Mandates Commission of the **League of Nations.**
4) The International Court of Justice at The Hague, the world's supreme international court of judicial appeal.
5) The Economic and Social Council, devoted to spreading welfare and culture.
6) The Secretariat, international in membership, which staffs services and organizes the whole from New York, with a subsidiary headquarters at Geneva.

M. R. D. Foot

UNITED NATIONS RELIEF AND REHABILITATION ADMINISTRATION (UNRRA).

The United Nations Relief and Rehabilitation Administration, a body as valuable as its name was cumbersome, was set up on November 9, 1943 by agreement among 44 nations. Its object was to help war-ravaged countries help themselves in repairing the destruction wrought by battle. It began work in North Africa in the winter of 1943-44, followed the Allied armies into Europe and was at its most active in 1945-46. Before it was phased out on June 30, 1947, handing its uncompleted work over to various **United Nations** agencies, it had assisted over 1,000,000,000 people and distributed a total of 24,000,000 tons of goods, including 9,000,000 tons of **food** and 11,000,000 tons of industrial equipment (of which **Italy** received over half). It was financed mainly by American money, with substantial British and Canadian help as well, and had an international staff of some 25,000. Its refugee camps, bleak though they

necessarily were, provided food and shelter of a sort for several million "displaced persons" from all over the continent (see **Evacuation and Resettlement**).

UNITED STATES.

To understand the United States' war effort one must look back to the late 1920s—actually, to October 18, 1929, during the administration of the Republican president Herbert Hoover. On that date a panic broke out in the New York Stock Exchange. In the days that followed 70 million shares were offered for sale. Very few buyers could be found, and prices dropped as much as 60 percent. It was the beginning of the Great Depression; from Wall Street it surged across the capitalist world. It also marked the logical end of a 10-year period of excessive laissez faire in the United States, a period of runaway **credit** and rampant speculation, overproduction in the face of inadequate demand, overinvestment, an uninhibited passion for machines and the reckless practice, on the part of the state as well as individuals, of living beyond one's means. The elections in 1932 staggered the Republican Party and turned out the Hoover administration, which for three years had grappled frantically but ineffectively with the nation's crisis.

The winner of the elections was **Franklin Delano Roosevelt**, who came to power the same year as **Hitler** and inherited a similarly crippled national economy. The mistakes this great president made toward the end of his life, after 1943, can never mar the record of exceptional service he rendered his country and the world until his death in 1945. Like his cousin Theodore, 30 years earlier, the new president brought to his office a fresh, inspiring air of competence and self-confidence. An aristocrat by birth as well as education, democratic by temperament, Roosevelt hoped to smash the power of the trusts—and the financial world. He was responsive to the demands of conservationists and tried to preserve the nation's mineral, agricultural and forest resources. Roosevelt recognized that the material riches of his country were limited and that only its spiritual wealth was inexhaustible.

At the beginning of 1933 14 million Americans were unemployed and six million farmers were unable to pay a total of $10 billion in mortgage loans. The prices of wheat and cotton were pitifully low, banks were failing by the hundreds after defaulting on bonds they had issued, panic-stricken depositors were storming the savings banks in frequently fruitless attempts to withdraw their nest eggs and "reputable" banks were compelled to confess extensive fraudulent procedures. The economic collapse was so severe that many observers feared widespread outbreaks of violence from ruined bank depositors and the unemployed.

From the moment of his inaugural address, Roosevelt proved willing to confront the disastrous state into which the country had fallen, the failure of its financiers and the deplorable, unlimited speculation of its citizens that had helped precipitate the crisis. It was a situation requiring enormous courage, which Roosevelt readily provided. Almost by surprise he launched his New Deal program. It was a revolutionary move, a startling departure from traditional American economic practice. To the wealthy few, it was an abomination; to most Americans it offered a regenerating hope. The New Deal brought the United States an era of controlled economic activity, with the controls operating from the White House rather than from Wall Street.

From a bewildered Congress ready to follow any strong leader, Roosevelt obtained unprecedented powers. In three months both houses passed more legislation at Roosevelt's initiative than his predecessor had succeeded in enacting in four years. From March 4, the day he took office, his campaign to restore the nation's self-confidence went into high gear. He halted the runs on savings banks by simply declaring a bank holiday lasting roughly two weeks; gold exports were banned; credit liquidation was suspended; and the speculators on Wall Street were placed under the strict supervision of the Securities and Exchange Commission. Political officeholders' salaries were cut by 10 percent. Prohibition, the ban on liquor that had been mandated by an amendment to the Constitution in 1920, was repealed. On April 19 the United States departed from the gold standard. The Thomas Amendment of May 12 permitted the president to devalue the dollar by 50 percent. This devaluation, together with the abolition of the gold standard, facilitated the payment of debts. The federal government took over part of the farm mortgages and lowered the interest rate. To shore up the price of farm products, the Department of Agriculture ordered the reduction of sown acreage. Unemployed youth were organized into forestry corps to assist in the conservation of the nation's timberland; many other idle workers were absorbed by public works programs. To keep the public utility giants in line, Roosevelt fixed power rates and initiated government utility enterprises such as the Tennessee Valley Authority. Not only did the authority distribute electric power at low rates, it also stimulated rural electrification and aided in the restoration of moribund farmland.

Roosevelt believed that the social structure of the country needed changing as well. He was adamant about maintaining individual profits, which he considered an indispensable force motivating most human activity. But he thought that the state did have the right to suggest the direction and coordination of individual efforts and to keep the trusts under control. He tried to ensure that laborers would have a greater stake in the goods they produced. This was the purpose of the National Industrial Recovery Act of June 16, 1933. A new body, the National Recovery Administration—better known as the NRA—was created and operated under a brain trust made up of intellectuals and academics of independent views, rather than management and labor representatives. The NRA had the power to institute social reforms with the agreement of industrialists and labor unions. Business leaders were asked to develop codes ensuring fair competition in each particular industry. These codes fixed salaries, working hours, health and safety conditions, hiring and firing practices, severance pay, procedures for choosing labor representatives and the like. The new law empowered the president to modify the code standards and to impose codes on those industries that had enacted none of their own.

There were outraged cries, to be sure. The "malefactors of great wealth," to use Roosevelt's phrase, reviled the New Deal. The Supreme Court, for its part, struck down the NRA as unconstitutional. The codes, the Court said, were laws and the Constitution does not authorize Congress to transfer its legislative prerogative to other branches of the government. But the spirit of the NRA persisted, and the codes, even if they were no longer the law, were often retained as collective contracts.

After a false start in 1934, the economic recovery became quite strong in 1935. Roosevelt was reelected on November 4, 1936 by a huge majority. The national economy maintained its growth at an increasing pace in the years that followed. And that fact was to have enormous impact on the outcome of World War II. Without the innovations President Roosevelt brought about, the United States could never have borne the staggering and decisive burden it assumed in the war.

When Roosevelt came to the White House in 1933, he plunged into a grim international situation. He very quickly understood the danger that Hitler's rise posed for the world. The problem that perplexed him was how to alert the country to this danger, especially since the inertia of the European democracies in the face of fascist aggression in **Ethiopia**, the Rhineland, **Austria** and **Czechoslovakia** disgusted a large part of the American public.

Congress passed three neutrality acts between 1935 and 1937 in an attempt to check the strength Roosevelt had demonstrated by imposing the New Deal on the nation. Basically these acts forbade the supply of armaments, munitions or other materiel to any belligerent nation and banned loans to any such nation.

The laws could only favor and encourage the aggressors.

Europeans failed to understand the Americans' hands-off attitude. But how could a citizen of Dallas or Des Moines regard the German menace in the same way as an inhabitant of Liege or Nancy? It was more likely, if less reasonable, for an American to worry about Tokyo than about Berlin. This feeling, perfectly understandable for a people protected by two massive oceans, must be borne in mind to perceive the odds against Roosevelt's eventually successful struggle to convince his people that the American flag should flap alongside Britain's Union Jack in the struggle against **Axis** oppression.

But the brutal policies of the fascist dictators after 1938 and their religious persecution, particularly the Nazis' **anti-Semitism**, smoothed the path for Roosevelt to join in common cause with the European democracies even before **Pearl Harbor**. In the spring of 1939 he refused to recognize the German Protectorate of **Bohemia-Moravia** or Italy's annexation of **Albania**. At that time he sent a long message to **Mussolini** and Hitler asking them to keep the peace. The ironic and malevolent response of the Fuehrer proved to be a fatal error, for a good many American isolationists, aware of the unanimous applause with which the French and British had greeted the president's message, now clearly understood which of the two blocs sincerely wanted peace. In September 1939 the majority of American public opinion was sympathetic to the Allies. A month earlier 200 Curtiss fighter planes had been delivered to France. The same year orders were accepted for 250 heavy Glenn-Martin bombers, 100 light Douglas bombers and 40 dive-bombers, but there were long delays between manufacture and delivery. Only a few of these aircraft managed to reach Casablanca by April and May 1940; most remained crated, and none were ever used in combat.

In March 1940 the neutrality acts were revised. The **United Kingdom** and France ordered 4,000 aircraft and 13,000 engines from the United States. Roosevelt's plan to furnish substantial aid to the democracies of Europe was on its way to fulfillment.

On August 27, 1940 Congress voted compulsory military service. The United States began preparing for war while it was still at peace. On November 5 Roosevelt's triumphant precedent-shattering reelection to a third term demonstrated his success in changing public opinion to wholehearted approval of his policies. It was a crushing blow for the isolationists.

In March 1941 Congress passed the **Lend-Lease** Act as well as a series of measures to ease the task of the Royal Navy (see **Atlantic, Battle of the**).

On December 7, 1941 the Japanese launched an attack on the U.S. fleet berthed at Pearl Harbor, without a preliminary declaration of war. The entire world was now aflame, with **Germany, Japan,** Italy and their satellites facing the United States, the United Kingdom, **China** and the other Allies. Although the **USSR** and Japan eyed each other furtively, they were to remain officially at peace until August 8, 1945. As a result the Soviet Union did not consider itself China's ally.

The gargantuan effort of the United States, which thus began in 1941, was to continue at an incredible pace until the end of hostilities. The American war effort produced enormous quantities of weapons and materiel. To take one example, in three years of operation, the battleship *North Carolina* sailed 260,000 miles, a distance equal to 10 circumnavigations of the globe, without a single pause for repairs.

From June 1940 until the Japanese surrender, more than 300,000 aircraft were built; the average weight of each plane rose during the course of the war from two tons to five tons. In that same period the United States produced 86,333 **tanks**, 104,891 armored cars, 12.5 million rifles and machine guns, 2.6 million automatic cannon, 800,000 artillery pieces (of which 216,000 were heavy and 50,000 motorized) and 2.5 million trucks.

From December 7, 1941 to August 15, 1945, American shipyards constructed 10 battleships, 13 heavy cruisers, 33 light cruisers, 27 aircraft carriers, 110 escort aircraft carriers, 352 destroyers, 498 destroyer escorts, 203 submarines and 109,642 small vessels (patrol boats, minesweepers, minelayers and **landing craft**), totaling nine million tons. To these figures the 35 million tons of merchant ships built and launched in the same period should be added. (See also **Warships**.)

Among the military innovations emerging from World War II were the following:

1) Self-propelled projectiles; bazookas; a revolutionary artillery weapon, the proximity fuse missile (see **Radar, V-1 and V-2**); recoilless cannon; 75-mm mortars, each capable of manual assembly and disassembly and possessing considerable destructive power in spite of its moderate weight (1,210 pounds); flame-throwing tanks capable of hurling 275 gallons of mixed fuels a distance of 500 feet—1,300 feet with an extension—in 60 fiery jets.

2) Semiautomatic rifles, which provided firepower.

3) Defense "in depth," using successive layers of troops to provide maximum protection together with freedom of movement.

4) Electric heating equipment for high-altitude flights.

5) Jeeps, which appeared in 1942, light, tough, easily handled vehicles with four-wheel drive, capable of crossing any kind of terrain at a maximum speed of 60 miles per hour. Often equipped with radio transceivers, jeeps sometimes carried light arms or special devices. They were excellent towing vehicles and were also used for transporting supplies and munitions.

6) Individually issued **food** rations, scientifically selected; impermeable wrapping and conservation of food. These innovations resulted in the elimination of field kitchens.

7) New means of landing troops, inspired in Britain but developed in the United States, including many varieties of ships with hulls capable of opening and closing, landing craft, amphibious vehicles and tanks, which, late in the war, weighed as much as 30 tons and were equipped with foam rubber floats fore and aft, jettisoned by explosive charges that detonated when they ran aground.

8) Submarines standardized on a single ocean model of 1,500 tons, capable of a surface speed of 20 knots and a speed of 10 knots while diving, with air-conditioned compartments for use in the tropics.

9) Floating dry docks for large ships, formed by placing independent units side by side and welding them together. These floating docks were capable of accommodating the heaviest battleships. Each unit of these dry docks had two elevating bridges about 33 feet thick and 55 feet high serving as the dock walls, two groups of 500 horsepower diesel motors, 200 horsepower ballast pumps, a 30-ton crane, public address systems, lighting equipment for night work, a workshop with the most modern machine tools and facilities for sleeping 60 men, with a kitchen and refrigeration equipment. Depending on the ships to be overhauled, a number of these units were arranged side by side. Ten combined to form a dock adequate for the repair of a 32,000-ton battleship and possessed a motive power equal to 10,000 horsepower—as much as that of a large factory. Docks like these, completely assembled, were submerged by filling their ballast tanks. The ship to be repaired was introduced between the walls, and the whole was then raised by the ballast pumps to duplicate the conditions of a genuine floating dry dock.

10) Floating power stations installed on board destroyer escorts for restoring port installations taken from the enemy to service when the local power centers had been devastated or sabotaged; power stations on rails; fully equipped mobile road stations riding on tires with diesel generators of 600 kilowatts to assure electrical service in primitive regions, such as Oceania.

11) Bulldozers and excavation equipment; rapid construction of airfields on every kind of terrain.

12) Rapid construction of heavy bridges.

13) And finally, the **production** and use of the **atomic bomb**.

In 1939 regular American forces totaled 500,000 men, including 241,000 in the Army comprising five activated divisions. Under the organizational genius of Gen. **George C. Marshall**, the three branches of the U.S. armed forces reached a strength of 12 million, including servicewomen, by 1945. Thirty-eight million civilians also contributed to the war effort. Thus some 50 million Americans, one-third the national population, participated.

U.S. ground forces were augmented greatly, reaching a strength of 89 divisions, 16 armored and 15 airborne, plus six Marine divisions by the end of the war.

There was growth in other respects as well. Improved psychological testing methods bore fruit. An effort was made to put every technician, intellectual or manual worker, in the rank where he would be most productive. A whole new methodology was worked out. There was a feeling for organization and a taste for logistical problems; a team spirit; a talent for brash initiative, as evidenced in the naval maneuvers in the Pacific between 1943 and 1945; and an ordered sense of large-scale planning, accompanied by sufficient flexibility to permit changes of established plan in the presence of the unanticipated. There was some overconfidence too—unsurprising from a powerful, relatively young nation—which was sometimes costly, as at Pearl Harbor, in the Kasserine Pass and in the **Battle of the Bulge**.

The Americans did not limit themselves to equipping their own armed forces; they dispatched arms and materiel to their allies and in particular to the USSR (see **USSR—Aid from the United States, the United Kingdom and Canada**). After 1943 they equipped eight divisions and 300 support units of French soldiers in North Africa. They also armed and provisioned three divisions and 40 auxiliary formations in France and supplied complete materiel to 19 air squadrons. By March 1, 1945 French troops were consuming 356,000 American rations per day. The freight load amounted to 3,250,000 tons at an expense of 793 billion francs. Moreover the **Office of Strategic Services** parachuted large amounts of materiel to **Resistance** groups in Europe.

The military power of the United States and Britain could not have been completely effective without close cooperation among the Allies. There was an interweaving process uniting the British and Americans in response to the need for fusing the armies of various Allied nations into a single mighty machine. In 1942 some land forces and an air complement that became increasingly powerful began to arrive in Britain. It was not until September 1943 that American naval power, relieved of the need for constant watch in the Mediterranean (see **Mediterranean and Middle Eastern Theater of Operations**), could concentrate its protective efforts on **convoys** to Britain. At the beginning of June 1944, the British Isles hosted 1.5 million Americans; from the beginning of the year, they had been arriving at the rate of 150,000 per month.

After the **Normandy landing** in June 1944, the Americans' field of operations was truly global. Not only was American military power deployed over the seas and skies of the earth, it constituted the bulk of the land forces in the northwestern European theater and practically half of those on the Italian front, in addition to its unaided land, sea and air activity in the Central Pacific and its presence, with Allied assistance, in the South Pacific. It was also active in **Burma**, and its formidable air arm in China lent indispensable support to the armies of **Chiang Kai-shek**.

H. Bernard

UNITED STATES—Aid to the USSR.
See **USSR—Aid from the United States, the United Kingdom and Canada.**

UNRRA.
See **United Nations Relief and Rehabilitation Administration.**

URQUHART, Robert (1901-   ).
Urquhart, a British general, participated in the North African campaign of 1941 and in the Sicilian and Italian operations of 1942-43. In September 1944 he was in command of the airborne raid on Arnhem, was encircled by German forces and, after resisting their attacks for a week, retreated across the Rhine on Gen. **Montgomery**'s order, with 2,400 men left out of the original 10,000 in the foray. On May 10, 1945 he landed in Oslo at the head of British and Norwegian **airborne troops**.

USSR.
While transforming itself from a backward peasant country into an industrial colossus and completely revamping its social structure, the USSR maintained its vast land area constant at about 8.25 million square miles until 1938. During the course of World War II the Soviet government acquired an additional 17,000 square miles from **Finland**; over 75,000 square miles in the western Ukraine and Belorussia, which were taken from **Poland**; the territories of Bessarabia and northern Bukovina, amounting to nearly 20,000 square miles, from **Rumania**, all of Lithuania, Estonia and Latvia (see **Baltic States**), amounting to nearly 65,000 square miles; and the formerly independent Tuva region, another 65,000 square miles in size, for

a grand total of some 242,000 square miles. At the close of the war, the Soviets also annexed nearly 10,000 square miles of East Prussia, including Memel, at German expense; the region known as Ruthenia, nearly 5,000 square miles in size, from **Czechoslovakia** and **Hungary**; and the southern half of the island of Sakhalin and the Kuril archipelago, totaling almost 20,000 square miles, from the Japanese; the whole amounted almost to 35,000 square miles. Thus, as of the summer of 1945, the USSR covered some 8.53 million square miles; its population, 170.5 million as of 1939, approached 190 million by the end of the war; and 32.8 percent of the people lived in urban areas. By 1939 the nation's boundaries enclosed some 60 different ethnic groups, including Slavs (78 percent) and Turks (9.5 percent), along with 100 smaller groups. Like czarist Russia in World War I, the USSR sustained enormous losses in World War II. More than seven million soldiers in the Red Army died, along with at least 18 million civilians; some 1.3 million Soviet citizens emigrated (see **USSR—War with Germany**).

A master plan to control the country's economy for the following 15 years, which was announced in 1941, just before the beginning of the war with Nazi **Germany**, was never applied. The conversion of the economy to the needs of the war was extremely difficult; a large part of the industrial area in European Russia was occupied by the enemy and the major manufacturing and agricultural centers were blocked. It was from these areas that the USSR obtained, in peacetime, about 46 percent of its total industrial **production** and 47 percent of its total area under cultivation. The Soviet government was forced by the headlong advance of the German armies to dismantle huge and complex machinery for reassembly in the east, a contingency for which it had prepared before the beginning of the conflict. Blast furnaces and steel plants had already been constructed in the Kuznetsk region, at Magnitogorsk in the Urals and in western Siberia. These were enlarged. According to Soviet data, the state operated more than 3,000 industrial complexes during the war. The war industries in the Urals manufactured more than 440,000 artillery pieces, 136,000 aircraft, 100,000 **tanks** and mechanized gun carriages between 1941 and 1945. Automotive fuel supplies were developed along the Volga, in the Urals and in the Far East. This expansion of heavy industry was accompanied by a drastic reduction in the production of consumer goods.

After the first tragic battles in 1941, **Stalin** repeatedly demanded that the Western Allies create a **Second Front**, but they were hardly in a position to mount such an intricate and costly operation. The American government, however, responded with im-

475

mediate assistance in materiel. In October 1941 there was a secret agreement between the **United States** and USSR, providing for quick shipments of 200 aircraft, 250 tanks, more than 5,000 jeeps and 85,000 trucks; the total value was $1 billion (see **USSR—Aid from the United States, the United Kingdom and Canada**). On November 7, 1941 Congress agreed to include the USSR in the **lend-lease** program. The agreements for assistance were expanded in the summer of 1942; 3.3 million tons of supplies arrived in the USSR through the ports of Murmansk and Arkhangelsk and another 4.4 million tons through roads in **Iran** that had just been completed. By the end of the war the United States had delivered more than 18,000 planes, 10,000 tanks and 10,000 cannon, respectively equivalent, according to Soviet sources, to 12 percent, 10 percent and two percent of Soviet war production.

Until the beginning of hostilities in 1939, the Soviets had displayed a defensive policy in their official diplomatic relations, founded on the threat of encirclement by the fascist powers. But this policy by no means diminished the ideological aggressiveness of the **Comintern**. In the meantime, however, the USSR took advantage of the international complications of the period, as we have seen, to gain buffer territory in the event of a German invasion. At the same time it profited from German military successes to expand its territorial holdings and push its ideological and economic projects. The Soviet leaders watched **Hitler** invade half of Europe without responding perceptibly. They even helped him materially until that fatal summer of 1941, when the Fuehrer, unable to break the unyielding spirit of the **United Kingdom**, turned on his unnatural ally Stalin. The economic accord of February 1940 between the Germans and the Soviets provided that the USSR would deliver, during the first year of the treaty, one million tons of cereals and dried vegetables, 100,000 tons of gasoline, 100,000 tons of cotton, 100,000 tons of chromium ore and 500,000 of manganese; the Reich would furnish machinery and war materiel in exchange. At the end of every six-month period, the amount of German goods delivered was to represent 80 percent of the Soviet goods delivered. The commercial accord of January 1941 further reinforced this economic cooperation. For the following 18 months it provided for exchanges of commodities valued at 620 to 640 million Reichsmarks. The USSR pledged to supply the Reich with 2.5 million tons of cereals. In November 1940 the USSR and Germany attempted, in the course of secret negotiations, to come to an understanding on the limits of their respective spheres of interest. However, the conditions that the USSR required before signing the **Tripartite Pact** indicated quite plainly the impossibility of any accord between

the two on a plan for partitioning Europe. The Soviet minister of foreign affairs, **Vyacheslav Molotov**, had made four unequivocal demands: total annexation of Finland; recognition of **Bulgaria** as part of the Soviet "zone of security"; reinforcement of the Soviet presence in Rumania by cession to the USSR of southern Bukovina; and the installation of air and naval bases in the Dardanelles, in Turkish territory. By way of more remote objectives, Molotov required recognition of **Sweden** as a neutral buffer state marking the limits of the Soviet orbit, settlement of the problem of freedom of navigation through the Baltic Sea and recognition of Soviet interests in Hungary, **Yugoslavia, Greece,** and western Poland.

The German attack on June 22, 1941 put this situation completely awry. During the "Great Patriotic War" the USSR fought with every possible means for its very existence as an independent nation. Unable to depend on any strength but its own, the Red Army bore the entire crushing burden of the war in Europe, fighting with fanatical desperation. The appeals of Stalin and the Communist Party quickly imbued the country with profound patriotism and an emotional determination to defend the country. They tapped a powerful source of energy that had accumulated over centuries of history, enabling the Soviet people to resist the invader. The patriotic exhortations of the nation's leaders stirred the population to action as the Nazis instituted their program of terror and extermination and flaunted their intentions of brutalizing the Slavic races. When the relentless **Blitzkrieg** ground to a halt at the gates of Moscow in December 1941, the USSR had overcome the deadliest threat in its history. The government and the diplomatic corps had already been evacuated to Kuibyshev on the Volga; no officials remained in Moscow other than a skeleton staff and Stalin himself. But the dreaded Blitzkrieg had not only been stopped in the USSR—it had been turned back.

The agreements with Britain on July 12, 1941 and on May 26, 1942, providing for cooperation over a 20-year period, and America's participation in the war after the end of 1941 offered Stalin a glimpse of final victory. In a meeting with British Minister of Foreign Affairs **Anthony Eden**, Stalin revealed his long-term objectives with unaccustomed frankness. He wanted the partition of Germany, weakening what had been the pivotal center of Europe and Allied recognition of Soviet annexations in eastern Europe. In reply **Churchill** reminded the Soviet leader of the **Atlantic Charter** of 1941 and indicated that he would prefer ironing out questions of frontier realignment in a peace conference. But in February 1942 Stalin publicly declared that his country desired nothing more from the war than to free its territory of the invaders and to destroy the entire Hitler clique, an excellent formula for the Communist **propaganda** machine since it distinguished between the German people and their Nazi masters.

In the meantime the Red Army was demonstrating to the world that it had not only found the key to the *Wehrmacht*'s "invincibility" but was also using it successfully. By the beginning of 1943 the Soviets had taken over the initiative on practically all fronts, and Stalin continued to speak frankly of his long-term objectives. To compensate for their inability to provide him with the promised Second Front, he expected certain territorial concessions from the Western Allies. At the same time he denied accusations that he coveted Poland, and even went so far as to dissolve the Comintern and, later, to conclude an "alliance" with the Russian Orthodox Church. In a further effort to soothe public opinion in the West, the USSR pledged, on October 30, 1943, that it had no political aims in the war and would not claim any nation's territory through force of arms. On November 6, 1943 Stalin insisted again that the USSR was fighting for the victory of the Allies over Nazi Germany, for the liberation of the oppressed peoples of Europe and for the right of those people to opt freely for their preferred national and social order. The USSR, he affirmed, was fighting primarily for a European system that would prevent any possibility of renewed aggression and that could encourage the economic, cultural and political cooperation of Europe's people.

However, the numerous secret conferences during the last few years of the war (see **Conferences, Allied**) as well as the actual behavior of the Soviet government in its dealings with the liberated nations of eastern Europe indicated clearly that the Communists had appointed themselves the strategic and ideological protectors of Europe, with the ultimate intention of assuming an international rather than merely a national role. In 1945 Stalin privately stated his ambitions: "This war differs from those of the past. The victor occupying a territory imposes his own social system on it. One's system follows one's army. It could not be otherwise." The methods of occupation the Soviets used, and the territorial claims they made, in Poland in 1939, in the occupied portion of Finland and after the annexation of the Baltic States pointed definitely in this direction even before the German invasion of the USSR. The first to succumb, these nations were totally incorporated into the Soviet Union. And from all indications the governments installed by the Soviets in Poland and Rumania in 1944-45 owed their loyalty to Moscow.

After 1943 the Polish question continued to weigh on the anti-Nazi coalition. At the beginning of March the Soviet authorities notified the Polish **government-in-exile** that postwar Poland was to have no jurisdiction over the eastern region, under Soviet rule since 1939. When the Germans discovered the mass graves at **Katyn** in April 1943 and there was no longer any doubt that the Polish officers captured by the Red Army had been liquidated, Stalin accused the prime minister in exile, **Wladyslaw Sikorski**, of complicity with "fascist" policy. It served as a pretext for breaking relations with the government-in-exile.

As Soviet forces approached Poland, resolution of the problem of the country's frontiers and especially of the composition of its future government became increasingly urgent. At the Teheran Conference, Stalin not only admitted that he wanted the German city of Koenigsberg (now Kaliningrad), but also insisted on the "ethnographic precision" of the **Curzon Line**, a boundary Stanislaw Mikolajczyk, the new prime minister of the Polish government-in-exile, refused to recognize. When the Red Army destroyed the German army group at the center of the front, Stalin considered his partition of Poland a fait accompli. In July 1944 the socialist Edward Osubka-Morawski formed a countergovernment—the so-called **Lublin Committee**—which Stalin recognized on July 27, 1944. The Soviet aims were coming into focus—to create a puppet Polish government under Stalin's wing, ready to accept any frontiers the USSR deemed acceptable.

Stalin apparently was playing a double game with Germany in 1942-43. On the one hand, he seemed to be using his secret negotiations with Germany in Stockholm to come to terms with his enemy—a proposition Hitler rejected. On the other, he put together the *National Komitee "Freies Deutschland"* (National Committee of Free Germany) at Krasnograd in the summer of 1943, composed of German Communist emigres and officers. He hoped that a national anti-Nazi movement would hasten Hitler's end, finish the war and bring about a new Soviet-German understanding on the model of the Treaty of Rapallo in 1921. But the committee proved a failure, and Stalin finally abandoned it at the end of the war.

Discussions in the Allied conferences touched on the fate of **Turkey**, Sweden, the Balkan states and **Austria**, but the question of Germany remained uppermost in all minds. The **European Consultative Commission**, in which the USSR actively participated, proposed solutions of problems that would arise after the war. In his first talks with the Western Allies, Stalin seemed to approve **Roosevelt**'s suggestion of guaranteeing the security of Europe by dividing Germany into five autonomous states. At the beginning Stalin had been in favor of partitioning the Reich but was willing to consider other solutions. In any case, on September 12, 1944 the Western nations approved the Soviet plan of cutting Germany up into occupation zones. To eliminate any reawakened German threat after the war, Stalin also concluded an alliance and mutual assistance pact with France on December 10, 1944.

At the end of the war, the dominating influence of the USSR was most clearly perceptible in Bulgaria, Hungary, Czechoslovakia and Rumania. Then, on May 9, 1945, to the bewilderment of his Western Allies, Stalin officially declared that he had no intention of splitting up Germany. At the Potsdam Conference he insisted that the defeated nation should be treated as a single economic unit during the period of its occupation. This conference confirmed the security of the Soviet grip on central and eastern Europe.

With regard to the Far East, the USSR had concluded a nonaggression pact with Japan on April 13, 1941, with clauses relating to the disposition of Manchuria and Outer Mongolia. At first the Soviets seemed only to procrastinate. At the Teheran Conference toward the end of 1943, however, Stalin indicated that the USSR was ready to declare war on Japan when Germany was defeated. By the end of 1944 he was already reinforcing his Siberian divisions. But it was not until the Yalta Conference that he definitely promised to attack Japan two or three months after the end of hostilities in Europe and to grant American forces some air bases in eastern Siberia. He also professed his willingness to conclude a pact of friendship and alliance with Gen. Chiang Kai-shek to ease the civil war in China. That pact was signed on August 14, 1945. But Stalin was determined to make the Japanese pay—not only for having chosen the wrong side in World War II, but also for the defeat their forebears had inflicted on czarist Russia in 1905. He claimed the Kurils and the south half of the island of Sakhalin and demanded the internationalization of the port of Dairen, the guarantee of Soviet interests in Chinese ports and the restoration of the czarist treaty providing for the leasing of Port Arthur. Stalin also called for the organization of the Soviet-Chinese enterprise to operate the railroad extending from eastern China to southern Manchuria and recognition of the People's Republic of Outer Mongolia. The Soviet intervention in the Pacific theater of operations thus considerably strengthened the positions of the USSR in the northwestern Pacific and on the Chinese frontier, at the expense not only of the Japanese enemy but also of the Chinese. On August 8, 1945 the USSR declared war on Japan, and on the next day Red Army troops crossed into Manchuria. The atomic bombs dropped by the United States and the general military situation forced the Japanese to surrender on September 2, 1945, and the war in the Pacific came to an end—but not before the Soviet Union had decisively tightened its grip on northeastern Asia.

H.-A. Jacobsen

USSR—Aid from the United States, the United Kingdom and Canada.

Beginning in the summer of 1941, the United Kingdom and the United States contributed the following materials to the USSR: 2,680,000 tons of steel; 170,400 tons of aluminum; 29,400 tons of tin; 240,000 tons of copper; 330,000 telephone sets and some one million miles of cable; 2,000 radar sets; 5,000 radio receivers; 900,000 tons of projectiles and explosives; 3,786,000 tires; 49,000 tons of leather; 18 million pairs of shoes; more than six million tons of provisions; three million tons of gasoline; 900,000 tons of chemical products; and 700,000 trucks. The Americans delivered the equipment for entire factories for the manufacture of sheet aluminum, rubber and pipelines. They also furnished 63 electric power stations on rails. After the British-Soviet occupation of Iran in August 1941, assembly shops were set up on the Persian Gulf to supply trucks and aircraft to the USSR, beginning in the spring of 1942.

In addition the United Kingdom, Canada and the United States delivered the materiel listed in the following table.

	UNITED KING-DOM AND CANADA	UNITED STATES
Aircraft	7,411	14,795
Tanks	5,128	7,056
Antitank weapons	4,932	
Antiaircraft guns		8,218
Machine guns	4,005	
Submachine guns		131,633
Jeeps		51,503
Tractors		8,071
Motorcycles		35,710
Locomotives		1,981
Trucks		11,115
Torpedo boats	9	
Submarines	4	
Minesweepers	14	

Goods were delivered to the USSR through the Arctic, by the Royal Navy, from bases in Iceland and from Spitsbergen; through Iran, by truck, both from the Persian Gulf and from India; and by air freight, from Alaska to Siberia. Because considerable losses were inflicted on the Royal Navy in the Arctic by German submarines, the figures given in the first column above—which represent the goods loaded on transports—should be reduced by seven to eight percent to arrive at the figures for supplies actually received by the USSR.

USSR—War with Germany.

From the time of his arrival on the political scene, **Hitler** regarded the **USSR** as the incarnation of "Judeo-Bolshevism" and consequently, in accordance with his racist principles, the enemy of **Germany**. This ideological hostility led him to formulate a "definitive solution" to the Soviet problem. Until 1940 strategic and economic considerations pushed this basic goal into the background, even leading Hitler to overcome his revulsion for the Soviets for the sake of a temporary accommodation with them. But he never abandoned his long-term aim: the annihilation of bolshevism and the acquisition of an enormous colonial territory in the East for his thousand-year Reich.

To neutralize the USSR while he pursued military operations in the west, Hitler signed the **Nazi-Soviet Pact** with **Stalin** on August 23, 1939, followed five days later by a second treaty concerning national frontiers, with a secret clause dividing **Finland**, the **Baltic States** and the Balkans into German and Soviet spheres of influence. After the partition of **Poland**, the occupation of **Denmark** and **Norway** and the German victory in the west (see *Fall Gelb*), the USSR occupied the Baltic countries on June 15-17, 1940 and annexed them in August. The Soviet desire for strategic bases in Finland for the defense of Leningrad led to the **Russo-Finnish Winter War**, which lasted from November 30, 1939 to March 12, 1940. The war gave the USSR control over part of Karelia and the naval base of Hangoe at the mouth of the Gulf of Finland. Soviet troops also occupied the Rumanian provinces of northern Bukovina and Bessarabia on June 26, 1940. Fearing simultaneous territorial grabs by neighboring **Hungary** and **Bulgaria**, **Rumania** turned to Germany for help. The second Vienna agreement of August 30, 1940 guaranteed Rumania's revised frontiers in return for economic and military concessions to the Germans. King **Carol II** of Rumania then fled the country, leaving Gen. **Ion Antonescu** in control of the government. A German army and air force mission arrived in October 1940 to ensure domestic political stability and maintain deliveries of motor fuel and agricultural products to the Reich. The Germans also reorganized the Rumanian army in preparation for the anticipated struggle against the USSR.

The defeat of the *Luftwaffe* in the **Battle of Britain** during the summer of 1940 and the likelihood that the British would be joined in their fight by the **United States**, which had already aided them through the **Lend-Lease** Act, forced Hitler to revise his plans. The Soviet Union's determined campaign in Finland and the Balkans, together with the threat of a Soviet alliance with the Western powers, convinced him in June 1940 that it was time to eliminate this "sword planted in the Continent." His original plan called for a campaign in the east to begin on August 4, 1940, reaching a line formed by the Don, the middle Volga and the Dvina within 17 weeks. A northern army group would drive along the northern limit of the Pripet Marshes to encircle and destroy Soviet forces at Minsk and Smolensk; it would then wheel north and advance toward Leningrad to cut off the northwestern corner of the USSR. With this operation completed in a short time, a second army group, concentrated at the center of the Soviet frontier, would advance directly on Moscow. A third army group at the southern end of the border would overrun the Ukraine and the Crimea. Finally a northern group, assisted by Finnish forces, would occupy Leningrad.

Finland meanwhile had begun negotiating with Germany for military and political support against the USSR, offering the German war industry access to badly needed nickel deposits in the Petsamo region. Beginning in March 1940 the chiefs of staff of the two nations conferred on procedures to be adopted in the prospective Soviet campaign.

On Nov. 12, 1940, while Soviet Foreign Minister **Vyacheslav Molotov** was visiting Berlin, Hitler signed General Directive No. 18, ordering the acceleration of military preparations in the east. Meanwhile the Soviets escalated their price for Nazi-Soviet cooperation in a memorandum dated November 25, demanding concessions in Finland, **Turkey** and Rumania. At the beginning of December, Hitler opted to put off the anticipated Soviet campaign until May 1941. His directive No. 21 regarding Operation **Barbarossa**, issued on December 18, 1940, outlined the objectives of the campaign and the sequence of operations; the starting date was set for May 15, 1941. Directive No. 32 on June 11, 1941 dealt with the period following the campaign, estimating that only 50 German divisions would remain in Russia as occupation troops after the autumn of 1941; the remainder of the army would presumably be available for other operations.

But the Yugoslavian coup of March 27, 1941, and the ensuing fighting in the Balkans again forced postponement of Operation Barbarossa, this time to June 22, 1941. Between the Russo-Finnish Winter War in 1939-40 and the Nazi invasion in 1941, the USSR followed a policy conforming to the Reich's in order to gain as many advantages as possible and especially to gain time to prepare for the apparently inevitable hostilities. The danger of Soviet confrontation with the Western powers vanished with the end of the Winter War and the German occupation of Norway. The differences between Soviet and German policies, however, became apparent when Molotov visited Berlin. Stalin claimed Finland, **Sweden** and the Baltic Sea for his sphere of influence, in addition to a large part of dismembered Rumania, naval and air bases in Turkey and more influence over Bulgaria and **Greece**. Evidently he expected Germany's defeat at the hands of the Western powers and was presenting his bill to Berlin in advance.

On Nov. 30, 1940 the Bulgarian government rejected a Soviet proposal for a mutual assistance pact that offered it territorial gains at Turkish, Rumanian and Greek expense. Ten weeks later Bulgaria concluded a friendship treaty with the Turks as a gesture of opposition to Soviet meddling in the region. These diplomatic maneuvers ended with Bulgaria's joining the **Axis** on March 1, 1941 and the entry of German troops into Bulgarian territory. The USSR responded on March 24 by assuring Turkey of its benevolence in case of war in the Balkans and concluded a friendship and nonaggression treaty with **Yugoslavia** on April 6. Soviet leaders also hastened to sign a treaty of neutrality with **Japan** on April 13, removing the danger of invasion from the east while their hands were full in the west.

The gathering of German troops along the Soviet border had gone too far to be ignored. Stalin's own intelligence reports were confirmed by warnings from Western diplomats. Stalin did not think Hitler would have the nerve to attack until the British were subdued. He did, however, order a hasty defensive deployment of the Red Army. Gen. **Georgi Zhukov**, head of the Soviet chiefs of staff since February 13, 1941, divided the defense zone into five military districts or "fronts." Economic preparations for the war had been in progress since 1938, but by 1941 they had not nearly reached the level required to defend the country against the Nazi threat. Nevertheless heavy industry, particularly armaments plants, had begun to be transferred from the European to the Asiatic part of the Soviet Union. In addition raw materials had been stockpiled for war industries.

On March 8, 1941 Red Army forces were redistributed and supplied with new equipment. Beginning at the end of March, reservists were systematically called up to reinforce the frontier zones. Some 170 newly activated divisions, augmented by 20 motorized corps, now manned the western border. Aircraft **production** accelerated and airstrips were constructed in the region. Soviet commanders anticipated a German attack on the Ukraine, with subsequent loss of the Donets Basin's coal, and made their plans on that basis in the spring of 1941. Stalin appointed himself president of the Council of People's Commissars on May 6, officially becoming head of the Soviet government as well as of the Communist Party.

On June 23, the day after the German invasion, the Soviet Supreme Command was placed under the Committee for Defense, of which Stalin also appointed himself president (see **Chain of Command, Soviet**).

In the days that followed, most of Germany's allies joined the battle. Rumania supplied 14 infantry divisions, three cavalry brigades and three brigades of mountain troops on June 24. Hungary sent five brigades on June 27; Slovakia, two divisions and one motorized brigade on June 24; and **Italy**, three expeditionary corps divisions on August 7, 1941.

Most of the Soviet air force was quickly destroyed on the ground or in air battles by the *Luftwaffe*. In the southern sector of the front, the German army group commanded by Gen. **Gerd von Rundstedt**, together with the 17th Army, the Sixth Army, the First Armored Army and Rumanian detachments overran Kiev to encircle and destroy large bodies of Soviet troops. The German 11th Army, left behind in Rumania to guard the Rumanian oil fields against an anticipated Soviet attack, marched on the Ukrainian city of Vinnitsa to join Army Group South after the Soviet threat failed to materialize.

German Army Group Center, consisting of the Fourth and Ninth armies together with the Second and Third Armored groups, easily broke through the disorganized Soviet defenses and encircled Minsk. At the same time part of its force was diverted in the direction of Leningrad to reinforce the thrust against the city. Sensing the rapid collapse of the Red Army, the German command accelerated the drive on Moscow. Field Marshal **Wilhelm von Leeb**, commanding the 16th and 18th armies plus the Fourth Armored Group in Army Group North, had the task of occupying the Baltic ports and opening the sea lanes to shipment of supplies from Germany. He later joined in the attack on Leningrad,.

Finnish troops under the command of Field Marshal **Carl Gustav von Mannerheim** conducted operations at the southern Soviet-Finnish border. After advancing to the limit of their former frontier, they waited until German troops crossed the Dvina and then joined them in the siege of Leningrad. In the north of Finland an army of German and Finnish detachments under the German high command in Norway was entrusted with occupying the territory of Petsamo and then marching on Murmansk. Operations in the Petsamo region began on June 22, and the offensive against Murmansk was unleashed June 29. Neither of these objectives was attained, however, and the front in the extreme north remained immobile almost until the Finnish surrender of 1944. It was a critical triumph for the Soviets, enabling them to keep open the railroad from Murmansk, practically the only warm-water port on the Arctic Ocean, to besieged Leningrad.

In the first days of the German offensive, the schedule set by *Wehrmacht* strategists was strictly followed. In the southern sector fighting intensified on June 23 around Lvov. Four days later the Red Army retreated, leaving behind a large concentration of troops and equipment caught in the German pocket. The German 11th Army concentrated its forces for a joint offensive with a Hungarian corps dispatched over the Carpathians to the Dniester. It succeeded in breaking through the Stalin line by July 9, but failed to encircle the bulk of the Soviet 12th Army, which escaped over the Dniester. Six Soviet armies on the southern and southwestern fronts then began an offensive aimed at halting the German advance west of the Dnieper, but they were encircled in a German pincer movement between July 18 and August 3. In the battle of Uman on August 7, most of the Soviet Sixth, 12th and 18th armies, amounting to more than 20 divisions, were encircled and captured. The German First Armored Group took Dnepropetrovsk, and the Sixth Armored Group established a bridgehead on the Dnieper north of Kiev, the capital of the Ukraine.

German forces in the center of the long front, the keystone of the entire offensive, sent two spearheads east to capture Smolensk and trap large detachments of Red Army troops in Bialystok, while German armor pushed towards Minsk. The Soviet Third and 10th armies were captured. On June 28 two German armored groups joined at Minsk to complete a second pincer movement on top of the first. Every man in these forces not engaged in mopping up the encircled Soviet troops in Minsk was then transferred to the assault on Smolensk, while the German armor went on to attack Moscow. The German Second and Ninth armies occupied the area between Orsha and Vitebsk. In the double encirclement of Smolensk beginning on July 13, the Germans bagged three Russian armies, including 17 artillery and six **tank** divisions that finally surrendered on August 5. The Smolensk operation, however, caused a delay in the German advance, which gave the Red Army an opportunity to activate new units and throw up defensive fortifications around Moscow.

The momentum of the Nazi armies to the north brought the offensive by June 26 to the bend in the Dvina. The German 16th Army took Kaunas and the 18th Army went on to capture Riga on June 29. By July 1 the campaign had attained its initial objectives, but no large bodies of Russian troops were caught by the encirclement **tactics** of the **Blitzkrieg**. Fighting on the central front also diverted part of the 16th Army, delaying the advance in the north. Only 20 divisions could be spared for the drive to Leningrad. The offensive launched from the bridgehead of Daugavpils and Yekabpils on July 2 took two days to reach the former Estonian frontier. By July 8 the first stage of the advance on Leningrad was completed on schedule. The German armies then regrouped for an attack between Pskov and Lake Ilmen.

On July 24 Hitler changed his orders for the sequence of operations. He proposed putting off the offensive against Moscow, abandoning the **strategy** of encircling and destroying the major part of the enemy forces in favor of economic objectives: seizure of the industrial Ukraine and the oil wealth of the Caucasus. This new plan called for rapid progress on the part of Army Group South, which had to advance along the Black Sea to take the industrial region west of the Donets. Kiev fell to the Germans on August 14. By the end of the month, the offensive had crossed the Dnieper. On September 25, large bodies of Soviet troops on the southwestern front were again cut off and destroyed. No obstacles now stood between the Germans and the Donets Basin. By mid-October the 11th Army had bypassed Melitopol and driven along the coast of the Black Sea to Mariupol (now Zhdanov), opening the way to the lower reaches of the Don. The battle of the Crimea began. After taking Rostov on the Don, the German armor was stalled by the onset of the rainy season, which turned the unpaved Russian roads into muddy swamps. By November 14, however, the Crimea was in Nazi hands. The invaders then had to fall back under the pressure of a Soviet counteroffensive at Rostov.

German Army Group Center contained three elements that July. The southernmost of the three pushed toward Kiev, the central remained stationary at the approaches to Moscow and the northernmost rejoined Army Group North for the attack on Leningrad. On August 1 Gen. **Heinz Guderian**'s army attacked Yaroslavl. It was shattered by the solid defense of Soviet forces under Field Marshal **Semion Timoshenko**, and with this defeat all German hopes of breaking Soviet resistance before autumn faded. Directive No. 25 of September 6, 1941 then ordered the armies at the center of the front to isolate and destroy Russian forces in the Yaroslavl-Smolensk-Vyazma triangle, opening the way for an offensive against Moscow. This drive, Operation Typhoon, was ordered to begin October 2.

The first stage of the German advance on Moscow ended on October 7 with the encirclement of three Soviet armies near Vyazma. The Second Panzer Army took Orel and pressed on to Bryansk, where it managed to strap three more armies. Elements of the German Second and Fourth armies, operating between the two encircled zones, moved on toward Moscow by way of

Sukhinichi and Yukhnov. Heavy autumnal rains hampered the regrouping of the German forces for a frontal assault on the capital; they then received orders to tighten the noose about it first. German strategists planned a two-pronged drive, with the Second Armored Group approaching Moscow from the direction of Tula and the Ninth Army and Third Panzer Army attacking from the north along the Volga canal. The Ninth Army actually reached the Volga, and the Third Panzer Army arrived at the canal, wheeled south and advanced to within 20 miles of Moscow. But on November 27, short of fuel and facing a numerically superior defense, it was forced to halt. The German Fourth Army was also stopped by determined defensive fighting. Nevertheless, the southern prong of the offensive took Kursk.

It became apparent to the German command by the beginning of December that the capture of Moscow was, at least for the moment, out of the question. The German troops had no choice but to endure the rigors of a Russian winter in the open field. Hitler ordered them to retain their positions at any cost and establish an advanced line on which to fall back. Angered by the failure to break Russian resistance before winter, Hitler also dismissed Field Marshal **Walther von Brauchitsch**, commander in chief of the German army, and personally took supreme command on December 19.

On the Moscow front the Red Army deployed 16 divisions and 14 brigades in addition to the existing defense force. Beginning on October 10, these troops were reinforced by 10 armies in concentrated formation. By the beginning of December the Soviets could throw a million men, 8,000 heavy guns and grenade launchers, 720 tanks and 1,370 aircraft into their impending counteroffensive. The city's defenses were held by 40 percent of the troops in the Red Army, with 33 percent of its heavy guns and grenade launchers, 40 percent of its tanks and the major part of the Red air force. On November 5 the 29th and 31st army groups went into action against the German Ninth Army at Kalinin near Moscow, while the Soviet First Army attacked the German Third Armored Corps. Stalin decided on December 20 that the German armies at the center of the front could be annihilated if pushed back some 150 miles within a month. On January 7, 1942 he ordered a full-scale offensive. But his plan involved so many complex turning maneuvers that the German forces had until the end of January to consolidate their positions. Both armies were so exhausted by then that they were incapable of intensive combat.

In the north the German invaders continued their offensive toward the end of July 1941, cutting the Moscow-Leningrad railway and penetrating the outer belt of the fortifications around Leningrad. In October the offensive took another turn, in the direction of Tikhvin, and cut the last highways and rail lines south of Leningrad. Beginning in January 1942 the German besiegers faced repeated Soviet efforts to cut the noose around the city. The German front astride the Volkhov broke under one of these attacks, and Soviet units retook the Novgorod-Leningrad railroad.

With these actions, the German offensive in the USSR ground to a halt. Hitler had failed to crush Soviet forces in a quick campaign. He also failed to reach the oil zone in the south or to take Leningrad in the north. The Red Army had recovered from its catastrophic defeats of the summer and fall of 1941 and was now being reinforced from the huge resources of the eastern Soviet territories. The losses suffered by the German army on the Soviet front, amounting to one million men, could not be made up. Its losses in materiel—4,200 tanks, more than 10,000 heavy vehicles, artillery pieces, aircraft and other equip-

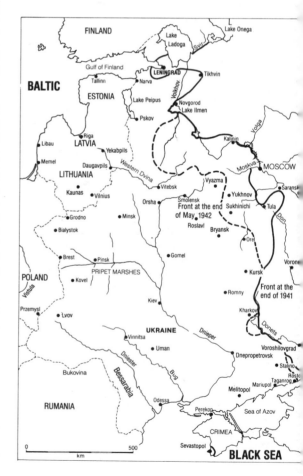

ment—forced the high command to set up strong points along the front to ensure the mobility of at least part of the German forces. The most serious shortcoming was lack of fuel, a problem that only the conquest of the Caucasus oil fields could solve. The Germans looked to the next campaign to furnish them with the requirements of their war economy: gasoline, **food** and raw materials.

On April 5, 1942 Hitler issued orders for the summer campaign, to be launched on June 28. The left wing of Army Group South jumped off from Kursk and advanced to the Don. For the second phase of the new offensive, Hitler divided the southern group into two sections, one assigned to move south and the other north as far as the limits of the central sector. On July 23 he directed three armies to seize the precious Caucasian oil wells while two armies were to take Stalingrad, a key industrial center on the Volga. The Rumanian Third Army, the German 17th Army and the First Panzer Army drove southward between the lower reaches of the Don and the Caucasus, entering Maikop at the beginning of August. From the southwest the Fourth Panzer Army approached Stalingrad and occupied the outer suburbs on September 3.

Gen. **Franz Halder**, German army chief of staff, lost his position at this time, as a result of differences of opinion among German strategists over the course of operations. As he had done the previous year, Hitler banned any retreat, and he ordered the construction of winter quarters while the attack on Stalingrad was still in progress. In mid-October the Sixth Army pushed into the city's ruins, battling the Soviets for every house and yard of territory.

The Red Army command threw all its resources into the defense of Stalingrad. Appointed by Stalin to liberate the city named after him, Gen. Georgi Zhukov hung on with the Soviet 62nd Army until reinforcements arrived in November to crush the entire southern wing of the German attack.

Soviet forces launched their general counterattack in the Stalingrad area on November 19, involving 11 armies, several corps, 13,500 artillery pieces, 900 tanks and 1,400 aircraft. With the aid of attacking troops further to the south, these units drove deep into the Rumanian lines and recaptured Kalach-na-Donu, to the west of Stalingrad. The German Sixth Army in Stalingrad, under the command of Gen. **Friedrich von Paulus**, was cut off from the rear, while Soviet forces in the city advanced to turn the German right flank. The maneuver was completed on November 24; the bulk of the German forces in the southern sector of the Soviet front, together with their allies, were trapped in the ruins of Stalingrad; a total of 200,000 men were encircled. The newly reorganized Army Group South, under the command of Field

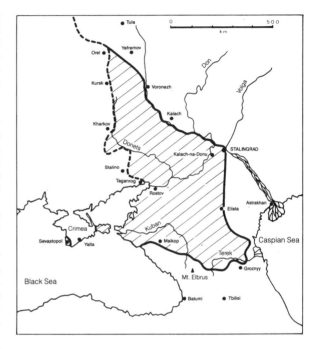

Marshal **Erich von Manstein**, tried to extricate them with what remained of the Fourth Panzer Army. The trapped Sixth Army, hoping for the success of Manstein's effort, continued its struggle until worn out by exposure and starvation. It finally surrendered on February 2, 1943. German troops in the Caucasus, threatened with isolation, retreated but regrouped to launch a counteroffensive south of Kharkov on February 22. A similar German withdrawal, followed by stabilization of the battle lines, also occurred in the central sector of the front.

On March 13, 1943 Hitler ordered the preparation of a new summer offensive after shortening the front to permit the transfer of some units to the west, where the possibility of an Anglo-American invasion had begun to loom. The renewed offensive against the Soviets, known as Operation *Zitadelle* (Citadel), began on July 5 but brought disappointing results. By July 9 units of Army Group Center were already on the defensive. Five days later Manstein, in the south, went on the offensive, but he had to fall back to his original position at the end of August. It was the end of the German advance in the USSR.

The Red Army then began a long-prepared offensive aimed at pinching off the German salient at Orel. Still stronger Soviet forces struck in the south, pushing the Germans back from their Kuban bridgehead. On October 31 German and Rumanian units were isolated in the Crimean Peninsula. Toward the end of September the Germans evacuated the Donets Basin. They lost Kiev by the beginning of November in a huge Soviet pincer movement, from south to north, which cut off an entire group of German armies in the southern sector. At the end of December the trapped German units were attacked in the center by the First Ukrainian Front, with four armies, west of Kiev. The attack broke through to the southwest, forcing the remaining German forces to evacuate the Dnieper bend.

Continuing Soviet gains in the southern sector brought the Red Army to the Dniester by the end of March 1944. Before the beginning of May the Soviet command formed a new front, starting from the northeast end of the Carpathians and stretching northward through Kovel, Minsk, Orsha, Vitebsk and Pskov to the western shore of Lake Peipus and Narva. The contour of this front indicates that the Red Army aimed the spearhead of its thrust at the Balkan states of Rumania and Hungary, in order to cut Germany off from the raw materials they furnished the Reich. In the meantime Soviet forces captured what remained of the German and Rumanian units in the Crimea and liberated the entire peninsula.

The final, giant offensive that was to sweep the USSR clean of the invaders began in May 1944. Its first phase was the destruction of the German armies at the center of the front, followed by the liberation of Minsk, the capital of Belorussia, on June 22. Operations on all four Soviet fronts were a complete success. German losses totaled 28 divisions or 350,000 men, an even worse blow to the German army than their losses at Stalingrad. In the north, Soviet troops of the First Baltic Front took Vilnius, isolating German forces in Estonia and Latvia. A German effort to reestablish contact with the remnants of Army Group North failed on August 16. Nevertheless the units trapped in Estonia managed to hold out until the war's end. The Soviet command simply bypassed them, concentrating on the central and southern sectors of the front.

On July 10, 1944 Soviet forces opened an offensive on the right wing of their southern sector. Troops of the Fourth Ukrainian Front drove back the German Fourth Panzer Army and the Hungarian First Army to the Beskids, while units of the First Ukrainian Front reached the northern bank of the Vistula. Further to the south, the German situation took a sudden turn for the worse when Rumania surrendered to the advancing Soviets and declared war on Germany on August 25. Soviet forces surrounded Belgrade on October 15, and troops of the Second Ukrainian Front attacked Budapest.

On January 12, 1945 the Red Army launched its final offensive. By the end of the month it had penetrated Silesia and cut East Prussia off from the remainder of the Reich. By mid-February, Soviet forces were fighting in the Prussian province of Pomerania. The Soviets reached the outskirts of Berlin in early April and attacked it on April 16. The city was surrounded by April 23, and three days later the Soviets reached the Elbe river. The war in Europe ended with the occupation of Berlin and the surrender of the *Wehrmacht* on May 7, 1945.

E. Klink

USTACHI.

This Croatian terrorist movement, founded in 1929, opposed the Yugoslavian monarchy, with support from **Italy** and **Hungary**. From 1941 to 1945 the Ustachis, under **Ante Pavelich**, controlled **Croatia**; while in power they massacred thousands of opponents. (See also **Yugoslavia**.)

V

V-1 AND V-2.

At the beginning of the war, **Germany** had many more aviators than their opponents. But beginning in 1942 the **United Kingdom**, the **United States** and their allies trained increasing numbers of aircraft pilots, allowing a lengthy training period, while the *Luftwaffe*'s ranks were thinning, resulting in a shorter and hastier conditioning process for new recruits. The Germans then turned to the development of "robot aircraft," initiating a new breed of giant rockets that is with us today. While the Allies were clearly ahead of the Germans in **radar** and atomic energy (see **Atomic Bomb**) throughout the war, it was the Reich's engineers, fired by the enthusiasm of **Wernher von Braun**, who developed the long-range rocket. Fortunately for the Allies, the practical realization of the new weapon occurred too late to alter the course of the war or even to prolong it.

The two principal "flying bombs" the Germans put into operation were the V-1, an airplane piloted by a robot, and the V-2, a true rocket. The "V" in these names stands for *Vergeltung*—the German word for reprisal—an expression of Nazi vindictiveness in the face of massive Allied bombardment of the Reich. The numbers in V-1 and V-2 indicate that these two models were to be only the precursors of a whole series of formidable weapons.

The V-1 used a liquid fuel but relied on oxygen in the air to support its combustion. Driven by a pulsed jet engine, the robot rocket was some 25 feet long, weighed five tons and contained 1,100 pounds of explosives. With a maximum speed of 400 miles per hour, it was slower than Allied fighter aircraft with internal combustion engines. Its maximum altitude was only about 3,000 feet and its range was limited to under 200 miles. This rather crude weapon was launched from ramps some 165 feet in length; its stability in flight was provided by a gyroscope. Reaching its objective, it was directed into a steep dive by a preset propeller-operated tachometer. Its range was consequently fixed. The moment its range limit was reached, its engine's supply of fuel was cut off; hence the characteristic abrupt silence signaling the rocket's descent.

An electrical contact detonated the drone's explosive when it hit the ground.

The V-2 was a much more advanced weapon. Like the V-1 it used a jet engine, with a methyl alcohol fuel; unlike it, however, it carried its own supply of combustion booster in the form of liquid oxygen—or "lox," as it is commonly known today. This novel feature lent the rocket a new dimension, the ability to cruise at high altitudes where atmospheric oxygen is sparse or nonexistent. It was 45 feet long and cigar-shaped; it weighed 13 tons and was capable of delivering a one-ton warhead a distance of over 200 miles. It was launched vertically and therefore required no special ramp. Fired straight upward to an altitude of 15 to 18 miles, it inclined to a trajectory of 40° in the desired direction under the action of graphite flaps at the level of the jet outlet and controlled by a preset gyroscope. Equipped with a radio receiver to take commands telecommunicated from a ground station, the V-2 soared to an altitude of 30 miles one minute after launch, reaching a speed of 3,600 miles per hour. At that moment its engine was halted by radio command. After launching it continued to rise to an altitude of more than 60 miles, then dropped in a free-fall, roughly parabolic path at a speed of about 2,200 miles per hour. Unlike its predecessor, the V-2 could not be heard. Moving faster than sound in the atmosphere, it had already fallen and done its damage before the buzzing it left behind could reach its victims' ears. One effect, however, robbed the bomb of some of its power—the wide dispersion of its shock wave. Many V-2s did not even hit their objectives.

In addition to the V-1, the V-2 and other improved weapons of this series, the Reich's factories produced a flow of smaller rockets with either self- or remote-controlled guidance—self-guidance being provided by a gyroscope and remote-controlled guidance by telecommunication from the ground or from an aircraft. Toward the end of the war, the Germans were launching remote-controlled bombs such as the HS-293 and SD-1400X against allied **convoys** in the Atlantic. In 1945 a spate of German air-surface, surface-air and air-air missiles were introduced; some of them were loosed in a final barrage before the end of the war. The worst of these for the Allied bombers was the *Wasserfall*, which had a maximum altitude of over 50,000 feet, carried a warhead of 225 pounds and was controlled by infrared rather than radio waves.

The information furnished to London by the European **Resistance**, especially the Czech, Belgian, French and Polish networks, pinpointed the principal **production** centers of the V weapons and their accessories—particularly **Peenemuende**, a port on the Baltic Sea. At the beginning of August 1943, the Danish Resistance on the island of Bornholm communicated precise, eyewitness information to London on the first experiments of V-1 launchings over water. On the night of August 17, 1943, the **Royal Air Force** made its famous raid on the Peenemuende plants. The German command panicked, according to **Goebbels'** diary. However, at the time the direct effects of the raid were overestimated by the Allies. The V-2 installations were heavily damaged, but the V-1 centers were only slightly affected.

The primary cause of the delay in the German V rocket offensive was the dispersion of the plants producing the bombs, a precaution to avoid a repetition of the August 17 disaster, rather than the bombings of the V-1 factories and launching ramps. Almost as fast as the Germans changed the launch sites of the rockets, their new locations were reported to London by French, Belgian and Dutch espionage agents or by aerial **reconnaissance**.

The V-1 launching ramps were located in France, arranged along the coast from the Belgian border to south of the Seine estuary in Normandy. In June and July 1944 many of the V-1s launched from the German bases on the Straits of Dover and the Somme went astray and destroyed parts of occupied Normandy.

On June 13, 1944, six days after the **Normandy landing**, the V-1 offensive against London began—much later than Hitler had anticipated. The first V-2 rockets began falling on the British in September. If, as **Eisenhower** said later, the Germans had been able to use these weapons en masse six months before the invasion against the landing points rather than against London, the Allies would have had to confront a formidable obstacle. Terrible as they were, the rockets arrived much too late. Furthermore, these strikes at the capital, during the rush hours of 7:00 to 9:00 a.m., 12:00 noon to 2:00 p.m. and 6:00 to 7:00 p.m., proved to be a serious psychological error on the part of the Nazis. Many Londoners were killed and thousands of buildings destroyed, but for a people who had triumphantly survived many worse moments in 1940 when victory was so uncertain, these new horrors meant little now that victory was so close. British

soldiers in Normandy outdid themselves in their thrusts to destroy as quickly as possible the sources of these weapons endangering their families. Goebbels was confounded in his hopes of daunting British **morale**. The rockets did, however, have the effect of diverting from the main Allied effort many fighter planes and antiaircraft guns, which were used for defense, and bombers, which were used for strikes on the launching sites.

Following the Normandy landing the major target of the V-1s and V-2s was the port of Antwerp, which had been liberated on September 4, 1944. It was opened to navigation on November 27, after Canadian troops captured Zeeland and freed the mouth of the Schelde. Understanding the port's strategic significance for the Allies, the Germans refused to part with it. Their final recourse was the flying bombs.

When U.S. Army Col. Clare H. Armstrong took command of the Antwerp group charged with countering the V-1 attacks, his instructions were to destroy 50 percent of the rockets to make the port safe for use by Allied ships. Armstrong decided to deploy his weapons in depth against pinpoint attacks based on the theory that since each V-1 launching ramp was difficult to construct, the mass of rockets converged on the city from isolated localities. Hence the attack channels could be covered by an economical deployment of antiaircraft guns in depth.

The first V-1s had arrived from the direction of Trier, in Germany. The defending guns were therefore deployed to counter that threat. Reinforced on November 10 by two American brigades, the American-British artillerists were organized for three barrages from the southeast. The V-1 attack increased in intensity; more than 50 V-1s from that direction pierced the Antwerp defenses.

The German offensive in the Ardennes, launched on December 16 and culminating in the **Battle of the Bulge**, brought a new torrent of V-1s on Antwerp. Rockets suddenly began pouring in from the northeast while the attack from the southeast continued. But Armstrong had taken pains to deploy his forces to cover any eventuality. Several hours later his units opened radar-controlled fire, and by December 18, 28 batteries, set up in depth, pointed in this new direction. Because of the shorter distance between the new launching sites and Antwerp, the V-1s from the northeast were 50 percent more accurate than those from Trier.

On January 11, 1945, when the German defeat in the Battle of the Bulge was no longer in doubt, the V-1 attacks from the northeast became heavier than those from the southeast. But more and more of the rockets were shot down by the in-depth **antiaircraft defense** employing the newly invented proximity fuses.

In the final days of January 1945 rockets began arriving from the north, from ramps near Rotterdam and the Hague. The defenses were at once deployed to counter this threat. From the moment the Germans comprehended the failure of their last great offensive, the V-1 rocket attacks increased, reaching a fierce climax on February 16, 1945, when 160 of the drones converged on Antwerp from three different directions.

Until the end of this prolonged V-1 assault on March 30, 1945, the defense remained strong in all three directions. By that day practically all the flying bombs had been shot down. However, no defensive measures were effective against their successors, the V-2s; the antimissile missile did not appear on the military scene until after the war was over.

Some 5,760 V-1 rockets were launched against Antwerp. Several went astray and 4,268 were destroyed in the air or shot down. 1,198 (628 V-1 and 570 V-2) fell within an approximate radius of four miles from the port, and 211 of these landed in the center of the city. Liege too was badly damaged, and several rockets were directed at Brussels. Together they claimed the lives of 3,470 Belgian civilians and 882 Allied soldiers.

By the end of the rocket attacks in March 1945, two American brigades, a British brigade and a Polish regiment—about 22,000 men—operating 72 antiaircraft searchlights and 524 guns, 336 of which were heavy, had fired 582,000 shells against the V-1s. At no time during the assault was there a halt in the work of the Antwerp dockers or the landing of Allied troops.

H. Bernard

VAN ACKER, Achille (1898-1975).
Van Acker was the leader of the underground Belgian Socialist Party. Through his secret contacts with labor unions and industrialists he prepared the social security system that was installed after **Belgium**'s liberation.

VAN HAMEL, Lodewijck (1915-1941) and Gerard (1911-1944).
Lodewijck, a Dutch naval officer, distinguished himself at Dunkirk. On August 27, 1940 he parachuted into **the Netherlands** to form an espionage network there. He was arrested and shot on June 16, 1941. His brother, Gerard, continued his profession as a diplomat but was himself arrested and died at Natzweiler.

VANIER, Georges (1883-1954).
From 1940 to 1942 Vanier, a Canadian general, was a member of the Common Defense Committee of the **United States** and **Canada**. In 1943 he represented Canada among the Allied governments in London

and with the Provisional Government of the French Republic in 1944. From 1944 to 1948 he was Canadian ambassador to France.

VASILEVSKI, Alexandr M. (1895-1977).
Vasilevski rose through the ranks of the Red Army to become chief of the general staff (1942) and Soviet marshal. He was one of **Stalin**'s close advisers, particularly at the beginning of the war. For brief periods in 1945 he commanded the Third Belorussian Front and led Soviet forces against the Japanese.

VATUTIN, Nikolai F. (1901-1944).
A Soviet general, Vatutin distinguished himself as commander in chief of the Voronezh Front during the battle of Stalingrad in 1942 (see **USSR—War with Germany**). In 1944 he commanded the First Ukrainian Front; he was killed that year, reportedly by Ukrainian nationalists.

VEMORK.
Located in **Norway**, Vemork was the site of the only industrial plant in German-held territory producing heavy water, which the Germans needed for their experiments aimed at producing an **atomic bomb**. In February 1943 Norwegian **Resistance** groups destroyed the plant and in February 1944 they sank a vessel on Lake Tinnsjoe carrying the only available supply of heavy water, thereby ending **Germany**'s program for developing such a bomb.

VENLO.
On November 9, 1939 two officers of **MI-6**, S. Payne Best and R. H. Stevens, were decoyed to the Dutch-German frontier crossing at Venlo, some 30 miles east of Eindhoven, and kidnapped by a party of **SS** under Alfred Naujocks, the man who had organized the **Gleiwitz** (Gliwice) incident of August 1939. Their Dutch companion was killed. One of the captives talked; the consequences for MI-6's work in western Europe were serious, and **the Netherlands** was lucky to escape charges of imperfect neutrality.

VERCORS.
The plateau in the French departments of Isere and Drome where, in June 1944, 3,500 patriots of Dauphine and various other regions gathered. Attacked by large numbers of **airborne troops** of the SS, they defended themselves courageously but were forced to disband after suffering heavy losses.

VERCORS (pseudonym of Jean Bruller) (1902-   ).
A French artist and writer, Vercors was the founder of the **French Resistance** press *Editions de Minuit* ("Mid-

night Editions''), to which many great French writers contributed. His book *La Silence de la mer* (1942) was the first volume issued by this **underground press**.

VICHY GOVERNMENT.
See **French State; Petain and the French State.**

VICTOR EMMANUEL III (1869-1947).
King of **Italy** since 1900, Victor Emmanuel's greatest fear was the loss of his crown. He provided the cover for **Mussolini**, who was constitutionally responsible for him, as long as **fascism** effectively guarded the monarchy. He accepted the title of emperor of **Ethiopia** in 1936 and king of **Albania** in 1939. Although disapproving the alliance with **Germany** and Italy's subsequent entry into the war, he lacked the courage to oppose them. He abandoned *Il Duce* in July 1943, when Mussolini was rejected by Italy's ruling caste, the army and part of the Fascist hierarchy. On June 5, 1944 he turned his powers over to his son Umberto of Savoy, who was promoted to ''lieutenant general of the kingdom.'' On May 8, 1946 he abdicated in favor of Umberto, who himself abdicated on June 16 when the referendum of June 2 demanded a republic.

VIET MINH.
The ''Vietnam League for Independence,'' founded in 1941 in southern **China** by Vietnamese Communists in exile, was led by **Ho Chi Minh**. In August 1945 it overthrew Bao Dai's Vietnamese **empire**, a puppet state set up by **Japan**. Ho proclaimed the Democratic Republic of Vietnam on September 2, 1945.

VIETNAM.
See **Indochina.**

VIVIAN, Valentine (''Vee Vee'') (1886-1948).
A British secret service staff officer, Vivian spent his early career in the Indian police, and he fought in France in World War I. As assistant chief of the **MI-6** in 1939-45, he looked with favor on **Harold Philby's** rise—not realizing whom he aided.

VLASOV, ANDREI A. (1901-1946).
After participating in the defense of Kiev and of Moscow, Vlasov, a Soviet general, was taken prisoner in August 1942. He then transferred his allegiance to the Germans and made speeches against **Stalin**. On December 27, 1942 he founded the Smolensk Committee—later, the Committee for the Liberation of the Peoples of Russia—and concluded an accord with **Heinrich Himmler** on September 16, 1944 to continue the battle against the Communists. He recruited Soviet **prisoners of war** to fight Stalin's forces. Captured by the Americans, Vlasov was turned over to the **USSR**, where he was condemned to death and hanged. (See also **Collaboration**.)

VOLKSSTURM.
In English, ''people's attack.'' Within the framework of total war, this word meant the mobilization of the ultimate in reserves. It was used in connection with **Hitler's** order of September 25, 1942 for the call-up of all Germans from 16 to 60 capable of bearing arms to defend **Germany** ''with all available means.''

VORONOV, Nikolai (1899-   ).
Voronov developed the **USSR's** artillery to a level of power, diversity and perfection that made it a particularly terrifying and efficient weapon. He held the title of marshal of the Soviet Union.

VOROSHILOV, Kliment E. (1881-1969).
As commissar for defense from 1925 to 1940, Voroshilov, a marshal of the **USSR**, was responsible for the lack of preparation of the Red Army in 1940. He commanded the Northern Front in 1941 and participated in the defense of Leningrad. As a member of the state committee for national defense, Voroshilov attended many of the Allied conferences (see **Conferences, Allied**).

VYSHINSKI, Andrei I. (1883-1954).
In 1939 Vyshinski was deputy commissar for foreign affairs of the **USSR** under **Vyacheslav Molotov** and a member of the Central Committee of the Communist Party. He was also a leading exponent of Soviet law.

W

WAKE.
An atoll in the Central Pacific under U.S. administration, Wake was conquered by the Japanese on December 23, 1941 after a valiant defense by a small garrison of Marines. **Japan** surrendered it to the **United States** in September 1945.

WALLACE.
Code name for the Rennes-to-Epinal operation of the Second British **Special Air Service** Division in August 1944.

WALLENBERG, Raoul (1912-?).
A Swedish diplomat and member of a banking family, Wallenberg devoted himself in 1944 to saving the Jews of occupied Europe (see **Anti-Semitism; Final Solution**). Residing in Budapest under the protection of the Swedish embassy, he organized a system for feeding and preserving the lives of Jews in the Budapest ghettos. He saved thousands of these people by providing them with Swedish "passports of protection." In September 1944 he concealed himself to escape **Gestapo** killers and got in touch with Soviet authorities when the Red Army arrived in **Hungary** in January 1945. Called to the headquarters of Marshal **Rodion Malinovski** on January 15, 1945, Wallenberg disappeared without a trace. In the late 1970s recurrent rumors that he was still alive in a Soviet prison camp spurred an international movement for his release, despite official Soviet protestations that he died shortly after the war.

WALLIS, Sir Barnes (1887-1979).
A British inventor, Wallis designed the R-100 airship and invented a geodetic system of fuselage construction used, for example, in the Wellington bomber. He also developed various exceptionally powerful nonnuclear bombs, such as those dropped by **Guy Penrose Gibson** and other **Royal Air Force** pilots on the Moehne and Eder dams.

WANG CHING-WEI (1885-1944).
A Chinese politician, Wang headed the Japanese puppet regime at Nanking from 1940 to 1944. Born in Kwangtung and educated at Hosei University in Tokyo, he joined the revolutionary T'ung Meng Hui and was imprisoned in 1910 for trying to bomb the Manchu prince regent in Peking. He served briefly as president of the Nationalist government after Sun Yat-sen died in 1925 but was ousted by his archrival, **Chiang Kai-shek**. An ambitious but weak-willed leader, Wang quit the Nationalists in late 1938, fled Chungking with Japanese aid and began creating a "reorganized" national government of disaffected Chinese Nationalists at Nanking. He accepted assistance from the Japanese army because of enmity for Chiang and an ambition to take power should **Japan** win the war against **China**. Formally established on March 30, 1940, his regime enjoyed scant popular support. Wang fell ill and died in Japan in 1944.

WANNSEE CONFERENCE.
The Nazi conference held at Wannsee in January 1942 for the purpose of effecting the "**final solution** of the Jewish question" (see **Anti-Semitism**).

WAR AT SEA.
See **Aleutian Islands; Atlantic, Battle of the; Badung Strait; Blockade; Cape Esperance; Combined Operations; Convoys; Coral Sea; Eastern Solomons; Frogmen; Landing Craft; Leyte; Midway; Pacific Theater of Operations; Pearl Harbor; Sonar; Task Force; U-Boat; Warships**.

WAR CRIMINALS.
After World War I, for the first time in human history, the conquering Allies wanted to prosecute German political and military leaders for the alleged perpetration of war crimes. A list of 895 such war criminals was established, carrying the names of Marshal Paul von Hindenburg, Gen. Erich von Ludendorff, Grand Adm. Alfred von Tirpitz and Air Force Capt. **Hermann Goering**. The Allies sought to extradite Kaiser Wilhelm II, a refugee in **the Netherlands**, but failed. Other such attempts were soon abandoned.

The crimes committed by the Nazis in the occupied

countries during World War II impelled the Allies to formulate a definition of war crimes.

Between October 1941 and June 1945, organizations developed by five inter-Allied agreements prepared for the prosecution of war criminals on a proper juridical basis. A special commission was created in London at the end of 1943. It began to accumulate evidence, and by the end of 1945, it had developed dossiers on 35,000 identified Nazis. On August 8, 1945 the governments of the **United Kingdom**, the **United States**, France and the **USSR** agreed to set up an international military tribunal. Nineteen other nations subscribed to this agreement.

Established at Nuremberg, the tribunal tried only 24 defendants, all of whom had occupied high government positions during the Nazi regime. One of the accused was **Robert Ley**, who took his own life in prison. Another, **Gustav Krupp von Bohlen und Halbach**, could not be tried because of poor health. A third, **Martin Bormann**, had escaped and so was judged in absentia. The crimes judged by the tribunal fell into three categories. The first category was *crimes against peace*—the preparation, direction and initiation of a war of aggression, the violation of international treaties etc. Next came *war crimes*, i.e., violations of the codes and covenants of war—assassinations, the persecution or deportation for forced labor of civilian populations in occupied territories (see **Forced Labor Battalions**), the murder or ill treatment of **prisoners of war**, the execution of hostages, the looting of public or private property, the pointless destruction of cities and villages, the devastation of areas of no military significance. And finally, there were *crimes against humanity*—extermination, enslavement, deportation or any inhuman act against civilian populations before or during hostilities or persecution for political, racial or religious reasons, including the attempted genocide of Jews and Gypsies as well as the extermination of the Polish intellectual elite, which had been decided upon in September 1939 and began in May 1940 with the massacre of academics at the universities of Krakow and Lublin.

The trials opened on November 20, 1945 and ended August 31, 1946. Twelve death sentences were pronounced: Goering committed suicide on the night of October 15, 1946, the eve of his scheduled execution; **Joachim von Ribbentrop, Ernst Kaltenbrunner, Fritz Sauckel, Alfred Rosenberg, Hans Frank, Wilhelm Frick, Julius Streicher, Wilhelm Keitel, Alfred Jodl** and **Arthur Seyss-Inquart** were hanged. The 12th, Bormann, was condemned to death in absentia. Seven defendants were given prison sentences: **Karl Doenitz**, 10 years; **Constantin von Neurath**, 15 years; Baldur von Schirach and **Albert Speer**, 20 years; **Rudolf Hess, Walter Funk** and **Erich Raeder**, life im-

prisonment. **Hjalmar Schacht, Franz von Papen** and Hans Fritzsche were acquitted.

The trials of the Nazi leadership at Nuremberg were followed by several series of trials aimed at war criminals other than those responsible for the Nazi state. The foremost of these trials, in 1947, prosecuted the doctors alleged to have performed criminal experiments on inmates of **concentration camps**. In 1948, 24 leaders of extermination groups presumed to have perpetrated innumerable massacres in eastern Europe were tried.

At the request of the Americans and British, a Far East military tribunal was organized to try war criminals active in the **Pacific theater of operations**. The trials, conducted in Tokyo, ended in death sentences for seven Japanese principals, one of whom was Gen. **Hideki Tojo**, prime minister of **Japan** from 1941 to 1944. The seven were executed, and eighteen others were sentenced to long terms in prison. Various tribunals sitting outside of Japan judged some 5,000 guilty, of whom more than 900 were executed.

In Germany Allied military tribunals judged numerous war criminals. American, British and French courts, working from 1947 to 1953, tried 10,400 people, pronounced 5,025 sentences and executed 806 prisoners.

After 1956 the Federal Republic of Germany continued the search for Nazi criminals. In 1958 a central office for seizure and classification of evidence was created at Ludwigsburg. It set up a dossier of more than 200,000 names, prosecuted almost 13,000 and obtained 6,000 convictions. Officials of the German Democratic Republic brought 12,821 war criminals to trial. The figures for the Soviet Union and other eastern European countries are unavailable, but it is thought that a total of at least 30,000 Nazis were tried.

Private organizations have also helped track down war criminals. The most celebrated instance is the Documentation Center created in Vienna by Simon Wiesenthal, who has unearthed war criminals in some of the most isolated corners of the globe.

Most countries have abandoned attempts to seek out and punish war criminals. The Federal Republic of Germany extended its statute of limitations for such crimes to 1970 and then stopped prosecutions completely in certain cases.

A good many war criminals have evaded prosecution. It is very unlikely that those who had given orders without participating directly in their execution will be brought to trial now or in the future. The greatest difficulties in prosecuting war crimes have been encountered in obtaining the extradition of suspected criminals living in a foreign country. France, for example, has never been able to extradite former

Gen. Heinz Lammerding, head of *Das Reich* Panzer division, condemned to death in absentia. One exception is Dr. Horst Schumann, the physician in charge of the Nazi **euthanasia** program and creator of the heinous medical experiments performed at **Auschwitz**. After the war Schumann took refuge in Ghana, where he became adviser to President Kwame Nkrumah, but was turned over to the Federal Republic of Germany when Nkrumah fell from power. Another is Franz Stangl, former commandant of the Treblinka concentration camp, who was handed over to the authorities of the Federal Republic by **Brazil**.

Adolf **Eichmann**, the "human symbol" of the genocide of the Jewish people, was charged at the beginning of 1942 with responsibility for the "**final solution** of the Jewish question" (see **Anti-Semitism**) in all of occupied Europe. He was kidnapped in May 1960 near Buenos Aires by Israeli agents, who thereby circumvented extradition procedures, and brought back to Israel. He was judged by a special ad hoc tribunal in two successive trials, condemned to death on December 15, 1961, hanged on June 1, 1962, then cremated. His ashes were thrown into the sea.

J. Delarue

WARSAW, Rebellions in.

The Jews in the Warsaw ghetto rebelled against their oppressors between April 19 and May 16, 1943. The brutal reaction of the **SS** and the German police caused the deaths of 60,000 people.

The Polish revolt conducted by Gen. **Tadeusz Bor-Komorowski** began on August 1, 1944. Failing to receive assistance from outside **Poland**, the rebels were forced to surrender on October 2.

WARSHIPS.

Battleships

Of all warships, battleships possessed the greatest destructive power in the most compact and durable form. They were indispensable for mastery of the sea, for bombarding coastal installations and for providing artillery support for military landing parties. Two weapons can, however, be used quite effectively against battleships: bombs and torpedoes.

There are several factors that particularly distinguish battleships from other warships. The first is the battleship's huge size. Its maximum beam width in World War II was limited primarily by the width of the Panama Canal at its narrowest point—110 feet. Next is its enormous displacement and the weight of its armor. World War II's most powerful battleships displaced 50,000 tons; armor typically made up more than 40 percent of a battleship's tonnage. The 35,000-ton

French battleship *Richelieu* had 15,000 tons of armor. The armor was 15.75 inches thick at the waterline and nearly 18 inches thick on the gun turrets.

Battleships are also characterized by their enormous firepower. The largest battleships had nine guns of 406 mm each, firing projectiles weighing some 2,600 pounds over a range of 20 miles or more, 148 semiautomatic anti-aircraft guns of 127 mm each and automatic "pom-pom" guns of 27 to 40 mm, which were capable of firing more than five tons of shells in 15 seconds. Firing precision was considerably sharpened by **radar**.

Battleships' top speed in World War II was typically 28 to 30 knots. Speed was considerably more important on the sea than for land vehicles—the faster ship in a naval confrontation has the option of accepting or refusing combat; when committed to battle it can choose the range best for it.

The final distinction between battleships and other warships is their high cost. The American battleship *Iowa*, for example, cost $100,000,000; its longevity, however, compensated for its cost.

Battle Cruisers

These were ships of more than 10,000 tons with 203-mm guns; they were designed as **reconnaissance** vessels. The British and Japanese had battle cruisers in 1940; the Americans, however, considered them useless, since battleships, with their more powerful engines, were faster.

Cruisers

The object of naval warfare is to gain control of the sea lanes. Cruisers—fast, relatively inexpensive ships with long radii of action and great firepower—contributed significantly to this effort in World War II. They were excellent for sea patrols and highly effective against armed merchant ships. In a battle fleet they could be used as scouting vessels or as a protective curtain against torpedo aircraft or torpedo boats. Their tonnage ranged from 5,000 to 13,000 tons. They carried from six to 15 guns of medium caliber, small anti-aircraft guns and torpedo launching tubes.

There are two classes of cruisers: heavy, with naval guns of 155 to 203 mm, and light, with guns smaller than 155 mm. World War II cruisers traveled at a relatively high speed—38 knots on the average. Some Italian cruisers were much faster, at 42 knots.

Aircraft

Aircraft (see **Aircraft—Characteristics**) were indispensable auxiliaries to battle fleets in World War II. They acted as a fleet's "eyes"—they furnished information about enemy vessels which were invisible to surface ships; observed the fleet's firing accuracy and supplied data to improve it; protected the fleet against attacks from the air, concealing it by laying down a smoke screen; augmented its firepower with bombs and torpedoes; etc. Among the types of aircraft cooperating with naval fleets were aircraft on carrier decks, seaplanes, land-based aircraft and pontooned planes catapulted from surface vessels.

Aircraft Carriers

Several types of aircraft carriers were used in World War II. Battle aircraft carriers of the *Midway* type displaced up to 45,000 tons; these were extremely expensive and, as a consequence, scarce. Three such American vessels remained in service at the end of the war; each was capable of carrying as many as 82 twin-engine and 153 single-engine planes. There were also standard aircraft carriers of the *Saratoga* type, displacing 33,000 tons and capable of carrying 78 planes, and light aircraft carriers.

Carriers are fast ships—in World War II the top speed of carriers was 30 knots or more. They were protected by heavy anti-aircraft armament and thick armor. Their offensive strength was even more noteworthy. They were capable of striking over ranges equal to the radii of action of the bombers and torpedo planes they carried. Carriers are, however, extremely vulnerable when isolated. Five of the six British carriers in service in 1939 were sunk during the first three years of the war. They are also highly flammable because of the huge quantities of gasoline they store to fuel the aircraft they carry. Aircraft carriers are much less vulnerable when they constitute part of a **task force**.

Escort Aircraft Carriers

There is not much resemblance between these ships and standard aircraft carriers. Escort carriers are not fighting ships; they simply provide support for aircraft. In World War II escort carriers were usually refitted merchant ships with little or no armor plating. They were used to protect **convoys** against enemy submarines, to provide air cover for landings on hostile coasts and to supply aircraft to land-based forces. With an average speed of 16-20 knots, the World War II escort carrier was a slow and vulnerable ship.

Destroyers

Destroyers are extremely versatile ships. In World War II they were used to guard battle fleets against torpedo attack and throw up smoke to veil them from the enemy, to launch torpedoes against enemy battleships and to protect convoys from enemy submarines. Destroyers are only lightly protected with armor. They were, in World War II, typically armed with four to eight guns ranging in size from 100 to 130 mm and

four to eight—in some instances up to 16—torpedo-launching tubes. Destroyers were found to be especially effective against submarines detected by **sonar**; they destroyed these submarines with depth charges.

The displacement of destroyers ranged, in World War II, from 1,050 to 2,200 tons. Their relatively small size, their speed (35 to 40 knots, on the average) and their maneuverability made them difficult to hit.

Submarines

World War II submarines varied in size from the two-man, 45-ton Japanese midget submarines used at **Pearl Harbor** to the *Surcouf*, which weighed 2,880 tons. They had an enormous radius of action—15,000 nautical miles on the average—and thus could travel across the entire Pacific. Submarines are redoubtable weapons because of their torpedoes (German **U-boats** carried four or five launching tubes and 12 torpedoes and British submarines, 10 or 11 tubes and 17 torpedoes), which can be used against ships of the line or convoy vessels. They are also equipped with anti-aircraft guns. A significant disadvantage of submarines in World War II was that they could not depend on speed to dodge enemy ships larger than themselves.

Destroyer Escorts or Corvettes

These ships were either manufactured by assembly-line methods or converted freighters. They were used to escort convoys, and were equipped to battle against submarines and aircraft.

Speedboats

Speedboats were useful primarily in surprise attacks and for night sorties in coastal regions. Within these limits the speedboat was more effective than the torpedo plane.

Troop Transports and Special Landing Craft

See **Combined Operations; Landing Craft**.

H. Bernard

WATSON-WATT, Sir Robert (Alexander) (1892-1973).

A British scientist, Watson-Watt invented radio direction finding—later renamed **radar**—in 1935. The use of radar contributed significantly to the British victory in the **Battle of Britain**.

WAVELL, Sir Archibald Percival, Viscount (later Earl) (1883-1950).

Wavell was one of the most accomplished British generals in World War II, if not the luckiest. He served in **South Africa** in 1901 and in France in 1914-16 (losing an eye at Ypres). In 1916-17 he was attached to the Russian army in **Turkey**, and in 1917-18 he fought under Gen. Edmund Allenby in **Palestine**. Between the wars he used his perceptive mind and phenomenal memory on problems of **tactics** and training; he commanded the British army's experimental brigade in 1930, and defined the ideal infantryman as a cross between a poacher, a gunman and a cat-burglar. In 1937-38 he commanded British troops in Palestine, and in July 1939 formed the Middle East command. By bluff, he kept the Italians at bay with much inferior forces in the summer of 1940; in the winter of 1940-41 he drove them from both Cyrenaica and **Ethiopia**. (See **Mediterranean and Middle Eastern Theater of Operations**.)

But in the spring of 1941 Wavell lost Cyrenaica, after being ordered to divert large forces to **Greece**, where they lost much equipment. Most of those who withdrew to Crete were lost also. Wavell was then ordered to operate simultaneously in **Iraq**, **Syria** and the Sahara though his forces were not strong enough for the task. The debacles of April-June 1941 were not his fault, but **Churchill** lost confidence in him; he changed places with **Claude Auchinleck**, commander in **India**.

Wavell had little help from home against the Japanese, and had to give up **Burma**, but he was already planning its reconquest before it was evacuated, and launched **Orde Wingate**'s **Chindits** early in 1943. In June, to his own surprise, he was made viceroy.

No doubt he was meant simply to keep India quiet until the end of the war. He nevertheless pursued his own initiatives, starting with a **reconnaissance** of the Bengal famine. In July 1945 he almost persuaded India's Hindus and Moslems to agree on terms for a united subcontinent, but their united obstinacy defeated him. In February 1947 he handed over his command to Lord **Mountbatten**, who had wider powers than he had ever wielded, and retired to writing and benevolence.

M. R. D. Foot

WELFARE STATE.

Long a familiar concept in Scandinavia and **New Zealand**, the welfare state became an issue in English politics when **Beveridge**'s report was accepted, rather faintheartedly, by the government in February 1943. In the only substantial party division between May 1940 and May 1945, Labor members of the House of Commons recorded 121 votes (against 338) in favor of stronger support for Beveridge's plans.

The theory of the welfare state is that the state should guarantee the citizen against the ill effects of unemployment, sickness and as many other social and industrial ills as the **society** concerned desires, in return, as a rule, for a statutory deduction from wages. The welfare state has been hailed as an aim of socialist policy. In fact, it seems to work best in a mixed capitalist-socialist economy and to be a comparatively unadventurous, materialist, even conservative aim.

WEREWOLF.

Code name for the German operation of April 7, 1945 in which 183 fighter planes attempted to stop American air attacks. On the German side there were a total of 133 losses and 78 pilots bailed out, as against 23 American four-engine bombers destroyed. (See also **Germany, Air Battle of**.) The same code name was applied to the German organization that was to continue the fight against the Allies behind their lines in 1945.

WESERUEBUNG.

Code name of the *Wehrmacht* operations for landing in and occupying **Denmark** and **Norway** on April 9, 1940 (see **Axis Combat Forces**).

WEYGAND, Maxime (1867-1965).

A French general and head of Marshal Foch's chiefs of staff in World War I, Weygand was head of the army chiefs of staff in 1930, inspector general of the army in 1935 and commander in chief of the armies on May 19, 1940. Estimating that the war was lost, he urged Marshal Petain, the successor to **Paul Reynaud**, to conclude the armistice with **Germany**, which was done on June 12, 1940 (see **French State**; **Marshal Petain and the French State**). As minister of national defense to Petain, he opposed **Laval** and became general delegate of the French government in Africa in September 1940, where he planned his revenge on the Laval government without at the same time ending his quarrel with Gen. **de Gaulle**. The Germans obtained his dismissal in November 1941 and then deported him across the Rhine, where he was found and liberated by American troops in May 1945. He was then turned over to the High Court of Justice, where the case against him was dismissed.

WHITTLE, Sir Frank (1907-   ).

A British flier and engineer, Whittle conceived the idea for **jet aircraft** in 1928. He produced the first Gloucester planes in May 1941.

WILHELMINA of Orange-Nassau (1880-1962).

Queen of the **Netherlands**, Wilhelmina succeeded to the throne in 1890, eight years before coming of age. She maintained Dutch neutrality in 1914-18 and protested vigorously the German invasion of May 10,

493

1940. She escaped a kidnap attempt and reached London on May 13 with her family and government (see **governments-in-exile**). She remained a symbol of Dutch **resistance** throughout the war by frequently broadcasting on Radio Oranje. She returned to her country in April 1945 and abdicated in September 1948. A deeply religious Protestant with a strong sense of duty, she was much loved by her people.

WILSON, Sir H. Maitland (later Lord) (1881-1964).
A British general, Wilson held commands in **Egypt** (1939-40), the Western Desert (1940-41) and **Greece** and **Syria** (1941). He was supreme Allied commander in the Mediterranean in 1944-45 and attended the Yalta and Potsdam conferences (see **Conferences, Allied**).

WILSON, Sir Horace John (1882-1972).
A British civil servant, Wilson was a confidant of **Chamberlain** and accompanied him to Munich in 1938. In 1939-40 he was head of the treasury and the civil service but had little influence thereafter.

WINGATE, Orde Charles (1903-1944).
British general. He was brought up a strict puritan and was throughout his life original and unconventional. He was a regular artillery officer in 1923. In **Palestine** he organized special Jewish night squads to combat Arab **sabotage** in 1936-38. At **Wavell**'s request he organized the irregular campaign in **Ethiopia** with striking success. Again under Wavell, he led long-range penetration groups (''Chindits'') on a six-week campaign behind Japanese lines in **Burma**, in February-March 1943. He was killed in an air crash, in command of a second penetration mission. Wavell said he ''had undoubtedly a high degree of military genius.''

WITZLEBEN, Erwin von (1881-1944).
German field marshal. In 1940 Witzleben commanded the First Army on the western front and in 1941-42 was commander of the German armies in the west. The participants in the **assassination attempt of July 20, 1944** against **Hitler** intended to name him head of the *Wehrmacht*. He was hanged on August 8, 1944.

WOLFF, Karl (1900-   ).
German **SS** general. In 1943-44 he commanded the German armies in north **Italy** and negotiated the German surrender with **Allen Dulles** on Swiss territory.

WOMEN.
Women have always played a part, often a leading part, in war. There is no reason to believe they are any less tough than men. World War II, nevertheless, took place near enough to the age of chivalry for men to take for granted that women had no place on a battlefield; very few women were to be found in action on the main infantry fighting fronts, except during sieges (Warsaw, Leningrad, the three days' tragedy of Naples—these were serious; Paris in 1944 looks more frivolous in retrospect, but seemed serious enough at the time).

All the same, the development of air bombardment of working-class housing areas as an instrument of strategic policy necessarily placed millions of women on the front lines: in the **Netherlands** in May 1940 (see also *Fall Gelb*); in the **United Kingdom** during the nightly raids on London all through the winter of 1940-41 (see also **Britain, Battle of**); in the Ruhr from 1942 to the end of the war (see also **Germany, Air Battle of**); in the industrial cities of **Japan** from 1943 on (see also **Japan, Air War Against**); and in many more places—wherever air attacks were launched against built-up areas. That **society** survived the war at all is quite as much due to these women's stubborn heroism as to the efforts of their menfolk.

Most of them did not only have themselves to think of; their first thoughts were for children or parents, and this encouraged planning and endurance. Those who did not already excel in the traditional feminine arts of the kitchen quickly learned to do their best or went hungry. In several countries where the bourgeoisie had been quite large before the war and even poor women had habitually employed servants to cook for them, the servants vanished—conscripted, or fled, or directed to factory labor, or sent to work in **Germany**—and the bourgeois women had to learn to cook themselves (Britain, France and **Belgium** provide examples).

British labor policy made more extensive use of women than in any other combatant country except the **USSR**. Soviet women made munitions, filled and laid sandbags, swept streets and cleared ruins on a basis of perfect equality with men; only in the high command of the party and the armed forces, and on actual battlefields, were they scarce. They participated fully in the partisan conflict, and several piloted combat aircraft. British women were much less used for heavy labor, but all of them between the ages of 17 and 45 were conscripted—that is, they were either brought into the auxiliary fighting forces, as clerks, nurses, drivers or other machine operators, or were directed to undertake some particular industrial work that would help the war effort. They took over, as the war went on, a large part of the responsibility for Britain's **anti-aircraft defenses**. The country indeed owes its survival as an independent state to about 150 young women who kept the **radar** stations along the coasts of Essex, Kent and Sussex working all through the Battle of Britain, in spite of a series of dive bombing attacks directed at them personally, and thus made the **Fighter Command**'s more famous pilots' victory feasible. **Ernest Bevin** made sure there was no trouble with the trade unions about "dilution of labour" in factories, which had been a great bone of contention in World War I.

In the **United States** women played a substantial, but not a compulsory, part in the armed forces, and took over a proportion of effort on the factory floor; they were less fully engaged in the war effort than their British opposite numbers.

The Germans, true to the Nazi doctrine that woman's place is in the nursery and the kitchen, took a quite different view. Every Aryan girl was expected to bear at least one male baby to an Aryan man (whether in wedlock or not, no Nazi official much cared). Otherwise, she was expected to cook. Not only was little use made of women's labor in German factories, even foreign labor; late in 1941, miscalculating the impending result of the war on the eastern front, the German labor ministry released several hundred thousand captured civilian women to work as domestic servants for Aryan housewives.

None of the leading politicians or commanders, on either side, were women. There was, however, one field of activity in which women took as important a part as men: clandestine war.

Over a quarter of the **Special Operations Executive**'s members were women; mostly, it is true, cipher operators and clerks, but including a number of powerful staff officers and some highly distinguished agents. One of the largest, longest-lasting, most secure and best informed of the **Special Intelligence Service**'s intelligence networks in France was run by a woman, **Marie-Madeleine Fourcade**. The huge "Comet" escape route was created by a Belgian girl in her early twenties, **Andree de Jongh**. Escape lines would not have been workable without the women who ran the safe houses, with all the fearsome risks involved.

After such acts of heroism far beyond the common run became known, it was no longer possible for men to pretend that theirs was necessarily the dominant sex; the road to a major social reconstruction lay open.

M. R. D. Foot

WORLD WARS.

Wars covering several continents and involving great efforts by several countries have been frequent since the 16th century and were not unknown before. Two have been fought so far in the 20th century, each more widespread, more fearsome and more a concern to more people than any known before. By a **United States** congressional decision, the war of 1914-18 is known as the First World War and that of 1939-45 as the Second World War. Weapon developments since 1945, particularly in the nuclear field, make it probable that another war on a world scale would be fatal to organized **society** and possible that it would shatter the human race's control of this planet.

WORLD WAR II—General Conduct.

The conduct of a war—in particular the relationship between a government and its military command—is an extremely complex affair. War aims derive to some extent from politics, but the pursuit of these aims, at least where the conduct of military operations is concerned, belongs exclusively to military commanders.

Everything would be simpler if each agency kept to its own area of responsibility. Political **strategy** is the business of government, which solicits advice from its military commanders in order to understand more fully how its aims might be realized. But final decisions concerning general strategy rest with the government itself. Operational strategy on the other hand, is the province of the commander-in-chief. As a result of this conflict, relations between governments and their commanders have been characterized by considerable friction throughout history, except when an absolute autocrat simultaneously directed both political and military strategy.

In a war fought by allies, the problem of relations among the various governments complicates matters even further. Divergent interests, language difficulties and the emotions that impel one ally to make a greater effort than another often lead to serious problems.

An examination of the efforts of each major nation in World War II to resolve this problem, first within the nation, then within the alliance, follows.

Within Individual Nations

In **Germany**, **Hitler** personally directed the course of the war, with the assistance of the *Oberkommando der Wehrmacht* (OKW) and the Chancellory of the Reich.

The chief of staff on the OKW was Gen. **Wilhelm Keitel**; **Alfred Jodl** headed the Bureau of Operations and Walter Warlimont, the *Abteilung Landesverteidigung*—the National Defense Section. Keitel and Jodl were only the Fuehrer's executive agents. In 1939-41, the OKW—commanded directly by Hitler rather than by Keitel—oversaw the *Oberkommando des Heeres* (OKH), under **Walther von Brauchitsch**, with **Franz Halder** as chief of staff, the *Oberkommando der Luftwaffe* (OKL), under **Hermann Goering**; and the *Oberkommando der Kriegsmarine* (OKM), under

WORLD WAR II

Adm. **Erich Raeder**.

After the German setback outside Moscow (see **USSR—War with Germany**), Hitler accepted Brauchitsch's resignation and took personal command of the German armies. The Fuehrer was henceforth to act as the commander of the OKW, with Keitel as chief of staff, and of the OKH, with Halder, **Kurt Zeitzler**, **Heinz Guderian** and Albert Krebs as successive chiefs of staff. In the OKM, Raeder gave way to **Karl Doenitz** on January 30, 1943. Only Goering, among the commanders of the various branches of the German armed forces, retained his office throughout the war.

The Chancellory of the Reich—whose adjutant, Gen. Rudolf Schmundt, was one of Hitler's favorites—was controlled by Hans Lammers. Its major subsections were Foreign Affairs, under **Joachim von Ribbentrop**; Party Affairs, under **Rudolf Hess** and, later, **Martin Bormann**, and its **SS** combat units, under **Heinrich Himmler**; the *Sicherheitspolizei*, under **Reinhard Heydrich**; the Ministry of **Propaganda**, under **Joseph Goebbels**; Armaments and Public Works; Labor Services; and the Administration of Conquered Territories (see also **Chain of Command, German**).

This organization should, it would seem, have been simple and convenient, Hitler, as political and military commander, should have been able to move faster than the Allied democracies, impeded as they were by the complexities of their national and interallied chains of command. Actually, the German command mechanism was faulty. It was not very obvious in 1939-40; the contrast most notable at that point was between Germany's strength and its adversaries' weakness. But after 1941 the flaws in the German chain of command began to make themselves known; eventually they would contribute to the collapse of the Nazi Reich.

There was little harmony between the OKW Chiefs of Staff and the Chancellory. In the Chancellory, Hitler made military decisions that were often impractical without consulting Keitel and Jodl—without, in fact, even giving them sufficient notice. Not only were the military chiefs informed too late of their duties; they were sometimes kept ignorant of political decisions that could affect military plans. Keitel and Jodl were unusually passive, always approving the most idiotic decisions of the Fuehrer. The opinions of the Chancellory personnel, meanwhile, invariably were paid greater heed than those of the OKW; similarly, **Nazi Party** hierarchs had more influence on policy than the Army. Moreover, the liaison and division of responsibilities between the OKW on the one hand and the ostensibly subordinate OKH, OKL and OKM on the other were poor.

Hitler often failed to do what he should have done. As frequently, he did what would have best been left undone. He constantly interfered in operational activity and assumed responsibilities that properly belonged to his military chiefs. The OKW never successfully coordinated land, air and naval operations, in large part because of Hitler's meddling. Once the Fuehrer made his decision, he left it to the OKH, OKL and OKM to work out the details among themselves. This often permitted Goering, as Hitler's confidant, to combine forces with Himmler and overbear the military.

From 1939 to the summer of 1940, the powerlessness of France and of the **United Kingdom** was reflected in their political and military conduct of the war. The coordination among the three branches of the armed forces in each country, moreover, was completely defective. The campaign in **Norway** was an obvious example.

On May 10, 1940, in London, **Winston Churchill** formed a national unity government that succeeded **Neville Chamberlain**'s Conservative government. The conduct of the war underwent a change. For the numerous and impotent agencies which had littered Whitehall, Churchill substituted a modest war cabinet of only five members, including the head of the Labour Party, **Clement Attlee**. Assuming the posts not only of prime minister but also of first lord of the treasury, minister of defense, president of the war cabinet and leader of the Conservative Party, which controlled a majority in the House of Commons, Churchill was actually to conduct the war, with the assistance of the war cabinet for important affairs, and with the military counsel of the Committee of Chiefs of Staff. He could count on unanimous support from England's three major parties. His exuberant personality extended his capabilities. The four chiefs of staff, working together with the war cabinet, were: first **John Dill** and then, beginning in November 1941, **Alan Brooke** for the land armies; **Dudley Pound** and then, after October 1943, **Andrew Cunningham** for the Royal Navy; Cyril Newall and then, after September 1940, **Charles Portal** for the **Royal Air Force**; and **Hastings Ismay**, military adviser to the prime minister. Alan Brooke later became chairman of the chiefs of staff; these latter executed the war cabinet's decisions.

In the **United States** the president is the commander in chief of all the armed forces. **Roosevelt**, who conducted the nation's political affairs as well, was assisted in his military deliberations by four men bearing the responsibility of assembling and deploying a military machine that was to be the most formidable in the world's history. Those men were Gen. **George Marshall**, army chief of staff; Adm. **Ernest King**, commander in chief of the navy; Gen **Henry Arnold**, commanding the Air Force; and Adm. **William Leahy**, personal chief of staff to the president. They comprised the Joint Chiefs of Staff, of which Leahy was chairman.

In the **USSR** the war was conducted at the highest echelon by the National Defense Committee. **Stalin** acted as president; **Vyacheslav Molotov, Kliment Voroshilov, Laurenti P. Beria** and Georgi Malenkov were members. The committee supervised the various peoples' commissars; the commissar of defense, who was in charge of general headquarters, which oversaw land, sea and air forces; the army political service, which served as the political and cultural general staff and as the liaison between the army and the Communist Party; the directors of services; the directors of arms; the directors of partisans, etc. In addition to his functions as president of the Council of Peoples' Commissars, secretary general of the Party and president of the National Defense Committee, Stalin was also named minister of defense by the Presidium of the Supreme Soviet on July 19, 1941. On August 7 he became commander in chief of all the armed forces. He was thus in complete control (see **Chain of Command, Soviet**).

Within Each Alliance

The Axis
See **Conferences of the Axis Powers**.

The Allies
From September 1939 to June 1940 there was no coordination of the Anglo-French military efforts, except for several governmental and military discussions between representatives of the two countries. There was, however, an agreement to transport British troops to France, with Lord **Gort** in command, under the orders of Gen. **Joseph Georges**, as long as their number did not exceed the size of one army—i.e., about a dozen divisions. The problem was to be reviewed when about 30 British divisions landed in France—in September 1940, according to the plan.

On May 12, 1940, two days after the Germans attacked **the Netherlands, Belgium** and **Luxembourg** (see *Fall Gelb*), the Conference of Casteau, was convoked near Mons. Those attending were **Leopold III** and his military adviser Gen. Raoul van Overstraeten; **Edouard Daladier**, minister of war in **Paul Reynaud**'s cabinet; Gen. Georges and his subordinate Gaston Billotte, head of the First Army Group; and Gen. **Henry Pownall**, chief of staff to Lord Gort. The decision of the conference was to coordinate the operations of French, British and Belgian forces under Billotte, acting for Gen. Georges. There was no mention of a single command. Billotte, in effect, secured a "command by persuasion."

On May 21, when the German armor reached Abbeville and the Allied forces in the north were encircled, **Maxime Weygand**, who had been promoted to commander in chief two days before, flew into the pocket to confer with King Leopold III and the King's military adviser, along with Billotte and Gort. At this Conference of Ypres—consisting of sporadic meetings for which no minutes were recorded—Billotte arrived late and Gort stayed away until Weygand left. With the Allied armies in their desperate state, the Conference failed to produce a workable plan. Billotte was killed in an accident after leaving the Conference. Gen. Georges Blanchard, commander of the First French Army, did not learn until May 25 that he had replaced Billotte on May 21. The three trapped armies were left to fight on alone and met their inevitable fate.

The organization of the joint Anglo-American command was established at the Arcadia Conference (see **Conferences, Allied**) in Washington, which began December 22, 1941, two weeks after **Pearl Harbor**. For the first time in history, the British and the Americans succeeded in combining the armed forces of two nations into one efficient, flexible and well-defined agency for conducting the war. The German officer Walter Warlimont has enviously contrasted the efficient and effective Allied command with the OKW. It should be noted, by the way, that so close an association between two different nations would have been almost inconceivable had they not shared the same language and common origins.

The Combined Chiefs of Staff consisted of the four British chiefs of staff and the four American chiefs of staff. However, since Alan Brooke and his British colleagues had to remain in England to fulfill their obligations as advisers to the war cabinet, they sent four "stand-ins" to Washington. These officers formed the British Joint Staff Mission and worked alongside the American chiefs of staff. The British delegation was headed by Field Marshal Sir John Dill, who had formerly been the head of the Imperial Chiefs of Staff and who played a major role in Anglo-American relations. Upon his death in November 1944, he was replaced by Sir **Henry Maitland Wilson**.

When Churchill and Roosevelt met at various conferences between 1942 and 1945 to plot the course of the war, the Combined Chiefs of Staff were at their side. The first echelon made strategic and logistical plans and the second arranged for their execution.

There were, of course, divergences in views between the "Big Two." There were, similarly, disagreements between the British and American chiefs of staff, as there were between Churchill and his own chiefs of staff. There were also occasions when decisions harmoniously arrived at went awry. But the system's efficiency was impressive. Once they made their decisions, Brooke, Marshall and their colleagues worked swiftly to develop the operations to execute them—their scheduling and the forces that would be deployed on the various fronts—while maintaining sufficient flexibility in their plans to allow for the initiative of theater commanders. These were, in 1944, **Dwight Eisenhower** in western Europe; H. Maitland Wilson and, after him, **Harold Alexander** in the **Mediterranean and Middle Eastern Theater of Operations**; Lord **Mountbatten** in Southeast Asia; **Chester Nimitz** in the central Pacific; and **Douglas MacArthur** in the South Pacific. Each of these commanders had both combined and integrated general staffs (an integrated staff was one on which officers of both nationalities served) and commanded the land, sea and air forces in his theater. The British and American strategic aircraft commanders (**Arthur Harris** and **Carl Spaatz**, respectively) were directly subject to the orders of the combined chiefs of staff, as was Max Horton, the commander of the naval power patrolling the Atlantic.

The conduct of the war was further complicated by the fact that if Anglo-American delivery of materiel to the Soviets was speedily executed (see **USSR—Aid from the United States, the United Kingdom and Canada**), operational coordination between the two was not. Moreover, the USSR was not yet at war with **Japan**. Also, while Churchill, Roosevelt and **Chiang Kai-shek** held some meetings and Churchill, Roosevelt and Stalin held others, never did all four men meet at the same time. But Stalin had enormous problems to cope with before he could attend one of these conferences for the first time, in November 1943.

Even before the United States entered the war, Roosevelt and Churchill conferred at sea, on the decks of the American warship *Augusta*. Over a period of six months **Lend-Lease** aid to Great Britain had been increasing. The United States Navy had been surveying the Atlantic and reporting to the British Admiralty any German fleet activity it encountered, assuming the further responsibility of protecting **convoys** between the American continent and Iceland. At the Augusta Conference Churchill asked for even greater assistance. The two leaders reviewed the general military situation, affirmed Anglo-American-Dutch solidarity in the event of Japanese aggression and signed the **Atlantic Charter**, which the representatives of all the Allied nations were later to sign in London as well.

The purposes of the subsequent Arcadia Conference were to consider the new situation created by Japanese aggression, to coordinate Allied efforts against Japan and to apportion the duties and zones of operation among American and British forces. At this conference, in the final days of 1941, the essential machinery of the Combined Chiefs of Staff was set in motion. At the same time, in the face of the first astonishing successes of the Rising Sun, Roosevelt and Churchill reaffirmed that Germany was the prime target of conquest. To his great credit, this decision was essentially Roosevelt's. It was to have fundamental importance for the conduct of the war. Roosevelt and Churchill alike considered Japan a minor accomplice of the master criminal, despite its own temporary victories. After the fall of the Reich, **Hirohito's empire** would collapse in its turn. In this Roosevelt courageously opposed American public opinion which, for the most part, favored concluding the war in the Pacific before intervening actively in Europe.

The next major step, after the initial decision to strike first at Germany, was to plan a landing on the French coast. This was Operation **Round-up**, first considered in April 1942 and finally launched during the summer of 1943. At Marshall's request a limited operation known as **Sledgehammer** was planned for the second half of 1942. This involved landing a small force on the French coast if the Soviets found themselves hard pressed and demanded the immediate opening of a **second front** on Germany's western flank.

But **Axis** victories that simultaneously threatened Suez and the Caucasus forced the Allied commanders to change their plans. It was necessary to ease the Soviets' situation as soon as possible and to save **Egypt** with a swift operation.

Alan Brooke had never liked Sledgehammer. With so few men and ships available, he thought, the time was not ripe for risking a landing in western Europe. It could end in disaster, especially since the enemy submarine offensive was at its height. More realistic than Marshall and more in touch with recent events, Brooke feared that the psychological consequences would be severe if Sledgehammer failed. Four times, he said, the Allies had been driven back into the sea—in Norway, at Dunkirk, in **Greece** and in Crete. Yet the occupied countries still had confidence in them, as the growing **Resistance** indicated. A significant defeat could, Brooke feared, forever destroy their faith.

Churchill argued for a landing in **French North Africa**. Roosevelt agreed with him and Alan Brooke, against the counsel of his own chiefs of staff.

On July 30, 1942, Sledgehammer was abandoned in favor of **Torch**, a plan for landings in Morocco and Algiers. Thus a second front would open before the end of 1942, and the Italo-German positions in Africa would be caught in the pincers formed by the landing troops on one side and the British Eighth Army on the other. The Mediterranean could then be opened and an enormous amount of shipping could once more plow through its waters. There was an additional military advantage—Germany's southern flank would be exposed.

The month of November 1942 marked the "turn of the tide," as Alan Brooke expressed it. With his victory at **El Alamein**, Gen. **Bernard Montgomery**, commander of the British Eighth Army, crushed the Italo-German army in Africa. From there he advanced to Tripoli, where he arrived January 23, 1943, after covering 1,400 miles in 80 days.

In the meantime the Americans and British initiated Operation Torch. Morocco and Algeria were easily taken, but enemy resistance stiffened in Tunisia. In March, 1943 the Italian and German troops faced the Americans to the east and the British Eighth Army to the south; both forces were assisted by the loyal French of North Africa.

The turning tide became a flood with the great Soviet victory at Stalingrad in early 1943 and the American conquest of **Guadalcanal** on November 15, 1942.

The Casablanca Conference began on January 12, 1943. In addition to Roosevelt, Churchill and their chiefs of staff, Lord Louis Mountbatten, chief of **combined operations**, and the commanders of the strategic air forces, Arthur Harris, Carl Spaatz and Ira Eaker, attended the conference. There it was agreed to begin the decisive phase of the anti-submarine campaign and to bomb Germany continuously from the air (Operation **Pointblank**). The priority of targets for bombing, allowing for unforeseen eventualities, was tentatively set as follows: first, sites where submarines were constructed and repaired, including plants where spare parts were manufactured; second, aircraft plants; third, ball-bearing factories; fourth, oil refineries; fifth, synthetic rubber plants; and sixth, automotive factories. (See also **Germany, Air Battle of.**) In the course of the discussions, Alan Brooke's support for operations in the Mediterranean won out over Marshall and his American colleagues, who wanted to concentrate all available forces for an assault on the French coast in 1943. The final decision was that a landing on the coast of France would have to wait until the spring of 1944 unless the Reich suddenly collapsed. 1943, meanwhile, was to see more limited activity, beginning with an invasion of Sicily— Operation **Husky**. It was further agreed to reconquer **Burma** and to augment the airlifts from northern **India** to **China** in order to provision that country. Finally, the conference formulated the demand for the **unconditional surrender** of Germany and its allies.

The second Washington conference, known as "Trident," began on May 13, 1943, the day General Alexander totally destroyed the Italo-German armies in Africa. The date for a landing on the coast of France was set for May 1944. With regard to **Italy**, two

viewpoints arose. The British chiefs of staff proposed an invasion of the Italian boot in 1943, while the Americans favored the conquest only of Sicily, Sardinia and Corsica, reserving the mass of troops for the landing in France.

With the African campaign nearly complete, the Allies prepared for the assault on **Fortress Europe**. The Anglo-American landing on Sicily began on July 10, 1943. Its objectives were to bring about Italy's surrender and liberate the Mediterranean, to pin down large bodies of German troops and so ease the situation for the Soviets and to construct air fields on the Italian peninsula from which strategic aircraft could strike southeastern Germany and the Ploesti oil wells in **Rumania**. The conquest of Sicily would, it was hoped, accelerate the disintegration of Italy itself. If added operations were necessary to bring that about, Eisenhower could execute them. He was cautioned, however, that he had only relatively small detachments for those pursuits and that he could not draw on the reserves earmarked for the landing on France the following year. This condition was imposed by the American chiefs of staff in exchange for the British acceptance of operations in the Mediterranean.

Sicily was completely subjugated on August 16, 1943. During this campaign, however, Eisenhower established his plan for an eventual landing on continental Italy. On August 15, the first Quebec Conference, bearing the code name "Quadrant," came to the following conclusions: first, to accept unconditional surrender of Italy, to obtain from it all possible assistance and to set up airfields on the peninsula to augment the bombing raids on Germany; second, to deprive the Germans of fuel by destroying Ploesti; third, to launch the major effort of the war with a landing on Normandy (Operation Overlord) before May 1, 1944; fourth, to effect a landing in the south of France (Operation **Anvil**) as a diversion to ensure the success of Overlord; fifth, to aid the Yugoslavian forces; sixth, to undertake concentric operations against Japan starting from the central Pacific, the South Pacific and the Indo-Burma frontier (this last offensive was intended to reestablish land communications with China and to facilitate airlifts to that country). It was also at the Quadrant Conference that Roosevelt and Churchill reached an agreement concerning the development of the **atomic bomb**.

By the end of 1943, the importance of the invasion of Italy became manifest. The Italian forces surrendered; but the Germans, having long been prepared for such an eventuality, reacted strongly. The Allies gained a foothold in southern Italy on September 3. Once the Italian campaign began, Marshall and his American colleagues demanded, as they had before, that amphibious equipment be used sparingly in the Mediterranean. This was why seven seasoned divisions and aviation groups from that theater were removed to Great Britain. The consequences of this caution soon became evident. The Allied land forces were stymied in the narrow and mountainous Italian terrain by a stubborn enemy. With enough ships, the Anglo-American forces could have accomplished miracles in the final months of 1943. But, with limited amphibious strength, the Anzio operation could not be consummated until January 1944. Meanwhile, Churchill was hesitant about Operation Anvil on the Cote d'Azur. He doubted its success; he would have preferred using the troops trained for that project in a tremendous offensive toward **Austria** to support the Yugoslavian forces at the North Italian border. He also favored such a drive to enter central Europe ahead of the Soviets.

Thus, in 1942-43, a clear difference appeared between American and British strategic ideas. Alan Brooke's indirect British strategy, in keeping with the tradition of the two Pitts and Wellington, was to "close the ring." The scenario called first for isolating Germany by depriving it of its Italian ally, then helping the Yugoslavs drive it out of the Balkans, thus to tempt **Turkey** into the war. The more direct American strategy was to accumulate as much hardware as possible in Great Britain for a quick and concerted attack on the west coast of France without spreading resources thin in secondary forays.

There were good reasons for these differences in opinion. For the British, the Mediterranean is a vital artery. For the Americans, the Mediterranean is of secondary importance. Marshall and his colleagues resigned themselves reluctantly to Torch; they had to agree to it since Roosevelt aligned himself with Churchill. They were later to resent the need for three successive landings—on Africa, on Sicily and on the Italian boot.

For the British, the landing in France had to have every chance of success, with a minimum of losses. This view was prompted by the recollection of Artois, the Somme, Ypres and Passendale. But for the Americans, whose losses in France in World War I were relatively light and who had an enormous population to draw from, the important thing was to win the war quickly, even if losses were high.

It would be wrong to conclude that misunderstandings split the "Big Two" and the chiefs of staff of the two nations. Their goals were alike; they simply disagreed on the best ways of attaining them. To be sure, there were errors and wrong-headedness. The British underestimated the Americans. Obsessed by the setbacks in the Kasserine Pass and in Tunisia, Alan Brooke and some of his staff suspected the American forces of lacking the necessary training to be thrown into so delicate a maneuver as a landing on a hostile coast against a battle-hardened enemy. By receiving secondary assignments, the British reasoned, American troops would have the opportunity to become seasoned. The Americans, on the other hand, accused Churchill and Brooke of losing interest in Overlord, a project which—along with Roosevelt—they preferred. When Gen. Marshall pointed out that economy of troops required a concentrated attack on the French coast, Brooke replied that, since that operation was not to begin until May 1944, there was nothing to prevent the use of some of the amphibious forces accumulated for Overlord in the Mediterranean. Thus, according to Brooke, many of the German units would be pinned down far from the major French front while the Allied air and naval forces could exploit the mobility they had achieved. Finally the Americans consented to May 1, 1944 as the target date for Overlord, guessing that Churchill would seek any pretext for delays. But the prime minister understood, no less than his allies, that the moment for a landing was approaching; he asked only for more elasticity in the timing, with less insistence on a particular date. If more profitable opportunities presented themselves in the meantime, there could be no great loss in putting the landing off four or six weeks.

At the end of November 1943 Churchill and Roosevelt met with Chiang Kai-shek at the Cairo Conference—code name "Sextant"—and then, for the first time, with Stalin, at the Teheran Conference ("Eureka"). The president and the prime minister then returned to Cairo for more talks with Chiang. At Teheran Stalin promised a large-scale offensive the moment Allied forces set foot on Normandy. But he insisted on the simultaneous execution of Operation Anvil in the South of France. His intention, though tacit, was clear: he wanted the Allies out of Italy. A decisive triumph of Anglo-American troops in the Italian peninsula could bring the Western powers into central Europe ahead of the Red Army. To Churchill's great regret, Roosevelt concurred with the Soviet dictator. Cleverly, Stalin assured the president that he would throw all the Soviet forces into action against Japan once Hitler was defeated. Roosevelt thus did not have to worry too much about the situation in the Pacific; he could as a consequence devote a maximum of manpower to both Overlord and Anvil. Thus Roosevelt and Stalin overcame Churchill. It was agreed to undertake Anvil as soon as possible, as the same time as Overlord, with no other operations in Europe that might endanger the two major projects. This double concession made to the Americans and the Soviets dismayed Alan Brooke.

At Cairo the decision which had been made in Quebec to concentrate Allied forces in the central and South Pacific for a drive toward the **Philippines** was confirmed, as was the land offensive planned in Burma. The Americans and Chiang Kai-shek had wanted the British to undertake an amphibious thrust at the Andaman Islands in the Indian Ocean (Operation Buccaneer) at the same time as the **Burma Campaign**. But Alan Brooke adamantly opposed it, and eventually won out. He pointed out that his Washington colleagues were not adhering to the principle they had advocated when the question of a Mediterranean front had arisen: to avoid diverting the amphibious power so necessary for the landing in France. As Brooke insisted, the operations against the Andaman Islands would absorb a good many ships of all types, more than the prize was really worth.

The differences of opinion between the British and American chiefs of staff notwithstanding, their method in attaining these complex goals deserves admiration. The vast deployment and distribution of personnel, of raw materials and of arms by every slender communications route on the planet and to all fronts was an astounding feat. The magnitude of their task was overwhelming. Curiously enough, their major problem was not men, guns or planes; these were plentiful by 1943. What constantly occupied their thoughts was the **landing craft**, both large and small, they would need. The war at that moment took on a completely unprecedented aspect: every military operation set in motion also demanded naval cooperation. They were all amphibious. Ships were always lacking. Errors in judgment were therefore inevitable. Furthermore, as we have seen, friction arose between forceful men with widely varying national interests and personalities on whose shoulders the heavy responsibilities of the war rested. Nevertheless, a review of these global operations as a whole and of the war's final result provides convincing evidence that the deployment and direction of men and materiel resulted in almost the maximum possible yield.

Churchill and Roosevelt agreed to appoint the American Gen. Eisenhower and the British Gen. H. Maitland Wilson commanders in chief of the Northwest European and Mediterranean theaters respectively. The first appointment was made December 6, 1943; the second, twelve days later.

Overlord in Normandy (see **Normandy Landing**) and the operation known first as Anvil and later as **Dragoon** in the South of France began on June 6 and August 15, 1944, respectively. By mid-September practically all of France and Belgium had been liberated. The Allies on the Italian front entered Rome on June 4 and occupied the Pisa-Ancona line. The Soviets overran **Poland** and the **Baltic States**. In the Balkans, Rumania and **Bulgaria** switched sides, and **Tito**'s army controlled 70% of **Yugoslavia**. The British were preparing for the amphibious and airborne liber-

ation of Greece: it was realized on October 3. Allied victories accelerated in the Far East as well: the Japanese were completely routed in Burma and the overland route to China was cleared. After their sensational advances in the Pacific, Gen. MacArthur and Admiral Nimitz combined forces for an assault on the Philippines.

It was in an atmosphere of euphoria, then, that Churchill, Roosevelt and their entourages assembled at the Second Quebec Conference—code word "Octagon"—on September 12, 1944. Gen. Eisenhower's plan for the decisive blow to destroy the German war machine was accepted. In Southeast Asia a huge amphibious operation was to be undertaken against Rangoon, leading to the complete encirclement of the Japanese, retreating before Lord Louis Mountbatten's land forces. The conference also heard a proposal for the occcupation of Germany, with zones assigned to each of the conquering powers as a basis for later negotiations with the Soviets and French.

Shortly after the conference in October 1944, Churchill traveled to Moscow to inform Stalin of the intentions of the Western Allies and to discuss future problems. Stalin was willing to accept the division of Germany and Austria into Soviet, American and British zones, but as Roosevelt had, he balked at giving one to the French. Churchill, however, insisted on it. It was agreed that Rumania and Bulgaria would be part of the Russian sphere of influence and Greece part of the British sphere, while the interests of the two great powers in Yugoslavia and **Hungary** were to be split equally. But Stalin refused to commit himself on the question of Poland.

The hymn of victory at the "Octagon" conference was shortly afterward sung in a slightly different key. There was no question of the final victory, of course. But the hope of ending the war in 1944 vanished with the reverse suffered in the airborne operation in Holland at the end of September. Nevertheless, the Western Allies won the southern part of the Netherlands and opened the port of Antwerp to navigation at the end of November. For the moment, however, they could not shake the German hold on the Dutch waterways or the Siegfried line. The Allied forces in Italy, deprived of the units liberating Greece, made only slow progress against the well-fortified German defenses. The Soviet advance halted between the end of October 1944 and the beginning of January 1945, a completely normal development after the previous energetic drive.

As a result of these European disappointments, one of the first measures the great powers took was to cancel the giant amphibious operation on the other side of the globe, in Rangoon. Lord Mountbatten could not be given the reinforcements in men and ships he asked for. He was told that Burma would have to be taken by land troops alone. He accomplished that feat in the first five months of 1945.

Octagon was the last of the major military conferences. The later Allied meetings—at Yalta in February 1945 and at Potsdam in July 1945—concerned the postwar world.

Germany surrendered May 7, 1945; Japan followed on August 15, 1945.

Thus the strategy plotted at the end of 1941 by Churchill and Roosevelt achieved its purpose. Germany was the first target. After it fell Japan could not hold out for long.

H. Bernard

Y–Z

YALTA CONFERENCE.
See **Conferences, Allied.**

YAMAMOTO, Isoruku (1884-1943).
A Japanese grand admiral, Yamamoto entered the Japanese navy in 1900 and was wounded in the Battle of Tsushima Straits in the Russo-Japanese War of 1904-05. During World War I he studied for two years at Harvard University. In 1925-27 he was naval attache in Washington, D.C.; in 1930 and 1934 he served as delegate to the London Naval Conference. He acquired a particular interest in aeronaval warfare quite early. In 1936 he became assistant naval minister, expressing his opposition to an alliance with **Germany**, although he was one of the principal advocates of war against the Anglo-Saxon powers. In 1939 he was commander in chief of the Combined Fleet and, despite the opposition of the admiralty, succeeded in making the surprise attack on **Pearl Harbor** part of the Japanese war plans. During the first 18 months of the war he directed **Japan**'s naval operations, including the unsuccessful attempt to destroy the U.S. fleet at **Midway**. On April 18, 1943 his aircraft was shot down by American fighter planes over **Bougainville**.

H.-A. Jacobsen

YEO-THOMAS, Forest Frederick Edward (1901-1964).
Yeo-Thomas was an agent of the **Special Operations Executive**. Fluent in French, he was able to help de Gaulle's followers to organize the Secret Army in France, in 1943. Arrested on his third mission to France (1944), he eventually escaped from Buchenwald in 1945. Yeo-Thomas was known, among other names, as the "White Rabbit."

YEREMENKO, Andrei (1892-1970).
As commander in chief of several Soviet army groups, or fronts, Yeremenko saw action at Bryansk, Stalingrad and Kalinin. He liberated the Crimea from German control, and at the end of the war, he was commander in chief of the Fourth Ukrainian Front. Yere-menko held the rank of marshal of the **USSR**.

YONAI, Mitsumasa (1880-1948).
A Japanese admiral, Yonai was minister of the navy at different times between 1937 and 1945 and premier from January to July 1940. Yonai spent two and a half years in **Germany** after World War I, read *Mein Kampf* and unswervingly opposed closer ties with the **Axis** because he knew it might drive **Japan** into a war against the **United Kingdom** and the **United States** that could not be won. In 1937 he tried vainly to obtain a prompt settlement of the fighting in **China**. His cabinet focused on southward expansion in early 1940, pressuring French **Indochina** and the Dutch East Indies. As minister of the navy during the last year of the war, he was a leading spokesman for peace.

YOSHIDA, SHIGERU (1878-1967).
Yoshida, a diplomat and politician, served as prime minister of **Japan** for seven years after World War II. A conservative by instinct and an aristocrat by upbringing, Yoshida served as ambassador to the **United Kingdom** in the 1930s, causing Japan's wartime leaders to suspect him of being a Churchillian liberal. He took part in the clandestine movement to unseat Prime Minister **Hideki Tojo** in 1943-44 and was jailed for mentioning the likelihood of defeat in April 1945. After the surrender he was the single most important leader of Japan as the country rebuilt its polity and economy under American military occupation.

Yoshida was born in Kochi prefecture, graduated from Tokyo Imperial University and served for three decades in the foreign ministry. The army blocked his appointment as foreign minister in the cabinet organized by **Koki Hirota** in March 1936 because of his conciliatory views. When the war bogged down in early 1943, Yoshida joined senior statesmen and members of the imperial family in a **resistance** movement against Tojo and, by implication, the entire military leadership. This group managed to unseat Tojo after the fall of **Saipan** in July 1944. When the military police seized a letter he had written to Prince **Fumimaro Konoe** urging that **Hirohito** seek peace, Yoshida was jailed for a short time. He became foreign minister two days after the surrender on August 15, 1945 and prime minister in May 1946.

T. R. H. Havens

YUGOSLAVIA.

On March 27, 1941, Yugoslavian air officers, supported by the British secret services and very likely by those of the **USSR**, succeeded in a bloodless coup against Prince Paul, the other regents and the government presided over by Diagisa Cvetkovich. They placed on the throne the adolescent **Peter II**, the son of King Alexander, who had been assassinated at Marseilles in 1934 along with the French foreign minister, Louis Barthou. The air general Dusan Simovich appointed members of all the important parties, with the exception of the illegal Communist Party, to the new cabinet.

Obviously, the putsch was the result of the vague popular sullenness provoked by Cvetkovich's signature of the **Tripartite Pact** in Vienna on March 25. On March 26 huge demonstrations erupted. They had been organized by the Communist Party to condemn the government's **treason** and to rouse the people to defend their nation's independence.

Although there had been no formal declaration to that effect, **Hitler** interpreted those demonstrations as

a popular denunciation of the Vienna agreement. That same day he signed an order to invade Yugoslavia on April 6, and invited **Mussolini**, as well as representatives of **Hungary** and **Bulgaria**, to participate in the military expedition. One result of the invasion would be a delay in the thrust into the Soviet Union, which was to have begun on June 15, according to the **Barbarossa** plan, but was deferred to June 22. That fatal delay was in part responsible for the failure of the offensive on Moscow in the fall of 1941—the first crack to show in the Nazi war machine (see **USSR— War with Germany**).

The descent of the *Wehrmacht* on Yugoslavia began on schedule on April 6 with an air raid on Belgrade. A crazy-quilt of various nationalities, politically unstable, economically underdeveloped, militarily unprepared and above all unassisted from the outside, the country was incapable of **resistance**. It was overwhelmed in 11 days by hordes of German, Italian, Hungarian and Bulgarian troops, 52 divisions in all, aided by a "**fifth column.**" King Peter, the Yugoslavian government and a dozen of its leaders fled through **Greece** and the Middle East to London. Yugoslavia's surrender to the Germans was signed at Belgrade, more than 300,000 officers and soldiers were taken prisoner and the country was torn apart. **Germany** and **Italy** shared Slovenia. The central part of the country, consisting of **Croatia** and Bosnia-Herzegovina, became the state of Croatia; it was placed in the hands of Dr. **Ante Pavelich**, head of the **Ustachi** movement, who was under the direct control of the Germans and Italians. Italy took the coast and some of the Dalmatian islands, and appointed a governor in Split. It also occupied Montenegro, while practically all of the Kosovo-Metohija region and Macedonia were integrated into greater **Albania**. Germany seized Serbia, along with the fertile Banat region. Bachka and Baranya went to Hungary, while Bulgaria took all of Macedonia east of the Vardar river.

The occupying troops aggravated the traditional religious and national differences. In Croatia, the Ustachis began exterminating the Serbs under their control, burning villages, destroying churches and murdering Orthodox clergy. In Bosnia-Herzegovina the Ustachis deepened the mutual antipathies of Serbs and Moslems by praising the latter as the "flower of the Croatian people." In Bachka the Hungarian fascists staged an unprecedented orgy of terror among the Serb population; the Germans did the same in Banat. In their zone, the Bulgarians began persecuting Serbs and Macedonians. The Albanian fascists did the same in their territory, which was under Italian control. In Serbia, beginning in August 1941, the Germans replaced their provisional commissariat, which had been subordinate to the military

command for Serbia, with a puppet government controlled by Gen. Milan Nedich.

It was in this way that the **Axis** powers hoped to take control of the Balkans with relatively small forces and to exploit, in "peace and order," such strategic resources as nonferrous metals in Serbia and Macedonia and bauxite in Croatia and Bosnia-Herzegovina. But hidden in these regions were two Resistance movements, one of them inspired by the Communist Party, the other by Col. **Dragolyub Mihailovich**. Although it was illegal the Communist Party had 8,000 adult members and 30,000 youth members; it collected arms, created underground committees and formed disciplined units to take up weapons at the propitious moment. Mihailovich, a royal army colonel who had refused to surrender and took refuge in the Serbian mountains to the east with a group of 26 officers, meanwhile set up the Chetnik organization. After June 1941 the Chetniks made contact through Istanbul with the Yugoslavian **government-in-exile** and the **Special Operations Executive**. They were instructed to take no armed action against the occupying troops, to keep calm, to consolidate their organization and to await the outcome of the war; later they would be expected to conduct an armed struggle to save the monarchy.

The German attack on the USSR on June 22, 1941, however, upset these plans, along with a good many others. To aid in the attack, the *Wehrmacht* pulled most of its forces out of Yugoslavia, leaving only a garrison of four divisions and some police units. The Communist Party took advantage of this weakness at the beginning of July by undertaking some diversionary actions. It formed a general staff for partisans of the Yugoslavia national liberation movement, with Josip Broz (**Tito**) as commander in chief. The small blaze begun by this organization spread through practically all the country's provinces; the partisans scored victory after victory. They liberated a huge chunk of Montenegro as well as parts of Serbia and Bosnia. By the fall of 1941 Tito's rebels numbered about 80,000. The guerrilla war began to taken on such dimensions that it forced occupying Axis troops and their collaborators to retire to the large cities and limit their operations to defending the principal communications arteries. The rest of the country was for the most part in the hands of the Resistance, allowing Tito to infuse the Yugoslavian peoples with the ideal of fraternity and to demand the renunciation of the fratricidal enmity that played into the hands of the Axis occupiers as it had played into the hands of the monarchy. He pledged a federated and democratic Yugoslav state and protected the peasantry against looting by occupation soldiers.

For his part, Mihailovich favored assassination on

the theory that the attacks he conducted on the occupying troops were in the nature of reprisals. He defended the interests of the monarchy and in general diverged ideologically from Tito's guerrillas to such an extent that, despite conferences between the two on September 19 and again on October 26-27, 1941, Mihailovich rejected all his rival's attempts to make common cause. In October 1941 a British mission arrived at Mihailovich's headquarters and established a liaison between the Chetniks on the one hand and the Yugoslavian government-in-exile and the SOE on the other. At the beginning of November 1941, on Mihailovich's orders, the Chetniks mounted an attack on Tito's stronghold in Uzice, also the site of an arms factory. It failed. Both parties now came openly to oppose each other. In 1941 the Chetniks allied themselves with the Italian occupation troops, who supplied them with arms, in Dalmatia, Herzegovina and Montenegro. In Serbia the Chetnik movement won the favor of the Nedich collaborationist government, under the approving eye of the German high command for Serbia. By this time the Chetniks were actively seeking direct contact with the Germans. On November 11, 1941 Mihailovich reached an accord with German officers. Although Hitler and **Himmler** generally frowned on such meetings, the German command on several occasions used the Chetniks as auxiliary weapons against Tito's guerrillas.

To blunt the constant threat from the Resistance, the Germans called on the 342nd Division, which had been stationed in France, and withdrew the 113th Division from the eastern front. Their combined forces launched a violent assault on the guerrillas. Forced to fall back under the weight of these numbers, the guerrillas split up, retreating to Serbia, Bosnia-Herzegovina and Montenegro. But that did not end their activity; in 1942 they not only continued to battle the Germans and their collaborators, but took on the Chetniks as well, meeting with considerable success—so much so that by the end of 1942 Tito had 150,000 men under arms.

A new military organization, the National Liberation Army of Yugoslavia, whose hierarchy resembled that of a formal army, was formed. It conquered various isolated points in the country, establishing bases for the national liberation movement in each. By the beginning of 1943 large portions of western Bosnia and eastern Croatia had been liberated. It was in these areas that the Anti-Fascist Council for the Liberation of Yugoslavia—known as the **AVNOJ**—was formed. The new organization was made up of a large network of local liberation committees. These replaced the district and regional committees that had served as tools of the occupier; they constituted the new local seats of power.

The defeat of the Axis powers in North Africa (see **Mediterranean and Middle Eastern Theater of Operations**) and at Stalingrad and the landing of American forces in the Mediterranean heightened the continuing drama in the Balkan theater. In anticipation of an Allied landing on the shores of the Adriatic, the Germans embarked on the first part of the two great operations, *Weiss* and *Schwarz*, in 1943, in the region beyond the Dalmatian coast. They were reinforced by additional divisions. The battle of Neretva was fought in March 1943. The partisans, who suffered some 4,000 casualties, succeeded in slipping the nucleus of their forces into Montenegro under the noses of the combined German, Italian, Ustachi and Chetnik forces. After bloody battles in Slovenia and Croatia in June 1943, the partisans managed to penetrate eastern Bosnia.

In the first half of 1943 the **United Kingdom** decided to seek out partisan supreme headquarters. The British missions, led by Capt. F. W. D. Deakin and Brigadier Gen. Fitzroy McLean, informed London of the partisans' tenacious and effective harassment of the Axis forces and of the Chetniks' defection to the enemy. Yet, in the second half of 1943, the British continued to assist both movements. It was not until the Teheran Conference of November 30-December 1, 1943 (see **Conferences, Allied**) that the decision was made to aid only the partisans. The British persisted in trying to save the monarchy, but it was too late.

At the second session of the AVNOJ in Jajce on November 29, 1943, the Yugoslavian National Liberation Committee was organized to act as a provisional government for a new Yugoslavia. The King, the session announced, was not to reenter the country until the people had decided the fate of the monarchy, and Yugoslavia was to be a federated state. By the end of 1943 the partisans commanded a disciplined army of 300,000. The surrender of Italy lent them even greater strength by adding the weapons they took from the disbanding Italian divisions to their arsenal. Tito's partisans were now in a position to act independently from both the British and Soviets.

In May 1944 Mihailovich lost the post of minister of the army and the navy in the Yugoslav government in exile, which he had held since January 1942. The British withdrew their military assistance from the Chetniks. On June 16, and again on November 1, 1944, the head of the Yugoslav government-in-exile, Ivan Subasich, signed an accord with Tito providing for a coalition to administer the liberated state. In the meantime, the Red Army had advanced as far as the eastern frontiers of Yugoslavia. The National Liberation Army began to receive additional aid from its eastern allies. In the fall of 1944 Belgrade, Serbia,

Voivodina and Macedonia fell to the Red Army, aided by the partisans. The National Liberation Army was then charged with establishing liaison between the Red Army and the Western Allied forces in Italy. By the beginning of 1945 the National Liberation Army cut off German forces in Hungary and Italy.

On March 7, 1945, the coalition government of the Federal People's Republic of Yugoslavia was formally established, with Marshal Tito at its head. At the war's end Yugoslavia had an army of 800,000 men. In the final operations in the northwest it took 150,000 prisoners, together with a mass of war booty. Stealing a march on the Allies, the Yugoslav army captured the prize city of Trieste; the question of that city's final disposition would create conflicts among the victors.

In the course of World War II, Yugoslavia lost some 1,700,000 people, or 10.8% of the total population.

J. Marjanovic

ZEITZLER, Kurt (1895-1958).

After serving as chief of staff of the First Panzer Group, Zeitzler replaced Gen. **Franz Halder** as chief of the general staff of the land armies in September 1942 and held that position until July 1944. He was responsible for the German offensive at Kursk in the summer of 1943. Zeitzler held the rank of general.

ZHUKOV, Georgi Konstantinovich (1896-1974).

Zhukov was a noncommissioned officer in the Russian Imperial Army in 1915. He joined the Communist Party in 1919. In 1938, as commander of an army corps, he defeated Japanese border troops in Manchuria and in 1940 assumed command of a group of armies defending Moscow. From 1942 to 1943 he directed the defense of Stalingrad and from 1944 to 1945 led the First Ukrainian Front and the First Belorussian Front. The forces under his command captured Warsaw, Lodz, Poznan and Berlin, where he received **Germany's unconditional surrender** on May 8, 1945. From 1945 to 1946 he commanded Soviet occupation forces in Germany. He was made minister of defense of the **USSR** in 1955 but was dismissed in 1958 by Nikita Khrushchev, who accused him of "Bonapartism." He held the rank of marshal of the Soviet Union.

ZITADELLE.

In English, "Citadel." Code name for the German offensive of July 1943 against the **USSR**.

CONCLUSION
IMMEDIATE AND LONG-RANGE
CONSEQUENCES OF THE WAR

When the German armies finally surrendered, the Allies focused their attention on two immediate problems: first, assuring the security of their occupying troops, and second, helping the citizens of Allied countries, profoundly scarred by four, five or even—in the case of Poland—six years of Nazi occupation.

The first problem, it soon became clear, was hardly a problem at all. The collapse of the defeated regime was as complete as it was ugly. All the youngsters mobilized at the last moment into the *Volkssturm*, who were at first suspected of having been hypnotized into fanaticism by Goebbels' propaganda, offered not the slightest resistance. Contrary to all expectations these boys and girls, who had been brought up under the swastika and who everybody assumed would fight on furiously against all odds, were completely apathetic.

An immense lassitude afflicted Germany, completely spent after a gigantic military effort whose final act had borne no resemblance whatever to a tragic "twilight of the gods" in the Wagnerian mode. Hitler's desperate prophecy, "when we perish we will crush the universe," had failed, like so much else he had promised, to come about. German civilians were primarily concerned with getting something to eat or a scrap of clothing to wear, or perhaps with finding some shelter against the rigors of the coming winter. The Americans, British and French did not have to face any resistance, nor did their soldiers have to keep an eye out for snipers hiding in the rubble.

In short, the Hitler nightmare ended with one enormous sigh. The German people waited meekly for judgment to be passed on them. The Germans' psychological state was indicated by a popular anecdote: an American soldier asks a German teenager, "Well, sonny, do you still want to shout 'Heil Hitler'?" "No," the boy answers, "now it's forbidden."

Naturally, the problem was quite different in eastern Germany.

While the Red Army entered what was to be the Soviet zone with a plan for systematic Bolshevization already prepared, the Western forces had no idea what their attitude would be toward the population. Actually, no master plan had been developed to replace the ill-conceived, and quickly abandoned, Morgenthau Plan. Germany was not to be reduced to an agrarian state; the concept was obviously unrealistic and even a bit repulsive. But how, then, could militarism be eradicated from the German mind and democracy substituted for it? That was the primary problem facing the Western powers in the years to come. In any event, even in the first few months after Germany's surrender, Allied troops could freely move through the ruined cities in complete safety.

The attitudes of the liberated peoples were much easier to understand. For them the last months of the occupation had been the hardest. The Netherlands in particular had endured a long period during which every comfort had been lacking: gas, electricity, heating fuel—the winter of 1944-45 had been especially bitter—and food of any kind.

In the large cities all stores had remained closed simply because there was nothing to sell. Anarchy was almost complete. The police were interested only in tracking down enemies of the regime, and the people were faced with the naked and ugly truth that only the rule of the strong prevailed. In the parks trees had been cut down for firewood in spite of German decrees that stealing wood was punishable by death. The residents of Amsterdam invaded abandoned houses in the Jewish quarter for anything that could be burned—doors, stairways, posts. Often ceilings caved in, killing the foragers. People who would not ordinarily stoop to pick up a banknote gladly soiled their hands gathering precious cinders from rail beds. Only the churches and the various Resistance networks retained a semblance of authority.

Under these conditions the first duty of the Allies was to procure and distribute food. This task was accomplished at first with the tacit consent of the Germans, by parachuting in enormous quantities of food. The "flying grocer" operations brought hope of better eating in the future; it was clear that the worst was over. These emergency relief missions were carried out efficiently by the relatively new United Nations Relief and Rehabilitation Administration.

The reestablishment of order was the next priority. Existing government agencies barely operated, either because their heads had collaborated with the enemy or, just as likely, because their personnel no longer appeared for work—they needed somehow to acquire food for their families. There was a third possibility, too—that the records dating from the Nazi occupation had been burned to keep them from being examined by Allied eyes. In addition, everything had to be rebuilt, even the telephone service, which was, not surprisingly, especially bad in the cities that had been heavily bombed.

In sum, the victors had to undertake the most urgent practical tasks rather than laying the groundwork for a new society. The Resistance failed to be of much help in this respect because, in most countries, it spent its time trying to purge former collaborators.

Actually, one of the most astonishing postwar phenomena was the swift political elimination of those who had worked in the Resistance during the occupation. Many of them, neither Communist nor apolitical, had drawn up elaborate plans for establishing or renewing democratic institutions. Movements or embryonic political parties with such plans arose in several countries, but nowhere did they succeed in winning over the public to their ideas.

In Italy, where the civil war had cost the lives of tens of thousands of anti-Fascists, national renewal was incarnated in the *Partito d'Azione*. In the first free election after the war's end it received a ridiculously small number of votes. Apparently the electorate wanted nothing more than to return to the traditions of the pre-1923 era. The *Mouvement Republicain Populaire* (MRP) in France was a comparable movement. The MRP, a "faithful party"—to de Gaulle, that is—took a completely unexpected path; it soon lost whatever prestige it had acquired by becoming a Christian Democratic party. Soon it disappeared altogether, leaving its heritage to the Democratic Center. In Belgium the *Union Democratique Belge* was also inspired by the ideals of the Resistance; it shared the fate of Italy's *Partito d'Azione*. A Dutch Popular Movement that had sprung up in the Netherlands refused to develop into a political party, preferring to remain a nonpartisan exponent of reform. It too faded away, although it did encourage the growth of the former Social Democratic Labor Party, which eventually became the present-day Labor Party. All in all, however, the European Resistance turned out to be politically sterile.

How can this general phenomenon be explained? Several factors were involved. First, someone who had demonstrated courage during the occupation did not necessarily possess political acumen, judicial sagacity or

administrative efficiency. Second, the zeal members of the Resistance displayed in political purges tended to spoil their appetite for the less exciting adventure of reconstruction. And finally, many former resisters found themselves doubting the value of simply rebuilding old institutions and wondered whether it would not be preferable to strike out in a new direction. Such thinking usually led to advocacy of a federalist Europe.

In any case, memories of the Resistance seemed to disappear from public consciousness in the liberated countries during the months after the war. Resistance groups lost their political cohesion, and they often continued to exist only as social or veterans' clubs.

And yet, such a summary does not do justice to the Resistance as a political force. The heroic adventures Resistance members had shared helped unite citizens of different political, philosophical or religious beliefs. Under the incredible stresses the war had created, labels had tended to disappear and traditional groupings had become meaningless. The atheist discovered that the pious Christian was not as myopic as he had seemed, and the Christian found that the "pagan" was, at the very least, intellectually sincere. For the first time socialists began to understand the logic of conservatives, who in turn were amazed to find how inspiring the socialist faith could be. While these awakening sympathies did not crystallize into total political solidarity, they nevertheless laid a foundation of sympathy and mutual understanding on which a solid political base could be built.

Moreover, the European Resistance movement might have paved the way for a reconciliation between post-Hitler Germany and the formerly occupied countries. Although many who had remained inactive during the occupation suddenly turned into bloodthirsty German-haters once the danger was over, the former resisters recalled that they had cooperated with German anti-Nazis who sometimes even wore the detested uniform, an experience enabling them to distinguish easily between Nazis and Germans. And what of the high-ranking German officers who had participated in the attempt of July 20, 1944 to assassinate Hitler and the exceptional courage they had displayed in resisting the hideous regime that threatened to destroy their country? Hadn't they successfully confronted the crises of conscience that had bothered few others in countries where patriotism and anti-Nazism should have coincided?

But before reconciliation could begin, Resistance members felt it necessary to carry out one of the most painful actions of the immediate postwar period—the purges. They took their revenge everywhere and achieved nothing by it, for a number of reasons.

At first, in the fever of the liberation, blood flowed

freely—more in some countries than in others. There was more bloodshed in the south than in the north, on the whole. But even in Scandinavia there were death sentences, although the summary executions the Resistance had secretly conducted in wartime were eschewed. The chief collaborators, the native Nazis, were shot. What was the justification? The question was not pondered deeply. Very likely the condemned men felt the same way about their fate as their judges; the most prominent collaborators never expected to be spared.

The element of arbitrariness in these sentences became more apparent as, with the passage of time, judgments became less stringent. The visceral demand for revenge diminished, and as passions cooled, tolerance increased. An important political criminal who managed to stay hidden for several months thus stood a good chance of saving his skin. In this respect the Resistance lost its reputation in peacetime after having maintained it throughout the war. It had been admired as long as it was making history, but it became annoying when it refused to turn the page. Very soon after the end of hostilities, its tribunals began to operate in increasing isolation from the people they professed to serve.

This insensitivity on the part of the Resistance became especially obvious in its handling of economic collaborators. The entrepreneurs who had helped the enemy build the machinery of war, reaping tremendous profits for themselves, for example, had to be punished. Yet, on the other hand, their managerial ability and equipment were very much needed for national reconstruction. There was much gossip about rich collaborators who spent their nights in jail, only to be taken to their offices to conduct business as usual during the day, this time for the Allies' benefit rather than the Germans'. After all, the Japanese continued to fight after the Germans surrendered in May 1945, and more ships had to be built to end the war completely.

In sum, these purges, which, to members of the Resistance, had begun simply as a matter of separating the sheep from the goats, turned into a bewilderingly complex process. Where they should have brought about a wholesale purification they only resulted in painful disappointments. The people had cried out for justice during the war; they were still seeking it after their liberation.

Such folly was universal in Europe, but it was particularly tragic where the collaborators had succeeded in fooling themselves into thinking that they were really patriotic. Such self-deception was especially common in the Balkans, whose peoples had, even before the war, rightly or wrongly considered themselves oppressed by the governments of the states in which they lived. Consequently, once freed of the German yoke, they demanded autonomy or even complete independence. Faced with such problems, the purges were carried to extremes, ultimately smashing the federalist dream. These abortive ethnic declarations of independence temporarily glamorized the Flemish, Breton, Slovak or Croatian collaborators; in the minds of many Europeans, their efforts had in fact been noble contributions to the national cause. Injustices of this kind could hardly ease the already difficult process of postwar reconstruction. The people's apparent unanimity in wartime abruptly vanished along with the occupation. All the old quarrels that had troubled the Continent before 1939 erupted again, often in a more virulent form, and the inevitable result was the complete absence of the joy that community renewal should have brought about.

Germany, of course, was a special case. Its citizens certainly could not be reproached for having "collaborated" with their Fuehrer after they had elevated him to that position. By serving in the *Wehrmacht* they were only fulfillng their duty as citizens. On the other hand, however, it seemed somehow perverse that proportionately more death sentences were levied in the liberated countries than in the country that had started it all. The decision was then made to judge the German criminals of war in the courts of Nuremberg. But there again arose problems that were anything but simple. Who, for example, was responsible for the bombing of open cities like Warsaw, Coventry or Rotterdam? Surely not the pilots who had dropped the bombs. But how deeply into the hierarchy of German warlords did the courts have to probe before ferreting out the true criminal? They naturally chose Goering, supreme commander of the *Luftwaffe*, but he defended himself by throwing comparable accusations back at his prosecutors. The Allies, he reminded them sharply, were guilty of similar attacks on civilians in Dresden, Hiroshima and elsewhere.

When the defendants in the Katyn incident were accused of brutal reprisals against civilians in occupied territory, they replied that they had found the huge common grave of Katyn, where Red Army soldiers had apparently murdered and buried a good portion of the Polish officer corps, in the portion of Poland that the Soviets had occupied. Soviet representatives at the Nuremberg court protested the countercharge, but it was nevertheless picked up by the Allied press, whose acid editorial comments called the dignity of the tribunal into question.

The situation confronted by the Soviets in their portion of occupied Germany was less complex than that in the west. Moscow was not so much interested in the political history of its new German subjects as in their readiness to work for the Communist cause.

Under the direction of former members of the *Kommunistische Partei Deutschlands* (KPD), who had often fought the Nazis heroically, along with experts sent in from the USSR, the German bureaucrats in the eastern provinces were only too happy to continue their professional careers. The political structure of the provinces was quickly reorganized under the aegis of the Communist Party, which fused with the reborn Social Democrats throughout the region, except in East Berlin. The labor unions, too, took up their work where they had left off, although this time they were but one part of a state planning apparatus. Burgomasters and local functionaries went back to work under Soviet protection. After the turmoil of war and the shock of defeat, East Germany began to experience the comfort of routine and order.

Matters were different in the three Western occupation zones, where nobody quite knew what his position was or what he was supposed to do. In the beginning the Western powers attempted simply to occupy the country as if it had no residents by ignoring them as much as possible; this policy was called "nonfraternization." But it soon became apparent that such an absence of contact could not possibly be maintained. The nonfraternization policy, for example, had a definite sexual connotation that the Allied soldiers resented. It soon gave way to a new policy of denazification.

This new formula had actually been in preparation—at least in a certain rudimentary way—for some time. The Americans had, during the war, talked at length to the prisoners whom they considered likely candidates to conduct their country's affairs after the war's end—Germans who were willing to "collaborate" with the Western occupying powers. Professor Walter Hallstein, for example, who in 1958 was to become the first president of the European Economic Community, was approached in this way. The British undertook a similar operation in an ancient mansion known as Wilton Park in the English countryside. In this serene atmosphere many ties were established that were to prove useful after May 1945.

But what exactly was denazification? Naturally, what remained of the Nazi ideology and Prussian militarism had to be uprooted at all costs. But to achieve that, some sort of brainwashing procedure was called for, and that, in turn, required a complete revision of the German school curriculum. The practical and moral advantages of "free" institutions had to be emphasized. The problem lay in defining these institutions and modifying German political attitudes accordingly. Was the American system, with its federalism and its presidential form of government, to be regarded as the model? Or was the English system the purer democracy? Or was, perhaps, the best in representative democracy the natural product of German history? But the only German democracy to date had been the Weimar Republic, which had left a sad legacy of weakness and confusion.

In any case, a new path had to be chosen, especially since the horrors wrought by the Nazis were gradually coming to light. It is certain that many Germans knew of, or at least suspected, the atrocities that were committed in the concentration camps. But most of them preferred not to think about the matter. What was the point in brooding on its morality if nothing could be done? But now that it was no longer *verboten* to ask questions, eyes began at last to open and answers to such questions to suggest themselves. The first photographs released of Bergen-Belsen evoked cries of revulsion; if many initially felt they were elaborate fakes, many more understood that millions of human beings had been massacred systematically in the name of the German people. Even those skeptics who shrugged those pictures off as American propaganda were shaken by the testimony that survivors of the concentration camps gave. How, they asked themselves, could these unspeakable acts be committed by Germans, the people of Beethoven, Schiller and Goethe? The conscience-stricken German populace wondered if it would not be better to examine their national history and traditions in an effort to identify the source of this criminal virus before giving any thought to the politics of the future. Perhaps, shuddered some individual German with a sense of national kinship, this same virus that poisoned Hitler's brain is also in my own!

This self-flagellation was pointless, however, and most Germans felt that their country ought to attempt a reconciliation with the countries the Nazis had occupied. But it would not be enough merely to sign some diplomatic paper and join the anti-Communist front as if nothing had really happened. Churchill's presentation of the German problem in his "European" speech of September 1946 in Zurich was too simplistic. Reconciliation was necessary, to be sure, but it was not possible, as he suggested, simply to forget the wrongs that had been done. Germans who were conscious of their national pride, their sense of belonging to the European community and their role in the restoration of national morality could not permit themselves the luxury of simply "turning the page." They had to do more.

Thus, in postwar Germany the problem of civic education was addressed. Some professors and educators undertook the staggering job of attacking the evil of nationalism at its roots. One of them was Georg Eckert, who founded a center in Brunswick to revise German history and geography textbooks. It was exceedingly delicate work, but he managed to transform hundreds of books in fairly radical fashion. The Council of Europe was later to recognize Eckert's center as authoritative. Another was Professor Golo Mann, who analyzed the origins of Nazism in depth by exposing the faults in the Second Reich that had generated the Third. Federigo Chabod made a similar effort, in a comparable spirit, in Italy. Chabod was impelled by intellectual honesty to reexamine the justification for the *Risorgimento*, a subject nobody had ever dared touch. When Mussolini considered himself the legatee of the nationalist movement, had he been altogether wrong?

But these attempts, based on national self-doubt, remained relatively rare. The occupying powers' efforts at denazification could hardly be effective, resulting as they did from Germany's defeat. Moreover, Germany in the "year zero" was at the nadir of its misery, which was only too readily attributable to the Allied occupation. If the conquered country was to be reintroduced into the community of civilized peoples, only a spontaneous effort from within to establish a new and democratic German state could accomplish the task.

Revitalizing Germany's economic and especially its industrial structure would require a comparable effort. Air raids from both the east and the west had practically destroyed the manufacturing and distribution centers. Furthermore, as if that was not enough, the occupying powers were depriving Germany of some of its still usable machinery. The same sort of scavenging operation had been carried out after World War I, with disastrous results for all involved; in 1945 the victors were once again defeating their own purpose. For one thing, they were burdening themselves with obsolete mechanical equipment; for another, the Ruhr valley, along with other German industrial areas, was facing imminent ruin due to unemployment and poverty.

The Allies were thus saddled with another problem. If Germany were allowed to rebuild its heavy industry, it might be tempted to initiate another military adventure. If, on the other hand, reconstruction were forbidden, the Allies would forever be obliged to support the idle German labor force, which would soon ruin their taxpayers.

The situation was rapidly coming to a head. The commander of the British occupation forces did not hesitate to inform London that if street demonstrations against the incipient famine broke out in his territory, he would not be capable of ordering his soldiers to fire into the crowd.

The German problem thus had two facets, political and economic. The Russians knew exactly what they intended to do in their zone, but the Western powers were still fumbling for a solution in their area. Time

was passing, however; some reasonable solution had to be found, and quickly. An aggravating factor was the growing conviction in 1947, the "crucial year," that cooperation among the Allies was difficult if not impossible. A conference at Moscow in February and another at London in November hardened the suspicion that the United Nations was only a political fiction, that its Security Council would perpetually be handcuffed by Soviet *nyets* and that the slogan One World or None had no relation to reality. In other words, the Cold War between East and West had broken out. In Fulton, Missouri, Churchill declared in apocalyptic tones that an "iron curtain" had descended across Europe "from Stettin to Trieste." On which side of this curtain would the Germans find themselves?

The answer to that question was not long in coming, at least as far as Berlin was concerned. When the Soviets decided to cut off all roads to the old German capital in 1948 and turn it into an island in a Soviet sea, the Berliners enthusiastically rallied to the Western nations. And the Americans began to airlift supplies into the beleaguered city on a regular basis.

It was now perfectly clear that the West could no longer consider the Germans vanquished enemies; they were allies in the Cold War. If this new situation took concrete political form, the whole occupation policy of the West would have to be reconsidered. The American, British and French zones had, first of all, to be combined into one. Given the understanding between Washington and London that had even survived the peace, the amalgamation of the zones they controlled was simple. But Paris, always sensitive to the risks of aiding a German renaissance, delayed joining the Anglo-Saxon "bi-zone." Besides, Gen. de Gaulle was still consumed with his notion of partitioning Germany—or "the Germanies," as he like to phrase it—and to his desire for German territory that would give France a sphere of influence in the Rhine valley. Since these ambitions proved illusory, France finally accepted the establishment of a German political entity in the west—but not before it had achieved a benchmark in cultural penetration with the creation of the University of Mayence (Mainz).

The folly of expecting political dividends from such an enterprise became apparent at once. The Saar alone was to remain, at least provisionally, a fief of Paris, as had been the case after 1918. In 1955, however, the Saar was returned to Germany, after a referendum that recalled a similar vote in 1936. But this time the advocates of the status quo made a better showing, in the hope that Saarbruecken would be the capital of the anticipated united Europe.

Thus the death knell sounded for the French postwar policy of depriving Germany of its capacity to "inflict pain" on its neighbors. It is even possible that the federated government imposed on West Germany in the hope of weakening it was actually one of the reasons for the "German miracle," the astonishing economic growth of the truncated country that followed the *Waehrungsreform*—currency reform—carried out by the financial wizard Ludwig Erhard.

There appeared the real prospect, welcomed or not, that the Federal Republic of Germany, with its 60 million inhabitants and its healthy economic potential, would become the leading industrial power on the Continent. (Much later, Chancellor Willy Brandt could confidently assert that his country would not always be "an economic giant and a political dwarf.") After 1950 the main question would be whether this dizzying upsurge, already inevitable, would be accomplished within the framework of a united Europe or that of the classical nation-state. By way of response the French National Assembly rejected the European Defense Community, which provided for political union in its Article 38, on April 30, 1954, thus declaring for the second alternative.

In any case, the German question thus found one solution: national independence in the absence of any guarantees other than those provided by a series of international agreements, the Atlantic Alliance in particular.

Germany was obviously the most pressing problem in Europe at the end of the war, but other countries were also to undergo changes at the hands of the Allies. The first of these was Austria. While the war was still in progress, the Allies had often debated the question of whether Hitler's annexation of "Ostmark" was not, regardless of the circumstances surrounding it, an irreversible historical fact. The final decision was that the Austrians were to be treated as the citizens of an occupied country, comparable to the Czechs. Considering the wave of enthusiasm that had swept Austria in response to the *Anschluss*, the decision was rather remarkable. Furthermore, in view of the massive population transfers to the interior of the Third Reich that had taken place, Austria could hardly qualify as a unique entity. But while it was true that Hitler had received huge support in some Austrian cities, the final merger of the two countries was not particularly convincing evidence in favor of the pan-German thesis. The Austrians had dissociated themselves from the Nazi adventure when they judged the time auspicious, and their national identity was never seriously questioned afterward. The Allies' judgment of the country's status was therefore correct.

Austria, too, was caught up in the Cold War. The Soviets imposed an occupation regime in Austria that was different from the one they had established in Germany. Even in the Soviet-controlled section of Vienna, where enormous portraits of Stalin were to embellish the public squares for some time, there was no forced uniformity, no straitjacketing as there was in East Germany. Under the eyes of the Red Army, the people freely indicated their loathing for the conquerors. Austria's Social Democratic Party, in particular, distinguished itself by its courage; this is why the Austrian people later gave it their overwhelming support.

Perhaps the Soviets' attitude was in some way related to the Americans' monopoly of atomic weaponry at the time. In any event it did the cause of communism no particular good. Noting finally that the local Communist Party was a total failure, Moscow dropped its interest in Austria after signing a treaty providing for the country's complete independence as long as it kept a strict neutrality.

Italy's situation was different. Mussolini had declared war on the Allies in 1940, directly after the fall of France. But instead of the easy rewards in territory and plunder he evidently expected, he found himself trapped in a long and bloody war as the tail to the Nazi dog. The same thing was obvious to his Fascist Party when the Allies invaded Sicily after their successes in Africa. Did *Il Duce* expect his people to rush patriotically to his support? Possibly. What is certain, however, is that the Fascist Grand Council eventually deposed him.

After a few weeks of uncertainty regarding Italy's position, the country finally declared war on Germany. As a result, Italy as much as Austria had the right to consider itself an occupied country liberated by common effort. The bloody war the Italian Resistance waged against the *Wehrmacht* and its Italian allies of the Fascist "Social Republic" in Salo supported this contention.

After the war Italy was at first administered by the Allies and thus regarded as no more than an associate ally. To that extent, at least, the resolutely anti-Communist attitude of Alcide de Gasperi's Christian Democratic government was consonant with the thinking of the Allies. King Victor Emmanuel III, on the other hand, had never expressed a forthright opinion concerning fascism; he could hardly be expected to create a new, democratic Italy. A referendum ended in the creation of a republic, solidly governed from the center and open to all kinds of Western assistance as well as invitations to integrate with the rest of Europe.

In the meantime, Japan continued to resist incessant military pressure from combined American, British and Australian forces for three months after Germany's surrender. The final blow that crushed the Japanese was the atomic bombs dropped on Hiroshima and Nagasaki. By themselves they might not have ended the fighting, but they were enough to convince most members of the war regime that their effort was lost. Was such a horrible weapon necessary to obtain an end to the conflict? That question will be debated for years to come. At any rate, the appearance of this new weapon triggered the Soviet Union's decision to declare war against Japan. On the other hand, this first use of the atomic bomb was just as much a warning to the Soviet Union and a possible reason why Moscow moderated its territorial demands. The USSR was the only power to obtain huge territorial gains, both in Asia and Europe, as a result of the war, amounting to some 270,000 square miles. Still, the Soviets did reduce their demands—if only partially—each time the United States raised objections. The nuclear risk was as unacceptable to Stalin then as it is to Soviet leaders today.

Japan was eventually occupied, just as Germany had been. Gen. MacArthur—the hero of the Philippines, which had been lost early in the war, later to be regained in fierce fighting—administered occupied Japan. He was to derive a great deal of glory from his "proconsulate."

There were in fact, close parallels between Japan and Germany. Both nations plunged into war with the aim of creating, each on its own continent, a "co-prosperity sphere," to use the Japanese phrase. The basic means of obtaining these spheres was the same in both cases—subjugation of conquered populations. Both countries fought with resolution and tenacity worthy of more noble aims; both mobilized all national forces at their disposal with an enthusiasm approaching mass mysticism; both surrendered almost incredulously, the structure of their regimes crumbling despite the apparent solidity of their ideological foundations; and both set to work directly after their defeat, astounding the world with their energy and faith.

In other ways there were considerable differences between the two. For one thing, the supreme head of the Japanese Empire was neither dishonored nor dead. Hirohito, emperor of the state throughout its agony, retained his throne after the surrender was signed. It was he, in the last phase of the war, who supported reason in the face of the diehard samurai. The state continued its existence under his aegis, and its rupture with the past was much less painful, all things considered, than the death of German Nazism. Furthermore, Japan suffered less from the war than did Germany. Although Japan, too, had undergone heavy bombardment, the Japanese landscape was not left as much a mass of ruins. More emotional than the Germans, the Japanese people had been more distressed by Japan's defeat, but they undertook the labor of reconstruction with more zest. They also had the advantage of an industrial plant that remained practically intact. They were not saddled with the added burden of having to examine their national conscience, at least not to the point the Germans felt necessary. Japan had had its grand imperial dreams; it had wanted to realize them by force; it had lost—yet the national ideal remained intact. True, Japan had adopted a parliamentary regime only because the occupation authorities had insisted upon it. But, at bottom, the Japanese were preparing for another bout, one in which the parliament could not interfere. By adapting themselves to Western standards even more than the victors required, they reasoned, they could drive once again toward world domination. This time, however, they would do it by means of industry and commerce. Nothing could be less Wagnerian.

Above all, Japan had to rearm with patience. It had to rebuild, to recover its national independence and regain, at least partially, the territories it had lost to the Americans and especially to the Soviets, who, merely by showing a little military force at the last moment, had rewarded themselves with so much. And all Japan required to accomplish these goals was a smile—a smile addressed to the entire world. To the Americans first, because they were nearest for the moment and because they had a wealth of technology to offer, and then to the Soviets and even to the Chinese, under whatever regime.

In short, while the war had been a tremendous risk, the peace would be a far better one. And so it proved, for a quarter of a century later the Japanese economy had surpassed those of the major European countries with the possible exception of the Federal Republic of Germany. Japan has become America's primary rival. But to achieve this glowing success, Japan had to sacrifice many of its greatest attractions. Nowhere were spiritual and physical traditions neglected so completely. Nowhere did capitalist concentration take such extreme forms—perhaps because the ancient familial traditions of Japan proved flexible and strong enough to insure the cohesion of enormous industrial and banking combines.

Thus the two countries that had launched the war demonstrated the inexhaustibility of their vital energies after their military collapse. Where the British suffered acute discomfort and the French were slow to recover, the conquered nations rebounded in unexpected and spectacular fashion.

Let us now return to a Europe split in two by the Iron Curtain that had implicitly been recognized in the Yalta agreement. Churchill subsequently told the story of his meeting with Stalin during which, on a scrap of paper, they sealed the fate of Europe: "You can have 80 percent influence here, but I must get 85 percent there." The exact frontiers between the two fragments of the Continent thus represented, to a large extent, the results of the hostilities.

Naturally, the lands the Red Army liberated from the Germans were annexed or dominated by the Russians. Coups began in some of these states with denunciations of alliances previously considered indispensable. In Rumania, for example, the young King Michael routed Ion Antonescu, the fascist dictator, greeted the Soviets as liberators and declared war on the Reich. In Slovakia the collaborationist regime was eradicated. But regardless of differences in detail, the general procedure was identical in all cases. First, a patriotic front was created to embrace all the so-called anti-fascist parties. Then allegations made against certain participants in these fronts discredited them before the public or accused them of fraternizing with the enemy. In this way non-Communist government leaders were forced to commit political suicide, leaving vacancies that were immediately filled by Communist loyalists. In Rumania, for instance, the agrarian leader Juliu Maniu was thrown into jail, dragged before a court, condemned for high treason and executed; Nikola Petkov met the same fate in Bulgaria. In this simple fashion a political figure with a large following would be eliminated.

Under these conditions—and with considerable assistance in the form of the military presence of the Red Army—"workers'" parties were forced to fuse. Sometimes a group of old Social Democrats would put up a fight; they were quickly cooled off in jail. One after the other, promises of a democratic administration evaporated. The exile of the young Rumanian king at the end of 1947 was just one of the more dramatic episodes in this dreary cycle. In political conferences between socialists and Communists, the latter invariably dictated the terms. As for the "bourgeois" parties, like the one representing small landowners in Hungary, they were first "purged" of elements suspected of having collaborated with the Germans, then bullied into submission, especially if they had some success with the electorate. If all else failed, the party was simply dissolved.

The British Labor Party bore a definite responsibility for this liquidation of the working-class movement. It was so closely wedded to its democratic philosophy that it had no inkling of the game Moscow and its central and eastern European allies were playing. It naively believed that a fusion with the Communists would simply provide socialists with a broader proletarian base, since there were many more socialists than Communists. Apparently they were still unaware of the characteristic disregard of a totalitarian regime for the voice of the majority.

The Labor Party advised its comrades in the Soviet orbit to accept Communist offers of political fusion and then attempt to become the majority faction.

Closer to the realities of the situation, local socialists eyed this advice skeptically. It seemed to them that either London was completely misinformed as to the actual situation in central Europe or the Labor Party was seeking pretexts for abandoning them to the Soviets. Such misunderstandings have occurred frequently in history; a country pulled painfully from one side to the other when caught between two opposing forces appears to outsiders only to be drifting aimlessly. This was true of many of the Balkan countries, including Greece, which fell finally into the Western camp, and Czechoslovakia, which ended up in the Eastern sector.

Greece had, early in the war, fought the Italian aggressors to a halt, defeating enemy forces superior in numbers but poorly equipped for combat in the glacial mountains of Epirus and Albania. Although the Greek army was in turn badly mauled by the *Wehrmacht*, the Greek Resistance continued to harry the Germans in a courageous campaign to which Communists contributed importantly. Once liberation arrived, however, the Communist fervor for nationalism veered suddenly toward internationalism. Believing their hour had arrived, the Greek Stalinists rose against the royal regime, which was supported by a British garrison, in the latter part of 1944. Two divisions of British troops raced to the scene to defeat the revolt, succeeding only after several days of vicious street fighting.

As for Czechoslovakia, it had been Hitler's first victim and therefore was entitled to special treatment. A government under the leadership of Eduard Benes was installed in Prague, with a legislative body including Communists, Agrarians, Social Democrats and members of Benes' own party. The Red Army remained, unobtrusive but nonetheless visible. It did not have the country to itself, since American troops had penetrated deeply into Czech provinces after liberating Plzen, where they were received with delirious joy. But they later retired in accordance with the decisions of the Yalta Conference. From that moment on, the Bolshevization of Czechoslovakia was only a matter of time.

The Communist Party occupied many seats in the Czech parliament, but it was in no position to take complete power by legal means or even with Soviet pressure. Slovakia was in the main hostile to communism, while Bohemia and Moravia were controlled by the Agrarian and Social Democratic parties, which both supported Benes. In February 1948 the Communists decided to take control by fomenting violent street demonstrations. There were also counterdemonstrations, calling on Benes to stand fast against the Red tide, but the Communists forced changes in the president's cabinet, pushing the country ineluctably into Moscow's arms. Benes, torn between the tradition of pan-Slavism and the certitude that the Western democracies could not be counted on, resigned himself to this situation. He was right; as in the Munich crisis, the West offered him only condolences. Nevertheless, the "Prague coup d'etat" alerted the West to the need for more forceful responses to the Soviet bloc and led, the following year, to the creation of the Atlantic Alliance.

Yugoslavia was another country caught in the grips of the West-East nutcracker. Between World War I and World War II, this little nation had been torn among its component nationalities. In 1945 it fell into the hands of the partisans, led by Tito, who were compelled to wage war simultaneously against the Chetniks of Gen. Dragolyub Mihailovich and the Axis armies. Yugoslavia alone, of all the occupied countries, was able to free itself of its invaders with no assistance from either the Western Allies or the Red Army. Tito himself, of course, was a hard-line Communist, but his victory was brought about by the patriotism of his countrymen rather than their passion for communism. Hence his independent attitude toward his Soviet "advisers" who attempted to cow Belgrade as they had every other capital in central Europe. Tension between Tito and the Kremlin gradually increased until Stalin lost his temper and kicked his old comrade out of the Communist family. Among the ranks of enemies of the Red cause, Tito was placed in the "fascist" category. After Krushchev's election as premier, Moscow came to accept Tito's version of "Yugoslavia's road to socialism."

In 1947 Stalin convoked a meeting of the Communist parties of central and eastern Europe, with some representatives from the west as well. Out of this meeting came the Cominform, organized, as its name suggests, to promote the exchange of information among Moscow's satellite states. Its general secretariat was established in Belgrade, where a weekly bulletin of its activities was published for some time. Why was Belgrade chosen? Most likely because the Kremlin anticipated using the Cominform as a leash to keep Tito under control, but to no avail. In 1948 the conflict between the two erupted in public and once again Tito found himself an outcast: the Yugoslavian Communist League was excluded from the Cominform. To the surprise of the watching world, Tito demonstrated his control of the situation by securing the support of orthodox Stalinists in his country. As further insurance against the long arm of Moscow, he made overtures to the United States without jeopardizing his freedom of action. Washington was perfectly willing to grant him economic aid with no strings attached. He remained the master of his own country and political party, silencing his opposition even if, as in the case of Milovan Djilas, its spokesmen were his most intimate friends. Truly nonaligned, Yugoslavia learned to play East against West and to escape being crushed between the two.

The establishment of the North Atlantic Treaty Organization (NATO) in 1949 represented a radical shift in the military policy of the Western powers. With the surrender of Japan, the citizens of Britain and the United States began clamoring for demobilization of their armed forces. In the USSR, where public opinion had always amounted to an inaudible whisper, no such activity took place. The result was that the military balance between East and West remained precarious, with the latter maintaining its monopoly on nuclear weaponry until 1949 while the former controlled a vastly greater force of seasoned troops. In the years that followed, both filled their respective gaps. But the focus of contention between them—Europe—was comparatively defenseless and therefore was compelled to seek shelter under the American military umbrella. The United Kingdom had, of course, by this time devised its own atomic bomb—with the assistance of the Americans who, in violation of the McMahon Act, had given British scientists an impressive amount of applicable data. The Fourth Republic of France was later to engage in a similar enterprise, but its *force de frappe* ("striking power") never benefited from American aid; France had not even requested it.

An equilibrium of "terror" was thus established in the world as a consequence of the scientific achievements of the East and the West.

World War II had caused, or rather foreshadowed and accelerated, the decline of "old" Europe, especially Great Britain. At the end of the war, however, it was widely believed that Britain held the key to Europe's future.

During the war a cabinet of Laborites and Conservatives had governed the United Kingdom, cooperating under Churchill's direction. The victory had barely been achieved when the voters turned their leader out of office, believing that the Labor Party could better institute the reforms required in peacetime. To a large extent, it was the armed forces that contributed to the defeat of the man who had inspired the military effort.

The first of the reforms in question was the dissolution of the British Empire. Actually, the war had dealt the final blow to the imperial structure, which had outlived its usefulness even before the beginning of hostilities in 1939. Not just the old colonies but the "white dominions" as well had tired of control by the Old World; they yearned for independence. As for the colonies, India presented the biggest problem. The subcontinent had escaped invasion by the Japanese thanks only to a supreme military effort. Faced with this threat, many Indian nationalists had begun to wonder how far their loyalty to the mother country extended. Mohandas Gandhi's disciples had no particular affection for Japan's authoritarian regime. Yet, since independence remained their primary objective, the idea of cooperating with another Asiatic nation had its attractions. Besides, the Japanese occupation authorities in Indonesia had lent substantial impetus to the goals of Sukarno and his supporters. With the defeat of Japan, to which the Indian Resistance had contributed on a large scale, the Hindu anticolonialist movement presented its bill to the London government. It was sympathetically considered, along with apprehension concerning the British public's reaction to a possible Tory charge of a "giveaway." But a series of dramatic events intervened, notably a naval mutiny at Karachi in the beginning of 1946, and the Attlee cabinet finally granted India its independence in 1947.

This prudent decision, however, could not solve the problems of the ex-colony, particularly the religious ones. Conflicts between Moslems and Hindus erupted at once. These became so violent that to avoid the potential loss of hundreds of thousands of lives, the formation of two autonomous republics, India and Pakistan, was proposed. India would be dominated by Hindus and Pakistan by Moslems. Like many political compromises, this plan created more problems than it solved. For one thing, it formed a geographical absurdity: the two parts of Pakistan were separated by a considerable distance. Furthermore, the religious enmity, augmented by linguistic differences, continued in force, with bloody consequences. On both sides, minorities with claims of discrimination against the central government appeared.

The problem no longer directly concerned London, which had shed the burden of settling India's vexatious squabbles. But the war had also sharpened the desire for autonomy in the white dominions that had, out of loyalty to Great Britain, declared war on the Axis at the same time it had. Thus Canada drifted further away from Europe and closer to its giant neighbor to the south, while the French-speaking minority in Quebec became even more indifferent to the British than before. Eventually Canada abandoned even the old Union Jack flag for an entirely new design with a red maple leaf in the middle.

At the other end of the world, Australia had learned the expensive and painful lesson of Singapore. With the once-powerful British navy unable to help it in time of trouble, Australia had nowhere else to turn but to the United States, whose strength had sustained it during the war. This new attitude even influenced the commercial proclivities of the former colony. Its

earlier preference for trade within the British Empire, which had been steadily dropping in the period between the two world wars, disappeared completely.

The loss of Australia was another situation to which the British public had to adapt itself. It required an effort. In fact, when Britain was faced with the question of closer cooperation with Europe, the sentimental impulse to remain within the Commonwealth kept London from jumping squarely into the European economic community. Nevertheless, the Attlee cabinet was intent on carrying out decolonization; in this it refused to be influenced by British attitudes concerning the Continent.

Actually, even if all its consequences could not as yet be grasped by the entire spectrum of public opinion, one reality had become obvious: World War II had put an end to the concept that Europe was the center of civilization. This new facet of postwar international relations requires further analysis, for it is of major significance and touches many more countries than just the United Kingdom.

Europe had been the source of the global voyages of exploration and the settlements that followed them. Western modes of living were introduced everywhere, in medicine as in industry, in education as in banking. The Christian missions that accompanied or followed the explorers flourished where they first landed or moved on as the explorers progressed. As time passed, Europeans came to believe ever more firmly that their civilization was the only one possible. Even the dissenters who fled the Old World prided themselves on the benefits of their civilization in overcoming the paganism, superstitions and inertia of the new lands.

The 20th century scattered modern technology, which had developed in Europe, all over the globe. Far from unifying the world on an economic and technological plane, however, this phenomenon isolated continental Europe from the rest of the world, which learned to get along without European products and "leadership." The Commonwealth then became, as an American journalist put it, "no more than an opportunity for the Queen to take trips to warmer climates." Even the "special relationship" between the United States and its former guardian came to be no more than a subject of polite conversation for Americans and of temporary illusions for Britons.

Other European countries were similarly affected. French political life, in particular, was to be profoundly influenced after the liberation by the continuing battles for independence in the colonies, as well as the desperate—and sometimes successful—efforts to maintain at least a cultural, linguistic and human presence there.

One of the consequences of any military conflict is that the belligerent nation accelerates its exploitation of its colonies' resources and cuts back the investments in capital and energy on which the native populations subsist. This neglect leads, in turn, to the loosening of ties between the home population and the colonialists; the political "strong man" of each colony typically profits from the situation. In the case of France, however, the picture was slightly skewed. While most of the colonial governors had supported the Vichy government, other territories had remained loyal to London and the Free French. The enmity between Petainists and Gaullists was virulent, leaving still other options for local nationalists. In the meantime, Gen. de Gaulle described decolonization as a historic imperative in his celebrated speech at Brazzaville—which did not prevent the leaders of the Fourth Republic from becoming entrapped in extended fighting, first in Indochina and then in Algeria. In both cases, independence was the only logical outcome. The initial concept of the "French Union" fizzled out, but the sense of unity among speakers of French remains a reality, even in the former colonies overseas.

The situation was not much different in Indonesia. There, too, a quirk in events altered long-range developments. After the occupation of the archipelago, the Japanese imprisoned the entire white population in camps. The governor-general, Tjarda van Starkenborch-Stachouer, was moved by a noble sense of kinship to submit to this hardship along with his family. "This is our home," he said simply, "and we will not desert it in time of danger." The mass of Indonesians felt no gratitude to him, but they were profoundly impressed by this astonishing spectacle of their former unchallenged masters being mistreated by Asiatics.

When the Japanese surrendered, tens of thousands of the Dutch who had dominated Indonesia tottered out from behind barbed wire fences, enfeebled by malnutrition and many months of privation in the tropical heat. Most of them were poorly prepared for the enormous task of rebuilding the colonial power after the long period of Indonesian "independence," declared by Sukarno with Japanese approval. There, too, the sun of an empire had begun to set. Fifteen years later it was the Belgian Congo's turn to free itself and become Zaire.

This done, the only remaining vestiges of European imperialism were the possessions of Portugal, which pretended to an Afro-Portuguese partnership. Portugal, of course, had been neutral in the war and so, at least for a time, escaped the agony of decolonization that unsettled the British, French and Dutch. Its turn finally came in 1974, after years of vain military campaigns in Angola and Mozambique as well as other, less important places.

Europe was everywhere retreating—not only from the former colonies. In February 1947 the British ambassador to Washington, Lord Kirkpatrick, was given a painful mission. In a conference at the White House with Truman, he told the president that his country was no longer capable, economically or militarily, of maintaining its positions in the Near East, particularly in Greece. Only a few months after their intervention in the Greek civil war, British troops had to be withdrawn. Truman at once obtained from Congress an appropriation of $400 million to provide Greece with military and economic aid, and the United States assumed the role of "world policeman," the traditional post of Great Britain.

Saddled with the job of administering a nation whose influence was declining, Attlee tried brilliantly to compensate for it with a tough domestic policy. He observed that most European nations were initiating some sort of social security system and followed suit. What was unique in Britain was that the whole reform structure was created with one stroke, inspired by a homogeneous party and cabinet moving uniformly in the same direction. Was it socialist reform? Strangely enough, the idea was conceived by a British radical Lord Beveridge, who was not even a member of the Labor Party. His vast project was a model of daring and realism, even if in its execution it was later to develop certain weaknesses, particularly in the Health Service, the free and complete medical insurance it provided. But that was not to prevent the Laborites from showing the way to other European countries. In this, at least, they felt very much at home.

The situation was different in international politics when the former labor unionist Ernest Bevin became the Labor Party's foreign minister. He was faced with two principal problems. The first was the question of a European union, which was later to come into prominence; the second, the problem of the Middle East.

There were three factors requiring London to confront this second problem—Arab nationalism, Zionism and the old French claims on this part of the world, which de Gaulle eloquently, and continuously, repeated. Before and during World War II, the Moslems had been unwilling to support the Allies, primarily because of their antipathy toward the Jews. From the beginning Arab leaders were openly sympathetic to Hitler; the Grand Mufti of Jerusalem, Amin el-Husseini, even took refuge, at one point, in Berlin. When an Arab revolt in Iraq seriously threatened British lines of communication during the war, London had to offer all sorts of concessions and promises in order to restore order—and in the anti-imperialist postwar world, such promises had to be kept.

The Balfour Declaration of 1917 was still in force in Palestine, but attempts to apply it had evoked such bloody battles between Zionists and Arabs that the British mandate had virtually been superseded by a reign of anarchy. But when Germany was occupied and the last surviving Jews were released from the concentration camps, it would have been the height of inhumanity to refuse them access to the Holy Land, where they hoped finally to find peace.

Yet that is exactly what the British mandate did. Tens of thousands of immigrants were brutally turned back in view of the land they already considered their home. Bevin's anti-Zionism met with bitter criticism from a great many militants in his Labor Party—not all of whom were Jews. But the efforts of the British to hold off the immigrant Zionists were not enough to win the Arabs' loyalty. The last British soldiers abandoned Palestine in 1948 and Israel was created, beginning its life as an independent nation at war with its neighbors. The Palestinian "partition" was not chosen by Great Britain; it was forced upon it. No other course could have been taken. But the whole affair added nothing to the reputation of Bevin, who had been an incomparable union organizer and an excellent minister of social affairs before failing in the Foreign Office, a post for which he was completely unprepared.

French intervention in this Middle Eastern drama could only be a nuisance. While French claims in the area dated back to the Crusades, economic aspirations, and national pride, contributed more directly to Gen. de Gaulle's insistence on France's "traditional rights" in Syria and Lebanon. Another factor was the contribution the Free French, under Gen. Georges Catroux, had made in 1941 to the defeat of the Vichy troops who had been covering German penetration into the Middle East and permitting the *Wehrmacht* the use of Syrian airstrips. France let the Arabs and the British know that it was ready for any eventuality. A rebellion in Damascus was violently quelled, and the controversy between Paris and London took on such bitterness that for a moment both sides were tempted to break diplomatic relations. Fortunately, however, neither had the means to back up their threats. In the end it was de Gaulle who gave in. Syria and Lebanon obtained their independence; when a Western power did intervene in Lebanon, it was neither France nor Britain but the United States.

Actually, as long as the Communist menace was the dominating factor in international politics, it was relatively easy for the United States to conduct a consistent foreign policy. The secretary of state in the mid-1950s was John Foster Dulles, who attempted everywhere to create military alliances that, apparently, nobody but he expected would discourage Soviet expansionism. Even after Stalin's death in March 1953, this simplistic approach to foreign policy persisted for some time; it seemed perfectly natural for Dulles to practice "brinkmanship," which he defined as "the ability to get to the verge [of war] without getting into the war." But once Stalin's successors had assumed control in the Kremlin, the duties of the non-Communist peoples were no longer quite so clear.

Under these circumstances unconditional adherence to an Atlantic coalition became more difficult for the Europeans. De Gaulle proposed a "Europeanized" continent independent of Washington after he became president of the Fifth Republic. He even tried to carry his notion of softening the Eastern and Western blocs behind the Iron Curtain until he was rudely shocked out of his proselytizing by the Soviet occupation of Czechoslovakia in 1968. Despite the various forces that strained and loosened the great alliances, these blocs remained intact.

The problems we have discussed so far resulted directly from the war. The war also left at least one positive legacy—the attempt to establish a legal order among the nations of the world. Beginning with their first meeting in 1941, Churchill and Roosevelt had pondered how this might be accomplished. The Atlantic Charter, born of these studies, sketched out a new organization, the United Nations. Or was it really new? Essentially, it amounted to a patched-up version of the League of Nations presented as an original work. Actually, it had to be presented in that way before the USSR would consent to join the U.N., for the Soviets had demonstrated a profound aversion to the league. Memories were still fresh in the Kremlin of the league's ostracism of the USSR after its attack on Finland in 1939. Besides, some new elements had been introduced into the new organization to make it more palatable. At the conference held in San Francisco after the war to hammer out the U.N. Charter, the new family of nations' ability to make decisions was apparently enhanced by the addition of a Security Council. The most important states were assigned permanent seats on the council, and others would be elected to temporary seats by the General Assembly.

In its time the League of Nations had been the subject of considerable controversy. It was supported by pacifists but derided as merely utopian by nationalists. Hence it depended on the support of public opinion. It was a high-level social movement but a movement all the same, one that would not shrink from a courteously conducted debate if one occurred.

But the United Nations could not develop into such a movement. Nobody was really opposed to the new organization, but few were under any illusions concerning its prospective effectiveness. It was born and lived in an atmosphere of indifference that only one of its secretaries-general, Dag Hammarskjold, was able to dissipate on occasion.

From the beginning, it was obvious that the veto, which was a privilege of permanent members of the Security Council, would be a favorite Soviet tactic. Later on it became equally obvious that the rule of unanimity was prized by all the great powers, regardless of their political orientation: none of them could ever be overridden on an important problem when a single vote was sufficient to block decisions they found unacceptable.

Only once was the U.N. flag carried in a large-scale military venture. That occurred in 1950, when the American intervention in Korea was endorsed by the United Nations. Actually, however, the world organization merely lent its name to the undertaking, and that only as the consequence of a misunderstanding on the part of the Soviet delegation, which walked out of the council chamber in a snit just before a vote was taken on Korea. The fact remains that nobody has ever seen the beginning of a true world order guaranteed by an army in the service of an international administration. It is true that certain countries dispatched expeditionary forces to the Far East during the conflict, but the principal military burden was borne by the United States, which received all the credit—or all the blame—for the action.

The U.N. has also intervened on several occasions when one part of the world or another has threatened to explode. In such situations everything depends on the resourcefulness and the political opinions of the secretary-general. On the eve of the Six-Day War in 1967, for example, U Thant permitted Egypt to close the Straits of Tiran at Sharm-el-Sheikh, an action Israel obviously would not tolerate. Thus the international force was withdrawn at exactly the moment it was most needed. Clearly, this intervention favored one of the possible belligerents; it was in no way likely to contribute to keeping the peace in the Middle East. Other instances can be cited. Gradually the U.N. became a neutral ground where enemies or potential enemies could meet. That was of some value, but it was certainly not the nucleus of juridical order the U.N.'s founders had envisaged.

In the face of this failure, many Europeans began to search for other possible solutions. An updated version of pan-Europeanism was one of them. After the ephemeral "One World or None," it became clear that the ideologies and interests of the two world blocs were too much in conflict to permit the construction of a supranational structure that would govern both. There was no choice but to fall back on somewhat more modest projects. Union of the European continent, it was hoped, would contribute importantly to world peace.

During the war there had been a great deal of talk on both sides about Europe as a distinct entity. For the Nazis it was an aspect of anti-Bolshevik propaganda; for some who collaborated with them in good faith, it was a source of illusions. For most Western leaders it represented a paradise forever lost. For those members of the Resistance who were neither Communists nor indifferent to the problems that would emerge after the end of the war, a united Europe was both a program and an ideal.

Only one official proposal had been drawn up. That was the "Benelux" project, initiated by Paul-Henri Spaak after his return from exile in London. But once the initial period of immediate reconstruction had passed and the governments of the three states were solidly back in place, little official enthusiasm was shown for even this miniature federation. Reluctantly, however, the three governments agreed to make the attempt.

It soon became obvious that imposing obstacles lay in that path. It would be relatively easy to open frontiers, ease border crossings and lower customs duties. But how could a truly multi-national economy be created if the unification process did not also affect tax systems and police controls? These factors also tended to keep the countries separate. In short, a good many details remained to be worked out.

Thus Benelux came into being as an experiment, a laboratory where various solutions to these problems could be tried out. Later the experiences of the Benelux countries would serve as models to be followed or avoided by the Common Market as it established its policies. But the operation proceeded slowly. All signs indicated that economic integration would proceed at a rather slow pace as long as it was inspired only by a temporary political situation. Members of the Resistance could no longer be counted on to provide that inspiration; their movement had rapidly disintegrated. It was therefore up to those in power to keep the Benelux experiment going. They had three quite serious problems to worry about, however: the Soviet threat, the uncertainty of the Western powers regarding the problem of Germany and the material difficulties presented by the reconstruction process. Each of these is worth closer examination.

Those who had thought that the USSR would emerge from the war with greater enthusiasm for democracy were, of course, wrong. The arguments they had adduced in support of their judgment had, however, seemed faultless. Hadn't the Americans and British helped their Soviet partner organize the feeding of the country? Hadn't the Red Army seen enough of Europe and particularly of Germany to realize that they weren't horrible dens of capitalist iniquity? And, above all, hadn't Stalin promulgated, in 1943, a whole series of measures presaging a more liberal policy? So it had seemed, for the churches in the USSR had obtained more benevolent treatment from the government, the Comintern had been dissolved and the USSR, which, up until that point, had been federalist only on paper, was actually on the verge of becoming a federation of partially autonomous entities.

These promises were as substantial as the air. True, the Russian Orthodox Church was allowed some liberties, but it still could not deliver its message freely to its communicants. True, the Comintern disappeared, but it had been moribund for a long time in any case. The Soviets had long suspected the Comintern, which they had launched so enthusiastically in 1919, as a source of potential confusion among Communists abroad, since it seemed to invite criticism of Soviet policy from foreign comrades. This was reason enough, in their eyes, to throw it on the junk pile, with appropriate ceremony—especially since its disbandment would please the Allies. As for the apparent decentralization of Soviet power implicit in the "federalization" of the Soviet Republics, not only was it bereft of any element of liberalization, it also provided Stalin with another ace up his sleeve by giving the USSR two additional seats in the U.N. and permitting the establishment abroad of more embassies, which could be used as espionage centers.

Nor could any changes really be expected as a result of the contacts that had developed between the Soviets and the British and the Americans, or the memories of Europe that Red Army soldiers retained. Even those Russians who, under orders, had negotiated the organization of convoys from the Allies to the USSR during the war found themselves under suspicion. In his *One Day in the Life of Ivan Denisovich*, Alexandr Solzhenitsyn relates the story of his encounter with one such naval officer in a concentration camp. The few Soviet prisoners who survived the miserable conditions in the German camps came home only to find themselves accused of disloyalty in Stalin's courts. As a result, unfortunate vacancies occurred in the ranks of the armed forces. Of all the promises the Soviets had made to the Allies for their cooperation in the war, none were kept.

Accompanying this internal political reaction was a disturbing external expansion. The frontiers of the USSR bulged considerably, as much toward the east as toward the west. Since Stalin wanted a naval base on the southern shore of the Baltic, the city of Koenigsberg was summarily annexed and its exclusively German population driven out. In the same way Poland was pushed westward, losing such traditionally Polish cities as Lvov. Provinces that had always been German were incorporated into the USSR, with no regard to the welfare of the displaced populations. We have

seen the fate awaiting those nations that became Soviet "satellites" while maintaining their de jure independence.

Step by step, Soviet power advanced toward the heart of Europe, and the world wondered when it would stop. When Paul-Henri Spaak made his speech before the General Assembly of the United Nations on the theme "We are afraid," he enunciated the fears of many Westerners. These fears contributed to a closer European union. Like a flock of sheep threatened by a storm, Europe sought courage by uniting.

But the movement towards union raised new questions about the future of Germany, a problem still uppermost in the minds of postwar Europeans. If the original plans for the "economic disarmament" of that country had been unrealistic, how could Germany be permitted to regain its self-confidence and at the same time be prevented from menacing its neighbors once again? How in fact could this be achieved without integrating Germany into a united Europe? Since the Federal Republic already existed and, as part of the Allied bloc, it could not be occupied by Allied troops indefinitely, only European federalism could provide a practical and durable solution.

The problem of reconstruction in Europe still remained to be solved. The United States and the United Nations Relief and Rehabilitation Administration had assumed responsibility for needs of the population in the immediate postwar period. But as time went on and the independent national governments reassumed control of public affairs, it became clear that the European economy would have to be organized on a sounder basis. One phrase haunted the minds of those in charge—the "dollar gap." To reconstruct the war-torn Continent, raw materials and machines were required. The only place they could come from at that particular moment was the United States, but means for repayment were terribly lacking. On the other hand, living from day to day on charity was equally out of the question. The only solution was to give European industry the initial shove it needed to get going once again, and the only country in a position to do that was the United States. In June 1947 Gen. George C. Marshall made his great speech at Harvard University in which he offered Europe American aid.

There were several motives for this offer. In the first place, there was the unquestionable emotional tie between America and Europe. To underestimate this factor would be to deny the moral idealism of the American people and their sense of responsibility to the populations they had just liberated. The Marshall Plan was to cost the United States astronomical sums of money, in addition to a tremendous public-relations campaign to prepare Americans for a task of that magnitude.

What was the economic justification for the Marshall Plan? The record on this point is less clear. To get Europe back on its feet meant, of course, to guarantee it profitable trade. The value of America's exports compared to its gross national product was relatively small—about 4%—while for the Benelux countries the comparable percentage was more than 30%. On the other hand, the clients were potential competitors. But it was important for the American economy to be assured of its markets, which required Europe's reconversion to a peacetime economy.

The principal motive, however, was political. The Marshall Plan certainly benefited from the anti-Communist wave in the United States during the postwar period. Actually, this development had been bewildering. Where Roosevelt saw in Stalin an "Uncle Joe" with whom contact, if not always easy, would always be possible, it now became plain that the USSR had already established its policy for the postwar world while still at war with Germany. Furthermore, many Americans came to suspect that Alger Hiss, one of Roosevelt's advisers, had been working for the Soviet secret service. The shock was overwhelming, and explains the fearful "witch hunt" conducted by Sen. Joseph McCarthy. Marshall, too, benefited from the popular indignation, since it was evident that the misery of Europe's population had to be alleviated to stop Communist infiltration there.

But Secretary of State Marshall was not content with promising Europe aid in money and goods. He also urged the various European countries to attempt to coordinate their plans. Europe had to be assisted "as a whole." Unfortunately, the European nations were slow to understand this reasonable language. They resented Uncle Sam for poking his nose into matters that did not concern him; they felt, that is, that he had no right to oversee how the money he was spending was being used. Nor did they want their neighbors to know what they were doing with it. And yet that was what Marshall seemed to insist on. When the governments of western Europe finally sent in their requests, it was apparent that the demands of one conflicted with the demands of another, even to the extent of oversupplying the different sectors. Washington impatiently sent these lists back, again admonishing the European nations to coordinate their requests. From that experience emerged the "Organization of European Economic Cooperation."

A new motive for the unification of Europe was thus added to the others: The United States was specifying coordination of the reconstruction efforts as a condition for supplying aid. Why was this aid given exclusively to the so-called "free" western European

nations? The Marshall Plan was, in fact, meant for all of Europe, but only the western nations took advantage of it. At a conference in Paris the Soviet minister of foreign affairs, Vyacheslav Molotov, rejected the plan disdainfully, and all the eastern European states followed his lead, regardless of their true feelings about the manna dropping from the American heavens. Poland, for example, hesitated a great deal at first, and finally refused. The government of Czechoslovakia, where the Communists had not yet solidified their control, at first accepted; later they reversed their decision under pressure from Moscow. Thus the Marshall Plan deepened the rift between the two parts of the Continent. When Czechoslovakia finally fell under Soviet control in February 1948, all possibility of independence among the "satellites" disappeared.

Faced with the German problem, the misery of hunger and the Soviet menace, the West returned to the idea so dear to the Resistance—a federalist Europe. But which country was to take the initiative? The movement could not be started simply by a group of militants, not even if they were joined by a few sympathetic politicians. It had to be led by an authoritative government. The question was, though, which one? Up until 1947, it could not have been France. It was too preoccupied with its purges; besides, the French cabinet was composed of assorted Resistance activists—Communists, Socialists and members of the Popular Republican Movement or Christian Democrats. De Gaulle presided over it, and his plans for Germany were completely at variance with the idea of a federated Europe. Furthermore, any limitation on France's sovereignty was alien to his sense of national pride. But even after he left the government in January 1946, any French initiative was still stalled by the attitude of the Communists. Just after the liberation, in fact, the Communist Party had issued a manifesto which was among the most nationalist in tone of that era. In their eyes, the martyrs of the Resistance had given their lives for the national independence, and to surrender any shred of French sovereignty was to betray them.

In 1947, however, Paul Ramadier eliminated the Communists from the French government. But by that time the consensus in Europe was that Great Britain should undertake the lead in establishing European federalism as the only former belligerent in Europe that had not known the humiliation of Nazi occupation. Britain's government was stable, and because it was composed of Laborites it was bound to be less inhibited by imperialist traditions than the Tories. And the clinching argument was that it had no Communists. France's turn could come later; at that point London had to take the lead.

London, however, did not budge. The British were too deeply engaged in the planning of a national "welfare state" to permit weakening it with pan-European considerations. Besides, it was the arch-Tory, Churchill himself, who had introduced the idea of a European federation in the first place. In the face of that final argument, foreign minister Ernest Bevin ignored Europe, leaving the decision up to France. And France took it.

The first step was the creation of a Council of Europe, a move that Churchill had recommended during the war and which French diplomacy promoted after a spectacular European conference at The Hague in May 1948. When this council, established in Strasbourg, quickly showed the limits of its capabilities, a second French initiative, more ambitious and perhaps more realistic, made its appearance. It was the Schuman Plan, proposing an end to the inter-Allied control of the Ruhr and the creation of a supranational authority to supervise the production of coal and steel, the key products of the modern economy, throughout Europe. Great Britain, which had continually restrained the Council of Europe from within, was kept out of the new Community; it even tried for some time to undermine it by starting alternative projects. But it was too late; the European Community seemed well on its way.

It was without question the most novel idea of the postwar period, at least in Europe. But it finally accomplished little of any importance compared with the initial hopes of its founders, men such as Konrad Adenauer, Alcide de Gasperi, Paul-Henri Spaak, J. W. Beyen and especially Robert Schuman. Yet the European idea, lame as it was, constituted a moment of hope in recent history, in Europe at any rate. But as we have seen, the history of the 20th century becomes less and less concerned with Europe.

We turn now to the Far East, where the disintegration of Japan left a gaping political vacuum. The major effect of the Allied victory was felt in China, the first and foremost victim of Japanese expansion in the 1930s. In some ways China's status was similar to Yugoslavia's. The war between the Chinese and the Japanese coexisted with the war between the Nationalist armies of Chiang Kai-shek and the Communist forces of Mao Tse-tung. Here again were two leaders who in a real sense could be considered pawns in the game between the giant rivals, the USSR and the United States. But it soon became apparent that the Chinese situation, at least for Mao, was taking a unique twist. He needed Soviet assistance and used it well, but managed to avoid paying the bill. China simply refused to be a Soviet satellite. Chiang's position, on the other hand, went from bad to worse. He continually gave ground and just as continually prided himself on his democratic principles and the support he said he was receiving from the Chinese masses. Until he was finally unmasked he continued to obtain American arms; a good part of them fell into the hands of the Reds when Nationalist soldiers either changed sides or simply deserted en masse, leaving their equipment behind.

Obviously, this mess had to be cleared up, especially since the "China lobby" vehemently cheering Chiang on from Washington was quite influential. What was to become of the legacy of several generations of Protestant missions to the Celestial Empire, as well as exports to China, if the Communists took control?

To find the answers to these questions, President Truman sent Gen. Marshall to China. After several months there, Marshall returned with a pessimistic report. He had found that Mao's victory over Chiang was only a matter of time, that the morale of the Communist troops was far better than the Nationalist army's and that the Communists enjoyed the support of the peasant masses, to whom they promised social emancipation. Marshall's view was surely correct—the Communist command was clearly cognizant of the civil war's sociopolitical nature. Mao told his troops that the People's Army needed to feel as much at home among the people as a fish does in water. The manner in which the Maoists treated their prisoners of war reflected the same concern for the people's welfare. It was not enough to conquer territory, Communist soldiers were instructed; its inhabitants must also be assisted in restoring it to fertility. This attitude was diametrically opposed to that of the warlords, the aristocratic Chinese bandits who descended on the peasants like locust hordes stripping them of everything. Sincere or not, such a spirit among the Communist army was certain to bring it to ultimate victory.

The United States was therefore constrained to abandon its old Pacific ally and to resign itself to Communist domination of China, with its hundreds of millions of inhabitants and its vast potential. No one as yet had the least inkling that the USSR would become apprehensive about the birth of a sister Marxist state on its southeast frontier. What remained of the Nationalist army eventually retreated across the Quemoy Strait to the large island of Taiwan, also known by its Portuguese name, Formosa, where Chiang maintained the fiction of the true Chinese Republic, a great Pacific power temporarily in eclipse. Chiang's government remained a member of the U.N. Security Council until 1971, when the People's Republic finally acquired the ultimate in diplomatic recognition: it replaced Taiwan in the United Nations.

Directly after his victory in 1949, Mao began making threatening gestures across the strait separating the two Chinese states, but staunch American support of Chiang dissuaded him. There were propaganda exchanges and even some artillery salvos, after which the Quemoy Strait ceased to be one of the world's "hot spots." Peking then took the opposite tack, appealing to the patriotism and ethnic brotherhood of the Taiwanese. The People's Republic even went to the extreme of invading the Indian subcontinent, pushing as far as Brahmaputra before retreating, to impress Taipei with their power in the Pacific. If that was the purpose of the Red adventure, it succeeded; many of Chiang's men were proud of their Communist counterparts' exploit.

An interval of stable equilibrium now settled on this portion of the world, and in that interval, the People's Republic of China began an immense drive for economic self-development which was to awe the Third World. After the break with the Soviet Union, which occurred during Khrushchev's rule, Red China blossomed into the USSR's rival as the chief interpreter of Leninism by going through the ritual purges and "cultural revolutions."

In its international activities the Peking regime was powerfully abetted by millions of Chinese patriots dispersed all over the world, particularly in Southeast Asia, where there were difficult confrontations with capitalist America. The British-dominated port of Hong Kong has served as an escape route to the West for many Chinese unhappy with the Communist regime, but it is also useful to the People's Republic for conducting trade with its rivals.

This may be the calm before new tempests in the Pacific. Everything depends on the area's economic and social development as well as the magnitude of the political vacuum left by departed colonists, like those formerly in Indochina.

It may be difficult to draw any firm conclusions from the many confusing aspects of the postwar global situation we have seen, but they can be classified into several categories in the following way:

The first and most obvious factor is the remarkable resurgence of the two major conquered countries. In 1974, Germany was by far the largest industrial power in Europe, while Japan deals with the huge Chinese land mass on an equal footing and successfully competes with all European and American exporters. The two nations have, moreover, undergone a fascinating transfiguration. Both have adapted themselves to parliamentary democracy with little trouble. By contrast, Italy has become increasingly mired in its own worst habits. Government by political deals is still in fashion, the Mafia is no less active and corruption is as widespread as ever. All of these threaten the economic

advances that for a while had seemed promising. But too many shocks to the smooth workings of business have been permitted. On the positive side, however, neo-Fascism has gained little favor among the voters.

The second phenomenon is the rapid decolonization or, more generally, the spread of anti-imperialism throughout the world. Former colonies are well aware of the weaknesses of the colonists. To the extent that the world is recrystallizing into a single community, it will not be based on old entities like the British Empire or the "French Union," which at one time seemed to have a future. The elements constituting a universal federation will instead be unified continents or linguistic, ethnic and religious fraternities like the Arab League. The fact of the matter is that the old structures of the 19th century are giving way to forms of cooperation based on voluntary integration and collaboration.

But this does not mean—and this is the third factor—that the tendency to hegemony is fading from the international scene. Quite the contrary. The USSR has its satellites, and the United States has its commercial clients; the USSR can control occasional brush fires of revolt, the United States can control occasional independence sprees—which have usually been only verbal, anyway. But both these countries realize that each must not interfere in the other's affairs and that respect for each other's spheres of influence is a condition of the status quo. Between the two are the nonaligned nations over which the rivals dispute and which try to sell their good graces as dearly as possible. Thus Indonesia, after having seemed to fall into the Communist camp, climbed out and began a flirtation with the United States after erasing its active leftists with a cruelty astonishing even in our era. At the other extreme, Cuba under Fidel Castro has become an encapsulated foreign body inside the American midriff. From now on, much will depend on the possibilities the USSR, the United States and China offer for exploiting the economic and social resources of the undeveloped nations. This rivalry may sometimes result in trial by weapons, more often in trial by financial legerdemain, but always in trial by ideas.

Europe, however, struggled out of the war considerably exhausted. Still on the way to economic recovery, it remains far behind America and has long since been enveloped in the dust trailing Japan. The conflict that once again broke out in Europe over a port on the Baltic inundated the entire planet and ended in the symbolic fraternization between a Red Army soldier and an American GI somewhere on the Elbe river in the Continent's heart. One chunk of Europe is trapped in the Soviet maw, the other in the American fist. Cut off from its empires overseas, Europe dreams from time to time of generating a

"Third Force" but has missed its chance; the union that could have been its zygote never formed. Hence the sterility of European anti-Americanism, most often nourished by chauvinist feelings rather than a clear perception of what Europe can still contribute to the world.

Given these premises, another conclusion emerges. World War II has shown, as did the worldwide economic crisis of the 1930s, that "the time for the end of the world has begun," in the words of the French poet Paul Valery. We all have the same problems at a time when suspicions, rivalries and ideological tensions blind us to their solution.

The UN is basically helpless. To be sure, the General Assembly provides a platform from which dozens of ministers make speeches, principally for internal consumption. In its tight little circle, the Security Council is the stage on which the major protagonists of the diplomatic world meet and take each other's measure. It occasionally resounds with clever formulas for compromises or face-saving. The secretary-general himself may exercise his personal influence, as did the brave and talented Dag Hammarskjold, an international favorite. On the other hand, his successor, U Thant, chose to recall the UN's peace-keeping troops—the so-called "Blue Berets"—from the Strait of Tiran at Egyptian Pres. Nasser's demand, thus precipitating the Six-Day War and depriving the world organization of most of its prestige. And shortly afterward it fell under the domination of the Third World, which used it to browbeat Israel, the victor in that war.

The UN thus remains a toothless watchdog over the world's precarious peace. It offers a mechanism but cannot force anyone to use it. Very likely it would act more effectively if the number of its members were drastically reduced and representatives of larger regional federations were invited to present their views. Even then the problems placed before it would be no more susceptible to solutions, and the frictions as well as conflicts of interest would still remain. But at least the disorder plaguing it could to some extent be reduced. As it stands, the UN is simply ungovernable.

For all their handicaps, neither the UN nor its predecessor, the League of Nations, has been completely impotent. As in the period after 1919, the "special agencies" have accomplished a great deal of value, as the organizations spun off by the UN continue to do.

The International Labor Organization (ILO) continues to operate as it has for more than half a century. The same is true of the World Health Organization (WHO), among others. UNESCO conducts several operations in the domains of education and culture, all of them receiving the blessings of East and West. It saved the ancient Egyptian sculptures in Nubia that were doomed to submersion in an artificial lake, restored the ruins of Khmer art in Cambodia and lent its aid to the exacting work of restoring the precious art works of Venice. If for nothing else, it deserves the world's gratitude for its efforts to eliminate illiteracy. Unfortunately it has not been able to escape political prejudice. UNICEF's attempts to make inquiries about the protection of children against endemic underdevelopment have been sharply rebuffed by the governments of a good many countries. Yet the agency enjoys the confidence of the public, as the universal popularity of its Christmas cards attests. Much less fortunate is UNCTAD, the agency responsible for promoting fair trade relations between rich and underdeveloped countries, which has had unfortunate duels with food suppliers.

Thus far the results achieved by the world organization are far below the level envisaged by its founders during the war. There is no need to prove the obvious, that the UN has been found wanting. But that judgment is by no means conclusive. Certainly there were opportunities that arose just after the end of hostilities that were snubbed or ignored and are not likely to offer themselves again. The national sovereignties that had always resisted progress in the world were reborn after the liberation along with their tenacious bureaucracies. But new phenomena may yet emerge—a dearth of raw materials, for example—demanding daring solutions that receive scant notice in "normal" times. But it was for abnormal times that the planners of supranational federations prepared during the torment of 1939 to 1945. Their utopias may yet become real. For it is only slowly and tortuously that humanity realizes the dreams of sages.

Hendrik Brugmans

CHRONOLOGY OF WORLD WAR II

September 18-19, 1931	Japan occupies Mukden, Manchuria; the war against China begins.
September 15, 1932	Japanese puppet state of Manchukuo established.
January 30, 1933	Hitler named German chancellor.
March 24, 1933	*Reichstag* gives supreme power to Hitler.
March 27, 1933	Japan leaves League of Nations.
October 21, 1933	Germany leaves League of Nations.
August 2, 1934	German President Paul von Hindenburg dies, Hitler named *Reichsfuehrer* and assumes duties of president and chancellor.
September 18, 1934	USSR joins League of Nations.
March 16, 1935	Germany reestablishes military draft.
April 14, 1935	Stresa accords on status quo in Europe signed by France, United Kingdom and Italy.
May 2, 1935	Franco-Soviet mutual assistance treaty signed.
June 18, 1935	Britain and Germany sign naval treaty without consulting France: German surface navy will not total more than 35 percent of Royal Navy.
October 3, 1935	Italy invades Ethiopia.
March 7, 1936	Rhineland reoccupied and remilitarized by Germany in violation of Versailles Treaty.
May 9, 1936	Italy annexes Ethiopia.
July 18, 1936	Spanish civil war begins.
October 14, 1936	Belgium adopts independent policy.
October 25, 1936	Treaty establishes Rome-Berlin Axis.
November 25, 1936	Anti-Comintern Pact signed by Germany and Japan.
July 7, 1937	Marco Polo Bridge incident, resumption of Sino-Japanese hostilities.
November 6, 1937	Italy joins Anti-Comintern Pact.
December 11, 1937	Italy leaves League of Nations.
March 13, 1938	*Anschluss* joins Austria to German Reich.
September 26, 1938	Germany sends ultimatum to Czechoslovakia.
September 29-30, 1938	Munich conference: Chamberlain, Daladier, Hitler and Mussolini sign Munich Pact dividing Czechoslovakia.
October 1, 1938	Germany annexes Sudetenland.
October 2, 1938	Poland annexes Teschen.
November 2, 1938	Hungary annexes Slovakian territory.
February 2, 1939	Pope Pius XI dies.
February 24, 1939	Hungary and Manchukuo join Anti-Comintern Pact.
March 2, 1939	Pope Pius XII elected.
March 14, 1939	Slovakia declares independence under Monsignor Yosef Tiso.
March 15, 1939	Hitler enters Prague.
March 16, 1939	Czechoslovakia becomes German Protectorate of Bohemia-Moravia.
March 22, 1939	Lithuania cedes Memel to Germany.
March 27, 1939	Spain joins Anti-Comintern Pact.
March 31, 1939	Britain offers guarantees to Poland, Greece, Turkey

	and Rumania, France backs Britain; German-Spanish Friendship Treaty concluded.
April 1, 1939	Franco announces end of Spanish civil war.
April 7, 1939	Italy invades Albania.
April 28, 1939	Hitler denounces British-Polish pact, claims Danzig.
May 8, 1939	Spain leaves League of Nations.
May 18, 1939	Britain reinstates military draft.
July 26, 1939	U.S. denounces trade treaty with Japan signed July 11.
August 21, 1939	Moscow talks begun August 11 between France, Britain and USSR suspended.
August 23, 1939	Nazi-Soviet Pact signed.
August 24, 1939	Britain announces general mobilization.
August 25, 1939	Britain and Poland sign mutual assistance treaty.
September 1, 1939	Germany invades Poland; Italy declares neutrality.
September 2, 1939	Henri Guisan becomes commander in chief of Swiss forces.
September 3, 1939	Britain, France, Australia and New Zealand declare war on Germany.
September 6, 1939	South Africa declares war on Germany.
September 8, 1939	President Roosevelt proclaims limited state of emergency.
September 9, 1939	Canada declares war on Germany.
September 15, 1939	Japan signs treaty with Moscow establishing cease-fire on Mongolian-Manchurian border.
September 17, 1939	USSR occupies eastern Poland.
September 24, 1939	Warsaw bombed.
September 27, 1939	Warsaw surrenders.
September 28, 1939	Polish army surrenders; Soviet-German friendship treaty partitioning Poland concluded; Soviet-Estonian mutual assistance treaty signed.

September 30, 1939	Polish government-in-exile under Marshal Wladyslaw Sikorski formed in Paris.
October 3, 1939	U.S. declares neutrality.
October 5, 1939	Soviet-Latvian mutual assistance treaty signed.
October 6, 1939	Hitler presents peace plan, which is rejected October 12 by Chamberlain.
October 8, 1939	Western Poland and Danzig incorporated into German Reich.
October 10, 1939	Soviet-Lithuanian mutual assistance treaty signed.
October 14, 1939	British battleship *Royal Oak* sunk at Scapa Flow by German *U-47*.
October 19, 1939	British-French-Turkish treaty concluded.
October 25, 1939	Hitler creates General Government for Occupied Poland; Hans Frank named governor-general November 8.
November 4, 1939	U.S. passes "cash and carry" amendment to Neutrality Act, allowing European democracies to buy weapons.
November 7, 1939	Mediation offer made by Netherlands Queen Wilhelmina and Belgian King Leopold III, rejected on November 12 by Britain and France and on November 14 by Germany.
November 9, 1939	Venlo incident.
November 30, 1939	USSR attacks Finland.
December 14, 1939	USSR ousted from League of Nations.
December 17, 1939	German pocket battleship *Admiral Graf Spee* scuttled in Uruguayan waters off Montevideo.
January 10, 1940	Mechlin incident.
January 19, 1940	French parliament bars Communists.
January 22, 1940	Vatican condemns German indemnity demand on Poland.
March 12, 1940	Soviet-Finnish peace treaty signed in Moscow.
March 20, 1940	French Foreign Minister Edouard Daladier replaced

	by Paul Reynaud.		sign oil pact assuring Germany all of Rumania's oil production.
March 28, 1940	French and British agree not to conclude a separate peace.	May 26-June 4, 1940	Over 300,000 British and French soldiers evacuated from Dunkirk; Belgian government flees to France.
March 30, 1940	Pro-Japanese Wang Ching-wei government installed in Nanking.		
April 9, 1940	Germany invades Denmark and Norway.	May 28, 1940	Belgian army surrenders, Leopold III taken prisoner; Narvik captured by French-Polish-British force.
April 15, 1940	British troops land in Norway, French and Polish troops arrive April 19.		
April 24, 1940	Hitler creates *Reichskommissariat* for Norway under *Gauleiter* Josef Terboven.	June 6, 1940	De Gaulle enters Reynaud cabinet as undersecretary of state for defense.
May 10, 1940	Germany attacks the Netherlands, Belgium and Luxembourg; French and British troops enter Belgium; British occupy Iceland; Switzerland undergoes general mobilization; Churchill replaces Chamberlain as prime minister, forms unity government.	June 7-10, 1940	French-British-Polish forces evacuate Narvik.
		June 9, 1940	Norwegians cease fire at midnight, Norwegian king and queen flee to Britain.
		June 10, 1940	Germans cross Seine at Rouen; French government flees Paris; Italy declares war on France and Britain; Allies evacuate Norway.
May 12, 1940	Casteau conference on general course of war attended by Daladier, Leopold III and Sir Henry Pownal.	June 12, 1940	Japan and Thailand sign friendship treaty.
		June 14, 1940	Paris surrenders.
		June 15-17, 1940	USSR occupies Estonia, Latvia and Lithuania.
May 13, 1940	Queen Wilhelmina reaches London, Dutch government follows; Germans cross Meuse near Dinant.	June 16, 1940	French front collapses, Reynaud resigns, Petain becomes president.
May 14, 1940	Rotterdam bombed; Germans break through French lines at Sedan.	June 17, 1940	Petain announces armistice negotiations with Germany.
May 15, 1940	Dutch army surrenders.	June 18, 1940	De Gaulle, in London, calls for struggle.
May 18, 1940	Hitler decrees return of Eupen, Malmedy and Moresnet to Reich; Reynaud brings Marshal Petain into French government.	June 22, 1940	German-French armistice signed at Rethondes (1.5 million French prisoners taken).
May 19, 1940	Gen. Maxime Weygand replaces Gen. Maurice Gamelin as commander in chief of Allied armies; Arthur Seyss-Inquart named *Reichskommissar* for the Netherlands.	June 24, 1940	Italian-French armistice signed in Rome.
		June 26-28, 1940	USSR demands cession of Bessarabia and northern Bukovina from Rumania, occupies territories July 2.
		June 28, 1940	Britain recognizes de Gaulle as leader of Free French.
May 20, 1940	Germans reach Abbeville.		
May 21, 1940	British counterattack at Arras.	July 1, 1940	French Vichy government established.
May 22, 1940	Germans and Rumanians	July 3, 1940	British destroy French navy

	at Mers el-Kebir.		to cede southern Dobruja
July 4, 1940	Italy attacks Sudan.		to Bulgaria.
July 5, 1940	Vichy government breaks diplomatic relations with Britain.	September 13, 1940	Italy enters Egypt, reaches Sidi Barani by September 15.
July 10, 1940	Battle of Britain starts; Petain given power by Vichy government, becomes head of state July 11.	September 15, 1940	Japanese issue ultimatum to France on naval bases in Indochina; French departments of the North and Pas-de-Calais joined to military administration under Alexander von Falkenhausen in Brussels.
July 12, 1940	Pierre Laval named vice-president.		
July 16, 1940	Hitler orders preparations for invasion of Britain, Operation Seeloewe ("Sea Lion").	September 17, 1940	Hitler cancels Operation Seeloewe; Franco-Japanese Hanoi agreement concluded.
July 21, 1940	Switzerland makes defense preparations.	September 23, 1940	Japanese attack Lang Son (northern Indochina).
July 22, 1940	New Hebrides joins Free France, Ivory Coast joins July 26, Chad joins August 26, French Equatorial Africa joins August 28, French governments in Pacific join September 2, French West Indies joins September 9, New Caledonia joins September 24.	September 23-25, 1940	British-Free French operation in Dakar defeated.
		September 25, 1940	U.S. reduces oil exports to Japan.
		September 26, 1940	Japanese land in Tonkin.
		September 27, 1940	Tripartite Pact signed by Italy, Germany and Japan; Germans issue decree on status of Jews in occupied France.
August 3, 5 and 6, 1940	Estonia, Latvia and Lithuania incorporated into USSR.	September 28, 1940	Thailand attacks Indochina.
August 4, 1940	Italy occupies British Somaliland.	October 3, 1940	Belgian government in London officially established by Camille Gutt and Albert De Vleeschauwer, government formed October 31 upon arrival of Pierlot and Spaak.
August 7, 1940	Alsace-Lorraine incorporated into German Reich.		
August 24, 1940	Belgian ministers Hubert Pierlot and Paul-Henri Spaak detained by Spanish en route to London, escape October 22.		
		October 7, 1940	German troops enter Rumania under accord with Antonescu.
August 27, 1940	U.S. votes compulsory military service.	October 12, 1940	Japanese political parties abolished and National Movement to Serve the Throne created.
August 30, 1940	Vienna negotiations held; Germany and Italy force Rumania to cede Transylvania to Hungary.		
		October 18, 1940	Vichy enacts Jewish Statute.
September 3, 1940	U.S. gives Britain 50 destroyers in exchange for bases in British territory.	October 22, 1940	Hitler and Laval hold talks.
September 4, 1940	Ion Antonescu takes power in Rumania.	October 23, 1940	Hitler and Franco hold talks at Hendaye.
September 6, 1940	Rumanian King Carol abdicates in favor of son Michael.	October 24, 1940	Hitler and Petain hold talks at Montoire.
September 7, 1940	Germany forces Rumania	October 27, 1940	De Gaulle establishes French Empire Defense

	Council in Brazzaville.		support of Jews arrested February 22 and 23.
October 28, 1940	Italy attacks Greece; Hitler and Mussolini hold talks at Florence; first laws against Jews in Belgium implemented.	February 26, 1941	British African troops take Mogadishu.
		March 1, 1941	Gen. Leclerc captures Koufra; Bulgaria joins Tripartite Pact.
November 5, 1940	Roosevelt reelected to a third term.	March 2, 1941	Germans supply Bulgaria.
November 11-12, 1940	British victory over Italian fleet at Taranto.	March 2-4 1941	British and Norwegian commandos attack Lofoten Islands.
November 14, 1940	Germans carry out mass bombing of Coventry.	March 11, 1941	U.S. votes Lend-Lease Act.
November 15, 1940	Germans seal off Jews in Warsaw ghetto.	March 24, 1941	Gen. Wavell completes reconquest of Somalia.
November 20, 1940	Hungary joins Tripartite Pact, Rumania and Slovakia follow on November 23 and 24.	March 25, 1941	Yugoslavia joins Tripartite Pact.
		March 26-29,1941	British naval victory over Italians at Cape Matapan.
November 30, 1940	Japan signs pact with Nanking government.	March 27, 1941	Yugoslav Regent Paul ousted by Peter II.
December 9, 1940- February 11, 1941	Gen. Wavell's successful Egyptian and Libyan campaign starts.	March 30, 1941	Roosevelt orders seizure of German ships in U.S. ports.
December 13, 1940	Petain dismisses and arrests Laval.	March 31, 1941	Rommel begins offensive from El Agheila in Cyrenaica.
December 18, 1940	Hitler orders preparation for Soviet invasion (Operation Barbarossa).	April 3, 1941	British evacuate Benghazi.
		April 5, 1941	British liberate Addis Ababa; USSR and Yugoslavia sign friendship and nonagression treaty.
December 22, 1940	Eden replaces Lord Halifax as British foreign minister.		
December 23, 1940	Chiang Kai-shek outlaws Communist Party.	April 6, 1941	Yugoslavia invaded by Germans, Italians and Bulgarians; Germans invade Greece (Operation Marita).
December 29, 1940	London firebombed.		
January 5, 1941	U.S. appoints Adm. William Leahy ambassador to Vichy government.		
		April 6-7, 1941	Belgrade bombed, 20,000 killed.
January 10, 1941	Nazi-Soviet Pact renewed.	April 10, 1941	Croatia declared independent.
January 19, 1941	British offensive in Ethiopia and Eritrea starts.	April 12, 1941	Belgrade surrenders.
January 20, 1941	Japan mediates Franco-Thai conflict.	April 13, 1941	Soviet-Japanese neutrality pact signed.
January 26, 1941	British offensive in Somalia begins.	April 18, 1941	Yugoslavia surrenders, is divided; U.S. declares Greenland and Iceland in its sphere of influence.
January 30, 1941	Armistice between Thailand and Indochina concluded.		
		April 21, 1941	Greek army surrenders at Epirus and Macedonia.
February 8-10, 1941	Adm. Francois Darlan appointed Petain's deputy and minister of foreign affairs.	April 26, 1941	U.S. representative Robert Murphy concludes agreement with Gen. Weygand on supplying French North Africa.
February 12, 1941	Rommel invades Libya.		
February 25, 1941	General strikes held in Amsterdam, Zaandam, Hilversum and Utrecht in	April 27, 1941	Athens surrenders.

April 30-May 2, 1941	British evacuate Greece.
May 2-30, 1941	Anti-British revolt in Iraq led by Rashid Ali.
May 9, 1941	Tokyo treaty between France and Japan concluded: Indochina territory ceded to Thailand, Japan gets Haiphong port privileges.
May 11, 1941	Rudolph Hess, Hitler's designated successor, parachutes into Scotland.
May 12, 1941	Hitler and Darlan hold talks; Germans permitted to use Syrian airports.
May 18, 1941	Bulgaria seizes Greek and Yugoslav Macedonia; Italian Croatian border agreement signed.
May 19, 1941	Italian troops surrender in Ethiopia; Ho Chi Minh creates Viet Minh.
May 20, 1941	German aircraft attack Crete.
May 24-27, 1941	Germans and British engage in naval battle: *Hood* sunk by *Bismarck* May 24, *Bismarck* sunk May 27; German warships withdraw from Atlantic.
May 27, 1941	Roosevelt proclaims unlimited state of emergency.
May 28-31, 1941	British evacuate Crete; Greek king and government flee to Cairo.
June 2, 1941	Vichy enacts second Jewish Statute.
June 8-July 14, 1941	British and Free French fight Gen. Henri-Fernand Dentz in Syria and Lebanon, ended by armistice of Saint-Jean-d'Acre; U.S. force relieves British troops in Iceland.
June 12, 1941	Allies affirm mutual assistance: Britain and its dominions, Free France, Belgium, the Netherlands, Poland, Greece, Czechoslovakia, Yugoslavia.
June 14, 1941	U.S. freezes German and Italian assets after American ship torpedoed.
June 15, 1941	Croatia joins Tripartite Pact.
June 16, 1941	German-Turkish nonagression treaty signed.
June 22, 1941	Germany and Rumania invade USSR, Finland joins attack June 26, Hungary joins June 27, Italy, Slovakia and Albania join June 30.
June 30, 1941	Vichy France breaks diplomatic relations with USSR.
July 4, 1941	Yugoslav Communist Party decides to revolt.
July 5, 1941	Germans reach Dnieper.
July 12, 1941	British-Soviet mutual assistance treaty signed.
July 16, 1941	Luxembourg absorbed into Reich.
July 26, 1941	U.S. freezes Japanese assets.
July 28, 1941	Japanese land in Cochin China.
July 29, 1941	Vichy-Tokyo agreements on joint defense of Indochina concluded.
July 30, 1941	USSR resumes diplomatic relations with Polish government-in-exile.
July 31, 1941	Goering puts Reinhard Heydrich in charge of deporting all Jews from Europe.
August 1, 1941	U.S.-USSR accord signed.
August 9-12, 1941	Roosevelt and Churchill meet at Atlantic Conference; Atlantic Charter proclaimed (August 9).
August 11, 1941	Japan calls general mobilization.
August 14, 1941	Soviets evacuate Smolensk.
August 25, 1941	Soviet and British troops enter Iran.
September 3, 1941	Rumania retakes Bukovina.
September 9, 1941	Siege of Leningrad begins.
September 16, 1941	Riza Pahlavi abdicates Iranian throne in favor of his son Mohammed Riza Pahlavi.
September 17, 1941	British and Soviet forces occupy Teheran.
September 19, 1941	Germans take Kiev.
September 24, 1941	French National Council created in London; USSR

	joins United Nations pact.
September 25, 1941	Germans launch Crimea offensive.
September 27, 1941	Gen. Georges Catroux, de Gaulle's envoy, offers independence to Syria and Lebanon, reserving French right to maintain bases.
October 2-December 5, 1941	Battle of Moscow.
October 4, 1941	U.S. suspends oil deliveries to Japan.
October 9, 1941	Pro-German Panamanian government overthrown.
October 14, 1941	Decree drafting Luxembourg citizens from age 17 to 25 for labor service issued (applied only to age 21).
October 16, 1941	Tojo cabinet formed in Japan.
October 21, 1941	Kragujevac massacre.
November 11, 1941	U.S. extends lend-lease to Free France.
November 13, 1941	Roosevelt amendments to Neutrality Act passed.
November 15, 1941	Germans take Yalta, control Crimea except Sevastopol.
November 18-December 30, 1941	German-Italian forces retreat from Bardia to El Agheila before British Eighth Army.
November 25, 1941	Bulgaria, Denmark, Croatia, Finland, Rumania and Slovakia join Anti-Comintern Pact; Spanish, French, Belgian and Dutch volunteers called to fight against communism.
November 27, 1941	Wavell's capture of Gonder completes liberation of Ethiopia.
December 4, 1941	Polish-Soviet defense and friendship treaty signed.
December 5, 1941	Soviet counteroffensive launched from Moscow.
December 7, 1941	Japanese attack Pearl Harbor; Britain declares war on Finland, Hungary and Rumania.
December 8, 1941	Britain and U.S. declare war on Japan; Japanese land in Thailand and Malaya.
December 9, 1941	Franco-Japanese military pacts on Indochina concluded; Japanese invade Gilbert Islands; Free France declares war on Japan.
December 10, 1941	Japanese invade Guam; Japanese sink British flagships *Prince of Wales* and *Repulse*.
December 11, 1941	Germany and Italy declare war on U.S.; Japanese invade southern Luzon.
December 15, 1941	Ireland declares neutrality.
December 16, 1941	Germans retreat along Moscow front.
December 17, 1941	Japanese invade northern Borneo.
December 19, 1941	Gen. Walther von Brauchitsch resigns OKW command, Hitler takes personal control; Britain raises draft age limit to 51, female conscription enacted.
December 20, 1941	Japanese invade Mindanao.
December 21, 1941	Japanese invade Lingayen Bay.
December 22, 1941-January 14, 1942	Arcadia Conference held in Washington: Roosevelt and Churchill organize united military effort, create committee of heads of major states, among others.
December 24, 1941	Free French land on St. Pierre and Miquelon, which Roosevelt puts under U.S. control; Japan occupies Wake Island.
December 25, 1941	Hong Kong surrenders.
December 26, 1941	British-U.S.-China military alliance concluded; British raid Lofoten Islands for second time.
December 26-28, 1941	British-Norwegian force raids Vaagso.
December 28, 1941	Japan invades Sumatra.
January 1, 1942	United Nations Declaration signed in Washington by U.S., United Kingdom USSR, China, Australia, Belgium, Canada, Costa

	Rica, Cuba, Czechoslovakia, Dominican Republic, El Salvador, Greece, Guatemala, Haiti, Honduras, India, Luxembourg, the Netherlands, New Zealand, Nicaragua, Norway, Panama, Poland, South Africa and Yugoslavia.	March 1-8, 1942	Japanese capture Java.
		March 3, 1942	British conduct operation in Diego Suarez.
		March 7, 1942	Rangoon captured; Japanese land in New Guinea.
		March 7-15, 1942	Last battle for control of Singapore fought.
		March 10, 1942	Allied air victory over Japanese ships at Salamaua.
January 9, 1942	Allied declaration on war criminals signed.	March 12, 1942	British retreat from Andaman Islands.
January 15-28, 1942	Rio de Janeiro conference held (Latin America, except for Argentina and Chile, break relations with Axis powers).	March 21, 1942	Hitler orders Fritz Sauckel to recruit forced labor from occupied countries to free Germans to fight.
January 16, 1942	Japanese begin Burma offensive.	March 28, 1942	British raid Saint-Nazaire.
		March 28-29, 1942	RAF conducts mass bombing of Lubeck.
January 20, 1942	Wannsee Conference of chief German ministers held, concentration camps for ''Final solution of Jewish question'' examined.	April 5, 1942	Japanese attack on Colombo defeated.
		April 7, 1942	Japanese complete capture of Sumatra.
		April 9, 1942	U.S. forces on Bataan surrender.
January 21, 1942	Rommel launches last offensive in Libya.	April 18, 1942	Laval returns to Vichy government (named president and foreign affairs and interior minister); U.S. conducts first air raid on Tokyo.
January 25, 1942	Thailand declares war on Britain and U.S.		
January 26, 1942	Japanese invade northern Solomon Islands.		
January 29, 1942	Anglo-Soviet-Iranian treaty signed.	April 27, 1942	U.S. recalls Vichy ambassador.
February 1, 1942	Norwegian *Reichskommissar* Terboven names Quisling premier-president.	May 1, 1942	Mandalay captured; Burma-China route cut.
		May 4-8, 1942	Battle of Coral Sea, Adm. Nimitz's forces victorious in first aircraft carrier battle.
February 8, 1942	Albert Speer named minister of armaments and war production.		
February 15, 1942	British base at Singapore captured by Japanese.	May 5, 1942	British land in Madagascar.
February 16, 1942	Palembang in Sumatra captured by Japanese.	May 8, 1942	U.S. forces on Corregidor surrender.
February 18, 1942	Japanese invade Bali.	May 9, 1942	Soviets launch Kharkov offensive.
February 20, 1942	Japanese invade Timor.		
February 27, 1942	Japanese defeat Allied naval force in battle of Java Sea; British with Free French and Resistance forces raid German radar station at Bruneval.	May 11, 1942	U.S. forces on Mindanao surrender.
		May 12, 1942	First mass gasing of Jews at Auschwitz.
		May 16, 1942	Germans take Kerch in Crimea.
February 27- March 14, 1942	Leclerc's forces raid Fezzan.	May 17, 1942	Kharkov counteroffensive launched.
		May 24, 1942	Heydrich shot in Prague,

	dies May 26.	August 30, 1942	Luxembourg citizens drafted by Germans.
May 26, 1942	Twenty-year Anglo-Soviet mutual assistance pact signed.	August 31, 1942	German-Italian forces defeated at Alam el Halfa.
May 26-June 30, 1942	Successful German-Italian offensive launched in Libya.	September 1, 1942	Germans reach Volga.
		September 4, 1942	Vichy institutes labor conscription.
May 28, 1942	Mexico declares war on Tripartite signatories.	September 5, 1942	Novorossisk surrenders.
May 30-31, 1942	First RAF mass bombing raid (1,000 planes) launched against Germany (Cologne).	September 6, 1942	Battle of Stalingrad begins.
		September 12, 1942	Japanese advance on Port Moresby halted.
		September 23, 1942	British occupy Tananarive (Madagascar).
June 3-7, 1942	Battle of Midway, decisive U.S. air and naval victory over Japanese.	October 8, 1942	Germans chain British prisoners from Dieppe, prisoners unchained December 12 following British reprisals.
June 5, 1942	U.S. declares war on Rumania and Bulgaria.		
June 10, 1942	Lidice massacre.		
June 11, 1942	U.S. extends lend-lease to USSR.	October 9, 1942	Soviet army abolishes political commissars.
June 15, 1942	Japanese land in Aleutians.	October 10, 1942	U.S. and Britain renounce extraterritorial privileges in China.
June 24, 1942	De Gaulle's ''French Charter'' published, sealing union between Free French and Resistance.	October 23-November 4, 1942	Montgomery launches successful offensive at El Alamein.
June 28, 1942	German general offensive in Russia launched.		
July 1, 1942	Italian-German forces reach El Alamein.	October 26, 1942	Battle of Santa Cruz Islands.
July 2, 1942	Sevastopol surrenders.	November 7-8, 1942	Anglo-U.S. forces land in Morocco and Algeria; Vichy breaks relations with U.S.
July 2-4, 1942	First battle of El Alamein, decisive blow to Rommel.		
July 4, 1942	First U.S. air raids against Germany carried out.	November 9, 1942	Hitler and Laval hold talks at Berchtesgaden; German-Italian forces land in Tunisia.
July 20, 1942	Soviets beat back Germans at Don near Voronezh.		
July 27, 1942	Germans take Rostov.	November 10, 1942	Adm. Darlan and Gen. Mark Clark sign French North African armistice.
August 7, 1942	U.S. Marines land on Guadalcanal, capture Japanese-held airfield on August 8.		
		November 11, 1942	Germans and Italians occupy Vichy zone; Vichy army dissolved; French Resistance group *Organisation de resistance de l'armee* created; Gen. Eugene Delestraint takes command of *Armee secrete*, another Resistance group.
August 8, 1942	U.S. Marines take Tulagi.		
August 8-9, 1942	Battle of Savo Island.		
August 17, 1942	Churchill, Averell Harriman and Stalin confer in Moscow.		
August 19, 1942	Anglo-Canadian force raids Dieppe.		
August 22, 1942	Brazil declares war on Germany.	November 12-15, 1942	Japanese navy defeated at Savo and Guadalcanal.
August 23-25, 1942	Battle of Stewart Islands in Pacific.	November 13, 1942	Darlan-Clark accords recognize Darlan's

	authority in French North Africa; Darlan appoints Henri Giraud military chief of French North Africa.		and Japanese surrender; first de Gaulle-Giraud meeting held.
		January 23, 1943	British forces under Montgomery enter Tripoli.
November 15, 1942	Battle of Guadalcanal, decisive U.S. naval victory.	January 28, 1943	Civilians called up in Germany.
November 18, 1942	Petain gives Laval supreme power.	January 30, 1943	Vichy establishes Militia under Laval as chief and Joseph Darnand as secretary-general.
November 19, 1942	Germans begin encircle-ment at Stalingrad.		
November 20, 1942	Sir William Beveridge's Welfare State Plan issued; Soviet offensive launched in central Caucasus.	February 1, 1943	Soviet offensive launched on Azov Sea and Ukraine.
		February 2, 1943	Field Marshal Friedrich von Paulus surrenders at Stalingrad.
November 23, 1942	French West Africa backs Darlan.	February 8, 1943	Soviets recapture Kursk.
November 26, 1942	Anti-Fascist Council for the Liberation of Yugoslavia created.	February 9, 1943	Japanese evacuate Guadalcanal.
		February 12, 1943	Ferhat Abbas issues "Manifesto of the Algerian People."
November 27, 1942	French fleet at Toulon scuttled.		
December 1, 1942	Soviet offensive between Don and Volga launched.	February 14, 1943	Soviets recapture Rostov and Voroshilovgrad.
December 2, 1942	First atomic reaction achieved at Chicago laboratory.	February 16, 1943	Vichy calls up 40-to-42-year-olds for national labor service; Soviets retake Kharkov.
December 4, 1942	Darlan becomes chief of state at Algiers.	February 28, 1943	Norwegian Resistance destroys heavy water factory at Vemork.
December 14, 1942	Franco-British pact re-establishes French sovereignty over Madagascar and its dependencies.		
		March 1, 1943	"Union of Polish Patriots" created in Moscow.
		March 1-3, 1943	U.S. and Australian planes destroy key Japanese convoy in Bismarck Sea.
December 16, 1942	Soviets advance between Don and Donets.		
December 24, 1942	Darlan assassinated by F. Bonnier de la Chapelle; U.S. recognizes Gen. Giraud as high commissioner of French North Africa and commander in chief.	March 14, 1943	Japan restores territorial concessions in China to Nanking government.
		March 15, 1943	Soviets evacuate Kharkov.
		March 20-27, 1943	British Eighth Army breaches Mareth Line, opening way to Tunisia.
December 27, 1942	Gen. Andrei Vlasov creates Smolensk Committee for "liberation of the peoples of Russia."	March 24, 1943	Giraud and de Gaulle hold talks at Casablanca.
		April 7, 1943	British Eighth Army and U.S. First Army link up in Tunisia.
January 1, 1943	Soviet offensive on Black Sea coast launched.		
January 14-24, 1943	Anfa Conference, attended by Roosevelt and Churchill, held at Casa-blanca, decision taken to accept nothing short of unconditional German	April 11, 1943	Sauckel-Laval pact makes French prisoners of war free laborers for Germany.
		April 13, 1943	Germans reveal discovery of Katyn massacre.
		April 19-May 16, 1943	Warsaw ghetto uprising.
		April 25, 1943	Stalin breaks relations with

	Polish government-in-exile.		independent under Japanese protection.
May 6-13, 1943	Gen. Harold Alexander defeats Italian-German forces in Tunisia (Tunis and Bizerte captured May 7, remaining Axis forces surrender May 13).	August 2, 1943	Lebanon freed from French mandate.
		August 4, 1943	Soviets recapture Orel.
		August 5, 1943	British capture Catania.
		August 14-24, 1943	Quadrant Conference held in Quebec; U.S.-British accord on atomic research reached.
May 12-25, 1943	Trident Conference held in Washington.		
May 15, 1943	Comintern dissolved.	August 17, 1943	U.S.-British capture of Messina ends German resistance in Sicily.
May 16, 1943	RAF bombs dams along Mohne and Eder.		
May 18-June 1, 1943	Hot Springs Conference convened; U.N. Relief and Rehabilitation Administration created.	August 18, 1943	Start of secret armistice talks between Badoglio and Britain; Portuguese agree to allow Anglo-U.S. bases on Faial and Terceira in Azores.
May 27,1943	*Conseil national de la resistance* created under Jean Moulin.	August 23, 1943	Soviets recapture Kharkov.
May 31, 1943	French squadron at Alexandria under Adm. Rene Godfroy defects to Giraud.	August 24, 1943	Himmler named minister of interior.
		August 26, 1943	U.S., Britain and USSR recognize *Comite francais de liberation nationale.*
June 3, 1943	French Imperial Council and French National Council united at Algiers; *Comite francais de liberation nationale* created under Giraud and de Gaulle.	August 28, 1943	Bulgarian King Boris III dies mysteriously after talks in Germany with Hitler; Germany takes direct control of Denmark after Danes refuse to suppress anti-German activity.
June 10-13, 1943	British take Pantelleria, Linosa and Lampedusa Islands.	September 3, 1943	British land in Calabria; Stalin meets with Russian Orthodox Church officials in Moscow.
June 21, 1943	Moulin arrested, dies July 8 following torture.		
June 23, 1943	Daladier decree abolishing Communist Party annulled at Algiers.	September 8, 1943	Italian army surrenders.
		September 9, 1943	Anglo-U.S. forces land in Salerno.
July 10, 1943	British-U.S. forces land in Sicily.	September 10, 1943	Germans occupy northern Italy and Rome.
July 12-13, 1943	*National Komitee "Freies Deutschland"* created in USSR.	September 11-October 5, 1943	Corsica liberated by French and Resistance forces.
July 15, 1943	Offensive on Orel launched.	September 12, 1943	Mussolini freed by Otto Skorzeny.
July 17, 1943	Allies carry out first bombing of Rome.	September 13, 1943	Chiang Kai-shek elected president of Chinese Republic.
July 24, 1943	Mussolini defeated in Fascist Grand Council.		
July 25, 1943	Mussolini's arrest ordered by Victor Emmanuel III; Marshal Pietro Badoglio creates new government.	September 14, 1943	Australian-U.S. forces capture Salamaua in New Guinea.
August 1, 1943	Burma declared	September 16, 1943	U.S.-Australian forces capture Lae in New

Guinea; Soviets liberate Novorossisk.

September 17, 1943 — Provisional Consultative Assembly created in Algiers; Bryansk liberated.

September 23, 1943 — Mussolini establishes Social Republic of Italy at Salo.

September 25, 1943 — Smolensk liberated.

September 27, 1943 — Giraud gives up political posts.

October 1, 1943 — Allies enter Naples.

October 7, 1943 — Soviets cross Dnieper; Allies enter Capua.

October 13, 1943 — Italy declares war on Germany.

October 14, 1943 — Japan proclaims Philippine independence.

October 18, 1943 — Moscow Conference (with Eden and Cordell Hull) held; European Consultative Commission created.

October 25, 1943 — Japanese air force destroyed at Rabaul; Dnepropetrovsk liberated.

November 3, 1943 — Resistance Consultative Assembly holds inaugural meeting at Algiers.

November 6, 1943 — Kiev liberated.

November 9, 1943 — Giraud resigns from *Comite francais de liberation nationale*, de Gaulle remains sole president.

November 22-26, 1943 — Sextant Conference in Cairo attended by Chiang Kai-shek, Churchill and Roosevelt.

November 28-December 1, 1943 — Eureka Conference in Teheran attended by Churchill, Roosevelt and Stalin.

November 29, 1943 — Yugoslav Anti-Fascist Council creates provisional government under Tito.

December 2-16, 23-29, 1943 — RAF bombs Berlin.

December 4-6, 1943 — Cairo Conference with Roosevelt, Churchill and Ismet Inonu, president of Turkey.

December 12, 1943 — Friendship treaty between USSR and Czech government-in-exile signed.

December 20, 1943 — Franco dissolves *Falange*.

December 22, 1943 — France begins handing over power to Syrian and Lebanese governments.

December 26, 1943 — German battle cruiser *Scharnhorst* scuttled.

January 5, 1944 — Berdichev liberated.

Janaury 12, 1944 — De Gaulle-Churchill conference held at Marrakesh.

January 14, 1944 — Belgian Resistance leader Walthere Dewe shot in Brussels.

January 15, 1944 — G Group sabotages all major power lines in Belgium.

January 22, 1944 — Anglo-U.S. forces land at Anzio.

January 24, 1944 — Eisenhower appointed supreme commander of Allied forces in Europe.

January 27, 1944 — Liberia declares war on Germany and Japan.

January 30-February 8, 1944 — Brazzaville conference on French colonial policy convened.

January 31, 1944 — U.S. forces land on Marshall Islands.

February 1944 — Various French Resistance groups unite under *Forces francaises de l'interieur*, including *Armee secrete, Organisation de resistance de l'armee* and *Partisans francais*, under Gen. Marie Pierre Koenig.

February 5, 1944 — Free French leader Pierre Brossolette arrested, kills himself February 22 to keep from talking.

February 6-22, 1944 — Apostolovo, Nikopol and Krivoy Rog liberated.

February 14, 1944 — Leningrad siege lifted, Novgorod liberated.

February 15, 1944 — Monte Cassino bombed.

February 20, 1944 — Norwegian Resistance sinks ferry carrying heavy water from Vemork.

February 23, 1944 — U.S. occupies Eniwetok.

March 4, 1944 — U.S. conducts first daytime air raids on Berlin.

March 3, 10, 14, 1944 — Allies bomb Rome.

March 5, 1944 — Decree grants "French Moslems" citizenship, in Algeria.

March 10, 1944 — Greek Provisional National

	Liberation Committee comprising all Resistance groups created.	June 16, 1944	Battle of Montmouchet between *Forces françaises de l'interieur* and Germans.
March 15, 1944	Soviets cross Bug; Germans and Vichy Militia attack *Glieres Partisans.*	June 26, 1944	Vitebsk liberated.
		June 26-July 3, 1944	General strike conducted in Denmark.
March 19, 1944	Soviets cross Dnieper; Germans occupy Hungary.	June 27, 1944	U.S. forces take Cherbourg.
March 25, 1944	U.S. invades Hollandia in New Guinea.	July 1-22, 1944	Bretton Woods Conference held.
March 29, 1944	Soviets cross Prut.	July 5, 1944	Minsk liberated.
March 30, 1944	Soviets capture Chernovtsy.	July 9, 1944	British take Caen.
April 2, 1944	Asq massacre.	July 12, 1944	Ministers at Vichy hold last meeting.
April 10, 1944	Odessa liberated.	July 16, 1944	Soviets take Vilna.
April 11-18, 1944	All Crimea, except Sevastopol, liberated.	July 18, 1944	Americans liberate Saint-Lo.
May 9, 1944	Sevastopol liberated.	July 20, 1944	Failure of attempted assassination of Hitler led by Col. Count Claus Schenk von Stauffenberg at Fuehrer's *Wolfsschanze* headquarters (Rastenburg).
May 12, 1944	Allies launch offensive toward Rome.		
May 14, 1944	Allies breach Gustav Line in southern Italy.		
May 18, 1944	British take Cassino, Poles take Monte Cassino.		
June 3, 1944	*Comite francais de liberation nationale* ("French National Liberation Committee") renames itself *Gouvernement provisoire de la Republique francaise* ("Provisional Government of French Republic").	July 21, 1944	Americans land on Guam.
		July 21-23, 1944	French Expeditionary Corps withdraws from Italy.
		July 21-27, 1944	Germans attack French Resistance at Vercors.
		July 23, 1944	Creation in Lublin of the Polish National Committee (the so-called Lublin Committee) recognized by Stalin.
June 4, 1944	Allies enter Rome.		
June 5, 1944	Prince Umberto of Savoy named lieutenant general of Italian kingdom.	July 31, 1944	Americans liberate Avranches; Soviets retake Lvov and Brest Litovsk.
June 6, 1944	Allies land in Normandy; general Resistance action launched in France, sabotage in Belgium, general strikes in Denmark, sabotage of communications in Norway.	August 1-October 2, 1944	General revolt of the Polish "hidden army" at Warsaw.
		August 2, 1944	Relations between Turkey and Germany severed.
		August 3, 1944	Germans in Brittany cut off from their bases.
June 7, 1944	Leopold III and family taken to Germany; German massacre at Tulle.	August 9, 1944	U.S. troops reach Le Mans; Provisional Government of French Republic restores liberated territory to its control.
June 8, 1944	Bayeux liberated.		
June 10, 1944	SS massacre at Oradour-sur-Glane.		
June 13, 1944	First V-bombs launched against Britain.	August 10, 1944	Railroad workers strike in Paris.
June 14, 1944	De Gaulle returns to France.	August 17, 1944	U.S. troops liberate Chartres and Orleans.

August 19, 1944	Montgomery completes defeat of German forces in Normandy with Falaise-Argentan maneuver; Paris rebels.	September 9, 1944	British cross Albert Canal; U.S. troops cross Moselle.
August 20, 1944	Petain transferred to Belfort, then to Sigmaringen September 9 by Germans.	September 10, 1944	French government abolishes Vichy legislature.
		September 11, 1944	Armistice between USSR and Bulgaria signed.
August 21-September 21, 1944	Dumbarton Oaks Conference attended by U.S., USSR and Britain.	September 11-19, 1944	Churchill and Roosevelt meet at Octagon Conference in Quebec.
		September 12, 1944	Le Havre taken; Luxembourg liberated; USSR, U.S. and United Kingdom sign armistice with Rumania.
August 21-31, 1944	Soviets take Constanza, Ploesti and Bucharest.		
August 22, 1944	Florence liberated.		
August 23, 1944	Bucharest rebels, Antonescu government overturned; Rumania surrenders, declares war on Germany.	September 13, 1944	Allies enter Germany.
		September 15, 1944	Tito's troops and Soviet forces meet at Negotin in Yugoslavia; French city of Nancy liberated.
August 24, 1944	Leclerc's armored division enters Paris.	September 17-28, 1944	British conduct airborne operation at Arnhem in the Netherlands.
August 25, 1944	Gen. Dietrich von Cholitz surrenders in Paris; Bulgarians demand German withdrawal, ask Anglo-American authorities for armistice.	September 18, 1944	U.S. forces take Brest.
		September 20, 1944	Prince Charles becomes regent in Belgium.
		September 22, 1944	Boulogne liberated.
		September 24, 1944	Decree integrating French Resistance forces into French army.
August 26, 1944	De Gaulle enters Paris.	September 25, 1944	Hitler mobilizes all men from 16 to 60 into *Volkssturm*.
August 28, 1944	Grenoble and Marseilles liberated.		
August 29, 1944	National uprising in Slovakia.	September 29-October 7, 1944	Second session of Dumbarton Oaks Conference attended by U.S., United Kingdom and China.
August 31, 1944	De Gaulle dissolves *Conseil national de la resistance*.		
September 3, 1944	French forces liberate Lyon and St. Etienne; British liberate Lille and Brussels.	September 30, 1944	Calais liberated.
		October 4, 1944	British land in Greece, Patras liberated.
September 4, 1944	British liberate Anvers, where Resistance preserves all harbor installations; Finland surrenders.	October 6, 1944	Soviets enter Hungary.
		October 7, 1944	Eastern Arab states sign Protocol of Alexandria, pattern for future Arab League.
September 5, 1944	Benelux accords signed in London by Belgium, the Netherlands and Luxembourg; USSR declares war on Bulgaria.	October 9-18, 1944	Moscow Conference attended by Stalin, Churchill and Harriman.
		October 13, 1944	Soviets take Riga.
September 8, 1944	Bulgaria declares war on Germany; U.S. troops liberate Liege; Canadians liberate Ostend; Pierlot and his cabinet return to Brussels.	October 14, 1944	British liberate Athens, where Papandreou forms government.
		October 15, 1944	Hungarian regent Adm. Horthy asks for armistice;

	Germans take power.	January 1-9, 1945	Germans begin counter-offensive in Alsace and Lorraine; Strasbourg threatened January 5, but de Gaulle refuses to abandon it.
October 18, 1944	Soviets attack East Prussia, enter Czechoslovakia.		
October 19, 1944	Anglo-Indian forces take Tiddim in Burma.		
October 20, 1944	Tito's National Liberation Army liberates Belgrade; U.S. Sixth Army lands on Leyte.	January 9, 1945	U.S. Sixth Army lands on Luzon.
		January 14-18, 1945	Soviets take Radom, Warsaw, Lodz and Krakow.
October 21, 1944	Americans take Aachen.		
October 22, 1944	U.S., USSR and United Kingdom award de jure recognition to Provisional Government of French Republic.	January 19-21, 1945	Soviets take Tilsit (Sovetsk), Insterburg (Chernyakhovsk), Allen-stein (Olsztyn) and Tannenberg (Stebark) in East Prussia.
October 24-26, 1944	Japanese fleet defeated at Leyte.		
October 28, 1944	All armed groups in France not belonging to army or police disbanded.	January 20, 1945	First French Army launches offensive in Vosges; armistice between Hungary and USSR signed in Moscow.
November 6, 1944	Greece liberated.		
November 7, 1944	Roosevelt reelected to fourth term.	January 23, 1945	Burma Road to China reopened.
November 12, 1944	*Tirpitz* sunk by RAF in Tromso fjord.	January 24, 1945	Soviets take Gleiwitz (Gliwice) in Upper Silesia.
November 13, 1944	Soviets cross Danube.	January 26, 1945	Ardennes completely liberated.
November 18, 1944	Jean de Lattre liberates Montbeliard.		
November 23, 1944	Second Armored Division liberates Strasbourg.	January 27, 1945	Soviets liberate Auschwitz.
November 28, 1944	Action resumed in port of Anvers.	January 28, 1945	Soviets cross Pomerania and Brandenburg rivers.
December 2-10, 1944	Conference held in Moscow between Stalin and de Gaulle to sign Franco-Soviet pact.	February 4-24, 1945	Americans liberate Manila.
		February 4-12, 1945	Churchill, Roosevelt and Stalin meet at Yalta, draw up plans for full defeat of Germany.
December 16, 1944	Germans launch offensive in Ardennes, start of Battle of Bulge.	February 6, 1945	Soviets cross Oder south-east of Breslau (Wroclaw).
December 22, 1944	Vietnam Liberation Army organized under Vo Nguyen Giap.	February 8, 1945	Anglo-Canadian offensive between Meuse and Rhine rivers launched.
December 26, 1944	Soviets begin siege of Budapest; Germans begin retreat from Ardennes after U.S. army relief unit arrives at Bastogne.	February 9, 1945	First French Army and American 21st Corps liquidate Colmar pocket.
		February 13, 1945	Soviets take Budapest; U.S. First Army crosses Rhine.
January 1, 1945	Lublin Committee pro-claims itself Poland's provisional government, recognized by USSR on January 5; U.S. troops land on Mindoro.	February 13-16, 1945	Dresden bombed.
		February 15, 1945	Soviets besiege Breslau (Wroclaw).
		February 19, 1945	U.S. Marines land on Iwo Jima.
January 1-3, 1945	British occupy Rathedaung and Akyab in Burma.	February 23, 1945	Soviets take Poznan; Turkey declares war on Germany; two U.S. armies

	carry on offensive at Aachen toward Rhine.	March 28, 1945	Collapse of German army in west.
February 25, 1945	Americans take Dueren and Juelich.	March 29, 1945	Americans take Frankfurt and Mannheim; Soviets enter Austria.
February 27-March 6, 1945	Communist Groza government established in Rumania.	March 30, 1945	Soviets take Danzig.
		April 1, 1945	U.S. forces land on Okinawa, conquering it completely by June 21; 21 German divisions are encircled in Ruhr.
February 27, 1945	Syria declares war on Axis powers.		
March 1, 1945	Japanese on Corregidor surrender; most of Philippines liberated.	April 2, 1945	Gen. Harold Alexander launches final offensive in Italy.
March 1-6, 1945	Americans take Muenchen-Gladbach, Krefeld, Treves and Cologne.	April 5, 1945	Americans cross Weser; USSR renounces its non-aggression pact with Japan.
March 4, 1945	Finland declares war on Germany.		
March 7, 1945	U.S. forces take bridge at Remagen and cross Rhine; Federal People's Republic of Yugoslavia established with Tito as president.	April 6, 1945	Yugoslavs take Sarajevo; British and Canadians begin general offensive in the Netherlands.
		April 9, 1945	Soviets take Koenigsberg.
March 9, 1945	U.S. First and Third armies meet up to encircle some 10 German divisions; Japan assumes power in Indochina, Emperor Bao Dai proclaims end of French protectorate there.	April 10, 1945	U.S. forces take Hanover.
		April 11, 1945	U.S. forces take Essen; discovery of Buchenwald hardens Allied attitude; Yugoslavia and USSR sign assistance and friendship pact.
March 10-13, 1945	U.S. Third and Seventh armies maneuver to encircle Palatinate, thereby trapping German armies.	April 12, 1945	Roosevelt dies, Truman succeeds him; King Norodom Sihanouk proclaims independence of Cambodia.
March 14-15, 1945	Norwegian Resistance undertakes 1,000 acts of railroad sabotage.	April 13, 1945	Soviets take Vienna.
		April 14, 1945	British liberate Arnhem.
March 16, 1945	U.S. Marines take Iwo Jima.	April 16, 1945	RAF sinks the *Luetsov*; battle of Berlin begins.
March 17-21, 1945	Americans take Koblenz, Worms, Saarbruecken and Ludwigshafen.	April 21, 1945	First French Army enters Berchtesgaden.
March 20, 1945	Anglo-Indian forces take Mandalay in Burma; Yugoslav army under Tito begins final offensive.	April 23, 1945	Allies reach Po river.
		April 24, 1945	Gen. Raffaele Cadorna signals general insurrection of Italian Resistance; Himmler proposes Germans surrender to Western Allies alone.
March 22, 1945	Egypt, Iraq, Syria, Lebanon, Transjordan, Saudi Arabia and Yemen sign Arab League pact in Cairo.		
		April 25-June 26, 1945	San Francisco Conference convenes to write United Nations Charter.
March 23, 1945	British and American troops under Montgomery cross Rhine between Rees and Wesel.	April 26, 1945	U.S. and Soviet troops join at Torgau on Elbe river; Bremen surrenders to British; Milan liberated

	by Italian partisans; Italian partisans arrest Mussolini, execute him on April 28.	June 26, 1945	china. United Nations Charter signed.
April 27, 1945	U.S. troops take Genoa.	June 28, 1945	National Unity Government formed in Poland.
April 29, 1945	German armies in Italy and the Tyrol surrender.	June 30, 1945	French recognize Polish government of Warsaw.
April 30, 1945	Australians land on Tarakan.	July 4, 1945	Western Allies and Soviets recognize Austria.
April 30-May 2, 1945	Yugoslavs occupy Trieste.	July 5, 1945	Gen. MacArthur
May 1, 1945	Doenitz announces death of Hitler (a suicide the day before), declares himself successor.		announces liberation of Philippines, end of Philippine campaign; Britain and U.S. recognize Polish government of
May 2, 1945	Berlin surrenders to Soviets; Australians land on Borneo; British and Yugoslavs join forces near Trieste.	July 16, 1945	Warsaw. First experimental atomic bomb detonated in New Mexico; King Leopold III
May 3, 1945	British take Hamburg; Anglo-Indian forces in Burma take Rangoon and Prome; Japanese army in Burma no longer exists.	July 17-August 2, 1945	refuses to abdicate after liberation by Allies. Potsdam Conference, with Stalin, Truman, Churchill and Attlee, held on settle-
May 4, 1945	German forces in Denmark surrender to Resistance.	July 26, 1945	ment of German problems. Vietnam established; U.S.,
May 5, 1945	All German forces in the Netherlands and north-western Germany surrender to British; Prague revolt.		Britain and China send ultimatum to Japan; British Labor Party wins; Churchill resigns.
May 6, 1945	Rebellion at Damascus against French trusteeship.	July 27, 1945	Attlee forms British cabinet.
May 7, 1945	Unconditional surrender signed at Reims by Gen. Alfred Jodl and, on May 8, at Berlin by Field Marshal Wilhelm Keitel.	July 28, 1945 August 2, 1945 August 6, 1945	Tokyo rejects ultimatum. British liberate Burma. Atomic bomb dropped on Hiroshima.
May 9, 1945	Soviets enter Prague.	August 8, 1945	USSR declares war on
May 14, 1945	Austria declares its independence.		Japan; U.S., France, United Kingdom and
May 20, 1945	Anti-French riots occur in Beirut.		USSR agree to create international military tribunal.
May 23, 1945	Doenitz and members of his government arrested.	August 9, 1945	Atomic bomb dropped on Nagasaki; Soviet offensive
May 30, 1945	British force French to end their resistance to Syrian revolt.	August 10, 1945	launched in Manchuria. Japan asks for preliminary peace talks.
June 1-2 1945	British occupy Syria and Lebanon.	August 12, 1945	USSR occupies North Korea, Sakhalin and
June 5, 1945	Supreme Allied Command in Germany declares that "in view of Germany's defeat" it will assume all government powers.	August 14, 1945	Kurils. Sino-Soviet friendship and alliance treaty signed; Japan surrenders.
June 13, 1945	Chinese penetrate Indo-	August 15, 1945	Japan formerly announces surrender.

August 28, 1945	Chiang Kai-shek and Mao Tse-tung meet in Chunking.	October 24, 1945	United Nations Charter activated.
August 29, 1945	American forces begin occupation of Japan.	November 20, 1945	War crimes trials open before international tribunal in Nuremberg.
September 2, 1945	Japanese sign surrender; Bao Dai abdicates in Indochina, Ho Chi Minh proclaims the independent Republic of Vietnam.	May 3, 1946	War crimes trials open before international tribunal in Tokyo.
September 16, 1945	Spanish forces evacuate Tangier, officially established as international zone on September 26.	October 16, 1946	Hanging of those condemned to death by Nuremberg International Military Tribunal for war crimes and crimes against humanity.

BIBLIOGRAPHY

The work of historians of World War II has generally been characterized by objectivity and careful analysis. These scholars have freed themselves to a remarkable extent from the extreme chauvinism that mars the historical record of World War I. Aside from a few courageous—and isolated—efforts, the historiography of the period between the two wars has also been spoiled by a pernicious nationalism. The various official records of World War I and its aftermath are filled with legends and rancor.

The serious consequences of such blunders, particularly in France, are well known. Actually, they were anticipated in 1931 by a military commentator writing under the pseudonym "Three Stars." "Here in France," he wrote, "apart from a few pamphlets, nobody has as yet written a serious and objective military history of the Great War.... The High Command still balks at submitting to critical examination the manner in which it conducted the operations of 1914-18." The author warned against the problems such attitudes could create in the future. Thus the drama of 1940 came about. One of the principal reasons for France's defeat was the failure of French military experts to analyze properly the conduct of World War I prior to the German invasion of Poland in 1939. Much of the scholarship on World War II, on the other hand, is distinguished by its objectivity and precision. German, French, British and American works alike openly discuss the errors made by their own commanders and the failures of their nations' troops.

There are three basic reasons for this scholarship. First, the works and teachings of the great historians of the last three decades have set a rigorous standard for today's scholarship. The intelligent reader is increasingly inclined to examine the written record perceptively. Every sincere writer tries to abide by the rules of objective research, to satisfy both his own conscience and the demands of an increasingly informed readership. Second, governments need accurate information to permit them to make decisions for the future, and this has led them to encourage research work. And third, most historians believe that the history of World War II touches on all disciplines—in fact, that the war touched, and still touches, all aspects of civilized life. The war "began" long before the first shots were fired, which is why any effort to provide a complete overview of the war must go as far back as 1922 to analyze the events that led to Italy's participation in the war.

We know now that if a historian is to be thorough, he should not only examine the surface on which the subjects of his chronicle move—i.e., the geography of the battlefields—but should also study the people and their governments in depth; that is, he should look into their philosophy, sociology, psychology, economy and the like. Since the time period that any study of the war may cover is extremely variable, the historian must present his work within the broadest possible context. Military operations should occupy only a limited portion of the historian's attention; discussions of these operations should be subordinate to the investigation of motives, of the general conduct of the war and of its economic, social and cultural ramifications. Resistance, deportation, captivity and collaboration should be investigated and discussed as carefully as variations in public opinion inside and outside the theaters of operation and on both the opposing sides; no nuances should be ignored.

It is surely no secret that the true work of the historian comes with the critical examination of his sources, documents and artifacts. Yet that is where the greatest likelihood of failure lurks. There is a profusion of sources, and they are often scattered. Many are hidden and remain so indefinitely because they are confidential or secret. Some countries refuse all access to their war archives. Secret documents also tend to disappear; if they reveal too much, they are often deliberately destroyed; this was the fate of many German, Italian and Japanese papers during the war. Most countries, however, have published portions of their archives, but it may take another 20 to 30 years before this gigantic task is finished. The historian of World War II, then, has no choice but to go directly to unpublished sources. Nor should he limit himself to the various bibliographies on the subject; the books they list are often obsolete before they are published.

Any serious study must originate with official government documents, which are often written collectively rather than individually. It then should continue with a study of the "classic" works that have proposed original theses based on recent discoveries, and are supported by judicious bibliographies. Only through such an effort can the careful student arrive at an adequate understanding of World War II.

The notes below, though intentionally brief, are intended to guide his or her progress.

DOCUMENTS, RECORDS AND OTHER SOURCES

German archives are voluminous—thanks to their capture, almost intact, in 1945.

Adler-Bresse, M. *"Les sources allemandes de la Deuxieme Guerre mondiale"* [German Sources of the Second World War], *Revue d'histoire de la Deuxieme Guerre mondiale* [Historical Review of the Second World War] No. 41. Paris, 1961.

Akten zur deutschen auswaertigen Politik 1918-1945 [Events Marking German Foreign Policy 1918-1945] 10 vols. Baden-Baden, 1950-1963.

Hitlers Lagebesprechungen [Hitler's Discussions of the State of the German Nation]. Stuttgart, 1962.

Hitlers Tischgespraeche im Fuehrerhauptquartier 1941-1942 [Hitler's Table Conversations in His Headquarters 1941-1942]. Stuttgart, 1963.

Hubatsch, W. ed. *Hitlers Weisungen fuer die Kriegsfuehrung 1939-1945. Dokumente des Oberkommandos der Wehrmacht* [Hitler's Orders on the Conduct of the War of 1939-1945: Documents of the Wehrmacht High Command]. Frankfurt, 1962.

Jacobsen, H.-A., and W. Jochmann. *Ausgewaehlte Dokumente zur Geschichte des Nationalsozialismus* [Selected Documents in the History of National Socalism]. Bielefeld, 1961.

Schramm, P., ed. *Kriegstagebuch des Oberkommandos der Wehrmacht 1940-1945* [War Diary of the Wehrmacht High Command 1940-1945] 4 vols. Frankfurt, 1961-1965.

Most of the German archives captured during the war remain unpublished. However, parts of them have been microfilmed in the United States, and the National Archives has printed detailed catalogues of the material that is available. The microfilms can be obtained at no charge.

Since 1963 France has published a series of *Documents diplomatiques*. The items in the collections of the *Archives Nationales* and the *Service historique de l'Armee* are now being declassified. They will soon be available; some of the catalogues are now ready.

Great Britain has already published 30 volumes from various sources, concerned principally with foreign policy.

Italy has begun the preparation of a series entitled *Documenti diplomatici*, which will eventually include 100 volumes.

Similar work is being done in the United States on a continuing series entitled *Foreign Relations of the United States*. Forty of these volumes have already been published.

In 1965 the Vatican began publication of its archives, seven volumes of which have appeared under the title of *Acts and Documents of the Holy See Regarding World War II*, edited by P. Blet, R. A. Graham, A. Martini and B. Schneider (Vatican City, 1965).

For these states, as well as for others too numerous to mention in a brief list, see the publications of their official archives.

BIBLIOGRAPHIES

A list of miscellaneous references has been compiled by M. Gunzenhaeuser under the title of *Die Bibliographien zur Geschichte des Zweiten Weltkrieges* [Bibliographies on the History of the Second World War] in the *Jahresbibliographie der Bibliothek fuer Zeitgeschichte* [Annual Bibliography of the Library of Modern History], Vol. 33 (Stuttgart, 1961).

This may be supplemented by the following works: *Annotated Bibliography on the Second World War*. New York-London: Byron-Dexter, 1972.

Conzemius, V. *"Eglises chretiennes et Totalarisme national-socialist. Un bilan historiographique"* [Christian Churches and National Socialist Totalitarianism: an Historiographic Account]. *Bibliotheque de la Revue d'histoire ecclesiastique* Fascicle 49. Louvain, 1969.

Dornbusch, C. *Histories of American Army Units in World Wars I and II and the Korean Conflict*. Washington, 1956.

Koehler, K. *Bibliographie zur Luftkriegsgeschichte* [Bibliography for the History of Aerial Warfare]. Frankfurt, 1966.

Michel, H. *Bibliographie critique de la Resistance* [Critical Bibliography of the Resistance]. Paris, 1971.

Michel, H., and J.-M. D'Hoop. *Bibliographie critique de l'histoire de la Deuxieme Guerre mondiale a l'usage des professeurs d'histoire* [Critical Bibliography of the History of the Second World War Intended for History Professors]. Brussels, 1964.

Pochepko, G., and I. Frolova. *Soviet Bibliography*. Moscow, 1967.

Roberts, H. *Foreign Affairs Bibliography: a Selected*

and Annotated List. New York, 1955.

Saggio bibliografico sulla seconda guerra mondiale [Bibliographic Study of the Second World War]. 8 vols. Rome, 1955.

White, A. A Bibliography of Regimental Histories of the British Army. London, 1965.

Ziegler, J. World War II: an International Bibliography of Bibliographies. Los Angeles, 1964 (a list of 200 national bibliographies).

Current bibliographies are often appended to specialized reviews. The largest of these is the Revue d'histoire de la Deuxieme Guerre mondiale [Historical Review of Second World War], edited by the French Committee on the History of World War II, in the form of a world survey. More than 90 issues have appeared so far, most of them around a central theme with a critical account of several recent books and an extensive bibliography established by the Bibliotheque de documentation internationale contemporaine [Library of Contemporary International Documentation]. The card catalogues of the committee, at 32, Rue de Leningrad, Paris, are the principal research instrument in French-speaking countries.

The second, in order of world reputation, is the Jahresbibliographie der Bibliothek fuer Zeitgeschichte [Annual Bibliography of the Library of Contemporary History] published in Frankfurt since 1961. It is a continuation of the Buecherschau des Weltkriegsbuecherei [Review of Books on the World War] from 1953 to 1960. This monumental work must be consulted as a supplement to the preceding source.

Researchers should consider the bulletins and catalogues issued by most of the American, German, French and British universities. The Imperial War Museum in London contains a treasure of documents and has compiled selected bibliographies on a large number of subjects. Since 1952 East Germany has published the Jahresberichte fuer deutsche Geschichte [Annual Reports on German History].

Finally, we should cite the following reviews comprising a voluminous bibliographic listing: Allgemeine Schweizerische Militaerzeitschrift [General Swiss Military Journal], the Journal of Contemporary History, Militaergeschichtliche Mitteilungen [Military History Bulletin], Military Review, Vierteljahreshefte fuer Zeitgeschichte [Quarterly Reports on Contemporary History], Revue historique de l'Armee [Army Historical Review], Zeitschrift fuer Militaergeschichte [Military History Journal] and War and Society Newsletter.

OFFICIAL HISTORIES

A collection of these histories, through 1962, can be found in J. C. Allmayer-Beck, Die internationale Kriegsgeschichtschreibung ueber den Zweiten Welt-

krieg [The International Military History of the Second World War], Vol. 34. Another, through 1964, is given in H.-A. Jacobsen, Zur Konzeption einer Geschichte des Zweiten Weltkrieges [Thesis for the History of the Second World War] (Stuttgart, 1964). These should be supplemented with current bibliographies (see above).

Germany: The series Wehrwissenschaeftliche Forschungen, Abteilung Militaergeschichtliche Studien [Scientific Research in Weaponry, Military History Studies Section] published by the Militaergeschichtliches Forschungsamt [Military History Research Office] of Freiburg im Breisgau, of which 18 volumes have appeared; details and commentary given in the Militaergeschichtliche Mitteilungen [Military History Reports], the review of this institute.

The series Schriften des Bundesarchiv [Documents of the Federal Archives] is published by the National Archives of the Federal Republic of Germany.

France: Since 1970 the historical service of the army has published the following:

de la Barre de Nanteuil, Gen. Les Historiques des unites combattantes de la Resistance en IV region militaire [History of the Fighting Resistance Units in the Fourth Military Region].

Boulle, Lt. Col., Le Corps expeditionnaire francais en Italie, 1943-1944 [The French Expeditionary Corps in Italy, 1943-1944]. 2 vols.

Constantini, Col. L'Union sovietique en guerre [The Soviet Union at War]. 3 vols.

Evan, Commandant, and Gen. de Nanteuil. Les Ordres de bataille des groupes d'armee D et G de la Wehrmacht [Order of Battle of the Wehrmacht Army Groups D and G].

Le Goyet, Col. La Participation francaise a la campagne d'Italie [French Participation in the Italian Campaign].

Les Grandes Unites francaises de la guerre 1939-1945 [The Large French Units of the 1939-1945 War]. 5 vols. with atlas.

Great Britain and the Commonwealth: Offical History of the Second World War, consisting of three sections: Civil Series, Medical Series, Military Series. Almost 80 volumes have already appeared under the aegis of Her Majesty's Stationery Office.

United States: The Department of Defense has completed the monumental United States Army in World War II. Seventy-two volumes in this series have appeared out of 99 planned.

Craven, W., et al. The Army Air Force in World War II. 7 vols. Chicago, 1948-58.

Morison, S. History of United States Naval Operations in World War II. 15 vols. Boston, 1947-62.

USSR: The Soviets are continually re-editing their

History of the Great Patriotic War.

Similar efforts were made in the following countries: Australia, Canada, Denmark, Finland, Greece, India, Italy, the Netherlands, New Zealand, Norway, Poland and Yugoslavia. Notably absent from the list are Belgium and the eastern European countries in general.

SYNTHESES

Bernard, H. *Guerre totale et guerre revolutionnaire* [Total War and Revolutionary War]. 3 vols. with atlas. Brussels, 1965-67.

Calvocoressi, P., and G. Wint. *Total War*. London, 1972.

Dahms, H. *Der zweite Weltkrieg* [The Second World War]. 2nd edition. Berlin, 1960.

Goerlitz, W. *Der zweite Weltkrieg 1939-1945.* 2 vols. Stuttgart, 1951-1953.

Jacobsen, H.-A. *La Seconde Guerre mondiale* [The Second World War]. 2 vols. Paris, 1968.

Jacobsen, H.-A., and J. Rohwer, *Decisive Battles of World War II*. New York, 1965.

Michel, H. *La Seconde Guerre mondiale* [The Second World War]. 2 vols. Paris, 1969.

Tippelskirch, K. von. *Geschichte des zweiten Weltkrieges* [History of the Second World War]. 2nd edition. Bonn, 1956.

Tosti, A. *Storia della seconda guerra mondiale* [History of the Second World War]. Milan, 1961.

Wright, G. *The Ordeal of Total War*. New York, 1968.

Note: All these works contain detailed bibliographies.

MEMOIRS

With the warning that these sources should be handled judiciously, the researcher should look into the first-hand accounts in the memoirs of the following major figures of the war: Alexander, H.; Arnold, H.; Bradley, O.; Brooke, A.; Cavallero, U.; Churchill, W.; Ciano, G.; Doenitz, K.; Eden, A.; Eisenhower, D.; Gamelin, M.; de Gaulle, C.; Gisevius, H.; Guderian, H.; Halder, F.; Hayashi, S.; Kesselring, A.; King, E.; Leahy, W.; Macmillan, H.; Manstein, E.; Marshall, G.; Montgomery, B.; Patton, G.; Raeder, E.; Rommel, E.; Roosevelt, F.; Ruge, F.; Schmidt, P.; Shigemitsu, M.; Slim, W.; Spaak, P.-H.; Speer, A.; Speidel, H.; Stettinius, E.; Stilwell,

J.; Togo, S.; Truman, H.; Weygand, M,; and Zhukov, G.

In addition, there is the fundamental work of W. Warlimont, *Im Hauptquartier der deutschen Wehrmacht 1939-1945* [In the Headquarters of the German Wehrmacht 1939-1945] (Frankfurt, 1962).

TRIAL RECORDS

Proces des grands criminels de guerre devant le tribunal international [Trial of the Major War Criminals Before the International Military Tribunal]. 1947-49. 42 vols. Nuremberg. Indispensable to those desiring to explore the monstrous mechanism of the Nazi system. It should be supplemented by publications regarding the numerous trials conducted by each of the victorious nations. The testimonies, pleadings, and indictments in all of the trials should be treated with special care.

CHRONOLOGIES

Chronologia della seconda guerra mondiale [Chronology of the Second World War]. Rome, 1959.

Chronologie van de tweede wereldoorlog [Chronology of the Second World War]. Baarn, 1965.

Hillgruber, A., and G. Huemmelchen. *"Vor zwanzig Jahren"* [Twenty Years Ago]. *Wehrwissenschaftliche Rundschau* [Review of Scientific Weaponry]. 1959-60.

Schramm, P., and O. Stange. *Geschichte des zweiten Weltkrieges* [History of the Second World War]. Bielefeld, 1951.

Survey of International Affairs 1939-1946. A. and V. Toynbee: London, 1953 et seq.

US Naval Chronology in World War II. Washington, 1955.

Williams, M. *Chronology 1941-1945, United States in World War II*. Washington, 1960.

FILMS

A list of centers having audio-visual collections can be found in J. de Launay, *Les grandes decisions de la Deuxieme Guerre mondiale* [Great Decisions of the Second World War], Vol. 3 (Geneva, 1975), with a very extensive bibliography.

J. L. Charles

EDITORIAL STAFF

Prepared under the direction of:

Marcel Baudot, secretary of the Commission on the History of the Resistance of the French Committee on the History of World War II; president of the Section on Modern and Contemporary History of the Committee on Historical and Scientific Studies in Paris.

Henri Bernard, professor emeritus at the Royal Military Academy in Brussels.

Hendrik Brugmans, rector emeritus of the College of Europe at Bruges; professor at the Catholic University of Louvain.

Michael R. D. Foot, former professor of modern history at the University of Manchester; former director of the European Discussion Centre.

Hans-A. Jacobsen, professor at the University of Bonn.

Principal contributors:

Uwe Dietrich Adam, instructor in political science and contemporary history at the Reutlingen Teachers' College.

Jean-Leon Charles, professor at the Royal Military Academy in Brussels.

Victor Conzemius, professor of theology at Lucerne; former professor at the University of Dublin.

Jacques Delarue, author of studies on the Gestapo and on the role of the police during the occupation of France.

Jules Gerard-Libois, director of the Center for Sociopolitical Research and Information in Brussels.

Roger Gheysens, secretary-general-adjunct of the International Commission for the Teaching of History.

Andreas Hillgruber, professor at the University of Cologne.

Francois Joyaux, professor at the National Institute of Oriental Languages and Civilizations in Paris.

Ernst Klink, scientific director of the Historical Service of the *Bundeswehr*.

Rene Lacour, former director of studies for the faculty of letters at Lyon; former director of teaching at Laval University in Quebec.

Branko Lazitch, former research associate at the Hoover Institution at Stanford.

Claude Levy, secretary-general-adjunct of the Committee on the History of World War II in Paris.

Jovan Marjanovic, professor at the University of Belgrade; vice president of the International Committee on the History of World War II; author of many studies on the Yugoslavian Resistance.

Bernd Martin, professor of modern and contemporary history at Freiburg im Breisgau.

Pierre Mermet, member of the research staff of the French Committee on the History of World War II.

Klaus-Jurgen Muller, professor of contemporary history at Hamburg.

Dietmar Petzina, professor of economics and social science at the University of Bochum.

Edmond Pognon, curator of the *Bibliotheque nationale* in Paris.

Josef Schroder, lecturer in contemporary history at the University of Bonn.

Waclaw W. Soroka, professor at the University of Wisconsin at Stevens Point.

Yves Ternon, former director of practical studies in medicine at the University of Paris.

Hans Umbreit, staff member of the Historical Service of the *Bundeswehr*.

Jean Vidalenc, professor of contemporary history at the University of Rouen; member of the French Commission on Military History and the French Committee on the History of World War II.

Translated from the French by:

Jesse Dilson, author and translator.

With additional material by:

Alvin D. Coox, professor of history at San Diego State University, and Thomas R. H. Havens, professor of history at Connecticut College.